PERGAMON GENERAL PSYCHOLOGY SERIES
EDITORS
Arnold P. Goldstein, Syracuse University
Leonard Krasner, Stanford University & SUNY at Stony Brook

HANDBOOK OF BEHAVIOR THERAPY AND PSYCHOLOGICAL SCIENCE
(PGPS-164)

Pergamon Titles of Related Interest

Bellack/Hersen BEHAVIORAL ASSESSMENT: A Practical Handbook, Third Edition
Goldstein/Hersen HANDBOOK OF PSYCHOLOGICAL ASSESSMENT, Second Edition
Hersen/Bellack DICTIONARY OF BEHAVIORAL ASSESSMENT TECHNIQUES
Hersen/Last HANDBOOK OF CHILD AND ADULT PSYCHOPATHOLOGY: A Longitudinal Perspective
Higginbotham/West/Forsyth PSYCHOTHERAPY AND BEHAVIOR CHANGE: Social, Cultural and Methodological Perspectives
Kanfer/Goldstein HELPING PEOPLE CHANGE: A Textbook of Methods, Fourth Edition
Kazdin CHILD PSYCHOTHERAPY: Developing and Identifying Effective Treatments
Schwartz/Johnson PSYCHOPATHOLOGY OF CHILDHOOD: A Clinical-Experimental Approach, Second Edition
Winkler/Brown/van Keppel/Blanchard CLINICAL PRACTICE IN ADOPTION

Related Journals
(Free sample copies available upon request.)

ADVANCES IN BEHAVIOUR RESEARCH AND THERAPY
BEHAVIORAL ASSESSMENT
BEHAVIOUR CHANGE
BEHAVIOUR RESEARCH AND THERAPY
CLINICAL PSYCHOLOGY REVIEW
JOURNAL OF BEHAVIOR THERAPY AND
   EXPERIMENTAL PSYCHIATRY

HANDBOOK OF BEHAVIOR THERAPY AND PSYCHOLOGICAL SCIENCE

An Integrative Approach

Edited by
PAUL R. MARTIN
University of Western Australia

PERGAMON PRESS
Member of Maxwell Macmillan Pergamon Publishing Corporation
New York • Oxford • Beijing • Frankfurt
São Paulo • Sydney • Tokyo • Toronto

Pergamon Press Offices:

U.S.A.	Pergamon Press, Inc., Maxwell House, Fairview Park, Elmsford, New York 10523, U.S.A.
U.K.	Pergamon Press plc, Headington Hill Hall, Oxford OX3 0BW, England
PEOPLE'S REPUBLIC OF CHINA	Pergamon Press, Xizhimenwai Dajie, Beijing Exhibition Centre, Beijing, 100044, People's Republic of China
GERMANY	Pergamon Press GmbH, Hammerweg 6, D-6242 Kronberg, Germany
BRAZIL	Pergamon Editora Ltda, Rua Eça de Queiros, 346, CEP 04011, Paraiso, São Paulo, Brazil
AUSTRALIA	Pergamon Press Australia Pty Ltd., P.O. Box 544, Potts Point, NSW 2011, Australia
JAPAN	Pergamon Press, 8th Floor, Matsuoka Central Building, 1-7-1 Nishishinjuku, Shinjuku-ku, Tokyo 160, Japan
CANADA	Pergamon Press Canada Ltd., Suite 271, 253 College Street, Toronto, Ontario M5T 1R5, Canada

Copyright © 1991 Pergamon Press, Inc.

All rights reserved. No part of this publication may be reproduced, stored in a retrieval system or transmitted in any form or by any means: electronic, electrostatic, magnetic tape, mechanical, photocopying, recording or otherwise, without permission in writing from the publishers.

Library of Congress Cataloging in Publication Data

Handbook of behavior therapy and psychological science : an
  integrative approach / edited by Paul R. Martin.
    p.   cm. -- (Pergamon general psychology series : 164)
  Includes index.
  ISBN 0-08-036129-3 :
  1. Behavior therapy. 2. Psychology. I. Martin, Paul R., 1951–
  II. Series.
    [DNLM: 1. Affective Disorders--therapy. 2. Behavior Therapy.
  3. Cognition Disorders--therapy. 4. Human Development.
  5. Psychological Theory.   WM 425 H2356]
  RC489.B4H364 1990
  616.89 '142--dc20
  DNLM/DLC
  for Library of Congress   90-7302
                                                                      CIP

Printing: 1 2 3 4 5 6 7 8 9 10   Year: 1 2 3 4 5 6 7 8 9 0

Printed in the United States of America

∞™ The paper used in this publication meets the minimum requirements of American National Standard for Information Sciences—Permanence of Paper for Printed Library Materials, ANSI Z39.48-1984

For Fiona M. Martin

No theory is good except on condition that one use it to go beyond.
André Gide, *Journals*, 1918.

CONTENTS

Preface xi

Chapter

1 Theoretical and empirical foundations of behavior therapy — Paul R. Martin — 1

PART I. DEVELOPMENTAL PSYCHOLOGY

2 Toward the integration of human developmental and therapeutic change — Richard M. Lerner, Laura E. Hess, Katherine Nitz — 13

3 Developmental psychopathology: An integrative framework — Ann S. Masten, Lauren Braswell — 35

4 Developmental factors in child behavioral assessment — Thomas H. Ollendick, Neville J. King — 57

5 Clinical-childhood-developmental interface: Implications for treatment — Grayson N. Holmbeck, Philip C. Kendall — 73

PART II. COGNITIVE PSYCHOLOGY AND NEUROPSYCHOLOGY

6	Theoretical cognitive psychology and mood disorders	Michael W. Eysenck	103
7	Cognitive-experimental approaches to the emotional disorders	Colin MacLeod Andrew M. Mathews	116
8	Contributions of cognitive psychology to assessment and treatment of anxiety	Michelle G. Craske David H. Barlow	151
9	Contributions of cognitive psychology to assessment and treatment of depression	Steven D. Hollon Mary Shelton	169
10	Clinical decision making	Steven Schwartz	196
11	Cognitive psychology applied to the treatment of acquired language disorders	Max Coltheart	216
12	Behavior therapy in the treatment of neurologically impaired adults	Barbara Wilson	227

PART III. SOCIAL PSYCHOLOGY

13	History and theories of social psychology: Their relevance to behavior therapy	John H. Harvey Mary L. Burgess Terri L. Orbuch	255
14	Psychosocial determinants of disorder: Social support, coping and social skills interactions	Rolf A. Peterson	270
15	Social cognition in behavioral assessment and behavior therapy	Frank D. Fincham Thomas N. Bradbury	283
16	Psychotherapy as a social process	Christopher Peterson	308

PART IV. PSYCHOBIOLOGY AND PSYCHOPHYSIOLOGY

17	Psychobiological processes in the etiology of disease	Andrew Steptoe	325
18	Psychophysiology and behavioral assessment: Is there scope for theoretical frameworks?	Graham Turpin	348
19	Psychophysiological contributions to behavior therapy	Derek W. Johnston Paul R. Martin	383

PART V. CONDITIONING AND LEARNING

20	Selective associations in the origins of phobic fears and their implications for behavior therapy	Michael Cook Susan Mineka	413
21	A contextual analysis of fear extinction	Mark E. Bouton	435

PART VI. COMMUNITY PSYCHOLOGY AND PREVENTION

22	Incorporating the ecological paradigm into behavioral preventive interventions	Nancy S. Burgoyne Leonard A. Jason	457
23	Extending applications of behavior therapy to large-scale intervention	Richard A. Winett Abby C. King David G. Altman	473
24	Conclusion: Psychological science and behavior therapy	Paul R. Martin	491

Author Index   519

Subject Index   547

About the Editors and Contributors   559

PREFACE

The idea for organizing this handbook originally evolved out of the editor's term as president of the Australian Behaviour Modification Association; in particular, it took shape as a consequence of preparing a presidential address. This role necessitated thinking broadly about the field of behavior therapy, and considering whether it was progressing in profitable directions. Such deliberations led to mixed feelings. On the one hand, a great deal seemed to have been accomplished in a relatively short time, and innovative developments were still occurring. On the other hand, the field appeared to be losing its identity as it moved further and further away from its roots in empiricism and its emphasis on the scientific method.

The rationale of the handbook will not be discussed in detail here as this is the focus of the first chapter. Suffice to say that I became convinced the time was ripe for behavior therapy to reassess its relationship with psychology. What had the various branches of psychology contributed to behavioral theories of disorders, behavioral assessment, and behavioral treatment? More important, what could they contribute in the future?

Before discussing the structure of the handbook, a few words about its title and subject matter are appropriate. The title uses the term "behavior therapy", but alternative terms such as "cognitive behavior therapy" and "psychotherapy" were considered. The intent of the handbook is to adopt a broad perspective which includes all the variations of behavior therapy that have been identified (e.g., applied behavior analysis, social learning theory, and cognitive behavior modification). On the other hand, it seemed advantageous to focus on a particular approach to therapy that would provide some structure and limits to the handbook. Unfortunately, all the terms used for describing therapy have multiple meanings and connotations, so that there is always the danger of misleading potential readers.

It could be argued that the notion of integrating behavior therapy and psychological science makes little sense, as behavior therapy is the clinical application of psychological principles. There are, however, two responses to this criticism. First, not all would agree with this conceptualization of behavior therapy (e.g., some would view behavior therapy more as the application of learning theory). Second, even if behavior therapy is conceptualized in this way, the degree to which behavior therapy has, in actuality, involved the application of psychological science is debatable.

One eminent academic who reviewed a prospectus for the handbook commented that it seemed to be more devoted to the empirical study of abnormal psychology than to behavior therapy, but acknowledged these terms are rather arbitrary. This is a valid point, but I feel that the chosen title best conveys the central theme of the handbook.

The handbook begins with an introductory chapter that provides a rationale for the book and a discussion of relevant terms. The first part, "Developmental Psychology", includes a theoretical chapter, followed by three chapters that discuss contributions of developmental psychology to psychopathology, assessment, and treatment. Part Two, "Cognitive Psychology and Neuropsychology", begins by focusing on emotional disorders, an area in which cognitive psychology has made a major contribution. The first four chapters in this part consider theoretical contributions to emotional disorders, cognitive-experimental studies of emotional disorders, and contributions of cognitive psychology to the assessment and treatment of anxiety and depression. The fifth chapter discusses a different area in which cognitive psychology can contribute to behavior therapy—clinical decision making. The last two chapters focus on cognitive neuropsychology.

Part Three, "Social Psychology", begins with a theoretical chapter, followed by three chapters that discuss areas in which social psychology has contributed or could contribute to behavior therapy: psychosocial determinants of disorders; social cognition; and an analysis of the therapeutic process from a social psychological prospective.

Part Four, "Psychobiology and Psychophysiology", excludes a theoretical chapter because this area of psychology is less theoretically driven than others. The three chapters focus on contributions to psychopathology, assessment, and treatment.

"Conditioning and Learning", Part Five, is relatively brief because this area has been covered in considerable depth in previous volumes on the theoretical foundations of behavior therapy. Two chapters discuss recent developments in this area with important clinical implications, one focusing on acquisition the other on extinction.

Part Six, "Community Psychology and Prevention", compares alternative service delivery systems to those traditionally used in behavior therapy. This is an appropriate topic on which to end the handbook because it emphasizes the value of drawing from literature beyond psychological science, such as health promotion sciences, public health, economics, and political science. The concluding chapter attempts to summarize and integrate the preceding chapters.

I would like to express my appreciation to a number of individuals for their contributions to the handbook. The book was planned and organized in 1987 while I was on sabbatical leave in the Department of Psychology at St. George's Hospital Medical School, the University of London, and the Center for Stress and Anxiety Disorders at the State University of New York at Albany. The visits were arranged through Andrew Mathews and David Barlow, and I am very grateful to them for the resources they made available to me, and for the support, encouragement, and advice they offered. I am indebted to all who wrote chapters for the handbook. Many of them suggested potential topics or authors; I am particularly indebted to Thomas Ollendick and Christopher Peterson in this respect.

Finally, I would like to express my appreciation to Bill Martin for preparing the author index; Debbie Roodbeen for her secretarial work on the manuscript; and Fiona Martin for helping with a number of the tasks involved in completing this handbook.

Paul R. Martin
The University of Western Australia
January 1990

CHAPTER 1

THEORETICAL AND EMPIRICAL FOUNDATIONS OF BEHAVIOR THERAPY

Paul R. Martin

Few statements can be made without fear of contradiction, but to suggest that behavior therapy has become well established in the field of psychotherapy is one of them. Perhaps it does not hold as dominant a position as some of its more ardent supporters believe, and cogent criticisms have appeared periodically from its inception to the present day. Nevertheless, the evidence for the exponential growth of interest in behavior therapy is irrefutable.

Kazdin's classic history of behavior modification traces the scientific foundations in general areas of research: conditioning and reflexology in Russia, comparative psychology, the behaviorism of John B. Watson, and the psychology of learning in America (Kazdin, 1978). In the first article devoted to the topic of behavior therapy published in the *Annual Review of Psychology*, Krasner (1971) argued that 15 streams of development within the science of psychology came together during the 1950s and 1960s to form the approach to behavior change generally known as behavior therapy. The term *behavior therapy* apparently was first used by Lindsley, Skinner, and Solomon (1953) in their application of operant conditioning procedures with hospitalized psychotic patients.

However, this group did not extend their work beyond the confines of one particular ward. Lazarus (1958) next used the term to refer to the addition of objective laboratory-derived procedures to traditional psychotherapeutic methods, and Eysenck (1959) later referred to a new therapeutic approach based on the application of modern learning theory to the treatment of psychological disorders. The publication in 1958 of Wolpe's book, *Psychotherapy by Reciprocal Inhibition* (systematic densensitization), was clearly a landmark event in the history of behavior therapy.

In the years since these early writings, the research literature on behavior therapy has become voluminous. The first journal devoted exclusively to behavior therapy was founded in 1963 (*Behaviour Research and Therapy*), and the second, restricted to operant procedures, in 1968 (*Journal of Applied Behavior Analysis*). Two more specialist journals were founded in 1970: *Behavior Therapy* and *Journal of Behavior Therapy and Experimental Psychiatry*. The number of such journals had risen to 21 by 1979 (Barlow, 1980), and to 26 by 1983 (London, 1983). Of course, articles on behavior therapy also appear in many journals that are not dedicated to this particular field, such as

...ychotherapy, psychiatry, clinical psy-...al work, education, and abnormal psy-...teen years ago, Yates (1975) estimated tha... ...st 500 papers and 20 to 30 books were published annually on some area of behavior therapy. In addition, every year numerous tapes (audio and visual), and self-help manuals purporting to be based on behavioral principles are published. The proliferation of self-help manuals (sometimes referred to as bibliotherapy) has been a particularly notable phenomenon since the 1970s (Glasgow & Rosen, 1978, 1979, 1984).

Major behavior therapy associations have been founded across at least five of the seven continents. In the United States, the Association for the Advancement of Behavior Therapy (AABT) was formed in 1966, and currently has nearly 4,000 members. Most European countries have associations that are affiliated with the European Association for Behaviour Therapy (EABT). Large behavior therapy organizations also exist in Australia, Japan, and Latin America, as well as smaller groups elsewhere (Franks & Rosenbaum, 1983). The first World Congress on Behaviour Therapy was held in 1980, and attracted 1,200 delegates from some 30 countries. The second World Congress held three years later was attended by more than twice as many delegates.

Perhaps more significant than these academic developments, an increasingly high proportion of psychologists are identifying behavior therapy as their primary approach (O'Leary, 1984). For example, in a U.S. survey of pediatric psychologists, Tuma and Cohen (1981) reported that behavioral psychology was the primary orientation of 59% of their sample. A survey of clinical psychologists in Australia indicated that eclectic and behavioral approaches were equally favored by those working in the field, while the majority (51%) of clinical psychologists with academic affiliations identified with the latter (Martin, 1989).

Given that behavior therapy is expanding so rapidly, it is critical to question the directions in which it is developing. What are the foundations of behavior therapy, and do they provide a sound base on which to build in future decades? Few would deny that behavior therapy has a substantial record of accomplishment behind it (e.g., O'Leary & Carr, 1982; Wilson, 1982a), but will this continue in the future? The evolution of behavior therapy has involved such dramatic changes that some writers were talking of an identity crisis in the 1970s (e.g., Mash, 1974), a trend which continued into the 1980s (e.g., Franks, 1984).

Periodically, authors argue that the term behavior therapy should be retired (e.g., Bandura, 1969; Lazarus, 1977), and it has been suggested that the related (some would consider synonymous) term, *behavior modification*, is dead (Krasner, 1976). Some attention should be given to what is meant by *behavior therapy* before focusing on the current status of the field and its likely progress in the futrue.

DEFINITION AND THEORETICAL BASE

Many meanings have been attached to the term *behavior therapy* (Wilson, 1978). Some of the early pioneers of behavior therapy proposed elegantly simple definitions such as Eysenck (1964), who defined behavior therapy as "the attempt to alter human behaviour and emotion in a beneficial manner according to the laws of modern learning theory" (p.1), and Wolpe (1969), who defined it as "the use of experimentally established principles of learning for the purpose of changing unadaptive behavior" (p. vii). Such definitions clearly emphasized that their authors perceived learning theory to be the theoretical base of behavior therapy. Definitions of this nature have obvious appeal, as specification of a theoretical framework for an approach to therapy should help unify and delineate the field. Also, it is evident that learning theory has proven to have great heuristic value for the advancement of behavior therapy; many etiological theories of dysfunction are based on learning principles, and the inspiration for the development of numerous therapeutic techniques has come from theories and findings in the learning literature.

In contrast to such definitions, other authors have viewed tying behavior therapy to learning theory or conditioning as too limiting (e.g., Lazarus, 1971). The definition of behavior therapy currently adopted by AABT emphasizes links with the whole of experimental and social psychology rather than just learning theory. It reads as follows:

> Behavior therapy involves primarily the application of principles derived from research in experimental and social psychology for the alleviation of human suffering and the enhancement of human functioning. Behavior therapy emphasizes a systematic evaluation of the effectiveness of these applications. Behavior therapy involves environmental change and social interaction rather than the direct alteration of bodily processes by biological procedures. The aim is primarily educational. The techniques facilitate improved self-control. In the conduct of behavior therapy, a contractual agreement is usually negotiated, in

which mutually agreeable goals and procedures are specified. Responsible practitioners using behavioral approaches are guided by generally accepted ethical principles. (Franks & Wilson, 1975, p.1)

An alternative to the approach of seeking a theoretical base in learning theory, or psychological science generally, is the antitheoretical stance adopted by Skinner and his colleagues. Skinner (1950) argued that a science of behavior must eventually deal with behavior in its relation to certain manipulable variables, and that theories generally deal with the intervening steps in these relationships. Therefore, instead of encouraging us to search for and investigate more relevant variables, these intervening steps frequently serve only to provide verbal answers in place of the factual data we might find through further study. Skinner's antitheoretical position has influenced, and is still influencing, many behavior therapists.

On the other hand, the majority of researchers in psychology view theory as being critical to guiding scientific enquiry. For example, Levis (1982) has stated that:

> The function of theory is to provide a systematic expansion of knowledge mediated by specific empirical propositions, statements, hypotheses, and predictions that are subject to empirical tests . . . The utility of a theory lies essentially in its ability to serve as a guide for empirical studies. Unguided experimentation usually results in an unorganised mass of data. (p.40)

In the field of behavior therapy, Reiss and Bootzin (1985) have pointed out that advances in theory have often led to advances in treatment. For example, the view that anxiety is a conditioned Pavlovian response led to the development of systematic desensitization and implosive therapy; the theoretical position that depression is caused by irrational ideas and other faulty cognitions led to the development of cognitive therapy.

While the author supports the position adopted by AABT of linking behavior therapy with psychological science generally (and, in fact, this forms the basis for the current volume), it should be pointed out that such an approach seems more a statement of intent than a summary of what has occurred so far. The theoretical base of behavior therapy is a generally neglected area, and has been largely restricted to learning theory. Theoretical considerations are covered minimally in most popular behavior therapy texts (e.g., Gambrill, 1977; Goldfried & Davison, 1976; Goldstein & Foa, 1980; Hersen & Bellack, 1985; O'Leary & Wilson, 1987; Rimm & Masters, 1979; Turner, Calhoun & Adams, 1981). *The International Handbook of Behavior Modification and Therapy* (Bellack, Hersen & Kazdin, 1982) has an excellent chapter devoted to the experimental and theoretical foundations of behavior modification by Donald Levis, but this work is limited to learning theory plus a brief section on cognitive models of behavior change. An important but not widely known book on the theoretical and experimental bases of behavior therapy appeared in the mid-1970s (Feldman & Broadhurst, 1976), and included sections on biological, cognitive, and social psychology, in addition to the psychology of learning. Other major areas of psychological science, such as developmental psychology, were not represented, however.

Interest in theoretical issues in behavior therapy gained momentum in the 1980s. Three recent books have been devoted to this area (Eysenck & Martin, 1987; Franks & Wilson, 1982; Reiss & Bootzin, 1985), and although none attempt to draw widely from the various branches of psychological science, all go well beyond learning theory. In addition, many conferences have been given on the interface between behavior therapy and one or more areas of psychology. The EABT, for example, organized their 1984 conference on the basis of the relationship between behavior therapy and three branches of psychology—cognitive, social, and physiological (Eelen & Fontaine, 1986). The AABT conventions in 1986 and 1987 focused on the interface of behavior therapy with biological sciences and developmental psychology, respectively; and the 1990 convention adopted a much broader theme, similar to the theme of this handbook, ("Clinical applications of scientific knowledge").

NEW DIRECTIONS IN BEHAVIOR THERAPY

During the 30 to 40 year history of behavior therapy, a number of developments have occurred that have particular relevance for the theoretical framework of behavior therapy. Three such developments will be discussed briefly here: the broadening of the range of problems to which behavior therapy has been applied; the extension of the domain of behavior therapy from overt behavior to covert processes; and the trend towards integrating behavior therapy with other schools of psychotherapy.

Behavior therapy initially focused on a limited range of disorders. In view of the close relationship that existed between clinical psychology and psychi-

rly history of behavior therapy, it is ... that the first applications were ... uroses, psychoses, and intellectual handicap, although other problems such as tics, stuttering, enuresis, sexual disorders, and alcoholism also received early attention (Yates, 1970). Since the 1960s, the range of applications has expanded dramatically, and the current diversity of the field can be gauged by the terms in use, which include behavioral family therapy, behavioral group therapy, behavioral marital therapy, behavioral psychopharmacology, behavioral neuropsychology, environmental behavior therapy, behavioral genetics, behavioral ecology, community behavior therapy, behavioral economics, behavioral pediatrics, and behavioral toxicology. The largest growth area in the last decade has been the application of behavioral techniques to the promotion of "physical" health and the treatment of "physical" illness, a field usually referred to as behavioral health or behavioral medicine. This field has become so extensive it has spawned its own speciality societies and journals, in addition to numerous books (e.g., Pinkerton, Hughes & Wenrich, 1982; Pomerleau & Brady, 1979).

With respect to the domain of behavior therapy, the early emphasis was on overt behavior and autonomic responses (Martin, 1985). Many behavioral researchers believed that psychology could only become a science by designating as its subject matter behavior that was observable and quantifiable. Behavior therapy developed in part as a reaction against "mentalistic" forms of therapy, and the focus on overt behavior was seen as a unique feature of the new approach.

While some researchers have maintained this tradition, the majority have not. Since the late 1960s, an increasing number of behavior therapists have shown a keen interest in cognitive processes. The books by Mahoney (1974) and Meichenbaum (1974) on cognitive behavior modification have had a major impact on the field. Advocates of this approach, such as Kendall and Hollon (1979), argued that "behavior therapy . . . may have reduced its own effectiveness by ignoring those unobservable 'mentalistic' processes so inexorably intertwined in any phenomena involving human beings" (p.xv). A number of critiques of cognitive behavior therapy have been offered (e.g., Ledwidge, 1978; Greenspoon & Lamal, 1978), focusing on such issues as whether private events can be studied in a scientific manner (is the investigator able to reliably determine when the phenomenon occurs?). Despite such papers, this approach has continued to flourish.

In his presidential address to AABT, Wilson (1982b) posed the question, "If we began with overt behavior in the 1950s and 1960s then added cognition in the 1970s, can affect be far behind? In looking for a new emphasis in behavior therapy, it might be 'affect in the eighties'" (p. 298). He suggested this shift may occur because of recent writings which imply that affect played a more influential role in psychological functioning than previously attributed to it. Zajonc (1980), for example, challenged cognitive theorists who assume affect is largely "postcognitive", meaning that emotional reactions occur after perceptual and cognitive processing of information. He argued that a variety of experimental and clinical data suggested "affective judgements may be fairly independent of and precede in time the sorts of perceptual and cognitive operations commonly assumed to be the basis of these affective judgements" (p.151).

Recent writings by influential authors in the behavioral field suggest yet another shift in focus, this time to unconscious processes (Bowers & Meichenbaum, 1984; Mahoney, 1986). Mahoney (1980) argued that with the introduction of cognition into the behavioral camp the consideration of unconscious events became inevitable. As cognition has been used to refer solely to conscious cognitive processes, but at times also includes preconscious cognition (Moroz, 1972), it is difficult to argue with Mahoney's view. Unconscious processes are already represented in both the experimental literature on cognition (e.g., Bower, 1986) and the clinical literature on cognitive behavior therapy (e.g., Beck, Rush, Shaw & Emery, 1979).

The third development in behavior therapy to be discussed is the move towards integration. Attempts to integrate the various schools of psychotherapy date back some 50 years, but trends in this area appear to be gaining momentum recently. The journal, *Behavior Therapy*, published a miniseries on "Integrationism in Psychotherapy", edited by Philip Kendall in 1982 [13(5)]. The prospective union that has received most attention is between psychodynamic psychotherapy and behavior therapy. Those arguing for a rapprochement have included individuals trained in psychoanalysis (e.g., Wachtel, 1977), and individuals trained in behavior therapy (e.g., Goldfried, 1982). This trend is related to those already discussed, as Goldfried (1980) has proposed that modern cognitive psychology can pave the way for integration. Meichenbaum and Gilmore (1984) view their analysis of unconscious processes as an attempt to bridge the gap between behavioral and psychodynamic approaches at the point the gap is widest. Attempts at integrating or at least looking for commonalities between behavior therapy and other schools of psychology have appeared in the literature. For example, Thoresen (1973) suggested that many of the philosophical underpinnings associated with behaviorism and humanism were in agreement, and Wandersman, Poppen, and Ricks' (1976) *Humanism and Behaviorism* attempted to acknowledge points of potential integration.

TERMINOLOGY RECONSIDERED: BEHAVIOR THERAPY AND BEHAVIORISM

Consideration of the varied directions in which behavior therapy has expanded encourages further analysis of the nature of behavior therapy: Can such diverse developments be incorporated within a single approach to therapy? Most behavior therapists seem to have moved away from the position that the theoretical base should be limited to learning theory (some never held this view), and from the position that overt behavior is the only valid target for assessment and treatment. How then can the field be defined? One alternative approach for seeking to delineate the field is to identify it with a particular philosophy or doctrine. In the case of behavior therapy a number of writers have followed this course by identifying behavior therapy with behaviorism. Wolpe (1968), for example, stated that "a behavior therapist is a behaviorist who does behavior therapy" (p.1). Locke (1969) defines behaviorism as "the doctrine that the behavior of man and animal can be fully understood without the use of explanatory concepts referring to states or actions of consciousness, namely by studying only observable behavior" (pp. 1000–1001). According to Locke (1971):

> The basic premises of behaviorism are (a) determinism: the doctrine that all of mans actions, thoughts, beliefs, etc. are ultimately determined by forces outside his control (typically by environmental forces); (b) epiphenomenalism: the doctrine that conscious states (e.g., ideas), if they exist at all, are merely by-products of physical events in the body and/or in the external world—that they are end points in a causal chain and have no effect on either the individual's subsequent actions or his subsequent ideas; and (c) the rejection of introspection as a scientific method. (p. 318)

Locke (1971) went on to argue that the therapeutic methods of Wolpe contradicted all three premises of behaviorism. Whether or not this view is accepted, it is clear from the previous section that much of what is currently called behavior therapy does not remotely conform to behaviorism as delineated by Locke. However, Franks (1984) has pointed out that there are at least two major forms of behaviorism: metaphysical and methodological.

Metaphysical or radical behaviorism denies the very existence of mental states (this being the type of behaviorism on which Locke focused). It is nonmediational, antimentalistic, never inferential, and favors induction over hypothesis testing. By contrast, methodological behaviorism or neobehaviorism is mediational, often mentalistic, and inferential, and usually employs hypothetico-deductive methodology. Metaphysical behaviorism tends to prefer single subject designs while methodological behaviorism lends itself to group designs. Individuals such as Watson and Skinner were metaphysical behaviorists whereas Hull, Eysenck, Bandura, and most contemporary behavior therapists are more appropriately viewed as methodological behaviorists.

Considerations such as these only emphasize the breadth and diversity of the field the term behavior therapy currently encompasses, rather than help define it. They do clarify why identity confusion and calls for abandoning use of the term have occurred. Writers seem to have responded to this situation in two main ways. One is to structure the field by identifying a number of distinct approaches within it. Kazdin and Wilson (1978), for example, divided the different approaches to behavior therapy into five categories as follows: (a) *applied behavior analysis* (a radical behaviorist approach involving the application of operant principles in a wide range of clinical and social institutions); (b) *neobehavioristic mediational S-R model* (involves the application of the principles of classical conditioning); (c) *social learning theory* (an approach developed by Bandura emphasizing cognitive mediational processes as well as external stimuli and reinforcement, and "reciprocal determinism"— the interaction between the individual's behavior and the environment); (d) *cognitive-behavior modification* (an approach emphasizing the importance of, and focusing on, cognitive processes and private events as mediators of behavior change); (e) *multimodal behavior therapy* (an approach developed by Lazarus characterized by a variety of assessment and intervention procedures spanning the seven areas [summarized by the acronym *BASIC ID*) of behavior, affect, sensation, imagery, cognition, interpersonal relations, and drugs].

The other response to the increasing diversity of the field seems to be for writers to merely characterize the field rather than attempting to formally define it.

Krasner (1982), for example, argues that the field of behavior modification (behavior therapy) is defined by "the behavior of those professionals who identify with it and by the historical context within which these people work" (p. 17). This statement probably feels quite comfortable to those professing a behavioral orientation, but is not very illuminating for those who do not. Kazdin and Hersen (1980) suggest four characteristic features of behavior therapy:

> (i) A strong commitment to empirical evaluation of treatment and intervention techniques; (ii) A general belief that therapeutic experiences must provide opportunities to learn adaptive or prosocial behavior; (iii) Specification of treatment in operational and, hence, replicable terms; (iv) Evaluation of treatment effects through multiple-response modalities with particular emphasis on overt behavior. (p. 287)

This list goes a long way towards capturing the current ethos of behavior therapy. The characteristics it enumerates are not unique to behavior therapy, however.

HOW RESEARCH AND THEORY DIFFER FROM PRACTICE

The widely accepted definition of behavior therapy quoted earlier included the statement that it "involves primarily the application of principles derived from research in experimental and social psychology . . ." (Franks & Wilson, 1975, p.1). A number of authors have suggested, however, that the gap between theory and research on the one hand and application on the other may be widening (e.g., Franks & Rosenbaum, 1983). This may be true in two respects: First, researchers using theories and research from psychological science in the development of theories of dysfunction, and new assessment, and treatment techniques; and second, behavior therapists using available theories and findings to guide their clinical practice.

On the research side, Ross (1985) made the interesting observation that inspection of the first volume of *Behavior Therapy* included references to the writings of numerous experimental psychologists and citations of studies in the *Journal of Comparative and Physiological Psychology*, the *Journal of Experimental Psychology*, the *Psychological Bulletin*, and the *Journal on the Experimental Analysis of Behavior*. Today the situation is quite different and references to basic research have practically disappeared from articles in *Behavior Therapy*. A longitudinal content analysis for the first 10 volumes of *Journal of Applied Behavior Analysis* by Hayes, Rincover and Solnik (1980), revealed that this journal too reflected less and less interest in conceptual questions and more and more purely technical concerns.

On the clinical side, the scientist-practitioner split has been well documented by Barlow, Hayes and Nelson (1984). In a survey of leading clinicians by Bergin and Strupp (1972), Matarazzo commented ". . . even after 15 years, few of my research findings affect my practice. Psychological science per se doesn't guide me one bit" (p. 340). Swan and MacDonald (1978) surveyed 353 members of AABT and reported a number of discrepancies between behavior therapy as presented in research and behavior therapy as reportedly practiced. Kanfer (1972) asked 30 leaders about assessment practices when functioning as therapists rather than researchers: The relationship between clinical and laboratory methods was minimal.

GOALS OF THIS HANDBOOK

It has been argued in this chapter that the field of behavior therapy has achieved a great deal in its short history, and has become well established as an important approach to treating a wide range of human disorders. A number of problems have been identified, however. The theoretical underpinnings of behavior therapy have received insufficient attention. Controversy exists concerning whether behavior therapy should draw from a relatively narrow and cohesive theoretical base (learning theory) or a more broad and diffuse literature (psychological science). Another problem discussed was the widening gap between research and theory on the one hand and application on the other.

Also considered in this chapter were some major trends in behavior therapy, specifically the ever-increasing range of disorders encompassed by the field, the inclusion of covert processes within its subject matter, and moves towards integration with other schools of psychotherapy.

The goal of this handbook is to look broadly at the field of psychological science in relation to behavior therapy (defined in its broadest sense), with a view to contributing to resolving the identified problems, and providing a context for evaluating current trends and possible future directions. What can psychological science offer behavior therapy? What have fields such as developmental psychology, cognitive psychology, social psychology, and psychophysiology, contributed to behavioral models of dysfunction, behavioral assessment, and behavioral treatment; and how can theories, models, concepts, principles, methodologies, paradigms, procedures, and findings from these fields contribute to behavior therapy in the future? It is hoped that consideration of questions such as these will extend and strengthen the theoretical and empirical foundations of behavior therapy. It is also hoped that such a review will help close the gap between theory and research versus practice. This aim seems likely to be fulfilled on the research side (researchers in behavior therapy using theory and research from psychological science), and may be fulfilled on the clinical side (behavior therapists using available theories and findings) if the review reveals theories and findings with clear clinical utility.

Are there implications in the psychological literature for the directions in which behavior therapy should be advancing? Trends which are currently emerging include the broadening of the domain of behavior therapy to include covert processes and attempts to integrate behavior therapy with other schools of psychotherapy. A review of the interface between the various fields of psychological science and behavior therapy may contribute to an evaluation of these trends but may also suggest quite new directions.

The handbook could be conceptualized as a trawling exercise, searching the psychological literature for material with clinical utility. This is not to argue against the development of original behavioral theories or innovations arising from clinical practice, but only to suggest that there are vast resources available but, as yet, largely untapped.

REFERENCES

Bandura, A. (1969). *Principles of behavior modification*. New York: Holt, Rinehart & Winston.

Barlow, D. H. (1980). Behavior therapy: The next decade. *Behavior Therapy, 11*, 315–328.

Barlow, D. H., Hayes, S. C., & Nelson, R. O. (1984). *The scientist-practitioner: Research and accountability in clinical and educational settings*. Elmsford, NY: Pergamon Press.

Beck, A. T., Rush, A. J., Shaw, B. F., & Emery, G. D. (1979). *Cognitive therapy of depression*. New York: Guilford Press.

Bellack, A. S., Hersen, M., & Kazdin, A. E. (Eds.). (1982). *International handbook of behavior modification and therapy*. New York: Plenum Press.

Bergin, A., & Strupp, H. (1972). *Changing frontiers in the science of psychotherapy*. Chicago: Aldine.

Bower, G. H. (1986). Prime time in cognitive psychology. In P. Eelen & O. Fontaine (Eds.), *Behavior therapy: Beyond the conditioning framework* (pp. 22–47). Leuven/Hillsdale, NJ: Leuven University Press and Lawrence Erlbaum Associates.

Bowers, K. S., & Meichenbaum, D. (Eds.). (1984). *The unconscious reconsidered*. New York: John Wiley & Sons.

Eelen, P., & Fontaine, O. (Eds.). (1986). *Behavior therapy: Beyond the conditioning framework*. Leuven/Hillsdale, NJ: Leuven University Press and Lawrence Erlbaum Associates.

Eysenck, H. J. (1959). Learning theory and behaviour therapy. *Journal of Mental Science, 105*, 61–75.

Eysenck, H. J. (1964). The nature of behaviour therapy. In H. J. Eysenck (Ed.), *Experiments in behaviour therapy* (pp. 1–15). Oxford: Pergamon Press.

Eysenck, H. J., & Martin, I. (Eds.). (1987). *Theoretical foundations of behavior therapy*. New York: Plenum Press.

Feldman, M. P., & Broadhurst, A. (Eds.). (1976). *Theoretical and experimental bases of the behaviour therapies*. London: John Wiley & Sons.

Franks, C. M. (1984). *New developments in behavior therapy: From research to clinical application*. Binghamton, NY: Haworth Press.

Franks, C. M., & Rosenbaum, M. (1983). Behavior therapy: Overview and personal reflections. In M. Rosenbaum, C. M. Franks, & Y. Jaffe (Eds.), *Perspectives in behavior therapy in the eighties* (pp. 3–14). New York: Springer.

Franks, C. M., & Wilson, G. T. (1975). *Annual Review of Behavior Therapy: Theory and Practice, 3*, New York: Brunner/Mazel.

Franks, C. M., & Wilson, G. T. (Eds.). (1982). *Contemporary behavior therapy: Conceptual and empirical foundations*. New York: Guilford Press.

Gambrill, E. D. (1977). *Behavior modification: Handbook of assessment, intervention and evaluation*. San Francisco: Jossey-Bass.

Glasgow, R. E., & Rosen, G. M. (1978). Behavioral bibliotherapy: A review of self-help behavior therapy manuals. *Psychological Bulletin, 85*, 1–23.

Glasgow, R. E., & Rosen, G. M. (1979). Self-help behavior therapy manuals: Recent developments and clinical usage. *Clinical Behavior Therapy Review, 1*, 1–20.

Glasgow, R. E., & Rosen, G. M. (1984). Self-help behavior therapy manuals: recent developments and clinical usage. In C. M. Franks (Ed.), *New developments in behavior therapy: From research to clinical application* (pp. 525–570). Binghamton, NY: Haworth Press.

Goldfried, M. R. (1980). Toward the delineation of therapeutic change principles. *American Psychologist, 35*, 991–999.

Goldfried, M. R. (1982). On the history of therapeutic integration. *Behavior Therapy, 13*, 572–593.

Goldfried, M. R., & Davison, G. C. (1976). *Clinical behavior therapy*. New York: Holt, Rinehart & Winston.

Goldstein A., & Foa, E. B. (Eds.). (1980). *Handbook of*

behavioral interventions: A clinical guide. New York: John Wiley & Sons.

Greenspoon, J., & Lamal, P. (1978). Cognitive behavior modification: Who needs it? *Psychological Record, 28,* 343–357.

Hayes, S. C., Rincover, A., & Solnik, J. V. (1980). The technical drift of applied behavior analysis. *Journal of Applied Behavior Analysis, 13,* 272–285.

Hersen, M., & Bellack, A. S. (Eds.). (1985). *Handbook of clinical behavior therapy with adults.* New York: Plenum Press.

Kanfer, F. H. (1972). Assessment for behavior modification. *Journal of Personality Assessment, 36,* 418–423.

Kazdin, A. E. (1978). *History of behavior modification: Experimental foundations of contemporary research.* Baltimore, MD: University Park Press.

Kazdin, A. E., & Hersen, M. (1980). The current status of behavior therapy. *Behavior Modification, 4,* 283–302.

Kazdin, A. E., & Wilson, G. T. (1978). *Evaluation of behavior therapy: Issues, evidence and research strategies.* Cambridge, MA: Ballinger.

Kendall, P. C., & Hollon, S. D. (Eds.). (1979). *Cognitive-behavioral interventions: Theory research and procedures.* New York: Academic Press.

Krasner, L. (1971). Behavior therapy. *Annual Review of Psychology, 22,* 483–532.

Krasner, L. (1976). On the death of behavior modification: Some comments from a mourner. *American Psychologist, 31,* 387–388.

Krasner, L. (1982). Behavior therapy: On roots, contexts, and growth. In G. T. Wilson & C. M. Franks (Eds.), *Contemporary behavior therapy: Conceptual and Empirical foundations* (pp. 11–62). New York: Guilford Press.

Lazarus, A. A. (1958). New methods of psychotherapy: A case study. *South African Medical Journal, 32,* 660–663.

Lazarus, A. A. (1971). *Behavior therapy and beyond.* New York: McGraw-Hill.

Lazarus, A. A. (1977). Has behavior therapy outlived its usefulness? *American Psychologist, 32,* 550–554.

Ledwidge, B. (1978). Cognitive behavior modification: A step in the wrong direction? *Psychological Bulletin, 85,* 353–375.

Levis, D. J. (1982). Experimental and theoretical foundations of behavior modification. In A. S. Bellack, M. Hersen, & A. E. Kazdin (Eds.), *International handbook of behavior modification and therapy* (pp. 33–56). New York: Plenum Press.

Lindsley, O. R., Skinner, B. F., & Solomon, H. C. (1953). *Studies in behavior therapy* (Status report I). Waltham, MA: Metropolitan State Hospital.

Locke, E. A. (1969). Purpose without consciousness: A contradiction. *Psychological Reports, 25,* 991–1009.

Locke, E. A. (1971). Is "behavior therapy" behavioristic? (An analysis of Wolpe's psychotherapeutic methods). *Psychological Bulletin, 76,* 318–327.

London, P. (1983). Science, culture, and psychotherapy: The state of the art. In M. Rosenbaum, C. M. Franks, & Y. Jaffe (Eds.), *Perspectives on behavior therapy in the eighties* (pp. 17–32). New York: Springer.

Mahoney, M. J. (1974). *Cognition and behavior modification.* Cambridge, MA: Ballinger.

Mahoney, M. J. (1980). Psychotherapy and the structure of personal revolutions. In M. J. Mahoney (Ed.), *Psychotherapy process* (pp. 157–180). New York: Plenum Press.

Mahoney, M. J. (1986). Personal knowing processes. In P. Eelen & O. Fontaine (Eds.), *Behavior therapy: Beyond the conditioning framework* (pp. 48–58). Leuven/Hillsdale, NJ: Leuven University Press and Lawrence Erlbaum Associates.

Martin, P. R. (1985). Trends in behaviour therapy: Progression or regression? *Behaviour Change, 2,* 119–128.

Martin, P. R. (1989). The scientist-practitioner model and clinical psychology: Time for change? *Australian Psychologist, 24,* 71–92.

Mash, E. J. (1974). Has behaviour modification lost its identity? *Canadian Psychologist, 15,* 271–280.

Meichenbaum, D. H. (1974). *Cognitive behavior modification.* Morristown, NJ: General Learning Press.

Meichenbaum, D., & Gilmore, J. B. (1984). The nature of unconscious processes: A cognitive-behavioral perspective. In K. S. Bowers & D. Meichenbaum (Eds.), *The unconscious reconsidered.* New York: John Wiley & Sons.

Moroz, M. (1972). The concept of cognition in contemporary psychology. In J. R. Royce & W. M. Rozeboom (Eds.), *The psychology of knowing* (pp. 177–214). New York: Gordon & Breach.

O'Leary, K. D. (1984). The image of behavior therapy: It is time to take a stand. *Behavior Therapy, 15,* 219–233.

O'Leary, K. D., & Carr, E. G. (1982). Childhood disorders. In G. T. Wilson & C. M. Franks (Eds.), *Contemporary behavior therapy: Conceptual and empirical foundations* (pp. 445–504). New York: Guilford Press.

O'Leary, K., & Wilson, G. T. (1987). *Behavior therapy: Application and outcome* (2nd ed.). Englewood Cliffs, NJ: Prentice-Hall.

Pinkerton, S. S., Hughes, H., & Wenrich, W. W. (1982). *Behavioral medicine: Clinical applications.* New York: John Wiley & Sons.

Pomerleau, O. F., & Brady, J. P. (1979). *Behavioral medicine: Theory and practice.* Baltimore, MD: Williams & Wilkins.

Reiss, S., & Bootzin, R. R. (Eds.). (1985). *Theoretical issues in behavior therapy.* Orlando, FL: Academic Press.

Rimm, D. C., & Masters, J. C. (1979). *Behavior therapy: Techniques and empirical findings* (2nd ed.). New York: Academic Press.

Ross, A. O. (1985). To form a more perfect union: It is time to stop standing still. *Behavior Therapy, 16,* 195–204.

Skinner, B. F. (1950). Are theories of learning necessary?

Psychological Review, 57, 193–216.
Swan, G. E., & MacDonald, M. L. (1978). Behavior therapy in practice: A national survey of behavior therapists. *Behavior Therapy, 9,* 799–807.
Thoresen, C. E. (1973). Behavioral humanism. In C. E. Thoresen (Ed.), *Behavior modification in education* (pp. 385–421). Chicago: University of Chicago Press.
Tuma, J. M., & Cohen, R. (1981). *Pediatric psychology: An investigation of factors relative to practice and training.* Unpublished manuscript, Louisiana State University, Baton Rouge.
Turner, S. M., Calhoun, K. S., & Adams, H. E. (Eds.). (1981). *Handbook of clinical behavior therapy.* New York: John Wiley & Sons.
Wachtel, P. L. (1977). *Psychoanalysis and behavior therapy.* New York: Basic Books.
Wandersman, A., Poppen, P. J., & Ricks, D. F. (Eds.), (1976). *Humanism and behaviorism: Dialogue and growth.* Elmsford, NY: Pergamon Press.
Wilson, G. T. (1978). On the much discussed nature of the term "behavior therapy". *Behavior Therapy, 9,* 89–98.
Wilson, G. T. (1982a). Adult disorders. In G. T. Wilson & C. M. Franks (Eds.), *Contemporary behavior therapy: Conceptual and empirical foundations* (pp. 505–562). New York: Guilford Press.
Wilson, G. T. (1982b). Psychotherapy process and procedure: The behavioral mandate. *Behavior Therapy, 13,* 291–312.
Wolpe, J. (1958). *Psychotherapy by reciprocal inhibition.* Stanford: Stanford University Press.
Wolpe, J. (1968). Presidential message. *Newsletter of the Association for Advancement of Behavior Therapy, 3,* 1–2.
Wolpe, J. (1969). *The practice of behavior therapy.* Elmsford, NY: Pergamon Press.
Yates, A. J. (1970). *Behavior therapy.* New York: John Wiley & Sons.
Yates, A. J. (1975). *Theory and practice in behavior therapy.* New York: John Wiley & Sons.
Zajonc, R. (1980). Feeling and thinking. *American Psychologist, 35,* 151–175.

PART I
DEVELOPMENTAL PSYCHOLOGY

CHAPTER 2

TOWARD THE INTEGRATION OF HUMAN DEVELOPMENTAL AND THERAPEUTIC CHANGE

Richard M. Lerner
Laura E. Hess
Katherine Nitz

Therapeutic strategies and/or human developmental interventions are predicated on the belief that human functioning is flexible, and that the processes involved in human change are plastic or malleable ones (Kendall, Lerner, & Craighead, 1984; Lerner, 1984). However, the changes studied and/or sought by interventionists are, at least in part, influenced by another type of individual change: development. As such, any attempt to design and implement interventions should of necessity deal with the topic of development (Lerner, Hess, & Nitz, in press; Lerner & Tubman, in press). Development, however, is a complex concept.

While development always involves change, not all changes are developmental ones. Typically, developmentalists reserve the term *development* for application only to particular sets or types of changes. The specific changes considered developmental vary in relation to different philosophical and theoretical positions or, in other words, models of development. Historically, definitions of development have been derived from "organismic" and "mechanistic" models (Lerner, 1976, 1986; Overton & Reese, 1973; Reese & Overton, 1970). The organismic model is associated with conceptions of development that stress: (a) movement towards a final end-state (i.e., teleology), and (b) the predetermined bases (usually hereditary or maturation in character) of developmental changes (e.g., Erikson, 1959; Freud, 1949; Gesell, 1946). The mechanistic model is associated with approaches to development that stress: (a) the primacy of organism–extrinsic (e.g., environmental) determinants of behavior, and (b) elementaristic influences (e.g., S–R units) which, through continuous, quantitative additions, shape behavior. These influences may be either proximal environmental events (e.g., conditioning processes; Bijou & Baer, 1961) or distal, macrosociological institutional effects (Meyer, 1988).

Developmental psychology has seen increasing criticism of conceptions of development associated with organismic and mechanistic models, especially

---

The writing of this chapter was supported in part by a grant to Richard M. Lerner and Jacqueline V. Lerner by the William T. Grant Foundation and by NIMH Grant MH39957.

over the last two decades. For instance, organismic conceptions have been criticized for: philosophical problems associated with teleology (Nagel, 1957), and accordingly with a nonempirically supportable belief in unidirectionality in development (Baltes, 1987; Lerner & Kauffman, 1985); an empirically inappropriate rigid, nonplastic view of biological processes (Gollin, 1981; Gottlieb, 1970, 1983; Lerner, 1984; Tobach & Schneirla, 1968); a lack of needed attention to social, cultural, and historical variations in development (e.g., Bronfenbrenner, 1977, 1979); and an inappropriately pessimistic, too limited view of the potential for intervention to alter undesired or maladaptive behavior patterns (Baltes & Baltes, 1980; Brim & Kagan, 1980; Lerner, 1984).

In turn, mechanistic conceptions have been criticized for: a philosophical and theoretical elementarism and reductionism that have been inadequate to deal with qualitative changes across life (Piaget, 1950; von Bertalanffy, 1933, 1969); an inability to deal with phenomena at multiple levels of analysis (Riegel, 1975, 1976); and an inattention to the active, constructivist role of the person in his or her own development (Lerner, 1982; Lerner & Busch-Rossnagel, 1981; Liben, 1981).

Because of the philosophical, theoretical, and empirical problems with conceptions of development associated with the organismic and the mechanistic models, increasing attention has been given to other models, for example, dialectical and contextual ones (Lerner, Hultsch, & Dixon, 1983). Developmentalists have considered conceptions of development associated with these latter models (e.g., Dixon, 1986; Riegel, 1976). In addition, some developmentalists have forwarded conceptions involving integrations of ideas associated with two or more models (e.g., Overton, 1984). These latter, integrative efforts have attempted to overcome limitations of the respective models when they are employed separately. Through a synthesis of selected features of each model, attempts have been made to develop a potentially more useful concept of development.

Of increasing prominence over the last two decades has been an integrative perspective—developmental contextualism—involving a synthesis of the active organism in organicism and the active context in contextualism. This perspective, emphasizing the relation between person and context, conceives of development as involving systematic, successive, and "aptive" (Gould & Vrba, 1982) changes within and across all life periods in the structure, function, and/or content of the person's mental (e.g., cognitive, emotional), behavioral (e.g., activity level, threshold of responsivity), and interpersonal/social (e.g., approach–withdrawal, institutional affiliational) characteristics (Lerner, 1984; Lerner & Lerner, 1983). (Following Gould and Vrba [1982] we use the term "aptive" to describe changes that allow the organism to meet the demands of its context, instead of the more usual term "adaptive." The prefix "ad" in adaptive indicates that the changes have been shaped by natural selection to allow the developing organism to fit its environment. We do not necessarily make any inferences about the evolutionary shaping of the changes across ontogeny, which we study; thus, we use the more neutral term "aptive.").

This conception of development has direct import for understanding the development of both aptive and malaptive human functioning across the life span. From a developmental contextual perspective, malaptive behavior exists and develops when, and only when, an inadequate *relation* exists between psychological and social functioning, that is, between an individual and his or her context.

We should emphasize that this relational, developmental contextual view is compatible with those of other developmentalists studying malaptive functioning (e.g., Cicchetti, 1984, 1987; Harkness & Super, in press; Magnusson, 1987; Magnusson & Oehman, 1987; Super, 1987; Wapner & Demick, 1988; see too Lerner et al., in press, for another presentation of the present authors' perspective). To illustrate, Cicchetti (1987), writing about psychopathology during human infant development, notes:

> It is inappropriate to focus on discrete symptomatology to infer the presence of nascent or incipient infant psychopathology. Rather, disorders in infancy are best conceptualized as *relational psychopathologies*, that is, as consequences of dysfunction in the parent-child-environment system. (p. 837)

A similar stress on the relational and developmental contextual character of maladjustment is made by Super (1987), who considers "disorders of development as a class of phenomena that reveal something of the nature of our children and also of the nature of the worlds we make for them" (p. 2). Indeed, he notes that:

> The settings, customs, and psychology of caretakers not only regulate the healthy emergence of human potential, they also shape the possibilities of disorder. At every stage of the etiology, expression, course, intervention, and final outcome of developmental problems, human culture structures the experience and adjusts the odds. (Super, 1987, p. 7)

In a corresponding vein, Oehman and Magnusson (1987) indicate that:

> Any disease must be understood as resulting from a multiplicity of causal events spanning observational levels from biochemistry to sociology. Thus, any single-factor, linear causal model is unrealistic for understanding disease in general, and mental disorders in particular. Instead, multiple interacting causal factors that often change in their effect over time must be postulated (p. 18) (see, too, Magnusson, 1987; Magnusson & Allen, 1983; Super & Harkness, 1982, 1986).

Given, then, the apparent prominence of ideas pertinent to a developmental contextual perspective for understanding development across the life span and, for present purposes, the pertinence of this perspective for intervening to optimize human functioning across the life span, it is useful to discuss the features of developmental contextualism.

DEVELOPMENTAL CONTEXTUAL PERSPECTIVE

An interest in the context of human development has a long history in philosophy and social science (for reviews see Dixon & Nesselroade, 1983; Kaplan, 1983). Contextualist philosophy (Pepper, 1942) was conceived of as an orientation that considered the import for human functioning of multiple, qualitatively distinct levels of existence—ranging from the individual through the sociocultural—all changing historically (Lerner et al., 1983). This philosophy began to attract increasing interest from psychologists during the late 1960s (e.g., see Bandura, 1978; Bronfenbrenner, 1977, 1979; Jenkins, 1974; Kuo, 1967; Mischel, 1977; Rosnow, 1983; Rosnow & Georgoudi, 1986; Rosnow & Rosenthal, 1984; Sarbin, 1977). One basis for this interest was the growing theoretical and empirical literature which suggested that it was necessary to forego an exclusively psychological analysis of individual development, and instead seek explanations which emphasize the multilevel bases of human functioning *and* the connections among levels (e.g., Baltes, 1987; Bronfenbrenner, 1979; Elder, 1975; Kuo, 1967; J. Lerner, 1983; Lerner, 1984; Lerner & Busch-Rossnagel, 1981; Novikoff, 1945a, 1945b; Magnusson & Allen, 1983; Tobach, 1981; Tobach & Greenberg, 1984).

Levels, in this literature, are conceived of as integrative organizations. That is:

> The concept of integrative levels recognizes as equally essential for the purpose of scientific analysis both the isolation of parts of a whole and their integration into the structure of the whole. It neither reduces phenomena of a higher level to those of a lower one, as in mechanism, or describes the higher level in vague nonmaterial terms which are but substitutes for understanding, as in vitalism. Unlike other "holistic" theories, it never leaves the firm ground of material reality. . . . The concept points to the need to study the organizational interrelationships of parts and whole. (Novikoff, 1945a, p. 209)

Moreover, Tobach and Greenberg (1984) stress that:

> The interdependence among levels is of great significance. The dialectic nature of the relationship among levels is one in which lower levels are subsumed in higher levels so that any particular level is an integration of preceding levels. . . . In the process of integration, or fusion, *new* levels with their own characteristics result. (p. 2)

If the course of human development is the product of the processes involved in the "fusions" (or "dynamic interactions;" Lerner, 1978, 1979, 1984) among integrative levels of functioning, then the processes of development are more plastic than often previously believed (cf. Brim & Kagan, 1980). That is, because the process of development is seen as emerging from individually distinct interactions between a changing person and his or her changing context, there exist multiple pathways (or potential person–context combinations) along which development may proceed.

To a great extent the developmental literature that suggests these ideas has been associated with the life span view of human development (e.g., Baltes, 1987; Brim & Kagan, 1980; Featherman, 1983; Hetherington, Lerner, & Perlmutter, 1988; R. Lerner, 1984; Lerner et al., 1983; Sorensen, Weinert, & Sherrod, 1986). Within this perspective, the context for development is not seen merely as a simple stimulus environment, but rather as an "ecological environment . . . conceived topologically as a nested arrangement of concentric structures, each contained within the next" (Bronfenbrenner, 1979, p. 22) and including variables from biological, psychological, physical, and sociocultural levels, all changing interdependently across history (Riegel, 1975, 1976). This life span, ecological conception of development raised by developmental contextualism underscores the point made above regarding the relational nature of psychopathology: Behavior, either functional or malfunctional, develops as a consequence of historically and socioculturally moderated relations between people and their contexts. Thus, a temporal perspective is requisite for the understanding of psychopathology, given this historical embeddedness. As a consequence, both conceptually and methodologically a longitudinal approach to the study of psychopathology is necessary in order to capture the temporality of psychopathological phenomena.

Not only must this longitudinal perspective encompass the life span, because change (history) is ceaseless, but it must be comparative as well. Comparisons must be made to nonpsychopathological developments, because both pathological and nonpathological developments are of the "same clothe", differing only in the person–context relational characteristics involved. In addition, comparisons must be made with other contextual conditions (e.g., proximal ones, such as family types, versus more distal ones, such as cultural mores), because such contextual conditions represent an important source of variation into the human psychosocial system (Magnusson & Oehman, 1987). Finally, the longitudinal perspective central to this set of ideas requires an age–comparative perspective, one which, as noted, involves the entire life span. From a developmental contextual perspective one must ask what person variables (e.g., what biological attributes), in relation to what contextual variables (e.g., what family types, educational systems, or cultural standards), at what age levels (e.g., childhood, adolescence, adulthood) are associated with particular instances of pathological or nonpathological behaviors?

The longitudinal, life span perspective associated with developmental contextualism leads to a concern with issues of the relations between evolution and ontogeny (given the idea of historical embeddedness); of life course constancy and change, of human plasticity (given the person–context relational character of development); and of the role the developing person plays in his or her own development (given the concern with the active organism and of its relation to an active context) (Baltes, 1987; Lerner, 1982; Lerner & Busch-Rossnagel, 1981; Scarr & McCartney, 1983; Tobach, 1981). These issues are linked by the idea that reciprocal relations (i.e., dynamic interactions; R. Lerner, 1978, 1979) between individuals and the multiple contexts within which they live characterize human development (Bronfenbrenner, 1979). Thus, the issues raised by this perspective are derived from a common appreciation of the basic role of the changing context in developmental change. It is the functional significance of this changing context that requires adoption of what Gottlieb (1970, 1983) termed a "probabilistic epigenetic" view of an organism's development.

Features of Probabilistic Epigenetic Development

Since its inception as a specialization within the discipline, developmental psychology—or, as it was initially termed, "genetic psychology" (e.g., Hall, 1904)—has been dominated by a biological model of change. Indeed, the concept of development is biological in its scientific origin (Harris, 1957; von Bertalanffy, 1933). Although the particular version of biological change that has influenced developmental psychology has been and remains Darwinian in character (White, 1968), this common heritage has nevertheless led to the formulation of quite diverse models of development (Dixon & Lerner, 1988). For instance, both the mechanistic conceptions of developmental change (e.g., Bijou, 1976; Bijou & Baer, 1961) and the organismic ones (e.g., Freud, 1949) noted earlier may be interpreted as derived from this Darwinian heritage (Dixon & Lerner, 1988).

However, despite this range of interpretations of the contribution of biology to psychological development, the organismic versions have been predominant in developmental psychology, and in fact have been termed "strong" developmental models (e.g., Reese & Overton, 1970). Thus, to the field of psychology in general, and perhaps to the scholarly community as a whole, the organismic theories of Freud (1949), Erikson (1959), and Piaget (1950) are typically held to be the classic, prototypic, or exemplary ones within developmental psychology (e.g., see Emmerich, 1968; R. Lerner, 1976, 1986).

These instances of organismic theory, especially those of Freud and of Erikson, have been labeled *predetermined epigenetic* (Gottlieb, 1983). As indicated, in this type of theory biology is seen as the prime mover of development: Intrinsic (e.g., maturational) changes are seen to essentially unfold, and although environmental or experiential variables may speed up or slow down these progressions they can do nothing to alter the sequence or quality (e.g., the structure) of these hereditarily predetermined changes (e.g., see Gesell, 1946; Hamburger, 1957).

However, another view of biological functioning exists, one which sees biological and contextual factors as reciprocally interactive; as such, developmental changes are probabilistic in respect to normative outcomes, due to variation in the timing of the biological, psychological, and social factors that provide interactive bases of ontogenetic progressions (e.g., Schneirla, 1957; Tobach, 1981). It is this *probabilistic epigenetic* (Gottlieb, 1983) view of development that is represented by the developmental contextual perspective and provides the theoretical underpinning of the life span view of human development (R. Lerner & Kauffman, 1985).

In essence, a probabilistic epigenetic formulation emphasizes not the intrinsically predetermined or inevitable time tables and outcomes of development; instead, such a formulation stresses that the influence of the changing context on development is to make the trajectory of development less certain with respect to the applicability of norms to the individual (Gottlieb, 1970, 1983; Tobach, 1981). Thus, such a conception emphasizes the probabilistic character of development and in so doing admits of more plasticity in development than do predeterministic conceptions. Indeed, the term *probabilistic epigenesis* was used by Gottlieb:

> To designate the view that the behavior development of individuals within a species does not follow an invariant or inevitable course, and, more specifically, that the sequence or outcome of individual behavioral development is probable (with respect to norms) rather than certain. (Gottlieb, 1970, p. 123)

Moreover, Gottlieb explains that this probable, and not certain, character of individual development arises because:

> Probabilistic epigenesis necessitates a bidirectional structure-function hypothesis. The conventional version of the structure-function hypothesis is unidirectional in the sense that structure is supposed to determine function in an essentially nonreciprocal relationship. . . . The bidirectional version of the structure-function relationship is a logical consequence of the view that the course and outcome of behavioral epigenesis is probabilistic: It entails the assumption of reciprocal effects in the relationship between structure and function whereby function (exposure to stimulation and/or movement of musculoskeletal activity) can significantly modify the development of the peripheral and central structures that are involved in these events. (Gottlieb, 1970, p. 123)

This bidirectional relation between structure and function denoted by the concept of probabilistic epigenesis implies that a developmental contextual perspective promotes a very dynamic view of the nature of organism–context relations. Given the bidirectionality involved in developmental contextualism, a general assumption is that the functional significance of behavior and of any particular developmental trajectory lies neither in the organism nor in the context; rather, it is the nature of the relation, of the interaction, between person and context that establishes the meaning for aptation of any given behavior or developmental pattern. As we have noted already, this conception indicates that neither aptive nor malaptive functioning are attributes of either people or contexts. Rather, it is the nature of the interaction between these two elements of the human psychosocial system that provides a given behavior with its functional significance. The developmental contextual notion of interaction is, therefore, quite an important one to consider.

The Role of "Interaction" in Developmental Contextualism

A developmental contextual perspective captures the complexity of a multilevel context: (1) without ignoring the active role of the organism in shaping, as well as being shaped by, the context; and (2) without sacrificing commitment to useful prescriptive, universal principles of developmental change. These two foci are integrated within the contextual orientation at the level of the presumed *relation* between organismic and contextual processes. The developmental contextual conceptualization of this relation differs substantially from those of the organismic and mechanistic perspectives (R. Lerner, 1985). That is, a *strong* concept of organism–environment interaction (Lerner & Spanier, 1978, 1980; Overton, 1973), transaction (Sameroff, 1975), or dynamic interaction (R. Lerner, 1978, 1979) is associated with probabilistic epigenesis. As suggested earlier, this version of interaction stresses that organism and context are always embedded in each other (Lerner et al., 1983), that the context is composed of multiple levels changing interdependently across time (i.e., historically), and that because organisms influence the context that influences them, they are efficacious in playing an active role in their own development (Lerner & Busch-Rossnagel, 1981; Tobach, 1981).

Moreover, because of the mutual embeddedness of organism and context, a given organismic attribute will have different implications for developmental outcomes in the milieu of different contextual conditions. This relationship arises because the organismic attribute is only given its functional meaning by virtue of its relation to a specific context. If the context changes significantly, as it may over time, then the same organismic attribute will have a different import for development. Embedded in one social context, a psychopathological condition may develop; yet in another contextual situation, the same organismic characteristics may result in healthy or aptive psychological development. In turn, the same contextual condition will lead to alternative developments when different organisms interact with it. Stating this position in stronger terms, a given organismic attribute only has meaning for psychological development by virtue of its timing of interaction, i.e., its relation to a particular set of time-bound, contextual conditions. In turn, the import of any set of contextual conditions for psychosocial behavior and development can only be understood by specifying the context's relations to the specific, developmental features of the organisms within it. This central role for the timing of organism–context interactions in the determination of the nature and outcomes of development is, of course, the probabilistic component of probabilistic epigenesis (Gottlieb, 1970; Kuo, 1967; Scarr, 1982; Scarr & McCartney, 1983; Tobach, 1981). But, what does such probabilism mean for the ways in which individuals can, through influencing their context, produce their own development? More important, for the ultimate worth of the developmental contextual view of development and, for present purposes, for conceptualizing and implementing therapeutic interventions, we may ask what such probabilism means for the empirical study of malaptive or psychopathological behavior.

To address these issues we reiterate that taking the probabilistic character of development seriously means focusing on the *relation* between organism and context and not on either element in the relation per se. The context enveloping a person is composed of, for example, a specific physical ecology and the other individually different and developing people with whom the person interacts (e.g., parents and peers). This context is as unique and changing as is the person lawfully, individually distinct as a consequence of his or her particular genotype–environment interaction history. One cannot say completely in advance what particular features of the context will exist at a specific time in a given person's life. As a consequence, it is only possible to speak probabilistically of the effects that a given person may have on his or her context; of the feedback the person is likely to receive from the context; and of the nature of the person's development that will therefore ensue.

Thus, the probabilism of development represents a formidable challenge for theory and research. To gain understanding of how people may influence their own development, and of their relations to a changing, multilevel context, we obviously need to do more than just have a conceptualization of the nature of individual characteristics or processes. In addition, we need to conceptualize and operationalize the features of the context, or of the ecology, wherein significant interactions occur for the person. Next, we must devise some means, or model, by which personological and contextual features can be integrated. Then a last—and by no means unidimensional—task is to translate all this conceptualization into methodologically sound, longitudinal research.

There is no laboratory within which all the preceding tasks have been fully accomplished. However, progress has been made in developing models that begin to address such tasks. Data pertinent to the models derive from work in several laboratories, and in presenting the general features of some of these models, some of this research is noted. The findings from this research underscore quite clearly the relational and comparative features of the development of psychopathology about which we have spoken.

PERSON-CONTEXT INTERACTION IN DEVELOPMENTAL CONTEXTUALISM

Both life span developmental and ecological developmental psychologists have described several intraindividual, interindividual, familial, social network, sociocultural, and historical variables presumed to be involved in the dynamic interactional processes described within developmental contextualism (e.g., Baltes, 1987; Bronfenbrenner, 1979; Featherman & Lerner, 1985; R. Lerner, 1984; Riegel, 1976; Schneirla, 1957). The resulting view of the range of the variables involved in development and of complexity of interrelations among them, is—to say the least—formidable. Figure 2-1 is a good representation of the integrated and interdependent, that is, dynamically interactive, levels of organization first spoken of by Novikoff (1945a, 1945b), developed further by Schneirla and his collaborators (e.g., Lehrman, 1970; Tobach, 1981; Tobach & Schneirla, 1968; Schneirla, 1956, 1957), and elaborated within developmental psychology by proponents of the life span perspective (e.g., Baltes, 1987; Featherman, 1983, 1985; R. Lerner, 1976, 1984, 1986; R. Lerner & Kauffman, 1985).

To illustrate the empirical use in the extant developmental literature of the conception of integrative,

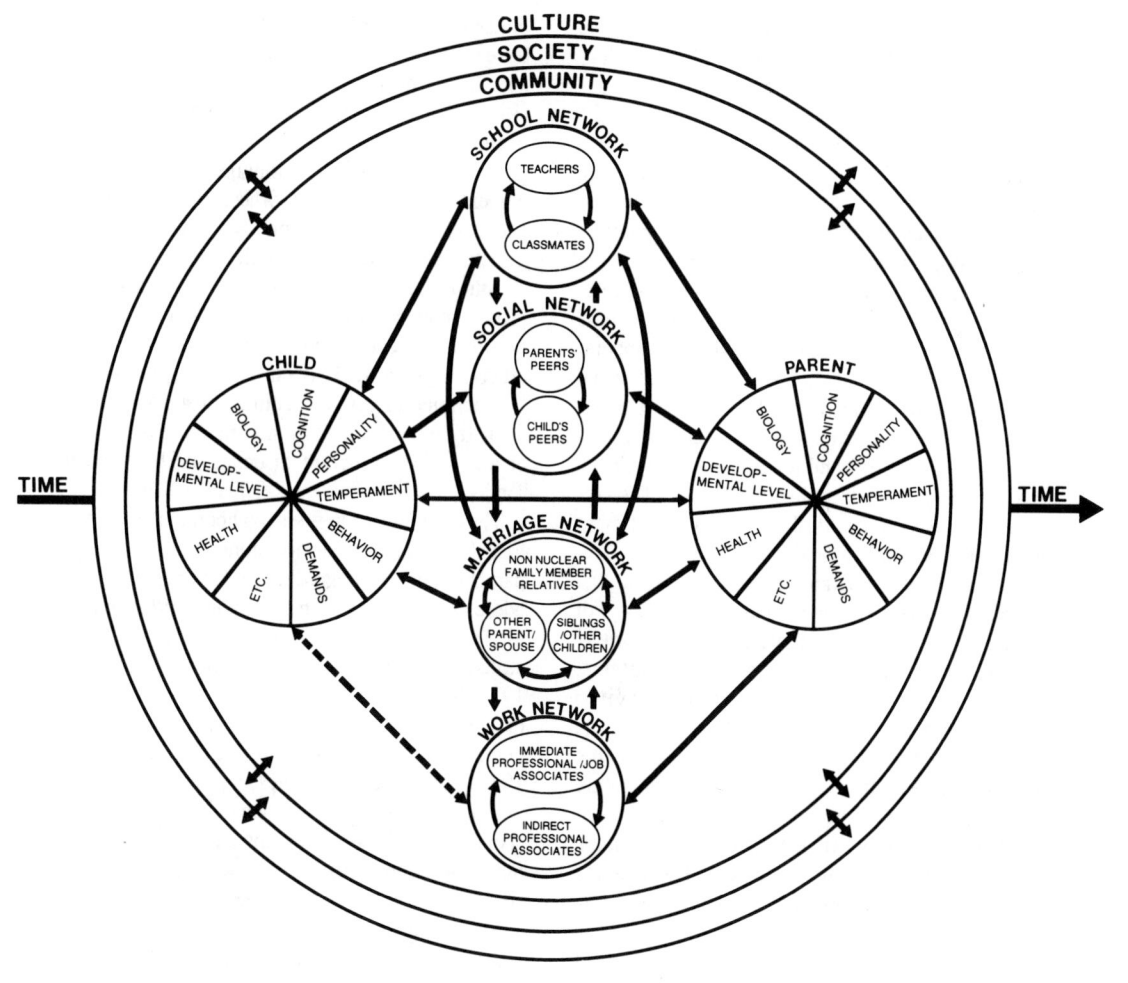

Figure 2.1. A dynamic interactional model of child and parent development (Lerner, 1986).

dynamically interactive levels depicted in Figure 2–1, let us draw on two examples of pertinence to developmentalists; one involves characteristics of behavioral individuality, in regard to behavioral style or temperament, and the other involves characteristics of physical individuality, in regard to physical maturation and physical attractiveness. In regard to temperament, the child development literature contains studies examining the relation, within-the-child, between temperament and other characteristics of individuality, such as personality (Buss & Plomin, 1975) or cognitive status variables (such as "social referencing"; Campos, 1980-81; Feinman & Lewis, 1983). In turn, other studies examine how the child's temperamental individuality influences the parent—typically the mother-child relationship (Crockenberg, 1981) and/or the mother's emotional adjustment (Brazelton, Koslowski, & Main, 1974). Such studies provide data constituting "child effects" on their significant others—others that, to developmental psychologists (Belsky et al., 1984), represent a component of the child's context, here an interpersonal one. These studies comprise one portion of the bidirectional effects (child⟶parent) discussed in the child development literature (e.g., Bell, 1974; Belsky, 1984; Belsky et al., 1984; Lerner & Spanier, 1978; Lewis & Rosenblum, 1974; Scarr & McCartney, 1983).

These child⟶parent studies contrast those that examine how parental characteristics—such as temperament (Thomas, Chess, & Birch, 1970), demands or expectations placed on the child regarding the child's temperament (Thomas, Chess, Sillan, & Mendez, 1974), or cognitive status (e.g., stage of cognitive development; Sameroff, 1975)—influence the child; such studies are parent⟶child ones, and provide the other direction of effect to complement child⟶parent studies. Other studies in the temperament literature examine the influence of the parent's social network on the child's temperament, on the mother's characteristics, or on the parent-child relationship (e.g., Crockenberg, 1981); in turn, some studies examine how children with different temperaments "produce" different responses in their social (e.g., school) network (East, Lerner, & Lerner, 1988). Still other studies examine how child-temperament ⟷ parent-demand relationships vary in relation to their embeddedness in different social classes or communities (Thomas et al., 1974) or in different cultural settings (Super & Harkness, 1981).

Together, these temperament studies indicate that the relation between a given temperament attribute of the child (e.g., sleep arrhythmicity or high activity level) and problem behaviors or, in the extreme, psychopathology is not universal. In turn, any given feature of the context (e.g., particular family types; such as authoritarian or permissive ones) are also not linked invariably to disorders. Instead, this literature indicates that the presence of psychopathology depends on the relation between particular temperament attributes and such contextual factors as: The meaning or interpretation of temperament maintained by a child's parents or teachers (Thomas & Chess, 1977); the demands or expectations regarding temperament prevalent in a given societal or cultural setting (Super & Harkness, 1981); the social support network within which the child-mother relation is embedded (Crockenberg, 1981); and the parent's pattern of embeddedness in nonfamilial social interactions (e.g., as occurs with mothers employed outside the home; J. Lerner & Galambos, 1985).

To illustrate the representation of the developmental contextual perspective found in Figure 2-1 in regard to characteristics of physical individuality, let us focus on a variable—menarche—that has been a central one in the study of biological-psychosocial interrelations in early adolescence (Brooks-Gunn & Petersen, 1983; Hamburg, 1974; Petersen, 1983; Ruble, 1977; Ruble & Brooks-Gunn, 1982). The adolescent developmental literature contains studies examining the relation, within-the-person, of menarche (e.g., whether it occurs early, on time, or late) and other characteristics of individuality, for example, perceptions of self (Tobin-Richards, Boxer, & Petersen, 1983), cognition (Hamburg, 1974; Petersen, 1983), or the experience of menstrual discomfort (Brooks-Gunn & Ruble, 1980). In turn, other studies examine how the occurrence of menarche influences a girl's relations with the significant others in her context (for example, with her parents and/or her peers) (e.g., Brooks-Gunn & Matthews, 1979; Lynch, 1981; Simmons, Blyth, & McKinney, 1983; Westney, Jenkins, & Benjamin, 1983). Such studies provide data constituting "adolescent effects" on that portion of their social context composed of significant others, and as such comprise one portion of the bidirectional effects (here an adolescent ⟶ social context one) discussed in this literature (e.g., Belsky et al., 1984; Lerner & Spanier, 1978; Petersen & Taylor, 1980).

These "adolescent ⟶ social context" studies contrast those that examine how contextual features—like parental demands regarding desired behavior in their adolescent children (e.g., Anthony, 1969; Windle et al., 1986), continuities or discontinuities in school structure (Blyth, Simmons, & Bush, 1978; Hamburg, 1974; Simmons, Blyth, Van Cleave, & Bush, 1979), or cultural beliefs regarding menstruation (Brooks-Gunn & Ruble, 1980; Ruble & Brooks-Gunn, 1979)—influence the adolescent undergoing the biopsychosocial transition of menarche. Such studies are social context ⟶ adolescent ones, and provide the other direction of effect to complement the adolescent ⟶ social context one.

Still other studies in the adolescent development literature examine how adolescent menarche ⟷ social context relations (e.g., in regard to adolescents and their peers) vary in relation to their embeddedness in more molar levels of the context, such as different social classes (e.g., Hamburg, 1974; Simmons, Brown, Bush, & Blyth, 1978), cultures (Hamburg, 1974; R. Lerner, Iwawaki, Chihara, & Sorell, 1980; Mussen & Bouterline-Young, 1964; Paige, 1983), or historical eras (Elder, 1974).

The import of these studies in regard to developmental contextualism is that an attribute of biological/physical individuality—as represented by menarche—does not exert a direct link to problematic or disordered behaviors. Rather, whether such a linkage exists depends on contextual conditions. For example, when a female adolescent undergoes a transition in social institutions (e.g., from elementary school to junior high school) at the same time she is experiencing menarche she is at enhanced risk for low self-esteem and for a diminution in academic performance

(Simmons et al., 1979, 1987). In turn, when a girl experiencing menarche is in a particular type of peer group (an athletically competitive one, as compared to an athletically noncompetitive one) she is at greater risk for eating disorders (Brooks-Gunn, 1987). Finally, when the adolescent is embedded in a culture having a negative belief system regarding the meaning of menarche, she is at greater risk for experiencing dysmenorrhea (Ruble & Brooks-Gunn, 1982).

In summary, several of the interrelations illustrated in the model in Figure 2–1 are found in the extant literature on behavioral and physical individuality. Whereas relatively few of the studies in this literature assess both directions of relation between one component (or level) of the model and another (cf. Bell, 1974; Lewis & Lee-Painter, 1974), the bidirectionality of relations discussed in this literature (e.g., Bell, 1974; Belsky et al., 1984; Lerner & Spanier, 1978; Lewis & Rosenblum, 1974) emerges when studies are integrated within a representation like the one presented in Figure 2–1. Furthermore, by helping to integrate extant studies of the person–context relational character of development, the model also points to other instances of such relations that have not been investigated but that may be of potential importance.

This use of the model for furthering research points out other features of the model that should be stressed. It probably would not be useful or even possible to do research testing the model as a whole. Instead, this or similar representations (e.g., Baltes, 1987) of person–context relations can guide the selection of individual and ecological variables in one's research, and provide parameters for generalizing about one's findings. That is, this representation should serve as a reminder that we need to consider whether the results of a given study may be generalized beyond the particular individual and ecological variable studied herein and applied to other community, societal, cultural, and historical contexts.

To illustrate how the model of Figure 2–1 can be used as a guide for selecting variables from the individual and contextual levels depicted (i.e., the interpersonal and physical features of the settings within which one lives), we show how our research is based on selected components of the model. Figure 2–2 shows the "restricted" or "reduced" model used in our research on individual context relations.

The studies we conducted have focused on how the demands regarding characteristics of behavioral or physical individuality (e.g., temperament or physical attractiveness, respectively) held by a child's or an adolescent's parents, teachers, or peers are associated with different levels of aptation, or adjustment, among children with various repertoires of temperamental individuality or characteristics of physical attractiveness (e.g., East, Lerner, & Lerner, 1988; J. Lerner, 1983; Lerner, Lerner, & Zabski, 1985; Lerner, Delaney, Hess, Jovanovic, & von Eye, 1988; Lerner, Lerner, Jovanovic, Schwab, Talwar, Hess, & Kucher, 1988; Talwar, Nitz, Lerner, & Lerner, 1988; Talwar, Schwab, & Lerner, 1988; Windle et al., 1986). The rationale for this focus comes from our interest in testing a model derived from the conception of integrated, dynamically interactive levels represented in Figure 2–1. It is termed the *goodness-of-fit* model and provides a useful link between the study of human development and the practice of intervening to improve or enhance human functioning throughout the life span. It is useful, then, to turn to a presentation of this model.

THE GOODNESS OF FIT MODEL OF ORGANISMIC INDIVIDUALITY–SOCIAL CONTEXT RELATIONS

Although several different theoretical models associated with the developmental contextual perspective exist, one model has received extensive attention within psychology, education, and psychiatry. This notion—the goodness-of-fit model of person–context relations—is derived from the view that the person–context interactions depicted within developmental contextualism involve "circular functions" (Schneirla, 1957). These functions are person–context relations predicated on others' reactions to a person's characteristics of individuality: As a consequence of their characteristics of physical and behavioral individuality people evoke different reactions in their significant others; these reactions constitute feedback to people and influence their further interactions (and thus their ensuing development). The goodness-of-fit concept allows the valence of the feedback involved in these circular functions to be understood (Lerner & Lerner, 1983, 1987; Thomas & Chess, 1977).

It is through the establishment of such functions in ontogeny that people may be conceived of as producers of their own development (Lerner & Busch-Rossnagel, 1981). However, this circular functions idea needs to be extended. In and of itself the notion is mute regarding the specific characteristics of the feedback (for example, its positive or negative valence) a child will receive as a consequence of its individuality. What provides a basis for the feedback?

Just as a child brings his or her singular character-

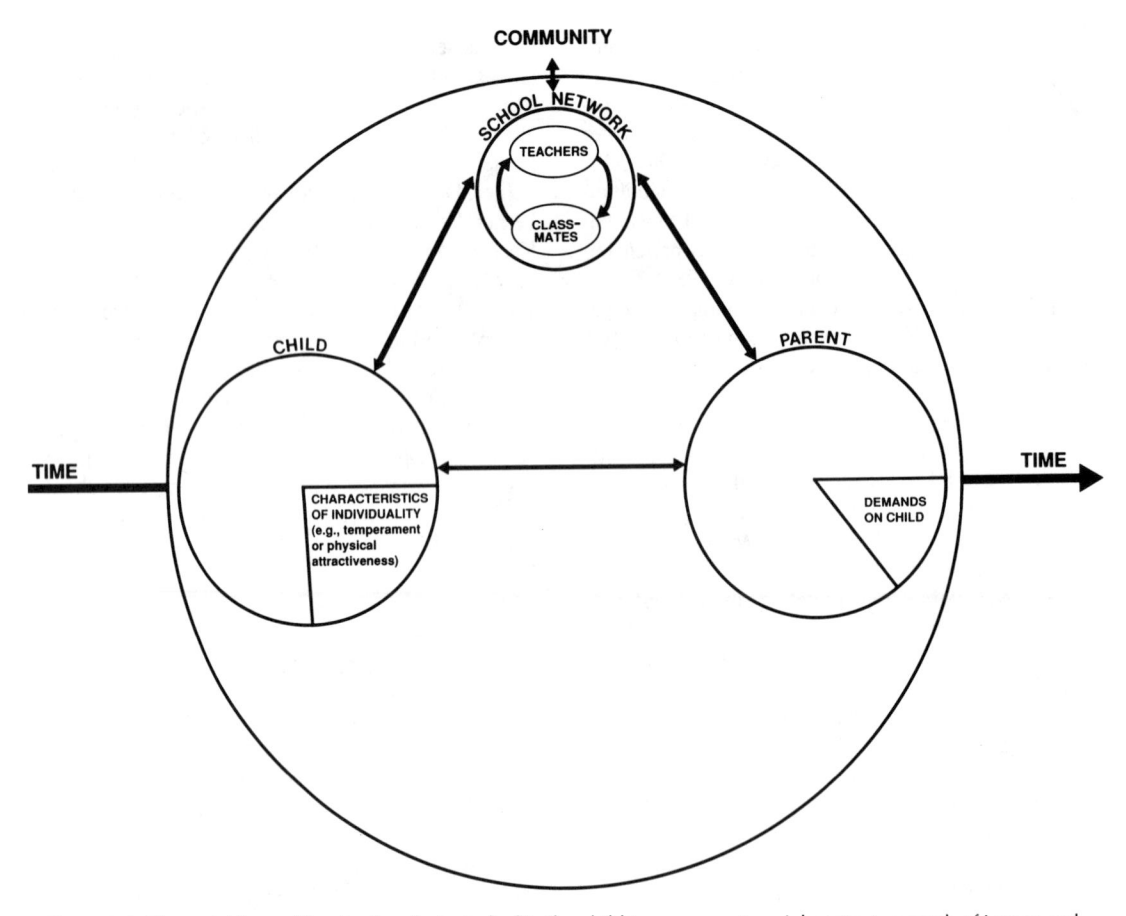

Figure 2.2. The variables and levels of analysis studied in the child temperament–social context research of Lerner and Lerner (1987).

istics to a particular social setting, there are demands placed on the child by virtue of the physical and/or by the social components (i.e., by the significant others) in the setting (Lerner & Lerner, 1983). According to Super and Harkness (1981), the developing person's context is structured by three kinds of influences: The physical and social setting; culturally regulated customs involved in socialization; and the "psychology" of the caregivers or the other significant people with whom the developing person interacts. This psychology is termed an *ethnotheory* (Super & Harkness, 1980, 1981, 1988), that is, significant others' beliefs, attitudes, expectations, or values regarding the meaning or significance of particular behaviors. Together, the three types of influence comprise the *developmental niche* of a person, that is, the set (or sets) of structured demands on the developing person (Super & Harkness, 1981). It is these demands that provide the functional significance for a given characteristic of individuality; if congruent with the demands of a significant other (e.g., a parent), this characteristic should produce a positive adjustment (aptation). If that same attribute is incongruent with such demands, a negative adjustment would be expected.

To illustrate, consider the case of the child in a family context and of the psychosocial and physical climate promoted by the parents. Parents can vary in their cognitive and behavioral attributes (e.g., in regard to their child-rearing attitudes and parenting styles; Baumrind, 1971); parents can vary, too, in the physical features of the home they provide. These parent-based psychosocial and physical characteristics constitute presses for, or demands on, the child for adaptation. Simply, parent characteristics are "translated" or "transduced" into demands on the child.

The child's individuality in differentially meeting

these demands provides a basis for the feedback he or she receives from the socializing environment. For example, considering the demand "domain" of attitudes, values, or expectations, teachers and parents may have relatively individual and distinct expectations about behaviors desired of their students and children, respectively. Teachers may want students who show little distractibility, because they do not want attention diverted from a lesson by the activity of children in the classroom. Parents, however, might desire their children to be moderately distractible—for example, when they require their children to move from television watching to the dinner table or to bed. Children whose behavioral individuality was either generally distractible or generally not distractible would thus differentially meet the demands of these two contexts.

Similarly, Parke (1978) has argued that the attitudes, values, and expectations for behavior held by a child's significant others represent a highly important basis for interaction. According to Parke (1978), the same behavior from a child may have a very different meaning in various settings, and this difference may reflect the demand structure of the context, a structure comprised in part of attitudes, values, and expectations. Thus, attitudes, values, or expectations about particular child behaviors—or, in the terms of Super and Harkness (1981), the ethnotheory about particular behaviors—represent one set of contextual demands to which children must adjust if they are to successfully meet the challenges present in their world. In other words, problems of adjustment to school demands or to home demands might develop as a consequence of a child's lack of match, or goodness-of-fit, in either or both settings.

There is both laboratory and clinical evidence that supports the use of the goodness-of-fit model for understanding the bases of healthy and unhealthy developmental patterns, and for designing intervention strategies aimed at optimizing person-context relations across the life span. Thus, we turn now to a review of this literature.

Tests of the Goodness-of-Fit Model

Much of the research literature supporting the use of the goodness-of-fit model is derived either directly from the Thomas and Chess (1977) New York Longitudinal Study (NYLS) of the functional significance of temperament, or is associated with independent research that has adopted their conceptualization of temperament. Temperament in this literature has been conceived of as behavioral style—that is, how a child does whatever it does (Thomas & Chess, 1977). For example, because all children engage in eating, sleeping, and toileting behaviors, the absence or presence of such contents of the behavior repertoire would not differentiate among them. But whether these behaviors occur with regularity (i.e., rhythmically), or with a little or a lot of intensity might serve to differentiate among children. We consider first the contribution of the NYLS data set.

The NYLS

Within the NYLS data set, information relevant to the goodness-of-fit model exists as a consequence of the multiple samples present in the project. First, the NYLS core sample is composed of 133 white, middle-class children of professional parents. This sample, which was studied originally in 1956, is still being followed at this writing. In addition, a sample of 98 New York City Puerto Rican children of working-class parents has been followed for about 14 years. Each sample subject was studied from at least the first month of life onward. Although the distribution of temperamental attributes in the two samples was not different, the import of the attributes for psychosocial adjustment was quite disparate. Two examples may suffice to illustrate this distinction.

First to be considered is the impact of low regularity or rhythmicity of behavior, particularly in regard to sleep-wake cycles. The Puerto Rican parents studied by Thomas and Chess (1977; Thomas, Chess, Sillan & Mendez, 1974) were very permissive. No demands in regard to rhythmicity of sleep were placed on the infant or child. Indeed, the parents allowed the child to go to sleep any time the child desired, and permitted the child to awaken any time as well. The parents molded their schedule around the children. Because the parents were so accommodating, there were no problems of fit associated with an arrhythmic infant or child. Indeed, neither within the infancy period nor throughout the first 5 years of life did arrhythmicity predict adjustment problems. In this sample arrhythmicity remained continuous and independent of aptive implications for the child (Korn, 1978; Thomas et al., 1974).

In white, middle-class families, however, strong demands for rhythmic sleep patterns were maintained. Thus, an arrhythmic child did not fit with parental demands, and consistent with the goodness-of-fit model, arrhythmicity was a major predictor of problem behaviors both within the infancy years and across time through the first 5 years of life (Korn, 1978; Thomas et al., 1974).

It should be emphasized that there are at least two ways of viewing this finding. First, consistent with the idea that children influence their parents, it may be noted that sleep arrhythmicity in their children resulted in problems in the parents [e.g., reports of stress, anxiety, anger (Chess & Thomas, 1984; Thomas et al., 1974)]. Such an effect of child temperament on the parent's own level of adjustment has been reported in other data sets wherein, for instance, infants who had high thresholds for responsiveness to social stimulation and thus were not soothed easily by their mothers evoked intense distress reactions in their mothers and a virtual cessation of maternal caregiving behaviors (Brazelton et al., 1974). Therefore, it is possible that the presence of such child effects in the NYLS sample could have altered previous parenting styles in a way that constituted feedback to the child that was associated with the development of problem behaviors in him/her.

In turn, a second interpretation of this finding arises from the fact that problem behaviors in the children were identified initially on the basis of parent reports. It may be that irrespective of any problem behavior evoked in the parent by the child and/or of any altered parent–child interactions that thereby ensued, one effect of the child on the parent was to increase the probability of the parent labeling the child's temperamental style as problematic and reporting it to the NYLS staff psychiatrist. Unfortunately, the current state of analysis of the NYLS data does not allow us to discriminate between these obviously nonmutually exclusive possibilities.

However, the data in the NYLS do allow us to indicate that the parents in the middle-class sample took steps to change their arrhythmic children's sleep patterns; and as most of these arrhythmic children were also adaptable, low rhythmicity tended to be discontinuous for most children. That the parent behaved to modify their child's arrhythmicity is also an instance of a child effect on its psychosocial context. That is, the child "produced" in his or her parents alterations in parental care-giving behaviors regarding sleep. That these "child effects" on the parental context fed back to the child and influenced his or her further development is consistent with the finding above that sleep arrhythmicity was discontinuous among these children.

Thus, in the middle-class sample early infant arrhythmicity tended to be a problem during this time of life but proved to be neither continuous nor predictive of later problems of adjustment. In turn, in the Puerto Rican sample, infant arrhythmicity was not a problem during this time of life but was continuous and—because in this context it was not involved in poor fit—was not associated with adjustment problems in the child in the first five years of life. Of course, this is not to say that the parents in the Puerto Rican families were not affected by their children's sleep arrhythmicity; as was the case with the parents in the middle-class families, it may be that the Puerto Rican parents had problems of fatigue and/or suffered marital or work-related problems due to irregular sleep patterns produced in them as a consequence of their child's sleep arrhythmicity. However, the current nature of data analysis in the NYLS does not allow an investigation of this possible "child effect" on the Puerto Rican parents.

Yet, the data do underscore the importance of considering fit with the demands of the psychosocial context of development by indicating that arrhythmicity did begin to predict adjustment problems for the Puerto Rican children when they entered the school system. Their lack of a regular sleep pattern interfered with their obtaining sufficient sleep to perform well in school and, in addition, often caused them to be late to school (Korn, 1978; Thomas et al., 1974). Thus, before age 5 only one Puerto Rican child presented a clinical problem diagnosed as a sleep disorder. However, almost 50% of the Puerto Rican children who developed clinically identifiable problems between ages 5 and 9 were diagnosed as having sleep problems.

Another example may be given to illustrate how the differential demands existing between the two family contexts provide different presses for aptation. This example pertains to differences in the demands of the physical contexts of the families.

As noted by Thomas et al. (1974), as well as by Korn (1978), overall there was a very low incidence of behavior problems in the Puerto Rican sample children in their first five years of life, especially when compared to the corresponding incidence among the core sample children. However, if a problem was presented at this time among the Puerto Rican sample it was most likely to be a problem of motor activity. In fact, across the first nine years of their lives, of those Puerto Rican children who developed clinical problems, 53% were diagnosed as exhibiting problematic motor activity. Parents complained of excessive and uncontrollable motor activity in such cases. However, in the core sample's clinical group only one child (a child with brain damage) was characterized in this way. It may be noted here that the Puerto Rican parents' reports of "excessive and uncontrollable" activity in their children does constitute, in this group, an example of a child effect on the parents. That is, a major value of the Puerto Rican parents in the NYLS was child "obedience" to authority (Korn, 1978). The type of motor activity shown by the highly active children of these parents evoked considerable distress in them, given their perception that their children's behavior was inconsistent with what would be expected of obedient children (Korn, 1978).

Of course, if the middle-class parents had seen their children's behavior as excessive and uncontrollable, it may be that—irrespective of any major salience placed on the value of child obedience—problems would have been evoked in the middle-class parents, and feedback to the child, derived from such an evocation, would have ensued. Thus, an issue remains as to why the same (high) activity level should evoke one set of appraisals among the Puerto Rican parents but another set among the middle-class parents (i.e., in the latter group no interpretation of "excessive and uncontrollable" behavior was evoked). Similarly, it may be asked why high activity level is highly associated with problem behavior in the Puerto Rican children and not in the middle-class children. The key information needed to address these issues may be related to the *physical* features of the respective groups' homes.

In the Puerto Rican sample the families usually had several children and lived in small apartments. Even average motor activity tended to impinge on others in the setting. Moreover, and as an illustration of the embeddedness of the child-temperament–home-context relation in the broader community context (see Figures 2–1 and 2–2), it may be noted that even in the case of the children with high activity levels, the Puerto Rican parents were reluctant to let their children out of the apartment because of the actual danger of playing on the streets of East Harlem. In the core sample, however, the parents had the financial resources to provide large apartments or houses for their families. There were typically suitable play areas for the children both inside and outside the home. As a consequence, the presence of high activity levels in the homes of the core sample did not cause the problems for interaction that they did in the Puerto Rican group. Thus, as Thomas et al. (1968, 1974) emphasize, the mismatch between temperamental attribute and physical environmental demand accounted for the group difference in the import of high activity level for the development of behavioral problems in the children.

In sum, data from the NYLS are not fully consonant with the methodology required for a direct and complete test of the goodness-of-fit model. For example, measures of temperament were not directly related to measures of the context. However, in spite of such limitations, the NYLS data set provides results compatible with the goodness-of-fit model. One may conclude from the NYLS data that it is the relation between individual and context which provides opportunities for and/or constraints on the development of aptive or malaptive behaviors. Data independent of the NYLS, from our own laboratory, lend additional support to this conclusion.

Research from the Lerner and Lerner laboratory

J. Lerner, R. Lerner, and their students, have tested the goodness-of-fit model quite extensively, and this work has been summarized in several articles and chapters (e.g., Lerner, 1984; Lerner & Lerner, 1983; Lerner & Lerner, 1987, 1989; Lerner et al., 1986; Windle & Lerner, 1986; Windle et al., 1986). Here, then, are some recent findings derived from the Lerner and Lerner Pennsylvania Early Adolescent Transitions Study (PEATS), a short-term longitudinal study of approximately 150 northwestern Pennsylvania early adolescents, studied from the beginning of sixth grade across the transition to junior high school and to the end of the seventh grade.

In one study derived from the PEATS, East, Lerner, and Lerner (1988) determined the overall fit between adolescents' temperament and the demands of their peers regarding desired levels of temperament. Based on the circular functions notion involved in the goodness-of-fit model, East et al. predicted that while no significant direct paths would exist between adjustment and either temperament, measured alone, or temperament–demands fit, fit would influence adolescent–peer social relations which, in turn, would influence adjustment. In short, significant mediated paths, but insignificant direct paths, were expected. These expectations were supported. For 9 of the 12 measures of adjustment employed (involving parents' ratings of behavior problems; teachers' ratings of scholastic competence, social acceptance, athletic competence, conduct adequacy, and physical appearance; and students' self-ratings of scholastic competence, social acceptance, athletic competence, conduct adequacy, physical appearance, and self-worth), both of the two mediated paths (between adolescent–peer group fit and peer relations, and then between peer relations and adjustment) were significant; in no case, however, was a significant direct path found. Figure 2–3 presents diagrammatically one representa-

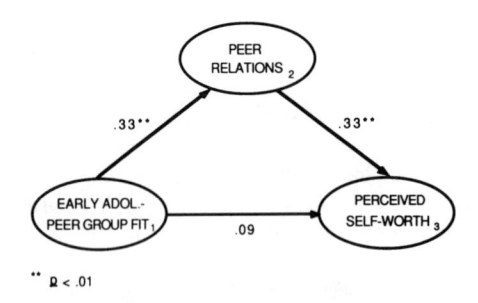

Figure 2.3. Path analysis of early adolescent-peer group fit, peer relations, and perceived self-worth. Higher scores reflect a good fit, positive peer relations, and favorable perceived self-worth.

tive finding, involving the adjustment outcome of self-rated (or perceived) self-worth, from the East et al. (1988) study.

Nitz, Lerner, Lerner, and Talwar (in press) found similar results regarding temperamental fit with parental demands and adolescent adjustment. Although at the beginning of sixth grade the number of significant relations between the adjustment measures and temperament–demands fit did not exceed the number of significant relations between temperament alone and adjustment, at both the middle and the end of sixth grade the percentage of significant relations between fit and adjustment scores was significantly greater than the corresponding percentages involving temperament alone. Moreover, and underscoring the interconnections among the child–family relation and the other key contexts comprising the ecology of human development, Nitz et al. found virtually interchangeable results when fit scores with the peer demands were considered.

In a related study, Talwar, Nitz, Lerner, and Lerner (1988) found that poor fit with parental demands (especially in regard to the attributes of mood and approach-withdrawal) at the end of sixth grade was associated in seventh grade with low teacher-related academic and social competence and negative peer relations. Corresponding relations were found in regard to fit with peer demands. Moreover, and again underscoring the importance of considering the context within which organismic characteristics are expressed, goodness-of-fit scores (between temperament and demands) were more often associated with adjustment than were temperament scores alone; this was true in regard to both peer and parent contexts at the end of sixth grade, and for the peer context after the transition to junior high school (at the beginning of seventh grade). Finally, Talwar et al. grouped the PEATS subjects into high vs. low overall fit groups. Adolescents in the low fit group in regard to peer demands received lower teacher ratings of scholastic competence, and more parent ratings for conduct and school problems, than did the adolescents in the high fit group in regard to peer demands. Comparable findings were found in regard to groups formed on the basis of low versus high fit with parent demands.

In a related temperament study, Talwar, Schwab and Lerner (1988) assessed whether the links among temperament and the PEATS subjects' academic competence, as indexed by Grade Point Average (GPA) and by standardized achievement test scores on the California Achievement Test, Form C (CAT/C), are (1) direct ones; or (2) are mediated by social appraisals (by the teacher) of the adolescent's scholastic competence and by the adolescent's appraisal of his/her own scholastic competence. From a developmental contextual perspective, these latter links would be expected to be significant. In turn, however, within a personological, acontextual view of temperament-psychosocial functioning relations (Plomin & Daniels, 1984; Sheldon, 1940, 1942) only a direct link (or path) between temperament and academic competence should exist.

Talwar et al. used data from the end of the sixth grade and the end of the seventh grade to test these alternative models of the functional significance of temperament. In addition to the adolescents' self-ratings of temperament several other measures of the adolescents were used. Their grade point averages for the sixth and for the seventh grades; their total CAT/C scores for the sixth grade; teachers' ratings of the subjects' scholastic competence, on the Teacher Behavior Rating Scale (Harter, 1983); and the subjects' ratings of their scholastic competence, on the Harter (1983) Self Perception Profile, were involved in these data analyses.

For the purpose of data reduction, the nine temperament variables measured on the Revised Dimensions of Temperament Survey (DOTS-R; Windle & Lerner, 1986) were first factor analyzed. Three second-order factors emerged. Factor one was labelled *Task Rhythmicity*, and was composed of the four DOTS-R attributes of task-orientation and rhythmicity in eating, in sleeping, and in daily habits. The second factor was labelled *Activity*, and was composed of the two DOTS-R attributes of sleep activity level and of general activity level. The third factor was labelled *Adaptation*, and was composed of the three DOTS-R attributes of flexibility, approach behaviors, and positive mood.

Analyses subsequent to this factor analysis resulted in corresponding findings for all three of the above-noted temperament factors. For instance, the temperament factor of Adaptation was correlated significantly with GPA and CAT/C scores at the end of sixth grade and with GPA at the end of seventh grade. However, these correlations were *not* found to be the outcome of the direct influence of Adaptation on academic competence. Using the path analytic procedures illustrated in Figure 2–4, Talwar et al. compared: (1) the direct link between temperament and academic competence; with (2) the indirect paths that included the teacher's rating of scholastic competence and the adolescent's self conception of his/her scholastic functioning. The data indicated that there were no significant paths between Adaptation and either GPA or CAT/C scores. However, significant paths were found between this temperament factor, teacher ratings, self ratings, and GPA and CAT/C scores at the end of sixth grade. Corresponding findings involving GPA occurred at the end of seventh grade. In respect to the Task Rhythmicity and the Activity factors, indirect paths were also found between these factors, adolescent self-ratings, and the outcome measures of GPA and CAT/C scores. As with the Adaptation factor, no direct paths were found between these latter two temperament factors and either GPA and CAT/C scores at either grade level.

These findings, then, lend further support to the developmental contextual view of the nature of the relation between adolescent temperament and psychological characteristics: Links between temperament and adjustment are contingent on the character of the prevalent temperament-context relations. Positive adjustment ensues from good person-context fits; negative adjustment follows from poor fits.

Moreover, to illustrate that support for the developmental contextual, goodness-of-fit model is not limited to temperamental individuality, we note some findings from the PEATS related to the functional implications of characteristics of physical individuality, specifically physical attractiveness. Lerner et al. (1990) found that the circular functions component of the goodness-of-fit model was supported in regard to links between physical attractiveness (PA) and academic achievement. Based on the presence of a "what is beautiful is good" stereotype (Langlois, 1986), teachers were expected to differentially evaluate adolescents who differed on PA. These different evaluations should influence the achievements of adolescents and their self-evaluations of their academic competence; these self-perceptions should, in turn, influence achievement. In both cases, however, it was expected that these indirect paths between PA and achievement would be significant whereas direct paths between PA and achievement would not. The results of Lerner et al. (1990) confirm these expectations in respect to the two indices of achievement noted above, grade point average and the standardized achievement test scores on the CAT/C. These findings are illustrated in Figures 2–5 and 2–6, in respect to GPA and CAT/C scores, respectively.

Given this support for the developmentally contex-

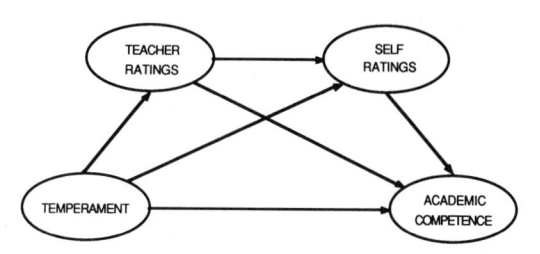

Figure 2.4. The path model linking temperament, teacher ratings, self ratings, and academic competence used in the Talwar, Schwab, and Lerner (1988) study.

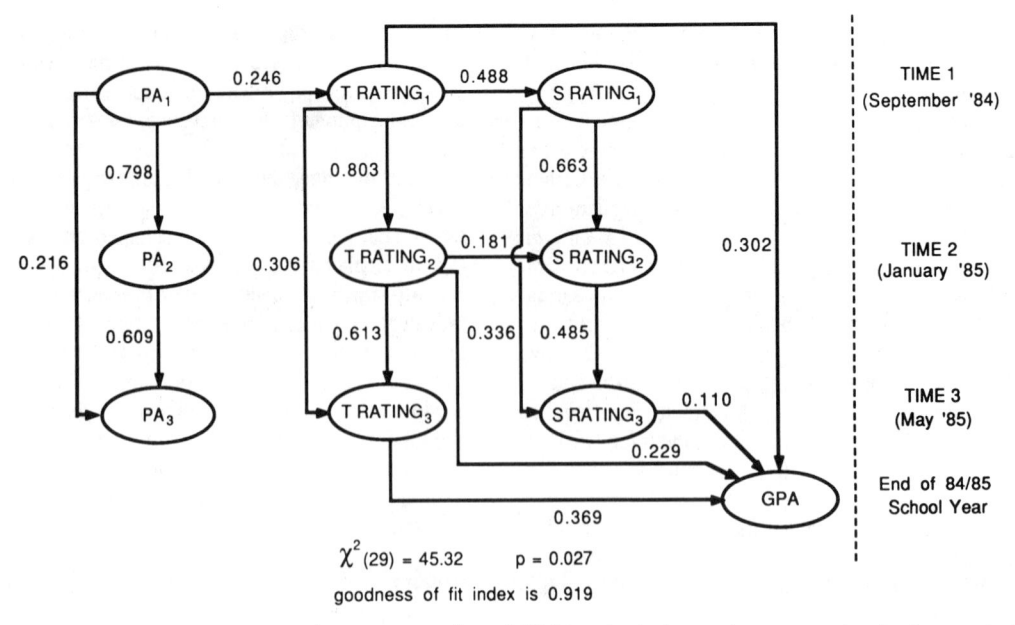

Figure 2.5. Developmental contextual perspective path model linking physical attractiveness, teachers' ratings, and self ratings, measured at three points in time, and grade point average (all paths are significant) (Lerner et al., 1988).

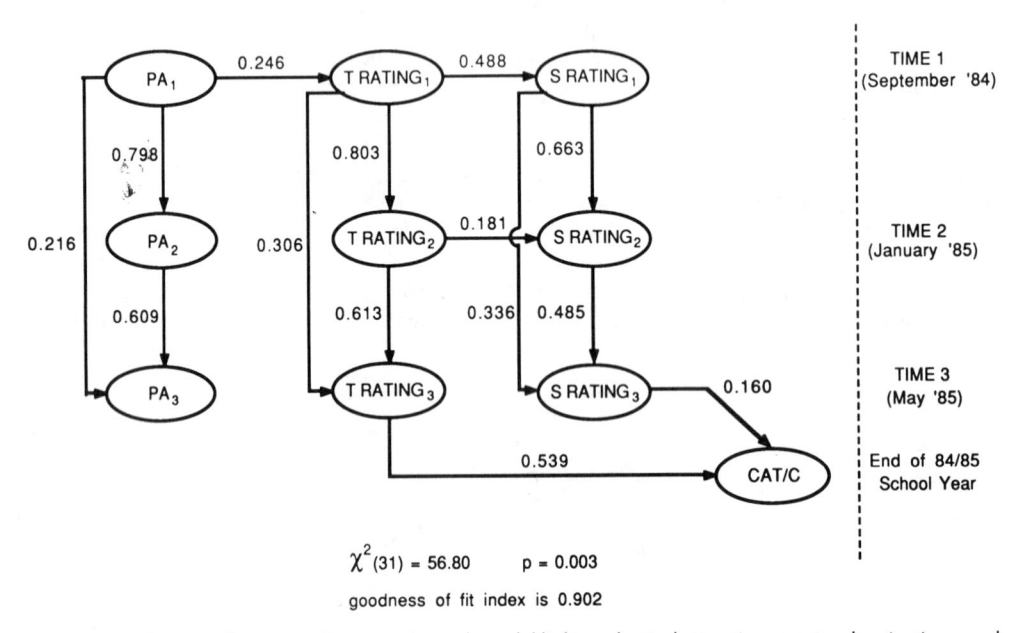

Figure 2.6. Developmental contextual perspective path model linking physical attractiveness, teachers' ratings, and self ratings, measured at three points in time, and achievement test scores (all paths are significant) (Lerner et al., 1988).

tually derived goodness-of-fit model, as well as the support found in other studies from our laboratory (e.g., see J. Lerner, 1984; Lerner & Lerner, 1983; Lerner & Lerner, 1987, 1989, it is useful to make some final statements regarding the future role of ideas associated with this approach for fostering a productive synthesis between developmental and clinical psychologists.

CONCLUSIONS

The concepts of person, context, and of the relations between the two found in a probabilistic epigenetic, developmental contextual perspective are, as a set quite complex ones, ones that impose formidable challenges on those who seek to understand the developmental bases of psychopathology and of nonpsychopathologic behavior; to derive feasible research from this perspective; and to use this conception and its associated research for the design and implementation of interventions. As we have argued, this developmental contextual perspective leads to an integrated, multilevel concept of development, one in which the focus of inquiry is the organism–environment dynamic interaction. Furthermore, such an orientation places an emphasis on the potential for intra-individual change in structure and function—for plasticity—across the life span.

As Kendall et al. (1984) note, plasticity provides the basis of interventions, and indeed makes such efforts rational. Thus, it is crucial that interventionists attempt to understand how individual behavioral attributes, as well as contextual demands regarding these attributes, change across a person's life span. Such understanding will facilitate the design of therapeutic strategies aimed at helping individuals: (1) be more flexible; (2) change themselves to meet new contextual presses; and/or (3) change the context to better meet their own objectives. In other words, interventions should provide individuals with the necessary skills to actively create a good fit for themselves, and thus enhance their own development.

We believe that the integration of a developmental contextual perspective into the design and implementation of therapeutic interventions has important implications for the advancement of both developmental psychology and clinical practice. As pointed out by Kendall et al. (1984):

> Interventionists will come to understand better why their techniques do not have equipotentiality across life and how one portion of life circumscribes possibilities for change in succeeding ones. On the other hand, developmentalists will come to recognize that the prototypic developmental course is more open to change than previously or generally thought and that, because of the plasticity of human developmental processes, the potential for substantial flexibility remains present for more of life than previously believed.
>
> Together, developmentalists and interventionists may contribute to clarifying a major issue in psychology today, the issue of constancy and change over the life course (Brim & Kagan, 1980). From such collaboration we may come to know better the conditions under which we observe constancy and under which we see or precipitate change, and we may learn how we can best balance these two ubiquitous features of life to improve the human condition. (p. 79)

In sum, a future including the sort of integration we have suggested should enrich greatly our understanding of the precise conditions promoting and constraining the development of both adjusted and maladjusted functioning. In addition, such integration should further our abilities to conceptualize and develop interventions designed to ameliorate malaptive person–context relations, both as they exist concurrently at the time of intervention and in the future development of the person. Given then, the present literature, and the promise we see for tomorrow, we believe there is reason for great optimism about the future use of the developmental contextual view of person–context relations for both scientific and clinical purposes.

REFERENCES

Anthony, J. (1969). The reaction of adults to adolescents and their behavior. In G. Caplan & S. Lebovici (Eds.), *Adolescence: Psychological perspectives* (pp. 54–78). New York: Basic Books.

Baltes, P. B. (1987). Theoretical propositions of life-span developmental psychology: On the dynamics between growth and decline. *Developmental Psychology, 23,* 611–626.

Baltes, P. B., & Baltes, M. M. (1980). Plasticity and variability in psychological aging: Methodological and theoretical issues. In G. E. Gurski (Ed.), *Determining the effects of aging on the Central Nervous System* (pp. 41–60). Berlin: Schering AG, (Oraniendruck).

Bandura, A. (1978). The self system in reciprocal determinism. *American Psychologist, 33,* 344–358.

Baumrind, D. (1971). Current patterns of parental authority. *Developmental Psychology Monographs, 4* (No. 1, Part 2).

Bell, R. Q. (1974). Contributions of human infants to caregiving and social interaction. In M. Lewis & L. A. Rosenblum (Eds.), *The effect of the infant on its caregiver* (pp. 1–20). New York: John Wiley & Sons.

Belsky, J. (1984). The determinants of parenting: A process model. *Child Development, 55,* 83–96.

Belsky, J., Lerner, R., & Spanier, G. (1984). *The child in the family.* Reading, MA: Addison-Wesley.

Bijou, S. W. (1976). *Child development: The basic stage of early childhood.* Englewood Cliffs, NJ: Prentice-Hall.

Bijou, S. W., & Baer, D. M. (1961). *Child development: A systematic and empirical theory* (Vol. 1). New York: Appleton-Century-Crofts.

Blyth, D. A., Simmons, R. G., & Bush, D. (1978). The transition into early adolescence: A longitudinal comparison of youth in two educational contexts. *Sociology of Education, 51,* 149–162.

Brazelton, T. B., Koslowski, B., & Main, M. (1974). The origins of reciprocity: The early mother–infant interaction. In M. Lewis & L. A. Rosenblum (Eds.), *The effect of the infant on its caregivers* (pp. 49–76). New York: John Wiley & Sons.

Brim, O. G., Jr., & Kagan, J. (Eds.). (1980). *Constancy and change in human development.* Cambridge, MA: Harvard University Press.

Bronfenbrenner, U. (1977). Toward an experimental ecology of human development. *American Psychologist, 32,* 513–531.

Bronfenbrenner, U. (1979). *The ecology of human development.* Cambridge, MA: Harvard University Press.

Brooks-Gunn, J. (1987). Pubertal processes and girls' psychological adaptation. In R. M. Lerner & T. T. Foch (Eds.), *Biological-psychosocial interactions in early adolescence: A life-span perspective* (pp. 123–153). Hillsdale, NJ: Lawrence Erlbaum Associates.

Brooks-Gunn, J., & Matthews, W. S. (1979). *He and she: How children develop their sex role identity.* Englewood Cliffs, NJ: Prentice-Hall.

Brooks-Gunn, J., & Petersen, A. C. (Eds.). (1983). *Girls at puberty: Biological and psychosocial perspectives.* New York: Plenum Press.

Brooks-Gunn, J., & Ruble, D. N. (1980). Menarche: The interaction of physiology, cultural, and social factors. In A. J. Dan, E. A. Graham, & C. P. Beecher (Eds.), *The menstrual cycle: A synthesis of interdisciplinary research* (pp. 141–159). New York: Springer.

Buss, A. H., & Plomin, R. (1975). *A temperament theory of personality development.* New York: John Wiley & Sons,

Campos, J. J. (1980–81). Human emotions: Their new importance and their role in social referencing. *Annual Report for the Research and Clinical Center for Child Development.* Sapporo, Japan: Hokkaido University, Faculty of Education.

Chess, S., & Thomas, A. (1984). *The origins and evolution of behavior disorders: Infancy to early adult life.* New York: Brunner/Mazel.

Cicchetti, D. (1984). The emergence of developmental psychopathology. *Child Development, 55,* 1–7.

Cicchetti, D. (1987). Developmental psychopathology in infancy: Illustration from the study of maltreated youngsters. *Journal of Consulting and Clinical Psychology, 55,* 837–845.

Crockenberg, S. B. (1981). Infant irritability, mother responsiveness, and social support influences on the security of infant–mother attachment. *Child Development, 52,* 857–865.

Dixon, R. A. (1986). Contextualism and life-span developmental psychology. In R. L. Rosnow & M. Georgoudi (Eds.), *Contextualism and understanding in behavioral science* (pp. 125–144). New York: Praeger.

Dixon, R. A., & Lerner, R. M. (1988). A history of systems in developmental psychology. In M. H. Bornstein & M. E. Lamb (Eds), *Developmental psychology* (2nd ed.) (pp. 3–50). Hillsdale, NJ: Lawrence Erlbaum Associates.

Dixon, R. A., & Nesselroade, J. R. (1983). Pluralism and correlational analysis in developmental psychology: Historical commonalities. In R. M. Lerner (Ed.), *Developmental psychology: Historical and philosophical perspectives* (pp. 113–145). Hillsdale, NJ: Lawrence Erlbaum.

East, P. L., Lerner, R. M., & Lerner, J. V. (1988). *Early adolescent peer group fit, peer relations, and adjustment.* Unpublished manuscript, The Pennsylvania State University, University Park.

Elder, G. H., Jr. (1974). *Children of the great depression.* Chicago: University of Chicago Press.

Elder, G. H., Jr. (1975). Age differentiation and the life courses. In A. Inkeles, J. Colemen, & N. Smelser (Eds.), *Annual review of sociology* (Vol. 1, pp. 165–190). Palo Alto, CA: Annual Reviews.

Emmerich, W. (1968). Personality development and concepts of structure. *Child Development, 39,* 671–690.

Erikson, E. H. (1959). Identity and the life-cycle. *Psychological Issues, 1,* 18–164.

Featherman, D. L. (1983). Life-span perspectives in social science research. In P. B. Baltes & O. G. Brim, Jr. (Eds), *Life-span development and behavior* (Vol. 5, pp. 1–57). New York: Academic Press.

Featherman, D. L. (1985). Individual development and aging as a population process. In J. R. Nesselroade & A. von Eye (Eds.), *Individual development and social change: Explanatory analysis* (pp. 213–241). New York: Academic Press.

Featherman, D. L., & Lerner, R. M. (1985). Ontogenesis and sociogenesis: Problematics for theory about development across the lifespan. *American Sociological Review, 50,* 659–676.

Feinman, S., & Lewis, M. (1983). Social referencing at ten months: A second-order effect on infants' responses to strangers. *Child Development, 54,* 878–887.

Freud, S. (1949). *Outline of psychoanalysis.* New York: W W Norton.

Gesell, A. L. (1946). The ontogenesis of infant behavior. In L. Carmichael (Ed.), *Manual of child psychology* (pp. 295–331). New York: John Wiley & Sons.

Gollin, E. S. (1981). Development and plasticity. In E. S.

Gollin (Ed.), *Developmental plasticity: Behavioral and biological aspects of variations in development* (pp. 231–251). New York: Academic Press.

Gottlieb, G. (1970). Conceptions of prenatal behavior. In R. Aronson, E. Tobach, D. S. Lehrman, & J. S. Rosenblatt (Eds.), *Development and evolution of behavior: Essays in memory of T. C. Schneirla* (pp. 111–137). San Francisco: W H Freeman.

Gottlieb, G. (1983). The psychobiological approach to developmental issues. In M. M. Haith & J. J. Campos (Eds.), *Handbook of child psychology: Infancy and developmental psychobiology* (4th ed.; pp. 1–26). New York: John Wiley & Sons.

Gould, S., & Vrba, E. (1982). Exaptation: A missing term in the science of form. *Paleobiology, 8*, 4–15.

Hall, G. S. (1904). *Adolescence: Its psychology and its relations to physiology, anthropology, sociology, sex, crime, religion, and education* (Vols. 1 and 2). New York: Appleton.

Hamburg, B. (1974). Early adolescence: A specific and stressful stage of the life cycle. In G. Coelho, D. A. Hamburg, & J. E. Adams (Eds.), *Coping and adaptation* (pp. 101–125). New York: Basic Books.

Hamburger, V. (1957). The concept of development in biology. In D. B. Harris (Ed.), *The concept of development* (pp. 49–58). Minneapolis: University of Minnesota Press.

Harkness, S., & Super, C. M. (in press). Culture and psychopathology. In M. Lewis & S. Miller (Eds.), *Handbook of developmental psychopathology*. New York: Plenum Press.

Harris, D. B. (Ed.). (1957). *The concept of development*. Minneapolis: University of Minnesota Press.

Harter, S. (1983). *Supplementary description of the self-perception profile for children: Revision of the perceived competence scale for children*. Denver: University of Denver.

Hetherington, E. M., Lerner, R. M., & Perlmutter, M. (Eds.). (1988). *Child development in life span perspective*. Hillsdale, NJ: Lawrence Erlbaum Associates.

Jenkins, J. J. (1974). Remember that old theory of memory: Well forget it. *American Psychologist, 29*, 785–795.

Kaplan, B. (1983). A trio of trails. In R. M. Lerner (Ed.), *Developmental psychology: Historical and philosophical perspectives* (pp. 185–239). Hillsdale, NJ: Lawrence Erlbaum Associates.

Kendall, P. C., Lerner, R. M., & Craighead, W. E. (1984). Human development intervention in childhood psychopathology. *Child Development, 55*, 71–82.

Korn, S. (1978, September). *Temperament, vulnerability, and behavior*. Paper presented at the Louisville Temperament Conference, Louisville, KY.

Kuo, Z. Y. (1967). *The dynamics of behavior development*. New York: Random House.

Langlois, J. H. (1986). From the eye of the beholder to behavioral reality: The development of social behaviors and social relations as a function of physical attractiveness. In C. P. Herman (Ed.), *Physical appearance, stigma, and social behavior: The Ontario Symposium on Personality and Social Policy* (pp. 23–51). Hillsdale, NJ: Lawrence Erlbaum Associates.

Lehrman, D. S. (1970). Semantic and conceptual issues in the nature–nurture problem. In L. R. Aronson, E. Tobach, D. S. Lehrman, & J. S. Rosenblatt (Eds.), *Development and evolution of behavior: Essays in memory of T. C. Schneirla* (pp. 17–52). San Francisco: W H Freeman.

Lerner, J. V. (1983). A "goodness of fit" model of the role of temperament in psychosocial adaptation in early adolescents. *Journal of Genetic Psychology, 143*, 149–157.

Lerner, J. V. (1984). The import of temperament for psychosocial functioning: Tests of a "goodness of fit" model. *Merrill-Palmer Quarterly, 30*, 177–188.

Lerner, J. V., & Galambos, N. L. (1985). Maternal role satisfaction, mother–child interaction, and child temperament. *Developmental Psychology, 21*, 1157–1164.

Lerner, J. V., & Lerner, R. M. (1983). Temperament and adaptation across life: Theoretical and empirical issues. In P. B. Baltes & O. G. Brim, Jr. (Eds.), *Life-span development and behavior* (Vol. 5, pp. 197–230). New York: Academic Press.

Lerner, J. V., Lerner, R. M., & Zabski, S. (1985). Temperament and elementary school children's actual and rated academic performance: A test of a "goodness of fit" model. *The Journal of Child Psychology and Psychiatry, 26*, 125–136.

Lerner, R. M. (1976). *Concepts and theories of human development*. Reading, MA: Addison-Wesley.

Lerner, R. M. (1978). Nature, nurture and dynamic interactionism. *Human Development, 21*, 1–20.

Lerner, R. M. (1979). A dynamic interactional concept of individual and social relationship development. In R. Burgess & T. Huston (Eds.), *Social exchange in developing relationships* (pp. 271–305). New York: Academic Press.

Lerner, R. M. (1982). Children and adolescents as producers of their own development. *Developmental Review, 2*, 342–370.

Lerner, R. M. (1984). *On the nature of human plasticity*. New York: Cambridge University Press.

Lerner, R. M. (1985). Adolescent maturational change and psychosocial development: A dynamic interactional perspective. In J. Brooks-Gunn, A. C. Petersen, & D. Eichorn (Eds.), Timing of maturation and psychological adjustment. *Journal of Youth and Adolescence, 14*, 355–372.

Lerner, R. M. (1986). *Concepts and theories of human development* (2nd ed.). New York: Random House.

Lerner, R. M., & Busch-Rossnagel, N. (1981). Individuals as producers of their development: Conceptual and empirical bases. In R. M. Lerner & N. A. Busch-Rossnagel (Eds.), *Individuals as producers of their development: A life-span perspective* (pp. 1–36). New York: Academic Press.

Lerner, R. M., Delaney, M., Hess, L. E., Jovanovic, J., & von Eye, A. (1990). Early adolescent physical attractiveness and academic competence. *Journal of Early Adolescence, 10*, 4–20.

Lerner, R. M., Hess, L. E., & Nitz, K. (in press). A developmental perspective on psychopathology. In M. Hersen & C. G. Last (Eds.), *Handbook of child and adult psychopathology: A longitudinal perspective*. Elmsford, NY: Pergamon Press.

Lerner, R. M., Hultsch, D. F., & Dixon, R. A. (1983). Contextualism and the character of developmental psychology in the 1970s. *Annals of the New York Academy of Sciences, 412*, 101–128.

Lerner, R. M., Iwawaki, S., Chihara, T., & Sorell, G. T. (1980). Self-concept, self-esteem, and body attributes among Japanese male and female adolescents. *Child Development, 51*, 847–855.

Lerner, R. M., & Kauffman, M. B. (1985). The concept of development in contextualism. *Developmental Review, 5*, 309–333.

Lerner, R. M., & Lerner, J. V. (1983). Temperament-intelligence reciprocities in early childhood: A contextual model. In M. Lewis (Ed.), *Origins of intelligence: Infancy and early childhood* (2nd ed., pp. 399–421). New York: Plenum Press.

Lerner, R. M., & Lerner, J. V. (1987). Children in their contexts: A goodness of fit model. In J. B. Lancaster, J. Altmann, A. S. Rossi, & L. R. Sherrod (Eds.), *Parenting across the life span: Biosocial dimensions* (pp. 377–404). Chicago: Aldine.

Lerner, R. M., & Lerner, J. V. (1989). Organismic and social contextual bases of development: The sample case of adolescence. In W. Damon (Ed.), *Child development today and tomorrow.* (pp. 69–85). San Francisco: Jossey-Bass.

Lerner, R. M., Lerner, J. V., Jovanovic, J., Schwab, J., Talwar, R., Hess, L., & Kucher, J. S. (1988). Physical attractiveness, body type, and psychosocial functioning among early adolescents. Manuscript submitted for publication.

Lerner, R. M., Lerner, J. V., Windle, M., Hooker, K., Lenerz, K., & East, P. P. (1986). Children and adolescents in their contexts: Tests of a goodness of fit model. In R. Plomin & J. Dunn (Eds.), *The study of temperament: Changes, continuities, and challenges* (pp. 337–404). Hillsdale, NJ: Lawrence Erlbaum Associates.

Lerner, R. M., & Spanier, G. B. (1978). A dynamic interactional view of child and family development. In R. M. Lerner & G. B. Spanier (Eds.), *Child influences on marital and family interaction: A life-span perspective* (pp. 1–22). New York: Academic Press.

Lerner, R. M., & Spanier, G. B. (1980). *Adolescent development: A life-span perspective*. New York: McGraw-Hill.

Lerner, R. M., & Tubman, J. (in press). Plasticity in development: Ethical implications. In C. B. Fisher & W. W. Tryon (Eds.), *Ethics in applied developmental psychology*. Norwood, NJ: Ablex.

Lewis, M., & Lee-Painter, S. (1974). An interactional approach to the mother–infant dyad. In M. Lewis & L. A. Rosenblum (Eds.), *The effect of the infant on its caregivers* (pp. 21–48). New York: John Wiley & Sons.

Lewis, M., & Rosenblum, L. (Eds.). (1974). *The effect of the infant on its caregiver*. New York: John Wiley & Sons.

Liben, L. S. (1981). Individuals' contributions to their own development during childhood: A Piagetian perspective. In R. M. Lerner & N. A. Busch-Rossnagel (Eds.), *Individuals as producers of their development: A life-span perspective* (pp. 117–148). New York: Academic Press.

Lynch, M. E. (1981). *Paternal androgeny, daughters' physical maturity level, and achievement socialization in early adolescence*. Unpublished doctoral dissertation, Cornell University.

Magnusson, D. (1987). Individual development from an interactional perspective. Volume 1. In D. Magnusson (Ed.), *Paths through life*. Hillsdale, NJ: Lawrence Erlbaum Associates.

Magnusson, D., & Allen, V. L. (Eds.). (1983). *Human development: An interactional perspective*. New York: Academic Press.

Magnusson, D., & Oehman, A. (Eds.). (1987). *Psychopathology: An interactional perspective*. New York: Academic Press.

Meyer, J. W. (1988). The social construction of the psychology of childhood: Some contemporary processes. In E. M. Hetherington, R. M. Lerner, & M. Perlmutter (Eds.), *Child development in life-span perspective* (pp. 47–65). Hillsdale, NJ: Lawrence Erlbaum Associates.

Mischel, W. (1977). On the future of personality measurement. *American Psychologist, 32*, 246–254.

Mussen, P. H., & Bouterline-Young, H. (1964). Relationships between rate of physical maturing and personality among boys of Italian descent. *Vita Humana, 7*, 186–200.

Nagel, E. (1957). Determinism in development. In D. B. Harris (Ed.), *The concept of development* (pp. 15–24). Minneapolis: University of Minnesota Press.

Nitz, K., Lerner, R. M., Lerner, J. V., & Talwar, R. (in press). Parental and peer demands, temperament, and early adolescent adjustment. *Journal of Early Adolescence*.

Novikoff, A. B. (1945a). The concept of integrative levels of biology. *Science, 62*, 209–215.

Novikoff, A. B. (1945b). Continuity and discontinuity in evolution. *Science, 101*, 405–406.

Oehman, A., & Magnusson, D. (1987). An interactional paradigm for research on psychopathology. In D. Magnusson & A. Oehman (Eds.), *Psychopathology: An interactional perspective* (pp. 3–19). Orlando, FL: Academic Press.

Overton, W. F. (1973). On the assumptive base of the nature–nurture controversy: Additive versus interactive conceptions. *Human Development, 16*, 74–89.

Overton, W. F. (1984). World views and their influence on psychological theory and research: Kuhn-Lakatos-Lauden. In H. W. Reese (Ed.), *Advances in child development and behavior* (Vol 18, pp. 191–225). New York: Academic Press.

Overton, W. F., & Reese, H. W. (1973). Models of development: Methodological implications. In J. R. Nesselroade & H. W. Reese (Eds.), *Life-span developmental psychology: Methodological issues* (pp. 65–86). New York: Academic Press.

Paige, K. E. (1983). A bargaining theory of menarchael responses in preindustrial cultures. In J. Brooks-Gunn & A. C. Petersen (Eds.), *Girls at puberty* (pp. 301–322). New York: Plenum Press.

Parke, R. (1978). Parent–infant interaction: Progress, paradigms, and problems. In G. P. Sackett (Ed.), *Observing behavior. Vol. 1: Theory and implications in mental retardation* (pp. 69–95). Baltimore: University Park Press.

Pepper, S. C. (1942). *World hypotheses*. Berkeley: University of California Press.

Petersen, A. C. (1983). Pubertal change and cognition. In J. Brooks-Gunn & A. C. Petersen (Eds.), *Girls at puberty* (pp. 179–198). New York: Plenum Press.

Petersen, A. C., & Taylor, B. (1980). The biological approach to adolescence: Biological change and psychological adaptation. In J. Adelson (Ed.), *Handbook of adolescent psychology* (pp. 117–155). New York: John Wiley & Sons.

Piaget, J. (1950). *The psychology of intelligence*. New York: Harcourt Brace Jovanovich.

Plomin, R., & Daniels, D. (1984). The interaction between temperament and environment: Methodological considerations. *Merrill-Palmer Quarterly, 30*, 149–162.

Reese, H. W., & Overton, W. F. (1970). Models of development and theories of development. In L. R. Goulet & P. B. Baltes (Eds.), *Life-span developmental psychology: Research and theory* (pp. 115–145). New York: Academic Press.

Riegel, K. F. (1975). Toward a dialectical theory of development. *Human Development, 18*, 50–64.

Riegel, K. F. (1976). The dialectics of human development. *American Psychologist, 31*, 689–700.

Rosnow, R. L. (1983). Von Osten's horse, Hamlet's question, and the mechanistic view of causality: Implications for a post-crisis social psychology. *The Journal of Mind and Behavior, 4*, 319–338.

Rosnow, R., & Georgoudi, M. (Eds.), (1986). *Contextualism and understanding in behavioral research*. New York: Praeger.

Rosnow, R. L., & Rosenthal, R. (1984). *Understanding behavioral science: Research methods for research consumers*. New York: McGraw-Hill.

Ruble, D. N. (1977). Premenstrual symptoms: A reinterpretation. *Science, 197*, 291–292.

Ruble, D. N., & Brooks-Gunn, J. (1979). Menstrual symptoms: A social cognition analysis. *Journal of Behavioral Medicine, 2*, 171–194.

Ruble, D. N., & Brooks-Gunn, J. (1982). The experience of menarche. *Child Development, 53*, 1557–1566.

Sameroff, A. (1975). Transactional models in early social relations. *Human Development, 18*, 65–79.

Sarbin, T. R. (1977). Contextualism: A world view for modern psychology. In J. K. Cole, & A. W. Lundfield (Eds.), *Nebraska symposium on motivation, 1976* (pp. 1–41). Lincoln: University of Nebraska Press.

Scarr, S. (1982). Development is internally guided, not determined. *Contemporary Psychology, 27*, 852–853.

Scarr, S., & McCartney, K. (1983). How people make their own environments: A theory of genotype-environment effects. *Child Development, 54*, 424–435.

Schneirla, T. C. (1956). Interrelationships of the "innate" and the "acquired" in instinctive behavior. In P. P. Grass (Ed.), *L'instinct dans le comportement des animaux et de l'homme* (pp. 387–452). Paris: Maxon et Cie.

Schneirla, T. C. (1957). The concept of development in comparative psychology. In D. B. Harris (Ed.), *The concept of development* (pp. 78–108). Minneapolis: University of Minnesota Press.

Sheldon, W. H. (1940). *The varieties of human physique*. New York: Harper & Row.

Sheldon, W. H. (1942). *The varieties of temperament*. New York: Harper & Row.

Simmons, R. G., Blyth, D. A., & McKinney, K. L. (1983). The social and psychological effects of puberty on white females. In J. Brooks-Gunn & A. C. Petersen (Eds.), *Girls at puberty* (pp. 229–272). New York: Plenum Press.

Simmons, R. G., Blyth, D. A., Van Cleave, E. F., & Bush, D. M. (1979). Entry into early adolescence: The impact of school structure, puberty, and early dating on self-esteem. *American Sociological Review, 44*, 948–967.

Simmons, R. G., Brown, L., Bush, D. M., & Blyth, D. A. (1978). Self-esteem and achievement of black and white early adolescents. *Social Problems, 26*, 86–96.

Simmons, R. G., Carlton-Ford, S. L., & Blyth, D. A. (1987). Predicting how a child will cope with the transition to junior high school. In R. M. Lerner & T. T. Foch (Eds.), *Biological-psychosocial interactions in early adolescence: A life-span perspective* (pp. 325–375). Hillsdale, NJ: Lawrence Erlbaum Associates.

Sorensen, B., Weinert, E., & Sherrod, L. R. (Eds.). (1986). *Human development and the life course: Multidisciplinary perspectives*. Hillsdale, NJ: Lawrence Erlbaum Associates.

Super, C. M. (1987). The role of culture in developmental disorder. In C. M. Super (Ed.), *The role of culture in developmental disorder* (pp. 2–7). San Diego: Academic Press.

Super, C. M., & Harkness, S. (1980). Anthropological perspectives on child development. *New Directions for Child Development* (No. 8). San Franciso: Jossey-Bass.

Super, C. M., & Harkness, S. (1981). Figure, ground, and gestalt: The cultural context of the active individual. In R. M. Lerner & N. A. Busch-Rossnagel (Eds.), *Individuals as producers of their own development: A life-span perspective* (pp. 69–86). New York: Academic Press.

Super, C. M., & Harkness, S. (1982). The infant's niche in rural Kenya and metropolitan America. In L. L. Adler (Ed.), *Cross-cultural research at issue* (pp. 47–56). New York: Academic Press.

Super, C. M., & Harkness, S. (1986). The developmental niche: A conceptualization at the interface of child and culture. *International Journal of Behavioral Development, 9*, 1–25.

Super, C. M., & Harkness, S. (1988). *The development niche: Culture and the expressions of human growth.* Unpublished manuscript.

Talwar, R., Nitz, K., Lerner, J. V., & Lerner, R. M. (1988, April). *Temperamental individuality, fit with parent and peer demands, and personal and social adjustment across the transition to junior high school.* Paper presented at the Fifty-ninth Annual Meeting of the Eastern Psychological Association, Buffalo, NY.

Talwar, R., Schwab, J., & Lerner, R. M. (1988). *Early adolescent temperament and academic competence.* Unpublished manuscript, the Pennsylvania State University, University Park.

Thomas, A., & Chess, S. (1977). *Temperament and development.* New York: Brunner/Mazel.

Thomas, A., Chess, S., & Birch, H. (1968). *Temperament and behavioral disorders in childhood.* New York: New York University Press.

Thomas, A., Chess, S., & Birch, H. G. (1970). The origin of personality. *Scientific American, 223*, 102–109.

Thomas, A., Chess, S., Sillan, J., & Mendez, O. (1974). Cross-cultural study of behavior in children with special vulnerabilities to stress. In D. F. Ricks, A. Thomas, & M. Roff (Eds.), *Life history research in psychopathology* (pp. 53–67). Minneapolis: University of Minnesota Press.

Tobach, E. (1981). Evolutionary aspects of the activity of the organism and its development. In R. M. Lerner & N. A. Busch-Rossnagel (Eds.), *Individuals as producers of their development: A life-span perspective* (pp. 37–68). New York: Academic Press.

Tobach, E., & Greenberg, G. (1984). The significance of T. C. Schneirla's contribution to the concept of levels of integration. In G. Greenberg & E. Tobach (Eds.), *Behavioral evolution and integrative levels* (pp. 1–7). Hillsdale, NJ: Lawrence Erlbaum Associates.

Tobach, E., & Schneirla, T. C. (1968). The biopsychology of social behavior of animals. In R. E. Cooke & S. Levin (Eds.), *Biologic basis of pediatric practice* (pp. 68–82). New York: McGraw-Hill.

Tobin-Richards, M. H., Boxer, A. M., & Petersen, A. C. (1983). The psychological significance of pubertal change: Sex differences in perceptions of self during early adolescence. In J. Brooks-Gunn & A. C. Petersen (Eds.), *Girls at puberty* (pp. 127–154). New York: Plenum Press.

von Bertalanffy, L. (1933). *Modern theories of development.* London: Oxford University Press.

von Bertalanffy, L. (1969). *General systems theory.* New York: George Braziller.

Wapner, S., & Demick, J. (1988, October). *Some relations between developmental and environmental psychology: An organismic-developmental systems perspective.* Paper presented at the "Visions of Development, the Environment, and Aesthetics: The Legacy of Joachim Wohlwill" conference, The Pennsylvania State University, University Park.

Westney, O. E., Jenkins, R. R., & Benjamin, C. A. (1983). Sociosexual development of preadolescents. In J. Brooks-Gunn & A. C. Petersen (Eds), *Girls at puberty* (pp. 273–300). New York; Plenum Press.

White, S. H. (1968). The learning–maturation controversy: Hall to Hull. *Merrill-Palmer Quarterly, 14*, 187–196.

Windle, M., Hooker, K., Lenerz, K., East, P. L., Lerner, J. V., & Lerner, R. M. (1986). Temperament, perceived competence, and depression in early- and late-adolescents. *Developmental Psychology, 22*, 384–392.

Windle, M., & Lerner, R. M. (1986). Reassessing the dimensions of temperamental individuality across the life-span: The Revised Dimensions of Temperament Survey (DOTS-R). *Journal of Adolescent Research, 1*, 213–230.

CHAPTER 3

DEVELOPMENTAL PSYCHOPATHOLOGY: AN INTEGRATIVE FRAMEWORK

Ann S. Masten
Lauren Braswell

Developmental psychopathology, rapidly emerging as the organizational framework for the study of behavior problems in children and adolescents, has as its goal the understanding of psychopathology in the full context of human development. This framework represents the integration of several scientific traditions in child psychology and experimental psychopathology, as well as clinical traditions in psychiatry and psychology. The purpose of this chapter is to delineate the central assumptions of this approach and to examine its implications for clinical practice and research, particularly for behavior therapy. The origins, tenets, and potential applications of developmental psychopathology will be described. Although a developmental perspective is important across the life span, this chapter will focus on childhood and adolescence—periods of human life when the pace and nature of change are often dramatic.

Advances in the fields of child development, psychiatry, clinical psychology, and behavior genetics have laid a scientific foundation on which a synthesis can be built (Cicchetti, 1984; in press). The impetus for integration, however, has come both from research questions that necessitated interdisciplinary thinking and collaboration and from a growing recognition of the shortcomings of assessment and intervention methods for children and adolescents. By their attention to rigorous measurement and therapy outcome evaluation, behaviorists have played a significant role in highlighting the limitations of their own and other strategies of behavioral assessment and change.

Although first rate clinicians who treat children and their parents probably have always implicitly considered the developmental status of the individual child in their methods of assessment and intervention, the benefits of a systematic developmental approach have not been explicitly acknowledged until very recently. The neglect of developmental psychology in the theory and practice of psychotherapy has been particularly evident in behavior therapy (Furman, 1980; Gelfand & Peterson, 1985; Mahoney & Nezworksi, 1985; Masten, 1986; McMahon & Peters, 1985). The potential of integrating behavioral and developmental models to improve assessment and treatment has been well articulated by McMahon and Peters (1985) in their introduction to the volume resulting from the fifteenth Banff International Conference on Behavior Sciences, which focused on these issues. Similarly, Delprato (1987) has argued that behaviorists can best understand both behavioral difficulty and intervention

---

Preparation of this chapter was supported in part by a McKnight-Land Grant Professorship from the University of Minnesota to Dr. Masten.

in a context of developmental interactionism rather than more restrictive learning and conditioning accounts.

Developmental psychology offers a rich source of theory and data about continuities and discontinuities in human behavior over time that can be used more effectively by behaviorists to enhance their theory and methods of behavior change. Both clinicians and researchers have much to contribute to the knowledge base of developmental psychopathology, which will in turn improve both interventions and theory (Garmezy & Masten, 1986).

ORIGINS OF DEVELOPMENTAL PSYCHOPATHOLOGY

The origins of the developmental psychopathology perspective cannot be fully explored here (see Cicchetti, 1990); however, three key influences will be discussed briefly: (1) attachment theory, (2) psychiatric classification, and (3) risk research. In each case, recent advances have led to a more integrative and developmental approach to investigating psychopathology in children.

Attachment theory and research has played an important role in bringing together ideas from psychoanalytic theory, Darwinian theory, and mainstream child development (Bowlby, 1969, 1973, 1980; Sroufe, 1979; Sroufe & Waters, 1977). For a long time, academic child psychology was focused primarily on laying out the principles and patterns of normative development. Attachment theorists and researchers, however, were interested in qualitative differences in the relationships between infants and their caregivers and the significance of these differences for subsequent development. John Bowlby's ideas about attachment, referring to the bond that develops between infants and caregivers beginning in the first year of life, were grounded in clinical observations of the effects of separation and loss on children and the theory he developed had many implications for the possible origins of some forms of psychopathology (Bowlby, 1988; Sroufe & Waters, 1977).

The acceptance of the attachment theory into mainstream academic child psychology was greatly facilitated by the development of an experimental method, the strange situation procedure, to measure attachment and test hypotheses generated by the theory (Ainsworth, Blehar, Waters, & Wall, 1978). Researchers were able to examine the long and short term significance of attachment differences for later competence and psychopathology (Bretherton & Waters, 1985). The ideas and questions generated by attachment theory have spurred a greater interest in deviant development within traditional child psychology.

A second major influence on developmental psychopathology has been the psychiatric tradition of classifying and diagnosing diseases. Modern child psychiatry developed largely through the downward extension of adult psychiatry and, perhaps as a consequence, the classification and diagnosis of disorders in children was carried out with little attention to developmental issues (Garber, 1984). This appears to be changing, however, as a function of more and better research on disorders in children.

The changing perspective of psychiatry is well represented by the evolution over the past four decades of the standard classification system, the Diagnostic and Statistical Manual (DSM) of the American Psychiatric Association. The first manual, DSM-I, published in 1952, included two basic categories for children: adjustment reactions and schizophrenia-childhood type. The 1968 revision, DSM-II, expanded the child sections to include six behavior disorders of childhood, including "hyperkinetic reaction" and "runaway reaction." In 1980, DSM-III was published, marking a watershed in psychiatry. Most remnants of psychoanalytic terminology, such as "neurosis," were eliminated and an attempt was made to systematize the process of diagnosis by the introduction of multiaxial classification and clear diagnostic criteria modeled on the Research Diagnostic Criteria developed at Washington University in St. Louis. In DSM-III, (APA, 1980) the child section was greatly expanded and reframed in terms of "disorders usually first evident" during childhood. For example, five eating disorders were included. More recently, the child section was further revised in DSM-III-R (APA, 1987).

Although DSM-III has been criticized, it was a marked improvement over earlier versions, with notable developmental features (Achenbach, 1980; Cantwell & Baker, 1988; Rutter & Shaffer, 1980). In DSM-III, it was acknowledged that disorders arising in childhood may persist in adulthood (e.g., Residual Autism) and that some disorders may be found in children as well as adults (e.g., schizophrenia). Within disorders, the developmental course was often described. DSM-III also distinguished three types of developmental problems: pervasive developmental disorders, specific developmental disorders, and mental retardation. Subsequently, in DSM-III-R, these classes of disorders were grouped separately on Axis II (as recommended by a number of critics) along with personality disorders, in order to emphasize that these patterns of behavior usually have childhood onset and relatively stable form.

Within disorders, age-related symptoms were described and diagnostic criteria often included age limits. For example, Functional Enuresis required the following: "Chronologic age at least five, and mental age at least four." Some criteria required age norms. For example, criteria for Attention-Deficit Hyperactivity Disorder not only included onset before the age of 7, but also noted: "Consider a criterion met only if the behavior is considerably more frequent than that of most people of the same mental age." Unfortunately, DSM-III does not set forth norms for such behaviors, nor does it describe normal behavior, developmental tasks, or milestones as a context for understanding psychopathology. In contrast, the classification system proposed by the Group for the Advancement of Psychiatry (1966), though much less comprehensive than DSM-III, did define a normal developmental context.

Nevertheless, the evolution of better classification systems with clearly specified diagnostic criteria in psychiatry has played a major role in intervention and in research. A driving force behind the adoption of diagnostic criteria was the need of researchers to identify more homogeneous as well as more replicable groups for research. The current surge of research on depression in children is only one example of efforts to systematize and understand a set of clinical phenomena in children (Rutter, Izard, & Read, 1986).

The third influence on developmental psychopathology arose from the research of psychiatrists, psychologists and behavior geneticists on the origins of specific mental illnesses, most notably schizophrenia. The study of children at risk for schizophrenia was pioneered in clinical studies by Bender (1937) and Fish (1957) and, on a larger scale more systematically, by Mednick and Schulsinger (1968). The "high risk" strategy (Garmezy, 1974; Garmezy & Streitman, 1974; Goldstein & Tuma, 1987; Watt, Anthony, Wynne, & Rolf, 1984) for studying the origins of schizophrenia depended on longitudinal studies, requiring a developmental perspective. These risk studies gave considerable impetus to the emergence of developmental psychopathology (Masten, 1989). Risk investigators had to choose meaningful and predictive measures of a functioning across different age periods. They also had to decide what were the most informative comparison groups for high risk children. These questions encouraged a generation of investigators to discuss continuities and discontinuities in development and also continuities between normal and abnormal behavior, two central concerns of developmental psychopathology. Interdisciplinary research was fostered by the need for combining expertise in child development, experimental psychology, psychiatry, and behavior genetics.

Another legacy of the risk studies was an increased interest in the positive side of adaptation, in terms of competence and resilience, the latter referring to successful adaptation despite risk or adversity (Masten, 1989). It became clear in a variety of high risk studies that many children develop well despite their risk status. Subsequently, a number of investigators turned their attention to the study of competence and resilience (Anthony & Cohler, 1987; Garmezy, 1981, 1987; Garmezy & Rutter, 1983; Rutter, 1987; Werner, in press).

Within the last two decades these three influences, as well as others, began to converge as a function of greater attention to child psychopathology. In the first edition of his textbook called *Developmental Psychopathology*, Achenbach (1974) opened with the comment that "This is a book about a field that hardly exists yet." Yet, in the last ten years this perspective has taken hold, as evidenced by numerous books, special issues of journals, and articles on the topic and in the initiation of new graduate training programs with this focus (Cicchetti, 1984). The rapid ascendance of this perspective suggests that the groundwork was already laid and the time was ripe for a new synthesis.

EVOLVING TENETS OF DEVELOPMENTAL PSYCHOPATHOLOGY

Developmental psychopathology has underlying assumptions that focus the attention of its proponents on certain issues, phenomena, and methodology. Because this framework is still forming, these may change, but we believe it is informative to identify the major assumptions and focal themes of developmental psychopathology at this time.

Tenet 1. *Psychopathology occurs in a developing organism.*

Developmental psychopathology begins with the premise that psychopathology occurs in a developing organism. Particularly in childhood and adolescence, when developmental changes are pronounced, it is essential to consider the role of development in the origins, symptoms, and course of psychopathology, and, concomitantly, in classification, assessment, and treatment of childhood disorders.

It is predicted from this assumption that developmental changes will be evident in age patterns of behavior problems and the incidence of syndromes. Suicidal behavior, for example, extremely rare before adolescence, rises sharply in incidence in early to mid-adolescence (Masten, 1988). This phenomenon probably reflects developmental changes in the organism as well as changes in the social milieu. Anorexia nervosa, schizophrenia, and major depression disorders show marked changes in prevalence in adolescence (Masten, 1988; Rutter, 1988). Etiological theories of these disorders must account for these age patterns.

The utility of examining age of onset and age-related patterns of behavior is illustrated by the differentiation of autism and schizophrenia from what was once globally described as childhood psychosis or childhood schizophrenia. Examined from the perspective of age, the data on symptoms, familial incidence, course and prognosis showed two distinct patterns: an early onset disorder with features Kanner (1943) had identified with autism and a later onset pattern very much like schizophrenia in adults but occurring earlier (Hanson & Gottesman, 1976; Rutter, 1974).

There are also significant age patterns of psychopathology related to sex. There is a preponderance of boys in many of the earlier onset disorders, including autism, hyperactivity, and conduct disorder. In some disorders associated with adolescence, there are relatively more females, as in anorexia nervosa, or more balanced sex ratios, as in schizophrenia. The sex ratio appears to shift around adolescence in some disorders; in major depression, for example, girls begin to significantly outnumber boys during adolescence (Rutter, 1986).

The course and prognosis data for different disorders can also be viewed as developmental data. Not only is earlier age of onset often associated with worse prognosis, as in schizophrenia or conduct disorder, but there are changes in the nature and patterns of symptoms in children identified as having a given disorder, such as autism (Schopler & Mesibov, 1983) or attention deficit hyperactivity disorder (Weiss & Hechtman, 1986). These data provide clues as to the etiological and developmental processes in psychopathology.

It is also predicted from this first tenet that the nature and meaning of behavioral problems (symptoms) will reflect developmental and age differences. Not only is the normative context important (see Tenet 2), but symptoms are expected to vary by age and syndromes to have age-specific manifestations. Thus, even disorders that appear to have impressive cross-age and cross-cultural similarities would be expected to vary in their features according to the developmental level of the person. Very young children with major depression or post-traumatic stress disorder, for example, would be expected to show age-specific forms of symptoms such as anhedonia or traumatic re-experiencing. DSM-III-R has adopted this view for some disorders by indicating age-related features. On the other hand, it is assumed that different symptoms may result from the same processes at different points in development (Garber, 1984; Sroufe & Rutter, 1984). For example, bedwetting is more common in reaction to psychic trauma in preschoolers than teenagers (Eth & Pynoos, 1985), while suicidal thinking is more common in depressed teenagers than depressed preschoolers (Rutter, 1986). The disease process of schizophrenia may produce externalizing symptoms, attentional problems, or social isolation in middle childhood and the classical symptoms of schizophrenia in adulthood (Garmezy & Streitman, 1974; Rutter, 1988).

Tenet 2. *Psychopathology is defined by reference to normative patterns of development in normative environmental contexts.*

The second major assumption of developmental psychopathology is that deviance is defined by normative behavior and expectations within a culture that are developmentally based. Normative development is a critical context for defining psychopathology: Is this behavior unusual for children of this age, mental age, or level of biological maturation? One of the most salient features of many symptoms and disorders is their developmental inappropriateness. For example, frequent crying, eating nonfoods, bedwetting, hitting and tantrums, nightmares, fear of monsters and animals, impulsiveness, short attention span, distractability, and talking aloud to imaginary friends are common behaviors at some ages and deviant at other ages. Some symptoms are uncommon or bizarre at any age, but these are fewer in number, such as self-injury or hallucinations.

Adaptation generally refers to biological and cultural fitness, the degree to which an organism is able to survive and develop. "Success" can be defined from different perspectives. From a biological perspective, success is measured in terms of genetic transmission. From a cultural perspective, success is measured in terms of contributions to society. From a humanistic perspective, success is measured in terms of a personal sense of fulfillment, mastery, efficacy, or self-actualization, all referring to psychological well-being. Most definitions of "mental illness" require either that the person is ineffective in meeting of basic needs or feels miserable.

In developmental psychopathology, adaptation is often defined in terms of developmental tasks. The notion of developmental tasks was popularized by Robert Havighurst, initially through a pamphlet he created in 1948 as a teacher at the University of Chicago, and later in publications (Havighurst, 1972). The basic idea is that in order for a person to adapt, there are developmental challenges that must be met. Some arise through biological maturation, others are imposed by families and society, while others arise from the developing self. Successes in these tasks are taken as markers of competence, akin to milestones of psychomotor development, such as sitting, crawling, or walking. Some tasks appear to be universal (e.g., attachment to caregivers) while others vary more by culture (e.g., school adjustment).

The concept of developmental tasks is related to stage notions of development and the idea of "salient developmental issues" that serially serve to organize behavior proposed by those with the structuralist-organizational perspective (Cicchetti, in press; Greenspan, 1981; Sander, 1975; Sroufe, 1979). A seminal contribution to this perspective was the work of Erik Erikson (1950) who articulated the "Eight Ages of Man" in terms of such issues. The first issue was "Basic trust versus basic mistrust," which Erikson construed as the first task of the ego, nurtured by the parent. Even if a sense of basic trust is established, through responsive caregiving in early infancy, such an issue is never totally resolved. It may re-emerge as a prominent issue at any point in development, as when a major loss or betrayal occurs or when a later issue closely related to trust arises, such as intimacy. Erikson outlined a progression of such issues, describing a picture of the usual sequences and times at which these issues are particularly salient, although all issues remain active throughout life. Adaptive responses to each major issue or task were hypothesized to provide a foundation for coping with later tasks. Sander (1975), Sroufe (1979), and others have more recently postulated the processes by which trust and dependence of the infant in the infant-caregiver relationship might lead to self-regulation and autonomy in successive periods of development.

Developmental psychopathology predicts that referral patterns will reflect developmental tasks, as defined by a given cultural context, as will age patterns of disorder or symptoms in epidemiological data. Examples of commonly cited developmental tasks in American society are provided in Table 3-1. One would expect problems to become salient in the minds of parents and society soon after children are expected to have mastered one of these tasks. In this way, many symptoms of psychopathology can be viewed as maladaptation in the context of developmental expectations indicated by such tasks.

The tasks of early infancy have been detailed by Greenspan (1981; Greenspan & Lourie, 1981), Sander (1975), Sroufe (1979), and Santostefano (1978). Difficulties with these tasks are reflected in such diagnoses as "Failure to Thrive" or "Reactive Attachment Disorder." Parents expect their babies to develop attachment behaviors during the first year. They are likely to become concerned if their infants fail to smile responsively, avoid physical contact, and

Table 3-1. Examples of Developmental Tasks in Childhood and Adolescence

INFANCY
Smooth physiological regulation (eating, sleeping patterns)
Transition from reflex to voluntary behavior
Attachment to caregiver
Separation/individuation of the self

TODDLER AND PRESCHOOL
Independent toileting, other self-care
Language
Self-control, compliance
Gender identity formation

MIDDLE CHILDHOOD
School adjustment (e.g., attendance, appropriate behavior, peer acceptance)
Academic achievement (e.g., learning to read, mastering basic mathematics)
Friendships with peers; Peer acceptance
Morals (following rules of home, school and moral conduct for the society)

ADOLESCENCE
Adjustment to pubertal changes
Transition to secondary schooling
Herterosexual friendships and dating
Identity (achieving coherent sense of self)

never develop a preference for parents over strangers. Pervasive developmental disorders such as autism may be detected early because they are associated with absences, gross distortions, or great delay in these expected attainments.

By preschool age, parents are attentive to delays or problems with a new set of expected achievements, including those related to language, toileting, and self-control. Parents are likely to check with their doctors if children show little progress in these areas. Parents may seek the help of professionals complaining of such concerns as tantrums, noncompliance, or stuttering. For boys, behaviors such as expressions of wishes to be a girl or dressing like a girl become an increasing concern as gender identity is expected to be fairly solid by school age. Girls have somewhat more room for cross-sex behavior than do boys in American society, although parents would be concerned by exclusively "boyish" interests or consistent beliefs by a girl that she was really a boy.

In many societies, a major task beginning in middle childhood is schooling. At school, children are expected to behave in acceptable ways (to go and stay in the classroom, to separate from parents for the day, to listen to teachers, to follow rules, to get along with the other pupils, etc.) and to learn academic skills, such as reading and arithmetic. Behavioral problems that shadow these tasks include school refusal, disruptive/aggressive behavior, and learning disabilities. Parents also become increasingly concerned about peer relations, including bully or victim issues, social isolation, and peer rejection. Moral development in terms of behavior and conscience become salient. Increasingly, children are expected to not only obey rules but to make morally correct judgments, to know what is wrong and refrain from doing it. Lying and stealing for example gradually become intolerable.

With adolescence comes a new set of challenges. Sexual maturity must be assimilated or accommodated by all young people. Adolescents must adjust to physical changes, including new shapes and growth spurts, as well as changing social expectations by parents, peers, and teachers. Sexual maturity also brings increased attention to sexual friendships and dating.

In the United States, adolescence ushers in a whole new style of schooling as well. The family-like milieu of elementary schools is usually replaced by one less personal, larger, more complicated, more demanding, and less supportive. Roberta Simmons and her colleagues (Simmons & Blyth, 1987) have shown how self-esteem plummets, especially in girls, following the transition to junior high school. They suggest that too many changes often come too close together in the conjunction of early adolescent tasks with entry into secondary school.

One of the challenges facing the adolescent is to sort out the meaning of these changes, a task Erik Erikson described as identity versus role diffusion. A new focus on reflection in adolescence may be provoked by the changes mentioned above and by maturing cognitive capabilities. Adolescents are more interested and better at examining where they have been and where they may be going. They can contemplate greater spans of their lives, projecting into the future. Adolescents are also better able to consider hypotheticals. Intense self-focus may be accompanied by a (perhaps protective) illusion of uniqueness or invulnerability in some adolescents (Lerner, 1988) while others suffer miserable feelings or even depression (Masten, 1988). The adolescent's world expands with more independence and unmonitored time, greater mobility, and greater expectations for responsible behavior.

Accompanying the challenges and opportunities of adolescence come new kinds of behavior problems and different parental and societal concerns, including: trying out adult behaviors too soon (e.g., early sexual activity or alcohol consumption), negative identity and role models (e.g., "punk" or gang associations), family conflicts over rules, or an upsurge in truancy. Common developmental tasks and challenges may account for the increases and intercorrelations of delinquency, promiscuity, drug use, and running way. (Donovan & Jessor, 1985; Donovan, Jessor, & Costa, 1988).

Depression and suicidal behavior become much more common with adolescence. Although it is not clear why these behaviors increase in early adolescence, it is likely that changes associated with puberty, cognitive development and the stress of cumulative challenges in adolescence play a role in these problems (Masten, 1988). Attempting and completing suicide show particularly strong age patterns, with rates of both climbing sharply in adolescence (Carlson & Cantwell, 1982; Fowler, Rich, & Young, 1986; Garfinkel & Golombek, 1983; Masten, 1988; Petzel & Cline, 1978; Shaffer, 1986). Preadolescent children appear to be protected from such behaviors to a large degree by their own immaturity, while adolescents become dramatically more vulnerable to self-destructive behavior. For example, preadolescent children may be less able to sustain a hopeless cognitive set or to execute a suicide plan and have less access or exposure to methods, opportunities, and examples of suicide. There are also striking sex differences in these phenomena with girls showing many more suicide attempts while boys continue to outnumber girls in completed suicides (Hawton, 1986; Pfeffer, 1986).

Clearly the transition to adolescence is an important period to study very closely if we are to understand why some forms of psychopathology show sharp increases at this time. Increasing attention is being paid to the importance of such *developmental transitions* (Rutter, 1989). Some are marked by maturation (e.g., puberty) and others by experiences (e.g., birth of a child). Periods of transition may offer a window through which to view developmental processes and also an opportunity to guide individuals toward one set of paths rather than another, with long term consequences.

Tenet 3. *All psychopathology is influenced by complex interactions of gene expressions and the environmental context of development and behavior.*

Developmental psychopathologists recognize the importance of experiences in shaping behavior and the importance of the individual's role in shaping the environment that will in turn influence his or her life. For example, the growing child's environment is profoundly influenced by parental behavior, which is itself the product of complex genetic and environmental interactions and which is influenced by the characteristics of the child (Bell, 1968; Plomin, Loehlin, & DeFries, 1985; Sameroff & Chandler, 1975; Scarr & McCartney, 1983). Eisenberg (1977) has argued that development is the unifying process by which genes and experience result in individual behavior, both normal and abnormal.

In developmental psychopathology, it is also assumed that some behavior is the product of evolution, genetically influenced and naturally selected because it enhanced survival. Attachment, for example, is widely viewed as a product of evolution as well as learning. John Bowlby (1969), based on extensive observations of infant responses to separations or reunions with mothering figures and to the approach of strangers, concluded that this behavioral system has evolved because of its survival value for infants in the environments of human evolution. Older infants in whom attachment bonds have been well established seek proximity and cling to the caregiver and signal for help in other ways when they feel insecure or threatened. While there appears to be a strong inborn tendency to develop this type of special relationship, attachment theorists have argued that an infant's experiences will influence the quality and nature of this behavioral system, which in turn will influence later social development (Bretherton & Waters, 1985; Sroufe, 1979).

An important corollary of this assumption is that behavior always has a *context*. The most elaborated perspective within this view is systems theory, which points to the multilayered, interrelated systems in which human behavior is embedded (Gunnar & Thelen, 1989). Bronfenbrenner (1979) has described the microsystems, mesosystems, and macrosystems in which we all live and reminds us of their influence. Increasingly, investigations of child functioning take into account some of these contexts by assessing behavior at home, at school, with peers, and from multiple perspectives of parent, child, teacher, peers, and trained observers. Elder (1979; Elder, Caspi, & Burton, 1988) similarly has argued persuasively for the importance of historical context in human development and learning. Lerner, Hess, and Nitz, in this volume, describe an integrative developmental-contextual perspective in detail.

Tenet 4. *Because most forms of psychopathology result from multiple causal influences (sometimes including a necessary but not sufficient cause), rarely from a single cause, it is useful to describe psychopathology in terms of deviant pathways or trajectories of development.*

The growing acceptance of multicausal models of disorders such as anorexia nervosa or conduct disorder has followed in the wake of diathesis–stressor models of psychopathology, most notably schizophrenia (Gottesman & Shields, 1982). In the latter case, for example, the divergent development of identical twins provided evidence that simple genetic models cannot account for the development of such disorders.

The idea that individual development follows a path influenced continually by genes and environment has been eloquently advanced by Waddington (1966). Waddington described the individual as traveling along an "epigenetic landscape" in constant flux from dynamic changes in gene expression (at a given point only some genes are "turned on") and environmental conditions. Some paths are "canalized" or strongly determined by genetic constraints while others are more open to experiential pulls in many directions. Gottesman (1974; Gottesman & Shields, 1972) proposed a polygenetic model of schizophrenia, which would explain how identical twins may have divergent developmental trajectories while nonrelatives may have convergent trajectories. Twins with identical genetic risk for schizophrenia could end up discordant for the disorder owing to different experiences (beginning in utero). Unrelated people with different initial vulnerabilities could have experiences that lead them both across the threshold for triggering schizophrenia.

In these symbolic landscapes, there is a generally healthy direction for development (defined over time in terms of a range of adaptive behavior) as well as directions that tend toward poor outcomes. Bowlby (1988) has recently described pathways of development toward anxious attachment and depression versus hostility and delinquency, deviating from a range of healthy pathways.

Although there are many potential paths individuals follow, and each life course is unique, these models assume that there are important patterns that can be identified: (1) final common pathways, where various paths lead eventually to the same pattern, or (2) developmental patterns, where there is a similarity over time in the pathway some children follow. For example, major depression (Akiskal & McKinney, 1975) and anorexia nervosa (Garner & Garfinkel, 1985) have been described as psychobiological final common pathways. On the other hand, some investigators have differentiated patterns of antisocial behavior that may represent distinct patterns (Loeber, in press; Masten, 1988). Two such patterns that go by various names are the undersocialized, aggressive pattern and the socialized, delinquent pattern. In the former, children appear to go off the normative developmental track very early. These children are aggressive and isolated. They begin to stand out as socially deviant when most children are becoming more compliant and less physically aggressive during the early childhood years. Their behavior looks relatively worse as time goes on, as other children become increasingly socialized in their conduct. It may be very informative for psychopathologists interested in these patterns to consider the development of self-regulation in the preschool years (e.g., Kopp, 1982; Vaughn, Kopp, & Krakow, 1984), as well as the microdevelopmental family processes that contribute to an escalating cycle of antisocial behavior (Patterson & Bank, 1989). Moreover, because these children are notably solitary, it is important to ask how early social bonding influences the development of self-regulation.

The socialized pattern, on the other hand, is associated with the transition to adolescence, a time when unsupervised, vulnerable children may be spending time in the presence of delinquent peers, or searching for a viable identity. These young people appear to have more skills essential to social life although they may act against society at large. The prognosis for this pattern appears to be better in many cases, with more desistance (Henn, Bardwell, & Jenkins, 1980).

Tenet 5. *The study of adaptation in all its forms, successful and unsuccessful, is important to understanding psychopathology.*

Developmental psychopathology is fundamentally concerned with the study of adaptation. Studies of *competence* and *resilience* are as important to understanding adaptation as are studies of extreme deviance and maladaptation. Competence in this sense refers broadly to the quality of effective functioning in the environment. Waters and Sroufe (1983) have defined the competent individual as "*one who is able to make use of environmental and personal resources to achieve a good developmental outcome*" (p. 81). They emphasize that current adaptation relates to competence only insofar as it indicates good developmental outcome present and future.

Resilience refers to successful adaptation under adverse conditions or to recovery from stress or trauma. The recent surge of interest in resilience grew out of studies of children at risk due to a variety of genetic, developmental, or environmental disadvantages that revealed quantitatively a phenomenon that long had been observed in case histories, namely that there were marked individual differences in outcome (Masten, 1989).

Studies of resilience consistently point to individual, family, socioeconomic, and school factors that appear to moderate the relations of adversity to outcome. These include: 1) dispositional vulnerability to stress, sometimes referred to in terms of difficult versus easy temperament; 2) cognitive or problem-solving abilities; 3) a strong relationship with an effective adult parent, role model, or mentor; 4) socioeconomic advantage or disadvantage; and 5) the quality of the school milieu (Garmezy, 1981; Garmezy & Rutter, 1983; Masten, Garmezy, Tellegen, Pellegrini, Larkin & Larsen, 1988; Rutter, 1985; Werner, in press).

The study of competence and resilience is important to developmental psychopathology for a number of reasons. If elucidating the developmental processes of adaptation will provide crucial clues for improving intervention and prevention efforts, knowing how it is that some children avoid problems or turn in a more positive direction provides as much information as do maladaptive patterns. For example, much research over the years focused on risk factors for delinquency, without a great deal of yield for intervention programming. Very recently, Mulvey (1985; Mulvey & LaRosa, 1986) and others have begun to examine the developmental phenomenon of *desistance* from delinquent behavior in order to learn how many young people turn away from these behavior patterns. Such information may be very informative to efforts in redirecting the life-streams of other adolescents in a more positive direction. Similarly, those who want to help children at risk due to poverty and high crime neighborhoods or to those trying to improve American schools are turning to successful poor families and successful schools for guidance.

Tenet 6. *The study of deviant development contributes to the study of normative child development.*

In developmental psychopathology, it is assumed that normal and abnormal development are both critical parts of understanding human behavior and that the study of one informs our knowledge of the other. Thus, a better understanding of deviant behavior is expected to contribute to knowledge of normative development. For example, the development of babies with Down's syndrome has contributed to our basic knowledge of cognitive and affective development (e.g., Cicchetti & Sroufe, 1978). More recently, social and language development in children with pervasive developmental disorders such as autism are beginning to provide insights into the processes underlying attachment and human communication (Cohen, Donnellan, & Paul, 1987).

IMPLICATIONS

Developmental psychopathology has many implications for theories, research, and applications pertaining to adaptation and behavioral problems in children and adolescents. Only a few ideas can be presented here. Other chapters in this section focus on additional implications. In the remainder of this chapter, we will explore implications for classification and diagnosis, treatment, prevention, and research, trying to find common ground between behavior therapy and developmental psychopathology.

Classification and Diagnosis

It is necessary, for many reasons, to describe behavior problems in an orderly fashion. This need is shared by clinicians and researchers alike. Clinicians must be able to access and add to a body of knowledge relevant to helping individuals. Similarly, in order to coordinate findings, researchers must be able to describe how subjects in their study are like and unlike the subjects of other studies.

Behaviorists, however, have neglected the enterprise of formal classification and diagnosis. Kazdin (1983) has asserted that behavior therapists have either conceptualized clinical dysfunction in terms of behavioral excesses, deficits, and approach or avoidance reactions or performed functional analyses of behavior. He suggested that behavior therapists tend to equate the concept of target behavior with the descriptive psychopathologist's concept of symptom, but with no equivalent for the traditional psychiatric notions of syndrome or disorder, thereby failing to consider the greater patterning of behaviors. Kazdin concluded that, with few exceptions, there has been little attention to the hierarchical organization of behavior. Yet this need not be the case (see Powers, 1984). The strengths of behavior theory can be used to improve current approaches to classification and diagnosis that can benefit from the observational rigor and functional perspective of behavioral analysis.

There have been two major approaches to classification in childhood behavior problems: the categorical tradition and the dimensional tradition. Categorical approaches derive from the classical medical tradition of organizing illnesses by describing symptoms that distinguish one class from another. These systems list disorders or syndromes that have been observed to differ qualitatively in terms of salient characteristics. The DSM system of classification, described earlier, is an example of pooled expertise derived from both clinical practice and research, although the system has been criticized for not indicating the sources of conclusions presented as diagnostic criteria. The dimensional tradition, on the other hand, arose from psychometric studies of how behaviors cluster together and is essentially a quantitative approach, although dimensions can be used to generate "types" or profiles that resemble diagnostic categories.

Each of these approaches when applied to children has required some accommodation to development, although the resulting age-related features of these systems are sometimes implicit rather than explicit. For example, as mentioned above, DSM-III has a number of developmental features, including age-based inclusion and exclusion criteria. The rationale for such features is not always explicitly articulated, however. Why does "Enuresis" not apply to a 2-year-old? Because this system assumes that bedwetting is normative in a 2-year-old. It is the timing of the behavior that is crucial, within the context of normative developmental trends. Why is it noted for the category "attention deficit hyperactivity disorder" that the definitive behaviors have to be "considerably more frequent than that of most people of the same mental age"? First, it is because this category is explicitly described in terms of degrees of behavior that are "developmentally inappropriate." Implicitly, this category requires the assumption that the symptoms are not in and of themselves qualitatively deviant, but rather quantitatively deviant in frequency or intensity from that of other children at the same level of development. This disorder also requires onset before 7 years of age, indicating an implicit recognition that as a developmental pattern of behavior, something has gone awry fairly early in areas such as attention, impulse control, and restraint.

As its name implies, the dimensional approach is an attempt to delineate the major dimensions along which individuals vary and may be described. Its roots lie in psychometric psychology and personality assessment. Probably the most widely used assessment tools in this tradition are behavior checklists developed by Achenbach and his colleagues for children 2 to 18 years old (Achenbach & Edelbrock, 1983, 1987; Achenbach & McConaughy, 1987). With data from large clinical and normal samples, this group has identified by factor analytic techniques a hierarchical set of dimensions that describe behavior problems in children of a particular sex and age range. Two pervasive global dimensions have been called "internalizing" and "externalizing." At a finer level of analysis, there are more dimensions, termed narrow-band syndromes, such as "depressed" or "somatic complaints." Norms within sex and age groups are provided for each dimension of behavior problems in keeping with the psychometric tradition (cf. intelligence test norms).

Achenbach's system also provides cluster profiles—a set of prototype profiles derived from cluster analyses of data from large samples of children. A child's profile of scores on the various dimensions can be compared to these prototypes, a process of quantitative diagnosis. These multidimensional types reflect patterns across dimensions of behavior. These patterns often strongly resemble disorders derived from more clinically derived systems (Achenbach, 1980; 1985).

In addition to these two major approaches to classification, there have been efforts to create more developmentally based systems. Garber (1984) has argued that a developmental approach to the classification of children's disorders is best accomplished by attending to the expression of organized patterns of behavior over long periods. Greenspan and Lourie (1981), for example, have suggested a classification system for infancy and early childhood from a developmental structuralist approach. For example, the first task described in their proposed system is homeostasis, referring to the maintenance of internal regulation that leads to smooth routines of sleeping, feeding, and easy soothability. Maladaptation takes the form of difficulty regulating, either hyperexcitable or withdrawn, apathetic behavior. Difficulties at each stage can arise either from the child's inability to organize behavior or a lack of environmental support.

Recently, Tanguay (1984) has suggested another developmental approach to classification, specifically applied to pervasive developmental disorders, that is related to Anna Freud's (1963) notion of developmental lines. He suggested that serious psychopathology such as autism in children could be better understood and differentiated in terms of a profile of progression along several major relevant lines of cognitive and motor development. As yet, however, these developmental lines and profiles have not been substantiated by research.

In deciding that a particular pattern of behavior or specific behavioral target represents a problem worthy of classification (or treatment), Garber (1984) has posed this critical question: "How long is too long?" She argued that in order to answer this question, one must consider age and sex norms for given behavior patterns in given situations. Such a question highlights the need for a classification of what is developmentally normal to complement the classification of psychopathology.

There has been some discussion of creating a "Manual of Development" but as yet no group appears willing to undertake this formidable task in the same way that the American Psychiatric Association undertook the *Diagnostic and Statistical Manual of Mental Disorders*. A manual of normal development would be an important step toward a more comprehensive classification system.

Attention to context is a basic feature of both developmental psychopathology and behavior therapy, yet extant classification systems give little attention to context. Whereas behaviorists have tended to conceptualize the context of a behavioral difficulty in strict formulations of the immediate antecedents and consequences of behavior, more recently there has been greater attention to the role of family factors such as marital discord and divorce, maternal depression, and maternal interaction outside of the home, in the expression of deviant child behavior and in outcome of behavioral treatment (Kazdin, 1983). Whalen and Henker (1980), for example, have provided a model for behaviorists in their analysis of the social ecology of hyperactive boys. From their work they have concluded that hyperactivity is most accurately conceptualized as a child-by-situation interaction and have offered analyses of which contexts are hardest for these children.

We need a comprehensive system that describes both normal and deviant behavior in the same system. As Tanguay (1984) argued in regard to the label "autism", patterns of functioning in children who meet the DSM-III criteria for this disorder vary so greatly that it is impossible to plan treatment without much more information on cognitive, language, social, and motor functioning.

What might a comprehensive system look like? What follows are some speculations with the goal of illustrating the implications of developmental psychopathology in this regard.

First of all, a comprehensive system would undoubtedly be multifaceted, an extension of the current trend toward multiaxial classifications evident in efforts by the American Psychiatric Association and the World Health Organization. One area should index cognitive development, both in terms of general intellectual functioning and academic achievement. This would allow children with specific learning disabilities to be identified by a pattern of normal general cognitive ability and impaired development in specific areas of achievement.

Another area should index social adaptation and development in terms of expected conduct for age, sex, and society, reflecting competence in typical environments. Composite scores of total problems (as on the Achenbach & Edelbrock, 1983 & 1987, checklists) or general ratings of adaptive functioning (as on Axis V of DSM-III-R) can be used to index this area, but they lose useful information. For example, empirical data suggest that there may be two major dimensions of social behavior in young children: (1) Engaged/interested versus disengaged/withdrawn and (2) prosocial/socialized/well-behaved versus aggressive/disruptive/antisocial. When assessments contain only negative items or problems, these emerge as "Internalizing" and "Externalizing" dimensions (e.g., Achenbach & Edelbrock, 1983). Broader assessments that include positive social behaviors reveal the bipolar nature of these dimensions (Kohn, 1977; Masten, 1989).

Much work is needed to develop norms for both development and society. The concept of developmental tasks may prove very useful in defining adaptive behavior and establishing age and sex norms.

Another area should describe current mood or distress level. Here again, two dimensions might be needed, because the literature suggests that mood and emotionality reflect two major bipolar dimensions, usually called *positive affect* and *negative affect* (Tellegen, 1985; Watson & Clark, 1984; Watson, Clark, & Carey, 1988). Depressed mood, for example, particularly reflects low levels of positive affect while anxiety or general distress reflects high negative affect. These mood states or traits seem to covary widely across many disorders or patterns of behavior and would seem to warrant a separate axis.

Other areas of the system might describe known causal influences that contribute to observed behavior. Known organic contributing factors could be noted on one axis, including brain damage or diseases with behavioral symptoms, as in Axis III "Physical Disorders and Conditions" of DSM-III-R. Eventually, these might include known markers of vulnerability to mental disorder (Masten & Garmezy, 1985). Another part of the classification would allow for environmental influences, indexing trauma, life events, psychosocial disadvantage, and possibly family dysfunction (akin to Axis IV on DSM-III-R), although it is unclear at this time how best to index psychosocial stressors.

Mental disorders could be grouped according to whether the disorder is defined by a distinct configuration of symptoms versus developmental patterns of deviance. A trend in this direction is already evident in the DSM-III-R system in which developmental and personality disorders are separated from other disorders because they "generally begin in childhood or adolescence and persist in a stable form . . . into adult life" (1987). Disorders with highly reliable and distinctive configurations of symptoms (i.e., syndromes) would include disorders such as schizophrenia, bipolar depression, and anorexia nervosa. Disorders defined primarily by developmental delays, distortions, or deviance would include such disorders as pervasive developmental disorders, personality disorders, conduct disorders, and hyperactivity. It might be possible to delineate subtypes of disorders such as conduct disorder according to more specific developmental patterns (e.g., an early onset, aggressive, solitary pattern, as discussed earlier).

Efforts could be made to reduce such a system to a workable number of axes without ignoring multiple causes and domains of behavior. Eventually, strong patterns across dimensions might be noted, adding to the list of well-defined syndromes and developmental patterns of deviance. Treatment needs and resources should become clearer with diagnoses based on such a system. This speculative exercise also points to the need for a broader view of assessment.

Implications for Assessment

If a classification system were developed, either in comprehensive form or in the form of a developmental manual supplementing available manuals of mental disorders, describing a person's behavior in terms of the system would require a broader view of assessment than common up to now. Researchers interested in competence and adaptation, especially those involved in longitudinal studies, have already had to come to terms with these implications and have attempted to measure adaptive behavior as well as maladaptation.

We need methods of assessment possessing age and sex norms. Moreover, assessment must address all of a child's behavior in salient developmental areas of functioning rather than focus exclusively and narrowly on symptoms. For example, social competence may be as important for understanding and helping a person as are problems on a "misbehavior" checklist.

Waters and Sroufe (1983) have argued that competence should be assessed by broad-based measures suited to the developmental issues of a given age group. Such measures would be expected to change because the central developmental tasks change and because the same observable behavior may have very different meanings at different ages.

At present, our assessment tools are more effective in the traditional areas of interest, pertaining to the perceived needs of education and clinical practice, such as intellectual functioning, academic achievement, and behavioral problems, than they are in terms of developmental tasks, social competence, or contextual variables such as stressors or resources. Extant instruments to assess development tend to focus on infants and preschoolers (e.g., Brazelton Neonatal Behavioral Assessment Scale, Denver Developmental Screening Test, Bayley Scales of Infant Development, Gesell Developmental Schedule).

Behavior therapy has a long tradition of objective, systematic assessment. Behaviorists attend closely to context and measuring environmental factors. Yet, as previously noted, it is only in recent years that behaviorists have begun to move beyond narrow formulations of antecedents and consequences of individual behaviors. In their discussion of ecological behavior analysis, Martens and Witt (1988) have called for behaviorists to move towards a more molar focus that addresses behavioral systems in addition to traditional molecular focus on individual events. This exhortation echoes Patterson's (1981) earlier call for a behavioral systems methodology, as exemplified in his time series analyses of parent and child behavior (Patterson, 1982). There is great potential for applying this expertise to create better methods of assessing social competence and adaptation as defined in developmental and environmental context.

A developmental perspective has many implications for how assessments are conducted by the individual practitioner. For example, while behaviorists have traditionally favored interviewing parents to obtain data about a child, recent data show that there is often little agreement across informants about child behavior and that the child may provide unique information (Achenbach, McConaughy, & Howell, 1987). Herjanic and Reich (1982) observed that while mothers and children may agree on specific, observable symptoms or events, mothers tend to report more behavior problems and children report more somatic complaints and symptoms of subjective emotional distress.

Cognitive-behaviorists have recommended interviewing the child to obtain a sense of the child's expectancies, beliefs, self-statements, and problem-solving capacities regarding the difficulties in question (Kendall & Braswell, 1985; Meichenbaum, Bream, & Cohen, 1985). But these recommendations are typically not accompanied by suggestions for developmentally appropriate methods of obtaining such information. Bierman (1983) and Harris and Ferrari (1983) suggested attending to differences in how children may interpret words and questions in interviews. Bierman (1983) advised that with children younger than approximately 7 years of age, it is advisable to present structured rather than open-ended questions and provide response alternatives, as well as visual referents for responses.

Implications for Treatment

The advantages of a developmental perspective for meeting the goal of more effective, individualized treatments has been articulated by a number of behaviorists (Furman, 1980; Harris & Ferrari, 1983; Kendall, Lerner, & Craighead, 1984; McMahon & Peters, 1985; Phillips & Ray, 1980). Examined in this section are implications of developmental psychopathology for treatment issues such as deciding whether and when to intervene, the goals of intervention, specific targets of change, concerns with specific behavioral techniques, and the context of treatment. Finally, an example is provided of recent developmental research with important implications for intervention.

Logically, the first question in examining treatment applications is whether it is appropriate or desirable to intervene in a specific instance. Garber (1984) argued that in addition to considering how long is too long when defining the presence of a problem, the clinician must ask how long is too long before treatment is advisable. Both the behaviorist and the developmental psychopathologist would be comfortable with the notion of examining the consequences of action or inaction; however, the developmental psychopathologist would be expected to conceive of consequences in a broader context. For example, the more developmentally oriented clinician would consider possible long-term effects even if the specific difficulty resolves itself in a limited time frame. Garber (1984) noted that while the primary symptoms of a disorder such as depression may resolve in a circumscribed period, the associated features such as poor peer relations and poor school adjustment may have more long term consequences for the child. Achenbach (1987) has also discussed the need to distinguish situations in which at-risk children are best served by a "wait and see" attitude from those situations in which intervention clearly produces better outcomes.

Better data on the natural history of cognitive, emotional, and behavioral difficulties would enable clinicians to make empirically based decisions regarding whether or not to intervene. It would also yield data important for the better timing of interventions.

Developmental psychopathologists are united in the goal of carefully matching the timing of the intervention with the state of the organism (Achenbach, 1987; Harter, 1982). By definition, this paradigm emphasizes the unfolding of a developmental process that requires environmental input, but, as Achenbach (1987) noted, the effect of the environment is assumed to depend upon the organization's current level of development: "As a consequence, manipulations of environmental stimuli are thought unlikely to bring about advanced developmental levels unless the organism has reached the appropriate preliminary level" (p. 120). Relevant to the current practice of self-control training in children, research indicates that young children do not have the ability or, alternatively, the interest in focusing on themselves as an object of evaluation or criticism (Harter, 1982). Typically this capacity and/or interest develops around the age of 6 to 8 years. Such findings have direct implications for the timing of therapies that assume the capacity for self evaluation.

Yet the timing of intervention involves more than determining whether the child has the requisite abilities to benefit from a particular form of therapy. Interventions can occur too late as well as too early in the developing organism. It has become increasingly clear in the area of antisocial behavior that prevention and very early intervention are extremely important, because antisocial child behavior often escalates, becomes increasingly stable in childhood, and is resistant to change; there may be critical periods of malleability for altering antisocial pathways (Loeber & Stouthamer-Loeber, 1987).

The choice of targets for intervention also could benefit from a more developmental perspective. Behavioral conceptualizations of childhood problems have focused almost exclusively on specific symptoms or target behaviors, with a lack of concern for how a specific behavior might relate to a larger constellation of issues (Kazdin, 1983; Phillips & Ray, 1980). This narrow focus has made behavior therapy vulnerable to accusations that selected treatments are unimportant, inappropriate, and/or unethical (Furman, 1980). Thus, volumes central to the practice of behavioral therapy, such as Mash and Terdal's (1981, 1988) *Behavioral Assessment of Childhood Disorders*, have called for behaviorists to look to developmental theories in preparing behavioral assessment and treatment plans. Furman (1980) has discussed cogently the implications of developmental research for the selection of target behaviors in social skills training that takes into account the developmental status of the child and the child's ecological context.

To be fair, many behavior therapists do operate with an implicit sense of developmental appropriateness of a given problem behavior. Gelfand and Peterson (1985) note that even the earliest early conditioning targeted concerns appropriate to the child's level of development, such as excessive crying in infants (Williams, 1959), enuresis in school-age children (Mowrer & Mowrer, 1938) and delinquent behavior in adolescents (Schwitzgebel & Kolb, 1964). This implicit approach, however, tends to ignore the wealth of data from the literature on normal development that offers greater accuracy than a given behaviorist's highly individualized internal norms.

The different approaches to the selection of the target behaviors offered by developmental and behavioral perspective reflect an underlying difference in how these viewpoints conceptualize the goals of intervention. Historically, behavioral formulations have emphasized the resolution of specific target behaviors or, alternately, the increase of selected desirable behaviors, such as increasing attempts at initiating social play in withdrawn children. Whereas it was assumed that such changes would aid the present and future functioning of the child, there was little or no consideration given to how the desired changes would specifically affect the child's ability to negotiate developmental tasks or influence the developmental trajectory of the child. The emergence of competence models and coping skills orientations to intervention within behavior therapy are more congruent with developmental viewpoints, because they attempt to increase the child's ability to meet current and future developmental challenges.

Developmental psychopathology has implications for the methods of intervention as well. Given the focus of this volume on behavior therapy, examples will be drawn from methods of behavioral and cognitive-behavioral therapy. It should be noted, however, that in some situations a thorough analysis of developmental concerns might result in the selection of an intervention approach that falls outside the bounds of behavioral or cognitive-behavioral approaches.

The implications of developmental findings for the key behavioral tools of reward, punishment, and observational learning have been clearly detailed by Furman (1980), who advised the researcher or clinician implementing a program involving positive reinforcement to be aware of the developmental changes in the value of social approval, accuracy feedback, mastery incentives, and tangible versus symbolic reinforcers. Furman's review offers guidelines for selecting reinforcers that are not unduly distracting or likely to cause maintenance difficulties. Concerning the use of aversive contingencies, Furman cited data that clarifies developmental changes in the value of providing a rationale for punishment and discusses how the provision of a rationale can, at certain developmental levels, heighten the effectiveness of even delayed, low intensity punishment. Furman's discussion of developmental changes in the process of observational learning or modeling is particularly valuable for the behaviorist because it is commonly assumed that modeling is an effective mode of intervention with even very young children (Wasserman, 1983). Although Furman also supports the use of modeling with young clients, his review clarifies the marked developmental changes in the quantity and quality of the information children acquire through observational learning.

When implementing approaches that include a more complex combination of components, such as systematic desensitization, it may be even more crucial to consider developmental concerns and avoid direct downward extensions of methods found successful with adults. Data on the efficacy of systematic desensitization with children is much more equivocal than is the case with adults (Graziano, DeGiovanni, & Garcia, 1979; Hatzenbuehler & Schroeder, 1978). It is widely recognized that children are capable of vivid images and that such imagery can be used to aid recall (Hayes & Birbaum, 1980; Purkel & Bornstein, 1980), but questions remain regarding whether or not children can use imagery as a means of changing complex behaviors (Wasserman, 1983). Ollendick (1979) has argued that the available literature suggests that children profit more from graduated *in vivo* exposure to feared stimuli than to imaginal presentations. A number of reviews of behavioral intervention methods with children (Harris & Ferrari, 1983; Ollendick, 1979; Wasserman, 1983) have recommended using a creative approach to selecting counter conditioning agents, such as the Lazarus and Abramovitz (1962) procedure of having children imagine themselves in the company of their favorite superhero when encountering the feared stimulus. Greater recognition of the key role of a warm, supportive relationship with the trainer (whether therapist or a parent) as the primary counter conditioning agent has also been urged (Ollendick, 1979) and such relationship factors would seem to play a primary and sometimes underrecognized role in some accounts of successful densensitization attempts (e.g., Osborn, 1986).

The cognitive–behavioral approach of verbal self-instructional training has achieved tremendous popularity both as an object of study and as a mode of intervention with both children and adults (see Braswell & Kendall, 1987). Compared to other behavioral methods, it was more rooted in developmental theory. Meichenbaum and Goodman (1971) based the format of their verbal, self-instructional training methods on the theory of the development of verbal control over behavior proposed by Vygotsky (1962) and elaborated by Luria (1959, 1961).

Although self-instructional interventions have achieved positive outcomes in treating a variety of childhood difficulties, this method, like many traditional behavioral interventions, has been plagued with problems of poor maintenance and limited generalization of gains, particularly when applied with samples manifesting clinically significant levels of impairment (see reviews by Abikoff, 1987; and Braswell & Kendall, 1987). In an effort to understand these problems, some investigators have explored the impact of developmental variables (see review by Copeland, 1982).

For example, research addressing the role of age and cognitive level suggests that younger, lower IQ, and/or pre-operational children benefit from simple task-oriented self-instructions in terms of improved task performance but are unlikely to generalize across tasks. Children who are older, have higher IQs, and/or have developed more logical thinking (in Piagetian terms, concrete operational thinking) seem to benefit from more generalized self-instruction, both in terms of task performance and generalization across tasks (Bender, 1976; Kendall & Wilcox, 1980; Thackwray, Meyers, Schleser, & Cohen, 1985). Optimal outcomes with concrete operational children have been achieved with interventions combining both specific, task-oriented statements and general strategy statements (Schleser, Meyers, & Cohen, 1981).

These efforts to understand the interaction between aspects of the child and methods of conducting verbal self-instructional training represent important steps toward greater recognition of developmental factors; however, Mahoney and Nezworski (1985) have challenged that cognitive-behavioral formulations must move away from their "portrayal of the nervous system as an isolated island of (albeit mediated) adaptation" (p. 472) to a greater recognition of the role of family and affectional systems in shaping the development of the difficulties in question, whether one is addressing issues of self-control, problem-solving, or social interaction. Implicit in the Mahoney and Nezworski (1985) critique is the view that cognitive-behaviorists attempt to accomplish in a few weeks of isolated training, capacities that, in the healthy individual, develop over the course of years of social interaction and exchange with people of great emotional significance. According to this view, effective intervention would not only need to involve addressing family and other significant relationships, but would need to plant the seeds for change that would be accomplished over a time frame much longer than is typical for behavioral and cognitive-behavioral treatments. Interventions that address shifting the family's style of problem-solving, and making the home and school environments more rewarding of reflective behavior, in addition to teaching the child verbal self-instructional training represent beginning efforts at meeting this challenge (Bloomquist & August, 1988; Bloomquist & Braswell, 1987).

Implicit in the discussion to this point is the importance of the environmental context of treatment as well as the developmental context. It seems ironic that behavioral interventions that grew out of theory addressing the significance of the context of behavior have tended to focus so narrowly on the immediate context and ignored other contextual systems in which behavior occurs, such as family and peer relationships, school, and community. The case for broadening the context of concern in behavior therapy has been articulated by Craighead, Meyers, and Craighead (1985). The power of a contextual view is well illustrated by recent research on the treatment programs for delinquency (e.g., Henggeler, Rodick, Borduin, Hanson, Watson, & Urey, 1986) and younger conduct disordered children (Webster-Stratton, 1985).

Recent theory and ground breaking research on the role of beliefs in behavior provides a striking example of developmental work with implications for intervention. For example, Ellen Skinner and her colleagues (Skinner, in press; Skinner, Chapman, & Baltes, 1988) have proposed an integrative model of perceived control linking beliefs, actions, and outcomes in a system that develops in children. They propose that at a microdevelopmental level, greater perceived control produces more sustained efforts to achieve an outcome or to engage the task. Success tends to increase one's beliefs in control although the evaluation of success depends both on one's means–ends beliefs, or beliefs about the causes of outcomes (e.g., luck, effort, ability) and agency beliefs, or beliefs about one's self in regard to those causes (e.g., I am lucky, I can try hard, or I am smart). This system, however, emerges and develops in children. It becomes increasingly self-regulatory and less influenced by the environment. Beliefs about causes shift from known-versus-unknown to internal-versus-external to ability-versus-lack of ability. For example, belief in luck as a cause of success decreases in middle childhood. In younger children, who are less self-regulatory, and whose beliefs are more influenced by outcomes, there are many ways to change perceived control and influence beliefs. One can promote action or provide contingent outcomes that are set up to be positive and that suggest causes to the children that increase their perceived control. Older children, however, especially by adolescence, have highly self-regulating systems where beliefs are much less influenced by such environmental manipulations. The same strategies won't work, or may even decrease beliefs in perceived control. To change the beliefs of an adolescent or adult will be more challenging, as no doubt cognitive-behavioral therapists will attest. This model also suggests that early intervention is important for motivational problems. Although this model is itself still developing, it seems clear that here is an area of thinking and research where developmentalists and cognitive-behaviorists are coming together to produce an integrative model with profound implications for intervention.

Implications for Prevention

It is fundamental for prevention and early intervention efforts to understand the etiology and course of maladaptive patterns of behavior and the contrasting patterns of desired adaptation. All the points outlined above with regard to intervention apply as much and more so to prevention efforts. Especially in a rapidly developing organism, such as a child, it is important to know how successful and deviant patterns arise and unfold in order to design the best—most effective, efficient, and timely—interventions to prevent the onset or improve the outcome of incipient disorder. Developmental psychopathology has a number of key implications for prevention that only will be outlined here as there is another chapter in this book devoted entirely to the subject.

To begin, if psychopathology is conceptualized as a multidetermined path that has gone too far from the spectrum of adaptive pathways identified as normative or "OK" for current and future adaptation, then the question of prevention becomes one of knowing when and how to deflect development in such a way that a deviant fork in the road is avoided or a person's path is turned in more adaptive directions early enough to avoid the worst outcomes. Central to these goals is an understanding of developmental patterns, crucial forks in the road, methods of deflecting movements along a path, and the best times to concentrate efforts at intervention so as to achieve maximal effects in terms of adaptive developmental trajectories.

Thus, in order to achieve the goals of prevention, we must have a strong foundation of knowledge both about processes of adaptive development and processes of psychopathology. It is not enough to know the risk factors and processes that lead to deviant patterns. It is also necessary to understand and know how to facilitate the processes that produce more adaptive outcomes. For the latter goal, normative developmental processes can provide many clues, but the best clues may come from similarly high risk children who avoided deviance or children whose developmental patterns reveal a turning away from deviance back toward adaptation. Developmental psychopathologists who study competence in high risk children, recovery from adversity, "desistance" or turning away from deviant behavior patterns, and other forms of moving toward adaptive development aim to provide this kind of knowledge. Behaviorists have argued the same case when they brought attention to the importance of simultaneously increasing desirable behaviors while decreasing undesirable behaviors by altering environmental contingencies. Treatment outcome research that examines who has the best outcomes or the mechanisms of change for the better serves this goal as well.

At this time, we are just at the beginning stages of integrating all that is known about development, patterns of psychopathology, and recovery in order to apply this knowledge to prevention programming. Yet there are examples of prevention programs that draw effectively on such developmental knowledge. Gelfand and Peterson (1985), for example, have described behavioral language skills training programs designed with a developmental perspective. Similarly, programs to prevent antisocial behavior in school-age children focus increasingly on the preschool years when the underpinnings of compliance and self-regulation are developing (e.g., Patterson & Bank, 1989). Programs to prevent adolescent behavior problems such as smoking, drug use, suicide, as well as behaviors associated with high risk for AIDS increasingly are focused in the elementary years before these patterns develop. Prevention aimed at the teenage mind now appears to focus on immediate teenage concerns (attractiveness for example) rather than long range, adult concerns such as cancer (Creswell, Stone, Hoffman, & Newman, 1971).

Delinquency researchers not only have turned their attention toward the phenomenon of desistance (e.g., Mulvey, 1985; Mulvey & LaRosa, 1986), they have also begun to examine possible critical periods for all out intervention effects in early adolescence that precede the period when delinquency patterns appear to crystallize and become much more difficult to deflect. Much research still is needed to improve the design and timing of prevention programs.

CONCLUSIONS

Developmental psychopathology is just emerging as a framework for the science and practice of psychology as applied to behavior problems. Hence, the research agenda is full and the evolving tenets described herein provide a guide to the research directions taking shape within this framework. There is much to be done in regard to classification and assessment, examining the etiological patterns and course of psychopathology, designing developmentally sensitive intervention and prevention programs, and integrating the existing and previously largely separate data on normative and deviant behavior in children and adolescents. Although a full examination of this research agenda is beyond the scope of this chapter, we will consider the potential role of behavior therapy in this effort. The collaboration of developmentally and behaviorally oriented researchers could yield information of tremendous value to all professionals involved in the study and treatment of childhood psychopathology. Whereas the possibilities for productive collaboration are unlimited, a few key areas provide examples in which united efforts would be of particular importance.

There is a great need for better normative data on the behavior of children and adolescents that is pertinent to developmental tasks, adaptation, and maladaptation. Epidemiological data are especially crucial (Rutter, 1988). Developmentalists and behavior therapists have a strong tradition of careful empirical observation that in combination could yield data that are more informative to both. We need normative data that reflects both the concern with developmental change and age differences of the former, and the concern with function and context of the latter group of empirical observers.

Similarly, there is a great need for new assessment methods that capture the important aspects of behavior in a given period of development while enabling one to monitor adaptation over time and developmental change. The same context that is valid for 3-year-olds is unlikely to be meaningful for the assessment of adolescents. Indeed, the same behavior is likely to have a different meaning and significance altogether. Yet developmental theory and research suggests that there are coherent patterns of behavior with great significance over time if assessment tools capture the salient lines of developmental change (Waters & Sroufe, 1983). Behavior therapy has a lot to offer in the design and evaluation of such new assessment tools.

One of the great contributions of behavior therapy to the science and practice of psychology has been systematic outcome research. The maturing of developmental psychopathology is going to require a great deal more work evaluating new developmentally-oriented treatment and prevention efforts. Similarly, age and developmental status must become a central focus of new outcome research in behavior therapy. Just as mainstream academic child developmentalists originally focused on setting forth general principles of development, academic behaviorists were initially concerned with establishing the generality of the laws of learning, rather than attending to factors, such as individual differences in developmental status, that moderate the effects of learning paradigms. Fortunately, individual differences in responsiveness to various techniques is now a highly accepted topic of study within behavior therapy. With this greater recognition and acceptance of individual differences in treatment response, behaviorists may now be ready to incorporate assessments that can fully address the diversity of outcomes following intervention. Such an approach would demand the inclusion of longitudinal measures that assess the child's developmental status along a number of dimensions.

In this chapter, we have attempted to set forth the basic assumptions and some implications of an emerging developmental framework for understanding psychopathology. We believe that the theoretical, methodological, and technological strengths of behavior therapy have much to offer to this integrative model and that, concomitantly, behavior therapy has much to gain from the developmental perspective. In many ways, development has been a missing ingredient in the endeavors of behavior therapists, although there are encouraging signs of change. We hope that this chapter provides a glimpse of the tremendous potential in merging behavioral and developmental models of psychopathology.

REFERENCES

Abikoff, H. (1987). An evaluation of cognitive behavior therapy for hyperactive children. In B. B. Lahey & A. E. Kazdin (Eds.), *Advances in clinical child psychology*, (Vol. 5, pp. 171–216). New York: Plenum Press.

Achenbach, T. M. (1974). *Developmental psychopathology*. New York: Ronald Press.

Achenbach, T. M. (1980). DSM-III in light of empirical research on the classification of child psychopathology. *Journal of the American Academy of Child Psychiatry*, *19*, 395–412.

Achenbach, T. M. (1985). *Assessment and taxonomy of child and adolescent psychopathology*. Beverly Hills, CA: Sage Publications.

Achenbach, T. M. (1987). The developmental study of psychopathology: Implications for psychotherapy and behavior change. In S. L. Garfield & A. E. Bergin (Eds.), *Handbook of psychotherapy and behavior change* (3rd ed., pp. 117–154). New York: John Wiley & Sons.

Achenbach, T. M., & Edelbrock, C. (1983). *Manual for the Child Behavior Checklist and Revised Child Behavior*

Profile. Burlington: University of Vermont, Department of Psychiatry.
Achenbach, T. M., & Edelbrock, C. (1987). *Manual for the Youth Self-Report and Profile.* Burlington: University of Vermont, Department of Psychiatry.
Achenbach, T. M., & McConaughy, S. H. (1987). *Empirically-based assessment of child and adolescent psychopathology: Practical implications.* Newbury Park, CA: Sage Publications.
Achenbach, T. M., McConaughy, S. H., & Howell, C. T. (1987). Child/Adolescent behavioral and emotional problems: Implications of cross-informant correlations for situational specificity. *Psychological Bulletin, 101,* 213–232.
Ainsworth, M. D. S., Blehar, M. C., Waters, E., & Wall, S. (1978). *Patterns of attachment: A psychological study of the Strange Situation.* Hillsdale, NJ: Lawrence Erlbaum Associates.
Akiskal, H. S., & McKinney, W. T. (1975). Overview of recent research in depression: Integration of ten conceptual models into a comprehensive clinical frame. *Archives of General Psychiatry, 32,* 285–305.
American Psychiatric Association (1980). *Diagnostic and statistical manual of mental disorders.* (3rd ed.). Washington, DC: Author.
American Psychiatric Association (1987). *Diagnostic and statistical manual of mental disorders.* (3rd ed., Revised.) Washington, DC: Author.
Anthony, E. J., & Cohler, B. J. (Eds.). (1987). *The invulnerable child.* New York: Guilford Press.
Bell, R. (1968). A reinterpretation of the directions of effects in studies of socialization. *Psychological Review, 75,* 81–95.
Bender, L. (1937). Behavior problems in the children of psychotic and criminal parents. *Genetic Psychology Monographs, 19,* 229–339.
Bender, N. (1976). Self-verbalization versus tutor verbalization in modifying impulsivity. *Journal of Educational Psychology, 68,* 347–354.
Bierman, K. L. (1983). Cognitive development and clinical interviews with children. In B. B. Lahey & A. E. Kazdin (Eds.), *Advances in clinical child psychology* (Vol. 6, pp. 217–250). New York: Plenum Press.
Bloomquist, M. L., & August G. (1988). *A comparison of comprehensive versus focused cognitive-behavioral treatment and methylphenidate versus placebo status with attention deficit-hyperactivity disordered children.* Unpublished manuscript, University of Minnesota Hospitals, Department of Child and Adolescent Psychiatry, Minneapolis.
Bloomquist, M. L., & Braswell, L. (1987). *Comprehensive child and family intervention for attention deficit-hyperactivity disordered children.* Unpublished manuscript.
Bowlby, J. (1969). *Attachment and loss: I. Attachment.* New York: Basic Books.
Bowlby, J. (1973). *Attachment and loss: II. Separation: Anxiety and anger.* New York: Basic Books.
Bowlby, J. (1980). *Attachment and loss: III. Loss: Sadness and depression.* New York: Basic Books.
Bowlby, J. (1988). Developmental psychiatry comes of age. *American Journal of Psychiatry, 145,* 1–10.
Braswell, L., & Kendall, P. C. (1987). Cognitive–behavioral methods with children. In K. S. Dobson (Ed.) *Handbook of cognitive–behavioral therapies* (pp. 167–213). New York: Guilford Press.
Bretherton, I., & Waters, E. (Eds.) (1985). Growing points of attachment theory and research. *Monographs of the Society for Research in Child Development, 50,* (1–2, Serial No. 209).
Bronfenbrenner, U. (1979). *The ecology of human development: Experiments by nature and design.* Cambridge, MA: Harvard University Press.
Cantwell, D. P., & Baker, L. (1988). Issues in the classification of child and adolescent psychopathology, *Journal of the American Academy of Child and Adolescent Psychiatry, 27,* 521–533.
Carlson, G. A., & Cantwell, D. P. (1982). Suicidal behavior and depression in children and adolescents. *Journal of the American Academy of Child Psychiatry, 21,* 361–368.
Cicchetti, D. (1984). The emergence of developmental psychopathology. *Child Development, 55,* 1–7.
Cicchetti, D. (1990). An historical perspective on the discipline of developmental psychopathology. In J. Rolf, A. Masten, D. Cicchetti, K. Nuechterlein, & S. Weintraub (Eds.), *Risk and protective factors in the development of psychopathology* (pp. 2–28). New York: Cambridge University Press.
Cicchetti, D., & Sroufe, L. A. (1978). An organizational view of affect: Illustration from the study of Down's syndrome infants. In M. Lewis & L. Roseblum (Eds.), *The development of affect* (pp. 309–350). New York: Plenum Press.
Cohen, D. J., Donnellan, A. M., & Paul, R. (Eds.). (1987). *Handbook of autism and pervasive developmental disorders.* New York: John Wiley & Sons.
Copeland, A. P. (1982). Individual difference factors in children's self-management: Toward individualized treatments. In P. Karoly & F. H. Kanfer (Eds.), *Self-management and behavior change: From theory to practice* (pp. 207–239). Elmsford, NY: Pergamon Press.
Craighead, W. E., Meyers, A. W., & Craighead, L. W. (1985). A conceptual model for cognitive-behavior therapy with children. *Journal of Abnormal Child Psychology, 13,* 331–342.
Creswell, H. W., Stone, D. B., Hoffman, W. J., & Newman, I. M. (1971). Anti-smoking education study at the University of Illinois. *Health Services and Mental Health Administration Health Reports, 86,* 565–576.
Delprato, D. J. (1987). Developmental interactionism: An integrative framework for behavior therapy. *Advances in Behavior Research and Therapy, 9*(4), pp. 173–205.
Donovan, J. E., & Jessor, R. (1985). Structure of problem

behavior in adolescence and young adulthood. *Journal of Consulting and Clinical Psychology, 53*, 890–904.

Donovan, J. E., Jessor, R., & Costa, F. M. (1988). Syndrome of problem behavior in adolescence: A replication. *Journal of Consulting and Clinical Psychology, 56*, 762–765.

Eisenberg, L. (1977). Development as a unifying concept in psychiatry. *British Journal of Psychiatry, 131*, 225–237.

Elder, G. H., Jr. (1979). Historical change in life patterns and personality. In P. B. Baltes & O. G. Brim, Jr. (Eds.), *Life span development and behavior*. (Vol. 2, pp. 117–159). New York: Academic Press.

Elder, G. H., Caspi, A., & Burton, L. M. (1988). Adolescent transition in developmental perspective: Sociological and historical insights. In M. R. Gunnar & W. A. Collins (Eds.), *Development during the transition to adolescence: Minnesota Symposia on Child Psychology* (Vol. 21, pp. 151–179). Hillsdale, NJ: Lawrence Erlbaum Associates.

Erikson, E. H. (1950). *Childhood and Society*. New York: W. W. Norton.

Eth, S., & Pynoos, R. S. (Eds.) (1985). *Post-traumatic stress disorder in children*. Washington, DC: American Psychiatric Press.

Fish, B. (1957). The detection of schizophrenia in infancy. *Journal of Nervous and Mental Disease, 125*, 1–24.

Fowler, R. C., Rich, C. L., & Young, D. (1986). San Diego suicide study: II. Substance abuse in young cases. *Archives of General Psychiatry, 43*, 962–965.

Freud, A. (1963). The concept of developmental lines. *Psychoanalytic Study of the Child, 18*, 245–265.

Furman, W. (1980). Promoting social development: Developmental implications for treatment. In B. B. Lahey & A. E. Kazdin (Eds.), *Advances in clinical child psychology*, (Vol. 3, pp. 1–40). New York: Plenum Press.

Garber, J. (1984). Classification of childhood psychopathology: A developmental perspective. *Child Development, 55*, 30–48.

Garfinkel, B. D., & Golombek, H. (1983). Suicidal behavior in adolescence. In B. D. Garfinkel & G. H. Golombek (Eds.), *The adolescent and mood disturbance*, (pp. 189–217). Toronto, Ontario: International University Press.

Garmezy, N. (1974). Children at risk: The search for the antecedents to schizophrenia: Part II. Ongoing research programs, issues and intervention. *Schizophrenia Bulletin, 9*, 55–125.

Garmezy, N. (1981). Children under stress: Perspectives on antecedents and correlates of vulnerability and resistance to psychopathology. In A. I. Robin, J. Aronoff, A. M. Barclay, & R. A. Zucker (Eds.), *Further explorations in personality* (pp. 196–269). New York: John Wiley & Sons.

Garmezy, N. (1987). Stress, competence, and development: Continuities in the study of schizophrenic adults, children vulnerable to psychopathology, and the search for stress-resistant children. *American Journal of Orthopsychiatry, 57*, 159–174.

Garmezy, N., & Masten, A. S. (1986). Stress, competence, and resilience: Common frontiers for therapist and psychopathologist. *Behavior Therapy, 17*, 500–521.

Garmezy, N., & Rutter, M. (Eds.) (1983). *Stress, coping, and development in children*. New York: McGraw-Hill.

Garmezy, N., & Streitman, S. (1974). Children at risk: The search for the antecedents to schizophrenia: Part I. Conceptual models and research methods. *Schizophrenia Bulletin, 8*, 14–90.

Garner, D. M., & Garfinkel, P. E. (Eds.) (1985). *Handbook of psychotherapy for anorexia nervosa and bulimia*. New York: Guilford Press.

Gelfand, D. M., & Peterson, L. (1985). *Child development and psychopathology*. Beverly Hills, CA: Sage Publications.

Goldstein, M. J., & Tuma, A. H. (Eds.) (1987). Special section on high-risk research. *Schizophrenia Bulletin, 13* (3).

Gottesman, I. I. (1974). Developmental genetics and ontogenetic psychology: Overdue detente and propositions from a matchmaker. In A. D. Pick (Ed.), *Minnesota Symposia on Child Psychology*, Vol. 8 (pp. 55–80). Minneapolis, MN: University of Minnesota Press.

Gottesman, I. I., & Shields, J. (1982). *Schizophrenia: The epigenetic puzzle*. New York: Cambridge University Press.

Graziano, A. M., DeGiovanni, I. S., & Garcia, K. A. (1979). Behavioral treatment of children's fears: A review. *Psychological Bulletin, 86*, 804–830.

Greenspan, S. I. (1981). *Psychopathology and adaptation in infant and early childhood: Principles of clinical diagnosis and preventive intervention*. New York: International Universities Press.

Greenspan, S., & Lourie, R. S. (1981). Developmental structuralist approach to the classification of adaptive and pathologic personality organizations: Infancy and early childhood. *American Journal of Psychiatry, 138*, 725–735.

Group for the Advancement of Psychiatry (1966). *Psychopathological disorders in childhood: Theoretical considerations and a proposed classification*. New York: Author.

Gunnar, M. R., & Thelen, E. (Eds.) (1989). *Systems and development: The Minnesota Symposia on Child Psychology* (Vol. 22). Hillsdale, NJ: Lawrence Erlbaum Associates.

Hanson, D. R., & Gottesman, I. I. (1976). The genetics, if any, of infantile autism and childhood schizophrenia. *Journal of Autism and Childhood Schizophrenia, 6*, 209–245.

Harris, S. L., & Ferrari, M. (1983). Developmental factors in child behavior therapy. *Behavior Therapy, 14*, 54–72.

Harter, S. (1982). A developmental perspective on some parameters of self-regulation in children. In P. Karoly & F. H. Kanfer (Eds.), *Self-management and behavior*

change: From theory to practice (pp. 165–204). Elmsford, NY: Pergamon Press.
Hatzenbuehler, L. C., & Schroeder, H. E. (1978). Densensitization procedures in the treatment of childhood disorders. *Psychological Bulletin, 85*, 831–844.
Havighurst, R. J. (1972). *Developmental tasks and education* (3rd ed.). New York: Longman.
Hawton, K. (1986). *Suicide and attempted suicide among children and adolescents*. Beverly Hills, CA: Sage Publications.
Hayes, D. S., & Birbaum, D. W. (1980). Preschoolers retention of televised events: Is a picture worth a thousand words? *Developmental Psychology, 16*, 410–416.
Henggeler, S. W., Rodick, J. D., Borduin, C. M., Hanson, C. L., Watson, S. M., & Urey, J. R. (1986). Multisystemic treatment of juvenile offenders: Effects on adolescent behavior and family interaction. *Developmental Psychology, 22*, 132–141.
Henn, F. A., Bardwell, R., & Jenkins, R. I. (1980). Juvenile delinquents revisited: Adult criminal activity. *Archives of General Psychiatry, 37*, 1160–1163.
Herjanic, B., & Reich, W. (1982). Development of a structured psychiatric interview for children: Agreement between child and parent on individual symptoms. *Journal of Abnormal Child Psychology, 10*, 307–324.
Kanner, L. (1943). Autistic disturbances of affective contact. *Nervous Child, 2*, 217–250.
Kazdin, A. E. (1983). Psychiatric diagnosis, dimensions of dysfunction, and child behavior therapy. *Behavior Therapy, 14*, 73–99.
Kendall, P. C., & Braswell, L. (1985). *Cognitive-behavioral theory for impulsive children*. New York: Guilford Press.
Kendall, P. C., Lerner, R. M., & Craighead, W. E. (1984). Human development and intervention in childhood psychopathology. *Child Development, 55*, 71–82.
Kendall, P. C., & Wilcox, L. E. (1980). A cognitive-behavioral treatment for impulsivity: Concrete versus conceptual training in non-self-controlled problem children. *Journal of Consulting and Clinical Psychology, 48*, 80–91.
Kohn, M. (1977). *Social competence, symptoms and underachievement in childhood: A longitudinal perspective*. Washington, DC: V. H. Winston & Sons.
Kopp, C. B. (1982). Antecedents of self-regulation: A developmental perspective. *Developmental Psychology, 18*, 199–214.
Lazarus, A. A., & Abramovitz, A. (1962). The use of "emotive imagery" in the treatment of children's phobias. *Journal of Mental Science, 108*, 191–195.
Lerner, R. M. (1988). Early adolescent transitions: The lore and laws of adolescence. In M. D. Levine & E. R. McAnarney (Eds.), *Early adolescent transitions* (pp. 1–21). Lexington, MA: D. C. Heath.
Loeber, R. (1990). Development and risk factors of juvenile antisocial behavior and delinquency. *Clinical Psychology Review, 10*, 1–41.

Loeber, R., & Stouthamer-Loeber, M. (1987). Prediction. In H. C. Quay (Ed.), *Handbook of juvenile delinquency* (pp. 325–382). New York: John Wiley & Sons.
Luria, A. R. (1959). The directive function of speech in development and dissolution. *Word, 15*, 341–352.
Luria, A. R. (1961). *The role of speech in the regulation of normal and abnormal behaviors*. New York: Liveright.
Mahoney, M. J., & Nezworski, M. T. (1985). Cognitive-behavioral approaches to children's problems. *Journal of Abnormal Child Psychology, 13*, 467–476.
Martens, B. K., & Witt, J. C. (1988). Ecological behavior analysis. In M. Hersen, R. M. Eisler, & P. M. Miller (Eds.), *Progress in behavior modification* (Vol. 22, pp. 115–140). Newbury Park, CA: Sage Publications.
Mash, E. J., & Terdal, L. G. (Eds.) (1981). *Behavioral assessment of childhood disorders*. New York: Guilford Press.
Mash, E. J., & Terdal, L. G. (Eds.) (1988). *Behavioral assessment of childhood disorders*. (2nd ed.). New York: Guilford Press.
Masten, A. S. (1986). Developmental psychopathology: The promise continues. [Review of R. J. McMahon & R. DeV. Peters (Eds.), *Childhood disorders: Behavioral-developmental approaches*.] *Contemporary Psychology, 31*, 884.
Masten, A. S. (1988). Toward a developmental psychopathology of early adolescence. In M. D. Levine & E. R. McAnarney (Eds.), *Early adolescent transitions* (pp. 261–278). Lexington, MA: D. C. Heath.
Masten, A. S. (1989). Resilience in development: Implications of the study of successful adaptation for developmental psychopathology. In D. Cicchetti (Ed.), *The emergence of a discipline: Rochester symposium on developmental psychopathology* (Vol. 1) (pp. 261–294). Hillsdale, NJ: Lawrence Erlbaum Associates.
Masten, A. S., & Garmezy, N. (1985). Risk, vulnerability and protective factors in developmental psychopathology. In B. B. Lahey & A. E. Kazdin (Eds.), *Advances in Clinical Child Psychology*, (vol. 8, pp. 1–52). New York: Plenum Press.
Masten, A. S., Garmezy, N., Tellegen, A., Pellegrini, D. S., Larkin, K., & Larsen, A. (1988). Competence and stress in school children: The moderating effects of individual and family qualities. *Journal of Child Psychology and Psychiatry*.
McMahon, R. J., & Peters, R. DeV. (Eds.). (1985). *Childhood disorders: Behavioral-developmental approaches*. New York: Brunner/Mazel.
Mednick, S. A., & Schulsinger, F. (1968). Some premorbid characteristics related to breakdown in children with schizophrenic mothers. In D. Rosenthal & S. S. Kety (Eds.), *The transmission of schizophrenia* (pp. 267–291). Oxford: Pergamon Press.
Meichenbaum, D. H., Bream, L. A., & Cohen, J. S. (1985). A cognitive-behavioral perspective of child psychopathology: Implications for assessment and training. In R. J. McMahon & R. DeV. Peters (Eds.), *Childhood disor-

ders: *Behavioral–developmental approaches* (pp. 36–52). New York: Brunner/Mazel.

Meichenbaum, D., & Goodman, J. (1971). Training impulsive children to talk to themselves: A means of developing self-control. *Journal of Abnormal Psychology, 77,* 115–126.

Mowrer, O. H., & Mowrer, W. M. (1938). Enuresis: A method for its study and treatment. *American Journal of Orthopsychiatry, 8,* 436–459.

Mulvey, E. P. (1985). *Toward a theory of delinquency cessation.* Paper presented at the annual meeting of the American Psychological Association, Los Angeles.

Mulvey, E. P., & LaRosa, J. F. (1986). Delinquency cessation and adolescent development: Preliminary data. *American Journal of Orthopsychiatry, 56,* 212–224.

Ollendick, T. H. (1979). Fear reduction techniques with children. In M. Hersen, R. M. Eisler & P. M. Miller, (Eds.), *Progress in Behavior Modification,* (Vol. 8. pp. 127–168). New York: Academic Press.

Osborn, E. L. (1986). Effects of participant modeling and contact desensitization on childhood warm water phobia. *Journal of Behavior Therapy and Experimental Psychiatry, 17,* 117–119.

Patterson, G. R. (1981). Foreword. In E. J. Mash & L. G. Terdal (Eds.), *Behavioral assessment of childhood disorders* (pp. vii–viii). New York: Guilford Press.

Patterson, G. (1982). *A social learning approach: Vol. 3. Coercive family process.* Eugene, OR: Castalia Publishing.

Patterson, G. R., & Bank, L. (1989). Some amplifying mechanisms for pathological processes in families. In M. R. Gunnar & E. Thelen (Eds.), *Systems and development: Minnesota Symposia on Child Psychology* (Vol. 22, pp. 167–209). Hillsdale, NJ: Lawrence Erlbaum Associates.

Petzel, S. V., & Cline, D. W. (1978). Adolescent suicide: Epidemiological and biological aspects. In S. C. Feinstein & P. L. Giovacchini (Eds.), *Adolescent psychiatry: Developmental and clinical studies,* (pp. 239–266). Chicago: University of Chicago Press.

Pfeffer, C. R. (1986). *The suicidal child.* New York: Guilford Press.

Phillips, J. S., & Ray, R. S. (1980). Behavioral approaches to childhood disorders: Review and critique. *Behavior Modification, 4,* 3–34.

Plomin, R., Loehlin, J. C., & DeFries, J. C. (1985). Genetic and environmental components of "environmental" influences. *Developmental Psychology, 21,* 391–402.

Powers, M. D. (1984). Syndromal diagnosis and the behavioral assessment of childhood disorders. *Child and Family Behavior Therapy, 6,* 1–15.

Purkel, W., & Bornstein, W. H. (1980). Pictures and imagery both enhance children's short-term and long-term recall. *Developmental Psychology, 16,* 153–154.

Rutter, M. (1974). The development of infantile autism. *Psychological Medicine, 4,* 147–163.

Rutter, M. (1985). Resilience in the face of adversity: Protective factors and resistance to psychiatric disorder. *British Journal of Psychiatry, 147,* 598–611.

Rutter, M. (1986). The developmental psychopathology of depression: Issues and perspectives. In M. Rutter, C. E. Izard, & P. B. Read (Eds.), *Depression in young people: Developmental and clinical perspectives* (pp. 3–30). New York: Guilford Press.

Rutter, M. (1987). Psychosocial resilience and protective mechanism. *Journal of Orthopsychiatry, 57,* 316–331.

Rutter, M. (1988). Epidemiological approaches to developmental psychopathology. *Archives of General Psychiatry, 45,* 486–495.

Rutter, M. (1989). Pathways from childhood to adult life. *Journal of Child Psychology and Psychiatry, 30,* 23–51.

Rutter, M., Izard, C. E., & Read, P. B. (1986). *Depression in young people: Developmental and clinical perspectives.* New York: Guilford Press.

Rutter, M., & Shaffer, D. (1980). DSM-III: A step forward or back in terms of the classification of child psychiatric disorders? *Journal of the American Academy of Child Psychiatry, 19,* 371–394.

Sameroff, A. J. & Chandler, M. J. (1975). Reproductive risk and the continuum of caretaking casualty. In F. D. Horowitz, M. Hetherington, S. Scarr-Salapetek & G. Siegel (Eds.), *Review of child development research* (Vol 4, pp. 187–243). Chicago: University of Chicago Press.

Sander, L. W. (1975). Infant and caretaking environment: Investigation and conceptualization of adaptive behavior in a system of increasing complexity. In E. James Anthony (Ed.), *Explorations in child psychiatry,* (pp. 129–166). New York: Plenum Press.

Santostefano, S. (1978). *A biodevelopmental approach to clinical child psychology: Cognitive controls and cognitive control therapy.* New York: John Wiley & Sons.

Scarr, S., & McCartney, K. (1983). How people make their own environments: A theory of genotype→environment effects. *Child Development, 54,* 424–435.

Schleser, R., Meyers, A., & Cohen, R. (1981). Generalization of self-instructions: Effects of general versus specific content, active rehearsal, and cognitive level. *Child Development, 52,* 335–340.

Schopler, E., & Mesibov, G. B. (Eds.) (1983). *Autism in adolescents and adults.* New York: Plenum Press.

Schwitzgebel, R., & Kolb, D. A. (1964). Inducing behavior change in adolescent delinquents. *Behaviour Research and Therapy, 1,* 297–304.

Shaffer, D. (1986). Developmental factors in childhood and adolescent suicide. In M. Rutter, C. E. Izard, & P. B. Read (Eds.), *Depression in young people: Developmental and clinical perspectives* (pp. 383–396). New York: Guilford Press.

Simmons, R. G., & Blyth, D. A. (1987). *Moving into adolescence: The impact of pubertal change and school context.* Hawthrone, NY: Aldine de Gruyter.

Skinner, E. A. (in press). Individual trajectories of perceived control: A developmental model of context and action. In

M. Gunnar (Ed.), *Self-processes in development: Minnesota Symposia on Child Psychology* (Vol. 23). Hillsdale, NJ: Lawrence Erlbaum Associates.

Skinner, E. A., Chapman, M., & Baltes, P. B. (1988). Control, means–ends, and agency beliefs: A new conceptualization and its measurement during childhood. *Journal of Personality and Social Psychology, 54,* 117–133.

Sroufe, L. A. (1979). The coherence of individual development: Early care, attachment, and subsequent developmental issues. *American Psychologist, 34,* 834–841.

Sroufe, L. A., & Rutter, M. (1984). The domain of developmental psychopathology. *Child Development, 55,* 17–29.

Sroufe, L. A., & Waters, E. (1977). Attachment as an organizational construct. *Child Development, 48,* 1184–1199.

Tanguay, P. E. (1984). Toward a new classification of serious psychopathology in children. *Journal of the American Academy of Child Psychiatry, 23,* 373–384.

Tellegen, A. (1985). Structures of mood and personality and their relevance to assessing anxiety, with an emphasis on self-report. In A. H. Tuma & J. D. Maser (Eds.), *Anxiety and the anxiety disorders* (pp. 681–716). Hillsdale, NJ: Lawrence Erlbaum Associates.

Thackwray, D., Meyers, A., Schleser, R., & Cohen, R. (1985). Achieving generalization with general versus specific self-instructions: Effects on academically deficient children. *Cognitive Therapy and Research, 9,* 297–308.

Vaughn, B. E., Kopp, C. B., & Krakow, J. B. (1984). The emergence and consolidation of self-control from eighteen to thirty months of age: Normative trends and individual differences. *Child Development, 55,* 990–1004.

Vygotsky, L. (1962). *Thought and language.* New York: John Wiley & Sons.

Waddington, C. H. (1966). *Principles of development and differentiation.* New York: Macmillan.

Wasserman, T. H. (1983). The effects of cognitive development on the use of cognitive behavioral techniques with children. *Child and Family Behavior Therapy, 5,* 37–50.

Waters, E., & Sroufe, L. A. (1983). Social competence as a developmental construct. *Developmental Review, 3,* 79–97.

Watson, D., & Clark, L. A. (1984). Negative affectivity: The disposition to experience aversive emotional states. *Psychological Bulletin, 96,* 465–490.

Watson, D., Clark, L. A., & Carey, G. (1988). Positive and negative affectivity and their relation to anxiety and depressive disorders. *Journal of Abnormal Psychology, 97,* 346–353.

Watt, N. F., Anthony, E. J., Wynne, L. C., & Rolf, J. E. (Eds.) (1984). *Children at risk for schizophrenia: A longitudinal perspective.* New York: Cambridge University Press.

Webster-Stratton, C. (1985). Predictors of treatment outcome in parent training for conduct disordered children. *Behavior Therapy, 16,* 223–243.

Weiss, G., & Hechtman, L. T. (1986). *Hyperactive children grown up: Empirical findings and theoretical considerations.* New York: Guilford Press.

Werner, E. E. (in press). Protective factors and individual resilience. In S. J. Meisel & M. Shonkoff (Eds.), *Handbook of early intervention.* Cambridge: Cambridge University Press.

Whalen, C. K., & Henker, B. (Eds.). (1980). *Hyperactive children: The social ecology of identification and treatment.* New York: Academic Press.

Williams, C. D. (1959). The elimination of tantrum behavior by extinction procedures. *Journal of Abnormal and Social Psychology, 59,* 269.

CHAPTER 4

DEVELOPMENTAL FACTORS IN CHILD BEHAVIORAL ASSESSMENT

Thomas H. Ollendick
Neville J. King

Child behavioral assessment, which may be described as being in its "childhood" state, has seen considerable growth in recent years. Befitting its childhood status, we would be remiss if we did not point out that much remains to be achieved. In this chapter, we shall attempt to illustrate both the problems and promises of child behavioral assessment from a developmental perspective. Much of what we discuss will be embedded in current theory and extant research; the remainder will be based on speculation derived from our clinical experience in working with children, adolescents, and their families over the past several years. Our goal in this chapter is to address the theory, research, and practice of child behavioral assessment in an integrated fashion.

We begin with a brief overview of child behavioral assessment in order to set the stage for the remainder of the chapter. We also examine developmental theory, and the various implications and issues it raises for child behavioral assessment. Finally, we attempt to integrate developmental theory and behavioral assessment.

CHILD BEHAVIORAL ASSESSMENT

Two primary features characterized early developments in child behavioral assessment: (a) adherence to an operant perspective that placed heavy emphasis on observable events, current behavior, the situational determinants of behavior, and intra-individual comparisons (Bijou & Peterson, 1971; Mash & Terdal, 1981); and (b) relative inattention to developmental processes and normative comparisons (Ciminero & Drabman, 1977; Evans & Nelson, 1977; Ollendick & Cerny, 1981). Although these early developments had shortcomings (Ollendick & Hersen, 1984), they provided the necessary foundation for an *empirical* approach to the assessment of behavioral problems in childhood.

More recently, child behavioral assessment has been described as an "exploratory, hypothesis-testing process in which a range of procedures is used to understand a given child, group, or social ecology and to formulate and evaluate specific intervention strategies" (Ollendick & Hersen, 1984, p. 6). As such, it entails more than the identification of specific target behaviors and their controlling variables. While the importance of direct observation of target behaviors should not be underestimated (in fact, it remains the hallmark of child behavioral assessment), recent advances have incorporated a range of procedures including interviews, self-reports, ratings by others, self-monitoring, physiological measurement, *and* behavioral observation. One way to combine these procedures is best described as a multimethod one in which a composite "picture" of the child is obtained.

Two other features have been proposed to characterize child behavioral assessment procedures (Ollendick & Hersen, 1984). First, they should be validated empirically, and second, they should be sensitive to developmental changes seen in children.

Regarding the first point, many clinicians and researchers working with children have used assessment methods of convenience without due regard for their psychometric characteristics, including their reliability, validity, and clinical utility. Although child behavioral assessors have fared somewhat better in this regard, they too have tended to design and use highly idiosyncratic tools for assessment. The advancement of an assessment technology, let alone an understanding of child behavior disorders, is not realized with such an idiosyncratic approach. Further, a comparison of findings across studies is extremely difficult, if not impossible.

Just as child behavioral assessment procedures must be empirically validated, they must also be developmentally sensitive. Probably the most distinguishing characteristic of children is change. Whether such change is based on hypothetical stages of growth or demonstrated principles of learning (a point we will discuss later), it has implications for the selection of specific assessment devices and their subsequent use in treatment evaluation. Behavioral interviews, self-reports, other-reports, self-monitoring, physiological measurement, and behavioral observation are all potentially affected by changing developmental processes. Further, some of these procedures may be more useful at one age period over another. To illustrate briefly, interviews may be more difficult to conduct and self-reports may be less reliable with young children, whereas self-monitoring and behavioral observation may be more reactive with older children. Although these speculations await empirical evaluation, it should be obvious that age-related constraints are evident and that they should be taken into consideration when selecting specific methods of assessment.

Whereas a multimethod approach that is based on empirically validated and developmentally sensitive procedures is proposed, it should be evident that a "test battery" approach is not espoused. The specific procedures to be used depend on a host of factors including the age of the child, the referral question posed, and the personnel, time, and resources available (Ollendick & Cerny, 1981; Ollendick & Greene, 1990). Nonetheless, given the limitations of the different procedures, as well as the desirability of obtaining a "complete" picture of the child, a multimethod assessment should be attempted whenever possible. Any single procedure, including behavioral observation, is not sufficiently complete to provide this composite view. The multimethod approach is not only helpful in assessing specific target behaviors and in determining response to behavior change, but also in understanding child behavior patterns.

Based on these characteristics, one can see that child behavioral assessment has advanced considerably from its early beginnings. Although some continue to debate the merits of these advances and, in fact, do not view these developments as "advances" (cf. Cone & Hoier, 1986), there is little doubt that recent attention to psychometric issues and developmental factors has increased our awareness of the many issues involved in assessing children. We will now turn our attention to important developmental considerations and will return to the issues raised in this brief overview in later sections.

DEVELOPMENTAL CONSIDERATIONS

As noted by Lerner (1986) and others, the field of developmental psychology is one that is characterized by considerable theoretical controversy. How to conceptualize the many changes observed in individuals as they grow across the life span is not at all straightforward . . . nor obvious. Clearly, one's conception of development is embedded deeply in philosophical as well as theoretical issues. Whereas some posit what has come to be known as the "mechanistic" model (e.g., Baer, 1982; Bijou, 1976; Skinner, 1938), others propose an "organismic" model (Erikson, 1968; Freud, 1949; Piaget, 1950). In brief, the mechanistic model stresses that changes over time in the behavior of organisms result from alterations in stimuli impinging on the organism. The principles of classical and operant conditioning are invoked to explain behavioral development. In this model, at least from a historical perspective, behavioral development over time becomes the "mechanical mirror" (Langer, 1969) of environmental stimulation; and the organism, regardless of age, is viewed primarily as reactive, passive, or responsive to such input. In sharp contrast, the organismic model views the organism as inherently active, as a constructor of the events around it rather than a passive responder. Implicit in the organismic model is the notion of basic structures and functions associated with particular stages of growth. Further, these structures are thought to change across age (e.g., Piaget's stages of cognitive development) and to reflect emerging, qualitatively different ways of interacting with the environment (the doctrine of epigenesis; see Gottlieb, 1970). The extent to which these structures are thought to be dependent on learning for their expression is the source of much controversy. In its purest form, the organismic model proposes a rather "predetermined epigenesis" (Gottlieb, 1970; Lerner, 1986) in which behavioral development results from maturational processes that are determined by inherited, intrinsic factors and not anything closely akin to learning.

In many respects, these two models represent polar opposites. Although both have valuable contributions to make, in their pure forms they are incomplete ways of viewing the developing organism. In recent years, a synthesis of these two views has occurred in what has come to be known as "contextualism." In contextualism, behavioral development occurs as a consequence of reciprocal relations between an active organism and an active environmental context (Lerner, 1986). Just as the context changes the individual, the individual alters the context. As such, by being both products and producers of their contexts, organisms affect their own development (cf. Bell, 1968). This view, articulated most forcefully by Lerner and his colleagues, is remarkably similar to that put forth by Bandura in his social learning theory (1977, 1986). Thus, from both a developmental perspective and a clinical perspective, a synthesis has occurred that views the human organism as both determining, and determined by, an active, changing environment. A bidirectional process is evident in such theorizing.

Regardless of one's theoretical position on these matters, nearly all developmentalists agree that the concept of development implies "systematic and successive changes over time in an organism" (Lerner, 1986, p. 41). Inclusion of descriptors such as "systematic" and "successive" indicate that these changes should be orderly and that changes seen at one point in time should be influenced, at least in part, by changes that occurred at an earlier point in time. In this sense, behavioral development is not viewed as random or capricious nor, for that matter, disconnected. Changes that occur at an early age (whether due to learning, an unfolding of basically predetermined structure, or some complex, interactive process) have an impact on subsequent development. In the least, the diversity of changes possible at a later time are constrained by those that occur at an earlier time (Lerner, 1986). These changes in behavioral development create special problems in selecting appropriate methods of assessment, as well as in identifying specific target behaviors for change.

Despite a general consensus that the assessment of children *should* be different from that with adults, remarkably little attention has been paid to this issue. Thus, we have many assessment methods—both behavioral and traditional—that are simply downward extensions of those used with adults (Ollendick & Hersen, 1984). In most of these cases, not only are the methods of assessment the same, but so too are the underlying assumptions about using these methods. The use of a self-report instrument to describe feelings of depression or a behavioral approach test to capture avoidant behavior in fearful persons are but two of many examples of this practice. Can we really expect children and adults to respond similarly to these diverse methods? Further, can we expect our observations to mean similar things? That is, does a child's self-report of depressed mood mean the same thing as depressed mood reported by an adult? In addition, as noted by Edelbrock (1984), even the measures designed specifically for "children" may be problematic. Typically, these measures are designed for children and adolescents who vary between 4 and 18 years of age. Quite obviously, a 4-year-old's world and his/her interpretation of it is different from a 16-year-old's. The behavior of "children" depends to a large degree on age, experience, and other factors associated with development.

Moreover, the expectations we have for children vary with age, as do the norms associated with certain behaviors. Several studies have described "normal age trends" associated with certain behavioral problems (cf. Edelbrock, 1984). Specific fears and phobias, for instance, have been shown to occur with regularity during the course of adjustment. Most infants show a startle-like response to loss of support or to sudden and loud noises. Later, during the first year of life, infants evidence a fear of strangers in which they react with fear-like panic to unfamiliar people and unfamiliar situations. Between 2 and 3 years of age, fear of animals emerges with fear of the dark being increasingly evident between 3 and 4 years of age. School fears characteristically occur upon entry to school (as well as subsequent changes in schools or grade levels), while evaluative fears and social fears develop during middle childhood and continue on into adolescence. Presence of such predictability in fears, of course, does not "explain" their occurrence. Undoubtedly, emerging cognitive abilities (e.g., Bauer, 1976) as well as specific situational events (Miller, Barrett, & Hampe, 1974; Ollendick, 1979) interact to occasion their presence. The point here is simply that awareness of these developmental trends may guide us in the selection of target behaviors and the interpretation of their significance. What is viewed as "normal" at one age may be perceived as "abnormal" at a different age.

In the next part of this chapter, we will present a normative–developmental perspective on behavioral development and its implications for child behavioral assessment (Edelbrock, 1984; Ollendick & Hersen, 1984). Critical differences between the behavioral and developmental approaches will be highlighted, and ways of integrating the two will be illustrated.

DEVELOPMENTAL-BEHAVIORAL SYNTHESIS

According to Edelbrock (1984), the developmental point of view can best be described as a "normative–developmental" perspective because it involves two basic principles. The "developmental" principle calls our attention to the importance of accounting for quantitative and qualitative changes that occur with development. As noted earlier, these changes are usually systematic and successive. Further, they are usually orderly and build upon one another. Yet, at other times, these changes may be rapid and uneven. Importantly, the developmental principle suggests that current behavior be viewed in a context that includes consideration of events preceding and following it.

According to the "normative principle," it is helpful to evaluate children's behavior with respect to appropriate reference groups. Most generally, this reference group involves children of the same age (Edelbrock, 1984). Obviously, age is a crude index of developmental level; yet it can yield potentially important comparative information along a number of important dimensions including the child's emotional, cognitive, behavioral, and social functioning. Ideally, normative information related to gender, socioeconomic status, race, and culture would also be available. Only in this way can we be assured that the comparison group is truly a representative one. Given baselines for "normal" changes in the reference group, we could then identify those behaviors in our targeted child that are clearly outside the normal range. For example, important developmental deviations in social behavior could be recognized with such an approach. In fact, such observations frequently lead to the referral of children who display socially withdrawn or aggressive behavior. However, we should hasten to add that the behaviors viewed as problematic in one setting (e.g., rural, middle-class community) may not be viewed as such in a different setting (e.g., urban, lower-class community). Such referral practices demonstrate the importance of local norms, as well as the relativity involved in determining what behaviors are problematic and when children evincing those behaviors should be referred for evaluation. The contextual aspects of behavior are readily evident in such practices. Out of context, any one behavior may or may not be problematic.

Thus, the normative–developmental perspective emphasizes the central importance of change over time and the need for relevant norms against which children can be compared. In doing so, this nomothetic approach relies on deductive reasoning to conceptualize, design, implement, and evaluate interventions for children. Its primary goal is to establish general "laws" that pertain to large groups of children. Thus, even with our example of a rural, middle-class, 10-year-old boy who exhibits "aggressive" behavior, the tendency here would be to seek general principles that would account for this behavior in similar children and how such "explanations" might differ for children of differing backgrounds and developmental characteristics. The behavioral perspective, on the other hand, places its emphasis elsewhere. Here, the primary emphasis is on inductive reasoning which leads to a largely idiographic approach. This idiographic-nomothetic distinction is an important one. As Mash and Terdal (1981) and Ollendick and Hersen (1984) point out, child behavior assessors have typically been more interested in intraindividual change than interindividual differences. As child behavioral assessors, we are most likely to be concerned with the behaviors of individual children. We are likely to design interventions for individual children and evaluate their outcome in terms of specific, individual behavior change. The direct relevance of normative comparisons is less clear with such an approach (Cone & Hoier, 1986).

Cone and Hoier (1986) offer another important

limitation of the deductive, nomothetic approach in which norms are used as the significant criterion by which judgments are made regarding the appropriateness of a given behavior. In its place, they argue for a criterion-referenced approach. To illustrate this point, they provide an example of a handicapped child who was withdrawn and devoid of close friends and social interactions. In particular, she was below the normal level of social interaction on "verbal initiations," "proximity," and "sharing." Following intervention, she was found to exhibit "normal" levels of interaction on all three of these measures; yet, systematic observations revealed that the other children were still not interacting with her. Her initiations were not reciprocated, and she failed to establish close friendships. Being normal was not enough. As Cone and Hoier (1986) point out, the failure of their intervention to achieve its desired effects may have stemmed from an inadequate assessment of the meaning of interpersonal competence in this child's unique social context. What was needed was an analysis of the behaviors required of the target child to produce social acceptance by *her* peers (and we might add an analysis of the broader context to prompt and reinforce such behaviors). According to Cone and Hoier, the better criterion to be used is one that can be evaluated by measuring the effects of the intervention on the environment, not just whether the intervention brings the child up to a normal rate of interchange. Social competence likely means different things in different contexts. An idiographic analysis would facilitate investigation of such a possibility. We shall return to this idiographic-nomothetic distinction later.

Voeltz and Evans (1982) raise yet another characteristic of child behavioral assessment that differentiates it, at least historically, from the developmental perspective. In general, behavioral assessment places heavy emphasis on the description and quantification of discrete behaviors. In fact, as we noted earlier, selection of specific target behaviors is the hallmark of child behavioral assessment. In contrast, much developmental research has been focused on the identification of patterns of covariation among behaviors. This distinction, however, has been less evident in recent years. Voeltz and Evans (1982), for instance, speak of the importance of response-response relationships in child behavioral assessment, whereas Harris and Powers (1984) address important issues related to diagnostic considerations from a behavioral perspective. Further, recent factor-analytic studies (Achenbach & Edelbrock, 1989; Ollendick, King, & Frary, 1989) have shown that certain behavior problems co-occur and form distinct patterns. Thus, it is evident that child behavior assessors are cognizant of patterns of behavior, which they usually refer to as "response covariation." Still, developmentalists may tend to take an even broader perspective on this issue, asserting that even a given response cluster needs to be understood in terms of a developmental progression that has direct implications for future behavior as well as current behavior (Lerner, 1986).

Finally, the developmental and behavioral perspectives differ in terms of the emphasis placed on the current environment in determining behavior (Edelbrock, 1984; Ollendick & Hersen, 1984). The behavioral perspective places emphasis on the current environment in producing behavior change, whereas the developmental perspective includes greater consideration of developmental precursors or the historical antecedents of current functioning. As mentioned above, greater emphasis is placed on "behavior over time in context." It is important to note, however, that the developmental approach does not ignore the current environment or dismiss the situational specificity of behavior. Similarly, it is important to note that the behavioral perspective does not ignore the context of behavior nor its bidirectionality. Rather, the emphases have simply been different. A blurring of these two distinctions is currently occurring, making a rapprochement between the developmental and behavioral perspectives increasingly more likely. In brief, it has been proposed that developmental theory can play a key role in formulating behavioral assessment and treatment plans for children (Gelfand & Peterson, 1985; Hartmann, Roper, & Bradford, 1979; Mash & Terdal, 1981; Ollendick & Hersen, 1984).

Though the value of incorporating developmental theory into child behavioral assessment may seem obvious, the ways of doing so are less clear. How might we go about this process? What would we have to do differently? Surprisingly, as indicated by Edelbrock (1984), the answers to these questions can be found in the differences between the developmental and behavioral perspectives that we have just reviewed. Inherent in these differences are the grounds for a synthesis of the two fields. In the remainder of this section, we will examine areas of research that blend the developmental perspective with a contemporary behavioral assessment perspective. In doing so, we will follow the lead of Edelbrock (1984) and review three primary areas: (a) the development and use of normative guidelines for behavior, (b) the determination of age differences in the patterning of behaviors, and (c) the study of stability and change in behavior over time. In particular, we will explore these issues as they relate to anxious and phobic behavior in children, although examples in other areas abound as well.

Normative Baselines

As previously noted, one often major difference between the developmental and behavioral perspectives is the use of a nomothetic approach versus an idiographic approach. From the outset it is important to point out that these two approaches are not *necessarily* incompatible. That is, it is possible to evaluate an individual child's behavior within a normative context (Edelbrock, 1984; Ollendick & Hersen, 1984). In doing so, as child behavior assessors we need not depart from our allegiance to a behavior-analytic framework; rather, we can conduct our analysis and place it into a context by comparing our results to those observed in children who are members of an appropriate reference group. One simple example may help to illustrate this possibility. Recently, we were asked to complete an evaluation of a kindergarten child who was described by his teacher as "overly active, always out of his seat, and disruptive of other children." A functional analysis of the child's behavior revealed the importance of both antecedent and consequent events. The behaviors occurred with increasing frequency at certain times of the day; namely, around midmorning and midafternoon after the child had been attending for a relatively long period of time. Further, the child's peers tended to "reinforce" the target child by laughing when he made "funny" noises or spoke out of turn during structured activities. Following such "disruptive" behaviors, he was observed getting out of his seat and walking around the classroom. It appeared as if he was seeking additional attention from other children on these occasions. Thus, the analysis was fairly straightforward. Yet when we observed a subset of children in the classroom, we detected a similar pattern in behavior. Nearly all of the children were "restless" at these times (albeit in different ways; e.g., dropping materials, slouching in chair, gazing outdoors, etc.). Yet it was obvious to us that *this* child was being singled out by the teacher as particularly problematic. This simple observation led us to conceptualize the target child's problem as largely being a "normal" one for that classroom and, perhaps, being related to the teacher's unrealistic expectations for that individual child. We used this "normative" information to provide feedback to an otherwise capable and energetic teacher who realized that her expectations for the child, who was viewed as her "favorite," were unrealistic. On rearranging her schedule and adjusting her expectations, many of the problematic behaviors were significantly reduced. It was not necessary for us to view the targeted child as deviant or different with such an analysis. Classroom behavioral norms for children this age led us to a different conclusion and intervention.

Establishing norms, however, is not an easy task. As noted by Edelbrock (1984), this would require the development of comprehensive data bases describing the behavior of large representative samples of clinic-referred and nonreferred children. As we indicated earlier, ideally, such representative samples would also include data related to gender, race, socioeconomic status, and culture in addition to age. In this way, the contribution of these contextual variables to obtained differences in the referred and nonreferred children could be evaluated more critically. In the least, if we are to admit normative information into our thinking about child behavioral patterns, we will have to develop specific age and gender norms (although we continue to recognize the need for racial, cultural, and socioeconomic norms as well).

Fortunately, a few clear examples of the use of age and gender norms in child behavioral assessment exist. We shall illustrate the potential value of such norms for a parent rating form (Child Behavior Checklist; Achenbach & Edelbrock, 1981), a self-report questionnaire (Fear Survey Schedule for Children, Revised; Ollendick, 1983), and a behavioral observation schedule (Katz, Kellerman, & Siegel, 1980). First, we will turn our attention to the Child Behavior Checklist (CBC). The CBC is composed of 20 social competence and 118 behavioral problem items (e.g., acts too young, fears own impulses, argues a lot, gets in fights). Social competency items assess the child's participation in social organizations, activities, and school. The behavior problem items are rated on a three-point scale as to how well each describes the child (0 indicates that the problem is *not true* of the child, 1 indicates that the problem is *somewhat* or *sometimes true,* and 2 indicates it is *very* or *often true*). The inclusion of social competency and behavior problem items permits a comprehensive analysis of both the child's strengths (supports) and weaknesses (stresses). For our purposes here, it is important to note that different norms have been developed for boys and girls aged 4 to 5, 6 to 11, and 12 to 16 (Achenbach, 1978; Achenbach & Edelbrock, 1979; Edelbrock & Achenbach, 1980). In an unusually well-controlled investigation, Achenbach and Edelbrock (1981) collected CBC data on 1,300 children referred for mental health services and a matched sample of 1,300 randomly selected nonreferred children. Fifty boys and 50 girls at each age from 4 through 16 were rated in the referred and nonreferred samples. Further, within each group, there was approximately equal representation of lower, middle, and upper socioeconomic levels and a ratio of 4:1, white to black children. Cultural variables were not described.

Concerning age differences, several interesting findings emerged. For example, 84 of the 118 behavior problem items showed significant age effects. For the most part, these age effects reflected a linear decrease in prevalence of the item as a problem from 4 through 16 years of age. Representative items that showed this linear decreasing trend were acting too young, hyperactivity, whining, nightmares, poor peer relations, and demanding attention. On the other hand, 19 of the behavior problem items showed a linear *increase* in prevalence over age (4 through 16 years). Representative items of this trend were fears school, preferring to be alone, headaches, running away from home, and suicidal talk. Still, a few behavior problems were found to show nonlinear age trends (e.g., is teased, feels worthless, daydreams, and confused). Middle-age children were reported to have these problems more frequently than younger or older children. Examples of these differential prevalence rates are shown in Figure 4-1 for the referred and nonreferred boys and girls of varying ages.

In reference to gender, significant differences between boys and girls were obtained for 51 of the 118 behavioral problem items. Of these, 25 reflected higher prevalence among boys whereas 26 showed a higher prevalence among girls. In general, the problems reported for boys were associated with "externalizing" behaviors (e.g., aggression, hyperactivity, and delinquency) whereas those reported for girls were typical of "internalizing" problems (e.g., depression, withdrawal, and somatic complaints). Although these gender effects accounted for less variance than those associated with age (Edelbrock, 1984), they do reveal clinically useful information. (In addition, significant SES [socio-economic status] differences were noted for 53 of the 118 behavior problems, with 49 reflecting higher prevalence for the lower-class children. No discernible pattern in race differences was obtained.)

Thus, on the CBC, important age and gender differences were evident in both referred and nonreferred children. We will return to a discussion of how to use this normative information following our review of equally interesting findings for a self-report and a behavioral observation measure.

The Fear Survey Schedule for Children, Revised (Ollendick, 1983; Ollendick, Matson & Helsel, 1985) is a self-report instrument for the assessment of fear in children and adolescents. A revision of an inventory originally designed by Scherer and Nakamura (1968), it consists of 80 fear stimuli to which children are instructed to report their level of fear (none, some, or a lot). Representative items include "being called on by teachers," "going to bed in the dark," "getting a cut or injury," "getting lost in a strange place," and "taking tests." In the original studies, a five-factor solution was determined: Fear of Failure and Criticism, Fear of the Unknown, Fear of Injury and Small Animals, Fear of Danger and Death, and Medical Fears. In addition to the five factor scores, a total fear score and the total number of fears endorsed as producing "a lot" of fear can be generated.

In a recent study (Ollendick, King, & Frary, 1989), the FSSC-R was administered to a total of 1,185 children and adolescents: 572 girls and 613 boys. The youths ranged in age from 7 to 16; 395 were between 7 and 10 years of age, 449 between 11 and 13 years of age, and 341 between 14 and 16 years of age. Five hundred ninety-four of the children and adolescents were from the United States, and 591 were from Australia. Although specific information about socioeconomic status was not obtained, limited detail about the occupations of the heads of households indicated a fairly even distribution of occupations ranging from professional to service worker. The youths were drawn from urban, suburban, and rural areas. Over 97% of the children and adolescents in both countries were Caucasian.

Analyses revealed clear age and gender differences, but not nationality differences. Concerning age, the 7- to 10-year-olds reported significantly more fear (total score) than either the 11- to 13-year-olds or the 14- to 16-year-olds, who also differed significantly from one another. These overall age differences were reflected on four of the five factor scores as well. The younger group of children reported more fear than the two older groups on the Failure and Criticism, Unknown, Injury and Small Animals, and Danger and Death factors. Only on the Medical Fears factor did the three age groups not differ from one another. Of additional interest, the youngest group of children reported "a lot" of fear to more stimuli (17) than either the middle (13) or oldest (12) groups of children. Finally, and somewhat surprisingly, 8 of the 10 most common

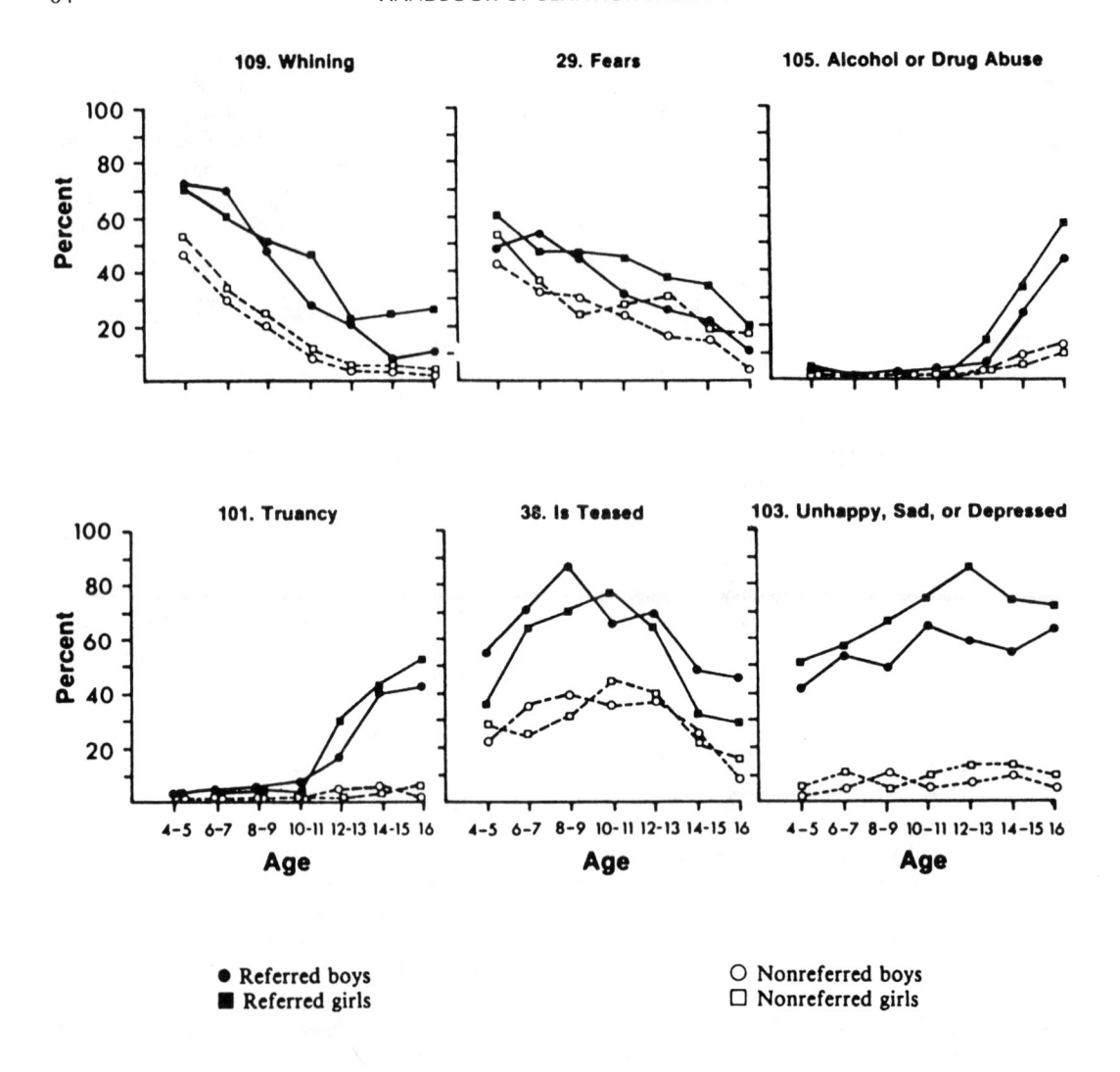

Figure 4.1. Prevalence of various parent-reported behavior problems for referred and nonreferred boys and girls aged 4–16. From Edelbrock, C. S. (1984). Developmental considerations. In T. H. Ollendick & M. Hersen (Eds.), *Child behavioral assessment*. Elmsford, NY: Pergamon Press. Reprinted by permission.

fears were the same for all three age groups: being hit by a car or truck, not being able to breathe, bombing attacks, fire/getting burned, falling from a high place, a burglar breaking into our house, earthquakes, and death.

Regarding gender, girls reported significantly more fear on the total score and on each of the five factor scores. Further, they reported "a lot" of fear to more stimuli (18) than did the boys (10). Finally, 9 of the 10 most common fears were the same for both boys and girls.

Of course, we do not know whether these age and gender differences in self-report are "real" differences in fear or if they simply reflect the tendency of young children and girls to report more veridically on such scales than adolescents and boys. Regardless, the findings are consistent with other ones that find higher levels of fear in girls than in boys and in younger than older children. Again, we will return to a discussion of the use of these normative findings following our review of normative data obtained from a behavioral observation measure to which we now turn our attention.

Katz et al. (1980) can be credited with one of the first clinical efforts to determine, via a behavioral observation system, the effects of age and gender on the expression of anxiety in children and adolescents. Specifically, they set out to develop a behavioral rating scale that would be reliable and valid for the measurement of anxiety in children who were undergoing bone marrow aspirations *and* to investigate developmental aspects of such anxiety. Bone marrow aspirations (BMAs) were studied since they were observed to cause distress in children and because they are given repeatedly as a diagnostic test to children with acute leukemia. Thus, BMAs provided a standard medical procedure with which to study acute anxiety across a wide age range of boys and girls.

In this study, the BMA procedure was broken down into 12 steps, encompassing four phases: an anticipatory phase, a preparatory phase, a procedure phase, and a recovery phase. Although 25 discrete behaviors were identified and operationally defined, only 13 were used in the actual study (the other 12 did not occur with sufficient frequency). The 13 behaviors coded were: cry, cling, fear verbal, pain verbal, scream, stall, carry, flail, refusal position, muscular rigidity, emotional support, and requests termination. Muscular rigidity, for example, was defined as "any of the following behaviors: clenched fists, white knuckles, gritted teeth, clenched jaw, wrinkled brow, eyes clenched shut, contracted limbs, and body stiffness" (Katz et al., 1980, p. 359). Each of the 13 behaviors was coded as to their occurrence/nonoccurrence during each phase of the BMA procedure. The study sample consisted of 115 children with cancer, randomly selected from oncology patients undergoing BMAs in an outpatient hematology–oncology clinic. They were divided into thirds by age: 38 children with a mean age of 3 years 10 months (range: 8 months to 6 years, 4 months), 38 with a mean age of 7 years 5 months (range: 6 years 6 months to 9 years 11 months), and 39 with a mean age of 12 years 7 months (range: 10 years 10 months to 17 years 9 months).

As with the findings associated with parent ratings on the CBC (Achenbach & Edelbrock, 1981) and with child self-report ratings on the FSSC-R (Ollendick et al., 1989), some rather interesting age and gender effects were observed. First, younger children displayed greater behavioral anxiety than older children for each of the four phases and across phases. For the most part, the two older groups did not differ from one another (except during the third phase when the two younger groups were both significantly more anxious than the oldest group). The presence of more signs of distress and anxiety in the younger group should not have been unexpected. What was of more interest, however, from a developmental standpoint was the qualitative differences that were observed with regard to age. Children in the youngest group were most likely to exhibit their anxiety by crying, screaming, needing to be physically restrained, and expressing pain verbally. The middle group, however, did not require physical restraint and was more likely to express their anxiety verbally. Furthermore, signs of muscular rigidity began to appear in this age group. Children and adolescents in the oldest group relied on two primary modes of expressing their anxiety: verbal expressions of pain and muscular rigidity. Thus, as described by Katz et al. (1980, p. 361), "what was observed was a developmental tendency toward less diffuse vocal protest and skeletal activity and greater emphasis on verbal expression along with increased muscle tension." Confirming this picture, muscular rigidity was observed to increase among the three age groups (31%, 57%, and 64%, respectively). In contrast, screaming was observed to systematically decrease (72%, 50%, and 8%, respectively) as was flailing (33%, 15%, and 13%, respectively). The general picture was that of increased body control accompanied by constriction of the musculature with increasing age.

In reference to gender, and consistent with findings obtained on parent rating scales and self-report questionnaires, girls displayed greater behavioral anxiety than boys for all phases. Furthermore, when the individual items were examined for differences, three items (crying, clinging, and requesting emotional support) were more frequently observed for girls whereas one item was more frequent for boys (stalling). Interestingly, significant gender by age effects were not found, suggesting that these differences were evident at an early age. These behavioral findings, as well as those on the self-report and parent report measures, are consistent with those obtained in sex role studies (cf. Maccoby & Jacklin, 1974). Apparently, girls are more likely to display and report affective behavior than are boys.

At this stage, having reviewed age and gender differences for parent report, self-report, and behavioral measures, the reader might well want to know of what specific use are such norms. We have alluded to a variety of uses throughout our earlier comments. Here, we shall limit ourselves to brief mention of three primary purposes. In doing so, we borrow heavily from our earlier work (King, Hamilton, & Ollendick, 1988; Ollendick & Francis, 1988; Ollendick & Hersen, 1984) as well as others (Edelbrock, 1984; Hartmann et al., 1979; Mash & Terdal, 1981). First, such normative information can help determine what behavior problems represent clinically significant areas of concern. For example, the presence of whining or crying in a 4- or 5-year-old is not unexpected. However, if such behaviors were to continue into middle childhood or early adolescence, they would be viewed as problematic and likely targets of behavior change. Thus, normative information can be useful in helping us determine what constitutes a behavior problem for a certain age child and, relatedly, determine what behaviors to target for change. However, we must hasten to acknowledge Cone and Hoier's (1986) admonition to not be ruled blindly by such normative findings. A behavior can be distressing even though a large number of children exhibit it and it is viewed as "normal" for that age. The emergence of suicidal thoughts in preadolescence is one potent example.

Second, normative information can be used to address the appropriateness of a referral. Frequently, referrals are made by parents and teachers who are potentially biased observers. Thus, for example, a parent who is particularly sensitive to anxiety in his child due to his own generalized anxiety might well "see" anxiety when there is none or when what is seen is "normal" for the child's age. Norms can help determine whether the problem lies "in the child" or in the parent's perception (Edelbrock, 1984). If there is a biased perception or a misperception, it may be more constructive to deal with the parent's sensitivity than the child himself. Similarly, many parents refer children who are simply displaying the behaviors of childhood that are appropriate for a given age (e.g., normal fears, normal activity level). Again, it would be better to provide the parent with information about normal development and perhaps to teach the parent effective parenting skills than to admit the child into treatment directly.

Third, and finally, normative information can play a crucial role in the evaluation of treatment effectiveness. Kazdin (1977), Wolf (1978), and Walker and Hops (1979) have referred to use of normative information when used in this way as "social validity." In effect, social validity addresses whether or not the change associated with treatment is meaningful. A given treatment may reduce a problem behavior significantly, but its rate or severity may still exceed normal or acceptable limits. In this sense, norms can be used to establish benchmarks for determining the applied or social significance of the effects of treatment.

Patterning of Behaviors

A second way in which developmental principles can be integrated into child behavioral assessment is to identify age differences in the relations or patterns among behaviors (Edelbrock, 1984). Identifying such differences is, of course, central to developmental psychology (Lerner, 1986). Again, whether these qualitative differences are due to hypothesized structural changes associated with stage theory or empirical laws of behavioral acquisition associated with learning theory and reflected in age-contingent learning histories is less critical for our current purposes. What is significant is that qualitative changes in patterns of behavior are expected from a developmental standpoint.

In the previous section, we alluded to some distinct patterns of behavior that were age-related. In the Katz et al. (1980) behavioral observation study, we concluded that a developmental trend was present in the response of children with leukemia about to undergo bone marrow aspirations. The youngest children tended to express their anxiety largely through more diffuse activity: crying, screaming, flailing, and needing to be carried into the treatment room and restrained. In contrast, the oldest children tended to express their anxiety by verbal reports of pain and muscular rigidity. The general picture was that of increased body control accompanied by constriction of the musculature with age. Such would be expected from a developmental standpoint.

Additional support for the integration of developmental theory into child behavioral assessment comes from the extensive research on the Child Behavior Checklist (CBC), aspects of which we reviewed earlier (Edelbrock, 1984; Achenbach & Edelbrock, 1978). In these studies, checklists completed on clinically referred children were submitted to factor analyses (principal components analysis followed by orthogonal and oblique rotations) to determine the nature of behavioral patterns present. Sample sizes for this analysis were large and representative: 450 for boys and girls aged 6 to 11 and 12 to 16, and 250 for boys and girls aged 4 to 5. The specific groupings of behaviors were described as "behavioral problem syndromes" which, in turn, were submitted to second-order factor analyses designed to arrive at global broad-band factors. Consistent with earlier studies, two broad-band factors—internalizing and externalizing—were confirmed. Of interest to our purposes here, these two broad-band factors were found across age levels, suggesting their descriptive utility and robustness. Of greater interest, some of the narrower-band (first-order) factors differed across age. To illustrate, for boys and girls aged 6 to 11, definitive factors of depression were found that were not obtained for boys and girls aged 12 to 16. For the older children, indicants of depression were viewed more as "social withdrawal" in girls and described as signs of "uncommunicativeness" in boys. Thus, a "purer" form of depression was evident in the middle age group. Of course, this does not mean that older children do not show signs of depression; to the contrary, their "depression" is just expressed differently. This latter consideration is consistent with developmental expectations.

The role of developmental factors is even more evident in a recent study of Francis, Last, and Strauss (in press). In this study, Francis et al. examined the role of age (and gender) in the behavioral expression of Separation Anxiety Disorder (APA, 1987). Although behaviorists have generally eschewed the diagnostic process, current advances in behavioral assessment have argued for the utility of such a process in assessment and treatment planning (see Harris & Powers, 1984; Nelson & Barlow, 1981, for a full discussion of these issues). Briefly, it has been argued that diagnoses provide useful indices of the relationship among various behaviors in the child's repertoire, a point not inconsistent with Voeltz and Evans' (1982) notion of response covariation or response-response relationships.

Francis et al. were interested in looking at these interrelationships in a sample of 45 children who had been reliably diagnosed as Separation Anxiety Disorder, a disorder characterized by excessive distress upon separation from major attachment figures and persisting beyond the age at which it is normally expected to occur (i.e., beyond 2–3 years of age). The specific diagnostic criteria for this disorder include at least three of the following (APA, 1987):

1. unrealistic worry about possible harm befalling major attachment figures or fear that they will leave and not return
2. unrealistic worry that an untoward calamitous event will separate the child from a major attachment figure, for example, the child will be lost, kidnapped, killed, or be the victim of an accident
3. persistent reluctance or refusal to go to school in order to stay with major attachment figures or at home
4. persistent reluctance or refusal to go to sleep without being next to a major attachment figure or to go to sleep away from home
5. persistent avoidance of being alone in the home and emotional upset if unable to follow the major attachment figure around the home
6. repeated nightmares involving theme of separation
7. complaints of physical symptoms on school days, for example, stomachaches, headaches, nausea, vomiting
8. signs of excessive distress on separation or when anticipating separation from major attachment figures, for example, temper tantrums or crying, pleading with the parents not to leave and
9. social withdrawal, apathy, sadness, or difficulty concentrating on work or play when not with a major attachment figure.

The presence or absence of each of these "symptoms" was determined through a structured diagnostic process and confirmed by behavioral observations, self-report, and parent report.

For purposes of analysis, the children were divided into three age groups (ages 5–8, 9–12, and 13–16), and the percentage of children in each group who met each of the nine criteria was determined. Several interesting age trends were observed. First, consistent with some of the other studies reviewed earlier, the youngest group of children presented with the most symptoms, followed in order by the middle-age and older children. Second, interesting linear trends were found with several of the items. For example, worry that a calamitous event might separate the child from the attachment figure was observed in 70% of the youngest and 44% in both the middle group and the oldest group. Similarly, separation nightmares were evident in 60% of the youngest group and only 13% and 22% respectively of the two older groups. Physical complaints on school days, however, were noted in 100% of the oldest group, 69% of the middle group, and only 58% of the youngest group. As a result of these differential trends, clear patterns in symptom expression were evident: the oldest group was characterized primarily by physical complaints on school days and reluctance or refusal to go to school; in contrast, the youngest group was characterized by excessive worries about separation or harm befalling the attachment figure and resulting nightmares associated with such possible separations. As we have argued elsewhere (Ollendick & Huntzinger, 1990), such a pattern speaks for qualitatively different "disorders" at these age groups.

In sum, there are several lines of converging evidence that children of differing ages show distinct patterns in their expression of anxiety and depression (and we propose for other emotions as well). These patterns have direct implications for the assessment and treatment of various child behavior problems. As stated early on by Voeltz and Evans (1982), knowledge of the relationships among behavioral response classes is useful in identifying meaningful response-response units, their controlling variables, and the evaluation of treatment outcomes. For purposes of assessment, such knowledge provides valuable guidelines for selecting target behaviors. For treatment, such knowledge provides a basis for predicting and determining related treatment effects. Inasmuch as these relationships vary across age, developmental principles in understanding these changes is critical.

Continuity/Discontinuity

A third way in which developmental principles can be integrated into child behavioral assessment is to explore the implications of developmental theory for the continuity-discontinuity of behavior as well as its stability-instability. Here we will have less empirical data with which to assert the importance of these issues; rather, we will rely on a brief discussion of the theoretical issues involved. The direct implications of these issues for child behavioral assessment are less clear at this time.

The continuity-discontinuity issue pertains to issues of change as it occurs within an individual (Lerner, 1986). Basically, this issue can be addressed from two vantage points, a descriptive one and an explanatory one. From a descriptive standpoint, we are interested in determining whether a behavior seen at one point in time in the life span can be described in the same way as behavior at another point in time. If it can be described in the same way, *descriptive continuity* is said to exist; if it cannot, *descriptive discontinuity* is said to obtain. We are simply asking, does the behavior look the same or is it different? Does it take the same form over time? For example, if 4-year-old, 8-year-old, and 12-year-old children all emitted the same behaviors to gain entry in a social group, we would conclude that descriptive continuity exists. Similarly, if children at these three age levels all expressed anxiety or depression in the same way, we would conclude that descriptive continuity is present. Of course, we have already shown in the preceding section that some differences exist in the way children of varying ages express their emotions and the behaviors which accompany those emotions (cf. Achenbach & Edelbrock, 1981; Katz et al., 1980; Ollendick et al., 1989). Such a conclusion supports descriptive discontinuity; for most of us, this makes intuitive sense. Simply observing children and adolescents reveals that they engage in behaviors that change over time and which are closely related to their age (as well as important contextual variables). Yet our current diagnostic systems and ways of thinking about child behavior do not fully take this principle of discontinuity into consideration. For example, DSM-III-R (APA, 1987) posits nine diagnostic criteria for Separation Anxiety Disorder, all of which are the same regardless of the child's or adolescent's age. Can we really expect "unrealistic worry about harm befalling a major attachment figure" to mean the same thing for a 4-year-old child as a 16-year-old adolescent? Surely, the understanding that these two individuals have of "harm" must differ, let alone what must constitute "unrealistic worry" for them. The patterning among the nine criteria, reported by Francis et al. (in press) supports the notion of discontinuity, although it does not fully establish it (a longitudinal study would be required to do so).

Similar limitations are evident in our parent rating scales and self-report questionnaires. On the Child Behavior Checklist (Achenbach & Edelbrock, 1981), for example, parents are requested to rate items such as "refusing to talk," "fears school," and "daydreams." What constitutes daydreaming for a young child may differ greatly from daydreaming in an adolescent. Further, as we noted earlier, the perceptions of parents undoubtedly differ at these varying ages. Similar limitations are evident in self-report measures. On our revised fear survey schedule, for instance, we ask children and adolescents between 7 and 16 years of age to tell us how much fear they have to specific stimuli such as "taking tests," "having a burglar break into your house," and "falling from a high place." Although we have noted age-related differences in the self-report of fear, we are not at all sure what they mean. Are young children really more fearful? Or might it be that younger children are interpreting the stimuli differently and/or unable to make fine discriminations about "how much" they fear specific stimuli? A fuller understanding of observed age differences on these types of measures is clearly needed and awaits further study.

To some extent, the use of behavioral observation procedures circumvents many of these problems. By operationalizing a specific behavior (and obtaining reliability regarding its measurement), we are able to observe the same behavior over time *and* across individuals of varying age. Yet behavioral observations are not immune to issues of continuity-discontinuity. Assume for the moment that Katz et al. (1980) had limited their measures of "anxiety" to verbal reports of worry and pain and signs of muscular tension in their children undergoing bone marrow aspirations. Had they done so, "anxiety" as determined by these two measures would have been largely nonexistent in their younger sample of children. As defined by these two measures, anxiety would have been observed to begin to occur in their middle-age group and to be clearly evident only in their oldest group. Using this restricted measure, we would have concluded something quite different from what we did in an earlier section; namely, that anxiety is present but in a different form at these various ages.

In brief, descriptive continuity refers to the issue of whether the behavior being described takes the same form over time. Does it look the same? We have concluded that oftentimes it does not and that descriptive discontinuity exists. The changes that are observed, of course, can occur for many reasons. If the same explanations are used to account for behavior over time, then that behavior is interpreted as involving unchanging laws or rules and *explanatory continuity* is said to exist. However, if different explanations are used to account for changes in behavior over time, then there is *explanatory discontinuity* (Lerner, 1986). For the most part, clinicians and researchers who espouse a behavioral perspective believe that changes over time are due to a set of learning principles that are largely the same across the child's life span. No new principles are needed. In partial contrast, developmental theorists comfortably reside in either camp. If a theoretical position is adopted that stresses a progressive, hierarchical interpretation of the organism, the development will be viewed as continuous. On the other hand, if one stresses the progressive differentiation of the organism, development will be viewed as discontinuous (Gagne, 1958; Lerner, 1986). As indicated by Langer (1970) and Werner (1957), there are both continuous and discontinuous aspects of development (i.e., differentiation and integration). Clearly, discussion of the issues associated with explanatory continuity–discontinuity is well beyond the scope of this chapter. It is important to note, however, that one's theoretical stance on this issue may have direct implications for assessment and treatment. For assessment, if we assume explanatory discontinuity, we might likely select very different instruments to measure change over time (e.g., cognitive development across concrete and formal operational "stages"). If we were to assume continuity, however, we would likely assume that similar processes (e.g., learning principles) underlie the behavior we are measuring. Accordingly, we would likely use sophisticated measures that would detect change over time. For treatment, of course, we might design qualitatively different interventions to address the differences inferred by our theoretical stance.

In sum, although the exact implications of *both* descriptive and explanatory continuity for child behavioral assessment are not clearly spelled out at this time, it is evident that there are important theoretical issues that *may* have a direct bearing on the practice of child behavioral assessment. Much work remains to be done in this area. For example, from simply a descriptive standpoint, we know precious little about age-related manifestations of a variety of problem behaviors or how they change over time. Further, we know even less about how emerging cognitive abilities affect these behavioral expressions. Much remains to be learned before a true integration of continuity–discontinuity issues and child behavioral assessment can be said to occur. We might look to the emerging field of developmental psychopathology to provide us with heuristic guidelines in this synthesis (cf. Cichetti, 1984; Lewis & Miller, 1990; Wenar, 1982; also see Chapter 3 this volume).

CONCLUSION

In this chapter we have explored the utility of developmental principles for contemporary approaches to child behavioral assessment. On the one hand, the marriage of these two seemingly compatible bedmates seems a "natural." Yet on the other hand, basic philosophical and theoretical differences remain that necessarily make the marriage a difficult and rivalrous one. Bones of contention center around nomothetic-idiographic issues, whether patterns of behavior or specific target behaviors should be studied, and whether we should place primary emphasis on the organism or the environment in the assessment enterprise. In our pursuit of "developmental-behavioral assessment," we have proposed that these differences might paradoxically serve as the grounds for a mutually satisfying and long-lasting relationship. The use of normative comparisons, assessment of behavior in a context over time, and the prevailing issues of continuity–discontinuity, illustrate the possibilities for rapprochement.

Yet this rapprochement is tenuous at best. We really do not have a firm conceptual or empirical base in which to embed this merger. In many respects, this state of affairs exists because we do not yet have an integrated behavioral theory of development. As noted by Horowitz (1988), the traditional behavioral view paid little theoretical attention to the length of time an individual has lived, or to the age of the individual. Time or age was of no consequence in itself. It simply reflected the accrual of a specific response repertoire with little acknowledgement for the regularities found in the course of behavioral development or the qualitative differences in behavior at different ages. It should be pointed out, however, that the behaviorist was not necessarily being simplistic; rather, changes in behavior over time were understood as being contextually embedded and understood by examining the history of the learned behaviors and their relationship to the remainder of the child's behavioral repertoire.

Recently, Horowitz (1988) has proposed a structural/behavioral model of development that addresses many of the shortcomings associated with our earlier theories. In this model, she proposes that the laws of behavioral acquisition can be found in the laws of learning *and* in the laws of development. Implicit in the model is the notion that human development proceeds according to a mixed model—one that is neither wholly mechanistic nor wholly organismic in character. The implications of this model for child behavioral assessment are not fully understood at this time. Still, it is precisely this type of theorizing that is needed before significant integration of developmental principles and behavioral assessment principles can occur. The emergence of "developmental-behavioral assessment" is on the horizon. We are at an exciting juncture; additional theorizing and empirical research in the next few years should determine whether the merger is a productive and lasting one.

REFERENCES

Achenbach, T. M. (1978). The Child Behavior Profile: I. Boys aged 6–11. *Journal of Consulting and Clinical Psychology, 46,* 478–488.

Achenbach, T. M., & Edelbrock, C. S. (1978). The classification of child psychopathology: A review and analysis of empirical efforts. *Psychological Bulletin, 85,* 1275–1301.

Achenbach, T. M., & Edelbrock, C. S. (1979). The Child Behavior Profile: II. Boys aged 12–16 and girls aged 6–11 and 12–15. *Journal of Consulting and Clinical Psychology, 47,* 223–233.

Achenbach, T. M., & Edelbrock, C. S. (1981). Behavioral problems and competencies reported by parents of normal and disturbed children aged 4 through 16. *Monographs of the Society for Research in Child Development, 46* (1, Serial No. 188).

Achenbach, T. M., & Edelbrock, C. S. (1989). Diagnostic, taxonomic, and assessment issues. In T. H. Ollendick & M. Hersen (Eds.), *Handbook of child psychopathology* (2nd Ed.). New York: Plenum Press.

American Psychiatric Association. (1987). *Diagnostic and Statistical Manual of Mental Disorders* (3rd ed, Rev). Washington, DC: Author.

Baer, D. M. (1982). Behavior analysis and developmental psychology: Discussant comments. *Human Development, 25,* 357–361.

Bandura, A. (1977). *Social learning theory.* Englewood Cliffs, NJ: Prentice-Hall.

Bandura, A. (1986). *Social foundations of thought and action: A social cognitive theory.* Englewood Cliffs, NJ: Prentice-Hall.

Bauer, D. (1976). An exploratory study of developmental changes in children's fear. *Journal of Child Psychology and Psychiatry, 17,* 69–74.

Bell, R. Q. (1968). A reinterpretation of the direction of effects in studies of socialization. *Psychological Review, 75,* 81–85.

Bijou, S. W. (1976). *Child development: The basic stage of early childhood.* Englewood Cliffs, NJ: Prentice-Hall.

Bijou, S. W., & Peterson, R. F. (1971). The psychological assessment of children: A functional analysis. In P. McReynolds (Ed.), *Advances in psychological assessment* (Vol. 3, pp. 27–61). Palo Alto, CA: Science and Behavior Books.

Cichetti, D. (1984). The emergence of developmental psychopathology. *Child Development, 55,* 1–7.

Ciminero, A. R., & Drabman, R. S. (1977). Current developments in the behavioral assessment of children. In B. B. Lahey & A. E. Kazdin (Eds.), *Advances in clinical child psychology* (Vol. 1, pp. 47–82). New York: Plenum Press.

Cone, J. D., & Hoier, T. S. (1986). Assessing children: The radical behavioral perspective. In R. J. Prinz (Ed.), *Advances in behavioral assessment of children and families* (Vol. 2, pp. 1–27). Greenwich, CT: JAI Press.

Edelbrock, C. S. (1984). Developmental considerations. In T. H. Ollendick & M. Hersen (Eds.), *Child behavioral assessment: Principles and procedures*. Elmsford, NY: Pergamon Press.

Edelbrock, C. S., & Achenbach, T. M. (1980). A typology of Child Behavior Profile patterns: Distribution and correlates for disturbed children aged 6–16. *Journal of Abnormal Child Psychology, 8,* 441–470.

Erikson, E. H. (1968). *Identity, youth, and crisis*. New York: W W Norton.

Evans, I. M., & Nelson, R. O. (1977). Assessment of child behavior problems. In A. R. Ciminero, K. S. Calhoun, & H. E. Adams (Eds.), *Handbook of behavioral assessment* (pp. 603–681). New York: Wiley-Interscience.

Francis, G., Last, C. G., & Strauss, C. C. (in press). Expression of Separation Anxiety Disorder: The roles of age and gender. *Child Psychiatry and Human Development*.

Freud, S. (1949). *Outline of psychoanalysis*. New York: W W Norton.

Gagne, R. M. (1958). Contributions of learning to human development. *Psychological Review, 75,* 177–191.

Gelfand, D. M., & Peterson, L. (1985). *Child development and psychopathology*. Beverly Hills, CA: Sage Publications.

Gottlieb, G. (1970). Conceptions of prenatal behavior. In L. R. Aronson, E. Tobach, D. S. Lehrman, & J. S. Rosenblatt (Eds.), *Developmental evolution of behavior: Essays in memory of T. C. Schneirla* (pp. 111–137). San Francisco: W H Freeman.

Harris, S. L., & Powers, M. D. (1984). Diagnostic issues. In T. H. Ollendick & M. Hersen (Eds.), *Child behavioral assessment: Principles and procedures* (pp. 38–57). Elmsford, NY: Pergamon Press.

Hartmann, D. P., Roper, B. L., & Bradford, D. C. (1979). Some relationships between behavioral and traditional assessment. *Journal of Behavioral Assessment, 1,* 3–21.

Horowitz, F. D. (1988). *Exploring developmental theories: Toward a structural/behavioral model of development*. Hillsdale, NJ: Lawrence Erlbaum Associates.

Katz, E. R., Kellerman, J., & Siegel, S. E. (1980). Behavioral distress in children with cancer undergoing medical procedures: Developmental considerations. *Journal of Consulting and Clinical Psychology, 48,* 356–365.

Kazdin, A. E. (1977). Assessing the clinical or applied importance of behavior change through social validation. *Behavior Modification, 1,* 427–452.

King, N. J., Hamilton, D. I., & Ollendick, T. H. (1988). *Children's phobias: A behavioural perspective*. Chichester: John Wiley & Sons.

Langer, J. (1969). *Theories of development*. New York: Holt, Rinehart, & Winston.

Langer, J. (1970). Werner's comparative organismic theory. In P. H. Mussen (Ed.), *Carmichael's manual of child psychology* (Vol. 1, pp. 733–771). New York: John Wiley & Sons.

Lerner, R. M. (1986). *Concepts and theories of human development* (2nd ed.). New York: Random House.

Lewis, M., & Miller, S. M. (Eds.). (1990). *Handbook of developmental psychopathology*. New York: Plenum Press.

Maccoby, E. E., & Jacklin, C. N. (1974). *The psychology of sex differences*. Stanford, CA: Stanford University Press.

Mash, E. J., & Terdal, L. G. (1981) (Eds.), *Behavioral assessment of childhood disorders*. New York: Guilford Press.

Masten, A. S. & Braswell, L. (1990). Developmental psychopathology. In P. R. Martin (Ed.), *Handbook of behavior therapy and psychological science: An integrative approach*. Elmsford, NY: Pergamon Press.

Miller, L. C., Barrett, C. L., & Hampe, E. (1974). Phobias of childhood in a prescientific era. In A. Davids (Ed.), *Child personality and psychopathology: Current topics* (pp. 89–134). New York: John Wiley & Sons.

Nelson, R. O., & Barlow, D. H. (1981). Behavioral assessment: Basic strategies and initial procedures. In D. H. Barlow (Ed.), *Behavioral assessment of adult disorders*. New York: Guilford Press.

Ollendick, T. H. (1979). Fear reduction techniques with children. In M. Hersen, R. M. Eisler, & P. M. Miller (Eds.), *Progress in behavior modification* (Vol. 8, pp. 127–168). New York: Academic Press.

Ollendick, T. H. (1983). Reliability and validity of the Revised Fear Survey Schedule for Children (FSSC-R). *Behaviour Research and Therapy, 21,* 685–692.

Ollendick, T. H., & Cerny, J. A. (1981). *Clinical behavior therapy with children*. New York: Plenum Press.

Ollendick, T. H., & Francis, G. (1988). Behavioral assessment and treatment of childhood phobias. *Behavior Modification, 12,* 165–204.

Ollendick, T. H., & Greene, R. W. (1990). Child behavioral assessment. In G. Goldstein & M. Hersen (Eds.), *Handbook of psychological assessment* (2nd Ed.). Elmsford, NY: Pergamon Press.

Ollendick, T. H., & Hersen, M. (1984). An overview of child behavioral assessment. In T. H. Ollendick & M. Hersen (Eds.), *Child behavioral assessment: Principles and procedures* (pp. 3–19). Elmsford, NY: Pergamon Press.

Ollendick, T. H., & Huntzinger, R. M. (1990). Separation anxiety disorders in childhood. In M. Hersen & C. G. Last (Eds.), *Handbook of child and adult psychopathology: A longitudinal perspective*. Elmsford, NY: Pergamon Press.

Ollendick, T. H., King, N. J., & Frary, R. B. (1989). Fears in children and adolescents in Australia and the United States. *Behaviour Research and Therapy, 27,* 19–26.

Ollendick, T. H., Matson, J. L., & Helsel, W. S. (1985). Fears in children and adolescents: Normative data. *Behaviour Research and Therapy, 23,* 465–467.

Piaget, J. (1950). *The psychology of intelligence*. London: Routledge & Kegan Paul.

Scherer, M. W., & Nakamura, C. Y. (1968). A Fear Survey Schedule for Children (FSS-FC): An analytic comparison with manifest anxiety (CMAS). *Behaviour Research and Therapy, 6,* 173–182.

Skinner, B. F. (1938). *The behavior of organisms.* New York: Appleton.

Voeltz, L. M., & Evans, I. M. (1982). The assessment of behavioral interrelationships in child behavior therapy. *Behavioral Assessment, 4,* 131–165.

Walker, H. M., & Hops, H. (1979). Use of normative peer data as a standard for evaluating classroom treatment effects. *Journal of Applied Behavior Analysis, 9,* 159–168.

Wenar, C. (1982). Developmental psychology: Its nature and models. *Journal of Clinical Child Psychology, 11,* 192–201.

Werner, H. (1957). The concept of development from a comparative and organismic point of view. In D. B. Harris (Ed.), *The concept of development* (pp. 125–148). Minneapolis: University of Minnesota Press.

Wolf, M. M. (1978). Social validity: The case for subjective measurement or how behavior analysis is finding its heart. *Journal of Applied Behavior Analysis, 11,* 203–213.

CHAPTER 5

CLINICAL-CHILDHOOD-DEVELOPMENTAL INTERFACE: IMPLICATIONS FOR TREATMENT

Grayson N. Holmbeck
Philip C. Kendall

Imagine that any psychological treatment could be applied to children and adolescents with equal effectiveness regardless of the age or developmental level of the treatment recipient. If this were the case, then it would follow that developmental differences do not play a role in determining whether or not a particular treatment is effective. Given that children and adolescents do develop and that they do so in rather dramatic, and often predictable ways, most clinicians who work with youthful clients would maintain that different treatments will be differentially effective as a function of developmental level.

Although it may seem obvious that a variety of individual difference variables (in both the child and therapist) can have a moderating effect on treatment outcome, psychotherapy outcome researchers have been repeatedly criticized for their assumption (implicit in their research designs) that, at the start of treatment, patients and therapists are more alike than they are different (termed the patient and therapist *uniformity myths;* Kiesler, 1966; see also Garfield & Bergin, 1978). More recently, Kendall (1984) suggested that child-clinical psychologists be cautious not to endorse what he referred to as the "developmental uniformity myth". For example, it would be unwise for treatment providers and researchers of treatment outcome to implicitly believe that children 5 to 15 years of age are a homogeneous group, that treatments for one type of child problem are also appropriate for other childhood difficulties, or that treatments for young and latency-aged children should have direct applicability to young adolescents. Universal applicability has not been demonstrated and probably will not be demonstrated given the important developmental differences across ages 5 to 15 years (e.g., Kendall, Lerner, & Craighead, 1984).

Accordingly, one purpose of this chapter is to present an overview of the normative intra-individual developmental changes of childhood and adolescence that may have an effect on therapeutic process. In addition, we will discuss the normative developmental changes that take place in the various contexts in which we find children and adolescents (i.e., family, peers, school, and work). In short, childhood and adolescence is marked by change and this should be taken into account when devising and implementing clinical interventions.

Although there is a decided lack of information

concerning the effects of developmental level on treatment outcome (e.g., see Belsky & Nezworski, 1988; Furman, 1980; Ivey, 1986; Kendall et al., 1984; Nannis & Cowan, 1988; Pine, 1985; Shirk, 1988), the related field of developmental psychopathology (e.g., Achenbach, 1982; Cicchetti, 1984; Cicchetti & Schneider-Rosen, 1984; Gelfand & Peterson, 1985; Masten, 1988; Masten & Garmezy, 1985; Rutter & Garmezy, 1983) has seen much activity with the introduction of a new journal (i.e., *Development and Psychopathology*), a special issue of *Child Development* (Vol. 55, No. 1; Cicchetti, 1984), and an increase in research output (see Rutter & Garmezy, 1983, for a review). Why the lack of interface between developmental psychology and psychological treatment? Developmental psychopathology is an extension of developmental psychology insofar as the former is concerned with variations in the course of normal development (Rutter & Garmezy, 1983). Because clinical treatment and treatment outcome research have grown out of the field of clinical psychology, it presumably has taken longer for developmental psychologists and those concerned with child and adolescent treatment to become interested in each other's work. Given the paucity of treatment approaches that take advantage of this potential overlap (Rutter, 1983), we will discuss the implications that developmental psychology has for treatment of child and adolescent disorders, focusing in particular on the importance of knowledge in the following areas: developmental norms, developmental transitions, developmental level, developmental predictors, and developmental psychopathology.

The interface between developmental psychology and clinical treatment can take other forms as well. Some researchers have attempted to demonstrate that a child's developmental status can be the object of treatment if such development is delayed or at variance with one's age peers. Others have demonstrated the utility of employing peers as intervention agents. We will consider a number of these efforts. Finally, we will focus on research and training issues that are relevant to the interface between development and treatment.

NORMATIVE INTRA-INDIVIDUAL CHANGES

From infancy until late adolescence, children experience dramatic intra-individual changes across a number of domains, namely, physical, psychological, and social (Hill, 1980b; Petersen & Hamburg, 1986).

It is critical to note at the outset that changes within and across these domains are asynchronous and vary between individuals both in terms of rate and pattern. When appropriate, we will consider the implications these changes have for psychopathology and psychotherapy. Changes in one's environment will be considered in another section.

Physical Changes

Intra-individual physical changes are most dramatic during infancy and early adolescence. During infancy and the preschool years, the clinician will primarily be concerned with whether a child has acquired developmental milestones at a time that is age appropriate. The changes are many and primarily fall within the categories of perceptual and motor development. In the normal infant, intersensory differentiation abilities and information-processing capacity both increase over time, allowing the infant to make fine distinctions between stimuli, and to process more and different types of information (Bower, 1977). In addition, the development of language abilities begins in infancy and continues throughout childhood. As with milestones in other areas of infant development, there are language-based milestones (Hetherington & Parke, 1975) that are of concern to the clinician. In autism, for example, language deficits are typically present and are often the focus of treatment (Lovaas, 1987). In short, given the vast number of physical changes in early childhood and the (normal) immaturity of certain abilities during this period, it is critical that the clinician be aware of both the limitations of the normal infant or child as well as age-appropriate abilities of the child.

More than any other stage of life except the fetal/neonatal period, adolescence is a time of substantial physical growth and change. Tanner (1962) has charted most of the characteristics of these changes in males and females. Changes in body proportions, facial characteristics, voice, body hair, strength, and coordination are found in males. Changes in body proportions, body hair, and menarcheal status are found in girls. Crucial to the understanding of this process is the knowledge that the peak of pubertal development occurs two years earlier in the modal female than in the modal male and that there are substantial variations between individuals in the time of onset, the duration, and the termination of the pubertal cycle. Thus, not only is there intra-individual variation in terms of the onset of the different pubertal changes but there is interindividual variation in the many parameters of these changes as well. Both pubertal status (an individual's placement in the sequence of predictable pubertal changes) and pubertal timing (timing of changes relative to one's age peers) should be taken into account (Petersen, 1988).

Unlike the newborn, adolescents are aware of these changes and this awareness may be pleasing or horrifying; lack of information about puberty/sexuality can contribute to emotional upset (e.g., Ruble & Brooks-Gunn, 1982; see also Tobin-Richards, Boxer, & Petersen, 1982). Most of the psychological effects of pubertal changes are probably not direct, but rather, are mediated by the responses of the individual or significant others to such changes (Petersen, 1988; Petersen & Taylor, 1980; Richards & Petersen, 1987). Significant others may assume, for example, that physical changes indicate development in psychological areas. This is not the case.

Cognitive and Psychological Changes

Perhaps most relevant to a discussion of the interface between developmental psychology and treatment is the potential moderating effect of the child's cognitive and psychological changes. As will be discussed later, efforts have been made at taking cognitive development into account when designing treatments (e.g., Kendall, 1984; Shirk, 1988). Others have attempted to promote development in this area in order to increase social adjustment (e.g., Enright & Sutterfield, 1979; Gordon, 1988; Niles, 1986; Russo, 1986).

Piaget's Theory of Cognitive Development

Piaget (1970) has provided us with a comprehensive theory of cognitive development that has general applicability to infants, children, and adolescents. Piaget has enumerated a series of four stages of cognitive development, each of which is assumed to be (1) qualitatively different than the stage before or after, (2) a structured whole in a state of equilibrium, (3) universal across cultures, and (4) part of an invariant set of stages (Ginsburg & Opper, 1969; Miller, 1983; Piaget, 1970). The *sensorimotor period* (birth to 2 years of age) involves a series of substages whereby the infant develops from "a bundle of reflexes" to one who can physically manipulate his/her world with a set of organized, and progressively more advanced set of behaviors. *Preoperational* children (2 to 7 years of age) can now use mental images to represent events but are limited (in comparison to older children) in that they tend to be highly "egocentric." These children do not view others as having perspectives different from theirs and their speech is not tailored to the listener (Miller, 1983). Given that children in this age range are often seen in therapy, it is critical that the therapist be aware of these age appropriate limitations, rather than attributing them to some sort of deficit. Other limitations characteristic of this stage are rigidity of thought, semilogical reasoning, and limited social cognition (see "Social Cognition"). The thinking of children in the *concrete operational period* (ages 7 to 11 years) is more dynamic and involves what Piaget refers to as cognitive *operations*. Thought is more in tune with the environment and is increasingly logical and flexible.

Reviews of the literature on cognitive changes during adolescence have been provided by Hill and Palmquist (1978), Keating (1980), and Neimark (1975). Though less overtly observable, cognitive changes in adolescence are probably as dramatic as the physical changes. Piaget (1970, 1972) is credited with the identification of adolescence as the period of *formal operational* thinking where adult-level reasoning can take place. Some adolescents can, for example, begin to think about their own thinking (metacognition). However, this new skill is not without potential difficulties. Elkind (1967) suggested that the adolescent may become obsessed with this new ability. Even if not obsessed, the adolescent is not fully developed in a social cognitive sense and may misperceive others as equally interested in his/her own thoughts and actions (i.e., the imaginary audience) and yet perceive them as unable to understand his/her emotional experiences. Other changes associated with the advent of formal operations and the implications such changes have for adolescent psychopathology and psychotherapy have been detailed by Gordon (1988), Hains (Hains & Miller, 1980; Hains & Ryan, 1983), and Russo (1986).

Social Cognition

Piaget was a constructivist insofar as he maintained that individuals "actively participate in the construction of the known reality" (Reese & Overton, 1970, p. 134). Thus, development does not occur in a vacuum, but rather, is fostered or hindered through interactions with the social world. This viewpoint has led several researchers to explore the interface between cognitive development and social relations (i.e., *social cognitive development*; see Flavell &

Ross, 1981; Higgins, Ruble, & Hartup, 1983; Overton, 1983; Shantz, 1975, 1983). Of interest here are the child's socially relevant cognitions (Higgins et al., 1983) such as one's understanding of significant others and their behaviors. The development of role-taking and empathy skills, the role of affect in understanding people versus things, attributional processes in social situations, and prosocial behavior are a few of the research areas that have interested developmental and social psychologists working in this area. Many maintain that certain developmental pathways are "healthier" than are others, suggesting that such social cognitions could be the target of treatment efforts or at least provide a theoretical basis for treatment approaches (e.g., see Kendall, 1984; Urbain & Kendall, 1980, for reviews of treatment studies in the area of perspective-taking).

Psychological Development

Although too numerous to discuss in detail, theories of psychological development have been suggested and are clearly relevant to the child-clinical psychologist. Moral development (Gilligan, 1982; M. Hoffman, 1970; Kohlberg, 1967, 1969), for example, has been implicated in the onset of a number of antisocial disorders. Kohlberg describes six stages of moral reasoning with two stages comprising each of three levels: preconventional, conventional, and principled (or postconventional). Persons at lower stages tend to be rule- and obedience-bound whereas persons at higher stages recognize the arbitrary nature of rules and laws; and that such laws can be changed if they are unjust. These postconventional individuals base their decisions on a universal set of ethical principles as well as on their own conscience. Kohlberg's notions are social-cognitive in nature in that experiences with the social world shape development. As has been the case with perspective-taking, therapists have attempted to stimulate moral development (particularly with samples of delinquents and predelinquents) with group therapy approaches (e.g., Blatt & Kohlberg, 1975; Niles, 1986). Of course, it is critical, in research of this kind, to assess changes in outcome behaviors as well as changes in developmental level.

Loevinger's (1976; see Hauser, 1976, for a review) theory of ego development is also relevant here. Again, this is a stage theory and involves increasing levels of maturity. Stages differ along dimensions of impulse control, maturity of interpersonal relations, and cognitive style. Research with Loevinger's Sentence Completion Test has revealed, for example, that adolescents at higher levels of ego development evidence less psychopathology (e.g., Noam et al., 1984).

Sense of Self and Identity Formation

An excellent review of the development of the self-system during infancy and childhood has been provided by Harter (1983). Relevant here is the construction of self during infancy and childhood, the continuity of such conceptions over time, the development of self-esteem, and issues concerning self-control. Many of the constructs that Harter discusses (i.e., self-concept, self-esteem, and self-control) are related (in the directions expected) to psychopathology during childhood. Despite the rather extensive literature in this area, it has not been until recently that writers have explicitly discussed the relevance of these constructs for child psychotherapy (Harter, 1988).

A major psychological task of adolescence is believed to be the development of an identity (Erikson, 1968; Sprinthall & Collins, 1984). Although the notion that all adolescents experience identity crises appears to be a myth (Rutter, 1980), identity development is recognized as an adolescent issue. A related issue is the development of a sense of self-governance and a feeling of autonomy (however defined; Douvan & Adelson, 1966; Hill & Holmbeck, 1986; Rutter, 1983; Steinberg & Silverberg, 1986). Research with healthy adolescents (e.g., Kandel & Lesser, 1972) suggests that autonomy from parents does not develop at the expense of relationships with parents and that the values of parents and the values of one's peer group are usually more alike than different (Hartup, 1970).

Changes in Social Role

A variety of changes in the social status of children occur during adolescence (Hill, 1980b; Steinberg, 1985). Although such social redefinition is universal, the specific changes vary greatly across different cultures. In some nonindustrial societies, public rituals (i.e., rites of passage) take place soon after the onset of pubertal change. Norms for appropriate social behaviors are altered at this time and the adolescent is now viewed as an adult. In Western industrialized societies, the transition is less clear, but analogous changes in social status do take place. Steinberg (1985) cites changes across four domains: interpersonal (e.g., changes in familial status), political (e.g., late adolescents are eligible to vote), economic (e.g., adolescents are allowed to work), and legal (e.g., late adolescents can be tried in adult court systems). In addition, adolescents are able to obtain a driver's permit and can get married. Leaving home in late adolescence (e.g., Moore, 1987) also serves to redefine one's social role.

Such changes in social role have clinical implications. Adolescents' ability to adapt to changing adult expectations for acceptable behavior will vary. Expected roles are less clear in this culture than is the case in less industrialized societies; there is little consensus about what constitutes normal behavior for adolescents in Western culture (e.g., conflicting messages concerning sexuality and substance abuse are frequently presented on television). Given a lack of role clarity, psychopathology may be a frequent outcome of failure to sort through conflicting expectations.

We have discussed the normative intra-individual developmental changes of childhood and adolescence. We now turn our attention to environmental or contextual changes that typically occur during the first two decades of life.

NORMATIVE CONTEXTUAL AND ENVIRONMENTAL CHANGES

As noted by Hill (1980b) and Petersen and Hamburg (1986), contextual changes during childhood and adolescence can occur in the following domains: family, peers, school, and work (also see Barth, 1986; Bronfenbrenner, 1979). Changes in each domain will be reviewed, in turn.

Changes in Family Relations

Not only does the family play a principle role in the socialization of a child, but there are developmental changes in this role as well (Maccoby & Martin, 1983). Recent research suggests that *both* parents and siblings appear to play significant and unique roles in this process (e.g., Furman & Buhrmester, 1985). The role of fathers in child development is beginning to receive attention (e.g., Lamb, Pleck, & Levine, 1985) as are the effects of divorce (e.g., Guiduebaldi, Perry, & Cleminshaw, 1984; Hetherington, 1981; Kurdek, 1983; Wallerstein & Kelley, 1980) and maternal employment (Hoffman, 1974, 1979) on child adjustment.

Beginning our discussion with family relations during infancy, Ainsworth's (e.g., Ainsworth & Bell, 1969) and Sroufe's (e.g., Sroufe & Fleeson, 1986; Sroufe & Waters, 1977) work on infant-mother attachment has informed us about the importance and predictive utility of early primary relationships. Sroufe (1983; Sroufe & Fleeson, 1986) has shown, for example, that children with secure mother-infant attachments are more socially competent in preschool.

Also relevant here is the importance of child-rearing behaviors. Although family therapists have shown an interest in dimensions of parenting and family functioning (e.g., Olson, Russell, & Sprenkle, 1983), an extensive developmentally-oriented literature exists that concerns parenting behaviors and their corresponding child outcomes. Based on factor-analytic studies of parental power and control (e.g., Becker, 1964; see Maccoby & Martin, 1983, for a review), a two dimensional classification scheme of parenting has been developed that includes the following parenting patterns: authoritarian-autocratic, indulgent-permissive, authoritarian-reciprocal, and indifferent-uninvolved (Maccoby & Martin, 1983).

Baumrind (1968) has argued that authoritative parents are similar to authoritarian parents in their emphasis upon explicit standards and guidelines, the difference being that the former are likely to be more affectionate and to permit more say in the construction and application of rules. Permissive parents are those that do not clearly state or explain their rules and are more likely to submit to their children's demands. Regarding socialization outcomes, authoritarian and authoritative parenting have been found to have a negative and a positive impact, respectively, on children's (and especially boys') social competence, initiative, spontaneity, moral development, motivation for intellectual performance, self-esteem, and locus of control. Permissive parents tend to have children who are more aggressive and impulsive (DiLalla, Mitchell, Arthur, & Pagliocca, 1988; Maccoby & Martin, 1983; Steinberg, 1987a).

As highlighted by Petersen and Hamburg (1986) and Hill (1980a), adolescence is a time of transformation in family relations (also see Grotevant & Cooper, 1983). Changes in adolescent attachment and autonomy (e.g., Steinberg & Silverberg, 1986; see Hill & Holmbeck, 1986, for a review) as well as changes in the life circumstances of the parents themselves have an impact on the adolescent and the family system. Although the family must continually adapt throughout childhood, transformations in family relations may be particularly dramatic during the adolescent years. Families with young adolescents are more likely to conflict over mundane issues (rather than basic values) than are families with older or younger children (Montemayor, 1983); they tend to have about two conflicts every three days (Montemayor & Hanson, 1985). On the other hand, most adolescents do negotiate this period without severing ties with parents or developing serious disorders (see Holmbeck & Hill, 1988; for a review). The therapist should be aware that transformations in attachments to parents are to be expected during adolescence and that some normative familial problems may arise because of difficulties in managing this transition.

Changes in Peer Relations

A number of writers have maintained that peer relations "contribute uniquely to the growth of the individual—to the capacity to relate to others, to the development of social controls, and to the acquisition of social values" (Hartup, 1983, p. 103). Most now agree that child-child relationships are necessities and not luxuries and that these relationships have positive effects on cognitive, social-cognitive, linguistic, sex role, and moral development (see Parker & Asher, 1987, for a recent review). Indeed, Parker and Asher (1987) conclude their review of the literature on peer relations and later personal adjustment by arguing that there is support for the hypothesis that children with poor peer relations are at risk for later difficulties (e.g., dropping out of school and criminality).

One might argue that if children have quality relations with their parents that these parent-child relationships can take the place of peer relations or at least buffer any negative effects of problematic relations with other children. On the other hand, Piaget (1932/1965; see Likona, 1976; Turiel, 1983; Youniss, 1980, for a more detailed review and critique of Piaget's theory of children's morality) has argued that it is only through interactions with age-mates that an individual is able to attain a morality of cooperation (or autonomous morality). Initially, children believe that rules are external to themselves and that such rules are a function of the types of behaviors that adults in their lives forbid or allow (heteronomous morality). That is, parent-child relationships are inherently hierarchical in nature. It is through interactions with peers that a child comes to see that "rules are social agreements accepted by all members of a group as a basis for cooperative action" (Maccoby, 1980, p. 303). Through relations with peers, children become aware that they can develop their own rules based upon mutual understanding and agreement (i.e., symmetrical reciprocity; Youniss, 1980). In parent-child relations, however, such mutuality rarely exists because, as Youniss (1980) points out, "(heteronomous) morality is engendered by relations of unilateral constraint in which persons in authority are seen as possessing privileged knowledge to which others must then adhere" (p. 281). In short, peer relationships appear to provide a unique contribution to child adjustment.

Peer relations during childhood and adolescence appear to evolve through a series of developmental stages (e.g., Asher & Gottman, 1981; Berndt, 1981, 1983; Selman, 1980; Youniss, 1980). Selman (1980, 1981), for example, presents a theory of the growth of interpersonal understanding, the stages of which correspond to developmental levels of social perspective taking. For example, according to Selman's scheme, at the point that children are able to be self-reflective concerning their own thought from another's perspective (Level 2 of social perspective taking) they are at the "fair weather cooperation" stage of their understanding of close dyadic friendships. At this stage, the child's friendship is two-way as "exemplified by concerns for coordinating . . . the specific likes and dislikes of self and other" (Selman, 1981, p. 250). (Clinical implications of Selman's theory will be provided later.)

Sullivan (1953) has also provided a stage theory of the development of peer relations. As does Piaget, Sullivan stresses the importance of interpersonal relationships and the differences between child-child and parent-child relations (Youniss, 1980). He argues that an individual's personality is best understood by examination of his/her interpersonal interactions. Sullivan describes his notion of "chumship" and maintains that this (typically) same-sex friendship is a critical developmental accomplishment. It is with this relationship that the child presumably learns about intimacy, and this friendship serves as a basis for later close relationships. Thus, we again see that the nature of children's friendships changes with increasing maturity and, more generally, that child-child relationships are of critical developmental importance.

Although we have stressed, as have others, that family and peers provide unique contributions to development and adjustment, it is also true that the family can provide a secure base for a child's exploration into the world of peers. Hartup (1983), based on his review of the literature on peer relations, has noted that healthy family relations are a necessary basis for the development of healthy peer relations, especially in light of the following findings: (a) children and adolescents usually adhere to their parents' values even during increases in peer involvement, (b) parent and peer values are typically quite similar, especially with regard to important issues, and (c) differences between parent and peer values are more likely when children have distant relations with their parents *and* when they associate with peers who endorse antisocial behaviors. Thus, we must be careful not to treat the world of peers and the world of the family as separate. Each affects the other with both contributing uniquely to development and adjustment.

Effects of the School Context

Another context of child development is the child's school. As argued by Minuchin and Shapiro (1983), we should not only be interested in the school's effect on cognition and achievement, but that we should also look at the school "as an environment for individual development . . . (that has an effect on) . . . the sense of self, the belief in one's own competence, images of life possibilities as a male or female, relationships to other people, and views of justice and morality" (p. 198).

With increasing age, children are exposed to more complex school environments (Minuchin & Shapiro, 1983). Movement between schools (such as between an elementary school and a junior high school) can be viewed as a stressor, with multiple school transitions producing more deleterious effects (Petersen & Hamburg, 1986; Simmons & Blyth, 1987). Simmons and Blyth (1987) have found, for example, that children (and particularly girls) who switch from an elementary school into a junior high school (as opposed to staying in a K–8 school) will show significant self-esteem decrements and that recovery in self-esteem is not likely for a sizable number of these girls. Boys and girls who make such a transition evidence decrements in grade point average and extracurricular activities. Presumably, these decreases in self-esteem are due, at least in part, to movement from a protected environment (i.e., elementary school) to an impersonal environment (junior and senior high school) and to the detrimental effects of unsuccessful school transitions.

Not only do school transitions have an impact on development, but the school environment does as well. Physical setting, limitations in resources, philosophies of education, teacher expectations, curriculum characteristics, and interactions between teacher and student have been found to be related to a variety of child outcomes (Minuchin & Shapiro, 1983; Rutter, Maughan, Mortimore, & Ouston, 1979), and these findings are maintained even after social background is held constant. For example, elementary school children appear to profit from open school environments (in terms of social development and self-reliance) and high school students appear to profit from nonauthoritarian teaching approaches (Rutter et al., 1979). We know that smaller schools and less authoritarian school environments promote commitment on the part of the student (i.e., fewer students drop out) and that the high rate of drop outs in some school districts indicate that environment and student needs have not been well matched.

Others have attempted to use the school environment as a context for moral and affective development (see Minuchin & Shapiro, 1983, for a review). The former concerns issues of values, responsibility to the community, and delinquent behaviors whereas the latter concerns issues of self-awareness, being supportive to others, and attentive listening. Although the implications of such approaches for prevention of child psychopathology are many, they have not been thoroughly researched nor has generalization (to other environments outside of the classroom) or maintenance of effects been adequately demonstrated. Also lacking are comprehensive studies of peer relations in the classroom environment. Finally, "schools offer an untapped potential for studying the child's relationship to non-parental authorities at different developmental stages" (Minuchin & Shapiro, 1983, p. 253).

Effects of Working

The last context that we will consider is the work environment (primarily relevant for adolescents). Most of the work in this area has been reviewed by Greenberger and Steinberg (1986; also see Lewko, 1987). Although more than 80% of all high school students in this country work before they graduate (Steinberg, 1985) and many government agencies have recommended that adolescents work, little research has been done on the effects of such work on adolescent development and the adolescents' relationships with significant others.

Based on Greenberger and Steinberg's (1986) review, however, it seems clear that the work environment has important positive and negative effects on adolescent development. Although adolescents who work tend to develop an increased sense of self-reliance, they also tend to: (a) develop cynical attitudes about work, (b) spend less time with their families and peers and are less involved in school, (c) be more likely to abuse drugs or commit delinquent acts, and (d) have less time for self-exploration and identity development. The primary problem here seems to be the monotonous and stressful nature of adolescent jobs. As with our reviews of the research concerning the other contexts of child development, we again see the types of environmental characteristics that are associated with problem behavior and psychopathology.

BIDIRECTIONAL EFFECTS BETWEEN INTRA-INDIVIDUAL AND CONTEXTUAL CHANGES

Thus far we have been primarily concerned with presenting an overview of the separate intra-individual and contextual changes that occur during childhood and adolescence as a background to the discussion that follows on the interface between developmental psychology and child/adolescent treatment. It is also worth noting, however, that intra-individual changes do appear to have an impact on the child's environment and that such effects appear to be bidirectional (i.e., context also impacts on intra-individual change).

For example, recent work on associations between adolescent pubertal maturation and familial relationships suggests that there is a period of temporary perturbation or agitation in parent-adolescent relations shortly after the onset of pubertal change (e.g., Hill & Holmbeck, 1987; Hill, Holmbeck, Marlow, Green, & Lynch, 1985a, 1985b; Papini & Sebby, 1987; Steinberg, 1987b, 1988, 1989; Steinberg & Hill, 1978). These effects occur for pubertal status independently of chronological age and pubertal timing and appear to be most pronounced in adolescent-mother dyads. Findings for pubertal status have been replicated by several investigators with a variety of methodologies and measures of pubertal change. Finally, there is some evidence that pubertal timing has an impact on family relations. For example, and in line with much of the rest of the literature, Hill et al. (1985a) found that early-maturing girls may be at risk for chronic (rather than temporary) familial disruption. In addition to there being evidence for effects in the direction of pubertal change to family, there also appear to be effects in the opposite direction as well. Steinberg (1988) has found with longitudinal data that certain characteristics of family relations appear to have an impact on the onset of pubertal change for girls. That is, it appears that increased distance in the mother-child relationship, as indexed by measures of mother-adolescent conflict, accelerates female pubertal development and that closeness in the mother-adolescent dyad may slow this developmental process. Thus, it appears that rather than employing biological change solely as an independent variable, investigators should begin to search for reciprocal effects between social environmental and biological maturation.

Although not investigated in depth, it also appears that there is some effect of cognitive development on the contexts of childhood and adolescence. We have already discussed Selman's model of interpersonal understanding whereby friendship conceptions (as well as conceptions about the family) appear to develop as a function of social perspective taking. In fact, one of the goals of those working in the field of social cognitive development is to examine interactions between cognitive development and social development (see earlier discussion). Also of relevance is Hauser's (e.g., Hauser et al., 1984) work on the relations between ego development and familial contexts of adolescence. Adolescent ego development scores were positively related to adolescent problem solving and empathy behaviors in family interaction and negatively related to devaluing and withholding behaviors. Parent behaviors in the interaction sessions were related to adolescent *and* parent ego development scores. Finally, Santilli and Furth (1987) have examined developmental changes in adolescent's perceptions of work. Effects of age and logical reasoning have been found for adolescents' perceptions of employment and unemployment.

As is probably clear from this section, much of this type of research (on interactions between intra-individual change and contexts) has been done on adolescents. In part, this may be because there are more intra-individual changes during adolescence than in childhood (excluding infancy). On the other hand, we cannot assume that children 5 to 11 years of age (i.e., the elementary school years) are a homogeneous group that undergo relatively few intra-individual or contextual changes. Thus, more attention needs to be paid to "change" during this earlier age period.

IMPLICATIONS OF DEVELOPMENTAL PSYCHOLOGY FOR TREATMENT OF CHILDREN AND ADOLESCENTS

Following a rationale for examining the interface between developmental psychology and treatment, we examine three types of knowledge that appear to have implications for the treatment of children and adolescents and for treatment-based research in this area: (a) knowledge of developmental norms, level, and transitions, (b) knowledge of developmental predictors, and (c) knowledge of developmental psychopathology. In a later section, we review literature dealing with attempts to promote development and the literature pertaining to the inclusion of peers in treatment programs and evaluations.

Rationale

As argued earlier, some child-clinical psychologists have mistakenly endorsed the developmental uniformity myth (i.e., the assumption that children and adolescents of different ages and developmental level are more alike than they are different and that all can be handled similarly in the treatment setting). Regarding the use of developmental principles in *behavior therapy,* Rutter (1983) argues that the notion of the child as a developing organism "has always received lipservice and often much more than that in psychodynamic therapies, but until very recently it has been steadfastly ignored by many behavior therapists" (p. 144; see also Furman, 1980; Kendall et al., 1984). Similarly, Gelfand & Petersen (1985) noted that, in 1938, Skinner argued that "the basic premise of behavioral psychology (was) that all organisms, human and subhuman, young and old, were subject to the same law of effect (principle of reinforcement) and could be studied in the same basic manner" (p. 27), and, therefore, developmental process was viewed as unimportant. Although systematic desensitization has been applied to children and adolescents across a wide age range (in literally hundreds of studies), only a few studies have examined the effects for age (Hampe, Noble, Miller, & Barrett, 1973; Hatsenbuehler & Schroeder, 1978; Katz, Kellerman, & Siegel, 1980; Ollendick, 1979; A. Rodriguez, M. Rodriguez, & Eisenberg, 1959; Tasto, 1969). This observation is even more surprising because the nature of anxiety varies across age level.

Lourie (1987) sums up the state of the interface between developmental psychology and treatment, in general, by stating that "therapies have not been modified to make them developmental-stage specific . . . " (p. 85). Selman (1980) echoes these concerns by stating that "what appears to be missing, at least in the case of children, is clear acknowledgment of the important role of developmental level as a foundation for determining how variables interact and what path therapy might most productively follow" (p. 255). Finally, Kendall et al. (1984) argue that "development means that the same experience—the same intervention—occurring or implemented at distinct points in the life course will be processed differently and may, as a consequence, have different effects . . . thus, developmental theories and data offer guideposts for the selection of an intervention" (p. 73). Given the concern with the lack of interface between developmental psychology and treatment (also see Cicchetti, Toth, Bush, & Gillespie, 1988; Shirk, 1988), it is surprising that so few developmentally gauged treatments have been designed. Thus, our review of the relevant literature, in the next section, is unfortunately quite brief.

One example of an attempt to incorporate developmental psychology into an intervention program is Feindler and Ecton's (1986) cognitive-behavioral treatment of adolescent anger control. Although they do acknowledge that developmental issues should be incorporated into treatment planning, their treatment is not fully "developmental-stage specific." Mention of adolescent development is included, yet there is no mention of social cognitive development nor do they consider the ways in which pubertal change may impact on expressions of anger. Though the authors are moving in the right direction, developmental level could have been considered more when designing the treatment. For example, future efforts could consider the following questions: Are there developmental differences between early adolescents and late adolescents in the effectiveness of the treatment or specific components of the treatment? Do pre- and postpubertal children respond to the treatment differently? Does the adolescent's understanding of family and peer relationships (a la Selman, 1980), impact upon treatment effectiveness?

Regarding the interface between developmental psycho*pathology* and treatment, Santostefano (1980) reports that "a look at the literature of child psychopathology and of developmental psychology suggests that each is segregated, for the most part, from child clinical practice" (p. 2). Santostefano is even critical of Achenbach's text entitled "Developmental Psychopathology" (1974; a researcher whom Cicchetti justifiably describes as a "pioneer" in the field of developmental psychopathology) for merely paying lipservice to the concept of development and for not organizing sections concerning psychopathology and intervention around developmental theory. Santostefano is equally critical of handbooks of developmental psychology. Finally, Kovacs and Paulauskas (1984) are critical of the research literature on childhood depression for ignoring developmental psychology since it appears that "developmental stage determines the manifest symptom picture" (p. 61; also see Rutter, Izard, & Read, 1986).

Thus, it appears that knowledge of developmental psychology and developmental psychopathology have not been routinely used as a basis for treatment planning for children or adolescents. Although developmental psychology and psychopathology have been brought together in the new field of developmental psychopathology, there is room for greater consideration of treatment issues—we now turn to our discussion of the interface between developmental psychology and child/adolescent treatment.

Using Knowledge of Developmental Norms, Level, and Transitions

In the first half of this chapter we discussed a variety of normative intra-individual and contextual changes that occur during childhood and adolescence. Given the primacy of change during the first two decades of life, we argue that both the researcher and therapist who is knowledgeable about normal and maladaptive development is at a great advantage when attempting to design a treatment, determine the conditions under which a treatment is efficacious, and/or apply a given treatment. In short, we hypothesize that the quality of child and adolescent treatment is likely to "move up a notch or two" when knowledge of developmental psychology is taken into account.

Although we have thus far been critical of the existing clinical literature for not being attentive to the literature concerning normal development, this does not mean that efforts that do take developmental factors into account do not exist. For example, Craighead (1986), in an introduction to a miniseries in *Behavior Therapy*, reported that review papers that emphasized the study of adolescence from a developmental perspective were among those invited for the series. In this section, we review both research efforts and discussions of clinical practice that have attempted to take developmental norms, level, and transitions into account in the design, assessment, or implementation of treatment approaches.

Developmental Norms and Treatment

Knowledge of developmental norms serves as a basis for making sound diagnostic judgments, assessing the need for treatment, and selecting the appropriate treatment. In terms of diagnosis, both overdiagnosis and underdiagnosis can result from a lack of or erroneous knowledge of developmental norms. For example, Achenbach and Edelbrock (1981) reported that 52% of parents of 4- to 5-year-olds stated that their child was "disobedient at home." Thus, in the case of a 5-year-old who is disobedient, a clinician who lacks the knowledge that such a behavior is typical of this age period is much more likely to overdiagnosis and to inappropriately refer such a child for treatment.

With regards to underdiagnosis, it is a common belief that adolescents have stormy and stressful relations with their parents and that "detachment" from parents is the norm (Holmbeck & Hill, 1988). On the other hand, research has not supported this notion—it appears that approximately 20% (rather than 100%) of adolescents have such relations with their parents (see Holmbeck & Hill, 1988, for a review). It is interesting to speculate about the clinical implications of such erroneous "storm and stress" beliefs. Offer, Ostrov, and Howard (1981) have warned that "adolescents and their parents are not helped when experts tell them not to worry about their problems because the problems are a normal part of adolescence that will disappear with time . . . Adolescents in the midst of severe identity crises or emotional turmoil are *not* just experiencing a part of normal growing up" (p. 127–128). A problem results, then, when clinicians underdiagnose psychopathology during adolescence owing to storm and stress beliefs.

Some changes during adolescence are normal and these have implications for the selection of treatments. Given the adolescent's normal developmental trend toward greater autonomous functioning (Steinberg & Silverberg, 1986), certain treatments are more appropriate for this age group. Self-control strategies (e.g., Feindler & Ecton, 1986; see Harter, 1983, for a review of the developmental changes in self-control abilities) are probably more useful with older adolescents than are behavioral programs where parents are employed as behavior change agents (Kendall & Williams, 1986). Similarly, the work of Spivack and Shure (Shure & Spivack, 1978, 1980; Spivack, Platt, & Shure, 1976) suggests that different cognitive-problem solving strategies are relevant at different ages. Children 4 or 5 years of age are able to generate alternative solutions but it is not until 8 to 10 years of age that a child is able to employ means-end thinking. Their work capitalizes on these normative differences between children of different ages.

Cognitive Developmental Level and Treatment

The importance of cognitive development as a moderator of treatment effectiveness has been stressed by many (e.g., Bobbitt & Keating, 1983; Furman, 1980; Henggeler & Cohen, 1984; Kendall, 1977; Kendall & Braswell, 1985; Kendall et al., 1984) but has rarely received empirical attention. In one illustrative study, Schleser, Cohen, Meyers, and Rodick (1984; also see Schleser, Meyers, & Cohen, 1981) found with a sample of 6-year-olds that self-instructional training led to improvement on their dependent measures but only for those children in the concrete operational group. Those in the preoperational group did not improve (also see W. Craighead, Meyers, L. Craighead, & McHale, 1983). Studies such as these are rare. Given that most efforts thus far have been in the form of theoretical discourse, rather than empirical study, it appears that this is a new research area that shows great promise for the future (Kendall & Braswell, 1985; Shirk, 1988).

Henggeler and Cohen (1984) provide an important contribution by discussing the role of child and adolescent cognitive development in family-oriented treatments. They argue that "the child's level of cognitive development is an important factor in determining optimal treatment strategies. The effectiveness of an intervention often varies with the child's cognitive maturity" (p. 183). They then apply these notions to a variety of clinical examples, such as adjustment to sexual abuse and divorce.

In the case of sexual abuse, Henggeler and Cohen argue that treatment for the preoperational child will be quite different than treatment for the concrete operational child. They note that past research suggests that there are fewer negative effects for younger (and presumably less cognitively mature) children than for older children (Tsai, Feldman-Summers, & Edgar, 1979). Preoperational children are less at risk because: (a) they tend to not be aware of the negative social consequences of abuse, (b) they tend to feel less guilt, depression, and loss subsequent to the abusive act, and (c) are less aware of the potential impact that the abuse may have on future heterosexual relationships. Behavioral approaches may be helpful for these less cognitively mature children because they may fear specific individuals or situations. For the concrete operational child, on the other hand, the abuse is more likely to generate feelings of guilt and, as a result, emotional support may be more useful with such children. Peer relations may have to be addressed given that embarrassment may drive them to avoid social interaction.

Regarding relations between cognitive development and child adjustment to divorce, preoperational children may be primarily concerned with the loss of parental attention and behavior problems may result (Henggeler & Cohen, 1984). Again, behavioral techniques may be helpful in altering the consequences (i.e., rewards & punishments) of the child's behaviors. More cognitively mature children (and especially those who have role-taking skills) are able to understand that the lack of attention from parents may be a function of considerable marital stress as well as stress from other aspects of their parents' lives. They may also be aware that their behavior is capable of exacerbating this level of stress. Given the developmental differences between children with regard to role-taking, the therapist would not want to be blind to such developmental differences.

Although Henggeler and Cohen have noted the developmental differences in children's and adolescents' understandings of important life events, we need more information concerning the actual type of intervention strategy to employ. What is needed are developmentally gauged, step-by-step strategies that could be employed after assessment of a child's cognitive developmental level. It would be helpful if clinicians developed alternate forms of their treatments that could be appropriately applied to those of varying developmental level.

In the area of adolescent pregnancy (see Bolton, 1980; Chilman, 1983; Lancaster & Hamburg, 1986; Ooms, 1981; Stuart & Wells, 1982, for reviews of the adolescent pregnancy literature), few intervention programs have considered the developmental level, or more specifically, the cognitive developmental level of the treatment recipient. Given the availability of contraception and sex education classes, many are puzzled by the irrationality of adolescent contraception nonuse (Cvetkovich, Grote, Bjorseth, & Sarkissian, 1975; Lancaster & Hamburg, 1986; Morrison, 1985). Although teenage pregnancy and adolescent motherhood continue to be serious problems for our society, the onset of the AIDS epidemic coupled with the high rate of sexually transmitted diseases in the adolescent population underscores the need to examine adolescent sexual behaviors. One barrier to reducing the rate of adolescent pregnancy that has been repeatedly cited (Byrne & Fisher, 1983; Chilman, 1983; Cobliner, 1974; Cvetkovich et al., 1975; Jorgensen, 1981; Lancaster & Hamburg, 1986; Morrison, 1985; Pestrak & Martin, 1985; Urberg, 1982), but not studied, is the level of adolescent cognitive development. In fact, Morrison (1985), in her review of the adolescent contraceptive literature, has argued that "a relatively new and promising area for research in contraceptive use is the application of developmental and stage models" (p. 563). Put another way, Jorgensen (1981) maintains that "certain cognitive skills are developmental prerequisites to adequate internalization and integration of information bearing on . . . contraception" (p. 44). The reasoning behind the link between adolescent cognitive development and contraceptive use (see Cvetkovich et al., 1975; Jorgensen, 1981) involves the notion that adolescents who are less cognitively mature may not appreciate the seriousness of contraceptive nonuse, anticipate the difficulties that will be encountered in the future if pregnancy results, or properly evaluate the probability of pregnancy. The less cognitively mature male may also not take the role of his partner and, as a consequence, may not take seriously the risk of pregnancy or the consequences for the female if she should become pregnant.

In a recent effort, Holmbeck, Gasiewski, and Crossman (1988) examined the relations between adolescent cognitive development, egocentrism, *and* contraceptive knowledge, attitudes, and behavior. They found that adolescent cognitive development (as assessed with a measure of concrete and formal operational thought; Gray, 1976; Gray & Hudson, 1984) was related to knowledge of both contraceptive use and venereal diseases and that self-esteem and a measure of egocentrism were related to contraceptive attitudes and behaviors. These investigators are currently investigating the link between cognitive development and responsiveness to sex education, actual contraceptive behaviors, and family planning decisions. We would argue that different sex education programs are appropriate for children at different cognitive developmental levels. With less mature individuals, more immediate risks should be stressed as well as thorough education in the probability of pregnancy. With more cognitively mature students, role-taking skills and future risks could be emphasized.

Selman's (1980) work on the implications of children's social cognitions for therapy are also relevant to the discussion of the interface between cognitive development and treatment. He provided an interesting analysis of the frequent mismatch between therapist intervention and child understanding of the intervention (perhaps due to what he refers to as "adultocentrism") and he provides recommendations on how to avoid such a mismatch. Selman maintains that therapists' statements vary along a developmental hierarchy and should be matched with the level of social cognitive development of the child. Although Selman's therapeutic orientation differs from some of those discussed here, we see the utility of gauging treatment to the child's developmental level.

Shirk's (1988) edited volume *Cognitive Development and Child Psychotherapy* provides a current consideration of the "implications of children's cognitive and social cognitive development for existing forms of child psychotherapy" (p. x). In accordance with Selman (1980), Shirk (1988) argues that children's behavior in psychotherapy is not merely a function of their psychopathology, but is also related to their level of social-cognitive development. In this volume, all of the following are viewed as having implications for child psychotherapy: emotional understanding (Nannis, 1988), developmental changes in self-concept, self-development, and self-understanding (Harter, 1988; Noam, 1988b; Schorin & Hart, 1988; also see Noam, 1988a), causal reasoning (Shirk, 1988), interpersonal negotiation strategies (Selman & Schultz, 1988), and conceptions of social relationships (Bierman, 1988; also see Bierman, 1983). Many of the chapters present case summaries where development and treatment are adequately integrated, whereas other chapters tend to emphasize either development or treatment.

What is missing in many of these chapters (Shirk, 1988) and what is sorely needed are detailed recommendations concerning how developmental level can guide treatment choice. Knowledge of developmental level could be used in a number of ways to modify treatment strategies. First, such knowledge could be used to establish treatment goals, as is the case with Schorin and Hart's (1988) therapeutic approach involving the development of self-understanding.

Second, developmental level could provide a basis for designing alternate versions of the same treatment. For example, Bierman's (1988) discussion of changes in children's conceptions of social relationships could be broadened to include specific recommendations regarding different treatment approaches that may be relevant at each stage of these conceptions. More generally, a variety of existing treatments (e.g., behavioral, cognitive-behavioral, family) could be altered depending on the developmental level of the child. Certainly, family therapy interventions should vary depending upon the developmental level of the child's conceptions of social relationships. To her credit, Bierman (1988) does provide a brief discussion of these issues in the closing paragraphs of her chapter. For example, she notes that there are developmental changes in the nature of reinforcers used in behaviorally-oriented treatment, with an increase in the importance of "social" reinforcers with increasing age (also see Gelfand & Peterson, 1985; Furman, 1980).

Third, knowledge of developmental level may guide the stages of treatment. When teaching a child increasingly more complex levels of social interaction as part of social skill training, for example, the therapist could follow the developmental sequence of social play (i.e., ranging from isolated play to reciprocal play; Romanczyk, Diament, Goren, Trunell, and Harris, 1975; cited in Gelfand and Peterson, 1985). Finally, treatments can be applied directly toward advancing the developmental level of the child or adolescent (see discussion in later section).

Less a bias, and more a reflection of the extant literature, we have focused on the implications of *cognitive* development for child psychotherapy. For example, we found no studies that have examined the differential utility of treatments as a function of pubertal level (but see Kovacs & Paulauskas, 1984, for a discussion of differences in the manifestation of depressive symptomatology across pubertal status levels). Some work has been done in the area of family therapy with regard to developmental level (e.g., Kaye, 1985; Mirkin & Koman, 1985; also see Steinberg, 1987a, for a discussion of developmental differences in familial antecedents to delinquency), but again much of the work is in the area of developmental psychopathology. The use of peers in child therapy has seen much attention and will be the focus of a later section. We now turn to a discussion of the implications of developmental transitions for child treatment.

Developmental Transitions and Treatment: The Importance of Prevention Efforts

A significant contribution in the area of developmental transitions is the work of Simmons and Blyth (1987). In their work with early adolescents, they have tested the hypothesis (Coleman, 1974; Simmons, Blyth, Van Cleave, & Bush, 1979) that a child who must confront multiple life changes that occur simultaneously is at risk for adjustment difficulties.

The changes or transitions that they studied were as follows: school change (e.g., movement into a junior high school), pubertal change, early dating, geographical mobility, and major family disruption. Their research results support their hypothesis insofar as the number of transitions tended to be negatively related to outcomes such as grade point average and extracurricular activities. They postulate that adolescents who experience multiple life changes are unable to "withdraw to a more comfortable, accustomed sphere or relationship when the latter is changing as well" (p. 304; e.g., a child who has just moved to a new school will be unable to seek support at home if his/her parents are going through a divorce—two life changes that are frequently associated).

What implications do these findings have for treatment? The results of Simmons and Blyth's (1987) work suggest that prevention efforts are needed for children who are about to experience multiple transitions. Kendall et al. (1984) argue that the focus of such prevention should be on the development of appropriate coping strategies to deal with upcoming transitions. Here the focus would be on coping with *future events* rather than focusing on coping with current stressors. Indeed, how often is a sixth grader prepared (in any way) for their upcoming move to junior high school? More to the point, could we not easily target children who are about to experience multiple life changes? Finally, are different coping strategies going to be helpful with children and adolescents at different developmental levels?

Prevention could be applied more broadly to anticipation of changes in developmental level as well. The obvious application of this notion is to sex education. If they are cognitively ready, should we not educate pre-adolescents about sexuality and contraception *before* they are reproductively mature? We will return to the issue of prevention in the next section on developmental predictors.

In sum, although there has been much more discussion of the interrelatedness of developmental level and child psychotherapy than actual research, it appears plausible that "the psychological treatment of children can be informed, and advanced, by the introduction of developmental principles into clinical concepts and techniques" (Shirk, 1988, p. 14). The use of age, rather than developmental level, is not always appropriate given that children of the same age can vary widely with respect to developmental level. It is time to begin using developmental level as a "client variable" (Garfield & Bergin, 1978) insofar as it serves as a "moderator between intervention procedure and therapeutic outcome" (Shirk, 1988, p. 328).

Using Knowledge of Developmental Predictors

A clinician's knowledge of *developmental predictors* has a number of implications for the treatment of children and adolescents. By developmental predictors, we mean behaviors at some time 1 that reliably predict behaviors at some later time 2. For example, what do we know about the types of behaviors (relationships, disturbances, maturational deviations, etc.) early in childhood that predict certain forms of behavioral disturbance later in childhood, adolescence, or adulthood (e.g., Furman, 1980)? We acknowledge that this type of question is of concern to those who work in the field of developmental psychopathology (the focus of our next section) but we have chosen to highlight the issue of developmental predictors in a separate section given that it seems to have particular relevance to the interface between developmental psychology and treatment.

Knowledge of developmental predictors is of great use in treatment, especially in relation to prevention efforts. If we know, based on longitudinal studies, that a specific set of behavioral deficits, for example, is related to more serious pathology later in the individual's life, we can then treat the antecedent, and presumably less severe, disturbance before having to deal with the more serious subsequent disturbance. This is, of course, the goal of all prevention efforts (Cicchetti et al., 1988; Gelfand & Peterson, 1985; Kendall et al., 1984; Rickel & Lampi, 1984). Earlier we noted that prior knowledge of changes in developmental level and developmental transitions can aid in providing anticipatory interventions that circumvent the development of serious problems subsequent to the transition or change in developmental level. We also believe that knowledge of developmental antecedents and consequences is critical in establishing coherent prevention efforts.

The Complexity of Developmental Antecedents: The Case of Peer Acceptance

Unfortunately, the establishment of "time 1/time 2" connections does not necessarily inform us about what intervention effort is appropriate, as the following example will demonstrate. The literature on peer relations and later personal adjustment suggests that poor peer relations early in childhood (e.g., lack of peer acceptance, aggressiveness, shyness, withdrawal) place the child at risk for developing later adjustment difficulties (see Parker & Asher, 1987, for a review). The effects have been particularly strong for low peer acceptance and aggressiveness as predictors of criminality and dropping out of school. As noted by Parker and Asher (1987), however, there are a variety of possible causal links between these time 1 and time 2 behaviors. We do not know, for example, whether poor peer relations actually play a causal role in the development of later maladjustment. If such relationships did play a causal role, it may be that low peer acceptance limits socialization opportunities which, in turn, leads to maladjustment. Alternatively, it may be that maladjustment results from an underlying disturbance and that peer relations difficulties are merely a symptom (but useful as an indicator of pathology) of this underlying process. It may also be that either process could occur with differing adult outcomes.

To make the picture even more complex, there are a variety of different types of child-child relationships, each of which vary in terms of potential risk or benefit. We have the distinction between neglected and rejected children, the issue of peer acceptance versus peer friendship, the issue of single-setting versus multiple-setting peer rejection, and the distinction between peer and nonpeer social relations (Parker & Asher, 1987). Finally, we have the developmental changes in peer relations that must also be taken into account (i.e., the nature of peer acceptance changes with age and, as a result, there will be developmental discontinuity in how difficulties in peer relations are manifested; Parker & Asher, 1987). In short, the number of factors that must be considered in any intervention effort in this area are numerous. However, as argued by Parker and Asher (1987), we can test the various risk hypotheses cited earlier by examining whether treatment of peer relations difficulties leads to an improvement in later adjustment (see Ladd & Asher, 1985). Of course, follow-up data would have to be gathered at intervals much longer than are traditionally employed. Given that we have now reviewed some of the complexities in establishing links between time 1 and time 2 behaviors, and in devising relevant intervention efforts, we will now consider additional examples of how childhood difficulties have been linked with later adjustment problems.

The Berkeley Guidance Study: Childhood Temper Tantrums

One of the more productive longitudinally oriented research groups has been the Berkeley Guidance Study, a life-course longitudinal investigation that was initiated in 1928 with a sample size of over 200 individuals (McFarlane, Allen, & Honzik, 1954). Of the original sample, 87 males and 95 females have been followed into adulthood. We would like to focus on one of the studies that has come out of this group (Caspi, Elder, & Bem, 1987). As Caspi et al. (1987) point out, it makes sense that adaptive behaviors will demonstrate continuity over time, given the assumption that "behavior is largely sustained by its consequences" (p. 308). But why would maladaptive behaviors also demonstrate such continuity? These researchers maintain, as do others (e.g., Scarr & McCartney, 1983), that an individual's personality characteristics serve a "niche-picking" role in that these characteristics select the individual into an environment that reinforces the underlying dispositions. These environments "react" in such a manner as to provide short-term reinforcement of the behaviors that selected these individuals into these environments in the first place.

Caspi et al. (1987) chose as their developmental antecedent the occurrence of severe childhood temper tantrums. In men, childhood tantrums were predictive of divorce, erratic work experiences, and downward occupational status. Similarly, in females, tantrums during childhood were related to the likelihood of divorce, low occupational status, and ill-tempered parenting. They conclude that maladaptive personality dispositions are maintained "by the progressive accumulation of their own consequences (cumulative continuity) and by evoking maintaining responses from others during reciprocal social interaction (interactional continuity)" (p. 313). Thus, it appears that there is continuity of maladaptation as well as continuity of adaptive behaviors. Given these outcome data, it may be useful to develop prevention efforts to address early childhood tantrum behaviors.

Mother-Infant Attachment Relationships

As we noted earlier, problems with the mother-child attachment relationship often precede other later difficulties (Sroufe, 1983, 1988; also see Belsky & Nezworski, 1988). For example, level of empathy in preschool is predicted from the nature of the mother-infant attachment; more securely attached infants are more empathic preschool children. As Sroufe (1988) has argued, however, anxious attachment is not necessarily a *cause* of subsequent pathology, but rather, it is a *risk factor* that tends to predict behavioral problems when it occurs in conjunction with other risk factors.

Sroufe and Fleeson (1986) maintain that, as a result of early caregiving, the mother-child *relationship* is internalized and predictive of later relationships. That is, "each partner 'knows' all 'parts' of the relationship and each is motivated to recreate the whole in other circumstances, however different the required roles and behavior might be" (Sroufe & Fleeson, 1986, p. 61). The notion that children are motivated to recreate a familiar relationship pattern is used to explain a number of child behavior problems that develop subsequent to problematic mother-infant relationships. As an example, they maintain that the abused child carries forth the role of the exploited as well as the role of the exploiter. They report their findings that abusing children ("bullies") tend to have been abused themselves, and that they now appear to be acting out the opposite side of the relationship that they have internalized. Similarly, the rejected child may "pull" rejection from the environment in order to recreate this familiar scenario. Thus, it appears that prevention efforts could also be applied to relationships (especially parent-child relationships), as well as to problem behaviors, that are predictive of future problems.

Regarding the development of conduct problems, Greenberg and Speltz (1988) have argued that "conduct problems can be viewed as strategies for gaining the attention or proximity of caregivers who are unresponsive to the child's other signals" (p. 206). Presumably, the conduct disordered child must resort to such strategies because this was the most adaptive response to insensitive caregiving. They go on to propose a treatment approach that combines operant parent-training skills with an attachment-based skill training (e.g., helping the child to appropriately regulate parental caregiving, providing practice with parent-child reunion situations, teaching the child to label and express internal states). We would argue that prevention efforts in this area may be quite useful given that screening for disorders of attachment can be done at an early age. Again, it seems more fruitful to work with the antecedent behaviors rather than with the subsequent (more serious) maladaptation. (Other treatment plans for disorders of attachment have also been offered; see Belsky & Nezworski, 1988).

Protective Factors

Thus far, we have discussed how certain behaviors in childhood are predictive of maladaptation in later childhood, adolescence, or even adulthood. A number of writers have also stressed the notion that there are certain protective factors that make the child less likely to develop problem behaviors later in life. In part, protective factors are merely the reverse of risk factors (e.g., secure attachment appears to make a child more, rather than less, able to cope with stressors, such as divorce; Sroufe, 1988; Greenberg & Speltz, 1988). Protective factors are typically isolated based upon epidemiological studies, studies of normal children experiencing a traumatic event, and studies of at-risk samples (Masten & Garmezy, 1985). Garmezy (1985) discusses three categories of protective factors that seem to make the child most resilient: dispositional characteristics of the child, family cohesion, and the availability of external resources. Clinicians would benefit from a reading of this literature given that knowledge about protective factors can strengthen treatment endeavors. Knowledge of risk factors is not enough given that some child protective characteristics, such as coping style, are not merely the reverse of risk factors. Therefore, clinicians and treatment outcome research can contribute to this literature by adding to our understanding of how children develop effective coping strategies (e.g., Compas, 1987).

In sum, it appears that knowledge of developmental antecedents of later, more maladaptive, behaviors, is useful—especially in regard to prevention efforts. Simply said, prevention efforts will enable the therapist to ultimately deal with a younger and less seriously disturbed clinical population. Given a lack of professional attention and a cumulation of negative consequences (e.g., Caspi et al., 1987), disturbed children are likely to "choose" those environments that do not facilitate improvement and that often exacerbate the existing pathology.

Using Knowledge of Developmental Psychopathology

Developmental psychopathology is concerned with the continuity and discontinuity of certain psychological maladies (i.e., the developmental transformations in the types and nature of psychopathology; e.g., Achenbach, 1982, 1985; Cicchetti, 1984; Cowan, 1988; Masten, 1988; Rutter, 1980, 1985; Rutter & Garmezy, 1983; Sroufe & Rutter, 1984) and these data have important implications for treatment. We will not summarize all of the relevant findings, because another chapter in this volume (Masten & Braswell) further addresses this topic.

The nature and frequency of most disorders appear to vary across age level. Achenbach (Achenbach, 1982; 1985; Achenbach & Edelbrock, 1981; 1983) has found, for example, that attention deficit hyperactivity disorder (ADHD) varies with age, with the various components of the disorder (i.e., impulsivity, inattention, and hyperactivity) being exhibited in varying degrees at different ages and in males versus females. Inattention appears to peak at 8 and 9 years of age for boys and gross motor disturbance is more likely in younger children. Regarding depression, adolescent girls tend to exhibit symptoms of withdrawal, whereas younger depressed girls are less likely to exhibit this symptom. Similar age differences have been noted for other disorders falling within both the externalizing and internalizing categories (e.g., conduct disorders, anxiety).

Just as there is discontinuity across age in the manifestation of certain disorders, there is considerable continuity as well. Depressed individuals (adults and children) evidence distortions in their perceptions of their own abilities (Kendall, Stark, & Adam, 1988) and they tend to make attributions for negative events that are both internal and global (see Seligman & Peterson, 1986, for a review). Thus, at least for depression, it may be that there is cognitive continuity and behavioral discontinuity. Similarly, children with ADHD tend to manifest similar symptoms with increasing age (Weiss, 1983). Inattentiveness and impulsivity tend to persist and immaturity, poor school performance, and social maladjustment become frequently reported problems. Weiss argues that medication alone cannot be expected to produce changes in the wide range of problems typically manifested by the ADHD child. For these children, cognitive interventions (e.g., Kendall & Braswell, 1985) may be useful as an adjunct to medication treatment, given that these strategies would be useful across the lifespan and in many situations encountered.

Rutter (1980, 1985) has summarized the changes that occur in behavior disorders from childhood to adolescence and concluded that roughly half of all adolescent disorders are continuations of those seen in childhood. Those that are new during adolescence (e.g., anorexia) tend to be quite different than those that began during childhood. There are increases in the rates of the following disturbances during adolescence, relative to rates during childhood: depression, bipolar affective disorders, attempted suicide, completed suicide, and schizophrenia. There are increases in the frequency of antisocial activities but not in the number of individuals involved. Animal phobias become less common during adolescence and agoraphobia and social phobias become more common. Incidence of enuresis and encopresis is also less during adolescence. It is critical to note, however, that most adolescents do not develop mental disorders and that the actual percentage of adolescents who do show symptoms (most estimates are between 10 and 20%; Hill & Holmbeck, 1986; Holmbeck & Hill, 1988; Rutter, 1980) is only slightly higher (perhaps less than 5% higher) than the rates for children or adults.

Rutter (1985) suggests that antisocial behavior tends toward continuity insofar as antisocial adults have "almost always" been antisocial children. Depressed adults tend not to have been depressed children—with the onset of depression being less common in childhood. Finally, schizophrenia disorders are often not preceded by psychotic disorders during childhood, but, in a study of youth in St. Louis, MO, Robins (1966) found that multiple contacts with mental health professionals for antisocial acts were predictive of adult schizophrenia.

In short, there is not a simple continuous relationship between childhood and adolescent disorders. The clinician would want to have this knowledge of developmental psychopathology to enable him/her to develop hypotheses about the course of a given child's disturbance. Is it likely that the disturbance will change or abate or stay the same over time? Is the disturbance typical of the problems that are usually seen for a child of that age? Without answers to these questions, the therapist may be prone to apply inappropriate treatments or to be overly concerned about the presence of certain symptoms. If a therapist, for example, was asked to see an antisocial adolescent, it would be important to understand the age changes (or, in this case, lack of changes) in the patterning of this disorder, as well as the healthy components of the disorder that should be maintained (e.g., high energy levels of antisocial adolescents).

Additional Treatment Issues

Additional treatment considerations that are derived from the interface of developmental psychology and child/adolescent treatment will be examined. Specifically, we discuss: (a) involvement of peers in child and adolescent treatment, and (b) facilitating development in children and adolescents as a treatment strategy.

Involving Peers in Child and Adolescent Treatment

Although both families and peers have been involved in the treatment of children and adolescents (as alternatives to individual treatment), we focus here on interventions involving peers, because this is a relatively new area and because numerous volumes are available on relevant family interventions (e.g., Gurman & Kniskern, 1981; L'Abate, 1985; Mirkin & Koman, 1985; Pittman, 1987; Robin & Foster, 1989). As we suggested earlier, peer relations provide unique contributions to the development of children and adolescents, and therefore it makes sense that peers could participate as behavior change agents.

Strain (1985; Strain & Fox, 1981; Strayhorn & Strain, 1986) has provided a number of excellent reviews and empirical efforts on the use of peers as intervention agents for their withdrawn and isolated classmates (also see Lyman & Selman, 1985, for an alternative strategy). Peers have also been employed as models of prosocial behavior (see Barton, 1986, for a review). Strain and Fox (1981) describe four types of peer-mediated intervention strategies for withdrawn children: peer prompting and reinforcement, peer social initiations, peer modeling, and incidental peer influence.

With the peer prompting and reinforcement strategey (which differs from the direct prompt and reinforcement strategy wherein teachers work directly with the withdrawn child), confederate peers are prompted by teachers to interact with their socially withdrawn classmate. They review research that suggests that social responsiveness is increased with such strategies. The next strategy, peer social initiations, gives peers more responsibility (i.e., the teacher no longer prompts the children to interact with the withdrawn child). Results of studies investigating this approach suggest that peers are often able to carry out an intervention with little supervision (but see the more recent review by Howard & Kendall, 1988). Peer modeling of appropriate behaviors has also proved successful, but appears to be most useful for withdrawn children who are already capable of exhibiting the desired behaviors, but who do so at low frequencies. In sum, it appears that peers do help in increasing the rate of social interactions among the socially withdrawn. However, Strain and Fox point out that the more serious the withdrawal problem, the less the child will improve with peer interventions.

Howard and Kendall (1988) point out in their more recent review of the peer intervention literature that the available interventions are still applied primarily to socially withdrawn children. As noted in the review by Strain and Fox (1981), maintenance and generalization of effects had been a problem in most studies concerned with such interventions and Howard and Kendall maintain that these problems still persist in this literature. It appears that interventions often have to be re-introduced into each new setting (due to lack of generalization) and that peers tend to have to be prompted by teachers (in order to maintain a reasonable level of treatment initiations). On the other hand, Howard and Kendall found modeling studies where generalization and maintenance were achieved. Bierman (1986; Bierman & Furman, 1984; see Howard & Kendall, 1988, for a review) has combined social skills training with group experiences (similar to the incidental peer influence strategy noted above) and has demonstrated that each has strong but differential impacts on social behavior. The skills training appears to have produced long-term improvement in skills but not in peer acceptance. The group activities produced short-term improvement in sociometric status (i.e., peer acceptance). Thus, it appears that combinations of the various "peer" strategies can lead to additive increases in levels of skills, with each treatment component apparently complementing the other (also see Telch, Killen, McAlister, Perry, & Maccoby, 1982, for another example of a model peer intervention approach).

Problems with the current peer intervention literature include: lack of follow-up data, often inappropriate dependent measures, the selection of social skills behaviors based on face validity evidence (rather than on their ability to discriminate between skilled and unskilled children), and the lack of attention to developmentally gauged treatment strategies. Finally, Greenwood (1981), Howard and Kendall (1988), and Strain and Fox (1981) have noted a number of important considerations in the use of peers as behavior change agents:

1. the selection and training of peer therapists
2. parental permission for both the child therapists and child clients
3. the learning of maladaptive behaviors by peer change agents after working closely with their less well-adapted classmates

4. negative peer group consequences directed toward the peer intervention agent
5. payment of peer change agents for their services
6. issues of confidentiality

Although, the power of peer influence may be an as yet untapped positive mental health intervention, these concerns must be addressed before the power of this intervention can be harnessed fully.

Promotion of Development as a Treatment Strategy

A popular developmentally oriented treatment approach concerns the facilitation of normal developmental processes. The idea here is that treatment can aid a child or adolescent, whose developmental level is not commensurate with his or her age peers in taking "the next step that the child needs to take in his or her journey to more complex levels" (Selman, 1980, p. 258) of development.

A variety of strategies have been suggested to accomplish this task. Early approaches tended to stress facilitation of moral or social reasoning in school and correctional settings (Selman, 1980). A recent use of the moral development strategy (Niles, 1986; also see Gibbs, 1986), was initiated to increase the moral reasoning abilities of institutionalized delinquent and predelinquent adolescents. The findings of this investigation illustrate one of the problems that has tended to plague these endeavors, namely, that the adolescents tend to evidence improved moral reasoning skills relative to control groups, *but* that they did not tend to improve on measures of classroom behaviors. Enright (1980) employed a treatment approach designed to improve social cognitive skills and has found impressive increases in developmental level. His study, however, was not with a clinical sample and included only developmental dependent measures. From a clinical perspective, and according to Selman (1980), the therapist working on a child's social cognitive skills will need to assess the level of perspective-taking as well as the stage of interpersonal understanding. In fact, Selman (1980) provides a number of useful clinical examples that illustrate the use of his model in therapy. He recommends that the therapist discuss personal and hypothetical social dilemmas or play "social-cognitive games" that demand higher levels of social perspective-taking. He does caution, however, that applications of his stage model should be viewed as a supplement to more traditional methods of therapy rather than as a substitute.

Kendall (1981, 1984; also see Furman, 1980) has reviewed many of the studies where the focus has been on improvement of perspective-taking or role-taking skills. He concluded his review by stating that "egocentricity can be overcome through social interactions in which a therapist provides practice in taking the perspective of others" (p. 124). Again, a problem with these studies is that many of them have been done on nonclinical samples where the goal is often the improvement of normal development. Chandler's (e.g., 1973; also see Russo, 1986) studies are an exception, since he found that perspective-taking training has improved these social skills with delinquents as well as having an effect on the number of crimes committed. Unfortunately, it is not clear if such improvement in perspective-taking skills aided the delinquents in "getting away" with more crimes, because the outcome measure was "known" delinquencies. Thus, the implications of increases in such skills in clinical samples is not known.

Finally, strategies have also been developed that focus on the modification of mother-infant attachment relationships (e.g., Belsky & Nezworski, 1988), formal operations skills during adolescence (Gordon, 1988), identity development (Enright, Ganiere, Buss, Lapsley, & Olson, 1983), and children's development of prosocial behavior (e.g., Barton, 1986) and social skills (e.g., Argyle, 1985). A prototype of this form of therapy was proposed by Ivey (1986). He refers to his therapeutic approach as *developmental therapy,* and defines it as follows: "developmental therapy focuses on both the process and outcome of development and suggests specific therapeutic techniques that may be employed to facilitate growth and change . . . The therapist can first assess the client's developmental level and then use developmentally appropriate interventions to facilitate personal growth" (p. 2). Despite all of the enthusiasm for these approaches, there are critics. Noam (1988a, 1988b) has argued, as we have implied, that "structural transformation does not necessarily produce more mental health, better adaptation, and strength for the self. Furthermore, therapeutic work that produces more self-complexity but not mental health can hardly be viewed as successful treatment" (1988a, p. 117). He then goes on to provide clinical examples to support his claims. In short, it appears that the meaning of therapeutic changes in developmental level merits further investigation.

Given such criticisms, it may be helpful for clinicians working in this area to view their role as being less directive than has previously been the case. Therapists should perhaps direct their efforts at allowing children to grow and develop rather than "pushing" the child to develop to higher developmental levels. They also need to articulate how increases in developmental level will, at the same time, result in positive changes in mental health—given that this is the ultimate goal of any intervention.

CONCLUSION

Gelfand and Peterson (1985) have noted that "because developmental level could not be manipulated, it was not viewed (by early behaviorists) as an independent variable worthy of research attention" (p. 27). Although we seem to have come a long way since this belief was held by a majority of behavior therapists, it does appear that there is still an appreciable lack of interface between developmental psychology and clinical treatment—and this applies to those who do research as well as those who do clinical work with children and adolescents. Much of the work is theoretical rather than empirical (but this is a good place to start). Although it would be a great improvement if researchers assessed the differential effectiveness of treatments as a function of child age (Furman, 1980), this approach will ultimately provide less payoff than an approach where developmental level is employed as a moderator between intervention and outcome (Shirk, 1988), because children of the same age can differ dramatically in terms of developmental level.

For research to be advanced, it appears that a number of general steps need to be taken. We need to:

1. determine what types of developmental variables play a moderating role in therapy and for what treatments
2. design appropriate and structured treatments for children with specific disorders *at specific developmental levels* and alter existing treatments to take developmental level into account
3. determine what treatments effectively promote development and in what areas, as well as the implications of improvement in developmental level for mental health
4. differentiate between changes due to treatment versus those due to development

We may need to rethink how we provide treatment. That is, it may be that *intermittent* developmentally gauged treatments may be more effective than *contin-*

uous treatment, given that relapse of problem behaviors may occur during periods of developmental transition.

We have stressed the importance of knowledge in the following areas, for both researcher and therapist alike: knowledge of developmental norms, level, and transitions, knowledge of developmental predictors, and knowledge of developmental psychopathology. Yet, one may ask: How does one gain such knowledge in a clinical training program? It is recommended that: (a) a curriculum of developmental psychology coursework be incorporated into child/adolescent clinical training programs (e.g., Temple University), (b) clinical/developmental research be encouraged at the graduate level (which would also bring colleagues from these two disciplines together), and (c) a subdiscipline of adolescent clinical psychology be developed and promoted with training programs that produce clinicians who specialize in this area. In short, we must teach clinicians to "think developmentally" for the integration of these two areas to proceed.

Parents, teachers, and school administrators can also be trained to think developmentally so as to achieve a number of goals. We should attempt to: (a) aid parents and teachers in making an accurate assessment of the age-appropriateness of behaviors, so that they will be more inclined to bring a child who needs treatment to the proper service, (b) instruct school personnel as to the importance of this type of research, (c) provide schools with up-to-date information about available treatments, so that they become more willing to engage in creative approaches, such as peer intervention strategies, and (d) aid them in becoming more prevention-minded. This type of work is critical given that parental knowledge of child development has been related to a number of parenting difficulties. Most noteworthy is the negative relationship between such knowledge and child abuse (e.g., deLissovoy, 1973; Steele, 1975; Terr, 1970; cited in Maccoby & Martin, 1983). If parental expectations are inappropriate, then there is a poor fit between the child and his/her environment (J. Lerner, Baker, & R. Lerner, 1985; J. Lerner & R. Lerner, 1983). Thus, our efforts to integrate developmental psychology and clinical psychology should not stop with the researcher and the clinician but should also involve those who work closely with children and adolescents, namely, the parents and the teachers.

REFERENCES

Achenbach, T. M. (1974). *Developmental psychopathology*. New York: John Wiley & Sons.

Achenbach, T. M. (1982). *Developmental psychopathology* (2nd ed.). New York: John Wiley & Sons.

Achenbach, T. M. (1985). *Assessment and taxonomy of child and adolescent psychopathology* (Vol. 3; Developmental Clinical Psychology and Psychiatry). Beverly Hills, CA: Sage Publications.

Achenbach, T. M., & Edelbrock, C. S. (1981). Behavioral problems and competencies reported by parents of normal and disturbed children aged 4 to 16. *Monographs of the Society for Research in Child Development, 46* (Serial No. 188).

Achenbach, T. M., & Edelbrock, C. S. (1983). *Manual for the Child Behavior Checklist and Revised Child Behavior Profile*. Burlington, VT: University of Vermont, Department of Psychiatry.

Ainsworth, M. D. S., & Bell, S. M. (1969). Some contemporary patterns of mother-infant interaction in the feeding situation. In A. Ambrose (Ed.), *Stimulation in early infancy*. New York: Academic Press.

Argyle, M. (1985). Social behavior problems and social skills training in adolescence. In B. H. Schneider, K. H. Rubin, & J. E. Ledingham (Eds.), *Children's peer relations: Issues in assessment and intervention*. New York: Springer-Verlag.

Asher, S. R., & J. M. Gottman (1981). *The development of children's friendships*. New York: Cambridge University Press.

Barth, R. P. (1986). *Social and cognitive treatment of children and adolescents: Practical strategies for problem behaviors*. San Francisco: Jossey-Bass.

Barton, E. J. (1986). Modification of children's prosocial behavior. In P. S. Strain, M. J. Guralnick, & H. M. Walker (Eds.), *Children's social behavior: Development, assessment, and modification* (pp. 331–372). New York: Academic Press.

Baumrind, D. (1968). Authoritarian vs. authoritative control. *Adolescence, 3*, 255–272.

Becker, W. C. (1964). Consequences of different kinds of parental discipline. In M. L. Hoffman & L. W. Hoffman (Eds.), *Review of child development research* (Vol. 1). New York: Russell Sage Foundation.

Belsky, J., & Nezworski, T. (1988). *Clinical implications of attachment*. Hillsdale, NJ: Lawrence Erlbaum Associates.

Berndt, T. J. (1981). Relations between social cognition, nonsocial cognition, and social behavior: The case of friendship. In J. H. Flavell & L. Ross (Eds.), *Social cognitive development: Frontiers and possible futures* (pp. 176–199). New York: Cambridge University Press.

Berndt, T. J. (1983). Social cognition, social behavior, and children's friendships. In E. T. Higgins, D. N. Ruble, & W. W. Hartup (Eds.), *Social cognition and social development: A sociocultural perspective* (pp. 158–189). New York: Cambridge University Press.

Bierman, K. L. (1983). Cognitive development and clinical interviews with children. In B. B. Lahey & A. E. Kazdin (Eds.), *Advances in clinical child psychology* (Vol. 6; pp. 217–250). New York: Plenum Press.

Bierman, K. L. (1986). Processes of change during social skills training with preadolescents and its relation to treatment outcome. *Child Development, 57,* 230–240.

Bierman, K. L. (1988). The clinical implications of children's conceptions of social relationships. In S. R. Shirk (Ed.), *Cognitive development and child psychotherapy* (pp. 247–272). New York: Plenum Press.

Bierman, K. L., & Furman, W. (1984). The effects of social skills training and peer involvement on the social adjustment of preadolescents. *Child Development, 55,* 151–162.

Blatt, M., & Kohlberg, L. (1975). Effects of classroom moral discussions upon children's levels of moral judgment. *Journal of Moral Education, 4,* 129–162.

Bobbitt, B. L., & Keating, D. P. A. (1983). A cognitive–developmental perspective for clinical research and practice. In P. C. Kendall (Ed.), *Advances in cognitive behavioral research and therapy* (Vol. 2; pp. 198–241). New York: Academic Press.

Bolton, F. G., Jr. (1980). *The pregnant adolescent: Problems of premature parenthood.* Beverly Hills, CA: Sage Publications.

Bower, T. G. R. (1977). *A primer of infant development.* San Francisco: W. H. Freeman.

Bronfenbrenner, U. (1979). *The ecology of human development.* Cambridge, MA: Harvard University Press.

Byrne, D., & Fisher, W. A. (1983). *Adolescents, sex, and contraception.* Hillsdale, NJ: Lawrence Erlbaum Associates.

Caspi, A., Elder, G. H., Jr., & Bem, D. J. (1987). Moving against the world: Life-course patterns of explosive children. *Developmental Psychology, 23,* 308–313.

Chandler, M. (1973). Egocentrism and antisocial behavior: The assessment and training of social perspective-taking skills. *Developmental Psychology, 9,* 326–333.

Chilman, C. S. (1983). *Adolescent sexuality in a changing American society: Social and psychological perspectives for the human services professions.* New York: John Wiley & Sons.

Cicchetti, D. (1984). The emergence of developmental psychopathology. *Child Development, 55,* 1–7.

Cicchetti, D., & Schneider-Rosen, K. (Eds.). (1984). *Childhood depression:* No. 26; New Directions for Child Development. San Francisco: Jossey-Bass.

Cicchetti, D., Toth, S. L., Bush, M. A., & Gillespie, J. F. (1988). Stage-salient issues: A transactional model of intervention. In E. D. Nannis & P. A. Cowan (Eds.), *Developmental psychopathology and its treatment* (No. 39; New Directions for Child Development; pp. 123–146). San Francisco: Jossey-Bass.

Cobliner, W. G. (1974). Pregnancy in the single adolescent girl: The role of cognitive functions. *Journal of Youth and Adolescence, 3,* 17–29.

Coleman, J. C. (1974). *Relationships in adolescence.* Boston: Routledge & Kegan Paul.

Compas, B. E. (1987). Coping with stress during childhood and adolescence. *Psychological Bulletin, 101,* 393–403.

Cowan, P. A. (1988). Developmental psychopathology: A nine-cell map of the territory. In E. D. Nannis & P. A. Cowan (Eds.), *Developmental psychopathology and its treatment* (No. 39; New Directions for Child Development; pp. 5–30). San Francisco: Jossey-Bass.

Craighead, W. E. (1986). Adolescence: Developmental, prevention, and treatment issues. *Behavior Therapy, 17,* 478–479.

Craighead, W. E., Meyers, A. W., Craighead, L. W., & McHale, S. M. (1983). Issues in cognitive–behavior therapy with children. In M. Rosenbaum, C. M. Franks, & Y. Jaffe (Eds.), *Perspectives on behavior therapy in the eighties.* New York: Springer.

Cvetkovich, G., Grote, B., Bjorseth, A., & Sarkissian, J. (1975). On the psychology of adolescents' use of contraception. *The Journal of Sex Research, 11,* 256–270.

deLissovoy, V. (1973). Child care by adolescent parents. *Children Today, 14,* 22.

DiLalla, L. F., Mitchell, C. M., Arthur, M. W., & Pagliocca, P. M. (1988). Aggression and delinquency: Family and environmental factors. *Journal of Youth and Adolescence, 17,* 233–246.

Douvan, E., & Adelson, J. (1966). *The adolescent experience.* New York: John Wiley & Sons.

Elkind, D. (1967). Egocentrism in adolescence. *Child Development, 38,* 1025–1034.

Enright, R. D. (1980). An integration of social cognitive development and cognitive processing: Educational applications. *American Educational Research Journal, 17,* 21–41.

Enright, R. D., Ganiere, D. M., Buss, R. R., Lapsley, D. K., & Olson, L. M. (1983). Promoting identity development in adolescents. *Journal of Early Adolescence, 3,* 247–255.

Enright, R. D., & Sutterfield, S. J. (1979). Treating the regular class child in the mainstreaming process: Increasing social cognitive development. *Psychology in the Schools, 16,* 110–118.

Erikson, E. (1968). *Identity: Youth and crisis.* New York: WW Norton.

Feindler, E. L., & Ecton, R. B. (1986). *Adolescent anger control: Cognitive–behavioral techniques.* Elmsford, NY: Pergamon Press.

Flavell, J. H., & Ross, L. (1981). *Social cognitive development: Frontiers and possible futures.* New York: Cambridge University Press.

Furman, W. (1980). Promoting social development: Developmental implications for treatment. In B. B. Lahey & A. E. Kazdin (Eds.), *Advances in clinical child psychology* (Vol. 3; pp. 1–40). New York: Plenum Press.

Furman, W., & Buhrmester, D. (1985). Children's perceptions of the qualities of sibling relationships. *Child Development, 56,* 448–461.

Garfield, S. L., & Bergin, A. E. (Eds.). (1978). *Handbook of psychotherapy and behavior change: An empirical analysis* (2nd ed.). New York: John Wiley & Sons.

Garmezy, N. (1985). Stress-resistant children: The search for protective factors. In J. E. Stevenson (Ed.), *Aspects of current child psychiatry research* (Journal of Child

Psychology and Psychiatry Book Suppl. No. 4, pp. 213–233). Oxford: Pergamon Press.
Gelfand, D. M., & Peterson, L. (1985). *Child development and psychopathology.* Beverly Hills, CA: Sage Publications.
Gibbs, J. C. (1986). Sociomoral-cognitive developmental treatment for antisocial youth. In A. R. Siffman & R. A. Feldman (Eds.), *Advances in adolescent mental health: Treatment methods and issues* (Vol. 2). Greenwich, CT: JAI Press.
Gilligan, C. (1982). *In a different voice: Psychological theory and women's development.* Cambridge, MA: Harvard University Press.
Ginsburg, H., & Opper, S. (1969). *Piaget's theory of intellectual development: An introduction.* Englewood Cliffs, NJ: Prentice-Hall.
Gordon, D. E. (1988). Formal operations and interpersonal and affective disturbances in adolescents. In E. D. Nannis & P. A. Cowan (Eds.), *Developmental psychopathology and its treatment* (No. 39; New Directions for Child Development; pp. 51–74). San Francisco: Jossey-Bass.
Gray, W. M. (1976). *How is your logic?* (Experimental ed., Form A). Boulder, CO: Biological Sciences Curriculum Study.
Gray, W. M., & Hudson, L. M. (1984). Formal operations and the imaginary audience. *Developmental Psychology, 20,* 619–627.
Greenberg, M. T., & Speltz, M. L. (1988). Attachment and the ontogeny of conduct problems. In J. Belsky & T. Nezworski (Eds.), *Clinical implications of attachment* (pp. 178–218). Hillsdale, NJ: Lawrence Erlbaum Associates.
Greenberger, E., & Steinberg, L. (1986). *When teenagers work: The psychological and social costs of adolescent employment.* New York: Basic Books.
Greenwood, C. R. (1981). Peer-oriented behavioral technology and ethical issues. In P. S. Strain (Ed.), *The utilization of classroom peers as behavior change agents.* New York: Plenum Press.
Grotevant, H. D., & Cooper, C. R. (1983). *Adolescent development in the family* (No. 22 New Directions for Child Development). San Francisco: Jossey-Bass.
Guidubaldi, J., Perry, J. D., Cleminshaw, H. K. (1984). The legacy of parental divorce: A nationwide study of family status and selected mediating variables on children's academic and social competencies. In B. B. Lahey & A. E. Kazdin (Eds.), *Advances in clinical child psychology* (Vol. 7; pp. 109–155). New York: Plenum Press.
Gurman, A. S., & Kniskern, D. P. (Eds.). (1981). *Handbook of family therapy.* New York: Brunner/Mazel.
Hains, A., & Miller, D. (1980). Moral and cognitive development in delinquent and nondelinquent children and adolescents. *Journal of Genetic Psychology, 137,* 21–35.
Hains, A., & Ryan, E. (1983). The development of social cognitive processes among juvenile delinquents and nondelinquent peers. *Child Development, 54,* 1536–1544.

Hampe, E., Noble, H., Miller, L. C., & Barrett, C. L. (1973). Phobic children one and two years posttreatment. *Journal of Abnormal Psychology, 82,* 446–453.
Harter, S. (1983). Developmental perspectives on the self-system. In P. H. Mussen (Ed.), *Handbook of child psychology* (Vol. IV; E. M. Hetherington, volume editor; 275–386). New York: John Wiley & Sons.
Harter, S. (1988). Developmental and dynamic changes in the nature of self-concept: Implications for child psychotherapy. In S. R. Shirk (Ed.), *Cognitive development and child psychotherapy* (pp. 119–160). New York: Plenum Press.
Hartup, W. W. (1970). Peer interaction and social organization. In P. H. Mussen (Ed.), *Carmichael's manual of child psychology* (Vol. 2; pp. 361–456). New York: John Wiley & Sons.
Hartup, W. W. (1983). Peer relations. In P. H. Mussan (Ed.), *Handbook of child psychology* (Vol. IV; pp. 103–196). New York: John Wiley & Sons.
Hatsenbuehler, L. C., & Schroeder, H. E. (1978). Desensitization procedures in the treatment of childhood disorders. *Psychological Bulletin, 85,* 831–844.
Hauser, S. T. (1976). Loevinger's model and measure of ego development: A critical review. *Psychological Bulletin, 83,* 928–955.
Hauser, S. T., Powers, S. I., Noam, G. G., Jacobson, A. M., Weiss, B., & Follansbee, D. J. (1984). Familial contexts of adolescent ego development. *Child Development, 55,* 195–213.
Henggeler, S. W., & Cohen, R. (1984). The role of cognitive development in the family–ecological systems approach to childhood psychopathology. In B. Gholson & T. L. Rosenthal (Eds.), *Applications of cognitive-developmental theory* (pp. 173–189). New York: Academic Press.
Hetherington, E. M. (1981). Children and divorce. In R. Henderson (Ed.), *Parent-child interaction: Theory, research, and prospects.* New York: Academic Press.
Hetherington, E. M., & Parke, R. D. (1975). *Child psychology: A contemporary viewpoint.* New York: McGraw-Hill.
Higgins, E. T., Ruble, D. N., & Hartup, W. W. (Eds.), (1983). *Social cognition and social development: A sociocultural perspective.* New York: Cambridge University Press.
Hill, J. P. (1980a). The family. In M. Johnson (Ed.), *Toward adolescence: The middle school years* (pp. 32–55). Chicago: University of Chicago Press.
Hill, J. P. (1980b). *Understanding early adolescence: A framework.* Carrboro, NC: Center for Early Adolescence.
Hill, J. P., & Holmbeck, G. N. (1986). Attachment and autonomy during adolescence. In G. J. Whitehurst (Ed.), *Annals of Child Development* (Vol. 3; pp. 145–189). Greenwich, CT: JAI Press.
Hill, J. P., & Holmbeck, G. N. (1987). Familial adaptation to biological change during adolescence. In R. M. Lerner & T. T. Foch (Eds.), *Biological–psychosocial interac-*

tions in early adolescence (pp. 207–224). Hillsdale, NJ: Lawrence Erlbaum Associates.

Hill, J. P., Holmbeck, G. N., Marlow, L., Green, T. M., & Lynch, M. E. (1985a). Menarcheal status and parent–child relations in families of seventh-grade girls. *Journal of Youth and Adolescence, 14*, 301–316.

Hill, J. P., Holmbeck, G. N., Marlow, L., Green, T. M., & Lynch, M. E. (1985b). Pubertal status and parent–child relations in families of seventh-grade boys. *Journal of Early Adolescence, 5*, 31–44.

Hill, J. P., & Palmquist, W. (1978). Social cognition and social relations in early adolescence. *International Journal of Behavioural Development, 1*, 1–36.

Hoffman, L. (1974). Effects of maternal employment on the child: A review of research. *Developmental Psychology, 10*, 204–228.

Hoffman, L. (1979). Maternal employment: 1979. *American Psychologist, 34*, 859–865.

Hoffman, M. L. (1970). Moral development. In P. H. Mussen (Ed.), *Carmichael's manual of child psychology* (Vol. 2; pp. 261–359). New York: John Wiley & Sons.

Holmbeck, G. N., Gasiewski, E., & Crossman, R. (1988). *Cognitive development, egocentrism, and adolescent contraceptive knowledge, attitudes, and behavior*. Unpublished manuscript, Loyola University of Chicago.

Holmbeck, G. N., & Hill, J. P. (1988). Storm and stress beliefs about adolescence: Prevalence, self-reported antecedents, and effects of an undergraduate course. *Journal of Youth and Adolescence, 17*, 285–306.

Howard, B. L., & Kendall, P. C. (1988). *Child interventions: Having no peers?* Unpublished manuscript, Temple University, Philadelphia.

Ivey, A. E. (1986). *Developmental therapy*. San Francisco: Jossey-Bass.

Jorgensen, S. R. (1981). Sex education and the reduction of adolescent pregnancies: Prospects for the 1980's. *Journal of Early Adolescence, 1*, 38–52.

Kandel, D., & Lesser, G. S. (1972). *Youth in two worlds*. San Francisco: Jossey-Bass.

Katz, E. R., Kellerman, J., & Siegel, S. E. (1980). Behavioral distress in children with cancer undergoing medical procedures: Developmental considerations. *Journal of Consulting and Clinical Psychology, 48*, 356–365.

Kaye, K. (1985). Toward a developmental psychology of the family. In L. L'Abate (Ed.), *The handbook of family psychology and therapy* (Vol. 1; pp. 38–72). Chicago: Dorsey Press.

Keating, D. P. (1980). Thinking processes in adolescence. In J. Adelson (Ed.), *Handbook of adolescent psychology* (pp. 211–246). New York: John Wiley & Sons.

Kendall, P. C. (1977). On the efficacious use of verbal self-instructional procedures with children. *Cognitive therapy and research, 1*, 331–341.

Kendall, P. C. (1981). Cognitive-behavioral interventions with children. In B. B. Lahey & A. E. Kazdin (Eds.), *Advances in clinical child psychology* (Vol. 4; pp. 53–90), New York: Plenum Press.

Kendall, P. C. (1984). Social cognition and problem solving: A developmental and child-clinical interface. In B. Gholson & T. L. Rosenthal (Eds.), *Applications of cognitive-developmental theory* (pp. 115–148). New York: Academic Press.

Kendall, P. C., & Braswell, L. (1985). *Cognitive–behavioral therapy for impulsive children*. New York: Guilford Press.

Kendall, P. C., Lerner, R. M., & Craighead, W. E. (1984). Human development and intervention in childhood psychopathology. *Child Development, 55*, 71–82.

Kendall, P. C., Stark, K. D., & Adam, T. (1988). *Cognitive deficit or cognitive distortion in childhood depression?* Manuscript submitted for publication, Temple University, Philadelphia, PA.

Kendall, P. C., & Williams, C. L. (1986). Therapy with adolescents: Treating the "Marginal Man." *Behavior Therapy, 17*, 522–537.

Kiesler, D. J. (1966). Some myths of psychotherapy research and the search for a paradigm. *Psychological Bulletin, 65*, 110–136.

Kohlberg, L. (1967). Moral and religious education and the public schools: A developmental view. In T. Sizer (Ed.), *Religion and public education*. Boston: Houghton-Mifflin.

Kohlberg, L. (1969). Stage and sequence: The cognitive-developmental approach to socialization. In D. A. Goslin (Ed.), *Handbook of socialization theory and research* (pp. 347–480). Chicago: Rand McNally.

Kovacs, M., & Paulauskas, S. L. (1984). Developmental stage and the expression of depressive disorders in children: An empirical analysis. In D. Cicchetti & K. Schneider-Rosen (Eds.), *Childhood depression* (No. 26; pp. 59–80). San Francisco: Jossey-Bass.

Kurdek, L. A. (Ed.) (1983). *Children and divorce* (No. 19, New Directions for Child Development). San Francisco: Jossey-Bass.

L'Abate, L. (Ed.) (1985). *The handbook of family psychology and therapy*. Homewood, IL: Dorsey Press.

Ladd, G. W., & Asher, S. R. (1985). Social skills training and children's peer relations. In L'Abate & M. Milan (Eds.), *Handbook of social skills training and research* (pp. 219–244). New York: John Wiley & Sons.

Lamb, M. E., Pleck, J. H., & Levine, J. A. (1985). The role of the father in child development: The effects of increased paternal involvement. In B. B. Lahey & A. E. Kazdin (Eds.), *Advances in clinical child psychology* (Vol. 8; pp. 232–266). New York: Plenum Press.

Lancaster, J. B., & Hamburg, B. A. (1986). *School-age pregnancy and parenthood: Biosocial dimensions*. Hawthorne, NY: Aldine De Gruyter.

Lerner, J. V., Baker, N., & Lerner, R. M. (1985). A person-context goodness of fit model of adjustment. In P. C. Kendall (Ed.), *Advances in cognitive-behavioral research and therapy* (Vol. 4). New York: Academic Press.

Lerner, J. V., & Lerner, R. M. (1983). Temperament and adaptation across life: Theoretical and empirical issues. In P. B. Baltes & O. G. Brim, Jr. (Eds.), *Life-span development and behavior* (Vol. 5; pp. 198–233). New York: Academic Press.

Lewko, J. H. (Ed.). (1987). *How children and adolescents view the world of work* (No. 35, New Directions for Child Development). San Francisco: Jossey-Bass.

Likona, T. (1976). Research on Piaget's theory of moral development. In T. Likona (Ed.), *Moral development and behavior: Theory, research, and social issues* (pp. 219–240). New York: Holt, Rinehart, & Winston.

Loevinger, J. (1976). *Ego development: Conceptions and theories*. San Francisco: Jossey-Bass.

Lourie, I. S. (1987). New approaches in mental health services for adolescents. *The Clinical Psychologist, 40,* 85–87.

Lovaas, O. I. (1987). Behavioral treatment and normal educational and intellectual functioning in young autistic children. *Journal of Consulting and Clinical Psychology, 55,* 3–9.

Lyman, D. R., & Selman, R. L. (1985). Peer conflict in pair therapy: Clinical and developmental analyses. In M. W. Berkowitz (Ed.), *Peer conflict and psychological growth* (No. 29, New Directions for Child Development; pp. 85–102). San Francisco: Jossey-Bass.

Maccoby, E. E. (1980). *Social development: Psychological growth and the parent–child relationship*. New York: Harcourt Brace Jovanovich.

Maccoby, E. E., & Martin, J. A. (1983). Socialization in the context of the family: Parent-child interaction. In P. H. Mussen (Ed.), *Handbook of child psychology* (Vol. IV; E. M. Hetherington, Volume editor; pp. 1–102). New York: John Wiley & Sons.

Masten, A. S. (1988). Toward a developmental psychopathology of early adolescence. In M. D. Levine & E. R. McAnarney (Eds.), *Early adolescent transitions* (pp. 261–278). Lexington, MA: Lexington Books.

Masten, A. S., & Garmezy, N. (1985). Risk, vulnerability, and protective factors in developmental psychopathology. In B. B. Lahey & A. E. Kazdin (Eds.), *Advances in clinical child psychology* (Vol. 8, pp. 1–52). New York: Plenum Press.

McFarlane, J. W., Allen, L., & Honzik, M. P. (1954). *A developmental study of the behavioral problems of children between twenty-one months and fourteen years*. Berkeley: University of California Press.

Miller, P. H. (1983). *Theories of developmental psychology*. New York: W H Freeman.

Minuchin, P. P., & Shapiro, E. K. (1983). The school as a context for social development. In P. H. Mussen (Ed.), *Handbook of child psychology* (Vol. IV; E. M. Hetherington, Volume editor; pp. 197–274). New York: John Wiley & Sons.

Mirkin, M. P., & Koman, S. L. (Eds.). (1985). *Handbook of adolescents and family therapy*. New York: Gardner Press.

Montemayor, R. (1983). Parents and adolescents in conflict: All families some of the time and some families most of the time. *Journal of Early Adolescence, 3,* 83–103.

Montemayor, R., & Hanson, E. (1985). A naturalistic view of conflict between adolescents and their parents and siblings. *Journal of Early Adolescence, 5,* 23–30.

Moore, D. (1987). Parent-adolescent separation: The construction of adulthood by late adolescents. *Developmental Psychology, 23,* 298–307.

Morrison, D. M. (1985). Adolescent contraceptive behavior. A review. *Psychological Bulletin, 98,* 538–568.

Nannis, E. D. (1988). A cognitive–developmental view of emotional understanding and its implications for child psychotherapy. In S. R. Shirk (Ed.), *Cognitive development and child psychotherapy* (pp. 91–115). New York: Plenum Press.

Nannis, E. D., & Cowan, P. A. (Eds.). (1988). *Developmental psychopathology and its treatment* (No. 39, New Directions for Child Development). San Francisco: Jossey-Bass.

Neimark, E. E. (1975). Intellectual development in adolescence. In F. D. Horowitz (Ed.), *Review of child development research* (Vol. 4; 541–593). Chicago: University of Chicago Press.

Niles, W. J. (1986). Effects of a moral development discussion group on delinquent and predelinquent boys. *Journal of Counseling Psychology, 33,* 45–51.

Noam, G. G. (1988a). A constructivist approach to developmental psychopathology. In E. D. Nannis, & P. A. Cowan (Eds.), *Developmental psychopathology and its treatment* (No. 39, New Directions for Child Development; pp. 91–122). San Francisco: Jossey-Bass.

Noam, G. G. (1988b). The theory of biography and transformation: Foundation for clinical–developmental therapy. In S. R. Shirk (Ed.), *Cognitive development and child psychotherapy* (pp. 273–318). New York: Plenum Press.

Noam, G. G., Hauser, S. T., Santostefano, S., Garrison, W., Jacobson, A. M., Powers, S. I., & Mead, M. (1984). Ego development and psychopathology: A study of hospitalized adolescents. *Child Development, 55,* 184–194.

Offer, D., Ostrov, E., & Howard, K. I. (1981). *The adolescent: A psychological self-portrait*. New York: Basic Books.

Ollendick, T. H. (1979). Fear reduction techniques with children. In M. Hersen, R. M. Eisler, & P. M. Miller (Eds.), *Progress in behavior modification Vol. 8*. New York: Academic Press.

Olson, D. H., Russell, C. S., & Sprenkle, D. H. (1983). Circumplex model of marital and family systems: VI. Theoretical update. *Family Process, 22,* 69–83.

Ooms, T. (Ed.). (1981). *Teenage pregnancy in a family context: Implications for policy*. Philadelphia: Temple University Press.

Overton, W. F. (Ed.). (1983). *The relationship between social and cognitive development*. Hillsdale, NJ: Lawrence Erlbaum Associates.

Papini, D. R., & Sebby, R. A. (1987). Adolescent pubertal status and affective family relationships: A multivariate

assessment. *Journal of Youth and Adolescence, 16,* 1–15.
Parker, J. G., & Asher, S. R. (1987). Peer relations and later personal adjustment: Are low-accepted children at risk? *Psychological Bulletin, 102,* 357–389.
Pestrak, V. A., & Martin, D. (1985). Cognitive development and aspects of adolescent sexuality. *Adolescence, 20,* 981–987.
Petersen, A. C. (1988). Adolescent development. In M. R. Rosenzweig, & L. W. Porter (Eds.), *Annual Review of Psychology* (Vol. 39; 583–608. Palo Alto, CA: Annual Reviews Inc.
Petersen, A. C., & Hamburg, B. A. (1986). Adolescence: A developmental approach to problems and psychopathology. *Behavior Therapy, 17,* 480–499.
Petersen, A. C., & Taylor, B. (1980). The biological approach to adolescence: Biological change and psychosocial adaptation. In J. Adelson (Ed.), *Handbook of adolescent psychology* (pp. 117–155), New York: John Wiley & Sons.
Piaget, J. (1932/1965). *The moral judgment of the child.* Glencoe, IL: The Free Press.
Piaget, J. (1970). Piaget's theory. In P. H. Mussen (Ed.), *Manual of child psychology* (3rd ed.). (pp. 703–732). New York: John Wiley & Sons.
Piaget, J. (1972). Intellectual evolution from adolescence to adulthood. *Human Development, 15,* 1–12.
Pine, F. (1985). *Developmental theory and clinical process.* New Haven, CT: Yale University Press.
Pittman, F. S. (1987). *Turning points: Treating families in transition and crisis.* New York: WW Norton.
Reese, H. W., & Overton, W. F. (1970). Models of development and theories of development. In L. R. Goulet & P. B. Baltes (Eds.), *Life-span developmental psychology: Research and theory* (pp. 116–145). New York: Academic Press.
Richards, M, & Petersen, A. C. (1987). Biological theoretical models of adolescent development. In V. B. Van Hasselt & M. Hersen (Eds.), *Handbook of adolescent psychology* (pp. 34–52). Elmsford, NY: Pergamon Press.
Rickel, A. U., & Lampi, L. A. (1984). Prevention of childhood dysfunction. In B. B. Lahey & A. E. Kazdin (Eds.), *Advances in clinical child psychology* (Vol. 7; pp. 295–350). New York: Plenum Press.
Robin, A. L., & Foster, S. L. (1989). *Negotiating adolescence: A behavioral family systems approach.* New York: Guilford Press.
Robins, L. (1966). *Deviant children grown up.* Baltimore: Williams & Wilkins.
Rodriguez, A., Rodriguez, M., & Eisenberg, L. (1959). The outcome of school phobia: A follow-up study based on 41 cases. *American Journal of Psychiatry, 116,* 540–544.
Romanczyk, R. G., Diament, C., Goren, E. R., Trunell, G., & Harris, S. L. (1975). Increasing isolated and social play in severely disturbed children: Intervention and past intervention effectiveness. *Journal of Autism and Childhood Schizophrenia, 5,* 57–70.
Ruble, D. N., & Brooks-Gunn, J. (1982). The experience of menarche. *Child Development, 53,* 1557–1566.
Russo, T. J. (1986). Cognitive counseling for adolescents. *Journal of child and adolescent psychotherapy, 3,* 194–198.
Rutter, M. (1980). *Changing youth in a changing society: Patterns of adolescent development and disorder.* Cambridge, MA: Harvard University Press.
Rutter, M. (1983). Psychological therapies. In S. B. Guze, F. J. Earls, & J. E. Barrett (Eds.), *Childhood psychopathology and development* (pp. 139–164). New York: Raven Press.
Rutter, M. (1985, July). *Some notes on psychopathology in adolescence.* Paper presented at a workshop sponsored by the Committee on Child Development Research and Public Policy, National Academy of Sciences, Woods Hole, MA.
Rutter, M., & Garmezy, N. (1983). Developmental psychopathology. In P. H. Mussen (Ed.), *Handbook of child psychology* (Vol. IV; E. M. Hetherington, Volume editor; 775–912). New York: John Wiley & Sons.
Rutter, M., Izard, C. E., & Read, P. B. (Eds.). (1986). *Depression in young people: Developmental and clinical perspectives.* New York: Guilford Press.
Rutter, M., Maughan, B., Mortimore, P., & Ouston, J. (1979). *Fifteen thousand hours: Secondary schools and their effects on children.* Cambridge, MA: Harvard University Press.
Santilli, N. R., & Furth, H. G. (1987). Adolescent work perception: A developmental approach. In J. H. Lewko (Ed.), *How children and adolescents view the world of work* (No. 35, New Directions for Child Development; pp. 33–50). San Francisco: Jossey-Bass.
Santostefano, S. (1980). Clinical child psychology: The need for developmental principles. In R. L. Selman & R. Yando (Eds.), *Clinical–developmental psychology* (No. 7; New Directions for Child Development; pp. 1–20). San Francisco: Jossey-Bass.
Scarr, S., & McCartney, K. (1983). How people make their own environments: A theory of genotype environment effects. *Child Development, 54,* 424–435.
Schleser, R., Cohen, R., Meyers, A., & Rodick, J. D. (1984). The effects of cognitive level and training procedures on the generalization of self-instructions. *Cognitive Therapy and Research, 8,* 187–200.
Schleser, R., Meyers, A., & Cohen, R. (1981). Generalization of self-instruction: Effects of general versus specific content, active rehearsal, and cognitive level. *Child Development, 52,* 335–340.
Schorin, M. Z., & Hart, D. (1988). Psychotherapeutic implications of the development of self-understanding. In S. R. Shirk (Ed.), *Cognitive development and child psychotherapy* (pp. 161–186). New York: Plenum Press.
Seligman, M. E. P., & Peterson, C. (1986). A learned helplessness perspective on childhood depression: The-

ory and research. In M. Rutter, C. E., Izard, & P. B. Read (Eds.), *Depression in young people: Developmental and clinical perspectives* (pp. 223–250). New York: Guilford Press.

Selman, R. L. (1980). *The growth of interpersonal understanding: Developmental and clinical analyses.* New York: Academic Press.

Selman, R. L. (1981). The child as a friendship philosopher. In S. R. Asher & J. M. Gottman (Eds.), *The development of children's friendships* (pp. 242–272). New York: Cambridge University Press.

Selman, R. L., & Schultz, L. H. (1988). Interpersonal thought and action in the case of a troubled early adolescent: Toward a developmental model of the gap. In S. R. Shirk (Ed.), *Cognitive development and child psychotherapy* (pp. 207–246). New York: Plenum Press.

Shantz, C. U. (1975). The development of social cognition. In E. M. Hetherington (Ed.), *Review of child development research* (Vol. 5; 257–324). Chicago: University of Chicago Press.

Shantz, C. U. (1983). Social cognition. In P. H. Mussen (Ed.), *Handbook of child psychology* (Vol. III; J. H. Flavell, & E. M. Markman, volume editors; 495–555). New York: John Wiley & Sons.

Shirk, S. R. (Ed.). (1988). *Cognitive development and child psychotherapy.* New York: Plenum Press.

Shure, M. B., & Spivack, G. (1978). *Problem-solving techniques in childrearing.* San Francisco: Jossey-Bass.

Shure, M. B., & Spivack, G. (1980). Interpersonal problem-solving as a mediator of behavioral adjustment in preschool and kindergarten children. *Journal of Applied Developmental Psychology, 1,* 29–43.

Simmons, R. G., & Blyth, D. A. (1987). *Moving into adolescence: The impact of pubertal change and school context.* Hawthorne, NY: Aldine de Gruyter.

Simmons, R. G., Blyth, D. A., Van Cleave, E. F., & Bush, D. M. (1979). Entry into early adolescence: The impact of school structure, puberty, and early dating on self-esteem. *American Sociological Review, 44,* 948–967.

Skinner, B. F. (1938). *The behavior of organisms.* New York: Appleton-Century-Crofts.

Spivack, G., Platt, J. J., Shure, M. B. (1976). *The problem solving approach to adjustment.* San Francisco: Jossey-Bass.

Sprinthall, N. A., & Collins, W. A. (1984). *Adolescent psychology: A developmental view.* Reading, MA: Addison-Wesley.

Sroufe, L. A. (1983). Infant-caregiver attachment and patterns of adaptation in preschool: The roots of maladaptation and competence. In M. Perlmutter (Ed.), *Minnesota symposia on child psychology* (Vol. 16; pp. 41–84). Hillsdale, NJ: Lawrence Erlbaum Associates.

Sroufe, L. A. (1988). The role of infant-caregiver attachment in development. In J. Belsky & T. Nezworski (Eds.), *Clinical implications of attachment* (pp. 18–38). Hillsdale, NJ: Lawrence Erlbaum Associates.

Sroufe, L. A., & Fleeson, J. (1986). Attachment and the construction of relationships. In W. W. Hartup & Z. Rubin (Eds.), *Relationships and development* (pp. 51–72). Hillsdale, NJ: Lawrence Erlbaum Associates.

Sroufe, L. A., & Rutter, M. (1984). The domain of developmental psychopathology. *Child Development, 55,* 17–29.

Sroufe, L. A., & Waters, E. (1977). Attachment as an organizational construct. *Child Development, 48,* 1184–1199.

Steele, B. F. (1975). *Working with abusive parents from a psychiatric point of view* [U.S. Department of Health, Education, and Welfare Publication No. (OHD) 75–70]. Washington, DC: U.S. Government Printing Office.

Steinberg, L. (1985). *Adolescence.* New York: Knopf.

Steinberg, L. (1987a). Familial factors in delinquency: A developmental perspective. *Journal of Adolescent Research, 2,* 255–269.

Steinberg, L. (1987b). The impact of puberty on family relations: Effects of pubertal status and pubertal timing. *Developmental Psychology, 23,* 451–460.

Steinberg, L. (1988). Reciprocal relation between parent–child distance and pubertal maturation. *Developmental Psychology, 24,* 122–128.

Steinberg, L. (1989). Pubertal maturation and family relations: Evidence for the distancing hypothesis. In G. Adams, R. Montemayor, & T. Gullotta (Eds.), *Advances in adolescent development* (Vol 1; pp. 71–97). Beverly Hills, CA: Sage Publications, Inc.

Steinberg, L. D., & Hill, J. P. (1978). Patterns of family interaction as a function of age, the onset of puberty, and formal thinking. *Developmental Psychology, 14,* 683–684.

Steinberg, L. D., & Silverberg, S. B. (1986). The vicissitudes of autonomy in early adolescence. *Child Development, 57,* 841–852.

Strain, P. S. (1985). Programmatic research on peers as intervention agents for socially isolate classmates. In B. H. Schneider, K. H. Rubin, & J. E. Ledingham (Eds.), *Children's peer relations: Issues in assessment and intervention.* New York: Springer-Verlag.

Strain, P. S., & Fox, J. J. (1981). Peers as behavior change agents for withdrawn classmates. In B. B. Lahey & A. E. Kazdin (Eds.), *Advances in clinical child psychology* (Vol. 4; pp. 167–198). New York: Plenum Press.

Strayhorn, J. M., & Strain, P. S. (1986). Social and language skills for preventive mental health: What, how, who, and when. In P. S. Strain, M. J. Guralnick, & H. M. Walker (Eds.), *Children's social behavior: Development, assessment, and modification* (pp. 287–330). New York: Academic Press.

Stuart, I. R., & Wells, C. F. (Eds.). (1982). *Pregnancy in adolescence: Needs, problems, and management.* New York: Van Nostrand Reinhold.

Sullivan, H. S. (1953). *The interpersonal theory of psychiatry.* New York: W W Norton.

Tanner, J. (1962). *Growth at adolescence* (2nd ed.). Springfield, IL: Charles C Thomas.

Tasto, D. L. (1969). Systematic desensitization, muscle relaxation, and visual imagery in the counterconditioning of a four-year-old phobic child. *Behaviour Research and Therapy, 7,* 409–411.

Telch, M. J., Killen, J. D., McAlister, A. L., Perry, C. L., & Maccoby, N. (1982). Long term follow-up of a pilot project on smoking prevention with adolescents. *Journal of Behavioral Medicine, 5,* 1–8.

Terr, L. C. (1970). A family study of child abuse. *American Journal of Psychiatry, 127,* 665–671.

Tobin-Richards, M. H., Boxer, A. M. N., & Petersen, A. C. (1982). The psychological significance of pubertal change: Sex differences in perceptions of self during early adolescence. In J. Brooks-Gunn & A. C. Petersen (Eds.), *Girls at puberty: Biological and psychosocial perspectives* (pp. 127–154). New York: Plenum Press.

Tsai, M., Feldman-Summers, S., & Edgar, M. (1979). Childhood molestation: Variables related to differential impacts on psychosexual functioning in adult women. *Journal of Abnormal Psychology, 88,* 404–417.

Turiel, E. (1983). *The development of social knowledge: Morality and convention.* New York: Cambridge University Press.

Urbain, E. S., & Kendall, P. C. (1980). Review of social-cognitive problem solving interventions with children. *Psychological Bulletin, 88,* 109–143.

Urberg, K. A. (1982). A theoretical framework for studying adolescent contraceptive use. *Adolescence, 17,* 528–540.

Wallerstein, J., & Kelley, J. (1980). *Surviving the breakup: How children and parents cope with divorce.* New York: Basic Books.

Weiss, G. (1983). Long-term outcome: Findings, concepts, and practical implications. In M. Rutter (Ed.), *Developmental neuropsychiatry* (pp. 422–436). New York: Guilford Press.

Youniss, J. (1980). *Parents and peers in social development: A Sullivan–Piaget perspective.* Chicago: University of Chicago Press.

PART II
COGNITIVE PSYCHOLOGY AND NEUROPSYCHOLOGY

CHAPTER 6

THEORETICAL COGNITIVE PSYCHOLOGY AND MOOD DISORDERS

Michael W. Eysenck

The term *cognitive psychology* is used increasingly in a very broad and imprecise sense to refer to almost everything that used to be known as experimental psychology. As Eysenck (1984) pointed out, "Virtually all those interested in perception, learning, memory, language, concept formation, problem solving, or thinking call themselves cognitive psychologists, despite the great diversity of experimental and theoretical approaches to be found in these various areas" (p. 1). However, what cognitive psychologists have in common is an interest in investigating the processes and structures that intervene between stimulus and response. This interest was given formal recognition in Tolman's (1932) notion that behavior is determined jointly by the independent variable (some aspect of the environment) and by intervening variables that are neither stimuli nor responses.

Meehl and MacCorquodale (1948) pointed out that the term *intervening variable* was used in more than one sense. They proposed a distinction between intervening variables, which are merely ways of stating empirical laws correlating independent variables with dependent variables, and hypothetical constructs, which refer to postulated internal states, processes, or structures. If one uses their terminology, then one could argue that cognitive psychology attempts to identify the intervening variables and hypothetical constructs that mediate between stimuli and responses.

It is possible to divide cognitive psychology into various subcategories, yet some of these subcategories are of little relevance to theory and research within clinical psychology. However, a subcategorization that is of particular importance, as pointed out by Brewin (1988), is the distinction between experimental cognitive psychology and cognitive social psychology. In general terms, experimental cognitive psychologists use laboratory tasks to understand psychological processes such as attention, perception, learning, and memory; whereas cognitive social psy-

---

Many thanks are due to the Wellcome Trust for their generous support to Professor Andrew Mathews and myself, which enabled us to research some of the information reported in this chapter.

chologists concentrate on self-report measures of attitudes, beliefs, and expectancies of which there is conscious awareness.

A fundamental difference between experimental cognitive psychologists and cognitive social psychologists is their attitudes concerning the relevance of conscious awareness and introspection to an understanding of human behavior. Experimental cognitive psychologists generally claim that introspective evidence can be of value, but that performance measures are of paramount importance. In contrast, cognitive social psychologists typically accord much greater significance to conscious awareness. As a consequence, they make much use of self-report questionnaires and introspective evidence.

We will not enter into a detailed analysis of the advantages and disadvantages of relying on introspective evidence. However, it seems important to indicate briefly why introspective evidence should be used circumspectly. First, there is strong evidence that stimulus information can be processed in the complete absence of conscious awareness (see Dixon, 1981, for a review). An example of this is the phenomenon of "blindsight." Weiskrantz (1986) discussed in detail a patient (D. B.) who reported being unable to see visual displays. In spite of his lack of conscious awareness of seeing, he could nevertheless make reasonably accurate perceptual judgements about the location and orientation of visual objects within those displays. Reliance on conscious awareness as the sole criterion for perception would have led to the erroneous conclusion that D. B. had no visual perception at all.

Second, Nisbett and Wilson (1977) argued forcibly (with substantiating evidence) that people generally have no conscious awareness of the processes involved in determining their behavior. For example, subjects asked to select the best pair of stockings from five essentially identical pairs exhibited a strong tendency to select the pair presented at the right end of the display. However, when they were asked to explain why they had chosen a particular pair, they never mentioned the position in the display as having influenced their choice.

What appears to be the case, as Ericsson and Simon (1980) pointed out, is that introspective evidence is especially fallible when it is collected retrospectively, when it requires interpretation of a situation, and when it refers to information that is not in focal attention. These are precisely the circumstances prevailing in most of the studies Nisbett and Wilson (1977) cited in support of their position. In contrast, according to Ericsson and Simon (1980), introspections are most likely to be valid when they relate to current events, when they describe what the individual is attending to or thinking about, and when the information provided is in focal attention.

Third, introspective evidence in the form of self-reports can manifestly be distorted in various ways. For example, patients who have recovered from anxiety or depression may well have a strong vested interest in maintaining that they are now free of negative and self-defeating thoughts whether that is actually the case or not.

Research on mood disorders from the cognitive perspective has considered numerous different aspects of cognitive functioning. However, most research interest has been in memory processes, followed by attentional and perceptual phenomena. Accordingly, the coverage of cognitive psychology in this chapter will reflect this. It should be pointed out that clinical anxiety and clinical depression will generally be discussed as if they were both unitary mood disorders. That is obviously a substantial oversimplification, but is justified because the emphasis in this chapter is on broad theoretical considerations rather than the detailed differences in cognitive functioning found in various subgroups of clinically anxious or depressed patients.

THE MEMORY SYSTEM

Theoretical approaches to human memory have tended to draw a distinction between process and structure. While it is generally agreed that both process and structure are vital to the functioning of the memory system, there are nevertheless substantial differences among theorists as to the relative importance accorded to them. For example, the multistore model proposed by Atkinson and Shiffrin (1968) and others is primarily a structural theory, whereas the levels-of-processing theory put forward by Craik and Lockhart (1972) emphasizes process at the expense of structure.

Structural Aspects of Memory

At the structural level, Atkinson and Shiffrin (1968) argued that there are three qualitatively different kinds of memory store; sensory or modality-specific stores; a short-term memory store; and a long-term memory store. The distinction between short-term and long-term memory stores was regarded as being of crucial significance. According to Atkinson and Shiffrin (1968), the short-term memory store has very limited capacity, short temporal duration of storage, and forgetting occurs via displacement (i.e., new information replaces old information). In contrast, the long-term memory store has essentially unlimited capacity, there is no time limit on the duration of storage, and forgetting occurs through interference in memory traces.

There is general agreement that there is, indeed, a valid distinction between short-term and long-term memory (see Eysenck, 1984, for a review). However, there is also general agreement that the kind of theoretical approach favored by Atkinson and Shiffrin (1968) is grossly oversimplified. In particular, it no longer appears tenable to assume that there are unitary short-term and long-term stores. So far as short-term memory is concerned, the unitary short-term store has been replaced by the working memory system (Baddeley, 1986). According to this conceptualization, at least three different components of working memory need to be identified:

1. the central executive, which is a modality-free, limited capacity system resembling attention;
2. the articulatory loop, which is organized in a temporal and serial fashion, and processes information in terms of its phonemic characteristics;
3. the visuo-spatial sketch pad, which processes information in terms of its visual and/or spatial qualities.

Episodic and Semantic Memory

The notion that the long-term memory store is unitary has been challenged by several theorists. For example, Tulving (1972) proposed that there are at least two different long-term memory systems: episodic memory and semantic memory. Episodic memory is essentially autobiographical in nature. It contains information about specific events or episodes of a personal nature, and the time and place these events occurred. In contrast, semantic memory contains most of our knowledge of the world. In Tulving's (1972) words:

> It is a mental thesaurus, organized knowledge a person possess about words and other verbal symbols, their meanings and referents, about relations among them, and about rules, formulas, and algorithms for the manipulation of these symbols, concepts and relations. Semantic memory does not register perceptible properties of inputs, but rather cognitive referents of input signals. (p. 386)

Tulving's (1972) theoretical distinction has not commanded universal acceptance. It is obvious that episodic and semantic memory differ in terms of content, but it is much less clear that they differ in terms of their underlying processes. It is also obvious that episodic and semantic memory are typically interdependent in their functioning, which tends to obscure the distinction between them.

Despite cognitive psychologists' skepticism about the theoretical value of distinguishing between episodic and semantic memory, the distinction has played some role in attempts to understand clinical phenomena from a cognitive perspective. A number of clinical theorists (e.g., Kuiper, MacDonald, & Derry, 1983) have argued in favor of the notion of a self-schema, which could be regarded as consisting of organized information from episodic memory. It seems entirely reasonable in some ways that it should be the autobiographical and personal episodic memory that is relevant to mood disorders rather than the more impersonal, knowledge-based semantic memory. However, as we will discuss shortly, there are some complications with that view.

According to Tulving (1972), episodic memory is relatively unorganized, with one of the few organizing principles being the time dimension (i.e., how long ago each episode happened). In addition, the information in episodic memory is specific, in the sense that each episodic memory trace refers to a single event or episode. Neither of these characteristics seems to apply to the self-schema. The self-schema is usually thought of as containing highly organized information about oneself, and this information is often in a relatively general and abstract form (e.g., "Success always eludes me").

Clinical psychologists might find it valuable to consider in more detail precisely how the self-schema develops over time. At a first approximation, the self-schema is initially formed on the basis of a series of personal experiences that are represented in long-term memory by episodic memory traces. In ways that are not clear at present, much more general semantic memory traces are then formed from collections of related episodic memory traces. The self-schema itself develops as these semantic memory traces become increasingly interconnected. If this account is along the right lines, then it suggests that both episodic and semantic memory are substantially involved in the evolution of the self-schema.

If there were greater understanding of how the self-schema evolves, and of how the self-schemata of mood-disordered individuals come to differ from those of normal individuals, there would probably be implications for therapy. For example, cognitive therapy often involves providing new information that is inconsistent with the information contained in a patient's negative self-schema. The type of information that is optimal for changing such a self-schema presumably depends upon the precise structure of the existing self-schema.

Procedural and Declarative Knowledge

An alternative theoretical distinction was offered by Cohen and Squire (1980) and by Cohen (1984). Their starting point was the distinction between two kinds of knowledge (knowing that and knowing how), which was offered by the philosopher Ryle (1949). According to Cohen (1984), procedural knowledge is involved when "experience serves to influence the organization of processes that *guide* performance without access to the knowledge that *underlies* the performance" (p. 96). On the other hand, declarative knowledge is employed "in a system quite compatible with the traditional metaphor of experimental psychology, in which information is said to be first processed or encoded, then stored in some explicitly accessible form for later use, and then ultimately retrieved upon demand" (p. 96). Thus, procedural knowledge corresponds to Ryle's (1949) knowing how and declarative knowledge corresponds to his knowing that.

Cohen and Squire (1980) regarded episodic memory and semantic memory as different aspects of declarative knowledge. They argued that previous theorists had tended to focus on declarative knowledge to the relative exclusion of procedural knowledge. Procedural knowledge can take many different forms, but representative examples are motor skills such as piano playing or touch-typing.

One of the problems with the theoretical distinction between procedural and declarative knowledge is that it is defined in a rather amorphous fashion. In addition, there are complexities at the empirical level. Consider a motor skill such as playing golf. This appears at first glance to be based squarely on procedural learning. However, many golfers make use of declarative knowledge in the form of golfing tips they have learned (e.g., "Keep your head still"; "Never up, never in"), and so golf skills actually represent an amalgam of procedural and declarative knowledge. As yet, no satisfactory techniques are available for disentangling the relative contributions of procedural and declarative knowledge to complex performance.

In spite of these problems, the distinction between procedural and declarative knowledge has proved useful in describing the pattern of memory performance observed in many amnesic patients (see Parkin, 1987, for a review). In essence, amnesic patients typically experience considerable difficulties with the acquisition and subsequent retention of declarative knowledge (whether involving episodic or semantic memory), but often exhibit a normal ability to acquire procedural skills. This reasonably clear separation between impaired declarative learning and intact procedural learning in amnesics provides the strongest empirical evidence that these are independent learning systems located in different parts of the brain.

The procedural-declarative distinction may be of some relevance to an understanding of some aspects of patients' performance. For example, it has often been observed (e.g., Craske & Craig, 1984) that anxious individuals or individuals in a stressful situation fail to respond concordantly in terms of their pattern of behavioral, physiological, and verbal data. In other words, some kinds of data may indicate a high level of anxiety whereas others taken at the same time do not. Some of the discordances between verbal and behavioral data may be explicable if one assumes that the declarative knowledge system is involved in the production of verbal data, whereas the procedural knowledge system is involved in the production of some behavioral data.

The distinction between procedural and declarative knowledge is also useful in that it helps to clarify why it is that introspective evidence often provides very partial and inadequate information. Because there is no conscious awareness of the procedural knowledge underlying performance, it follows that introspective evidence is intrinsically limited. Despite these limitations, experimental clinical psychologists have traditionally investigated declarative knowledge in mood-disordered patients, and have only rarely considered procedural knowledge.

Semantic Networks

One way of conceptualizing long-term memory (e.g., Anderson & Bower, 1973) is in terms of a semantic network. The basic idea is that concepts are represented as nodes within an interconnected network. Activation of any node leads to activation of those nodes that are related to it. Bower (1981) extended this notion of a semantic network to include emotions by assuming that emotions are also represented as nodes within the semantic network. As a consequence, activation of an emotion node (e.g., depression) typically produces activation of a range of depression-related nodes throughout the network. The way activation spreads through the network has been likened by Bower (1981) to an electrical circuit in which the application of voltage at one terminal spreads to adjacent terminals along interconnecting wires of different resistances. This basic theory was extended by Bower and Cohen (1982) and by Gilligan and Bower (1984) to include a blackboard control structure (resembling the working memory system proposed by Baddeley, 1986) and stored conditional (i.e., "if . . . . , then . . . ") rules.

The semantic network theory proposed by Bower (1981) has been applied to memory for emotionally toned material in depressed and anxious patients. As the review by Singer and Salovey (1988) makes clear, the results are often consistent with expectations from Bower's (1981) theory. However, there are a number of findings that are puzzling from the perspective of semantic network theory. For example, suicide attempters did not differ from normal controls in their ability to recall memories to negative cue words (Williams & Broadbent, 1986) although according to the semantic network theory their negative mood state should have facilitated the recall of negative memories.

To a greater extent than is generally realized, there are major difficulties with nearly all network theories. First, while the spread of activation among nodes may play some part in memory, it can hardly be the whole story. Concepts can be related to each other in numerous different ways, and this diversity is not captured by the simple notion of activation spread. Second, the assignment of meaning to environmental stimuli is obviously crucial in learning and memory, but semantic network theories tell us little or nothing about how this occurs. Third, most semantic network theories are designed primarily to account for the learning and retention of rather small units of information (e.g., individual words). Such theories typically omit the larger units of organized stored information (e.g., schemata), which are increasingly believed to form an important part of long-term memory.

Schemata

Definitions of schemata vary, but in essence they are organized collections of knowledge representing information about objects, situations, events, or people. For example, according to Bartlett (1932), who was the first psychologist to explore systematically the properties of schemata, a schema is "an active organisation of past reactions, or past experience."

In theory, schemata should influence a range of processes, including those involved in perception, learning, and memory. In practice, however, most research has focussed on memory (see Alba and Hasher, 1983, for a review). It has generally been assumed (e.g., Bartlett, 1932) that memory is determined by the to-be-learned material and by the relevant schema or schemata. As a consequence, long-term memory will often be distorted to a greater or a lesser extent.

Several theorists (e.g., Beck, Rush, Shaw, & Emery, 1979; Beck & Clark, 1988; Kuiper, MacDonald, & Derry, 1983) have made use of the "schema" construct in order to account for clinical phenomena associated with mood disorders. Beck and Clark (1988) have adopted a schema-theory perspective for depression and anxiety. So far as depression is concerned, they proposed the following schema theory: "The schematic organization of the clinically depressed individual is dominated by an overwhelming negativity . . . . As a result of . . . negative maladaptive schemas, the depressed person views himself as inadequate, deprived and worthless, the world as presenting insurmountable obstacles, and the future as utterly bleak and hopeless" (p. 26). For anxiety, Beck and Clark (1988) put forward a somewhat different schema theory:

> The maladaptive schemas in the anxious patient involve perceived physical or psychological threat to one's personal domain as well as an exaggerated sense of vulnerability . . . different schematic themes are evident in the various subtypes of anxiety. With generalized anxiety disorder (GAD) a variety of life situations are viewed as threatening to one's self-concept; in panic disorder (PD) bodily or mental experiences are interpreted as catastrophic; with simple phobias danger is attributed to specific avoidable situations; and in agoraphobia panic attacks are associated with external situations and so reinforce avoidance behaviour. (pp. 26-27)

If one compares research into schemata by clinical researchers with that carried out by cognitive psychologists into nonclinical populations, various interesting differences become apparent. As Blaney (1986) and Singer and Salovey (1988) make clear in their reviews of the literature on affect and memory, it is typical in the clinical literature for researchers to use a relatively high level of retention of schema-relevant stimulus material as the main empirical support for schema theory. This approach can be contrasted with some of the findings obtained by cognitive psychologists. For example, Graesser, Woll, Kowalski, and Smith (1980) discovered that recognition memory was actually better for information that did not conform to a schema than for information that did conform. This finding was replicated by Smith and Graesser (1981), who also found the opposite pattern of results for recall. This difference between recall and recognition may occur because schemata guide the retrieval process in recall to a much greater extent than in recognition memory.

More evidence against the notion that schema-relevant information is necessarily well retained in long-term memory was obtained by Friedman (1979). She found that objects that are inconsistent with the current frame or schema receive more attention than those that are consistent. Furthermore, subjects only occasionally failed to notice missing, new, or partially changed schema-consistent objects, but performed excellently with deletions or replacements of schema-inconsistent objects.

We have seen that there are good reasons for doubting whether enhanced recall of a particular kind of stimulus material provides strong evidence for the existence of a related underlying schema. Within cognitive psychology, there has been much reliance on schema-relevant distortions and intrusions in recall as an indication of an underlying schema. For example, this was the main evidence used by Bartlett (1932). While schema-relevant distortions are an important source of evidence about schemata, care obviously has to be taken that such distortions do not merely reflect response bias.

In sum, the use of memory paradigms to investigate schemata in patients with mood disorders is less straightforward than is generally assumed. In particular, the results obtained can depend substantially on the form of retention test used. Consideration should be given to taking more than one measure of memory performance (e.g., schema-relevant distortions as well as level of recall).

Some clarification of the reasons why substantial differences between memory tests are often found was provided by Morris, Bransford, and Franks (1977). They discovered that a learning task that required processing of the meaning of list words led to better long-term memory than one that required processing of rhyme when a standard recognition test was used. In contrast, the pattern of results was precisely the opposite when the recognition test required decisions based on rhymes. According to Morris et al. (1977), these findings can be interpreted in terms of a transfer-appropriate processing of long-term memory. Different learning tasks or individual differences in underlying schemata lead to differences in the kinds of stimulus information that are stored in long-term memory. Performance on a subsequent retention test is based upon the *relevance* of that stored information to the kind of memory test that is used. In their experiment, storing information about the meanings of the words was essentially irrelevant when the recognition test required the identification of words rhyming with list words.

Memory Processes

It is obviously important to clinical psychologists to establish the kinds of information that patients tend to remember and to forget, because information remembered from the past may well influence future behavior. There are numerous theories of memory that have emphasized the role played by processing strategies in determining what is learned and remembered. In this chapter, however, we will consider one major theoretical approach focussing on processes occurring at the time of learning (Craik and Lockhart's, 1972, levels-of-processing theory), and one theoretical approach more concerned with processes occurring at the time of retrieval (based on Schacter's, 1987, distinction between explicit and implicit memory).

Levels-of-Processing Theory

According to Craik and Lockhart (1972), long-term memory depends very much on the kinds of processing of the to-be-remembered stimulus material that are carried out at the time of acquisition. More specifically, they emphasized the importance of the depth of processing, by which they meant the extent to which the stimulus material was processed in terms of its meaning. There are numerous experimental findings that appear to support the view that semantic processing is crucial for memory, but the theory is demonstrably inadequate in several ways (see Eysenck, 1984, for a discussion).

Of particular relevance here, elaboration or extensiveness of processing has been found to be at least as important a determinant of long-term retention (e.g., Johnson-Laird, Gibbs, & de Mowbray, 1978). However, the popular view that there is a direct relationship between the number of elaborations and the probability of long-term retention is erroneous. Bransford, Franks, Morris, and Stein (1979) presented their subjects with similes, some of which involved minimal elaboration (e.g., "A mosquito is like a doctor because they both draw blood") and others of which involved multiple elaborations (e.g., "A mosquito is like a raccoon because they both have heads, legs, jaws"). Subsequent recall of the simile to the first nouns presented as a cue was considerably higher for the sentences involved fewer elaborations, presumably because the similes were more distinctive in those sentences.

The depth and elaboration of processing are under conscious control to some extent. It follows that the extent to which mood-disordered patients learn and remember threatening or negatively toned stimulus material may well be affected by their decisions concerning the appropriate depth of processing and amount of elaboration. These strategic decisions have scarcely been studied within a clinical context, but need to be for a full understanding of differences between patient groups and normal controls in retention of negative and neutral stimulus material.

Explicit and Implicit Memory

A theoretical distinction that is becoming increasingly important is that between explicit and implicit memory. In 1985, Graf and Schacter provided the following definitions of those terms: "Implicit memory is revealed when performance on a task is facilitated in the absence of conscious recollection; explicit memory is revealed when performance on a task requires conscious recollection of previous experiences" (p. 501).

All of the traditional measures of memory (e.g., free recall; cued recall; recognition) involve instructions to retrieve information that was stored previously, and thus qualify as forms of explicit memory. Implicit memory is often assessed by means of a word-completion test. First, a list of words is presented to some of the subjects. Subjects are given word fragments (e.g., BAR---) and simply instructed to write down the first word that occurs to them. Implicit memory is measured by comparing the number of word completions corresponding to words on the list previously presented written down by those subjects who did or did not see or hear the list.

The distinction between explicit and implicit memory has proved particularly useful in amnesia research (see Schachter, 1987, for a review). There are numerous studies showing that amnesic patients perform poorly on tests of long-term explicit memory. Indeed, a severe impairment of long-term memory is one of the criteria customarily used to define the "amnesic syndrome." However, several recent studies have shown that amnesic patients are at little or no disadvantage to control subjects when a test of implicit memory is used (e.g., Graf, Squire, & Mandler, 1984).

In addition to amnesia research, Schachter (1987) reviews other lines of research with normal subjects that have demonstrated that several experimental manipulations have very different effects on explicit and implicit memory. It has been established, therefore, that there are important qualitative differences between explicit and implicit memory. What remains unclear are the processes and mechanisms underlying explicit and implicit memory. For example, some theorists (e.g., Graf et al., 1984) argue that implicit memory depends upon automatic activation of the internal representation of a word when it is presented to a subject; this activation may persist for hours or days. In contrast, Roediger and Blaxton (1987) argued that data-driven processes (i.e., those initiated directly by external stimuli) generally underlie performance on tests of implicit memory, whereas conceptually driven processes (i.e., those initiated by the subject) usually underlie performance on explicit memory tests.

The available evidence does not indicate the clear superiority of any one theoretical approach to the explicit-implicit memory distinction. It is beginning to appear that the term implicit memory may actually refer to a number of somewhat separate phenomena, and that in consequence no single theory will turn out to be adequate to account for all of the data.

Nearly all memory research on patients with mood disorders has made use of tests of explicit rather than implicit memory. Why might it be valuable for researchers to investigate implicit memory in anxious and depressed patients? One important reason is that tests of implicit memory may provide more direct information than tests of explicit memory about underlying schemata. Consider, for example, research attempting to demonstrate a negative memory bias in generalized anxiety disorder patients when presented with a mixture of threatening and nonthreatening stimulus words. No evidence of such a negative memory bias has been found in several studies (e.g., Mogg, Mathews, & Weinman, 1987) using explicit memory tests.

Mathews, Mogg, May, and Eysenck (in press) also failed to observe a negative memory bias in generalized anxiety disorder patients when an explicit memory test (cued recall) was used. However, the results were quite different on a test of implicit memory (word-completion test). Anxious patients produced more word completions than normal controls corresponding to list words, but the opposite was the case for nonthreatening words. What may be happening here is that the internal representations of threatening words in anxious patients are either more strongly activated or more long-lastingly activated than those of normal controls by the presentation of the corresponding words, and this produces the effects on implicit memory. For explicit memory, the anxious patients may have adopted the strategy of curtailing elaborative processing of threatening information, and this prevented them from demonstrating a negative recall bias in cued recall.

This study shows very clearly the advantages to be obtained from assessing implicit memory. On the basis of the explicit memory data alone, it would have been concluded that there were no differences between anxious patients and normal controls in their processing of threatening and nonthreatening words. The implicit memory data indicate that drawing that conclusion would have been erroneous.

PERCEPTION AND ATTENTION

There has been much less clinical research on perception and attention than on memory. Perhaps as a consequence, there are fewer theoretical constructs from within cognitive psychology that have been applied to the mood disorders. What follows is a very selective discussion of some theoretical notions that have potential relevance to an understanding of mood disorders.

Date-Driven and Conceptually Driven Processes in Perception

There is a very basic theoretical distinction between data-driven (or bottom-up) processes and conceptually driven (or top-down) processes. The distinction has relevance to many areas of cognitive functioning, but is perhaps most associated with perceptual phenomena. In essence, data-driven processes are those that are guided or driven entirely by external stimuli, whereas conceptually driven processes are those that depend upon stored knowledge and expectations.

A study by Warren and Warren (1970) provides a good example of the influence of conceptually driven or top-down processes on perception. Their subjects received one of the following sentences presented auditorily (the asterisk indicates a deleted portion of the sentence);

1. It was found that the *eel was on the axle.
2. It was found that the *eel was on the shoe.
3. It was found that the *eel was on the table.
4. It was found that the *eel was on the orange.

Since "*eel" was identical in every sentence, the data-driven processes initiated by it must presumably have been the same in every case. However, subjects listening to the first sentence usually reported hearing "wheel," whereas those hearing the other sentences heard "heel," "meal," and "peel," respectively. Perception varied systematically in this way because the contextual information within each sentence biased the conceptually driven or top-down processing.

Any differences in perceptual processing between mood-disordered patients and normal controls are far more likely to involve conceptually driven than data-driven processes. If anxious and depressed patients differ substantially from normals in their schematic knowledge (e.g., Beck & Clark, 1988), then this will influence perceptual processing in many circumstances. Conceptually driven processes are especially likely to influence perception when (as in the study by Warren and Warren, 1970) the stimulus input is ambiguous, because data-driven processes on their own cannot resolve the ambiguity.

There have been remarkably few clinical studies of the perception of ambiguous stimuli. An exception is a study by Mathews, Richards, and Eysenck (in press). They asked patients with generalized anxiety disorder, recovered anxious patients, and normal controls to write down the spelling of several auditorily presented homophones with threat-related and neutral or nonthreatening interpretations (e.g., die, dye; guilt, gilt). There were substantial differences among the groups. The percentage of threat-related homophone spellings was 85.4% in the currently anxious group, 77.1% in the recovered anxious group, and 69.9% in the control group.

In sum, there appear to be good reasons for maximizing the involvement of conceptually driven processes and minimizing the involvement of data-driven processes in studies of perceptual functioning in clinical patients. Data-driven processes can be minimized by presenting stimuli for very brief periods of time or by presenting ambiguous stimuli. Conceptually driven processes can be maximized by presenting stimuli that are related directly to an individual's underlying concerns and knowledge.

Automaticity

Several theorists have drawn a distinction between automatic and attentional or controlled processing. For example, Shiffrin and Schneider (1977) and Schneider and Shiffrin (1977) proposed that controlled processes are of limited capacity, require attention, and are used flexibly, whereas automatic processes have no capacity limitations, do not require attention, and are not readily modifiable. They carried out a series of experiments in which they discovered that prolonged practice under the same learning conditions led to the development of fast and automatic responses, whereas changing conditions were associated with relatively slow controlled processes.

The development of automaticity with practice has been demonstrated in several other studies (see Eysenck, 1984, for a review). However, there has been relatively little progress at a theoretical level in terms of understanding the mechanisms involved. It has often been assumed (e.g., Shiffrin & Schneider, 1977) that automaticity develops with practice because processing demands decrease, but this does not explain why the processing demands decrease.

The most promising theoretical approach is that of Logan (1988). He argued that every experience with a situation leads to the establishment of new memory traces. Prolonged practice in a given situation leads to a substantial increase in the knowledge base, and this in turn permits rapid retrieval of appropriate responses to the stimulus situation. In Logan's (1988) words, "Automaticity is memory retrieval: performance is automatic when it is based on a single-step direct-access retrieval of past solutions from memory" (p. 493). Without practice, on the other hand, subjects typically respond to stimuli only after the application of thought and/or rules.

Logan's (1988) theoretical approach helps to make sense of the major characteristics of automaticity. Automatic responses are fast because there is no problem of retrieval. They do not reduce processing capacity because immediate retrieval of the appropriate response does not require any capacity. Finally, automatic responses are unavailable to conscious awareness because no processes intervene between presentation of the stimulus and the retrieval of the response.

Cognitive theories of anxiety and depression (e.g., Beck et al., 1979; Beck & Emery, 1985) have often been closely associated with particular forms of cognitive therapy. The emphasis with respect to both theory and therapy has been on conscious thoughts, and on ways in which these thoughts may be maladaptive. Beck (1967) obtained evidence that the thinking of depressed individuals frequently involves themes of negative self-evaluation, hopelessness, and a pessimistic view of the world, and various questionnaires have been designed since then in order to assess these aspects of conscious thought processes. These questionnaires include the Automatic Thoughts Questionnaire, Cognitions Checklist, and the Crandell Cognition Inventory.

Hibbert (1984) investigated conscious thought context in anxious patients. He discovered that reported thoughts involved physical or social dangers. When he divided his sample into those with and without panic attacks, he found that those with panic attacks were more likely to have catastrophic thought content, especially relating to sudden death or severe disease.

Despite this emphasis on conscious thoughts, Beck has recognized that depressed patients are frequently unaware of the rules that influence their behavior. For example, Beck et al. (1979) proposed the existence of "core assumptions," which are unarticulated rules used to make sense of experience. The use of these core assumptions may correspond to the kinds of automatic processing we have been discussing.

Is it important for clinical psychologists to consider automatic processes as well as conscious processes? The answers to that question have been quite diverse. One extreme position was adopted by Sacco and Beck (1985), who came to the following conclusion: "The concept of unconscious processes is largely irrelevant to cognitive therapy" (p. 5).

The position adopted here is diametrically opposed to that of Sacco and Beck (1985). One reason is that it is probable that many conscious processes have automatic processes as antecedents, and so even to understand conscious processing in mood disorders it will be necessary to focus on automatic processes as well. For example, suppose we find (e.g., MacLeod, Mathews, & Tata, 1986) that anxious patients selectively attend to threatening stimuli rather than neutral stimuli, whereas normal controls do not. It could be argued that this simply reflects differences in conscious processes between the two groups. However, the *decision* as to which of two or more stimuli to attend to is probably taken at a pre-attentive level. If that were not the case, it would be necessary to attend to all environmental stimuli in order to decide to which stimulus to attend!

Vulnerability

At a more theoretical level, there is another very important reason for considering automatic or pre-attentive processes. One of the goals of cognitive research into mood disorders is to distinguish between those non-normal cognitive processes and mechanisms in mood-disordered patients that might form part of a cognitive vulnerability factor and those that reflect anxious or depressed mood state. While the reality is almost certainly more complex than this, it is tempting to assume that non-normal automatic processes are more likely to be part of a vulnerability factor, whereas non-normal conscious processes are more likely to reflect current mood state. Those non-normal processes forming part of a vulnerability factor must, by definition, remain largely unchanged over long periods of time, and a major characteristic of automatic processes is their relative unmodifiability. In contrast, conscious processes are readily modified, and thus seem less likely candidates to be involved in a vulnerability factor.

Much of the available evidence on cognitive vulnerability factors in depression and in anxiety is consistent with the above assumptions. Several investigators have studied conscious processes in depression, and have been unable to obtain any evidence of a cognitive vulnerability factor. For example, Lewinsohn, Steinmetz, Larson, and Franklin (1981) conducted a prospective study in which conscious attitudes and cognitions were assessed by means of questionnaires. They arrived at the following pessimistic conclusion: "Prior to becoming depressed, ... future depressives did not subscribe to irrational beliefs, they did not have lower expectancies for positive outcomes or higher expectancies for negative outcomes, they did not attribute success experiences to external causes and failure experiences to internal causes, nor did they perceive themselves as having less control over the events of their lives . . . . People who are vulnerable to depression are not characterized by stable patterns of negative thinking of the type postulated by the cognitive therapists" (p. 218).

The issue of a cognitive vulnerability factor in depression has also been investigated in studies that have used recovered depressed patients. The basic rationale is that those cognitive measures reflecting stable characteristics associated with vulnerability to depression should distinguish the normal controls from currently depressed patients and recovered depressed patients, whereas cognitive measures reflecting current depressed mood state should distinguish currently depressed patients from recovered depressed patients and normal controls.

The strategy of investigating cognitive vulnerability by using recovered depressed patients has more problems associated with it than the prospective study approach. For example, if recovered depressed patients do not differ in their cognitive performance from currently depressed patients, then the simplest explanation is that they have not really recovered. Another possibility is that suffering from clinical depression may affect the cognitive system in such a way that it never returns to the state that it was in beforehand. In that case, recovered depressed patients may not resemble a premorbid group.

In spite of the interpretative problems, the studies themselves have shown fairly consistently that conscious cognitions form no more than a very small part of a cognitive vulnerability factor, and possibly no part at all. Segal and Shaw (1986) reviewed studies on conscious negative cognitions in recovered depressed patients. In nearly every study it was found that those individuals who had recovered from depression had fewer and less intense negative cognitions than currently depressed patients. However, there were some minor differences across the studies in terms of whether the negative cognitions of recovered depressed patients had improved to the level of normal controls.

In sum, both prospective studies and studies with recovered depressed patients have yielded very little evidence of a cognitive vulnerability factor in depression. The same conclusion is applicable to studies of negative recall bias, where the bias typically disappears in patients who have recovered (see Brewin, 1988, for a review). It is not possible to be certain of the reasons for these regular failures to demonstrate a vulnerability factor. However, on the basis of the theoretical distinction between automatic and conscious processes, it seems strangely limited that virtually all of the cognitive measures taken in these studies have been measures of conscious processes. At the very least, it would seem desirable to base statements on cognitive vulnerability in depression on a much broader range of empirical evidence. This is especially the case when, as we have seen, there are reasonable theoretical grounds for assuming that automatic processes are more likely than conscious processes to form part of a cognitive vulnerability factor.

The best evidence that the distinction between automatic and conscious or controlled processes is a valuable one has emerged from studies of patients with generalized anxiety disorder. This is not the place to consider all of the available evidence. Instead, consideration will be given to three studies that are of particular interest. Eysenck, Mogg, Richards, and

Mathews (unpublished) investigated the vulnerability issue in a study in which subjects were presented with ambiguous sentences (e.g., "The two men watched as the chest was opened") which could be interpreted in either a threatening or a non-threatening fashion. Subjects were then given a recognition test in which they had to decide whether reworded versions of these sentences were the same in meaning as the sentences they had seen originally. Anxious patients differed from controls in that they recognized relatively more of the threatening interpretations, and recovered anxious patients closely resembled normal controls.

The findings of Eysenck et al. (unpublished) suggest that the interpretative bias shown by currently anxious patients is a reflection of their mood state, and does not form part of a cognitive vulnerability factor. Unfortunately, there is no clear understanding of all the processes involved in the comprehension and subsequent retrieval of ambiguous material. However, it is clear that several conscious processes are involved at the time of acquisition and at the time of retrieval.

The second study to be considered is the one by Mathews et al. (in press) on explicit and implicit memory which was discussed earlier in this chapter. In that study, a further group of individuals who had recovered from generalized anxiety disorder was run. On the test of implicit memory, the performance of this group was intermediate between that of the currently anxious group and the normal control group. This suggests, in a preliminary way, that the negative bias effect in implicit memory demonstrated by currently anxious patients may reflect current mood state combined with a vulnerability factor. However, this conclusion must be very tentative given that the recovered anxious group did not differ significantly from either of the other two groups.

Of particular theoretical interest here is that performance on the word-completion task used to assess implicit memory in the study by Eysenck et al. (unpublished) may very well depend primarily on automatic processes (Graf et al., 1984). If so, it might be expected that implicit memory would be more likely than explicit memory to provide evidence of a vulnerability factor. It would be interesting to test that expectation across a range of explicit and implicit memory tasks.

The third study to be considered is that of Mathews, May, Mogg, and Eysenck (submitted). They investigated distractibility in patients with a diagnosis of generalized anxiety disorder using both neutral and threat-related distracting stimuli. The anxious patients were more distractible than the normal controls, and this enhanced distractibility was more evident with threat-related distractors than with neutral distractors. In other words, anxious patients exhibit a general tendency to be distracted by task-irrelevant stimuli, and they also have a more specific tendency to have their attention captured by threat-related stimuli. Recovered anxious patients were similar in performance to normal control subjects when neutral distractors were used, but they were significantly more distractible than controls when threat-related distractors were presented.

The findings indicate that the tendency of anxious patients to have their attention captured by threat-related distracting stimuli forms part of a cognitive vulnerability factor. It seems reasonable that those individuals who are especially likely to attend to mildly threatening stimuli should be vulnerable to generalized anxiety disorder. The exact processes involved in attentional capture are not known, but it is probable that relatively automatic processes play an important part in determining which aspects of the visual environment will receive attention.

CONCLUSION

From the perspective of cognitive psychology, the most striking characteristic of research on cognitive factors in mood disorders is the narrow range of experimental paradigms that have been used. At a general level, most of the research has focussed on conscious processes. The memory research has concentrated on explicit memory for declarative knowledge, with recall being preferred to recognition as the retention test.

Common sense suggests that a full understanding of the role of cognition in mood disorders is unlikely to be forthcoming from such a narrowly focussed approach. More importantly, there are reasons for assuming that mood-disorder patients may differ from normal controls in theoretically significant ways on some of the aspects of cognitive processing that have received very little attention (e.g., automatic processes; implicit memory). For example, it may well be the case that automatic processes are more likely to form part of a cognitive vulnerability factor than are conscious processes, and yet it is conscious processes that have been extensively investigated.

At the most general level, the search for cognitive vulnerability factors underlying clinical anxiety and depression should be theoretically motivated. The evidence increasingly indicates that some aspects of cognitive functioning may form part of a cognitive vulnerability factor whereas other aspects may simply reflect clinical mood states. In order to make progress, we need to understand why it is that only some aspects of cognitive functioning apparently reflect a vulnerability factor. It is possible that the automatic-conscious process distinction will be of value in this connection.

REFERENCES

Alba, J. W., & Hasher, L. (1983). Is memory schematic? *Psychological Bulletin. 93*, 203–231.

Anderson, J. R., & Bower, G. H. (1973). *Human associative memory*. Washington, DC: Winston.

Atkinson, R. C., & Shiffrin, R. M. (1968). Human memory: A proposed system and its control processes. In K. W. Spence & J. T. Spence (Eds.), *The psychology of learning and motivation: Vol. 2*. London: Academic Press.

Baddeley, A. D. (1986). *Working memory*. Oxford: Clarendon.

Bartlett, F. C. (1932). *Remembering: A study in experimental and social psychology*. Cambridge: Cambridge University Press.

Beck, A. T. (1967). *Depression: Causes and treatment*. Philadelphia: University of Pennsylvania Press.

Beck, A. T., & Clark, D. A. (1988). Anxiety and depression: An information processing perspective. *Anxiety Research, 1*, 23–36.

Beck, A. T., & Emery, G. (1985). *Anxiety disorders and phobias: A cognitive perspective*. New York: Basic Books.

Beck, A. T., Rush, A. J., Shaw, B. F., & Emery, G. (1979). *Cognitive therapy of depression*. New York: John Wiley & Sons.

Blaney, P. H. (1986). Affect and memory: A review. *Psychological Bulletin, 99*, 229–246.

Bower, G. H. (1981). Mood and memory. *American Psychologist, 36*, 129–148.

Bower, G. H. & Cohen, P. R. (1982). Emotional influences in memory and thinking: Data and theory. In M. S. Clark & S. T. Fiske (Eds.), *Affect and cognition: The 17th annual Carnegie symposium on cognition*. Hillsdale, NJ: Lawrence Erlbaum Associates.

Bransford, J. D., Franks, J. J., Morris, C. D., & Stein, B. S. (1979). Some general comments on learning and memory research. In L. S. Cermak & F. I. M. Craik (Eds.), *Levels of processing in human memory*. Hillsdale, NJ: Lawrence Erlbaum Associates.

Brewin, C. R. (1988). *Cognitive foundations of clinical psychology*. London: Lawrence Erlbaum Associates.

Cohen, N. J. (1984). Preserved learning capacity in amnesia: Evidence for multiple memory systems. In L. R. Squire & N. Butters (Eds.), *Neuropsychology of memory*. New York: Guilford Press.

Cohen, N. J., & Squire, L. R. (1980). Preserved learning and retention of pattern-analyzing skill in amnesia: Dissociation of knowing how and knowing that. *Science, 210*, 207–210.

Craik, F. I. M., & Lockhart, R. S. (1972). Levels of processing: A framework for memory research. *Journal of Verbal Learning and Verbal Behavior, 11*, 671–684.

Craske, M. G., & Craig, K. D. (1984). Musical performance anxiety: The three-systems model and self-efficacy theory. *Behaviour Research and Therapy, 22*, 267–280.

Dixon, N. F. (1981). *Preconscious processes*. Chichester: John Wiley & Sons.

Ericsson, K. A., & Simon, H. A. (1980). Verbal reports as data. *Psychological Review, 87*, 215–251.

Eysenck, M. W. (1984). *A handbook of cognitive psychology*. London: Lawrence Erlbaum Associates.

Eysenck, M. W., Mogg, K., Richards, A., & Mathews, A. (Unpublished). Interpretation of ambiguity in anxiety states.

Friedman, A. (1979). Framing pictures: The role of knowledge in automatised encoding and memory for gist. *Journal of Experimental Psychology: General, 108*, 316–355.

Gilligan, S. G., & Bower, G. H. (1984). Cognitive consequences of emotional arousal. In C. Izard, J. Kagen, and R. Zajonc (Eds.), *Emotions, cognition, and behavior*. New York: Cambridge University Press.

Graesser, A. C., Woll, S. B., Kowalski, D. J., & Smith, D. A. (1980). Memory for typical and atypical actions in scripted activities. *Journal of Experimental Psychology: Human Learning and Memory, 6*, 503–515.

Graf, P., & Schacter, D. L. (1985). Implicit and explicit memory for new associations in normal and amnesic subjects. *Journal of Experimental Psychology: Learning, Memory, and Cognition, 11*, 501–518.

Graf, P., Squire, L. R., & Mandler, G. (1984). The information that amnesic patients do not forget. *Journal of Experimental Psychology: Learning, Memory, and Cognition, 10*, 164–178.

Hibbert, G. A. (1984). Ideational components of anxiety: Their origin and content. *British Journal of Psychiatry, 144*, 618–624.

Johnson-Laird, P. N., Gibbs, G., & de Mowbray, J. (1978). Meaning, amount of processing, and memory for words. *Memory & Cognition, 6*, 372–375.

Kuiper, N. A., MacDonald, M. R., & Derry, P. A. (1983). Parameters of a depressive self-schema. In J. Suls & A. G. Greenwald (Eds.), *Psychological perspectives on the Self, Vol. 2*. Hillsdale, NJ: Lawrence Erlbaum Associates.

Lewinsohn, P. M., Steinmetz, J. L., Larson, D. W., & Franklin, Y. (1981). Depression related cognitions: Antecedents or consequences. *Journal of Abnormal Psychology, 90*, 213–219.

Logan, G. D. (1988). Toward an instance theory of automatization. *Psychological Review, 95*, 492–527.

MacLeod, C., Mathews, A., & Tata, P. (1986). Attentional

bias in emotional disorders. *Journal of Abnormal Psychology, 95*, 15–20.

Mathews, A., May, J., Mogg, K., & Eysenck, M. W. (Submitted). Attentional bias in anxiety: Selective search or defective filtering?

Mathews, A., Mogg, K., May, J., & Eysenck, M. W. (in press). Implicit and explicit memory biases in anxiety states. *Journal of Abnormal Psychology*.

Mathews, A., Richards, A., & Eysenck, M. W. (in press). The interpretation of homophones related to threat in anxiety states. *Journal of Abnormal Psychology*.

Meehl, P. E., & MacCorquodale, K. (1948). On a distinction between hypothetical constructs and intervening variables. *Psychology Review, 55*, 243–261.

Mogg, K., Mathews, A., & Weinman, J. (1987). Memory bias in clinical anxiety. *Journal of Abnormal Psychology, 96*, 94–98.

Morris, C. D., Bransford, J. D., & Franks, J. J. (1977). Levels of processing versus transfer appropriate processing. *Journal of Verbal Learning and Verbal Behavior, 16*, 519–533.

Nisbett, R. E., & Wilson, T. D. (1977). Telling more than we can know: Verbal reports on mental processes. *Psychological Review, 84*, 231–259.

Parkin, A. J. (1987). *Memory & amnesia*. Oxford: Blackwell.

Roediger, H. L., III, & Blaxton, T. A. (1987). Retrieval modes produce dissociations in memory for surface information. In D. S. Gorfein & R. R. Hoffman (Eds.), *Memory and cognitive processes: The Ebbinghaus centennial conference*. Hillsdale, NJ: Lawrence Erlbaum Associates.

Ryle, G. (1949). *The concept of mind*. London: Hutchinson.

Sacco, W. P., & Beck, A. T. (1985). Cognitive therapy of depression. In E. E. Beckham & W. R. Leber (Eds.), *Handbook of depression: Treatment, assessment and research*. Homewood, IL: Dorsey Press.

Schacter, D. L. (1987). Implicit memory: History and current status. *Journal of Experimental Psychology: Learning, Memory, and Cognition, 13*, 501–518.

Schneider, W., & Shiffrin, R. M. (1977). Controlled and automatic human information processing: I. Detection, search and attention. *Psychological Review, 84*, 1–66.

Segal, Z. V., & Shaw, B. F. (1986). Cognition in depression: A reappraisal of Coyne & Gotlib's critique. *Cognitive Therapy and Research, 10*, 671–694.

Shiffrin, R. M., & Schneider, W. (1977). Controlled and automatic human information processing: II. Perceptual learning, automatic attending, and a general theory. *Psychological Review, 84*, 127–190.

Singer, J. A., & Salovey, P. (1988). Mood and memory: Evaluating the network theory of affect. *Clinical Psychology Review, 8*, 211–251.

Smith, D. A., & Graesser, A. C. (1981). Memory for actions in scripted activities as a function of typicality, retention interval, and retrieval task. *Memory & Cognition, 9*, 550–559.

Tolman, E. C. (1932). *Purposive behavior in animals and men*. New York: Century.

Tulving, E. (1972). Episodic and semantic memory. In E. Tulving & W. Donaldson (Eds.), *Organization of memory*. London: Academic Press.

Warren, R. M., & Warren, R. P. (1970). Auditory illusions and confusions. *Scientific American, 223*, 30–36.

Weiskrantz, L. (1986). *Blindsight: A case study and its implications*. Oxford: Oxford University Press.

Williams, J. M. G., & Broadbent, K. (1986). Autobiographical memory in suicide attempters. *Journal of Abnormal Psychology, 95*, 144–149.

CHAPTER 7

COGNITIVE-EXPERIMENTAL APPROACHES TO THE EMOTIONAL DISORDERS

Colin MacLeod
Andrew M. Mathews

Despite our universal familiarity with the experience of anxious and depressed mood states, the factors that mediate these emotions have been a topic of debate for many decades. One central forum for this debate has developed around the study of these moods when they occur at sufficient levels of intensity or frequency to represent clinical conditions. The prevalence rates for such emotional problems are extremely high. Anxiety disorders are experienced by between 4% and 8% of the population each year (Lader & Marks, 1973; M. Weissman, 1985), whereas approximately 12% of all adults will require treatment for depression at some time in their life (Klerman, 1975, 1978).

Whereas traditional psychiatric accounts have attributed these conditions to various hypothetical biochemical imbalances, or have conceptualized the emotional disorders in terms of psychodynamic conflicts among hypothetical subsystems within the personality, clinical psychologists have primarily approached the emotional disorders from a behaviorist perspective. The clinical importance of the treatment approaches that have been derived from this behavioral approach can scarcely be overestimated. Indeed the development of successful behavioral interventions, such as flooding and systematic desensitization (Wolpe, 1958, 1973), which represent the direct applications of laboratory based learning principles, have been major factors in establishing clinical psychology as an applied science and have thus laid the foundations for the professional development of the discipline.

Nevertheless, despite such therapeutic advances, behaviorists have always had some difficulty in offering a comprehensive theory of anxiety or depression, in view of the fact that the central symptomatology of the emotional disorders is essentially subjective. Classical conditioning may well account for learned associations between particular types of setting and the experience of emotional distress, while instrumental learning may explain some behavioral correlates of these emotions, but neither mechanism can serve to illuminate the subjective aspects of such disorders.

Excessive worry and pervasive apprehension are not mere epiphenomena to the generalized anxiety patient, they are the disorder. Similarly, negative ruminations and self-deprecation are central definitive features of depression, and yet cannot even be represented within a behavioral model of the condition.

The theoretical limitations of behaviorism have therefore been a source of growing discomfort for those psychologists who would attribute greater significance to mental events in the emotional disorders.

It is not surprising, therefore, that the new wave of cognitivism that has swept through clinical psychology over the past decade has found greatest acceptance among those involved in the study of depression and anxiety. After many fallow years the field of mentalism is proving exceedingly fertile, as any cursory glance over the major contemporary clinical journals will readily confirm.

However this "cognitive revolution" (Mahoney, 1977) which has so transformed clinical psychology has not gone uncriticized (e.g., H. J. Eysenck, 1972; Wolpe, 1976). A major concern shared by most critics is that any return to mentalism must inevitably be accompanied by a reduction in scientific rigour. For example, H. J. Eysenck (1972) rejects the investigation of mental events with the claim ". . . for methodological reasons they cannot be made the objects of proper scientific study." While we dispute the logic of this argument, we nevertheless believe that it should be taken very seriously.

Behaviorism developed in response to the recognized inadequacies of introspection as an acceptable investigative procedure. Self-reports on cognitive processes fail to meet the minimal scientific requirement that a data base must have demonstrable reliability and validity. Indeed Nisbett and Wilson (1977) have reviewed a great deal of evidence indicating that, although subjects will readily provide such self-report, these reports are commonly inaccurate.

If a return to mentalism were to involve a return to an exclusive reliance upon the introspective method then this would indeed represent a retrograde step. Fortunately, however, the path upon which clinical theorists now find themselves has been paved in advance by the experimental psychologist, who made the transition from behaviorism to cognitivism some three decades ago. Clearly the development of cognitive-experimental psychology has not involved the compromising of scientific rigor.

Two factors have made this possible. First, a framework has been constructed, borrowing concepts from information technology, that permits the development of precise theoretical models capable of generating highly specific predictions. Second, a range of experimental procedures have been developed that are capable of testing such predictions, without recourse to introspection. Indeed the majority of cognitive-experimental paradigms employ objective behavioral measures, such as response latencies or recall scores, and infer mental processes by relating such data to theoretical models. Cognitive-experimental psychology therefore offers the clinical theorist a valuable precedent.

In this chapter we consider research that has adopted the information processing paradigm, and used cognitive-experimental research techniques to investigate the cognitive characteristics of anxiety and depression. Until recently the application of the information processing approach to the study of these emotions was restricted to the investigation of associated cognitive deficits, and this research will be reviewed in the next section. We will then go on to consider how the cognitive-experimental approach has been extended to directly address more recently clinically motivated hypotheses concerning the role of cognitive factors in the emotional disorders.

AFFECT-RELATED COGNITIVE IMPAIRMENTS

Few clinicians are unfamiliar with emotionally disordered clients' common claim that their general cognitive abilities are functioning at a reduced level. Indeed at times it may be difficult to isolate these concerns from the affective symptoms themselves, as anxious or depressed mood often appears to be intensified in response to this perceived cognitive impairment. Reducing such deficits could therefore represent a therapeutic goal in many cases, and potential intervention procedures may usefully be informed by detailed investigation into the actual nature of the cognitive deficits that characterize the emotional disorders. In this section we will review the literature separately for depression and anxiety, and will attempt not only to indicate the nature of the deficits that are found, but also to consider the information processing mechanisms that are likely to be implicated.

Cognitive Deficits in Depression

Depressed patients do indeed perform poorly, relative to nondepressed control subjects, on a variety of higher level cognitive tasks, ranging from abstracting ability (e.g., Donnelly, Waldman, Murphy, Wyatt, & Goodwin, 1980; Sprock, Braff, Saccuzzo, & Alkinson, 1983) through proverb interpretation (e.g., Gorham, 1956), to general problem solving ability (e.g., Silberman, Weingartner, & Post, 1983). Perhaps the simplest explanation for impaired performance on such tasks attributes deficits to the general slowing of reaction time that often accompanies depression (e.g., Payne & Hewlett, 1960; W. Miller, 1975). According to this position, depressed subjects obtain poorer scores because they take a long time to respond. Weckowicz, Nutter, & Cruise (1972) provide supportive evidence for this view by demonstrating that tests related to speed of performance best discriminate depressives from controls. On the basis of such results Weckowicz et al., and others (e.g., Hale & Strickland, 1976; Harness, Bental, & Carmon (1977), argue that deficits in depression may solely reflect psychomotor retardation.

However it appears that, while depression is certainly associated with slowing, this retardation is not restricted to the psychomotor system. Byrne (1976), for example, subdivided tasks into a preparatory, or decision phase, and an execution phase, and measured these independently in both control subjects and depressed patients. He found that the execution phase was indeed slower in depressed subjects. However, he found that psychotic depressives showed a slowing in the preparatory phase also, indicating the presence of cognitive retardation in addition to psychomotor retardation. Similar results, employing a different methodology, have also been reported by Cornell, Suarez, & Berent, 1984).

It therefore appears that the performance deficits in depression cannot simply be attributed to psychomotor slowing. Central cognitive operations are also involved. Much research has attempted to identify the component of the cognitive system that contributes most towards impaired functioning, and a great deal of evidence points towards memory performance as an important locus of such deficits in depression. Performance on free-recall tasks in particular have been shown to be frequently impaired in depressed subjects.

Such memory deficits have been reported in depressed patients, for example, by Breslow, Kocsis, & Belkin (1980) using the Wechsler Memory Scales (Wechsler, 1945), by Silberman, Weingartner, Lorcia, Byrnes, and Post (1983) using an incidental recall task, and by Coughlan and Hollows (1984) using list learning and design learning paradigms. Much of this evidence has been reviewed recently by Johnson and Magaro (1987) and by Ellis and Ashbrook (1987).

There are three lines of evidence which suggest that memory impairment is related directly to depressed mood, rather than representing a stable trait in individuals prone to depressive disorders. First, similar deficits can be produced in normal subjects by inducing a depressed mood (e.g., Leight & Ellis, 1981; Ellis, Thomas, & Rodriguez, 1984).

Second, degree of memory impairment is often found to be correlated with the level of depressed mood across a patient population (e.g., Frith et al., 1983; Pettinati & Rosenberg, 1984; Warren & Groom, 1984). Finally, fluctuations in depressed mood within individual depressive patients is associated with fluctuations in the severity of their memory impairment. Henry, Weingartner, & Murphy (1971) have demonstrated such an association between mood and memory deficit in bipolar patients whose moods show daily fluctuations.

Additional studies have charted a reduction in memory problems as patients recover from their depressive episode, and shown that the degree of improvement in memory is highly correlated with the magnitude of improvement in the level of depressed mood. Such patterns of association between mood and memory deficit have been found following treatment with electroconvulsive therapy (ECT) (e.g., Cronholm & Ottoson, 1961; Stomgren, 1977; Frith et al., 1983; Warren & Groom, 1984; Pettinati & Rosenberg, 1984), with tricyclics (e.g., Sternberg & Jarvik, 1976), and with amphetamine (e.g., Reus, Silberman, Post, & Weingartner, 1979). It therefore seems fairly clear that it is depression as a state, rather than as a personality trait, which is implicated in the development of memory problems.

There has been more controversy concerning the actual cognitive basis of the impaired performance shown by depressed subjects on memory tasks. One suggestion has been that memory itself is not actually impaired but, rather, that depressed subjects omit reporting available information. There are two schools of thought concerning why this may be so.

According to one view, depressed subjects are characterized by a general output paucity due to their unwillingness to invest effort in producing their responses (Henry, Weingartner, & Murphy, 1973; Whitehead, 1973, 1974). However, Watts and Sharrock (1987) found no support for this hypothesis in a direct test, which manipulated the output requirements in a memory test by comparing free recall with cued recall—the latter requiring only single word or short phrase responses. Depressed subjects were even more impaired on the "low output" version of the task, leading Watts and Sharrock to conclude that a general unwillingness to produce effortful responses was unlikely to be the basis of their poor memory performance.

An alternative view is that paucity of responding in depression may reflect an elevation of confidence thresholds, leading subjects to adopt very stringent criteria. Thus depressed subjects may simply omit items from their output unless they are absolutely certain that these items were indeed presented, whereas normal subjects are more willing to guess with less certainty. This possibility has been investigated experimentally by examining hit rates (i.e., items presented at learning and accurately remembered) and false alarm rates (i.e., items not presented at learning but inaccurately "remembered" as having been presented). If depressed subjects are poor on memory tasks only because they adopt elevated confidence levels then both hit rates and false alarm rates should be reduced, but the relative ratio of hits to false alarms should remain constant. A number of studies have indeed found depression related reductions in false alarm rates (e.g., Larner, 1977; E. Miller & Lewis, 1977; Zuroff, Colussy, & Wielgus, 1983). Silberman, Weingartner, & Post, (1983), however, have found that depression impairs hit rate more than false alarm rate. Furthermore Watts, Morris, and MacLeod (1987) have shown that hit rate is disproportionately low in depressed subjects even under conditions that *increase* false alarm rates specifically in those depressed subjects (a manipulation achieved by requiring subjects to vocalize words on presentation during learning).

Finally, studies that force subjects to respond by guessing if they are uncertain (and hence eliminate the influence of subjective confidence criteria on performance), have still found lowered memory scores in depressed subjects (e.g., Leight & Ellis, 1981). Therefore, the evidence suggests that depressed subjects may indeed adopt an elevated confidence criterion, but that this is not a sufficient explanation for their poor performance on memory tasks.

Additional evidence against explanations in terms of general paucity of responding comes from the observation that equivalent deficits are not shown by depressed subjects on all types of memory task. Depressives show little deficit on immediate recall of trigrams, for example, but show greater deficits with increasing retention intervals (Cohen, Weingartner, Smallberg, Pickar, & Murphy, 1982). They are less impaired on tasks involving recognition memory rather than free recall (Calev & Erwin, 1985; Weingartner, Cohen, Murphy, Martello, & Gerdt, 1981), and show the greatest degree of impairment on recall tasks that require effortful elaborative processing and analysis of information (Ellis et al., 1984; Weingartner & Silberman, 1982).

One way this pattern of findings has been accommodated within an information processing framework involves the proposal that depression does not affect "automatic" processes that proceed effortlessly without imposing capacity demands, but impairs "strategic" processes that are under voluntary control and draw upon the limited pool of cognitive resources available to the subject. Roy-Byrne, Eingartner, Bierer, Thompson, & Post (1986) have presented evidence consistent with this theoretical position. Depressed patients and control subjects were presented with word lists in which some words were repeated. Previous research has demonstrated that, whereas the learning of items in a word list involves strategic processes, the registration of frequency information occurs quite automatically (Hasher & Zacks, 1984). Consistent with this hypothesis, depressed subjects were found to be impaired on the recall of words, but were at least as good as normals in their recall of frequency information. High level structured organization of experimental stimuli in memory, plausibly a product of the strategic processing of this material is notably absent in depressed subjects. For example, depressed patients fail to show normal semantic clustering of related items during recall of word lists (Russell & Beekhuis, 1976; Calev & Erwin, 1985), and fail to show the normal recall advantage for propositions central to the underlying structure of narrative text (Watts & Sharrock, 1987).

The argument that depression affects strategic operations, but not automatic cognitive processes fits nicely with Ellis and Ashbrook's (1987) proposal that depression impairs performance by depleting available cognitive resources. Such a depletion would indeed affect specifically those cognitive operations that make demands for such resources (i.e., strategic processes), while leaving unaffected those operations that run independently from capacity requirements (i.e., automatic processes).

The pattern of deficits which characterize depression are quite consistent with such an account. Indeed Krames and McDonald (1985) have shown that the profile of deficits found in depression are comparable to those found in normal subjects whose processing capacity is reduced by having them simultaneously perform a secondary task. The explanation offered by these researchers for the reduction in processing capacity that depressed subjects appear to allocate to the experimental task is that some capacity is "syphoned off" by task irrelevant processing, specifically the processing of information concerning their depressive state. This position is very similar to the one outlined by Foulds (1952), who explained the paradoxical finding that depressive subjects performance on a maze task is improved by a secondary task involving digit repetition, whereas normal subjects are impaired by this manipulation (Foulds, 1952; Campbell, 1957).

Foulds suggested that the secondary task disrupted depressive preoccupations, and thus freed processing capacity, which could be used for the primary task.

Cognitive Deficits in Anxiety

The majority of studies investigating the possibility that cognitive functioning may be impaired in anxious subjects have not employed patient populations. Some have compared groups of normal subjects high and low in trait anxiety, while others have investigated the effects of elevated state anxiety in a normal sample. The results have been less straightforward than those for depression, though deficits in high anxious subjects have been reported in anagram task performance (e.g., Zarantonello, Slaymaker, Johnson, & Petzel, 1984), analogical reasoning (e.g., Leon & Revelle, 1985), mental arithmetic (e.g., Calvin, Koons, Bingham, & Fink, 1955), general problem solving (e.g., Eliatamby, in M. W. Eysenck, 1982) and a wide range of memory tasks including digit span (e.g., Knox & Grippaldi, 1970), paired associate learning (e.g., Spence & Spence, 1966), alphabet searching (e.g., Eysenck, 1985) and free recall of learned words (e.g., Mueller, 1976). Such deficits are, however, less reliable than those shown by depressed subjects. For example, studies examining the influence of high and low trait anxiety on memory functioning have produced discrepant results.

Although high trait anxiety has often been shown to be associated with poor recall performance (e.g., Mueller, 1977; Mueller & Overcast, 1976; Zatz & Chassin, 1983, 1985; Darke, 1988b), some studies have failed to find any such impairment (e.g., Finch, Anderson, & Kendall, 1976). Indeed a number of researchers have reported a positive relationship between trait anxiety and memory performance (e.g., Haynes & Gormly, 1977). Occasionally, even more complex results emerge, such as the findings of Hodges and Durham (1972), who report a positive relationship between trait anxiety and digit span for high intelligence subjects and a negative relationship for low intelligence subjects.

At least part of the reason for this confusion appears to reflect the fact that trait anxiety is imperfectly correlated with current level of anxious state, and it is the latter which appears to be most directly involved in producing memory deficits. Studies examining the influence of state anxiety produce more consistent results, with M. W. Eysenck (1982) reporting a significant digit span deficit in 11 out of the 12 studies he reviewed that specifically examined high levels of anxious mood. The suggestion that such deficits are state specific is further reinforced by Hodges and Spielberger's (1969) finding that reduced digit span can be induced by stress, but span does not differ in high and low trait subjects. It seems possible therefore that the inconsistency of results when comparing high and low trait subjects may reflect the fact that this distinction may only sometimes be confounded with different levels of state anxiety.

There is also evidence that the presence or absence of a processing deficit will depend upon the level of task difficulty. Spence and Spence (1966) have presented findings from a range of tasks that demonstrate that anxiety impairs performance most profoundly on difficult tasks, while relatively easy tasks are unaffected, or indeed may be improved, by elevated levels of anxiety. While a precise definition of "difficulty" poses a continuing problem for this position, experimental support for this general notion is now widespread. M. W. Eysenck (1982) reports over twenty studies that have confirmed this pattern of interaction between anxiety and task difficulty, with anxiety actually facilitating performance on the easy task version in eight of those experiments.

A number of alternative theories have been proposed to account for differential effects of anxiety on easy and hard tasks. Spence and Spence (1966) adopted a Hullian position, suggesting that anxiety acts as a nonspecific drive state that, in any situation, will make responses with the greatest habit strength disproportionately likely to occur. Spence and Spence conceptualized easy tasks as those in which the correct response has no effective competitor, whereas difficult tasks are those in which the correct response must be discriminated from competing responses with stronger habit strengths. Elevated anxiety will therefore increase the probability of the wrong response in the latter tasks only. While elegant, this account lacks predictive power, since there is no reliable way of determining the number and relative habit strengths of all available responses in advance. A high degree of circularity is therefore inevitable.

Easterbrook's (1959) account of the relationship between arousal and information processing has also been employed to accommodate the observed relationship between task difficulty and performance deficits in anxious subjects. According to Easterbrook, anxiety serves to reduce the range of cues a subject will use when performing a task. Specifically, highly anxious subjects will restrict their consideration to only a few central cues during processing. Whether or not this will result in a performance deficit depends upon the nature of the task. If the task is relatively simple in the sense that it can be performed accurately with few cues, then by eliminating processing of irrelevant cues, anxiety may serve to facilitate performance. In contrast, if the task is complex in that it requires the coordinated processing of a wider range of cues, then anxiety will lead to a performance decrement.

Some problems with potential circularity in defining task difficulty also occur for this account. However, some empirical support for the general position can be found in dual task studies, which typically confirm the prediction that anxiety impairs performance on the secondary (peripheral) task, rather than on the primary (central) task. Also, when additional cues are provided during a learning task, anxious subjects have been found to show less beneficial effects of task relevant cues, and less adverse effects of irrelevant cues than normals (e.g., Bruning, Capage, Kozuh, Young, & Young, 1968; Zaffy & Bruning, 1966). Despite these positive findings, however, there is a great deal of evidence that on many tasks anxious subjects are characterized by elevated levels of distractability (e.g., Dornic, 1977; Dornic & Fernaeus, 1981; M. W. Eysenck, 1988; Pallack, Pittman, Heller, & Munson, 1975). Such findings are inconsistent with accounts that predict a general decrease in distractability for anxious subjects.

The dominant current view concerning the cognitive basis of processing deficits in anxiety, bearing a striking similarity to the theoretical account of depression related deficits just considered, attributes these impairments to a reduction in the capacity of resources allocated to task relevant processing (M. W. Eysenck, 1979, 1981, 1982, 1985, 1988; Mandler & Sarason, 1952; Wine, 1971). M. W. Eysenck specifically implicates the working memory system as the locus of the restriction in capacity.

According to Baddeley (Baddeley, 1979, 1986; Baddeley & Hitch, 1974), working memory is a limited capacity system that shares its available capacity between processing functions and temporary information storage functions. It is centrally involved in a great many strategic processes, though not involved in automatic processes, which run without capacity requirements.

M. W. Eysenck argues that the kind of task difficulties that exaggerate deficits in anxious subjects will be those that impose an increased demand upon working memory resources. There is growing evidence to support this position. Certainly, high level organizational processing, plausibly dependent upon capacity consuming strategies, are particularly impaired in anxious subjects (Mueller, 1976, 1978), whereas retrieval operations that occur automatically, such as the accessing of antecedents for anaphoric terms during text comprehension, are unaffected by anxiety (Darke, 1988a).

In general, memory tasks that use the working memory system are those on which anxious subjects show the greatest deficit. For example, Darke (1988b) points out that working memory will be more important in tasks that simultaneously demand both storage and processing operations, and compared such a task against one requiring only storage operations. Digit span was used in the "storage only" condition, while a task requiring subjects to process sentences and recall the last word in each sentence (introduced by Daneman & Carpenter, 1980, as a test of working memory capacity) was employed in the "processing plus storage" condition. Anxious subjects were most impaired on the latter task; consistent with the hypothesis that their capacity deficit was located in working memory.

M. W. Eysenck (1985) has conducted analyses of task microstructure when presenting subjects with letter transformation problems, such as changing the string of letters "DRLK" to the string of letters four positions later in the alphabet (i.e., HVPO). Overall high anxiety subjects performed worse than low anxiety subjects. However, when he separately examined 12 component processing stages in this task, M. W. Eysenck found that this impairment was restricted to the rehearsal and temporary storage of information (i.e., the operations conducted by the working memory system), and was not evident on such measures as speed of access to letter codes or transformation speed.

As in depression, therefore, it seems plausible that anxiety impairs performance on strategic processing because of a reduction in available cognitive capacity, possibly within the working memory system. Again, it has been argued that this reflects the fact that anxious subjects engage in task irrelevant processing of anxiety relevant information, which usurps this capacity (M. W. Eysenck, 1988; Paulman & Kennelly, 1984; Wine, 1971).

Perhaps the most subjectively obvious manifestation of this capacity consuming task irrelevant processing in anxiety is worry, which Borkovec, Robinson, Prujinsky, & DePree (1983) describe as "a chain of thoughts and images, negatively affect-laden and relatively uncontrollable" (p. 10). Whereas it is consistent with considerable data, this account does not predict the processing advantage occasionally shown by anxious subjects on relatively simple cognitive tasks. M. W. Eysenck accommodates this by proposing that anxiety is associated also with an increase in the amount of effort that subjects will exert on task performance. The concept of effort is not fully elaborated, but in some ways can be considered a motivational variable.

Thus, the actual pattern of performance will depend upon the combined influence of two factors in anxious subjects, a restriction in available processing capacity and an increase in motivation. On tasks that are not highly capacity demanding, therefore, the facilitating effect of the motivational increase may predominate; whereas on tasks requiring more working memory capacity, impairment will be the dominant effect.

Summary of Cognitive Deficits in Emotional Disorders

In summary then, both depressed and anxious subjects show a variety of cognitive impairments, and these appear to be directly related to the level of depressed or anxious affect rather than to trait variables. Memory operations are particularly implicated. Depressed subjects often show some general response deficit, which may be attributable to a motivational deficit. Whereas anxious subjects, in contrast, may be characterized by an increased motivation or effort, but the performance patterns that are found cannot be fully accounted for by response styles.

The aspects of memory that appear to proceed automatically are relatively preserved in both negative affective states, whereas strategic aspects of memory, particularly those which make heavy demands on processing resources, are most disrupted. It therefore appears plausible that depressives and anxious populations may have restricted processing capacity available for many demanding experimental tasks; and a common explanation for this is that some capacity has been diverted to the processing of task irrelevant information related to mood relevant concerns.

Given that levels of anxiety and depression are often highly correlated, one might reasonably ask whether depressed subjects may show such deficits because of their typically elevated anxiety levels, or anxious subjects because of their commonly elevated level of depression, rather than each mood state independently impairing cognition. Little research on cognitive impairment has explicitly focused on dissociating the correlates of these two moods. However, in one exception to this Zarantonello et al. (1984) found that although both depressed subjects and anxious subjects reported elevated cognitive interference during an anagram task, and showed impaired performance, this was related significantly only to the anxiety factor common to both groups of subjects. It remains unclear to what extent these results may be generalized to other aspects of impairment associated with depression.

The "task irrelevant processing" account of cognitive impairments holds that anxious subjects and depressives perform poorly on certain experimental tasks because they are preferentially engaging in other lines of processing. The argument is that the processing of task relevant information is impaired because the processing of mood relevant, but task irrelevant, information takes precedence. This position implies that the emotional valence of the experimental material may be critical in mediating the influence of affective state on performance. As we shall see in the remainder of this chapter, there is indeed considerable evidence that both depression and anxiety are associated with relative processing advantages for information that is emotionally congruent with these conditions.

MODELS OF AFFECT CONGRUENT INFORMATION PROCESSING

The hypothesis that depressed and anxious subjects will show processing advantages for material that shares the same emotional valence as their affective condition has in fact been made explicit by two different theoretical frameworks. The first model, proposed by Beck (1976; Beck, Emery, & Greenberg, 1986; Beck, Rush, Shaw, & Emery, 1979) to accomodate patterns of thinking reported by mood disordered patients, is based primarily on clinical observation. The second model, offered by Bower (1981, 1983, 1985, 1987), was developed in response to empirical data in normal subjects undergoing mood induction procedures in the laboratory. Although these two models were developed independently from different data bases, and are dissimilar in many ways, they nevertheless make parallel predictions concerning the relationship between affective status, and the processing of affectively valenced information. In this section we will examine the central features of each model and consider these predictions in more detail.

Beck's Schema Theory of Mood and Cognition

Central to Beck's formulation is the proposal that the cognitive system "filters" environmental information through pre-existing memory representations known as schemata, which impose their own structure on this new information. This idea can be traced back to the work of Bartlett (1932), and schema based theories enjoy current popularity for a variety of information processing operations including, for example, perception (e.g., Goldstein & Chance, 1985), comprehension (e.g., Galambos & Rips, 1982; White & Carlston, 1983) and memory (e.g., Griggs & Green, 1983). Although different theorists define the construct in subtly different ways, all would agree that a schema is a stored body of knowledge that interacts with the encoding, comprehension, and/or retrieval of new information within its domain, by guiding attention, interpretation, and memory search (Alba & Hasher, 1983; Graesser & Nakamura, 1982). Most would also agree that schemata embody generic knowledge of prototypical environmental regularities, and impose a correspondingly stereotypical organization on new information. Schemata have been proposed to exist for a wide range of complex information including personal stereotypes (e.g., Hamilton, 1983), spatial scenarios (e.g., Biederman, 1982); stereotyped actions (e.g., Nelson, 1977) and complex narratives (Thorndyke, 1977). Novel examples of such stimuli will therefore be processed using the appropriate schematic structure as a blueprint to guide the intake of information, impose structure, resolve ambiguities, and provide supplementary information. At any time, certain schemata may be active in guiding information processing while others remain latent. Ultimately, the integrated representation that is stored will be heavily influenced by the active schema used during encoding. A more complete account of schematic processing is provided by Williams, Watts, MacLeod, and Mathews (1988).

Beck suggests that mood disordered individuals are characterized by overactive idiosyncratic schemata that lead to particular types of processing biases. According to this account, depressive individuals possess "depressogenic schemata," perhaps constructed during earlier life to accommodate important traumatic events involving loss or failure. Essentially, these schemata embody prototypical information concerning such loss events. A parallel account for anxiety suggests that anxious patients possess "danger schemata," again perhaps initially constructed to accommodate genuinely threatening life episodes, but ultimately embodying prototypical information concerning threat events. Although such schemata may remain inactive, or "latent" for many years, they become overactive during episodes of mood disorder; and begin to exert an active influence over information processing, resulting in several types of processing bias. They will direct processing resources towards schema congruent elements of the environment, impose schema consistent interpretations on ambiguous information, and facilitate access to schema congruent memories. Thus, according to Beck, depressed patients will show increased attention to depression congruent stimuli, will resolve ambiguity in a manner that yields the most depressing interpretation, and will recall depression congruent information with disproportionate ease. Similarly, anxious patients will show equivalent biases favoring the processing of threat related material.

Bower's Network Model of Mood and Cognition

In a series of articles Bower (1981, 1987; Bower & Cohen, 1982; Gilligan & Bower, 1984) has independently developed a rather different model of the relationship between affect and information processing, which represents an extension of earlier network theories of human memory. Fundamental to this account is the assumption that memory can be modeled as a large system of interrelated nodes. Each node contains information regarding specific semantic concepts, or elements of events, and related nodes share associative connections. Models of this type have a long and respectable history within the field of cognitive psychology (e.g., Anderson & Bower, 1973; Collins & Loftus, 1975; Collins & Quillian, 1969), and have certain characteristic properties. Accessing information involves activating the relevant memory nodes (which receive inputs from both perceptual processors and a central executive mechanism), beyond some critical threshold level. Such activation will spread through associative connections, to partially activate related nodes. These "primed" nodes will thus be rendered more available, because they will now require less input to exceed the critical level of activation required for access. Associative priming effects of this type have been demonstrated on a wide range of experimental paradigms (e.g., Blank & Foss,

1978; Broadbent & Broadbent, 1979; Morton, 1964, 1981; Neely, 1977).

Bower extended this general framework by suggesting that basic mood states are represented within this associative network by corresponding "emotion nodes." An emotion node is activated when the subject enters that particular mood state. Thus a node corresponding to depression will be activated by the depressed mood state, whereas a node corresponding to anxiety is activated by anxious mood. Over time each emotion node will come to develop associative connections with other nodes in memory space.

Specifically, Bower proposes that those nodes containing information causally related to the occurrence of any particular mood state will develop associative linkages with the corresponding emotion node. Thus nodes concerning negatively valenced concepts and events, such as loss and failure, will develop connections in associative memory with the depression node; nodes containing threat relevant information will share linkages with the anxiety node; those containing positively valenced information will become linked to the node corresponding to happiness, and so on. In general, therefore, any mood node will share associative linkages with those nodes in memory space that contain mood congruent information.

Consider the properties of this associative network. Entering any particular mood state will activate the corresponding emotion node in memory space. This activation will spread through the network to partially activate those nodes sharing associative linkages with this emotion node, which will tend to contain mood congruent information. In this manner, information congruent with current mood will be rendered disproportionately available from memory. Although this network model locates the mechanism underlying mood congruent processing biases in the memory system, it nevertheless predicts the occurrence of such biases on a broad range of cognitive operations. Any processing task that requires access to stored information should be relatively facilitated when this information is congruent with current emotional state.

Bower identifies three large categories of mood congruent processing biases predicted by the model. First, mood should influence relative ability to retrieve emotionally valenced information from memory, with mood congruent material being disproportionately available. Second, it should influence how readily emotional stimuli are perceived (because perception involves mapping an input onto the appropriate stored representation in long term memory), and thus will determine the degree to which such stimuli capture attention. A stimulus that is emotionally consistent with current mood should have a reduced perceptual threshold, and hence a correspondingly increased ability to recruit selective attention. Third, comprehension processes, which involve imposing meaning (accessed from long-term memory) on complex or ambiguous information, should also be biased by emotional state with mood consistent interpretations being favored over alternatives inconsistent with affective state.

Comparing the Schema and Network Models

The two models that have been outlined here differ greatly in important ways. The schema model suggests that mood congruency effects will occur in an active "top down" manner. That is, the differences in information processing are attributed to differences in complex interpretative structures that operate at a high level within the cognitive system to actively guide, control and organize lower level aspects of cognition. Hence, mood congruent biases "filter down" through the system, ultimately producing distortions in basic cognitive operations such as memory and attention.

In contrast, the network model accounts for mood congruency effects in a passive "bottom up" manner. The basic process producing these effects is sited within the single low level mechanism of associative priming, which functions passively and only moderates the relative availability of basic information. However, mood related biases at this low level do "percolate up" through the processing system, ultimately producing mood congruency effects in complex high level cognitive operations such as comprehension and interpretation.

The former account may be more compatible than the latter with Beck's concurrent argument that mood disordered individuals can, through the use of intentional strategies, actively modify these processing biases, but both accounts give rise to remarkably similar predictions concerning the type of mood congruency effects that are likely to exist.

Another distinguishing feature of the two models is their relative emphasis on trait and state aspects of emotion, which may reflect the subject samples considered by each theorist. Beck's account, developed through observation of clinical samples, attributes individual differences in information processing to differences in the nature of the long term representational structures that organize the encoding of new information. Clearly, individual differences in such structures are most likely to be relatively stable, and hence are most easily related to trait aspects of emotion.

On the other hand, Bower's formulation, derived primarily from mood induction studies on normal populations, implicates the current state of activation of any particular emotion node in determining the pattern of processing biases that occur. Because this level of activation is determined solely by present mood, the model deals most easily with the relationship between mood state and information processing.

Despite this difference in emphasis, however, each model has potential mechanisms for accommodating both trait and state emotional influences on cognition. Consider first the schema model. Individuals may differ not only in the range of schemata they possess, which represents a trait variable; but also in the degree to which any particular schema is active at a given time, which represents a state variable. The extent of processing bias observed would thus reflect an interaction of both trait and state emotion.

Depressed mood many activate the most "depressogenic" schema available to any individual. While this may produce state related processing biases, favoring negative information, in all subjects, such biases will be most pronounced in those subjects possessing the most intensely depressogenic schemata. That is, those with a trait vulnerability to depression. Turning to the network model, individuals will differ not only in the degree to which a particular emotion node is currently active (clearly a state variable), but also in the richness of the associative connections that link the emotion node to other nodes containing emotionally congruent information—a structural difference that must therefore represent a trait variable.

Individuals with a common history of experiencing any particular emotion (i.e., those who are high trait for that emotion) will have a richer and stronger network of associative connections between the corresponding emotion node and congruent information in memory. This will reflect the fact that, on each occurrence of the mood, new associative linkages will have been created or old ones strengthened between the emotion node and those nodes containing information related to the cause of the mood on that occasion.

Consequently, according to the network model, emotionally linked processing biases will be determined by an interactive function of both state and trait variables. Specifically, increases in state anxiety may lead to processing biases favoring threat related materials in all subjects to some degree, but this mood will be associated with particularly strong biases in those individuals high on trait anxiety, who will show stronger and more extensive priming of mood congruent information in associative memory.

In summary, although the schema and network accounts represent very different types of models, each developed independently in response to quite separate domains of data, they nevertheless show a remarkable degree of convergence in the predictions that they generate. According to both accounts, an individual's affective status should be associated with pervasive biases, favoring emotionally congruent information, throughout the processing continuum.

The cognitive processes involved should be essentially equivalent for all emotions, with congruency effects occurring, quite automatically, during the encoding of information (i.e., biased perceptual and attentional processes), during comprehension (i.e., biased interpretative processes) and during recall (i.e., biased retrieval processes).

State and trait variables may both be involved, with intensified mood state being associated with the greatest mood congruency effects in individuals having a high trait disposition for that emotion. This predicted relationship between emotion and cognition has potentially important clinical implications. Because the model of the world we construct is ultimately the product of those processing operations, these postulated biases would inevitably lead to internal representations of the environment that are affectively congruent with an individual's emotional state and disposition.

Cognitive models of psychopathology are based on the assumption that individuals respond emotionally, not directly to external events, but to their internal representations of such events. Clearly this leads to the possibility that mood congruent information processing biases, if indeed they do exist, may play a functional role in the development and maintenance of emotional disorders. Teasdale (1983), for example, argues that a reciprocal relationship may exist between emotional condition, and current pattern of information processing. According to this view, an emotion such as anxiety or depression not only elicits mood congruent processing biases, but that mood itself is intensified by the products of that distorted processing, and the processing biases are in turn further magnified by this intensification of mood state. An individual showing sufficiently strong mood congruency effects on any particular emotion would therefore be vulnerable to frequent escalations of that emotional state, mediated by this reciprocal relationship between mood and information processing.

We will now turn to studies that have attempted to evaluate these parallel predictions derived from both schema based and associative network models of emotion and information processing.

EVIDENCE FOR MOOD CONGRUENT INFORMATION PROCESSING

A conceptual distinction has often been drawn between cognitive processes and cognitive products (e.g., Nisbett & Ross, 1980; Rakover, 1983). Although the precise formalization of this distinction has given rise to considerable debate (e.g., Smith & Miller, 1978; White, 1980, 1988), most researchers would agree that consciously accessible thoughts and beliefs represent the products of underlying, low level, cognitive processes. Indeed it has been argued that conscious access is restricted to cognitive products, while the underlying processes themselves defy accurate introspective appraisal (Nisbett & Wilson, 1977). A considerable amount of evidence now exists, gathered primarily through introspection, that suggests that such cognitive products tend to be affect congruent in nature. Whereas this is consistent with the hypothesis that underlying processes, including perception, attention, comprehension, and retrieval, do show emotionally linked biases, the introspective method offers little prospect of adequately investigating this possibility directly (MacLeod, 1987).

Recent research has, however, adopted and adapted experimental paradigms developed within the field of cognitive psychology to investigate the relationship between information processing and emotion. We will first briefly consider some of the findings concerning cognitive products, such as conscious thoughts and accessible beliefs, then go on to examine in more detail recent research on cognitive processes that has employed experimental methods derived from the information processing paradigm.

Cognitive Products in Depression and Anxiety

Depression

Beck (1967) had 50 clinically depressed patients report their predominant thoughts, and noted that themes concerning negative self evaluation, hopelessness, and negative interpretations of the environment were particularly pronounced. These basic findings have been replicated many times (e.g., Blackburn, Jones & Lewin, 1986; Dobson & Shaw, 1986; Eaves & Rush, 1984; Hollon, Kendall, & Lumry, 1986; Ross, Gottfredson, Christensen, & Weaver, 1986) in methodologically improved studies employing more structured assessment instruments such as the Automatic Thoughts Questionnaire (ATQ; Hollon & Kendall, 1980), or the Crandell Cognition Checklist (CCC; Crandell & Chambless, 1986).

In reviewing this literature, Beck and Clark (1988) conclude that the cognitive products of depression are typically automatic thoughts concerning failure, which usually take the form of self-statements. The occurrence of such thoughts tends to be correlated with depressed mood states (Harrell, Chambless, & Calhoun, 1981; Wickless & Kirsch, 1988), and they appear specific to depression rather than characteristic of psychopathology in general.

Thus, for example, Hollon et al. (1986) found that scores on the ATQ, measuring such negative self-statements, were elevated in clinically depressed patients, but not in schizophrenic samples or in other nondepressed psychiatric controls. Similarly, Ingram, Kendall, Smith, Donnell, & Ronan (1987) found elevations of negative automatic thoughts concerning failure in depressed, but not in anxious subjects.

There is some evidence that depressed subjects are also characterized by an increased number of dysfunctional attitudes; that is, essentially irrational beliefs that are depressogenic in content. Scores on the Dysfunctional Attitudes Scale (DAS; Weissman & Beck, 1978) and the Irrational Beliefs Test (IBT; Jones, 1968) often have been found to be highly correlated with severity of depression in a variety of subject samples (e.g., Cook & Peterson, 1986; Hollon et al., 1986; Norman, Miller, & Dow, 1988). Beck (1967) argues that such beliefs pre-exist depression and are involved in the generation and maintenance of depressed mood state.

Similarly, Hollon et al. (1986) suggest that the attitudes assessed by the DAS represent "stable trait-like phenomena." DAS scores are not, however, invariant for any given individual. Recovery from a depressive episode is correlated with a reduction in reported irrational beliefs (Eaves & Rush, 1984; Persons & Rao, 1985; Simons, Garfield, & Murphy, 1984). Even more striking evidence that expression of dysfunctional attitudes may be state-sensitive is the demonstration by Miranda and Persons (1988) that DAS scores can be reliably manipulated by temporarily induced negative mood state. Subjects with a history of vulnerability for depression showed an increase in DAS score as depressed mood state was increased, whereas subjects with no such history of depressive vulnerability showed no relationship between mood state and DAS score.

Thus, the availability of depressogenic beliefs appears to be determined by the interactive influence of both trait and state aspects of depression, a finding consistent with the predictions of both theoretical models of mood and cognition outlined here.

Anxiety

Like depression, anxiety has been found to be associated with an increased prevalence of mood congruent thoughts that, in general, appear to be related to social or physical dangers. Beck, Laude, and Bohnert (1974) interviewed 32 clinically anxious patients and reported the presence of thoughts concerning the anticipation of physical harm, and/or psychosocial trauma in all subjects. In this study the degree of anxiety associated with such thoughts was directly related to a patient's evaluation of their credibility.

Hibbert (1984), also using interview assessments of clinically anxious subjects, has more recently reported similar findings, with thoughts concerning personal danger being particularly common in patients experiencing intense episodes of state anxiety. Using more reliable structured questionnaires this general finding (that anxious subjects do indeed experience mood congruent threat related thoughts) has been widely replicated with a variety of anxiety linked disorders such as Simple Phobias, Agoraphobia, Social Phobia, Panic Disorder and Generalized Anxiety Disorder (e.g., Chambless, Caputo, Bright, & Gallagher, 1984; Ganellen, Matuzas, Uhlenhuth, Glass, & Easton, 1986; Mizes, Landolf-Fritsche, & Grossman-McKee, 1987; Sutton-Simon & Goldfried, 1979).

Furthermore, this association between anxiety and threat related cognitive content is not restricted to clinical samples, but has been demonstrated in normal samples including students (e.g., Davison, Feldman, & Osborn, 1984; Sewitch & Kirsch, 1984), schoolchildren (Fox, Houston, & Pittner, 1983; Zatz & Chassin, 1985), and mothers under stress (Parkinson & Rachman, 1981). The finding that threat related thoughts can be induced by stress indicates that thought content is at least partially associated with level of state anxiety. However, no studies have attempted to directly evaluate the relative roles of trait and state variables when investigating the content of thought in anxious subjects.

The thoughts that characterize anxiety can be distinguished from those that are associated with depression. Sewitch and Kirsch (1984) had 70 students keep detailed journals concerning their state anxiety levels and thoughts. They found that elevated anxiety was associated with thoughts concerning threat, rather than with thoughts concerning loss. This pattern was unchanged in subgroups of subjects explicitly "trained" to expect thoughts concerning loss when anxious, thus reducing the probability that the results reflect demand characteristics of the study. Wickless and Kirsch (1988) extended this approach by having subjects record moods other than anxiety, in addition to their thoughts, which were subsequently subdivided into those concerning threat and those concerning loss. Multiple regression analysis confirmed that anxiety alone was uniquely predicted by thoughts of threat, whereas thoughts of loss were predictors of depression. Beck, Brown, Steer, Eidelson, and Riskind (1987) have shown a similar dissociation between the subtypes of thoughts characteristic of depression and anxiety. Thus the content of thinking appears to be mood congruent in nature.

There is less evidence that anxious and depressed subjects can be reliably distinguished on the basis of underlying beliefs. Irrational beliefs have been less extensively evaluated in anxiety than in depression. But, there is reasonable evidence that high trait anxiety subjects show a pattern of elevated irrational beliefs, relative to low trait anxiety controls, similar to that shown by depressives (Deffenbacher, Zwemer, Whisman, Hill, & Sloan, 1986; Zwemer & Deffenbacher, 1984).

Furthermore, as with depression, it appears that induced anxious mood can inflate reported irrational beliefs. Thus, for example, Davison, Feldman, and Osborne (1984) found elevated scores on the Irrational Beliefs Test for normal subjects subjected to an anxiety mood induction procedure. Whereas state anxiety is implicated in the degree to which irrational beliefs are reportable, there is insufficient research to determine whether for anxiety, as in depression, state induced elevations in irrational belief scores are disproportionately great in high trait subjects.

In summary, introspective self-report data do indeed suggest that the content of thought tends to be mood congruent in nature. Cognitive content can therefore be distinguished in depressed and anxious subjects, with the former individuals characterized by sad thoughts concerning loss and failure, and the latter by fearful thoughts concerning threat and danger. Irrational beliefs are, however, elevated in both groups. Such elevations have been found in samples high in vulnerability for each emotion (i.e., in high trait samples), and can also be produced by induced mood state.

With depression there is evidence that state induced elevations in the report of irrational beliefs is greatest in trait vulnerable individuals, though this issue has not been investigated for anxiety. These results are generally consistent with the models of mood congruent information processing addressed here, but this type of experimental approach has severe limitations. It requires that subjects provide accurate reports of their actual thinking. There is considerable literature claiming to demonstrate that individuals are generally extremely poor at providing accurate report through introspection (cf. Nisbett & Wilson, 1977). They may nevertheless show great willingness to comply with the request to supply such information despite this inaccuracy.

There is a real possibility that artifacts, such as perceived experimenter demand, may influence self-reports of this type, and the above data must therefore be viewed with some caution. Furthermore, even if we assume that such self-report data are valid, the existence of mood congruent cognitive content need not imply that fundamental cognitive processes are biased in ways that favor mood congruent information, as both theoretical models claim.

Introspection was discredited as an adequate experimental technique for the investigation of cognitive processes more than 60 years ago and, consequently, the entire study of mental events was dismissed as an acceptable focus of scientific psychological investigation for the next 30 years. The return to mentalism, which began in the 1950s and has ultimately led to the current dominance of the information processing approach within experimental psychology, was only made possible by the development of objective experimental paradigms that permitted predictions concerning cognitive processes to be tested without recourse to introspection. In recent years such paradigms have been used to test predictions concerning mood congruent information processing.

Cognitive Processes in Depression and Anxiety

In this section, we will review research that has used paradigms adopted or adapted from information processing psychology to investigate affect congruent processing biases in memory, comprehension, and attention. Each type of cognitive operation will be considered in turn, and its relationships with both depression and anxiety will be described and compared. Whenever possible, we will attempt to isolate the relative contributions of state and trait emotion to any biases that occur, and to relate the pattern of findings to the two theoretical models under consideration.

Memory

Since the early 1900s, it has been observed that the emotional valence of stimulus material may potentially affect its memorability (e.g., Baxter, Yamanda, & Washburn, 1917; Morgan, Mull, & Washburn, 1919). In normal populations the most common finding is that pleasant information is more accessible than unpleasant information, and can thus be recalled more accurately and more rapidly, though Lishman (1972a, 1972b, 1974) has found that this bias may be reduced in the subjects who score high on the neuroticism scales.

Indeed Lloyd and Lishman (1975) found a significant correlation between neuroticism score and the recall speed of negative relative to positive information. Because the personality trait of neuroticism is correlated with trait and state anxiety, and with depression, this finding is consistent with the above predictions that affectively congruent information will be disproportionately accessible from memory. When we turn to more recent studies, which have examined memory for affectively toned material in depression and anxiety separately, we find that there is considerably more supportive evidence from work on depression than from research on anxiety. We will consider each emotion in turn.

Depression. There is extensive evidence that depressed subjects do show retrieval advantages for negatively valenced information, thus reversing the normal advantage for positive material shown by nondepressed subjects. This pattern of mood congruent recall in depression has been found for stimulus materials ranging from real life autobiographical memory (e.g., Rholes, Riskind, & Lane, 1987; Teasdale & Fogarty, 1979; Teasdale, Taylor, & Fogarty, 1980; Williams & Broadbent, 1986a), to lists of phrases (e.g., Forgas & Bower, 1987; Laird, Wagener, Halal, & Szegda, 1982), sets of words (e.g., Bradley & Mathews, 1983; D. A. Clark & Teasdale, 1985; Dobson & Shaw, 1987; McDowell, 1984), or even nonsense trigrams differing in rated likeability

(Slife, Miura, Thompson, Shapiro, & Gallagher, 1984).

Some of this research has contrasted populations of clinically depressed patients with normal control subjects. Clark and Teasdale (1982) presented both groups with neutral words as "cues" and asked subjects to report the first memory elicited in association to this word. By subsequently having these responses categorized according to their hedonic tone, they were able to show that the depressed patients recalled more negatively valenced memories, whereas the control produced more positive memories. Williams and Broadbent (1986a) confirmed that this selectivity does indeed appear to reflect an increased ability to recall mood congruent events, rather than simply a preference to do so when given a choice. Williams and Broadbent presented suicide attempters and normal controls with emotionally valenced cues, such as "happy" or "hurt," and required them to report a personal memory hedonically related to this cue. Even when the type of memory required was thus constrained, the suicide attempters exhibited shorter latencies to produce specific negative memories than specific positive memories, whereas this pattern was reversed in control subjects.

One could argue that these effects may not be caused by differences in retrieval processes, but may rather reflect differences in past experience. That is, the subject groups may actually differ in the distributions of memories that they possess, with the relative accessibility of negative events from episodic memory in depressed subjects reflecting the greater number of such events stored in those subjects' memory. However, similar memory biases have been reported in depressed patients when recall for experimentally presented material is tested. The precise nature of the encoding task may be of considerable importance in determining whether such effects occur.

Roth and Rehm (1980) found no difference between depressed patients and control subjects in their relative abilities to recall pleasant and unpleasant words they had previously encountered in an incidental learning task in which they rated each word's "likeability." Frith et al. (1983) also failed to find differential recall of pleasant and unpleasant words by clinically depressed patients following a similar incidental learning task involving assigning a pleasantness rating to each item.

However, McDowell (1984) argued that such rating tasks provide strong recall cues that mask the effect of depression. McDowell presented a list consisting of similar words to clinically depressed subjects and nondepressed controls and gave free recall instructions. Mood congruent recall patterns were then quite clear, with the depressed patients recalling more of the unpleasant words, and the controls recalling more pleasant words.

The most reliable mood congruent recall effects have been found using trait adjectives in an incidental recall paradigm in which subjects initially rate the degree to which each word is self-destructive. A great many studies have found that subsequent recall is relatively improved for trait adjectives that are mood congruent. Thus depressed patients, unlike nondepressed controls, show a relative recall advantage for the negative trait words (e.g., Bradley & Mathews, 1983, 1988; Derry & Kuiper, 1981; Mathews & Bradley, 1983).

In contrast, when the incidental learning task involves deciding the degree to which each word is descriptive of some specified individual other than the self, no such mood congruency recall occurs.

McDowell (1984) has argued that depressed subjects recall more negative items from a word list because, while learning the list, these items are processed selectively, at the expense of mood incongruent items. Consistent with this account, he has shown that depressed patients only show mood congruent recall when they have been presented with a "mixed" list of words, containing both pleasant and unpleasant items. If the words are presented in two separate lists, each containing items of a singel valence, then both lists are recalled equally.

Not all findings are entirely consistent with McDowell's account, however. For example, using the self-referent encoding paradigm, Derry and Kuiper (1981) had subjects present themselves with each word at a self-paced rate. Although depressed subjects recalled the negative trait words disproportionately well, they actually spent *less* time looking at these items than the positive words during encoding.

Even more powerful evidence that emotionally congruent recall effects in depression cannot be attributed solely to individual differences in past experience, comes from the common observation that relative ability to retrieve positive and negative information is affected by mood changes that follow the encoding of this information. State linked changes in mood congruent recall have been observed in clinically depressed patients (e.g., Bradley & Mathews, 1988; Clark & Teasdale, 1982; Dobson & Shaw, 1987; Slife et al., 1984).

Clark and Teasdale (1982) studied patients who showed diurnal fluctuations in their level of depression. They found that the probability of a subject offering a negative autobiographical memory in response to a neutral cue word increased, whereas the probability of offering a positive memory decreased as that subject's level of depression intensified during the day.

Similarly, studies that have examined recovery from clinical depression have found a reduction or reversal of the negative recall bias as mood improves. Thus, for example, Slife et al. (1984) found that the recall advantage for trigrams rated as "disliked" over those rated as "liked," shown by 23 elderly depressives, disappeared as their mood improved during therapy. On completion of therapy, however, these subjects showed the same recall advantage for "liked" trigrams as was shown by nondepressed controls.

Dobson and Shaw (1987) tested and retested clinical depressives undergoing treatment. These patients recalled more negative words than control subjects at test time 1. For the subgroup of patients showing no mood improvement at time 2, this recall pattern remained unchanged. However, on this second test occasion, those patients showing a remission of their depression now produced the same recall profile as the nondepressed controls.

Further evidence that the retrievability of valenced information is associated with depressed mood state comes from research using mood induction procedures, in normal populations. For example, Teasdale and his colleagues have found that induced depression in college students reduces their retrieval latency for negative information relative to positive information, and increases the relative probability of their recalling negative events from autobiographical memory in response to neutral cue words (Teasdale & Fogarty, 1979; Teasdale & Russell, 1983; Teasdale, Taylor, & Fogarty, 1980).

Typically, such mood inductions have employed the Velten procedure, in which subjects read mood descriptive statements and attempt to establish a congruent mood state (Velten, 1968). Rholes, Riskind, and Lane (1987) have found that, while somatic statements such as "I feel tired and listless" and cognitive self-evaluative statements such as "I am worthless" both induced equivalent depressed mood, negative recall biases are more likely for the latter form of induction. However, such memory biases have been induced by a range of more subtle inductions. For example, Laird et al. (1982) were able to influence the relative recall of affectively toned phrases, in a mood congruent manner, by a facial muscle manipulation which, although its function was disguised by a cover story, resulted in a smiling, or pouting expression.

This discussion provides a small sample of the research that has demonstrated a memory bias favoring the retrieval of negative information in depression. Although it is clear that depressed mood plays a role in mediating this bias, the relative role of state and trait variables remains largely untested. In a large part, this reflects a failure to adequately discriminate these two constructs in depression, with no consensus view having been adopted concerning which questionnaire scores represent trait or state measures (cf. Mayer & Bower, 1985). Nevertheless, the general pattern of findings is clearly consistent with the predictions that arise from both the network and schema theories of the relationship between emotion and cognition.

Anxiety. Both the network and schema models predict the relationship between memory and anxiety should essentially parallel that found with depression, though the retrieval advantage should be demonstrated on anxiety congruent information. In contrast to the extensive supportive literature for this prediction in the area of depression, however, very little empirical support exists for the prediction that anxious subjects will show facilitated memory for threat related information. Indeed, the paucity of published experimental work on memory for valenced information in anxiety is striking, given the voluminous research on this topic in depression, the very considerable literature on other aspects of information processing in anxiety, and the salience of the prediction that biased emotional recall should be observed in anxious subjects.

One plausible explanation is that other researchers pursuing such hypothetical recall biases for threat related information in anxiety have come up with the same null results as we have repeatedly encountered in our own laboratory. There are, nevertheless, a few published studies on this topic that we will consider in some detail. Two experiments that could be taken as providing supportive evidence for the mood congruency hypothesis have important methodological flaws. In contrast, most of the studies without flaws suggest that anxiety is not associated with facilitated retrieval of threat related information.

The first study claiming to have demonstrated facilitated recall of emotionally threatening information in anxious subjects was conducted by Nunn, Stevenson, and Whalan (1984), and involved a comparison of agoraphobic patients and nonanxious controls. Both groups of subjects were presented with word lists that, according to Nunn et al., contained both threatening and nonthreatening items. All subjects were then given a memory test for these words. The agoraphobic subjects, unlike the control subjects, showed facilitated recall for the threatening words. Superficially, this would appear to support the hypothesis that anxiety is associated with enhanced memory for threatening information. However, a closer look at the stimulus materials employed by Nunn et al. (1984) casts considerable doubt on the necessity of this conclusion.

The problem arises because the threatening words used in this experiment consisted of such items as *cinema, travel,* and *street*. Whereas these may be threatening stimuli for the agoraphobic group, they constitute neutral stimuli for the control subjects. This study cannot, therefore, compare the relative retrievability of threatening stimuli across the two groups, as only one group encountered any threat stimuli. The observed experimental results may simply reflect the well established fact that memory, under certain conditions, is generally better for emotional than for neutral information (e.g., Bower, 1981; Strongman & Russell, 1986), because in Nunn et al.'s study the threat words were emotional for the agoraphobic subjects only. Furthermore, a recent attempt by Pickles and van den Broek (1986) to replicate Nunn et al.'s results, with appropriate methodological refinements, failed to find any evidence of facilitated recall for emotionally congruent information in an agoraphobic population.

A more recent experiment by Greenberg and Beck (1989) also appears to offer support for the mood congruency hypothesis with anxious patients, whereas in fact this is only illusory. These researchers employed an encoding task similar to that used in studies on depression (e.g., Bradley & Mathews, 1983; Derry & Kuiper, 1981), requiring subjects to decide whether or not trait adjectives were descriptive of themselves, the world, or the future. In an unexpected recall task, Greenberg and Beck appeared to show that anxious patients, but not normal controls, remembered more anxiety related traits words, such as *disturbed* or *frightening,* than nonanxiety words such as *worthy* and *optimistic*.

A closer look at this study, however, reveals that recall was only scored for words that had received a "yes" response during encoding, and that the anxious patients had endorsed a disproportionate number of anxiety relevant items at this time. Thus the pool of anxiety related words that *could* be scored as recalled was disproportionately great for the anxious patients, leading inevitably to an artificially inflated recall score for such items in this subject group. No memory bias can be inferred therefore from the findings.

In fact, when a methodologically appropriate self-referent task employing threat relevant and neutral traits was conducted on generalized anxiety patients, with a subsequent incidental memory task testing recall for all the words presented, Mogg, Mathews, and Weiman (1987) found no evidence to support the mood congruency hypothesis. Indeed, exactly the opposite results were produced, with the anxious patients alone showing disproportionately poor memory for the anxiety relevant traits.

A signal detection analysis demonstrated that this impaired memory for mood congruent information in anxious subjects was due to a genuine reduced sensitivity for such information (i.e., there was a significant d' effect) rather than occurring because of a different response bias across the subject groups (i.e., there was no β effect).

This finding of a reverse memory bias in anxiety, impairing retrieval of threat related information, has also been reported elsewhere in the literature. Watts, Trezise, and Sharrock (1986) obtained similar results with spider phobics who, relative to control subjects, showed impaired recognition memory for large, card mounted spiders, in an incidental learning paradigm.

Even more recently, Foa, McNally, and Murdock (1989) have conducted a careful investigation of the relationship between anxiety and emotional memory. Using the self-reference incidental encoding paradigm that has yielded such powerful mood congruency effects with depression, these researchers tested recall in speech anxious subjects undergoing a state anxiety induction procedure. Anxiety level was systematically elevated, by leading subjects to believe they would be required to give a speech, either during learning, during recall, or on both occasions. Though each of these manipulation conditions reliably increased physiological measures of anxiety, such as heart rate, this was never associated with a relative increase in the number of anxiety relevant words that were subsequently recalled. Indeed, the anxiety words were recalled least often by those subjects who showed the greatest increase in heart rate.

Before leaving this section, we should mention one study that has found improved memory for threat words in anxious subjects. McNally, Foa, and Donnell (1988), once again using the self-reference encoding paradigm, investigated incidental memory for anxiety related and nonanxiety related words in panic disorder patients and normal controls. Panic disorder subjects alone did indeed show a tendency to recall mostly anxiety words, whereas the control subjects showed the opposite effect, recalling less anxiety related than neutral words.

However, as this single supportive finding stands in contrast to the results of most previous research on anxiety, including their own, it seems most likely, as McNally et al. suggest, that the memory bias may be a characteristic of panic disorder alone, rather than a general feature of elevated anxiety. If so, although interesting, this finding cannot be taken as adequate support for the general models of emotion and information processing currently under consideration. We conclude, therefore, that mood congruent recall is not a universal feature of all emotional conditions. Whereas it occurs reliably with depressed subjects, this is not the case with generalized anxiety or phobic subjects. Mogg (1988) has reported a long series of failures to find mood congruent recall effects in generalized anxiety patients, using a wide range of stimulus materials including not only words but also emotionally valenced short stories and pictures.

As we have seen, with the exception of McNally et al.'s study of panic disorder, significant effects in methodologically sound experiments tended to occur in the opposite direction of that predicted by network and schema theory, with memory for mood congruent information being relatively impaired in anxiety. So far, the relative contribution of trait and state anxiety to any such impairment has not been adequately investigated.

It also remains uncertain whether any of the described emotional memory effects, associated with either depression or anxiety, are *automatic,* in the sense that they operate unconsciously without volition, or are *controlled,* reflecting deliberately adopted strategies. This issue has not yet been addressed explicitly by appropriate research. However, the finding that mood congruent retrieval effects in depression are dependent on the types of encoding tasks used suggests that strategic factors may be of some importance.

Comprehension

Both the network model and the schema model predict that comprehension will be biased by a subject's emotional status, such that emotionally congruent interpretations of ambiguous information will be disproportionately probable. This general prediction has been tested for both depression and anxiety, and the general findings are predominantly supportive. Many of the paradigms used, however, do require that subjects explicitly report their interpretation of ambiguous stimulus information. The problems associated with such data already have been discussed. Various experiments have overcome these problems to differing degrees. Once again we will consider research on depression and anxiety in turn.

Depression. The most transparent measure of interpretative bias that often has been used to study comprehension in depression is the Cognitive Bias Questionnaire (CBQ; Krantz & Hammen, 1979). This instrument provides a brief description of events, and asks subjects to choose one of four possible responses. The chosen response is considered to indicate the degree to which a negative interpretation was initially imposed on the event. Numerous studies have shown that depressed patients show elevated CBQ scores, consistent with the possibility that they are showing a negative interpretative bias for the original event (e.g., Hamilton & Abramson, 1983; Miller & Norman, 1986; Norman, Miller, & Dow, 1988; Norman, Miller, & Klee, 1983).

A pattern of negatively distorted interpretations has been shown by depressed subjects on many other experimental tasks also. Such distortions are often found on evaluative judgments made by subjects when assessing their own performance. For example, Cane and Gotlib (1985) videotaped two groups of subjects, differing in naturally occurring level of depression, while they performed a social skills type of task. Independent blind raters judging the tapes gave equivalent ratings for the performance of each group of subjects. When judging their own performance, however, the high depression group gave poorer evaluations than did the independent raters, whereas the low depression group's self-ratings were consistent with these independent ratings. Distorted evaluations of one's own performance appears to be related to depression as a state, rather than representing a stable personality variable. Thus such negatively biased interpretations can be elicited by mood induction procedures.

Forgas, Bower, and Krantz (1984) videotaped short interviews with student subjects who returned the following day and, following the induction of a happy or sad mood, rated their performance from this recording. Using a time sampling method, they judged at 5 second intervals whether they were engaged in neutral, prosocial or antisocial behaviors. Subjects in an induced happy mood gave mainly prosocial ratings, whereas those in the sad mood gave disproportionately high numbers of antisocial ratings. Once again, objective judges rated the actual performance of both groups to be equivalent.

Whereas the finding that negative evaluation of self-efficacy and performance is increased in depressed moods appears to be quite reliable (Bandura, 1986; Kavanagh & Bower, 1985), the possibility that it may reflect demand effects is difficult to dismiss, especially in those studies that explicitly manipulate mood state. However, similar interpretative biases are found in studies examining types of judgments less likely to be influenced by demand, and employing subtle mood manipulations unlikely to be detected by the subject.

One such study, which examined happy rather than sad mood, was conducted by Isen, Shalker, Clark, and Carp (1978). These researchers induced a positive affective state in subjects in a shopping mall by presenting them with a free pen, supposedly as an advertising promotion. Elsewhere in the mall, subjects and controls who had received no gift, were asked to take part in a consumer survey on cars and television sets. Subjects in the happy mood induction condition gave reliably more positive evaluations of their own car and television set, than did the subjects in the control condition.

Schwartz and Clore (1983) have used similarly subtle procedures to induce sad moods (e.g., by manipulating the attractiveness of the testing room) or have taken advantage of naturally occurring negative mood inductions (e.g., by testing subjects on days when the weather is particularly poor). Such inductions are associated with an increase in the degree to which a wide range of personal circumstances, including one's life as a whole, are evaluated negatively. Demand-based explanations of these effects may seem unlikely given the inconspicuous nature of the mood induction procedures. The improbability of such accounts is further increased by Schwartz and Clore's (1983) additional finding that alerting the subject to the mood induction variable actually eliminated its effect on evaluative judgments. That is, if the experimenter commented on the bad weather before testing then subjects showed no more negative evaluations than did those subjects tested when the weather was better.

These findings are clearly inconsistent with an explanation attributing the biased evaluations to experimenter demand, because highlighting the critical variable could only plausibly serve to increase this demand. The finding is, however, consistent with Schwartz and Clore's (1983) claim that mood will only influence judgement if people consider their affective state to be a source of information relevant to the judgment they are asked to make—an assumption often erroneously made by default. When asked to evaluate their marriage, for example, subjects may use their affective state as a source of information to make this judgment (implicitly reasoning, perhaps, "if I feel happy then I must have a good marriage"). Highlighting an alternative source of this positive affective state serves to reduce the probability of subjects erroneously considering it relevant to the judgement task.

Anxiety. There is also considerable evidence that supports the existence of an anxiety linked bias in complex comprehension processes, leading to distortions in the evaluation of risk and in the interpretation of ambiguous stimuli. Typically, when anxious subjects are asked to estimate the risk of various types of uncertain events actually occurring to them—a judgement that requires the application of fairly complex cognitive heuristics (Tversky & Kahneman, 1974, 1982)—they provide inflated estimates of the probability that they will experience negative events (Butler & Mathews, 1983, 1987). This does not reflect a general inflation of probability estimates, because anxiety is not associated with an increase in the perceived probability of experiencing positive events or with any modification of probability estimates for either positive or negative events occurring to people other than oneself.

This effect has been recorded in generalized anxiety patients by Butler and Mathews (1983), who had subjects give probability ratings for a list of specified events. Anxious patients gave risk estimates for positive events that were equivalent to those given by normal controls. However the patients inflated their estimated probability for personally experiencing the negative events.

A subsequent study by Butler and Mathews (1987) clearly demonstrated that this increase in subjective risk for negative events is mediated by both trait and state anxiety. Students showing an increase in state anxiety across two test sessions, which differed in proximity to an important examination (i.e., one month before vs. one day before this exam), also showed an increase in subjective risk judgements for personally experiencing negative, but not positive, events. The breadth of this distortion, however, was moderated by level of trait anxiety. In low trait subjects the increased risk was restricted to the subcategory of negative events related to the source of state anxiety (i.e., anticipated examination performance), such as the possibility of misunderstanding an exam question. For the high trait group alone, however, these inflated risk estimates were generalized to negative events unrelated to exam performance, such as the possibility of being involved in a motor vehicle accident.

Thus state anxiety increases were associated with distorted risk estimates over a wider domain in the high trait anxiety subjects. It will be recalled that this is the precise pattern predicted by both the schema account and the network account described earlier. According to Beck's model, state anxiety may activate "danger schemata," but the degree to which such schemata will be extensively elaborated—and hence will produce the wide ranging distortions in information processing when active—will depend upon level of trait anxiety.

Bower's network theory also attributes the distortions to the spread of activation from the anxiety node in memory space, with the original activation in this node reflecting level of state anxiety. However, the richness of associative connections from this anxiety node, and hence the semantic scope of the mood's priming effect, will represent a trait variable.

Research employing ambiguous stimuli has supported the hypothesis that anxious subjects show interpretative biases favoring threat related meanings. Again, self-report has sometimes been employed. For example, Butler and Mathews (1983) asked anxious patients and controls to indicate their probable interpretations of short ambiguous scenarios, such as being awakened in the night by a noise. The patients ranked threatening interpretations as being more likely to come to mind (such as the presence of a burglar) than did the nonanxious controls.

Subsequent performance measures, with less salient demand characteristics, have been consistent with this kind of finding. For example, we presented subjects with a spelling test, disguised among other psychometric measures, in which they were to write down words as they were spoken on tape (Eysenck, MacLeod, & Mathews, 1987). Distributed within this word list was a pool of twenty-eight homophones (i.e., words with one sound but two different meanings), each with a threatening and a neutral interpretation that differed in spelling. Examples included: dye/die, pane/pain, grown/groan, and gilt/guilt.

Subjects' spellings revealed the interpretation that they had imposed on these ambiguous auditory stimuli. A highly significant correlation was found between trait anxiety score and the number of threat spellings produced. Thus, the trait anxious subjects were more likely to impose the threatening meaning upon these ambiguous words. The correlation between state anxiety and this interpretative bias was less pronounced, but trait and state measures were so highly correlated that it was impossible to distinguish clearly their relative contribution in this study.

A more recent study by Mathews, Richards, and M. W. Eysenck (1989), using the same paradigm, suggests that state anxiety may indeed play some role in mediating this effect. Clinically anxious patients were found to produce more threat spellings, for the homophone stimuli, than did normal control subjects. A group of recovered anxiety patients were also included in this study, however, and their tendency to produce threat spellings fell in between the current patients and the control subjects.

It seems possible, therefore, that this anxiety linked interpretative bias, to some extent, is attenuated as mood improves during recovery. Nevertheless, in this second study, correlations of this effect were consistently greater with trait than with state anxiety. Therefore, it seems probable that a real association does exist between trait anxiety and interpretative bias.

We are currently extending our investigation of these anxiety linked biases in comprehension, using more complex materials (i.e., sentences or short passages) and more subtle dependent variables (i.e., false recognition or comprehension latency). In an unpublished study, M. W. Eysenck, Mathews, and Richards (reported in Williams et al., 1988, p. 141) presented subjects initially with a taped list of sentences including ambiguous items with a threat related and a neutral interpretation, such as *The men watched as the chest was opened* or *Working behind bars gave Sam a new view of life*. In a subsequent recognition memory test, these subjects encountered one disambiguated version of each sentence, that could retain either the neutral or the threat meaning, such as *The men watched as the box was opened,* or *Working in jail gave Sam a new view of life.*

Clinically anxious patients endorsed more of the threat versions in this recognition test than did nonanxious control subjects. The potential role of state anxiety was again implied by the observation that recovered anxiety patients showed equivalent results to control subjects, differing significantly from their currently anxious counterparts.

The existence of a mood congruent interpretative bias in anxiety is thus well supported by experimental research, with considerable evidence indicating that a similar effect also occurs in depression. Mood state appears to play some role in mediating interpretation of emotionally valenced ambiguous stimuli though it also appears, particularly in the anxiety research, that trait differences may also be influential. Indeed, investigation of anxiety linked distortions to subjective risk estimations has shown that the actual pattern of probability judgments given for positive and negative events depends upon the joint function of trait and state anxiety.

Attention/Perception

Turning to work on encoding processes, we also find considerable evidence supporting the existence of mood congruent attentional bias. However, this bias does not appear with equal consistency in anxiety and depression. The situation with attention represents a reversal of that found with memory, in that anxious subjects show reliable mood congruency effects that are more difficult to obtain with depressed subjects. For this reason we will review the work on anxiety first, before going on to consider attentional processes in depression.

Anxiety. Consistent with both network and schema theory, it has been claimed that anxiety is associated with an enhanced ability to detect fear relevant words under conditions where these are not readily identifiable. Experimental evidence for this claim has been provided by studies examining anxiety related clinical disorders such as agoraphobia and social phobias (Burgess et al., 1981), and obsessional disorders (Foa & McNally, 1986). These studies have presented fear relevant and neutral words to the unattended ear of a dichotic listening task, while requiring subjects to "shadow," or repeat aloud, information presented to the other ear.

The anxious subjects demonstrated an increased ability to detect the fear relevant stimuli. This enhanced sensitivity to such stimuli appears to vary with mood state. Foa and McNally, for example, found that it was eliminated following successful treatment of their obsessional subjects.

Conversely, Parkinson and Rachman (1981) have found that a similar effect is shown by normal subjects when they are experiencing stress. Mothers who were in a high state of anxiety because their children were about to undergo surgery, showed a disproportionate ability to identify fear relevant, but not neutral, words embedded in white noise.

Although these results are consistent with the mood congruency hypothesis, they are vulnerable to an alternative explanation attributing the effects to a guessing bias. In the above studies, all subjects would plausibly obtain partial information about the experimental stimuli, from which they could guess at each word's identity. Thus, for example, all subjects may perceive a sound something like "... .ick" in the unattended ear or embedded in the white noise. If anxious subjects tend to produce mood congruent guesses, then they may be more inclined than nonanxious subjects to guess that the word is "sick", rather than "pick" or "chick". Such a guessing bias would lead to the observed pattern of results without indicating that anxiety actually leads to enhanced perceptual sensitivity for threat related material.

However, other paradigms have produced convergent evidence for the mood congruency hypothesis in anxious subjects without requiring that these subjects attempt to identify the experimental stimuli. Indeed some studies explicitly require that subjects ignore emotionally valenced distractor stimuli during performance of some central task, and indirectly measure whether anxiety is associated with difficulty ignoring threat related distractor stimuli.

One methodology used for this purpose has adapted the color naming paradigm introduced by Stroop (1938). Subjects are required to rapidly name the ink color in which various words are written, while ignoring the meaning of these words. Stroop found that subjects could not completely avoid processing the meaning of the words, and that color naming latencies were increased when the word itself was a color name incongruent with the ink color (e.g., the word *red* written in blue ink).

Subsequent research has shown that such color naming latencies are increased by manipulations that serve to make the word's meaning more difficult to ignore (e.g., Warren, 1972; Geller & Shaver, 1976). The hypothesis that subjects will selectively attend to mood congruent stimuli thus leads to the prediction that anxious subjects should be disproportionately slow to color name threat related words, and experimental evidence generally confirms this hypothesis. Ray (1979) demonstrated that college students approaching an important examination were slower to color name exam related than unrelated words. This effect was particularly pronounced in those subjects showing the greatest levels of state anxiety.

Research has confirmed this general finding with a variety of anxiety related clinical disorders. Watts, McKenna, Sharrock, and Trezise (1986) found that spider phobics showed increased color naming latencies for fear related words such as *web*. Again this effect appears likely to have been mediated by mood state, as it disappeared following successful treatment.

Mathews and MacLeod (1985) report that generalized anxiety patients, but not normal controls, show elevated color naming latencies for words related to both social threat (e.g., *failure* or *lonely*) and physical threat (e.g., *coffin* or *disease*), with the relative slowing across these two classes of threat stimuli being determined by a subject's relative preoccupation with social or physical domains of worry. Mogg, Mathews, and Weinman (1989) subsequently replicated this effect, and also found that the degree to which generalized anxiety patients were slow to color name each class of threat word, was mediated by their particular domain of worry.

Specifically, patients primarily reporting worries of a physical nature showed increased latencies to color name the physical threat words, relative to neutral words, and yet weren't slow to color name the social threat words. Conversely, patients whose most common worries were of a social nature were disproportionately slow to color name the social threat words, but not the physical threat words. Consistent with this pattern of specificity, Ehlers, Margraf, Davies, and Roth (1988) have found that panic disorder patients, who are characterized by primarily physical concerns, are disproportionately slow to color name only those words related to physical threat.

Whereas the studies by Mathews and MacLeod (1985), and by Mogg et al. (1989), report very similar group differences, their findings concerning the relative roles of state and trait anxiety are not entirely consistent. In Mogg et al.'s study, the degree to which subjects were slowed when color naming the threat words was predicted best by trait anxiety. The correlation between this selective interference effect, and level of trait anxiety, remained significant after the effect of state anxiety had been partialled out. However, Mathews and MacLeod found that the relative slowing to color name threat words was best predicted, across all subjects, by level of state anxiety. Though trait anxiety score, and score on the Beck Depression Inventory, were also correlated with the effect, such correlations disappeared when the influence of state anxiety was partialled out.

In contrast, the correlation with state anxiety remained after the influence of these two variables had been statistically removed. When Mathews and MacLeod (1985) considered their two subject groups separately, however, a significant correlation between the interference effect on threat words and level of state anxiety was found only in the patient sample, who also showed high levels of trait anxiety. Thus, state anxiety was found to be most closely associated with this mood congruent attentional bias in those subjects with a high level of trait anxiety.

Although the results of these studies are consistent with the hypothesis that anxious subjects selectively attend to threat related stimuli, the experiments represent only an indirect test of this possibility. Their conclusions rest on the inference that subjects are slow to color name certain words because they are selectively attending to those words' meanings. Other possible explanations exist that are not necessarily consistent with the mood congruency hypothesis. One could even suggest that anxious subjects avoid processing the stimulus item completely if it contains threat related information, perhaps by looking away, with their impaired color naming latencies for the threat words reflecting this avoidance.

More direct measures of attentional deployment, however, provide further evidence threat material does indeed recruit attentional resources in anxious subjects. For example we have simultaneously presented threatening and neutral words to upper and lower locations on a video display screen for brief exposure durations (500 ms). Following each presentation, the ensuing distribution of visual attention was measured by recording latency to detect small dot probes subsequently appearing in either location on this display (MacLeod, Mathews, & Tata, 1986).

Previous research has established that detection latencies are reliably reduced for such probes when they appear in attended areas of a display (e.g., Navon & Margalit, 1983). Consistent with predictions, we found that generalized anxiety patients detected the dot probes in each location fastest when the threat word, rather than the neutral word, had just been presented to that same location. Thus these patients had shifted attentional resources towards the screen location where threat stimuli had appeared, resulting in disproportionately rapid detection of probes in those same locations.

Nonanxious control subjects, in contrast, showed a strong tendency in the opposite direction, detecting probes in each location more slowly if the threat word had just been presented to this area of the screen. These findings suggest that the control subjects selectively moved attentional resources away from the location where the threat stimuli had been presented.

In subsequent research, employing this same paradigm, we have attempted to dissociate the relative contribution of trait and state variables, by testing groups of high and low trait students well before an important exam, when state anxiety was relatively low, and again in the week before this exam, when state anxiety was elevated (MacLeod & Mathews, 1988).

Once again, the results indicate that the bias is best predicted by neither trait nor state anxiety alone but by the joint functioning of these two factors. At test time 1, when the subjects were not stressed, the low and high trait students showed no significant attentional response either towards or away from exam relevant threat words. Both groups showed an equivalent increase in state anxiety as the examination approach. However this was associated with distinctly different attentional correlates in high and low trait subjects.

The high trait students now showed the pattern of probe detection latencies that had previously characterized the patient sample, indicating that they were selectively shifting attention towards the screen locations where stress relevant threat stimuli had just appeared. Probes occurring in the screen locations where threat stimuli had just appeared were thus detected with disproportionate speed.

In contrast, the equivalent state anxiety increase in the low trait students was associated with exactly the opposite effect. As these low trait subjects became more state anxious, so they increased their tendency to move attentional resources away from those same threat stimuli that now recruited attentional resources in the high trait subjects. Thus, the low trait subjects under stress became selectively slower to detect probes occurring in the same location as exam related threat stimuli.

Using the same probe detection paradigm, Broadbent and Broadbent (1988) have also found that the attentional response to threat related information is best predicted by this interactive function involving both state and trait anxiety. High levels of state anxiety were most strongly associated with selective attentional orientation towards threat stimuli in those subjects who were high on trait anxiety also.

Although the general finding that mood congruency effects will be mediated by a joint function of both state and trait variables is predicted by both the network and the schema model, the specific pattern of results described above are not easily accommodated by either model. These models may lead to the expectation that cognitive biases favoring the processing of emotionally congruent information will be most powerfully elicited by elevations in state emotion in those individuals who are also high trait for this emotion. Low trait subjects should perhaps show more modest processing biases at any given level of state emotion, or perhaps may even show no measurable mood congruency effects whatsoever.

However, neither model leads to the prediction that state elevations will exaggerate reverse biases in low trait subjects. This empirical finding is quite inconsistent with either theoretical account.

On the other hand, the prediction made by both models that mood congruent processing biases should occur quite automatically, originating at a very early stage in the processing continuum, has received substantial support from our own research on attentional operations in anxiety. Even when the emotionally valenced material is presented in such a manner that it does not become consciously represented, there is evidence that threat related information recruits disproportionate processing resources.

Thus, for example, we presented threat or neutral word lists to the unattended ear on a dichotic listening task, and determined the degree to which this material recruited processing resources by measuring residual capacity using a simple reaction time index (Mathews & MacLeod, 1986). Neither generalized anxiety patients nor control subjects were able to identify any words in the unattended ear, either in recall or recognition tests or in check trials where the tape was halted and the content of the unattended channel interrogated.

Nevertheless, the anxious patients showed a slowing on the simultaneous reaction time measure when threat rather than neutral words were appearing in the unattended ear, indicating that processing capacity was being diverted in those trials. In contrast, the reaction times for the nonanxious control subjects were unaffected by the valence of these unattended words.

More recently, we have demonstrated (Mathews, MacLeod, & Tata, 1990) that the increased latencies shown by generalized anxiety patients when color naming threat words continue to occur even when the semantic content of the words is eliminated from awareness using a backward pattern masking procedure (cf. Neisser, 1967). In contrast, nonanxious control subjects were consistently faster to color name threat rather than neutral words, even when this masking procedure prevented conscious representation of the words' content.

These results suggest that this anxiety linked orientation of the selective system towards threat related information is initiated prior to conscious awareness of such stimuli. Clearly, therefore, this attentional bias must indeed occur quite automatically, without requiring that an intentional strategy is implemented in response to the perceived threat.

Depression. Both Beck's schema theory and Bower's associative network model of emotion and cognition clearly predict that equivalent effects will occur with depression, leading to an attentional bias towards mood congruent stimuli. Negatively valenced stimuli should selectively recruit processing resources, and should thus be disproportionately difficult to ignore and disproportionately easy to detect in depressed subjects.

In contrast to anxiety, however, there is a striking sparsity of research that offers unequivocal suport for this prediction. Though negative findings are probably most underrepresented in the published literature, there are nevertheless a number of published studies that have failed to support the above predictions. Furthermore, supportive studies often have methodological flaws, and typically fail to exclude the possibility that the occurrence of such biases in depressed subjects may actually be mediated by concomitant elevations in anxiety levels.

First, we will consider research that has failed to find evidence of an attentional bias operating to favor the intake of negative information in depression. In our own research, we have tested a group of clinical depressives on the dot probe paradigm that demonstrated attentional orientation towards threat in anxious patients. However, the position of emotionally negative words on the video display screen had no effect on the relative detection latencies for dot probes in either location on this screen, indicating that these depressed patients showed no selective attentional response to negative words (MacLeod et al., 1986). This was the case even when the negative words were closely congruent with depressive concerns, such as *failure, lonely,* or *rejected;* despite the fact that such stimuli have consistently been associated with recall advantages in depressed subjects.

More recently Gotlib, McLachlan and Katz (1988) have also studied the attentional response shown to emotionally toned stimuli by depressives, using a modified version of this paradigm. Subjects were exposed on a tachistoscope to word pairs that contained either a neutral and negative word, a neutral and positive word, or a positive and negative word, with each word being simultaneously presented to different spatial locations. Following every exposure, each word was replaced by a color bar, either red or green. Although the onset of the color bars was in fact simultaneous, subjects were told they were asynchronous and had to report which bar appeared first.

Gotlib et al. (1988) cite previous research to support the claim that the bar that occurs in the more attended area of the screen will be perceived as appearing earlier than the bar in the less attended area. The bar reported as occurring first was therefore taken as an indication of the word in each pair that had recruited the subject's attention to the greater degree. In contrast to their prediction, Gotlib et al. (1988) found that depressed subjects showed no tendency whatsoever either to move attention towards the negative, or away from the positive stimuli.

Thus, those experimental paradigms that have attempted to directly measure visual attention have found evidence for mood congruent biases both in anxiety and in positive mood states, but have been unable to demonstrate such effects in depression.

Research on the perception of emotional stimuli in depression has often investigated the relative speed with which subjects can identify emotionally toned words. Again the results are predominantly inconsistent with the hypothesis that depression selectively facilitates the perception of negatively valenced words. Gerrig and Bower (1982) measured tachistoscopic recognition thresholds for negative and positive words, in subjects undergoing hypnotic mood induction. In contrast to their predictions, induced happiness did not differentially influence the recognition threshold for emotionally congruent and incongruent words.

Clark, Teasdale, Broadbent, and Martin (1983) have employed the lexical decision paradigm to address this same issue, using a depression and elation mood induction. The lexical decision paradigm requires subjects to decide as rapidly as possible whether letter strings are, or are not, real words. Their reaction time to correctly respond *yes* to a word thus provides a measure of the speed with which that word can be processed. Clark et al. (1983) found that the relative lexical decision latencies for positive, neutral and negative words remained unchanged by the induction of either depressed or elated mood states.

More recently, Challis and Krane (1988) conducted a similar lexical decision study employing positive or negative trait adjectives as their stimulus materials. Three mood manipulation conditions were included, to induce neutral, elated, or depressed affect. Although induction of elation led to a relative speeding for decision on positive as compared with negative adjectives as predicted, the results for depression induction were contrary to predictions. As in Clark et al.'s (1983) study, Challis and Krane found that induced depression had no effect whatsoever on the relative decision latencies for positive and negative words.

Powell and Hemsley (1984) have argued that facilitated perceptual processing of mood congruent stimuli, such as negatively toned words, may be associated with depression as a trait rather than as a state. Consequently, they suggest that this processing bias may occur in clinical depressives, even if it cannot be induced by elevating depressed mood in normals.

To test this hypothesis, they tachistoscopically presented clinical depressives and nondepressed control subjects with neutral and negative words, at brief exposure durations that were calculated individually to permit approximately 50% accuracy. Subjects had to guess at the words' identity, even if they were not sure. Clinical depressives were shown to correctly identify more negative words than did the control subjects, though the groups did not differ in their ability to identify neutral words. While these results are consistent with Powell and Hemsley's (1984) hypothesis, they could easily be attributed to a guessing bias, rather than to a difference in perceptual processing. All subjects may have insufficient information at these exposure latencies to identify the words with certainty, and the instructions explicitly encourage guessing. If depressed subjects favor mood congruent guesses, then they will be disproportionately accurate on the negative words. Clearly, however, this would not represent perceptual facilitation.

The lexical decision paradigm does not require that an emotionally valenced response be made, nor does it require that subjects supply the words' identity. It can therefore provide a measure of a word's processing speed that is unaffected by any such guessing bias. We have tested clinically depressed patients, and nondepressed controls on the lexical decision task, employing the same neutral and negative stimulus words as were used by Powell and Hemsley (1984), and including an additional pool of positive words (MacLeod, Tata, & Mathews, 1987). All subjects were significantly affected by the emotional valence of the stimulus words, showing the fastest decision latencies on positive words and the slowest on negative words.

However, there was no trace of support for the hypothesis that decisions on negative words would be relatively facilitated in the depressed patients. Indeed, these patients showed a (nonsignificantly) greater tendency than did control subjects to process the negative words slower than the positive words. The weight of evidence, therefore, is clearly against the hypothesis that depression facilitates the perceptual processing of negative stimuli.

There is, nevertheless, some evidence that task performance may be selectively disrupted in depressed subjects by the presentation of mood congruent, rather than incongruent, distractor stimuli. (This has been demonstrated using the modified Stroop (1938) type paradigm and has already been described in the discussion on anxiety.) Depressed subjects have been found to show increased latencies to name the ink color of words that have an emotionally negative semantic content, suggesting that depression congruent content may indeed selectively recruit attentional resources in this population.

Gotlib and McCann (1984), for example, found that students who scored high on the Beck Depression Inventory were slower to color name negative, as compared with neutral or positive, words. Students scoring low on this depression measure, however, showed no differential latencies on these different classes of words. Williams and Nulty (1986) have reported similar results with depressed subjects volunteering to participate in a study on "worry".

We have found clinical depressive patients to show this selective slowing to color name mood congruent words in our own research (Mathews, MacLeod, & Tata, 1990). Of course, because naturally occurring levels of anxiety and depression are commonly highly correlated, it seems possible that anxiety levels may also have been elevated in these depressed subjects, and may have contributed to their attentional bias. Indeed in our own color naming study clinical depressives reported state anxiety levels that were even higher than our clinical anxiety patients.

Neither Williams and Nulty (1986), nor Gotlib and McCann (1984) report anxiety scores for their college students high on naturally occurring depression, and so the potential role of anxiety cannot be assessed. However Williams and Nulty do report that half of their "depressed" sample had previously received treatment for anxiety, and all were self-defined "worriers." Gotlib and McCann report that the deliberate induction of depressed mood, which may have resulted in a very specific elevation of this target mood state alone, was not associated with any relative increase in the color naming latency of negative, as compared with positive or neutral, words.

Clearly, therefore, the potential role of anxiety cannot be excluded from these studies. Nevertheless, Williams and Broadbent (1986b) have found a fairly clear association between depression and color naming interference for certain negatively valenced words in a sample of suicide attempters, hospitalized after having taken a drug overdose. This disruption correlated with level of current depressed mood rather than with anxiety level.

It is, however, worth noting that the overdose patients only showed more color naming interference than the control subjects on those negative words that were directly related to the recent suicide attempt (e.g., words such as *overdose* or *drug*). Words that were clearly mood congruent, but were not specifically related to this attempted suicide (such as *unhappy* or *helpless*) were not associated with disproportionately elevated color naming latencies in these patients.

In summary, therefore, while there is considerable empirical support for the hypothesis that anxiety is indeed associated with an attentional bias favoring mood congruent stimuli, the evidence is far less convincing for depression. A number of direct negative findings have been reported. Most positive findings with depressed subjects have failed to exclude the potential role of anxiety. Even the apparently supportive effects shown by overdose patients may demonstrate attentional orientation towards *concern* congruent, rather than *mood* congruent information. It therefore seems reasonable to conclude that mood congruent attentional biases are far more characteristic of anxiety than of depression.

CONCLUSION

The preceding review clearly provides a great deal of support for the existence of processing biases, in both anxiety and depression, which operate to favor mood congruent information. These effects may indeed be mediated by an interactive function of both trait and state variables, with elevated state emotion being most closely associated with mood congruent processing in those subjects who are also high trait for this emotion.

In general this is consistent with the theoretical accounts of the relationship between mood and cognition offered by Beck and by Bower. However, such mood congruency effects are less ubiquitous than predicted by either the schema or the network model. Furthermore, the pattern of effects that characterize anxiety do not simply parallel those that are found in depression, as would have been anticipated on the basis of these models. Rather, each emotion appears primarily to be associated with biases in specific types of cognitive operation. Table 7-1 summarizes the pattern of findings associated with each emotion.

As studies have shown, depressed subjects show mood congruency effects that are primarily restricted to retrieval operations, leading to facilitated memory for negative information. In contrast, there is little evidence for mood congruent retrieval in anxious

Table 7-1. Summary of Research Findings Concerning the Relationship Between Emotion and Cognition

	ANXIETY	DEPRESSION
Perception/ Attention	Reliable evidence for mood congruency effects, from wide range of studies employing objective experimental techniques. These effects appear to be associated with state anxiety in high trait subjects. The opposite effects are sometimes associated with state elevations in low trait subjects.	No convincing evidence for mood congruency effects in perceptual or attentional processes. Many direct tests of this hypothesis, but all adequate experimentation has produced null results.
Comprehension	Fair evidence for mood congruent interpretative biases. Both introspective methods and more objective measures have been employed, with trait anxiety having been most clearly implicated. Response bias accounts do, however, remain possible.	Considerable evidence to support the existence of mood congruency effects in evaluative, and interpretative processes. Studies have, however, relied exclusively on self report data. Demand characteristics of the task, and response bias accounts, therefore remain possible alternative explanations.
Retrieval	No convincing evidence for mood congruent retrieval associated with either trait or state anxiety. Many null results, with a number of significant effects in the reverse direction.	Very substantial body of research supporting the existence of mood congruent retrieval biases. Both depression as a transient state, and as a more stable personality characteristic, have been implicated in such effects.

subjects. These anxious subjects, however, do show striking effects at the "front end" of the cognitive system, with mood congruent material recruiting disproportionate processing resources even prior to conscious awareness of such stimuli.

Additionally, there is a lack of consistent evidence supporting the existence of such attentional biases towards mood congruent stimuli for depressed subjects. Neither Beck's schema theory nor Bower's network model can easily handle this pattern of findings, because both attribute mood congruency effects across all emotional conditions to a common cognitive mechanism.

The results reviewed here, however, suggest that mood congruency effects are mediated by different cognitive mechanisms in anxiety and in depression. This position is consistent with the view of Oatley and Johnson-Laird (1987), who conceptualize each primary emotion as corresponding to a unique mode of cognitive organization. Each cognitive mode facilitates the specific types of information processing operation that are most likely to be adaptive under the conditions that elicited that emotion. Although any specific cognitive mode would therefore be associated with characteristic processing biases, the particular profile of such biases would be unique to that mode.

Whereas their general account is consistent with the reviewed findings, Oatley and Johnson-Laird (1987) do not go into detail concerning the underlying characteristics of those cognitive modes associated with anxiety and depression. Elsewhere, however, together with M. Williams and Watts, we have attempted to integrate these diverse findings (Williams, Watts, MacLeod, & Mathews, 1988), with reference to a distinction drawn between two types of cognitive operation by Graf and Mandler (1984).

These researchers identify two processes that operate on mental representations. The first, which we shall call *activation* (in preference to the more ambiguous term *integration,* originally employed by Graf and Mandler) involves a temporary strengthening of a representation's internal organization, which thus renders it more *accessible*. This does not mean that the recall of such a representation will be facilitated, but rather that a representation in a high state of activation will be more readily produced (or seen or heard) when only some of its features have been fully processed, due to the increased cohesiveness of the representation's internal structure. Activation is an automatic operation, which therefore occurs at a very early processing stage.

The second operation that may act on a representation is, however, a more strategic process that Graf and Mandler refer to as *elaboration*. This involves the formation and strengthening of associations between this representation and other associated representations in memory. A highly elaborated representation will come to share multiple associative connections within memory, and will thus be rendered more *retrievable,* as each such connection may serve as a possible retrieval path.

Thus, a highly activated representation will be disproportionately accessible, and hence easy to perceive and difficult to ignore. Whereas a highly elaborated representation will be disproportionately retrievable, and hence easy to remember. We have suggested that mood congruency effects in anxiety are localized in the process of activation, whereas in depression they are localized in the process of elaboration.

According to this account, anxious subjects are characterized by an increased tendency to selectively activate mood congruent representations, but possibly with a reduced tendency to elaborate such representations. This results in a very early automatic processing bias involving the facilitated detection of threat relevant stimuli (as found by Burgess et al., 1981; Foa & McNally, 1986; and Parkinson & Rachman, 1981), an attentional orientation towards threat related stimuli (as reported, for example, by Broadbent & Broadbent, 1988 and MacLeod et al., 1986), and a reduced ability to avoid processing threat related distractor material (as found, for instance, by Ehlers et al., 1988 and Mathews & MacLeod, 1985). Because the process of activation occurs automatically, the influence of this bias would be detectable prior to conscious awareness (as demonstrated by Mathews & MacLeod, 1986; and Mathews et al., submitted). However, no parallel mood congruency effects would be anticipated at retrieval.

Indeed if, as suggested, the elaboration of such representations is inhibited in anxious subjects, then a memory deficit for threat related material could occur simultaneously with these processing advantages for such material (as reported, for example, by Watts et al., 1986; Mogg et al., 1987; and Foa et al., 1989).

In contrast, our proposal that depression is associated with mood congruency effects in elaborative processing, would lead to precisely the reverse effects. If mood congruent material is disproportionately elaborated in depressed subjects then this information should show a recall advantage, as has been well documented in a wide range of studies (e.g.,

Teasdale et al., 1980; Clark & Teasdale, 1985; Williams & Broadbent, 1986a). The finding that the self-referent encoding task is associated with particularly strong mood congruent recall effects in depression (e.g., Bradley & Mathews, 1983, 1988; Derry & Kuipers, 1981; Mathews & Bradley, 1983), may reflect the exaggerated potential for such elaborative processing offered by this encoding task, that explicitly requires that subjects attempt to establish associative connections between the stimulus item and an existing memory structure.

Selective elaboration of mood congruent material would not, however, increase the accessibility of such representations, and hence would not lead to the types of mood congruent attentional biases that, though commonly observed in anxiety, have proven so elusive with depressed subjects (e.g., Gotlib et al., 1988; MacLeod et al., 1986).

Within this model, we consider trait emotion to reflect a relatively permanent disposition to selectively increase or inhibit activation (i.e., high vs. low trait anxiety), or selectively increase or inhibit elaboration (i.e., high vs. low trait depression), of representations produced by negatively valenced stimuli. Because this selectivity is sensitive to the emotional valence of the stimulus being processed, it is preceded by a decision mechanism that establishes the affective status of this stimulus. We propose that state emotion exerts its influence on this affective decision mechanism. Elevated levels of state anxiety or state depression serve to increase the negativity value assigned to any stimulus during this decision phase.

Consider the properties of this hypothetical system. Any given mood congruency effect will be loosely associated with both trait and state emotion, but these effects would be best predicted by the interactive functioning of both trait and state variables. If a stimulus representation were judged to be affectively negative then trait anxiety level would determine whether an individual shows enhanced activation, and trait depression level determine whether that individual shows increased elaboration, of that representation. Level of state emotion, however, determines the probability that any given stimulus input will indeed be judged to be affectively negative. Thus the model predicts that elevated levels of state emotion will only elicit mood congruency effects in those individuals who are also high trait for that emotion, whereas reverse effects may be elicited by the same state elevation in low trait subjects. The model therefore accommodates this pattern of experimental findings (e.g., Broadbent & Broadbent, 1988; MacLeod & Mathews, 1988).

Though tentative at this stage, the model is capable not only of accommodating current research findings in this field, but of generating highly specific novel predictions. For example, Graf and Mandler (1984) have found that, whereas performance on explicit memory tasks such as recognition and recall may reflect the degree to which a stimulus representation has been elaborated, there are other types of memory tests, usually referred to as implicit memory tasks (cf. Schacter, 1987), which appear primarily sensitive to the level of activation of this stimulus representation.

Thus, when subjects are quite unable to explicitly recall words from a previous learned list, they still show a tendency to complete word fragments to form words that they have seen on this list, rather than equally frequent words that were not previously presented. Graf and Mandler (1984) claim that this implicit memory for unrecallable words reflects the increased activation (and hence accessibility) of these words, produced by previous exposure. If anxious subjects do indeed show disproportionate levels of activation for representations of threat related stimuli, then this suggests that they may show mood congruency effects on implicit memory tasks, such as word stem completion, even though these mood congruency effects will not be found on explicit memory tasks, such as recall or recognition.

Mathews, Mogg, May, and Eysenck (in press) therefore presented generalized anxiety patients and nonanxious control subjects with threat related, and neutral, stimulus words in a self-referent encoding paradigm, and measured both explicit and implicit memory for this material. Neither the anxiety nor the control subjects showed any differential ability to recall threat and neutral words. In contrast, on the implicit memory task the predicted interaction was indeed significant. Both groups tended to complete word fragments to form words that had been presented more often than unpresented words, indicating implicit memory for the previously seen material.

However the anxious subjects showed this effect to a greater degree for the threat related rather than the neutral words, while this pattern was reversed in the control subjects. As predicted by the model, therefore, mood congruency effects occurred on the implicit, but not the explicit, memory task, suggesting disproportionate activation of threat related representations in anxiety, but no increased elaboration of these representations.

Despite progress over the past few years, researchers have barely started to explore the full potential of adopting the information processing approach to evaluate and refine cognitive models of the emotional disorders. Important issues remain to be addressed. For example, although we know that certain patterns of information processing are *associated* with anxiety and depression, it remains uncertain to what extent these information processing styles *mediate* these emotional conditions. We are exploring this issue in the laboratory, employing both subjective and physiological mood measures to examine the emotional consequences of these different cognitive styles when processing affectively valenced information. Of course, we must also consider to what extent we can generalize from single word stimuli to the types of naturalistic events that are commonly associated with anxiety and depression in real life.

One way we are currently addressing this issue is by investigating the degree to which individuals' pattern of emotional reactions to one specific real life event—the diagnosis of cervical cancer—can be predicted prior to diagnosis, on the basis of attentional and memory tests employing emotionally valenced words. Ultimately, however, the most clinically salient question must concern our eventual capacity to modify the types of information processing biases that are implicated in the development and maintenance of anxiety and depression. Direct objective information processing measures may enable us not only to identify the particular pattern of biases that produce emotional disorders, but also to formulate and evaluate specific cognitive techniques designed to reduce these various biases.

Suppose, for example, that depression is indeed maintained through distorted retrieval operations that reflect the selective elaboration of negative events in memory. A plausible intervention procedure may involve the deliberate strategic elaboration of positive events, by directly drawing explicit associations between these events and existing representations. Such an approach may have little therapeutic value in the case of anxiety, however, if this disorder reflects the increased activation, rather than the increased elaboration of negative representations.

Despite its demonstrated efficacy, (e.g., Hollon & Beck, 1986; Meichenbaum, 1986) there is, as yet, no direct evidence that cognitive therapy operates by changing the way in which information is processed. Nevertheless, it is highly probable that the scientific credibility of cognitive therapy will ultimately depend upon the degree to which the underlying concepts can be operationalized and objectively measured, and the theoretical rationale experimentally validated.

In this chapter we have attempted to illustrate how we believe these goals may best be pursued. The information processing paradigm offers a flexible and extensive range of objective techniques for investigating the cognitive characteristics of anxiety and depression, for assessing such disorders clinically, and for evaluating alternative intervention approaches designed to produce cognitive change.

Furthermore, it provides a powerful theoretical framework that permits these findings to be integrated into precise formal models. These models are not only capable of considerable explanatory power, but also generate specific predictions that may translate into novel therapeutic procedures. It is both probable and desirable, therefore, that the information processing approach will exert a steadily increasing influence on those of us who welcome cognitivism into our psychology clinic, without being prepared to see our older ally, scientific rigour, driven out the back door.

REFERENCES

Alba, J. W., & Hasher, L. (1983): Is memory schematic? *Psychological Bulletin, 93,* 203–231.

Anderson, J., & Bower, G. H. (1973): *Human associative memory*. Washington, DC: Winston.

Baddeley, A. D. (1979). Working memory and reading. In P. Kolers, M. Wrolstad, & H. Bouma (Eds.). *Processing of visible language*. New York: Plenum Press.

Baddeley, A. D. (1986). *Working memory*. Oxford: Oxford University Press.

Baddeley, A. D., & Hitch, G. J. (1974). Working memory. In G. H. Bower (Ed.). *Recent advances in learning and motivation*. New York: Academic Press.

Bandura, A. (1986). Self-efficacy mechanism in physiological activation and health-promoting behavior. In J. Madden, S. Matthysse, & J. Barchas (Eds.). *Adaptation. learning and affect*. New York: Raven Press.

Bartlett, F. C. (1932). *Remembering*. Cambridge: Cambridge University Press.

Baxter, M. F., Yamanda, K., & Washburn, M. F. (1917). Directed recall of pleasant and unpleasant experiences. *American Journal Psychology, 28,* 155–157.

Beck, A. T. (1967). *Depression*. New York: Hober Medical.

Beck, A. T. (1976). *Cognitive therapy and the emotional disorders*. New York: International Universities Press.

Beck, A. T., & Clark, D. A. (1988). Anxiety and depression: An information processing perspective. *Anxiety Research, 1,* 23–36.

Beck, A. T., Emery, G., & Greenberg, R. C. (1986).

Anxiety disorders and phobias: A cognitive perspective. New York: Basic Books.
Beck, A. T., Laude, R., & Bohnert, M. (1974). Ideational components of anxiety neurosis. *Archives of General Psychiatry, 31,* 319–325.
Beck, A. T., Rush, A. J., Shaw, B. F., & Emery, G. (1979). *Cognitive therapy of Depression: A treatment manual.* New York: Guilford Press.
Beck, A. T., Brown, G., Steer, R. A., Eidelson, J. I., & Riskind, J. H. (1987). Differentiating anxiety and depression utilizing the Cognitions Checklist. *Journal of Abnormal Psychology, 96,* 179–186.
Biederman, I. (1982). On the semantics of glance at a scene. In N. Kubovsky & J. R. Pomerantz (Eds.). *Perceptual organisation.* Hillsdale, NJ: Lawrence Erlbaum Associates.
Blackburn, I. M., Jones, S., & Lewin, R. J. P. (1986). Cognitive style in depression. *British Journal of Clinical Psychology, 25,* 241–251.
Blank, M. A., & Foss, D. J. (1978). Semantic facilitation and lexical access during sentence processing. *Memory and Cognition, 6,* 644–652.
Borkovec, T. D., Robinson, E., Prujinsky, T., & DePree, J. A. (1983). Preliminary exploration of worry: Some characteristics and processes. *Behaviour Research and Therapy, 21,* 9–16.
Bower, G. H. (1981). Mood and memory. *American Psychologist, 36,* 129–148.
Bower, G. H. (1983). Affect and cognition. *Philosophical Transactions of the Royal Society.* London, *B302,* 387–402.
Bower, G. H. (1985, September). *A review of research on mood and memory.* Paper presented at Symposium on Affect and Cognition, Cognitive Psychology Section, British Psychological Society, Oxford.
Bower, G. H. (1987). Commentary on mood and memory. *Behaviour Research and Therapy, 25,* 443–456.
Bower, G. H., & Cohen, P. R. (1982). Emotional influences on memory and thinking: Data and theory. In S. Fiske, & M. Clark (Eds.), *Affect and cognition.* Hillsdale, NJ: Lawrence Erlbaum Associates.
Bradley, B., & Mathews, A. (1983). Negative self-schemata in clinical depression. *British Journal of Clinical Psychology, 22,* 173–182.
Bradley, B., & Mathews, A. (1988). Memory bias in recovered clinical depressives. *Cognition and Emotion, 2,* 235–246.
Breslow, R., Kocsis, J., & Belkin, B. (1980). Memory deficits in depression: Evidence utilizing the Wechsler Memory Scale. *Perceptual and Motor Skills, 51,* 541–542.
Broadbent, D. E., & Broadbent, M. H. P. (1979). Priming and the passive/active model of word recognition. *Attention and Performance, 8,* 419–434.
Broadbent, D. E., & Broadbent, M. H. P. (1988). Anxiety and attentional bias: State and trait. *Cognition and Emotion, 2,* 165–183.

Bruning, J. L., Capage, J. E., Kozuh, G. F., Young, P. F., & Young, W. E. (1968). Socially induced drive and range of cue utilization. *Journal of Personality and Social Psychology, 9,* 242–244.
Burgess, I. S., Jones, L. N., Robertson, S. A., Radcliffe, W. N., Emerson, E., Lawler, P., & Crow, T. J. (1981). The degree of control exerted by phobic and non-phobic verbal stimuli over the recognition behaviour of phobic and non-phobic subjects. *Behaviour Research and Therapy, 19,* 223–234.
Butler, G., & Mathews, A. (1983). Cognitive processes in anxiety. *Advances in Behaviour Research and Therapy, 5,* 51–62.
Butler, G., & Mathews, A. (1987). Anticipatory anxiety and risk perception. *Cognitive Therapy and Research, 91,* 551–565.
Byrne, D. G. (1976). Choice reaction times in depressive states. *British Journal of Social and Clinical Psychology, 15,* 149–156.
Calev, A., & Erwin, P. G. (1985). Recall and recognition in depressives: use of matched task. *Journal of Abnormal Psychology, 93,* 127–128.
Calvin, A. D., Koons, P. B., Bingham, J. L., & Fink, H. H. (1953). A further investigation of the relationship between manifest anxiety and intelligence. *Journal of Consulting Psychology, 19,* 280–282.
Campbell, D. (1957). A study of some sensory-motor functions in psychiatric patients. Unpublished doctoral dissertation, University of London.
Cane, D. B., & Gotlib, I. H. (1985). Depression and the effects of positive and negative feedback on expectations, evaluations and performance. *Cognitive Therapy and Research, 9,* 145–160.
Challis, B. H., & Krane, R. V. (1988). Mood induction and the priming of semantic memory in a lexical decision task: Asymmetric effects of elation and depression. *Bulletin of the Psychonomic Society, 26,* 309–312.
Chambless, D. L., Caputo, G. C., Bright, P., & Gallagher, R. (1984). Assessment of fear in agoraphobics: The body Sensations Questionnaire and the Agoraphobic Cognitions Questionnaire. *Journal of Consulting and Clinical Psychology, 52,* 1090–1097.
Clark, D. A., & Teasdale, J. D. (1982). Diurnal variations in clinical depression and accessibility of memories of positive and negative experiences. *Journal of Abnormal Psychology, 91,* 97–95.
Clark, D. A., & Teasdale, J. D. (1985). Constraints on the effects of mood on memory. *Journal of Personality and Social Psychology, 48,* 1598–1608.
Clark, D. M., Teasdale, J. D., Broadbent, D. E., & Martin, M. (1983). Effects of mood on lexical decisions. *Bulletin of the Psychonomic Society, 21,* 175–178.
Cohen, R. M., Weingartner, H., Smallberg, S. A., Pickar, D., & Murphy, D. L. (1982). Effort and cognition in depression. *Archives of General Psychiatry, 39,* 593–597.
Collins, A. M., & Loftus, E. F. (1975). A spreading

activation theory of semantic processing. *Psychological Review, 82,* 407–428.
Collins, A. M., & Quillian, M. R. (1969). Retrieval time from semantic memory. *Journal of Verbal Learning and Verbal Behaviour, 8,* 240–248.
Cook, M. L., & Peterson, C. (1986). Depressive irrationality. *Cognitive Therapy and Research, 10,* 293–298.
Cornell, D. G., Suarez, R., & Berent, S. (1984). Psychomotor retardation in melancholic and non melancholic depression: cognitive and motor components. *Journal of Abnormal Psychology, 93,* 150–157.
Coughlan, A. K., & Hollows, S. E. (1984). Use of memory tests in differentiating organic disorders from depression. *British Journal of Psychiatry, 145,* 164–167.
Crandell, C. J., & Chambless, D. L. (1986). The validity of an inventory for measuring depressive thoughts: The Crandell Cognitions Inventory. *Behaviour Research and Therapy, 3,* 291–298.
Cronholm, B., & Ottoson, J. (1961). Memory function in endogenous depression: Before and after electroconvulsive therapy. *Archives of General Psychiatry, 5,* 193–199.
Daneman, M., & Carpenter, P. (1980). Individual differences in working memory and reading. *Journal of Verbal Learning and Verbal Behaviour, 19,* 450–456.
Darke, S. (1988a). Anxiety and working memory capacity. *Cognition and Emotion, 2,* 145–154.
Darke, S. (1988b). Effects of anxiety on inferential reasoning task performance. *Journal of Personality and Social Psychology, 55,* 499–505.
Davison, G. C., Feldman, P. M., & Osborn, C. E. (1984). Articulated thoughts, irrational beliefs, and fear of negative evaluation. *Cognitive Therapy and Research, 8,* 349–362.
Deffenbacher, J. L., Zwemer, W. A., Whisman, M. A., Hill, R. A., & Sloan, R. D. (1986). Irrational beliefs and anxiety. *Cognitive Therapy and Research, 10,* 281–292.
Derry, P. A., & Kuiper, N. A. (1981). Schematic processing and self-reference in clinical depression. *Journal of Abnormal Psychology, 90,* 286–297.
Dobson, K. S., & Shaw, B. F. (1986). Cognitive assessment with major depressive disorders. *Cognitive Therapy and Research, 10,* 13–29.
Dobson, K. S., & Shaw, B. F. (1987). Specificity and stability of self-referent encoding in clinical depression. *Journal of Abnormal Psychology, 96,* 34–40.
Donnelly, E. F., Waldman, I. N., Murphy, D. L., Wyatt, R. J., & Goodwin, F. K. (1980). Primary affective disorder: thought disorder in depression. *Journal of Abnormal Psychology, 89,* 315–319.
Dornic, S. (1977). Mental load, effort, and individual differences, (No. 509). Reports from the Department of Psychology, The University of Stockholm.
Dornic, S., & Fernaeus, S. E. (1981). Individual differences in high load tasks: The effect of verbal distraction. (No. 569). Reports from the Department of Psychology, The University of Stockholm.

Easterbrook, J. A. (1959). The effect of emotion on cue utilization and the organization of behavior. *Psychological Review,* 183–201.
Eaves, G., & Rush, A. J. (1984). Cognitive patterns in symptomatic and remitted unipolar major depression. *Journal of Abnormal Psychology, 93,* 31–40.
Ehlers, A., Margraf, J., Davies, S., & Roth, W. T. (1988). Selective processing of threat cues in subjects with panic attacks. *Cognition and Emotion, 2,* 201–220.
Ellis, H. C., & Ashbrook, P. W. (1987). Resource allocation model of the effects of depressed mood states on memory. In K. Fiedler & J. Forgas (Eds.). *Affects, Cognition and Social Behaviour.* Toronto: Hogrefe.
Ellis, H. D., Thomas, R. L., & Rodriguez, I. A. (1984). Emotional mood states and memory: elaborative encoding, semantic processing and cognitive effort. *Journal of Experimental Psychology: Learning Memory and Cognition, 69,* 237–243.
Eysenck, H. J. (1972). Behaviour therapy is behaviouristic. *Behavior Therapy, 3,* 609–613.
Eysenck, M. W. (1979). Anxiety, learning and memory: A reconceptualization. *Journal of Research in Personality, 13,* 363–385.
Eysenck, M. W. (1981). Learning, memory and personality. H. J. Eysenck (Ed.). *A model for personality.* London: Springer.
Eysenck, M. W. (1982). *Attention and arousal: Cognition and performance.* Berlin: Springer-Verlag.
Eysenck, M. W. (1985). Anxiety and cognitive task performance. *Personality and Individual Differences, 6,* 579–586.
Eysenck, M. W. (1988). Anxiety and attention. *Anxiety Research, 1,* 9–15.
Eysenck, M. W., MacLeod, C., & Mathews, A. (1987). Cognitive functioning in anxiety. *Psychological Research, 49.* 189–195.
Finch, A. J., Anderson, J., & Kendall, P. C. (1976). Anxiety and digit span performance in emotionally disturbed children. *Journal of Consulting and Clinical Psychology, 44,* 874–892.
Foa, E. B., & McNally, R. J. (1986). Sensitivity to feared stimuli in obsessive-compulsives: a dichotic listening analysis. *Cognitive Therapy and Research, 10,* 477–486.
Foa, E. B., McNally, R., & Murdock, T. B. (1989). Anxious mood and memory. *Behaviour Research and Therapy, 27,* 141–147.
Forgas, J. P., & Bower, G. H. (1987). Mood effects in person perception. *Journal of Personality and Social Psychology, 53,* 53–60.
Forgas, J. P., Bower, G. H., & Krantz, S. E. (1984). The influence of mood perception. *Journal of Experimental Social Psychology, 20,* 497–513.
Foulds, G. A. (1952). Temperamental differences in maze performance II: The effect of distraction and of electroconvulsive therapy on psychomotor retardation. *British Journal of Psychiatry, 43,* 33–41.

Fox, J., Houston, B. K., & Pittner, M. S. (1983). Trait anxiety and children's cognitive behaviours in an evaluative situation. *Cognitive Therapy and Research, 7,* 149–154.

Frith, C. D., Stevens, N., Johnstone, E. C., Deakin, P. L., Lawler, P., & Crowe, T. J. (1983). Effects of ECT and depression on various aspects of memory. *British Journal of Psychiatry, 142,* 610–617.

Galambos, J. A., & Rips, L. J. (1982). Memory for routines. *Journal of Verbal Learning and Verbal Behaviour, 21,* 260–281.

Ganellen, R. J., Matuzas, W., Uhlenhuth, E. H., Glass, R., & Easton, C. R. (1986). Panic disorder, agoraphobia, and anxiety-relevant cognitive style. *Journal of Affective Disorders, 11,* 219–225.

Geller, V., & Shaver, P. (1976). Cognitive consequences of self-awareness. *Journal of Experimental Psychology, 12,* 99–108.

Gerrig, R. J., & Bower, G. H. (1982). Emotional influences on word recognition. *Bulletin of the Psychonomic Society, 19,* 197–200.

Gilligan, S. C., & Bower, G. H. (1984). Cognitive consequences of emotional arousal. In C. Izard, J. Kagan, & R. Zajonc (Eds.). *Emotions, cognitions and behaviour.* New York: Cambridge University Press.

Goldstein, A. J., & Chance, J. E. (1985). Effects of training on Japanese face recognition: reduction of other-race effect. *Bulletin of the Psychonomic Society, 23,* 211–214.

Gorham, D. R. (1956). A proverbs test for clinical and experimental user. *Psychological Reports, 2,* 1–12.

Gotlib, I. H., & McCann, C. D. (1984). Construct accessibility and depression: an examination of cognitive and affective factors. *Journal of Personality and Social Psychology, 47,* 427–439.

Gotlib, I. H., McLachlan, A. L., & Katz, A. N. (1988). Biases in visual attention in depressed and nondepressed individuals. *Cognition and Emotion, 2,* 185–200.

Graesser, A. C., & Nakamura, G. V. (1982). The impact of a schema on comprehension and memory. *Psychology of Learning and Motivation, 16,* 59–109.

Graf, P., & Mandler, G. (1984). Activation makes words more accessible, but not necessarily more retrievable. *Journal of Verbal Learning and Verbal Behaviour, 23,* 553–568.

Greenberg, M. S., & Beck, A. T. (1989). Depression versus anxiety: A test of the content specificity hypothesis. *Journal of Abnormal Psychology, 98,* 9–13.

Griggs, S. S., & Green, D. W. (1983). How to make a good cup of tea: Exploring the scripts of thought-disordered and non-thought-disordered patients. *British Journal of Medical Psychology, 56,* 125–133.

Hale, W. D., & Strickland, B. R. (1976). The induction of mood states and their effect on cognitive and social behaviour. *Journal of Consulting and Clinical Psychology, 44,* 155.

Hamilton, V. (1983). *The cognitive structures and processes of human motivation and personality.* Chichester: John Wiley & Sons.

Hamilton, E. W., & Abramson, L. Y. (1983). Cognitive patterns and major depressive disorders: A longitudinal study in a hospital setting. *Journal of Abnormal Psychology, 92,* 173–184.

Harness, B. Z., Bental, E., & Carmon, A. (1977). Comparison of cognition and performance in patients with organic brain damage and psychiatric patients. *Acta Psychiatrica Belgium, 77,* 339–347.

Harrell, T. H., Chambless, D. L., & Calhoun, J. F. (1981). Correlational relationships between self-statements and affective states. *Cognitive Therapy and Research, 5,* 159–173.

Hasher, L., & Zacks, R. T. (1984). Automatic processing of fundamental information: the case of frequency of occurrence. *American Psychologist, 39,* 1372–1388.

Haynes, J., & Gormly, J. (1977). Anxiety and memory. *Bulletin of the Psychonomic Society, 9,* 191–192.

Henry, G., Weingartner, H., & Murphy, D. (1971). Idiosyncratic patterns of learning and word association during mania. *American Journal of Psychiatry, 128,* 564–573.

Henry, G. M., Weingartner, H., & Murphy, D. L. (1973). Influence of affective states and psychoactive drugs on verbal learning and memory. *American Journal of Psychiatry, 130,* 966–971.

Hibbert, G. A. (1984). Ideational components of anxiety: Their origin and content. *British Journal of Psychiatry, 144,* 618–624.

Hodges, W. F., & Durham, R. L. (1972). Anxiety, ability, and digit span performance. *Journal of Personality and Social Psychology, 24,* 401–406.

Hodges, W. F., & Spielberger, C. D. (1969). Digit span: an indicant of trait or state anxiety? *Journal of Consulting and Clinical Psychology, 33,* 430–434.

Hollon, S., & Beck, A. T. (1986). Research on cognitive therapies. In S. L. Garfield, & A. E. Bergin (Eds.), *Handbook of Psychotherapy and Behavior Change.* (3rd ed.) New York: John Wiley & Sons.

Hollon, S. D., & Kendall, P. C. (1980). Cognitive self statements in depression: Development of an automatic thoughts questionnaire. *Cognitive Therapy and Research, 4,* 383–395.

Hollon, S. D., Kendall, P. C., & Lumry, A. (1986). Specificity of depressotypic cognitions in clinical depression. *Journal of Abnormal Psychology, 95,* 52–59.

Ingram, R. E., Kendall, P. C., Smith, T. W., Donnell, C., & Ronan, K. (1987). Cognitive specificity in emotional distress. *Journal of Personality and Social Psychology, 53,* 52–59.

Isen, A. M., Shalker, T. E., Clark, M., & Carp, L. (1978). Affect, accessibility of material in memory, and behavior: A cognitive loop. *Journal of Personality and Social Psychology, 36,* 1–12.

Johnson, M. H., & Magaro, P. A. (1987). Effects of mood

and severity on memory processes in depression and mania. *Psychological Bulletin, 101,* 28–40.

Jones, R. J. (1968). A factored measure of Ellis' irrational belief system with personality and maladjustment correlates. *Unpublished doctoral dissertation.* Texas Technical College.

Kavanagh, D. L., & Bower, G. H. (1985). Mood and self-efficacy: impact of joy and sadness on perceived capabilities. *Cognitive Therapy and Research, 9,* 507–525.

Klerman, G. L. (1975). Overview of depression. In A. M. Freedman, H. S. Kaplan, & B. J. Sadock (Eds.). *Comprehensive Overview of Psychiatry, Vol. 3,* Baltimore: Williams and Wilkins.

Klerman, G. L. (1978). Affective disorders. In A. M. Nicholi (Ed.), *The Harvard Guide to Modern Psychiatry.* Cambridge, MA: Belknap.

Knox, W. J., & Grippaldi, R. (1970). High levels of state or trait anxiety and performance on selected verbal WAIS subtests. *Psychological Reports, 27,* 375–379.

Krames, L., & McDonald, M. R. (1985). Distraction and depressive cognition. *Cognitive Therapy and Research, 9,* 561–573.

Krantz, S., & Hammen, C. (1979). Assessment of cognitive bias in depression. *Journal of Abnormal Psychology, 88,* 611–619.

Lader, M. H., & Marks, I. (1973). *Clinical anxiety.* New York: Grune and Stratton.

Laird, J. D., Wagener, J. J., Halal, M., & Szegda, M. (1982). Remembering what you feel: The effects of emotion on memory. *Journal of Personality and Social Psychology, 42,* 646–657.

Larner, S. (1977). Encoding in senile dementia and elderly depressives: a preliminary study. *British Journal of Social and Clinical Psychology, 16,* 379–390.

Leight, K. A., & Ellis, H. D. (1981). Emotional mood states, strategies and state dependency in memory. *Journal of Verbal Learning and Verbal Behaviour, 20,* 251–266.

Leon, M. R., & Revelle, W. (1985). Effects of anxiety on analogical reasoning: A test of three theoretical models. *Journal of Personality and Social Psychology, 49,* 1302–1315.

Lishman, W. A. (1972a). Selective factors in memory. Part 1: Age, sex and personality attributes. *Psychological Medicine, 2,* 121–138.

Lishman, W. A. (1972b). Selective factors in memory. Part 2: Affective disorders. *Psychological Medicine, 2,* 248–253.

Lishman, W. A. (1974). The speed of recall of pleasant and unpleasant experiences. *Psychological Medicine, 4,* 212–218.

Lloyd, G. C., & Lishman, W. A. (1975). Effects of depression on the speed of recall of pleasant and unpleasant experiences. *Psychological Medicine, 5,* 173–180.

MacLeod, C. (1987). Cognitive psychology and cognitive therapy. In H. Dent, (Ed.), *Clinical psychology: Research and development.* New York: Croom Helm.

MacLeod, C., & Mathews, A. (1988). Anxiety and the allocation of attention to threat. *Quarterly Journal of Experimental Psychology: Human Experimental Psychology, 38,* 659–670.

MacLeod, C., Mathews, A., & Tata, P. (1986). Attentional bias in emotional disorders. *Journal of Abnormal Psychology, 95,* 15–20.

MacLeod, C., Tata, P., & Mathews, A. (1987). Perception of emotionally valenced information in depression. *British Journal of Psychology, 26,* 67–68.

Mahoney, M. J. (1977). Reflections on the cognitive-learning trend in psychotherapy. *American Psychologist, 32,* 5–13.

Mandler, G., & Sarason, S. B. (1952). A study of anxiety and learning. *Journal of Abnormal and Social Psychology, 47,* 166–173.

Mathews, A., & Bradley, B. (1983). Mood and the self-reference bias in recall. *Behaviour Research and Therapy, 21,* 233–239.

Mathews, A., & MacLeod, C. (1985). Selective processing of threat cues in anxiety states. *Behaviour Research and Therapy, 23,* 563–569.

Mathews, A., & MacLeod, C. (1986). Discrimination of threat cues without awareness in anxiety states. *Journal of Abnormal Psychology, 95,* 131–138.

Mathews, A., MacLeod, C., & Tata, P. (1990). *Interference from subliminal emotional words.* Manuscript submitted for publication.

Mathews, A., Richards, A., & Eysenck, M. (1989). Interpretation of homophones related to threat in anxiety states. *Journal of Abnormal Psychology, 98,* 31–34.

Mathews, A., Mogg, K., May, J., & Eysenck, M. W. (in press). Implicit and explicit memory bias in anxiety. *Journal of Abnormal Psychology.*

Mayer, J. D., & Bower, G. H. (1985). Naturally occurring mood and learning: Comment on Hasher, Rose, Zacks, Sanft and Doren. *Journal of Experimental Psychology: General, 14,* 396–403.

McDowell, J. (1984). Recall of pleasant and unpleasant words in depressed subjects. *Journal of Abnormal Psychology, 93,* 401–407.

McNally, R. J., Foa, E. B., & Donnell, C. D. (1989). Memory bias for anxiety information in patients with panic disorder. *Cognition and Emotion, 3,* 27–44.

Meichenbaum, D. (1986). Cognitive behavior modification. In F. H. Kanfer, & A. P. Goldstein (Eds.). *Helping people change* (3rd ed.) Elmsford, NY: Pergamon Press.

Miller, W. R. (1975). Psychological deficits in depression. *Psychological Bulletin, 82,* 238–260.

Miller, E., & Lewis, P. (1977). Recognition memory in elderly patients with depression and dementia. *Journal of Abnormal Psychology, 86,* 84–86.

Miller, I. W., & Norman, W. H. (1986). *Maladaptive cognitions in depression.* Paper presented at the meeting of the Association for the Advancement of Behavior Therapy, Philadelphia.

Miranda, J., & Persons, J. B. (1988). Dysfunctional attitudes are mood state dependent. *Journal of Abnormal Psychology, 97,* 76–79.

Mizes, J. S., Landolf-Fritsche, B., & Grossman-McKee, D. (1987). Patterns of distorted cognitions in phobic disorders. *Cognitive Therapy and Research, 11,* 583–592.

Mogg, K. (1988). *Cognitive processing in anxiety.* Unpublished doctoral dissertation, University of London.

Mogg, K., Mathews, A., & Weinman, J. (1987). Memory bias in clinical anxiety. *Journal of Abnormal Psychology, 96,* 94–98.

Mogg, K., Mathews, A., & Weinman, J. (1989). Selective processing of threat cues in anxiety states: a replication. *Behaviour Research and Therapy, 27,* 317–323.

Morgan, E., Mull, H. K., & Washburn, M. F. (1919). An attempt to test moods or temperaments of cheerfulness and depression by directed recall of emotionally toned experiences. *American Journal of Psychology, 30,* 302–304.

Morton, J. (1964). The effects of context on the visual duration threshold for words. *British Journal of Psychology, 55,* 165–180.

Morton, J. (1981). Facilitation in word recognition: Experiments causing change in the logogen model. In P. A. Kolers, M. E. Wrolstad, & H. Bouma (Eds.), *Proceedings of the conference on the processing of visible language.* New York: Plenum Press.

Mueller, J. H. (1976). Anxiety and cue utilization in human learning and memory. In M. Zuckerman & C. D. Spielberger (Eds.), *Emotions and anxiety: New concepts, methods and applications.* Hillsdale, NJ: Lawrence Erlbaum Associates.

Mueller, J. H. (1977). Test anxiety, input modality, and levels of organization in free recall. *Bulletin of the Psychonomic Society, 9,* 67–69.

Mueller, J. H. (1978). The effects of individual differences in test anxiety and type of orienting task on levels of organisation in free recall. *Journal of Research in Personality, 12,* 100–116.

Mueller, J. H., & Overcast, T. D. (1976). Free recall as a function of test anxiety, concreteness, and instructions. *Bulletin of the Psychonomic Society, 8,* 194–196.

Navon, D., & Margalit, B. (1983). Allocation of attention according to informativeness in visual recognition. *Quarterly Journal of Experimental Psychology, 35,* 497–512.

Neely, J. H. (1977). Semantic priming and retrieval from lexical memory: Roles on inhibitionless spreading activation and limited capacity attention. *Journal of Experimental Psychology: General, 106,* 226–254.

Neisser, U. (1967). *Cognitive psychology.* New York: Appleton-Century-Crofts.

Nelson, K. (1977). Cognitive development and the aquisition of concepts. In R. C. Anderson, R. J. Spiro, & W. D. Montague (Eds.), *Schooling and the acquisition of knowledge.* Hillsdale, NJ: Lawrence Erlbaum.

Nisbett, R. E., & Ross, L. (1980). *Human inferences: Strategies and shortcomings of social judgment.* Englewood Cliffs, NJ: Prentice-Hall.

Nisbett, R. E., & Wilson, T. D. (1977). Telling more than we can know: verbal reports on mental processes. *Psychological Review, 84,* 231–259.

Norman, W. H., Miller, I. W., & Dow, M. G. (1988). Characteristics of depressed patients with elevated levels of dysfunctional cognitions. *Cognitive Therapy and Research, 12,* 39–52.

Norman, W. H., Miller, I. W., & Klee, S. (1983). Assessment of cognitive distortion in a clinically depressed population. *Cognitive Therapy and Research, 7,* 133–140.

Nunn, J. D., Stevenson, R., & Whalan, G. (1984). Selective memory effects in agoraphobic patients. *British Journal of Clinical Psychology, 23,* 195–201.

Oatley, K., & Johnson-Laird, P. (1987). Towards a cognitive theory of emotions. *Cognition and Emotion, 1,* 29–50.

Pallack, M. S., Pittman, T. S., Heller, J. F., & Munson, P. (1975). The effect of arousal on Stroop color-word task performance. *Bulletin of the Psychonomic Society, 6,* 248–250.

Parkinson, L., & Rachman, S. (1981). Speed of recovery from an uncontrived stress. *Advances in Behaviour Research and Therapy, 3,* 119–123.

Paulman, R., & Kennelly, K. (1984). Test anxiety and ineffective test taking: different names, same constructs? *Journal of Educational Psychology, 76,* 279–288.

Payne, R. W., & Hewlett, J. H. G. (1960). Thought disorders in psychotic patients. In H. J. Eysenck (Ed.), *Experiments in Psychology, Vol. 2.* London: Routledge and Kegan Paul.

Persons, J. B., & Rao, P. A. (1985). Longitudinal study of cognitions, life events, and depression in psychiatric inpatients. *Journal of Abnormal Psychology, 94,* 51–63.

Pettinati, H. M., & Rosenberg, J. (1984). Memory self-ratings before and after electroconvulsive therapy: Depression vs ECT induced. *Biological Psychiatry, 19,* 539–548.

Pickles, A. J., & van den Broek, M. D. (1988). Failure to replicate evidence for phobic schemata in agoraphobic patients. *British Journal of Clinical Psychology, 27,* 271–272.

Powell, M., & Hemsley, D. R. (1984). Depression: a breakdown of perceptual defence? *British Journal of Psychiatry, 145,* 358–362.

Rakover, S. (1983). Hypothesizing from introspections: A model for the role of mental entities in psychological explanation. *Journal for the Theory of Social Behaviour, 13,* 211–230.

Ray, C. (1979). Examination stress and performance on a colour word interference test. *Perceptual and Motor Skills, 49,* 400–402.

Reus, V. I., Silberman, E., Post, R. M. & Weingartner, H. (1979). D-Amphetamine: Effects on memory in a depressed population. *Biological Psychiatry, 14,* 345–356.

Rholes, W. S., Riskind, J. H., & Lane, J. W. (1987). Emotional states and memory biases: Effects of cognitive priming and mood. *Journal of Personality and Social Psychology, 52,* 91–99.

Ross, S. M., Gottfredson, D. K., Christensen, P., & Weaver, R. (1986). Cognitive self-statements in depression: Findings across clinical populations. *Cognitive Therapy and Research, 10,* 159–166.

Roth, D., & Rehm, L. P. (1980). Relationships among self-monitoring processes, memory, and depression. *Cognitive Therapy and Research, 4,* 149–157.

Roy-Byrne, P. J., Eingartner, H., Bierer, L. M., Thompson, K., & Post, R. M. (1986). Effortful and automatic processes in depression. *Archives of General Psychiatry, 43,* 265–267.

Russell, P. W., & Beekhuis, M. E. (1976). Organizatin in memory. *Journal of Abnormal Psychology, 85,* 527–534.

Schacter, D. L. (1987). Implicit memory: History and current status. *Journal of Experimental Psychology: General, 13,* 501–518.

Schwartz, N., & Clore, G. L. (1983). Mood, misattribution, and judgments of well-being: Informative and directive functions of affective states. *Journal of Personality and Social Psychology, 45,* 513–523.

Sewitch, T. S., & Kirsch, I. (1984). The cognitive content of anxiety: Naturalistic evidence for the predominance of threat related thoughts. *Cognitive Therapy and Research, 8,* 49–58.

Silberman, E. K., Weingartner, H., & Post, R. M. (1983). Thinking disorder in depression. *Archives of General Psychiatry, 40,* 775–780.

Silberman, E. K., Weingartner, H., Lorcia, M., Byrnes, S., & Post, R. M. (1983). Processing of emotional properties of stimuli by depressed and normal subjects. *Journal of Nervous and Mental Disorders, 171,* 10–14.

Simons, A. D., Garfield, S. L., & Murphy, G. E. (1984). The process of change in cognitive therapy and pharmacotherapy for depression. *Archives of General Psychiatry, 41,* 45–51.

Slife, B. D., Miura, S., Thompson, L. W., Shapiro, J. L., & Gallagher, D. (1984). Differential recall as a function of mood disorder in clinically depressed patients: Between- and within-subject differences. *Journal of Abnormal Psychology, 9,* 391–400.

Smith, E. R., & Miller, F. D. (1978). Limits on perception of cognitive processes: A reply to Nisbett and Wilson. *Psychological Review, 85,* 355–362.

Spence, J. T., & Spence, K. W. (1966). The motivational component of manifest anxiety: Drive and drive stimuli. In C. D. Spielberger (Ed.). *Anxiety and behaviour.* New York: Academic Press.

Sprock, J., Braff, D. L., Saccuzzo, D. P., & Alkinson, J. H. (1983). The relationship of depression and thought disorder in pain patients. *British Journal of Medical Psychology, 56,* 351–360.

Sternberg, D. E., & Jarvik, M. E. (1976). Memory functions in depression. *Archives of General Psychiatry, 33,* 219–224.

Stomgren, L. S. (1977). The influence of depression on memory. *Acta Psychiatrica Scandinavia, 56,* 109–128.

Strongman, K. T., & Russell, P. N. (1986). Salience of emotion in recall. *Bulletin of the Psychonomic Society, 24,* 25–27.

Stroop, J. R. (1938). Factors affecting speed in serial verbal reactions. *Psychological Monographs, 50,* 38–48.

Sutton-Simon, K., & Goldfried, M. R. (1979). Faulty thinking patterns in two types of anxiety. *Cognitive Therapy and Research, 3,* 193–203.

Teasdale, J. D. (1983). Negative thinking in depression: Cause, effect, or reciprocal relationship? *Advances in Behaviour Research and Therapy, 5,* 3–26.

Teasdale, J. D., & Fogarty, S. J. (1979). Differential effects of induced mood on retrieval of pleasant and unpleasant events from episodic memory. *Journal of Abnormal Psychology, 88,* 248–257.

Teasdale, J. D., & Russell, M. L. (1983). Differential effects of induced mood on the recall of positive, negative and neutral words. *British Journal of Clinical Psychology, 22,* 163–172.

Teasdale, J. D., Taylor, R., & Fogarty, S. J. (1980). Effects of induced elation-depression on the accessibility of memories of happy and unhappy experiences. *Behaviour Research and Therapy, 18,* 339–346.

Thorndyke, P. W. (1977). Cognitive structures in comprehension and memory of narrative discourse. *Cognitive Psychology, 9,* 77–110.

Tversky, A., & Kahneman, D. (1974). Judgement under uncertainty: heuristics and biases. *Science, 185,* 1124–1131.

Tversky, A., & Kahneman, D. (1982). Judgement under uncertainty: heuristics and biases. In D. Kahneman, P. Slovic, & A. Tversky (Eds.), *Judgement under uncertainty: Heuristics and biases.* Cambridge: Cambridge University Press.

Velten, E. (1968). A laboratory task for induction of mood states. *Behaviour Research and Therapy, 6,* 473–482.

Warren, R. E. (1972). Stimulus encoding and memory. *Journal of Experimental Psychology, 94,* 90–100.

Warren, E. W., & Groom, D. H. (1984). Memory test performance under three different waveforms of ECT for depression. *British Journal of Psychiatry, 144,* 370–378.

Watts, F. N., & Sharrock, R. (1987). Cued recall in depression. *British Journal of Clinical Psychology, 26,* 149–150.

Watts, F. N., Morris, L., & MacLeod, A. K. (1987). Recognition memory in depression. *Journal of Abnormal Psychology, 96,* 273–275.

Watts, F. N., Trezise, L., & Sharrock, R. (1986). Processing of phobic stimuli. *British Journal of Clinical Psychology, 25,* 253–261.

Watts, F. N., McKenna, F. P., Sharrock, R., & Trezise, L. (1986). Colour naming of phobia related words. *British Journal of Psychology, 77,* 97–108.

Wechsler, D. (1945). A standardised memory scale for clinical use. *Journal of Psychology, 19,* 87–95.

Weckowicz, T. E., Nutter, R. W., & Cruise, D. G. (1972). Speed in test performance in relation to depressive illness and age. *Journal of the Canadian Psychiatric Association, 17,* 241–250.

Weingartner, H., & Silberman, E. (1982). Models of cognitive impairment: cognitive changes in depression. *Psychopharmalogical Bulletin, 18,* 27–42.

Weingartner, H., Cohen, R. M., Murphy, D. L., Martello, J., & Gerdt, C. (1981). Cognitive processes in depression. *Archives of General Psychiatry, 38,* 42–47.

Weissman, A. N., & Beck, A. T. (1978). Development and validation of the Dysfunctional Attitudes Scale: A preliminary investigation. Paper presented at the meeting of the American Educational Research Association, Toronto, Canada.

Weissman, M. W. (1985). The epidemiology of anxiety disorders: rates, risks, and familial patterns. In A. H. Tuma, & J. D. Maser (Eds.), *Anxiety and the anxiety disorders.* Hillsdale, NJ: Lawrence Erlbaum Associates.

White, P. (1980). Limitations on verbal reports of internal events: A refutation of Nisbett and Wilson and of Bem. *Psychological Review, 87,* 105–112.

White, P. A. (1988). Knowing more than we can tell: Introspective access and causal report accuracy 10 years later. *British Journal of Psychology, 79,* 13–45.

White, J. D., & Carlston, D. E. (1983). Consequences of schemata for attention, impressions, and recall in complex social interactions. *Journal of Personality and Social Psychology, 45,* 538–549.

Whitehead, A. (1973). Verbal learning and memory in elderly depressives. *British Journal of Psychiatry, 123,* 203–208.

Whitehead, A. (1974). Factors in the learning deficit of elderly depressives. *British Journal of Social and Clinical Psychology, 13,* 201–208.

Wickless, C., & Kirsch, I. (1988). Cognitive correlates of anger, anxiety and sadness. *Cognitive Therapy and Research, 12,* 367–377.

Williams, J. M. G., & Broadbent, K. (1986a). Autobiographical memory in attempted suicide patients. *Journal of Abnormal Psychology, 95,* 144–149.

Williams, J. M. G., & Broadbent, K. (1986b). Distraction by emotional stimuli: Use of a Stroop task with suicide attempters. *British Journal of Clinical Psychology, 25,* 101–110.

Williams, J. M. G., & Nulty, D. D. (1986). Construct accessibility, depression and the emotional Stroop task: Transient mood or stable structure? *Personality and Individual Differences, 7,* 485–491.

Williams, J. M. G., Watts, F. N., MacLeod, C., & Mathews, A. (1988). *Cognitive psychology and the emotional disorders.* Chichester: John Wiley & Sons.

Wine, J. (1971). Test anxiety and direction of attention. *Psychology Bulletin, 76,* 92–104.

Wolpe, J. (1958). *Psychotherapy by reciprocal inhibition.* Stanford, CA: Stanford University Press.

Wolpe, J. (1973). *The practice of behavior therapy.* (2nd ed.). Elmsford, NY: Pergamon Press.

Wolpe, J. (1976). Behavior therapy and its malcontents. *Journal of Behavior Therapy and Experimental Psychiatry, 7,* 109–116.

Zaffy, D. J., & Bruning, J. L. (1966). Drive and the range of cue utilization. *Journal of Experimental Psychology, 71,* 382–384.

Zarantonello, M., Slaymaker, F., Johnson, J., & Petzel, T. (1984). Effects of anxiety and depression on anagram performance, ratings of cognitive interference, and the negative subjective evaluation of performance. *Journal of Clinical Psychology, 40,* 20–25.

Zatz, S., & Chassin, L. (1983). Cognitions of test anxious children. *Journal of Consulting and Clinical Psychology, 51,* 526–534.

Zatz, S., & Chassin, L. (1985). Cognitions of test anxious children under naturalistic test taking conditions. *Journal of Consulting and Clinical Psychology, 53,* 393–401.

Zuroff, D. C., Colussy, S. A., & Wielgus, M. S. (1983). Selective memory and depression: a cautionary note concerning response bias. *Cognitive Therapy and Research, 7,* 223–232.

Zwemer, W. A., & Deffenbacher, J. L. (1984). Irrational beliefs, anger, and anxiety. *Journal of Counseling Psychology, 31,* 391–393.

CHAPTER 8

CONTRIBUTIONS OF COGNITIVE PSYCHOLOGY TO ASSESSMENT AND TREATMENT OF ANXIETY

Michelle G. Craske
David H. Barlow

This chapter reviews evidence for the role of cognitive processes in anxiety disorders and presents assessment and treatment implications. Issues such as conscious appraisal and preawareness mechanisms, primacy of affect or cognition, and cognitive schemata as causal or consequential to the development of anxiety, are reviewed in the introduction. In addition, the tendency for conscious appraisals characteristic of anxiety states to center upon perceived danger and uncontrollability, is described. This description includes a discussion of state and trait dimensions of danger schemata, and a safety signal perspective of agoraphobic reactions. Evidence (or lack of) for mood dependent recall biases specific to anxiety is reviewed, with brief coverage of network models of memory. It also discusses the possible mitigation of measurable recall biases by avoidance strategies and reviews evidence for selectivity of attention, and preawareness perceptual biases. Self-focusing of attention is described as a specific feature of selectivity of attention, which serves to intensify emotional experiences. The potential impact of various attentional mechanisms (such as avoidant cognitive strategies) upon fear/anxiety reduction is described.

Given the strong action tendency to avoid what characterizes states of fear and anxiety, distraction strategies are typically employed, which are believed to result in strong vascillation between self-focus and external focus of attention. Attentional shifting may impede naturally occurring fear/anxiety reduction. The ways in which different attentional foci may mitigate habituation processes is elaborated upon. Finally, assessment and treatment implications that arise from recognition of the different cognitive biases are presented.

INTRODUCTION

Cognitive processes have been incorporated extensively in recent conceptualizations of anxiety disorders (Barlow, 1988; Beck & Emery, 1985; Butler & Mathews, 1987; Clark et al., 1988). The two general approaches to the investigation of anxious cognition have been, first, examination of cognitive content; and second, examination of cognitive processes such as selectivity of attention, and accessing and retrieval of information.

Cognitive content has been assessed on the basis of self-ratings, and the effects observed from instructional manipulations. For example, different foci of concern have been discerned across different anxiety groups on the basis of thought descriptions (Beck & Rush, 1975). In addition, provision of different instructional sets, which influence levels of perceived predictability and safety of exposures to feared stimuli, have been shown to alter reported levels of distress and thought content markedly (Ehlers & Margraf, 1989; Rapee, Mattick, & Murrell, 1986).

However, reliance upon self-report of conscious appraisals is limited by response biases associated with demand and expectancy (Mathews & Eysenck, 1987). Furthermore, such findings should not lead to the assumption that emotional responding is influenced only by conscious thought processes.

Definition of Cognition

Consideration of whether the definition of cognitive processes should include unconscious processes is one of several issues that arise in discussion of cognitive principles in anxiety states. Other issues include the primacy of affect or cognition, and the extent to which cognitive processes observed in anxiety disorders are predispositional and/or consequential to the disorder.

The oversimple conceptualization of cognition as conscious appraisal encounters difficulty in attempting to explain "irrational" anxiety, or, anxiety that reportedly occurs without recognizable cause. The temptation to then assume that specific elaborated cognitions direct emotional responding from a level that is below conscious awareness becomes potentially nontestable and purely speculative.

A more scientifically observable and testable position is to consider biasing in information processing as primarily concordant with variations in emotional state. Information processing biases not only influence conscious thought content but also operate outside of the individual's conscious awareness.

Primacy of Affect and Cognition

In light of the definition of cognitive processes as encompassing pre-awareness mechanisms, it has been argued that they are no longer cognitive in nature (Zajonc, 1984). Zajonc espouses potential independence of the cognitive and affective systems, such that affective responding can, under some circumstances, occur without cognitive involvement. However, the debate over the primacy of affect or cognition has been viewed as being largely dependent on the way in which cognition is defined (Williams, Watts, MacLeod, & Mathews, 1988). Williams et al. suggest that Zajonc's argument is based on a definition of cognition that is limited to conscious processes. Hence, the evidence that suggests that information can be encoded affectively without conscious cognitive evaluation (see Derryberry & Rothbart, 1984) is not viewed as evidence of the absence of cognitive processes in such encoding but rather as evidence for more basic cognitive processes.

Similarly, Mathews and Eysenck (1987) state that the development of an emotional reaction without conscious awareness of precipitants is not evidence for noncognitive processing. Rather, they suggest that two levels of cognitive processing exist, such that emotional responding may be activated through direct means or through higher level processing. Direct elicitation (which occurs through less elaborated but still cognitive processes) of emotional responding is believed to occur once an association is established between an event and an emotion, whereas the initial association is believed to incorporate higher level elaboration of meaning.

Williams et al. (1988) describe the stage model presented by Leventhal (1984), which resembles the notion of levels as described by Mathews and Eysenck (1987). According to Williams et al. (1988), Leventhal recognizes three cognitive levels: sensorimotor, which operates without volitional effort; schematic, which involves concrete representations of specific emotional events and experiences; and conceptual, which operates by conscious volition. Similarly, Williams et al. distinguish between automatic and controlled cognitive processing in which *automatic* refers to processing without need for attention or conscious effort. Automatic processing implies a coherent set of associative connections that are either innately determined or based on extensive training and experience. *Controlled* cognitive processing, on the other hand, refers to processing with attentional effort, and therefore is subject to attentional capacity limitations. Hence, what Zajonc (1984) recognizes as noncognitive, others recognize as cognitive at a level that is "direct" or sensorimotor or automatic.

The strongest contrast to Zajonc's (1984) position concerning the primacy of affect is represented by the Schacter and Singer (1962) model. The latter considers emotion to be experienced differentially depending on appraisal of the context and attribution of cause following awareness of a state of generalized, undifferentiated arousal. However, in addition to methodological problems and difficulty replicating the Schacter and Singer study, it has been demonstrated since that unexplained arousal is perceived negatively regardless of environmental cues (Barlow, 1988). In addition, anxiety is sometimes reported in the absence of arousal, and hence discordance among the response systems is observed (Rachman & Hodgson, 1974).

Emotion and cognition are both given central significance in Lang's (1977, 1984, 1985) bioinformational model. Emotion is conceptualized as an action tendency stored in memory and accessed in a variety of ways, all of which involve the processing of information. Lang speculates that emotional dispositions or acts are stored in data files comprising stimulus propositions, response propositions and meaning propositions.

The strength of the associative links between these propositions depends on the intensity or coherence of the emotion. Accessing of the associative network is accomplished by presenting information that matches the memory data files. Weak or incomplete matching may result in elicitation of only part of the emotional response, especially if the emotion is not very coherent in its associative structure. On the basis of Lang's model, "emotional responses are directly accessed without intervening appraisal if enough propositions are matched. Of course, meaning propositions, which are basically interpretations, come very close to the concept of attributions as elaborated by Schacter (1964), but attributions are seen as simply one type of proposition among many, not as necessary antecedents" (Barlow, 1988, p. 43). That is, the bioinformational model does not specify the necessity of elaborated cognitive schemata for the elicitation of an emotional response at any given time.

However, the data in support of the bioinformational model are limited mostly to studies with small Ns and analogue populations (Barlow, 1988). Zander and McNally (1988) attempted to test the response of panic disorder subjects to scripts containing either stimulus propositions, stimulus and response propositions, or stimulus, response and meaning propositions. It was assumed that the third type of script would produce the strongest fearful emotional reaction given the assumed more complete accessing of the relevant fear structure.

Unfortunately for the theory, equal amounts of fear and physiological response were elicited by each type of script, and in fact, very little physiological arousal was evoked overall. The authors concluded that the results may reflect difficulty devising scripts that match the fear structure of panic disorder individuals. Alternatively, the data may suggest a fallability of the hypotheses generated from the bioinformational model.

More recently, the polarity of the primacy of affect and cognition debate has lessened as information processing principles are incorporated more fully into the definition of cognition and regarded as important components of emotional states (Barlow, 1988; Eysenck & Mathews, 1987; Williams et al., 1988).

Cause or Consequence

Given cognitive biases that are characteristic of anxiety disorders, whether conscious or unconscious, and whether driven by affect or preceding affect at any given time, the question becomes whether such biases predispose to the development of anxiety disorders, or are the consequence of anxiety disorders. Investigators of congitive processes have used normal populations and clinically anxious populations, with the assumption that cognitive processes associated with anxiety are comparable across the two groups (Mathews & Eysenck, 1987). However, Bower (1987) has pointed to examples of apparent lack of generalization across such groups, although it is unclear whether group differences are qualitative or quantitative in nature.

Investigation of why some individuals experience unexplainable bursts of autonomic arousal and accompanying bodily symptoms, and yet do not subsequently develop anxious apprehension in association with such somatic events is pertinent to this issue. Several studies have independently reported ratios in the range of 10 to 15% of a nonclinical population as having experienced panic attacks in any given year (Norton, Dorward, & Cox, 1986; Rapee, Ancis, & Barlow, 1988; Salge & Beck, 1988). Yet, the prevalence of panic disorder is in the range of 3 to 6%.

More recently, Telch, Lucas, and Nelson (in press) found, from a large college sample, that individuals who experienced infrequent panic attacks differed from those who experienced frequent panic attacks, and met diagnostic criteria for panic disorder, in terms of level of anxious apprehension focused on future panic attacks. This finding pertains to the interaction between trait and state anxiety that will be discussed in a later section.

Furthermore, some individuals experience unexplainable bodily symptoms but do not interpret them as frightening at the time. Katon, Vitaliano, Russo, Jones, and Anderson (1987) assessed primary-care physicians' patients to find that many reported past episodes of rushes of different types of physical symptoms without reporting the experience of panic. Similarly, Beitman et al. (1987) examined cardiology patients and found that approximately 32% experienced nonfearful panic attacks (or, discomfort without fear in the presence of four or more panic bodily sensations). Does the development of anxious apprehension and anxiety disorders such as panic disorder depend on predispositional information processing biases and specific cognitive schemata?

Lang's bioinformational model targets only the maintenance of unadaptive anxiety. In contrast, Beck and Emery (1985) propose the etiological significance of distorted cognitive schemata for the development of anxiety disorders. Specifically, they suggest that danger schemata serve as predispositional cognitions, such that information about the world, self, and future is processed within a framework of automatic thoughts and images of danger. Distortion in processing of information is therefore believed to result in higher level distortions or perceptions of threat. Similarly, Mathews and Eysenck (1987) state that vulnerability to anxiety disorders resides in "systematic biases in the cognitive input to the emotional evaluative system" (p. 221). They emphasize processes of preattentive biases, selective attention and preferential encoding in memory in addition to specific cognitive schemata that result from such biases.

It is conceivable that measures of "neuroticism" or "arousability" on the one hand, and of threat biased cognitive processes on the other may represent different facets of the same predispositional factor: that arousability is as central to trait anxiety as is threat biased cognition. However, the data are not yet available to determine whether such biases precede or follow the development of anxiety disorders (Barlow, 1988).

Nevertheless, whether informational processing biases are causal or not, they are evident in anxiety disorder populations, are most likely significant to the maintenance of anxiety disorders, and seem to be important variables to consider in the assessment and treatment of anxiety.

In the following sections, data pertaining to information processing biases in anxiety will be reviewed. It should be noted that a complete model of anxiety, which could include reference to biological predispositional factors, life events and somatic events, will not be presented. Throughout the review it is assumed that the same biases are operative across the different anxiety disorders, but are manifested differentially depending on the nature of the foci of concern. For example, narrowing of attention upon an external phobic stimulus may have little impact upon the state of the stimulus, whereas focusing of attention upon an internal stimulus (thoughts, images or bodily sensations) may affect the intensity of the stimulus. In addition, it is assumed that all of the information processing effects to be discussed are intricately bound to the action tendencies associated with the states of anxiety (vigilance, preparation, and anticipatory avoidance) and fear (escape) (Barlow, 1988).

CONSCIOUS APPRAISAL

Aspects of information processing that have been highlighted as relevant to anxiety include selectivity of attention, narrowing of attention, and retrieval of information. Before presenting the evidence for such processes in anxiety states, evidence for the bias in conscious appraisal resulting from the assumed processes will be reviewed. Conscious appraisal has been studied using self-report and measurement of the effects of instructional manipulations.

The most predominant characteristic of the conscious appraisal associated with anxiety states is perceived threat and danger, as was mentioned briefly above in reference to the model outlined by Beck and Emery (1985). Reiss (1987) and colleagues (Reiss, Peterson, & Gursky, 1988; Reiss, Peterson, Gursky, & McNally, 1986) have pointed to one specific aspect of an anxious cognitive schemata that they label as anxiety sensitivity: or, the belief that anxiety symptoms have harmful consequences apart from their immediate unpleasantness (Holloway & McNally, 1987). To assess this construct, which resembles the "fear of fear" construct postulated by Goldstein and Chambless (1978), the Anxiety Sensitivity Index was developed. One difference between the concepts of anxiety sensitivity and "fear of fear" lies in the assumed causal basis: Goldstein and Chambless (1978) assumed that fear of fear develops subsequent to the experience of panic attacks (via interoceptive conditioning) whereas anxiety sensitivity is believed to emerge from factors such as biological constitution, and personality factors such as needs to avoid embarrassment, avoid illness or maintain control.

Anxiety sensitivity is hypothesized to predispose towards the development of anxiety disorders (Reiss, 1987). Within the anxiety sensitivity model, the specific cognitive schemata that is labeled anxiety sensitivity is assumed to underlie biases of selective attention, or increased alertness to signals of becoming anxious.

Various studies have been conducted to examine the construct validity of anxiety sensitivity, as measured by the Anxiety Sensitivity Index, including differential response to hyperventilation tests (Holloway & McNally, 1987), and prediction of number of situations feared (McNally & Lorenz, 1987; Reiss, Peterson, & Gursky, 1988). However, despite the assertion that anxiety sensitivity is a construct separable from trait anxiety, the precise relationship between trait anxiety and anxiety sensitivity remains unclear.

This is especially the case, given the emphasis upon fear of bodily symptoms within the anxiety sensitivity construct, and given that the presence of bodily symptoms is closely linked to levels of trait anxiety or arousability. In addition, as with previously cited references to specific cognitive schemata, longitudinal research is needed to determine whether anxiety sensitivity precedes or follows the development of anxiety disorders.

Another method of detecting conscious danger appraisal in anxiety states has been to assess the self-reported valence/threat value and probability of negative events. Butler and Mathews (1983) have shown that anxious and depressed patients rate the risk of negative events, especially self-referent events, as higher than do groups of normals. On the other hand, estimates of the risk of positive events do not differentiate the groups. In 1987, Butler and Mathews tested probability estimates for positive and negative events in relation to state anxiety (comparing one month and one day before an exam in a college population) and trait anxiety. State anxiety was associated with increased subjective risk of exam failure, whereas level of general anxiety was related to estimates of risk for all negative events.

In an investigation of a related topic, McNally, Foa, and Donnell (1989) tested whether panic disorder individuals interpreted ambiguous information regarding physiological arousal as more threatening and associated events as more likely than did either nonanxious controls or treated panic disordered subjects. In addition, they tested whether the untreated panic disorder group rated information related to ambiguous arousal as more negative and associated events as more likely than if information was related to ambiguous external stimuli, because the latter were considered less relevant to the fear structure of panic disorder. Indeed, they found that events associated with arousal were rated as more negative and more likely to occur than external event-related information, in the group of untreated panic disordered individuals in comparison to the other two groups.

Clark et al. (1988) posit that panic attacks are associated with a relatively enduring tendency to interpret certain bodily sensations in a catastrophic fashion, which in turn leads to hypervigilance (or, selectivity and narrowing of attention). It is not clearly stated whether they propose that the cognitive distortions precede or follow the development of maladaptive anxiety.

Clark et al. (1988) found that when given four types of ambiguous information (panic bodily sensations, ambiguous social events, other ambiguous events, and other bodily sensations), a panic disorder group interpreted the first type of information as more threatening than did groups of anxious nonpanickers and controls.

These data converge with other data to suggest the presence of cognitive schemata that are most likely strongly associated with the process of anxiety. Furthermore, the schemata seem to be specific to different anxiety disorders. The predictive validity of an information processing model of anxiety disorders depends upon demonstration of specificity of biases to foci of concern as opposed to no more than a generalized danger schemata that is apparent across different anxiety disorders to the same degree.

Butler and Mathews (1987) hypothesized that both generalized and specific biases are operative. That is, trait anxiety is associated with a general threat schemata that is pervasive and encompasses a wide range of threatening information. In the presence of ambiguous information, the activation of such schemata would result in the experience of anxiety and worry. In addition, state anxiety results in increased access to specific information pertaining to a current threat and leads to specific risk perception inflation.

Chambless and Graceley (1989) compared specific fears of bodily sensations and catastrophic events (physical injury and loss of control) among groups of panic disorder, social phobia, obsessive compulsive disorder, generalized anxiety disorder, major depressive disorder, dysthymia, and nonanxious controls. They found that fears of physical anxiety symptoms were stronger in panic disorder individuals, whereas fears of loss of control and of behavioral and social consequences of anxiety were relatively equal across groups of anxious and depressed subjects. In concordance with an information processing view, panic disordered individuals should evidence more selectivity of attention to physical symptom cues than would the other anxious and depressed groups. Similarly, selectivity of attention to such cues might be expected to vary in relation to expectancy of panicking and/or the recent experience of panic.

A related but somewhat different perspective to the issue of conscious awareness of danger emphasizes overt vigilance for safety (Rachman, 1984). It is hypothesized that, on the basis of initial danger schemata, safety signals are sought, and awareness of their accessibility is viewed as a major determinant of approach-avoidance behavior. In other words, the presence of conscious threat/danger schemata can be assessed in ways other than ratings of threat and danger. In addition, Rachman's safety signal perspective of agoraphobia suggests that vigilance for the presence or absence of safety may develop over time somewhat independently of vigilance for danger.

One implication might be that within a specific anxiety disorder, cognitive appraisals vary over time and accordingly, specificity of biases also vary. Obviously, treatment changes can be viewed from an information processing perspective also, such that perceived danger associated with specific cues reduces with successful anxiety and fear reduction.

Interestingly, Bouton (1988) discusses this issue within the framework of Pavlovian conditioning paradigms and terminology. Bouton hypothesizes that following extinction, the previous CS becomes an ambiguous CS as opposed to a non-CS. Future responses to the ambiguous CS are influenced strongly by the meaning of the context in which the CS occurs. Bouton proposes that if the context is frightening, then fear of an extinguished CS is relatively likely to return. That is, fearful learning (or, in information processing terms, an association between events and the emotion of fear) is never lost, but simply becomes more difficult to retrieve, until combined with frightening contexts. Of relevance to mood-state dependency theories is Bouton's suggested inclusion of mood states in the list of contextual cues believed to influence responses to an extinguished CS.

RECALL BIASES

Mood-biases in information processing include mood-congruity in learning, selectivity of attention and attention narrowing, and development of memory representations. Bower (1981) defined *mood congruity* as attending to and learning more about events that match an ongoing emotional state. *Mood state dependent retention* refers to more accurate recall when recall is assessed during reinstatement of the emotion present at the time of learning, and more accurate recall of information consistent with the original mood than of information inconsistent with the original mood.

Whereas most of the research has been conducted on the basis of induction of happy and sad mood states, the same principles are assumed to operate in anxious mood states. Negative cognitions and judgements are believed to be more readily retrieved when depressed because they were originally learned and encoded in memory when in a depressed mood state. Bower's (1981) associative network model is therefore consistent with Lang's bioinformational model, in which the recurrence of depressed mood is assumed to cue other related propositions such as specific cognitive content (Barlow, 1988). That is, network models of memory assume that emotions act as retrieval cues resulting in a spread of activation to events with which the emotions were associated, rendering the events more accessible for short term memory (Alexander & Guenther, 1986).

Furthermore, because a sad mood renders examples of negative events more accessible (due to the associative network), the perceived probability of such events is assumed to increase, because probability estimation, as described by Kahneman, Slovic and Tversky (1982), is determined by the ease with which examples of a class of events can be brought to mind. This phenomenon is referred to as the *availability heuristic*. Hence, the induced moods serve as a schema for interpreting and organizing elements associated with an event.

Therefore, at the time of retrieval, any cue to recall an event is likely to bring to mind the mood congruent elements. "The basic idea is that arousal of an emotion by whatever means primes into readiness concepts and categories that are congruent with how one is feeling. These primed categories are then used to describe the somewhat ambiguous social events that go on around us . . ." (Bower, 1987, p. 444). It is noteworthy, however, that Williams et al. (1988) suggest that the availability heuristic does not affect judgments of frequency and probability.

Rachman, Lopatka, and Eich (unpublished manuscript) tested whether mood dependent retrieval was dependent on specific moods, by examining whether pain also increased access to sad memories. They assessed subjects in pain and pain free states by providing lists of words for which subjects were to retrieve past real life experiences. They found that while recall of unhappy experiences was more common during pain states, the bias was attributable to ratings of level of sadness at the time of recall. In other words, the retrieval of sad memories seemed to be specific to the emotion of sadness.

Nunn, Stevenson, and Whalan (1984) reported that panic disorder groups recalled more propositions from passages containing phobic material than neutral passages, in contrast to normals. However, their results were confounded by differential word familiarity and a response bias favoring all negative material (Mathews & Eysenck, 1987).

Norton, Schaefer, Cox, Dorward, and Wozney (1987) used word lists containing danger, hostile, and neutral words in nonclinical subjects who reported either no experience of panic or infrequent experience of panic. Subjects were primed before the learning phase by reading passages that were related to either panic, anger, or neutral material. Differences in recall between the groups were only present when subjects underwent certain priming paragraphs: the panic group who read the panic paragraph recalled more anxious words than nonpanickers who read the same paragraph, and than panickers who read the anger or neutral paragraphs.

The results suggest specificity of effects to the provocation of a relevant fear structure (the panic paragraph for the panic group). This reflects, most likely, mood congruity (i.e., selective attention to information that matches an ongoing mood state) rather than mood dependent retrieval, because the effect of mood at the time of recall was neither manipulated nor assessed.

Mogg, Mathews, and Weinman (1987) concluded that there was no evidence for memory bias in anxiety states. They were unable to find evidence for a recall effect favoring negative or threatening words in anxious subjects in the short term. Mathews and Eysenck (1987) reviewed several other pieces of evidence suggesting lack of biased recall in anxious states, at least in terms of short term recall. They suggested that, "Unlike depressives, anxious subjects may tend to adopt secondary cognitive avoidance strategies, such as selective ignoring or failure to rehearse, which could inhibit or delay elaborative encoding" (p. 226). That is, the avoidant action tendency associated with anxious anticipation might mitigate the bias towards threat recall.

Williams et al. (1988) distinguish between passive retrieval and active retrieval. *Passive retrieval* refers to processes believed to underlie the memories that present without obvious prompting, and actually reflect the fact that "more highly primed material will come to mind more readily when only partial [unrecognized] cues are available" (p. 173). In contrast, *active retrieval* involves elaborated encoding, which, Williams et al. suggest, may be inhibited in anxious states.

The notion of inhibition of active retrieval of threat related material is very consistent with an emphasis upon the action tendencies associated with some anxious states (Barlow, 1988). That is, attentiveness and passive retrieval processes, which are less dependent on higher level cognitive elaboration, may reflect the action tendency of preparation and vigilance for danger. Active retrieval processes that involve cognitive elaboration may be affected by the tendency to avoid.

Although recognizing potential secondary avoidance in active retrieval, both Matthews and Eysenck (1987) and Williams et al. (1988) conclude that memory biases are less implicated in anxiety states than in depressive states. Yet, the hypothesized role of avoidance in selective memory for threat related material is highly significant. A less directly measurable memory effect does not necessarily imply a lesser memory effect, but may imply a memory effect that is mediated by a process central to the psychopathology of anxiety states (i.e., avoidance).

Of final note to this section is Bower's (1987) recent conclusion that mood dependent retrieval in depressed moods is proving unreliable and may be limited to occasions in which the person attributes their emotion to the event at time of learning. Should the same attributional principle apply to anxious mood, then mood dependent retrieval effects may be observable in anxiety states only under conditions in which individuals remember, at times when anxious, past events that were linked with anxious mood at the time of learning.

SELECTIVITY OF ATTENTION

The evidence for selectivity of attention in anxious states is quite strong; that is, anxious individuals display a bias in perceiving mood congruent material, because mood congruent material has more perceptual salience. Parkinson and Rachman (1981) found that mothers of children in surgery responded to significantly more stress-related words than control subjects in the presence of distracting auditory information. The dichotic listening task is used to assess for bias in access to semantic or emotional content that occurs without awareness.

It is assumed that information with emotional or personal significance can intrude into consciousness from a previously unattended source, and physiological reactions can occur in response to the emotional stimuli without awareness of the presence of the stimuli. In other words, attentional bias may precede conscious awareness. However, the above experiment did not control for differential familiarity with the stimuli presented to the unattended channel.

A series of studies have since demonstrated selectivity of attention to threat related material after controlling for word familiarity in anxious patients. Mathews and MacLeod (1985) found that generalized anxiety disorder subjects responded more slowly to color naming tasks when the words were related to threat in contrast to nonanxious controls, which they assumed to reflect greater attentional demands. MacLeod, Mathews, and Tata (1986) demonstrated that the same type of anxiety patients shifted their attention toward threat words during visual detection tasks.

In an attempt to examine more closely the extent to which processing occurred at a preconscious level, Mathews and MacLeod (1986) compared generalized anxiety disorder subjects and normals using dichotic listening tasks, and tested recall of the words presented to the unattended channel. Despite failure to recall the content of the unattended channel (i.e., lack of conscious recall), the groups responded differently. However, it is still possible that the threatening words were recognized during the course of the task. In addition, ambiguous but potentially threatening stories were used for shadowing, which may have differentially influenced the responding of the two groups. Therefore it is still unclear whether the results reflect unconscious processes, and the effects of state and trait anxiety are still confounded. Nevertheless, the authors interpreted the results as suggestive of a bias in preattentive mechanisms that determine allocation of processing resources to threat cues. The results were assumed to reflect either a selection of threat cues for additional processing or a demand on resources necessary to inhibit awareness of threat, although they favored the former interpretation.

Williams et al. (1988) cite results from dichotic listening tasks as evidence for "automatic" biasing (as opposed to elaborated biasing) to elements that are potentially threatening to the individual. On the other hand, Martin, Williams, and Clark (1988) argue that the bias observed in selective processing may be a function of emotionality as opposed to a specific threat perception. By matching positive and negative words in terms of emotionality, they found that anxious patients responded equally slowly to both types of words in comparison to neutral, nonemotional words, whereas nonanxious individuals responded equally to all three types of words.

MacLeod et al. (1986) suggest that probe detection (which does not produce differential responses relevant to an individual's particular foci of concern) reflects earlier stages of processing and a general bias to threat, whereas color naming (which does reflect specificity to particular foci of concern) reflects more elaborate stage processing. However, according to the conclusions drawn by Martin et al. (1988), the MacLeod et al. speculations are limited by virtue of failure to control the emotionality of the different word stimuli used in their tests.

The most stringent method of examining threat bias, therefore, is to compare equally negative emotional words and assess for effects specific to the individual's fears. This has already been demonstrated with spider phobics, where response to emotional words specific to spiders was greater than response to other equally emotional words (Watts, McKenna, Sharrock, & Trezise, 1986).

The evidence is consistent with the clinical observation of the ease with which anxious patients notice threat cues relevant to their own fears. For example, Van den Hout et al. (1988) found that panic disorder subjects were much faster and more accurate in determining whether they had been given yohimbine (an alpha-adrenergic antagonist) or placebo in contrast to nonanxious controls. The authors attributed the findings to level of interoceptive awareness (but also mentioned the possible confound of the experience of more symptoms due to the combination of yohimbine and high levels of chronic arousal in the panic disorder group).

On the other hand, Borkovec and O'Brien (1977) found that autonomic perception (measured using the Autonomic Perception Questionnaire) was quite variable in a group of speech anxious subjects. Yet, the variability might be due to the possibility that interoceptive cues are less reliably fear provoking for speech anxious individuals than for panic disorder individuals.

Interestingly, Ehlers, Margraf, Roth, Taylor, and Birbaumer (1988) found that panic disorder groups and controls did not differ in terms of accuracy of heart rate perception, although the panic disorder group were more fearful of the heart rate symptoms as measured in a false physiological feedback design. It is likely that fearfulness is associated more strongly with reported awareness of heart rate than with accuracy of heart rate detection. The relationship between selectivity of attention and cognitive schemata is unclear.

Williams et al. (1988) describe two basic hypotheses; first, that selectivity of attention produces differential processing; and second, that selectivity is the consequence of differential processing. They suggest that the former hypothesis is subject to the tautology of selectivity producing selectivity, whereas the second hypothesis can be understood logically as selectivity occurring as a function of priming of certain processing structures. The priming may occur on a chronic basis or acutely. That is, selectivity of attention is believed to be influenced by the schemata that an individual has developed through learning experiences.

Williams et al. (1988) describe a cyclical model, in which once a stimulus is perceived, the reaction is dependent upon an affective decision process that incorporates schemata, with a resulting direction of attention towards or away from the stimulus (i.e., selectivity of attention), all of which occurs at a preattentive stage. It is further speculated that once stimuli have received such attentional allocation, their representations become primed, and therefore more likely to generate negative items into consciousness. Hence, trait anxiety, which results in direction of attention towards threat, increases state anxiety, and so on.

SELF-FOCUSED ATTENTION

Two models that describe information processing effects in terms of trait anxiety have been posited. First, trait anxiety is associated with a tendency to selectively attend to threat related stimuli, and to attach threatening meaning to ambiguous stimuli, resulting in susceptibility to high levels of state anxiety (MacLeod et al., 1986). Second, the perception of threat in general that characterizes trait anxiety reflects emotionality, whereas state anxiety may be associated with specific selectivity of attention. In either case, it is speculated that selectivity of attention (at a trait and/or state level) is influenced by cognitive schemata of danger or threat (Williams et al., 1988).

In addition, there is a natural tendency to self-focus following the perception of physiological arousal (Barlow, 1988) that seems to be a process closely related to selective attention. For example, Wegner and Giuliano (1980) compared states of relaxation and physical activity, and found that the latter resulted in production of more self-referent words in a subsequent word task. Not only is arousal accompanied by self-focus, but self-focus is believed to lead to an increased sensitivity to proprioceptive sensations and more intense emotions.

Review of the literature provides evidence to suggest that self-focused attention results in increased sensitivity to internal experiences and intensification of relevant emotions (cf. Barlow, 1988). It has been shown that individuals with chronically high levels of self-focused attention experience laboratory induced emotions with more intensity than less focused individuals. That is, they experience greater subjective intensity of the emotion once the emotion is elicited. In addition, more distress is experienced if attention is directed towards affective versus mechanical qualities of one's own response (Barlow, 1988). Furthermore, self-focused attention tends to slow the rate of habituation to external stimuli (Scheier & Carver, 1983).

It is believed that a self-focused shift of attention is one component of pathological anxiety and that some patients with chronic hyperarousal have learned to attend to internal states and have become preoccupied with affective qualities of those sensations. Initially, increases in negative affect result in a self-focusing of attention, but eventually the self-focus becomes an integral part of the negative affect (Barlow, 1988).

In a cyclical process, such self-focus intensifies and perpetuates the emotional experience. It may be the case that in either trait or state anxiety the focus of attention shifts rapidly between the focus of threat and one's internal reaction in a selective fashion, contributing to a spiraling of affect.

NARROWING OF ATTENTION

It is hypothesized that the self-focus of attention that occurs as a function of arousal associated with negative affect is matched by a narrowing of attention, which also increases as a function of arousal. Easterbrook (1959) described this process as a preoccupation with mood congruent material during emotional reactivity, thus reflecting the process of selectivity of attention. The number of cues used decreases as the emotional intensity increases. Therefore, while some view selectivity of attention as primarily a function of cognitive schemata (Eysenck & Mathews, 1987; Williams et al., 1988), it is also conceivable to view selectivity of attention as primarily arousal driven (Barlow, 1988). Alternatively, danger-laden cognitive schemata and arousal may be viewed as different facets of the same state that "drives" selectivity of attention.

Korchin (1964) described the effect of attention narrowing and exclusion of focus upon external stimuli as resulting in an inability to respond adaptively (a state of disarray). Attention narrowing may underlie the Yerkes-Dodson (1908) law of the relationship between arousal and performance. For example, the psychopathology of sexual dysfunction can be viewed as excessive focusing upon task irrelevant cues, such as negative consequences of not performing sexually, which results in increased arousal, increased focus upon performance cues, and ultimately, dysfunctional performance (Barlow, 1986). The precursors to self-focused attention, arousal, and negative affect are believed to be accompanied by a dispositional sense of uncontrollability (Barlow, 1988), which further narrows attention toward the content of the apprehension, specific to the individual. That is, initial selectivity of attention is followed by increased narrowing of attention.

Perceived uncontrollability has been posited as central to the psychopathology of anxiety, being acquired from learning history experiences with uncontrollable events, and serving to predispose towards the development of anxiety disorders (Barlow, 1988). Animal research has shown that whereas exposure to uncontrollable aversive events is more distressing than exposure to controllable aversive events, the threshold for distress in response to the former is influenced by prior experience of mastery and control (Mineka, Gunnar, & Champoux, 1986). Those with more mastery experience tend to demonstrate less distress in response to uncontrollable aversive events. Extrapolating from animal based data, it is suggested that cognitive sets of lack of control or helplessness exist as predispositional cognitive schemata that emerge under stress (Barlow, 1988). Certainly, provision of a sense of control, where control refers to means of escape from, or termination of, an aversive event, alleviates distress. This has been demonstrated in terms of exposure to in vivo situations that are feared (Rachman, Craske, Tallman, & Solyom, 1986) and exposure to interoceptive feared stimuli (Sanderson, Rapee, & Barlow, 1990). Litt (1988) also emphasized the role of perceived control, and self-efficacy to implement control, in terms of response to stress.

It is also conceivable, in view of the action tendencies of avoidance and escape associated with anxiety and fear, that excessive narrowing of attention upon fear relevant cues is alternated with attempts to distract and avoid elaboration upon the meaning of the cue. Such shifting could at least partly account for the failure of extinction to occur naturally in cases of pathological anxiety. Rapid shifting of attention is also suggested by Eysenck and Mathews (1987) in their criticism of Easterbrook's (1959) model, as the reason why it is unlikely that attention is focused on only one cue in a situation, but rather that attentional focus is indeed narrow but also variable, resulting in distractability. If one also considers the likelihood of attentional shifting from external to internal states, the potential for distractability is multiplied.

Recognition of the significance of (pre)attentive focusing upon and of distraction (at higher levels of cognitive elaboration) from relevant cues is in some ways paralleled by recognition of information seeking tendencies from a social psychological perspective. Individual styles of preference for amount of control and information in the face of objective threat have been identified. Some individuals seem to develop cognitive styles of avoiding information as a means of helping to blunt the psychological impact of stressful events. Miller and Birnbaum (1988) suggest that if the situation is uncontrollable, those who monitor (or, seek information) will experience more stress and arousal than those who attempt to avoid. For example, high monitors reportedly show less habituation across trials of uncontrollable shock presentations than do low monitors.

On the other hand, it seems that such individual styles are not related directly to levels of state or trait anxiety or depression, but that in situations of high stress, high monitors experience more distress (Miller & Birnbaum, 1988). Miller, Brody, and Summerton (1988) suggest that high monitors not only show faster reaction time to negative internal and external stimuli, but also may attend to potentially more negative consequences of those stimuli than do low monitors. This area of research highlights the importance of remembering to place information processing biases effects within the broader context of individual historical variables and learned methods of coping. Such individual styles may interact with information processing biases to determine level of distress experienced.

HABITUATION AND REPRESENTATIONS

Models of memory representations are relevant to the understanding of how narrowing of attention upon fear relevant cues impedes fear reduction. Whitlow (1975) has described the process of habituation as one in which the matching of a stimulus representation in short term memory yields further corresponding stimulus presentations as less effective. Habituation only occurs, however, if the priming representation (one that is retrieved from long term memory or is present in short term memory as a result of very recent presentations of the stimulus) matches the stimulus presentation. In addition, retrieval of representations from long term memory occurs through associative learning with contextual cues. Wagner (1981) posits a similar habituation model.

Accordingly, if individuals limit their attention to specific fear relevant aspects and or vascillate between narrow attentional focus upon the feared cue(s) and distraction, it is conceivable that the stimulus representations will not match the actual stimulus or that retrieval of the stimulus representation will be impeded, and fear reduction therefore mitigated. Watts, Trezise, and Sharrock (1986) hypothesized also that by failing to focus attention fully upon phobic stimuli, phobics develop poor cognitive representations of the relevant stimuli, which in turn interferes with fear reduction through exposure for the reasons described above. Their hypothesis does not contrast with the notion that attentional resources are recruited by presentation of anxiety stimuli, but rather that the stimuli are poorly processed. They suggest that the focus is typically upon responses of anxiety (self-focused attention), which interferes with focus upon the stimuli.

Watts et al. (1986) tested this assumption by asssessing recall of objective characteristics of spiders in spider phobics and found that phobics showed poorer recognition recall than nonphobics. On the other hand, when instructed to identify two distinctive features of the presented spiders, only a weak correlation between level of fear and memory was obtained.

ASSESSMENT AND TREATMENT IMPLICATIONS

Assessment

Anxiety based cognitive biases yield significant implications for at least three issues in the assessment of anxiety: (1) identification of targets for therapeutic change, (2) designation of markers of therapeutic change, and (3) validity of the method of assessment. First, the assessment of conscious appraisals, including specific foci of concern or beliefs, and the associated negative valence and risk estimates, serves to identify targets for therapeutic change that may be essential to successful outcome. Similarly, the perception of unpredictability and uncontrollability of events and/or emotional reactions is a suitable target for modification through treatment.

Second, appropriate measures of the degree to which therapeutic change has taken place might include negative valence and risk estimates for specific foci of concern, and selectivity of attention. Third, the method of assessment is likely to be influenced by variables such as potential mood dependent memory effects, and state versus trait differences in terms of estimates of perceived threat.

Identification of Targets for Therapeutic Change

Three methods of assessment of conscious cognitive appraisals are available. First, self-report instruments have been developed, to assess conscious appraisals of danger and other misinterpretations, for the different anxiety disorders. Examples of such instruments include the Anxiety Sensitivity Index (Reiss et al., 1986), the Agoraphobia Cognitions Questionnaire (Chambless, Caputo, Bright, & Gallagher, 1984), and the Fear of Negative Evaluation scale (Watson & Friend, 1969).

Recently, Gursky and Reiss (in press) have developed scales pertaining to estimates of perceived danger for various simple phobic situations. In addition to standardized self-report schedules, individually tailored self-report instruments that target negative valence and risk estimation for specific foci of concern can be used. An example would be a visual analogue, 0- to 100-point scale, of the certainty with which "going crazy" or "dying" will result from panicking, where 0 equals no chance, and 100 equals will definitely happen. These types of individually tailored scales may be more appropriate for repeated measurement, and may also be more sensitive indicators of treatment progress than standardized instruments. Thought sampling techniques have been used also (e.g., Kenardy, Evans, & Oei, 1989), although such procedures are more cumbersome than visual analogue scales.

Unfortunately, self-report instruments assume accurate self-awareness of biases or misinterpretations, in addition to their susceptibility to response demand biases. Frequently, a verbal report of the specific focus of distress is unobtainable. In addition, the precipitant to any given episode of distress is often unrecognized.

The extent to which clients reportedly experience anxiety or fear without noticeable precipitants is important to assess and modify, given the heightened distress resulting from perceived unpredictability. Even within situationally cued anxiety or fear, such as social situations for socially phobic individuals or trapped situations for agoraphobic individuals, the precise cues that elicit responses at any given time may not be obvious to the individual. This occurs because the cues are often very subtle (such as minor fluctuations in somatic state, or specific cognitive images), and because perceptual selectivity may occur at a preawareness level of attention.

A second method of assessing conscious cognitive appraisals entails performance based tasks. Measurement of differential responding dependent upon manipulations of contextual features during behavioral testing may serve to identify specific features of cognitive biases for a given individual. For example, the presence of others may yield differential fear patterns depending on whether the individual's focus of apprehension is upon physical danger or negative social evaluation. Similarly, the degree to which distraction strategies are employed in response to different contextual settings (such as the comparison between quiet and noisy surroundings) may serve to identify relevant features of danger schemata (such as fears of going crazy resulting from self-focus of attention when in a quiet environment, or fears of becoming inappropriately aggressive resulting from feeling physiologically aroused when in a noisy environment).

Differential use of help seeking behaviors (such as leaning against a wall for support) can be measured in the same way as distraction strategies. Hence, the dependent variables from performance based tasks can be level of fear experienced in given settings or time/event sampling of different behaviors (such as distraction strategies or help seeking behaviors) in given settings. Performance based tasks overcome many of the limitations of self-report assessments, although they are more time consuming.

A third method of assessment of conscious cognitive appraisals is physiological assessment in which different stimuli (real or imagined) are presented to the individual, and physiological responding is concurrently monitored. This method of assessment is advocated by proponents of the bioinformational model, in which the most sensitive method of assessment is believed to be physiological monitoring of response to different imaginal scenarios that include stimulus, response and meaning propositions. However, technological limitations and complexities of physiological responding result in many influences from sources irrelevant to the target of interest, hence limiting the validity of physiological output as a direct measure of cognition.

Markers of Therapeutic Change

Suitable markers of therapeutic change include measures of selectivity of attention to signals of perceived danger, and negative valence and risk estimates. (Measurement of valence and risk, in terms of conscious appraisals, was described earlier.) Given that selectivity of attention is likely to operate at a level of awareness that is "preconscious", methods of assessment that tap aspects of functioning such as reaction time and latency of response, have been devised. These include dichotic listening tasks, probe detection latencies, and color naming tasks, in which the effect of material (which pertains more or less to an individual's foci of apprehension) upon attentional resources is asssessed. Because the dependent variables are performance, as opposed to self-report, many of the limitations of self-report are overcome. Nevertheless, the intricacies of attentional focus raise questions about the extent to which a direct parallel exists between performance on such tasks and cognitive biases.

An example of such intricacies includes the recent recognition of the need to control for word familiarity and word emotionality when conducting these forms of assessment (Mathews & MacLeod, 1985; Martin et al., 1988). Other methods of assessing selectivity of attention to signals of perceived threat include measurement of perceptual threshold for the relevant signals. In the case of panic disorder, where the signal of impending danger is usually a physiological sensation, tasks of autonomic perception are appropriate (Ehlers & Margraf, 1989).

In the case of social phobia, where the signal of impending threat is typically verbal/nonverbal cues from others, tasks of social perception may be appropriate. That is, responses to the presentation of feared stimuli are assessed, as opposed to responses to words that symbolize the feared stimuli (as in the case of dichotic listening tasks, color naming tasks or probe detection latencies).

Validity of Methods of Assessment

The final implication of cognitive principles in the assessment of anxiety is to recognize the degree to which methods of assessment may be invalidated as a result of cognitive biases. Given the tendency to attend to mood congruent stimuli, and for conscious appraisals to differ across states of high state anxiety and low state anxiety, assessment while in the presence of the feared stimulus is likely to yield results different from assessment within the office setting.

The research by Butler and Mathews (1987), for example, has shown how estimates of risk inflate as state anxiety increases. Therefore, assessment of negative valence and risk estimation in the presence of the stimulus would yield a more accurate reflection of pre- to post-treatment change than assessment of negative valence and risk estimation in general.

This may be achieved through concurrent self-monitoring of negative valence and risk during naturalistic encounters, or by measurement during forced exposures to specific events. Similarly, given the possible tendency to recall more anxious, mood congruent stimuli, and to recall information more accurately when mood at time of recall is similar to the mood at time of learning, assessment may yield more sensitive results if conducted in the presence of provocative stimuli.

Treatment

The obvious treatment implication from the recognition of biased conscious appraisals in anxiety states is to attempt to modify such appraisals. However, the issue of appraisal modification seems to be much more complex than assumed initially. Anxiety or fear can be associated with conscious misappraisals that the individual does not recognize as being erroneous. Examples include the interpretation of chest pain as heart attack in the absence of disconfirmatory medical evidence, and the interpretation of certain benign noises during flight as indicative of impending crashing. Anxiety and fear generated by such conscious misappraisals may be responsive to the provision of corrective information.

On the other hand, anxiety or fear associated with conscious misinterpretations that the individual also recognizes as being potentially erroneous (such as the interpretation of chest pain as heart attack despite knowledge of disconfirmatory medical evidence) would seem to reflect the process of irrational anxiety associated with anxiety disorders.

Cognitive restructuring, as opposed to provision of corrective information, has therefore been implemented to target the irrational appraisal process. In addition to modification of misinterpretations, cognitive restructuring (and other methods of altering cognitive biases) should include self identification of subtle cues that trigger emotional responding. Generalized perceptions of unpredictability and uncontrollability, that appear to be very significant to the maintenance of anxious apprehension, are likely to decrease upon development of awareness of cues.

Questions that then arise include the following: (1) Does cognitive restructuring reliably modify conscious appraisals in the presence of provocative stimuli? (2) Does modification of conscious appraisals also correct associated perceptual biases? Can change in conscious appraisals and selectivity of attention occur desynchronously, and what would be the implications of continuing selectivity of attention, in the absence of consciously perceived threat or danger, for short term and long term anxiety and fear reduction? (3) Is cognitive restructuring the most effective method of modifying information processing biases, and does the efficacy of cognitive restructuring interact with the particular content area or foci of concern? For example, is social anxiety more responsive to cognitive restructuring than is obsessive compulsive disorder, and if so, how is a differential response accounted for from an information processing perspective? (4) Is modification of information processing biases necessary for anxiety/fear reduction, or strongly predictive of degree of anxiety/fear reduction?

Evidence for Cognitive Change

Unfortunately, very few treatment studies have included assessment of information processing biases as a pre- to postmeasure. Therefore, it is difficult to address the above issues due to limited data. However, Clark et al. (1988) and McNally, Foa, & Donnell (1989) reported that successful treatment of panic disorder was associated with marked reductions in the tendency to perceive ambiguous material related to arousal as threatening.

Investigations of the extent to which information processing biases are modified differentially by different therapeutic procedures, and the extent to which such modifications predict treatment outcome, are yet to be performed. Most of the available evidence concerns the efficacy of cognitive restructuring in terms of measures of anxiety or fear reduction, without assessment of hypothesized processes of anxiety/fear reduction. Therefore, mechanisms of change are unclear. Furthermore, the comparison between cognitive restructuring and exposure procedures is usually confounded, as the procedures overlap extensively.

In most studies of the treatment of phobias, exposure treatments have been shown to be more effective than cognitive restructuring (Biran & Wilson, 1981; Emmelkamp, Kuipers, & Eggeraat, 1978). In addition, cognitive therapy seems to add little to the effectiveness of exposure therapy, with the exception of reducing the rate of attrition (Emmelkamp & Mersch, 1982; Michelson, Mavissakalian, & Marchione, 1985; Williams & Rappoport, 1983).

On the other hand, in one study cognitive therapy was found to add to the effectiveness of exposure therapy for the treatment of social phobia (Butler, Cullington, Mumby, Amies, & Gelder, 1984). In addition, instructional manipulations have been shown to have marked impact upon response to exposure procedures (Kirsch, 1985). Mathews and Eysenck (1987) suggest that imagery may lead to cognitive changes that resemble processes of change that occur during exposure in vivo. Vivid imagination has been shown to influence the judged probability of events occurring (Gregory, Cialdini, & Carpenter, 1982, cited in Mathews & Eysenck, 1987). Exposure procedures may be more effective means for altering information processing biases than pure cognitive restructuring.

It is conceivable that cognitive therapy is of limited value not only because of the impotency of verbal procedures, but because the procedures do not directly address the action tendencies of escape or avoidance that are characteristic of anxious and fearful responding. In other words, rational elaboration may not be sufficient to alter anxious information processing biases, which may have more to do with the affective system that the cognitive system (to the extent these systems are qualitatively different). Alteration of these biases may be best accomplished through behavioral change, as was suggested by Bandura (1977). The question would then become how can modification of cognitive biases be maximized using exposure procedures, assuming that their modification is essential to outcome.

Exposure Type and Cognitive Change

From the research concerning selectivity of attention, self-focused attention, and attention to affective qualities of the stimulus-response complex, it might be predicted that instructions to focus attention on mechanical aspects of the situation (while preventing escape action tendencies) would be beneficial. On the other hand, predictions from the bioinformational model include the detrimental effect of distraction during exposure, because exposure is believed to proceed most effectively when the fear memory or representation is activated fully.

Such activation necessitates presentation and focus of attention upon stimulus, response, and meaning propositions. Therefore, distraction, which is consistent with the action tendency to avoid or escape and is most likely used typically by anxious patients, should impede processing. Focusing on the mechanical aspects of an exposure exercise may serve as a distraction.

Research regarding the efficacy of distraction, conducted mostly with obsessive-compulsive clients, has suggested that distraction produces immediate reduction in level of anxiety but impedes long term or between session reduction (Foa & Kozak, 1986; Grayson, Foa & Steketee, 1982, 1986). Craske, Street, and Barlow (1989) found that distraction instructions during in vivo exposure resulted in less improvement beyond the end of treatment than did focus instructions, with agoraphobic subjects. A similar pattern of results has been observed when distraction is employed as a coping technique to deal with stressful events (Suls & Fletcher, 1985). However, the weaker long term results from distracted exposure as contrasted to focused exposure is not necessarily antithetical to the above prediction that focus upon affective qualities of responding is a less effective treatment than is focusing upon more mechanical aspects of responding.

Focus upon mechanical aspects of responding may not constitute distraction, but rather more effective focusing of attention. For example, subjects who focus on the emotional quality of pain experience more distress and less endurance than those who focus upon objective physical sensations (McCaul & Haugtuedt, 1982).

The poor long term efficacy of "distracted" exposure is consistent with the stimulus representational models of habituation cited earlier, which specify the necessity of the development of stimulus representations that match actual stimulus presentations accurately. Foa and Kozak (1986) suggest a more "meaning proposition" oriented model of the reasons for which focused exposure is more beneficial than distracted exposure. They speculate that, after accessing the relevant fear memory, information that is incompatible with some elements of the fear structure are realized and therefore a new memory is formed. Specifically, the connections between stimulus and response are changed as a result of within session habituation, which leads to information concerning the absence of arousal responses in the presence of the stimulus. In addition, a reduction in the probability and valence of the stimulus (the meaning proposition) occurs as a result of long term habituation that occurs following within session habituation. Consequently, persistent high levels of arousal may interfere with changes in the meaning proposition, because within session habituation will be impeded.

Indeed, Borkovec and Sides (1979) found that relaxation prior to exposure yielded more effective results than exposure alone, which they attributed to increased attention during exposure associated with more extensive within session response strength reduction. On the other hand, it seems clear that anxiety must be elicited during exposure for therapeutic change to take place (Barlow, 1988).

The effect of information that is incompatible with an existing expectational set has been demonstrated by Rachman and colleagues (Rachman & Levitt, 1985; Rachman & Lopatka, 1986; Rachman, Lopatka, & Levitt, 1988). These investigators have observed that negative incompatible information has a stronger impact than positive incompatible information. That is, underprediction of fear or panic has been shown several times to yield more influential effects on subsequent levels of anticipation than does overprediction. Hence, disconfirmation of stimulus-response connections requires several trials of "less fearful than expected" exposure, whereas reinstatement of anticipation can occur after only one trial of "more fearful than expected" exposure.

While Foa and Kozak (1986) suggest that the most effective method of altering meaning propositions is to experience full exposure, it is also conceivable that disassociations between stimuli and arousal responding, and reduced negative valence and risk estimations, occur through any procedure that instills in the individual a sense of control. It has been argued that perceptions of control are best attained through preventing the action tendency of escape or avoidance in the case of fear (Barlow, 1988). Therefore performance accomplishments, regardless of level of anxiety experienced during the task, may be essential.

In accord with this prediction, controlled escape instructions for exposure were found to be as effective as instructions to remain in the feared situation until fear levels reduced (Rachman et al., 1986). In the escape conditions, subjects were allowed to escape and thereby prevent the experience of high levels of fear, but were required to repeatedly re-enter the situation. Hence, subjects in the escape condition experienced less anxiety/fear during exposures but accomplished behavioral approach.

CONCLUSION

In conclusion, research on basic cognitive processes in anxiety is only just beginning in earnest and many exciting discoveries lie ahead of us. But we must not make the mistake of concluding that the phenomenon of emotion can be reduced to the study of cognition in the same way that some in biology have attempted to reduce behavior to the action of neurotransmitters. We await adequate conceptualizations of how best to integrate emotion and cognition in some sort of hierarchical fashion and further elucidation of the role of information processing in this complex phenomenon.

Also, it is becoming increasingly clear that cognitive therapy, as currently conceptualized, probably has little to do with the cognitive phenomena that are the subject of cognitive psychology and this chapter. We also await more adequate models of therapy for emotional disorder (affective therapy, Barlow, 1988) that take into account the complexity of the cognitive-affective structures with which we are confronted.

REFERENCES

Alexander, L., & Guenther, R. K. (1986). The effect of mood and demand on memory. *British Journal of Psychology, 77,* 343–350.

Bandura, A. (1977). Self-efficacy: Toward a unifying theory of behavioral change. *Psychological Review, 84,* 191–215.

Barlow, D. H. (1986). Causes of sexual dysfunction: The role of anxiety and cognitive interference. *Journal of Consulting and Clinical Psychology, 54,* 140–148.

Barlow, D. H. (1988) *Anxiety and its disorders: Nature and treatment of anxiety and panic.* New York: Guilford Press.

Beck, A. T., & Emery, G. (1985). *Anxiety disorders and phobias: A cognitive perspective.* New York: Basic Books.

Beck, A. T., & Rush, A. J. (1975). A cognitive model of anxiety formation and anxiety resolution. In I. Sarason & C. Spielberger (Eds.), *Stress and anxiety: Vol. 2.* New York: Halstead Press.

Beitman, B. D., Basha, I., Flaker, G., DeRosear, L., Mukerji, V., & Lamberti, J. (1987). Non-fearful panic disorder: Panic attacks without fear. *Behaviour Research and Therapy, 25,* 487–492.

Biran, M., & Wilson, G. T. (1981). Treatment of phobic disorders using cognitive and exposure methods: A self-efficacy analysis. *Journal of Consulting and Clinical Psychology, 49,* 886–899.

Borkovec, T. D., & O'Brien, G. T. (1977). Relation of autonomic perception and its manipulation to the maintenance and reduction of fear. *Journal of Abnormal Psychology, 86,* 163–171.

Borkovec, T. D., & Sides, J. K. (1979). The contribution of relaxation and expectancy to fear reduction via graded, imaginal exposure to feared stimuli. *Behaviour Research and Therapy, 17,* 529–540.

Bouton, M. E. (1988). Context and ambiguity in the extinction of emotional learning: Implications for exposure therapy. *Behaviour Research and Therapy, 26*, 137–149.

Bower, G. H. (1981). Mood and memory. *American Psychologist, 36*, 129–148.

Bower, G. H. (1987). Commentary on mood and memory. *Behaviour Research and Therapy, 25*, 443–456.

Butler, G., & Mathews, A. (1983). Cognitive processes in anxiety. *Advances in Behaviour Research and Therapy, 5*, 51–62.

Butler, G., & Mathews, A. (1987). Anticipatory anxiety and risk perception. *Cognitive Therapy and Research, 11*, 551–565.

Butler, G., Cullington, A., Mumby, M., Amies, P., & Gelder, M. (1984). Exposure and anxiety management in the treatment of social phobia. *Journal of Consulting and Clinical Psychology, 52*, 642–650.

Clark, D. M., Salkovskis, P. M., Gelder, M., Koehler, C., Martin, M., Anastasiades, P., Hackmann, A., Middleton, H., & Jeavons, A. (1988). Tests of a cognitive theory of panic. In I. Hand & H.U. Wittchen (Eds.), *Panic and Phobias II*. Berlin: Springer-Verlag.

Chambless, D. L., Caputo, G. C., Bright, P., & Gallagher, R. (1984). Assessment of fear in agoraphobics: The Body Sensation Questionnaire and the Agoraphobic Cognitions Questionnaire. *Journal of Consulting and Clinical Psychology, 52*, 1090–1097.

Chambless, D. L., & Gracely, E. J. (1989). Fear of fear and the anxiety disorders. *Cognitive Therapy & Research, 13*, 9–20.

Craske, M. G., Street, L., & Barlow, D. H. (1989). Instructions to focus upon or distract from internal cues during in vivo exposure for the treatment of agoraphobic avoidance. *Behaviour Research and Therapy, 27*, 663–672.

Derryberry, D., & Rothbart, M. K. (1984). Emotion, attention, and temperament. In C. E. Izard, J. Kagan, & R. B. Zajonc (Eds.), *Emotions, cognition, and behavior*. New York: Cambridge University Press.

Easterbrook, J. A. (1959). The effect of emotion on cue utilization and the organization of behavior. *Psychological Reviews, 66*, 183–201.

Ehlers, A., & Margraf, J. (1989). The psychophysiological model of panic attacks. In P. M. G. Emmelkamp (Ed.), *Anxiety disorders: Annual series of European research in behavior therapy; Vol. 4*. Amsterdam: Swets.

Ehlers, A., Margraf, J., Roth, W. T., Taylor, C. B., & Birbaumer, N. (1988). Anxiety induced by false heart rate feedback in patients with panic disorder. *Behaviour Research and Therapy, 26*, 1–11.

Emmelkamp, P. M. G., & Mersch, P. P. (1982). Cognition and exposure in vivo in the treatment of agoraphobia: Short term and delayed effects. *Cognitive Therapy and Research, 6*, 77–88.

Emmelkamp, P. M. G., Kuipers, A. C. M., & Eggeraat, J. G. (1978). Cognitive modification versus prolonged exposure in vivo: A comparison with agoraphobics as subjects. *Behaviour Research and Therapy, 16*, 33–41.

Eysenck, M. W., & Mathews, A. (1987). Trait anxiety and cognition. In H. J. Eysenck & I. Martin (Eds.), *Theoretical foundations of behavior therapy*. New York: Plenum Press.

Foa, E. B., & Kozak, M. (1986). Emotional processing of fear: Exposure to corrective information. *Psychological Bulletin, 99*, 20–35.

Foa, E. B., McNally, R., & Murdock, T. B. (1989). Anxious mood and memory. *Behaviour Research and Therapy, 27*, 141–147.

Goldstein, A. J., & Chambless, D. L. (1978). A reanalysis of agoraphobia. *Behavior Therapy, 9*, 47–59.

Grayson, J. B., Foa, E. B., & Steketee, G. (1982). Habituation during exposure treatment: Distraction vs. attention-focusing. *Behaviour Research and Therapy, 20*, 323–328.

Grayson, J. B., Foa, E. B., & Steketee, G. S. (1986). Exposure in vivo of obsessive-compulsives under distracting and attention-focusing conditions: Replication and extension. *Behaviour Research and Therapy, 24*, 475–479.

Gursky, D. M., & Reiss, S. (in press). Identifying danger and anxiety expectancies as components of common fears. *Journal of Behavior Therapy and Experimental Psychiatry*.

Holloway, W., & McNally, R. J. (1987). Effects of anxiety sensitivity on the response to hyperventilation. *Journal of Abnormal Psychology, 96*, 330–334.

Kahneman, D., Slovic, P., & Tversky, A. (1982). (Eds.), *Judgement under uncertainty: Heuristics and biases*. Cambridge: Cambridge University Press.

Katon, W., Vitaliano, P. P., Russo, J., Jones, M., & Anderson, K. (1987). Panic disorder: Spectrum of severity and somatization. *The Journal of Nervous and Mental Disease, 175*, 12–19.

Kenardy, J., Evans, L., & Oei, T. P. (1989). Cognitions and heart rate in panic disorders during everyday activity. *Journal of Anxiety Disorders, 3*, 33–43.

Kirsch, I. (1985). Response expectancy as a determinant of experience and behavior. *American Psychologist, 40*, 1189–1202.

Korchin, S. (1964). Anxiety and cognition. In C. Scheerer (Ed.), *Cognition: Theory, research and promise*. New York: Harper & Row.

Lang, P. J. (1977). Imagery in therapy: An information processing analysis of fear. *Behavior Therapy, 8*, 862–886.

Lang, P. J. (1984). Cognition in emotion: Concept and action. In C. Izard, J. Kagan, & R. B. Zajonc (Eds.), *Emotion, cognition, and behavior*. New York: Cambridge University Press.

Lang, P. J. (1985). The cognitive psychophysiology of emotion: Fear and anxiety. In A. H. Tuma & J. D. Maser

(Eds.), *Anxiety and the anxiety disorders*. Hillsdale, NJ: Lawrence Erlbaum Associates.

Litt, M. D. (1988). Cognitive mediators of stressful experience: Self-efficacy and perceived control. *Cognitive Therapy and Research, 12,* 241–261.

MacLeod, C., Mathews, A., & Tata, P. (1986). Attentional bias in emotional disorders. *Journal of Abnormal Psychology, 95,* 15–20.

Martin, M., Williams, R., & Clark, D. (1988, September). *Does anxiety lead to selective processing of threat-related information?* Paper presented at the World Congress of Behaviour Therapy. Edinburgh, Scotland.

Mathews, A., & Eysenck, M. W. (1987). Clinical anxiety and cognition. In H. J. Eysenck & I. Martin (Eds.), *Theoretical foundations of behavior therapy*. New York: Plenum Press.

Mathews, A., & MacLeod, C. (1985). Selective processing of threat cues in anxiety states. *Behaviour Research and Therapy, 23,* 563–569.

Mathews, A., & MacLeod, C. (1986). Discrimination of threat cues without awareness in anxiety states. *Journal of Abnormal Psychology, 95,* 131–138.

McCaul, K. D., & Haugtuedt, C. (1982). Attention, distraction, and cold-pressor pain. *Journal of Personality and Social Psychology, 43,* 154–162.

McNally, R. J., & Lorenz, M. (1987). Anxiety sensitivity in agoraphobics. *Journal of Behaviour Therapy and Experimental Psychiatry, 18,* 3–11.

McNally, R. J., Foa, E. B., & Donnell, C. D. (1989). Memory bias for anxiety information in patients with panic disorder. *Cognition and Emotion, 3,* 27–44.

Michelson, L., Mavissakalian, M., & Marchione, K. (1985). Cognitive and behavioral treatments of agoraphobia: Clinical, behavioral, and psychophysiological outcomes. *Journal of Consulting and Clinical Psychology, 53,* 913–925.

Miller, S. M., & Birnbaum, A. (1988). Putting the life back into 'life events': Toward a cognitive social learning analysis of the coping process. In S. Fisher & J. Reason (Eds.), *Handbook of life stress, cognition and health*. New York: John Wiley & Sons.

Miller, S. M., Brody, D. S., & Summerton, J. (1988). Styles of coping with threat: Implications for health. *Journal of Personality and Social Psychology, 54,* 142–148.

Mineka, S., Gunnar, M., & Champoux, M. (1986). Control and early socio-emotional development: Infant rhesus monkey reared in controllable versus uncontrollable environments. *Child Development, 57,* 1241–1254.

Mogg, K., Mathews, A., & Weinman, J. (1987). Memory bias in clinical anxiety. *Journal of Abnormal Psychology, 96,* 94–98.

Norton, R. G., Dorward, J., & Cox, B. J. (1986). Factors associated with panic attacks in non-clinical subjects. *Behavior Therapy, 17,* 239–252.

Norton, R. G., Schaefer, E., Cox, B. J., Dorward, J., & Wozney, K. (1987, November). *Selective memory effects in non-clinical panickers*. Paper presented at the Association for the Advancement of Behavior Therapy 21st Annual Conference, Boston, MA.

Nunn, J. D., Stevenson, R. J., & Whalan, G. (1984). Selective memory effects in agoraphobic patients. *British Journal of Clinical Psychology, 23,* 195–201.

Parkinson, L., & Rachman, S. (1981). Speed of recovery from an uncontrived stress. *Advances in Behaviour Research and Therapy, 3,* 119–123.

Rachman, S. (1984). Agoraphobia—A safety-signal perspective. *Behaviour Research and Therapy, 22,* 59–70.

Rachman, S. J., Craske, M. G., Tallman, K., & Solyom, C. (1986). Does escape behavior strengthen agoraphobic avoidance? A replication. *Behavior Therapy, 17,* 366–384.

Rachman, S., & Hodgson, R. J. (1974). Synchrony and desynchrony in fear and avoidance. *Behaviour Research and Therapy, 12,* 311–318.

Rachman, S., & Levitt, K. (1985). Panics and their consequences. *Behaviour Research and Therapy, 23,* 585–600.

Rachman, S. J., & Lopatka, C. (1986). Match and mismatch in the prediction of fear. *Behaviour Research and Therapy, 24,* 387–393.

Rachman, S. J., Lopatka, C., & Eich, E. (Unpublished manuscript). *The recall of unhappy memories during pain*. University of British Columbia.

Rachman, S., Lopatka, C., & Levitt, K. (1988). Experimental analyses of panic-II. Panic patients. *Behaviour Research and Therapy, 26,* 33–40.

Rapee, R. M., Ancis, J., & Barlow, D. H. (1988). Emotional reactions to physiological sensations: Comparison of panic disorder and non-clinical subjects. *Behaviour Research and Therapy, 26,* 265–269.

Rapee, R., Mattick, R., & Murrell, E. (1986). Cognitive mediation in the affective component of spontaneous panic attacks. *Journal of Behavior Therapy and Experimental Psychiatry, 17,* 245–253.

Reiss, S. (1987). Theoretical perspectives on the fear of anxiety. *Clinical Psychology Review, 7,* 585–596.

Reiss, S., Peterson, R. A., & Gursky, D. M. (1988). Anxiety sensitivity, injury sensitivity, and individual differences in fearfulness. *Behaviour Research and Therapy, 4,* 341–345.

Reiss, S., Peterson, R. A., Gursky, D. M., & McNally, R. J. (1986). Anxiety sensitivity, anxiety frequency and the prediction of fearfulness. *Behaviour Research and Therapy, 24,* 1–8

Salge, R. S., & Beck, J. G. (1988). A community survey of panic. *Journal of Anxiety Disorders, 2,* 157–167.

Sanderson, W. C., Rapee, R. M., & Barlow, D. H. (1990). The influence of an illusion of control on panic attacks induced via inhalation of 5.5% carbon dioxide-enriched air. *Archives of General Psychiatry, 46,* 157–162.

Schacter, S. (1964). The interaction of cognitive and physiological determinants of emotional state. In L. Berkowitz

(Ed.), *Advances in experimental social psychology: Vol. 1.* New York: Academic Press.

Schacter, S., & Singer, J. (1962). Cognitive social and physiological determinants of emotional state. *Psychological Review, 69,* 379–397.

Scheier, M. F., & Carver, C. (1983). Two sides of the self: one for you and one for me. In J. Suls & A. G. Greenwald (Eds.), *Psychological perspectives on the self: Vol. 2.* Hillsdale, NJ: Lawrence Erlbaum Associates.

Suls, J., & Fletcher, B. (1985). The relative efficacy of avoidant and nonavoidant coping strategies: A meta-analysis. *Health Psychology, 4,* 249–288.

Telch, M. J., Lucas, J. A., & Nelson, P. (in press). Nonclinical panic in college students: An investigation of prevalence and symptomatology. *Journal of Abnormal Psychology.*

van den Hout, M. A., Albus, M., Pols, H., Griez, E., Zahn, T., Breier, A., & Uhde, T. W. (1988). Differential discrimination of yohimbine and panic disorder patients versus normal controls. *British Journal of Psychiatry.* Manuscript submitted for publication.

Wagner, A. R. (1981). SOP: A model of automatic memory processing in animal behavior. In N. E. Spear & R. R. Miller (Eds.), *Information processing in animals: Memory mechanisms.* Hillsdale, NJ: Lawrence Erlbaum Associates.

Watson, D., & Friend, R. (1969). Measurement of social-evaluative anxiety. *Journal of Consulting and Clinical Psychology, 33,* 448–457.

Watts, F. N., Trezise, L., & Sharrock, R. (1986). Processing of phobic stimuli. *British Journal of Clinical Psychology, 25,* 253–259.

Watts, F. N., McKenna, F. P., Sharrock, R., & Trezise, L. (1986). Colour naming of phobia related words. *British Journal of Psychology, 77,* 97–108.

Wegner, D. M., & Giuliano, T. (1980). Arousal-induced attention to the self. *Journal of Personality and Social Psychology, 38,* 719–726.

Whitlow, J. W., Jr. (1975). Short-term memory in habituation and dishabituation. *Journal of Experimental Psychology, 104,* 189–206.

Williams, S. L., & Rappoport, J. A. (1983). Cognitive treatment in the natural environment for agoraphobics. *Behavior Therapy, 14,* 299–313.

Williams, J. M. G., Watts, F. N., MacLeod, C., & Mathews, A. (1988). *Cognitive psychology and emotional disorders.* New York: John Wiley & Sons.

Yerkes, R. M., & Dodson, J. D. (1908). The relation of strength of stimulus to rapidity of habit-formation. *Journal of Comparative Neurology and Psychology, 18,* 459–482.

Zajonc, R. B. (1984). On the primacy of affect. *American Psychologist, 39,* 117–123.

Zander, J. R., & R. J. McNally (1988). Bio-information processing in agoraphobia. *Behaviour Research and Therapy, 26,* 421–429.

CHAPTER 9

CONTRIBUTIONS OF COGNITIVE PSYCHOLOGY TO ASSESSMENT AND TREATMENT OF DEPRESSION

Steven D. Hollon
Mary Shelton

In his controversial and classic treatise, *Clinical versus Statistical Prediction*, Paul Meehl (1954) observed that the diagnostic and prognostic judgments of clinicians were subject to many of the same logical errors as the descriptions and predictions of lay people. Furthermore, he noted that the "judgment" errors of clinicians—like those of lay people—were not limited to decision-making biases, but were predetermined by biases in implicit judgments, such as selective perception and selective memory. Although such apparently universal processing errors had been studied for many years by cognitive and social cognitive psychologists (e.g., Bartlett, 1932; Menzies, 1935; Turner & Barlow, 1951; Waters & Leeper, 1936), this literature had never penetrated the clinical field. Meehl's study of clinical judgment—along with Heider's (1958) concurrent work on lay inference processes—turned the attention of clinical psychologists to the study of normal distortions in perception, memory, and decision-making.

The exploration and consequent blurring of the bounds of normative and pathological information processing has continued over the last two decades. In the process, the concerns of cognitive, social cognitive, and clinical research have increasingly overlapped; and cognitive theory and methods have had a delayed but powerful impact on clinical research and practice (e.g., Kahneman, Slovic, & Tversky, 1982; Nisbett & Ross, 1980). More importantly, over the last two decades clinical psychology has been reshaped by a paradigmatic shift from a radical-behavioral to a cognitive mediation perspective (e.g., Mahoney, 1974, 1977). This new perspective supports causal complexity and demands the integration of normative and pathological phenomena and experimental and clinical paradigms.

This recent convergence of cognitive and clinical issues has coincided with an upsurge of interest in the etiology and maintenance of depression, a disorder with a significant cognitive dimension and for which the gradations between "normal" and "pathological" are apparently continuous and complex (e.g., Ruehlman, West, & Pasahow, 1985). Although there are currently a number of behavioral, social, and biological theories of depression, to date some of the most influential approaches have been the cognitive theories, especially those of Beck (1963, 1967, 1976) and Seligman and associates (Abramson, Metalsky, &

Alloy, 1989; Abramson, Seligman, & Teasdale, 1978).

In this chapter, we describe the major cognitive theories of depression and examine them from the context of recent advances in cognitive and social-cognitive psychology. Next, we turn to a discussion of major methods for assessing beliefs and information processing strategies relevant to depression. We close with a consideration of strategies designed to reverse or prevent depression that have been developed from a cognitive perspective.

COGNITION AND DEPRESSION

Cognitive Theories of Depression

Beck's Cognitive Theory

According to Beck (1963, 1967, 1976), depression is precipitated by "... psychological stress, biochemical imbalance, hypothalamic stimulation, or whatever ..." that activates a prepotent depressogenic schema defined as an "... underlying predisposition (personality trait or cognitive structure) ..." (Kovacs & Beck, 1978, p. 1570). These schemata then guide the screening, encoding, interpretation, and recall of the depressed individual's experience in a selectively negative fashion, producing what Beck calls the *negative cognitive triad*, consisting of generalized negative evaluations of the self, the world, and the future. In addition to such prepotent information processing biases (*schemata*) and specific depressive thoughts (*cognitive triad*), Beck proposes that depression is characterized by ongoing *cognitive errors*, or systematic information processing errors such as arbitrary inference and selective abstraction.

Seligman's Helplessness Theory and Subsequent Revisions

Beck's theory of depression was originally developed on the basis of clinical observations (Beck 1963, 1967, 1976), whereas Seligman's (1975) theory was based on psychopathology research. Seligman (1975) originally advanced a learned helplessness model of depression in which that disorder was seen as the result of the individual's perception that life event outcomes were not contingent upon his or her responses. The reformulated helplessness theory (Abramson et al., 1978) emphasized the role of the attributions that are made as to the causes of these outcomes. Depressed individuals typically display a *depressogenic attributional style*, that is, they make internal (self-caused), global (general, nonsituational), and stable (permanent, likely to recur) causal attributions for their failures and losses, whereas they make external, specific, and unstable causal attributions for their successes.

The most recent reformulation of the learned helplessness theory, now called the hopelessness theory (Abramson et al., 1989) describes a specific subtype of depression caused by a complex interaction of *life events, preexisting cognitive biases*, and *information* regarding the situation from the environment. After experiencing a negative life event (the stress), people seek information from the environment before arriving at causal attributions and forming expectations for the future.

A depressogenic attributional style (the diathesis) may be constrained or reinforced by situational cues. For example, a person would be more likely to make internal, stable, and global attributions for a particular failure if situational information suggested that the event was low in *consensus* (others do not fail), high in *consistency* (he or she typically experiences this type of failure) and low in *distinctiveness* (he or she typically fails in other areas, as well). Thus, when a negative life event occurs, and if it is considered to be an important event, and if depressogenic attributions are subsequently made, and if other factors influencing expectations (e.g., social support, perceived resources) are also negatively weighted, then "hopelessness depression" will develop.

All subsequent versions of the helplessness model (Abramson et al., 1978, 1989; Seligman, 1975) suggest that depression is characterized by at least three major symptoms that are generally associated with learned helplessness: (1) retarded initiation of voluntary responses (motivational symptom); (2) difficulty in seeing that one's responses control outcomes (cognitive symptom); and (3) sad affect (emotional symptom). When individuals feel that others would be able to control the negative outcomes that they are experiencing, lowered self-esteem will also be present.

Other Cognitive Models

Although Beck's and Seligman's theories have had the greatest impact on research and practice, there are at least three other partially cognitive theories of depression. For example, Rehm (1977) has proposed that depression results from deficits in several self-control areas, including: (1) selective monitoring of negative events; (2) selective monitoring of immediate as opposed to delayed consequences of behavior; (3) stringent self-evaluative criteria; (4) inaccurate attributions of responsibility; (5) insufficient self-reward; and (6) excessive self-punishment.

Self-referent cognition and behavior are also the focus of Kuiper and colleagues' theory of depression (Kuiper, Derry, & MacDonald, 1982; Kuiper, Olinger, & MacDonald, 1988). Kuiper's group has investigated and extended Beck's (1963, 1967, 1976) depressive schemata concept through a series of social cognitive experiments investigating the self-schema as an important component of the human information-processing system (Kuiper & Derry, 1981). A major tenet of this model is that one's degree of depression largely determines both the *content* of the self-schema and the *efficiency* of information processing through the self-schema (Kuiper et al., 1982). Nondepressives' self-schemata contain nondepressive information and are efficient information processors; mild depressives' self-schemata contain both nondepressive and depressive information and are inefficient processors; and clinical depressives' self-schemata contain depressive information and are efficient processors. Kuiper et al. (1982) have proposed that mild levels of depression are accompanied by a disruption of the well-developed, organized, and consistent view of self, which is normally positively biased. In more severe levels of depression, the self-schema has been reorganized to facilitate the processing of depressive information through a well-developed, consistent negative bias.

Although Kuiper's model—and other self-schema based models of depression (e.g., Davis & Unruh, 1981; Higgins, Klein, & Strauman, 1985; Linville, 1985)—have strong theoretical and methodological ties to social cognitive and cognitive-experimental psychology, they are not really as explicitly "cognitive" in nature as the most recent information processing models of depression. For example, Ingram (1984) proposes that the initial experience of depression may result from the activation of an affective structure referred to as a "depression-emotion node" (p. 443). Once this unit is activated, depressive cognitions recycle through the individual's cognitive networks, thus maintaining the depressive affect. Depression thus is seen as a product of affective learning that is characterized by a feedback loop of cognitive and emotional responses.

It should be obvious from this overview of the major cognitive theories of depression that the concepts and techniques of cognitive psychology are revitalizing the study of depression. The influence of the cognitive-experimental lab is growing, ironically bringing depression research closer to its roots in neuropsychiatry. In this chapter, we will explore the links and overlap between cognitive psychology and the research, assessment, and treatment of depression.

An Operational Perspective on Cognitive Factors in Depression

With the development of cognitive-behavioral theories and interventions, many researchers and clinicians have become interested in understanding the basic cognitive factors that operate in both normal and clinical populations. In explaining these factors, some researchers have borrowed concepts from cognitive and social-cognitive approaches to experimental psychology, whereas others have developed new concepts. We discuss the various constructs that have been proposed later in this chapter.

Here, we will be discussing cognitive factors of three types, namely structures, products and processes (see Hollon & Kriss, 1984). Basic to all three is the notion of information present in the central nervous system, whether that information is factual or procedural, readily accessible or not. Whereas cognitive processes, structures, and products will later be discussed as separate construct domains, it is apparent that these three domains are part of a dynamic system in which each influences and is influenced by the others.

In brief, cognitive *structures*, or knowledge structures, are basic theories that contain knowledge regarding how environmental stimuli are organized and structured. Cognitive *products* are the results or output of information-processing. Cognitive *processes* are the mechanisms by which incoming information and existing knowledge structures are combined to produce cognitive products. Until recently, depression research and intervention has focused most intensively on cognitive products and least on cognitive processes. Now it appears that this imbalance is being redressed. Recent work with information-processing models appears to be leading cognitively oriented depression researchers "back to the basics" with respect to matters pertaining to cognitive psychology.

Network Models

One of the most important principles in cognitive psychology is the notion that information is stored in a series of networks. This includes not only deliberate or relatively accessible judgments, such as causal attributions and expectations, but normally automatic, unaccessible information. In both normals and depressives, limited information-processing capacities and short-term memory space necessitate the use of primarily nonconscious information-processing regarding environmental and internal stimuli. The problem is this: Of all the available information, what should be perceived, what should be attended to or further processed, and what should be remembered? As Alba and Hasher (1983) describe in regard to a schema theory of memory, these judgments concerning stimuli are made on the basis of four central encoding processes: (1) *selection*, a process that chooses only some of all incoming stimuli for internal representation; (2) *abstraction*, a process that stores the meaning or core of the message without "extraneous" details; (3) *interpretation*, a process by which relevant prior knowledge is accessed to aid comprehension; and (4) *integration*, a process by which a single percept or memory representation is formed from the products of the previous three operations.

A Framework for Evaluating Cognitive Factors

Both the content (e.g., what to perceive or remember) and the structure (e.g., complexity, affective quality) of normal and depressive judgments are determined by the interaction of several factors. These factors can be economically represented by considering a model that Jenkins (1979) developed to clarify the complex, contextually dependent relationships found in studies of learning and memory. The model extracts four factors that are found in any cognitive-experimental situation: (1) subject characteristics (e.g., interests, knowledge); (2) characteristics of learning materials (e.g., verbal or visual, meaningfully organized or unorganized); (3) criterial tasks (e.g., recall, recognition, problem-solving); and (4) information-processing activities of the subjects (e.g., whether they rehearse auditorially, image, elaborate, ask questions).

In adapting the Jenkins' model to an operational analysis of cognition in depression, the four factors might be represented as: (1) individual characteristics (e.g., whether one is nondepressed, dysthymic, or clinically depressed; one's current affect; the types of knowledge structures that one possess); (2) the nature of the environmental or internal information available for processing (e.g., events that are positive or negative, ambiguous or unambiguous, unique or familiar); (3) criterial tasks (e.g., perception, recall, interpretation, attribution, prediction, problem-solving); and (4) information-processing activities (e.g., whether one selects, abstracts, interprets, integrates, or recalls information automatically or strategically, unconsciously or deliberately).

Individual Characteristics

Of the four factors, *individual characteristics* have been by far the most thoroughly researched. For example, although theorists have at various times stated that in comparison to those of nondepressed people, depressed people's self-evaluations (Beck, 1967; Rehm, 1977), attributions (Abramson et al., 1978), and expectancies (Beck, Weissman, Lester, & Trexler, 1974; Radloff & Rae, 1979) are more pessimistic *and* less accurate, other studies have suggested that nondepressed individuals are equally or more inaccurate in each of these judgments (e.g., Alloy & Abramson, 1979; Kuiper et al., 1982; Ruehlman et al., 1985). Normal nondepressive cognition is characterized by overly positive self-evaluations, exaggerated perceptions of control or mastery, and unrealistic optimism (Taylor & Brown, 1988). Mildly depressed individuals tend to display unbiased and thus more accurate response patterns in each of these areas. Severely depressed individuals may have an unrealistically negative bias, and they may be particularly inaccurate in processing information directly related to themselves, but they may differ from normals only in the direction, not the existence, of bias.

Nature of the Information

Examples of the depression-related effects of the *nature of the information* to be processed are found in the literature on attributions and self-schemata. The attributional bias in depressed individuals is reflected in a tendency to judge that negative life events have been caused by internal, global, and stable factors (Abramson et al., 1978) and that positive life events have been caused by external, specific, and unstable factors (Seligman, Abramson, Semmel, & von Baeyer, 1979). Similarly, negative self-references are more readily recalled than positive self-references by clinically depressed individuals; positive self-references are more readily recalled than negative self-references by nondepressed individuals; and mildly depressed individuals recall positive and negative self-referents equally well (Kuiper et al., 1982).

Critical Tasks

There has been some controversy regarding the effects of *critical tasks* in depressive and nondepressive information-processing. It has been shown that the depression-related error pattern described in the paragraph above is seen across several criterial tasks, including judgments of contingency, attributions, and expectancies (Ruehlman et al., 1985). It should be noted, however, that although these interpretive and predictive judgments are distinct criterial tasks, they have the same central strategy and goal, that is, evaluating information from one's experience of a particular event in order to fill in missing information about that event. There is tentative evidence that depression has different effects on somewhat less similar criterial tasks. For example, Peeters (1986) has observed that episodic memory (i.e., autobiographical, *experienced* memory, Tulving, 1972) is much more affected by an individual's mood than is semantic memory (i.e., memory of conceptual and generic information: Tulving, 1972).

Information-Processing Activities

Both Beck (1976) and Weingartner (1986) focus less on the effects of criterial tasks on information-processing in depression than on the effects of *information-processing* activities. Beck (1976) states that depressotypic thinking is characterized by (a) broad changes in the processing rules for inference and interpretation (see cognitive errors, such as arbitrary inference or selective abstraction) and (b) a reliance on previously latent cognitive structures for information organization and retrieval (see depressotypic schemata). Weingartner states that a wide range of criterial tasks can be significantly affected by depression, and that the degree of the effect depends on the amount of processing effort that the task requires. Researchers have recently distinguished between two types of information-processing: *automatic* (or nondeliberate, nonconscious) and *effortful* or *deliberate* (Schneider & Shiffrin, 1977; Roy-Byrne, Weingartner, Bierer, Thompson, & Post, 1986).

Effortful processing requires much more effort, time, and cognitive energy. It is less likely to involve the use of heuristics, and it is less likely to produce processing errors than is automatic processing. Automatic processing, on the other hand, is more likely to be used when the individual is experiencing low motivation, low energy, or is highly distracted due to concurrent distress. Processing effort effects might explain differences attributed to criterial tasks and information type. For example, it could be that episodic memory is easier to access than semantic memory because it tends to be more elaborated, and mood-congruent information may be easier to retrieve than mood-incongruent information because it does not involve accessing new affect-emotion nodes (see Ingram, 1984).

Two Models of Accessibility

Whether one focuses on individual characteristics, information characteristics, criterial tasks, or information-processing activities, there is more to be learned about cognitive factors in depression. At present, the most original, promising research involves *access bias*, or the interface between individual characteristics and information-processing activities. One branch of this endeavor approaches access bias from a meaning system perspective. It examines the functioning of cognitive schemata, along with other aspects of theory-driven cognition. The other branch approaches access bias from an operational perspective. It examines the functioning of psychobiological factors in cognition, including affect and motivation. Although the exploration of access bias from a clinical-experimental perspective is less than 10 years old, there are already several empirically based models of the phenomenon.

Meaning-Based Access

The purest example of a meaning system-based model of access bias is that of the depressive self-schema (see review by Kuiper et al., 1982). As mentioned earlier, a self-schema consists of an organized cluster of stored knowledge, beliefs, and assumptions regarding aspects of an individual and his or her world. Its content is built up and organized from day-to-day experiences, and it can be considered a master copy or prototype against which an individual bases perceptions and judgments about stimuli that are even tangentially self-related. According to Beck (1976), the depressive's self-schema tends to involve themes characterizing him or her as a loser, and this prototype is responsible for the systematic biases and negative distortions that are seen in these individuals. Kuiper and MacDonald (1980) have demonstrated that the access bias operating through depressive and nondepressive self-schema takes the familiar pattern of positive distortion by normals, neutral or mixed by mild depressives, and negative distortion by clinical depressives. A weakness of the self-schema approach to access bias is that there has been little or no research on how the depressive self-schema develops. Beck (1967) proposed that the depressive self-schema develops in childhood and is dormant until activated by the initial onset of depressive symptoms. Davis and Unruh (1981) have suggested that negative self-referent events may, over time, disconfirm a positive self-schema and establish a negative one, but the cognitive mechanisms for this process have not been described.

Operational Perspectives on Access

One of the earliest examples of an operationally based model of access bias comes from Bower's (1981) classic discussion of "mood and memory" (see also Blaney, 1986; Bower, 1986; Johnson & Magaro, 1987). The mood-based perspective assumes that an individual's concurrent mood state determines how an experience is encoded for storage in long-term memory (Bower, 1981, 1986; Ingram, 1984; Isen, 1984). During the encoding process, the subjective feeling, characteristic physiological changes, and characteristic nonverbal gestures associated with the present mood state serve as a distinctive context for memories. This context subsequently functions as a retrieval cue for specific memories. Bower (1981) and others have suggested that the similarity between the mood state at the time of retrieval and the mood state at the time of encoding largely determines how easily specific information can be accessed, including target information and related (i.e., other mood-congruent) information.

Ingram (1984) has elaborated this model as follows in regard to clinical depression: (1) Depressives may have pre-existing self-concept differences that enhance the mnemonic effects of depressed moods; (2) these differences strengthen the vicious cycle in which dysphoria activates negative cognitions, which in turn evoke dysphoria; and (3) these differences mitigate the natural decay of mood-congruent reverberations and so prolong the dysphoric state. The difficulty with Ingram's (1984) mechanism for explaining exaggerated access-bias effects in depression is that pre-existing schematic differences between depression-vulnerable normals and nonvulnerable normals have never been observed (Kuiper, Olinger, MacDonald, & Shaw, 1985). It may be that the exaggerated access-bias is related to psychobiologically based cognitive deficits. For example, short-term memory in depressives may be more limited than that in nondepressed individuals because of distraction by depressive rumination (Krames & MacDonald, 1985); and processing capacity may be more limited because of physiologically based cognitive deficits (Roy-Byrne et al., 1986). Or perhaps low neurophysiological arousal and low motivation lead to an increase in automatic processing (see Silberman, Weingartner, & Post, 1983) and hence an over-reliance on distortion-prone processing short cuts. Whatever the mechanisms, it is clear that the problem of access-bias is representative of the overall study of cognitive factors in depression.

This problem cannot currently be resolved from a meaning systems or operational perspective, but will require an integration of old and new approaches. In an interesting amalgamation of the meaning-system and operational perspectives on cognitive factors in depression, Riskind (1989) has proposed that mood-congruent access bias is an example of the implicit priming of a cognitive schema. A given mood is characterized by a typical cognitive set and by individual cognitive schemata and ideational themes, such as negative views of the world and self. These associated cognitions serve as implicit retrieval cues that prime mood-congruent—but not, technically, mood-state dependent-memory.

A Meaning Systems Perspective on Cognitive Factors in Depression

In this section, we will be discussing cognitive structures, products, and processes; how cognitive processes transform environmental and internal stimuli into cognitive products through the mediation of knowledge structures; and how these components appear and operate in depression.

Knowledge Structures

Knowledge structures are organizational entities that contain all of an individual's knowledge at any given moment about a particular focus of experience, such as himself or herself, others, or the world (Nisbett & Ross, 1980).

Schemata are cognitive structures that contain specific information (e.g., "yesterday it rained"), general information in the form of rules (e.g., "it rains more often when it is cloudy") or prototypic information (e.g., "all rainy days are wet, cool, uncomfortable, and depressing") (Turk & Speers, 1983). Schemata are apparently constructed from information that was received and processed in the past, and they are strengthened when similar information is processed and stored in the same schema (Markus, 1977). They can be altered when discrepant information is received, but this is more difficult as the schema becomes more elaborated; more often the discrepant information is altered. In fact, it was this propensity for information distortion that first brought them to the attention of social cognitive researchers (Bartlett, 1932). Although organizing and storing old information are important functions, the primary purpose of the schema is to process new information by determining which information will be attended to and which ignored, how much importance to attach to various stimuli, and how to structure information (Markus, 1977; Neisser, 1967, 1976; Turk & Speers, 1983). They make information-processing more economical and coherent by providing "default" values for information that is not actually present or observed in the environment.

As research on knowledge structure has progressed, schema have been categorized according to the type of information they organize. Markus (1977) and others have presented empirical evidence in support of a self-schema that actively processes, organizes, and stores self-referent information. The person prototype (Cantor, 1981) or persona (Nisbett & Ross, 1980) contains information about a certain type of person, such as a "conservative," a "boss," or a "woman." It plays a role in the persistence of personal biases and cultural stereotypes. Organized knowledge regarding behavioral routines and familiar events has been referred to, respectively, as "scripts" (Abelson, 1981) and "frames" (Minsky, 1975).

The self-schema appears to be most relevant to depression research. The evaluative dimension has been most frequently studied, with the familiar pattern of results in nondepressed, mildly depressed, and clinically depressed individuals (see Kuiper et al., 1982; Ruehlman et al., 1985). However, it has also been found that the specific contents and structural complexity of schemata are relevant to depression. For example, structural complexity in the self-schema (e.g., multiplicity of roles) seems to decrease vulnerability to depression by buffering against particular failures and losses.

In addition, whether an individual is "schematic" (i.e., equipped with a well-organized prototype) or "aschematic" on a particular dimension largely determines his or her vulnerability to depression following distressing life-events in that dimension. For example, high achievement orientation increases vulnerability to failure; and high affiliative orientation increases vulnerability to interpersonal loss (Hammen, Marks, deMayo, & Mayol, 1985; Hammen, Marks, Mayol, & deMayo, 1985). Finally, a significant discrepancy between one's "real" and "ideal" self-schema may be associated with greater vulnerability to depression (Higgins et al., 1985).

Nisbett and Ross (1980) distinguish between two different forms of knowledge structure: schemata and theories (or beliefs). They use schemata to mean more or less generic knowledge that is organized in a sort of "laundry list" fashion. (For example: a tree has leaves, branches, trunk; stands in earth; needs water; gives shade; is pleasant.) They include frames, personae, prototypes, and scripts in the category of schemata. Theories differ from schemata in that they are more propositional in nature, involving two or more concepts and the perceived relationships. (For example: "Dogs make good pets"; "Mother is a strong woman"; "Ending a relationship means I am no good.") Some types of theories have been found to be strongly associated with depression and appear to increase vulnerability to depression in individuals who endorse them (Dent & Teasdale, 1988; Silverman, Silverman, & Eardley, 1984). For that reason, these theories and their verbalized "products" are generally referred to as "maladaptive attitudes" or "dysfunctional attitudes" (Rush, Weissenberger, & Eaves, 1986; Weissman & Beck, 1978).

Cognitive Products

Cognitive products are similar to cognitive structures in that both contain information; but whereas cognitive structures are the raw data stored in the central nervous system, cognitive products are the results or output of information-processing (see Hollon & Garber, 1988; or Turk & Speers, 1983). Cognitive products are largely accessible to the individual, whereas the presence and content of knowledge structures can only be inferred (Nisbett & Wilson, 1977).

Linguists refer to this type of distinction as the difference between surface structure and deep structure (Chomsky, 1957). Surface structure represents what is actually said, thought, or done by the individual, whereas deep structure represents the meaning system that organizes that statement or act. Cognitive processes parallel what linguists call "transformational rules" (Chomsky). Their role is to actively create cognitive products from cognitive structures, or to manifest surface structure through operations. It is an important principle that an individual's statement (product) can have several different meanings (structure), and that a meaning can be expressed in many different statements (Thorndyke & Hayes-Roth, 1979). It is also important to recognize that cognitive products only hint at the nature of an individual's knowledge structures and cognitive processes.

Researchers have referred to cognitive products as beliefs (Ellis, 1962), self-statements (Meichenbaum, 1977), and automatic thoughts (Beck, 1970; Hollon & Kendall, 1980). These terms are basically synonyms, although subtle differences do exist. Hollon and Bemis (1981) have suggested a taxonomy of cognitive products of an inferential nature, which includes characteristic ascriptions, causal attributions, and expectations or expectancies. These three types of products overlap with the three domains seen by Ross (1977) as representing the main foci of study for attributional theory; they represent the most basic forms of judgment regarding environmental and internal stimuli. *Characteristic ascriptions* refer to inferences regarding a particular feature of a person, object, or situation, for example, "I am a bad employee." It has been found that clinically depressed individuals ascribe significantly more negative characteristics than positive characteristics to themselves, whereas nondepressed individuals do the opposite (Ruehlman et al., 1985).

Causal attributions refer to inferences regarding the causes of events, including behaviors. It has been found that clinically depressed individuals make internal, stable, and global attributions for self-related negative events and external, unstable, and specific attributions for self-related positive events, whereas nondepressed individuals exhibit the reverse pattern (Peterson & Seligman, 1984). *Expectations* refer to inferences about the outcomes of actions or future events. The expectations of clinically depressed individuals are significantly more pessimistic than those of nondepressed individuals (Hollon & Garber, 1988; Lewinsohn, Larson, & Muñoz, 1982).

Whereas clinical researchers have focused on the differences between the cognitive products of normal and disturbed individuals, cognitive and social psychologists have focused more on the accuracy of cognitive products. Ross (1977) suggests that for each type of inference made by an individual, it is theoretically possible to specify what constitutes a "normative" or accurate inference under conditions of uncertainty—that is, an inference based on a logical synthesis of all the available information. Cognitive and social psychologists (Kahneman et al., 1982; Nisbett & Ross, 1980) have documented many examples of "nonnormative" references drawn by nonpathological groups. These findings are theoretically interesting because of their implications for models of depression, such as Beck's (1976) and Weingartner's (1986), which strongly contrast normal and depressive cognition on the basis of cognitive errors. In addition, the failure to find simple differences in inferential accuracy opens up the field for the more refined, complex study of pathological and nonpathological inferential processing.

Cognitive Processes

As described earlier, *cognitive processes* are responsible for changing deep structure into surface structure, or knowledge structures into cognitive products (Kihlstrom & Nasby, 1981; Nisbett & Ross, 1980). More specifically, they are the transformational rules for using knowledge structures to manipulate information, turning environmental and internal input into judgments. Like computer software, cognitive processes determine how incoming information is perceived, encoded, stored, combined, and altered with respect to information and structures already present in the system; how that existing information is retrieved; and how those existing structures are engaged, disengaged, or altered (Hollon & Garber, 1988; Kihlstrom & Nasby, 1981). It should be noted that "cognitive processes" are essentially the same as the "central encoding processes" discussed earlier; the terminology reflects a meaning-system versus an operational perspective on cognitive factors.

Assimilation, Accommodation, and Activation-Deactivation

Two important principles, *assimilation* and *accommodation* (Piaget, 1952, 1954) describe the reciprocal relationship between information and structure that is mediated by these processes. When an individual is presented with information that is discrepant with an existing schema for that type of information, one of two outcomes can occur. The stimulus may be altered or assimilated so that it becomes consistent with the pre-existing schema, or the schema may be modified to accommodate the discrepant information (Nisbett & Ross, 1980). Most of the literature in cognitive psychology suggests that the process of assimilation occurs much more frequently than accommodation (Nisbett & Ross, 1980; Ross, 1977). This is the more efficient alternative in terms of processing effort, and quite frequently existing knowledge structures provide a highly accurate (if not perfect) guide to external reality.

However, assimilation is more likely to lead to inaccurate cognitive products (at least in the short-run) than is accommodation, because incoming information is selectively processed to promote consistency with internal structures over fidelity to external reality. For example, clinical depressed individuals may fail to register, misinterpret, or immediately forget positive feedback about themselves because it conflicts with their self-schemata (Ruehlman et al., 1985). For the same reason, nondepressed individuals tend to "miss" negative feedback (Ruehlman et al., 1985). On the other hand, accommodation may also be important to depression. It has been suggested that the normal person's positive self-schema is transformed into the depressed person's negative self-schema through a process of incremental accommodations (Davis & Unruh, 1981; Kuiper et al., 1982). Particularly significant, severe or repeated failures or losses may gradually erode a positive self-schema, until both positive and negative information are processed without bias. If the negative events continue, then the self-schema may resolidify around a negative core. At that point, the accommodation process will be complete, and positive information will thereafter be transformed into negative information via the process of assimilation.

Hollon and Garber (1988) have speculated that there may be a third possible outcome of encountering schema-discrepant information. The stimulus might lead to the deactivation of the currently operating schema and the activation of a schema that is more consistent with the discrepant information. The newly activated schema may have been dormant for minutes or even years, but the "switch" may seem no more remarkable than the transformation that often occurs when an employed adult goes from being a professional to being a parent upon returning home, or when a grown adult re-experiences adolescent conflicts upon returning to his or her parent's home for a visit. This proposition implies an externally cued rather than internally cued example of access bias. The situational or state-dependency nature of schematic activation may thus be a research issue of particular importance.

Judgmental Heuristics

Why does assimilation occur more frequently than accommodation, and why does it lead to nonnormative inferences or cognitive products? Tversky and Kahneman's (1974) work on human judgment under uncertainty has supplied some answers to these questions. They suggest that under conditions of uncertainty, individuals use *heuristics*, or information-processing short cuts, in order to generate inferential judgments. Heuristics are information-processing strategies that reduce complex judgmental tasks to simpler operations. They are automatic processes presumably operating outside of conscious awareness. Tversky and Kahneman (1974) describe three types of heuristics that are commonly used: availability, representativeness, and anchoring with adjustment.

Availability

The *availability* heuristic is a short-cut for making judgments about the frequency or probabilities of certain events. Judgments are made on the basis of how quickly or easily similar instances of the event are remembered, rather than on the event's true or expected base rate (Tversky & Kahneman, 1973). For example, a car owner may reject a generally reliable model on the basis of his or her experience with a particular car that was a "lemon," or a depressed person may expect failure in a job on the basis of a previous setback, in spite of a generally successful employment history. Several stimulus factors could influence the availability of information. Ease of retrieval from memory may be due to vividness or concreteness (Borgida & Nisbett, 1977), importance or meaning (Alba & Hasher, 1983), or frame of reference of the perceiver (Taylor & Fiske, 1975, 1978). Ease of retrieval may also be influenced by individual factors, as is proposed in schema theories of memory (Alba & Hasher, 1983) and in discussions of mood-state dependent memory (e.g., Bower, 1986).

Representativeness

The second heuristic, *representativeness*, refers to the process of making judgments regarding stimuli based on knowledge of a more familiar stimulus category to which they appear similar (Kahneman & Tversky, 1972). For example, an inexperienced adolescent who is asked for a "rain check" on a proposed date may interpret this as a rejection on the basis of its resemblance to the more familiar "maybe later" response of parents; or an adult who is laid off a job may experience low self-esteem because he or she thinks of the lay-off as a disciplinary firing.

Anchoring with Adjustment

The third heuristic, *anchoring with adjustment*, refers to the failure of individuals to revise (or adjust) their beliefs (anchors) after being given disconfirming evidence. For example, the person who believes that he or she is disliked or rejected will persist in this belief, regardless of the amount of praise and affection others may give.

According to Tversky and Kahneman (1974), these heuristics can produce accurate inferences but more often produce inaccurate ones, primarily because many pieces of relevant information (e.g., base rates, correlational data) are ignored. Other biases in information processing are also common, such as the tendency to overlook regression to the mean, failure to recognize inadequate sample size, and the influence of illusory correlations. Beck (1967) has compiled a list of "depressotypic" information-processing errors, such as: *arbitrary inference* (i.e., in the absence of evidence or in apposite of contradictory evidence); *selective abstraction* (focusing on a detail taken out of context, ignoring more salient features); *over generalization*; *magnification* and *minimization* (in evaluating the magnitude or significance of an event); *personalization* (relating events to the self when there is no basis for a connection); and *absolutist, dichotomous thinking* (all-or-none thinking). It may well prove that these processing errors are not limited to depressed populations and that they may, in fact, be reducible to the more universal heuristics described by Tversky and Kahneman (see Evans & Hollon, 1988).

Information-Processing and Depression

It appears that among nondepressed adults assimilation occurs readily and heuristics—which are based on the principle of assimilation—are used routinely (Hollon & Kriss, 1984). This appears to reflect the fact that human beings cannot possibly conduct the complex information processing necessary to constantly draw normative inferences. As described previously, normal information processing occurs in two forms, automatic processing and effortful (or deliberate) processing. Automatic processing is more error-prone, and, in depression, these errors serve to maintain depressive cognitions and moods. Cognitive therapies for depression generally seek to replace automatic processing with effortful processing, at least to a more adaptive level (e.g., Beck, 1976).

In fact, both automatic processing and effortful processing were indirectly introduced in the earliest cognitive theories of depression and intervention for depression (e.g., Beck, 1967), albeit under quite different terms. This is just one example of the steady infusion of cognitive-experimental theory and methods into depression research. This cognitive influence on research in depression promises to revitalize theory, assessment, and treatment by bringing together research in depression from a meaning-system perspective and from an operational perspective.

ASSESSMENT OF COGNITION IN DEPRESSION

As interest in cognitive processes in depression has grown, there has been a corresponding growth in interest in the methods of cognitive assessment as they relate to depression (cf. Hollon & Bemis, 1981; Kendall & Hollon, 1981; Merluzzi, Glass, & Genest, 1981; Parks & Hollon, 1988). This interest is predicated on the notion that a thorough understanding of the principles governing information-processing and memory can be used to construct assessment procedures that yield reliable and accurate information (Ericsson & Simon, 1980). As Mahoney (1977) has argued, it is not unscientific to entertain constructs not directly observable by others so long as those phenomena are themselves directly tied to observables.

There are, of course, limits to what can be expected. People may be quite inaccurate at describing the processes they have followed to arrive at a judgment (Nisbett & Wilson, 1977), even though they typically can report the products of those judgments. Further, some critical aspects of information processing may occur outside of conscious awareness (Shevrin & Dickman, 1980). Finally, memory retrieval may be largely reconstructive, meaning that successive instances of retrieval may produce cumulative modifications in the existing memory trace (Loftus & Loftus, 1980). These issues are discussed in greater detail elsewhere (Hollon & Bemis, 1981; Parks & Hollon, 1988).

Methods of Assessment

Recording Methods

A variety of methods exist for assessing cognition relevant to depression. *Recording methods* allow the investigator to assess beliefs by virtue of sampling verbal productions generated in relevant contexts. Examples include "think aloud" procedures, in which subjects are asked to verbalize whatever comes to mind while engaged in some task (Genest & Turk,

1981), recordings of private speech, in which unobtrusive measurements are made of barely audible, noncommunicative speech (Vygotsky, 1962), and articulated thoughts, a more structured version of the above developed by Davison and colleagues (Davison, Feldman, & Osborn, 1984; Davison, Robins, & Johnson, 1983).

Endorsement Methods

Endorsement methods involve presenting subjects with a predetermined set of items. Ratings or responses are then made. Endorsement methodologies can be roughly divided into those instruments developed rationally versus those generated empirically via contrasting known groups. Endorsement methods in the form of self-report inventories are among the most prevalent methods of cognitive assessment. Such methods are convenient and facilitate replication across subjects, but, because they rely heavily on recall and self-report, may be particularly susceptible to unintended inaccuracy and dissimulation.

Production Methods

Production methods such as thought listing (Cacioppo & Petty, 1981; Petty & Cacioppo, 1977), thought sampling (Hurlburt, 1976, 1979, 1980; Klinger, 1978; Klinger, Barta, & Maxeiner, 1981), and event recording (Hollon & Kendall, 1981) involve asking subjects to list thoughts currently in the sensorium. This may be done in the context of structured situations as in the case of thought listing; at random or preprogrammed intervals as in the case of thought sampling; or in the context of target life events as in the case of event recording. These methods have the advantage of not contaminating recall with recognition processes, but do require the development of structured scoring systems.

Inferential Methods

Inferential methods involve the use of tasks drawn from basic cognitive research in the study of cognitive structures and processes (Goldfried & Robins, 1982, 1983; Hollon & Kriss, 1984; Turk & Salovey, 1985; Turk & Speers, 1983). Frequently, these efforts are directed at uncovering various aspects of schematic processing. Typically, these methodologies are indirect in nature. That is, the purpose of the assessment is not readily discernable from the procedures. One such method, the identification of *features of social categories* (Cantor, 1980a, 1980b; Cantor & Mischel, 1979; Rosch, 1978), asks subjects to list the attributes of a target category. Common features are then held to define a consensual prototype.

Another method asks subjects to make *category judgments*. Specific features (or instantations) are presented to a subject, who is then asked to determine whether or not the features belong to a general category. Measures of simple endorsement (Markus, 1977), latency (there appears to be a curvilinear relationship between prototypicality and categorization latency; Fazio, Sanbonmatsu, Powell, & Kardes, 1986; Kuiper & Derry, 1981), or the use of false recognition (Canter & Mischel, 1977; Dodge & Frame, 1982; Rogers, Rogers, & Kuiper, 1979; Tsujimoto, 1978) can all be used to identify underlying cognitive structures.

Finally, *incidental recall tasks* have been used to identify schematic structures. Subjects are asked to process various descriptive adjectives under varying levels of self-reference. Those instantations with the greatest self-referential meaning are typically most readily recalled (Craik & Lockhart, 1972; Craik & Tulving, 1975). Depressives typically appear to have more negative self-referential schema (Hammen, Marks, Mayol, & DeMayo, 1985; Kuiper & Derry, 1981), but there is little evidence that this tendency is anything other than state-dependent. *Organization in free recall* is based on the tendency of subjects to recall randomly presented stimuli in an order determined by patterns of subjective organization (Sternberg & Tulving, 1977). *Autobiographical memory* tends to follow patterns of internal categorization, and can be used to study differences between depressed and nondepressed cognition (Hammen, Marks, Mayol, & DeMayo, 1985; Teasdale, Taylor, & Fogarty, 1980). In addition, recent efforts have suggested that *multidimensional scaling* can be used to map psychological space (Landau & Goldfried, 1981).

Specific Assessment Instruments

A variety of instruments have been developed across these various methodological domains, particularly with regard to endorsement-based instruments. We turn next to a brief review of several of the prominent assessment devices.

Automatic Thoughts Questionnaire

The Automatic Thoughts Questionnaire (ATQ: Hollon & Kendall, 1980) is a 30 item endorsement-type inventory designed to assess the relatively accessible surface level depressotypic cognitions found in depression. This instrument possesses good psychometric properties (Dobson & Breiter, 1983; Harrell & Ryon, 1983) and readily discriminates depressed from nondepressed psychopathological or normal controls (Dobson & Shaw, 1986; Eaves & Rush, 1984; Harrell & Ryon, 1983; Hollon, Kendall, & Lumry, 1986; S. Ross, Gottfredson, Christensen, & Weaver, 1986). It is, however, largely state-dependent (DeRubeis et al., in press; Eaves & Rush, 1984; Hollon et al., 1986; Simons, Garfield, & Murphy, 1984), normalizing as depression normalizes, regardless of the intervening form of treatment. Further, there is little reason to believe that scores on the ATQ in euthymic individuals predicts vulnerability to subsequent depression (Evans, et al., 1989; Simons et al., 1984). Thus, it appears to be a good measure of the construct of "surface-level" depressotypic ruminations, but the construct itself appears to be largely a state-dependent consequence of depression, rather than a cause.

Dysfunctional Attitudes Scale (DAS)

The Dysfunctional Attitudes Scale (DAS: Weissman & Beck, 1978) consists of a pair of parallel-form 40 item inventories designed to identify attitudes held by individuals at risk for depression (Beck, 1963, 1967, 1976). Psychometric properties are adequate (Oliver & Baumgart, 1985) and the instrument appears to readily discriminate depressed from nondepressed controls (Eaves & Rush, 1984; Giles & Rush 1982; Hamilton & Abramson, 1983; Hollon et al., 1986; Silverman et al., 1984; Zimmerman & Coryell, 1986; Zimmerman, Coryell, Corenthal, & Wilson, 1986). Specificity is somewhat suspect, as two studies have found comparable elevations in nondepressed schizophrenics (Hollon et al., 1986; Zimmerman et al., 1986). The DAS does appear to be less wholly state-dependent than is the ATQ, but not so stable as might be expected were it to be a marker of a cognitive-diathesis. In some studies, scores have remained somewhat elevated following remission (DeRubeis et al., in press; Dobson & Shaw, 1986; Eaves & Rush, 1984; Rush et al., 1986), whereas in others, full normalization has been evidenced (Hamilton & Abramson, 1983; Silverman et al., 1984). Similarly, while DeRubeis et al. (in press) found the DAS at least somewhat more affected by cognitive therapy than by pharmacotherapy, Simons and colleagues (Simons et al., 1986) did not. Evidence in support of any predictive status with regard to subsequent episodes is, at best, weak (Evans et al., 1989; Rush et al., 1986). Olinger, Kuiper and Shaw (1987) have suggested that a modification of the DAS, in which subjects are questioned about just how important each of the domains is to them, enhances predictive capacity. Overall, the DAS appears to provide an adequate assessment of attitudes associated with depression, but only a marginal measure of attitudes contributing to the onset of the disorder. Whether this reflects a failing of the measure, an error in the theory, or some as yet unrecognized problem in assessment (e.g., accessibility) remains to be determined.

Attributional Styles Questionnaire (ASQ)

The Attributional Styles Questionnaire (ASQ: Seligman et al., 1979) represents an effort to assess the depressogenic attributional style targeted as playing a causal role in the etiology of depression by the reformulated helplessness model (Abramson et al., 1978). Subjects are asked to respond to each of 12 hypothetical events (6 positive and 6 negative), supplying a probable cause for each, and rating those causes for internality, globality across situations, and stability over time. The tendency to be more internal, global, and stable for negative as opposed to positive events is considered to be depressogenic. Psychometric properties are generally acceptable (Peterson, Semmel, von Baeyer, Abramson, Metalsky, & Seligman, 1982) and the instrument appears to discriminate depressed from nondepressed controls (see Peterson & Seligman, 1984; or Sweeney, Anderson, & Bailey, 1986, for reviews). Specificity is not so clearcut, as one study has found comparable elevations in nondepressed schizophrenics (Zimmerman et al., 1986). Several studies have suggested that it has predictive utility for determining who is at risk for subsequent depression (Cutrona, 1983; Evans et al., 1989; Metalsky, Abramson, Seligman, Semmel, & Peterson, 1982; Metalsky, Halberstadt, & Abramson, 1987; O'Hara, Rehm, & Campbell, 1982), although instances of null findings have also been reported (e.g., Manly, McMahon, Bradley, & Davidson, 1982; O'Hara, Neunaber, & Zekoski, 1984; Rush et al., 1986).

Also troubling is the fact that efforts to assess the attributional construct by means other than the ASQ have typically not supported a causal role for the construct in the onset of subsequent depression(e.g., Barthe & Hammen, 1981; Gong-Guy & Hammen, 1980; Hammen & Cochrane, 1981; Hammen & deMayo, 1982; Hammen, Krantz, & Cochran, 1981; Harvey, 1981; Lewinsohn, Steinmetz, Larson, &

Franklin, 1981). Whereas the ASQ remains one of the most promising measures of cognitions playing a predispositional role in depression, this status is by no means free of continuing controversy (see Coyne & Gotlib, 1983; and Peterson, Villanova, & Raps, 1985, for a discussion).

Given that the ASQ is the most successful measure of cognitive-diathesis to date, it is interesting that it is the only measure that "primes" respondents by providing hypothetical negative life events to which to respond. Our sense is that the issue of accessibility of latent constructs is a major methodological constraint with which few of the existing assessment devices have adequately dealt (Riskind & Rholes, 1984).

Other Measures

A variety of other measures exist that deserve at least passing mention. The Cognitive Response Test (CRT: Watkins & Rush, 1983) is a production-type instrument that asks subjects to complete a series of sentences relevant to depression. Although the instrument appears to perform adequately as a measure of state-dependent cognition (Dobson & Shaw, 1986; Simon, Murphy, Levine, & Wetzel, 1986; Wilkinson & Blackburn, 1981), it requires much more effort to score than do other comparable alternatives. The Hopelessness Scale (HS: Beck et al., 1974; Beck, Kovacs, & Weissman, 1975) is a 20 item true-false inventory assessing pessimism. It is perhaps the closest approximation to a pure measure of expectations currently available, but is more generic than might be desired. In general, although it also discriminates depressed from nondepressed controls, it too appears to be largely state-dependent (DeRubeis et al., in press; Rush, Beck, Kovacs, Weissenberger, & Hollon, 1982; Wilkinson & Blackburn, 1981).

At least two efforts have been made to assess irrationality in process. First, Hammen and colleagues (Hammen & Krantz, 1976; Krantz & Hammen, 1979) developed an endorsement-type inventory designed to assess the propensity for distorted thinking. In general, depressives appear to evidence the predicted types of distortions (Hammen, 1978; Hammen & Krantz, 1976; Krantz & Hammen, 1979; Michael & Funabiki, 1985; Miller & Norman, 1986; Norman, Miller, & Klee, 1983). Little is known, however, about the proclivity of people at risk for future depressions to evidence such distortions during the euthymic state. Second, Cook and Peterson (1986) assessed the logical basis for the evidence subjects provided to justify particular attributions for recent life events.

Depressed subjects were more likely to be rated as showing distortions in information processing. Again, no evidence is available linking this propensity to risk for subsequent depression.

Issues in Assessment

Overall, there appear to be a variety of ways of assessing cognition relevant to depression. Across these various procedures, depressives appear to be reliably discriminable from nondepressives with respect to the content, structure, and process of cognition. What is less clear is whether any of these differences are evident in people at risk for depression not currently in the depressed state. Such evidence is, of course, necessary to support any claim for an etiologic role for cognition in depression. At least two issues are relevant in this regard. First is the issue of accessibility (Riskind & Rholes, 1984). None of the major cognitive theories postulate that people at risk for depression think differently from nondepressives in general; rather, they all posit that such individuals have a propensity to process information differently when under stress (see, for example, Abramson et al., 1989, or Beck, 1963, 1967). Adequate assessment of any purported cognitive-diathesis would therefore require priming with negative life events before the differential information processing would be accessible. Just such a strategy, involving the use of various challenge tests, appears to be useful in mapping out biological predispositional factors (Depue, Kleinman, Davis, Hutchinson, & Krauss, 1985). In this regard, it is of interest that the ASQ, the assessment method most nearly providing a "prime," has produced the strongest (albeit mixed) evidence of cognitive-diathesis status.

The second issue is what we have elsewhere labeled the issue of "isomorphism" (Parks & Hollon, 1988). Depression researchers have typically assumed that aberrant cognition in people at risk for depression should be similar in nature to the aberrations noted in the thinking of those same individuals when depressed. As pointed out by Kuiper et al. (1988), although this may be a reasonable assumption, it is by no means a necessary one. Future efforts at assessment might profitably be guided by theoretically driven speculations about the nature of such diatheses (should they exist) or by empirical contrasts between populations at risk but not currently depressed and populations not at risk.

Overall, it is clear that differences in cognition and information-processing exist between depressed and nondepressed populations and that these differences can be reliably measured. What is not so clear is whether such differences play any role in the etiology of the disorder. Some evidence does exist, but it is by no means robust. Future efforts, particularly those taking into account the issues of accessibility and isomorphism, will be needed to resolve this controversy.

COGNITION AND THE TREATMENT OF DEPRESSION

There exist several effective interventions for the treatment of depression. Although the pharmacotherapies remain the standard of treatment against which all novel interventions still need to be compared (cf. Klein & Davis, 1969; Morris & Beck, 1974), the last two decades have seen the development of cognitive and cognitive-behavioral interventions that have evidenced great promise (see Hollon & Beck, 1986, or Hollon & Najavits, 1988, for recent reviews). Chief among these is Beck's cognitive therapy (Beck, 1964, 1967; Beck, Rush, Shaw, & Emery, 1979). Predicated on a model that views abberations in cognition as playing a causal role in a larger diathesis-stress model of depression (cf. Beck, 1963; Kovacs & Beck, 1978), this intervention seeks to ameliorate acute depression and to reduce the risk for subsequent relapse/recurrence by virtue of changing the way people think. These changes are viewed as taking place not only at the level of cognitive products, but also in terms of underlying structure and processes. Central to this theory of change is the notion that alterations are produced in the underlying cognitive schemata; that is, that cognitive therapy will produce profound changes in underlying cognitive structures and their associated processes. As we shall see, although there is good evidence supporting the efficacy of cognitive therapy in the treatment of depression and the prevention of relapse/recurrence, the data are still not conclusive with regard to precisely how this change is brought about.

Efficacy of Cognitive Therapy

Acute Response

There is considerable evidence that cognitive therapy is comparable to tricyclic pharmacotherapy in the treatment of nonpsychotic nonbiopolar depressives (virtually nothing is known about its efficacy with bipolar or psychotic populations). In general, most controlled trials have demonstrated comparability to tricyclic pharmacotherapy (cf. Blackburn, Bishop, Glen, Whalley, & Christie, 1981, psychiatric outpatient population; Hollon et al., 1989; Murphy, Simons, Wetzel, & Lustman, 1984). In the two trials that have evidenced superiority for cognitive therapy over pharmacotherapy (Blackburn et al., 1981, general medical population; Rush, Beck, Kovacs, & Hollon, 1977), factors were present that temper any strong claims for differential efficacy. In Rush et al. (1977), treatment differences did not become pronounced until after medications were withdrawn, and in Blackburn et al.'s (1981) general medical population, the overall response to pharmacotherapy (14%) was so low as to bring into question the adequacy of the implementation of this approach. Similarly, although cognitive therapy failed to exceed placebo in the National Institute of Mental Health (NIMH) Treatment of Depression Collaboration Research Project and pharmacotherapy did, the two active treatments did not significantly differ (Shea, Elkin, & Hirschfeld, 1988). In addition, this somewhat poorer showing for cognitive therapy occurred in the context of a very sparse supervision schedule for therapists newly trained in the approach.

Prevention of Relapse/Recurrence

Cognitive therapy also appears to provide protection against subsequent relapse or recurrences following successful treatment for depression. In five studies, patients treated to remission with cognitive therapy and then followed treatment-free evidenced about one-half the rate of subsequent relapse/recurrence as did patients treated pharmacologically until remission and then withdrawn from medications (Blackburn, Eunson, & Bishop 1986; Evans et al., 1989; Kovacs, Rush, Beck, & Hollon, 1981; Simons et al., 1986). This preventive impact appeared to be roughly comparable to that produced by keeping patients on continuation medications (Evans et al., 1989). Thus, it appears that cognitive therapy is not only effective in treating depression, but it also appears to provide protection against subsequent symptomatic return.

Mechanisms of Change

Establishing the efficacy of cognitive therapy, although consistent with a cognitive theory of change, does not necessarily establish the validity of that model. Similarly, establishing a preventive impact for the intervention does not necessarily mean that that effect was mediated by changes in cognition. In each instance, additional corroboration of theory-relevant changes in cognition are required in order to test the respective formulations. Such tests of mediational models are notoriously difficult to accomplish (Hollon, DeRubeis, & Evans, 1987). The tricyclic antidepressants have been established for over 30 years and as yet no consensual explanation exists as to precisely how they work (cf. McNeal & Cimbolic, 1986). When viewed in such a context, it is clear that efforts to use treatment outcome studies to test mediational causal theories are complex, to say the least.

Elsewhere (DeRubeis et al., in press), we have argued that any purported mediator of treatment efficacy must meet three conditions: (1) it must change during treatment, (2) it should be relatively specific with respect to other interventions believed to operate through different mechanisms, and (3) change in the mediator should precede change in the dependent variable of interest. The first principle is simply that of covariation. The second is specificity, and the third temporal antecedence, each expanded to incorporate the concept of change. These are precisely the three conditions typically held to be necessary (but not sufficient) to infer causality from correlational data (Kenny, 1979).

Activation-deactivation

There are at least three models that can be invoked to explain the observed efficacy of cognitive therapy, both with respect to acute treatment and with respect to the prevention of relapse (Hollon, Evans, & DeRubeis, 1988). These are *activation-deactivation*, *accommodation*, and *compensation*. In a manner similar to that previously described, under activation-deactivation, cognitive therapy is seen as producing change in depression by facilitating a switch from an operative depressotypic schema to a latent nondepressive one. Neither cognitive structure is changed in the process; one is simply substituted for the other, much as an employee stops thinking like an employee and starts thinking like a parent when he or she receives a call at work that a child has become ill at school. Arguing against the sole operation of this deactivation-activation model is the fact that cognitive therapy appears to exert a preventive impact. It is hard to account for the stability of its effect over time if its sole mechanism of action is to deactivate an existing depressive schema, with that schema left unchanged in a latent state to await the next negative life event.

Accommodation

Also as described earlier, accommodation refers to a process in which some alteration is made in existing cognition, probably at the level of structure and/or process. Under such a model, the underlying depressogenic schema would be seen as being altered in some profound way. This is clearly the model preferred by most cognitive theorists (cf., Beck, 1970; Beck, 1984). Under such a model, one should expect to see changes in cognition, certainly at the level of product, usually at the level of structure, and possibly at the level of process.

Compensation

Compensation refers to the development of skills and strategies that offset the effects of pernicious cognitive proclivities. In this model, therapy is not seen so much as producing changes in those aspects of cognition that predispose people to depression, as introducing additional skills and abilities that influence the end-point judgments in a more benign direction. For example, underlying depressotypic schema may remain unmodified, but an additional reevaluative process, akin to Lazarus' (1966) concept of *reappraisal*, may still compensate for and correct judgements that would otherwise have been more depressogenic.

As shown in Table 9-1, although these three models are not necessarily mutually exclusive, they should be discriminable. As was previously noted, schema activation-deactivation alone can hardly account for cognitive therapy's preventive effect. Nonetheless, such a model might well predict a rather discontinuous course to therapy. It should prove possible to examine individual response curves for evidence of discontinuity in change. Accommodation would be expected to produce change in deep structures, and perhaps in process as well, although we are by no means as sure of that. Compensation would *not* be expected to produce such change in deep structures, but should produce detectable gains in compensatory skills. All three models would be expected to produce change in surface level cognitive products, and all three would be expected to produce change in depression, although only the latter two would be predicted to produce long-term prevention.

Sequential Compensation-Accommodation Model

Elsewhere (Evans & Hollon, 1988), we argued that cognitive therapy might not so much lead depressed patients to *think* like nondepressives, as to lead them to process information in a very atypical fashion that serves to protect against dysphoric affect and behavioral passivity. If we define "normative" thinking not

Table 9-1. Discriminating Among Three Models of Change in Depression Produced by Cognitive Therapy

MODEL	STRUCTURE	PROCESS	PRODUCT	SYMPTOM REDUCTION	PREVENTION OF RELAPSE/ RECURRENCE
Activation-deactivation	No (deactivation only)	No	Yes	Yes (discontinuous course)	No
Accommodation	Yes	No (?)	Yes	Yes	Yes
Compensation	No	Yes (use of more "normative" information processing)	Yes	Yes	Yes

in terms of the way most people think (a statistical definition), but rather in terms of a fashion of which a logician would approve (an ideal definition), then there is considerable evidence that most nondepressives are anything but normative. As was previously described, it is well established that the typical nondepressed person holds numerous beliefs that overestimate their own stature in others' eyes, distort information in a positive or self-enhancing fashion, and engage in heuristic-governed information processing (cf. Kahneman et al., 1982; Nisbett & Ross, 1980; Taylor & Crocker, 1981). Earlier in the chapter (Evans & Hollon, 1988), we suggested that cognitive therapy may work, in the short run, not by having depressives engage in the same type of nonnormative information processing. Rather, we speculated that depressives might be led to process information in a far more deliberate, nonheuristic governed fashion, at least across the bulk of the active treatment period. This model would predict that recently remitted patients in cognitive therapy should evidence a real difference in information-*processing*, relative to either nondepressives, untreated depressives, or remitted depressives treated by other means (e.g., pharmacotherapy). This is the form that we expect the compensation model to take, with depressed patients treated cognitively acquiring skills that facilitate the reappraisal of their initial schema- and heuristic-driven cognitive propensities. Further, we think it is quite likely that such a process may be a transitional one, with such initial efforts at compensation increasing the likelihood of long-term accommodation. Under such a sequential model, initial compensation, comprised of an atypical but highly "normative" reliance on careful evidence gathering, hypothesis-testing, and deliberate information processing, is seen as ultimately leading to accommodation in deep structures. As that occurs, the treated individual can increasingly dispense with such deliberate compensatory strategies, as the more efficient schema-driven heuristics can safely be used without risking the production of depressogenic beliefs.

Table 9-2 contrasts cognitively treated depressives with normal controls, untreated depressives, and pharmacologically treated depressives. As can be seen, under the sequential compensation-accommodation model, cognitively treated depressives would be seen as evidencing atypical "normative" information processing, differing from all other three groups, then later showing changes in underlying deep structures. The other three groups are seen as differing in terms of underlying structures; normals with nondepressive schemas only, depressives with depressive schemas (and latent nondepressive ones), and pharmacologically treated depressives with nondepressed schemas (but latent depressed ones).

What can be seen from these two successive tables is that, in order to test these respective models, measures and measurement procedures are needed that will allow such differential assessment. As discussed previously, there are currently an abundance of measures of cognitive products (e.g., the ATQ, HS, and CRT). But, as shown in Tables 9-1 and 9-2, measures of products do not differentiate between any of the interesting theoretical contrasts. Similarly, whereas some initial efforts have been made to develop measures of deep structure (e.g., "depth of processing" or DAS), such efforts may prove unproductive until the twin issues of accessibility and isomorphism are taken into account. In this regard, it is of interest that the ASQ provides a partial prime and, in at least one study, evidenced differential

Table 9-2. Sequential Compensation-Accommodation Model

GROUP	STRUCTURE	PROCESS	PRODUCT	STATUS	LONG-TERM RISK
Normal Controls	Nondepressed	Heuristic-driven	Nondepressed	Low	Low
Depressives	Depressogenic (nondepressed latent)	Heuristic-driven	Depressotypic	High	High
Pharmacologically treated Depressives	Nondepressed (but latent depressogenic)	Heuristic-driven	Nondepressed	Low	Low
Cognitively treated Depressives:					
-Early	Depressogenic (Nondepressed latent)	Normative (deliberative)	Nondepressed	Low	Low
-Late	Nondepressed	Heuristic-driven (but can be normative if desired)	Nondepressed	Low	Low

change over time in different treatments (DeRubeis et al., in press) and predicted relapse following successful treatment (Evans et al., 1989).

However, what is needed are measures of process and/or compensatory skills; the coding systems developed by Cook and Peterson (1986) or Hammen and colleagues' CBQ (Hammen, 1978; Hammen & Krantz, 1976) represent initial efforts, although neither appears to be wholly adequate. DeRubeis and colleagues (Barber & DeRubeis, 1989) have recently developed a system for ascertaining what patients have learned in treatment and/or the impact that such learning has had on the way they process information. While preliminary validity studies are just now underway, if successful, this system or others like it might prove particularly useful in testing hypotheses related to the change process in cognitive therapy.

Practice of Cognitive Therapy from a Social-Cognitive Perspective

Cognitive therapy consists of the systematic application of empirical procedures to the cognitive, behavioral, and affective processes of depressed patients (see Beck et al., 1979, for a detailed description of the treatment process). The practice of cognitive therapy can be likened to the conduct of any scientific inquiry. Beliefs, assumptions, and expectations are treated as "hypotheses" to be tested. Emphasis is placed on formulating rigorous tests of these beliefs based on sound methodological principles. The main strategy that underlies the interactions between client and therapist is one of *collaborative empiricism* (Hollon & Beck, 1979). Both client and therapist act as active collaborators in the identification of problem areas and in the design and execution of tests of the various beliefs. The data generated by these tests, rather than simple therapist credibility or authority, are relied on to provide insight and to produce change. Thus, the client is not so much persuaded to change by the therapist as he or she is led to use a series of unbiased experiments to generate evidence that speaks for itself. For this reason, we have always considered cognitive therapy to be, despite its name, an integration of cognitive and behavioral procedures (cf. Hollon & Beck, 1979, 1986; Hollon & Kendall, 1979; Kendall & Hollon, 1979).

In an important paper, Ross (1977) outlined three methods for producing changes in existing beliefs. These three strategies were derived from several decades of basic social-cognitive experimentation with nonclinical populations (e.g., Fischhoff, 1975; Fischhoff & Beyth, 1975; Lord, Ross & Lepper, 1979; Nisbett & Ross, 1980; Ross, Amabile, & Steinmetz, 1977; Ross & Lepper, 1980; Ross, Lepper, & Hubbard, 1975; Ross, Lepper, Strack, & Steinmetz, 1977). As outlined by Ross, the three methods for producing changes in existing beliefs that are particularly relevant to cognitive therapy are: (1) the "brute" force of consistently disconfirming evidence, (2) wholesale assaults on the rationale underlying an existing belief system, with the goal of discrediting that existing rationale and replacing it with an alternative explanatory system, and, (3) insight into aberrations in the processes followed to collect, store, retrieve, and combine information.

As we have discussed in detail elsewhere (Hollon & Garber, 1988), each of these three processes is quite relevant to cognitive therapy. In that approach, efforts to produce change can typically be divided into seven sequential stages. These include: (1) setting the rationale, (2) training in self-monitoring, (3) behavioral activation, (4) identifying beliefs, (5) evaluating beliefs, (6) uncovering underlying assumptions, and (7) preparing for termination and relapse prevention. Across each of these stages, Ross' three principles occur repeatedly in the provision of change. We discuss each in turn.

Setting the Rationale

The first task in cognitive therapy involves providing a rationale for the approach to be taken. In many instances, depressed individuals enter treatment with some type of stable trait theory about why they are in distress (e.g., "My wife left me because I'm unlovable," or "I lost my job because I am incompetent"). These individuals often have recent experience of interpersonal loss or failure in the achievement domain. These events are typically explained in terms of some stable flaw within the self that is likely to affect all other areas of life and likely to remain with them over time. In terms of the reformulated helplessness model, these individuals are prone to make internal, global, stable attributions for negative life events.

In most cases, the provision of an alternative rationale involves suggesting that these difficulties need not have arisen solely as a consequence of some pervasive, immutable personal flaw, but may have been the consequence of some combination of chance, inadequate behavioral skills, or the operation of self-fulfilling prophesies, in which negative expectations lead to the choice of behaviors that guarantee a particular nondesired consequence (cf. Darley & Fazio, 1980). All of these are correctable. Examples are sought of recent instances of negative life experiences and carefully examined to see if multiple causal explanations are possible. This effort is not an end in itself; the goal is not so much to produce change as to set the stage for its later realization. Cognitive therapists typically maintain a profound suspicion of change that is achieved solely on the basis of a conversion from one ideology to another. Such conversions are notoriously susceptible to later reversal (Ross, 1977). But the multiple alternative explanations provide the basis for subsequent hypothesis-testing, because the two or more competing constructs will typically yield different predictions in a number of readily specifiable situations.

Thus, for the depressed client who has been out of work for six months and has come to believe that he or she is unemployable, one can readily specify the competing hypothesis that he or she is indeed employable but, by virtue of not looking, (or looking ineffectually), has reduced the odds of finding a job. With this contrast in mind, it is then quite clear what needs to be done; the client needs to engage in an active job search, suspending disbelief in its positive conclusion and examining closely the adequacy of his or her actual behavioral efforts, in order to fairly test the accuracy of his or her belief. In this fashion, Ross' second principle (providing an alternative rationale) is used to set the stage for Ross' first principle (the application of empirical evidence) in the service of producing change in beliefs. As should be evident, such a process is neither solely rational nor solely empirical. Rather, it is one in which careful attention to the a priori logic involved is used to guide the design of experiments that contrast the accuracy of the two or more competing explanatory models. The process is, in fact, a rationally-guided empirical one, much like the application of the scientific method in any broader context.

Closely related is the provision of a basic cognitive model of affect and behavior. In this model, one's affective and behavioral responses to particular life events are not seen solely as a consequence of that event. Rather, the interpretations one makes and the meanings one ascribes to those antecedents are seen as mediating their impact and determining the individual variability in response across people to those situations (Beck, 1963, 1967, 1976; Ellis, 1962; Mahoney, 1977). This role of cognition as a partial mediator of response to life events in the context of a broader cognitive-diathesis stress model is the essence of a cognitive theory of disorder (cf. Abramson et al., 1989; Hollon & Garber, 1980). In cognitive therapy, one does not question the appropriateness of a client's affective reactions. Rather, the therapist seeks to help the client evaluate the accuracy of his or her beliefs. If, according to the cognitive model, one's depressogenic beliefs are found to be inaccurate, then affect should improve and efforts at coping with life stresses should become more effective. To continue with our earlier example, if the out-of-work client can succeed in getting a job by virtue of persistent and more competent efforts, he or she not only disproves the original belief in unmodifiable incompetence, he or she also dispels distress and sets the stage for more effective behaviors in the future.

Self-Monitoring Skills

Early in treatment, usually before the end of the first session, the client is trained in the use of explicit self-monitoring skills (see Beck et al., 1979; Hollon & Beck, 1979; or Hollon & Kendall, 1981, for examples). The basic rationale is to gather specific information regarding affective states, life events, behavioral activities, and (typically later) specific cognitions. Particular care is taken to teach clients how to gather information in a descriptive fashion relatively uninfluenced by the operation of biasing schemas. In general, the less one relies on memory, the less one's observations are contaminated by systematic distortions (Alba & Hasher, 1983). Such self-monitoring serves both to provide a wealth of information to the therapist about the specific measures of the client's life, thus serving as a basis for hypotheses about the sources of his or her difficulties, and, more importantly, as a source of evidential data that can subsequently be used for empirical hypothesis testing. In either case, the more abstract, asynchronous, and inferential the data-gathering task requested of the client, the more heavily influenced the product of the task is likely to be by schematic biases and heuristic-driven information-processing.

Behavioral Activation

A variety of behavioral activation strategies are subsumed within cognitive therapy (another reason why we consider it a cognitive-behavioral, rather than a purely cognitive, intervention; Hollon & Beck, 1986). Specific procedures include such steps as breaking large tasks down into their discrete components and then proceeding one step at a time, starting with the least difficult step ("chunking"), engaging in some relatively easily accomplished task prior to initiating a more difficult one ("success therapy"), scheduling specific activities so as to reduce indecision ("activity scheduling"), and planning particularly challenging or gratifying tasks ("mastery and pleasure"). More detailed accounts of these and other procedures are available elsewhere (cf. Beck et al., 1979; Hollon & Beck, 1979). The key point for our current discussion is that these more nearly behavioral activation principles are not implemented in isolation from the cognitive change techniques. Rather, they are executed in unison with them. Thus, specific activity scheduling and "chunking" might be used to increase the likelihood that an overwhelmed parent will plan and execute a family outing for the purposes of testing the beliefs that (a) he or she can't and, (b) he or she wouldn't enjoy it even if he or she could. In many instances, the various behavioral activation strategies can be used to describe a set of behaviors that are not only more likely to produce the desired results, but that generate evidence that prior failures were more nearly the consequence of an unfortunate choice of strategies rather than some permanent internal flaw. In this way, the behavioral activation process not only facilitates getting the client moving (thus overcoming behavioral passivity and response initiation deficits, Miller, 1975), but also furthers the process of empirical hypothesis-testing.

Identifying Beliefs

Considerable attention is devoted to helping clients identify the specific beliefs they entertain in specific concrete situations. This process provides the raw data needed to engage in the empirical hypothesis-testing process. Quite often, assessing and attending to such cognitions is a relatively new skill that needs to be acquired. A variety of techniques, including modeling, direct inquiry, role playing, imaginal reenactment, or *in vivo* experience can be used to help change the client's skills in this regard.

Cognitive therapists differentiate between *automatic thoughts*, the relatively accessible, relatively specific beliefs that seem to arise unbidden in concrete situations and *underlying assumptions*, the purported deeper structures that are presumed to organize and underlie within-individual consistency across situations. Automatic thoughts can be either verbal-ruminative or imagery-based in nature, the former being more often the case when depression is involved and the latter being more common in anxiety (Beck & Emery, 1985; Beck, Laude, & Bohnert, 1974). Further, most clients experience their affective reactions before they are aware of their cognitive interpretations in a situation. Whether this reflects a basic flaw in the cognitive model (Zajonc, 1980) or simply a process of differential speed of accessibility (Lazarus, 1982) remains somewhat controversial. Finally, it is often necessary to inquire precisely what a client expects or what a situation means in order to ascertain how a client perceives that situation. Automatic thoughts do not necessarily pass through conscious awareness in all situations.

Even after collecting specific beliefs about a specific situation, it is frequently useful to make further inquiries about precisely what those surface-level beliefs mean or imply to the client. This is the process of exploring the client's meaning system (also known as the "downward arrow" technique, Burns, 1980), and is most readily accomplished by simply asking the client "what would it mean to you if . . . ." This process is continued until each of the affects apparent in the situation can be accounted for, both in terms of nature and intensity. For example, if a client reports feeling both anxious and depressed, it is important to continue this mapping out of meaning systems until cognitions associated with each affect are identified. Typically, the further one proceeds down the "downward arrow," the more likely one is to move from concrete automatic thoughts to more abstract underlying assumptions.

Evaluating Beliefs

Once a belief or set of beliefs has been identified, it can be subjected to critical scrutiny. There are three questions that appear to have considerable heuristic utility in evaluating the validity of these beliefs. These questions are:

1. "What is the evidence for that belief?"—the *evidence* question.
2. "Is there any other way of looking at this?"—the *alternative explanations* question.
3. "Even if it is true, is it as bad as it seems?"—the *implications* question.

The therapist typically begins by raising these questions and guiding the discussion in the early sessions. Over time, the client is encouraged to use these questions himself or herself, increasingly automatizing their application through the use of self-instructional procedures (Meichenbaum, 1977).

The use of the evidence question nicely reflects Ross' first principle, disconfirmation via contradictory evidence. Frequently, a review of existing evidence is sufficient, but, at times, it becomes apparent that the generation of additional evidence via prospective information gathering or experimentation is needed. The alternative explanations question eventually generates multiple hypotheses for some prior event. Generation of such multiple hypotheses logically leads one back to the evidence question. The implications question essentially represents an extension of the evidence question down the hierarchy of meanings associated with the original beliefs. As such, it also leads quite logically to an evidentiary-based examination of the likely future outcomes of a given event. In all instances, every effort is made to encourage the client to review all available information in an even-handed fashion; the emphasis is on reality-testing, not positive thinking. Similarly, whenever possible this reality-testing process is grounded in the collection of empirical observations.

Identifying Underlying Assumptions

Cognitive therapists typically wait until later in the course of therapy before attempting to articulate the underlying assumptions that organize their clients' belief systems. In general, these assumptions are more abstract and general in nature than the concrete automatic thoughts identified in specific situations. As previously noted, the application of the "downward arrow" procedures to such specific cognitions earlier in therapy can often facilitate the identification of such underlying assumptions. In most instances, clients do not readily recognize the existence of such generic beliefs in their own meaning systems. Thus, collecting multiple examples of the operation of such assumptions across multiple situations is typically advisable before engaging the client in their consideration.

It is at this stage that historical reconstruction is often useful. The typical underlying assumption, often, but not invariably propositional in nature (e.g., "I must be successful in everything I do in order to be worthwhile," or "the people important to me should approve of every thing I do"). Historical reconstruction, often keyed to a recollection of the earliest situation eliciting the particular pattern of affect associated with the particular assumptive system, frequently uncovers contexts in which it was eminently reasonable to have drawn the inference drawn. Once articulated, these assumptive systems can then be evaluated in precisely the same manner described earlier.

Preparation for Terminations and Relapse Prevention

In most instances, eventual termination is a topic of discussion from the very first session. This facilitates using treatment time efficiently and helps make salient the importance of skills acquisition by the client. In addition to this heightened salience, the typical reduction in session frequency in midtreatment is presented as a trial run for eventual termination.

Relapse-prevention is facilitated by the ongoing emphasis on skills-training. In addition, time is typically set aside late in therapy to practice handling particularly stressful life events. Clients are encouraged to imagine precisely the sorts of events that might be most likely to get them depressed. In these imaginal role plays, clients first create a vivid imaginal situation, then rehearse the concrete steps they would pursue if confronted by such a state of affairs. This process not only provides the client with an opportunity to practice handling stressful life events while the therapist is still available for consultation, but also communicates a perspective in which the return of subsequent symptoms is treated as only a manageable nuisance rather than an overwhelming calamity. In view of cognitive therapy's apparent preventive effect, it would appear that something appropriate is occurring over the course of treatment with respect to the development of changes and/or that survive the end of the formal treatment.

CONCLUSION

There is no question that cognitive factors are intimately involved in the phenomenon of depression. Whether these processes are causal, as has been hypothesized, remains a subject of controversy. At the very least, it is apparent that attention to the subtle nuances of information-processing will enhance our understanding of the nature of depression.

Similarly, the assessment of cognition remains an uncertain process, but one that has shown clear strides over the past two decades. A variety of measurement methods exist, ranging from the direct to the indirect. Virtually all tend to differentiate depressives from nondepressives, but few, if any, are more than state-dependent. Among the more promising constructs is that of attribution styles, which appears to predict both onset and relapse/recurrence following successful treatment.

Finally, it is clear that, despite the uncertain epistomologic status of cognitive theories of depression, treatment interventions based on such models have been notably successful, both with respect to acute reponse and long-term prevention. Although the precise mechanisms involved remain unclear, it seems quite likely that changing beliefs may play a central role in both treatment reponse and prevention. It is this therapeutic success that fuels interest in both assessing cognitive phenomena and relating those phenomena to the etiology of depression. Whether these possibilities will be realized remains an empirical question, but clearly there is a phenomenon there to be explained.

REFERENCES

Abelson, R. P. (1981). Psychological status of the script concept. *American Psychologist, 36*, 715–729.

Abramson, L. Y., Metalsky, G. I., & Alloy, L. B. (1989). Hopelessness depression: A theory-based subtype of depression. A metatheoretical analysis with implications for psychopathology research. *Psychological Review, 96*, 358–372.

Abramson, L. Y., Seligman, M. E. P., & Teasdale, J. (1978). Learned helplessness in humans: Critique and reformulation. *Journal of Abnormal Psychology, 87*, 49–74.

Alba, J. W., & Hasher, L. (1983). Is memory schematic? *Psychological Bulletin, 93*, 203–231.

Alloy, L. B., & Abramson, L. Y. (1979). Judgment of contingency in depressed and nondepressed students: Sadder but wiser? *Journal of Experimental Psychology: General, 108*, 441–485.

Barber, J. P., & DeRubeis, R. J. (1989). On second thought: Where the action is in cognitive therapy for depression. *Cognitive Therapy and Research, 13*, 441–457.

Barthe, D. G., & Hammen, C. L. (1981). The attributional model of depression: A naturalistic extension. *Personality and Social Psychology Bulletin, 7*, 53–58.

Bartlett, F. C. (1932). *Remembering: A study in experimental and social psychology*. London and New York: Cambridge University Press.

Beck, A. T. (1963). Thinking and depression: I. Idiosyncratic content and cognitive distortions. *Archives of General Psychiatry, 9*, 324–333.

Beck, A. T. (1964). Thinking and depression: II. Theory and therapy. *Archives of General Psychiatry, 10*, 561–571.

Beck, A. T. (1967). *Depression: Clinical, experimental, and theoretical aspects*. New York: Harper & Row.

Beck, A. T. (1970). Role of fantasies in psychotherapy and psychopathology. *Journal of Nervous and Mental Diseases, 150*, 3–17.

Beck, A. T. (1976). *Cognitive therapy and the emotional disorders*. New York: International Universities Press.

Beck, A. T. (1984). Cognition and therapy. *Archives of General Psychiatry, 41*, 1112–1114.

Beck, A. T., & Emery, G. (1985). *Anxiety disorders and phobias*. New York: Basic Books.

Beck, A. T., Kovacs, M., & Weissman, A. (1975). Hopelessness and suicidal behaviors: An overview. *Journal of the American Medical Association, 234*, 1146–1149.

Beck, A. T., Laude, R., & Bohnert, M. (1974). Ideational components of anxiety neurosis. *Archives of General Psychiatry, 31*, 319–325.

Beck, A. T., Rush, A. J., Shaw, B. F., & Emery, G. (1979).

Cognitive therapy of depression. New York: Guilford Press.
Beck, A. T., Weissman, A., Lester, D., & Trexler, L. (1974). The measurement of pessimism: The Hopelessness Scale. *Journal of Consulting and Clinical Psychology, 42,* 861–865.
Blackburn, I. M., Bishop, S., Glen, A. I. M., Whalley, L. J., & Christie, J. E. (1981). The efficacy of cognitive therapy in depression: A treatment trial using cognitive therapy and pharmacotherapy, each alone and in combination. *British Journal of Psychiatry, 139,* 181–189.
Blackburn, I. M., Eunson, K. M., & Bishop, S. (1986). A two-year naturalistic follow-up of depressed patients treated with cognitive therapy, pharmacotherapy and a combination of both. *Journal of Affective Disorders, 10,* 67–75.
Blaney, P. H. (1986). Affect and memory: A review. *Psychological Bulletin, 99,* 229–246.
Borgida, E., & Nisbett, R. (1977). The differential impact of abstract vs. concrete information on decisions. *Journal of Applied Social Psychology, 7,* 258–271.
Bower, G. (1981). Mood and memory. *American Psychologist, 36,* 129–148.
Bower, G. H. (1986). Prime time in cognitive psychology. In P. Eelen & O. Fontaine (Eds.), *Behavior therapy: Beyond the conditioning framework* (pp. 22–47). Hillsdale, NJ: Lawrence Erlbaum Associates.
Burns, D. D. (1980). *Feeling good: The new mood therapy.* New York: William Morrow.
Cacioppo, J. T., & Petty, R. E. (1981). Social psychological procedures for cognitive response assessment: The thought-listing technique, In T. V. Merluzzi, C. R. Glass, & M. Genest (Eds.), *Cognitive Assessment* (pp. 309–342). New York: Guilford Press.
Cantor, N. (1980a). A cognitive-social analysis of personality. In N. Cantor & J. F. Kihlstrom (Eds.), *Personality, cognition, and social interaction* (pp. 23–44). Hillsdale, NJ: Lawrence Erlbaum Associates.
Cantor, N. (1980b). Perceptions of situations: Situation prototypes and person-situation prototypes. In D. Magnusson (Ed.), *The situation: An interactional perspective* (pp. 229–244). Hillsdale, NJ: Lawrence Erlbaum Associates.
Cantor, N. (1981). A cognitive-social analysis of personality. In N. Cantor & J. F. Kihlstrom (Eds.), *Personality, cognition, and social interaction* (pp. 23–44). Hillsdale, NJ: Lawrence Erlbaum Associates.
Cantor, N., & Mischel, W. (1977). Traits as prototypes: Effects on recognition memory. *Journal of Personality and Social Psychology, 35,* 38–48.
Cantor, N., & Mischel, W. (1979). Prototypes in person perception. In L. Berkowitz (Ed.), *Advances in experimental social psychology* (Vol. 12). New York: Academic Press.
Chomsky, N. (1957). *Syntactic structures.* The Hague: Mouton.
Cook, M. L., & Peterson, C. (1986). Depressive irrationality. *Cognitive Therapy and Research, 10,* 293–298.

Coyne, J. C., & Gotlib, I. H. (1983). The role of cognition in depression: A critical appraisal. *Psychological Bulletin, 94,* 472–505.
Craik, F. I. M., & Lockhart, R. S. (1972). Level of processing: A framework for memory research. *Journal of Verbal Learning and Verbal Behavior, 11,* 671–684.
Craik, F. I. M., & Tulving, E. (1975). Depth of processing and the retention of words in episodic memory. *Journal of Experimental Psychology: General, 104,* 268–294.
Cutrona, C. E. (1983). Causal attributions and perinatal depression. *Journal of Abnormal Psychology, 92,* 161–172.
Darley, J. M., & Fazio, R. H. (1980). Expectancy confirmation processes arising in the social interaction sequences. *American Psychologist, 35,* 867–881.
Davis, H., & Unruh, W. R. (1981). Development of self-schema in adult depression. *Journal of Abnormal Psychology, 90,* 125–133.
Davison, G. C., Feldman, P. M., & Osborn, C. E. (1984). Articulated thoughts, irrational beliefs and fear of negative evaluation. *Cognitive Therapy and Research, 8,* 349–362.
Davison, G. C., Robins, C., & Johnson, M. K. (1983). Articulated thoughts during simulated situations: A paradigm for studying cognition in emotion and behavior. *Cognitive Therapy and Research, 7,* 17–40.
Dent, J., & Teasdale, J. P. (1988). Negative cognition and the persistence of depression. *Journal of Abnormal Psychology, 97,* 29–34.
Depue, R. A., Kleiman, R. M., Davis, P., Hutchinson, M., & Krauss, S. P. (1985). The behavioral high-risk paradigm and bipolar affective disorder, VIII: Serum free cortisol in nonpatient cyclothymic subjects selected by the general behavior inventory. *American Journal of Psychiatry, 142,* 175–181.
DeRubeis, R. J., Evans, M. D., Hollow, S. D., Garvey, M. J., Grove, W. M., & Tuason, V. B. (in press). How does cognitive therapy work? Cognitive change and symptom change in cognitive therapy and pharmacotherapy for depression. *Journal of Consulting and Clinical Psychology.*
Dobson, K. S., & Breiter, H. J. (1983). Cognitive assessment of depression: Reliability and validity of three measures. *Journal of Abnormal Psychology, 92,* 107–109.
Dobson, K. S., & Shaw, B. F. (1986). Cognitive assessment with major depressive disorders. *Cognitive Therapy and Research, 10,* 13–29.
Dodge, K. A., & Frame, C. L. (1982). Social cognitive biases and deficits in aggressive boys. *Child Development, 53,* 620–635.
Eaves, G., & Rush, A. J. (1984). Cognitive patterns in symptomatic and remitted unipolar major depression. *Journal of Abnormal Psychology, 93,* 31–40.
Ellis, A. (1962). *Reason and emotion in psychotherapy.* Secaucus, NJ: Lyle Stuart.
Ericsson, K. A., & Simon, H. A. (1980). Verbal reports as data. *Psychological Review, 87,* 215–251.

Evans, M. D., & Hollon, S. D. (1988). Patterns of personal and causal inference: Implications for a cognitive therapy of depression. In L. B. Alloy (Ed.), *Cognitive processes in depression* (pp. 344-377). New York: Guilford Press.

Evans, M. D., Hollon, S. D., DeRubeis, R. J., Piasecki, J. M., Grove, W. M., Garvey, J. J., & Tuason, V. B. (1989). *Relapse/recurrence following cognitive therapy and pharmacotherapy for depression.* Manuscript submitted for publication.

Fazio, R. H., Sanbonmatsu, D. M., Powell, M. C., & Kardes, F. R. (1986). On the automatic activation of attitudes. *Journal of Personality and Social Psychology, 50,* 229-238.

Fischhoff, B. (1975). Hindsight = foresight: The effect of outcome knowledge on judgement under uncertainty. *Journal of Experimental Psychology: Human Perception and Performance, 1,* 288-299.

Fischhoff, B., & Beyth, R. (1975). "I knew it would happen"—Remembered probabilities of once-future things. *Organizational Behavior and Human Performance, 13,* 1-16.

Genest, M., & Turk, D. C. (1981). Think-aloud approaches to cognitive assessment. In T. V. Merluzzi, C. R. Glass, & M. Genest (Eds.), *Cognitive assessment* (pp. 233-269). New York: Guilford Press.

Giles, D. E., & Rush, A. J. (1982). Relationship of dysfunctional attitudes and dexamethasone in endogenous and nonendogenous depression. *Biological Psychiatry, 17,* 1303-1314.

Goldfried, M. R., & Robins, C. (1982). On the facilitation of self-efficacy. *Cognitive Therapy and Research, 6,* 361-380.

Goldfried, M. R., & Robins, C. (1983). Self-schema, cognitive bias, and the processing of therapeutic experiences. In P. C. Kendall (Ed.), *Advances in cognitive-behavioral research and therapy* (Vol. II, pp. 33-80). New York: Academic Press.

Gong-Guy, E., & Hammen, C. (1980). Causal perceptions of stressful life events in depressed and nondepressed clinic outpatients. *Journal of Abnormal Psychology, 89,* 662-669.

Hamilton, E. W., & Abramson, L. Y. (1983). Cognitive patterns and major depressive disorders: A longitudinal study in a hospital setting. *Journal of Abnormal Psychology, 92,* 173-184.

Hammen, C. L. (1978). Depression, distortion, and life stress in college students. *Cognitive Therapy and Research, 2,* 189-192.

Hammen, C., & Cochrane, S. (1981). Cognitive correlates of life stress and depression in college students. *Journal of Abnormal Psychology, 90,* 23-27.

Hammen, C., & deMayo, R. (1982). Cognitive correlates of teacher stress and depressive symptoms: Implications for attributional models of depression. *Journal of Abnormal Psychology, 91,* 96-101.

Hammen, C. L., & Krantz, S. (1976). Effect of success and failure on depressive cognitions. *Journal of Abnormal Psychology, 85,* 577-586.

Hammen, C., Krantz, S. E., & Cochran, S. D. (1981). Relationships between depression and causal attributions about stressful life events. *Cognitive Therapy and Research, 5,* 351-358.

Hammen, C., Marks, T., deMayo, R., & Mayol, A. (1985). Self-schemas and risk for depression: A prospective study. *Journal of Personality and Social Psychology, 49,* 1147-1159.

Hammen, C., Marks, T., Mayol, A., & deMayo, R. (1985). Depressive self-schemas, life stress, and vulnerability to depression. *Journal of Abnormal Psychology, 94,* 308-319.

Harrell, T. H., & Ryon, N. B. (1983). Cognitive behavioral assessment of depression: Clinical validation of the Automatic Thoughts Questionnaire. *Journal of Consulting and Clinical Psychology, 51,* 721-725.

Harvey, D. (1981). Depression and attributional style: Interpretations of important personal events. *Journal of Abnormal Psychology, 90,* 134-142.

Heider, F. (1958). *The psychology of interpersonal relations.* New York: John Wiley & Sons.

Higgins, E. T., Klein, R., & Strauman, T. (1985). Self-concept discrepancy theory: A psychological model for distinguishing among different aspects of depression and anxiety. *Social Cognition, 3,* 51-76.

Hollon, S. D., & Beck, A. T. (1979). Cognitive therapy for depression. In P. C. Kendall & S. D. Hollon (Eds.), *Cognitive-behavioral interventions: Theory, research, and procedures* (pp. 153-203). New York: Academic Press.

Hollon, S. D., & Beck, A. T. (1986). Cognitive and cognitive-behavioral interventions. In S. L. Garfield & A. E. Bergin (Eds), *Handbook of psychotherapy and behavior change: An empirical analysis* (3rd ed., pp. 443-482). New York: John Wiley & Sons.

Hollon, S. D., & Bemis, K. M. (1981). Self-report and the assessment of cognitive functions. In M. Hersen & A. S. Bellack (Eds.), *Behavioral assessment: A practical handbook* (2nd. ed., pp. 216-252). Elmsford, NY: Pergamon Press.

Hollon, S. D., DeRubeis, R. J., & Evans, M. D. (1987). Causal mediation of change in treatment for depression: Discriminating between nonspecificity and noncausality. *Psychological Bulletin, 102,* 139-149.

Hollon, S. D., Evans, M. D., & DeRubeis, R. J. (1988). Preventing relapse following treatment for depression: The Cognitive Pharmacotherapy Project. In T. M. Field, P. M. McCabe, & N. Schneiderman (Eds.), *Stress and coping across development* (pp. 227-243). Hillsdale, NJ: Lawrence Erlbaum Associates.

Hollon, S. D., DeRubeis, R. J., Evans, M. D., Wiemer, M. J., Garvey, M. J., Grove, W. M., & Tuason, V. B. (1989). *Cognitive therapy, pharmacotherapy, and combined cognitive-pharmacotherapy in the treatment of depression.* Manuscript submitted for publication.

Hollon, S. D., & Garber, J. (1980). A cognitive-expectancy theory of therapy for helplessness and depression. In J. Garber & M. E. P. Seligman (Eds.), *Human helpless-*

ness: Theory and applications (pp. 173–195). New York: Academic Press.

Hollon, S. D., & Garber, J. (1988). Cognitive therapy. In L. Y. Abramson (Ed.), *Social cognition and clinical psychology* (pp. 204–253). New York: Guilford Press.

Hollon, S. D., & Kendall, P. C. (1979). Cognitive-behavioral interventions: Theory and procedure. In P. C. Kendall & S. D. Hollon (Eds.), *Cognitive-behavioral interventions: Theory, research, and procedure*, (pp. 445–454). New York: Academic Press.

Hollon, S. D., & Kendall, P. C. (1980). Cognitive self-statements in depression: Development of an automatic thoughts questionnaire. *Cognitive Therapy and Research, 4*, 383–395.

Hollon, S. D., & Kendall, P. C. (1981). In vivo assessment techniques for cognitive-behavioral processes. In P. C. Kendall & S. D. Hollon (Eds.), *Assessment strategies for cognitive-behavioral interventions* (pp. 21–35). New York: Academic Press.

Hollon, S. D., Kendall, P. C., & Lumry, A. (1986). Specificity of depressotypic cognitions in clinical depression. *Journal of Abnormal Psychology, 95*, 52–59.

Hollon, S. D., & Kriss, M. R. (1984). Cognitive factors in clinical research and practice. *Clinical Psychology Review, 4*, 38–78.

Hollon, S. D., & Najavits, L. (1988). Review of empirical studies on cognitive therapy. In A. J. Frances & R. E. Hales (Eds.), *American Psychiatric Press Review of Psychiatry* (Vol. 7, pp. 643–666). Washington, DC: American Psychiatric Press.

Hurlburt, R. T. (1976). *Self-observation and self-control*. Unpublished doctoral dissertation, University of South Dakota.

Hurlburt, R. T. (1979). Random sampling of cognitions and behavior. *Journal of Research in Personality, 13*, 103–111.

Hurlburt, R. T. (1980). Validation and correlation of thought sampling with retrospective measures. *Cognitive Therapy and Research, 4*, 235–238.

Ingram, R. E. (1984). Toward an information processing analysis of depression. *Cognitive Therapy and Research, 8*, 443–447.

Isen, A. M. (1984). Toward understanding the role of affect in cognition. In R. S. Wager & T. K. Srull (Eds.), *Handbook of social cognition*, (Vol. 3, pp. 179–236). Hillsdale, NJ: Lawrence Erlbaum Associates.

Jenkins, J. J. (1979). Four points to remember: A tetrahedron model of memory experiments. In L. S. Cermak & I. M. Craik (Eds.), *Levels of processing in human memory* (pp. 429–426). Hillsdale, NJ: Lawrence Erlbaum Associates.

Johnson, M. H., & Magaro, P. A. (1987). Effects of mood and severity on memory processes in depression and mania. *Psychological Bulletin, 101*, 28–40.

Kahneman, D., Slovic, P., & Tversky, A. (Eds.), (1982). *Judgment under uncertainty: Heuristics and biases*. Cambridge, England: Cambridge University Press.

Kahneman, D., & Tversky, A. (1972). Subjective probability: A judgment of representativeness. *Cognitive Psychology, 3*, 430–454.

Kendall, P. C., & Hollon, S. D. (Eds.), (1979). Cognitive-behavioral interventions: Current status. In P. C. Kendall & S. D. Hollon (Eds.), *Cognitive-behavioral interventions: Theory, research, and procedures*, (pp. 1–9). New York: Academic Press.

Kendall, P. C., & Hollon, S. D. (Eds.), (1981). *Assessment strategies for cognitive-behavioral interventions*. New York: Academic Press.

Kenny, D. A. (1979). *Correlation and causality*. New York: John Wiley & Sons.

Kihlstrom, J. F., & Nasby, W. (1981). Cognitive tasks in clinical assessment: An exercise in applied psychology. In P. C. Kendall & S. D. Hollon (Eds.), *Assessment strategies for cognitive-behavioral interventions* (pp. 287–317). New York: Academic Press.

Klein, D. F., & Davis, J. M. (1969). *Diagnosis and drug treatment of psychiatric disorders*. Baltimore: Williams & Wilkins.

Klinger, E. (1978). Modes of normal conscious flow. In K. S. Pope & J. L. Singer (Eds.), *The stream of consciousness: Scientific investigations into flow of human experience* (pp. 225–258). New York: Plenum Press.

Klinger, E., Barta, S. G., & Maxeiner, M. E. (1981). Current concerns: Assessing therapeutically relevant motivations. In P. C. Kendall & S. D. Hollon (Eds.), *Assessment strategies for cognitive-behavioral interventions* (pp. 161–196). New York: Academic Press.

Kovacs, M., & Beck, A. T. (1978). Maladaptive cognitive structures in depression. *American Journal of Psychiatry, 135*, 525–533.

Kovacs, M., Rush, A. J., Beck, A. T., & Hollon, S. D. (1981). Depressed outpatients treated with cognitive therapy or pharmacotherapy: A one-year follow-up. *Archives of General Psychiatry, 38*, 33–39.

Krames, L., & MacDonald, M. R. (1985). Distraction and depressive cognitions. *Cognitive Therapy and Research, 9*, 561–573.

Krantz, S., & Hammen, C. L. (1979). Assessment of cognitive bias in depression. *Journal of Abnormal Psychology, 88*, 611–619.

Kuiper, N. A., & Derry, P. A. (1981). The self as a cognitive prototype: An application to person perception and depression. In N. Cantor & J. Kihlstrom (Eds.), *Personality, social interaction, and cognition* (pp. 215–232). Hillsdale, NJ: Lawrence Erlbaum Associates.

Kuiper, N. A., Derry, P. A., & MacDonald, M. R. (1982). Self-reference and person perception in depression: A social cognition perspective. In G. Weary & H. L. Mirels (Eds.), *Integrations of clinical and social psychology* (pp. 79–103). New York: Oxford University Press.

Kuiper, N. A., & MacDonald, M. R. (1980). Self-reference and person perception in depression. Unpublished manuscript, University of Western Ontario.

Kuiper, N. A., Olinger, L., & MacDonald, M. (1988). Depressive schemata and the processing of personal and social information. In L. Alloy (Ed.), *Cognitive processes in depression*. New York: Guilford Press.

Kuiper, N. A., Olinger, L. J., MacDonald, M. R., & Shaw, B. F. (1985). Self-schema processing of depressed and nondepressed content: The effects of vulnerability to depression. *Social Cognition, 3,* 77-93.

Landau, R. J., & Goldfried, M. R. (1981). The assessment of schemata: A unifying framework for cognitive, behavioral, and traditional assessment. In P. C. Kendall & S. D. Hollon (Eds.), *Assessment strategies for cognitive-behavioral interventions* (pp. 363-399). New York: Academic Press.

Lazarus, R. S. (1966). *Psychological stress and the coping process.* New York: McGraw-Hill.

Lazarus, R. S. (1982). Thoughts on the relations between emotion and cognition. *American Psychologist, 37,* 1019-1024.

Lewinsohn, P. M., Larson, D. W., & Muñoz, R. F. (1982). The measurement of expectancies and other cognitions in depressed individuals. *Cognitive Therapy and Research, 6,* 437-446.

Lewinsohn, P. M., Steinmetz, J. L., Larson, D. W., & Franklin, J. (1981). Depression-related cognitions: Antecedent or consequences? *Journal of Abnormal Psychology, 90,* 213-219.

Linville, P. W. (1985). Self-complexity and affective extremity: Don't put all of your eggs in one cognitive basket. *Social Cognition, 3,* 94-120.

Loftus, E. F., & Loftus, G. R. (1980). On the permanence of stored information in the human brain. *American Psychologist, 35,* 409-420.

Lord, C. G., Ross, L., & Lepper, M. R. (1979). Biased assimilation and attitude polarization: The effects of prior theories on subsequently considered evidence. *Journal of Personality and Social Psychology, 37,* 2098-2109.

Mahoney, M. J. (1974). *Cognition and behavior modification.* Cambridge, MA: Ballinger.

Mahoney, M. J. (1977). Reflections on the cognitive learning trend in psychotherapy. *American Psychologist. 32,* 5-13.

Manly, P. C., McMahon, R. B., Bradley, C. F., & Davidson, P. O. (1982). Depressive attributional style and depression following childbirth. *Journal of Abnormal Psychology, 91,* 245-254.

Markus, H. (1977). Self-schemata and processing information about the self. *Journal of Personality and Social Psychology, 35,* 63-78.

McNeal, E. T., & Cimbolic, P. (1986). Antidepressant and biochemical theories of depression. *Psychological Bulletin, 99,* 361-374.

Meehl, P. E. (1954). *Clinical versus statistical prediction: A theoretical analysis and a review of the evidence.* Minneapolis: University of Minnesota Press.

Meichenbaum, D. (1977). *Cognitive-behavior modification: An integrative approach.* New York: Plenum Press.

Menzies, R. (1935). The comparative memory values of pleasant, unpleasant, and indifferent experiences. *Journal of Experimental Psychology, 18,* 267-279.

Merluzzi, T. V., Glass, C. R., & Genest, M. (Eds.), (1981). *Cognitive assessment.* New York: Guilford Press.

Metalsky, G. I., Abramson, L. Y., Seligman, M. E. P., Semmel, A., & Peterson, C. (1982). Attributional styles and life events in the classroom: Vulnerability and invulnerability to depressive mood reactions. *Journal of Personality and Social Psychology, 43,* 612-617.

Metalsky, G. I., Halberstadt, L. J., & Abramson, L. Y. (1987). Vulnerability to depressive mood reactions: Toward a more powerful test of the diathesis-stress and causal mediation components of the reformulated theory of depression. *Journal of Personality and Social Psychology, 52,* 386-393.

Michael, C. C., & Funabiki, D. (1985). Depression, distortion, and life stress: Extended findings. *Cognitive Therapy and Research, 9,* 659-666.

Miller, I. W. III., & Norman, W. H. (1986). Persistence of depressive cognitions within a subgroup of depressed inpatients. *Cognitive Therapy and Research, 10,* 211-224.

Miller, W. R. (1975). Psychological deficit in depression. *Psychological Bulletin, 82,* 238-260.

Minsky, M. (1975). A framework for representing knowledge. In P. H. Winston (Ed.), *The psychology of computer vision* (pp. 211-280). New York: McGraw-Hill.

Morris, J. B., & Beck, A. T. (1974). The efficacy of anti-depressant drugs: A review of research, 1958-1972. *Archives of General Psychiatry, 30,* 667-674.

Murphy, G. E., Simons, A. D., Wetzel, R. D., & Lustman, P. J. (1984). Cognitive therapy and pharmacotherapy, singly and together in the treatment of depression. *Archives of General Psychiatry, 41,* 33-41.

Neisser, U. (1967). *Cognitive psychology.* New York: Appleton-Century-Crofts.

Neisser, U. (1976). *Cognition and reality: Principles and implications of cognitive psychology.* San Francisco: Freeman.

Nisbett, R. E., & Ross, L. (1980). *Human inference: Strategies and shortcomings of social judgment.* Englewood Cliffs, NJ: Prentice-Hall.

Nisbett R. E., & Wilson, T. D. (1977). Telling more than we can know: Verbal reports on mental processes. *Psychological Review, 84,* 231-259.

Norman, W. H., Miller, I. W. III., & Klee, S. H. (1983). Assessment of cognitive distortion in a clinically depressed population. *Cognitive Therapy and Research, 7,* 133-140.

O'Hara, M. W., Neunaber, D. J., & Zekoski, E. M. (1984). Prospective study of postpartum depression: Prevalence, course, and predictive factors. *Journal of Abnormal Psychology, 93,* 158-171.

O'Hara, M. W., Rehm, L. P., & Campbell, S. B. (1982). Predicting depressive symptomatology: Cognitive-behavioral models and postpartum depression. *Journal of Abnormal Psychology, 91,* 457-461.

Olinger, L., Kuiper, N., & Shaw, B. (1987). Dysfunctional attitudes and negative life events: An interactive model of depression. *Cognitive Therapy and Research, 11,* 25-40.

Oliver, J. M., & Baumgart, E. P. (1985). The Dysfunctional

Attitudes Scale: Psychometric properties and relation to depression in an unselected adult population. *Cognitive Therapy and Research, 9,* 161–167.

Parks, C., & Hollon, S. D. (1988). Cognitive assessment. In M. Hersen & A. S. Bellack (Eds.), *Behavioral Assessment: A practical handbook* (3rd ed., pp. 161–212). Elmsford, NY: Pergamon Press.

Peeters, R. (1986). Mood effects in episodic and semantic memory. In P. Eelen & O. Fontaine (Eds.), *Behavior therapy: Beyond the conditioning framework,* (pp. 69–85). Hillsdale, NJ: Lawrence Erlbaum Associates.

Peterson, C., & Seligman, M. E. P. (1984). Causal explanations as a risk factor in depression: Theory and evidence. *Psychological Review, 91,* 347–374.

Peterson, C., Semmel, A., von Baeyer, C., Abramson, L. Y., Metalsky, G. I., & Seligman, M. E. P. (1982). The Attributional Style Questionnaire. *Cognitive Therapy and Research, 6,* 287–299.

Peterson, C., Villanova, P., & Raps, C. S. (1985). Depression and attributions: Factors responsible for inconsistent results in the published literature. *Journal of Abnormal Psychology, 94,* 165–168.

Petty, R. E., & Cacioppo, J. T. (1977). Forewarning, cognitive responding, and resistance to persuasion. *Journal of Personality and Social Psychology, 35,* 645–655.

Piaget, J. (1952). *The origin of intelligence in children.* New York: International Universities Press.

Piaget, J. (1954). *The construction of reality in the child.* New York: Basic Books.

Radloff, L. S., & Rae, D. S. (1979). Susceptibility and precipitating factors in depression: Sex differences and similarities. *Journal of Abnormal Psychology, 88,* 174–181.

Rehm, L. P. (1977). A self-control model of depression. *Behavior Therapy, 8,* 787–804.

Riskind, J. H. (1989). The mediating mechanisms in mood and memory: A cognitive priming formulation. *Journal of Social Behavior and Personality, 4,* 173–184.

Riskind, J. H., & Rholes, W. S. (1984). Cognitive accessibility and the capacity of cognitions to predict future depression: A theoretical note. *Cognitive Therapy and Research, 8,* 1–12.

Rogers, T. B., Rogers, P. J., & Kuiper, N. A. (1979). Evidence for the self as a cognitive prototype: The "false alarms effect." *Personality and Social Psychology Bulletin, 5,* 53–56.

Rosch, E. (1978). Principles of categorization. In E. Rosch & R.B. Lloyd (Eds.), *Cognition and categorization.* Hillsdale, NJ: Lawrence Erlbaum Associates.

Ross, L. (1977). The intuitive psychologist and his shortcomings. In L. Berkowitz (Ed.). *Advances in experimental social psychology* (Vol. 10, pp. 173–220). New York: Academic Press.

Ross, L., Amabile, T. M., & Steinmetz, J. L. (1977). Social roles, social control, and biases in social perception processes. *Journal of Personality and Social Psychology, 35,* 485–494.

Ross, S. M., Gottfredson, D. K., Christensen, P., & Weaver, R. (1986). Cognitive self-statements in depression: Findings across clinical populations. *Cognitive Therapy and Research, 10,* 159–165.

Ross, L., & Lepper, M. R. (1980). The perseverance of beliefs: Empirical and normative considerations. In R. A. Schweder (Ed.), *New directions for methodology of behavioral science: Fallible subjects in behavioral research* (pp. 32–48). San Francisco: Jossey-Bass.

Ross, L., Lepper, M. R., & Hubbard, M. (1975). Perseverance in self-perception and social perception: Biased attributional processes in the debriefing paradigm. *Journal of Personality and Social Psychology, 32,* 880–892.

Ross, L., Lepper, M. R., Strack, F., & Steinmetz, J. (1977). Social explanations and social expectation: Effects of real and hypothetical explanations on subjective likelihood. *Journal of Personality and Social Psychology, 35,* 817–829.

Roy-Byrne, P. P., Weingartner, H., Bierer, L. M., Thompson, K., & Post, R. M. (1986). Effortful and automatic cognitive processes in depression. *Archives of General Psychiatry, 43,* 265–267.

Ruehlman, L. S., West, S. G., & Pasahow, R. J. (1985). Depression and evaluative schemata. *Journal of Personality, 53,* 46–92.

Rush, A. J., Beck, A. T., Kovacs, M., & Hollon, S. D. (1977). Comparative efficacy of cognitive therapy versus pharmacotherapy in outpatient depressives. *Cognitive Therapy and Research, 1,* 17–37.

Rush, A. J., Beck, A. T., Kovacs, M., Weissenberger, J., & Hollon, S. D. (1982). Comparison of the effects of cognitive therapy on helplessness and self concept. *American Journal of Psychiatry, 139,* 862–866.

Rush, A. J., Weissenberger, J., & Eaves, G. (1986). Do thinking patterns predict depressive symptoms? *Cognitive Therapy and Research, 10,* 225–235.

Schneider, R. M., & Shiffrin, W. (1977). Controlled and automatic information processing: I. Detection, search, and attention. *Psychological Review, 84,* 1–66.

Seligman, M. E. P. (1975). *Helplessness: On depression, development, and death.* San Francisco: Freeman.

Seligman, M. E. P., Abramson, L. Y., Semmel, A., & von Baeyer, C. (1979). Depressive attributional style. *Journal of Abnormal Psychology, 88,* 242–247.

Shea, T. M., Elkin, I., & Hirschfeld, R. M. A. (1988). Psychotherapeutic treatment of depressives. In A. J. Frances & R. E. Hales (Eds.), *American Psychiatric Press Review of Psychiatry* (Vol. 7, pp. 235–255). Washington, DC: American Psychiatric Press.

Shevrin, H., & Dickman, S. (1980). The psychological unconscious: A necessary assumption for all psychological theory? *American Psychologist, 35,* 421–434.

Silberman, E. K., Weingartner, H., & Post, R. M. (1983). Thinking disorder in depression: Logic and strategy in an abstract reasoning task. *Archives of General Psychiatry, 40,* 775–780.

Silverman, J. S., Silverman, J. A., & Eardley, D. A. (1984).

Do maladaptive attitudes cause depression? *Archives of General Psychiatry, 41*, 28-30.

Simons, A. D., Garfield, S. L., & Murphy, G. E. (1984). The process of change in cognitive therapy and pharmacotherapy for depression. *Archives of General Psychiatry, 41*, 45-51.

Simons, A. D., Murphy, G. E., Levine, J. L., & Wetzel, R. D. (1986). Cognitive therapy and pharmacotherapy for depression: Sustained improvement over one year. *Archives of General Psychiatry, 43*, 43-49.

Sternberg, R. J., & Tulving, E. (1977). The measurement of subjective organization in free recall. *Psychological Bulletin, 84*, 539-556.

Sweeney, P. D., Anderson, K., & Bailey, S. (1986). Attributional style in depression: A meta-analytic review. *Journal of Personality and Social Psychology, 50*, 974-991.

Taylor, S. E., & Brown, J. D. (1988). Illusion and well-being: A social psychological perspective on mental health. *Psychological Bulletin, 103*, 193-210.

Taylor, S. E., & Crocker, J. (1981). Schematic basis of information processing. In E. T. Higgins, C. P. Herman, & M. P. Zanna (Eds.), *Social cognition: The Ontario symposium* (Vol. 1, pp. 89-134. Hillsdale, NJ: Lawrence Erlbaum Associates.

Taylor, S. E., & Fiske, S. T. (1975). Point of view and perceptions of causality. *Journal of Personality and Social Psychology, 32*, 439-445.

Taylor, S. E., & Fiske, S. T. (1978). Salience, attention, and attribution: Top of the head phenomena. In L. Berkowitz (Ed.), *Advances in experimental social psychology* (Vol. 11, pp. 250-258). New York: Academic Press.

Teasdale, J. D., Taylor, R., & Fogarty, S. J. (1980). Effects of induced elation-depression on the accessibility of memories of happy and unhappy experiences. *Behavior Research and Therapy, 18*, 339-346.

Thorndyke, P. W., & Hayes-Roth, B. (1979). The use of schemata in the acquisition and transfer of knowledge. *Cognitive Psychology, 11*, 83-106.

Tsujimoto, R. N. (1978). Memory bias toward normative and novel trait prototypes. *Journal of Personality and Social Psychology, 36*, 1391-1401.

Tulving, E. (1972). Episodic and semantic memory. In E. Tulving & W. Donaldson (Eds.), *Organization of memory*, (pp. 381-403). New York: Academic Press.

Turk, D. C., & Salovey, P. (1985). Cognitive structures, cognitive processes, and cognitive-behavior modification: I. Client issues. *Cognitive Therapy and Research, 9*, 1-18.

Turk, D. C., & Speers, M. A. (1983). Cognitive schemata and cognitive processes in cognitive-behavioral interventions: Going beyond the information given. In P. C. Kendall (Ed.), *Advances in cognitive-behavioral research and therapy* (Vol. II, pp. 3-31). New York: Academic Press.

Turner, R. H., & Barlow, J. A. (1951). Memory for pleasant and unpleasant experiences: Some methodological considerations. *Journal of Experimental Psychology, 42*, 189-196.

Tversky, A., & Kahneman, D. (1973). Availability: A heuristic for judging frequency and probability. *Cognitive Psychology, 5*, 207-232.

Tversky, A., & Kahneman, D. (1974). Judgment under uncertainty: Heuristics and biases. *Science, 185*, 1124-1131. [Reprinted in D. Kahneman, P. Slovic, & A. Tversky (Eds.), *Judgment under uncertainty: Heuristics and biases*. Cambridge: Cambridge University Press.]

Vygotsky, L. (1962). *Thought and language*. Cambridge, MA: Massachusetts Institute of Technology Press. (Originally published 1934).

Waters, R. H., & Leeper, R. (1936). The relation of affective tone to the retention of experiences of daily life. *Journal of Experimental Psychology, 19*, 203-215.

Watkins, J. T., & Rush, A. J. (1983). Cognitive response test. *Cognitive Therapy and Research, 7*, 425-435.

Weingartner, H. (1986). Automatic and effort-demanding cognitive processes in depression. In L. W. Poon, T. Crook, K. L. Davis, C. Eisdorfer, B. J. Gurland, A. W. Kaszniak, & L. W. Thompson, *Handbook for clinical memory assessment of older adults*, (pp. 218-225). Washington, DC: American Psychological Association.

Weissman, A., & Beck, A. T. (1978, November). *Development and validation of the Dysfunctional Attitude Scale (DAS)*. Paper presented at the 12th annual meeting of the Association for the Advancement of Behavior Therapy, Chicago.

Wilkinson, I. M., & Blackburn, I. M. (1981). Cognitive style in depressed and recovered patients. *British Journal of Clinical Psychology, 20*, 283-292.

Zajonc, R. (1980). Feeling and thinking: Preferences need no inferences. *American Psychologist, 35*, 151-175.

Zimmerman, M., & Coryell, W. (1986). Dysfunctional attitudes in endogenous and nonendogenous depressed inpatients. *Cognitive Therapy and Research, 10*, 339-346.

Zimmerman, M., Coryell, W., Corenthal, C., & Wilson, S. (1986). Dysfunctional attitudes and attribution style in healthy controls and patients with schizophrenia, psychotic depression, and nonpsychotic depression. *Journal of Abnormal Psychology, 95*, 403-405.

CHAPTER 10

CLINICAL DECISION MAKING

Steven Schwartz

Psychologists are continually making decisions that affect the lives and well-being of others. Although many of these decisions are routine, others are characterized by uncertainty; information is never perfectly reliable, the outcomes of treatment strategies are rarely perfectly predictable. Even reasonably straightforward cases require sophisticated clinical judgments. Understanding how clinicians make decisions (and the role that subjective values play in clinical judgment) has been the subject of intensive psychological research over the past 15 years. This chapter contains a review of the research on clinical judgment and decision making. Because not all topics can be covered in a single chapter, the focus is on the cognitive strategies and heuristics clinicians use to make everyday judgments. (For more general reviews, see Schwartz & Griffin's 1986 work as well as the appropriate chapters in Turk & Salovey, 1988).

The chapter is divided into four sections. The first consists of a hypothetical case history followed by a short quiz. The purpose of this quiz is to give the reader a first-hand idea of the phenomena studied by decision making researchers. Because all clinical relationships begin with an information-gathering stage, section two is concerned with acquiring and interpreting clinical data. Combining several, potentially conflicting, items of information can often prove difficult and errors can occur. The sources of these errors—judgment heuristics and biases—are discussed in section three. Attempts to help clinicians make better judgments, through the use of decision models and decision aids, are reviewed in section four.

This paper was completed while I was a Royal Society visiting scientist in the Biomedical Computing Unit, Imperial Cancer Research Fund Laboratories. I am indebted to the Australian Academy of Science, Royal Society of London, British Council, Australian Research Commission, International Computers Limited, and the University of Queensland International Collaborative Grants Programme for research support.

THE CASE OF A. C.

A. C., a medical student in his final year of training, lost interest in his studies and his clinical duties. Instead of attending lectures and ward rounds he stayed in his room working endlessly at arranging his stamp collection. His roommate convinced him to seek help at the university counseling center but A. C. missed many appointments and soon refused to attend at all. There seemed little alternative to hospitalization.

On the ward, A. C. seemed listless and preoccupied. From A. C.'s parents, the ward psychologist learned that their son was always an excellent student who was never active socially. He had few friends and never dated. Neither A. C.'s parents nor his roommate could think of any specific event that may have triggered his present behavior.

At first, A. C. refused to talk with the psychologist but she was persistent and after a while he opened up. He confessed to feelings of self-doubt and inadequacy. A. C. believed that his previous academic successes were not the result of his own ability but rather just good luck. He thought it highly unlikely that he would ever be able to function as a doctor. Except for brief talks with the psychologist, A. C. kept almost entirely to himself. Most of his time was spent either lying in bed or arranging his stamps.

A. C. received a battery of psychological tests including an adult intelligence scale, a memory scale, a personality inventory, a suicide prediction instrument and a self-esteem questionnaire. The psychologist noted that A. C. was slow and methodical and that he needed considerable reassurance about his performance. (He frequently interrupted the testing to ask whether his answers were "correct".) On several occasions, A. C. asked to return to earlier questions so that he could change his answers. The testing yielded 3 IQ scores, rankings on 12 personality dimensions, 5 memory measures, a suicide potential score and a self-esteem score. The test results indicated that A. C.'s overall IQ was well above average with a verbal IQ score in the top 1% of the population. The personality inventory showed distinct signs of depression and a tendency toward obsessiveness. He was also found to have low self-esteem and he was classified a suicide risk.

The clinical team, which consisted of the pychologist, psychiatrist, social worker and psychiatric nurse, agreed that A. C. was depressed. Despite the test results, they believed that suicide was unlikely; indeed they thought it was rare in such cases. After considering several alternatives, the team decided to treat A. C. with a combination of antidepressant medication and behavior therapy. The latter involved cognitive restructuring aimed at raising A. C.'s low self-esteem and a program of rewards for participation in interpersonal activites. His tendency toward obsessiveness was considered partly the result of his depression and was not treated directly.

After a few weeks on the ward, A. C.'s behavior began to improve rapidly and after six weeks, he was discharged from the hosptial. The clinical team believed that there was a high (greater than 90%) probability that A. C. would maintain his contact with the hospital but, although he kept up his antidepressant medication for the next six months, he did not attend scheduled follow-up visits with his psychologist.

Quiz

Please answer the following questions as best you can given the admittedly incomplete information provided in the case study. In the discussions to follow, the questions will be used to exemplify important issues in the psychology of decision making.

1. If, during his hospitalization, A. C. was asked to draw a picture of a person, which of the following would he be most likely to draw:
   a. A person looking at the sky.
   b. A person staring down at the floor.
   c. A person reading a book.
2. The suicide potential test administered to A. C. accurately identifies 90% of patients who later attempt suicide (true-positive rate = 90%). It also classifies as suicidal 10% of those who never attempt suicide (false positives). If 5% of hospitalized depressed patients attempt suicide, then was the clinical team justified in ignoring the test results?
3. The treatment team believed that suicide was *unlikely*. Indeed, they thought such an outcome to be *rare* in such cases. Assign a probability between 0% (no chance) and 100% (absolute certainty) that corresponds to the term *unlikely* as it is used in this case study. Now do the same for *rare*.
4. If A. C. decided to change careers, which of the following do you think he would pursue?
   a. scientific research
   b. clinical psychology
   c. business
5. A year after his discharge, A. C._____ (rank order the following events according to their respective likelihood):
   a. was rehospitalized.
   b. attempted suicide.
   c. joined a monastery.
   d. attempted suicide and was rehospitalized.
   e. attempted suicide and joined a monastery.
   f. was rehospitalized and joined a monastery.
6. If A. C.'s IQ was retested one year after discharge, would you expect his verbal IQ to:
   a. increase
   b. decrease
   c. remain unchanged.

7. The clinical team believed that there was a greater than 90% probability that A. C. would return for outpatient therapy, but he did not. If you were a member of the clinical team how would you have estimated the chances of A. C.'s returning? (Use a probability from 0 to 1.00.)

As noted, the preceding questions were specially designed to illustrate some of the important difficulties inherent in clinical judgment and decision making. To appreciate the significance of these questions, you need to know more about decision making research. The present chapter was designed with that goal in mind. During the course of the various discussions, the importance of the preceding questions will become clear as will the "correct" answers.

DATA ACQUISITION AND INTERPRETATION

If we are ever to develop a general theory of clinical decision making, we must first have some idea of the questions such a theory should be able to answer. For example, a theory of clinical decision making should be able to describe the process by which clinical data are acquired and analyzed. At present, there is a great deal about data acquisition and interpretation that we do not know. For example, how did A. C.'s psychologist decide which tests to administer? Did she begin with a likely hypothesis about A. C. and then choose the psychological tests best able to confirm her hypothesis or did she administer them as part of a routine test "battery"? Is one approach better than the other? It is also important to know whether the psychological tests were administered because their results had potential treatment implications. If the results had no influence on how A. C. was treated, then why were the tests used? Were test reliability and validity considered? Should they have been?

Although it may not be possible to give complete answers to all these questions, decision researchers, as will be shown, have made a good start. In this section, several factors that influence clinical data gathering and evaluation are described and discussed.

Sources of Uncertainty: Client Reports

Clinical data are often imprecise and uncertain. This is especially true of client reports. Although they often constitute the main source of clinical data, client reports are notoriously unreliable. This does not mean that clients consciously set out to deceive the clinician (although some do). Unreliability may arise in more subtle ways. For instance, clients do not always interpret a clinician's questions correctly. Medical researchers have found that patients vary greatly in their definitions of pain (Schwartz & Griffin, 1986). When the doctor palpitates part of a patient's body and asks if it feels painful, it is the patient's definition of pain that determines whether the answer is yes or no. Two patients with precisely the same condition may answer differently if they have different subjective ideas about pain. Similarly, psychologists who enquire about anxiety may expect considerable variability in the replies they receive.

Some clients provide misleading information because they are genuinely unaware of their own behavior; others exaggerate their problems. There is also client ignorance to consider. A striking example was provided by Lilienfeld and Graham (1958) who reported that 35% of their sample of 192 men answered the question, "Are you circumcised?" incorrectly.

Client perceptions, therefore, are an important source of uncertainty (and inaccuracy) in clinical data. How clients interpret psychologists' questions, their background, education, and attitudes toward psychological problems can all affect the quality of clinical data. But not all the uncertainty in the clinic derives from client reports. Psychological tests can also produce ambiguous data.

Psychological Test Validity

Each year, many thousands of psychological tests are performed at a cost of millions of dollars. Tests should be performed because they help the psychologist to formulate a diagnosis or to produce a treatment plan. However, as in A. C.'s case, some tests appear to be administered simply because they are available—to have them "on the record." Although there are no specific data on how psychological tests are used in clinical practice, a study of the laboratory tests ordered by 111 California doctors (Wertman, Sostrin, Pavlova, & Lundberg, 1980) found that 32% of the tests produced absolutely no change in diagnosis, prognosis, therapy, or understanding of the patient's condition. There is little reason to believe that psychological tests are any different.

Even when the data provided by tests are potentially relevant, test use may not be justified because many psychological tests have low predictive validity (see Winters, Weintraub, & Neale, 1981, for example). Nevertheless, they continue to be used. At least part of the explanation for their continued popularity is a phenomenon called *illusory correlation*.

Chapman and Chapman (1969) investigated illusory correlations by asking people to evaluate the relationship between responses to a psychological test and specific personality characteristics. Imagine yourself as a subject in this experiment. You are told that, when shown the Rorschach inkblots, a young man saw: feminine clothing, food, rectum and buttocks, maps, a figure, part man—part woman, sexual organs, monsters, a figure, part animal—part human. You are asked to judge the relationship of each of these responses to homosexual tendencies. If you think a response is highly related to homosexuality then you are asked to give it a rating of 6; if a response is not related to homosexuality, give it a rating of 1. All others should be given ratings between these two extremes. Now, compare your ratings with those obtained by Chapman and Chapman (Table 10-1). Responses are divided into three categories. The first contains responses rated as highly associated with homosexuality but have no direct research evidence to support them. The second category contains unpopular, but valid, signs that have been found to be associated with homosexuality and the third category contains filler items that are totally unrelated to homosexuality. As shown in the table, the highest ratings went to the popular, but invalid, responses. Chapman and Chapman concluded that untested stereotypes influence our ratings. We base our "strength of association" estimates on relationships we believe *ought* to exist rather than on true empirical covariation.

Table 10-1. Mean Association Strength Between Rorschach Responses and Homosexuality (from Chapman & Chapman, 1969)

RESPONSE	RATED STRENGTH
POPULAR INVALID SIGNS	
Rectum and buttocks	4.38
Figure, part man-part woman	3.53
Feminine clothing	3.12
Sexual organs	4.47
UNPOPULAR VALID SIGNS	
Figure, part animal-part human	1.93
Monsters	1.68
FILLER ITEMS	
Food	1.09
Maps	1.09

At this point, you may want to reconsider your answer to question 1 in the quiz presented at the beginning of this chapter. If you are like most respondents, you chose alternative *b* ("a person staring down at the floor"). Clinical psychologists frequently make the same choice. Unfortunately, the correlation is illusory, depressed patients do not produce such pictures any more frequently than other patients; the three alternatives presented in question 1 are all equally likely.

Because of illusory correlations, symptoms and diagnoses (as well as treatment and outcomes) may appear to covary even when they are unrelated (Arkes, 1981). Indeed, illusory correlations appear to be responsible for the persistence of many unwarranted beliefs (tuberculosis is caused by the night air, "insanity" is related to the lunar cycle). Put another way, illusory correlations introduce "noise" into the diagnostic system thereby reducing the quality and certainty of test data.

Behavioral Assessment

Although clinical decision making research has been concerned with the evaluation of treatment outcomes (as will be shown later in this chapter), it is fair to say that the primary focus has been on the related issues of assessment and diagnosis. Because behavior therapists have been traditionally less concerned with these issues than other clinicians, many may believe that the problems discussed here are not relevant to their practice. Nothing could be further from the truth.

Of course, there are differences between behavior therapists and other clinicians. For example, behavior therapists make much less use of psychological tests. Their stated preference is for a functional analysis of the variables controlling behavior. In recent years, the emphasis on observing and measuring behavior has given way to checklists and self-reports which are, superficially at least, similar to traditional forms of assessment (Barrios, 1988). However, even traditional behavior assessment is subject to uncertainty. Because they choose specific target behaviors to observe, behavior therapists, like other clinicians, are prone to a "confirmatory" bias. They concentrate on behavioral evidence that is likely to support their clinical hypothesis and they ignore disconfirming evidence. Such selective attention to supportive evidence provides a fertile environment for the development of illusory correlations. These may be responsible for the persistence of some forms of behavioral treatment even when they have been shown to be ineffective (Foa & Emmelkamp, 1983). The remainder of this chapter will show that clinical judgment is inherently difficult—both behavior therapists and nonbehavioral clinicians suffer under similar handicaps.

Prevalence and Uncertainty

Another source of uncertainty in clinical data is indirect—the prevalence of a particular behavior in the population. The importance of prevalence to the interpretation of clinical data is illustrated by quiz question 2. The test administered to A. C. classified him as a suicide risk. According to the information given in question 2, we expect 5% of hospitalized, depressed patients to attempt suicide. This is the prevalence of suicide for this population. If we administer the test to 1,000 hospitalized depressed patients, we will obtain the results contained in Table 10-2. Specifically, out of 1,000 patients, 50 will attempt suicide. The test successfully identifies 90% of these or 45 true-positive cases (.90 × 50). Thus, five of those who attempt suicide will be "missed." The remaining 950 people will not attempt suicide but because the test has a 10% false positive rate, 95 people (950 × .1) will be falsely classified as suicidal. The percentage of true positives out of the total number of positives (the test's predictive value) is 32% (45/140). This means that *even after a positive test result*, the odds are still more than 2 to 1 against A. C. attempting suicide. So, the correct answer to question 2 is that the clinical team was wise to ignore the test results.

Now consider what happens if instead of hospitalized depressed patients, the test is administered to a population even more likely to attempt suicide—patients who have made previous attempts. The prevalence of suicide attempts in this population is, say,

Table 10-2. Outcome of the Administration of a Hypothetical Suicide Potential Test to 1,000 Depressed Patients (Prevalence = 5%)

	PATIENTS' ACTUAL BEHAVIOR		
TEST RESULTS	SUICIDE ATTEMPT	NO ATTEMPT	TOTAL
Predict Attempt	45	95	140
Predict No Attempt	5	855	860
Total	50	950	1000

Table 10-3. Outcome of the Administration of a Hypothetical Suicide Potential Test to 1,000 Previous Attempters (Prevalence = 15%)

	PATIENTS' ACTUAL BEHAVIOR		
TEST RESULTS	SUICIDE ATTEMPT	NO ATTEMPT	TOTAL
Predict Attempt	135	85	220
Predict No Attempt	15	765	780
Total	150	850	1000

15%. This means we would expect 150 suicide attempts out of a population of 1,000 previous attempters. The results expected from using the same test used on A. C. on this new population are contained in Table 10-3. It shows that the test correctly identifies 135 and misses 15 suicidal patients. Of the remaining 850, 85 are false-positives and the others are correctly classified as nonsuicidal. The percentage of true-positives out of all positives is 61%, a great improvement over that obtained in the population with lower prevalence. In this high risk population, 3 out of 5 patients with a positive result may be expected to attempt suicide. Clearly, prevalence is an important factor influencing the value of test results. However, as will be shown later in this chapter, clinicians often ignore prevalence when making judgments about behavior.

Interpreting Numbers and Words

Although many tests yield numerical data, it is customary for clinicians to communicate using verbal labels rather than numbers. Terms such as "unlikely" and "rare" which appeared in A. C.'s case history are common in clinical reports. Unfortunately, investigations of how people view the relationship between numbers and labels have found large inter-individual variability. For example, Bryant and Norman (1980) asked a sample of hospital-based clinicians to indicate on a scale of 0 to 100% the meaning of 30 commonly used probability labels. They found little agreement. For example, "sometimes" meant a 5% chance to one clinician and a 75% chance to another! The range of estimates exceed 50% for more than half the terms surveyed. Similar results have been reported by others (Budescu, Weinberg, & Wallsten, 1988; Haynes, Sackett, & Tugwell, 1983; Robertson, 1983). Given this variability, there are clearly no universally agreed on "correct" answers to quiz question 3. Indeed, this is the whole point of including the question.

Nakao and Axelrod (1983), and most other writers on the subject, recommend that clinicians replace frequency adjectives with actual numbers (50%, 30%, and so on). They believe this will eliminate the ambiguity produced by verbal probability labels. However, indications are that their faith may be misplaced. Berwick, Fineberg, and Weinstein (1981) found that medical clinicians had difficulty interpreting numerical estimates of probability as well (see also, Pollatsek, Well, Konold, Hardiman, & Cobb, 1987).

Information Overload

Thus far, it has been shown how clients' beliefs, unreliable data gathering, invalid inferences and inconsistent use of terms combine to make clinical data decidedly fuzzy. One factor that has not yet been emphasized is the sheer amount of information available to the clinician. It is generally agreed among clinicians that more information leads to better judgments than less information. This is one reason why new psychological tests are constantly being developed. However, clinicians have difficulty interpreting and integrating information from many different sources. Some psychologists have suggested that, like computers, there are inherent limitations to the amount of information that human beings are capable of handling (Simon, 1957). When a complex decision task makes cognitive demands that are beyond our information-processing capacity, we create simplified "problem representations" (subjective models of the real world) that permit us to handle the task with our available cognitive resources (see Newell & Simon, 1972).

Our limited cognitive capacity has particular relevance for clinical decision making because clinicians have always been taught to gather as much information as possible providing, of course, that gathering this information produces no harm. The problem with this approach (in addition to the expense) is aptly illustrated by the case of A. C. The large volume of test findings makes them difficult to use. Perhaps this is why medical clinicians have been found to ignore laboratory tests even though they ordered them (Dixon & Lazlo, 1974). (A. C.'s psychologist seemed to behave in a similar fashion, interpreting only a small number of her test results.)

Clinicians faced with a bewildering array of data often have no systematic way of using them. Fortunately, several studies have shown that a carefully selected subset of information is often as useful as the voluminous data collected by an exhaustive approach (Keighly, Hoare, & Horrocks, 1976). Indeed, at least one study has shown that providing clinicians with too much information can lead to lower diagnostic accuracy than providing them with what appears at first to be too little data (Sisson, Schoomaker, & Ross, 1976).

In addition to simplified problem representations, cognitive load can be reduced by using stereotyped decision making strategies. These simplifying procedures, or rules of thumb, are known in the literature as *judgment heuristics*. Judgment heuristics normally lead to good decisions, but under certain circumstances they can lead the decision maker astray. When this happens we say that judgment has been *biased*. Over the past 20 years, psychologists have described several general judgment heuristics (see the chapters in Kahneman, Slovic, & Tversky, 1982, for detailed reviews). Some of these heuristics are discussed in the next section.

JUDGMENT HEURISTICS AND BIASES

Availability

Clinicians are often called on to estimate probabilities from their own experience. For example, the clinical team predicted that A. C. was unlikely to attempt suicide. This estimate was based on their experience with similar people. Indeed, unless epidemiological data were available, there is nothing else on which to base such estimates. There is nothing inherently wrong with clinicians making subjective probability estimates. But, it is possible that clinicians with different backgrounds (hospital versus clinic-based psychologists, for example) may make different probability estimates. Studies of the effect of experience on probability judgments suggests that people use an "availability" heuristic in which easy-to-imagine events are thought more likely to occur than those that are difficult to imagine or recall. For example, people asked to estimate the probability that a marriage will end in divorce do so by trying to recall the cases of divorce with which they have first-hand experience (as well as those they have read about). People who are acquainted with many cases of divorce estimate a higher probability that a marriage will end in divorce than those who have rarely encountered divorce (Kozielecki, 1981).

Ordinarily, events that are easy to recall (more available) are also more likely to have occurred, so the availability heuristic leads to accurate probability estimates. However, this is not always the case. In some circumstances, availability is not directly related to probability. For example, Tversky and Kahneman (1973) asked people whether the letter "k" appeared more often as the first or third letter of a word. Although twice as many words have "k" as the third letter than the first, most people judged "k" to be more frequent as a first letter. It is evidently easier to think of words beginning with "k" than words with "k" as the third letter. The subjects in this experiment ignored the true probabilities because the availability heuristic suggested a different answer.

Another factor that can exert a strong effect on availability is the amount of attention events receive. For example, Slovic, Fischhoff, and Lichtenstein (1979) asked subjects to estimate the risk of dying from different causes. They found that people overestimated the risk of death from "sensational" causes such as homicide and storms while underestimating the probability of death from more insidious causes such as asthma and diabetes. Slovic et al. concluded that subjects were using the availability heuristic. Sensational events are easier to recall (and they receive more media coverage) than the more common causes of death.

Research reported by Christensen-Szalanski, Beck, Christensen-Szalanski, and Koepsell (1983) showed that medical clinicians also rely on the availability heuristic to estimate probabilities. They asked doctors to estimate the mortality of diseases. They found that doctors overestimated the lethality of diseases that received substantial journal coverage. They concluded that journal coverage makes a disease more "available" which, in turn, increases its subjective frequency.

Data-gathering sequences can also influence subjective probability estimates. For example, Friedlander and Stockman (1983) sequentially presented psychiatrists, psychologists, and social workers with case material for two patients. One was suffering from anorexia nervosa and one from suicidal depression. The materials were arranged so that definitive diagnostic information appeared either early or late in the sequence. The researchers found that early information served as an anchor for later diagnosis. That is, those clinicians who received misleading information early in the sequence took longer to reach the correct diagnosis than those who received appropriate information at the outset. Presumably, the early misleading information caused incorrect diagnostic hypotheses to become more "available" than the correct ones.

The availability heuristic may also be responsible for illusory correlations such as the one illustrated in quiz question 1. Because the association between depression and "staring down at the floor" is more available, we believe it to be more common than the other choices—we perceive correlations where none really exist.

These examples demonstrate how a cognitive strategy can lead to biased judgments. Availability—the ease with which instances can be recalled—is generally a valid way to estimate probability. In certain circumstances, however, the strategy breaks down and leads to biased judgments. The same is true of the next heuristic to be described, representativeness.

Representativeness

Representative thinking relies on stereotypes. That is, the probability of an event or outcome is estimated by the degree to which it fits an existing cognitive stereotype (or schema). Consider, for example, a casino roulette wheel. You observe and record the outcome of 12 spins of the wheel. Assuming the wheel is honest, which of the following sequences are you more likely to observe (R = red, B = black)?

1. RBRBBRRBRBRB
2. BBBBBRRRRRRR

Although, mathematically, the two sequences are equally likely (as are all other possible sequences), most readers will choose sequence "A" because it more closely resembles a stereotyped "random" sequence.

Although representativeness is sometimes a useful guide to probability, like the availability heuristic, it can lead to cognitive biases and errors. Tversky and Kahneman (1974) identified six cognitive errors associated with the representativeness heuristic: insensitivity to prior probabilities, insensitivity to sample size, misconceptions about randomness, insensitivity to predictability, the illusion of validity, and misconceptions about statistical regression. As will be shown, each can produce clinically significant errors.

Insensitivity to Prior Probabilities

Kahneman and Tversky (1973) provided subjects with anonymous personality descriptions of people who were supposed to be either lawyers or engineers. Subjects were asked to rate the probability that a sketch described a member of one profession or the other. Half the subjects were told that the population from which subjects were drawn consisted of 30 engineers and 70 lawyers; the other half were told that there were 70 engineers and 30 lawyers. This population base-rate (prevalence) information had little effect on either group's responses; it was largely ignored. Instead, subjects assigned probabilities by judging how similar each sketch was to a stereotyped engineer ("he likes building things") or a lawyer ("he is a good debater"). That is, they relied on the representativeness heuristic. It should be obvious that this strategy only works if the personality sketch is a perfect predictor of occupation. If some engineers have "lawyers' " personalities or vice versa—that is, if false-positives are possible—then population base-rates need to be taken into account (see Tables 10-1 and 10-2). A failure to attend to false-positive results and population base-rates can lead to what Beyth-Marom and Fischhoff (1983) call *pseudodiagnosticity*, a misplaced belief in the diagnostic value of imperfect, case-specific, information.

Pseudodiagnostic thinking is common in clinical evaluations (Kern & Doherty, 1982). Sometimes, good outcomes result. For example, A. C.'s clinical team accurately assessed his suicide potential based on how closely he resembled previous suicidal patients. But, representativeness can also lead one astray. Quiz question 4 is a good example. Based on his training in medicine, it may seem likely to many readers that A. C. would become a scientist (option *a*). Alternatively, his depressive illness may have led him to a career in psychology (option *b*). Both these choices involve representative thinking and both ignore the fact that there are more people in business (option *c*) than scientists or clinical psychologists. In the absence of any definitive information, the best guess is the one with the highest base-rate probability or option *c*.

Representative thinking can also produce unrealistically high probability estimates for combinations of events and inappropriately low estimates for atypical single events. This phenomenon was demonstrated by Tversky and Kahneman (1983). They presented subjects with the following information about a hypothetical woman:

> Linda is 31 years old, single, outspoken, and very bright. She majored in philosophy. As a student, she was deeply concerned about issues of discrimination and social justice, and also participated in antinuclear demonstrations.

Tversky and Kahneman (1983) asked their subjects to estimate the likelihood of various other facts about Linda including: "Linda is a bank teller" and "Linda is a bank teller and active in the feminist movement." Because the second possibility includes and extends the first, it cannot be more probable. Put another way, the probability that Linda is a bank teller cannot be lower than the probability that she is *both* a bank teller and active in the feminist movement. Yet, most subjects believed it *more* likely that Linda is both a bank teller and in the feminist movement than simply a bank teller. Although feminism was not mentioned in the description, it would seem that the stereotype it elicited was consistent with being a feminist and somehow not compatible with being simply a bank teller. The representativeness heuristic led to illogical probability estimates. Those readers who ranked any of the multi-outcome options *d*, *e* or *f* as more likely than options containing only one of their possible outcomes behaved in a similar illogical manner.

Insensitivity to Sample Size and Misconceptions About Randomness

Kahneman and Tversky (1972) presented subjects with the following problem:

> A certain town is served by two hospitals. In the larger hospital about 45 babies are born each day, and in the smaller hospital about 15 babies are born each day. As you know, about 50 per cent of all babies are boys. The exact percentage of boys, however, varies from day to day. Sometimes it may be higher than 50 per cent, sometimes lower. For a period of one year, each hospital recorded the days on which more than 60 per cent of babies born were boys. Which hospital do you think recorded more such days? (p. 443)

The most common response to this problem is that the two hospitals are equally likely to record days when the percentage of births exceeded 60% while the correct answer is the smaller hospital. Subjects did not perceive the size of the hospital as important even though the larger hospital, which records many more births, *represents* a larger sample of the population (50% boys and 50% girls). Subjects appeared to believe that any sample, no matter how small, is equally "representative" of the population.

A misplaced faith in the representativeness of small samples is responsible for misconceptions about randomness. This is illustrated by the "roulette wheel" example given earlier. In the long run, the wheel should produce an equal number of black and red responses. But, using the representativeness heuristic, we believe that *every* sample, no matter how small, should show a roughly alternating sequence of black and red. The gambler who has just seen red come up five spins in a row, and who invokes the (mythical) "law of averages" to predict that the next spin will be black, is relying on the representativeness heuristic. So, too, are Lotto players who avoid regular sequences such as 1,2,3,4,5,6 because they believe them to be less likely than more "random" sequences such as 2,9,22,31,4,14 (Kozielecki, 1981). So, if you want to maximize your Lotto payout, choose the regular sequences that others avoid. If your numbers come up, you will not have to share your winnings.

Misconceptions about randomness may lead to unwarranted causal attributions. For example, a clinician may be tempted to conclude that any change in the frequency of a behavior from baseline is the result of treatment when the change may simply be a random fluctuation. Reliance on the representativeness heuristic can also result in unrealistic predictions. This was shown by Detmer, Fryback, and Gassner (1977; cited by Hogarth, 1980), who told surgeons that the yearly mean postoperative complication rate is normally 20% and that the rate for the first six months of the current year is 14%. The surgeons were then asked to predict the rate for the rest of the year. Roughly half the clinicians predicted a rate of around 25%. That is, they believed that this year's sample should equal the annual mean of 20% so they predicted a higher than normal rate for the second half of the year to compensate for a lower than normal rate in the first six months.

Insensitivity to sample size and misconceptions about randomness can lead to improper inferences. But, an even more important bias that can be introduced by representative thinking is a belief in invalid predictors. The source of this bias is discussed next.

Insensitivity to Predictability and the Illusion of Validity

Clinicians who work with tests are often interested in predicting behavior. For example, A. C.'s psychologist administered a test designed to predict the likelihood that A. C would attempt suicide. As indicated in quiz question 2, the suicide potential test correctly identifies 90% of those who attempt suicide. A. C. scored in the "positive" range. Does this mean that he has a 90% chance of attempting suicide? We have already seen from the earlier discussion of question 2, that the answer is no. The actual probability that A. C. will attempt suicide, given a positive result on the suicide potential test, is only around 32%. Unfortunately, few clinicians would reach this conclusion without statistical training. The majority would estimate A. C.'s suicide potential to be 90% thereby confusing a test's retrospective accuracy with its predictive accuracy.

A test's retrospective accuracy is determined by administering it to an already identified population. Thus, in a population of suicidal patients, the test administered to A. C. would be expected to identify correctly 90%. In probability terms, the retrospective accuracy of the test is equal to the conditional probability (p) of a positive test (test$^+$) given that the person is suicidal (suicidal) or p (test$^+$/suicidal) = .90.

A test's predictive accuracy is the reverse probability, p (suicidal/test$^+$) = .32. There is no doubt that clinicians would prefer to know a test's predictive accuracy; unfortunately, the information typically available is a test's retrospective accuracy. Many clinicians appear to be unaware of the difference and use the two interchangeably. Eddy (1982), for example, found that doctors equate the probability that a woman with breast cancer will have a positive mammogram with the probability that a woman with a positive mammogram will have cancer. In reality, these probabilities are completely different. Saying they are the same is equivalent to claiming that the probability of a woman being pregnant given that she has had intercourse is the same as the probability that she has had intercourse given that she is pregnant. The latter probability is, of course 1.00 (ignoring artificial insemination) while the former probability is (fortunately, for many) much lower.

Clinical psychologists make similar errors. For example, Dawes (1986) quotes Branden (1984, p. 12) who writes: "I cannot think of a single psychological problem—from anxiety and depression, to fear of intimacy or of success, to alcohol or drug abuse, to spouse battery or child molestation—that is not traceable to the problem of poor self-esteem." In our terminology, Branden has found a high probability that people with psychological problems have low self-esteem. However, by claiming that psychological problems are traceable to low self-esteem, he is arguing that the reverse probability (the probability that people with low self-esteem are most likely to have psychological problems) is also high. Branden really has no information about this second probability because his clients come to him because of their problems not because of their low self-esteem. Many low self-esteem people may never develop psychological problems.

Failing to distinguish between predictive and retrospective accuracy can lead to serious clinical errors. For example, in a notorious British child abuse case, a physical sign found in some sexually abused children (a change in the muscles of the rectum) was interpreted to mean that children who show this sign had a high probability of having been sexually abused. In reality, the latter probability was unknown; only abused children, not normal children, had been studied. Yet, many children were removed from their homes because retrospective and predictive probabilities had been equated.

Psychological signs can also be misunderstood. To use one of many examples cited by Dawes (1986), child abusers have often been abused themselves as children. That is, the probability that an adult will abuse a child given that he or she was abused as a child is high. This fact was transformed by a self-help group as follows: "*about half the people who were physically abused as children end up mistreating their own children*" (italics in the original, cited by Dawes, 1986, p. 430). This statement is completely unjustified. Because data are only available on suspected abusers, we have no idea how many abused children grow up to be loving, nonabusing parents. Using a history of abuse as a child to predict future child abuse can lead to errors as serious as those produced by relying on an unvalidated sign.

The confusion of predictive and retrospective accuracy results from reliance on the representativeness heuristic. Because low self-esteem and psychological problems "go together" in the clinic, the relationship is seen as predictive. The rest of the population, who are not clients, are not even considered. So long as a test yields results that appear representative, the actual predictive accuracy of the test is overlooked. Such tests develop the "illusion of validity" and continue to be used even when they have low predictive value. This is a serious consequence of relying on representativeness to estimate probability.

Misconceptions About Statistical Regression

Tall fathers have sons that are, on average, not quite so tall. Short fathers tend, on average, to have somewhat taller sons. The reason is not mysterious, it is statistical. Parent-child heights are not perfectly correlated, so we cannot predict one exactly from the other. Because there are more people around average height than at the extremes, we find that heights "regress" toward the statistical mean.

Psychological test scores are also not perfectly reliable. Random fluctuations can produce deviations from the "true" score. Because random fluctuations are, by definition, unlikely to be repeated, a second testing will also show regression toward the mean. Quiz question 6 was designed to test knowledge about statistical regression. A. C.'s verbal IQ score was in the top 1%; on statistical grounds alone, his score would be expected to decrease on a second testing.

A failure to appreciate the importance of regression can lead to serious misjudgments. For example, Tversky and Kahneman (1974) described how flight instructors would praise trainee pilots after very good flights only to find that their next flights were not quite so good. Scolding them after bad flights, however, led to better performance the next time around. The flight instructors concluded that punishment works better than praise for teaching trainees to fly. The failure to appreciate regression is the result of the representativeness heuristic. The flight instructors believed that every flight was equally representative of their student's flying ability.

Clearly, ignoring regression can lead to unwarranted conclusions. For example, fluctuations in the frequency of an unwanted behavior are common. If a treatment is instituted for a behavioral excess, which consequently decreases, it is entirely possible that regression, and not the treatment, is responsible. On this point, Dawes (1986) notes that electroshock is only administered to severely depressed people who have not responded to other treatments. Because depression changes over time, an illusory, regression-based improvement may be responsible for the changes that are observed. The only way to be certain that the treatment was responsible is to use adequate controls.

Overconfidence

As noted, human information-processing capacity is limited and easily overloaded. When this happens, judgment heuristics are used and errors can easily occur. Yet, the more information they have available, the more confident decision makers become in the accuracy of their judgments. The relationship between the amount of information available and confidence is the subject of a frequently cited study by Oskamp (1965). He presented clinical psychologists with increasing amounts of case material. At various stages, Oskamp tested the psychologists' understanding of the case. He found that subjects became more convinced that they understood the case as the amount of information available to them increased even though the tests showed them to be no better at predicting outcomes than they were with fewer items of information.

One particularly interesting form of overconfidence has become known as "hindsight bias" (see Fischhoff, 1982). This bias occurs when our present knowledge is allowed to influence our estimates of the likelihood of previous events. Hindsight bias leads us to overestimate our own abilities by convincing us that we "knew it all along". Fischhoff (1975) illustrated hindsight bias using clinical case histories. One group of subjects, the "foresight" group, judged the likelihood of four possible outcomes based on the case material. The "hindsight" group also read the same material but were told which of the four outcomes actually occurred. The latter group's task was to give the probability they *would* have assigned to outcomes if they had not known it had occurred. Fischhoff found that the hindsight group assigned higher probabilities to the actual outcomes than the foresight group. He concluded that outcomes seem more likely in hindsight than in foresight (see also, Arkes, Wortmann, Saville, & Harkness, 1981). Quiz question 7 illustrates a similar point. With the benefit of hindsight, almost all readers will rate the probability that A. C. would return for outpatient psychotherapy as less than 90%. Clinicians asked to give second opinions or to take over cases previously managed by someone else are especially likely to succumb to hindsight bias. The result is overconfidence in one's ability to make accurate predictions.

Hindsight bias has proved difficult to eliminate (Fischhoff, 1977). An approach with some promise, however, was reported by Arkes, Guilmette, Faust and Hart (1988). They asked neuropsychologists given case histories and diagnostic outcomes not only to indicate their retrospective belief in the ultimately correct outcome but also to give reasons why the other diagnoses might have been correct. This procedure was found to markedly reduce hindsight bias. In a sense, Arkes, et al. forced their clinicians to consider "negative" information and thereby improved their performance.

Clinical Implications of Research on Judgment Heuristics

The picture of human judgment presented thus far is dismaying. Judges have been described as unaware of invalid tests and illusory correlations, ignorant about such things as base rates, conditional probabilities and statistical regression and overconfident in their own abilities. Is this an overstatement? Some writers believe it is (Edwards, 1983; Jungerman, 1983; and Wallsten, 1983). From their viewpoint, decision biases are difficult to demonstrate except in contrived laboratory experiments. Whereas it may be possible to design more clinically realistic experiments (see Rock, Bransford, Maisto, & Morey, 1987, for some suggestions), many researchers would still argue that such biases are relatively unimportant in clinical situations. Reinforcing this view, Christensen-Szalanski (1985) showed that judgment heuristics have only a small effect on actual clinical outcomes and that correcting them may not be worth the considerable trouble involved.

The critics of the judgment heuristic literature have an important point. As noted earlier, judgment heuristics are adopted in the first place because they usually work; they help decision makers reach useful conclusions. There are occasions when using heuristics leads to biased judgments but these are more common in the laboratory than they are in the clinic. Nevertheless, the examples given in the preceding discussion amply demonstrate that real-world clinical decisions (in child abuse cases and the case of A. C., for example) are also affected by judgment heuristics. All the factors determining when bias will occur are not known, but is seems certain that information overload plays an important role. Too much information can lead to simplified information processing, the adoption of judgment heuristics and, sometimes, to biased judgments. Attempts to teach people how to avoid cognitive biases have not been notably successful (see Schwartz & Griffin, 1986, for a review). For this reason, attempts have been made to provide clinicians with external decision aids. Some of these are described in the next section.

DECISION MODELS AND DECISION AIDS

Like it or not, we live in an age of specialization. In almost every line of work, practitioners can be said to know more and more about less and less. Although we often have no choice but to rely on expert judgments, our faith is shaken by technological disasters such as thalidomide-induced birth defects and the Chernobyl nuclear power plant leak. Such events always produce calls for better experts. Over the past 20 years, attempts have been made to develop decision aids to improve experts' judgments. This work has been carried out by psychologists, computer scientists working in artificial intelligence and decision analysts. Although there has been little interaction among these research communities, their aims are similar. All three wish to model and improve expert judgment in uncertain situations and all believe that they can develop computerized decision aids that will allow expertise to be generalized to a variety of novel problems. These similarities in research goals do not extend to research methods or theories.

Hammond (1987) lists 15 differences between the artificial intelligence and the psychological approaches alone. Although all Hammond's points are important, the crucial differences between the various approaches revolve around the related issues of knowledge encoding and knowledge manipulation. Artificial intelligence researchers are concerned with capturing an expert's knowledge of a particular domain (usually as a complex set of rules). They also wish to know how this knowledge is manipulated, analyzed, synthesised, or otherwise used to produce judgments and decisions. Psychologists, on the other hand, have opted for statistical representations of judgment strategies. These are usually, but not always, expressed as multiple regression equations. The decision analysts have mainly been concerned with applying a particular theory of decision making, subjective expected utility (SEU), to clinical situations. They have had little to say about where the data required by the theory come from.

All three research traditions agree that clinicians must integrate information from diverse sources and then use these data to make diagnostic and treatment decisions. How clinicians accomplish these tasks— and how they should do them—have been important areas of psychological research for many years. This research traces its beginnings to 1954, the year in which Paul Meehl began what has come to be known as the "clinical versus statistical prediction" debate.

Clinical Versus Statistical Prediction

Meehl (1954) distinguished between "clinical" and "statistical" reasoning. Although neither approach was precisely defined, Meehl thought of clinical reasoning as largely intuitive and certainly nonquantitative whereas the statistical approach was exactly that—reasoning based on some sort of actuarial formula. Einhorn (1988) provides the following example of the difference between clinical and statistical prediction:

Clinician: *The couple fights over money, control of the children, and has problems of intimacy. The husband is domineering and refuses to listen to his wife's opinion. She, on the other hand, resents giving up her career to stay home and take care of the children. The hostility in the relationship needs to be aired since both partners have difficulty expressing anger. Indeed, the husband is an only child with a very domineering mother, making it difficult for him to . . . Therefore, a divorce is likely . .*
Statistician: *Let P = probability of a divorce, F = number of fights per week, and I = number of times the couple has sexual intercourse per week (with each other). Then assume the model, P = f(F − I) and thus, the larger the positive difference between F and I, the greater the probability of a divorce. (p. 63)*

The statistical model (derived from Howard & Dawes, 1976) is abstract and general, clinical reasoning is detailed and case specific. However, it is important to note that statistical and clinical reasoning do not differ in the data they use, but in the way data are combined and evaluated. Clinical reasoning involves making largely intuitive judgements based on a patient's history, present behavior and test results. The statistical approach requires that judgements be reached through the application of formal quantitative techniques and statistical formulae. Consider, for example, the prediction of A. C.'s suicide potential. The clinicians noted whether A. C. had made any threats or preparations, the severity of his depression, his score on the suicide prediction instrument and other potentially relevant behaviors and then concluded that he presented a low suicide risk. These clinicians were using "clinical" reasoning. The alternative, statistical, procedure requires setting up a decision rule that is independent of A. C.'s case. Signs that have been previously correlated with suicide are identified and weighted according to how well they predict performance. A. C. is then evaluated on each of these signs and if he scores above a certain cut-off, then he is classified as a suicide risk.

Meehl (1954) claimed that judgments ("Will this patient attempt suicide?") made by following statistical rules are at least as accurate, and sometimes more accurate, than clinical judgments. This claim was hotly contested and the debate raged on in the psychology literature for many years (see Kleinmuntz, 1984, for a review). Interestingly, writers on both sides of the debate agreed that clinical judgments are full of uncertainty. Both also admit that the relationship between signs and diagnoses and between treatment and outcome are never perfect. Where they differ is on what, if anything, needs to be done. Those in the clinical camp believe that intuitive judgments applied on a case-by-case basis will lead to effective decisions. Those favoring a statistical approach favor more general a priori decision rules. In most cases, these rules are derived from what has become known as a "linear model."

Linear Models

Linear judgment models consist of a set of predictor variables on the one hand and some criterion (the outcome to be predicted) on the other. Usually, the predictor variables are weighted so as to maximize the correlation between their weighted sum and criterion but linear models can be used for other purposes (such as to differentiate groups of patients.) As their name suggests, linear models are concerned only with linear relationships, not curvilinear ones. When linear models are being used to predict judgments, the statistical technique of multiple regression analysis represents a straightforward way to determine the weights to be assigned to the various predictors.

An example of how the linear multiple regression approach may be used to generate a model of clinical judgment comes from a study by Fisch, Hammond, Joyce, and O'Reilly (1981). They asked clinicians to judge the severity of depression in 80 patients for whom they had been given symptom profiles. A linear multiple regression analysis was used to calculate the relationship between the various symptoms and the criterion (severity of depression) for each clinician. The weights assigned to each symptom by each clinician constituted a linear model of the emphasis that each clinician placed on each predictor (symptom). Using these weights, it is possible to predict the severity rating that a clinician will assign to a new case of depression (not part of the original 80).

An important limitation to the multiple regression approach is the assumption that all relevant predictors (symptoms, signs, behaviors, test results) are known. The squared multiple correlation, which reflects the amount of explained variance in a clinician's predictions, can serve as a guide to whether the clinician's judgments are reliable. If the squared multiple correlation is high, we can feel secure that we have captured the clinician's judgment model. If it is low, the clinician is either inconsistent in his or her weighting of predictors or one or more important predictor variables have been omitted.

The bulk of the relevant research (Dawes & Corrigan, 1974) shows that Meehl was indeed correct—statistical linear models are better than unaided clinical judgments in predicting clinical outcomes. This does not mean that linear models mimic how decision makers think. The parameters of the regression equation are not meant to represent the expert's knowledge in any serious way. Instead, they are chosen because, when aggregated according to a predetermined—normally additive—combination rule, these parameters produce "accurate" judgments and predictions. It is also possible to reach the same conclusion as the model without weighting and summing a set of cues. This is why linear judgment models are generally described as "paramorphic" representations of human judgment (Hoffman, 1960). They are abstract idealizations of cognition rather than concrete theories of how human beings process information.

Although linear models are not theories of cognition, they are excellent decision making devices. Indeed linear models can often out-perform the human decision makers upon which they were based. That is, a linear model using the predictor variables specified by the decision maker—and the decision maker's own weights—will often do a better job of predicting a criterion (for new cases, for example) than the decision maker on whom it is based (see Dawes & Corrigan, 1974, for examples). This phenomenon is known as *bootstrapping*. The statistical model is superior because it is more reliably applied. Boredom, fatigue, distraction, and illness can affect human judgments, but the model is immune to such things. Because the model captures experts' principles but eliminates their unreliability, it is often superior. Linear models are such good predictors that even those models with unweighted predictors (that assign each predictor a weight of one) can still outperform human judges (Dawes, 1979). As long as the relationship between predictors and the criterion is linear, all we need to know to make good predictions is "what variables to look at and how to add" (Dawes & Corrigan, 1974, p. 105).

Linear models may be used to design decision aids. In medicine, these usually take the form of a precisely formulated set of predictor-criterion relationships. Lindberg and Feyno (1987), for example, developed a set of five signs which, when weighted and summed, can tell a casualty room doctor whether a patient with acute abdominal pain is likely to have appendicitis (for many other examples see Schwartz & Griffin, 1986). Such decision aids are easy to computerize and many form the basis of the computerized psychological test interpretation programs that are becoming so popular among clinical psychologists (Lanyon, 1987). The main advantages of statistical models is their ease of use and their explicit nature. However, decision aids based on linear models do have limitations. An important one is that they are costly to develop and maintain. This can be best illustrated by an example.

Suppose we wished to construct a linear regression model to predict a depressed patient's response to therapy. There are a multitude of possibly relevant predictors on which to base this prediction. Age, race, sex, previous episodes, severity of depression, activity level, tobacco and alcohol consumption, work and family stress, and many other variables are all potential candidates. Choosing a subset requires that we determine which predictors are at least conditionally independent and how well various combinations of predictors account for therapeutic response. To pick the best predictors, we will have to study a representative sample of depressed patients who vary on the possible predictors and see how they are affected by therapy. Because no single predictor exerts an overwhelming influence on therapeutic response, the sample will have to be large to generate stable data. Large, reliable, data bases are not available for many clinical problems. Thus, the designers of statistical systems must gather the data themselves. As you may imagine, collecting relevant information from genuine patients can be enormously costly and time-consuming. Even the simple statistical models underlying many of the currently popular psychological test interpretation programs have been accumulated across many years (and may still be unreliable according to Lanyon, 1987).

Not only are statistical systems costly to construct, they are also expensive to modify. Because they are based mainly on empirical relationships between a set of signs on the one hand and some criterion on the other, modifying statistical systems usually means repeating the normative studies on which they are based. For example, the Minnesota Multiphasic Personality Inventory (MMPI) was originally created by examining how patients with different psychiatric diagnoses responded to sets of true-false type questions. It was found that patients with different diagnoses produced different patterns of answers. These data were used to produce a set of statistical relationships which have been computerized. Considerably more is known about psychiatric syndromes today than when the MMPI was first developed. Yet, there is no valid way—short of renorming the entire test—to incorporate this new knowledge into the statistical test-interpretation systems.

Linear models fare best when they are used to make predictions (or diagnoses) for specific problems. Because they can only provide information about the likelihood of prespecified hypotheses given a specific set of predictors, linear models cannot help the clinician identify previously unrecognized causal variables nor are they capable of suggesting new hypotheses or of explaining their own decisions. They are also difficult to apply to problems that originate in complex social contexts and do not have neat algorithmic solutions (such as the decision to remove a potentially battered child from his or her home). Such problems have prompted the development of expert systems which are discussed.

Expert Systems

Expert systems are computer programs that solve problems and give advice by making inferences from the available data. Unlike the equally "intelligent" computer systems that control manufacturing or laboratory equipment, expert systems operate interactively. For expert systems to behave like experts, they need to have two kinds of knowledge: public and private (Hayes-Roth, Waterman, & Lenat, 1983). Public knowledge includes the type of information found in textbooks: definitions, facts, and theories. Private knowledge consists of the rules-of-thumb that enable experts to make educated guesses when necessary, to recognize promising approaches to problems, and to deal effectively with uncertain data. Like a human expert, an expert system must know whether its knowledge base contains information relevant to a particular task (as well as the reliability and completeness of the stored information). It must be able to decide whether a decision should be made immediately or postponed and it must be able to "reflect" on its own decision process. These capabilities permit expert systems to be used as general clinical aids. In theory, at least, expert systems can assist the clinician to structure a problem, suggest potential hypotheses, point out logical weaknesses and evaluate decisions. None of these functions can be performed by statistical systems. (See Fox, O'Neil, Glowinski, & Clark, 1988, for more details.)

Expert systems are currently popular items. No doubt there is a large element of exaggeration in all the publicity. Nevertheless, a computer that "thinks" like an expert has significant appeal. Unlike statistical systems, expert systems are easily modified as new public knowledge becomes available. Private knowledge can also be updated. Rules can be added to the knowledge base and confidence ratings can be adjusted. (For a review of clinical expert systems see Kleinmuntz & Elstein, 1987.)

Because they can explain the basis for their recommendations—they can trace through their reasoning process—expert systems can also serve in a teaching role. The quote below shows what happens if a clinician asks a neuropsychological expert system the question "why?" ("why are you asking me for this information?"). The system explains the reasoning behind its question by tracing backward through its rules. Many computer scientists and most psychologists believe that an ability to provide convincing explanations will ultimately determine how acceptable computer consultants are to clinicians.

> *Computer:* Is patient's illness progressive?
> *Clinician: Why?* (Why do you want to know this?)
> *Computer:* This will help to determine whether the patient's illness is psychogenic.
> *Clinician:* Explain
> *Computer:* If: (1) The illness is not progressive and (2) Remissions occurred and (3) Onset was gradual
> THEN: It is probable that the illness is psychogenic.

One important goal of many clinical expert systems is to suggest hypotheses that might otherwise go unconsidered. No one is sure how clinicians generate hypotheses from clinical data but there is no doubt that hypotheses are formulated (Elstein, Schulman, & Sprafka, 1978). One way that expert systems generate hypotheses is by a type of backward inference in which current observations are connected to underlying "causes". As more information is gathered (say, from psychological tests) hypotheses may be altered. They can be made more general or more focused. Linear statistical models lack this capability; they require preformulated hypotheses and specific types of data. Of course, there is no reason expert systems cannot include linear models in their knowledge bases where required. A method of combining expert systems with linear models has been suggested by Hammond (1987; see also Spiegelhalter & Knill-Jones, 1984).

On the negative side, compared with human experts, expert systems often display an amazing lack of "common sense". This is known as the "plateau and cliff" effect. Systems perform well in a circumscribed problem area, but once they are asked to perform outside their limited domain, there is not a graceful decline but rather a sudden and dramatic drop in performance. For example, a system may be good at neuropsychological diagnosis but be unable to recognize that a patient is schizophrenic. Expert systems also tend to be slower than human experts and to give considerably more complicated explanations of their thinking processes than humans do (Alvey, 1983).

Although both linear statistical models and expert systems can serve as decision aids, ultimately the clinician will have to make a decision—to administer one test rather than another, to institute a specific therapeutic intervention, or, sometimes, to do nothing at all. Providing a rational basis for making such choices is the goal of decision analysis.

Decision Analysis

Decision analysis (Kassirer, Moskowitz, Lau, & Pauker, 1987) is a set of procedures for making decisions under conditions of uncertainty. It proceeds by breaking down complex decisions into smaller, more tractable, problems and then combining the answers to these into an overall measure of outcome attractiveness. Axiomatic to decision analysis is that clinicians must consider both the probability and the *utility* (subjective value) of all possible outcomes. The probability of each outcome is multiplied by its utility and the choice that leads to the highest expected utility (probability × utility) is usually taken at best. When the probabilities involved are objective (based on epidemiological data, for example), this approach to decision making is known as *expected utility theory*. When the probabilities really reflect a clinician's subjective belief in the likelihood of an outcome, the approach is called *subjective expected utility theory* (SEU).

An example of the subjective expected utility approach appears in Figure 10-1 which contains a simplified *decision tree* representation of the process of deciding whether a potentially suicidal patient should be placed in a secure ward. Decision trees should be read from left to right; a square represents a specific choice while a circle indicates that two or more outcomes can take place. In Figure 10-1, each choice can result in two possible outcomes: the client attempts suicide or the client does not attempt suicide. The probability of the first outcome is P and the probability of the second outcome is $1-P$ (the probabilities of all outcomes associated with each branch must sum to one). Each outcome has been assigned a utility represented by the letters, A, B, C and D. Although no numbers have been assigned to these utilities, it is safe to assume that for most clinicians false-positives (incorrectly classifying someone suicidal) are less serious than false-negatives (misclassifying someone

| ACTION | OUTCOME | PROB. | UTILITY |

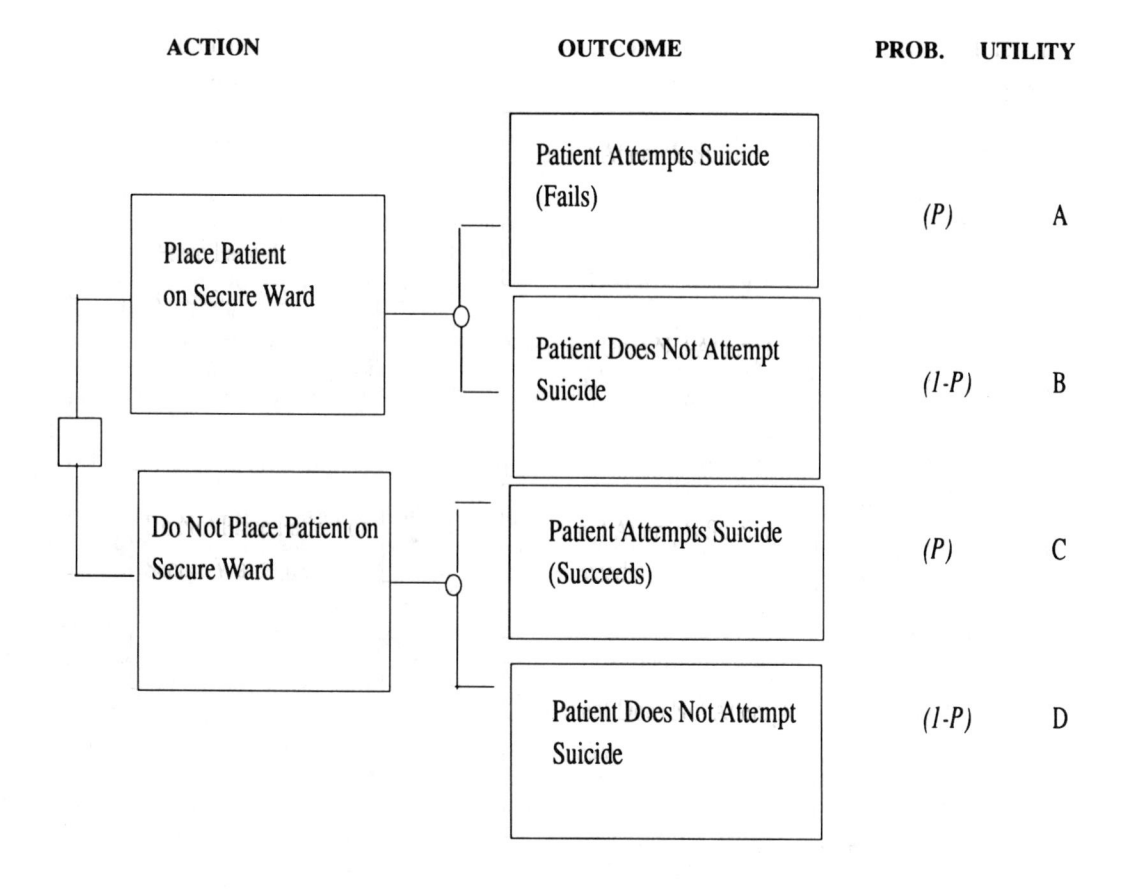

```
Place Patient          Patient Attempts Suicide
on Secure Ward         (Fails)                        (P)        A

                       Patient Does Not Attempt
                       Suicide                        (1-P)      B

Do Not Place Patient on   Patient Attempts Suicide
Secure Ward               (Succeeds)                  (P)        C

                          Patient Does Not Attempt
                          Suicide                     (1-P)      D
```

EXPECTED UTILITIES

(1) EU OF PLACING PATIENT ON SECURE WARD = (P)A + (1-P)B

(2) EU OF NOT PLACING PATIENT ON SECURE WARD = (P)C + (1-P)D

DECISION RULE

IF 1 > 2 THEN PLACE PATIENT ON SECURE WARD

IF 2 > 1 THEN DO NOT PLACE PATIENT ON SECURE WARD

Figure 10.1. A decision tree representation of a diagnostic problem. The initial square represents an action; the circles are possible outcomes of the action. The utilities for the final outcomes are expressed arbitrarily as the letters A, B, C, and D.

as nonsuicidal) which can possibly result in death. Of course, the utilities for both are lower than for assigning patients appropriately.

SEU theory requires decision makers to maximize their expected utility. This does not mean that clinicians should always choose the most likely alternative. Depending on the utilities assigned to each outcome, even an unlikely outcome can wind up maximizing the clinician's utilities. Examples of possible decision rules are given at the bottom of Figure 10-2. In addition to making decisions about diagnosis and treatment, SEU theory can help with the allocation of scarce resources ("Should this client be put on a waiting list or must she be seen immediately?") It may also be used to compare the risks and benefits of various actions (Weinstein & Fineberg, 1980).

SEU theory is known as a "normative" theory. Unlike linear statistical models or expert systems that are idealized *descriptions* of expert decision makers, normative theories offer *prescriptions* for how decisions "should" be made.

Although SEU-based decision analysis provides a powerful technology for clinical decision making (see, for example, the series on clinical decision making appearing in the journal *Medical Decision Making*) it does have drawbacks. First, the information—the probabilities and utilities—required may not be available. As already mentioned, reliable data bases are unavailable for many or perhaps most clinical problems. Second, despite their normative status, psychological research has established that people do not always behave as SEU theory claims they should (see Schwartz & Griffin, 1986, for a review). One conclusion is that people act irrationally; and no doubt sometimes they do. However, in many situations, SEU axioms are violated because they conflict with how people think about probabilities and utilities. For example, McNeil, Pauker, Sox, and Tversky (1982) asked people to choose between two treatments for lung cancer. Subjects were told that with one treatment "68 per cent of patients survive 5 years" whereas with the other "32 per cent die within 5 years". Both patients and doctors preferred the former treatment to the latter even though from an SEU viewpoint, the outcomes are exactly the same (see also, Tversky & Kahneman, 1981).

A second drawback to SEU theory is the measurement of utility. Although utility is an integral aspect of SEU theory, it is not easy to quantify. A particular problem is that preferences for various outcomes are often unstable. Christensen-Szalanski (1984), demonstrated how preferences for pain reduction in childbirth can change over time. He found that women questioned before childbirth preferred to avoid anaesthesia but the same women preferred to avoid pain (and receive anaesthesia) during childbirth. A month after delivery, their preference again turned against anaesthesia. If preferences (and utilities) change from time to time, then so may the outcome of a decision analysis.

Finally, there is a question of practicality. Even doctors trained in use of decision analysis find it difficult to use its techniques in their everyday work (Elstein, 1984). It would seem that decision analysis is too time-consuming for routine clinical application.

Reaction to Decision Aids

Because clinicians are prone to the judgment errors, they may improve their clinical decision making by using decision aids. Many different types of aids have been developed. Some are based on linear statistical models, others are based on the knowledge of experts and still others employ the techniques of decision analysis. Although all three types of aids have been shown to be valuable in different contexts, all clinicians, not just behavior therapists, have been slow to adopt them. Except for automated psychological test interpretations, clinicians have preferred to hang on to clinical reasoning. Among the reasons advanced for this is the feeling that the research on clinical judgment has not been entirely fair. Holt (1978), for example, argued that statistical decision rules are only applicable to some aspects of clinical practice (diagnosis, for example) and that these may not be the most important. Other objections are more practical. Clinicians are always pressed for time and most decision aids require that data be systematically collected and scored. Similarly, because they require that data be collected across many people, decision rules are difficult to formulate.

Although all these objections have some merit, by far the most important is the feeling that reliance on the "numbers" used by external aids diminishes the importance of the clinician and devalues the individual patient. The statistical approach, by definition, refers to groups of patients whereas clinicians are always interested in a specific case. Base rates, regression equations and decision analysis appear far removed from living, breathing people.

These reactions must be taken into account if the results of decision making research are ever to be incorporated into clinical practice. Ultimately decision aids will be acceptable if they are perceived as increasing the utility of current clinical practice. The dimensions on which the utility of clinical decision aids may be judged are summarized in the following list:

1. Improvements in efficiency
2. Reductions in cost
3. Patient attitudes
4. Clinicians' attitudes
5. Hardware reliability
6. Diagnostic accuracy

However, little research using these dimensions to evaluate the utility of decision aids in the clinic has been conducted. Clinical decision making researchers are beginning to perform studies on the practical value of decision aids. As such studies begin to appear, decision making research will begin to make its deserved impact on clinical pratice.

REFERENCES

Alvey, P. (1983, December). *The problems of designing a medical expert system*. Paper presented at the Expert Systems Conference, Cambridge, UK.

Arkes, H. R. (1981). Impediments to accurate clinical judgment and possible ways to minimize their impact. *Journal of Consulting and Clinical Psychology, 49*, 323–330.

Arkes, H. R., Guilmette, T. J., Faust, D., & Hart, K. (1988). Eliminating the hindsight bias. *Journal of Applied Psychology, 73*, 305–307.

Arkes, H. R., Wortmann, R. L., Saville, P. D., & Harkness, A. R. (1981). Hindsight bias among physicians weighing the likelihood of diagnoses. *Journal of Applied Psychology, 66*, 252–254.

Barrios, B. A. (1988). On the changing nature of behavioral assessment. In A. S. Bellack & M. Hersen (Eds.), *Behavioral assessment*. (3rd. ed., pp. 3–41.) Elmsford, NY: Pergamon Press.

Berwick, D. M., Fineberg, H. V., & Weinstein, M. C. (1981). When doctors meet numbers. *The American Journal of Medicine, 71*, 991–998.

Beyth-Marom, R., & Fischhoff, B. (1983). Diagnosticity and pseudodiagnosticity. *Journal of Personality and Social Psychology, 45*, 1185–1195.

Branden, N. (1984). In defense of self. *Association for Humanistic Psychology Perspectives*, August-September, 12–13.

Bryant, G. F., & Norman, G. R. (1980). Expressions of probability: Words and numbers. *New England Journal of Medicine, 302*, 411.

Budescu, D. V., Weinberg, S., & Wallsten, T. S. (1988). Decisions based on numerically and verbally expressed uncertainties. *Journal of Experimental Psychology: Human Perception and Performance, 14*, 281–294.

Chapman, L. J., & Chapman, J. P. (1969). Illusory correlation as an obstacle to the use of valid diagnostic signs. *Journal of Abnormal Psychology, 74*, 271–287.

Christensen-Szalanski, J. J. J. (1984). Discount functions and the measurement of patient values: Women's decisions during childbirth. *Medical Decision Making, 4*, 41–48.

Christensen-Szalanski, J. J. J. (1985, August). *Toward an understanding of human judgment: Medical pills for psychological ills*. Paper presented at the 10th International Research Conference on Subjective Probability, Utility and Decision Making, Helsinki, Finland.

Christensen-Szalanski, J. J. J., Beck, D. E., Christensen-Szalanski, C. M., & Koepsell, T. D. (1983). The effect of journal coverage on physician's perception of risk. *Journal of Applied Psychology, 68*, 278–284.

Dawes, R. M. (1979). The robust beauty of improper linear models in decision making. *American Psychologist, 34*, 571–582.

Dawes, R. M. (1986). Representative thinking in clinical judgment. *Clinical Psychology Review, 6*, 425–441.

Dawes, R. M., & Corrigan, B. (1974). Linear models in decision making. *Psychological Bulletin, 81*, 95–106.

Dixon, R., & Lazlo, J. (1974). Utilization of clinical chemistry services by medical house staff. *Archives of Internal Medicine, 134*, 1064–1067.

Eddy, D. M. (1982). Probabilistic reasoning in clinical medicine: Problems and opportunities. In D. Kahneman, P. Slovic, & A. Tversky (Eds.), *Judgment under uncertainty: Heuristics and biases.* (pp. 249–267.) Cambridge, UK: Cambridge University Press.

Edwards, W. (1983). Human cognitive abilities, representativeness, and ground rules for research. In P. Humphreys, O. Svenson, & A. Vari (Eds.), *Analysing and aiding decision processes.* (pp. 507–513). Amsterdam: North-Holland.

Einhorn, H. J. (1988). Diagnosis and causality in clinical and statistical prediction. In D. C. Turk & P. Salovey (Eds.), *Reasoning, inference and judgment in clinical psychology.* (pp. 51–70.) New York: Free Press.

Elstein, A. S. (1984). *Symposium on teaching applications* (audio tape). Presented at the Judgment and Decision Making Meeting, San Antonio, Texas.

Elstein, A. S., Schulman, L. F., & Sprafka, S. A. (1978). *Medical problem solving: An analysis of medical reasoning*. Cambridge, MA: Harvard University Press.

Fisch, H. U., Hammond, K. R., Joyce, C. R. B., & O'Reilly, M. (1981). An experimental study of the clinical judgment of general physicians in evaluating and prescribing for depression. *British Journal of Psychiatry, 138*, 100–109.

Fischhoff, B. (1975). Hindsight is not equal to foresight: The effect of outcome knowledge on judgment under uncertainty. *Journal of Experimental Psychology: Human Perception and Performance, 1*, 288–299.

Fischhoff, B. (1977). Perceived informativeness of facts. *Journal of Experimental Psychology: Human Perception and Performance, 3*, 349–358.

Fischhoff, B. (1982). For those condemned to study the past: Heuristics and biases in hindsight. In D. Kahneman, P. Slovic, & A. Tversky, (Eds.), (pp. 335–354.) *Judgment under uncertainty: Heuristics and biases*. Cambridge, UK: Cambridge University Press.

Foa, E. B., & Emmelkamp, P. M. G. (1983). *Failures in behavior therapy*. New York: John Wiley & Sons.

Fox, J., O'Neil, M., Glowinski, A. J., & Clark, D. (1988). *A logic of decision making*. Paper presented at the Illinois Interdisciplinary Workshop on Decision Making. University of Illinois.

Friedlander, M. L., & Stockman, S. J. (1983). Anchoring and publicity effects in clinical judgment. *Journal of Clinical Psychology, 39*, 637–643.

Hammond, K. R. (1987). Toward a unified approach to the study of expert judgment. In J. Mumpower, L. D. Phillips, O. Renn, & V. R. R. Uppuluri. (Eds.), *Expert judgments and expert systems*. (pp. 1–16.) Heidelberg: Springer-Verlag.

Hayes-Roth, F., Waterman, D. A., & Lenat, D. B. (1983). An overview of expert systems. In F. Hayes-Roth, D. A. Waterman, & D. B. Lenat (Eds.), *Building expert systems*. (pp. 3–29) Boston: Addison-Wesley.

Haynes, R. B., Sackett, D. L., & Tugwell, P. (1983). Problems in the handling of clinical and research evidence by medical practitioners. *Archives of Internal Medicine, 143*, 1971–1975.

Hoffman, P. J. (1960). The paramorphic representation of clinical judgment. *Psychological Bulletin, 47*, 116–131.

Hogarth, R. M. (1980). Judgment, drug monitoring and decision aids. In W. H. W. Inman (Ed.), *Monitoring for drug safety*. (pp. 439–475). Lancaster, UK: MTP Press.

Holt, R. R. (1978). *Methods in clinical psychology: Prediction and research* (Vol. 2). New York: Plenum Press.

Howard, J. W., & Dawes, R. M. (1976). Linear prediction of marital happiness. *Personality and Social Psychology Bulletin, 2*, 478–480.

Jungerman, H. (1983). Two camps of rationality. In R. W. Scholz (Ed.), *Decision making under uncertainty*. (pp. 63–86). Amsterdam: Elsevier.

Kahneman, D., & Tversky, A. (1972). Subjective probability: A judgment of representativeness. *Cognitive Psychology, 3*, 430–454.

Kahneman, D., & Tversky, A. (1973). On the psychology of prediction. *Psychological Review, 80*, 237–251.

Kahneman, D., Slovic, P., & Tversky, A. (Eds.). (1982). *Judgement under uncertainty: Heuristics and biases*. Cambridge, UK: Cambridge University Press.

Kassirer, J. P., Moskowitz, A. J., Lau, J., & Pauker, S. G. (1987). Decision analysis: A progress report. *Annals of Internal Medicine, 106*, 275–291.

Keighly, M., Hoare, A., & Horrocks, J. (1976). A symptomatic discriminant to identify recurrent ulcers in patients with dyspepsia after gastric surgery. *Lancet, 2*, 278–279.

Kern, L., & Doherty, M. E. (1982). 'Pseudodiagnosticity' in an idealized medical problem solving environment. *Journal of Medical Education, 57*, 100–104.

Kleinmuntz, B. (1984). The scientific study of clinical judgment in psychology and medicine. *Clinical Psychology Review, 4*, 111–126.

Kleinmuntz, B., & Elstein, A. S. (1987). Computer modeling of clinical judgment. *CRC Critical Reviews in Medical Informatics, 1*, 209–228.

Kozielecki, J. (1981). *Psychological decision theory*. Warsaw: PWN-Polish Scientific Publishers.

Lanyon, R. I. (1987). The validity of computer-based personality assessment products: recommendations for the future. *Computers in Human Behavior, 3*, 225–238.

Lilienfeld, A., & Graham, S. (1958). Validity of determining circumcision status by questionnaire as related to epidemiological studies of cancer of the cervix. *Journal of the National Cancer Institute, 21*, 713–770.

Lindberg, G., & Feyno, G. (1987). *Algorithmic diagnosis of acute appendicitis using Bayes' theorem and logistic regression*. Paper presented at the annual meeting of the Society for Medical Decision Making, Philadelphia.

McNeil, B. J., Pauker, S. G., Sox, H. E., & Tversky, A. (1982). On the elicitation of preferences for alternative therapies. *New England Journal of Medicine, 306*, 1259–1262.

Meehl, P. E. (1954). *Clinical versus statistical prediction: A theoretical analysis and review of the evidence*. Minneapolis: University of Minnesota Press.

Nakao, M. A., & Axelrod, S. (1983). Numbers are better than words: Verbal specifications of frequency have no place in medicine. *The American Journal of Medicine, 74*, 1061–1065.

Newell, A., & Simon H. A. (1972). *Human problem solving*. Englewood Cliffs, NJ: Prentice-Hall.

Oskamp, S. (1965). Overconfidence in case-study judgments. *Journal of Consulting Psychology, 29*, 261–265.

Pollatsek, A., Well, A. D., Konold, C., Hardiman, P., & Cobb, G. (1987). Understanding conditional probabilities. *Organizational Behavior and Human Decision Processes, 40*, 225–269.

Robertson, W. O. (1983). Quantifying the meaning of words. *Journal of the American Medical Association, 249*, 2631–2632.

Rock, D. L., Bransford, J. D., Maisto, S. A., & Morey, L. (1987). The study of clinical judgment: An ecological approach. *Clinical Psychology Review, 7*, 645–661.

Schwartz, S., & Griffin, T. (1986). *Medical thinking: The psychology of medical judgment and decision making*. New York: Springer-Verlag.

Simon, H. A. (1957). *Models of man: Social and rational*. New York: John Wiley & Sons.

Sisson, J. C., Schoomaker, E. B., & Ross, J. C. (1976). Clinical decision analysis: The hazard of using additional data. *Journal of the American Medical Association, 236*, 1259–1263.

Slovic, P., Fischhoff, B., & Lichtenstein, S. (1979). Rating the risks. *Environment, 21*, 14–20, 36–39.

Spiegelhalter, D., & Knill-Jones, R. (1984). Statistical and knowledge-based approaches to clinical support systems with an application in gastroenterology. *Journal of the Royal Statistical Society, 147*, 35–77.

Turk, D. C., & Salovey, P. (1988). *Reasoning, inference, and judgment in clinical psychology*. New York: Free Press.

Tversky, A., & Kahneman, D. (1973). Availability: A heuristic for judging frequency and probability. *Cognitive Psychology, 4*, 207–232.

Tversky, A., & Kahneman, D. (1974). Judgment under uncertainty: Heuristics and biases. *Science, 185*, 1124–1131.

Tversky, A., & Kahneman, D. (1981). The framing of decisions and the psychology of choice. *Science, 211*, 453–458.

Tversky, A., & Kahneman, D. (1983). Extensional versus intuitive reasoning: The conjunction fallacy in probability judgment. *Psychological Bulletin, 90*, 293–315.

Wallsten, T. S. (1983). The theoretical status of judgment heuristics. In R. W. Scholz (Ed.), *Decision making under uncertainty*, (pp. 21–37). Amsterdam: Elsevier.

Weinstein, M. C., & Fineberg, H. V. (1980). *Clinical decision analysis*. Philadelphia: Saunders.

Wertman, B. G., Sostrin, S. V., Pavlova, Z., & Lundberg, G. D. (1980). Why do physicians order laboratory tests? A study of laboratory test request and use patterns. *Journal of the American Medical Association, 243*, 2080–2082.

Winters, K. C., Weintraub, S., & Neale, J. M. (1981). Validity of MMPI codetypes in identifying DSM-III schizophrenics, unipolars and bipolars. *Journal of Consulting and Clinical Psychology, 49*, 486–487.

CHAPTER 11

COGNITIVE PSYCHOLOGY APPLIED TO THE TREATMENT OF ACQUIRED LANGUAGE DISORDERS

Max Coltheart

A person who has suffered an injury to the brain will often be left with some form of cognitive impairment, in the sense that one or more of the basic cognitive functions can no longer be accomplished with normal ease. What I mean by the term *basic cognitive functions* are activities such as recognizing objects, naming objects, understanding spoken or written language, producing spoken or written language, planning actions, storing new information in memory, or retrieving old information from memory. Cognitive psychology is the study of these activities. Cognitive neuropsychology is a branch of cognitive psychology.

The specific feature that defines *cognitive* neuropsychology (Ellis & Young, 1988; Shallice, 1988) is the study of the relationships between the pattern of impaired performance of the brain-damaged individual on cognitive tasks and what cognitive psychologists have learned about how the cognitive task in question is *normally* carried out. In contrast, neuropsychology itself is concerned with establishing relationships between patterns of performance and neurological data such as information about etiology or site of lesion.

Many cognitive neuropsychologists are interested in the treatment as well as the theoretical analysis of cognitive impairments after brain damage (Howard & Hatfield, 1987; Coltheart, 1990). According to the cognitive-neuropsychological approach to treatment, before attempting to treat any cognitive impairment—for instance, a difficulty in naming seen objects—one should first understand what has caused it. Of course, there is a sense in which one already knows what has caused it—the brain damage. But this is not what the cognitive neuropsychologist has in mind here. When you or I correctly name an object, we make use of a particular mental information-processing system—one that can accept as input a visually presented object and that yields as output the correct name of that object. If naming has been impaired by brain damage, then some component or components of this system no longer are functioning normally. Discovering which of the information-processing components of the naming system are impaired and which are still intact is what the cognitive neuropsychologist means by "understanding the cause of the patient's naming difficulty." Therefore, one needs to have in mind a model of how naming is normally achieved before one can begin to seek to understand impairments of naming consequent upon brain damage; and one needs this understanding before one can determine what kinds of treatment could be appropriate.

As far as the cognitive neuropsychologist is concerned, this point applies to all aspects of cognition, not just to naming. If one were considering how to treat an amnesic patient, for example, the cognitive neuropsychologist would at a minimum want to know whether the patient's failure to show any evidence of acquiring new memories was because new information was not being registered in memory, or because it was being registered in memory adequately but was not being retained, or because it was being registered and retained but could not be retrieved.

Issues of this kind must often be set aside in the initial stages of managing a person with a brain injury. If a patient is utterly disoriented in space and time, is violent or suicidal, or is suffering from major seizures, treatment would be focused on these general problems rather than any specific disorders of basic cognitive processes. However, many brain-damaged patients after emerging from an acute phase of this kind are left with persistent specific cognitive disorders. It is at this point that cognitive-neuropsychological rehabilitation becomes relevant.

For any form of rehabilitation, two distinct questions emerge: what to treat, and how to treat it. Behavior theory or behavior therapy has much to say about the second question—there is a great deal of literature on treatment techniques such as errorless learning, modeling, the use of various types of reinforcement schedules, and so on. Cognitive neuropsychology, on the other hand, has a lot to say about the first question, because it allows us to define with some precision exactly what aspects of cognitive functioning have been impaired by the brain damage. Unless this is done as a preliminary to embarking upon treatment, how can one avoid the risk of attempting treatment programs that are entirely misdirected?

Let us return to naming as an example: imagine a hypothetical group of patients, all of whom have great difficulty in naming objects that they see around them, to such a degree that everyday life is even affected. We would like to alleviate their situations by improving their ability to name, and so we seek to design an appropriate treatment program for them.

If we scrutinize what actually happens when the patients are tested for their ability to name objects, we might find something like the following: Presented with a cigarette and asked to name it, Patient A says "A piece of chalk"; Patient B says "A matchbox"; Patient C says "One of those things people smoke, it gives you lung cancer, I can't remember the name"; and Patient D says "A siket." (These are actual examples of naming errors produced by brain-damaged patients.) All four patients thus score zero on this item of the naming test. Indeed, they might all achieve the same total score on the test; but it is obvious that to regard them as having the same disorder, and so requiring the same treatment, must be wrong. There are four quite distinct disorders here.

Patient A can't name the objects he sees because he can't *recognize* them. He mistakes a cigarette for something that looks similar (a long narrow white cylinder). Patient B fails in naming because of a semantic impairment—he confuses semantically similar concepts, so that, though a cigarette is correctly recognized, at the stage of semantic processing the semantic distinction between cigarette and matchbox is not appreciated. Patient C recognizes the object, and processes it correctly at the semantic level, but cannot retrieve the spoken name of the object. Patient D gets as far as retrieving the spoken name, but can't produce it, because of an articulation problem—in this patient's attempts at speech, voiced consonants are devoiced, unstressed syllables are omitted, and consonant clusters can't be articulated. Here we have a visual agnosia, a case of semantic impairment, an anomia, and a dyspraxia. Is it conceivable that the same treatment of the naming difficulty would be appropriate in all four cases? Clearly not; and this shows how a cognitive-neuropsychological analysis is an essential preliminary to any consideration of treatment.

This analysis is cognitive-neuropsychological precisely in the sense that it is based upon a model of how object naming is *normally* performed. This model, sketched in Figure 11-1, proposes that naming involves a sequence of five different information-processing stages. Disruption of any one of these stages, or of any one of the pathways by which information is transmitted from one stage to another, will result in an impairment of the ability to name objects.

Here many cognitive neuropsychologists like to make the following point. Because there are five processing components and six pathways for information in this model of the naming function, there are $2^{11} - 1 = 16,383$ different distinct ways in which the naming system can be impaired, if brain damage can affect any component or any pathway. If so, what are the chances that any two patients with a naming difficulty will have the same pattern of impairment to

```
   seen object
       ↓
┌─────────────────┐
│ VISUAL-FEATURE  │
│    ANALYSIS     │
└─────────────────┘
       ↓
┌─────────────────┐
│  VISUAL OBJECT  │
│   RECOGNITION   │
└─────────────────┘
       ↓
┌─────────────────┐
│    SEMANTICS    │
└─────────────────┘
       ↓
┌─────────────────┐
│   SPOKEN WORD   │
│      FORMS      │
└─────────────────┘
       ↓
┌─────────────────┐
│   ARTICULATION  │
└─────────────────┘
       ↓
     speech
```

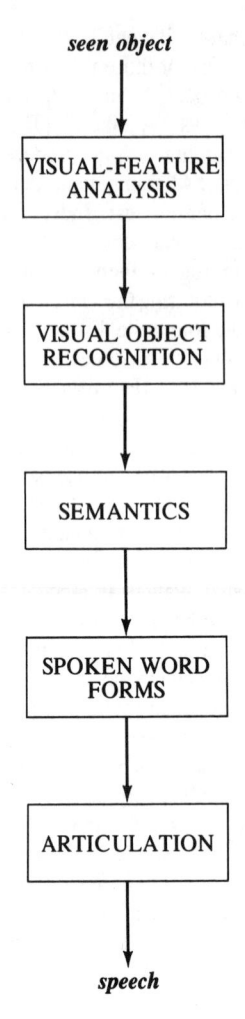

Figure 11.1. An information-processing model of object naming.

predilection for the single-case study approach to the investigation of treatment efficacy, and a concomitant interest in experimental designs and statistical methods tailored to the requirements of such an approach.

Cognitive-neuropsychological rehabilitation contrasts with behavior therapy in the basic target at which treatment is aimed. The traditional behavior therapist may think primarily about altering the behavior of the patient (though he or she may well be interested in any accompanying effects of treatment upon the patient's cognition). The cognitive behavior therapist will be more directly concerned with cognitive processing, but does not typically proceed with a particular model of the relevant kind of cognitive processing in mind. The cognitive neuropsychologist thinks primarily about altering the distorted "cognitive architecture" of the particular information-processing system that has been affected by brain damage (with the presumption that if this system can be restored to something like its premorbid configuration, behavior will change, in the sense that the patient's performance on the cognitive function in question will improve).

As we proceed through life, we acquire specific information-processing systems for carrying out specific cognitive functions, and it is clear that such systems are often tied to specific regions of the brain, because highly selective effects of brain damage upon cognition have been abundantly documented, particularly over the past decade. For example, not only can language difficulties after brain damage be restricted to impaired ability to produce names, but this naming difficulty can even be specific to the ability to produce *proper* nouns (Semenza & Zettin, 1988); impaired ability to understand words can be selective for particular semantic categories (Warrington & McCarthy, 1987); auditory recognition can be impaired for spoken words while still possible for environmental sounds (Goldstein, 1974); many other such selective cognitive deficits are discussed in the recent literature on cognitive neuropsychology (see Ellis & Young, 1988, for examples). If there is a considerable degree of localization of specific cognitive functions in specific brain regions, might this not mean that when permanent damage has been suffered in one region of the brain, the cognitive function in question could never be restored, because other, yet intact, parts of the brain are unsuitable as support for the particular types of information-processing needed to carry out that function?

This is an empirical question, and answers to it are provided by numerous recent reports of successful

the system? Infinitesimally small. If it is the case that what is an appropriate treatment for a patient with a naming difficulty depends upon what the specific underlying pattern of impairment actually is, then the chances that the same treatment is appropriate for any two patients with naming difficulties is infinitesimally small. This is why cognitive neuropsychologists consider that treatment—efficacy studies must be individual case studies. The point is a general one. Indeed, if it holds for a relatively simple and circumscribed function such as object naming, it will hold even more strongly for functions that require more complex processing systems, functions such as memory or language understanding. Thus cognitive neuropsychologists share with behavior therapists a strong

cognitive-neuropsychological rehabilitation. Among the cognitive functions that have responded to such rehabilitation are sentence comprehension (Byng, 1988), sentence production (Jones, 1986), reading (de Partz, 1985; Coltheart & Byng, in press), and writing (Hatfield, 1983; Behrmann, 1987). These results indicate that it is at least sometimes possible to use cognitive-neuropsychological rehabilitation to rebuild a damaged information-processing system, even when the region of the brain that formerly housed that system can no longer function.

Hence, what I will now describe in some depth are examples of this kind of rehabilitation. My aim is to indicate exactly how, in cognitive-neuropsychological rehabilitation, cognitive psychology is applied to the treatment of acquired disorders of language. I will consider only impairments of reading, because it is in this sphere that cognitive-neuropsychological rehabilitation is most advanced at present. However, the questions I will consider can be posed quite generally, in relation to the treatment of any kind of acquired cognitive impairment (which is not to say that the answers will always be the same).

I will discuss two studies. One (concerning patient E.E.) has already been published (see Byng & Coltheart, 1986; Coltheart & Byng, in press); the other (concerning patient Q.N.) is currently in progress.

IMPAIRED VISUAL WORD RECOGNITION

E.E., a mail-sorter in a postal depot, fell from a roof and suffered a severe closed head injury, which affected his language-processing in a variety of ways. In particular, his reading, writing, spelling, and ability to name objects were impaired. He had not been an avid reader before his accident, but even the limited amount of reading he was accustomed to doing was no longer possible. Reading was the focus of treatment.

Models of reading developed by cognitive psychologists seek to describe the various different information-processing components that make up the complex system we use when we read. Cognitive-neuropsychological rehabilitation of an acquired reading disorder must begin by applying such a model to the interpretation of the patient's reading difficulty. Which of the components of the reading system are still working normally? Which have been affected by the brain damage? A current version of such a model is given in full detail in Patterson and Shewell (1987) and Ellis and Young (1988). Not all these details were needed for interpreting the particular reading disorder exhibited by E.E.; it is sufficient to work with the simplified version of the model given in Figure 11-2.

For present purposes, there is one basic point about this description of the reading system that the reader needs to appreciate. The model incorporates two different procedures for reading aloud: the route from Visual Word Recognition to Spoken Word Production, and the Letter-Sound Rule system. The basic point is that neither of these two procedures is capable of reading aloud all types of printed input.

If the stimulus to be read aloud is a pronounceable nonword such as *vib*, the Letter-Sound Rule procedure can produce the correct response, but the alternative procedure can't. The reason is that the Visual Word Recognition component contains only representations of real words, those words known to the reader, and so, when the input string is not a real word, that component simply won't respond. Nor could the Spoken Word Production component *produce* the response "vib", because it can only produce *words*.

If the stimulus to be read aloud is one of the many words that violate the spelling-sound rules of English ("irregular" or "exception" words such as *yacht* or *pint* or *colonel*), the Letter-Sound Rule system will still produce a response, but it will be wrong: *yacht* will be pronounced as if it rhymed with *matched*, *pint* as if it rhymed with *sprint*, and the first *l* in *colonel* will be included in the response.

Normal readers can read nonwords aloud correctly, and they can read exception words aloud correctly. Hence both procedures are available to the normal reader. If reading aloud has been impaired by brain damage, then at least one of the processing components or pathways in Figure 11-2 is damaged. Cognitive psychology, having provided us with the model shown in this figure, also provides us with assessment methods allowing us to determine which parts of the system are still intact and which have been damaged. For example, if a patient can still read nonwords aloud correctly, then the Letter-Sound Rule system has been spared; if the patient can still read exception words aloud correctly then the Visual Word Recognition and Spoken Word Production components have been spared.

What about E.E.? Well, the errors quoted above, the misreadings of *yacht*, *pint* and *colonel*, are errors that E.E. actually made when reading aloud single words, under no time pressure. He also made many other such errors with exception words. In contrast, he was relatively good at reading aloud pronounceable nonwords (and also words that obey English letter-sound rules, such as *trout*, *rub* or *fresh*). Hence, we

```
                    print
                      │
                      ▼
            ┌──────────────────┐
            │     LETTER       │
            │  IDENTIFICATION  │
            └──────────────────┘
                  ╱        ╲
                 ▼          ▼
        ┌──────────────┐   ┌──────────────┐
        │ VISUAL WORD  │   │ LETTER-SOUND │
        │ RECOGNITION  │   │    RULES     │
        └──────────────┘   └──────────────┘
           ╱       ╲              │
          ▼         ▼              │
    ┌──────────┐    │              │
    │SEMANTICS │    │              │
    └──────────┘    │              │
          ╲         ▼              │
           ▼  ┌──────────────┐     │
              │ SPOKEN WORD  │     │
              │    FORMS     │     │
              └──────────────┘     │
                    │              │
                    ▼              ▼
                 speech         speech
```

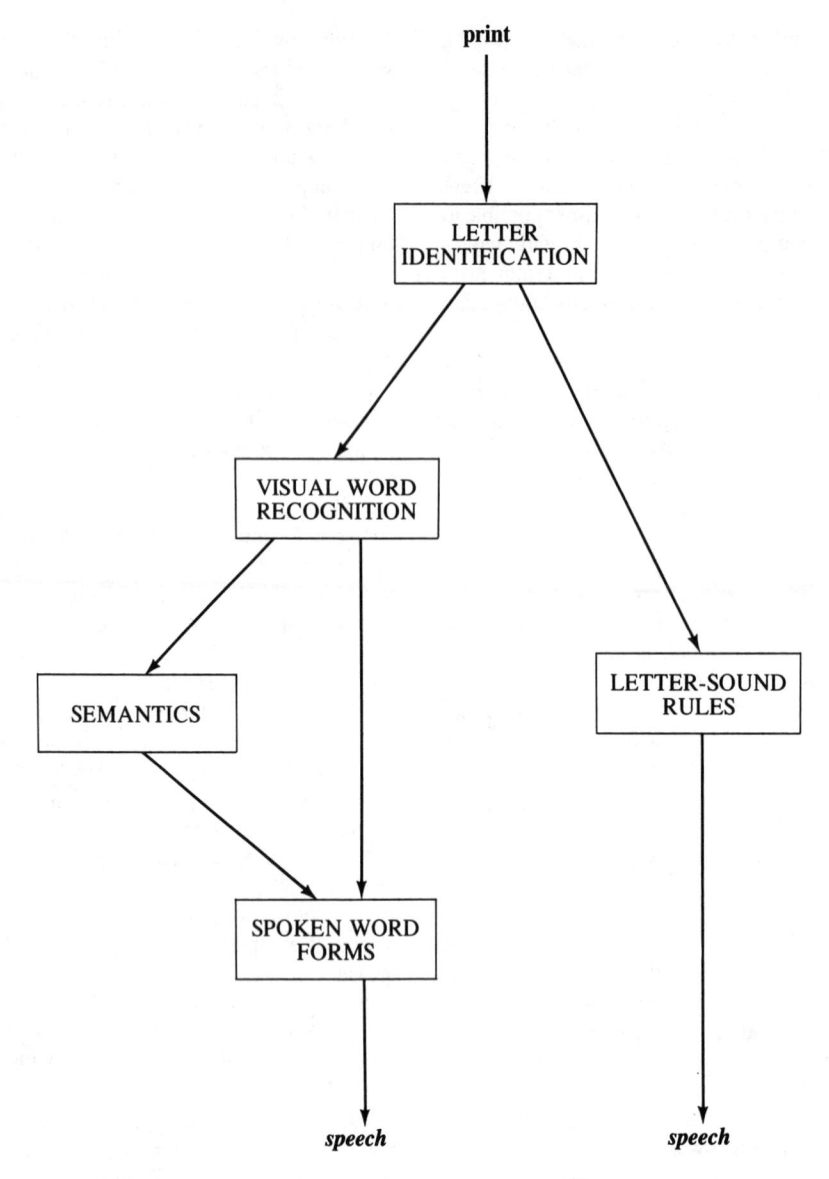

Figure 11.2. An information-processing model of reading.

can use Figure 11-2 to tell us that his reading problem was not so much to do with the ability to use letter-to-sound rules as to do with whole-word reading mechanisms. This immediately says something about rehabilitation: a phonics program, whereas it may be the right thing for some patients, is the wrong thing for E.E., because it is precisely this kind of processing that he can still accomplish—indeed, his reading errors result from using a phonic strategy to read aloud. Teaching him more about letter-sound rules could not possibly help his reading—it could only harm it, if there were any effect at all. E.E.'s case indicates that some kind of whole-word instruction is needed. That is what cognitive psychology tells us about treatment here.

This is not enough, however. If we accept that what is happening with E.E.'s reading is that he often is unable to use the route from Visual Word Recognition to Spoken Word Production when asked to read aloud, we still do not have a characterization of his reading problem that is sufficiently precise to serve as a guideline for the design of a rehabilitation program. Imagine two hypothetical patients, A and B. Patient A has impairment within the Visual Word Recognition component: if asked to read the word *yacht* aloud, A may not recognize it; if so he or she will have to use letter-sound rules to read it, and so will pronounce it as if it rhymed with *matched*. Patient B has an impairment within the Spoken Word Production component: if asked to read the word *yacht* aloud, Patient B will recognize it correctly, but may not be able to retrieve its pronunciation from the Spoken Word Production system; if so, he or she will have to use letter-sound rules to read the word aloud, and so will pronounce it as if it rhymed with *matched*. Here we have two patients with quite different impairments yet exactly the same symptom. Surely a difficulty in visual word recognition and a difficulty in retrieving spoken word forms would require different kinds of treatment? If so, we will have to decide just why E.E. reads *yacht* the way he does, before we can decide what treatment might be appropriate. How do we do this?

Further thought using the model of reading tells us how it can be done. Suppose I ask you to say what the printed word *beet* means. You respond that it means "a vegetable"; you don't say it means "to hit." But suppose you had a problem in the Visual Word Recognition component of your reading system, and you did not recognize *beet* as a familiar printed word. All you can do (because I am asking you to tell me what it means) is to use your intact Letter-Sound Rule system to work out how the word is pronounced and then decide what it means on the basis of its pronunciation. In this case, how can you tell whether it means "a vegetable" or "to hit?" You can't. Now consider the two hypothetical patients described in the previous paragraph. Patient A won't know whether to define the printed word *beet* as "a vegetable" or as "to hit," because the word won't be recognized by the Visual Word Recognition system, and so comprehension will have to be mediated by translating the word to its pronunciation using the letter-sound rule system. Patient B won't have this problem. He recognizes printed words correctly, so he will be able to get to their meanings in the system labeled semantics. His problem is later, at the Spoken Word Production level.

Thus before deciding how E.E. should be treated we need to know what he does when we ask him to tell us the meaning of printed homophones (words with different spellings, different meanings, and the same pronunciations—words like *beet*). When he was given this task, he frequently confused one homophone with its mate: for example, asked to say what the printed word *daze* meant, he said "six [sic] in a week", and he thought the printed word *I* referred to the thing we see with. The occurrence of this kind of error shows us that his reading problem is in fact a problem at the level of visual word recognition, and so treatment needs to be aimed at restoring his ability to recognize letter-strings as familiar words. A whole-word recognition treatment was thus initiated; details of the treatment method are given in Byng and Coltheart (1986) and Coltheart and Byng (in press). This treatment study was designed in such a way that, if at the end of treatment E.E.'s reading had improved, it would be possible to decide whether the improvement was due to the specific treatment used, rather than to spontaneous recovery, practice effects, or some general treatment effect. The treatment did improve E.E.'s ability to read, and the data from this treatment study were such that it was possible to claim that the effect was a specific treatment effect.

Specifically, the method used to improve E.E.'s impairment in visual word recognition was to pair a visual mnemonic with each of the words that was receiving treatment. For example, E.E. misread the irregular word *work*, reading it and comprehending it as *walk*, because the letter-sound rules of English prescribe that the letter sequence *or* has this pronunciation. E.E. was presented with an index card containing the word *work* accompanied by a drawing of a stamped envelope. He had worked as a mail-sorter, and this mnemonic was intended to indicate that the target word had something to do with postage, which led him away from the error *walk* and to the correct response *work*. Similarly, the target word *through* was presented with an arrow drawn through it, the target word *thus* (which he often misread as if it rhymed with *buzz*) inside a drawing of a bus, and the target word *often* was written on the card . . . often. These mnemonics enabled E.E. to work at home on his reading, trying to read a target word and then using the mnemonic to discover what the correct response actually was.

The treatment studies were set up as follows: a set of words that E.E. could not read correctly was chosen. This set was divided at random into two subsets: a Treated subset and an Untreated subset. Treated words were given visual mnemonics as described above, whereas Untreated words were displayed on their cards with no mnemonic. E.E. worked through all words at home, and was assessed weekly on all the words. In three separate treatment studies with three separate sets of words, his ability to read the Treated words improved significantly more than his ability to read the Untreated words. Thus one can claim that this mnemonic technique did have a specific effect upon E.E.'s impaired visual word recognition.

IMPAIRED MORPHOLOGICAL PROCESSING DURING READING

In contrast to E.E., Q.N. has been a highly literate person—an author, broadcaster, and university lecturer in English. He suffered a severe left-hemisphere stroke that produced a number of different cognitive impairments. His spelling and writing abilities were almost completely abolished, and his reading was seriously impaired. His ability to produce and to understand spoken language was affected considerably less than his ability to read and write. Not surprisingly, he is much more distressed than E.E. was by having a reading impairment. He reports that his reading of novels and poetry is now so slow and so painstaking—and so error-prone—that proper comprehension, let alone enjoyment, is impossible. This is obvious when he is asked to read prose aloud; his reading is extremely slow, arduous for him, and full of errors.

Close scrutiny of the errors he makes when he reads aloud shows that almost all of these involve the *ends* of words, reading *reading* as *read*, for example. He virtually never produces an error in which the beginning of the word is wrongly read. Being accurate at reading all parts of words except their ends is not of much value when reading prose in an inflected language like English in which the suffixes convey essential information for sentence comprehension.

What could go wrong with the reading system so as to produce errors of this sort? There are many possibilities, and each implies a different focus of treatment. Hence, as with E.E., we need to discover what aspect of the language system it is whose impairment is causing the reading difficulties before we can begin to think about designing an appropriate treatment.

A first possibility is that the problem is purely a perceptual one. Damage to certain parts of the left hemisphere can produce blindness in the right half of the visual field: someone who suffered from this impairment and was looking at the centre of a printed word would not be able to see the right half of the word. If this were the source of Q.N.'s reading difficulties, he would make errors with the right halves of any visual stimuli, including pictures or abstract patterns. This did not occur; the error pattern was specific to printed words.

What, then, causes him to read *reading* as *read*? Consideration of the kinds of reading errors made by various kinds of patients with various forms of acquired dyslexia suggests at least three possibilities:

1. **Semantic errors**: Patients with the form of acquired dyslexia known as "deep dyslexia" (Coltheart, Patterson, & Marshall, 1987) frequently produce semantic errors in reading isolated words under no time pressure, such as reading *hermit* as *recluse* or *canary* as *parrot*. The words *reading* and *read* are semantically related. So perhaps that is why Q.N. produces such errors.
2. **Visual errors**: Some patients with acquired dyslexia mainly produce reading errors that are visually related to the stimulus, such as reading *angle* as *angel* or *or* as *on*. The words *reading* and *read* are visually similar—is this why Q.N. produces such errors?
3. **Morphological errors**: It has been argued (e.g., Patterson, 1980) that there are some cases of acquired dyslexia in which the ability to read the prefixes and suffixes in morphologically complex words is what has been specifically impaired: errors such as reading *unreality* as *real* are interpreted as occurring because prefixes and suffixes are badly read whereas the root component of words is read well. Does Q.N. read *reading* as *read* because of a specific difficulty with reading suffixes?

These questions are of importance to theory (answers to them will tell us more about the nature of the normal reading system), and they are also important for treatment. Q.N.'s reading errors could be due to a semantic or a visual or a morphological problem affecting reading, and until we know which it is we won't know what kinds of treatment for his reading difficulties are appropriate.

Consider the words *reading* and *shilling*. Both end with the letter sequence–*ing*; but this is a suffix only in the word *reading*. If we could show that Q.N. omits the–*ing* in words like *reading* but not in words like *shilling*, this might be taken as evidence that his problem really is a morphological one: only if a letter sequence really is a suffix is it liable to error. This example should not convince us, however, because whereas *read* is a common word *shill* is not; and any inclination to omit the *ing* when attempting to read the word *shilling* might be defeated by the patient's realization that the potential response here is not a word. We need examples of words that end with letter sequences that could be, but are not suffixes. And, when the pseudosuffix is removed, what remains must still be a word—stimuli such as *quarter* or *wicked*—if we want to make adequate comparisons of Q.N.'s reading of such pseudosuffixed words with his reading of genuinely suffixed words such as *smarter* or *licked*. We also need to match the two types of words on frequency of occurrence in the English language (because this variable often affects the probability that a person with acquired dyslexia will read a word correctly). In addition, we need to match the two types of words on how concrete in meaning they are, because this variable, too, is often a potent determiner of reading success in acquired dyslexia.

Is this sufficient as a test for whether Q.N.'s difficulties with reading are truly morphological? No. Suppose he did tend to err with the *-ed* in genuinely suffixed words like *licked* but not with pseudosuffixed words like *wicked*, even when the two types of words are matched on frequency and concreteness. This might be because *lick* is more frequent, or more concrete, than *wick*, and so more available as a response. So, we need to match, not only the whole words, but also the relevant *components* of the words on frequency, and on concreteness. Only then will we have a set of materials that can tell us whether the reading problem is a genuinely morphological one.

We have Funnell (1987) to thank for performing the Herculean task of obtaining this material. She found 32 genuinely suffixed words (e.g., *builder*) and 32 pseudosuffixed words in which what remains after the suffix is removed is still a word (e.g., *quarter*), with the two sets of items matched as described in the previous paragraph. We gave these to Q.N. to read. He read correctly only 10 of the 32 genuinely suffixed words, but 29 of the 32 pseudosuffixed words. In other words, he is highly likely to misread *builder* as, say, *build*, but highly likely to read *quarter* correctly. So his reading problem is genuinely morphological.

But is it genuinely a *reading* problem? As discussed by Coltheart (1985), morphological problems in reading aloud, even when they are genuinely morphological, could be caused by any of the following three reasons:

1. **Input problem**: The Visual Word Recognition system is impaired in such a way that suffixes are poorly recognized when presented visually.
2. **Central problem**: The whole language system is impaired in such a way that *any* kind of processing of suffixes is impaired.
3. **Output problem**: It is the *production* of suffixes that is the difficulty, not their visual recognition or comprehension.

This is a reiteration of the point I made earlier: if we don't know which of these three very different disorders is present in Q.N., how can we decide what it is that we should be treating, when we are designing a rehabilitation program for Q.N.?

Another task described by Funnell (1987) provides the solution. It uses pairs of inflected words such as *dancer* and *dancing*, where one member of the pair refers to a category of person and the other does not. Suppose Q.N. were given such items in printed form, and asked which ones refer to persons. The correct answer can only be obtained if the suffixes are correctly recognized. If his problem were just in *producing* suffixes, he would be able to do this kind of reading task. However, he could not. He made numerous errors, such as classifying *secretarial* and *building* as persons, and *teacher* and *baker* as activities. So he doesn't have an output problem.

This doesn't tell us whether he has an input problem or a central problem. However, we can find this out simply by giving him the same test in spoken form. If he has a central problem, he will be no better at this than when the words are in printed form; if he has an input problem, he'll succeed with the spoken form of the test. The latter is what happened. When he hears *spoken* words like *baker* and *secretarial*, he performs almost without error on the person/nonperson classification.

Thus, we can finally characterize Q.N.'s reading problem with precision: his reading system is damaged in such a way that the recognition of suffixes in printed words is specifically impaired (so it is not surprising that his reading and comprehension of novels and poetry is slow and error-prone), even though *spoken* suffixes are processed normally, and even though the ends of words are read well when they are not suffixes. Knowing exactly what is wrong with his reading, we can design a treatment program that is directly aimed at correcting the problem.

Treatment programs in cognitive-neuropsychological rehabilitation, as I mentioned earlier, are almost invariably single-case in nature, and they are generally designed in such a way that their efficacy can be unambiguously evaluated. That is, if the patient improves, one can decide whether this was due to the specific treatment used, or to some other factor (a general treatment effect, practice, or spontaneous recovery). The program designed for Q.N. illustrates some of the ways in which this can be done.

It also illustrates another feature of cognitive neuropsychology that I have not referred to so far. At the beginning of this chapter, I mentioned that cognitive neuropsychologists seek to use data from studies of patients with cognitive impairments to test or develop or extend theories about normal cognitive processing. Exactly the same thing can be done with rehabilitation studies, because it is possible to design these studies in such a way that their results are capable not only of telling us whether the specific rehabilitation method used was responsible for an observed improvement in the patient's performance, but also of providing data relevant to theoretical ideas about normal cognitive processing. The program designed for Q.N. is intended to yield just such data.

Q.N.'s Treatment Program

We have determined that Q.N.'s acquired dyslexia is one in which the specific difficulty is in the visual recognition of suffixes in printed words. When he encounters a suffixed word while reading, he will very often read it as its unsuffixed form, or sometimes read it as a different suffixed form. Hence *likes* will often be read as *like*, sometimes as *liked*—and sometimes correctly. These facts hold true not only for reading aloud but also when Q.N. is reading silently for comprehension, as in the task of deciding whether a printed word refers to a person or not (*typist* versus *typing*). His difficulty is specific in the sense that it is confined to suffixes, but general in the sense that all kinds of suffixes are affected. We find that any kind of suffix (the various inflections of verbs, the plural for nouns, the comparative and superlative for adjectives, the *–ness* that makes an adjective a noun, the *–ly* that makes an adjective an adverb, the *–y* that makes a noun an adjective, and so on) are poorly recognized.

The treatment program for Q.N. does not involve all of these kinds of suffixes. Some are the focus of treatment, others will never appear in the treatment program. Table 11-1 illustrates this.

The material for the treatment study consists of 20 words in each of the 8 categories in Table 11-1, plus the 160 unsuffixed forms of each of these words. Q.N. was given all 320 words to read as a pretest. Given what we know about the nature of his reading difficulty, it was not surprising that his accuracy was very low. He correctly read fewer than half of the 320 words. For almost every error, the root of the word was read correctly, with the error affecting only the suffix. When the treatment program is completed, Q.N. will be given all 320 words to read as a posttest measurement.

Now, consider the plural *–s*. Twenty plural nouns have been selected. From these, 10 have been randomly chosen, and these are used in the treatment program along with their singular forms. The other 10 plural nouns and their singular forms are not used in the program itself, only in the pre- and posttests. Details of the methods that will be used to try to restore Q.N.'s ability to read the plural suffixes of the treated plural nouns need not concern us here. If these methods fail, that is that. If, however, they succeed—that is, if accuracy of reading of the 20 treated nouns is greater after the treatment than it is now—the design of this study allows us to ask (and answer) the following questions:

1. Is the treatment effect word-specific—that is, have we simply retaught Q.N. to read accurately the particular 20 nouns (10 plural and 10 singular) that were used in the treatment program? If this is so, the *other* 10 plural and 10 singular nouns that figure in the pre- and posttests, but not in the treatment study, will not have improved. His reading of these nouns will be no better at posttest than at pretest.
2. Is the treatment effect one in which the recognition of a particular *suffix*, namely the plural *–s*, has been retaught? If so, Q.N. should now be good at reading *all* plural nouns—not only the ones involved in the treatment, but also the ones that were

Table 11-1. Aspects of Q.N.'s Treatment Program

TREATED SUFFIXES	UNTREATED SUFFIXES
Plural-*s* (e.g., *frogs*)	Verb -*s* (e.g., *weeps*)
Comparative-*er* (e.g., *higher*)	Nominalizing -*er* (e.g., *dancer*)
Adjectival-*y* (e.g., *cloudy*)	Nominalizing -*ness* (e.g., *loudness*)
Adverbial-*ly* (e.g., *nicely*)	Superlative -*est* (e.g., *smallest*)

in the pre- and posttests, but not in the treatment itself.
3. Is the treatment effect one in which the recognition of the suffix *-s*, regardless of whether it is the plural or not, has been retaught? If so, Q.N. should now be good at reading not only all plural nouns, but also all inflected *verbs* where the inflection is the suffix *-s*, even though verbs were never used in the treatment program.
4. Has the treatment program made the whole suffix-recognition system work again? If so, Q.N. should now be good at reading every kind of suffixed word, even those that are very remote from the kinds of words used in the treatment program. For example, treatment involving plural nouns would generalize to the *-ness* that makes an adjective into a noun. This result would constitute very strong evidence that one component of the reading system is a subsystem specifically devoted to the job of recognizing suffixes in printed words. This is an example of the contributions rehabilitation studies can make to the development of theories about normal cognitive processing.

These examples relate to the use of the plural suffix in the treatment program. Similar considerations, plus some additional ones, arise in relation to the other three suffixes that will appear in the material of the treatment program. For example, suppose that at posttest Q.N. is now good at all plural nouns, all comparative adjectives, all adjectives derived from nouns by adding *-y*, and all *-ly* adverbs (that is, all the suffixes that were treated). But, he is no better at verbs with the *-s* inflection, nor at nominalized verbs like *dancer*, nor at nominalized adjectives like *loudness*, and he *is* better at superlative adjectives, even though these did not figure in the treatment. This would tell us that the treatment works on *classes of inflection*. That is, if you teach one adjectival inflection (the comparative), the effect generalizes to other inflections (the superlative), but not to derivational suffixes (the *-ly* that turns an adjective into an adverb). There are various other possible patterns of outcome that license many other kinds of theoretical inference.

The only outcome pattern that might be hard to interpret is one in which all kinds of words—the untreated and the treated—improve equally. As indicated above, this *might* mean that the treatment method has affected the entire suffix-recognition system, which would be good news. However, the result might also simply be due to spontaneous recovery. Neuropsychological patients sometimes do improve without getting any treatment at all. Might this be happening in Q.N.'s case?

One way to deal with this question is to use a multiple pretest design. Suppose we expect the treatment itself to take a month. In this case, we do two pretests, a month apart, before beginning the treatment. If there is no improvement between pretest 1 and pretest 2, but improvement after the treatment, that would seem to dispose of the possibility that the treatment effect is really a spontaneous recovery effect. Ethical considerations of various kinds preclude this in our case. First, it is quite possible that the sooner treatment begins after the brain injury, the better the chances are that it will be efficacious. Second, Q.N. himself is anxious to receive treatment for his reading problems immediately. So we need a different solution to the problem. Our solution is this: Q.N. has numerous cognitive deficits that were documented prior to the reading treatment. If, after the reading treatment, the only impaired function that has improved is reading, it is reasonable to claim that this is *not* because of spontaneous recovery. After all, wouldn't it be coincidental that, given all of his impairments, the only one that was recovering spontaneously was the one we chose to treat? If this argument seems too loose, here is another. Suppose Q.N.'s reading is better after the treatment, but other impaired functions that were not treated (e.g., spelling) do not change. Suppose spelling is now treated and it improves. That seems conclusive.

COGNITIVE NEUROPSYCHOLOGY AND TREATMENT METHODS

In this chapter I have discussed the ways in which cognitive neuropsychology can be used for the assessment of acquired language disorders, and how it can be used in designing treatment studies that are methodologically sound. After the assessment and the design, however, we need to decide upon a *method* of treatment, and here cognitive neuropsychology currently has much less to offer. The reason has to do with the state of development of the subject. We know that the model of reading as shown in Figure 11-2 is a reasonable one, so we know that it is reasonable to seek to determine which of the components of this model are still intact and which are damaged in a particular language-impaired person. But reading models have not advanced to a stage such that we can say how each of these components actually works. So, for example, we can claim that one component of the reading system is a Visual Word Recognition system, and that this system is damaged in E.E. But, because we do not know how this system actually works, the model does not provide us with ways in which to treat an impairment of the system. The particular mnemonic treatment method used with E.E. was not suggested by the model; because theory cannot be of great assistance at present, treatment methods have to be chosen in a relatively speculative and empirical way. Of course, the model is of *some* help: it can indicate which treatment methods are misdirected. For example, a phonics program for E.E. would be pointless, because it is precisely the use of letter-sound rules in reading words that is the cause of his reading errors. In other words, if assessments based on the model indicates that component X of the model is intact, that is, its functioning has not been affected by the brain damage, treatment directed at this intact component is not going to improve the patient's language functioning.

Hence, although we know *exactly* what Q.N.'s major difficulty with reading is—the visual recognition of suffixes—this does not automatically provide us with a treatment method. We have tried several different methods, including color-coding of the suffixed part of a word, or presenting root and suffix on different cards and gradually bringing these into juxtaposition. These studies follow upon a highly sophisticated assessment, and are designed with methodological rigor; but none has succeeded. Q.N's ability to read suffixed words has not improved. Is this because we have not yet hit upon the right treatment method? Is it because no other part of the brain is capable of the task of visual suffix recognition? Is it because Q.N.'s brain is damaged in such a way as to prevent *any* kind of new learning? One hopes that the cognitive neuropsychology of the future will give us ways of discovering the answers to such questions.

REFERENCES

Behrmann, M. (1987). The rites of righting writing: homophone remediation in acquired dysgraphia. *Cognitive Neuropsychology, 4*, 365–384.

Byng, S. (1988). Sentence processing deficits: Theory and therapy. *Cognitive Neuropsychology, 5*, 629–676.

Byng, S., & Coltheart, M. (1986). Aphasia therapy research: Methodological requirements and illustrative results. In E. Hjelmquist, & L. G. Nilsson (Eds.). *Communication and Handicap*. (pp. 191–213). Amsterdam: North Holland.

Coltheart, M. (1985). Cognitive neuropsychology and the study of reading. In M. I. Posner, & O. S. M. Marin (Eds.). *Attention and Performance, 11*, (pp. 3–37). Hillsdale, NJ: Lawrence Erlbaum Associates.

Coltheart, M. (1990). Cognitive neuropsychology and aphasia therapy. In A. Bennett & K. M. McKonkey, (Eds.) *Cognition in Individual and Social Contexts*. (pp. 529–544). Amsterdam: North Holland.

Coltheart, M., & Byng, S. (in press). A treatment for surface dyslexia. In X. Seron, (Ed.) *Cognitive Approaches in Neuropsychological Rehabilitation*. London: Lawrence Erlbaum Associates.

Coltheart, M., Patterson, K. E., & Marshall, J. C. (Eds.) (1980). *Deep Dyslexia*. London: Routledge and Kegan Paul.

de Partz, M. P. (1985). Re-education of a deep dyslexic patient: rationale of the method and results. *Cognitive Neuropsychology. 3*, 149–177.

Ellis, A. W., & Young, A. (1988). *Human Cognitive Neuropsychology*. London: Lawrence Erlbaum Associates.

Funnell E. (1987). Morphological errors in acquired dyslexia: a case of mistaken identity. *Quarterly Journal of Experimental Psychology, 39A*, 497–540.

Goldstein, M. N. Auditory agnosia for speech ("pure word deafness"): A historical review with current implications. *Brain and Language, 1*, 195–204.

Hatfield, F.M. (1983). Aspects of acquired disorthographia and implications for re-education. In C. Code, & D. Muller (Eds.). *Aphasia Therapy* (pp. 163–179). London: Edward Arnold

Howard, D., & Hatfield, F. M. (1987). *Aphasia Therapy*. London: Lawrence Erlbaum.

Jones, E. (1986). Building the foundations for sentence production in a non-fluent aphasic. *British Journal of Disorders of Communication, 21*, 63–82.

Patterson, K. E. (1980). Derivational errors. In M. Coltheart, K. E. Patterson, & J. C. Marshall (Eds.). *Deep Dyslexia*. (pp. 286–306). London: Routledge and Kegan Paul.

Patterson, K. E., & Shewell, C. (1987). Speak and spell: Dissociations and word-class effects. In M. Coltheart, G. Sartori, & R. Job. *The Cognitive Neuropsychology of Language* (pp. 181-198). London: Lawrence Erlbaum Associates.

Semenza, C., & Zettin, M. (1988). Generating proper names: a case of selective inability. *Cognitive Neuropsychology, 5*, 711–722.

Shallice, T. (1988). *From Neuropsychology to Mental Structure*. Cambridge: Cambridge University Press.

Warrington, E. K., & McCarthy, R. (1987). Categories of knowledge: Further fractionation and an attempted integration. *Brain, 110*, 1273–1296.

CHAPTER 12

BEHAVIOR THERAPY IN THE TREATMENT OF NEUROLOGICALLY IMPAIRED ADULTS

Barbara Wilson

This chapter is concerned with the application of behavior therapy and behavior modification to the treatment of patients with neurological problems. Traditionally, treatments offered to these people were administered by occupational, speech, and physiotherapists. In some centers, neuropsychologists would be involved in diagnosis and intellectual assessment but rarely with treatment. Times are changing however, and it is now more common to find clinical psychologists and some neuropsychologists attempting to alleviate problems resulting from neurological damage.

Treatment oriented psychologists have found that principles and practices of behavior therapy can be applied to much of their work. Errorless learning, graded practice, modeling, and reinforcement have been used in conjunction with occupational and physiotherapy to speed recovery of motor skills and activities of daily living. Behavior modification programs, which are widely employed in psychiatric and mental handicap settings, can be applied effectively to head injured patients whose behavior problems may be preventing them from making the best use of various therapies. Techniques for teaching severely retarded people can be adapted or modified to enable brain damaged patients either to regain some of their lost cognitive skills or manage without them.

Contents of this chapter will begin with a description of the common neurological conditions of head injury, cerebral vascular accident, dementia, multiple sclerosis, encephalitis, tumor and spinal cord injury. Motor, sensory, behavioral, cognitive and emotional problems arising from these conditions will be discussed in the following section. A third section offers a brief resumé of the history of behavioral techniques used in the treatment of patients with neurological disorders, and a discussion of the limitations of behavioral approaches in the treatment of patients with these conditions. This discussion will refer to patients who have memory or language problems that preclude them from using some of the strategies of behavior therapy, and other patients who have muscle tone disorders that prevent tense-and-release exercises in relaxation training.

A fourth section concentrates on behavioral assessment of neurologically impaired people and considers its relevance to the treatment of disabling problems manifested in normal, everyday activities. Direct observation and self-report measures are discussed, and references made to some recently developed assessment procedures claiming to be ecologically valid. This section also refers to benefits that can be gained from combining behavioral and neuropsychological assessments. It is argued that the latter is necessary for determining cognitive strengths and weaknesses that need to be taken into account when devising and implementing behavioral strategies.

Section 5 describes treatment techniques and provides examples of programs for (a) decreasing problem behaviors such as yelling, swearing and undue apprehension, and (b) increasing positive behaviors such as attending, recognizing and remembering in people with disorders in memory, movement, language, and self-care.

A sixth section discusses the importance and relevance of single-case experimental designs in neurological rehabilitation. The limitations of group studies are reviewed in the light of a number of factors such as the rarity of many of the syndromes and the multiplicity of deficits experienced by many patients.

Section 7 considers ways in which behavior therapy in the treatment of neurologically impaired people has been influenced by the disciplines of neuropsychology and cognitive psychology. It is suggested that the most successful approaches to treatment appear to be those that combine principles, methodologies, and concepts from the three disciplines of behavioral, cognitive, and neuropsychology.

COMMON NEUROLOGICAL CONDITIONS

Most patients with neurological dysfunctions who are seen by clinical psychologists or neuropsychologists are likely to be experiencing or have experienced one of the following conditions:

Severe head injury

Cerebral vascular accident (stroke)

A degenerative disease (such as Alzheimer's disease, Parkinson's disease, multiple sclerosis, Huntington's chorea, or dementia associated with HIV infection)

Cerebral or spinal tumor

Trauma to the spinal cord

Infection (e.g., encephalitis)

Anoxia (e.g., following myocardial infarction, carbon monoxide poisoning, anaesthetic accident or as secondary to a severe head injury)

Korsakoff's syndrome (following chronic alcohol abuse and poor nutrition).

The occurrence of neurological impairment is surprisingly high in industrial societies and is rarely if ever anticipated by sufficient treatment or rehabilitative measures. Very few neurologically impaired people will see a psychologist. In England and Wales, alone, about 7,500 people sustain a severe head injury each year (Royal College of Physicians Report, 1986). In the United States the number is between 50,000 and 60,000 each year. At a conservative estimate some 15% will never lead an independent life. Figures like these mean that, for example, we can expect between 10,000 and 15,000 severely disabled people in England and Wales in the next decade (British Psychological Society [BPS] Report, 1989). Most severely head-injured people sustain their brain damage before the age of 25 years and, should they survive the acute stage, can expect to live a normal life span despite crushing effects on the quality of life they experience.

In addition, about 10% of populations over the age of 65 years will have dementia (some 800,000 in Britain alone). There are approximately 130,000 stroke patients with significant impairment living in the community in Britain (BPS Report, 1989). AIDS related dementia is growing (Navia, Jordan, & Price, 1986). About 50,000 Britons and 500,000 Americans are estimated to have multiple sclerosis, and more than 100,000 people in Britain have Parkinson's disease. When the figures of Korsakoff patients, people surviving suicide attempts involving carbon monoxide poisoning, encephalitis, Huntington's disease, and a range of other problems are included, neurological impairment takes on epidemic proportions requiring much fuller responses than have so far been forthcoming from governments.

Because of the author's experience and expertise, this chapter will focus on treatment and rehabilitation of patients with nonprogressive brain damage, particularly those surviving head injury, stroke, encephalitis, and anoxia from various causes. This is not to deny, of course, the importance of the application of behavioral principles to the treatment of other groups outside the author's experience.

Problems Faced by People with Neurological Damage

People with damage to the central nervous system (CNS) are likely to experience a wide range of cognitive, emotional, social, behavioral, sensory, and motor problems, all of which psychologists may be expected to tackle. Although motor problems are likely to be best understood and treated by physiotherapists who are trained to prevent deformities and contractures resulting from severe head injury, psychologists can assist physiotherapists by enhancing response to rehabilitation. They can achieve this by bringing their knowledge of behavioral assessment, task analysis, and behavioral strategies to improve learning and evaluation of intervention procedures. Examples of such collaborative treatment programs are described in Wilson (1987a). These include exercising in physiotherapy for a young head injured woman, cooperation with a skin care regime in a man with a spinal cord injury, and teaching self-care activities to a woman with apraxia.

McKinlay, Brooks, Bond, Martinage, and Marshall (1981) say that many brain damaged patients make a good physical recovery if assessed by functional mobility. However, focal lesions following, for example, stroke or tumor can lead to permanent and intractable physical impairments. Severely head injured people with diffuse brain damage may show complex syndromes including upper motor neuron signs, increased spasticity, problems with the initiation of movement, tremor, and so forth.

Sensory impairments are also common after CNS damage. Hemiplegic stroke patients frequently lose sensation in their paralyzed limbs and may consequently injure themselves through catching an arm in the spokes of a wheelchair or burning a leg by keeping it too close to a radiator. Spinal patients may also lose sensation below the lesion and are at risk of developing pressure sores because they do not change position frequently enough and thus lose circulation to buttocks, heels, and other parts of the anatomy. Carr and Wilson (1983) describe a successful behavioral program to increase lifting in a spinal patient.

Apart from tactile sensation, visual sensory deficits are common sequelae of a range of neurological conditions including cerebral tumors, strokes, and head injuries. Patients can be taught to compensate for visual field loss and even taught to reduce myopia. Although studies have been reported showing improvement in myopia for nonbrain damaged people (e.g., Collins, Ricci, & Burkett, 1981), as far as I know only one has demonstrated this for a brain damaged person. This was a study carried out by David Thomas and reported in Wilson (in press a). Thomas worked with a 21-year-old head injured woman three months after she had been involved in a motor cycle accident. She was thrown backwards from the pillion seat and sustained damage to her occipital lobes. Her right eye was closed due to a third nerve palsy and she had restricted vision in her left eye. A shaping procedure was used to teach her to read words in three quarter inch high print (previously she could read only 3 inch high words), and to reduce her handwriting from letters between 4 to 6 inches high to letters one half inch high.

Auditory sensory problems are less frequently encountered, although occasionally head injured people become deaf as a result of their accident. It is sometimes possible to teach these people sign language or other alternative communication systems. Typically such programs would be implemented by speech therapists but there is no reason why psychologists should not join forces with speech therapists. As with physiotherapists, bringing behavioral principles to treatment should enhance learning.

Cognitive problems are usually present after severe head injury and frequently follow other causes of brain damage. Brooks (1984) suggests that disorders of learning and memory, information processing, planning and organizational problems, slowness of intellectual activity and communication are all common after traumatic brain damage. Less common are the agnosias, dyspraxias, and global aphasias although these are found often after stroke and some tumors.

Clinical and neuropsychologists are becoming increasingly interested in the management and remediation of cognitive deficits (Diller & Gordon, 1981; Gray & Robertson, 1987; Trexler, 1982; Uzzell & Gross, 1986; Wilson, 1987b). Some cognitive problems respond to specially tailored programs even several years after the injury has occurred. One young man described by Wilson (1987b), for example, was taught to read again five years after a gunshot wound left him totally alexic. Another man, a 65-year-old stroke patient, was taught to communicate through visual symbols 5 years after a hemorrhage left him unable to comprehend at the level of a two-year-old child (Wilson, in press b).

Emotional difficulties can be expected in perhaps the majority of people sustaining injury to the brain. McKinlay et al. (1981), for example, say that two thirds of patients with traumatic brain damage will have problems with depression and anxiety. Stroke patients may also show emotional changes. Those with right hemisphere lesions are likely to show denial or indifference to their plight whereas those with left hemisphere damage are more likely to show a "catastrophic reaction." Patients with brain stem strokes may well show extreme emotional lability (Ross, 1983). Of course, emotional problems may occur for nonorganic reasons such as fear of what might happen in the future or grief over role-loss or loss of function.

All clinical psychologists are taught anxiety management procedures, methods for treating depression and other emotional disturbances that can also be used with brain damaged people, although we need to find out to what extent the emotional problems result from cognitive deficits. Extreme fear, for example, can be due to loss of distance and depth perception rather than an emotional disorder per se (Wilson, 1989). Marked irritability may be a secondary result of loss of perceptual constancy so that the patient "sees" something different each time he or she looks at an object or array. This may lead the person to think staff or relatives are playing tricks which in turn leads to the irritability.

Many brain injured people are likely to return home to their families at the end of the day, often causing social problems. Few severely head injured people maintain a good network of friends. Social isolation is common for both victims and relatives (Talbott, 1989). Stress in such families is high. Livingstone, Brooks, and Bond (1985) tell us that families of head injured people report more than twice the level of psychiatric dysfunction than is to be expected in the general population. Family therapy and social skills training might be beneficial in these cases.

Once the acute period is over, behavior problems, along with cognitive and emotional problems, are usually the most handicapping and cause most stress to families and care-givers (Brooks, 1984). A British Psychological Society Report (in press) claims that if not treated well, emotional and behavioral deficits show a worsening over time. These problems are often associated with frontal lobe damage. The frontal and temporal lobes are particularly vulnerable to severe head injury.

The growing awareness of the importance of behavioral management programs is reflected in a number of publications in recent years (for example, Ince, 1969, 1976; Powell, 1981; Wood, 1984, 1988). Common problems associated with severe head injury include yelling and swearing. Perhaps less common, but more difficult to manage are physical violence and sexually offensive behaviors. Such problems may be the reason why a proportion of brain injured people are admitted to long term psychiatric care. Even very severe behavior disturbance can respond however to behavior modification regimes (Eames, 1989; Wood, 1984; Wood & Eames, 1981).

BEHAVIORAL TECHNIQUES IN THE TREATMENT OF NEUROLOGICALLY IMPAIRED ADULTS

Lane (1977) published an account of Itard's work in the eighteenth century with Victor, the wild boy of Aveyron in which he states (p. 165) that Itard's range of methods " . . . anticipated that of modern behavioral modification by nearly two centuries." Itard used shaping, task analysis, chaining, prompting, and fading. He taught imitation skills and was concerned with the issues of generalization. His is perhaps the first account of behavioral methods used to improve functioning. However, Victor was not an adult, being between 12 and 15 years old when found, nor can we say whether he was or was not neurologically impaired. Certainly, behavioral methods have been extensively used with children with mental handicap, many of whom have neurological deficits.

The question remains when were the first behavioral treatments employed in the treatment of adults whose neurological problems occurred after childhood? The answer is difficult to provide because people using these methods did not necessarily refer to them as "behavioral." In 1963, for example, Luria advocated behavior therapy techniques without describing them as such. Luria, Naydin, Tsvetkova and Vinarskaya (1969) used a combination of pharmacological agents and shaping techniques to "deblock" or "de-inhibit" depressed areas of the central nervous system. One of the examples given in their 1969 chapter is that of patients deafened as a result of concussion following explosions who were asked to read sentences (which, of course, they were able to do without difficulty). At the same time, the patients "listened" to sentences being read aloud. Being deaf they could not hear the sentences. Gradually the written sentences became more illegible although the spoken sentences remained loud and clear. Those patients whose learning impairments were caused by inhibition or shock or secondary damage became able to hear the sentences even when the written words became illegible. This approach can be seen as analogous to shaping and prompting with fading approaches used with children with mental handicap.

One of the first people to advocate behavioral techniques with brain injured adults was Goodkin who published two papers (1966 and 1969) describing operant conditioning programs. The first describes methods of improving wheelchair pushing, handwriting, and machine operating in three stroke patients and one patient with Parkinson's Disease. The second describes language improvement in a dysphasic stroke patient. Ince (1969) reports on the value of positive reinforcement in encouraging stroke patients to attend therapy sessions.

During the 1970s behavioral treatments became established for brain injured people. Taylor and Persons (1970) and Booraem and Seacat (1972) used behavior modification techniques in rehabilitation settings to improve disruptive behaviors such as complaining and refusing to exercise. Ince (1976) in his book on behavior modification in rehabilitation concentrated on reduction of problem behaviors although he also included suggestions on how behavioral principles could be used in other areas of rehabilitation. Lincoln (1978) continued the theme of using behavior modification to improve exercising in physiotherapy when she described three programs for stroke patients. The following year she reported on the applications of behavior therapy to language retraining in aphasic stroke patients (1979). This was one of a few papers prior to 1980 reporting on behavioral methods applied to cognitive problems.

Others who touched on aspects of cognitive impairment were Goodkin (1969) and Diller, and his colleagues in New York, working with patients who suffered from visuospatial and visuoperceptual problems resulting from right cerebral vascular accidents (Diller & Weinberg, 1977; Weinberg et al., 1979). The New York group incorporated behavioral principles into their programs although they are not described as such by the authors. They believe it is necessary to establish the problem, obtain a baseline, and start training with easy tasks before progressing to more complex ones. They also point out the importance of providing cues and environmental supports in the early stages before fading these out as treatment progresses. Feedback and evaluation are also considered crucial aspects of training. Thus they are following the behavioral principles of task analysis, observation and recording of the problem behaviors, shaping, reinforcement, and monitoring or evaluation of treatment effectiveness, all of which are components of behavioral assessment and treatment programs.

The application of behavior therapy techniques to cognitive problems continued throughout the 1980s. Ince's (1980) book contained a chapter by Diller on cognitive remediation. Wilson (1981a) published a survey of behavioral treatments carried out at a rehabilitation centre and she included a number of cognitive programs as well as programs for the remediation of behavioral, social, and emotional problems. Powell (1981), Wood & Eames (1981), Miller (1984), Wilson and Moffat (1984), and Wilson (1987b) are some of the numerous publications that have appeared in the past 10 years indicating that behavior therapy in the treatment of neurologically impaired adults has become well established. A good review of neuropsychology and behavior therapy can be found in Horton and Miller (1985).

Despite the undoubted value of a behavioral approach, the neurological and neuropsychological status of each individual patient must be taken into account when designing treatment programs or management regimes. It may be impossible, for example, for memory impaired people to remember behavioral contracts, delayed reinforcement or explanations no matter how carefully structured the program. Dysphasic patients may be unable to comprehend the written or spoken word. The lesson here is that behavioral targets for physically handicapped people must be within their physical capabilities. Take the example of FE, a severely brain injured young man who was about 30 pounds overweight. His physiotherapist requested help from the clinical psychologist and a goal was devised for FE to lose 28 pounds.

When the psychologist first saw FE she intended to ask him to record everything he ate or drank during the first week. FE, however, had lost the ability to read and write as a result of his head injury. Undaunted, the psychologist decided to lend FE a tape recorder and asked him to record his food and drink intake on it. However, FE's severe memory impairment made it impossible for him to remember what he had consumed by the time he came to record, and he was also likely to forget where he had placed the hospital's tape recorder. The psychologist considered asking FE to telephone the hospital each time he ate or drank but abandoned this idea partly because of the memory problems again and partly because it was impractical to ensure there was always someone on hand to take down the information from the telephone calls. Finally, a solution was reached when FE's father agreed to record his son's food and drink intake. FE went on to lose the 28 pounds when a powerful reinforcer was identified: he was allowed an extra half day of rehabilitation each week if he lost at least 2 pounds in the previous week. This case illustrates how behavioral treatments are not always perfectly geared to their clients and that sometimes considerable alterations have to be made to achieve precise targeting and the means to achieve goals.

Another example of a behavioral program was that designed for use with BH, a 65-year-old man who had a hemorrhage in the left cerebral hemisphere 5 years earlier. This left him with a right hemiplegia and global aphasia. He was unable to say any words, could only make one sound, and his comprehension of single words was at a two-year-old's level. BH had received speech therapy soon after his stroke and a year later an attempt had been made to teach him sign language. No improvements were noted and both treatment programs were abandoned by the speech therapists when it became obvious that BH was experiencing distress during sessions. After 5 years, BH was referred to a clinical psychologist to see if some communication system could be devised, particularly for application to the home setting where both BH and his wife were experiencing considerable anger and frustration at their lack of communication.

A visual symbol system based on one described by Gardner, Zurif, Berry, and Baker (1976) was devised

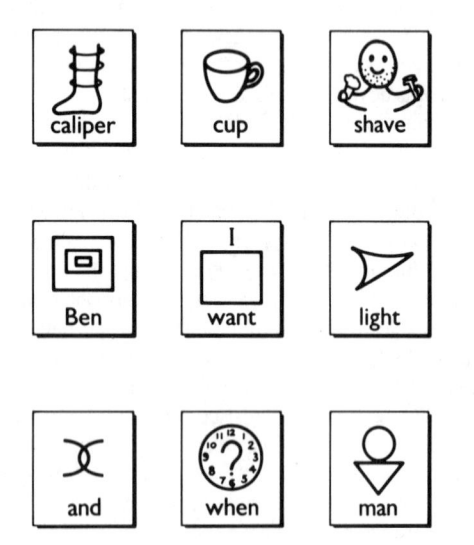

Figure 12.1. Visual symbols used in alternative communication program.

in which symbols were drawn on cards and were either abstract or pictorial.

A modeling procedure, together with positive reinforcement in the form of praise and attention, was employed to teach BH the symbols, many of which he learned to comprehend with some degree of ease. He began to use the cards spontaneously only for expressive communication after a period of nine months. Nevertheless, because they were so helpful in comprehension, life became easier for BH and his wife at home. Certain words continued to cause great difficulty. Some verbs could only be learned when they were drawn pictorially; others were not learned at all. In contrast, he was able to learn both pictorial and abstract nouns with little trouble.

Despite a successful teaching method (modeling), positive reinforcement, and a high level of motivation, BH's expression never matched his comprehension and he remained better at nouns than verbs. The neuropsychology of language may be able to offer us an explanation for these outcomes. We know that the right hemisphere of the brain is better at understanding speech than expressing it, and that it can comprehend nouns better than verbs (for example, Searleman, 1977; Zaidel, 1977). BH appeared to be using the language capabilities of his right hemisphere and although the behavioral approach was able to improve these residual skills it could not develop new skills or restore the damaged abilities of the language areas in the left hemisphere.

From these few examples it should be clear that behavioral psychologists must proceed with caution both during the design stages of their treatment programs and during their implementation. One should be sensitive to the needs, capabilities and indeed personal styles of each patient and be ready to change any aspect of a program should it show signs of ineffectiveness or produce any kind of unease in the client.

Caution is required when using anxiety reduction techniques with brain injured people. The widely used relaxation training involving tense-and-release exercises can cause adverse effects with some hemiparetic, hemiplegic, and ataxic patients, or those with increased muscle tone as the tensing of muscles can trigger or increase spasticity. Physiotherapists should, wherever possible, be involved in these programs.

All behavioral treatments with patients suffering from CNS damage should be modified in the light of neurological and neuropsychological considerations. If such considerations are ignored dangerous errors can be made in diagnosis which in turn can lead to treatment that, at best, is ineffective and, at worst, is harmful. As a student, the author remembers seeing a woman who was unable to walk without holding on to walls or other supports. Neurological causes were ruled out and, perhaps because there had been a previous psychiatric history, she was wrongly diagnosed as having a hysterical condition. A desensitization program was introduced and was well under way when treatment ceased for a week over the Easter holiday. On returning after the Easter break, it was learned that the woman had been moved to another hospital as a spinal tumor had been discovered.

BEHAVIORAL ASSESSMENT OF NEUROLOGICAL PATIENTS

Assessment has been defined as "the systematic collection, organization and interpretation of information about a person and his (her) situation" (Sundberg & Tyler, 1962, p. 81). There are many ways of obtaining this information, two of which are particularly important in the treatment of neurologically impaired adults, namely neuropsychological and behavioral assessments. Neuropsychology is the study of the relationship between brain and behavior. Goldstein (1984) says ". . . neuropsychological assessment is, in essence, the assessment of cognitive, perceptual, and motor abilities." (p. 11) He goes on to suggest that there is a relative lack of interest in behavioral, social, and emotional aspects despite the fact that these are just as likely to be affected by brain injury.

Neuropsychological assessments nevertheless provide valuable information about the general level of intellectual functioning, probable premorbid level of functioning, cognitive strengths and weaknesses, and the nature of the cognitive disorders. For example, whether there is global or material specific memory impairment or whether an acquired disorder of reading is more typical of deep dyslexia, surface dyslexia, phonological dyslexia, or letter-by-lettter reading.

Additionally, neuropsychological assessments can tell us whether a patient's score is in the abnormal range, how the patient compares with others in the general population, whether the problems are more likely to be due to organic or functional causes, and perhaps which part of the brain is most likely to be affected.

Important as this information is, it is in itself not sufficient to design a treatment program. For example, it does not help us answer such questions as "What kind of problems occur in everyday life?" or "How does the patient cope with these problems?" or "Can this person return to work or college?" Nor do neuropsychological assessments help a great deal in determining what kind of treatment we should offer. After all, we do not treat an inability to learn paired associates or a failure to perform a block design task within a given period of time. Even though some neuropsychologists use paired associates and block designs as outcome measures, they are not the best ways to determine the success of an intervention or treatment plan. People can improve on neuropsychological tasks yet remain unable to function in their own environment and, conversely, they can improve on everyday functions without showing an improvement on standardized tests.

The relationship between performance on real life tasks and performance on psychological tests is usually unclear. Most tests are not representative of the everyday demands faced by neurologically impaired people. Some recently developed tests have, however, attempted to make the assessment items analagous to real life tasks. The Rivermead Behavioral Memory Test (RBMT; Wilson, Cockburn, & Baddeley, 1985) and the Behavioral Inattention Test (BIT; Wilson, Cockburn & Halligan, 1987) are both standardized tests yet include items similar to real life tasks.

The RBMT, for example, requires subjects to remember an appointment, deliver a message, learn a new short route, and recognize faces shown to them earlier. There are 12 items in this test which takes about 25 minutes to administer. It has good face validity as well as being a valid test of everyday memory failures, and has high inter-rater and parallel form reliability (Wilson, Cockburn, Baddeley, & Hiorns, in press).

The BIT is similar in its approach but tries to predict which people will have everyday problems arising from unilateral visual neglect. Items include picture scanning, telephone dialing, sorting coins, and reading a menu. A few other ecologically valid tests are appearing including the Cognitive Competency Test (Wang & Ennis, 1986) and the Test of Functional Communication for Aphasic Adults (Holland, 1980).

Whereas these new trends in testing are to be welcomed, it would be wrong to believe that progress can be made without behavioral assessments as such. The latter have a crucial role to play in planning treatment for neuropsychological patients. Clearly, neuropsychological tests are needed to ensure that, cognitively, we are not asking the impossible, they enable us to find out which cognitive strengths can be used to by-pass cognitive weaknesses, and to find out whether a patient can understand, remember, read, and perceive the information we offer. Equally clearly, we need behavioral assessments to help identify ways in which impairments are manifested in the behavior of patients, we need them in order to measure problematic behaviors, and we need them in order to find out whether our intervention strategies and treatment procedures are helping to change behaviors beneficially.

When defining problems we might do well to follow principles that guide others working with different groups such as people with mental handicap. Problems should be specified as precisely as possible and where necessary an operational definition should be used. One of the most frequent referrals from occupational therapists to psychologists is for help with a patient's concentration problems. One such patient was Paul, a 21-year-old who had sustained both a head injury and a stroke. His occupational therapist (O.T.) asked the psychologists to design a program to improve Paul's concentration. Questioning revealed that the O.T.s had formed their opinion of Paul's lack of concentration because he would not work for more than a few minutes in occupational therapy before walking out, making a fuss, or refusing to continue. Concentration in this case was operationally defined as inability to work for more than 3 minutes. Paul was assessed in psychology and observed in occupational therapy for several days. He was too impaired for the usual neuropsychological tests which included tests for nonhandicapped children. He was able to cooperate with the Merrill-Palmer, a test for mentally handicapped children, and he could manage some memory and perceptual tests. Much of his intellectual functioning was equivalent to that of a three-year-old child. Even though the occupational therapists knew Paul was cognitively impaired they had no idea just how impaired he was. Consequently, the tasks they were setting him were too difficult. This was confirmed by direct observation in the O.T. department.

The first goal was to see if Paul could work for 5 minutes in O.T. before having a rest. "Treatment" consisted of setting very simple tasks, telling Paul how long he had worked for the previous session, asking him to do better, and giving him verbal and visual feedback. Paul achieved the first goal within a week of this program. .

Many, perhaps most, referrals from other staff express problem behaviors inappropriately. Terminology may be used imprecisely or incorrectly thereby creating mistaken views as to what is possible and what is not. For example, psychologists may find that they are being asked to "do some memory retraining" or "cognitive retraining" with brain injured adults. Ways in which a patient's difficulties are manifested need to be specified as unambiguously and precisely as possible.

Inappropriate definitions of behavior would include "poor memory," "frontal lobe deficits," or "poor body image." Appropriate definitions would include "difficulty in finding the way round the rehabilitation center," or "repeats the same question 20 times an hour," or "fails to put on the wheelchair brakes when transferring to the bed or a chair." With the former we are left with no directions for future action, whereas the latter suggest actions we might take to overcome problems. Thus goals for the problems specified above might be: "takes shortest route to (a) ward, (b) canteen, and (c) physiotherapy"; "asks each question no more than once a day"; "always puts on wheelchair brakes when transferring."

Defining problems can be achieved in a number of ways. We can obtain both documentary and observational data from staff of course. Behavioral interviewing of patients and their relatives may help, although in the case of the former it should be kept in mind that brain injured patients are often confused, have poor insight and may also be unrealistic. Severely memory impaired people are, for example, likely to underestimate the extent of their memory problems (Wilson, Cockburn, & Baddeley, 1989); not remember what it is they cannot remember, that is, be unable to tell you how the memory problems manifest themselves in daily life; and may expect complete restoration of memory functioning either by natural recovery or some special treatment.

We can administer checklists, rating scales, and questionnaires to identify problem behaviors and a number of these exist. Cautela (1981), for example, provides several survey schedules that can be used with neurologically impaired adults. Wood (1987) describes a number of behavior rating scales for assessing social skills, sexual behavior, aggression, and other interactive behaviors exhibited by brain injured people. Wilson et al. (1989) describe a therapists's checklist for noting memory failures of brain injured adults based on the work of Sunderland, Harris, and Gleave (1984). Most studies attempting to measure everyday memory problems by self-report measures with patients have found poor agreement between these and traditional or laboratory tasks.

Interviewing relatives may provide clearer perspectives (Sunderland et al., 1984).

Despite the limitations concerning patients' views of their own problems, their opinions are an important dimension that should not be overlooked in the process of diagnosis. Patients should be asked to complete self-report measures in order to find out how much insight they have into their problems. After all, brain injured people are not unique in showing a discrepancy between what they think and what they do. Hammond (1987) videotaped rheumatoid arthritis patients completing two tasks before and after attending a group to learn joint protection techniques. She also asked them to complete a questionnaire at the end of the group training. All patients thought they had changed their behavior in the tasks in order to protect their joints but analysis of the videotapes showed that in many cases actual behavior had not changed.

The behavioral recording methods of measurement of permanent product, automatic recording, frequency counts, duration recording, interval recording, and momentary time sampling have a place in defining problems and in taking baselines. Automatic recording can be used, for example, in physiotherapy to measure the number of revolutions on an exercise cycle or the distribution of weight between the left and right leg when carrying out standing practice. A medical engineering department will probably be needed to build the right equipment.

Measurement of permanent product could be used in occupational therapy or speech therapy. The permanent product might be the number of lines typed or the number of words written in a given session. An example from my own experience involved measurement of permanent product to assess whether a particular drug could reduce excessive dribbling in a severely head injured boy. The permanent product was the weight of all bibs and tissues required to mop up the saliva produced each day.

Frequency counts are perhaps the most widely used of behavioral recording methods although these can be very unreliable in a high frequency behavior. A group of 20 physiotherapists and occupational therapists at Southampton General Hospital (England) was asked to note the number of shouts and the number of times swearing occurred in a 5 minute videotape sequence of a head injured girl. The range for shouts was 2–8 and for swearing it was 15–27. Often it is simply impossible to count the number of times a problem behavior occurs. Wilson (1981a), for example, describes a young head injured man who called out "nurse, nurse" for most of his waking hours. Although this sounds a trivial problem, the stress on staff was intolerable. In this case it was necessary to use an interval recording procedure.

One example of a frequency count is reported in Wilson (1986) with a head injured dysphasic man who used one phrase "nice to see you" very frequently.

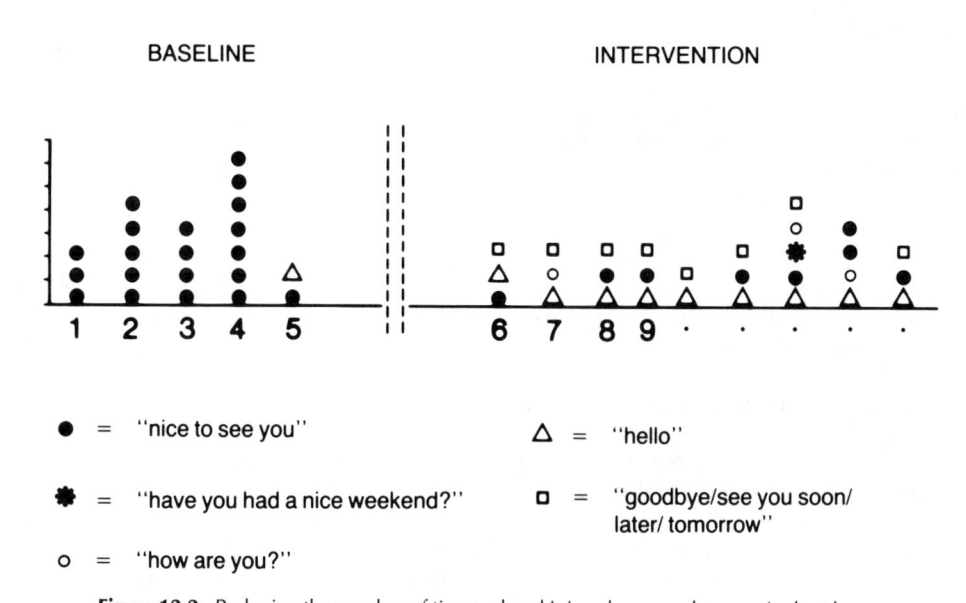

Figure 12.2. Reducing the number of times a head injured man spoke a particular phrase.

Again, this sounds trivial but it was used with such frequency that it affected others adversely. Frequency counting enabled the psychologist to see if intervention strategies actually reduced repetition of the single phrase and encouraged the use of other phrases.

Interval recording is often the most practical and reliable method of recording although it is poor at reflecting the true extent of the behavior (Murphy & Goodall, 1980). The 20 therapists referred to earlier achieved a much higher level of agreement when using a 20 second interval to record whether any swearing had occurred. However, their agreed level of 70% was a gross overestimate. It is quite possible that although interval recording promotes high interrater reliability and encourages greater staff cooperation it nevertheless loses something in terms of fine grained detail.

Momentary time sampling appears to be used infrequently with neurological patients. It is less accurate with infrequent behavior and infrequent sampling than other methods (Foster & Cone, 1986).

BEHAVIORAL TREATMENT STRATEGIES FOR DECREASING BEHAVIORS

Behavioral excesses are common after some kinds of neurological damage. Schuerman (1983), for example, looked at the hospital notes of 25 head injured patients over a period of 7 years and found 635 complaints of excessive behaviors and 257 complaints of behavioral deficits.

Powell (1981) describes a number of behavioral treatment strategies that can be used to reduce or eliminate problem behaviors. All of these are potentially helpful with brain injured people. Relaxation and systematic desensitization have, for example, been used to reduce fear of water in a stroke patient (Wilson, in press a). Stimulus control could prove to be effective in decreasing extreme distractability; extinction and positive reinforcement together have been employed successfully to reduce aggression (Wood, 1987) and yelling (Wilson, 1981a) in head injured people.

Time out has probably been the most frequently employed punishment procedure when dealing with aggressive behaviors (Goll & Hawley, 1989; Wood, 1987). Cognitive restructuring or cognitive behavior modification has, however, still to make its mark in treatment programs for neurologically impaired people. Depression, for example, is common after head injury, stroke, and other conditions. Survivors of these conditions may feel life is not worth living as they struggle with impairments such as a paralyzed limb or inability to read or reduced intellectual capacity. It is possible that cognitive therapy could be adapted to their circumstances.

Four examples of successful programs for decreasing problem behaviors in stroke and head injured patients are discussed here. Wood (1987) also describes a number of behavioral programs for reducing behaviors in brain injured people.

Reducing anxiety in a stroke patient: F.G. was a 39-year-old woman who had a subarachnoid hemorrhage some 5 months before referral for treatment. The physiotherapist referred F.G. to the clinical psychologist to improve her ability to walk unaided. F.G. had no major language or perceptual impairments although she was attending a daily memory group to assist her with impaired memory. Her physical functioning was good and it was difficult to explain why she was so anxious about her walking. When traveling between one department and another in the rehabilitation unit, F.G. clung to anybody nearby, and if unable to do this, she clung to walls. She refused to go out alone and would not cross a road even when accompanied.

Baselines were taken for 2 weeks on four target behaviors. First, F.G. was asked to walk from the ward to physiotherapy without holding on to anyone or anything. This was a journey of about 20 meters. The second behavior was climbing a flight of stairs without holding on to anyone and without stopping. She was allowed to touch the wall with one hand. The third behavior was to cross the road with one person accompanying her but without physical contact. The fourth behavior was to walk 40 meters to a shop unaccompanied but without having to cross any roads. Each behavior was recorded on a pass/fail basis. F.G. had to complete the whole task in order to pass.

F.G. failed all tasks consistently over the 3 week period. At the beginning of the second week a target was set after discussion between F.G., her physiotherapist and the psychologist. F.G. was asked to try and achieve the target as quickly as possible. Her efforts were recorded on a chart and she was allowed a free half hour at the end of the physiotherapy session if she achieved the target. A new goal was set each week. The results can be seen in Figure 12–3.

Reducing yelling in a head injured man: M.D. was a 29-year-old man who had sustained a severe head injury 11 months earlier. He had been unconscious for 8 weeks and, like many people having such a long period of coma, was impaired in several ways and

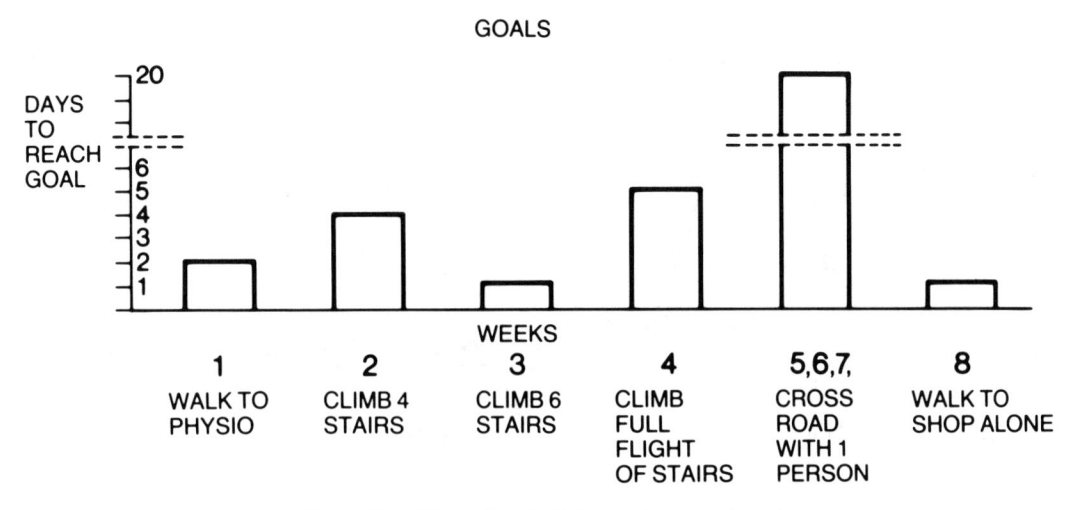

Figure 12.3. Time taken for F.G. to achieve each goal.

exhibited many problem behaviors, the most troublesome for staff and fellow patients being his disruptiveness in therapy sessions. He would shout for attention from his therapists several times during each session and this would upset everyone present.

A neuropsychological assessment revealed that although M.D. had considerable perceptual and visuospatial difficulties he was in other respects of average ability and had reasonably intact verbal memory skills. A behavioral program was devised with a number of objectives aimed at reducing what were regarded by those around M.D. as problem behaviors. Although these objectives may appear narrow to critics, their achievement would lead to a much happier environment in which therapy could continue for several patients, and this in itself might lead to more successful therapy. Ultimately, it could be argued that success in achieving these objectives would lead to M.D. becoming more socially skillful and thus more socially acceptable. However, such broad goals were not the province of the program designers at the outset: starting from such goals would lead us nowhere. However, we would hope ("intend" would be too strong a word) that the achievement of small steps might lead to the attainment of such broad goals. The program for M.D. is contained in Table 12–1 below; results appear in Figure 12–4.

Reducing the number of questions asked by a stroke patient: A.F. was a 59-year-old man who had a right hemisphere stroke 4 months prior to being admitted to a rehabilitation center. He had no physical problems and was able to attend as a day patient. His wife collected him each afternoon at 4:30 p.m. A.F. was a very anxious person who feared his wife was going to leave him. This idea dominated his thoughts and manifested itself during his hours at the rehabilitation center in continuous and urgent questioning of all members of staff with whom he came into contact. He

Table 12-1. A Behavior Program for M.D.'s Calling Out

STAGE	
1. define behavior/stage goals	stop M.D. calling out during therapy sessions
2. observe and record (baseline)	(i) problems—sometimes M.D. called out for good reason (ii) unnecessary calling out between 1 and 7 times per session
3. identify reinforcers	(i) verbal and visual feedback (ii) pub lunch
4. plan treatment	(i) explain to M.D. (ii) records kept (iii) pub lunch for 2 days without any unnecessary calling out
5. begin treatment	treatment begun
6. monitor and evaluate progress	calling out decreases other desirable side effects
7. change procedure if necessary	fading out of reinforcers

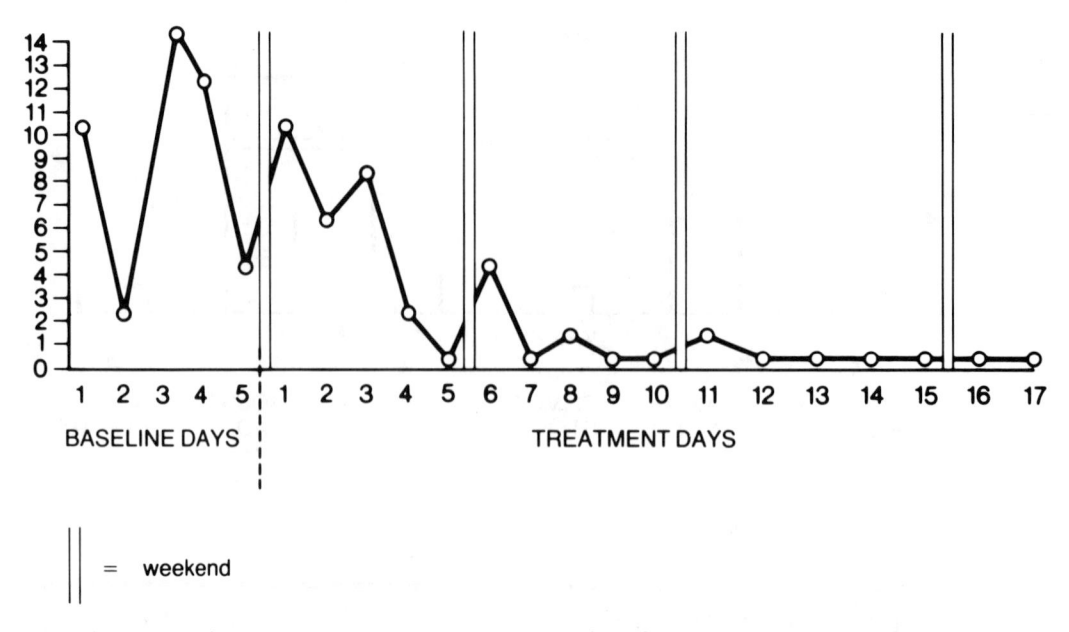

Figure 12.4. The frequency of M.D.'s calling out during physiotherapy sessions (two sessions per day).

would say, "Is my wife coming for me today?" or "What time is my wife coming today" His wife was always on time. Although continuous questioning like this was difficult enough for staff to tolerate it must have been almost unbearable for A.F.'s wife.

Records taken over a 3 day period showed that A.F. asked these sorts of questions over 40 times a day. In the treatment stage he was asked to record in a notebook each time he asked a question about his wife. In addition to this self-monitoring, he was given relaxation and imaginal desensitization in which he was requested to imagine his wife arriving a few seconds later each day. Initially A.F. became very distressed at the imaginal desensitization (even imagining his wife being 2 seconds late caused him to say, "Please, don't make me do that"). Eventually, however, his questions dropped to an average of five a day. Whether the self-monitoring or the desensitization alone would have been equally effective as the two together remains an open question. No further claims can be made for this program except that life with A.F. for the staff who worked with him was made easier. Hopefully, a decline in extreme anxiety and a lessening in the number of questions was noticeable at home and made life easier for A.F.'s wife.

Decreasing the amount of time taken to walk a given distance: S.B. was a 25-year-old woman with a condition that proved difficult to diagnose. She had epilepsy and some cognitive impairments. She claimed, for example, that she had forgotten what certain words meant and could no longer read. The neurologists were puzzled by her behavior and suspected her of being hysterical. A problem that was making life difficult for S.B. was that she walked with a pronounced limp and excessively slowly. We decided to take her problems at face value as far as her walking was concerned and therefore devised a program to reduce the amount of time she took to walk from physiotherapy to occupational therapy, a distance of some 25 yards. S.B. was timed walking this distance and encouraged to "beat" her previous record each time she repeated the journey. There was a minimal decrease in time over the first 3 days and then a noticeable increase on the fourth day, possibly caused by the onset of menstruation. After that her times improved considerably (see Figure 12–5) until her program was unfortunately interrupted by the medical director who decided to discharge S.B. on the grounds of doubt about her neurological status.

BEHAVIORAL TREATMENT STRATEGIES FOR INCREASING BEHAVIORS

As a general rule, it is easier to teach people to do something than it is to teach them not to do something. The use of behavioral principles for increasing behav-

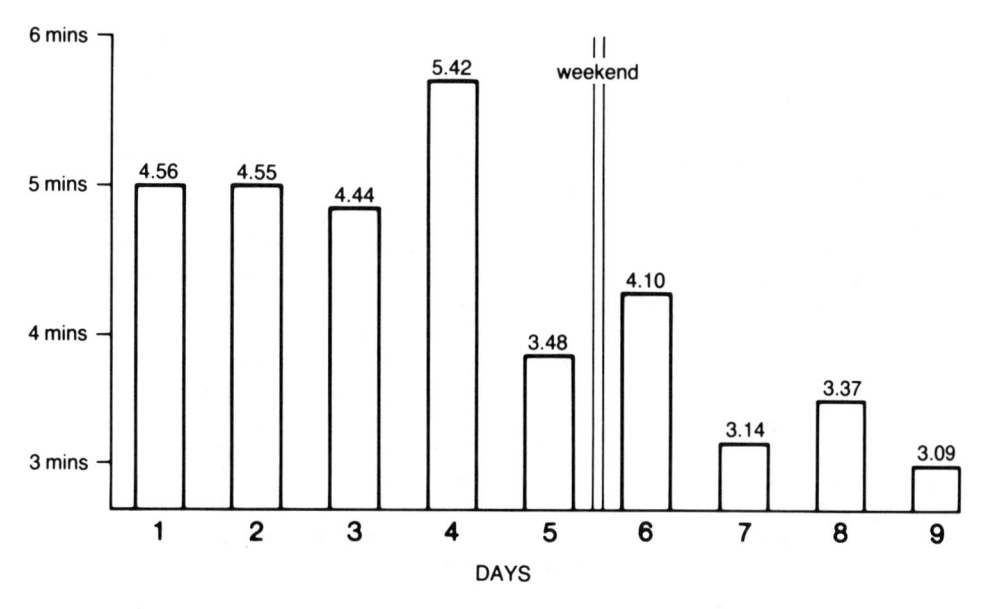

Figure 12.5. Time taken by S.B. to walk from physiotherapy to occupational therapy.

iors or teaching new behaviors has proved as valuable in the treatment of neurologically impaired adults as it has in the treatment of other learning disabled groups. The techniques that have proved most useful are prompting, method of vanishing cues (chaining), expanding rehearsal, positive reinforcement, and Portage. An example of each of these is provided here.

The use of prompting to teach self-care skills to a young woman with apraxia: S.H. was severely brain damaged at the age of 20 years as a result of an anaesthetic accident. She had a number of problems, the most handicapping being her complete inability to do anything for herself because of the apraxia. Apraxia is a disorder of movement which is not the result of paralysis, weakness, or poor comprehension. In order to diagnose apraxia, it is necessary to ensure the disabled person has a sufficient range of movements and sufficient strength to carry out a task, and that he or she understands what is required. S.H. could walk, move, grip, and carry out individual component movements of many tasks with a verbal prompt. Thus, for example, she could not demonstrate how to brush her teeth (either by gesture or with a real object), but she could lift her hand to her mouth, show her teeth, and hold a toothbrush when asked to do these things separately. The latter demonstrated that physical weakness was not preventing her from carrying out the everyday tasks she was failing to perform. Furthermore, S.H. could explain what she was trying to do and was obviously making attempts to complete the tasks requested of her. We could deduce from this that her failure was not due to a lack of understanding.

S.H.'s apraxia was so severe she could not feed or dress herself. A series of prompts was used to teach her to drink from a cup unaided. The task was broken down into a series of small steps, written as directions:

1. Put your hands flat on the table.
2. Keep your hand low.
3. Put your thumb through the handle.
4. Grasp the handle.
5. Lift the cup to your mouth.
6. Drink.
7. Put the cup down on the table.
8. Open your fingers.
9. Release your fingers and take your thumb out of the handle.

As S.H. tended to put the further rim of the cup to her mouth causing spillage, it was decided, after the seventh teaching session, to add another step between steps 5 and 6. This asked S.H. to look for the red rim that was painted on the side of the cup that was nearer to her mouth.

Breaking the task down like this looks like a chaining procedure but in S.H.'s case the steps were not taught one at a time. Instead, she was required to complete all steps by herself. A scoring procedure was devised whereby if S.H. completed a step without help she was awarded 1 point. If she was unable to do this, or made a wrong movement, a verbal prompt was given. If she succeeded with the verbal prompt she scored 2 points. If that failed she was given a slight physical prompt (in the form of a nudge in the right direction). This scored 3 points and, if all else failed, a full physical prompt was supplied (i.e., her hand was guided through the step). If this last form of prompt was given, S.H. scored 4 points. Results of this program can be seen in Table 12-2.

This program was initiated a year after S.H.'s accident. It is very unlikely that spontaneous recovery caused her success given that she had been receiving rehabilitation for several months and encouraged to complete such tasks for herself. S.H. learned only when the step-by-step procedure was introduced. The same approach was employed to teach S.H. other self-help skills (see Wilson, 1988, and in press a).

Apraxia has been explained as a disorder of planning (Liepman, 1920; Luria, 1973) and a disorder of the verbally mediated motor sequence selector (Heilman, 1979). Perhaps the step-by-step prompting provided a mediator for S.H. to plan her action.

The method of vanishing cues to teach severely amnesic patients computer skills: Glisky and Schacter have produced several accounts (1986, 1987; Schacter & Glisky, 1986) of teaching computer skills to amnesic patients. They employ a method described as "the method of vanishing cues" but this is in principle very similar to the chaining method used for a number of years to teach skills to people with mental handicap (for example, Yule & Carr, 1980).

Four amnesic patients were taught 15 computer related terms and their definitions (Schacter & Glisky, 1986) through a chaining procedure in which each letter of the word to be learned was one link in the chain. Subjects were provided with fragments of the word (letters), which were reduced gradually across trials. In this manner, the teaching of the definition of LOOP would be presented as "A repeated segment is called a LOOP." The letters in LOOP would gradually be reduced in the following manner. "A repeated segment is called a LOO-, LO--, L---, ----." The subject would be required to complete the segment. On each trial one less lettter would be provided than appeared in the previous trial. All four subjects in this study required fewer letters to complete the words both within and between trials. Furthermore, this method was superior to a repetition control method. Figure 12-6 demonstrates the number of letters required across trials for each of the four subjects.

Table 12-2. Teaching S.H. to Drink from a Cup

DAY	SESSIONS	STEPS								
		1	2	3	4	5	6	7	8	9
1	1	4	4	4	4	4	1	3	2	2
	2	2	2	2	2	1	1	2	2	2
	3	1	1	1	1	1	1	1	1	1
2	4	2	2	2	2	1	1	1	1	1
3	5	1	1	2	3	4	1	1	1	1
	6	1	2	2	4	4	1	1	1	1
	7	1	2	2	1	1*	1	1	2	1
4	8	1	2	1	3	4	1	2	1	1
	9	1	2	1	2	2	1	1	1	1
	10	1	2	1	2	2	1	1	1	1
	11	2	2	2	2	1	1	2	1	1
5	12	2	1	3	2	2	1	1	1	1
6	13	1	1	1	1	1	1	1	1	1
7	14	1	1	1	1	1	1	1	1	1
8	15	1	1	1	1	1	1	1	1	1

1 = complete step alone
2 = verbal prompt
3 = mild physical prompt
4 = physical guidance
* = additional step inserted

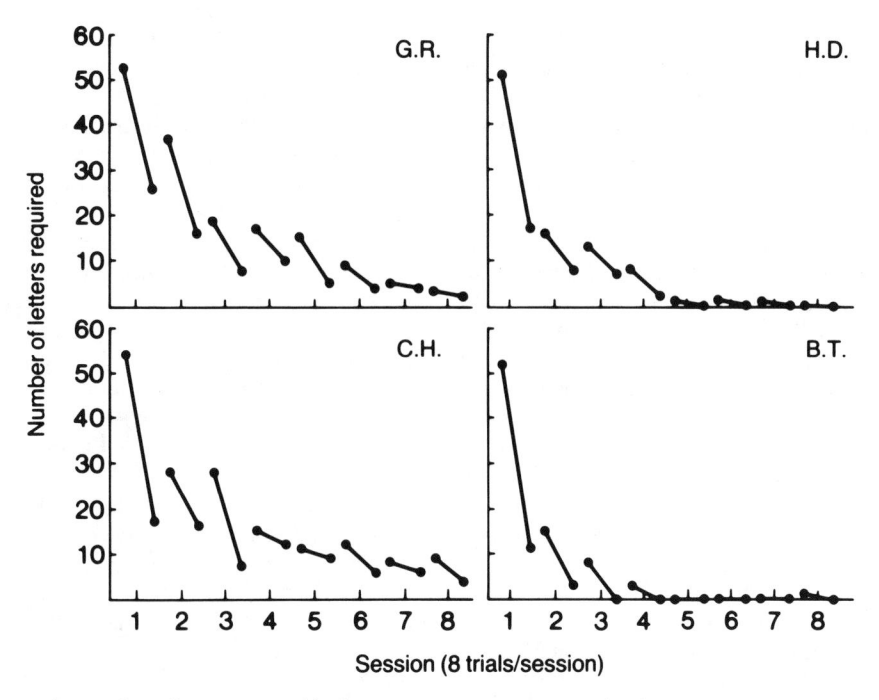

Figure 12.6. The number of letters required by four amnesic patients to complete fragments of computer-related words in the presence of their definitions. On a given trial, letters were added until the word was completed correctly. On the next trial, one less letter of the word was provided than was required for a correct response on the preceding trial. Sessions were conducted twice weekly. From "Learning and Retention of Computer-related Vocabulary in Memory Impaired Patients' Method of Vanishing Cues" by E. L. Glisky, D. L. Schacter, and E. Tulving, 1986, *Journal of Clinical and Experimental Neuropsychology*, 8, 292–312. Copyright 1982 by Swets and Zeitlinger. Reprinted by permission.

For one subject, C.H., Glisky and Schacter (1987) went on to teach her further computer skills with the result that she was able to obtain part-time work as a computer operator. Once the terminology had been learned through the method of vanishing cues, C.H. practiced this in order to speed up her responses to questions about the terminology.

A task analysis was then completed to determine what C.H. would need to learn in order to work at the job that was being offered to her. The task analysis identified the following steps:

1. Document discrimination.
2. Acquisition of rules and procedures.
3. Simulated job performance in the laboratory.
4. Performance in the workplace.
5. Task training on: 11 different documents; 14 different programs.

Over 250 individual items and components were taught using the method of vanishing cues. This took 6 months to complete but C.H. was able to carry out her work successfully even though she was unable to recount what her work entailed other than, "It's to do with computers."

The method of expanding rehearsal to teach names to a woman with dementia: The method of expanding rehearsal is employed to teach (or learn) new information. The information to be recalled (for instance, a new telephone number of a colleague's name) is presented to a subject who is then tested for recall immediately. Not surprisingly, success is virtually guaranteed provided immediate memory span is normal. The subject is then tested after a very brief delay of perhaps a few seconds, then after a slightly longer delay and so on. The gradual extension of delays frequently leads to better retention of information.

Landauer and Bjork (1978) demonstrated the superiority of expanding rehearsal over rote rehearsal (repetition) for normal subjects. Schacter, Rich, and Stampp (1985) demonstrated its effectiveness with amnesic patients. Although they called their method "spaced retrieval," it is identical to expanding rehearsal, and both procedures are similar to the shaping procedures of behavioral psychology whereby a final goal (in this case the learning of new information) is achieved through the gradual building up of behavior that becomes closer and closer to the optimum.

Moffat (in press) describes how a woman in her late 50s with Alzheimer's disease used the method of expanding rehearsal to reduce her nominal dysphasia. In addition to her word finding problems, Miss S. had generalized intellectual impairment and severe verbal memory deficits. The naming problem was the most noticeable deficit. She wrote down the names of any objects she could not recall in a test situation and practiced these items in between test sessions. She did not appear to retain the names for more than a few minutes, nor did she appear to be helped by first letter cues. Twenty pictures were given to Miss S. during each of five baseline sessions carried out prior to the expanding rehearsal program. She recalled very few of the 20 items (shown in Figure 12–7).

In the treatment stage Miss S. was given the name of a picture. Miss S. repeated the name and was tested on it after an interval of 2 minutes. If she named the picture correctly the retention interval was doubled, and if she was incorrect the interval was halved. Probe tests were conducted at regular intervals. The rapid increase in naming ability can also be seen in Figure 12–7. Furthermore, the latency of recall dropped from a mean of 30 seconds in the baseline to 8.5 seconds after nine training sessions.

Positive reinforcement in the form of computer feedback to improve exercising in children with cerebral palsy: Although this is a study with neurologically impaired children rather than adults it is included here as a good example of the use of positive reinforcement in rehabilitation and one which would be appropriate for use with adults. Lincoln (1978) claims that rest, praise, and feedback are the most powerful reinforcers in rehabilitation. (The use of feedback to decrease the amount of time taken to walk from one department to another was described earlier.)

Mackey (1989) was interested in the use of computer feedback for children with cerebral palsy. She worked with children who needed to perform spasticity inhibiting exercises daily. Mackey wanted to know whether feedback from a computer was superior to that provided by the child's physiotherapist. She conducted a series of ABA designs with six children, four boys and two girls, aged 4–12 years. In the baseline phase (the first A phase), each child was asked to carry out the spasticity inhibiting exercise, namely exerting pressure on a switch box connected to a computer. The optimal amount of pressure was the target to aim for. This optimal pressure was determined for each child. Too little would not inhibit

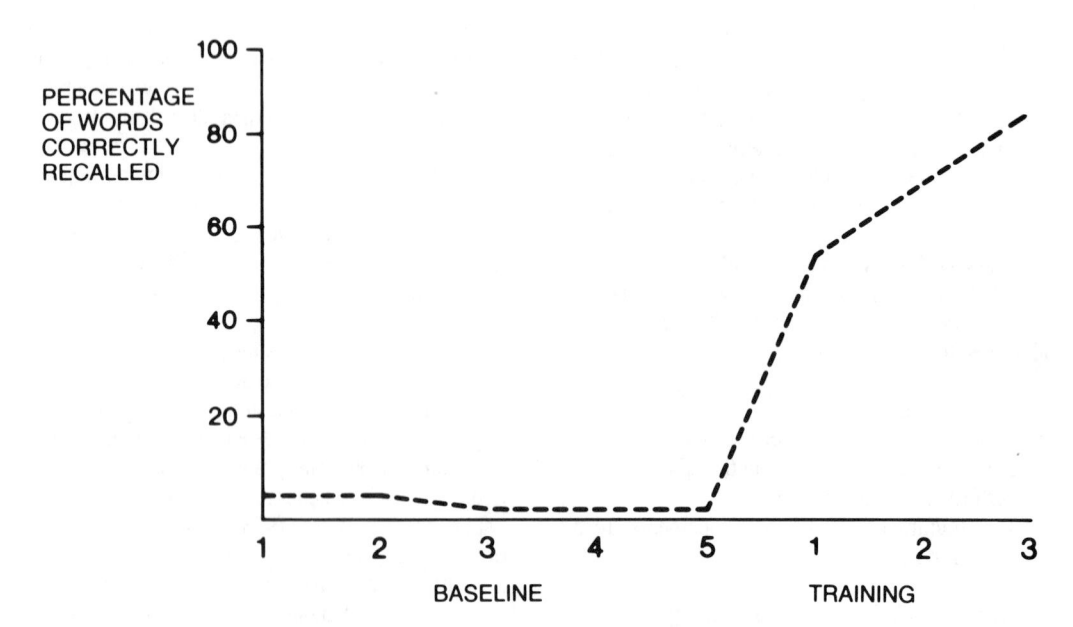

Figure 12.7. Retraining word retrieval with a dementia patient.

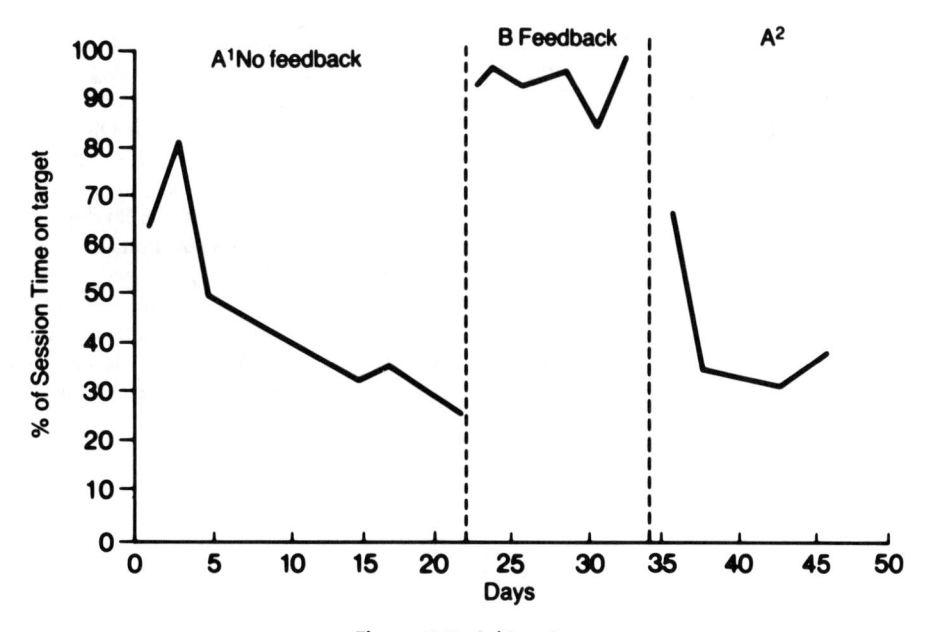

Figure 12.8. Subject C.

spasticity whereas too much could cause associated reactions. The amount of pressure exerted was recorded on computer and displayed on a monitor. The child was unable to see the computer, which was visible to the physiotherapist who was present throughout. The percentage of time-on-target for each child in each session was recorded on the computer. In the treatment phase (phase B) the child was able to see

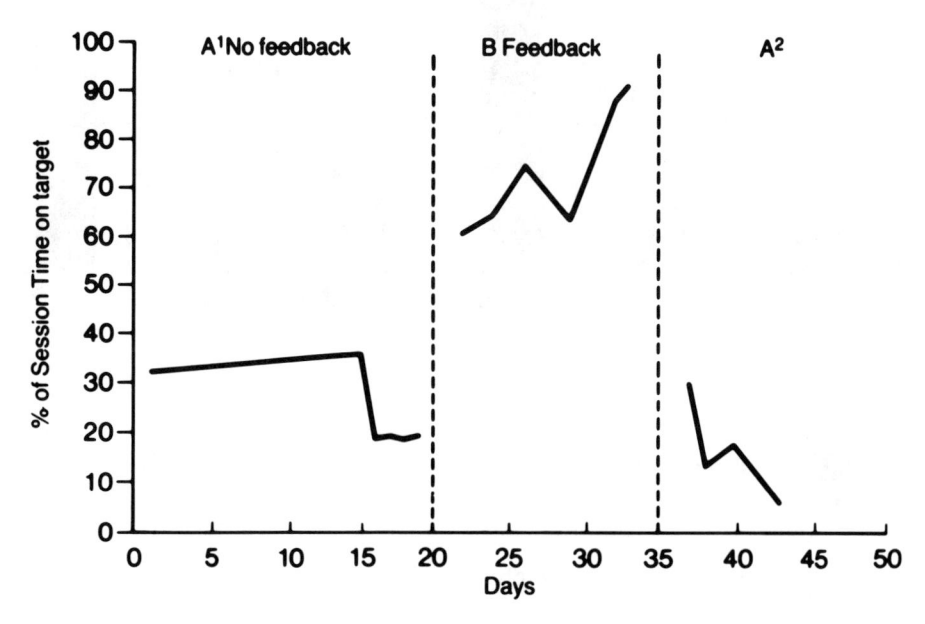

Figure 12.9. Subject D. Percentage of session time within target range. Data points are plotted from the percentage score and day of session. Vertical broken lines separate the A^1 (baseline), B (intervention) and A^2 (return to baseline) phases.

the results of his or her efforts on the screen. A colored column moved up the screen towards the target as pressure was exerted. Once the target was hit, a red and blue flashing light appeared. An audio cassette playing music was also triggered once the child reached the target area. In the second A phase the feedback was once again given by the physiotherapist. Figures 12–8 and 12–9 show the results of two of the six children. Every one showed a higher percentage of time-on-target under the computer feedback condition. This is confirmed by Figure 12–10. A one-way analysis of variance showed this was a significant difference (Table 12–3).

A modified Portage program to teach self-care skills to a quadriplegic woman: Portage, named after a town in Wisconsin, is a home-based teaching technique for parents of children with a mental handicap. It includes assessment that is carried out through the use of five developmental checklists and treatment programs that aim to "fill in" the developmental gaps. Wilson (1985) describes how Portage can be adapted for use with neurologically impaired adults.

A modified Portage program was first used by Wilson with this group in 1980 when asked to assess a woman who was left blind, dysphasic, hemiplegic, and apraxic as a result of an anaesthetic accident. The

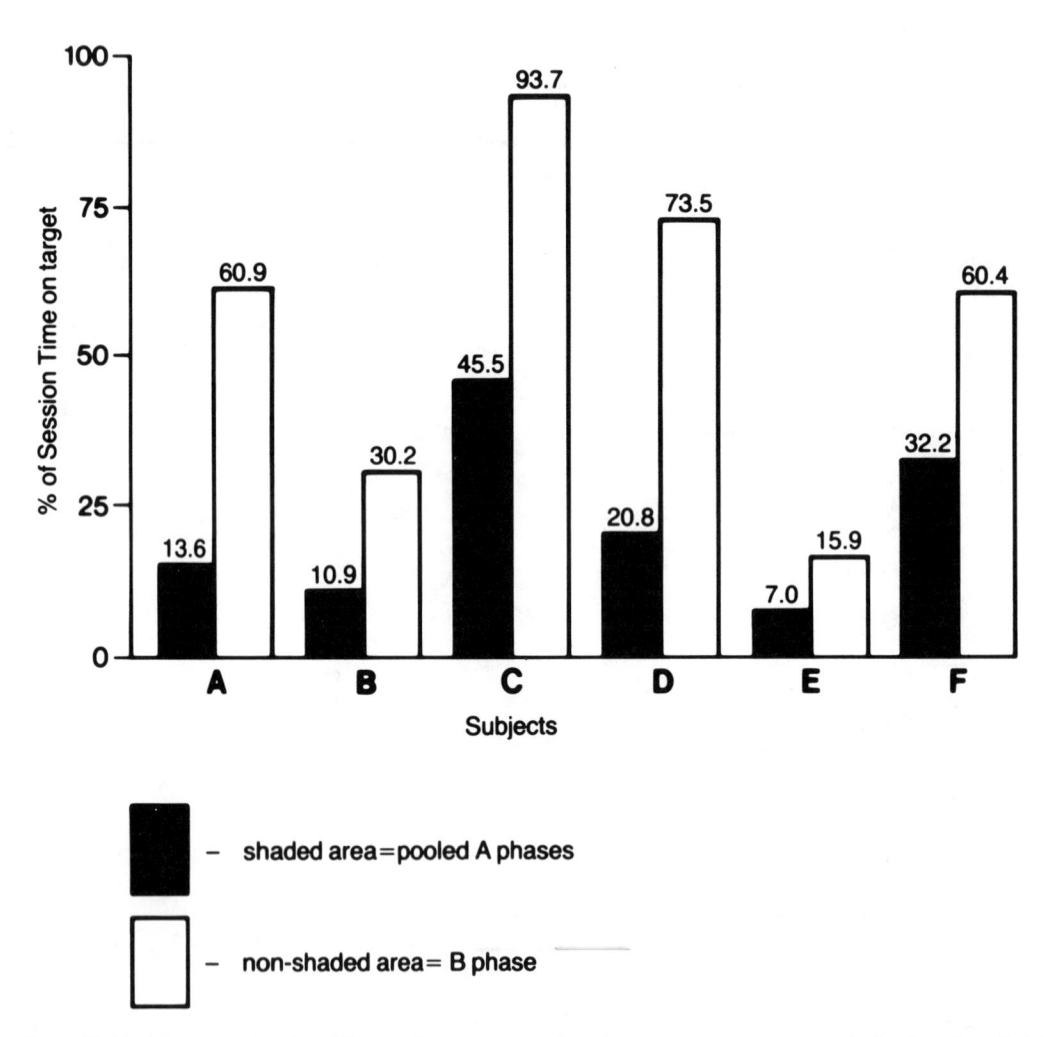

Figure 12.10. Histogram showing difference in percentage of session on target-mean scores during B and pooled A phases.

Table 12-3. One-Way Analysis of Variance Across Experimental Conditions

SUBJECT	F VALUES	LEVEL OF SIGNIFICANCE
A	107.65	$p < 0.001$
B	64.98	$p < 0.001$
C	15.55	$p < 0.001$
D	45.73	$p < 0.001$
E	10.21	$p < 0.01$
F	14.28	$p < 0.001$

rehabilitation staff wanted to know the level of her intellectual functioning. It is possible to administer psychological tests to people who cannot see, or cannot speak, or cannot move, but all the tests I know require at least one of these abilities. In the end I resorted to the Portage developmental checklist assessment that covers the areas of self-help, motor abilities, socialization, language, and cognition. The items range from birth to 6 years, and not all of them are appropriate for an adult, however extensive the handicap. Obviously categories such as "drinking from a bottle alone" and "waves goodbye in imitation of an adult" are unacceptable. However, the checklist offers one way of obtaining an objective score on the performance of very disabled people in a number of everyday life functions. The woman referred to here scored below the levels of a 2-year-old child on all five checklists. The first task selected for treatment was to teach her to "eat with a spoon independently."

Another young woman, L.H., was in her 30s when she developed brain stem encephalitis that left her with a quadriparesis and severe dysarthria. Cognitively, she had few problems but she could do very little for herself because of such severe weakness in her limbs. A modified Portage treatment approach was introduced. In the traditional Portage programs, parents act as teachers and one or two tasks are selected each week. The idea in selecting tasks is to ensure that the child is almost certain to succeed at something. The tasks are therefore small and achievable. The teaching procedure is carefully specified, reinforcers are identified, and correction procedures spelled out. When modifying Portage for adults, physiotherapists and occupational therapists can take the place of parents and the general principles of Portage can be followed.

The first task selected for L.H. was to teach her to drink half a cup of tea alone. She was to attempt this twice a day (at morning and afternoon breaks). The procedure was as follows:

1. L.H. to sit at the bench in the canteen.
2. Half a cup of tea to be placed in front of her and a bib attached to her front.
3. L.H. is to reach for the tea and drink alone. She can stop and start as she wishes, but should be finished by the end of tea break (15 minutes).

Success at the task, together with feedback charts, were considered to be sufficiently reinforcing. The correction procedure was: If L.H. cannot drink the tea alone (a) try verbal encouragement, (b) try a weighted cuff (this often helps people with very shaky hands), (c) guide her hand through the task. Figure 12–11 shows the progress of L.H. during the first week. From the chart we can see that L.H. did succeed in her first task by the end of the first week but another week was spent on this task before introducing a second task so as not to overtax her.

Although it might have seemed logical to set the next task of drinking two thirds or three quarters of a cup of tea, we did not do this as L.H.'s quadriparesis was sufficient to make the extra weight of the cup impossible for her to manage.

Eight further tasks were set over the following weeks. L.H. succeeded on six of these within the week. The two tasks failed were deemed by the psychologist and therapists to have been wrongly selected owing to the degree of severity they presented L.H. Table 12–4 shows the 10 tasks set during the 10 weeks the program was operating. The structured approach to treatment, selection of appropriate goals for widely differing individual needs, and the provision of feedback for patients, relatives, and staff make this behavioral approach eminently suitable for neurologically impaired adults.

	MON baseline	TUES	WEDS	THURS	FRI	MON post baseline
a.m.	√ 3	√ 3	√ 3	√ 1	√ √	√ √
p.m.	√ 3	√ 3	√ 3	√ 1	√ √	√ √

1 = verbal encouragement
3 = physical guidance
√ √ = without help

Figure 12.11. Teaching L.H. to drink half a cup of tea without assistance.

SINGLE-CASE EXPERIMENTAL DESIGNS IN THE TREATMENT OF NEUROLOGICAL PATIENTS

Single-case experimental designs in the treatment of humans originated with behavioral psychologists (for example, Skinner, 1938; Watson & Raynor, 1920), and it is not difficult to convince behavior therapists and behavior modifiers of their value. Problems occur, however, when attempts are made to persuade the medical profession, therapists, and other psychologists to adopt a similar attitude. Yet there are a number of very good reasons why reversal designs, multiple baseline designs, and other single-case experimental designs contribute to an accurate evaluation of treatment effectiveness with neurologically impaired people.

One of the major reasons why the more conventional group designs are limited is because it is so difficult to find homogeneous groups of neurological patients. People who have sustained a severe head injury, for example, will probably have a combination of problems and, furthermore, this combination is rarely matched in two individuals. If we want to find out which memory therapy or social skills training works best for head injured people as a group we need to take into account the physical, cognitive, behavioral, and emotional functioning. To find people with similar levels of deficit in these areas is virtually impossible.

In addition, some of the neuropsychological deficits seen in neurological patients are very rare. Take visual object agnosia, for example, a disorder of recognition that is not the result of poor visual acuity or language problems or severe generalized intellectual deterioration. Patients with this disorder are very rare yet can be helped by certain treatment procedures (see, for example, Wilson, in press a). However, if we waited for numbers of these patients to be gathered in order to conduct a group study then we would be waiting for a very long time indeed.

Table 12-4. Tasks Set in the Modified Portage Program for L.H.

WEEK	TASK	ACHIEVED
1	drink half cup of tea alone	yes
2	drink half cup of tea alone	yes
3	take off shoes	yes
4	put on shoes	no
5	wash and dry hands	yes
6	clean teeth alone	yes
7	maneuvre wheelchair round a table	yes
8	put on track suit trousers	yes
9	increase no. of times round the table	yes
10	open door into and out of workshops	yes (out) no (in)

It is the individual who is being treated and who needs to return home and to work, yet group studies rarely reveal insights into the problems of an individual within the group. Gianutsos and Gianutsos (1987) remind us that individuals risk becoming stuck in the tails of group designs. To illustrate, let us consider the following scenario: a group study is conducted to investigate the effect of a particular treatment on a number of stroke patients. Seventy per cent of subjects show an improvement of between 25–50% over baseline. A further 15% do better than that with an improvement over 50% above baseline. The remaining 15% show little or no improvement over baseline. It is this 15% who are likely to need help from clinical psychologists. The group study showed there was a significant effect of treatment and yet 15% failed to respond. What do we do? We have to find other solutions for these patients' problems and evaluate the effectiveness of these solutions through single-case designs. We need to carry out a behavioral analysis of each problem and monitor our intervention strategies.

It is difficult to do this with group designs as they tend to take only one or two readings per patient. Furthermore, the treatment is specified prior to the study taking place, and it is not possible to adjust treatment during the trials. If we had not been allowed to adjust treatment with S.H., described above, and inserted an extra step during her program, she would have continued to spill liquid down her dress for a long time.

It would be wrong to undervalue group studies, indeed answers to many questions can only be obtained through group studies. However, in treating individual neurological patients, group studies are of limited value. They do not help us answer the question: "Is my treatment the cause of this person's change?" To answer this question it is necessary to use a behavioral program and/or a single-case experimental design. These issues are discussed in more detail in relation to neurological patients in Wilson (1987c) and Gianutsos and Gianutsos (1987).

OTHER INFLUENCES ON THE TREATMENT OF NEUROLOGICAL PATIENTS

Although it would appear that behavioral psychology is perhaps the major source of treatment techniques for behavioral, cognitive, social, and emotional problems, there are other sources such as cognitive psychology and neuropsychology which have also been influential.

Cognitive psychology is valuable mainly because of its models of functioning of, for example, human memory (Baddeley, 1982), and the dual route model of reading (Coltheart, 1985). Such models allow us to conceptualize what is happening in a given disorder and help to explain where we are and where we are going.

Furthermore, ideas for treatment can come from the cognitive psychologist's explanations of breakdown in memory, reading, perception, or language. For example, three major theories have been offered to explain the human amnesic syndrome. (a) That it is a result of an encoding deficit; (b) that it is due to a storage deficit, and (c) that it is due to faulty retrieval. While none of these can explain all cases of the human amnesic syndrome, there are patients who have problems with encoding, others who have problems with storage, and still others who have problems with retrieval. We can improve encoding, storage, and retrieval in some cases through employing procedures developed by cognitive psychologists to lend support to their theories. In memory therapy, for example, we can simplify information, teach organization strategies and encourage deeper levels of processing based on the work of Craik and Lockhart (1972) when we need to help patients encode information. It may be advantageous to refer to the findings of encoding-specificity (Tulving, 1972) and context dependent learning (Godden & Baddeley, 1975) when attempting to increase generalization in therapy programs. Our patients could be taught in different contexts and situations to avoid encoding-specificity and context-dependent learning.

Cognitive psychologists have been interested for many years in the learning abilities of amnesic patients. A number of studies have shown that amnesic patients can learn some skills normally or almost normally despite having no conscious awareness of this learning (Brooks & Baddeley, 1976; Moscovitch, 1982; Warrington & Weiskrantz, 1973 and 1982). Graf & Schacter (1985) demonstrated the priming effect with amnesic subjects. Following on from this finding, Schacter and Glisky (1986) (described earlier) developed the method of vanishing cues.

We also know that amnesic people can learn some paired-associates if the pairs are phonemically or semantically related (Winocur & Weiskrantz, 1976). Thus a patient can learn cat-mat and up-down but not cat-down or mat-up. Psychologists can capitalize on this knowledge when teaching amnesic patients as Schacter and his colleagues have done. So, for example, if employing one of the mnemonic systems to teach information, we should not use bizarre images as Lorayne (1979) would have us do. Instead we should try for logical associations because they are easier to remember.

The dual-route model of reading proposed by Coltheart (1985) has been invoked to explain the success of two reading remediation programs (Wilson, 1987b), and it should certainly be possible to refer to the model to plan treatment programs for reading impaired people in the way that Byng (1988) has employed language models to identify and remediate specific deficits in dysphasic patients.

The discipline of neuropsychology has also contributed to the treatment of neurologically impaired people by increasing knowledge of the organization of the brain. Since the work of Broca and Dax in the 1800s, we have learned a considerable amount about the functions of different areas of the brain. Most right handed, severe dysphasics have left hemisphere lesions; people with bilateral hippocampal damage are likely to be severely amnesic; letter-by-letter readers will probably have a lesion in the left parieto-occipital area, and so forth. We can use our understanding of the human brain to help some of our patients. Wilson (1981b), for example, working with a man who had a left temporal lobe tumor removed, used a treatment procedure that involved the man's intact right hemisphere skills. Patients with right hemisphere lesions and visuo-spatial impairments can be taught to turn visual tasks into verbal ones to compensate. Other approaches to treatment that have come from neuropsychology include Brain Function Therapy described by Buffery (1976) in which he tried to develop language functioning in the right hemisphere of a patient who had sustained a left hemisphere lesion. Results were, however, equivocal (see Miller, 1984 for a discussion). This anatomical reorganization or finding alternative pathways in the brain is little understood, but Passingham (1988) argues that many systems in the brain are organized in parallel so the brain can cope with damage in part of a system by using other pathways. Again, Miller (1984) provides a discussion about anatomical reorganization.

Although we still have a long way to go before understanding the capacity of the brain to reorganize or strengthen existing but previously weak pathways, we can be fairly certain that efforts to comprehend such matters will be more successful if we draw upon the theories, models, and investigative research of the three disciplines I have outlined rather than simply relying upon one of them.

Recent interest in fetal transplants for Parkinson's patients may eventually lead to viable surgical procedures for helping the neurologically impaired. If this should happen, then it is likely that such procedures will be operated in conjunction with pharmacological agents and neuropsychological, cognitive, and behavioral rehabilitation.

CONCLUSION

This chapter focused mainly on patients with acquired nonprogressive brain damage sustained through traumatic injury, infection, or cerebral vascular accident. There are large numbers of these people surviving with one or more of the problems described in this chapter, yet little is provided to help survivors reduce, manage, or by-pass the problems they are left with once the acute stage is over. This failure to provide adequate rehabilitation is challenged by evidence suggesting that behavioral approaches can be effective in remediating a variety of problems even several years after initial insult.

It is likely that behavior therapists can contribute most fully to the treatment of neurological handicaps when they combine their skills with those of occupational, speech, and physiotherapists. Such teams are capable of maximizing the learning potential of their clients, they can formulate varied sets of specific objectives, they can offer a broad range of opportunities for developing skills, and can evaluate learning outcomes in both depth and detail.

Behavior therapy's major strength lies in its principles that are capable of being applied to almost any problem we are likely to encounter. Referrals to a clinical psychologist may be inappropriate. For example, I have been asked to "make this man into a nicer person"; "improve this woman's motivation"; "teach A.W. to read again"; and "memory retraining please." Applying the principles of behavior therapy to such ill-defined goals involves defining specific problem behaviors that can be tackled separately. The saying that "structure reduces anxiety" is as true for therapists as it is for patients. With the patient, whose behavior was quite violent and whose referral asked that he should be "made into a nicer person," an operational definition was used to ensure that he did not throw chairs at the nurses, did not swear, and did not leave the hospital grounds without informing someone and obtaining leave of absence. Once such objectives were agreed by the therapy team, we were able to take baselines and systematically try out various procedures to achieve the respective outcomes.

Direct observations and behavioral interviewing of the woman whose motivation needed improving revealed that her poor level of motivation was based on her feeling that she had not progressed despite several weeks at the rehabilitation center. The solution here was to demonstrate that she was indeed improving so an adapted Portage program was initiated to select appropriate tasks, chart progress, and provide feedback.

It is not always possible to teach a person to read if that person's dyslexia is the result of brain injury (Wilson, 1987 c). However, neuropsychological and behavioral assessments will enable us to find out what precise reading skills are intact and what are impaired. Some patients, for example, can read nouns but not verbs; others can read regular but not irregular words; others cannot read individual letters although they can tell if a letter is upside down or not, thus demonstrating that they can "see" the letter and have thus retained some knowledge of orthography. After a detailed assessment it might be possible to reteach certain letters or words or sound combinations. If this fails, it might be possible to teach reading through an alternative route. Some patients, for example, can read through a tactile route—by tracing with their fingers the letters of the words they read.

Whereas it might be demonstrated that people can improve on memory exercises they have been given, there is no evidence to support the notion that such exercises actually improve memory performance in general. Ericsson, Chase, & Falconer (1980), for example, gave some students practice on digit span tests. One student increased his digit span from the normal 7 plus 2 to a phenomenal 80 plus, yet when tested on a very similar letter span task his score returned to the normal 7 plus or minus 2. No transfer of learning had accurred. Although it appears to be the case that exercises themselves cannot improve general memory functioning, there are other means that can be used to offer real help to memory impaired people so that their lives are less fraught with accompanying difficulties. By using a behavioral framework we can define particular problems that result from an impaired memory system and tackle these through standard behavioral procedures, always bearing in mind, of course, the neuropsychological status of the patient.

Behavioral therapy techniques are now well established in rehabilitation regimes. The richness and complexity of multifaceted behavioral approaches make them ideally suited to the range and complexity of deficits shown by neurologically impaired people. Despite their acceptance by psychologists and other therapists we must still convince neurologists and others in the medical profession that rehabilitation is worthwhile. Because it is not often possible to restore lost functioning, many medical people believe that nothing can be done. This is manifestly untrue as can be seen in the many examples in this chapter. We need, I think, to follow the lead of many psychologists working in the field of mental handicap, who uphold a principle that suggests that if a person with a mental handicap cannot learn, it is because the psychologist has not found the right way to teach the person. Once the onus is on the teacher, it is possible to reformulate objectives and methods in the pursuit of real learning outcomes. It is surely insufficient to suggest (as some neurologists and neuropsychologists have done) that failure in learning is the end result of a physical injury such as a lesion in the hippocampus or a right parietal infarct. Behavioral psychologists have contributed the former principle to the scientific and medical world; they must now convince and indeed win over their fellow rehabilitationists so that neurological patients will be more widely helped to reduce the impact of their problems on their daily lives.

REFERENCES

Baddeley, A. D. (1982). Implications of neuropsychological evidence for theories of normal memory. *Philosophical Transactions of the Royal Society London, B, 298,* 59–72.

Booraem, C. D., & Seacat, G. F. (1972). Effects of increased incentive in corrective therapy. *Perceptual and Motor Skills, 34,* 125–126.

British Psychological Society (1989). *Report on psychology and physical disability.* Leicester, England: BPS.

British Psychological Society (in press). *Report on psychological services to young people with acquired brain damage.* Leicester, England: BPS.

Brooks, D. N. (1984). *Closed head injury: Psychological, social and family consequences.* Oxford: Oxford University Press.

Brooks, D. N., & Baddeley, A. (1976). What can amnesics learn? *Neuropsychologia, 14,* 111–122.

Buffery, A. W. H. (1976). Clinical neuropsychology: a review and preview. In S. Rachman (Ed.), *Contributions to medical psychology* (pp. 115–136). Oxford: Pergamon Press.

Byng, S. (1988). Sentence processing deficits: theory and therapy. *Cognitive Neuropsychology, 5,* 629–676.

Carr, S., & Wilson, B. (1983). Promotion of pressure relief exercising in a spinal injury patient: A multiple baseline across settings design. *Behavioural Psychotherapy, 11,* 329–336.

Cautela, J. R. (1981). *Organic dysfunction survey schedules.* Champaign, IL: Research Press.

Collins, F. L., Ricci, J. A., & Burkett, P. A. (1981).

Behavioural training for myopia: long term maintenance of improved acuity. *Behaviour Research and Therapy, 19*, 265–268.

Coltheart, M. (1985). Cognitive neuropsychology and the study of reading. In M. Posner & O. S. M. Marin (Eds.), *Attention and performance (Vol. 11)* (pp. 3–37). Hillsdale, NJ: Lawrence Erlbaum Associates.

Craik, F. I. M., & Lockhart, R. S. (1972). Levels of processing: a framework for memory research. *Journal of Verbal Learning and Verbal Behaviour, 11*, 671–684.

Diller, L., & Gordon, W. A. (1981). Rehabilitation and clinical neuropsychology. In S.B. Filskov & T.J. Boll (Eds.), *Handbook of clinical neuropsychology* (pp. 702–733). New York: John Wiley & Sons.

Diller, L., & Weinberg, J. (1977). Hemi-inattention in rehabilitation: the evolution of a rational remediation program. In E. A. Weinstein & R. P. Friedland (Eds.), *Advances in Neurology, Vol. 18*. New York: Raven Press.

Eames, P. (1989). Head injury rehabilitation: towards a 'model' service. In R. LL. Wood & P. Eames (Eds.), *Models of Brain Injury Rehabilitation* (pp. 48–58). London: Chapman.

Ericsson, K. A., Chase, W. G., & Falconer, S. (1980). Acquisition of a memory skill. *Science, 208*, 1181–1182.

Foster, S. L., & Cone, J. D. (1986). Design and use of direct observation procedures. In A. R. Ciminero, K. S. Calhoun & H. E. Adams (Eds.), *Handbook of Behavioural Assessment (2nd ed.)*. New York: John Wiley & Sons.

Gardner, H., Zurif, E. B., Berry, T., & Baker, E. (1976). Visual communication in aphasia. *Neuropsychologia, 14*, 275–292.

Gianutsos, R., & Gianutsos, J. (1987). Single-case experimental approaches to the assessment of intervention in rehabilitation. In B. Caplan (Ed.), *Rehabilitation Psychology Desk Reference*. Rockville, MD: Aspen Corporation.

Glisky, E. L., & Schacter, D. L. (1986). Long-term retention of computer learning by patients with memory disorders. *Neuropsychologia, 26*, 173–178.

Glisky, E. L., & Schacter, D. L. (1987). Acquisition of domain-specific knowledge in organic amnesia: training for computer-related work. *Neuropsychologia, 25*, 893–906.

Glisky, E. L., Schacter, D. L., & Tulving, E. (1986). Learning and retention of computer-related vocabulary in memory impaired patients' method of vanishing cues. *Journal of Clinical and Experimental Neuropsychology, 8*, 292–312.

Godden, D., & Baddeley, A. D. (1975). Context-dependent memory in two natural environments: on land and under water. *British Journal of Psychology, 66*, 325–331.

Goldstein, G. (1984). Methodological and theoretical issues in neuropsychological assessment. In B. A. Edelstein & E. T. Couture (Eds.), *Behavioural Assessment and Rehabilitation of the Traumatically Brain-Damaged*. New York: Plenum.

Goll, S., & Hawley, K. (1989). Social rehabilitation: the role of the transitional living centre. In R. L. Wood & P. Eames (Eds.), *Models of Brain Injury Rehabilitation*. London: Chapman & Hall.

Goodkin, R. (1966). Case studies in behavioural research in rehabilitation. *Perceptual and Motor Skills, 23*, 171–182.

Goodkin, R. (1969). Changes in word production, sentence production and relevance in an aphasic through verbal conditioning. *Behaviour Research and Therapy, 7*, 93–99.

Graf, P., & Schacter, D. L. (1985). Implicit and explicit memory for new associations in normal and amnesic subjects. *Journal of Experimental Psychology: Learning, Memory and Cognition, 11*, 501–518.

Gray, J., & Robertson, I. (1987). Remediation of attention and concentration deficits after brain injury using computerised procedures. *Neuroscience Letters Supplement, 29*, 132.

Hammond, A. (1987). *Joint protection behaviour of patients with rheumatoid arthritis following an education programme*. Unpublished Master's thesis, University of Southampton, England.

Heilman, K. M. (1979). Apraxia. In K. M. Heilman & E. Valenstein (Eds.), *Clinical Neuropsychology* (pp. 159–185). New York: Oxford University Press.

Holland, A. L. (1980). *Communicative Abilities in Daily Living*. Baltimore: University Park Press.

Horton, A. M., & Miller, W. G. (1985). Neuropsychology and behaviour therapy. In M. Hersen, R. M. Eisler & P. M. Miller (Eds.), *Progress in Behavior Modification, Vol. 19*. New York: Academic Press.

Ince, L. P. (1969). A behavioural approach to motivation in rehabilitation. *Psychological Record, 19*, 105–111.

Ince, L. P. (1976). *Behaviour Modification in Rehabilitation Medicine*. London: Williams & Wilkins.

Ince, L. P. (1980). *Behaviour Psychology in Rehabilitation Medicine*. Baltimore: Williams & Wilkins.

Landauer, T. K., & Bjork, R. A. (1978). Optimum rehearsal patterns and name learning. In M. M. Gruneberg, P. E. Morris, & R. N. Sykes (Eds.), *Practical Aspects of Memory*. London: Academic Press.

Lane, H. (1977). *The Wild Boy of Aveyron*. London: Paladin-Granada.

Liepman, H. (1920). Reported in K. M. Heilman & E. Valenstein (Eds.), 1979. New York: Oxford University Press.

Lincoln, N. B. (1978). Behaviour modification in physiotherapy. *Physiotherapy, 64*, 265–267.

Lincoln, N. B. (1979). *An investigation of the effect of the effectiveness of language retraining methods with aphasic stroke patients*. Unpublished doctoral dissertation, University of London.

Livingstone, M. G., Brooks, D. N., & Bond, M. R. (1985). Patient outcome in the year following severe head injury and relatives' psychiatric and social functioning. *Journal Neurology, Neurosurgery and Psychiatry 48*, 876–881.

Lorayne, H. (1979). *How to develop a super power memory*. Wellingborough, England: A. Thomas & Co.

Luria, A. R. (1963). *Recovery of Function after Brain Injury.* New York: Macmillan.

Luria, A. R. (1973). *The Working Brain.* New York: Basic Books.

Luria, A. R., Naydin, V. L., Tsvetkova, L. S., & Vinarskaya, E. N. (1969). Restoration of higher cortical function following local brain damage. In P. J. Vinken & G. W. Bruyn (Eds.), *Handbook of Clinical Neurology, Vol. 3.* Amsterdam: North Holland.

Mackey, S. (1989). The use of computer assisted feedback in a motor control exercise for cerebral palsied children. *Physiotherapy, 75,* 143–148.

McKinlay, W. W., Brooks, D. N., Bond, M. R., Martinage, D. P., & Marshall, M. M. (1981). The short term outcome of severe blunt head injured as reported by relatives of the injured person. *Journal of Neurology, Neurosurgery and Psychiatry, 44,* 527–533.

Miller, E. (1984). *Recovery and Management of Neuropsychological Impairments.* Chichester: John Wiley & Sons.

Moffat, N. (in press). Home based rehabilitation programmes for the elderly. In L. Poon, D. Rubin, & B. Wilson (Eds.), *Everyday Cognition in Adult and Later Life.* New York: Guilford Press.

Moscovitch, M. (1982). Multiple dissociation of function in amnesia. In L. Cermak (Ed.), *Human Memory and Amnesia.* Hillsdale, NJ: Lawrence Erlbaum Associates.

Murphy, G., & Goodall, E. (1980). Measurement error in direct observations: a comparison of common recording methods. *Behaviour Research and Therapy, 18,* 147–150.

Navia, B. A., Jordan, B. D., & Price, R. W. (1986). The AIDS dementia complex: 1. Clinical features. *Annals of Neurology, 19,* 517–524.

Passingham, R. (1988, February 11). Quoted in "Engineering for broken down brains," *New Scientist,* p. 33.

Powell, G. E. (1981). *Brain Function Therapy.* Aldershot, England: Gower Press.

Ross, E. D. (1983). Right-hemisphere lesions in disorders of affective language. In A. Kertesz (Ed.), *Localization in Neuropsychology* (pp. 493–508). New York: Academic Press.

Royal College of Physicians. (1986). Physical disability in 1986 and beyond. *Journal of the Royal College of Physicians, 20,* 160–194.

Schacter, D. L., & Glisky, E. L. (1986). Memory remediation: restoration, alleviation and the acquisition of domain-specific knowledge. In B. P. Uzzell & Y. Gross (Eds.), *Clinical Neuropsychology of Intervention,* (pp. 257–282). Boston: Martinus Nijhoff.

Schacter, D. L., Rich, S. A., & Stampp, M. S. (1985). Remediation of memory disorders: experimental evaluation of the spaced retrieval technique. *Journal of Clinical and Experimental Neuropsychology, 7,* 79–96.

Schuerman, J. A. (1983). *Rehabilitation of behaviour disorders in patients suffering from cerebral damage.* Paper presented at the first European conference of the Society for Research in Rehabilitation, Edinburgh.

Searleman, A. (1977). A review of right hemisphere linguistic capabilities. *Psychological Bulletin, 84,* 503–528.

Skinner, B. F. (1938). *The Behavior of Organisms.* New York: Appleton-Century-Crofts.

Sundberg, N. D., & Tyler, L. E. (1962). *Clinical Psychology.* New York: Appleton-Century-Crofts.

Sunderland, A., Harris, J. E., & Gleave, J. (1984). Memory failures in everyday life after severe head injury. *Journal of Clinical Neuropsychology, 6,* 127–142.

Talbott, R. (1989). The brain-injured person and the family. In R. L. Wood & P. Eames (Eds.), *Models of Brain Injury Rehabilitation* (pp. 3–16). London: Chapman & Hall.

Taylor, G. P., & Persons, R. W. (1970). Behaviour modification techniques in a physical medicine and rehabilitation center. *Journal of Psychology, 74,* 117–124.

Trexler, L. (1982). (Ed.), *Cognitive Rehabilitation, Conceptualization and Intervention.* New York: Plenum Press.

Tulving, E. (1972). Episodic and semantic memory. *Organization of Memory.* New York: Academic Press.

Uzzell, B. P., & Gross, Y. (1986). *Clinical Neuropsychology of Intervention.* Boston: Martinus Nijhoff.

Wang, P. L., & Ennis, K. E. (1986). Competency assessment in clinical populations: an introduction to the cognitive competency test. In B. P. Uzzell & Y. Gross (Eds.), *Clinical Neuropsychology of Intervention.* Boston: Martinus Nijhoff.

Warrington, E. K., & Weiskrantz, L. (1973). An analysis of short-term and long-term memory deficits in man. *The Physiological Basis of Memory,* (pp. 365–396). New York: Academic Press.

Warrington, E. K., & Weiskrantz, L. (1982). Amnesia: a disconnection syndrome? *Neuropsychologia, 20,* 233–248.

Watson, J. B., & Rayner, R. (1920). Conditioned emotional reactions. *Journal of Experimental Psychology, 3,* 1–14.

Weinberg, J., Diller, L., Gordon, W.A., Gerstman, L. J., Lieberman, A., Lakin, P., Hodges, G., & Ezrachi, O. (1979). Training sensory awareness and spatial organization in people with right brain damage. *Archives of Physical Medicine and Rehabilitation, 60,* 491–496.

Wilson, B. A. (1981a). A survey of behavioural treatments carried out at a rehabilitation centre for stroke and head injuries. In G. Powell (Ed.), *Brain Function Therapy.* Aldershot, England: Gower Press.

Wilson, B. A. (1981b). Teaching a patient to remember people's names after removal of a left temporal lobe tumour. *Behavioural Psychotherapy, 9,* 338–344.

Wilson, B. A. (1985). Adapting "Portage" for neurological patients. *International Rehabilitation Medicine, 7,* 6–8.

Wilson, B. A. (1986). Cognitive rehabilitation following severe head injury. In D. Glasgow & N. Eisenberg (Eds.), *Current Issues in Clinical Psychology.* Aldershot: Gower Press.

Wilson, B. A. (1987a). Clinical psychology and the care of the neurologically impaired. In H. Dent (Ed.), *Clinical Psychology Research and Developments* (pp. 310–316). London: Croom Helm.

Wilson, B. A. (1987b). *Rehabilitation of Memory*. New York: Gulford Press.
Wilson, B. A. (1987c). Single case experimental designs in neuropsychological rehabilitation. *Journal of Clinical and Experimental Neuropsychology, 9*, 527–544.
Wilson, B. A. (1988). Remediation of apraxia following an anaesthetic accident. In J. West & P. Spinks (Eds.), *Case Studies in Clinical Psychology*. London: John Wright & Sons.
Wilson, B. A. (1989). Models of cognitive rehabilitation. In R. L. Wood & P. Eames (Eds.), *Models of Brain Injury Rehabilitation*. London: Chapman & Hall.
Wilson, B. A. (in press a). Management of problems resulting from damage to the Central Nervous System. To appear in S. Pearce & J. Wardle (Eds.), *The Practice of Behavioural Medicine*. Oxford: Oxford University Press.
Wilson, B. A. (in press b). Cognitive rehabilitation for brain injured adults. To appear in B. Deelman (Ed.), *Traumatic Brain Injury*. Lisse, Netherlands: Swets & Zeitlinger.
Wilson, B. A., Cockburn, J., & Baddeley, A. D. (1985). *The Rivermead Behavioural Memory Test Manual*. Published by Thames Valley Test Co., 34 The Square, Titchfield, Hants, England.
Wilson, B. A., Cockburn, J., & Baddeley, A. D. (1989). Assessment of everyday memory following brain injury. In M. E. Miner & K. A. Wagner (Eds.), *Neurotrauma: Treatment, Rehabilitation and Related Issues 3*, (pp. 83–89). London: Butterworths.
Wilson, B. A., Cockburn, J., Baddeley, A. D., & Hiorns, R. (in press). The development and validation of a test battery for detecting and monitoring everyday memory problems. *Journal of Clinical and Experimental Neuropsychology*.
Wilson, B. A., Cockburn, J., & Halligan, P. (1987). The development of a behavioural test of visuospatial neglect. *Archives of Physical Medicine and Rehabilitation, 68*, 98–102.
Wilson, B. A., & Moffat, N. (1984). Rehabilitation of memory for everyday life. In J. Harris & P. Morris (Eds.), *Everyday Memory: Actions and Absent Mindedness*. London: Academic Press.
Winocur, G., & Weiskrantz, L. (1976). An investigation of paired-associate learning in amnesic patients. *Neuropsychologia, 14*, 97–110.
Wood, R. L. (1984). Attention training. In B. A. Wilson & N. Moffat (Eds.), *Clinical Management of Memory Problems*. London: Croom Helm.
Wood, R. L. (1987). *Brain Injury Rehabilitation: A Neurobehavioural Approach*. London: Croom Helm.
Wood, R. L. (1988). Attention disorders in brain injury rehabilitation. *Journal of Learning Disabilities, 21*, 327–333.
Wood, R. L., & Eames, P. G. (1981). Application of behavioural modification of traumatically brain injured adults. In G. Davey (Ed.), *Application of Conditioning Theory*. London: Methuen.
Yule, W., & Carr, J. (1987). (Eds.), *Behaviour Modification for the Mentally Handicapped* (2nd ed.). London: Croom Helm.
Zaidel, E. (1977). Unilateral auditory language comprehension on the Token Test following commissurotomy and hemispherectomy. *Neuropsychologia, 15*, 1–18.

PART III
SOCIAL PSYCHOLOGY

CHAPTER 13

HISTORY AND THEORIES OF SOCIAL PSYCHOLOGY: THEIR RELEVANCE TO BEHAVIOR THERAPY

John H. Harvey
Mary L. Burgess
Terri L. Orbuch

The question we have been asked to address is: How are social psychological theories related to behavior therapy? In the course of providing our answer, we will trace various historical developments in the field of social psychology that have been particularly relevant to events unfolding in behavioral theory and practice. At the outset, we should note our own predilections as scholars. The first two authors are psychological social psychologists, and the third is a sociological social psychologist. As a result of our backgrounds, we have chosen to inquire about possible linkages that may not have been discussed in previous analyses of social psychology's relevance for behavior theory and therapy (e.g., the reader is referred to a thoughtful treatment by Cantor & Kihlstrom, 1982). As one unique aspect of our presentation, we will describe Mead's (1934) conception of social behaviorism that has had an enduring impact in sociological social psychology (via the school of thought known as symbolic interactionism), but that has hardly been noticed in previous analyses of the relevance of social psychological theory to behavior therapy. We also will discuss the importance of extant, relevant work from psychological social psy-

chology such as Bem's (1972) theory of self-perception.

At the heart of social psychology's relevance to behavioral approaches are four decades of work in the field that have emphasized how learning theory may be applied to social behavior and perception. As part of the following historical sketch, we will trace the evolution of learning theory in the field from the 1940s to the cognitive revolution that swept the field in the late 1950s and early 1960s. Following our historical sketch, we will highlight major theoretical developments, first during the 1950s and 1960s and then in the last two decades, which have been dominated by cognitive theories.

DEFINITION AND HISTORICAL SKETCH

To begin, we should note that the field of social psychology always has been, above all else, a branch of general (and usually experimental) psychology. It is a broadly defined field, to wit G. Allport's (1968) classic definition: "an attempt to understand and explain how the thought, feeling, and behavior of individuals are influenced by the actual, imagined, or implied presence of others" (p. 3). Allport went on to say that "implied presence" refers to the many activities the individual carries out because of his or her position or role in a complex social structure or membership in a cultural group. Indeed, given the breadth of this definition, one may be hard pressed to imagine many instances of human behavior that do not have social psychological features or implications. In practice, however, as Allport was quick to acknowledge, there are many considerations of human nature that need to be solved apart from social psychological considerations, including: problems of psychophysics, sensory processes, memory processes, and the nature of personality integration. Nonetheless, a theme of this chapter will be that there still are many unexamined, or minimally investigated, interfaces between social psychological theory and research, and behavior therapy.

The Beginnings of Social Psychology

The formal study of social psychology is traced from the turn of the twentieth century when social psychological studies began in rather limited and halting ways. The first reported experiment was conducted by Triplett (1897). It concerned the effects on a bicyclist's speed when he was paced by another cyclist. Speed was found to increase when a pacer was present (the forerunner to later work on the social facilitation effect). In 1908, the first textbooks in social psychology were published separately by McDougall and Ross. McDougall's book emphasized the role of instinct in social behavior, an emphasis that dominated the field well into the 1920s. Ross's book emphasized the role of imitation (a concept that theorists using the learning approach later also emphasized) and "group mind." In 1921, the major journal of the field in the early years appeared in the form of the *Journal of Abnormal and Social Psychology* (JASP). This event signaled the beginning of a fertile alliance between clinical and social psychology that has mushroomed in the last decade and that we shall have more to say about later.

Morton Prince and his associate editor, Floyd Allport, created JASP from an earlier journal, the *Journal of Abnormal Psychology (JAP)*. JASP continued in existence until 1965 when it split into JAP, again, and the *Journal of Personality and Social Psychology*. This split was necessitated by the tremendous flood of papers being received by the journal at that time and by the increased specialization in research then occurring in psychology. But before we leave the journal development issue in our sketch, it is noteworthy to recall that Prince and F. Allport believed that an integration of the abnormal and social researches and literatures was needed in order to address the many problems in living and mental/behavioral disorders that were salient in their time and that had sprang from the violence and devastation created by World War I (see Hill & Weary, 1983, for an informative discussion of these developments).

The creation of valid and reliable measures of psychological states was a goal of early work in social psychology. Work on the development of attitude scales, which still are used to measure psychological states in contemporary psychology, was begun by social and quantitative psychologists in the 1920s and 1930s. Pioneering work on the development of scales to measure attitudes was done by Borgardus (1924), Thurstone (1928), Likert (1932), and Guttman (1950). Also, during this formative period for attitude measurement, Moreno (1934) developed the sociometric technique for measuring interpersonal attraction.

Mead's Social Behaviorism

As we implied initially, too often Mead's social behaviorism is not salient in considerations of the importance of social psychological theory in a variety of domains. But it clearly has had wide impact, particularly as it was translated into what was later called symbolic interaction theory (see House, 1977). Further, Mead's writing may have much more relevance for behavior theory and therapy in psychology than may have been recognized previously. For this reason, we will provide a relatively full summary of his ideas.

Mead lectured at the University of Chicago between 1893 and 1931, and books (Mead, 1932, 1934, 1938) based upon lecture notes taken by students in his classes were published after his death in 1931. The fullest exposition of Mead's arguments is given in his book *Mind, Self, and Society*. Like Watsonian radical behaviorism, Mead's approach focused on the observable actions of individuals. But unlike the Watson's position, Mead conceived "behavior" in broad enough terms to include *covert activity*. This inclusion was deemed necessary to understanding the distinctive character of human conduct, which Mead considered to be a qualitatively different emergent process as compared to the behavior of nonhumans. Mead felt that Watson's position reduced human behavior to the mechanisms found on the nonhuman level. Mead's research orientation usually is referred to as philosophical, meaning that he used findings from various sciences and apt illustrations from everyday life to try to make his case.

Mead's social behaviorism refers to the description of behavior at the distinctively human level. The basic datum is the social act, which may entail concern with covert activities. The concept of the social act implies that human conduct and experience have a fundamental dimension. Namely, that the social context is an inescapable element in distinctively human action. According to Mead, all group life is essentially a matter of cooperative behavior. Such cooperation can only be brought about by some process wherein: (a) each acting individual ascertains the intention of the acts of others (see later reference to attribution theory; this argument is similar to Jones & Davis' 1965 conception of how people make causal inferences) and (b) the individual makes his or her own response on the basis of that intention.

Mead's emphasis on the distinctive aspects of human symbolic behavior can be illustrated by reference to what he called the "conversation of gestures" used by many species of nonhumans. For example, when a mother hen clucks, her chicks will respond by running to her. This fact does not suggest that the chicks ascertain that the mother hen has an intention for them to run to her. Rather, clucking is a natural sign or signal, not a significant, meaningful symbol as is human speech.

One of the principal characteristics of the human in Mead's social behaviorism is the ability to respond to own gestures. This ability implies a *self* according to Mead. The human may praise, blame, or encourage self, become disgusted with self, punish self, and so on. Thus, the human may become the object of his or her own actions. The self is formed in the same way as other objects—through the *definitions* made by others (the definitions of others are quite similar to the *labels* others apply to persons perceived to be mentally ill, as labeling theory suggests, Scheff, 1966).

The mechanism whereby the individual becomes able to view self as an object is that of role-taking, involving the process of communication, especially vocal gestures. It is only by taking the role of others that the individual can come to see self as an object. The standpoint of others provides a platform for getting outside of self and thus viewing self. The development of the self is concurrent with the development of the ability to take on different roles.

Language plays a vital role in the creation of self and mind in Mead's conception. It is through language (symbolic symbols) that the child acquires the meanings and definitions of those around him or her. By learning the symbols of peer and other relevant groups, the child comes to internalize their definitions of events and things (in a sense, the child then can recapitulate society—the full cycle constantly is occurring for each human in the sequence of society-to self/mind-to society). That is, the possession of a self/mind makes the individual a society in miniature. In this subtle yet powerful unfolding of socialization, the child learns to visualize the intentions and expectations of several others. The child can do this visualization by abstracting a "composite" role out of the concrete roles of particular persons. In the course of associating with others, the child builds up a *generalized other*, a generalized role or standpoint from which he or she views self and own behavior. Having achieved this generalized standpoint, the individual can conduct self in an organized and consistent manner and essentially can uphold a consistent view of self across many diverse settings (Mead speaks of the Englishman who "dresses for dinner" in the wilds of Africa because he has this ability and is therefore emancipated from the pressures of the peculiarities of the immediate situation).

Mead conceived of the self as involving two distinct processes: the "I" and the "Me." The "I" is the impulsive tendency of the individual. It is the initial, spontaneous, unorganized aspect of human experience. The "Me," on the other hand, represents the incorporated other within the individual. It comprises the organized set of attitudes and definitions that have developed in the socialization process. Mead argued that every act begins in the form of an "I" and ends in the form of the "Me."

To Mead, mind is seen as developing correlatively with the self, constituting the self in action. Mind is viewed as a process which manifests itself whenever the individual is interacting with self by using significant symbols. The mind is social both in origin and function. It arises in the process of social communication. Through association with significant others, the individual comes to internalize the definitions transmitted through symbolic symbols, learns to assume the perspectives of others, and thereby acquires the ability to think. This process in turn enables the society to persist. The persistence of human society, in Mead's conception, depends upon consensus, and, in turn, consensus necessarily involves minded behavior.

Minded behavior is particularly apt to occur in the context of problems. It represents a temporary inhibition of action wherein the individual is attempting to prevision the future. The future is, thus, present in terms of images of prospective lines of alternative action from which the individual can make a selection.

The mental process, then, is one of delaying, organizing, and selecting a response to environmental stimuli. Further, the person constructs his or her act, rather than responding in predetermined ways.

Mead also provided intriguing ideas about the nature of the *act*. He believed that the act began with an impulse and involved cognitive constructive activity, comprising imagery, role-taking, and so on, eventuating in organized lines of response. It could involve a very specific response such as turning a page in a book or elaborate lifespan responses as in trying to achieve a successful career. Mead's logic here is not unlike that found in much contemporary theory in cognitive and lifespan psychology (e.g., it has qualities similar to those found in the *"Plans and the Structure of Behavior Approach"* outlined by Miller, Galanter, & Pribram, 1960).

In conclusion, Mead's social behaviorism is a rich brand of social psychological theory. Its value for psychology, in many areas, likely has not come close to being realized. In addition to the more contemporary concepts deriving from Meadian theory noted in our review, his ideas have much pertinence for influential social psychological ideas such as the self-fulfilling prophecy (see Darley & Fazio, 1980) and self-schema. Mead's most profound work occurred in the 1920s, culminating in the books derived from his lecture notes and published in the 1930s. We now will turn to a powerfully impactful event in the history of psychology that started to occur soon after Mead's death.

The Impetus Created by Pre- and Post-World War II Developments

No other singular event in the history of psychology as a whole was as important to the discipline's growth as was the prelude to and actual occurrence of World War II. That contention holds especially with regard to social psychology. Why? First, in the 1930s, probably the most systematic psychology in the world had developed in Europe and in particular at the University of Berlin Psychology Laboratory. The rise of the Nazi Movement, however, precipitated a massive exodus of scientists and scholars from Germany and surrounding countries to places where they hoped they would be safe from Nazi persecution. The mid- to late-1930s represent a critical period in this escape of scholars from the Nazi purge of the universities. The United States was the destination of many of these scholars, who at that time were at the top of their respective professions. In psychology alone, the emigres included such world famous scholars as Fritz Heider, Kurt Lewin, Kurt Koffka, Wolfgang Kohler, and Max Wertheimer. Heider and Lewin were social psychologists who made monumental contributions to the development of the field. Heider was the founder of the attribution approach and balance theory in attitudes work. His linking of basic and social perception ideas represents a classic contribution that still is affecting work on social perception in social psychology. His book *The Psychology of Interpersonal Relations* (1958) is within the elite ranks of the most important contributions of all time to social psychology. It was in this book that Heider outlined his ideas that later became attribution theory in social psychology and that still later led to a major contemporary genre of research on depression in clinical psychology.

Lewin is known as the founder of experimental social psychology. He pioneered studies on group processes and decision-making at the University of Iowa and, just prior to his early death by heart attack, founded the Research Center for Group Dynamics at MIT (Massachusetts Institute of Technology) in 1945. (In 1947, the center was moved to the University of Michigan and continues today as the foremost setting for many types of social psychological research in the country.) Lewin's (1935) ideas, packaged in the form of his field theory and topological psychology, were influential in the development of cognitive theories of social behavior in the 1950s and 1960s. But of Lewin's many assets, none had greater impact than his infectious zest for thinking, theorizing, and influencing young people to study social psychological processes. Two fine chronicles of Lewin's contributions are Marrow's (1969) biography of Lewin and Patnoe's (1988) narrative history of Lewin's influence as seen through the eyes of his students and their students—who, from the 1940s on, have represented the most influential group of scholars in social psychology.

It would be difficult to document here in any comprehensive way the major impacts of World War II on the development of social psychology. Clearly, in addition to the emigration to the United States of many of the most prominent social psychologists in the world, the war effort in the United States and Great Britian brought together many young psychologists (and soon-to-be psychologists) who worked for the military on various psychological projects such as personnel screening, basic perceptual processes, leadership, and group productivity and morale. The synergy established in these interactions and accomplishments led to a rush of new research and training programs right after the end of the war. Beyond these impacts, the federal government and a few private foundations began to make generous awards to social and personality psychological program development and research in the wake of World War II. The research foci included aggression, attitude change, prejudice, conformity and obedience, authoritarian personality, and altruism and helping behavior. As a civilized world, we wanted to know why these phenomena occurred and, in the case of those involving antisocial behavior, how to prevent them from occurring with such great destruction again.

After World War II, the world entered a "cold war" centering on relations between the United States and the U.S.S.R. and an unprecedented period of threat of total annihilation of the human species—the "atomic/nuclear age." This threat, too, was a catalyst for greater concern with social psychological processes and, consequently, greater funding for work and training in the area. Scores of social psychology training programs began to appear in the United States, and to a lesser degree in other English-speaking countries, as a function of the tremendous interest developing in achieving a better understanding of the human social condition and in training doctoral-level professionals to study this condition.

Early Learning Theory Applications in Social Psychology

Lewin, Heider, and their colleagues represented the Gestalt school of thought that was a precursor of much contemporary cognitive theory in social psychology. At the same time that they were making early important theoretical contributions, another school of thought in social psychology was associated with the then dominant learning theories. Learning theory applications were directed mainly toward language, attitudes, prejudice, and aggression. Neal Miller and John Dollard (1941) were instrumental in developing the learning approach to social behavior. They explained the acquisition of social drives and rewards essentially in terms of the notion that a neutral cue can acquire the property of a drive being connected or associated with a drive stimulus; it acquires rewarding properties by being associated with reduction of a drive stimulus. Thus, a child may learn to fear dogs after having been bitten by one, and the fear of dogs can thereafter motivate the child to make certain kinds of responses—such as running to mother—that reduce fear. The presence of the child's mother, in such a case, would take on reward value by being associated with fear reduction.

Miller and Dollard analyzed aspects of linguistic behavior in a similar way. The words "friendly" and "fierce" as applied to a dog discriminate between occasions of approach versus avoidance for the child. Verbal responses in language are especially useful cue-producing responses. They can be made overtly and covertly. Further, they are social in character. That is, one person's verbal responses, if made overtly, can function as cues both for self and other. Miller and Dollard (1941) also showed that social imitation plays a central role in the process of learning to talk and a considerable role in all social learning. Further, imitation is important in maintaining social conformity (as in group behavior). These theorists showed that imitation works when the individual is rewarded after he/she imitates and does not work when no reward is connected to imitating behavior.

Miller and Dollard's theory of imitation has been severely criticized as, in effect, requiring the person to be able to make a response before he/she can learn through imitation. Thus, Bandura (1962), one of the critics, argued that the theory implies that for a child to learn to say "symposium" imitatively, the child first would have to emit the word "symposium" in the course of random vocalization, match it with a model's verbal response, and be rewarded accordingly. Bandura concluded that the process of response acquisition is based on contiguity of sensory events, and that instrumental conditioning and reinforcement should be regarded as response-selection rather than response-acquisition.

Bandura went on to contend that models who are attractive, rewarding, prestigious, or powerful are likely to command more attention and therefore elicit more imitation than are models who lack these qualities. In other words, Bandura was arguing that reinforcement may serve as a causal agent in learning through imitation by augmenting the arousal and maintenance of the observing reaction. As we will discuss below, Bandura's argument later became part of his more general and influential theory of social learning and specifically linked to his idea of vicarious reinforcement.

Yale Communication Research Program

Another early influential approach was developed by Carl Hovland and his colleagues at Yale University in the late 1940s and 1950s. These investigators were concerned with the effects of different kinds of communication factors, communicator factors, and audience factors in affecting persuasion (Hovland, Janis, & Kelley, 1953). Their model has been referred to as an instrumental learning approach because it treats attentional dynamics in terms similar to those employed by Miller and Dollard. The central notion is that an opinion (an habitual judgment or prediction) or an attitude (an habitual evaluative orientation) becomes habitual because its overt expression or internal rehearsal is followed by the experience of satisfaction of positive reinforcement. These investigators argued that the techniques of opinion change involve obtaining the audience's attention, comprehension, and acceptance of the communication.

The Yale group studied experimentally how the process of persuasion is affected by communicator variables such as credibility, communication variables such as its one- or two-sidedness, and audience variables such as personality disposition (e.g., self-esteem). Cohen (1964) documents and summarizes much of this program of research. Later work in this tradition included Janis and Gilmore's (1965) argument that relatively large incentives (but not too large as to be blatant) associated with attitudinal messages create biased scanning for arguments favoring the new position advocated in the messages. As we will see later, their extension of learning theory to attitude change was challenged in a significant way by Lewin's student Leon Festinger (1957) who created the theory of cognitive dissonance to explain many attitude change phenomena.

THE CONTEMPORARY PERIOD IN THEORY DEVELOPMENT

We would suggest that the contemporary period in the development of social psychological theories as they relate to behavior therapy began in the late 1950s and early 1960s and is epitomized by the work of Leon Festinger and his colleagues and Albert Bandura and his colleagues.

Bandura and Colleagues' Early Work

Starting first with Bandura, his work has strong relevance for the present concern of how social psychology may inform behavior therapy. The work of Bandura and Walters (1959, 1963) was most important because they were learning theorists who had done most of their work with humans rather than nonhumans, and they successfully blended behavioristic and cognitive ideas in their formulations. Whereas Miller and Dollard assumed that imitated responses already are in an individual's behavioral repertoire, Bandura and Walters contended that novel response patterns can be acquired through observation. They also argued that the imitator can successfully imitate the model without performing any overt response and without receiving direct reinforcement. This argument not only was highly controversial at the time, but it also signaled a shift in the field toward theorizing about the more subtle nonbehavioral capacities of people as mediating their social behavior.

Bandura, Walters, and colleagues performed a series of nursery school studies in which children were exposed to different kinds of models (human adults in person, human adults on film, cartoon figures on film) who exhibited different patterns of behavior (aggressive or nonaggressive), which had different kinds of consequences for the model (rewarding or punishing).

The results indicated that children who observed aggressive models (as they hit, punched, and generally abused a large inflated doll—the "bobo doll") responded to subsequent frustration with considerable aggression. Much of this aggression imitated what they had previously observed. Equally frustrated children who had observed models displaying inhibited behavior, however, showed tendencies to exhibit inhibition of aggression. The viewing of cartoon figures and films of humans produced as much aggression in the test situation as did observing a physically present adult.

These findings suggest that children's behavior may be influenced by what they see on television programs and that this behavior may be interpreted in terms of vicarious reinforcement. Punished models did not elicit nearly as much imitation as rewarded models. Thus, in their theoretical conception, Bandura, Walters, and colleagues wed a central principle of learning theory the "law of effect" (that rewarded behavior is stimulated and punished behavior inhibited) with the principle that much of the action of imitation may occur in the mind of the potential imitator who may internalize the observed behavior and reinforcement and then at some later point exhibit similar behavior.

Bandura and Walters went on to theorize about the development of self-control. They argued and cited evidence suggesting that children not only imitate what adults and peers both do and do not do in relation to others, but also that they imitate the self-directed actions of others. If a model sets a high standard for behavior, the child likewise may set such a standard and continue to enforce that standard—now becoming a personal standard—even after the model is no longer present. In general, Bandura and Walters detailed five major ways of modifying behavior:

1. extinction—removal of positive reinforcement
2. counter-conditioning, which involves eliciting in the presence of the fear-arousing stimuli responses that are incompatible with fear reactions
3. positive reinforcement, which entails the use of rewards to increase the strength of a response tendency
4. social imitation
5. discrimination learning, which uses positive reinforcers to reward desired responses to given stimuli and negative reinforcers to punish undesired responses or lack of reward to extinguish them.

Festinger and Colleagues' Emphasis on the Cognitive-Justifying Human

The work of Bandura and colleagues continued to influence behavior theory and therapy. It might be argued, however, that the theoretical and empirical work of Leon Festinger and colleagues had no less impact on this and other areas of psychology because it focused attention on cognitions and a highly cognitive explanation for the workings of reward on behavior. Festinger developed two influential theories, his theory of social comparison (1954) and his theory of cognitive dissonance (1957). The latter theory is the one that has most relevance for our present analysis, and thus we will summarize it and its relevant implications here.

Festinger theorized that people have a drive to maintain consistency in their knowledge of the world. Specifically, people do not feel comfortable holding dissonant, or nonfitting, cognitions. This theory represents a consistency (or homeostasis—with such systems having a drive to resolve a tranquil state when a disorder occurs) model similar to then current theories of cognitive consistency such as Heider's (1946) theory of balance or Osgood and Tannenbaum's (1955) theory of attitudinal congruity. These positions assert that a person attempts to perceive, cognize, or evaluate the various aspects of the environment and of self in such a way that the behavioral implications of these perceptions will not be contradictory. Festinger's theory, in particular, emphasizes the consequences of decisions. The core of Festinger's theory is that (a) the existence of dissonance created by nonfitting relations among cognitive elements gives rise to pressures to reduce the dissonance and to avoid increases in dissonance; and (b) manifestations of the operation of these pressures include behavior changes, changes in cognition, and circumspect exposure to new information and new opinions.

In describing the reduction of dissonance, Festinger introduces a distinction between cognitive elements that refer to behavior or feelings (e.g., the belief that "I am going to a party today") and cognitive elements which refer to the environment (e.g., the belief that it is snowing). He indicates that environmental cognitions usually are more difficult to change than are beliefs about behavior. That is, it is easier to change one's beliefs about what one is going to do than one's beliefs about a tangible reality.

Unlike other consistency conceptions, Festinger makes a unique assumption that making a decision per se arouses dissonance and pressures to reduce the dissonance. According to Festinger, dissonance after decision results from the fact that the situation cognitively changes upon the making of the decision. Before the decision, there is more impartiality and conflict about the best option. But after the decision and the onset of dissonance-reduction processes, the decision-maker becomes partial in favor of the decision and believes that the option is the one that should have been chosen. A variety of interesting and nonobvious predictions stemmed from Festinger's theory of cognitive dissonance. Much of this work derived from the notion that if a decision produces insufficient rewards, the person will change his or her beliefs so as to make the decision seem more rewarding. Festinger (1961) wrote that rats and people come to love the things for which they have suffered. This idea was the catalyst for a study by Aronson and Mills (1959) which showed that people who had undergone a severe initiation to get into what turned out to be a boring group tended to like the group more than did people who had undergone a mild initiation to get into the same group.

In the classic study of the Festinger cognitive dissonance legacy, Festinger and Carlsmith (1959) predicted that the smaller the reward that is used to get someone to do something that is counter-attitudinal, the greater will be the dissonance upon the person's engaging in the task and consequently, the greater the liking for the task. One group of research participants was paid $1 to tell other participants that an intrinsically boring task they had completed actually had been quite interesting; another group of participants was paid $20 to tell the same lie; a third group was not asked to tell the lie. As predicted, those who deceived others for $1 rated the task as more enjoyable than did the other two groups which did not differ in their ratings of enjoyableness. Thus, the results support the counter-intuitive idea that a small reward may be more effective in producing attitude change than a large one.

Many criticisms have been directed at Festinger and Carlsmith's study over the years. Among them are the argument that the $20 group was suspicious (Chapanis & Chapanis, 1964) or felt like they were being bribed (Janis & Gilmore, 1965). However, the study and its theoretical logic have been supported in other work (e.g., Brehm & Cohen, 1962). Overall, despite considerable work aimed at establishing the parameters of when dissonance does or does not occur (see Aronson, 1968) in counterattitudinal advocacy and other situations, the influence of cognitive dissonance theory continues to the present, some four decades later.

In conclusion, Festinger's contributions to social psychology were monumental in stature. One aspect of his contributions that we should emphasize is that Festinger's theorizing liberated the field from the view that reward always enhances behavior (Aronson, 1989). In such theorizing, he significantly challenged the popular theorizing of the day in social psychology, such as that found in Hovland and colleagues' learning theory. Even as Bandura and colleagues' ideas represented a major revision in earlier learning theory analyses of social behavior, Festinger and colleagues' work represented a confrontation of the earlier dominant learning theory ethos regarding the explanation of social behavior. In addition to the emerging ideas from the cognitive revolution in psychology then starting to occur, Festinger provided interesting new propositions about the role of cognition in affecting behavior and about the tendency for humans to try to justify their behavior, particularly when it is problematic.

Bem's Challenge of Dissonance Theory

Cognitive dissonance occupied a preeminent theoretical position in social psychology until the early 1970s. At that point, attribution approaches were developing and began to become more dominant in stimulating theory and research (see Harvey & Smith, 1977). One of those approaches that Kelley (1967) first recognized as attributional in nature was Bem's (1965, 1972) influential analysis of self-perception. This analysis initially was developed to provide an alternative interpretation for phenomena that previously had been interpreted in terms of dissonance theory.

Bem proposed that the inverse relationship between attitude change and reward in the counter attitudinal advocacy situation can be explained in a relatively parsimonious manner without the positing of a motivational state like dissonance. He argued that people infer their attitudes on the basis of their self-perception of their actions and the context in which these actions occur. In this view, individuals are observers of themselves and can be expected to make inferences about their internal states that would agree with those made by an outside observer. That is, they are assumed to have the same public information with which to infer their own attitude as that possessed by anyone who happened to observe them acting in a situation that was relevant to the attitudinal issue.

How does Bem account for Festinger and Carlsmith's (1959) results? In the $1 condition, according to Bem, research participants should re-examine their behavior and its context (i.e., the inducement of receiving $1 to tell someone else that a task had been interesting) and conclude that the task must really be interesting since they had only been given $1 to tell others about it. On the other hand, in the $20 condition, research participants should look back at their behavior and the setting and conclude that they really did not enjoy it since they had to be given $20 to tell others about it. Thus, Bem suggested that adequate explanation for the main results could be found in the self-perception process and that there was no need to invoke a less parsimonious construct such as aversive motivation to explain the results.

In technical terms, Bem viewed himself as a behaviorist "eschewing" reference to internal states as explanatory mechanisms. He used the concepts of mand and tact from Skinner's (1957) analysis of verbal behavior to explain attitudinal behavior. A *mand* is defined as an attitudinal response under the control of the incentive conditions (e.g., the $20 incentive). A *tact* is defined as an attitudinal response not under the control of the incentive conditions (e.g., the $1 incentive) but instead controlled by the attitudinal query, "What is your attitude on this issue?" As Bem said, "It should be noted that self-perception theory lacks any motivational construct other than an implicit assumption that individuals are willing to answer inquiries concerning their internal states" (p. 44, 1972).

The most central form of evidence that Bem advanced to support his position derived from a set of simulation studies designed to test the idea that actors and observers would arrive at the same attitudinal inference if they both had access to information about the relevant behavior and its context. Bem sought to determine if people who are given information about the procedure involved in studies producing results interpretable in terms of dissonance theory can predict or estimate the research participants' attitudinal responses. In one of these studies, Bem gave observers details of the experimental conditions in a study by Cohen (1964). This study involved four incentive conditions, $.50, $1, $5, and $10, that were made contingent upon a request of research participants (Yale college students) to argue in favor of their college police department's recent and repressive actions against college students protesting on their campus (a strongly counterattitudinal position to take). Cohen found that as dissonance theory would predict, the lower the inducement offered, the greater the attitude change toward favoring the police department's actions. However, Bem also found that observers who were not experiencing dissonance estimated that participants in the $.50 condition had an attitude more in line with the discrepant action than did participants in the higher reward conditions. Thus, Bem concluded that no aversive motivation and dissonance-reducing process were necessary to explain these and similar data produced by scholars from the dissonance school of thought.

Bem's self-perception theory has continued to be important in social psychology throughout the last two decades even though critical tests of dissonance versus self-perception positions never proved conclusive. Instead, Bem's reasoning has been found to be useful as a guiding line of argument in a variety of substantive arenas including compliance behavior (Cialdini, 1985) and the treatment of heterosexual dating anxiety (Montgomery & Haemmerlie, 1986). As for whether people do indeed use prior behavior and context to infer present attitudes, it would appear from later work that such a tendency occurs mainly for weakly held or relatively unimportant attitudes (Taylor, 1975) For more important attitudes, they appear to be salient to people even after they have acted and thus enter into the chemistry of determining new attitudinal responses. Such reasoning is consistent with dissonance theory's emphasis on the nonfitting nature of past attitudes and present behavior, hence leading to a dissonance-arousing state and attempts to reduce this arousal. Overall, though, of all the ostensibly behavioral approaches in social psychology in the last two decades, Bem's position has been the most influential.

OTHER LEARNING/BEHAVIORALLY ORIENTED SOCIAL THEORIES

There were several other conceptions developed in the 1950s and 1960s that focused on learning processes as mediators of social behavior. Foremost among these conceptions were the works of another sociological social psychologist George Homans and of the eminent psychologists John Thibaut and Harold Kelley.

Homans' Elementary Social Behavior

Homans found in his colleague, B.F. Skinner, the system and ideas he desired to explain elementary social behavior. He was one of the only Skinnerian social psychologists in the history either of sociology or psychology. Homans made the bold assertion that the "ultimate explanatory principles in anthropology and sociology, and for that matter in history . . . (are) psychological" (Homans, 1962, p. 61). His choice of the Skinnerian system likely stemmed from his association with Skinner on the faculty at Harvard University.

One of Homans' classic contributions was his book *The Human Group* (1950) in which he detailed five field studies of human groups. These studies were conducted to try to determine into what basic classes the observations of groups can be divided and what propositions can be inferred about the relations among the classes of variables. It is beyond the scope of this chapter to try to summarize all of Homan's propositions and related evidence. One example, however, provides an illustration of the set of generalizations: "(The) more frequently persons interact with one another, the stronger their sentiments of friendship for one another are apt to be" (Homans, 1950, p. 135).

Homans elaborated on his Skinnerian position in his 1961 book. He said, "Briefly, behavioral psychology and elementary economics envisage human behavior as a function of its payoff: in amount and kind it depends on the amount and kind of reward and punishment it fetches" (p. 13, 1961). Homans detailed additional propositions in this book, including the following two: "The more often within a given period of time a man's activity rewards the activity of another, the more often the other will emit that activity" (1961, p. 54). "The more valuable to a man a unit of the activity another gives him, the more often he will emit activity rewarded by the activity of the other" (1961, p. 55). While Homans' ideas have ceased to be widely influential in contemporary social psychology, as we will see next, they have had considerable impact on important theoretical positions that do play an influential role in contemporary work.

Thibaut and Kelley's Social Psychology of Groups

Like Homans, Thibaut and Kelley (1959) explained social interaction found in groups, focusing particularly on the smallest group, the dyad, in terms of the outcomes of behavior. Also similar to Homans, they assumed that social behavior is unlikely to be repeated unless its rewards exceed its costs. The value that an individual places upon a given outcome, however, will be determined not by absolute magnitude of outcome, but by comparison against two standards. One standard called *comparison level* (CL) is defined as "some modal or average value of all the outcomes known to the person" (p. 81, 1959). The concept of CL was modeled after Helson's concept of "adaptation level" (Helson, 1948). The essential point of each idea is that what an individual experiences when he or she is exposed to a given stimulus will be determined by what he or she has become adapted to.

The second standard against which a person is conceived to evaluate outcomes is termed the "comparison level for alternatives," which is used in deciding whether or not to stay in a social relationship. It is the lowest outcome a person will accept in light of the best alternative opportunities available. If the outcome is perceived to be lower than this level, presumably the individual will leave the relationship in deference to other possible relationships.

As a way of characterizing social interaction, Thibaut and Kelley used a matrix approach to describe the outcomes of satisfaction or dissatisfaction to each participant in a dyad when the actions of each are known. The payoffs represented in these matrices are theorized to be the objectively available outcomes that the interactors would actually experience if they behaved in a given way. The full exposition of the Thibaut and Kelley logic is beyond our purposes, but the representation of social interaction by a matrix, which has its origins in mathematical game theory, has proved to be a useful tool for abstract descriptions of different types of social interdependences. These ideas have been particularly useful in later revisions of the origin theory of group interaction (Kelley & Thibaut, 1978) and of Kelley's influential work on close relationships (Kelley, 1979; Kelley et al., 1983). Also, continuing in Thibaut and Kelley's revision work on the dyad is their sophisticated notion of how people calculate reward-cost outcomes in interpersonal relations, which involves a combination of behavioral and cognitive considerations. Overall, their theoretical work has had the greatest impact on the literature of the social psychology of groups in the history of scholarship on this topic.

Other Behaviorally Oriented Attitude Theories

As a final historical note on 1950s and 1960s developments, we will briefly mention a couple of other theories in that attitude area. One argument was developed by Staats and Staats (1958) as an attempt to explain attitude formation by reference to classical conditioning processes. They suggested that if an object or recommendation is paired repeatedly with anything that elicits a favorable or an unfavorable response, the object or recommendation will come to elicit the same type of favorable or unfavorable response. Thus, an attitude will form regarding the object or recommendation.

Staats, Staats, and Crawford (1962) provided evidence for this position by illustrating the formation of negative attitudes by pairing words with stimuli (electric shocks or loud noises). Following repeated pairings with the unpleasant stimuli, the words alone were shown to research participants. For a measure of liking or evaluation, these investigators found that the words paired with the unpleasant stimuli were evaluated more negatively than control words, and additionally words paired with unpleasant stimuli evoked increased activity on a measure of galvanic skin response.

One of the principal debates surrounding this work is whether or not conditioning can occur without the individual's awareness of the process. The Staats' claimed that it can, whereas critics such as Page (1969) argued that participants had guessed the experimental hypothesis and were complying with that assumed hypothesis (i.e., they were exhibiting "experimental demand"). This debate ultimately faded as did continued work on a classical conditioning model of attitude formation. The Staats' work, however, is highly suggestive of a classical conditioning element in some attitude development.

Another group of scholars were busy in the 1950s and 1960s trying to test the general idea that attitudes are changed, and sometimes formed too, via operant conditioning principles. The idea was similar to the position developed in the Hovland, Janis, and Kelley (1953) approach, to wit: People come to adhere strongly to attitudes that yield rewards and to reject attitudes that result in punishment. These operant attitude theorists were stimulated by an early demonstration of verbal conditioning by Greenspoon (1955), who showed that people may increase the use of a plural noun simply as a function of the experimenter saying "mm-hmmm." As an illustrative attitude change study, Scott (1957) showed that the winners of a debate changed their attitudes in the direction of their advocacy. On the other hand, losers of the debate changed their attitudes away from the position they advocated.

The operant approach to attitude change did have some rippling impact in later attitude work (e.g., Insko & Cialdini, 1969). However, similar to work on the classical conditioning of attitudes, it has become inactive in the last decade that has involved the development of more highly sophisticated cognitive theories of attitude change (e.g., Fishbein & Ajzen, 1975; Petty & Cacioppo, 1986).

CONTEMPORARY ISSUES IN BEHAVIORALLY ORIENTED SOCIAL THEORIES

To a degree, social psychologists' work that is most relevant to behavior theory and therapy in the last two decades has continued in the same vein of scholarship that was starting in the 1950s and 1960s. Increasingly, this work also has been carried out by clinical-social scholars working close to the boundaries of social, clinical, and, to a lesser degree, cognitive, developmental, and counseling psychology. For example, attribution and social perception/cognition theoretical works (see chapter by Fincham and Bradbury in this volume) started to become prominent in the 1960s after Heider's (1958) seminal contribution and have continued to have great sway on developments in the field in the 1970s and 1980s, including work on depression (e.g., Abramson & Martin, 1981). In this last section of our treatment of history and theories in social psychology, we will mention some contemporary developments and work that are highly congenial to the interface of behavior therapy and social psychology. We also will note some future directions for theory and research that seem promising for this interface.

An Extensive Contemporary Social-Clinical Literature

There now is an extensive literature that has been the product of social and clinical (generically defined) scholars' cooperation in addressing problems of living and behavioral disorders. This development parallels and complements developments in behavior therapy, per se, in the last two decades. As Franks and Rosenbaum (1983) suggest, contemporary behavior therapy is no longer the "simplistic, cut-and-dried matter of the clinical application of something called modern learning theory that it was in the early 1960s . . . and (behavior therapy) is healthy . . . because of its variations and complexity" (p. 8). Part of that variety and complexity stems from a burgeoning interface of research that is being developed in clinical and social psychology.

Several recent edited volumes and textbooks have analyzed and summarized literature that shows how clinical and social approaches may be integrated (e.g., Goldstein, Heller, & Sechrest, 1966; Brehm, 1976; Weary & Mirels, 1982; Leary & Miller, 1986). In addition the *Journal of Social and Clinical Psychology*, was created in the early 1980s with the specific objective of stimulating theory and research at this boundary area (see Harvey, 1983). In addition, other journals regularly publish research that reflects the varied agenda of work being carried out by clinical and social psychologists usually focusing on social psychological processes underlying behavioral disorders and general psychological/health problems in people's lives.

A number of successful research programs also have been developed that reveal how this interface informs behavior therapy applications. As one example, Lewinsohn and colleagues have developed a behavioral analysis of depression that involves a concern with concepts of social interaction. In an illustrative paper, Lewinsohn, Youngren, and Grosscup (1979) advanced general hypotheses about the relationship between reinforcement and depression that defines reinforcement as the quality of the person's interactions with his or her environment. They suggested that those person/environment interactions with positive outcomes (i.e., outcomes that make the person feel good) constitute positive reinforcement and strengthen the person's behavior. They also hypothesized that the punishing events that are particularly important for the development and/or maintenance of depression include such social interaction events as marital discord, work hassles, and receiving negative interactions from others.

Similarly, Jacobson and Margolin (1979) developed an influential behavioral-exchange model of close relationship discord that emphasized the valence of social interactions. They suggested that a distressed relationship is one in which there is scarcity of positive outcomes available for each person in the relationship. In this model, couples generally are predicted to exchange low rates of rewarding interaction and high rates of punishing interaction (see Fincham and Bradbury's chapter in this volume for further discussion of this line of work). Probably the best examples of this interface have been aimed at exploring the difficulties married couples often experience early in their marriages. For instance, the research efforts of Jacobson and colleagues (e.g., Berley & Jacobson, 1984) and Fincham and colleagues (e.g., Fincham & Bradbury, in press) have provided some of the most sophisticated theoretical and empirical work available on links between social psychological concepts such as attribution and social cognition and behavior therapy with distressed couples.

Future Directions: Salient and Neglected Foci

As Martin (this volume) discusses, Krasner (1971) wrote an influential paper in which he outlined how 15 streams of development during the 1950s and 1960s converged to form the behavior therapy area in psychological science. Examination of this list of suggested streams of development reveals the long-term recognition of the role of social psychological processes in behavior change. The list includes, for example, the following developments: "Theoretical concepts and research studies of social role learning and 'interactionism' in social psychology and sociology . . . " and "Social influence studies of demand characteristics, experimental bias, hypnosis, subject and patient expectancy, and placebo effects" (Krasner, 1971, p. 3). In addition to such recognition, some behavior therapists have suggested that the field might benefit from consideration of some of the many theoretical conceptions being developed in social psychology (Franks & Rosenbaum, 1983). We agree. However, we think that the same point can be made about the value of exchanges with other areas of psychology and the social sciences in general in which rich theoretical perspectives have evolved.

It seems likely to us that in the future, these traditional avenues of exchange between behavior therapy and social psychology will continue to be pursued. The area of social influence and attitude change represents one such avenue. In particular, a broadly theoretical, contemporary view of social psychological research on attitude change processes (e.g., Petty & Cacioppo, 1986) likely has a lot to offer behavior therapists. This type of analysis speaks to the best evidence available on the roles of cognition, behavior, and affect in social influence phenomena.

Behavior therapists may find appealing the notion that a tendency to counterargue and become both cognitively and emotionally involved with some types of persuasion attempts, and not others, seems critical to whether or not attitude and behavior change occur.

A related social influence-type phenomenon that deserves scrutiny as it affects behavior change is that of self-presentation. Social psychologists have identified many dynamics associated with how people present themselves to others and toward what ends they make these presentations (e.g., Goffman's, 1959, classic analysis). Given the pervasiveness of self-presentation tactics and considerations in our daily life, behavior therapists might benefit from examination of contemporary work in the area (e.g., Jones & Pittman, 1982).

It seems ironic but perhaps the most neglected area of social psychological analysis in the field of behavior therapy concerns the literature of nonverbal behavior. This literature has grown in theoretical stature and methodological sophistication since the early years (e.g., when Moreno, 1934, developed the sociometric technique). A good example of this work is Ickes and colleagues' program of research on dyadic interaction (e.g., Ickes, 1983; Ickes, Tooke, Stinson, Baker, and Bissonnette, 1988). This approach involves video recordings of the unstructured verbal and nonverbal behavior of dyads—both same and mixed couples and including friends, lovers, and strangers. These investigators also have probed various personality tendencies of the research participants and have asked the participants to react to certain self-report measures. In essence, this technique involves one of the most comprehensive types of assessment of thought and behavior ever carried out in a laboratory setting. Other work along this line has been carrried out by attribution theorists (e.g., Yarkin, Harvey, & Bloxom, 1981) who have been concerned with showing the behavioral effects and correlates of attributions about others. Overall, research that focuses partially on nonverbal behavior, such as the foregoing programs, that is well integrated with work on topics within the broad field of cognitive social psychology may provide a rich base of data and theory for possible use by behavior therapists and theorists in the next decade.

CONCLUSION

This chapter summarized several major historical and theoretical developments in social psychology. Special emphasis was placed on developments that may be relevant to behavior theory and therapy. The field of social psychology started soon after the formal beginning of psychology, about 100 years ago, and began to develop a major literature and corps of workers particularly around the time of World War II. The chapter gives strong attention to the roles of pioneering scholars such as Lewin, Mead, Heider, Festinger, and Bandura in establishing a rich theoretical foundation for social psychology and related fields of inquiry about human social behavior.

We also note the influence of world and societal events (such as war) in hastening applied social research on how to influence people to change antisocial attitudes and negative lines of behavior. We trace the 1950s and 1960s development of the cognitive movement in social psychology and how this movement remains highly influential at present. Finally, examples of the extensive and developing literature at the interface of social and clinical psychology are given, and their relevance to behavior therapy is noted. Continuing and neglected foci for theoretical and research exchange between social psychology and behavior exchange also are discussed.

REFERENCES

Abramson, L. Y., & Martin, D. J. (1981). Depression and the causal inference process. In J. H. Harvey, W. Ickes, & R. F. Kidd (Eds.). *New Direction in Attribution Research* (Vol. 3, pp. 117–168). Hillsdale, NJ: Lawrence Erlbaum Associates.

Allport, E. W. (1968). The historical background of modern social psychology. In E. Lindzey & E. Aronson (Eds.). *The Handbook of Social Psychology* (2nd ed., pp. 1–80). Reading, MA: Addison-Wesley.

Aronson, E. (1968). Dissonance theory: Progress and problems. In R. P. Abelson, E. Aronson, W. J. McGuire, T. M. Newcomb, M. J. Rosenberg, & P. H. Tannenbaum (eds.). *Theories of Cognitive Consistency: A Sourcebook* (pp. 5–27). Chicago: Rand McNally.

Aronson, E. (1989). Memorial to Leon Festinger. Speech given at the meeting of the Society of Experimental Social Psychology, Los Angeles.

Aronson, E. & Mills, J. (1959). The effect of severity of initiation on liking for a group. *Journal of Abnormal and Social Psychology, 59*, 177–181.

Bandura, A. (1962). Social learning through imitation. In M. R Jones (Ed.) *Nebraska Symposium on Motivation*, (pp. 211–269). Lincoln: University of Nebraska Press.

Bandura, A., & Walters, R. H. (1959). *Adolescent Aggression.* New York: Ronald Press.

Bandura, A., & Walters, R. H. (1963). *Social Learning and Personality Development.* New York: Holt, Rinehart & Winston.

Bem, D. J. (1965). An experimental analysis of self-persuasion. *Journal of Experimental Social Psychology, 1*, 199–218.

Bem, D. J. (1972). Self-perception theory. In L. Berkowitz *Advances in Experimental Social Psychology* (Vol. 6, pp. 1–62). New York: Academic Press.

Berley, R. A., & Jacobson, N. S. (1984). Causal attributions in intimate relationships: Toward a model of cognitive-behavioral marital therapy. In P. C. Kendall (Ed.). *Advances in Cognitive-Behavioral Research and Therapy* (Vol. 3, pp. 1–60). Orlando, FL: Academic Press.

Borgardus, E. S. (1924). *Fundamentals of Social Psychology.* New York: Appleton-Century-Crofts.

Brehm, J. W., & Cohen, A. R. (1962). *Explorations in Cognitive Dissonance.* New York: John Wiley & Sons.

Brehm, S. S. (1976). *The Application of Social Psychology to Clinical Practice.* Washington: Hemisphere.

Cantor, N., & Kihlstrom, J. F. (1982). Cognitive and social processes in personality. In G. T. Wilson & C. M. Franks (Eds.). *Contemporary Behavior Therapy* (pp. 142–201). Washington, DC: Guilford Press.

Chapanis, N. P., & Chapanis, A. (1964). Cognitive dissonance: Five years later. *Psychological Bulletin, 61*, 1–22.

Cialdini, R. B. (1985). *Influence: Science and Practice.* Glenview, IL: Scott, Foresman.

Cohen, A. R. (1964). *Attitude Change and Social Influence.* New York: Basic Books.

Darley, J. M., & Fazio, R. (1980). Expectancy confirmation processes arising in the social interaction sequence. *American Psychologist, 35*, 867–881.

Festinger, L. (1954). A theory of social comparison processes. *Human Relations, 7*, 117–140.

Festinger, L. (1957). *A Theory of Cognitive Dissonance.* Evanston, IL: Row, Peterson.

Festinger, L. (1961). The psychological effects of insufficient reward. *American Psychologist, 61*, 1–11.

Festinger, L., & Carlsmith, J. M. (1959). Cognitive consequences of forced compliance. *Journal of Abnormal and Social Psychology, 58*, 203–211.

Fincham, F. D., & Bradbury, T. N. (in press). Cognition in marriage: A program of research on attributions. In D. Perlman & W. Jones (Eds.). *Advances in Personal Relationships* (Vol. 2). Greenwich, CT: JAI Press.

Fishbein, M., & Ajzen, I. (1975). *Belief, Attitude, Intention, and Behavior.* Reading, MA: Addison-Wesley.

Franks, C. M., & Rosenbaum, M. (1983). Behavior therapy: Overview and personal reflections. In M. Rosenbaum, C. M. Franks, & Y. Jaffe (Eds.). *Perspectives on Behavior Therapy in the Eighties* (pp. 3–14). New York: Springer-Verlag.

Goldstein, A. P., Heller, K., & Sechrest, L. B. (1966). *Psychotherapy and Psychology of Behavior Change.* New York: John Wiley & Sons.

Goffman, E. (1959). *The Presentation of Self in Everyday Life.* Garden City, NY: Doubleday-Anchor.

Greenspoon, J. (1955). The reinforcing effect of two spoken

sounds on the frequency of two responses. *American Journal of Psychology, 68*, 409–416.
Guttman, L. (1950). The basis for scalogram analysis. In S. A. Stouffer, L. Guttman, E. A. Schman, P. F. Lazasfelf, S. A. Star, & J. A. Gardner (Eds.). *Measurement and Prediction*. Princeton: Princeton University Press.
Harvey, J. H. (1983). The founding of *Journal of Social and Clinical Psychology*. *Journal of Social and Clinical Psychology*, 1–3.
Harvey, J. H., & Smith, W. P. (1977). *Social Psychology: An Attributional Approach*. St. Louis: C. V. Mosby.
Heider, F. (1946). Attitudes and cognitive organization. *Journal of Psychology, 21*, 107–112.
Heider, F. (1958). *The Psychology of Interpersonal Relations*. New York: John Wiley & Sons.
Helson, H. (1948). Adaptation-level as a basis for a quantitative theory. *Psychological Review, 55*, 297–313.
Hill, M. G., & Weary, G. (1983). Perspectives on the *Journal of Abnormal and Social Psychology*: How it began and how it was transformed. *Journal of Social and Clinical Psychology, 1*, 4–14.
Homans, E. C. (1950). *The Human Group*. New York: Harcourt, Brace and World.
Homans, E. C. (1961). *Social behavior: Its Elementary Forms*. New York: Harcourt, Brace and World.
Homans, E. C. (1962). *Sentiments and Activities: Essays in Social Science*. New York: Free Press.
House, J. S. (1977). The three faces of social psychology. *Sociometry, 40*, 161–177.
Hovland, C. I., Janis, I. L., & Kelley, H. H. (1953). *Communication and Persuasion*. New Haven: Yale University Press.
Ickes, W. (1983). A basic paradigm for the study of unstructured dyadic interaction. In H. Reis (Ed.), *New Directions for Methodology of Social and Behavioral Science* (pp. 5–21). San Francisco: Jossey-Bass.
Ickes, W., Tooke, W., Stinson, L., Baker, V. L., & Bissonnette, V. (1988). Naturalistic social cognition: Intersubjectivity in same-sex dyads. *Journal of Nonverbal Behavior, 12*, 58–84.
Insko, C. A., & Cialdini, R. B. (1969). A test of three interpretations of attitudinal verbal reinforcement. *Journal of Personality and Social Psychology, 12*, 333–341.
Jacobson, N. S., & Margolin, G. (1979). *Marital Therapy*. New York: Bruner/Mazel.
Janis, I. L., & Gilmore, J. B. (1965). The influence of incentive conditions on the success of role playing in modifying attitudes. *Journal of Personality and Social Psychology, 1*, 17–27.
Jones, E. E., & Davis, K. E. (1965). From acts to dispositions: The attribution process in person perception. In L. Berkowitz (Ed.), *Advances in Experimental Social Psychology* (Vol. 2, pp. 219–266). New York: Academic Press.
Jones, E. E., & Pittman, T. S. (1982). Toward a general theory of strategic self-presentation. In J. Suls (Ed.), *Psychological Perspectives on the Self* (pp. 231–262). Hillsdale, NJ: Lawrence Erlbaum Associates.
Kelley, H. H. (1967). Attribution theory in social psychology. In D. Levine (Ed.), *Nebraska Symposium on Motivation*. Lincoln: University of Nebraska Press.
Kelley, H. H. (1979). *Personal Relationships: Their structures and Processes*. Hillsdale, NJ: Lawrence Erlbaum Associates.
Kelley, H., Berscheid, E., Christensen, A., Harvey, J., Huston, T., Levinger, G., McClintock, E., Peplau, A., & Peterson, D. (1983). *Close Relationships*. San Francisco: W H Freeman.
Kelley, H. H., & Thibaut, J. W. (1978). *Interpersonal Relations: A Theory of Interdependence*. New York: John Wiley & Sons.
Krasner, L. (1971). Behavior therapy. *Annual Review of Psychology, 22*, 483–532.
Leary, M. R., & Miller, R. S. (1986). *Social Psychology and Dysfunctional Behavior*. New York: Springer-Verlag.
Lewin, K. (1935). *A Dynamic Theory of Personality*. New York: McGraw-Hill.
Lewinsohn, P. M., Youngren, M. A., & Grosscup, S. L. (1979). Reinforcement and depression. In R. A. Depue (Ed.), *The Psychobiology of the Depressive Disorders: Implications for the Effects of Stress*. New York: Academic Press.
Likert, R. (1932). A technique for the measurement of attitudes. *Archives of Psychology, 140*, 43–59.
Marrow, A. J. (1969). *The Practical Theorist: The Life and Work of Kurt Lewin*. New York: Basic Books.
McDougall, W. (1908). *Introduction to Social Psychology*. London: Methuen.
Mead, G. H. (1932). *The Philosophy of the Present*. Chicago: University of Chicago Press.
Mead, G. H. (1934). *Mind, Self, and Society*. Chicago: University of Chicago Press.
Mead, G. H. (1938). *Philosophy of the Act*. Chicago: University of Chicago Press.
Miller, G. A., Galanter, E., & Pribram, K. H. (1960). *Plans and the Structure of Behavior*. New York: Holt, Rinehart & Winston.
Miller, N. E., & Dollard, J. (1941). *Social Learning and Imitation*. New Haven: Yale University Press.
Montgomery, R. L., & Haemmerlie, F. M. (1986). Self-perception theory and the reduction of heterosexual activity. *Journal of Social and Clinical Psychology, 4*, 503–512.
Moreno, J. L. (1934). *Who Shall Survive?* Washington: Nervous and Mental Disease Publishing House.
Osgood, C. E., & Tannenbaum, P. H. (1955). The principle of congruity in the prediction of attitude change. *Psychological Review, 62*, 42–55.
Page, M. M. (1969). Social psychology of a classical conditioning of attitudes experiment. *Journal of Personality and Social Psychology, 11*, 177–186.

Patnoe, S. (1988). *A Narrative History of Experimental Social Psychology: The Lewin Tradition.* Berlin: Springer-Verlag.

Petty, R. E., & Cacioppo, J. T. (1986). *Communication and Persuasion: Central and Peripheral Routes to Attitude Change.* New York: Springer-Verlag.

Ross, E. A. (1908). *Social Psychology.* New York: Macmillan.

Scheff, T. (1966). *Being Mentally Ill: A Sociological Theory.* Chicago: Aldine.

Scott, W. A. (1957). Attitude change through reward of verbal behavior. *Journal of Abnormal and Social Psychology, 12,* 261–278.

Skinner, B. F. (1957). *Verbal Behavior.* New York: Appleton-Century-Crofts.

Staats, A. W., & Staats, C. K. (1958). Attitudes established on classical conditioning. *Journal of Abnormal and Social Psychology, 57,* 37–40.

Staats, A. W., Staats, C. K., & Crawford, H. L. (1962). First-order conditioning of meaning and the parallel conditioning of the GSR. *Journal of General Psychology, 67,* 159–167.

Taylor, S. E. (1975). On inferring one's attitudes from one's behavior: Some delimiting conditions. *Journal of Personality and Social Psychology, 31,* 126–131.

Thibaut, J. W., & Kelley, H. H. (1959). *The Social Psychology of Groups.* New York: John Wiley & Sons.

Thurstone, I. L. (1928). Attitudes can be measured. *American Journal of Sociology, 33,* 529–554.

Triplett, N. (1897). The dynamogenic factors in pacemaking and competition. *American Journal of Psychology, 9,* 507–533.

Weary, G., & Mirels, H. L. (1982). (Eds.). *Integrations of Clinical and Social Psychology.* New York: Oxford University Press.

Yarkin, R. L., Harvey, J. H., & Bloxom, B. M. (1981). Cognitive sets, attribution, and social interaction. *Journal of Personality and Social Psychology, 41,* 243–252.

CHAPTER 14

PSYCHOSOCIAL DETERMINANTS OF DISORDER: SOCIAL SUPPORT, COPING AND SOCIAL SKILLS INTERACTIONS

Rolf A. Peterson

The role of social support, coping style, and social skill have received a great deal of attention as potentially important factors in the development and treatment of psychopathology. Reviews by Cohen and McKay (1984), Kessler, Price, and Wortman (1985), Solomon and Rothblum (1986), and Wortman and Dunkel-Schetter (1987) have highlighted the complexity of each variable as well as the complex interplay between social support, coping, and social skill. The goal of this paper is to review the recent literature with the focus on social support as a determinant of behavioral disorders and the interaction of social support with coping style and social skill in producing adjusted and maladjusted behavior patterns. The primary question addressed is the impact of social support, social skill and coping style on the prevention and treatment of psychopathology. Before discussing psychosocial factors per se, a brief discussion of how psychosocial factors fit within the context of a behavioral/learning approach is necessary.

The general learning/behavioral approach to understanding human behavior involves the Stimuli-Organism-Response-Outcome chain. Thus, a problem behavior and/or intervention may be associated with any of the links within the chain, depending on the outcome of the behavioral analysis. Social support appears to be important in how the person (O) interprets and appraises stimuli as well as moderates and interprets the response. Thus, both the cognitive and emotional internal reactions may be influenced by social support. Social support can also be viewed as a stimulus (e.g., praise) for which the person's response to support can be evaluated. Coping and social skill (responses) are more easily identified as responses that can be evaluated in terms of outcome. The response is not independent of the person's cognitive interpretation of the stimuli nor the person's expectation of response and outcome efficacy (Bandura, 1977). Lazarus and Folkman (1984) have suggested the person's cognitive appraisal of the stimulus, and associated emotional reaction, determine the coping method selected by the individual.

The analysis of the entire S-R-Outcome chain, including the internal interpretation of the stimulus and the resulting cognitions and expectations, is necessary to determine the points in the process that are the most critical for change and therefore can be the most effectively changed. It is within this general context that the role of social support, coping and social skill as inter-related factors in the prevention and treatment of behavioral disorders will be evaluated.

SOCIAL SUPPORT DEFINITION

The scientific literature contains numerous articles which suggest social support may be an important factor in the prevention of psychological problems and in the reduction of psychological problems (Wortman & Dunkel-Schetter, 1987). One of the core problems with the concept of social support has been how to define and measure the variable (Lieberman, 1986; Monroe & Steiner, 1986).

Several conceptualizations of the types or functions of social support have been proposed. Caplan (1974) emphasized the informational aspects of social support. Caplan suggested social support provided feedback to the person about themselves and their view of the world. Cobb (1976) proposed a similar definition that emphasized the enduring social ties and the role of emotional/self-worth information. House (1981) suggested social support has a multi-function impact on the individual. The interpersonal transactions that function as social support may relate to emotional needs, material needs, general information, and self-appraisal information (House, 1981). Wortman and Dunkel-Schetter (1987) indentified seven types (roles) of support that have been reported in the literature. The seven types can be categorized as self-value feedback, belief and feeling validation, expression encouragement, information, material aid, task assistance, and network belongingness. These multitypes of support can be measured as tangible-objective events or as self-report perceived level of support and/or satisfaction with support received. Most studies measure only a few types of social support or some general global perception of received social support.

Several measures have been developed that can be used in research or for clinical assessment. The Perceived Social Support measure by Procidano and Heller (1983) provides a self-report on the availability and role of family and friends in the person's life. The Multidimensional Scale of Perceived Social Support (Zimet, Dahlem, Zimet, & Farley, 1988) assesses one's subjective evaluation of social support adequacy in regard to family, friend and significant other support. Both of these measures are 'perceived support' measures. Although tending to have the strongest association with mood state, it is important to note that self-reported perceived or satisfaction with support may in part be due to mood state (Cohen, Towbis & Flocco, 1988). Mood has little effect on report or actual social contacts or support events (Cohen et al., 1988). Measurement of perceived support is an important part of assessing the individual's cognitive perception of support and quality of life. Additionally, both the researcher and clinician need to assess actual social network and support events in order to determine how availability of support, type of support behaviors, and/or the person's perceptions and expectations are related to disordered functioning in a given case and in the general population. One extensive measure of social support availability and support events, as well as an assessment of satisfaction about the amount of support, is the Arizona Social Support Interview Schedule (Barrera, 1981). This interview schedule provides more of a self-report behavioral analysis than a norm based scales score. When measures of perceived support and social network are combined, a more accurate view of social support deficiencies may be provided than with a single approach.

Social support has been examined as a direct, main effect factor and as a buffering, interaction effect factor (Cohen & McKay, 1984). The main effect hypothesis postulates that level of social support is related to physical and mental health regardless of stressor/demand severity. The buffer hypothesis, (Cobb, 1976), states that social support level is only important for people under high stressor conditions. In other words, social support level is unrelated to psychopathology for individuals under low or normal demand conditions but high social support is important to preventing or reducing emotional problems for individuals under high demand/stressor conditions. The experimental data have been inconsistent, with both hypotheses receiving some support and disconfirmation (Cohen & McKay, 1984; Thoits, 1982; Wertlieb, Weigel, & Feldstein, 1987). The support and/or lack of support for a particular effect (main versus interaction) appears to depend on measurement and population factors.

To resolve some of the issues regarding the role of social support, Cohen and McKay (1984) proposed the "Stressor-Support Specificity Model of Buffering." In this model the effect of social support depends on the extent to which the support resources (e.g., tangible, appraisal) fit the stressor demand-threat conditions. Although this model is consistent with a logical interpretation of social support mechanisms, little research has been done that directly assesses the need-availability match hypothesis. Further, it is not clear that stressors always elicit specific needs. It may be that a particular need is primary, but under high threat conditions, the person has a complex reaction involving a variety of tangible and/or psychological needs. Thus, for more precise prediction and understanding of social support effects further work is needed to determine the best definitional and measurement approach for specific situations and populations. Still, even with the unresolved issues regarding definition and measurement (Monroe & Steiner, 1986; Cohen, Towbes & Flocco, 1988), a body of literature has developed that is relevant to understanding and preventing psychopathology.

SOCIAL SUPPORT AND PSYCHOPATHOLOGY

Several studies have looked at adjustment or amount of symptomatology as a correlate of social support within the general population. Hays and Oxley (1986) looked at adaptation to college among college freshmen as it related to network size and network functions (e.g., fun/relaxation, emotional support). A larger network was associated with fewer psychopathological symptoms and better self-reported adaptation to college (Hays & Oxley, 1986). Although network size was associated with adjustment, social competence may have been an underlying factor that predicted both network size and adjustment. Also, the primary functional aspect of the network which related to adaptation was the extent to which it provided fun/relaxation. Because all measurement was during the first semester, the pre-college family informal networks may have been more critical for emotional and appraisal support. Overtime, a negative aspect of network, was also noted. Negative interactions with network members increased over the semester and level of negative interaction was associated with greater symptoms and poorer college adaptation. As Hays and Oxley (1986) and Foorman and Lloyd (1986) point out, and as is indicated in a number of studies, a social support network may produce demands and be a stressor. The negative effects of social support (to be discussed later) appear to be especially strong when the network contains a conflicted close relationship.

Zimet, Dahlem, Zimet, and Farley (1988) looked at the correlation between sources of support and psychological symptoms in college students as part of the development of a social support scale. Perceived family support was negatively correlated with anxiety and depression, friend support was negatively related to depression, and significant other support was negatively correlated with depression scores. The perceived family support scale was the most strongly related over-all and this may explain why Hays and Oxley (1986) failed to find appraisal and emotional support as a factor in adjustment among beginning college students.

In a somewhat different vein, Hardy and Smith (1988) found that college students who score high on the Cook-Medley Hostility Scale reported less social support, as well as more negative life events, than the group low in hostility. Although the authors were focusing on vulnerability to health problems, hostility is also an important psychological adjustment variable and the correlation between social support and hostility is similar to the results of studies measuring anxiety and depression (Hays & Oxley, 1986; Zimet et al., 1988). Unfortunately, as with most of the studies on social support, the direction of causality of the association between psychopathology and social support cannot be determined. It is very possible that high hostility and the associated behaviors, produced low social support or prevented the development of a positive social support network.

The relationship between reported supportive transactions, network size, satisfaction with support and symptomatology was also evaluated within a college student sample by Sandler and Barrera (1984). Support satisfaction had a direct (main-effect) and an interactive (buffering) relationship with psychological symptoms. The size of the conflicted network was also related to symptomatology.

Studies focusing on adult, community populations also find social support related to psychopathology (Brown, Bhrolchain, & Harris, 1975; Warheit, Vega, Shimizu, & Meinhardt, 1982; Lehman, Ellard, & Wortman, 1986; Fiore, Coppel, Becker, & Cox, 1986; Pagel, Erdly, & Becker, 1987). In an early study on the topic, Brown et al. (1975) found that women aged 18-65 with an opposite sex confidant (a person they could confide in) were less likely to show increased psychiatric problems under high stress conditions than women without a confidant. No differences between the groups were present under low stress conditions. The interaction found by Brown et al. (1975), was consistent with the buffering hypothesis and indicated the importance of having a significant other for psychological support when faced with severe negative life events.

In a large epidemiological study, Warheit et al. (1982) failed to find a relationship between the presence of a family member network and mental health. However, among the Anglo and Mexican-American subsamples, the presence of a friend support network was associated with a lower number of psychological problems. Thus, Brown et al. (1975), and Warheit et al. (1982), found the same general social support–psychopathology relationship as has been reported for college populations (Sandler & Barrera, 1984; Zimet, et al., 1988).

Three studies focused on individuals dealing with high stress-demand situations. Both Fiore et al. (1988), and Pagel et al. (1987), studied spouses of individuals with Alzheimer's disease. Fiore et al. (1986) measured a wide variety of social support dimensions and types, and found 'satisfaction with support' to be the only social support index related to depression and psychopathology. In a prospective study with a 10 month follow-up, Pagel et al. (1987) found that reported degree of upset with the support network was associated with level of depression. The rating of degree to which the network member was perceived to be helpful was not independently associated with depression but did interact with network upset in accounting for significant variance in the prediction of depression. Fiore et al. (1986) used a measure of satisfaction with support, and thus the score may be related to network conflict, as suggested by the results of the Pagel et al. (1987) study.

Degree of network conflict appears to be a critical factor in the social support-psychological functioning relationship. To assess how individuals perceive the helpful and unhelpful aspects of interactions with network members, Lehman, Ellard, and Wortman (1986) interviewed 94 people who had lost a spouse or child in a motor vehicle accident. The two most helpful types of social support reported were interacting with someone with a similar misfortune and the opportunity to express feelings. Thus, information and acceptance were viewed as positive. On the other hand, direct advice giving and pressure to reduce bereavement were reported to be unhelpful types of support. It would appear the people who have suffered a tragic loss find communication with individuals with common experiences and unconditional acceptance of feelings by the network to be the most comforting sources of support. How effective these types of support are in reducing excessive negative mood and/or preventing unresolved bereavement were not assesssed (Lehman et al., 1986).

Family and friend perceived social support was compared for a chronic-psychiatric sample, a diabetic sample and college undergraduates by Lyons, Perrotta, and Hancher-Kvam (1988). The clinic psychiatric patients reported less perceived family social support than the diabetic subjects and students, but differed on friend support only from the student sample. Low support availability and/or the inability to elicit social support appears to be an important aspect of the chronic psychiatric patients' functioning level.

In an attempt to examine differences between early-onset dysthymia patients and nonchronic major depression patients, Klein, Taylor, Dickstein, and Harding (1988) compared these diagnostic groups on a variety of measures. Dysthymia (chronic moderate depression) patients reported significantly lower levels of appraisal support, belonging support, and tangible support. Additionally, although the groups were similar in terms of stressful life events, the dysthymics reported more chronic strain and perceived stress. Thus, perceived social support was associated with perceived level of stress but not reported negative life events, when comparing dysthymic patients with major depression patients.

Biglan et al. (1985) examined problem solving interactions among normal married couples and couples in which the wife was depressed. The depressed member couples displayed less self-disclosure than normal couples. When the depressed member couples were divided into marital distress versus no distress groups, the distress group performed less facilitative behavior. Self-disclosure and facilitation in problem solving can be viewed as social support behaviors, and, therefore, the Biglan et al. (1985) results are consistent with the expected poor social support–depression association. Similarly, Hersen, Bellack, Himmelhock, and Thase (1984) suggested that depressed individuals often lack a close and meaningful relationship with a significant other. Additionally, Biglan et al. (1985) suggested that the wife's depressive behavior operated to reduce interpersonal conflict and negative experiences while producing conditions which prevented the development of positive social support resources. The outcome for a given behavior (symptom) needs to be evaluated in terms of both positive and negative effects and immediate and long term effects.

Social support has been found to be associated with rate of recovery from psychiatric problems. Davies, Rose, and Cross (1983) assessed psychiatric symptoms among patients consulting a general practitioner at the time of the consultation and 6 months later. Higher levels of reported social support were associated with a reduction in psychiatric symptoms when no major negative life events were reported. Major negative life events, regardless of support level, resulted in a failure to improve and major positive life events were associated with improvement. Whereas the presence of major negative life events may have temporarily prevented improvement, positive social support may play an important role in recovery from psychiatric problems for the nonhighly stressed individual and also be important for recovery of the high stressor group at some later point after the occurrence of a highly negative life event.

Another group in which poor social support is associated with the disorder and recovery rate is Posttraumatic Stress Disorder (PTSD), (Foy, Resnick, Sipprelle, & Carroll, 1987; Solomon, Mikulincer, & Avitzur, 1988). Foy et al. (1987), in a review of factors associated with the development and maintenance of PTSD, note that studies have found problems with intimacy, sociability and marital adjustment among the PTSD samples. Solomon et al. (1988), and Solomon, Mikulincer, and Flum (1988), reported on Israeli soldiers involved in the 1982 Lebanon War and assessed individuals exhibiting PTSD over a 3-year time span. The severity of PTSD at each time period was associated with social resources and perceived social support. Social support also increased with improvement of PTSD but coping strategies were the best predictor of change over time. Social support was associated with coping style but failed to interact with locus of control, as the author's had expected (Solomon, Mikulincer, & Avitzur, 1988). The authors suggested the failure to find a social support locus of control interaction may have been due to the way social support was measured. Again, social support was associated with disorder severity and changed with improvement in disorder but the process of how social support influences psychopathology and change in psychopathology is unclear. The Solomon, Mikulincer, and Avitzur (1988) and the Solomon, Mikulincer, and Flum (1988) findings suggest coping style predicts change rather than level of social support. It is possible that social support operates through appraisal and coping strategy rather than directly on symptom type or level. This issue will be discussed in more detail in the section on coping and social support.

With depressed patients assessed at intake, Krantz and Moos (1988) found that a low quality "most important person" relationship and the use of avoidance coping strategies were among the risk factors for poor treatment outcome. Similarly, nonpsychotic depressed women were followed up at 6 months posthospitalization by Goering, Wasylenki, Lancee, and Freeman (1983) to assess factors associated with rehospitalization. Social support was the only factor related to readmission and, additionally, poor social support was related to poor symptom outcome and poor social adjustment. Unfortunately, measures of symptom level and social skills were not obtained at discharge so the reason for the existence of poor social support among re-admitted patients still needs to be elucidated.

The use of social support as a treatment modality suggests that increases in social support and social interaction assist in reducing relapse and hospital re-admission. Schoenfeld, Halevy, Hamley-Van-der-Velden, and Ruhf (1986) examined length of stay and rehospitalization rates for psychiatric inpatient participants and nonparticipants in network therapy. The therapy provided sessions with relatives and friends to develop an emotional and practical support system for the patients. The number of days hospitalized and the frequency of rehospitalizations fell dramatically for the participants as compared to nonparticipants. Likewise, Harris and Bergman (1985) reported significant deficits in the social networks of chronic psychiatric patients and presented case examples to illustrate the positive effect of social network intervention. Liberman, Mueser, and Wallace (1986) provided social skills training for schizophrenic inpatients at risk for nonrelease and/or rehospitalization postdischarge. The focus here was on social skills but it is important to note that social functioning improved, which should improve social support, and improvements were reported in level of severity of psychopathology and rehospitalization.

In most of the studies cited thus far, social support has had positive associations with adjustment. The other side of the support issue is negative support or the presence of conflict in the support network. As previously noted, demand and conflict appear to be negatively associated with adjustment (Hays & Oxley, 1986; Pagel et al., 1987; Krantz & Moos, 1988). A positive relationship and/or a conflictual relationship with a 'significant other' may be the critical factor in the role social support plays for some individuals (Coyne & DeLongis, 1986). This might be especially true for an individual who relies heavily on one or two people for their social support resources. Leavy (1983), in a review of social support effects, concluded that having a "confidant," a special trusted person, was critical for dealing with life's stressors. What is the effect if the relationship with a confidant is a conflicted or problem relationship? In Monroe,

Bromet, Connell, and Steiner (1986), social support functioned as a buffer against depression among healthy women in a nonconflicted marital relationship but when subjects with problem relationships were added to the sample the effects tended to wash out. Thus, the number of people in a given sample with conflicted significant social support relationships may determine the outcome effects for social support in a given study.

The psychological cost associated with perceived nonsupport by the spouse was shown in a study of mothers of developmentally disabled children by McKinney and Peterson (1987). Although mothers scoring more external in locus of control reported slightly more depression symptoms as a group, it was mothers who were internal in locus of control, and who reported a lack of expected support from the spouse who reported significant levels of depression, poor sense of competence, and greater over-all mood disturbance.

Ruehlman and Wolchick (1988) also found evidence that the behavior and support of a subject's most important person in their life strongly influenced the psychological state of the subject. The results of studies on the role of a "special significant other" suggest very careful behavioral analysis of close relationships is needed to determine both positive and negative social support influences. The interactions with a special, significant other are a particularly important source of support and source of distress (Coyne & DeLongis, 1986; Vinokur, Schul & Caplan, 1987). Behavioral assessment should include a careful evaluation of the support roles played by the people who are very important to the client.

In special situations, like medical illness, the significant sources of support may relate to the need-related important people in that situation. For example, Rosenberg, Peterson, Hayes, Hatcher, and Headen (1988) found that an important predictor of depression in medically ill, hospitalized patients was perceived physician support. For many chronic illness individuals, participation in a support group made up of individuals with a similar illness has positive psychological and physical effects (see Wortman & Dunkel-Schetter, 1987). Formally organized support groups for special crisis and/or illness groups have been demonstrated to be a highly effective procedure for preventing and/or reducing emotional problems (Bloom, 1988; Wortman & Dunkel-Schetter, 1987). This use of formal support groups for psychiatric patients has received little attention and has not been adequately evaluated. Group therapy and/or discussion groups have a long history as treatment approaches, but again, little formal outcome data are available.

Just as there has been an explosion in the use of professionally directed and/or organized formal support groups for medical illness groups, there has also been an explosion in the development of self-help support groups. Jacobs and Goodman (1989) estimate that 3.7% of adults in the United States are members of some form of self-help group. Almost every psychopathology type, chronic medical illness, and special need group (for example, parents of disabled, single mothers, spouses of psychiatrically ill, and phobics) have national and/or local support activities available for interested participants. Most of these groups are member-governed and focus on the special needs, and problems, of the identified group (Jacobs & Goodman, 1989). Although these groups fill a need unserviced by the mental health system, Jacobs and Goodman point out that we do not know how effective they are in preventing serious psychopathology and/or reducing psychopathology. Self-help and support groups are a major source of treatment for many people. The self-help group is usually identified by a common problem or common stressor situation and depends on both the main effects and buffer effects of the various types of social support to prevent and reduce psychological problems. We need to determine their effectiveness, identify the effective components and/or client groups and assist in developing effective self-help group models.

The use of social support as an adjunct or component in multifaceted treatment programs for behavior disorders has also increased in recent years. Barlow and Waddel (1985) have reported a positive clinical impression regarding the inclusion of spouse–patient discussion groups in the treatment of agoraphobics. Mermelstein, Cohen, Lichtenstein, Baer, and Kamarck (1986) found that partner support and perceived availability of support were associated with initial cessation of smoking as a function of smoking cessation treatment. On the other hand, Lichtenstein, Glasgow and Abrams (1986) reported on five studies that assessed the addition of social support treatment components to behavioral smoking cessation treatment programs and found mixed results. Lichtenstein et al. suggested further program development and evaluation of social support as a treatment component is needed. As with smoking cessation treatment, the formal inclusion of social support in behavioral treatment programs for a variety of disorders needs to be carefully evaluated to determine efficacy.

COPING STYLE AND SOCIAL SUPPORT

Coping style has been postulated to be an important predictor of mental health, quality of adjustment, and emotional reaction under negative stressor conditions (Lazarus & Folkman, 1984; Folkman & Lazarus, 1988; Moos & Billings, 1982). Lazarus and Folkman (1984) and Lazarus, Kanner, and Folkman (1980) have focused on a model of coping in which emotions and behavioral strategies are a result of the cognitive appraisal of the threat or demand. In the cognitive model the stimulus demand requires an appraisal of the severity of the threat, the strategies available, the ability to carry out the strategy, and the potential outcome of the strategy. The study of the appraisal process, the type of coping strategies used, and their association with adjustment is still in its infancy. In a recent review, Kessler et al. (1985) point out that although there is a great deal of interest in the concept of coping, how the concept should be defined and measured is still under debate. Issues regarding consistency in response across situations, accuracy and independence of self-report measures and the number and organization of coping behaviors continues to limit generalizations across studies and prevent strong conclusions regarding the role of coping (Folkman & Lazarus, 1988; Moos & Billings, 1982; Pearlin & Schooler, 1978).

Moos and Billings (1982) define three major coping dimensions (problem-focused coping, emotion-focused coping, and appraisal coping) that are consistent with the three dimensions that seem to encompass most of the proposed coping strategies (Kessler et al., 1985). For each general dimension, Moos and Billings (1982) define and measure several sub-factors. For example, problem-focused coping is made up of (a) seeking information or advice, (b) taking problem-solving action and (c) developing alternative rewards. Folkman, Lazarus, Dunkel-Schetter, DeLongis, and Gruen (1986) have proposed an eight dimension scale based of factor analysis. The resulting revised "Ways of Coping Questionnaire" includes confrontative coping, distancing, self-control, seeking social support, accepting responsibility, escape-avoidance, planful problem-solving, and positive reappraisal (Folkman & Lazarus, 1988). Folkman and Lazarus have provisionally categorized the scales as belonging to the problem focused, emotion-focused or a dual function dimension but emphasized the view that coping behaviors can vary in their coping functions depending upon the context of the behavior.

Most studies on coping use either the Moos and Billings' (1982) definition or the Folkman et al. (1986) definition of coping. Both measures provide useful research and clinical information. Also specialized measures have been developed for some populations, for example, the Coping Strategies Questionnaire (Rosenstiel & Keefe, 1983) for use with pain patients. With time, and the accumulation of studies, it will be possible to assess the best form of measurement for particular purposes. Indeed, several studies suggest coping may be an important factor in psychopathology. Thus, a variety of measurement approaches across situations and populations should be studied in order to develop a broad base of research from which conclusions can be drawn. The following brief review of selected studies will be used to indicate the general findings to date.

Severity and improvement in PTSD were associated with coping strategy in studies by Solomon, Mikulincer, and Avitzur (1988) and Solomon, Mikulincer, and Flum (1988) on an Israeli soldier sample. Severe PTSD was associated with distancing (denial) and emotion-focused coping (distress reduction), whereas problem-focused coping (problem solving) was associated with less severe PTSD. Also, negative life events produced a greater increase in PTSD symptomatology for subjects who engaged in high levels of distancing and emotion-focused coping. Negative life events and emotion-focused coping were associated, and as Solomon, Mikulincer, and Flum (1988) suggested, there may be a circular relationship between negative life events and negative coping styles with each causing more of the other.

Level of depression has also been associated with coping style. Rosenberg, Peterson, and Hayes (1987) found that medical inpatients scoring high on depression used more avoidance strategies whereas nondepressed patients used more active and problem solving strategies. Also, the nondepressed used more emotion-focused affective regulations than the depressed medical patients (Rosenberg et al., 1987). This is somewhat inconsistent with the expected depression and emotion-focused positive relationship but this relationship may depend on the subtype of emotion-focused stategy used and the particular stressor condition involved. Consistent with Rosenberg et al. (1987), Krantz and Moos (1988) found that avoidance coping strategies were associated with poor treatment outcome for a unipolar depression sample.

Sex differences have been found with women more often using passive or avoidance strategies (Solomon & Rothblum, 1986). Like Folkman and Lazarus

(1988), Solomon and Rothblum pointed out that different strategies may be effective with different demands/situations (e.g., active coping when control over the environment is possible) and overall adaptability may be associated with coping style flexibility rather than the frequency of use of a particular style. One coping style may be of value for a given set of circumstances and negative in another. In a study that examined the relationship between eight coping strategies and type of emotion experienced when dealing with an encounter for a middle aged adult sample and a sample of older (primarily over 65 years of age) subjects, Folkman and Lazarus (1988) found some differences associated with age. Planful problem solving was associated with positive emotional reactions as was positive reappraisal (an increased belief in self) in the middle-aged sample. Positive reappraisal was associated with negative emotions for the older sample. Confrontive coping (assertive behavior) was related to negative emotions in the younger sample and unrelated to emotions in the older sample. Whereas seeking social support had a positive effect among the older sample and was unrelated to emotion in the younger sample. The Folkman and Lazarus (1988) results are consistent with their view that a particular coping style is not always good or bad but depends on the type of demand and context of the demand.

COPING AND SOCIAL SUPPORT INTERACTION

Level of social support and type of coping style are both associated with psychopathology and appear to be associated with each other. Some studies have tried to determine the relationship between these variables and models of causality have been proposed (Heller, Swindle, & Dusenbury, 1986; Manne & Zautra, 1989). Holahan and Moos (1987), in a longitudinal study, found that positive family support was associated with a decrease in the use of avoidance coping over time in both a community and patient sample. Personality characteristics and coping style at time 1 were also strongly related to coping style at time 2. Thus, one of the determinants of coping style may be social support (Holahan & Moos, 1987), although it is not unreasonable to assume coping style may also contribute to level of support received. Consistent with Holahan and Moos, Manne and Zautra (1989) suggest a model (based on the path analysis model) in which spouse support influences type of coping strategies used by the partner. Both of the above results are consistent with a model proposed by Heller et al. (1986). This model proposes a circular relationship between social activity-support functions/activities and the person's appraisal process. Appraisal then interacts with the coping methods, with each influencing the other, and each independently contributing to health and mental health outcomes (Heller et al., 1986). This model will be difficult to test because of the interactive nature of variables but can serve as a useful guide to examining the roles of each variable and the interactions between variables, in mental health adjustment.

Thoits (1986), on the other hand, has offered a reconceptualization in which social support is a form of coping assistance. In her view, social support functions to change appraisal and reduce distress in the same way the coping strategies serve these functions. In other words, social support provides coping strategy assistance. From this perspective, therapy outcomes and assistance outcome rely heavily on the social support-coping assistance process. As suggested by Wortman and Dunkel-Schetter (1987), identifying the factors determining social support and how social support influences coping is important for the development of prevention and treatment models. Although the research to date suggests social support functions as a determinant of coping strategies, much more clarification of the process and situational problem type relationship is necessary before a clear guide is available.

SOCIAL SKILLS

In many of the studies cited thus far, one of the factors associated with psychopathology was social interaction problems, both in general social functioning and in developing a positive, intimate relationship. Social skill is one underlying mechanism which relates to the level of social support and/or the ability to obtain appropriate support from the support network (Wortman & Dunkel-Schetter, 1987; Kessler et al., 1985). Severe deficits in social skills may result in a chronic deficit in social support, which in turn may result in psychopathology or a vulnerability to psychiatric problems. Minor deficits in social skills may result in an inability to use or create special sources of support when special threats are present (relocation, family death, job loss, severe illness, termination of an important relationship).

Social skills have long been viewed as an important contributor to psychopathology (Phillips, 1978). Poor social skill is associated with isolation and loneliness (Jones, Hobbs, & Hockenbury, 1982; Vitkus &

Horowitz, 1987), social avoidance and poor social interaction (Dow, 1985; Strauss, Lahey, Frick, Frame, & Hynd, 1988). With children, level of competence, which includes social skill level, and social support, has been identified as a critical factor in reducing risk of psychological problems (Garmezy & Masten, 1986; O'Grady & Metz, 1987) and in defining strengths and improved prognosis within psychiatric samples (Cohen, Kershner, & Wehrspann, 1988). Similarly, social skill training has been an important treatment modality for chronic schizophrenics (Liberman, Mueser, & Wallace, 1986; Plienis et al., 1987), shyness and social phobias (Cappe & Alden, 1986; Christoff et al., 1985), and negative social behaviors and general psychiatric problems (Bierman, Miller, & Stabb, 1987; Tisdelle & St. Lawrence, 1988; Hersen, et al., 1984).

The goal of the brief review on social skill effects was not to provide an extensive review and discussion of the social skills literature, but, merely to indicate the important role of social skill as a potential determinant of social support availability, and, possibly coping strategy style. Social skill training programs usually deal with particular skills but often these skills (and skill deficits) can be defined as coping strategies, for example, problem solving (Christoff et al., 1985); communication and social feedback (Plienis et al., 1987). Thus, models that postulate social support and coping as determinants of psychopathology should include the role of social skill/social competence in determining social support level. For example, in the model proposed by Heller et al. (1986), which was discussed previously, social skill should be one variable that determines level of social/interpersonal functioning. As a logical precursor of social support, social skills should be included in psychosocial models of psychopathology and in the behavioral assessment of individuals with a behavioral problem.

CONCLUSION AND RECOMMENDATIONS

Research

Social support frequently has been found to be a correlate of amount of psychopathology and prevention or change in symptomatology. Social support has also been found to be correlated with coping style and social skill/social functioning. At this point it is necessary to intensify the effort to determine causal relationships and variable interaction patterns. With regard to social support, we need to further examine if and how social support influences appraisal and coping. The possible influences of social support should be expanded beyond the present models and hypotheses (Folkman & Lazarus, 1988; Moos & Billings, 1982; Heller et al., 1986) to include an assessment of how social support relates to other appraisal (cognitive) models. How is social support related to Beck's cognitive model of depression and anxiety (Beck, 1976; Beck, Rush, Shaw, & Emery, 1979), the attribution model of depression (Abramson, Seligman, & Teasdale, 1978), and Bandura's model of self-efficacy (Bandura, 1977)? Strauman (1989) has suggested self-discrepancies (actual, ideal, and ought to be self-view) are the important cognitive dimensions underlying psychopathology and Swallow and Kuiper (1988) make a strong case for negative cognitive social comparisons as an underlying factor in depression. With both of these processes, which seem to be part of the overall cognitive-appraisal style and psychopathology relationship, does social support (and if so, how) relate to self-discrepancies and social comparison? Both self-views and social comparison should be influenced by information, appraisal feedback and self-esteem support received by the individual. Additionally, models that have developed around specific appraisal situations, such as perception of illness (Peterson & Greenberg, 1989) need to be evaluated in terms of the casual relationships between social support, coping, expectations, and perception of environmental, social, and personal events. All of the above areas of research are important to developing a comprehensive theoretical framework from which to understand behavior and develop more effective forms of treatment.

On the applied side, relatively little research has been done on social support treatment and prevention effects with psychiatric and high risk groups even though social support and self help groups now play a major role in mental health services (Jacobs & Goodman, 1989). With the development of community programs, special interest group programs, and formal groups operated for medical and psychiatric patients, how effective different types of support groups are for different problem populations must be determined. A second very popular and effective approach to dealing with negative demands is stress management (Bloom, 1988). These programs often include cognitive restructuring (appraisal changes) and relaxation methods to control emotion. In my own experience, these groups also function as special social support groups and sometimes produce social groups that continue beyond the formal stress management training program. Frequently the difference between a social support group and stress management group is that the stress management group is more often time limited and may include formal relaxation training. The question to be answered is, how are these groups different and do they differ in their effectiveness for different populations and different types of stressors or intensity of stressor?

Another important applied area of research is the development and assessment of treatment programs aimed at producing the skills, and willingness, for the patient (client) to develop and expand his/her social support network. Treatment program (e.g., social skills, anxiety management) evaluation should include an assessment of change in social support and coping style and also evaluate the role of these variables in the maintenance of treatment gains.

Clinical

Behavioral assessment should include all aspects of the person-environment system. A detailed assessment of the problem stimuli – the social support – appraisal – cognitive interpretation – emotional reaction – coping methods, social skills response – outcome chain will provide the information to identify needed areas of intervention, and selection of methods of intervention with the best probability of success. This extended chain of assessment is an expansion of the triple mode response system suggested by Hollandsworth, Jr. (1986). In his model, he focuses on motoric, physiological, and cognitive responses. The extended chain mentioned above merely includes a greater emphasis on the assessment of stimuli/stressor, quantity and quality of social support, and coping strategy. In regard to social support and its use as a primary or secondary component of treatment, or when increased social support is a goal of treatment, perception of and satisfaction with social support should also be assessed in terms of the validity of the perception. From my own experience, it is often an unrealistic expectation about the amount of social support (e.g., sympathy, feedback, attention, and reinforcement) one should receive that results in a predetermined negative perception of social support. Thus, appraisal, interpretation of events, and expectations are not independent of social support, especially perceived support, and both the social support and cognitive systems, as well as their interaction, need careful assessment.

How to modify social support within the context of therapy has received little formal attention. The most common practice, usually with special-problem populations, has been to develop formal social support groups as the primary psychological intervention or as an adjunct to other treatment activities. The support group may consist of patients/clients or a combination of clients and relevant family members. The development of formal and social support groups with psychiatric clients is one recommended approach to assist in social support availability and network development. A second approach is to individually tailor the social support aspects of the treatment plan based on the assessment of perceived and network social support. Within the context of therapy (or as the therapy), social skills training, coping strategy assistance, and re-interpretation of social support and/or development of social support networks should be provided within the therapeutic interaction and through the use of homework assignments. In some cases, for example in cases of conflict with the person's most important support relationship, partners therapy and methods of dealing with interpersonal conflict will be the appropriate method of treatment.

Although we have a lot to learn about the role of social support, appraisal and coping, increases in social support generally result in a reduction in symptomatology or an increased ability to appropriately adapt to a negative event. For this reason, methods of increasing social support for preventative and treatment purposes should be considered an important component in the development of the treatment protocol.

REFERENCES

Abramson, L. Y., Seligman, M. E. P., & Teasdale, J. (1978). Learned helplessness in humans: Critique and reformulation. *Journal of Abnormal Psychology*, 87, 32–48.

Bandura, A. (1977). Self-efficacy: Toward a unifying theory of behavioral change. *Psychological Review*, 84, 191–215.

Barlow, D. H., & Waddel, M. T. (1985). Agoraphobia. In D. H. Barlow (Ed.), *Clinical handbook of psychological disorders* (pp. 1–68). New York: Guilford Press.

Barrera, M. (1981). Social support in the adjustment of pregnant adolescents. In B. H. Gottlieb (Ed.), *Social networks and social support* (pp. 69–96). Beverly Hills: Sage Press.

Beck, A. T. (1976). *Cognitive therapy and the emotional disorders*. New York: New American Library.

Beck, A. T., Rush, A. J., Shaw, B. F., & Emery, G. (1979). *Cognitive therapy of depression*. New York: Guilford Press.

Bierman, K. L., Miller, C. L., & Stabb, S. D. (1987). Improving the social behavior and peer acceptance of rejected boys: Effects of social skill training with instructions and prohibitions. *Journal of Consulting and Clinical Psychology, 55*, 194–200.

Biglan, A., Hops, H., Sherman, L., Friedman, L. S., Arthur, J., & Osteen, V. (1985). *Behavior Therapy, 16*, 431–451.

Bloom, B.L. (1988). *Health psychology: A psychosocial perspective.* Englewood Cliffs, NJ: Prentice-Hall.

Brown, G. W., Bhrolchain, M. N., & Harris, T. (1975). Social class and psychiatric disturbance among women in an urban population. *Sociology, 9*, 225–254.

Caplan, G. (1974). *Support systems and community health.* New York: Behavioral Publications.

Cappe, R. F., & Alden, L. E. (1986). A comparison of treatment strategies for clients functionally impaired by extreme shyness and social avoidance. *Journal of Consulting and Clinical Psychology, 54*, 796–801.

Christoff, K. A., Scott, W. O. N., Kelly, M. L., Schlundt, D., Baer, G., & Kelly, J. (1985). Social skills and social problem-solving training for shy young adolescents. *Behavior Therapy, 16*, 468–477.

Cobb, S. (1976). Social supports as a moderator of life stress. *Psychosomatic Medicine, 38*, 300–314.

Cohen, L. H., Towbes, L. C., & Flocco, R. (1988). Effects of induced mood on self-reported life events and perceived and received social support. *Journal of Personality and Social Psychology, 55*, 669–674.

Cohen, N. J., Kershner, J., & Wehrspann, W. (1988). Correlates of competence in a child psychiatric population. *Journal of Consulting and Clinical Psychology, 56*, 97–103.

Cohen, S., & McKay, G. (1984). Social support, stress and the buffering hypothesis: A theoretical analysis. In A. Baum, S. E. Taylor, & J. E. Singer (Eds.), *Handbook of psychology and health, Vol. IV* (pp. 253–267). Hillsdale, NJ: Lawrence Erlbaum Associates.

Coyne, J. C., & DeLongis, A. (1986). Going beyond social support: The role of social relationships in adaptation. *Journal of Consulting and Clinical Psychology, 54*, 454–460.

Davies, M. H., Rose, S., & Cross, K. W. (1983). Life events, social interaction and psychiatric symptoms in general practice: A pilot study. *Psychological Medicine, 13*, 159–163.

Dow, M. G. (1985). Peer validation and idiographic analysis of social skill deficits. *Behavior Therapy, 16*, 76–86.

Fiore, J., Coppel, D. B., Becker, J., & Cox, G. B. (1986). Social support as a multifaceted concept: Examination of important dimensions for adjustment. *American Journal of Community Psychology, 14*, 93–111.

Folkman, S., & Lazarus, R. S. (1988). Coping as a mediator of emotion. *Journal of Personality and Social Psychology, 54*, 466–475.

Folkman, S., Lazarus, R. S., Dunkel-Schetter, C., DeLongis, A., & Gruen, R. (1986). The dynamics of a stressful encounter: Cognitive appraisal, coping and encounter outcomes. *Journal of Personality and Social Psychology, 50*, 992–1003.

Foorman, S., & Lloyd, C. (1986). The relationship between social support and psychiatric symptomatology in medical students. *Journal of Nervous and Mental Disease, 174*, 229–239.

Foy, D. W., Resnick, H. S., Sipprelle, R. C., & Carroll, E. M. (1987). Premilitary, military, and postmilitary factors in the development of combat-related posttraumatic stress disorder. *The Behavior Therapist, 10*, 3–9.

Garmezy, N., & Masten, A. S. (1986). Stress, competence, and resilience: Common frontiers for therapist and psychopathologist. *Behavior Therapy, 17*, 500–521.

Goering, P., Wasylenki, D., Lancee, W., & Freeman, S. J. (1983). Social support and post hospital outcome for depressed women. *Canadian Journal of Psychiatry, 28*, 612–618.

Hardy, J. D., & Smith, T. W. (1988). Cynical hostility and vulnerability to disease: Social support, life stress, and physiological response to conflict. *Health Psychology, 7*, 447–459.

Harris, M., & Bergman, H. C. (1985). Networking with young adult chronic patients. *Psychosocial Rehabilitation Journal, 8*, 28–35.

Hays, R. B., & Oxley, D. (1986). Social network development and functioning during a life transition. *Journal of Personality and Social Psychology, 50*, 305–313.

Heller, K., Swindle, Jr., R. W., & Dusenbury, L. (1986). Component social support processes: Comments and integration. *Journal of Consulting and Clinical Psychology, 54*, 466–470.

Hersen, M., Bellack, A. S., Himmelhock, J. M., & Thase, M. E. (1984). Effects of social skill training, amitriptyline, and psychotherapy in unipolar depressed women. *Behavior Therapy, 15*, 21–40.

Holahan, C. J., & Moos, R. H. (1987). Personal and contextual determinants of coping strategies. *Journal of Personality and Social Psychology, 52*, 946–955.

Hollandsworth, Jr., J. G. (1986). *Physiology and Behavior Therapy.* New York: Plenum Press.

House, J. S. (1981). *Work stress and social support.* Reading, MA: Addison Wesley.

Jacobs, M. K., & Goodman, G. (1989). Psychology and self-help groups. *American Psychologist, 44*, 536–545.

Jones, W. H., Hobbs, S. A., & Hockenbury, D. (1982). Loneliness and social skill deficits. *Journal of Personality and Social Psychology, 42*, 682–689.

Kessler, R. C., Price, R. H., & Wortman, C. B. (1985). Social factors in psychopathology: Stress, social support and coping processes. In M. R. Rosenzweig & L. W. Porter (Eds.). *Annual review of psychology* (pp. 531–572). Palo Alto: Annual Reviews.

Klein, D. N., Taylor, E. B., Dickstein, S., & Harding, K. (1988). Primary early-onset dysthymia: Comparison with primary nonbipolar, nonchronic major depression on demographic, clinical, familial, personality, and socioenvironmental characteristics and short-term outcome. *Journal of Abnormal Psychology, 97*, 387–398.

Krantz, S. E., & Moos, R. H. (1988). Risk factors at intake predict nonremission among depressed patients. *Journal of Consulting and Clinical Psychology, 56*, 863–869.

Lazarus, R. S., & Folkman, S. (1984). Coping and adaptation. In W. D. Gentry (Ed.), *The handbook of behavioral medicine* (pp. 282–325). New York: Guilford Press.

Lazarus, R. S., Kanner, A. D., & Folkman, S. (1980). Emotions: A cognitive-phenomenological analysis. In R. Plutchik & H. Kellerman (Eds.), *Theories of emotion* (pp. 189–217). New York: Academic Press.

Leavy, R. L. (1983). Social support and psychological disorder: A review. *Journal of Community Psychology, 11*, 3–21.

Lehman, D. R., Ellard, J. H., & Wortman, C. B. (1986). Social support for the bereaved: Recipients' and providers' perspectives on what is helpful. *Journal of Consulting and Clinical Psychology, 54*, 438–446.

Liberman, R. P., Mueser, K. T., & Wallace, C. J. (1986). Social skills training for schizophrenic individuals at risk for relapse. *American Journal of Psychiatry, 143*, 523–526.

Lichenstein, E., Glasgow, R. E., & Abrams, D. B. (1986). Social support in smoking cessation: In search of effective interventions. *Behavior Therapy, 17*, 607–619.

Lieberman, M. A. (1986). Social supports—the consequences of psychologizing: A commentary. *Journal of Consulting and Clinical Psychology, 54*, 461–465.

Lyons, J. S., Perrotta, P., & Hancher-Kvam, S. (1988). Perceived social support from family and friends: Measurement across disparate samples. *Journal of Personality Assessment, 52*, 42–47.

Manne, S. L., & Zautra, A. J. (1989). Spouse criticism and support: Their association with coping and psychological adjustment among women with rheumatoid arthritis. *Journal of Personality and Social Psychology, 56*, 608–617.

McKinney, B., & Peterson, R. A. (1987). Predictors of stress in parents of developmentally disabled children. *Journal of Pediatric Psychology, 12*, 133–150.

Mermelstein, R., Cohen, S., Lichtenstein, E., Baer, J. S., & Kamarck, T. (1986). Social support and smoking cessation and maintenance. *Journal of Consulting and Clinical Psychology, 54*, 447–453.

Monroe, S. M., & Steiner, S. C. (1986). Social support and psychopathology: Interrelations with preexisting disorder, stress and personality. *Journal of Abnormal Psychology, 95*, 29–39.

Monroe, S. M., Bromet, E. J., Connell, M. M., & Steiner, S. C. (1986). Social support, life events, and depressive symptoms: A 1-year prospective study. *Journal of Consulting and Clinical Psychology, 54*, 424–431.

Moos, R. H., & Billings, A. G. (1982). Conceptualizing and measuring coping resources and processes. In L. Goldberger & S. Breznitz (Eds.), *Handbook of stress: Theoretical and clinical aspects* (pp. 212–230). New York: Free Press.

O'Grady, D., & Metz, J. R. (1987). Resilience in children at high risk for psychological disorder. *Journal of Pediatric Psychology, 12*, 3–23.

Pagel, M. D., Erdly, W. W., & Becker, J. (1987). Social networks: We get by with (and in spite of) a little help from our friends. *Journal of Personality and Social Psychology, 53*, 793–804.

Pearlin, L. I., & Schooler, C. (1978). The structure of coping. *Journal of Health and Social Behavior, 19*, 2–21.

Peterson, R. A., & Greenberg, G. D. (1989). The role of perception of illness. *The Health Psychologist, 11*, 2–3.

Phillips, E. L. (1978). *The social skills basis of psychopathology: Alternatives to abnormal psychology.* New York: Grune & Stratton.

Plienis, A. J., Hansen, D. J., Ford, F., Smith, Jr., S., Stark, L. J., & Kelly, J. A. (1987). Behavioral small group training to improve the social skills of emotionally-disordered adolescents. *Behavior Therapy, 18*, 17–32.

Procidano, M., & Heller, K. (1983). Measures of perceived social support from friends and from family: Three validation studies. *American Journal of Community Psychology, 11*, 1–24.

Rosenberg, S. J., Peterson, R. A., & Hayes, J. R. (1987). Coping behaviors among depressed and nondepressed medical inpatients. *Journal of Psychosomatic Research, 31*, 653–658.

Rosenberg, S. J., Peterson, R. A., Hayes, J. R., Hatcher, J., & Headen, S. (1988). Depression in medical in-patients. *British Journal of Medical Psychology, 61*, 245–254.

Rosenstiel, A. K., & Keefe, F. J. (1983). The use of coping strategies in chronic low back pain patients: Relationship to patient characteristics and current adjustment. *Pain, 17*, 33–44.

Ruehlman, L. S., & Wolchik, S. A. (1988). Personal goals and interpersonal support and hindrance as factors in psychological distress and well-being. *Journal of Personality and Social Psychology, 55*, 293–301.

Sandler, I. N., & Barrera, M. (1984). Toward a multimethod approach to assessing the effects of social support. *American Journal Community Psychology, 12*, 37–52.

Schoenfeld, P., Halevy, J., Hamley-Van-der-Velden, E., & Ruhf, L. (1986). Long-term outcome of network therapy. *Hospital and Community Psychiatry, 37*, 373–378.

Solomon, L. J., & Rothblum, E. D. (1986). Stress, coping and social support in women. *The Behavior Therapist, 9*, 199–204.

Solomon, Z., Mikulincer, M., & Avitzur, E. (1988). Coping, locus of control, social support, and combat-related posttraumatic stress disorder: A prospective study. *Journal of Personality and Social Psychology, 55*, 279–285.

Solomon, Z., Mikulincer, M., & Flum, H. (1988). Negative

life events, coping responses, and combat-related psychopathology: A prospective study. *Journal of Abnormal Psychology, 97*, 302–307.

Strauman, T. J. (1989). Self-discrepancies in clinical depression and social phobia: Cognitive structures that underlie emotional disorders. *Journal of Abnormal Psychology, 98*, 14–22.

Strauss, C. C., Lahey, B. B., Frick, P., Frame, C. L., & Hynd, G. W. (1988). Peer social status of children with anxiety disorders. *Journal of Consulting and Clinical Psychology, 56*, 137–141.

Swallow, S. R., & Kuiper, N. A. (1988). Social comparison and negative self-evaluations: An application to depression. *Clinical Psychology Review, 8*, 55–76.

Thoits, P. A. (1982). Life stress, social support and psychological vulnerability: Epidemiological considerations. *Journal of Community Psychology, 10*, 341–362.

Thoits, P. A. (1986). Social support as coping assistance. *Journal of Consulting and Clinical Psychology, 54*, 416–423.

Tisdelle, D. A., & St. Lawrence, J. S. (1988). Adolescent interpersonal probem-solving skill training: Social validation and generalization. *Behavior Therapy, 19*, 171–182.

Vinokur, A., Schul, Y., & Caplan, R. D. (1987). Determinants of perceived social support: Interpersonal transactions, personal outlook, and transient affective states. *Journal of Personality and Social Psychology, 53*, 1137–1145.

Vitkus, J., & Horowitz, L. M. (1987). Poor social performance of lonely people: Lacking a skill or adopting a role. *Journal of Personality and Social Psychology, 52*, 1266–1273.

Warheit, G., Vega, W., Shimizu, D., & Meinhardt, K. (1982). Interpersonal coping networks and mental health problems among four race-ethnic groups. *Journal of Community Psychology, 10*, 312–324.

Wertlieb, D., Weigel, C., & Feldstein, M. (1987). Stress, social support, and behavior symptoms in middle childhood. *Journal of Clinical Child Psychology, 16*, 204–211.

Wortman, C. B., & Dunkel-Schetter, C. (1987). Conceptual and methodological issues in the study of social support. In A. Baum & J. E. Singer (Eds). *Handbook of psychology and health, Vol. V* (pp. 63–108). Hillsdale, NJ: Lawrence Erlbaum Associates.

Zimet, G. D., Dahlem, N. W., Zimet, S. G., & Farley, G. K. (1988). The multidimensional scale of perceived social support. *Journal of Personality Assessment, 52*, 30–41.

CHAPTER 15

SOCIAL COGNITION IN BEHAVIORAL ASSESSMENT AND BEHAVIOR THERAPY

Frank D. Fincham
Thomas N. Bradbury

Is research on social cognition relevant to behavior therapy? The significance of this question is emphasized by the cognitive revolution in psychology and by the large body of knowledge that has accumulated on social cognition. Examination of this body of knowledge could potentially enrich our understanding of behavior therapy. Moreover, answering the question we pose might promote also the integration of social cognition research and clinical practice and thereby help arrest the growing schism between basic research and clinical application (see Chapter 1). Thus, the purpose of this chapter is to examine the relevance of the field of social cognition to behavior therapy and to suggest how an integration of these two areas might be best achieved. Before embarking on this task, we will define more precisely what is meant by the term behavior therapy and by the term social cognition.

ISSUES OF DEFINITION

The field of behavior therapy is a confluence of several intellectual traditions, including applied behavior analysis, the neobehavioristic stimulus-response approach, cognitive behavior modification, and social learning theory (Kazdin & Wilson, 1978). Furthermore, the broadening of the field to address a wider range of problems and aspects of human functioning has resulted in an extraordinary number of "behavior therapies." It is not possible in the present context to qualify each statement made about our initial question in terms of the various brands of behavior therapy, even though social cognition research may differ in its relevance to each. Instead, we will consider the relevance of social cognition to the "alleviation of human suffering and the enhancement of human functioning" by means of "environmental

---

*Frank Fincham was supported in the preparation of this chapter by a Faculty Scholar Award from the W. T. Grant Foundation and by Grant R01 MH44078-01 from the National Institute of Mental Health. Thomas Bradbury was supported by a grant from the National Science Foundation and a National Research Service Award from the National Institute of Mental Health.

change and social interaction," a concern that is shared by all behavior therapists (Franks & Wilson, 1975, p. 1).

Like behavior therapy, the term *social cognition* has a variety of referents, and "it is impossible to find two definitions that match" (Ostrom, 1984, p. 4). For example, Hamilton (1981, p. 136) considers the field to involve "all factors influencing the acquisition, representation, and retrieval of person information, as well as the relationship of these processes to judgments of the perceiver," whereas Forgas (1981, p. 259) sees social cognition as "devoted to the study of everyday knowledge and understanding." Similarly, social cognition has been equated with "person memory" (Wyer & Carlston, 1979), "how people think about people" (Wegner & Vallacher, 1977, p. vii), cognition "about people, groups, and social events and that colored by feelings, motives, attitudes, and emotional states" (Kosslyn & Kagan, 1981, p. 82), "the 'knowing of people'" (Higgins & Bargh, 1987, p. 370), and, most recently, as "an approach or set of assumptions guiding research in a variety of traditional domains within social psychology" (Sherman, Judd, & Park, in press, p. 1). The variety among definitions again creates a problem because the relevance of social cognition to behavior therapy may vary depending on what is denoted by this term. It therefore seems appropriate to discuss in more detail the nature of the field of social cognition; doing so provides important background information and will be used to structure the material presented in the remainder of the chapter.

THE REEMERGENCE OF SOCIAL COGNITION

There is consensus that social psychology became concerned with the study of cognition shortly after the first social psychological experiment conducted by Triplett in 1897. This initial research on social facilitation was behaviorally oriented but contradictory results showing that the presence of others sometimes inhibited rather than facilitated responding led researchers to embrace cognitive hypotheses (Farr, 1976). Social psychology therefore never fully adopted S-R psychology even though it was long regarded as the study of social *behavior*.

The early cognitive emphasis was reaffirmed and expanded in the founding of modern social psychology under the influence of Gestalt psychology (cf. Heider, 1958; Lewin, 1951). Indeed, Heider's highly influential work, *The Psychology of Interpersonal Relations*, was written partially in opposition to Skinner's behaviorism (Farr, 1981). Heider's concern is with the inferences a perceiver makes about another person from her observation of the person's behavior. In fact, the causal inferences the perceiver makes are considered fundamental to her understanding of the social world and gave rise to a voluminous literature on "attribution theory" that would come to dominate social psychology (Pleban & Richardson, 1979). In view of this cognitive orientation, Markus and Zajonc (1985) characterize modern social psychological research as reflecting an O-S-O-R orientation in which internal states of the organism (O) not only mediate responses (R) to environmental stimuli (S) but also determine the stimuli to which an individual attends. Thus, cognition pervades social psychological theory, the formulation of research problems, the selection of research methods, and even the evaluation of social psychological experiments (Zajonc, 1980). In short, modern social psychology might be more accurately described as "cognitive social psychology."

In view of these circumstances, it is surprising that the term "social cognition" apparently was first used in 1974 in the title of an empirical paper (Ostrom, 1984). Since then, there has been an explosion of interest in "social cognition" to the point where it has stimulated reviews in the *Annual Review of Psychology* for 3 of the last 5 years (Showers & Cantor, 1985; Higgins & Bargh, 1987; Sherman et al., in press). In particular, much of the recent interest in social cognition can be attributed to social psychologists' increasing attention to cognitive psychology.

The profound influence of cognitive psychology, especially at the level of methodology, has brought with it a change in the meaning of cognitive in social psychology; this factor may be at the root of the differing degrees of inclusiveness found in various definitions of social cognition. That is, the term *cognitive* has taken on the technical meaning ascribed to it in cognitive psychology and is used to refer to the cognitive *processes* involved in the representation and use of social knowledge. This emphasis thus contrasts with earlier work in social psychology where the focus was on particular cognitive *contents* (e.g., attitudes, attributions) and where the term *processes* was used more loosely to refer to the set of empirical and theoretical relations in the domain investigated (Ostrom, 1984).

The concern with cognitive processes was accompanied by a commitment "to promote the development of the information-processing metaphor as a common theoretical vehicle for the psychological sciences"

(Hastie et al., 1980, p. viii). This contrasts with the then dominant metaphor in social psychology of people as intuitive scientists seeking to understand the causes of behavior (cf. Kelley, 1967) and the metaphor to which it gave rise, that of people as "cognitive misers" (cf. Ross & Fletcher, 1985). These metaphors have far reaching implications because they influence the formal models that guide empirical inquiry and because they reflect a set of assumptions about human functioning that shapes psychologists' thinking about the questions they investigate and the manner in which they investigate them. Thus, although the metaphors are valuable in guiding research, they also impose limits on the understanding that arises from it.

From this brief historical sketch it can be seen that several factors might account for the lack of consensus regarding the definition of social cognition. First, researchers vary in the degree to which they identify social cognition solely with the information processing approach imported from cognitive psychology. Of particular relevance here is the extent to which such an approach is seen as a viable means of understanding persons as *social* beings (Forgas, 1981). Second, divergence may arise from acceptance of some of the imports from cognitive psychology (e.g., methodologies) but not others (e.g., the information-processing metaphor). Third, the recent emergence of the interface with cognitive psychology makes debate about its proper subject matter, approaches, and so on, appropriate.

The diversity outlined here reflects the vitality of the field of social cognition and is an important development in the evolution of social psychology. We consider this diversity to be healthy and view any attempt to choose a "correct" conception of social cognition as ill-advised because none can claim exclusive access to truth. This is not to suggest, however, that all viewpoints are equally relevant or useful for the behavior therapist. Thus, it is appropriate to examine differing conceptions of social cognition in the present chapter.

Our analysis of how social cognition is relevant to behavior therapy follows directly from the historical account outlined above. That is, we will examine the relevance for behavior therapy of research representative of the two dominant conceptual frameworks in social psychology over the last 20 years—namely, the attribution and information-processing frameworks. Both investigate peoples' understanding of their social world and constitute exemplars of the approaches taken prior to and subsequent to the influence of cognitive psychology, respectively.

The attributional and information-processing frameworks are considered in the next two sections of the chapter. Each begins with a description of the approach, then examines its application to behavioral assessment and behavior therapy, and concludes with a critique and set of recommendations for enhancing its contribution to clinical psychology. The chapter concludes by summarizing the major themes and outlines how an integration between social cognition research on the one hand, and clinical research and practice on the other, might be more fully achieved.

THE ATTRIBUTIONAL APPROACH

Description

The roots of the attributional approach (AA) are to be found in Heider's (1944, 1958) analysis of "naive" or common sense psychology. Heider emphasized the importance of common sense beliefs because they guide a person's behavior and contain many insights regarding human functioning. It follows that the AA is likely to be relevant to the clinician because maladaptive beliefs are often important in treating behavior dysfunction. Causal explanation or attribution is fundamental to Heider's analysis of common sense because "Attribution in terms of impersonal and personal causes, and with the latter, in terms of intent, are everyday occurrences that determine much of our understanding of and reaction to our surroundings" (Heider, 1958, p. 16).

Heider's observations provided the blueprint for later attribution models and research. For example, the distinction drawn between "personal factors" and "environmental factors" as causes (Heider, 1958, p. 82) remains fundamental to attribution research and dominates its application in clinical psychology (cf. Fincham, 1983). Similarly, the observation that people engage in a causal analysis that is "in a way analogous to experimental methods" (Heider, 1958, p. 297) was formalized by Kelley (1967) who proposed that perceived covariation between events is used to make casual inferences in a manner "akin to that employed in the analysis of variance" (Kelley, 1967, p. 195). This analysis of variance (ANOVA) model of causal attribution made salient the metaphor of persons as scientists that was already evident in the other major attempt to formalize some of Heider's ideas, namely, Jones and Davis' (1965; see also Jones & McGillis, 1976) model for making inferences about intentional behavior. Finally, it is noteworthy that Heider (1958) devoted much of his "naive analysis of action" to a consideration of how a perceiver understands the results or outcome of an action, a theme that is well developed in Weiner's (1985) attributional model of achievement motivation.

These models constitute the heart of attribution theory, a domain characterized by a set of loosely structured propositions (e.g., concerning the perspective of the naive scientist, the role of casual inference in mediating behavior) common to various models rather than a single, tightly knit theory. Numerous introductions to attribution models are available (e.g., Antaki, 1982; Hewstone, 1983a; Shaver, 1975) but because of the large number of studies conducted it is more difficult to gain an appreciation of the field of attribution research. Kelley and Michela (1980) uncovered over 900 references for the 10-year period prior to their review, and attribution research, particularly on applied topics, has since continued to thrive. More recent reviews of the field can be found in chapters (Harvey & Weary, 1984; Ross & Fletcher, 1985), edited volumes (Harvey, Ickes, & Kidd, 1981; Harvey & Weary, 1985; Hewstone, 1983b; Jaspars, Fincham, & Hewstone, 1983), and in an excellent, comprehensive book (Hewstone, in press).

Clinical Applications

Attempts to demonstrate the clinical relevance of attribution ideas began in the late 1960s (e.g., Ross, Rodin, & Zimbardo, 1969). However, the reintegration of social and clinical psychology (cf. Hill & Weary, 1983; Leary & Maddux, 1987), evidenced in the founding of a new journal and the appearance of several books devoted to this topic (e.g., Brehm, 1976; Leary & Miller, 1986; Maddux, Stoltenberg, & Rosenwein, in press; Weary & Mirels, 1982), has been accompanied by an explosion of clinical research using the AA. This research has been conducted in a variety of areas, including behavioral medicine (e.g., Watts, 1982), health psychology (e.g., Michela & Wood, 1986), learned helplessness and depression (e.g., Sweeney, Anderson, & Bailey, 1986), loneliness and social anxiety (e.g., C. Anderson & Arnoult, 1985), marital dysfunction (e.g., Fincham & Bradbury, in press), clinical child psychology (e.g., Fincham, 1985a), academic achievement (e.g., Forsterling, 1985), psychotherapy (e.g., Strong, 1982), and the maintenance of behavior change (e.g., Sonne & Janoff, 1982). Overviews of this research can be found in recent reviews (e.g., Brehm & Smith, 1986; Brewin & Antaki, 1987; Fincham, 1983; Harvey & Galvin, 1984; Lopez & Wolkenstein, 1990; Snyder & Higgins, 1988), in two books (Antaki & Brewin,

1982, Forsterling, 1988), and in a special issue of the *British Journal of Clinical Psychology* (Brewin, 1988).

The appeal of the AA in clinical research can be illustrated by its application in a case study. Johnson, Ross, and Mastria (1977) report the case of Mr. J, a man institutionalized because he claimed that he was being sexually aroused and brought to orgasm by a "warm form." These experiences were distressing to Mr. J. Although the psychiatric staff considered Mr. J to be schizophrenic (he was administered Thorazine), careful observation by Johnson et al. showed that he was inadvertently stimulating himself through leg movements. The "delusional behavior" disappeared when the patient was taught to attribute the cause of his sexual arousal to his leg movements and remained absent through the 6-month follow-up period (for other case studies see Davison, 1966; Skilbeck, 1974; Valins & Nisbett, 1971). The AA pervades this case study at several levels. These will become apparent in considering bodies of clinical research using the AA and their relevance to behavioral assessment and behavior therapy.

Behavioral Assessment

As the case of Mr. J illustrates, a client's beliefs about the cause of behavior can be dysfunctional. The absence of an understandable cause for the erotic experience resulted in misattribution ("delusional thinking"), and it is not uncommon in such situations for behaviors to be attributed to insanity (Farina & Fisher, 1982).

The phenomenon of misattribution, especially of physiological arousal, was the subject of many of the early clinically relevant studies stimulated by the AA. Studies on misattribution took two forms, investigation of perceived level of arousal and the perceived source of the arousal. These lines of research can be illustrated by two early investigations that became the prototype for later research. Valins and Ray (1967) provided snake phobics with bogus heart rate feedback while the subjects were viewing photographs of snakes and of the word "shock" accompanied by a mild shock. Misattribution subjects who heard steady heart beats for snake photographs but accelerated heart beats for shock photographs were more likely to approach and touch snakes than controls who thought the beating sound was extraneous noise. Second, Storms and Nisbett (1970) demonstrated that insomniacs who attributed their arousal to a neutral source (a pill), reported a reduction in the time it took to fall asleep as compared to subjects who could not attribute their arousal to the pill. These basic ideas have also been investigated in a variety of areas including speech anxiety, cigarette smoking, and social anxiety.

Although plagued by a host of problems (e.g., nonreplicability of the bogus feedback effect, Brehm 1976; the absence of attribution measures to support the misattribution interpretation, Fincham 1983), the ideas that prompted this research are applicable to behavioral assessment. That is, a thorough behavioral assessment should determine whether a client's presenting problem may result from misattribution. However, it is important to recognize the limited conditions under which misattribution carries implications for intervention. Most misattribution research has investigated subclinical problems rather than the more severe problems encountered in clinical practice, assumes that the client lacks information regarding the symptom, and that the therapist can easily provide information that results in a new, adaptive attribution. Thus, misattribution may be most relevant in regard to novel symptoms that do not yet constitute overlearned behaviors and for which a plausible nonarousing cause exists (e.g., symptoms resulting from self-attributions when the external sources of the symptoms are underestimated such as a job change, relocation, and so on) and symptoms that may be related to a lack of normative information (e.g., sexual behaviors that may reflect normal sexual functioning such as occasional erectile failure).

Thus, it is our contention that the misattribution literature represents a limited application of the idea that attributions may be related to dysfunctional behavior. More recent research has focused on multiple attribution dimensions and shows that attributions which do not specifically reflect lack of knowledge may be maladaptive. Thus, for example, there is considerable evidence that seeing oneself as the cause of a negative event, viewing the cause as stable or unlikely to change, and as global or affecting various areas of one's life is associated with several failures of adaptation (see Peterson & Seligman, 1984). The significance of attributions for relationship problems has also been investigated, and there is growing evidence that locating the causes of relationship problems in one's partner, and viewing the causes as stable and global is associated with dissatisfaction in the relationship (see Bradbury & Fincham, 1990; Fincham, Bradbury & Scott, 1990). In addition, attributions have been conceptualized in these literatures as stylistic and trait-like and not simply as discrete responses to specific events. Hence, for example, a distressed wife may tend to attribute all marital disagreements to her husband's selfishness (i.e., a disposition; an internal, stable, and global cause).

Broader application of the AA to dysfunctional behavior carries with it further implications for behavioral assessment. As before, it is necessary to determine whether the symptom results from dysfunctional attributions. Previously, as evidenced in the case of Mr. J, this approach would have sufficed. But now that attributions have been conceptualized in terms of a cross-situational tendency one might ask additionally whether the attribution reflects such an attributional style. If so, then changing the attribution for the symptom may be more difficult or even irrelevant unless changing the specific attribution is used as an approach to change the attributional style. Without a change in attributional style, similar attributions are likely to occur for future behaviors.

Alternatively, the attribution may not reflect an attributional style, in which case it is particularly important to examine whether the symptom has been maintained independently by current contingencies in the client's environment. The notion of an attributional style also alerts the clinician to the possibility that the dysfunctional behavior may be acquired independently but is maintained by the client's perceived cause for the behavior. Thus, attributions may be implicated in both the initiation and maintenance of the behavior. Finally, the level at which attributions occur needs to be determined. That is, do the attributions occur mindlessly and outside of awareness or, if the client is aware of the attributions, do they remain private or are they communicated to others? For communicated attributions, a functional analysis could be conducted to determine whether the attributions are maintained by environmental contingencies.

Although we have emphasized the implications that the client's attributions have for behavioral assessment, the case of Mr. J and the existence of a well-known attributional phenomenon highlight also the need to consider the clinician's attributions. Heider noted a tendency for the perceiver to attribute effects "entirely to persons" (1944, p. 361) and thereby underestimate the influence of other factors, a phenomenon that later became known as the "fundamental attribution error" (Ross, 1977). The importance of this phenomenon is apparent in assessing the role of attributions in clients' problems (e.g., a husband's dysfunctional anger due to his failure to recognize the situational factors contributing to his wife's negative behavior), but its significance for the attributions of behavioral clinicians may be underestimated. Langer and Abelson (1974) demonstrated that behavioral therapists, unlike their psychoanalytic counterparts, responded similarly to an interviewee when labeled as a job candidate and as a patient, a finding that is widely understood to reflect their adherence to data-based inferences and their lack of susceptibility to labeling effects. Davis (1979) offers an interesting reanalysis of these data using Bayes theorem to demonstrate that behavioral clinicians were not using base-rate information.

Historically, a behavioral orientation may have rendered clinicians less susceptible to the fundamental attribution error. However, the decreasing differences between traditional assessment and behavioral assessment in recent times (Barrios, 1988), and Snyder's (1977) demonstration that the psychoanalytic clinicians were more likely to make person attributions for the patient's difficulties, suggests that behavioral clinicians are increasingly likely to make person attributions. The implications of such a change are far reaching because it seems "clinically obvious that what we see as the cause of an event we want to change would heavily affect our next step" (Strong, 1978, p. 115). This is demonstrated in the case of Mr. J who was administered Thorazine as a result of his delusional behavior being attributed to schizophrenia. In addition, person attributions may also affect relapse. For example, Cohen and Streuning (1964) showed that clients treated by illness-oriented staff were rehospitalized earlier than patients treated by social-learning-oriented staff. In any event, it is important for the behavioral clinician to be continually aware of the fundamental attribution error not only because of its importance for understanding client attributions but because of its relevance to her own attributions.

In sum, the AA carries several implications for behavioral assessment. Specifically, a thorough behavioral assessment should include assessment of attributions in order to determine whether attributions (a) play a role in maintaining the dysfunctional behavior, (b) result from incomplete information, (c) should be the major target of intervention, (d) reflect an attributional style, and (e) are mindless, occur within awareness but remain private, or are communicated to others. The clinician also needs to monitor his or her own attributions for the client's behavior and evaluate whether he or she is falling prey to the fundamental attribution error.

Behavior Therapy

In view of the material presented thus far, it is not surprising to find that considerable emphasis has been placed on changing attributions in therapy; the case of Mr. J illustrates just how critical this task may be.

Strong (1978) has argued that changing causal attributions in therapy is a "key task" (p. 117) that is the "therapist's first order of business" (p. 127). Numerous analyses of how attributions might be changed in therapy are available for the treatment of individuals (e.g., Beach, Abramson, & Levine, 1981; Brehm & Smith, 1986; Forsterling, 1985, 1986, in press; Strong, 1978) and of dysfunctional relationships (e.g., Bagarozzi & Giddings, 1983; Fincham, 1985b; Holtzworth-Munroe, & Jacobson, 1987; Revenstorf, 1984). Attributionally oriented interventions may focus on changing attributions as an end in itself (e.g., when the attribution itself is a source of distress) or as a means by which to facilitate behavior change (e.g., when lack of social contact is inappropriately attributed to poor social skills).

Despite numerous papers outlining the implications of the AA for therapy, empirical evaluation of attributionally oriented interventions is rare. Indeed, the term *attribution therapy* was popularized almost two decades ago (Ross et al., 1969) but, with the possible exception of research on attributional retraining (see Forsterling, 1985 for a review), a distinct body of literature on attribution therapy has yet to emerge. Nonetheless, attribution retraining studies have demonstrated convincingly that inducing unstable attributions (e.g., lack of effort) for failure increases performance and persistence on achievement tasks.

Although promising, generalizing this finding to many therapy contexts is open to question because of the exclusive focus on changing attributions for academic or experimental tasks in nonclinical, child samples. Perhaps the most significant limitation of this literature is the use of clinically naive interventions in analogue studies. For example, in a widely cited study the 25-session intervention consisted of saying to a child after each experimentally induced failure "that means you should have tried harder" (Dweck, 1975). An attempt to use this intervention in a clinical context resulted in a child telling the experimenter in no uncertain terms, "I am sick of you telling me that I'm not trying and don't tell me that again" (Rhodes, 1977, p. 64). Moreover, the relative efficacy of such interventions is misleading because they are often not compared to more common clinical interventions. For example, Dweck (1975) compared the attribution intervention to one in which children received continual success. Thus, the alternative intervention consisted of "treating" a problem that involves reaction to failure by avoidance of failure.

In retrospect, the claims for an "attribution therapy" have been overstated and have detracted attention from the legitimate, but more restricted, role of attributions in therapy. With some exceptions (such as the case of Mr. J or the relatively infrequent instance where attributions are the presenting problem), the proper role of reattribution in therapy is as a technique used as part of a more broadly based intervention (e.g., as in cognitive therapy, Beck, Rush, Shaw, & Emery, 1979, or rational emotive therapy, Ellis & Greiger, 1977). In particular, clients' attributions for behavior change require attention if the effect of the change is to be maximized. For example, a depressed client who is induced to establish social contact with others may not change his negative beliefs about himself if he attributes the change to the therapist's skill, luck, or the friendliness of other people. Inducing the most functional attribution requires considerable skill. For example, the cause of the behavior change should be one that is plausible to the client (as in the case of Mr. J), should not be easily disconfirmed (without being deceptive), and should promote maintenance and generalization of the behavior change, a factor that has been considered the most important clinical implication of attribution research (Kopel & Arkowitz, 1975).

The efficacy of reattribution as an adjunctive therapy technique has received little attention. For example, the attributional reformulation of learned helplessness as a model of depression has stimulated a large literature (e.g., Sweeney et al., 1986, provide a meta-analysis of 75 studies on the attribution-depression relation) and even though the therapeutic implications of this model have been spelled out (e.g., Beach et al., 1981; Peterson, 1982), the utility of these implications remains untested. Some data on attribution techniques have emerged, however, from the recent application of the AA to marital dysfunction. For example, Baucom and Lester (1986) investigated the extent to which inclusion of an attributional treatment component increased the efficacy of marital behavior therapy. They found that while attributional training had specific effects on cognition, it did not increase marital satisfaction beyond that obtained from behavior therapy. Unfortunately, the attributionally oriented intervention was offered as a separate module of therapy and was not applied in the course of behavior therapy where it might have had the greatest impact. The evident need for such research on the utility of attribution techniques is matched only by the rarity with which it is found.

The lack of outcome research is underscored further by the need to understand the often differing explanations for client problems and therapeutic progress offered by client and therapist. According to Heider, the perceiver tends to "attribute his own reactions to the object world, and those of another, when they differ from his own, to personal characteristics" (1958, p. 157). This theme was elaborated by Jones and Nisbett (1971) and is now known as the "divergent perspectives hypothesis" or "actor-observer differences." Although the exact nature of actor-observer differences in attribution may be open to question (see Watson, 1982, for a review), the analogy to the client-therapist relationship emphasizes the fact that client and therapist are likely to reach different conclusions about the causes of the client's behavior and therapeutic outcome. This is important because it provides an intriguing perspective on the process that occurs in therapy. That is, successful therapy can be viewed as a process in which the client comes to believe the therapist's attributional analysis of his problems, whether it involves inappropriate reinforcement contingencies, faulty thinking or irrational beliefs, childhood experiences or anything else (Brewin & Antaki, 1982).

Traditionally, behavior therapy has eschewed causal analysis of the client's problem and has focused instead on functional analysis to determine the factors that maintain the problem. This does not mean that causal assumptions are absent in behavior therapy or that such assumptions are not, at the very least, implicitly conveyed to the client by the very nature of the intervention proposed. Moreover, it is quite possible that the client's rejection of the therapist's explanatory framework might account, in part, for dropout.

Our analysis suggests that the efficacy of behavior therapy might be enhanced by incorporating explicit discussion of the therapist's explanatory framework into the course of therapy and by careful monitoring of the client's reaction to and acceptance of this framework. This might prove to be a sufficient intervention when the dysfunctional behavior is maintained by the client's implicit or mindless attributions that occur outside of awareness. Making such attributions explicit and questioning their appropriateness is akin to some cognitive therapies (e.g., rational emotive therapy). Where the client is already aware of his attributions, the strategy we suggest seems particularly relevant as a precursor to intervention and is likely to facilitate the establishment of a collaborative set (Beck et al, 1979; Jacobson & Margolin, 1979). In fact, Hoffman and Teglasi (1982) found that providing shy clients with any causal attribution for their problem increased their motivation, involvement, and expectation of a successful therapeutic outcome beyond those of clients who were not given an explanation for their shyness.

In sum, claims for the therapeutic use of the AA have far outstripped their data base. This may be because the AA has often constituted a way of thinking in clinical psychology without being labeled as such. Indeed, it is difficult to imagine attributions being irrelevant to behavior therapy because "Whenever you cognize your environment you will find attribution occurring" (Heider, 1976, p. 18). This viewpoint, combined with the observations that attributions are intrinsic to language (Kanouse, Gumpert, & Canavan-Gumpert, 1981) and comprehension (Read, 1987), suggests that causal inferences are necessarily implicated in all interaction and thus their relevance to behavior therapy is not an empirical question. In any event, it is important to recognize that cognition is not limited to attributions. We have therefore argued that interventions which focus solely on attributions are rarely appropriate and that attributional techniques are best conceived as a "therapeutic adjunct in the armamentarium of the well-rounded clinician" (Fincham, 1983, p. 203).

Toward a More Complete Integration

Notwithstanding the valuable contribution the attributional approach makes to behavioral assessment and to behavior therapy, it is apparent from our analysis that little has changed since Harvey and Galvin (1984, p. 30) concluded that "the case for the application of attribution ideas to clinical phenomena still is quite incomplete." We therefore highlight three issues that will allow the potential contribution of the AA to be realized more fully.

Attributional Style

The notion that people exhibit an attributional style by making the same attributions across situations and time has been emphasized in theoretical analyses (e.g., Ickes, 1988) and clinical applications of the AA (e.g., Layden, 1982). However, the manner in which this construct has been investigated does not reflect adequately its potential significance. Most frequently, ratings of an individual attribution dimension (e.g., causal locus) for causes of several stimulus events are averaged and related to the phenomenon of interest. Less frequently, a composite attribution index reflecting an average score for the ratings of several attribution dimensions may be used (e.g., causal locus, stability, and globality). Both practices are unsatisfactory because average scores may arise in many ways and do not necessarily show consistency of response.

That is, the notion of attributional style emphasizes both the nature of attributions and variance in attributions. The variance can be applied to consistency of response within a particular dimension (e.g., seeing oneself as the cause of failure experiences) and consistency of response *across* dimensions (e.g., attributing failures to stable and global characteristics of the self, such as lack of ability).

Although attributional styles may be less pervasive than assumed (cf. Compas, Forsythe, & Wagner, 1988; Cutrona, Russel, & Jones, 1984), their investigation can yield information that is not available from the manner in which attributions are typically analyzed. For example, Baucom, Sayers, and Duhe (1989) show that the tendency to explain different spouse behaviors in a consistent manner is related inversely to marital satisfaction. The importance of this finding is apparent from its radical implication for marital therapy. Rather than focus solely on attributional content by inducing a spouse to make a particular, adaptive attribution for spouse behavior, the therapist might also try to increase the different types of attributions a spouse makes.

Two related issues need to be considered if the study of attributional style is to realize its full clinical potential. First, it is possible that attribution style is domain specific and it may prove fruitful to investigate domains defined at different levels of breadth (e.g., own interpersonal behaviors vs. behaviors of friends vs. behaviors of family members vs. spouse behaviors). Second, the event explained may affect the attribution offered (e.g., emotions vs. behaviors) and therefore require a taxonomy of what is being explained (cf. Lalljee & Abelson, 1983). Such research is important not only because it provides the clinician with normative information for evaluating client attributions, but also because it is likely to be related to the type of attribution offered.

Types of Attributions

Heider's naive analysis of action is applied largely to the outcomes of action rather than to the actions themselves. The tendency to overlook this distinction (cf. Lalljee & Abelson, 1983; Weiner, 1986) may be among the most significant barriers to the clinical application of the AA. Simply stated, explanations for outcomes (e.g., performance on an examination) do not focus attention on the actor's intentions whereas explanations for actions (e.g., a wife's criticism of her husband) frequently do. In fact, it has been shown that people take less time to infer intent than causality

(Smith & Miller, 1983), which suggests that perceived intent may be more critical, or at least rudimentary, in judging human action. These observations have profound implications because they lead one to question the type of attribution studied in clinical attribution research.

Consistent with the clinical attribution literature, we have focused on causal attributions. However, this becomes a problem when attention shifts to perceived intention as intent does not constitute a causal attribution dimension (Weiner, 1986). In the literatures on depression (Brewin, 1986), health psychology and criminal victimization (Shaver & Drown, 1986), and relationship dysfunction (Fincham, 1985b), distinctions have been drawn between causal, responsibility and blame attributions. Thus, a client may accept responsibility for his social isolation that is caused by increased work demands but may or may not engage in self-blame depending on whether the change in work load was voluntary and intentional (see Fincham & Bradbury, in press, and Shaver, 1985 for further discussion of these distinctions). As Shaver and Drown (1986) demonstrate, many studies report data that are difficult to interpret because they result from questions that include reference to more than one of the three types of attributions mentioned. Moreover, data are interpreted in terms of a particular type of attribution, usually causal attribution, even though the measures used to generate them ask about responsibility or blame.

Such practices are open to question. At the empirical level it has been found that people respond differently to questions regarding cause, responsibility, and blame. For example, Brewin (1984; Brewin, Robson, & Shapiro, 1983) has shown that causal judgments and judgments regarding a criterion underlying responsibility and blame attributions (perceived negligence) had independent effects on the outcome of rehabilitation. In a similar vein, Fincham, Beach, and Nelson (1987) provide data to suggest that distressed spouses may be more easily distinguished from nondistressed spouses on the basis of their responsibility attributions rather than their causal attributions.

Many clinically relevant symptoms (e.g., low self-esteem, spouse directed anger) result from an attribution (e.g., an internal attribution, a partner attribution) *and* the violation of some standard of behavior. Responsibility and blame attributions require consideration of such standards because these judgments only arise when something is done that violates what *ought* to be done. Clinically, this is extremely important because it changes the focus of attention. For example, it draws attention to guilt, perhaps one of the most neglected topics in behavior therapy despite its profound importance. Similarly, it shows that the standard contravened, rather than the attribution, is often the more appropriate target of intervention. These standards become salient when responsibility and blame, rather than causation, are considered in therapy. In fact, clinical attribution research on causal attributions may yield insights only because such attributions indirectly index responsibility and blame. As Orvis, Kelley, and Butler (1976, p. 379) note, "The *reasons* for behavior are learned as part and parcel of the *evaluation* of behavior." That is, a causal attribution in many circumstances reflects an evaluative judgment and is tantamount to a judgment of blame. It therefore behooves clinical researchers and practitioners to examine directly responsibility and causal attributions. Such application requires an understanding of what has already been documented in the attribution literature, an issue to which we now turn.

Models of Attribution

Of the classic analyses of attribution, Kelley's (1967) ANOVA model has had the most impact on clinical research. This model clearly influenced the attributional reformulation of learned helplessness (Abramson, Seligman, & Teasdale, 1978), and Forsterling (1986) has recently outlined how it can be applied in therapy. Other attribution models have had little, if any, impact on clinical research.

Unfortunately, there are a number of problems with Kelley's model that limit its clinical utility. First, it is rather abstract in terms of both the causes it predicts ("something" about the person, situation, etc.) and the antecedent information that determines attributions (perceived covariation of cause and effect along various dimensions). However, people give causal explanations that are usually quite concrete and specific and generate such explanations more quickly than the abstract attributions specified in the model (Druian & Omessi, 1983; Smith & Miller, 1983). Second, the model specifies that causal explanation can be achieved by simply observing co-occurrences of cause and effect and therefore depicts the person as a "mere statistician" (Ross, 1977). Although people can use such information in making causal judgments it is by no means clear that they engage naturally in such a process (Lalljee & Abelson, 1983). Third, the model does not predict responses for some configurations of stimulus information whereas more recent models do (e.g., Hewstone & Jaspars, 1987; Hilton & Slugoski, 1986). Finally, it cannot handle (a) situations where explanation requires numerous inferences based on our world-knowledge and where covariation information is unlikely to be helpful (e.g., "The Jewish Defence League sent a package of matzos to the Russian Embassy on Passover," see Leddo & Abelson, 1986; "The irate husband beat his wife"), and (b) sequences of actions, an important consideration because an action might be explained differently depending on what preceded it (cf. Read, 1987).

Although the limited impact of the classic attribution models reflects in part upon clinicians' lack of familiarity with them, it may also result from the fact that the analyses they offer seem unnatural and difficult to apply. Many, if not most, explanations of human action refer to the intent, goal, or purpose of the actor (Leddo & Abelson, 1986), yet attribution research has focused almost exclusively on causes rather than goals or responsibility attributions. Recognition of this fact has led recently to an analysis of explanation in terms of knowledge structures (e.g., goals, plans, scripts). From this perspective, explanation requires the construction of a scenario within which the action is embedded and causal inference is seen as analogous to story comprehension (Read, 1987). The construction of scenarios requires the person to determine (a) how individual actions form a plan, (b) what the goals of the sequence are, (c) how the particular plan achieves the person's goals, and (d) what conditions initiated the goal (Read, 1987).

This change in perspective from content-free models of attribution to those in which knowledge structures are central, has important implications. For example, the explanation of an event becomes the causal network within which it is embedded and is not exhausted by a single "why?" question. Rather the response to such a question will vary as a function of the particular knowledge structure used and the assumed knowledge of the questioner. This has given rise to a more natural, conversational analysis of explanation (Hilton, 1988). Clinically, this change in perspective focuses attention on the need to assess the appropriateness of knowledge structures (e.g., scripts, themes) used to generate explanations.

The knowledge structure analysis of causal reasoning clearly reflects the influence of cognitive psychology and the information processing approach. In fact, a computer program is available that can answer causal questions in the constructive manner that emerges from the application of knowledge structures (Wilensky, 1978). This development connects attribution research with more recent work in social cognition, a healthy development in view of Leddo and Abelson's (1986) observation that the existence of specialized cognitive processes solely for explaining events is both inefficient and implausible. Before turning to the information processing approach, it is worth noting that the limited overlap between basic attribution models and applied research occurs at a cost to both areas and that there is considerable potential for clinical application in the newer attribution models, specifically Weiner's (1986) attributional theory of motivation and emotion, Hilton's (1988) conversational analysis of attribution, and the knowledge structure approach to explanation (e.g., Lalljee & Abelson, 1983; Leddo & Abelson, 1986; Read, 1987).

THE INFORMATION PROCESSING APPROACH

Description

The information processing approach (IPA) emerged within experimental psychology in the 1950s and 1960s and is now a dominant force in psychology. At first glance, the task of characterizing the IPA appears overwhelming because it spans a "formidable array of populations, tasks, and conditions" (Lachman & Lachman, 1986, p. 32). This impression is reinforced by the fact that, unlike the attributional perspective, the IPA does not reflect the influence of a founding father such as Heider, but instead has multidisciplinary roots that include communication engineering and informational science, transformational linguistics, and computer science (Lachman, Lachman, & Butterfield, 1979).

Nevertheless, researchers who use the IPA share a common set of intellectual commitments and attitudes that shape their choice of theoretical perspectives, research problems, and methodological commitments. One of the commitments, a desire to understand cognitive processes, was mentioned earlier. This stands in contrast to research generated by the AA which focuses almost exclusively on attributions or judgments that are products of cognitive processes. However, it would be erroneous to conclude that the two approaches differ only on the dimensions outlined thus far because the IPA represents a broad attempt to elucidate how environmental and internal information is represented and used. More specifically, it entails consideration of (a) the interpretation and organization of information, (b) the integration of such information with existing knowledge to form a cognitive representation, (c) the storage of the representation in memory, (d) its retrieval, (e) determining the implications of the information for behavior, and (f) the generation of the behavior (Ottati & Wyer, in press). Thus, the IPA attempts to decompose a complex cognitive task into its various stages and then study these in relative isolation. Understanding complex tasks necessarily requires consideration of cognitive structures, processes, and products and their interrelations.

A factor gaining increasing prominence within the IPA is the role of artificial intelligence, a development that has led Neisser (1985, p. 18) to observe that "computer models may soon dominate it [the IPA] entirely." Whatever the cognitive model postulated, in principle it should be capable of computer simulation. According to Abelson and Black (1986), the criterion of computer simulation has three implications: (a) knowledge in the system needs to be organized in efficient chunks and this results in "top down" (theory driven) processing whereby the implications of what is already known to the system guide processing of new input relevant to that knowledge; (b) the system needs to be tailored to handle particular inputs and is thus content specific; and, (c) the system needs to be efficient and thus functionally flexible so that a variety of tasks can be handled with few mechanisms. Although computer simulation represents an ideal criterion, it has not yet been universally adopted and several influential frameworks (e.g., the propositional-network framework) in the IPA do not display the features outlined above. Nonetheless, even an approximation of this ideal requires conceptual precision, a necessary feature of any viable attempt to understand cognitive processes given the reliance on indirect measurement and inferential logic.

The absence of any referent to the term *social* in describing the IPA may appear to be curious. However, this reflects the perceived applicability of the IPA to all domains of cognition regardless of content. It represents a way of thinking, or in the words of J. Anderson and Bower (1973, p. 136), it is "a methodology for theorizing." Not surprisingly, therefore, research in social psychology using the IPA is very similar to that in cognitive psychology except for the use of person-relevant stimuli. That is, subjects tend to respond to word lists (comprising trait adjectives) and text (usually descriptive of a person and/or her actions). This is consistent with tradition in the area in which the IPA was first adopted and has remained most influential in social psychology, namely, person perception or impression formation (see Hastie & Carlston, 1980). However, the IPA is not limited to this area of research in social psychology and appreciation of its impact on social cognition can be gained from numerous sources, including reviews of the field, (e.g., Higgins & Bargh, 1987; Sherman et al., in press), a textbook on social cognition (Fiske & Taylor, in press), and the *Handbook of Social Cognition* (Wyer & Srull, 1984). More general introductions to the IPA are also available (e.g., Lachman et al., 1979; Lachman & Lachman, 1986).

Clinical Applications

Although the IPA has been used in experimental psychopathology research for some time (see Magaro, 1980), cognitively oriented behavior therapists began to pay attention to the IPA in the late 1970s (Landau & Goldfried, 1981). This is perhaps understandable insofar as cognitive psychopathologists tended to investigate possible malfunctions in the information processing systems of deviant populations and were therefore quite arbitrary in their choice of stimulus materials (e.g., geometric shapes, letters, digits). As Nasby and Kihlstrom (1986) note, however, most clients do not present with an overall breakdown of a cognitive function but with a problem that is specific to a particular domain, usually social cognition, that involves the content of the information in the domain or the way in which the information is used.

In the past decade, several writers have explored the implications of the IPA for clinical researchers and practitioners. This has occurred at the more general level (e.g., Bower, 1978; Ingram & Kendall, 1986; Kanfer & Hagerman, 1985; Merluzzi, Rudy, & Glass, 1981), in relation to specific cognitive constructs or phenomena (e.g., Goldfried & Robins, 1983; Hollon & Kriss, 1984; Laundau & Goldfried, 1981; Turk & Speers, 1983; Turk & Salovey, 1986), and in regard to particular disorders (e.g., Ingram & Reed, 1986; Litrownik & McInnis, 1986). In fact, the considerable momentum gained by clinical application of the IPA is evidenced by a recent book on the topic (Ingram, 1986) and a special issue of the journal *Cognition and Emotion* devoted to information processing and emotional disorders (Mathews, 1988).

Behavioral Assessment

The contribution to assessment, which was among the first clinical implications of the IPA to be recognized by behaviorally oriented clinicians, has focused on cognitive structures or organizations of conceptually related representations of items (e.g., attributes, objects, events, situations) and of sequences of events and actions. That the "schema" construct has dominated this analysis may be attributable, in part, to the central role accorded to it in both clinical (Beck, 1967) and cognitive psychology (Neisser, 1967). For example, Landau and Goldfried (1981) argue that the assessment of schemata provides a unifying framework for cognitive, behavioral, and traditional assessment, and they outline assessment strategies relevant to each type of schema analyzed. Such applications are useful because, as noted earlier, clients usually present in therapy problems relating to the content of their knowledge structures. As Abelson and Black (1986, p. 6) point out, however, the "schema concept is too easy to overextend" and both social and clinical psychologists have fallen prey to this temptation. (This is evidenced in attempts to classify schemata [see Hastie, 1980; Taylor & Crocker, 1981] and by the fact that schemata have rarely been defined independently of the effects they are presumed.) This is not to suggest that applications of the schema construct to behavioral assessment lack merit, especially in view of the fact that the term is often used to denote knowledge structures in general. Before considering such a contribution, a second clinical implication of the IPA that has gained attention in assessment, the use of cognitive heuristics, is briefly noted.

The metaphor of persons as "lay scientists" in the attribution literature formed a useful counterfoil for later research which showed that people use a number of shortcuts or heuristics in processing social information (Nisbett & Ross, 1980). This research, strongly influenced by work in cognitive psychology on judgments under uncertainty (for overviews see Kahneman, Slovic, & Tversky, 1982; Tversky & Kahneman, 1974), gave rise to the metaphor of the person as a "cognitive miser." The notion that clients' problems may reflect the use of such heuristics, the products of which were often labeled "errors" or "biases," led naturally to consideration of their clinical relevance (e.g., Achenbach, 1985; Hollon & Kriss, 1984; Turk & Salovey, 1985a, 1985b; Turk & Speers, 1983). The groundwork for this development can again be found in Beck's (1967) earlier analysis of depression in which he emphasized the notion of "faulty information processing."

The implications of the information processing perspective for behavioral assessment are rather obvious and can be illustrated by a clinical anecdote. In consulting at a school, the first author began an ongoing assessment by asking the teacher a general question about the target child's behavior over the last week. The teacher quickly responded that the child had "been awful" and went on to relate an incident in which he had turned the wastebasket upside down on her desk. The assessment then continued with questions about the child's behavior during the morning and the afternoon of each day during the preceding week. To the teacher's surprise, she found herself reporting that the child had behaved satisfactorily during each of these periods except for the incident reported. By the end of the questioning it was clear that the child's behavior had in fact improved over the last week. In short, the teacher had used the "availability heuristic" in response to the initial question. That is, she had estimated the frequency of the child's inappropriate behavior by the ease with which she could recall an instance of such behavior which, in this case, was probably related to its vividness.

The classes of problems to which the use of various heuristics can give rise are numerous (cf. Nisbett & Ross, 1980; Tversky & Kahneman, 1974) and should be evaluated carefully as the possible basis for a client's presenting complaint. A particularly valuable domain of application is in understanding referrals of children where the referring agent's perceptions play a critical role. Specifically, does the referral result from the adult's use of heuristics rather than from deviant child behavior? Finally, it should be noted that while heuristics represent a particular form of cognitive process, the literature on more general cognitive processes has received scant attention (for an exception see Nasby & Kihlstrom, 1986).

We have outlined only briefly the two major themes found in clinical discussions of recent cognitive and social psychological research using the IPA, namely, the discussion of schemata (cognitive structures) and heuristics (cognitive processes). Our treatment of these topics was limited, in part, to reduce redundancy with previous papers. More importantly, however, it reflects our belief that although the discussion of schemata and heuristics represents an important clinical application of the IPA, the most valuable contributions of this approach to behavioral assessment have yet to be realized. In the remainder of this section we consider three such contributions relating to the association between cognitive structure and process, methodology, and decision making, respectively.

Cognitive structure and process. The first contribution is primarily conceptual and lies in linking the two major themes found in clinical writings. Although it is recognized that cognitive structures and processes are inexorably linked (e.g., Turk & Salovey, 1985a), discussion of the precise nature of these links is conspicuous in its absence. Instead, the notion of "schematic processing" is simply accepted and the clinical implications of the various forms it might take are then explored. In this regard, clinical writers reflect the preoccupation with "theory driven" rather than "data driven" processing in social cognition research, a focus that may itself reflect an "availability heuristic bias" on the part of psychologists (Higgins & Bargh, 1987). Close examination of the data, however, can provide important insights into how knowledge structures are linked to cognitive processes, to the state of the perceiver, and to the nature of the information perceived. What emerges is a more balanced picture of a perceiver that is not predominantly theory driven or data driven but one "compelled by the relation *between* knowledge and events" (Higgins & Bargh, 1987, p. 387).

The significance of the relation between "theory" and "data" is apparent at various stages of processing. For example, the encoding of information cannot be considered independently of the events to which the perceiver has just been exposed. This is demonstrated in studies of priming where a knowledge structure made salient in one context is shown to influence the encoding of material in another context. Thus, for example, the valence of trait terms held in memory while naming the color in which a different word is presented affects later behavior in an ostensibly unrelated experiment; subjects' interpreted ambiguous target behavior in a manner that was consistent with the valence of the trait adjective to which they had earlier been exposed (Higgins, Rholes, & Jones, 1977; see also Srull & Wyer, 1979, 1980). Moreover, such priming effects occur even when the initial trait-relevant adjectives are presented subliminally (Bargh & Pietromonaco, 1982).

Such findings have profound implications for two reasons. First, most social information is somewhat ambiguous and therefore the relative accessibility of pertinent knowledge structures at the time of encoding will influence the meaning and interpretation of behavior. Thus, chronic exposure to a particular environment (e.g., via association with depressed friends, an aggressive manner of behaving that provokes aggression in others) can activate the consistent use of particular concepts (e.g., despair, aggression) in processing social information. Over time, the use of such concepts may ultimately result in maladaptive beliefs (e.g., a negative view of the world, that people are out to hurt you). Increased accessibility of a concept can also result from internal stimuli (e.g., negative thoughts). In any event, concepts can become chronically accessible and when this occurs the person becomes more sensitive to relevant stimuli even when the concept is not externally primed (Bargh, Bond, Lombardi, & Tota, 1986). Concepts relating to the self (e.g., persons' views of themselves as introvert, masculine, and so on) have been shown to be particularly relevant in processing social information (e.g., Markus, Smith, & Moreland, 1985) and are of considerable relevance clinically (see Kihlstrom & Nasby, 1981).

The importance of such priming effects on encoding is emphasized by a second consideration, the fact that what is stored in memory is the data to which the person has been exposed *as well as* an abstracted summary, judgment, or inference about the data. This is extremely important because the abstracted representation, rather than the original data, is often recalled when further judgments are made and can result in conclusions that are inconsistent with the original data (Wyer, Srull, & Gordon, 1984) even when the data are made available at the time of the later judgment (Schul & Burnstein, 1985). Not surprisingly, the strength of priming effects increases over time. Clinically, this suggests a need to evaluate the concrete details (data) regarding the events and circumstances surrounding the onset and maintenance of the presenting problem and the extent to which the client has drawn conclusions based on only part of the information (e.g., selective abstraction in depression may result from chronic accessibility of a self-relevant construct) or has drawn conclusions that were appropriate in the circumstances when the information was processed but are now maladaptive in the light of changed circumstances (e.g., fears related to a husband's behavior that arose in a prior abusive marriage).

In sum, the extent to which existing knowledge structures influence the processing of social information is at the heart of recent social cognition research (Sherman et al., in press) and should be used to inform clinical discussions of the IPA. However, the utility of clinical analyses of "schematic processing" will be enhanced to the extent that they are more specific (e.g., How do the effects operate? What are their implications when they affect different stages of processing such as encoding, storage, and retrieval?), include consideration of the circumstances under which "data driven" processing occurs, and are more closely informed by data rather than speculation (e.g., data from recall measures do not support the idea that schematic processing results in memory intrusions or distortions and most relevant findings are limited to the false recognition of foils that are schema consistent, see Higgins & Bargh, 1987; Markus & Zajonc, 1985). Finally, consideration of the stages of processing (e.g., encoding, storage, retrieval) not only forces a very precise clinical application of the IPA but also provides a general framework for behavioral assessment. Cognitive behavioral assessment and therapy have lacked a firm conceptual framework (Kanfer & Hagerman, 1985; Wilson, 1978), a weakness to which we believe the IPA can potentially speak.

Methodology. Methodology is the second level at which the IPA can contribute to behavioral assessment. Indeed, methodology has maintained the current resurrection of the schema construct in social psychology. Unlike previous eras (e.g., the New Look in social perception) where claims about the importance of hypotheses, sets, and so on soon dissipated in the wake of methodologically flawed research, the IPA brings with it impressive methodological advances. Of particular note is the fact that the cognitive phenomena under consideration are no longer limited to self-reported cognitions and include measures of how cognitions are organized (e.g., clustering in recall, sequence of retrieval) and processed (e.g., response time). The vagaries of self-reports have long vexed psychologists and are particularly troublesome in behavioral assessment because of the nature of the social context (the professional-client relationship) in which they are obtained. A further contribution of the IPA is the availability of multiple, disparate methods for assessing knowledge structures that lend themselves to the study of convergent validity (e.g., recall measures, similarity judgments, recognition measures).

These methodologies for "getting inside the head" include those that can be used to assess both the accessibility of a knowledge structure and its nature. For example, we have used the speed with which a spouse recalls positive versus negative characteristics of their partner during an interview as a rough index of the extent to which marital satisfaction has activated or made accessible affectively congruent knowledge structures relating to the partner. In a similar vein, it is possible to examine the characteristics reported for sequence, clustering, and quantity to gain information about the nature of the spouse's representation of their partner. Consider a wife who describes her husband's day-to-day behavior by listing five actions that she sees as selfish and then mentions appreciatively two chores he regularly completes. The order of the behaviors (negative before positive), clustering of "selfish" behavior, and the relative number of negative events suggest that she has a representation of her husband that is primarily negative and in which the trait "selfishness" is used to organize husband behavior. Taylor and Fiske (1981) provide an excellent overview of these methodologies and Kihlstrom and Nasby (1981) provide sophisticated examples of how their laboratory uses might be translated in clinical assessment procedures (see also Landau & Goldfried, 1981; Merluzzi et al., 1981). Unfortunately, these applications appear to have had little impact on behavioral assessment.

Decision-making. Decision-making is the third level at which the IPA can contribute to behavioral assessment. Barrios (1988, p. 35) has noted that in behavioral assessment "there has been a conspiracy of silence among us with regard to our decision-making strategies." This observation can be applied in three ways: (a) How do we decide the worth of a particular piece of data?; (b) How do we combine information to reach a decision?; and (c) How do we evaluate a decision once it has been made? As in our analysis of the AA, we thus apply our observations to the clinician.

In regard to the first question, Chapman and Chapman's (1967, 1969) elegant work on illusory correlation illustrates the operation of the availability heuristic among clinicians. For example, they showed that clinicians did not identify the empirically validated Rorschach signs associated with homosexuality but instead offered invalid signs that had high associative relations with homosexuality. In fact, undergraduates "discovered" characteristics of human figure drawings that clinicians believed to be associated with symptoms because both groups based their judgments on the associative strength between body characteristics and symptoms (e.g., eyes-paranoia, musculature-masculinity) rather than actual empirical relations with which they were presented. Awareness of our own use of heuristics is essential to evaluating the worth of any "data" we obtain regarding the client.

Second, how do we combine information to reach a judgment? Stated differently, what weights do we assign to various pieces of data and what rules (e.g., additive versus multiplicative) do we use to combine the information? By now it should be evident that the focus on process in the IPA makes it particularly suited to addressing such questions. However, their investigation predates the adoption of the IPA in research on social cognition and hence the considerable literature on decision making is also relevant here (e.g., N. Anderson, 1978; see Cantor, 1982).

Third, how are judgments tested once a decision has been made? Considerable attention has been devoted to this question and shows that lay people, in contrast to scientists, tend to seek confirmatory evidence when testing hypotheses (Snyder, 1981). Another relevant finding from this research is that schemata appear to have a greater influence on processing when the goal is to test a belief rather than when the goal is to form an impression (see Higgins & Bargh, 1987). Years ago, Meehl (1954) expressed concern about clinical judgment, and awareness of the potential impact of recently discovered heuristics on clinicians' cognitions has begun to receive attention (see Turk & Salovey, 1986).

In sum, application of the IPA to behavioral assessment has focused largely on the schema construct and on cognitive heuristics. Less attention has been paid to the precise nature of "schematic processing." The extensive knowledge base on the relation between cognitive structures and cognitive processes in social cognition was therefore identified as one area in which the IPA can potentially contribute a great deal to behavioral assessment. The range of methodologies within the IPA and its focus on process suggest that it may also be a particularly fruitful resource in view of the changing nature of behavioral assessment and the evident need to investigate decision-making processes in this domain.

Behavior Therapy

Although the goal of behavioral assessment is to inform behavior therapy, the therapeutic implications of an IPA-based assessment are not straightforward. This is because social cognition research is relatively silent on how schemata change (see Crocker, Fiske, & Taylor, 1984). The importance of this lacuna is emphasized by the fact that helping the client to adopt more adaptive schemata is an essential therapeutic task (Goldfried & Robins, 1983). In a similar vein, the wealth of information on the use of cognitive heuristics underlines the paucity of data on how to ameliorate adverse effects of heuristic processing or how to "inoculate" people against the difficulties to which such processing can give rise. These circumstances are exacerbated further by the fact that even though the IPA may provide insights regarding the manner in which a problem arises, the amelioration of the problem may require attention to entirely different processes. Despite the challenge posed by these circumstances, several attempts have been made to explore the implications of the IPA for behavior therapy (e.g., Goldfried & Robins, 1983; Hollon & Garber, 1988; Hollon & Kriss, 1984; Ingram & Hollon, 1986; Kanfer & Hagerman, 1985; Magaro, Johnson, & Boring, 1986; Turk & Salovey, 1986; Turk & Speers, 1983; Winfrey & Goldfried, 1986). These discussions are rich in suggestions for clinical intervention and, as in the previous section on behavioral assessment, we shall not repeat them here. Instead, we identify three major forms taken by contributions of the IPA to behavior therapy.

First, intervention can result directly from an IPA assessment of the presenting problem. For example, Magaro et al. (1986) outline a treatment program using intensive training on laboratory tasks similar to those used in assessing cognitive deficits associated with schizophrenia. The tasks, designed either to increase recognition of a broader range of stimulus inputs (i.e., to loosen rigid schemata in paranoid schizophrenia) or to facilitate processing of stimuli in terms of stable conceptual categories (i.e., create and strengthen schemata in nonparanoid schizophrenia), aim to remedy the deficits that emerge from an information processing analysis of the disorder. Consistent with the "high tech" flavor of IPA research, these tasks have been made available for administration on a microcomputer. Finally, it is noteworthy that this application cannot be attributed to social cognition research insofar as the analysis derives from cognitive psychology and is reflected in the stimuli of the recommended tasks (e.g., letter arrays, digit arrays).

The second form of contribution, one where findings and procedures emerging from the IPA are translated into therapeutic techniques, can be more easily related to social cognition research. For example, the preference for confirmatory evidence can lead people not only to ignore information discrepant with their knowledge structures, but to behave in ways that will result in feedback consistent with their existing knowledge structures when they are forced to attend to the discrepant information (e.g., Swann & Hill, 1982). In the therapy context this understanding of "resistance" leads to the suggestion that an ideal intervention strategy might be one that entails skillful questioning or exercises that will allow a client to negate one knowledge structure while simultaneously confirming a second one. For example, a client who began to view himself as incompetent after experiencing several panic attacks, was encouraged to confirm his view that he was a good father by teaching his son how to pilot the aircraft he had avoided flying since his first panic attack.

The relatively direct, "data driven" implications of the IPA outlined earlier appear to be less common than the third major form taken by behavior therapy applications of the IPA, namely, the analysis of existing interventions in terms of the IPA. For instance, the preference for confirmatory evidence has been related to behavior rehearsal as illustrated by Hollon and Kriss (1984). These authors provide examples from both their own and Beck's clinical work to demonstrate the need to ensure that depressed clients do not ask questions in a manner that is likely to negatively bias information to which they are exposed (e.g., "How badly did I do in the class discussion?") but that allows them to receive unbiased information (e.g., "How did I do in the class discussion?"). A number of additional therapeutic interventions have been analyzed in terms of the IPA (see Hollon & Garber, 1988; Ingram & Hollon, 1986). Such analyses are valuable because the fresh perspective they provide on well known procedures facilitates the creative use of these interventions.

Regardless of the form taken by IPA contributions to behavior therapy, a question that arises is the extent to which interventions should be metacognitive or focus on the client's knowledge of what factors influence his cognitions and how they do so. As Hollon and Kriss (1984) remind us, to assume that cognitive change requires the use of metacognitive interventions or that changes produced by such interventions are mediated by cognitive mechanisms is to fall prey to the representativeness heuristic (i.e., inferring a relationship based on the perceived similarity of problem and treatment). Thus even though an important implication of the IPA is that behaviors under the control of automatic processes (i.e., routine processes that require minimal or no conscious attention) need to occur in the context of controlled processing (i.e., be brought under conscious awareness), this does not imply the need for metacognitive interventions in which the client self consciously reflects on his or her cognitions. Indeed, several systems of individual and family therapy question the effectiveness of such interventions because explicit metacognitive intervention is presumed to result in resistance on the part of the client. It seems plausible to assume, however, that there are some conditions under which a metacognitive intervention is likely to be the treatment of choice (e.g., where rule learning regarding cognitive processes facilitates the generalization of behavior change). The lack of attention to this question is unfortunate in view of its significance for change in therapy and for the generalization of such change.

Finally, the IPA, like the AA, can be used to conceptualize the process of therapy. A central function of all therapies is to "present evidence" to help clients change existing misconceptions (Raimy, 1975), and close examination shows that most implications of the IPA involve either making particular information stored in memory more accessible to the client (e.g., past success experiences, competencies) or making available new information (largely, but not exclusively, via behavioral enactment) and guiding its processing. This view of therapy is supported by the promising, albeit limited, social cognition research on schema change which shows that the "major way in which knowledge representations change is through encountering new information" (Sherman et al., in press, p. 61).

In sum, analyses of the implications of the IPA for behavior therapy are somewhat speculative because relatively little is known about how schemata change or how cognitive processes can be altered. Nonetheless, it has been argued that the IPA can contribute to behavior therapy by using laboratory tasks in intervention, by devising interventions that are guided by its findings, and by analyzing existing interventions from the perspective of the IPA. Finally, the IPA, like the AA, can be used to conceptualize the therapeutic process.

Toward a More Complete Integration

Exploration of the implications of the information processing perspective for behavioral assessment and behavior therapy is in its infancy. The state of the art is captured succinctly by Hollon and Kriss (1984, p. 56) who describe their analysis as "a concatenation of extrapolations from the basic cognitive and social cognitive literatures and unstructured clinical experience." Nonetheless, they conclude that this interface is likely to be "the source of the next major breakthrough in clinical theory" (p. 68). The realization of this potential, however, requires some significant changes both in the nature of social cognition research conducted within the IPA and its application. In the remainder of this section we highlight three such changes.

An Ecological Perspective

Researchers using the IPA typically begin with the postulation of an internal mechanism and then conduct a tightly controlled experiment to test their hypothesis, usually using materials and procedures that are most convenient and/or lend themselves to high levels of experimental rigor. The underlying assumption is that cognitive phenomena investigated in this manner are also manifest in "real-life." Whether this assumption is tenable is an empirical question and relates to the issue of external validity. Although this is an important issue, the concern we wish to raise is not one of external validity but one that relates to the kind of phenomena studied when research begins with a model rather than with observation.

Neisser (1980, p. 364) has questioned whether the IPA as currently practiced can provide "significant insights into the human condition." He points out, for example, that progress in understanding concepts did not emerge from the research designed to investigate models of concept formation but from Rosch's analysis of the structure of concepts used in everyday life (Neisser, 1985). That is, the phenomena emerged from observation and analysis of categorization in relation to the environment in which it evolved. This ecological approach redefines what is studied in the laboratory because it attempts to "maintain the integrity of variables that matter in natural settings" (Neisser, 1985, p. 25).

Even a cursory survey of social cognition research using the IPA shows that this criterion has been ignored in favor of model testing and methodological rigor. For example, people typically process information to obtain some objective yet most studies on social cognition ignore this fact. Where goals are included they typically show strong effects (e.g., Showers & Cantor, 1985) but their use has been limited to comparing the goal of forming an impression with some nonsocial goal (e.g., remembering the stimulus material). It is important to emphasize that, as evidenced in the research that followed Rosch's work on categorization, an ecological perspective is not incompatible with model testing and methodological rigor. Such a perspective simply requires that the phenomena studied derive from observation and analysis of human functioning in its natural context. In the absence of an appreciation for the ecological perspective there is the very real danger that the phenomena studied (e.g., the robustness of a schema) may be epiphenomena of our methodologies (Markus & Zajonc, 1985). In any event, clinicians are likely to find the limited range of phenomena studied (mainly initial impressions) and the manner in which they are studied sterile in the absence of an ecologically guided research. Clinical relevance is also likely to be enhanced by greater attention to the inherently *social* nature of social cognition.

A Social Perspective

The reader may have noticed a disparity between earlier definitions of social cognition and the nature of the material discussed in our brief analysis of the IPA. In a similar vein, clinical writers often do not distinguish between cognitive and social psychological sources in exploring the clinical application of the IPA. Such observations prompt questions concerning what is unique about social cognition research using the IPA. Unfortunately, very little is unique because most studies resemble "the modal cognitive experiment with social stimuli" (Holyoak & Gordon, 1984, p. 42) in that they study socially isolated individuals performing on standard laboratory tasks that tend to exclude individual differences and noncognitive factors. Although individual differences and noncognitive factors are now receiving more attention, the IPA in social psychology remains largely asocial and there is a pressing need to reclaim its social heritage if it is to be more than a surrogate cognitive psychology (cf. Higgins, Kuiper, & Olson, 1981).

As attention is turned to the social nature of cognition, two points require reiteration. First, some aspects of social cognition (e.g., the cultural-collective representations studied by Moscovici, 1981) can not be reduced to individual cognition (Forgas, 1981). Nonetheless, we believe that much of the subject matter of social cognition can be studied with the IPA provided we begin to use the metaphor of the computer network rather than that of a single computer. Second, it is extremely important to acknowledge that people live in a moral world. Actions are often prescribed by the moral order and it is unlikely that such actions can be understood fully by any analysis that ignores this fact. This is critical from a clinical perspective because norms, rules, roles, and evaluations are intrinsic to the problems that confront the clinician. The ultimate viability of the IPA for clinical psychologists, however, also depends on the generation of clinically motivated research.

Clinically Motivated Research

Clinicians may vary in the extent to which they consider critical the need for an ecological perspective and for more socially oriented research. It appears that some discussions of the IPA make little reference to the findings generated using it and appear instead to use the approach as a heuristic device. From this perspective, the observations outlined above are unlikely to generate much concern even though their consideration might increase the heuristic utility of the

IPA. To the extent that clinical suggestions rest on research findings generated by the IPA, the concerns expressed above are particularly germane. Regardless of the perspective adopted, however, the need for clinically motivated research is the cornerstone on which the contribution of the IPA will ultimately stand or fall.

Just as cognitive psychologists have pointed out that their models are unlikely to be adequate in accounting for many aspects of social cognition (Holyoak & Gordon, 1984), so it behooves clinical psychologists to realize that IPA models and findings in social cognition are unlikely to meet their needs. For example, research showing that knowledge structures change simply as a result of attention (Sherman et al., in press) is likely to have little relevance to the modification of knowledge structures in therapy. Simply stated, the goals of social and clinical psychologists are necessarily different, and merely importing the traditions of the IPA used in social cognition research to study different groups of clinical populations is likely to be of limited value. Rather, the IPA should be molded to suit the needs of the clinician. For example, the cognitive contents of most concern to clinicians (e.g., self-statements, attributions, beliefs) have received little attention and their investigation may require modifications of the standard paradigms used by social psychologists (Ingram & Kendall, 1986). Such modifications are likely to require a more sophisticated understanding of the IPA, a development that we consider essential if the clinical utility of the IPA is to progress beyond that of a promissory note.

CONCLUSION

We have tried to answer our initial question by illustrating how research on social cognition can enhance behavior therapy. As shown by the structure of our chapter, we believe that this question is best pursued at the level of broad approaches used in social cognition research rather than in terms of specific theories or findings. This position is predicated, in part, on the view that wholesale borrowing from the field of social cognition is fraught with peril. The danger can be minimized by analysis of the approaches used in this field because it entails consideration of how the approaches are best adapted to the clinical context. These adaptations will result ideally in clinical research and it is on the basis of such research that the contribution of social cognition to behavior therapy ultimately rests.

In the absence of a solid body of clinical research relating to social cognition, the positive answer given to our initial question does not reflect unbridled enthusiasm for the contribution of social cognition research to clinical practice. The potential is clear but its realization awaits empirical evaluation. There are two more reasons for our more measured response. First, we believe that a sober appraisal of the potential contribution of social cognition research is more likely to facilitate sustained clinical research because consideration of the legitimate, albeit limited, contribution of social cognition research is less likely to result in the disappointment that inevitably occurs following overly enthusiastic claims. Second, recognition of the limitations of social cognition research is not only likely to foster more informative clinical research but may facilitate also the consideration of clinical findings by social cognition researchers. It is this link that is most often absent in the literature and that is critical to bridging the chasm between basic and applied research. The reasons for its absence are numerous and include insufficient attention to the utility of clinical studies for nonclinical researchers. Consequently, we discuss briefly the kind of clinical social cognition research that will circumvent this problem.

Ostrom (1984) has offered a 2 times 2 classification system for the differences between social and nonsocial knowledge using as dimensions properties of the entity (object of knowledge vs. perceiver) and sociality (being alone vs. with others). He concludes that whereas social interaction is at the heart of most definitions of the field, very little is known about the two cells in which the perceiver is with others. Indeed, virtually nothing is known about social cognition as it relates to interaction, especially in the close relationships that dominate most of our social lives.

Because behavior therapy operates through social interaction and often focuses on the social functioning of the client, an understanding of social cognition in social interaction is also critical to the behavior therapist. It is rather surprising that research has not been conducted on this topic in view of the behavior therapist's commitment to understanding how behavior therapy works (Franks & Wilson, 1975). The traditional focus on overt behavior in behavior therapy makes the behaviorally oriented researcher particularly suited to the investigation of social cognition in relation to social behavior. The necessity for such research is emphasized further by the relative lack of data on the relation between cognition and behavior (regardless of its social context) in the social cognition literature. Finally, it is important to note that current research yields virtually no information on how understanding emerges from social interaction, yet the negotiation of social knowledge often occurs through conversation. Thus, we suggest that the metaphor of persons as participants in a conversation might profitably be used in conducting the kind of research outlined above.

In sum, it has been argued that the attributional and information processing approaches used in social cognition research are relevant to behavior therapy. In fact, if one considers the three ways in which beliefs change—through the replacement of an existing explanatory system with a new one, from the brute force of raw evidence, and by insight into cognitive processes (Ross, 1977)—the attributional and information processing approaches were related to the first and second, respectively. The third was incorporated into discussions of both approaches. Throughout our analysis we have been guided by the need to integrate social and clinical research and have offered suggestions to facilitate this integration. Social psychologists fearing that the complexity of social functioning might lead to research paralysis have too often responded by studying phenomena that are minimally social. Clinical psychologists, on the other hand, confronted by the need for solutions have too often embraced what other branches of psychology have to offer without critical analysis or a sophisticated appreciation of what is embraced. It is only by greater mutual interchange between social and clinical psychologists regarding social cognition that each will develop the most adaptive means of coping with their respective maladies.

REFERENCES

Abelson, R. P., & Black, J. P. (1986). Introduction. In J. A. Galambos, R. P. Abelson, & J. B. Black (Eds). *Knowledge structures* (pp. 1–18). Hillsdale, NJ: Lawrence Erlbaum Associates.

Abramson, L. Y., Seligman, M. E. P., & Teasdale, J. (1978). Learned helplessness in humans: Critique and reformulation. *Journal of Abnormal Psychology, 87,* 49–74.

Achenbach, T. M. (1985). *Assessment and taxonomy of child and adolescent psychopathology.* Beverly Hills: Sage Publications, Inc.

Anderson, C. A., & Arnoult, L. H. (1985). Attributional models of depression, loneliness, and shyness. In J. H. Harvey & G. Weary (Eds.), *Attribution: Basic issues and applications* (pp. 203–234). New York: Academic Press.

Anderson, J. R., & Bower, G. H. (1973). *Human associative memory.* Washington, DC: Lawrence Erlbaum Associates.

Anderson, N. H. (1978). Cognitive algebra: Integration theory applied to social attribution. In L. Berkowitz (Ed.), *Cognitive theories in social psychology* (pp. 1–102). New York: Academic Press.

Antaki, C. (1982). A brief introduction to attribution and attributional theories. In C. Antaki & C. R. Brewin (Eds.), *Attributions and psychological change: Applications of attributional theories to clinical education and practice* (pp. 3–21). London: Academic Press.

Antaki, C., & Brewin, C. (Eds.) (1982). *Attributions and psychological change: Applications of attributional theories to clinical education and practice.* London: Academic Press.

Bagarozzi, D. A., & Giddings, C. W. (1983). The role of cognitive constructs and attributional processes in family therapy: Integrating intrapersonal, interpersonal, and systems dynamics. In L. R. Goldberg & M. L. Aronson (Eds.), *Group and Family Therapy* (pp. 207–219). New York: Bruner/Mazel.

Bargh, J. A., Bond, R. N., Lombardi, W. L., & Tota, M. E. (1986). The additive nature of chronic and temporary sources of construct accessibility. *Journal of Personality and Social Psychology, 50,* 869–878.

Bargh, J. A., & Pietromonaco, P. (1982). Automatic information processing and social perception: The influence of trait information presented outside of conscious awareness on impression formation. *Journal of Personality and Social Psychology, 43,* 437–449.

Barrios, B. A. (1988). On the changing nature of behavioral assessment. In A. S. Bellack & M. Hersen (Eds.), *Behavioral assessment* (3rd Ed., pp. 3–41). Elmsford, NY: Pergamon Press.

Baucom, D. H., & Lester, G. W. (1986). The usefulness of cognitive restructuring as an adjunct to behavioral marital therapy. *Behavior Therapy, 17,* 385–403.

Baucom, D. H., Sayers, S. L., & Duhe, A. (1989). Attributional style and attributional patterns among married couples. *Journal of Personality and Social Psychology, 56,* 596–607.

Beach, S. R. H., Abramson, L. Y., & Levine, F. (1981). Attributional reformulation of learned helplessness and depression: Therapeutic implications. In J. F. Clarkin & H. I. Glazer (Eds.), *Depression: Behavioral and directive intervention strategies* (pp. 131–145). New York: Garland STPM Press.

Beck, A. T. (1967). *Depression: Clinical, experimental and theoretical aspects.* New York: Hoeber.

Beck, A. T., Rush, A. J., Shaw, B. F., & Emery, G. (1979). *Cognitive therapy of depression.* New York: Guilford Press.

Bower, G. H. (1978). Contacts of cognitive psychology with social learning theory. *Cognitive Therapy and Research, 2,* 123–146.

Bradbury, T. N., & Fincham, F. D. (1990). Attributions in marriage: Review and critique. *Psychological Bulletin, 107,* 3–33.

Brehm, S. S. (1976). *The application of social psychology to clinical practice.* New York: Halstead Press.

Brehm, S. S., & Smith, T. W. (1986). Social psychological approaches to psychotherapy and behavior change. In S. L. Garfield & A. E. Bergin (Ed.), *Handbook of psychotherapy and behavior change* (pp. 69–115). New York: John Wiley & Sons.

Brewin, C. R. (1984). Attributions for industrial accidents: Their relationship to rehabilitation outcome. *Journal of Social and Clinical Psychology, 2,* 156–164.

Brewin, C. R. (1986). Internal attribution and self-esteem in depression: A theoretical note. *Cognitive Therapy and Research, 10,* 469–475.

Brewin, C. R. (Ed.) (1988). Clinical attribution research. Special issue of the *British Journal of Clinical Psychology, 27.*

Brewin, C. & Antaki, C. (1982). The role of attributions in psychological treatment. In C. Antaki & C. R. Brewin (Eds.), *Attributions and psychological change: Applications of attributional theories to clinical education and practice* (pp. 23–44). London: Academic Press.

Brewin, C. R., & Antaki, C. (1987). An analysis of ordinary explanations in clinical attribution research. *Journal of Social and Clinical Psychology, 5,* 79–88.

Brewin, C. R., Robson, M., & Shapiro, D. A. (1983). Social and psychological determinants of recovery from industrial injuries. *Injury: The British Journal of Accident Surgery, 14,* 451–455.

Cantor, N. (1982). "Everyday" versus normative models of clinical and social judgment. In G. Weary & H. L. Mirels (Eds.), *Integrations of clinical and social psychology* (pp. 27–47). New York: Oxford University Press.

Chapman, L. J., & Chapman, J. P. (1967). Genesis of popular but erroneous psychodiagnostic observations. *Journal of Abnormal Psychology, 72,* 193–204.

Chapman, L. J., & Chapman, J. P. (1969). Illusory correlation as an obstacle to the use of valid diagnostic signs. *Journal of Abnormal Psychology, 74,* 271–280.

Cohen, J., & Streuning, E. L. (1964). Opinions about mental illness: Hospital social atmosphere profiles and their relevance to effectiveness. *Journal of Consulting Psychology, 28,* 292–298.

Compas, B. E., Forsythe, C. J., & Wagner, B. M. (1988). Consistency and variability in causal attributions and coping with stress. *Cognitive Therapy and Research, 12,* 305–320.

Crocker, J., Fiske, S. T., & Taylor, S. E. (1984). Schematic bases of belief change. In R. Eiser (Ed.), *Attitudinal judgment* (pp. 197–227). New York: Springer-Verlag.

Cutrona, C. E., Russel, D., & Jones, R. D. (1984). Cross-situational consistency in causal attributions: Does an attributional style exist? *Journal of Personality and Social Psychology, 47,* 1043–1058.

Davis, A. (1979). What's in a name? A Bayesian rethinking of attributional biases in clinical judgment. *Journal of Consulting and Clinical Psychology, 47,* 1109–1114.

Davison, G. C. (1966). Differential relaxation and cognitive restructuring in therapy. *Proceedings of the American Psychological Association,* 177–179.

Druian, P., & Omessi, E. (1983). *A knowledge structure theory of attribution.* Unpublished manuscript, Grinnell College, IA.

Dweck, C. (1975). The role of expectations and attributions in the alleviation of learned helplessness. *Journal of Personality and Social Psychology, 36,* 951–962.

Ellis, A., & Greiger, R. (1977). *Rational-emotive therapy: A handbook of theory and practice.* New York: Springer-Verlag.

Farina, A., & Fisher, J. D. (1982). Beliefs about mental disorders: Findings and implications. In G. Weary & H. L. Mirels (Eds.). *Integrations of clinical and social psychology* (pp. 48–71). Englewood Cliffs, NJ: Prentice-Hall.

Farr, R. (1976). Experimentation: A social psychological perspective. *British Journal of Social and Clinical Psychology, 15,* 225–238.

Farr, R. (1981). The social origins of the human mind: A historical note. In J. Forgas (Ed.), *Social cognition: Perspectives on everyday understanding* (pp. 247–258). New York: Academic Press.

Fincham, F. D. (1983). Clinical applications of attribution theory: Problems and prospects. In M. Hewstone (Ed.), *Attribution theory: Social and functional extensions* (pp. 187–203). Oxford, England: Blackwell.

Fincham, F. D. (Ed.) (1985a). Disorders of childhood and adolescence. Special issue of *Journal of Social and Clinical Psychology, 3,* 385–507.

Fincham, F. D. (1985b). Attributions in close relationships. In J. H. Harvey & G. Weary (Eds.), *Attribution: Basic issues and applications* (pp. 203–234). New York: Academic Press.

Fincham, F. D., & Bradbury, T. N. (in press). Cognition in marriage: A program of research on attributions. In D. Perlman & W. Jones (Eds.), *Advances in Personal Relationships* (vol. 2). London: Kingsley Pub.

Fincham, F. D., Bradbury, T. N., & Scott, C. (1990). Cognition in marriage. In F. D. Fincham & T. N. Bradbury (Eds.), *The psychology of marriage* (pp. 118–149). New York: Guilford Press.

Fincham, F. D., Beach, S. R., & Nelson, G. (1987). Attribution processes in distressed and nondistressed couples: 3. Causal and responsibility attributions for spouse behavior. *Cognitive Therapy and Research, 11,* 71–86.

Fiske, S. T., & Taylor, S. E. (in press). *Social cognition* (2nd ed). New York: Random House.

Forgas, J. P. (1981). Epilogue: Everyday understanding and social cognition. In J. Forgas (Ed.), *Social cognition: Perspectives on everyday understanding* (pp. 259–272). New York: Academic Press.

Forsterling, F. (1985). Attribution retraining: A review. *Psychological Bulletin, 98,* 495–512.

Forsterling, F. (1986). Attributional conceptions in clinical psychology. *American Psychologist, 41,* 275–285.

Forsterling, F. (1988). *Attribution theory in clinical psychology.* New York: John Wiley & Sons.

Forsterling, F. (in press). Attributional therapies. In S. Graham & V. Folkes (Eds.), *Advances in Applied Social*

Psychology, (Vol. 5). Hillsdale, NJ: Lawrence Erlbaum Associates.

Franks, C. M., & Wilson, G. T. (1975). *Annual review of behavior therapy: Theory and practice, 3,* New York: Brunner/Mazel.

Goldfried, M. R., & Robins, C. (1983). Self-schemata, cognitive bias, and the processing of therapeutic experiences. In P. C. Kendall (Ed.), *Advances in cognitive-behavioral research and therapy* (Vol 2, pp. 33–80). NewYork: Academic Press.

Hamilton, D. L. (1981). Cognitive representations of persons. In E. Higgins, C. Herman, & M. Zanna (Eds.), *Social cognition: The Ontario Symposium.* (Vol. 1, pp. 121–134). Hillsdale, NJ: Lawrence Erlbaum Associates.

Harvey, J. H., & Galvin, K. S. (1984). Clinical implications of attribution theory and research. *Clinical Psychology Review, 4,* 15–33.

Harvey, J. H., Ickes, W., & Kidd, R. F. (Eds). (1981). *New directions in attribution research* (Vol. 3). Hillsdale, NJ: Lawrence Erlbaum Associates.

Harvey, J. H., & Weary, G. (1984). Current issues in attribution theory and research. *Annual Review of Psychology, 35,* 427–459.

Harvey, J. H., & Weary, G. (Eds.) (1985). *Attribution: Basic issues and applications.* New York: Academic Press.

Hastie, R. (1980). Memory for behavioral information that confirms or contradicts a personality impression. In R. Hastie, T. Ostrom, D. Hamilton, E. Ebbesen, R. Wyer, & D. Carlston (Eds.), *Person memory: The cognitive basis of social perception* (pp. 155–178). Hillsdale, NJ: Lawrence Erlbaum Associates.

Hastie, R., & Carlston, D. (1980). Theoretical issues in person memory. In R. Hastie, T. Ostrom, D. Hamilton, E. Ebbesen, R. Wyer, & D. Carlston (Eds.), *Person memory: The cognitive basis of social perception* (pp. 1–54). Hillsdale, NJ: Lawrence Erlbaum Associates.

Hastie, R., Ostrom, T., Hamilton, D., Ebbesen, E., Wyer, R., & Carlston, D. (1980). In R. Hastie, T. Ostrom, D. Hamilton, E. Ebbesen, R. Wyer, & D. Carlston (Eds.), *Person memory: The cognitive basis of social perception.* (Preface) Hillsdale, NJ: Lawrence Erlbaum Associates.

Heider, F. (1944). Social perception and phenomenal causality. *Psychological Review, 51,* 358–374.

Heider, F. (1958). *The psychology of interpersonal relations.* New York: John Wiley & Sons.

Heider, F. (1976). A conversation with Fritz Heider. In J. H. Harvey, W. Ickes, & R. F. Kidd (Eds.), *New directions in attribution research* (Vol. 1, pp. 3–18). Hillsdale, NJ: Lawrence Erlbaum Associates.

Hewstone, M. (1983a). Attribution theory and commonsense explanations: An introductory overview. In M. Hewstone (Ed.), *Attribution theory: Social and functional extensions* (pp. 1–26). Oxford, England: Blackwell.

Hewstone, M. (Ed.) (1983b). *Attribution theory: Social and functional extensions.* Oxford: Blackwell.

Hewstone, M. (in press). *Causal attribution: From cognitive processes to collective beliefs.* Oxford: Blackwell.

Hewstone, M., & Jaspars, J. M. (1987). Covariation and causal attribution: A logical model of the intuitive analysis of variance. *Journal of Personality and Social Psychology, 50,* 869–878.

Higgins, E. T., & Bargh, J. A. (1987). Social cognition and social perception. *Annual Review of Psychology, 38,* 369–425.

Higgins, E. T., Kuiper, N. A., & Olson, J. M. (1981). Social cognition: A need to get personal. In E. T. Higgins, C. P. Herman, & M. P. Zanna (Eds.), *Social cognition: The Ontario Symposium.* (Vol 1, pp. 395–420).

Higgins, E. T., Rholes, W. S., & Jones, C. R. (1977). Category accessibility and impression formation. *Journal of Experimental Social Psychology, 13,* 141–154.

Hill, M. G., & Weary, G. (1983). Perspectives on the *Journal of Abnormal and Social Psychology:* How it began and how it was transformed. *Journal of Social and Clinical Psychology, 1,* 4–14.

Hilton, D. (1988). *A conversational model of causal explanation.* Manuscript submitted for publication.

Hilton, D., & Slugoski, B. R. (1986). Knowledge-based causal attribution: The abnormal conditions focus model. *Psychological Review, 93,* 75–88.

Hoffman, M. A., & Teglasi, H. (1982). The role of causal attributions in counseling shy subjects. *Journal of Counseling Psychology, 19,* 238–240.

Hollon, S. D., & Garber, J. (1988). Cognitive-therapy: A social cognitive perspective. In L. Y. Abramson (Ed.), *Social cognition and clinical psychology: A synthesis.* New York: Guilford Press.

Hollon, S. D., & Kriss, M. R. (1984). Cognitive factors in clinical research and practice. *Clinical Psychology Review, 4,* 35–76.

Holtzworth-Munroe, A., & Jacobson, N. S. (1987). Attributional processes: Implications for marital therapy. In J. E. Maddux, C. D. Stoltenberg, & R. Rosenwein (Eds.), *Interfaces of social, clinical, and counselling psychology: A handbook of theory, research, practice, and professional issues* (pp. 153–170). New York: Springer-Verlag.

Holyoak, K. J., & Gordon, P. C. (1984). Information processing and social cognition. In R. S. Wyer, & Srull, T. K. (Eds.), *Handbook of social cognition.* (Vol 1, pp. 39–69). Hillsdale, NJ: Lawrence Erlbaum Associates.

Ickes, W. (1988). Attributional styles and the self-concept. In L. Y. Abramson (Ed.), *Social cognition and clinical psychology: A synthesis.* New York: Guilford Press.

Ingram, R. E. (Ed.) (1986). *Information processing approaches in clinical psychology.* New York: Academic Press.

Ingram, R. E., & Hollon, S. D. (1986). Cognitive therapy of depression from an information processing perspective. In R. E. Ingram (Ed.) *Information processing approaches in clinical psychology* (pp. 261–284). New York: Academic Press.

Ingram, R. E., & Kendall, P. C. (1986). Cognitive clinical psychology. Implications of an information processing perspective. In R. E. Ingram (Ed.) *Information processing approaches in clinical psychology* (pp. 3–22). New York: Academic Press.

Ingram, R. E., & Reed, M. R. (1986). Information encoding and retrieval processes in depression: Findings, issues and future directions. In R. E. Ingram (Ed.) *Information processing approaches in clinical psychology* (pp. 132–150). New York: Academic Press.

Jacobson, N. S., & Margolin, G. (1979). *Marital therapy: Strategies based on social learning and behavior exchange principles.* New York: Brunner/Mazel.

Jaspars, J. M., Fincham, F. D., & Hewstone, M. (Eds.) (1983). *Attribution theory and research.* New York: Academic Press.

Johnson, W. G., Ross, J. M., & Mastria, M. A. (1977). Delusional behavior: An attribution analysis of development and modification. *Journal of Abnormal Psychology, 86,* 421–426.

Jones, E. E., & Davis, K. E. (1965). From acts to dispositions: The attribution process in person perception. In L. Berkowitz (Ed.), *Advances in experimental social psychology* (Vol. 2, pp. 219–266). New York: Academic Press.

Jones, E. E., & McGillis, D. (1976). Correspondent inferences and the attribution cube: A comparative reappraisal. In J. H. Harvey, W. Ickes, & R. F. Kidd (Eds.), *New directions in attribution research* (Vol. 1, pp. 389–420). Hillsdale, NJ: Lawrence Erlbaum Associates.

Jones, E. E. & Nisbett, R. E. (1971). *The actor and the observer: Divergent perceptions of the causes of behavior.* Morristown, NJ: General Learning Press.

Kahneman, D., Slovic, P., & Tversky, A. (Eds.) (1982). *Judgment under uncertainty: Heuristics and biases.* Cambridge: Cambridge University Press.

Kanfer, F. H., & Hagerman, S. M. (1985). Behavior therapy and the information-processing paradigm. In S. Reiss & R. R. Bootzin (Eds.) *Theoretical issues in behavior therapy.* New York: Academic Press.

Kanouse, D. E., Gumpert, P., & Canavan-Gumpert, D. (1981). The semantics of praise. In J. H. Harvey, W. Ickes, & R. F. Kidd (Eds.), *New directions in attribution research* (Vol. 3, pp. 98–116). Hillsdale, NJ: Lawrence Erlbaum Associates.

Kazdin, A., & Wilson, G. T. (1978). *Evaluation of behavior therapy: Issues, evidence and research strategies.* Cambridge, MA: Ballinger.

Kelley, H. H. (1967). Attribution theory in social psychology. In D. Levine (Ed.), *Nebraska symposium on motivation* (Vol. 15, pp. 192–240). Lincoln, NE: University of Nebraska Press.

Kelley, H. H., & Michela, J. L. (1980). Attribution theory and research. *Annual Review of Psychology, 31,* 457–501.

Kihlstrom, J. F., & Nasby, W. (1981). Cognitive tasks in clinical assessment: An exercise in applied psychology. In P. C. Kendall & S. D. Hollon (Eds.), *Assessment strategies for cognitive-behavioral interventions* (pp. 287–317). New York: Academic Press.

Kopel, S. A., & Arkowitz, H. (1975). The role of attribution and self perception in behavior change. *Genetic Psychology Monographs, 92,* 175–212.

Kosslyn, S. M., & Kagan, J. (1981). "Concrete thinking" and the development of social cognition. In J. Flavell & L. Ross (Eds), *Social cognitive development: Frontiers and possible futures* (pp. 82–96). Cambridge: Cambridge University Press.

Lachman, R., & Lachman, J. L. (1986). Information processing psychology: Origins and extensions. In R. E. Ingram (Ed.) *Information processing approaches in clinical psychology* (pp. 23–49). New York: Academic Press.

Lachman, R., Lachman, J. L., & Butterfield, E. C. (1979). *Cognitive psychology and information processing: An introduction.* Hillsdale, NJ: Lawrence Erlbaum Associates.

Lalljee, M., & Abelson, R. P. (1983). The organization of explanations. In M. Hewstone (Ed.), *Attribution theory: Social and functional extensions* (pp. 65–80). Oxford: Blackwell.

Landau, R. J., & Goldfried, M. R. (1981). The assessment of schemata: A unifying framework for cognitive, behavioral, and traditional assessment. In P. C. Kendall & S. D. Hollon (Eds.), *Assessment strategies for cognitive-behavioral interventions* (pp. 363–399). New York: Academic Press.

Langer, E. J., & Abelson, R. P. (1974). A patient by any other name . . . : Clinical group differences in labelling bias. *Journal of Consulting and Clinical Psychology, 42,* 4–9.

Layden, M. A. (1982). Attributional style therapy. In C. Antaki & C. R. Brewin (Eds.), *Attributions and psychological change: Applications of attributional theories to clinical education and practice* (pp. 63–82). London: Academic Press.

Leary, M. R., & Maddux, J. E. (1987). Progress towards a viable interface between social and clinical-counseling psychology. *American Psychologist, 42,* 904–911.

Leary, M. R., & Miller, R. S. (1986). *Social psychology and dysfunctional behavior.* New York: Springer-Verlag.

Leddo, J., & Abelson, R. P. (1986). The nature of explanations. In J. A. Galambos, R. P. Abelson, & J. B. Black (Eds.), *Knowledge structures* (pp. 103–122). Hillsdale, NJ: Lawrence Erlbaum Associates.

Lewin, K. (1951). *Field theory in social science.* New York: Harper & Row.

Litrownick, A. J., & McInnis, E. T. (1986). Information processing and autism. In R. E. Ingram (Ed.) *Information processing approaches in clinical psychology* (pp. 169–195). New York: Academic Press.

Lopez, S., & Wolkenstein, B. (1990). Attributions, person perception, and clinical issues. In S. Graham & V. Folkes (Eds.), *Attribution Theory: Applications to*

achievement, mental health, and interpersonal conflict. Hillsdale, NJ: Lawrence Erlbaum Associates.
Maddux, J. E., Stoltenberg, C. D., & Rosenwein, R. (Eds.) (in press). *Interfaces of social, clinical, and counselling psychology: A handbook of theory, research, practice, and professional issues.* New York: Springer-Verlag.
Magaro, P. A. (1980). *Cognition in schizophrenia and paranoia: The integration of cognitive processes.* Hillsdale, NJ: Lawrence Erlbaum Associates.
Magaro, P. A., Johnson, M. H., & Boring, R. (1986). Information processing approaches to the treatment of schizophrenia. In R. E. Ingram (Ed.) *Information processing approaches in clinical psychology* (pp. 285–305). New York: Academic Press.
Markus, H., Smith, J., & Moreland, R. L. (1985). Role of the self-concept in the perception of others. *Journal of Personality and Social Psychology, 49,* 1494–1512.
Markus, H., & Zajonc, R. B. (1985). The cognitive perspective in social psychology. In G. Lindzey & E. Aronson (Eds.), *Handbook of social psychology.* (3rd ed., 137–230). New York: Random House.
Mathews, A. (Ed.) (1988). Information processing and the emotional disorders. Special issue of *Cognition and Emotion.*
Meehl, P. E. (1954). *Clinical versus statistical prediction: A theoretical analysis and a review of the evidence.* Minneapolis: University of Minnesota Press.
Merluzzi, T. V., Rudy, T. E., & Glass, C. R. (1981). The information-processing paradigm: Implications for clinical science. In T. V. Merluzzi, C. R. Glass & M. Genest (Eds.), *Cognitive assessment* (pp. 77–124). New York: New York University Press.
Michela, J. L., & Wood, J. V. (1986). Causal attributions in health and illness. In P. C. Kendall (Ed.), *Advances in cognitive-behavioral research and therapy* (Vol. 5, pp. 179–236). New York: Academic Press.
Moscovici, S. (1981). On social representations. In J. Forgas (Ed.), *Social cognition: Perspectives on everyday understanding* (pp. 181–210). New York: Academic Press.
Nasby, W., & Kihlstrom, J. F. (1986). Cognitive assessment of personality and psychopathology. In R. E. Ingram (Ed.) *Information processing approaches in clinical psychology* (pp. 219–240). New York: Academic Press.
Neisser, U. (1967). *Cognitive psychology.* Englewood Cliffs, NJ: Prentice-Hall.
Neisser, U. (1980). Three cognitive psychologies and their implications. In M. J. Mahoney (Ed.), *Psychotherapy process: Current issues and future directions* (pp. 363–367). New York: Plenum Press.
Neisser, U. (1985). Toward an ecologically oriented cognitive science. In T. M. Shlechter & M. P. Toglia (Eds.), *New directions in cognitive science* (pp. 17–32). Norwood, NJ: Ablex.
Nisbett, R. E., & Ross, L. (1980). *Human inference: Strategies and shortcomings of social judgment.* Englewood Cliffs, NJ: Prentice-Hall.
Orvis, B. R., Kelley, H. H., & Butler, D. (1976). Attributional conflict in young couples. In J. H. Harvey, W. Ickes, & R. F. Kidd (Eds.), *New directions in attribution research* (Vol. 1, pp. 353–388). Hillsdale, NJ: Lawrence Erlbaum Associates.
Ostrom, T. M. (1984). The sovereignty of social cognition. In R. S. Wyer, & T. K. Srull (Eds.), *Handbook of social cognition.* (Vol. 1, pp. 1–38). Hillsdale, NJ: Lawrence Erlbaum Associates.
Ottati, V. C., & Wyer, R. S. (in press). The cognitive mediators of political choice: Toward a comprehensive model of political information processing. In J. A. Ferejohn & J. H. Kuklinski (Eds.), *Information and democratic process.* Urbana, Il: University of Illinois Press.
Peterson, C. (1982). Learned helplessness and attributional interventions in depression. In C. Antaki & C. R. Brewin (Eds.), *Attributions and psychological change: Applications of attributional theories to clinical education and practice* (pp. 97–118). London: Academic Press.
Peterson, C., & Seligman, M. E. P. (1984). Causal explanations as a risk factor for depression: Theory and evidence. *Psychological Review, 91,* 347–374.
Pleban, R., & Richardson, D. C. (1979). Research and publication trends in social psychology: 1973–1977. *Personality and Social Psychology Bulletin, 5,* 138–141.
Raimy, V. (1975). *Misunderstandings of the self.* San Francisco: Jossey-Bass.
Read, S. (1987). Constructing causal scenarios: A knowledge structure approach to causal reasoning. *Journal of Personality and Social Psychology, 52,* 288–302.
Revenstorf, D. (1984). The role of attribution of marital distress in therapy. In K. Hahlweg & N. S. Jacobson (Eds.), *Marital interaction: Analysis and modification* (pp. 325–336). New York: Guilford Press.
Rhodes, W. A. (1977). *Generalization of attribution retraining.* Unpublished doctoral dissertation, University of Illinois.
Ross, L. (1977). The intuitive psychologist and his shortcomings: Distortions in the attribution process. In L. Berkowitz (Eds.), *Advances in Experimental Social Psychology* (Vol. 10, pp. 173–220). New York: Academic Press.
Ross, L., Rodin, J., & Zimbardo, P. G. (1969). Toward an attribution therapy: The reduction of fear through induced cognitive-emotion misattribution. *Journal of Personality and Social Psychology, 12,* 279–288.
Ross, M., & Fletcher, G. J. O. (1985). Attribution and social perception. In G. Lindzey & E. Aronson (Eds.), *Handbook of social psychology* (3rd ed., 73–122). New York: Random House.
Schul, Y., & Burnstein, E. (1985). The informational basis of social judgments: Using past impressions rather than trait description in forming a new impression. *Journal of Experimental Social Psychology, 21,* 421–439.
Shaver, K. G. (1975). *An introduction to attribution processes.* Cambridge, MA: Winthrop.
Shaver, K. G. (1985). *The attribution of blame: Causality, responsibility, and blameworthiness.* New York: Springer-Verlag.

Shaver, K. G., & Drown, D. (1986). On causality, responsibility, and self-blame: A theoretical note. *Journal of Personality and Social Psychology, 50,* 697–702.

Sherman, S. J., Judd, C. M., & Park, B. (in press). Social cognition. *Annual Review of Psychology.*

Showers, C., & Cantor, N. (1985). Social cognition: A look at motivated strategies. *Annual Review of Psychology, 36,* 275–305.

Skilbeck, W. M. (1974). Attributional change and crisis intervention. *Psychotherapy: Theory, research and practice, 11,* 371–375.

Smith, E. R., & Miller, F. D. (1983). Mediation among attribution inferences and comprehension processes: Initial findings and a general method. *Journal of Personality and Social Psychology, 50,* 697–702.

Snyder, C. R. (1977). "A patient by any other name" revisited: Maladjustment or attributional locus of problem? *Journal of Consulting and Clinical Psychology, 45,* 101–103.

Snyder, C. R., & Higgins, R. L. (1988). Excuses: Their effective role in the negotiation of reality. *Psychological Bulletin, 104,* 23–35.

Snyder, M. (1981). Seek and ye shall find: Testing hypotheses about other people. In E. T. Higgins, C. P. Herman, & M. P. Zanna (Eds.), *Social cognition: The Ontario symposium* (Vol. 1, pp. 227–304). Hillsdale, NJ: Lawrence Erlbaum Associates.

Sonne, J. L., & Janoff, D. S. (1982). Attributions and the maintenance of behavior change. In C. Antaki & C. R. Brewin (Eds.), *Attributions and psychological change: Applications of attributional theories to clinical education and practice.* London: Academic Press.

Srull, T. K., & Wyer, R. S. (1979). The role of category accessibility in the interpretation of information about persons: Some determinants and implications. *Journal of Personality and Social Psychology, 37,* 1660–1672.

Srull, T. K., & Wyer, R. S. (1980). Category accessibility and social perception: Some implications for the study of person memory and interpersonal judgments. *Journal of Personality and Social Psychology, 38,* 841–856.

Storms, M. D., & Nisbett, R. E. (1970). Insomnia and the attribution process. *Journal of Personality and Social Psychology, 16,* 319–328.

Strong, S. R. (1978). Social psychological approach to psychotherapy research. In S. L. Garfield & A. E. Bergin (Ed.), *Handbook of psychotherapy and behavior change.* (2nd ed., pp. 101–136). New York: John Wiley & Sons.

Strong, S. R. (1982). Emerging integrations of clinical and social psychology: A clinician's perspective. In G. Weary & H. L. Mirels (Eds.). *Integrations of clinical and social psychology* (pp. 181–213). Englewood Cliffs, NJ: Prentice-Hall.

Swann, W. B., Jr., & Hill, C. A. (1982). When our identities are mistaken: Reaffirming self-conceptions through social interaction. *Journal of Personality and Social Psychology, 43,* 59–66.

Sweeney, P. D., Anderson, K., & Bailey, S. (1986). Attributional style in depression: A meta-analytic review. *Journal of Personality and Social Psychology, 50,* 974–991.

Taylor, S. E., & Crocker, J. (1981). Schematic bases of social information processing. In E. T. Higgins, C. P. Herman, & M. P. Zanna (Eds.), *Social cognition: The Ontario symposium* (pp. 89–134). Hillsdale, NJ: Lawrence Erlbaum Associates.

Taylor, S. E., & Fiske, S. T. (1981). Getting inside the head: Methodologies for process analysis. In J. H. Harvey, W. Ickes, & R. F. Kidd (Eds.), *New directions in attribution research* (Vol. 3, pp. 459–506). Hillsdale, NJ: Lawrence Erlbaum Associates.

Turk, D. C., & Salovey, P. (1985a). Cognitive structures, cognitive processes, and cognitive-behavior modification: I. Client issues. *Cognitive Therapy and Research, 9,* 1–17.

Turk, D. C., & Salovey, P. (1985b). Cognitive structures, cognitive processes, and cognitive-behavior modification: II. Judgments and inferences of the clinician. *Cognitive Therapy and Research, 9,* 19–33.

Turk, D. C., & Salovey, P. (1986). Clinical information processing: Bias innoculation. In R. E. Ingram (Ed.) *Information processing approaches in clinical psychology* (pp. 305–323). New York: Academic Press.

Turk, D. C., & Speers, M. A. (1983). Cognitive schemata and cognitive processes in cognitive behavioral interventions: Going beyond the information given. In P. C. Kendall (Ed.), *Advances in cognitive-behavioral research and therapy* (Vol. 2, pp. 135–155). New York: Academic Press.

Tversky, A., & Kahneman, D. (1974). Judgment under uncertainty: Heuristics and biases. *Science, 185,* 1124–1131.

Valins, S., & Nisbett, R. E. (1971). *Attribution processes in the development and treatment of emotional disorders.* Morristown, NJ: General Learning Press.

Valins, S., & Ray, A. (1967). Effects of cognitive sensitization on avoidance behavior. *Journal of Personality and Social Psychology, 7,* 345–350.

Watson, D. (1982). The actor and observer: How are their perceptions of causality divergent? *Psychological Bulletin, 92,* 682–700.

Watts, F. (1982). Attributional aspects of medicine. In C. Antaki & C. R. Brewin (Eds.), *Attributions and psychological change: Applications of attributional theories to clinical education and practice* (pp. 135–156). London: Academic Press.

Weary, G., & Mirels, H. L. (Eds.). (1982). *Integrations of clinical and social psychology.* Englewood Cliffs, NJ: Prentice-Hall.

Wegner, D. M., & Vallacher, R. R. (1977). *Implicit psychology: An introduction to social cognition.* New York: Oxford University Press.

Weiner, B. (1985). An attributional theory of achievement motivation and emotion. *Psychological Review, 95,* 548–573.

Weiner, B. (1986). *An attributional theory of motivation and emotion*. New York: Springer-Verlag.

Wilensky, R. (1978). Why John married Mary: Understanding stories involving recurring goals. *Cognitive Science, 2*, 235–266.

Wilson, G. T. (1978). Cognitive behavior therapy: Paradigm shift or passing phase? In J. P. Foreyt & D. P. Rathjen (Eds.), *Cognitive behavior therapy: Research and applications* (pp. 7–32). New York: Plenum Press.

Winfrey, L. P., & Goldfried, M. R. (1986). Information processing and the human change process. In R. E. Ingram (Ed.) *Information processing approaches in clinical psychology* (pp. 241–260). New York: Academic Press.

Wyer, R. S., & Carlston, D. E. (1979). *Social cognition, inference, and attribution*. Hillsdale, NJ: Lawrence Erlbaum Associates.

Wyer, R. S., & Srull, T. K. (Eds.) (1984). *Handbook of social cognition*. Vols. 1–3. Hillsdale, NJ: Lawrence Erlbaum Associates.

Wyer, R. S., Srull, T. K., & Gordon, S. E. (1984). The effects of predicting a person's behavior on subsequent trait judgments. *Journal of Experimental Social Psychology, 20*, 29–46.

Zajonc, R. B. (1980). Cognition and social cognition: A historical perspective. In L. Festinger (Ed.), *Retrospections on social psychology*. New York: Oxford University Press.

CHAPTER 16

PSYCHOTHERAPY AS A SOCIAL PROCESS

Christopher Peterson

Perhaps because behavior therapy as an approach to alleviating human distress puts such great emphasis on particular techniques, it is easy for someone with but casual knowledge of this treatment to see it as a purely mechanical process. My thesis in the present contribution is just the opposite: behavior therapy, like all forms of psychotherapy, depends critically on the social interaction between the therapist and the client. Techniques per se cannot be effective unless deployed in the context of the ongoing relationship between the therapist and the client.

I write this chapter from the viewpoint of social psychology. The importance of the therapist-client relationship is well appreciated within the field of clinical psychology, by behavior therapists and others. What is not appreciated is that social psychology has much to say about the nature of the social relationship that characterizes psychotherapy in general and behavior therapy in particular. Indeed, not only have clinicians neglected the potential contribution to their field of social psychology, but so too have social psychologists lagged in pointing out this relevance.

Recent years have seen intriguing statements concerning the links between social psychology and clinical psychology (e.g., Brehm, 1976), and a journal has even been created that features the newest contributions here: that is, the *Journal of Social and Clinical Psychology*. However, the overwhelming thrust of this new melding of social psychology with clinical psychology is in terms of social cognition. The importance of social cognition is not to be argued against (see Chapter 15 of this volume), but social cognition is just an ingredient in the real business of social psychology, which is describing and explaining relationships between people.

Social cognition matters because social interaction in many ways is mediated by our cognitive representations of ourselves and each other. But contemporary social psychology has seemed reluctant to place social cognition in people and further to place people in relationships with one another. Various historical trends are no doubt responsible for the demise of the "social" within social psychology, and the methodological ease of studying disembodied social cognition as opposed to real people interacting has also contributed to this state of affairs. Nonetheless, the most important contribution that social psychologists have to make to clinical psychology concerns how to conceive the therapist-client relationship and what transpires between them in the course of psychotherapy.

With this strong statement made, I must acknowledge the limitations to be found in this chapter. Some are my own. I am, by the way, one of those social cognitive researchers whose work I just finished criticizing. Despite broad training long ago and far away in truly social social psychology, I have of late studied processes within people more frequently than I have studied those between them (cf. Coyne & Gotlib, 1983).

But other limitations here are those of social psychology and the field into which it has turned. Most of the theories I cite will seem dated, because the most powerful statements about social processes were made some time ago and have not really been updated. Relatedly, my strategy is necessarily to juxtapose research conducted by clinical psychologists with the theories proposed by social psychologists. Studies in a clinical setting have not been explicitly undertaken from the social psychological perspective that I sketch.

Here is the organization of this chapter. I begin with a general statement concerning the social relationship between the therapist and the client. This relationship and how it unfolds during therapy are what I wish to examine from the viewpoint of social psychology. Then I provide an overview of how social psychologists conceive relationships. My next section describes results from psychotherapy outcome studies. Findings concerning the initiation, continuation, termination, and success of therapy make a great deal of sense when looked at in terms of the social psychology of relationships. I close with some conclusions about the unique characteristics of behavior therapy when examined from social psychology.

THE RELATIONSHIP BETWEEN THERAPIST AND CLIENT

How should we characterize the therapist-client relationship? Let's start with a definition of psychotherapy that is intentionally general. I borrow the following from Bernstein and Nietzel (1980, p. 283):

1. Psychotherapy consists of an interpersonal relationship between at least two participants, one of whom (the therapist) has special training and expertise in handling psychological problems.

2. The other participant is a client who is experiencing some problem . . . and has entered the relationship in order to alleviate this problem.
3. The psychotherapeutic relationship is a nurturant but purposeful relationship in which several methods, largely psychological in nature, are employed to bring about the changes desired by the client and approved by the therapist.
4. These methods are based on some formal theory regarding psychological problems in general and the specific complaints of the client in particular.
5. . . . most therapists will employ several of the following intervention techniques: fostering insight, reducing emotional discomfort, encouraging catharsis, providing new information, assigning extratherapy tasks, and raising clients' faith in and expectancy for change.

To this characterization, I would like to add the explicit statement that psychotherapy is a relationship that develops over time and therefore has a temporal structure. That is, therapy has a beginning, middle, and ending.

Within this definition we can fit any of the 400-plus approaches to psychotherapy that have been described (Garfield & Bergin, 1986). But let us focus on psychoanalysis, because here is the approach that first specified the relationship between therapist and client as critical in determining therapy outcome. Indeed, the most sophisticated discussion of the relationship between therapist and client has taken place within the psychoanalytic literature, so it behooves us to see the distinctions drawn there. As this thinking has evolved, we see the relationship between therapist and client distinguished on three different levels (Stewart, 1980).

Transference and Countertransference

In classic psychoanalysis, *transference* is the client's mental construction of the relationship between him- or herself and the therapist. Characterizing this relationship is the "transfer" of previous thoughts and feelings from earlier and significant relationships onto the new relationship:

> What are transferences? They are new editions or facsimiles of the impulses or phantasies which are aroused and made conscious during the progress of the analysis, but . . . they replace some earlier person by the person of the physician. To put it another way: a whole series of psychological experiences are

revived, not as belonging to the past, but as applying to the person of the physician at the present moment. Some of these transferences have a content which differs from that of their model in no respect except the substitution. These then—to keep the same metaphor—are merely new impressions or imprints. Others are more ingeniously constructed; their content has been subjected to a moderating influence . . . by cleverly taking advantage of some real peculiarity of the physician's person or circumstances and attaching themselves to that. These, then, will no longer be new impressions, but revised editions. (Freud, 1953, p. 116)

The other side of this symbolic relationship of course is *countertransference:* the therapist's "transfer" of thoughts and feelings and styles of behaving from previous relationships to the current relationship with the client.

Therapeutic Alliance

However, more current psychoanalytic thinking posits that there must be more to the relationship between the therapist and the client than transference and countertransference. With the advent of ego psychology and the recognition within psychoanalysis that people actively cope with the problems they face, it became possible to acknowledge that another level of the relationship between client and therapist existed as well.

This has been called by various terms (e.g., therapeutic bond, helping alliance, and so on), but I'll use therapeutic alliance to describe the relationship between therapist and client that involves their joining together in the shared purpose of undertaking therapy. Necessary for this sort of relationship to form and succeed is that the client trust the therapist, perceive the therapist as competent, perceive himself or herself as competent as well, and that both have hope for the successful treatment.

As usually discussed, the therapeutic relationship is a strongly emotional one. The feelings that the therapist and client bring to the relationship may or may not be realistic. This point then leads to yet another level on which the relationship between therapist and client has been described.

Real Relationship

When therapists and clients interact, it is not just in terms of unconscious memories and habits and not just in terms of hopes and expectations and shared feelings. Interaction takes place as well within a so-called *real relationship* entered into freely by consenting adults who must acknowledge and deal with such matters as fees, appointments, and interruptions (Greenson, 1967). In the real relationship between therapist and client, their actual personality characteristics come into play. One may find the other to be objectionable or frustrating. Errors may be made. Bills must be paid.

In considering this level of the relationship between therapist and client, we must take into account a host of ascriptive characteristics. The client and the therapist are each a male or a female, of a particular age, from a particular socioeconomic and educational background. They have an ethnic or racial identity. These characteristics may mesh well or poorly.

Conclusions

Let me offer some conclusions about the relationship between therapist and client as it has been articulated within psychoanalytic thinking. First, quite obviously the very language used to describe these relationships is often at odds with how more behavioral psychologists conceive things.

Second, a longer view does find some commonalities. I find it useful, for instance, to think of transference as a bad habit (one with emotional and cognitive components, to be sure, like most bad habits) that is inappropriately generalized from previous relationships onto a new relationship, in this case with a therapist. "Working through" the transference can then be seen as throwing off the burden of past learning, distinguishing early situations from present situations, and acting appropriately in the here and now.

Third, the relationship between therapist and client is not a simple one. I've just discussed three levels on which it exists, and others would be possible to specify as well. Further, this relationship does not fall apart into components just because a theoretical discussion posits them. The levels of a relationship come together and must be considered together.

Fourth, the different levels of the therapist-client relationship influence each other. This was explicit in the quote from Freud, where a characteristic of the therapist (from the level of the "real relationship") is precisely the point at which the transference relationship takes off. And just as obviously, characteristics of the real relationship affect the therapeutic alliance. Consider for instance racial differences between therapist and client. If these are characterized by distrust or even just ignorance, they may get dragged into the therapeutic alliance, to its detriment.

Fifth, as I turn in the rest of this chapter to social psychology, we will find that social psychologists also make distinctions among various levels of social relationships but that they make different distinctions than those common within clinical psychology. We will have to grapple for a way to translate the social psychology language of relationships into the clinical psychology language. When we do so, we will find that not all of the clinical levels are equally well addressed within the social psychology literature.

THE SOCIAL PSYCHOLOGY OF RELATIONSHIPS

In this section, I wish to give an overview of social psychology and how it has gone about conceiving relationships. The first distinction I must make is between *psychological* social psychology and *sociological* social psychology. This distinction has existed as long as there has been a field of social psychology, because it can be traced to 1908 when the first two social psychology textbooks were published—one from the viewpoint of sociology by Ross and the other from the viewpoint of psychology by McDougall. Psychological approaches emphasize the individual, whereas sociological approaches concern themselves more with groups of people rather than individuals per se.

Definition of Social Psychology

I write here about psychological social psychology, which seems more applicable to understanding psychotherapy. This field can be defined with Gordon Allport's (1968) classical characterization:

> [Social psychology is] . . . an attempt to understand and explain how the thought, feeling, and behavior of individuals are influenced by the actual, imagined, or implied presence of others. (p. 3)

We can see that the different levels of the therapeutic relationship are included here. But we must be careful to remember that we are all "others" to everyone else in the world, which means that our individual focus is not to be misconstrued as one-way effects running from "others" to the individual. In psychotherapy, there is a temptation to look at the relationship as mainly one-way, because by definition, the therapist tries to do something that changes (influences) the client. However, in understanding any relationship, we must take into account both parties.

Indeed, the psychoanalytic stance of neutrality is cultivated precisely to make therapy a one-way interaction, but it is now seen to be a futile attempt, and the notion of countertransference was introduced to acknowledge the effect of the client on the therapist. For an example of a sophisticated psychodynamic view of psychotherapy as a relationship, we need only remember Sullivan's (1947) interpersonal psychiatry.

Describing Social Relationships

We can discern two general approaches within social psychology to describing the relationships between and among people. One way is in terms of a typology that specifies different sorts of relationships (e.g., acquaintances or friends) and their critical ingredients. The second approach is in terms of dimensions along which all relationships vary, such as liking, trust, power, or influence. These two approaches are of course compatible, because in making sense of a typology as a whole, we end up describing the interrelationships among its categories.

So, we can describe the psychotherapy relationship as a particular type of relationship and go on to specify where it falls along dimensions that distinguish various relationships from one another. Despite numerous attempts to reduce or interpret the relationship between therapist and client as "another" sort of relationship, like that between friends or that between religious leaders and their followers, I think at this point more is lost than gained in so doing. The relationship between client and therapist is sufficiently unique and well-defined within our society that a better strategy is to try simply to characterize it.

Studying Social Behavior

In this section, let me sketch the research strategy that many social psychologists traditionally have favored in studying relationships. Because of the nature of the research method, certain sorts of results have been obtained and not others, and we must appreciate that the social psychology of relationships applies to some aspects of the therapist–client relationship more than to others.

Psychological social psychologists often have employed laboratory experiments as a way of creating special social situations in which to study their subjects. I use the term *social analogue* to describe this special social situation, because researchers thereby try to capture only the essential characteristics of some social phenomenon.

Analogue research has many precedents within science and psychology. In particular, analogue studies have been useful within the investigation of psychopathology. So, although acknowledged as not identical to depression, learned helplessness is still thought to be similar enough that it provides a way to study depression in the laboratory (Seligman, 1975). The various social analogues that social psychologists devise are similarly acknowledged as not identical to social behavior outside the laboratory but still similar enough—presumably—to conformity or obedience to give the researcher a way to study these topics in the laboratory.

Here is an example from social psychology: Asch's (1946) approach to social perception and impression formation. He wanted to know how we combine different items of information about a person we meet into a coherent whole. This topic could be tackled in a number of ways. Certainly, an obvious—if difficult— strategy would require research subjects to meet different people, who would reveal different aspects of themselves according to the experimenter's instructions. After each interaction, the research subject would voice his or her overall impression of the person he or she has just met. But Asch took a simpler route. He gave subjects a list of personality traits and asked them what they would think of a person with these particular characteristics.

Here the list of traits is treated as analogous to an actual person. Consider the benefits and drawbacks of this research approach. On the plus side, social analogues make research simple. If a brief list of traits really can stand in for another human being for the purposes of studying social perception, then a social psychologist can study how an individual forms dozens of impressions in a matter of minutes. Indeed, because this particular social analogue can be implemented on sheets of paper, dozens of subjects can be studied simultaneously.

On the negative side, social analogues like these can be strained. We know from the start that these are not identical to "real" social phenomena. But some are better analogues than others. Think of the difference between paper people (like those studied by Asch) and honest-to-goodness people. Are these differences fatal to the validity of this social analogue? The answer depends on the researcher's purpose. A procedure like this might well capture the essence of what we go through as we scan the passengers in a train car to decide who we might sit next to. We check out a few characteristics of the passengers—like the presence or absence of weapons, communicable diseases, and cigars—and then make a rapid decision. But paper people procedures may fall short of capturing what we do when we choose a friend, a spouse, or an employee.

Theorizing in Social Psychology

Let me move on now to characterize the sort of theorizing that goes on within social psychology. Much of this is clarified if we remember the contributions of Kurt Lewin (1890–1947), the father of the modern discipline. Lewin was a German Jew, and he fled to the United States during the rise of Hitler. He brought with him the orientation of a gestalt psychologist and a keen interest in social problems. In combining these two, Lewin stamped social psychology with the character it still possesses.

I pause briefly at gestalt psychology, because it is important in understanding Lewin's (1951) contributions and thus the current face of social psychology. Several emphases define the gestalt approach:

- the idea that psychological phenomena are best described in terms of relationships among elements; these relationships are termed gestalts (meaning wholes, patterns, or configurations)
- the assumption that some relationships are more psychologically fundamental than others; these are called good gestalts
- field theory: the notion that people are self-regulating, dynamic systems that naturally seek out balance and harmony (i.e., people tend toward good gestalts)

The first gestalt psychologists concerned themselves with microscopic topics like perception and learning, but those who followed applied the gestalt perspective to larger topics in personality and social psychology. Here is where Kurt Lewin enters the picture. His theorizing began with the assumption that behavior is best understood in terms of the psychological field in which it takes place. He called this field the lifespace, the total of all forces acting on a person at a given time. Lewin defined a lifespace as the individual's construction of his or her relationship with the environment. The key term here is construction, which means that the lifespace is a psychological reality phrased in cognitive terms. The individual "lives" not in a physical world but in a psychological one.

Of course, the physical world bears on the psychological world, because many of our constructions have a basis in the physical world. Nevertheless, according to Lewin, psychologists should concern themselves not with "stimuli" but with someone's interpretations of them. By this view, strict behaviorists confuse their business with that of physicists and chemists, who are justifiably interested in physical reality. Lewin and other social psychologists believe that we must acknowledge perceived reality, because people only behave in terms of how they take the world to be.

Lewin believed that the lifespace was divided into regions, each with a particular valence. A particular region may be positive or negative for the individual, according to the forces operating at that particular moment. Sometimes these regions get out of kilter, and he is left in a state of disequilibrium. Within his lifespace, processes then are automatically set into motion to restore his equilibrium. Lewin described the lifespace and its reponse to disequilibrium with complicated terms like "forces" and "vectors" that never won much acceptance among his fellow psychologists. Nevertheless, his general statement that people strive to make their thoughts and feelings harmonious has been widely influential in social psychology.

Today, theorists don't speak explicitly of lifespaces, but the entire field of social psychology nonetheless concerns itself with the issues first phrased by Lewin: (a) how to describe the way people view themselves and others; and (b) how to explain the way people maintain and/or restore the balance among their thoughts and feelings following disturbance. It must be further added that Lewin was strongly committed to the use of psychology to solve social problems. He disagreed with the separation of "pure" and "applied" research, feeling instead that a particular investigation could serve both theoretical and practical purposes. The phrase *action research* reflects this approach to social psychology: the explicit attempt to make one's scientific investigations pertinent to larger social matters, like leadership style, group process, prejudice, aggression, and physical health. In sum, contemporary social psychology is very much Lewin's legacy. It is a cognitive endeavor that uses experiments in an attempt to shed light on socially relevant issues.

Models of Social Beings

Contemporary social psychologists don't phrase their theories in terms of forces and vectors. Instead, they use a variety of cognitive terms, many borrowed from experimental psychology's study of cognition. Indeed, social psychology is presently undergoing an explosion of cognitive theorizing. The general phrase social cognition is used to describe all the cognitive terms that play a part in this theorizing (Fiske & Taylor, 1984; Markus & Zajonc, 1985). Probably in the years to come we will see a consolidation of these units. But in the meantime, let me just call your attention to the heap of cognitive constructs that flourish in social psychology (see Chapter 15 of this volume). What they share in common is an attempt to capture how people represent their thoughts concerning the social world.

Social psychologists are interested not just with the basic units of social cognition but also with how people put these units together and deploy them in social behavior. Different styles of organizing one's thoughts about the self and others have been hypothesized. These styles reflect different views of human nature. Just as personality and clinical psychologists ascribe to various models, so too do social psychologists. Taylor (1981) distinguished three general views of people as social thinkers.

People as Consistency Seekers

The first model of social cognition to appear proposed that people seek consistency among their thoughts and feelings. This model stems directly from Lewin's concept of a person's lifespace: a self-regulating system that strives for harmony. In the 1950s and 1960s, many theories of cognitive consistency were proposed by social psychologists (see Abelson et al., 1968). Common to these theories were several related assumptions. First, consistency or inconsistency is to be understood from the point of view of the thinker. Second, when a person perceives an inconsistency among his thoughts, he experiences a negative feeling. Third, this aversive state motivates him to resolve the inconsistency in some way.

The best known of the consistency approaches is Festinger's (1957) cognitive dissonance theory. This theory concerns itself specifically with the case where a person perceives an inconsistency between his or her attitude toward some object and his or her behavior toward that object. In such an event, an unpleasant feeling (dissonance) results, and he or she casts about for a way to resolve the inconsistency. Often, an easy way to reduce dissonance is to change one's original attitude.

Consistency theories gave rise to research showing the irrational lengths to which people will go to maintain a balance among their beliefs. For example, Festinger, Riecken, and Schachter (1956) studied members of a doomsday cult who predicted that the world would end on a particular date. As believers, the cult members would be spirited away on a flying saucer by omnipotent space aliens. This did not happen on the appointed day, but the cult members did not relinquish their beliefs. Just the opposite happened. They decided that because of their sincerity, the world had been temporarily spared. So, they renewed their efforts to recruit new members.

People as Naive Scientists

An altogether different view arrived on the social cognition scene with the person as scientist metaphor (Gardner, 1985). Consistency was no longer considered the overarching purpose of our thoughts. Rather, theorists proposed that everyday people were much like scientists in their attempt to predict and control events in the world. The theories proposed during the 1970s emphasized the rationality of social cognition rather than its irrationality. And accuracy rather than harmony was viewed as the goal of the social thinker.

Kelley's (1973) theory of how people arrive at a particular causal explanation for some event is a good example of this second model. He suggested that people proceed exactly as a scientist would, by gathering information about how different factors relate to the event in question. To the degree that the presence or absence of a factor is associated with the subsequent occurrence or nonoccurrence of the event, then it is a likely cause. If you are trying to explain why you performed poorly on some task, you think of all the factors that might have influenced your performance. You figure out that the only factor that consistently distinguishes your good performances from your bad performances is the amount of time you devote to reviewing material. That becomes your causal attribution, and the process is clearly a rational one.

Kelley's attribution theory is a normative model, because it prescribes what a reasonable person interested in the truth should do. The problem with normative models of social cognition is that they do not always describe what people actually do. Although there are instances where the scientist model gets at what social cognition involves, there are also instances where the scientist metaphor falls short.

People as Misers

So, the third approach to people as social beings that we can discern within contemporary social psychology is descriptive, trying to get at what people actually do when they think about themselves and others (as opposed to what they should do if they are to be considered rational). Taylor (1981) summarized the findings of this approach by likening social thinkers to misers. In other words, people have limits in their ability to take all the information into account, and so they take shortcuts wherever possible by simplifying the cognitive tasks they face.

Well known within psychology is Kahneman and Tversky's (1973) research on judgment heuristics. Social psychologists in the 1980s have found these ideas extremely useful, and an avalanche of recent research has documented the use of these strategies in social cognition. For instance, the vividness bias refers to the tendency of people to base judgments, not on sober generalizations, but on striking examples (Borgida & Nisbett, 1977). Suppose you plan to buy a new car. You're thinking about a Ford Escort. An article in *Consumers Reports* summarizes the repair record for thousands of Escorts, and these results reflect well on the car. But your best friend once owned a beige 1982 Escort that was always in the shop, and she tells you in gory detail about one fuel pump transplant after another. What do you pay attention to? You know full well what you would do. Rationality be damned!

The Role of Motivation

Are people motivated to entertain particular beliefs and feelings, or do these simply occur granted that other thoughts are present? The importance of motivation in social psychology has been played up and played down during different eras. In the heyday of consistency theories, motivation was considered quite important. Cognitive dissonance theory, for instance, states quite clearly that perceived inconsistency motivates a person to resolve the discrepancy.

The person as scientist metaphor takes the opposite stance altogether, regarding social cognition as cool, calm, and collected, even when it is wrong. Intriguing work here explains prejudice (on the face of it a motivated phenomenon dripping with feeling and emotion) in strictly rational terms (e.g., Hamilton & Gifford, 1976). Granted that someone has particular beliefs, these "logically" give rise to other beliefs. Suppose you happen to believe, for whatever reason, that young males are loud and rude. This "theory" predisposes you to notice instances where it is confirmed and to overlook cases where it is disconfirmed. Motivational explanations are superfluous when it comes to your prejudice.

Another area where the role of motivation has been debated is the self-serving bias in attribution. To call this tendency "self-serving" is to imply that people are motivated to enhance their self-esteem, but it is possible to explain this bias solely in terms of the information available to a person. Usually when people undertake some activity, they expect to succeed because they believe they are competent. When they do succeed, explaining it in terms of their own characteristics makes a lot of sense. In contrast, when they fail, they look outside themselves and thus explain it in terms of external factors. Motivation is not responsible for the difference in how we explain our successes and failures—just the different information we pay attention to in the respective cases.

Conclusions

What does social psychology as sketched in this section have to do with psychotherapy? The main characteristics of social psychology include:

- A concern with effects of "others" on the individual.
- An approach to relationships in terms of interactions and the dimensions along which they vary.
- The use of social analogues in laboratory experiments.
- Theories derived from Lewin's gestalt approach and thus stresses cognitions and balance among them.
- Ambivalence about the role of motivation.

Needless to say, there are notable exceptions to this characterization of social psychology, but I think it a fair generalization, one that allows us to make sense of many of the particular theories, findings, and applications that comprise social psychology.

Here are some conclusions suggested by this review. First, many of the findings of social psychology's study of relationships apply to early stages in psychotherapy, and not so well to later stages. When therapist and client do not know each other well, they necessarily rely on the superficial social cues with which social psychologists have become expert. We should expect, therefore, that the initiation and continuation of therapy can be readily explained by social psychology findings.

Second and relatedly, social psychology speaks more to the real relationship between therapist and client and to the therapeutic alliance than to transference and countertransference. This probably reflects the Lewinian emphasis on contemporary factors defining the lifespace. However, there is no good reason why transference and countertransference, as social constructions, could not be accommodated within the approach of social cognition.

Third, social psychology does not have much to say about interaction between therapist and client, because—after all—the paper people used in social analogues do not react to our reactions. This is hardly what occurs in psychotherapy. Even the absence of a response by a real person is a response with significance.

Fourth, social psychology findings are necessarily stripped of the details and content that make psychotherapy what it is. Because much of social psychology is rendered content-free by its reliance on analogue methods, we should not expect these findings to tell us anything about the particular content of therapy. No light is shed on specific techniques or strategies. As you have noticed, my discussion so far in this chapter has been independent of the type of therapy that takes place. I will talk about behavior modification in particular later on, but the point here is that the contribution of social psychology is to an abstract relationship between client and therapist.

In sum, contemporary social psychology is thoroughly cognitive (see Chapter 15 of this handbook), even when the focus is on relationships between and among people. When individuals interact with each other it is via the thoughts and beliefs that they entertain. This is certainly compatible with the "cognizing" of psychoanalytic theory that object relations approaches represent, as well as the similar "cognizing" of learning theory by social learning theory. When social psychologists describe relationships, they stress the role played by balance or equity. If a relationship is harmonious, it continues and flourishes. If not, it is doomed.

PSYCHOTHERAPY RESEARCH AND SOCIAL PSYCHOLOGY

Whether or not the social psychology of relationships is useful to clinical psychology cannot be decided if we never stray from social psychology studies, a point that some social cognition researchers seem not to appreciate fully. Rather, we must grapple with clinical psychology. In this section, I will review some of the established findings from psychotherapy studies, and I will argue that they do make sense from a social psychological perspective. I borrow the organization of Garfield and Bergin's (1986) *Handbook of Psychotherapy and Behavior Change* to describe this research, dividing it into "client" studies, "therapist" studies, and "process" studies. However, remember my earlier comment that the real interest here is the relationship between client and therapist. These are convenient but artificial categories.

Research on Client Variables

Studies have looked at how particular characteristics of clients influence the course of therapy. Here are some generalizations from this body of work, arranged from the beginning to the ending of therapy (Garfield, 1986):

- Individuals seek out therapy when they are demoralized.
- Individuals who seek therapy receive it according to such factors as their socioeconomic class, education, race, age, and so on.
- The type of therapy a client receives also reflects these factors.
- The more similar the client to the therapist with respect to these characteristics, the more likely therapy is to be initiated and to be "psychological" in nature.
- Many clients terminate therapy after only a few sessions.
- Those who continue tend to be from a higher social class than those who do not, quite possibly because of mutuality of expectation on the part of the client and therapist.
- Therapy success is predicted by clients' subjective sense of change or improvement.

At each step along the way, these findings are compatible with social psychological thinking on relationships.

People seek out therapy when demoralized—which in Lewinian terms surely is an example of disequilibrium in their lifespace. They are "open" to a change. Once a potential client seeks out therapy, what transpires depends on the similarity between the client and the therapist. We may lament this bias, and we should try to combat it when it exists, but the fact of it makes sense in terms of the social psychology of relationships, which stresses similarity as an important factor in determining whether relationships actually begin.

The fact of frequent therapy termination before much progress is made also makes sense from a social psychological perspective. Here "equilibrium" has not been restored to the person. Demoralization continues, and so he or she stops. When expectations are compatible, therapy proceeds. We can find in these ideas a good rationale for beginning therapy with a contract and a role induction interview, where the nature of therapy is explained to the prospective client.

And therapy works to the degree that a client thinks it works! This sounds like double-talk, but it is a powerful affirmation of social psychology's emphasis on perceived reality. "Real" change follows "perceived" change, again because the individual seeks balance among his or her various parts.

Research on Therapist Variables

Let us turn our attention to the other partner in the therapeutic relationship. Again, a number of studies have investigated how different characteristics of the therapist influence the course and outcome of psychotherapy. Here are some representative conclusions from this line of work (Beutler, Crago, & Arizmendi, 1986):

- Therapist age has no strong relationship to outcome, although similarity of age between client and therapist works against early termination.
- Female therapists, first, and therapists of the client's gender, second, facilitate treatment.
- Ethnic similarity of therapist and client works against early termination.
- Findings on therapist personality are contradictory, but more specific attitudes like empathy, warmth, and trustworthiness are associated with improvement in therapy.
- However, these findings are stronger when they reflect the perceptions of the client as opposed to the judgment of "independent" observers.
- Therapist expectation for change predicts change.

Without belaboring the point, note again how most of these findings make good sense from a social psychological perspective that stresses the role of expectation, similarity, and likeableness in the origin and maintenance of relationships.

One finding—on the superiority of female therapists—is intriguing and not readily explicable. Social psychology has extensively studied how people differentially respond to males and females, and a fair summary of this work is that men fare better than women. Stereotypes about males are invariably more positive, and behaviors stemming from these stereotypes are thus more positive as well. Why should females end up as more effective therapists, on the average, than males? Perhaps the answer is to be found in the speculation by Beutler et al. (1986) that clients respond well to an egalitarian attitude on the part of the therapist. Perhaps women therapists are better able to achieve and act on this stance.

Research on Process Variables

A third line of psychotherapy research looks at what actually takes place during therapy sessions, trying to relate this to outcome. Once again, here is a summary of the major findings from this line of work (Orlinsky & Howard, 1986):

- Many ostensibly important variables—like individual versus group therapy, frequency of therapy sessions, and specification of length of treatment—have little affect on therapy outcome.
- Timeliness and consistency of implementing therapy are more important than the details of therapy.
- To the degree that the client participates actively in therapy, collaborates, and shares responsibility, therapy outcome is enhanced.
- The overall quality of the therapeutic alliance is consistently related to good outcome.

These results are easily summarized by saying that therapy works to the degree that the social relationship between client and therapist has the characteristics identified by social psychologists as leading to a good relationship between any two people.

BEHAVIOR MODIFICATION AND SOCIAL PSYCHOLOGY

I would like to conclude this chapter by addressing specifically behavior modification in light of social psychology. As I have noted several times, my discussion has been about therapy per se, with no special relevance to one form of treatment or another. This makes sense inasmuch as the client-therapist relationship is a common factor that cuts across all approaches. But can something more specific be said about behavior modification?

I believe so, because there is an intriguing convergence between social psychology findings on how best to ensure that attitude change leads to behavior change and some of the central tenets of behavioral therapy. Let me explain, starting again with Lewin and his interest in action research.

Attitude Change

Social psychology has long wanted to improve the human condition by eradicating discrimination, conflict, and the like. Granted the cognitive stance of social psychology, the favorite target of intervention has been one's attitude: presumably a pervasive cause of social behavior. If attitudes can be changed, a host of behaviors can be efficiently changed in the wake, so went the rationale. Social psychologists therefore have developed several specific strategies of changing one's attitudes.

Persuasive Communications

First is attitude change through messages explicitly designed for this purpose: persuasive communications. Hundreds of studies have looked at the process by which a person (or is not) persuaded to change his or her attitude by hearing a message urging this change (e.g., Hovland, Janis, & Kelley, 1953). Researchers break persuasion into steps. We can start with the source of the persuasive message: who urges the change in attitude? Change takes place to the degree that the source is credible, and credibility is served by expertise and trustworthiness (Brigham, 1986).

Next is the message itself. Should one advocate an extreme position to produce maximum attitude change? (Answer: Yes up to a point, after which extremity boomerangs; Sherif & Hovland, 1961.) Should one present arguments for and against the suggestion? (Answer: No, if the audience is already in general agreement; yes, if the audience is initially skeptical; Lumsdaine & Janis, 1953.) Should one appeal to fear? (Answer: Yes, if specific recommendations are provided for reducing it; Sutton, 1982.)

Finally, there is the target of the message: the person to be persuaded. Here the persuader can exercise the least control, because people usually exercise a lot of choice in the persuasive messages to which they expose themselves. As we well know (and as consistency theories predict), people usually pay attention only to messages with which they agree. Take campaign speeches by politicians. They quite obviously intend to change someone's attitude (and hence their voting), but speeches by particular candidates attract the attention mostly of voters already committed to them.

Social psychology researchers have investigated how self-esteem and intelligence of a listener predisposes attitude change following a persuasive communication. High self-esteem apparently works against attitude change (Cook, 1970). The effect of intelligence is more complicated. On the one hand, a degree of intelligence is needed to comprehend a message. But too much intelligence makes a person less likely to be persuaded by it (McGuire, 1968).

The various effects of persuasive communications are numerous and complicated, and a social psychologist friend calls this area of work "it depends" research, because this phrase captures the prevailing wisdom with regard to most lines of investigation. Nevertheless, some theorists have attempted a larger view of persuasive communications. Notable here is the work of Petty and Cacioppo (1986). They propose that persuasive communications change attitudes through two means. What they call the central route is change that results from people thinking actively about an issue. The peripheral route is change through cognitively irrelevant means, for example, because the source of a message is funny or cute. Petty and Cacioppo further say that attitude change through the central route is usually more enduring. In contrast, attitude change through the peripheral route is usually easier to accomplish, at least in the short run.

Counter-Attitudinal Behavior

An altogether different approach to attitude change comes from consistency theories. If a person has a particular attitude and can be induced to behave contrary to that attitude, then a state of dissonance should arise that can be readily reduced by changing her original attitude. One of the classic experiments in social psychology tested this hypothesized process. Festinger and Carlsmith (1959) recruited college students as subjects to perform a boring task: to stack spools on a tray, take them off, restack them, and so on for an hour. Each subject was then dismissed, but on the way out, the experimenter said something like, "Oops, it looks like my assistant didn't show up. I need some help. I need someone to tell the next subject what an interesting task this will be. Will you help me out? I'll be able to pay you."

The subject said yes, unaware that he was still participating in the experiment. The researcher then told the subject either that the payment would be $1 (small) or $20 (large). The subject then spoke to the next person, after which he or she again was dismissed. But there was one more step. The subject, still an unaware participant in the experiment, was interviewed by another researcher who asked him or her to rate how interesting the original task had been. According to dissonance theory, people should experience greater dissonance with the smaller reward, because it provides no decent rationale for the lie. And this is precisely what Festinger and Carlsmith (1959) found: more positive attitude for subjects paid $1 as opposed to those paid $20.

These findings have been challenged, and other explanations proposed. Appreciate their importance, though, in showing that one possible route to attitude change is through inducing a person to display counter-attitudinal behaviors. As seekers of consistency, we may try to bring our attitudes into line with the behavior we have already performed. There is an interesting implication here, as well. The smaller the inducement, so long as it is successful, the more attitude change should be produced.

Attitude-Value Confrontation

An intriguing version of consistency approaches to attitude change has been explicitly deployed by Rokeach (1971, 1979) in the attitude-value confrontation technique. By definition, values are more general than attitudes, so Rokeach tries to highlight inconsistencies between people's attitudes and values. He asks people to rank the importance of values, including freedom and equality. Among whites prejudiced against blacks, freedom is regarded as more important than equality, but in a simple intervention, Rokeach points out to these individuals that freedom and equality must go hand-in-hand; one way to serve freedom is to act in ways that serve equality. Prejudiced individuals exposed to this intervention indeed change their attitudes toward civil rights as well as their behavior.

Group Contact

Yet another approach to attitude change arranges matters so that people of different races interact in ways that produce positive thoughts and feelings. This work stemmed from an earlier notion called the contact hypothesis that proposed that mere contact between different groups would suffice to decrease prejudice. Subsequent research showed this to be an oversimplification. However, if the contact takes a particular form, then one's prejudice can be effectively combatted. In a series of important studies of actual work groups composed of whites and blacks, Cook (1970) delineated a number of the critical factors:

- Getting to know people as individuals (not simply as folks who fill rolls).
- Equal status.
- Norm of friendliness.
- Cooperative reward structure (rather than a competitive one).

- Personal characteristics of group members must be at odds with stereotypes.

All of these may sound completely obvious, but how many of our societal institutions—schools, clubs, work places, the armed forces, churches—are set up so that people of different races come into contact in these ways?

Attitude-Behavior Consistency

While research into attitude change was taking place, another line of work within social psychology was steadily undermining the premise of this research. Social psychologists became interested in attitudes in the first place because—by definition—they were thought to be general causes of behavior. But social psychology encountered a raging controversy over whether attitudes really did lead to behavior. More generally, the issue here is whether or not thoughts and actions are consistent with each other. This issue is akin to the one in clinical psychology about whether changes induced in therapy sessions will be carried out of the session by the client into his or her everyday life.

Most psychologists are well aware of the possibility that attitudes and behaviors are inconsistent. What may be less well known is that recent years have seen a resolution of this issue in favor of consistency under conditions that have been specified. My conclusion is that these conditions are quite similar to those that the behavior therapist tries to create.

Let me give you some background. LaPiere (1934) reported one of the most famous demonstrations of attitude-behavior inconsistency. He was a white male. For three months, he took an automobile trip with a Chinese-American couple, twice across the United States and up and down the West Coast. The three of them stopped at 251 different hotels and restaurants and were only once refused service. Later, LaPiere wrote to each of the 251 establishments and asked if they would accept Chinese patrons. About 50% wrote back, and of these 90% indicated that they would not. So, we have evidence of prejudiced attitudes on the part of people who ran hotels and restaurants in the United States during the 1930s. But we also know that these attitudes did not translate themselves into prejudiced behavior, because these establishments were precisely the ones that had recently rendered service to LaPiere and his traveling companions.

Findings like LaPiere's continued to accumulate until a crisis in social psychology occurred with regard to the issue. Some of the leading social psychologists despaired:

> Studies suggest that it is considerably more likely that attitudes will be unrelated to or only slightly related to overt behaviors than that attitudes will be closely related to actions. (Wicker, 1969, p. 65)

Some theorists even suggested that the attitude concept be abandoned altogether (e.g., Abelson, 1972; Wicker, 1971).

At the same time, there were many instances where attitudes and behaviors proved consistent:

- Among voters, attitudes toward political candidates predict actual voting for or against them.
- Among soldiers, attitudes toward combat predict actual performance under fire.
- Among whites, attitudes toward blacks predict participation in civil rights activities.
- Attitudes toward organ transplants predict the granting of permission to remove one's organs after death.
- Attitudes toward movies predict one's attendance at them.

The real task of the social psychologist is to explain when attitudes and behaviors are consistent and when they are not. Researchers have made great strides with this. Several factors not taken into account in earlier studies of attitudes and behavior now are seen as important in explaining the relationship between attitudes and behavior (Brigham, 1986). Let me describe these factors, and note in turn how each sheds light on LaPiere's findings.

First are the circumstances under which someone originally acquires a particular attitude. Attitudes stemming from direct experience are more consistent with our behavior than those acquired secondhand. Perhaps in the 1930s few of the hotel or restaurant proprietors had ever met a Chinese-American.

Second is the degree to which an attitude helps define a person's self-image. If who you are is tied up in your evaluation of a particular group or object, then you act quite consistently. Again, perhaps the subjects studied by LaPiere had little investment in their feelings about Chinese-Americans.

Third is whether the person is self-conscious while she is behaving. Sometimes a person needs to reflect on her attitudes before she behaves consistently with them. Mindless individuals, in contrast, behave inconsistently. Saying "no" in a letter is a more automatic (and much easier) task than doing so face-to-face.

Fourth is a person's evaluation of the particular behavior supposedly reflecting her attitude. If there is a strong norm for (or against) acting in a particular way, her attitude exerts little influence on her behavior. Here the individual is not inconsistent (with her attitudes) so much as consistent (with the expectations of others). Perhaps the people who ran the hotels and restaurants felt obliged to serve all who showed up at their door, even if they didn't like them.

Fifth is the generality of the attitude with regard to the behavior that's being predicted. Highly general attitudes toward the environment, for instance, do not predict particular behaviors like returning aluminum cans as well as more specific attitudes toward recycling. So, one's attitudes toward "Chinese" people in general may have little bearing on how one treats particular individuals.

Sixth is the scope of the behavior relevant to the attitude. Correlations between how one feels and how one acts can be boosted considerably if one's behavior is measured in various ways on various occasions. In LaPiere's study, only a single behavior was ascertained (serving the Chinese-American couple). Perhaps a wider range of observations would have turned up behaviors consistent with the expressed attitudes of the hotel and restaurant proprietors.

Do attitudes predict behavior? The answer is clearly yes, although the relationship is hardly as simple as researchers originally expected. A host of factors above and beyond people's evaluations of social groups determines how they act toward them. Now transpose these findings to the therapy sessions, where the therapist tries to help the client change an attitude (cognition, style, habit, whatever) in such a way that subsequent behaviors are consistent with the change. We are led quite simply to emphases on direct experience, on central characteristics of the individual, on consistency with prevailing rewards and punishments, on specific characteristics in a variety of settings. These are part of the behavioral agenda. The notion that mindfulness facilitates attitude-behavior consistency is compatible with recent modifications of behavior therapy in terms of cognitive theory (Bandura, 1986).

Conclusions

The behavioral approach to therapy, for all its important contributions and innovations, has lagged behind other therapeutic strategies in attending to the social relationship between the therapist and the client. My purpose in this chapter was to sketch one way to conceive psychotherapy as a social process, by using theory and research from social psychology's study of relationships. With a vocabulary to describe psychotherapy as a social process, perhaps future researchers and practitioners can move behavior therapy into the realm of truly "social" therapies.

In some ways, behavior therapy and social psychology are necessarily at odds. But they also converge in important ways, in particular stressing the importance of the context in which behavior change takes place. According to social psychology, the most important aspect of this context is other people (cf. Bandura, 1986). Behavior therapists should pay more attention to their relationship with clients, appreciating that their techniques are deployed only through social interaction. The success of any technique is bounded by the quality of the relationship that exists between therapist and client.

Social psychology research has shown that the success of relationships per se can be reliably predicted by factors that have clear counterparts in the realm of therapy. I predict that explicit attention to these factors by behavior therapists will take them a large step closer to the goal of helping as many troubled individuals as possible.

SUMMARY

Recent discussions of how social psychology applies to clinical psychology have focused almost exclusively on the role of social cognition. A broader applicability exists as well, and that is to conceiving psychotherapy as social process taking place at several levels. In this chapter, the social psychology of relationships is characterized and applied to the relationship between therapist and client with regard to the beginning, middle, and ending of therapy. The usefulness of the social psychology perspective is suggested by reviewing psychotherapy research findings. Almost all of the well-established findings in this line of work make good social psychological sense. I ended this chapter by pointing to a convergence between social psychology's findings on how to achieve consistency between people's attitudes and their behavior and behavior therapy's approach to treatment.

REFERENCES

Abelson, R. P. (1972). Are attitudes necessary? In B. T. King & E. McGinnies (Eds.), *Attitudes, conflict, and social change* (pp. 19–48). New York: Academic Press.

Abelson, R. P., Aronson, E., McGuire, W. J., Newcomb, T. M., Rosenberg, M. J., & Tannenbaum, P. H. (Eds.) (1968). *Theories of cognitive consistency: A sourcebook.* Chicago: Rand McNally.

Allport, G. W. (1968). The historical background of modern social psychology. In G. Lindzey & E. Aronson (Eds.), *The handbook of social psychology* (Vol. 1, 2nd ed, pp. 1–80). Reading, MA: Addison-Wesley.

Asch, S. E. (1946). Forming impressions of personality. *Journal of Abnormal and Social Psychology, 41,* 258–290.

Bandura, A. (1986). *Social foundations of thought and action.* Englewood Cliffs, NJ: Prentice-Hall.

Bernstein, D. A., & Nietzel, M. T. (1980). *Introduction to clinical psychology.* New York: McGraw-Hill.

Beutler, L.E., Crago, M., & Arizmendi, T. G. (1986). Research on therapist variables in psychotherapy. In S. L. Garfield & A. E. Bergin (Eds.), *Handbook of psychotherapy and behavior change* (3rd ed., pp. 257–310). New York: John Wiley & Sons.

Borgida, E., & Nisbett, R. E. (1977). The differential impact of abstract vs. concrete information on decisions. *Journal of Applied Social Psychology, 7,* 258–271.

Brehm, S. S. (1976). *The application of social psychology to clinical practice.* Washington, DC: Hemisphere.

Brigham, J. C. (1986). *Social psychology.* Boston: Little, Brown.

Cook, S. W. (1970). Motives in a conceptual analysis of attitude-related behavior. In W. J. Arnold & D. Levine (Eds.), *Nebraska symposium on motivation, Vol. 17* (pp. 179–231). Lincoln, NE: University of Nebraska Press.

Coyne, J. C., & Gotlib, I. H. (1983). The role of cognition in depression: A critical appraisal. *Psychological Bulletin, 94,* 472–505.

Festinger, L. (1957). *A theory of cognitive consistency.* Stanford: Stanford University Press.

Festinger, L., & Carlsmith, J. M. (1959). Cognitive consequences of forced compliance. *Journal of Abnormal and Social Psychology, 58,* 203–210.

Festinger, L., Riecken, H., & Schachter, S. (1956). *When prophecy fails.* Minneapolis: University of Minnesota Press.

Fiske, S. T., & Taylor, S. E. (1984). *Social cognition.* Reading, MA: Addison-Wesley.

Freud, S. (1953). Fragment of an analysis of a case of hysteria. In *Standard edition of the complete psychological works of Sigmund Freud, Vol. 7* (pp. 7–122). London: Hogarth.

Gardner, H. (1985). *The mind's new science: A history of the cognitive revolution.* New York: Basic Books.

Garfield, S. L. (1986). Research on client variables in psychotherapy. In S. L. Garfield & A. E. Bergin (Eds.), *Handbook of psychotherapy and behavior change* (3rd ed., pp. 213–256). New York: John Wiley & Sons.

Garfield, S. L., & Bergin, A. E. (Eds.) (1986). *Handbook of psychotherapy and behavior change* (3rd ed.) New York: John Wiley & Sons.

Greenson, R. R. (1967). *The technique and practice of psychoanalysis.* New York: International Universities Press.

Hamilton, D. L., & Gifford, R. K. (1976). Illusory correlation in interpersonal perception: A cognitive basis of stereotypic judgments. *Journal of Experimental Social Psychology, 12,* 392–407.

Hovland, C., Janis, I., & Kelley, H. H. (1953). *Communication and persuasion.* New Haven, CT: Yale University Press.

Kahneman, D., & Tversky, A. (1973). On the psychology of prediction. *Psychological Review, 80,* 237–251.

Kelley, H. H. (1973). The process of causal attribution. *American Psychologist, 28,* 107–128.

LaPiere, R. T. (1934). Attitudes and actions. *Social Forces, 13,* 230–237.

Lewin, K. (1951). *Field theory in social science: Selected theoretical papers.* New York: Harper.

Lumsdaine, A. A., & Janis, I. L. (1953). Resistance to "counter-propaganda" produced by one-sided and two-sided "propaganda" presentations. *Public Opinion Quarterly, 17,* 311–318.

Markus, H., & Zajonc, R. B. (1985). The cognitive perspective in social psychology. In G. Lindzey & E. Aronson (Eds.), *The handbook of social psychology* (Vol. 1, 3rd ed., pp. 137–230). New York: Random House.

McDougall, W. (1908). *Introduction to social psychology.* London: Methuen.

McGuire, W. J. (1968). Personality and susceptibility to social influence. In E. F. Borgatta & W. W. Lambert (Eds.), *Handbook of personality theory and research* (pp. 1130–1187). Chicago: Rand-McNally.

Orlinsky, D. E., & Howard, K. I. (1986). Process and outcome in psychotherapy. In S. L. Garfield & A. E. Bergin (Eds.), *Handbook of psychotherapy and behavior change* (3rd ed., pp. 311–381). New York: John Wiley & Sons.

Petty, R. E., & Cacioppo, J. T. (1986). The elaboration likelihood model of social persuasion. In L. Berkowitz (Ed.), *Advances in experimental social psychology* (Vol. 19, pp. 123–205). New York: Academic Press.

Rokeach, M. (1971). Long-range experimental modification of values, attitudes, and behavior. *American Psychologist, 26,* 453–459.

Rokeach, M. (Ed.) (1979). *Understanding human values.* New York: Free Press.

Ross, E. A. (1908). *Social psychology.* New York: Macmillan.

Seligman, M. E. P. (1975). *Helplessness: On depression, development, and death.* San Francisco: W H Freeman.

Sherif, M., & Hovland, C. (1961). *Social judgment: Assimilation and contrast effects in communication and attitude change.* New Haven, CT: Yale University Press.

Stewart, R. L. (1980). Psychoanalysis and psychoanalytic psychotherapy. In H. I. Kaplan, A. M. Freedman, & B. J. Sadock (Eds.), *Comprehensive textbook of psychiatry* (Vol. 2, 3rd ed., pp. 2113–2143). Baltimore: Williams & Wilkins.

Sullivan, H. S. (1947). *Conceptions of modern psychiatry.*

Washington, DC: William Alanson White Psychiatric Foundation.

Sutton, R. S. (1982). Fear-arousing communications: A critical examination of theory and research. In J. R. Eiser (Ed.), *Social psychology and behavioral medicine* (pp. 303–337). Chichester: John Wiley & Sons.

Taylor, S. E. (1981). The interface of cognitive and social psychology. In J. Harvey (Ed.), *Cognition, social behavior, and the environment* (pp. 189–211). Hillsdale, NJ: Lawrence Erlbaum Associates.

Wicker, A. W. (1969). Attitudes versus actions: The relationship of verbal and overt behavioral responses to attitude objects. *Journal of Social Issues, 25,* 41–78.

Wicker, A. W. (1971). An examination of the "other variables" explanation of attitude-behavior inconsistency. *Journal of Personality and Social Psychology, 19,* 18–30.

PART IV
PSYCHOBIOLOGY AND PSYCHOPHYSIOLOGY

CHAPTER 17

PSYCHOBIOLOGICAL PROCESSES IN THE ETIOLOGY OF DISEASE

Andrew Steptoe

The notion that psychophysiological processes are involved in the development and maintenance of human disease has a long but not always glorious history. The models formulated by researchers in the psychodynamically oriented psychosomatic tradition failed to convince the biomedical community at large, principally because they did not provide any convincing account of the mechanisms linking psyche with ill health (Alexander, 1950). Work stimulated by conditioning and learning theory has demonstrated that alterations of physiological function can be produced experimentally through the imposition of appropriate contingencies. Lachman (1972) has argued that such phenomena may provide a basis for the development of psychosomatic disorders. However, direct evidence for the conditioning of disease-related responses is rare. This is not to say that conditioning processes are entirely irrelevant, but that they are unlikely to explain human disease etiology (see Ader & Cohen, 1981; Levey & Martin, 1981).

Most research on psychobiological processes in disease etiology is now conducted within the general framework of stress-diathesis or stress-coping-vulnerability models, in which organic pathology can be seen to arise through an interaction between life stress or emotional processes and the specific biological vulnerabilities of the individual (Kagan & Levi, 1974). This chapter attempts to integrate recent developments in the understanding of psychobiological responses into the general framework of disease models based on stress-vulnerability interactions. The term *psychobiology* is used in preference to psychophysiology, because the latter has conventionally been concerned with autonomic and electrocortical phenomena. Psychobiology is more appropriate in reflecting our increasing knowledge of the links between behavior, autonomic physiology, endocrinology, immunology, and the genetic bases of disease. The problems with existing models relating stress with health have been detailed previously (Steptoe, 1980, 1984a). It will be argued that several different psychological pathways are involved in the etiology and maintenance of organic disease, and that the conceptual framework needs to be elaborated in order to accommodate these diverse processes. The evidence discussed in this chapter pertains primarily to disorders of physical health rather than to psychopathology, even at the risk of perpetuating a dualism that has been discredited by behavioral medicine. The reason for this approach is that psychopathological problems are evaluated elsewhere in this volume, and the contribution of stress-vulnerability models to the etiology of psychiatric conditions has been detailed by others (Depue & Monroe, 1986; Metalsky, Halberstadt, & Abramson, 1987; Neuchterlein & Dawson, 1984).

SOURCES OF EVIDENCE

The evidence relating psychosocial factors to the development of physical illness comes from several sources. Firstly, experimental studies in animals have documented the ways in which organic pathology can arise through exposure to aversive environments. For example, Kaplan, Manuck, Clarkson, Lusso, & Taub (1982) and Kaplan et al. (1983) have shown that coronary atherosclerosis develops more extensively in cynomolgus monkeys living in unstable, as opposed to stable, social groups. The role of psychosocial factors in the production of gastrointestinal lesions, hypertension, susceptibility to infections and malignancies, and pathologies such as renal failure, has also been illustrated by animal studies (Plaut & Friedman, 1981; Sklar & Anisman, 1981; Stephens & Santisteban, 1975; Von Holst, 1986; Weiss, 1977). Studies of this type provide valuable insight into psychobiological mechanisms, but two temptations must be resisted in their interpretation. The first is to avoid the assertion that because behavioral stress *can* lead to a particular pathology under controlled experimental conditions, the association is necessarily important either to humans, or indeed to naturally occurring clinical phenomena in animals. The second is not to be swayed by superficial similarities between the types of challenge that provoke pathological responses in animal models and the demands and stressors to which humans are exposed.

The second type of evidence relevant to psychological models stems from pathophysiological investigations of human disease. Studies of the metabolic and regulatory processes underlying clinical conditions may pinpoint mechanisms that are susceptible to disturbances of central nervous system activity. An example is the role of catecholamines and the sympathetic nervous system in the development of essential hypertension. Numerous comparisons of plasma catecholamine concentrations have been made between hypertensive and normotensive people, and these tend to show elevations among younger hypertensive groups (Goldstein, 1983). Studies using radiotracer techniques suggest that this is an effect of heightened sympathoadrenal activity in early hypertension, since norepinephrine release and spillover into the circulation is markedly increased among hypertensives younger than 40 years of age (Esler, Jennings, Biviano, Lambert, & Hasking, 1986).

The third source of information derives from studies of acute reactions to stress in humans. Experiments of this type are used to explore autonomic, endocrine and immunological adjustments to different types of challenge, and demonstrate that the mechanisms identified in animal experiments as relevant to the links between stress and pathology are indeed active in humans (e.g., Krantz & Manuck, 1984). The advantage of the laboratory experimental approach is that detailed physiological measurements can be made under controled conditions where extraneous sources of stimulation are eliminated. The limitations are that experiments are necessarily short term and cannot involve the type of stimulation that may provoke irreversible pathological reactions, and that the nature of the demands on the person may not accurately reflect real-life experience (see Steptoe, 1985, 1990b).

Observational studies of humans in everyday life conditions or those undergoing stressful experiences provide the fourth source of evidence. These studies frequently show disturbances in psychobiological processes relevant to disease, and links with modulating factors such as social support. For example, catecholamine excretion is elevated on work days in comparison with home days, with concomitant increases in blood pressure and heart rate (Lundberg, Hedman, Melin, & Frankenhaeuser, 1989). Chronic stress, as observed in women experiencing severe marital discord or in family members caring for people with Alzheimer's disease, is linked with suppression of immune function (Kiecolt-Glaser et al., 1987a; Kiecolt-Glaser et al., 1987b). Investigations of this type complement the laboratory studies, but again without proving clinical causality.

The fifth and final type of evidence derives from clinical and epidemiological studies showing links between disease occurrence and such factors as psychological state, job strain, sociocultural disturbance, and life events (e.g., Brown & Harris, 1989; Johnson & Hall, 1988; Kaplan & Reynolds, 1988; Ramirez et al., 1989; Vernon & Buffler, 1988). It can be argued that without evidence at this level, no amount of experimental or pathophysiological data can prove the case for psychobiological involvement in disease etiology. On the other hand, it must be recognized that clinical and psychosocial epidemiological studies are rarely completely conclusive, because of the impossibililty of random assignment of people to different experiences, and the difficulties in controlling for every confounding factor. Thus it is necessary to take all these levels of evidence into account when developing models of psychobiological influences on disease.

STRESS–COPING–VULNERABILITY MODELS

Models relating behavioral stress with disease must not only include credible psychobiological pathways, but must also account for two major individual differences. These are: *The variability issue*–How is it that two people may have very similar life experiences, yet one becomes ill while the other remains healthy, or one suffers a myocardial infarction while the other becomes depressed. *The intensity issue*–Why is it that groups who suffer from stress-related pathology often do not appear to have more stressful lives than those who remain healthy? This issue is frequently raised by physicians or others on the basis of "clinical experience." Although the evidence concerning life events and chronic difficulties can be marshaled in response to this question, it is nevertheless true that the world does not appear to be divided into two groups, one of which suffers from adverse life experience and a high incidence of illness, whereas the other contains people who lead uneventful lives and remain healthy.

These issues can be accommodated within the general stress-coping-vulnerability model that forms the basis for this discussion. This framework derives from transactional models that view psychobiological stress responses as arising from an imbalance between environmental demands on the one hand and the personal and social resources of the individual on the other (Cox, 1978; Lazarus & Folkman, 1984). Typically, the nature of the interaction is that demands exceed resources, but the reverse can sometimes be observed, particularly in monotonous working conditions where people are unable to utilize their skills effectively (Theorell, 1989). Figure 17–1 summarizes this model and shows those dimensions of psychosocial resource and demand that have been found to influence psychobiological stress responses. Details are provided elsewhere (Steptoe, 1990a), so only a brief summary will be given here.

Psychosocial Demands

Stage I involves the interaction between demands and resources. Situational factors such as the intensity and chronicity of psychosocial demands clearly influence the likelihood of sustained psychobiological reactions (Patterson & Neufeld, 1987). These relationships can most readily be observed in animal studies where exposure to aversive stimulation is carefully controled. They are less easy to demonstrate in humans because of difficulties in quantification and the modulation of responses by the psychosocial resources detailed below. However, the fact that many life event studies show links with pathology for severely threatening rather than less threatening events and difficulties indicates that intensity of stimulation is important (Brown & Harris, 1989; Creed, 1985). The association between intensity and reaction is also apparent in posttraumatic stress research, where the severity and duration of posttraumatic stress disorder can be correlated with the degree of exposure to both industrial and natural disasters (e.g., Shore, Tatum, & Vollmer, 1986; Weisaeth, 1989). Posttraumatic stress reactions in children whose school was subject to a fatal sniper attack showed links with proximity to violence (Pynoos et al., 1987).

The effects of chronic as opposed to acute stimulation may vary, depending on whether or not adaptation takes place. Although chronic demands may place progressive strain on psychobiological processes, there are studies in which reactions to aversive stimuli are more pronounced with single as opposed to multiple exposures (Sklar, Bruto, & Anisman, 1981). The favorable effects of predictable as opposed to unpredictable patterns of stimulation have been documented for a variety of response systems, although the explanation for this effect remains controversial (Abbott, Schoen, & Badia, 1984). Finally, behavioral or instrumental control over aversive stimulation has been shown to be beneficial for outcomes ranging from worker satisfaction to cardiovascular morbidity and immunological function (see Sauter, Hurrell, & Cooper, 1989; Steptoe & Appels, 1989). The pattern does, however, depend on the nature of the coping response required, and the individual's outcome and self-efficacy expectations (Öhman & Bohlin, 1989).

Psychosocial Resources

Psychosocial resources include those aspects of social milieu, personality and coping style that influence the person's response to life experience. Many of

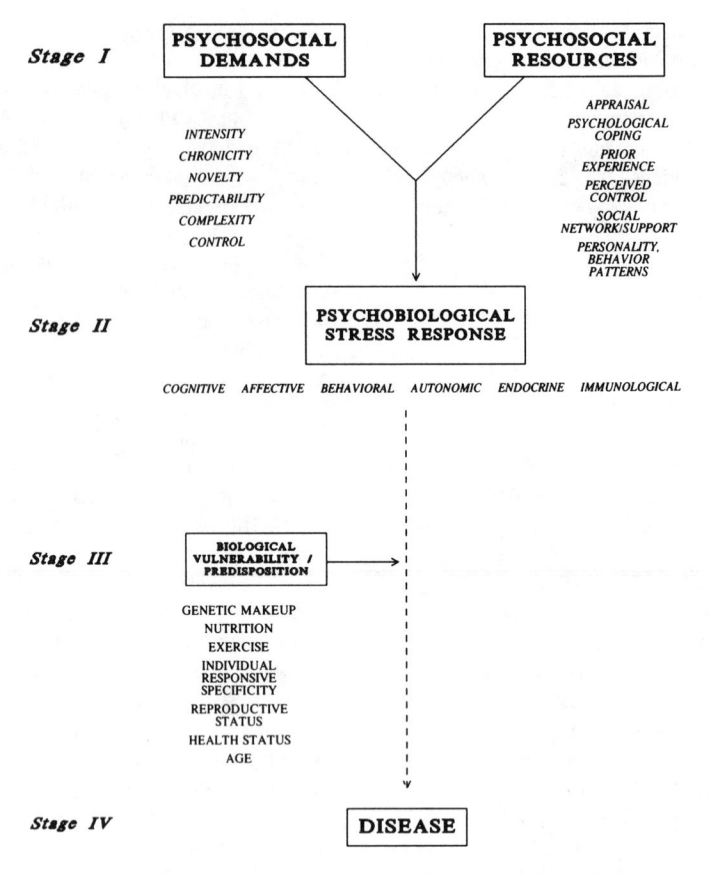

Figure 17.1. Stress–Coping–Vulnerability model of disease

these relationships are complex, and this is illustrated by the effects of previous experience of life stress on subsequent reactions. On the one hand, it has been argued that prior experience of stressful stimulation may increase tolerance of later life stress (Dienstbier, 1989; Gray, Davis, Feldon, Owen, & Border, 1981). On the other hand, early traumatic losses have been shown to increase vulnerability to later life stress (Brown, Harris & Copeland, 1977). In the laboratory, recent or concurrent life stress may increase psychophysiological reactions to demanding tasks (Fleming, Baum, Davidson, Rectanus, & McArdle, 1987; Gannon, Banks, Shelton, & Luchetta, 1989). Curvilinear patterns have also been observed, with lesser trauma in those who have undergone a moderate degree of prior life stress compared with those with high or low previous experience (Ruch, Chandler, & Harter, 1980). The effect may depend on the nature of the previous experience, with factors such as the degree of control and favorable family context being important (Mineka, Gunnar, & Champoux, 1986; Werner, 1989).

There is a long tradition of considering personality in relation to clinical disorders, and notions such as the arthritic personality, asthmatic personality, diabetic personality or even the "disease-prone" personality have been put forward (Friedman & Booth-Kewley, 1987). These ideas have, however, been subjected to severe criticism. Firstly, results have been extraordinarily inconsistent. By way of illustration, asthmatics have been characterized by such mutually exclusive traits as lacking in self-confidence, bossy, irritable, timid, aggressive, polite, rebellious and immature (Steptoe, 1984b). Different studies have described people with rheumatoid arthritis as depressed, dependent, neurotic, perfectionistic and unexpressive (Moos, 1964). The literature is plagued with a lack of appropriate chronic disease or normal population control groups and potentially biasing factors in the selection of participants. There has been an absence of attention to influential factors such as age, socioeconomic status, education, illness duration, and medication. Most such investigations have been retrospective in nature, with a concomitant difficulty in establishing cause-effect relationships. Chronic disorders often lead to social restrictions and disturbances in personal relationships that may have psychological consequences. The fact that the literature can be interpreted in terms of a disease-prone personality may simply be a reflection of the central role of negative affectivity in determining health complaints, subjective stress ratings, and medical referral practices (Watson & Pennebaker, 1989).

There may be greater promise in considering personal factors in relation to responses to environmental demands, viewing personality less as a trait than a style of responding to potentially stressful situations (Eysenck, 1989). In this context, hostility has been associated with coronary heart disease (Dembroski, MacDougall, Costa, & Grandits, 1989; Williams & Barefoot, 1988), the undemonstrative Type C personality with cancer (Temoshok, 1987), and difficulties in anger expression with high blood pressure (Julius, Harburg, Cottington, & Johnson, 1986). Other personal characteristics have been accorded more general roles in vulnerability to stress including hardiness (Hull, Van Treuren & Virnelli, 1987), locus of control (Parkes, 1984), self-esteem (DeLongis, Folkman, & Lazarus, 1988) and optimistic explanatory style (Peterson, 1988).

These factors are of course closely linked with the concepts of psychological coping and cognitive appraisal. Indeed, it can be argued that the processes just described influence peoples' ability to withstand psychological stimulation through their effect on coping. Psychological coping refers to the cognitive and behavioral responses displayed by people when attempting to avert or reduce the impact of potentially stressful events. They may have the effect of modifying the person's proximity to the events themselves or else the emotional reaction to these events. The early phase of psychological coping involves a cognitive appraisal process that determines the person's perception of the situation as threatening or nonthreatening. The allocation of attention to threat is affected by such factors as trait anxiety (Mathews & MacLeod, 1987). A meta-analysis by Suls and Fletcher (1985) of experimental studies suggested that in acute settings, avoidance and distraction are associated with lower distress and autonomic responsivity than is attention to threat. On the other hand, attention to threat may be more adaptive than distraction in the long term (Roth & Cohen, 1986). The coping responses mobilized in response to threat vary considerably between individuals, and in the same person on different occasions (Folkman & Lazarus, 1985). The deployment may depend on general factors such as self-efficacy and perceived control of the situation (Burger, 1989; Litt, 1988).

Although psychosocial demands and resources have been presented as independent components of the stress-coping-vulnerability model, they are of course closely related. The classic example of this is social support, which is frequently presented as a buffer of stressful life experience. Many of the life events that people experience involve alterations in social networks (loss of family members, relocation, etc.), so a change in the social environment may be considered as a psychosocial demand while simultaneously affecting psychosocial resources (Depue & Monroe, 1986). This has led to controversy over whether social networks and supports have main effects on health or buffering effects in relation to adverse life events (Berkman, 1985; Cohen, 1988).

Psychobiological Stress Responses

The psychobiological response systems (stage II) provide the pathways through which life stress may influence health. They will be discussed in detail below, but three general points need to be emphasized. First, psychobiological stress responses take several forms, as detailed in Figure 17-1. They include cognitive responses (changes in the mechanisms underlying information processing efficiency), affective responses, modifications in behavior and performance, autonomic responses, endocrine activation (principally release of corticosteroids and catecholamines, but also including other pathways), and alterations in cellular and humoral immunity. These systems do not necessarily respond in parallel, because patterns vary across individuals and situations.

Second, patterning of responses is observed within each system, running counter to Selye's (1976) notion of stress as the "non-specific response of the body to any demand." For example, it has been found that different types of stress have selective effects on stages of information processing such as selective attention, short term memory, and rapid decision making (Broadbent, 1971; Smith, 1990). The variety of stress response syndromes attests to the range of affective reactions that may arise (Horowitz, 1986).

At the neuroendocrine level, sustained corticosteroid and catecholamine release appear to be differentially associated with behavioral demands, with corticosteroids being activated by defeat, subordination, and behavioral helplessness, whereas catecholamines are linked with active challenge (see Henry, 1976). Some components of the neuroendocrine stress response may have the regulatory function of preventing overactivation of other pathways. Thus glucocorticoid release may prevent overshoot of inflammatory responses (Munck, Guyre, & Holbrook, 1984), whereas opioid peptides may modulate sympathoadrenal activation (Bouloux, 1987).

Thirdly, it must again be recognized that the model is not linear, because psychobiological responses themselves influence psychosocial demands and resources. For example, medical students who show the affective response of loneliness (Stage II) prior to important examinations (Stage I) appear at special risk of functional immunological suppression (Kiecolt-Glaser, Speicher, Holliday, & Glaser, 1984).

Biological Vulnerability

The model posits that whether psychobiological stress responses dissipate without lasting damage or increase the risk of ill health depends in large part on the biological vulnerability of the individual (Stage III). Biological vulnerability refers to the constitutional and background health characteristics relevant to the consequences of stress reactions. An important component of biological vulnerability is the family history and genetic make-up of the person. This has been studied extensively in relation to hypertension. The young offspring of hypertensive parents are prone to heightened cardiovascular reactivity during challenges evoking active coping behavior in comparison with the offspring of normotensives (Fredrikson & Matthews, 1990). These processes are manifest even though the offspring of hypertensives do not show any signs of elevated blood pressure themselves, and seem therefore to reflect increased vulnerability to cardiovascular disregulation in response to stress. More generally, it has been found that autonomic stress reactions display familial aggregation and patterns of association among monozygotic and dizygotic twins that strongly suggest a hereditary component (Ditto, France, & Miller, 1989; Smith et al., 1987).

One of the ways in which genetic factors may promote vulnerability to stress-related pathology is through individual-response specificity. This is the tendency for a person to respond maximally and consistently in one physiological parameter (Engel, 1960). For example, a person who carries out diverse tasks such as mental arithmetic, a public speech, watching an upsetting movie and a verbal reasoning task may consistently show his or her largest reactions in heart rate, whereas another responds maximally across experimental conditions in plasma cortisol. Establishing patterns of individual-response specificity is complicated, because comparisons across physiological systems involve mathematical transformation of responses onto a common metric. The evidence has been thoroughly reviewed by Fahrenberg (1986), and it appears that in studies of healthy young adults about one third show significant individual-response specificity in activation processes. It might then be predicted that these people will be particularly susceptible to stress-related illness, and that the type of disorder they experience will be linked with their *locus minoris resistentiae*.

Physical exercise is another factor that may contribute to resilience to stress pathology. Numerous comparisons have been made in the laboratory between physically active, or fit, and sedentary individuals, and lower reactivity in the former group is frequently observed (see Steptoe, 1989, for a review). Whether this is an effect of exercise per se or a reflection of biological differences between fit and unfit people is unclear, because longitudinal studies have demonstrated few changes in psychophysiological reactivity with exercise training (e.g., Seraganian, Roskies, Hanley, Oseasohn, & Collu, 1987; Sinyor, Peronnet, Brisson, & Seraganian, 1988). On the other hand, exercise may promote recovery from severe traumas such as surgery by maintaining muscle tone and flexibility.

Nutrition almost certainly plays a role as well, and this is being increasingly recognized in studies of cardiovascular etiology. Experiments with cynomolgus monkeys have shown that a combination of moderately atherogenic (cholesterol-containing) diet and social stress induces coronary artery atherosclerosis (Kaplan et al., 1982). Interactions between salt intake and stress-induced hypertensive processes have also been identified.

Anderson, Dietz, and Murphy (1987) demonstrated that hypertension developed in dogs subjected to avoidance conditioning in the presence of continuous saline infusion, whereas no such response was observed with saline infusion alone. The combination of hereditary predisposition, environmental stress, and salt intake produces changes in renal function characteristic of hypertension in rat models (DiBona, 1989). Outside the cardiovascular system, it should be recalled that the gastric pathology that was observed by Weiss (1977) in rats exposed to uncontrollable as opposed to controllable aversive stimulation was manifest in food deprived animals. Other ingested substances such as caffeine also affect stress responses, although the pattern of results and direction of effects is inconclusive at present (France & Ditto, 1989).

The role of endocrinological factors requires further clarification as well. A number of studies have been conducted comparing psychophysiological reactions in women at different phases of the menstrual cycle, but they have produced rather variable results (e.g., Polefrone & Manuck, 1988; Van den Akker & Steptoe, 1987). One argument is that the lower rates of coronary heart disease present in women over their reproductive years is dependent in part on modulation of stress reactivity by estrogen (Von Eiff & Peikarski, 1977). A comparison of reactions to mental stress in age-matched pre- and postmenopausal women lends some support to this notion, in that heart rate and blood pressure responses were larger following the menopause (Saab, Matthews, Stoney, & McDonald, 1989). However, the significance of these observations for disease incidence is not known.

One of the major biological influences on vulnerability is age. Most of the common forms of pathology to which behavioral and emotional factors may contribute are more frequent in the elderly, and vulnerability to stress may also increase. Many physiological systems have a functional reserve that enables them to respond to perturbations, but this adaptability becomes restricted with the decline in vitality (Strehler & Mildvan, 1960). Rodin (1986) has argued that the elderly are especially prone to stress-related pathology because their ability to cope with change at both the psychological and biological levels becomes restricted. Thus in comparison with young adults, elderly people show increased norepinephrine responses to laboratory tasks, and heightened blood pressure reactivity has also been observed (Barnes, Raskind, Gumbrecht, & Holter, 1982; Steptoe, Moses, & Edwards, 1990).

As with the other elements of the stress-coping-vulnerability model, the links between biological vulnerability and Stages I and II are not linear. Biological factors will influence the intensity of psychobiological stress responses, while also affecting peoples' exposure to different environments.

The Variability and Intensity Issues

The model presented in Figure 17-1 leads to a number of suggestions concerning the contentious issues of variabililty in response and intensity of stressful experience that were outlined earlier. The reason that people are variable in their response to aversive events may be because they differ in their psychosocial resources, so that one is better able to withstand adverse life experience than another. Alternatively, differences in biological vulnerability may be responsible, leading people to display different forms of pathology. Moreover, it would not be predicted that groups with stress-related pathology would necessarily have more 'stressful' lives, because their increased susceptibility might be accounted for by differences in coping ability or biological predisposition.

PATHWAYS TO DISEASE

The general stress–coping–vulnerability model described in the last section provides an adequate basis for understanding psychobiological processes in the etiology of disease, but it would benefit from greater refinement. Not surprisingly, the first two stages have been investigated in far more detail than stages III and IV, because the early phases are relevant to stress research in general, and not only to work on disease etiology. As described in Figure 17-1, the model has little to say about the variety of psychobiological pathways to disease, including the differences between causal and facilitatory processes, and the factors influencing the course of chronic disorder. In addition, the model is in danger of being untestable because it is unfalsifiable, given that almost any empirical result concerning the effect (or lack of effect) of stress on disease may be explained by postulating a particular combination of demands, resources, and vulnerabilities.

The remainder of this chapter is therefore devoted to an elaboration of the psychobiological processes. It is particularly concerned with the later stages (II, III and IV) of the stress-coping-vulnerability model, and with identifying the disease pathways through which psychobiological stress responses influence health. The conceptual framework for this discussion is summarized in Figure 17–2, where is is suggested that psychobiological stress responses may promote ill health through one of a number of cognitive-behavioral or physiological processes. The relevance

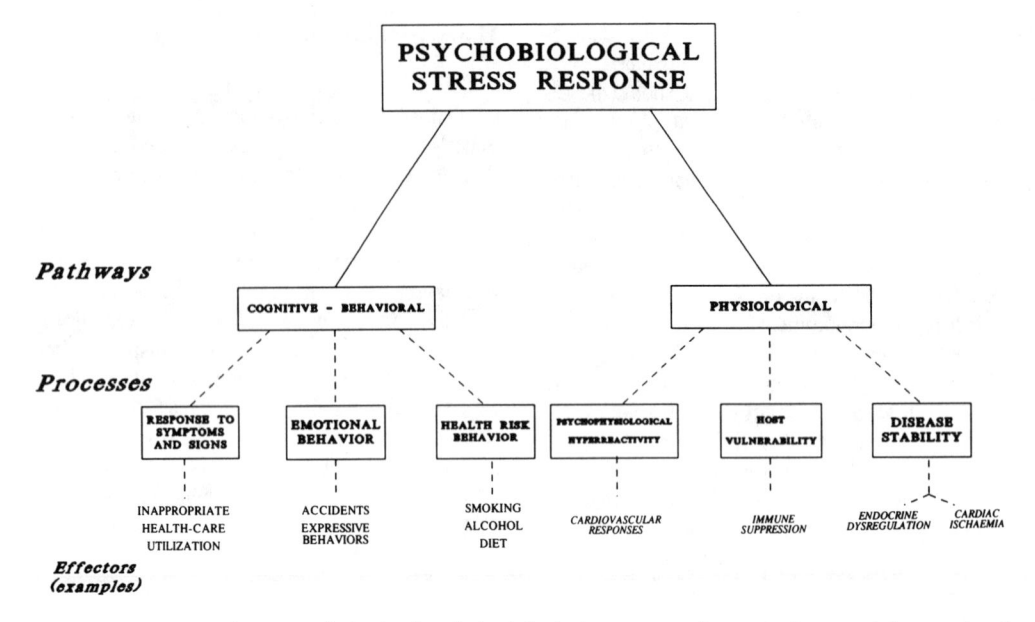

Figure 17.2. Summary of cognitive-behavioral and physiological processes relevant to disease etiology and maintenance

of these varies across disease conditions, and none of the processes are likely to be involved in a general way in all disorders.

Cognitive-Behavioral Pathways

A general distinction can be drawn between cognitive-behavioral and physiological pathways to disease. The first category implies that the cognitive, affective or behavioral changes that may be elicited as components of stress responses can influence health independently of any direct action of the central nervous system on the autonomic, endocrine or immune systems. At least three different processes may be relevant to links between stress and ill-health.

Response to Symptoms and Signs

It is well established that there is no simple linear correlation between physical pathology and the perception and appraisal of signs and symptoms (Pennebaker, 1982). People show quite variable responses to physical signs, and these influence subjective ratings of disability and medical consultation behavior (Barsky, Goodson, Lane, & Cleary, 1988; Miller, Brody, & Summerton, 1988). Responses are also affected by life stress, with people who report job pressures such as excessive workload also complaining of physical symptomatology that is out of proportion to objective heath status (House, McMichael, Wells, Kaplan, & Landerman, 1979). This association is generally regarded as a tiresome source of potential confound in research on health and life stress (Watson & Pennebaker, 1989).

It is nevertheless possible that a link between life stress and symptom interpretation of genuine importance is present, and that this has direct effects on health maintenance. There are, for example, a number of conditions in which serious consequences may be avoided by prompt action. A dramatic case is the delay between symptom onset and seeking medical treatment in acute myocardial infarction. This interval is crucial, since a high proportion of patients die within one to two hours of symptom onset, and these deaths might be avoidable with appropriate action (Gentry, 1975). That stress factors might be involved is suggested by a small study in which the delay before seeking treatment was positively correlated with perceived work demands (Matthews, Siegel, Kuller, Thompson, & Barat, 1983). Another illustration of referral behavior having damaging effects is in the identification of malignancies. Delay between detecting a lesion and a medical consultation is positively correlated with thickness of malignant melanomas

(Temoshok et al., 1985). It is possible that in the presence of life stress, regular body surveillance and response to symptoms is altered.

Emotional Behavior

The emotional behaviors that fall into this category include expressive acts that may precipitate physical pathology. At a trivial level, it is probable that accidents may arise through lapses of attention and judgment brought on by emotional distress. But perhaps the clearest example of this process is in the case of bronchial asthma, where bronchospasm can be induced by laughing or crying. Weinstein (1985) has shown that crying behavior in asthmatic children can precipitate symptoms, and that the pattern is related to non-specific bronchial hyperreactivity. This implies that the emotional behavior itself induces bronchospasm without the mediation of psychophysiological processes, possibly through hyperventilation or the irritant effect of cold air on the airways. Studies of family interaction suggest that persistent crying-induced asthma may be maintained by parental responses (Weinstein, 1987). In other cases, the influence of emotional expression on asthma may lead sufferers to suppress affective responses (Hollaender & Florin, 1983).

The role of emotional responses in mediating the association between life stress and ill health has also been examined at a more general level. Craig and Brown (1984) have argued that correlations between life events and somatic pathology may be dependent on the occurrence of an intervening affective disorder. Thus Murphy and Brown (1980) reported that recent physical symptoms were predated by severely threatening events only in subjects who experienced an intervening psychiatric disorder. Similarly, a comparison of patients with irritable bowel syndrome and organic gastrointestinal disorder showed that life events were associated with the irritable bowel in the presence of diagnosed psychiatric illness, but not in people free from affective disorder (Ford, Miller, Eastwood, & Eastwood, 1987). The literature therefore suggests a major role for emotional behavior, although whether the link with pathology is direct (as in the case of asthma) or is in turn mediated through psychophysiological processes is not known.

Health-Risk Behavior

It is widely acknowledged that a range of behaviors have a direct effect on physical health. These include substance use and abuse, diet, exercise, sexual behaviors, and risk-taking actions, together with preventive health behaviors like seat-belt use, immunization, and breast or testicular self-examination. The issue in the present context is not whether these actions are related to health, but whether their occurrence is altered with psychological stress. The area is controversial, because much of the evidence is retrospective, and reports may be biased through "effort after meaning" (Allan & Cooke, 1985). Nevertheless, there appears to be grounds for believing that adverse life experience can influence health-risk behavior. The use of alcohol and other substances is associated with life events and with chronic stressors (Budd, Eiser, Morgan, & Gammage, 1985; Baer, Garmetzy, McLoughlin, Pokorny, & Wernick, 1987; Brown, S., 1989). Data from ex-soldiers suggest that this is a long-term effect that persists for at least ten years (Branchley, Davis, & Lieber, 1984). Cigarette smoking may also increase following life events, at least in some groups (Lindenthal, Myers, & Pepper, 1972). Unemployment may be accompanied by increased cigarette smoking, although the effect on alcohol intake is inconsistent (Warr, 1987; Warr & Payne, 1983). The links between opportunities for employment and suicide remain controversial (Brenner, 1985). Another factor that may promote health risk behaviors such as smoking, consumption of alcohol, and tranquilizers is bereavement (Parkes & Brown, 1972).

A study that nicely illustrates the potential role of habitual behaviors in mediating stress-health associations was reported by DeFrank, Jenkins, and Rose (1987). Data were collected longitudinally from air traffic controllers over a 3 year period. During this time, a number of previously normotensive air traffic controllers became hypertensive, with psychosocial factors such as work anxiety and investment in the job being correlated with blood pressure. However, it was found that increased alcohol intake was the strongest predictor of blood pressure elevation and moderated the influence of stress on blood pressure. In this case therefore, there was no need to postulate an impact of psychosocial stress on psychophysiological pathways. These behavioral mechanisms deserve greater attention in future research.

Physiological Pathways

Research on stress and disease has traditionally focused on psychophysiological pathways rather than the cognitive-behavioral processes discussed in the last section. One reason for this is that in much psychosocial epidemiology, conventional risk factors (which may include smoking and diet-related measures) do not appear to account for associations between life experience and disease. By way of illustration, Marmot and Syme (1976) reported a relationship between acculturation and coronary heart disease among Japanese-Americans that persisted after controlling for smoking, dietary intake of fat, age, serum cholesterol, weight, and blood pressure. The influence of stressful working conditions on the blood pressure of manual workers was found by Matthews, Cottington, Talbot, Kuller, and Siegel (1987) to be independent of age, body mass index, alcohol intake, smoking, and family history. In the Alameda County, California, study, the association between social networks and mortality was only accounted for in part by health-risk behaviors (Berkman & Breslow, 1983). There is a strong implication in such investigations that psychophysiological processes must be responsible. There are however several different ways in which psychophysiological reaction patterns may contribute to the risk of illness.

Psychophysiological Hyperreactivity

The first possibility is that psychophysiological hyperreactivity is responsible for the increased risk of disease in stressed people. Hyperreactivity implies that biological reactions in susceptible individuals are larger than those in the remainder of the population, or that return to pre-stress levels is delayed. Psychophysiological hyperreactivity may arise from constitutional factors or previously learned response patterns and is not a general property, but may be restricted to the organ system under threat. Thus people with high blood pressure may show exaggerated pressor responses to active coping tasks compared with normotensives, without displaying abnormal reactions in noncardiovascular parameters such as skin conductance or respiration (Fredrikson, 1986). Two hypotheses underlie the notion that psychophysiological hyperreactivity is involved in etiology. The first is that people at risk will show larger responses in their vulnerable physiological system to psychological challenge than do others. The second is that repeated exposure to the psychosocial demands provoking hyperreactivity will be pathogenic.

Ideally, these hypotheses require testing in longitudinal studies relating psychophysiological hyperreactivity to later illness. Some of the most convincing evidence has emerged in animal studies of coronary atherosclerosis. Manuck, Kaplan, and Clarkson (1983) measured heart rate reactions to a standard challenge (threatened capture) in male cynomolgus monkeys housed in colonies and fed a moderately atherogenic diet. Coronary artery stenosis was subsequently found to be significantly more extensive in high heart rate reactors. This finding has since been replicated in female cynomolgus monkeys, with differences in atherosclerosis of the coronary arteries and the right carotid bifurcation (Manuck, Kaplan, Adams, & Clarkson, 1989). Corroborative evidence is provided by Beere, Glagov, and Zarins (1984) who showed that lowering heart rate by surgically ablating the sinoatrial node had a retarding effect on the development of coronary atherosclerosis.

Evidence of this type is difficult to obtain in humans, because an extended prospective period may be required before pathology emerges. Prospective studies have, however, been initiated into the predictive properties of cardiovascular hyperreactivity for the development of essential hypertension. These data (summarized in more detail in Steptoe, 1990b) indicate that hyperreactivity may predict subsequent blood pressure elevation, but primarily through interaction with other factors such as hypertensive family history or disturbed sodium metabolism (Borghi, Costa, Boschi, Mussi, & Ambrosioni, 1986; Falkner, Kushner, Onesti, & Angelakos, 1981).

In the absence of prospective data, the hyperreactivity hypothesis must be evaluated in cross-sectional designs. Evidence comparing people with a particular pathology and healthy controls is more plentiful. Flor and Turk (1989) have reviewed some 60 psychophysiological studies assessing reactivity patterns in patients with problems of pain (mostly headache and chronic low back pain). They conclude that stress-related reactions in headache sufferers tend to be exaggerated, with greater electromyographic (EMG) responses in tension headache compared with control, and more pronounced vascular responses in migraineurs. Disturbances in paraspinal muscle tension have been recorded in response to laboratory stress in chronic back pain patients. In all these cases, return to baseline following termination of the stress condition may be delayed.

In the gastrointestinal system, Kumar and Wingate (1985) demonstrated that patients with irritable bowel syndrome showed bowel motility abnormalities in response to a variety of stress tasks in comparison with healthy controls and sufferers from inflammatory bowel disease. Distinctions between asthmatics and nonasthmatics in airway responses to distressing movies have also been described (Levenson, 1979), as have differences in metabolic responses to experimental challenge in diabetics and nondiabetics (see Shillitoe, 1988). The evidence on stress reactivity in patients with rheumatoid arthritis is less consistent (e.g., Taylor, Gatchel, & Korman, 1982). However, Walker and Sandman (1977) observed greater reactions to stressful tasks in EMG recorded from an affected joint in arthritis as opposed to duodenal ulcer or healthy control volunteers, while delayed recovery in EMG following tasks was described by Anderson, Stoyva, and Vaughn (1982). Finally, there have been more than 60 studies (reviewed by Fredrikson, 1986) comparing blood pressure reactions in hypertensive and normotensive people. The majority demonstrate hyperreactivity in the former group with a variety of laboratory challenges. Delayed poststress recovery has also been observed.

These studies are consistent with the hyperreactivity hypothesis, but do not provide strong evidence for its involvement in etiology. The reason is that disturbances in reactivity to behavioral stress may be secondary to the pathological changes characteristic of the disease itself. Thus bronchial hyperreactivity is a general process in asthma that not only underlies responses to distressing events, but also reactions to exercise, cold, house dust mite, and other triggers (Nadel & Barnes, 1984). Changes in vascular geometry take place in hypertension, so that any challenge will provoke greater vasoconstriction irrespective of centrally induced hyperreactivity (Folkow, 1982). Similarly in chronic low back pain and rheumatoid arthritis, exaggerated reactivity may be an effect rather than cause of the condition.

One way to circumvent this problem of interpretation is to study people who are at risk for a particular disease before any manifestation of the condition. If hyperreactivity is present in such groups, it is possible to argue that the psychophysiological disturbance precedes disease and may therefore contribute to its development. This strategy has been used most extensively in the study of essential hypertension, mainly because the hereditary component to high blood pressure provides a readily accessible measure of "risk." Fredrikson and Matthews (1990) have reviewed studies comparing normotensives with and without a family history of hypertension. Their meta-analysis indicates that people with a positive history show greater blood pressure and heart rate responses to laboratory stress tests than negative history subjects. The pattern is more apparent when responses to actively challenging (active behavioral coping) tasks are studied, rather than passive stressors such as the cold pressor test. Some investigators have not found blood pressure hyperreactivity so much as disturbances in regional blood flow, catecholamine responses or renal dynamics (Anderson, Mahoney, Lauer, & Clarke, 1987; Lenders, Willemsen, De Boo, Lemmens, & Thien, 1989; Light, Koepke, Obrist, & Willis, 1983). Habitual styles of coping with stress and emotion may also have to be taken into account (Jorgensen & Houston, 1986).

The studies of hypertension provide perhaps the strongest evidence to date in humans concerning the etiological significance of psychophysiological reactivity. They must, nevertheless, still be interpreted with caution. First, as far as family history is concerned, it must be borne in mind that a number of potentially pathophysiological phenomena have been described in normotensive offspring. These include differences in left ventricular structure, sodium transport and venous distensibility (Ito, Takeshita, Higuchi, & Nakamura, 1986; Milner, Heagerty, Bing, Thurston, & Swales, 1984; Radice et al., 1986). Such factors may conceivably be involved in the augmentation of stress responses, implying that the psychophysiological mechanism is secondary rather than primary. Evaluation of stress responses in high risk groups other than those with an hereditary predisposition would therefore be valuable. Second, even if psychophysiological hyperreactivity does predict future hypertension, it may be a marker rather than causal factor. It may, for example, reflect some underlying pathophysiology that is not primarily psychophysiological in origin. Studies are therefore required in which psychophysiological reactivity patterns are modified, in order to discover whether the incidence of hypertension is changed.

Host Vulnerability

The second physiological process relevant to disease etiology concerns alterations in physical vulnerability that might render the person more susceptible to an invasive organism. This process is different from psychophysiological hyperreactivity in two important ways. First, it is not hypothesized that psychobiological stress responses cause illness, rather that they influence vulnerability. Second, it is not necessary to postulate that the person is exposed to intense, repeated stress in order for this process to be activated. Rather, heightened vulnerability for a single short period may be sufficient if it is contiguous with a critical stage of invasion.

The clearest illustration of this process involves the

immune system, where changes in immune status may increase or decrease the likelihood of infection taking hold. If immune function is modified by psychological stress, then in the presence of an infective agent physical health may be compromised. The change in immune status may on the other hand have no adverse consequences in the absence of concomitant infection or neoplasia.

This hypothesis is supported by studies in psychoneuroimmunology. It has for example been found that mitogen-induced lymphocyte proliferation and antibody production are modified by behavioral stress, and that these responses are influenced by such factors as controllability and the duration of aversive stimulation (Croiset, Heijnen, Veldhuis, De Wied & Ballieux, 1987; Laudenslager et al., 1988; Laudenslager, Ryan, Drugan, Hyson, & Maier, 1983; Monjan & Collector, 1977). Although it has frequently been assumed that this response is moderated through corticosteroid release, there is evidence that manipulations of predictability and controllability alter immune status without affecting steroid levels (Mormède, Dantzer, Michaud, Kelley, & Le Moal, 1988). Opioid responses, catecholamine release or mediation by neuropeptide Y have been implicated (Shavit & Martin, 1987; Mormède et al., 1988). In humans, there are as yet few experimental data. Nevertheless, a variety of life stressors such as bereavement, unemployment, marital discord, and caring for disabled relatives are accompanied by immune suppression (Arnetz et al., 1987; Kiecolt-Glaser et al., 1987a, 1987b; Schleifer, Keller, Camerino, Thornton, & Stein, 1983). By way of contrast, preliminary data suggest that relaxation may have the reverse effect, promoting the lymphocyte function and natural killer cell activity (Gruber, Hall, Hersch, & Du Bois, 1988). Modifications in immunoglobulin levels have also been documented, although their functional significance is unclear (Jemmott et al., 1983).

It might be argued that at least some of these responses are transient effects of no significance to health. Several studies have therefore been carried out in order to examine the relationship between stressful experience and susceptibility to viral agents (e.g., Friedman, Glasgow, & Ader, 1970). The successful implantation and subsequent growth of malignant tumors have also been shown to be influenced by behavioral stress, with uncontrollable stimulation having a greater impact than controllable conditions (Sklar et al., 1981; Visintainer, Volpicelli, & Seligman, 1982). In the clinical context, vulnerability to respiratory infections has been linked with everyday hassles and minor life events (Graham, Douglas, & Ryan, 1986; Meyer & Haggerty, 1962). Another illustration of this relationship can be seen in research on recurrent genital herpes infection. Retrospective studies suggest that the frequency and severity of herpes simplex virus recurrences are associated with life stress, mood disturbance and social support (Longo & Clum, 1989; VanderPlate, Aral, & Magder, 1988). The direction of causality in these investigations is not clear, however, because it is conceivable that frequent severe recurrences will have negative psychosocial consequences. Kemeny, Cohen, Zegans, and Conant (1989) therefore conducted a longitudinal study in which herpes recurrences were assessed monthly along with life stress indices, mood, and immune function. Overall, mood and life stress was not correlated with herpes recurrence. However, when participants who suffered from nongenital infections were excluded (leaving a generally healthier group) an association was found between herpes recurrence and depression. Interestingly, depression was not correlated with health behaviors such as alcohol intake and exercise that might affect recurrence rates. Stress and mood scores also covaried with helper and suppressor lymphocyte levels.

Disease Stability

The third process illustrated in Figure 17–2 by which physiological stress responses can influence disease is through modulation of the severity or progression of pre-existing pathology. This process is not exactly etiological, because it will only operate in the presence of an established disorder. The physiological reactions that arise from a stressful demand/ resource interaction may, nevertheless, affect the clinical stability of the illness, leading to disturbances of control in chronic conditions such as asthma or diabetes, or to acute and potentially life-threatening episodes in patients with coronary heart disease.

Hypotheses about the disease stability process are again different from those relevant to the psychophysiological hyperreactivity and host vulnerability mechanisms. First, the process will only be operative in people who already suffer from relevant pathophysiology. The pathophysiology need not, of course, have reached the stage of clinical diagnosis and management; for example, ventricular fibrillation might be brought on by acute sympathoadrenal activation in a person with subclinical coronary stenosis. Second, the influence of the psychobiological stress process may be manifest not only under conditions of extreme threat or distress, but also through the physiological correlates of relatively minor everyday fluctuations in mood and life experience. This may be particularly true of influences on chronic disease states. Third, the clinical significance of the disease stability process for an individual will depend not only on his or her life experience, but on the prominence of other nonpsychological influences. For instance, psychological distress can affect the clinical stability of asthma through bronchial hyperreactivity (Steptoe, 1984b). The importance of this process for the patient will depend on the frequency of such stressful episodes in relation to exposure to other triggers for bronchial constriction such as allergens and cold. For the sufferer from asthma who is frequently exposed to nonpsychological triggers, the psychobiological stress process may contribute only trivially to the variation in clinical state. On the other hand, an asthmatic who has little exposure to other sources of bronchial irritation may be manifestly susceptible to stress-related disturbances.

Studies over recent years have provided an experimental foundation for stress-related influences on disease stability by showing that autonomic and neuroendocrine function can fluctuate with daily life experience. Brantley, Dietz, McKnight, Jones, and Tulley (1988) collected urine samples daily from subjects for estimation of cortisol and vanillylmandelic acid (VMA), a catecholamine metabolite. Participants also completed stress inventories each day. A comparison of the two highest and two lowest stress days showed that cortisol and VMA levels were significantly greater on the high stress days. The background level of life stress may also influence acute physiological reactions to psychological challenge. Pardine and Napoli (1983) observed delayed recovery in systolic blood pressure following a mental stress task in students who reported high as opposed to low life stress over the previous 6 months. Greater cardiovascular reactions to mental stress and delayed recovery have also been documented in people living under chronically stressful crowded conditions compared with controls who live in less crowded streets (Fleming et al., 1987). A more recent experiment by Gannon et al. (1989) suggests that psychophysiological reactivity mediates the association between daily hassles on the one hand, and dependent variables such as depression and physical symptoms on the other.

The presence of a specific disease condition may magnify these relationships, leading to symptom-specific responses that influence clinical stability. One study of chronic rheumatoid arthritis patients involved completion of monthly inventories of major and minor life events (Zautra et al., 1989). It was found that major events were correlated with immune parameters such as a reduced helper/suppressor lymphocyte ratio, whereas minor incidents were associated with fluctuations in T and B cell counts. Steptoe and Holmes (1985) published a pilot study in which measures of mood and pulmonary function were obtained daily from bronchial asthmatics and nonasthmatic controls. Significant correlations between mood fluctuations and peak flow were found in most asthmatics but in few controls, with idiosyncratic patterns of association that varied across individuals. This result has subsequently been confirmed with more objective pulmonary function measures, where it also appears that mood changes may antedate physiological responses in some subjects (Butler & Steptoe, unpublished data). Similar studies have been carried out with chronic headache, with changes in mood that either precede or accompany headache activity (Arena, Blanchard, & Andrasik, 1984; Harrigan, Kues, Ricks, & Smith, 1984).

The significance of these processes in chronic disease is perhaps the object of rather more speculation than convincing empirical data. For instance, it has been suggested that peripheral vascular and sweat gland responses occurring during stress may influence itch thresholds, scratching and the subsequent severity of episodes of atopic dermatitis, but systematic evidence is lacking (Faulstich & Williamson, 1985). Several studies have related chronic stress and personal relationship problems with exacerbation of rheumatoid arthritis, but these are methodologically weak (see Anderson, Bradley, Young, McDaniel, & Wise, 1985). In the case of diabetes mellitus, Bradley (1979) has shown that life events may be associated with disturbances in control, including glycosuria. It was not clear from this study whether the pattern was mediated directly through endocrine and sympathetic nervous system disturbances, or through changes in health-related behaviors such as diet and exercise. However, Hanson and Pichert (1986) were able to control for variations in diet, exercise, and insulin administration in a study of insulin dependent diabetic adolescents at a summer camp. Stress measures completed daily were significantly correlated with blood glucose levels even after allowing for the effects of calorie consumption and exercise.

The possibility that the immune and endocrine components of psychobiological stress responses influence the course of cancer has been the focus of intense interest (Greer & Watson, 1985; Temoshok,

1987). The weight of the evidence suggests that psychosocial factors have a more important role in the progression rather than initiation of cancer (Fox, 1988). An additional factor that needs to be taken into account is lifespan, because the ability of the immune system to respond to invasion or neoplastic transformation may decline with advancing age (Ebbesen, 1986). Greer, Morris, and Pettingale (1979) reported that psychological reactions measured 3 months after surgery for breast cancer was associated with long-term survival, and a somewhat similar finding was described by Levy, Lee, Bagley, and Lippmann (1988). Ramirez et al. (1989) conducted life event interviews with women who had experienced a recurrence of breast cancer between 9 and 145 months following surgery. They were matched with women whose breast cancer was in remission. Women in the recurrence group were significantly more likely to have experienced a severely threatening event during this interval compared with controls.

In addition to the role of the disease stability process in chronic disorders, it was suggested earlier that transient psychophysiological responses may be important in acute episodes. An elegant illustration of the ability of psychological stress to cause transient, potentially damaging physiological responses in people with a pre-existing pathology is provided by research into myocardial dysfunction in patients with coronary heart disease. A study of 16 patients with angina using positron tomography found that 12 of the patients displayed abnormalities in regional perfusion of the heart muscle during mental arithmetic tests, probably due to neurogenically induced vasoconstriction of the coronary vessels (Deanfield et al., 1984). A controlled experiment was subsequently described by Rozanski et al. (1988). Thirty nine patients with coronary artery disease were studied, of whom 29 showed disturbances in myocardial wall motion during an exercise test. Of these, 21 displayed similar responses to mental stress, whereas only one of the 12 disease-free controls had this response. The wall motion abnormalities were manifestations of ischaemia resulting from transient occlusion of the coronary arteries. Interestingly, the myocardial ischaemia induced by mental stress in these studies was not accompanied by pain or other symptoms of angina, suggesting the psychological factors may influence coronary blood flow without the person being aware of it.

Clinical evidence for the role of psychological factors in spontaneous coronary spasm and cardiomyopathy is sparse at present. The action of catecholamines was demonstrated in an unusually well documented case of a 43-year-old man with normal coronary arteries who was administered epinephrine for pharyngitis (Ferry, Henry, & Kern, 1986). He abruptly developed an acute myocardial infarction. Pathological examinations of the victims of homicidal assaults who died without internal injuries have revealed myofibrillar degeneration and necrosis of cardiac tissue that may have resulted from pronounced autonomic stimulation and catecholamine release (Cebelin & Hirsch, 1980).

Two other potentially lethal cardiac disturbances have also been described, involving arrhythmias and thrombus formation in the coronary circulation. There is ample evidence from stimulation and lesion studies that cerebral mechanisms can influence cardiac rhythm (Skinner, 1988). Lown, Verrier, and Corbalan (1973) and Lown, Verrier, and Rabinowitz (1977) have shown in animals that the threshold for ventricular fibrillation can be lowered in susceptible organisms by aversive stimulation, hence increasing the possibility that acute cardiac sympathetic stimulation will induce a fatal arrhythmia. Tavazzi, Zotti, and Rondanelli (1986) reported that the vulnerability of the myocardium to ventricular fibrillation (as assessed by programmed ventricular stimulation) was increased in post-infarction patients during mental stress tests. Dangerous arrhythmias may therefore arise during psychological stress. This process may underlie cases in which sudden cardiac death occurs during periods of acute psychological trauma, even in people whose pre-existing heart disease is not severe (Reich, DeSilva, Lown, & Murawski, 1981). Studies using the new technology of transtelephonic ECG monitoring have also shown that ventricular arrhythmias are associated with psychological distress in vulnerable (post-infarction) patients (Follick et al., 1988).

As far as the thrombotic mechanism is concerned, increased platelet aggregability has been described during mental stress (Larsson, Hjemdahl, Olsson, Egberg, & Hornstra, 1989). The release of thrombotic substances from platelets within the coronary circulation has also been shown to correlate with the magnitude of psychophysiological responses (Fitchett, Toth, Gilmore, & Ehrman, 1983). Both these phenomena might increase the risk of thrombus formation within the coronary vasculature during mental stress, so this again is a process that could increase the likelihood of coronary thrombosis in susceptible individuals.

SYNTHESIS AND IMPLICATIONS FOR BEHAVIOR THERAPY

The integration of the stress–coping–vulnerability model with the pathways and processes discussed in the previous section leads to the framework summarized in Figure 17–3. The "moderating and external factors" in Figure 17–3 that are presumed to affect all stages include not only the biological vulnerabilities specified in Figure 17–1, but also habits and cultural background. They reflect the multidimensional nature of many of the elements of the model. For it would be quite wrong to assert that stress-related pathways are the sole, or even the main, determinants of components such as health-related behavior and responses to symptoms. There is, after all, a substantial literature in both areas documenting other influences on these components (Anderson, Davies, Kickbusch, McQueen, & Turner, 1988; Pennebaker, 1982).

The model described in this chapter lays no great claims to originality. Rather it is an attempt to systematize existing research on the relationship between psychosocial stress and physical pathology, using a general framework that acknowledges the diversity of pathways that may be involved. Although three distinct cognitive-behavioral and three physiological processes have been detailed in Figure 17–2, their activity is not mutually exclusive. Bronchial asthma may, for example, be influenced by autonomically mediated changes in bronchoconstriction, by emotionally expressive behaviors impinging on vulnerable regulatory systems, and by inappropriate self-medication and attention to symptoms. The impact of stress on diabetes may be mediated by several processes, including ineffective responses to symptoms, changes in health risk behavior, and endocrine influences on disease stability. In addition, severe life events may play a role in the early stages of the development of the condition (Robinson & Fuller, 1985). It is likely that multiple processes of this kind are involved in other types of disorder.

It is evident from this discussion that the specific hypotheses concerning links between life experience,

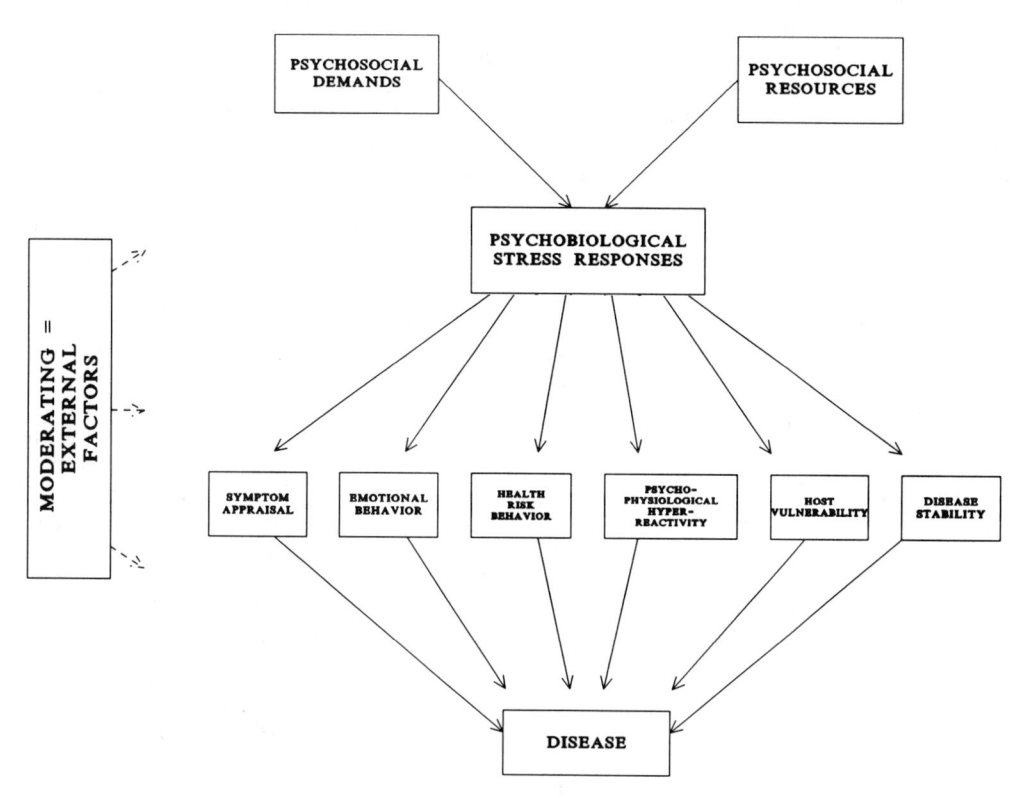

Figure 17.3. Modified framework for understanding Stress–Coping–Disease relationships

psychosocial coping resources and ill health will vary according to precisely which pathways are involved. Even within the psychophysiological domain, predictions will differ and the most appropriate type of study may not be the same. Thus the documentation of psychophysiological hyperreactivity processes will ultimately depend on prospective studies of initially healthy individuals, in which links can be tested between predispositions to hyperreactivity, exposure to environments that persistently elicit stress responses, and the development of disease. The relevance of host vulnerability processes on the other hand may be best delineated in studies in which the presence of infective agents at a subclinical level is monitored, together with immune and endocrine components of stress responses. It may then be possible to determine whether the presence of a pathogen during a period of stress-induced host vulnerability is likely to promote ill health. Finally, disease stability processes may be assessed through longitudinal studies of the covariation between disease quiescence or exacerbation, life stress, and intervening neuroendocrine or immune mechanisms, analyzed using time series techniques that take account of the autocorrelated nature of the data.

There are several implications of this formulation of stress-disease links for the use of behavioral management techniques. The first is that it serves to reemphasize the assertion made by theorists for the last two decades that stress processes are multifaceted. It cannot be assumed that a single pathway is involved, or that the relationship between adverse life experience and ill health will be the same in any two cases. It is all to easy to assume that once "stress" is identified as a "cause" that there is no more to be said, and that the course of action ("stress management") is clear. This view cannot be reconciled with the subtlety of connections identified in modern psychobiological research.

The second, related implication is that the various manifestations of stress frequently fail to covary. As can be seen from Figure 17-3, many factors are involved in the translation of life experience into illness, only some of which will be activated by a single transaction.

It is probably useful to view behavioral interventions in terms of the stages superimposed on Figure 17-1 (see Steptoe, 1989, for fuller discussion). Cognitive-behavioral techniques are generally directed at Stage I, and are intended either to alter the client's appraisals and coping resources, or to modify psychosocial demands (through time management, setting priorities, etc). Psychophysiological techniques such as relaxation and biofeedback are in contrast supposed to operate at Stage II, blunting the physiological and behavioral reactions to mental stress so that they no longer maintain symptoms. Hence a common outcome (reduced psychophysiological responsivity) may be arrived at through different approaches. For instance, the Type A behavior intervention program devised by Roskies et al. (1986) is designed to prevent autonomic and endocrine hyperactivation at the cognitive level, training people to perceive the environment in a differentiated and flexible fashion, instead of constantly appraising situations as competitive and challenging. The effects of relaxation training, on the other hand, may be mediated by reductions in autonomic and neuroendocrine function (e.g., Borkovec & Sides, 1979; Surwit & Feinglos, 1984). A third set of strategies is aimed at toughening biological resistance (Stage III), and include exercise training and nutritional balancing.

Whether these assertions about the mode of operation are warranted by the literature evaluting treatment processes is far from clear (Steptoe, 1989). In the case of relaxation for essential hypertension, for instance, Johnston (1986) has cogently argued that psychophysiological reactivity to mental stress is largely unaffected by treatment so cannot be responsible for therapeutic gains, and suggests that relaxation may operate at the cognitive level. Further research into these issues is urgently required because the question is an important one. The persistence of incorrect rationales and understanding of the processes responsible for the effectiveness of behavioral treatments will soon stifle therapeutic innovation.

The main implication for management using behavioral or other procedures is again that no single strategy will be adequate. Interventions may be directed at Stages I or II of the model outlined in Figure 17-1, using cognitive-behavioral or psychophysiological techniques. Methods aimed at toughening biological resistance (Stage III) such as exercise training or nutritional improvement may also be helpful (see Steptoe, 1989, for further discussion).

CONCLUSION

The field of psychobiological research into disease etiology is in a lively and empirically rich phase. The first generation of psychophysiological studies documenting links between stress or other physiological processes and disease has given way to more complex investigations that take account of individual differences at the psychological, psychophysiological and biological level. There is growing interest in individual differences in animal studies, together with an expanding database concerning the impact of social demands and challenges. Experimental research with humans is attempting to forge links between the responses displayed under carefully controlled conditions in the laboratory and the fluctuations in autonomic and endocrine function in field settings. Clinical research in behavioral medicine is mounting intervention studies on a broadening span of disease conditions. It is to be hoped that theoretical formulations will keep pace with clinical and experimental observation, so as to maintain the hypothesis-testing approach as a primary research strategy.

REFERENCES

Abbott, B. B., Schoen, L. S., & Badia, P. (1984). Predictable and unpredictable shock: Behavioral measures of aversion and physiological measures of stress. *Psychological Bulletin, 96*, 45–71.

Ader, R., & Cohen, N. (1981). Conditioned immunopharmacologic responses. In R. Ader (Ed.), *Psychoneuroimmunology* (pp. 281–319). New York: Academic Press.

Alexander, F. (1950). *Psychosomatic medicine.* New York: Naughton.

Allan, C. A. & Cooke, D. J. (1985). Stressful life events and alcohol misuse in women: A critical review. *Journal of Studies in Alcohol, 46*, 147–152.

Anderson, C. D., Stoyva, J. M., & Vaughn, L. J. (1982). A test of delayed recovery following stressful stimulation in four psychosomatic conditions. *Journal of Psychosomatic Research, 26*, 571–580.

Anderson, D. E., Dietz, J. R., & Murphy, R. (1987). Behavioral hypertension in sodium-loaded dogs is accompanied by sustained sodium retention. *Journal of Hypertension, 5*, 99–105.

Anderson, E. A., Mahoney, L. T., Lauer, R. M., & Clarke, W. R. (1987). Enhanced forearm blood flow during mental stress in children of hypertensive patients. *Hypertension, 10*, 544–549.

Anderson, K. O., Bradley, L. A., Young, L. D., McDaniel, L. K., & Wise, C. M. (1985). Rheumatoid arthritis: Review of psychological factors related to etiology, effects, and treatment. *Psychological Bulletin, 98*, 358–387.

Anderson, R., Davies, J. K., Kickbusch, I., McQueen, D. V., & Turner, J. (Eds.) (1988). *Health behaviour research and health promotion.* Oxford: Oxford University Press.

Arena, J. G., Blanchard, E. B., & Andrasik, F. (1984). The role of affect in the etiology of chronic headache. *Journal of Psychosomatic Research, 28*, 79–86.

Arnetz, B. B., Wasserman, J., Petrini, B., Brenner, S-O.,
Levi, L., Eneroth, P., Salovaara, H., Hjelm, R., Salovarra, L., Theorell, T., & Petterson, I-L. (1987). Immune function in unemployed women. *Psychosomatic Medicine, 49*, 3–12.

Baer, P. E., Garmetzy, L. B., McLoughlin, R. T., Pokorny, A. D., & Wernick, M. J. (1987). Stress, coping, family conflict, and adolescent alcohol use. *Journal of Behavioral Medicine, 10*, 449–466.

Barnes, R. F., Raskind, M., Gumbrecht, G., & Holter, J. B. (1982). The effects of age on plasma catecholamine responses to mental stress in man. *Journal of Clinical Endocrinology and Metabolism, 54*, 64–69.

Barsky, A. J., Goodson, J. D., Lane, R. S., & Cleary, P. D. (1988). The amplification of somatic symptoms. *Psychosomatic Medicine, 50*, 510–519.

Beere, P. A., Glagov, S., & Zarins, C. K. (1984). Retarding effect of lowered heart rate on coronary atherosclerosis. *Science, 226*, 180–182.

Berkman, L. F. (1985). The relationship of social networks and social support to morbidity and mortality. In S. Cohen & S. L. Syme (Eds.), *Social support and health* (pp. 241–278). New York: Academic Press.

Berkman, L. F. & Breslow, L. (1983). *Health and ways of living. The Alameda County study.* New York: Oxford University Press.

Borghi, C., Costa, F. V., Boschi, S., Mussi, A., & Ambrosioni, E. (1986). Prediction of stable hypertension in young borderline subjects: A 5-year follow-up study. *Journal of Cardiovascular Pharmacology, 8*, (Supp. 5), S138–S141.

Borkovec, T. D. & Sides, J. K. (1979). Critical procedural variables related to the physiological effects of progressive relaxation: A review. *Behaviour Research and Therapy, 17*, 119–125.

Bouloux, P. M. E. (1987). Cardiovascular responses to stress: The role of opioid peptides. *Baillière's Clinical Endocrinology and Metabolism, 1*, 439–465.

Bradley, C. (1979). Life events and the control of diabetes mellitus. *Journal of Psychosomatic Research, 23*, 159–162.

Branchley, L., Davis, W., & Lieber, C. S. (1984). Alcoholism in Vietnam and Korea veterans: A long-term follow-up. *Alcoholism: Clinical and Experimental Research, 8*, 572–575.

Brantley, P. J., Dietz, L. S., McKnight, G. T., Jones, G. N., & Tulley, R. (1988). Convergence between the daily stress inventory and endocrine measures of stress. *Journal of Consulting and Clinical Psychology, 56*, 549–551.

Brenner, N. H. (1985). Economic change and the suicide rate: A population model including loss, separation, illness, and alcohol consumption. In M. R. Zales (Ed.) *Stress in health and disease* (pp. 160–185). New York: Brunner/Mazel.

Broadbent, D. E. (1971). *Decision and stress.* New York: Academic Press.

Brown, G. W. & Harris, T. (1989). *Life stress and illness.* New York: Guilford Press.

Brown, G. W., Harris, T., & Copeland, J. R. (1977). Depression and loss. *British Journal of Psychiatry, 130,* 1–18.

Brown, S. A. (1989). Life events of adolescence in relation to personal and parental substance abuse. *American Journal of Psychiatry, 146,* 484–489.

Budd, R. J., Eiser, J. R., Morgan, M., & Gammage, P. (1985). The personal characteristics and life style of the young drinker: The results of a survey of British adolescents. *Drug and Alcohol Dependence, 16,* 145–157.

Burger, J. N. (1989). Negative reactions to increases in perceived control. *Journal of Personality and Social Psychology, 56,* 246–256.

Cebelin, M. S., & Hirsch, C. S. (1980). Human stress cardiomyopathy. *Human Pathology, 11,* 123–132.

Cohen, S. (1988). Psychosocial models of the role of social support in the etiology of physical disease. *Health Psychology, 7,* 269–297.

Cox, T. (1978). *Stress.* London: Macmillan.

Craig, T. K. J., & Brown, G. W. (1984). Life events, meaning and physical illness: A review. In A. Steptoe & A. Mathews (Eds.), *Health care and human behaviour* (pp. 7–39). London: Academic Press.

Creed, F. (1985). Life events and physical illness. *Journal of Pyschosomatic Research, 29,* 113–123.

Croiset, G., Heijnen, C. J., Veldhuis, H. D., De Wied, D., & Ballieux, R. E. (1987). Modulation of immune response by emotional stress. *Life Science, 40,* 775–782.

Deanfield, J. E., Shea, M., Kensett, M., Horlock, P. Wilson, R. A., De Landsheere, C. M., & Selwyn, A. P. (1984). Silent myocardial infarction due to mental stress. *Lancet, II,* 1001–1004.

DeFrank, R. S., Jenkins, C. D., & Rose, R. M. (1987). A longitudinal investigation of the relationships among alcohol consumption, psychosocial factors, and blood pressure. *Psychosomatic Medicine, 49,* 236–249.

DeLongis, A., Folkman, S., & Lazarus, R. S. (1988). The impact of daily stress on health and mood: Psychological and social resources as mediators. *Journal of Personality and Social Psychology, 54,* 486–495.

Dembroski, T. M., MacDougall, J. M., Costa, P. T., & Grandits, G. A. (1989). Components of hostility as predictors of sudden death and myocardial infarction in the Multiple Risk Factor Intervention Trial. *Psychosomatic Medicine, 51,* 514–522.

Depue, R. A., & Monroe, S. M. (1986). Conceptualization and measurement of human disorder in life stress research: The problem of chronic disturbance. *Psychological Bulletin, 99,* 36–51.

DiBona, G. F. (1989). Sympathetic nervous system influences on the kidney. *American Journal of Hypertension, 2,* 119s–124s.

Dienstbier, R. A. (1989). Arousal and physiological toughness: Implications for mental and physical health. *Psychological Review, 96,* 84–100.

Ditto, B., France, C., & Miller, S. (1989). Spouse and parent- off-spring similarities in cardiovascular response to mental arithmetic and isometric hand grip. *Health Psychology, 8,* 159–173.

Ebbesen, P. (1986). Age, immunity and cancer. In M. Bergener, M. Ermini, & H. B. Stähelin (Eds.), *Dimensions in aging* (pp. 97–104). London: Academic Press.

Engel, B. T. (1960). Stimulus-response and individual-response specificity. *Archives of General Psychiatry, 2,* 305–313.

Esler, M., Jennings, D., Biviano, B., Lambert, G., & Hasking, G. (1986). Mechanism of elevated plasma noradrenaline in the course of essential hypertension. *Journal of Cardiovascular Pharmacology, 8,* (Suppl. 5), s39–s43.

Eysenck, M. W. (1989). Personality, stress arousal, and cognitive processes in stress transactions. In R. W. J. Neufeld (Ed.) *Advances in the investigation of psychological stress* (pp. 133–160). New York: Wiley-Interscience.

Fahrenberg, J. (1986). Psychophysiological individuality: A pattern analytic approach to personality research and psychosomatic medicine. *Advances in Behaviour Research and Therapy, 8,* 43–100.

Falkner, B., Kushner, H., Onesti, G., & Angelakos, E. T. (1981). Cardiovascular characteristics in adolescents who develop essential hypertension. *Hypertension, 3,* 521–527.

Faulstich, M. E., & Williamson, D. A. (1985). An overview of atopic dermatitis: Toward a biobehavioral integration. *Journal of Psychosomatic Research, 29,* 647–654.

Ferry, D. R., Henry, R. L., & Kern, M. J. (1986). Epinephrine-induced myocardial infarction in a patient with angiographically normal coronary arteries. *American Heart Journal, 111,* 1193–1195.

Fitchett, D., Toth, E., Gilmore, N., & Ehrman, M. (1983). Platelet release of β-thromboglobulin within the coronary circulation during cold pressor stress. *American Journal of Cardiology, 52,* 727–730.

Fleming, I., Baum, A., Davidson, L. M., Rectanus, E., & McArdle, S. (1987). Chronic stress as a factor in psychologic reactivity to challenge. *Health Psychology, 6,* 221–237.

Flor, H., & Turk, D. C. (1989). Psychophysiology of chronic pain: Do chronic pain patients exhibit symptom-specific psychophysiological responses? *Psychological Bulletin, 105,* 215–259.

Folkman, S., & Lazarus, R. S. (1985). If it changes it must be a process: A study of emotion and coping during three stages of a college examination. *Journal of Personality and Social Psychology, 48,* 150–170.

Folkow, B. S. (1982). Physiological aspects of primary hypertension. *Physiological Review, 62,* 347–504.

Follick, M. J., Gorkin, L., Capone, R. J., Smith, T. W., Ahern, D. K., Stablein, D., Niaura, R., & Visco, J. (1988). Psychological distress as a predictor of ventricular arrhythmias in a post-myocardial infarction population. *American Heart Journal, 116,* 32–36.

Ford, M. J., Miller, P. M., Eastwood, J., & Eastwood, M. A. (1987). Life events, psychiatric illness and the irritable bowel syndrome. *Gut, 28,* 160–165.

Fox, B. H. (1988). Epidemiologic aspects of stress, aging, cancer and the immune system. *Annals of the New York Academy of Sciences, 521,* 16–28.

France, C., & Ditto, B. (1989). Cardiovascular responses to occupational stress and caffeine in telemarketing employees. *Psychosomatic Medicine, 51,* 145–151.

Fredrikson, M. (1986). Behavioral aspects of cardiovascular reactivity in essential hypertension. In T. H. Schmidt, T. M. Dembroski, & G. Blümchen (Eds.), *Biological and psychological factors in cardiovascular disease* (pp. 418–446). Berlin: Springer-Verlag.

Fredrikson, M., & Matthews, K. A. (1990). Cardiovascular responses to behavioral stress and hypertension: A meta-analytic review. *Annals of Behavioral Medicine, 12,* 30–39.

Friedman, S., Glasgow, L., & Ader, R. (1970). Differential susceptibility to a viral agent in mice housed alone or in groups. *Psychosomatic Medicine, 32,* 285–299.

Friedman, H. S., & Booth-Kewley, S. (1987). The "disease-prone personality." *American Psychologist, 42,* 539–555.

Gannon, L., Banks, J., Shelton, D., & Luchetta, T. (1989). The mediating effects of psychophysiological reactivity and recovery on the relationship between environmental stress and illness. *Journal of Psychosomatic Research, 33,* 167–175.

Gentry, W. D. (1975). Pre-admission behavior. In W. D. Gentry and R. B. Williams (Eds.) *Psychological aspects of myocardial infarction and coronary care* (pp. 53–62). St. Louis: C. V. Mosby.

Goldstein, D. S. (1983). Plasma catecholamines and essential hypertension. An analytical review. *Hypertension, 5,* 86–99.

Graham, N. N. H., Douglas, R. M., & Ryan, P. (1986). Stress and acute respiratory infection. *American Journal of Epidemiology, 124,* 389–401.

Gray, J. A., Davis, N., Feldon, J., Owen, S., & Border, M. (1981). Stress tolerance: Possible neural mechanisms. In M. J. Christie & P. Mellett (Eds.), *Foundations of psychosomatics* (pp. 153–167). Chichester: John Wiley & Sons.

Greer, S., Morris, T., & Pettingale, K. W. (1979). Psychological response to breast cancer: Effect on outcome. *Lancet, II,* 785–787.

Greer, S., & Watson, M. (1985). Towards a psychobiological model of cancer: Psychological considerations. *Social Science and Medicine, 20,* 773–777.

Gruber, B. L., Hall, N. R., Hersh, S. P., & Du Bois, P. (1988). Immune system and psychological changes in metastatic cancer patients using relaxation and guided imagery: A pilot study. *Scandinavian Journal of Behavior Therapy, 17,* 25–46.

Hanson, S. L., & Pichert, J. W. (1986). Perceived stress and diabetes control in adolescents. *Health Psychology, 5,* 439–452.

Harrigan, J. A., Kues, J. R., Ricks, D. F., & Smith, R. (1984). Moods that predict coming migraine headache. *Pain, 20,* 385–396.

Henry, J. P. (1976). Mechanisms of psychosomatic disease in animals. *Advances in Veterinary Science and Comparative Medicine, 20,* 115–145.

Henry, J. P., Stephens, P. M., & Santisteban, G. A. (1975). A model of psychosocial hypertension showing reversibility and progression of cardiovascular complications. *Circulation Research, 36,* 156–164.

Hollaender, J., & Florin, I. (1983). Expressed emotion and airway conductance in children with bronchial asthma. *Journal of Pyschosomatic Research, 27,* 307–311.

Horowitz, M. J. (1986). *Stress response syndromes.* Northvale, NJ: Jason Aronson.

House, J. S., McMichael, A. J., Wells, J. A., Kaplan, B. H., & Landerman, L. R. (1979). Occupational stress and health among factory workers. *Journal of Health and Social Behavior, 20,* 139–160.

Hull, J. G., Van Treuren, R. R., & Virnelli, S. (1987). Hardiness and health: A critique and alternative approach. *Journal of Personality and Social Psychology, 53,* 518–530.

Ito, N., Takeshita, A., Higuchi, S., & Nakamura, M. (1986). Venous abnormality in normotensive young men with a family history of hypertension. *Hypertension, 8,* 142–146.

Jemmott, J. B., Borysenko, J. Z., Borysenko, M., McClelland, D., Chapman, R., Meyer, D., & Benson, M. (1983). Academic stress, power motivation, and decrease in secretion rate of salivary secretory immunoglobulin A. *Lancet, I,* 1400–1402.

Johnson, J. E., & Hall, F. M. (1988). Job strain, workplace social support, and cardiovascular disease: A cross-sectional study of a random sample of the Swedish working population. *American Journal of Public Health, 78,* 1336–1341.

Johnston, D. W. (1986). How does relaxation training reduce blood pressure in primary hypertension? In T. H. Schmidt, T. M. Dembroski & G. Blümchen (Eds.), *Biological and psychological factors in cardiovascular disease* (pp. 550–567). Berlin: Springer-Verlag.

Jorgensen, R. S., & Houston, B. K. (1986). Family history of hypertension, personality patterns, and cardiovascular reactivity to stress. *Psychosomatic Medicine, 48,* 102–117.

Julius, M., Harburg, E., Cottington, E. M., & Johnson, E. H. (1986). Anger-coping types, blood pressure, and all-cause mortality: A follow-up in Tecumseh-Michigan (1971–1983). *American Journal of Epidemiology, 124,* 220–233.

Kagan, A. R., & Levi, L. (1974). Health and environment—psychosocial stimuli: A review. *Social Science and Medicine, 8,* 225–241.

Kaplan, G. A., & Reynolds, P. (1988). Depression and

cancer mortality and morbidity: Prospective evidence from the Alameda County study. *Journal of Behavioral Medicine, 11,* 1–14.

Kaplan, J. R., Manuck, S. B., Clarkson, T. B., Lusso, F. M., & Taub, D. B. (1982). Social status, environment, and atherosclerosis in cynomolgus monkeys. *Arteriosclerosis, 2,* 359–368.

Kaplan, J. R., Manuck, S. B., Clarkson, T. B., Lusso, F. M., Taub, D. B., & Miller, E. W. (1983). Social stress and atherosclerosis in normocholesterolemic monkeys. *Science, 220,* 733–735.

Kemeny, M. E., Cohen, F., Zegans, O. S., & Conant, M. A. (1989). Psychological and immunological predictors of genital herpes recurrence. *Psychosomatic Medicine, 51,* 195–208.

Kiecolt-Glaser, J. K., Fisher, L. D., Ogrocki, P., Stout, J. C., Speicher, C. E., & Glaser, R. (1987a). Marital quality, marital disruption, and immune function. *Psychosomatic Medicine, 49,* 13–34.

Kiecolt-Glaser, J. K., Glaser, R., Shuttleworth, E. C., Dyer, C. S., Ogrocki, B. S., & Speicher, C. E. (1987b). Chronic stress and immunity in family caregivers of Alzheimer's Disease victims. *Psychosomatic Medicine, 49,* 523–535.

Kiecolt-Glaser, J. K., Speicher, C. E., Holliday, J. E., & Glaser, R. (1984). Stress and the transformation of lymphocytes by Epstein-Barr virus. *Journal of Behavioral Medicine, 7,* 1–12.

Krantz, D. S., Manuck, S. B. (1984). Acute psychophysiologic reactivity and risk of cardiovascular disease: A review and methodologic critique. *Psychological Bulletin, 96,* 435–464.

Kumar, D., & Wingate, D. L. (1985). The irritable bowel syndrome. *Lancet, II,* 973–977.

Lachman, S. J. (1972). *Psychosomatic disorders: A behavioristic interpretation.* New York: John Wiley & Sons.

Larsson, P. T., Hjemdahl, P., Olsson, G., Egberg, N., & Hornstra, G. (1989). Altered platelet function during mental stress and adrenaline infusion in humans: Evidence for an increased aggregability in vivo as measured by filtragometry. *Clinical Science, 76,* 369–376.

Laudenslager, M., Ryan, S., Drugan, R., Hyson, R., & Maier, S. (1983). Coping and immunosuppression: Inescapable, but not escapable, shock suppresses lymphocyte proliferation. *Science, 221,* 568–570.

Laudenslager, M., Fleshner, M., Hofstadter, P., Held, P. E., Simons, I. L., & Maier, S. F. (1988). Suppression of specific antibody production by inescapable shock: Stability under varying conditions. *Brain, Behavior, and Immunity, 2,* 92–101.

Lazarus, R. S., & Folkman, S. (1984). *Stress, coping and appraisal.* New York: Springer-Verlag.

Lenders, J. W. M., Willemsen, J. J., De Boo, T., Lemmens, W. A. J., & Thien, T. (1989). Disparate effects of mental stress on plasma noradrenaline in young normotensive and hypertensive subjects. *Journal of Hypertension, 7,* 317–323.

Levenson, R. W. (1979). Effects of thematically relevant and general stressors on specificity of response in asthmatic and non-asthmatic subjects. *Psychosomatic Medicine, 41,* 28–39.

Levey, A. B., & Martin, I. (1981). The relevance of classical conditioning to psychosomatic disorder. In M. Christie & P. Mellett (Eds.), *Foundations of psychosomatics* (pp. 259–282). Chichester: John Wiley & Sons.

Levy, S. M., Lee, J., Bagley, C., & Lippmann, M. (1988). Survival hazards analysis in first recurred breast cancer patients: Seven-year follow-up. *Psychosomatic Medicine, 50,* 520–528.

Light, K. C., Koepke, J. P., Obrist, P. A., & Willis, P. W. (1983). Psychological stress induces sodium and fluid retention in men at risk for hypertension. *Science, 200,* 429–431.

Lindenthal, J. J., Myers, J. K., & Pepper, M. P. (1972). Smoking, psychological status and stress. *Social Science and Medicine, 6,* 583–591.

Litt, M. D. (1988). Cognitive mediators of stressful experience: Self-efficacy and perceived control. *Cognitive Therapy and Research, 12,* 241–260.

Longo, D. J., & Clum, G. A. (1989). Psychosocial factors affecting genital herpes recurrences: Linear versus mediating models. *Journal of Psychosomatic Research, 33,* 161–166.

Lown, B., Verrier, R., & Corbalan, R. (1973). Psychologic stress and the threshold for repetitive ventricular response. *Science, 183,* 834–836.

Lown, B., Verrier, R. L., & Rabinowitz, S. H. (1977). Neural and psychologic mechanisms and the problem of sudden cardiac death. *American Journal of Cardiology, 39,* 890–902.

Lundberg, U., Hedman, M., Melin, B., & Frankenhaeuser, M. (1989). Type A behavior in healthy males and females as related to physiological reactivity and blood lipids. *Psychosomatic Medicine, 51,* 113–122.

Manuck, S. B., Kaplan, J. R., & Clarkson, T. B. (1983). Behaviorally induced heart rate reactivity and atherosclerosis in cynomolgus monkeys. *Psychosomatic Medicine, 45,* 95–108.

Manuck, S. B., Kaplan, J. R., Adams, M. R., & Clarkson, T. B. (1989). Behaviorally elicited heart rate reactivity and atherosclerosis in female cynomolgus monkeys. *Psychosomatic Medicine, 51,* 306–318.

Marmot, M. G., & Syme, S. L. (1976). Acculturation and coronary heart disease in Japanese-Americans. *American Journal of Epidemiology, 104,* 225–247.

Mathews, A., & MacLeod, C. (1987). An information-processing approach to anxiety. *Journal of Cognitive Psychotherapy, 1,* 105–115.

Matthews, K. A., Cottington, E. M., Talbot, E., Kuller, L. H., & Siegel, J. M. (1987). Stressful work conditions and diastolic blood pressure among blue-collar factory workers. *American Journal of Epidemiology, 126,* 280–291.

Matthews, K. A., Siegel, J. M., Kuller, L. H., Thompson,

M., & Barat, M. (1983). Determinants of decisions to seek medical treatment by patients with acute myocardial infarction symptoms. *Journal of Personality and Social Psychology, 44,* 1144–1156.

Metalsky, G. I., Halberstadt, L. J., & Abramson, L. Y. (1987). Vulnerability to depressive mood reactions: Toward a more powerful test of the diathesis-stress and causal mediation components of the reformulated theory of depression. *Journal of Personality and Social Psychology, 52,* 386–393.

Meyer, R., & Haggerty, R. (1962). Streptococcal infections in families. *Pediatrics, 29,* 539–549.

Miller, S. M., Brody, D. S., & Summerton, J. (1988). Styles of coping with threat: Implications for health. *Journal of Personality and Social Psychology, 54,* 142–148.

Milner, M., Heagerty, A. M., Bing, R. F., Thurston, H., & Swales, J. D. (1984). Changes in leucocyte sodium transport in normotensive relatives of hypertensive subjects: Disassociation from blood pressure. *Hypertension, 6,* 369–373.

Mineka, S., Gunnar, M., & Champoux, M. (1986). Control and early socioemotional development: Infant rhesus monkeys reared in controllable versus uncontrollable environments. *Child Development, 57,* 1241–1256.

Monjan, A. A., & Collector, M. I. (1977). Stress-induced modulation of the immune response. *Science, 196,* 307–308.

Moos, R. H. (1964). Personality factors associated with rheumatoid arthritis: A review. *Journal of Chronic Diseases, 17,* 41–55.

Mormède, P., Dantzer, R., Michaud, B., Kelley, K. W., & Le Moal, M. (1988). Influence of stressor predictability and behavioral control on lymphocyte reactivity, antibody response and neuroendocrine activation in rats. *Physiology and Behavior, 43,* 577–583.

Munck, A., Guyre, P. M., & Holbrook, N. J. (1984). Physiological functions of glucocorticoids in stress and their relation to pharmacological actions. *Endocrine Review, 5,* 25–44.

Murphy, E., & Brown, G. W. (1980). Life events, psychiatric disturbance and physical illness. *British Journal of Psychiatry, 136,* 326–338.

Nadel, J. A., & Barnes, P. J. (1984). Autonomic regulation of the airways. *Annual Review of Medicine, 35,* 451–467.

Nuechterlein, K. H., & Dawson, M. E. (1984). A heuristic vulnerability/stress model of schizophrenic episodes. *Schizophrenia Bulletin, 10,* 300–312.

Ohman, A., & Bohlin, G. (1989). The role of controllability in cardiovascular activation and cardiovascular disease: Help or hindrance? In A. Steptoe & A. Appels (Eds.) *Stress, personal control and health* (pp. 257–276). Chichester: John Wiley & Sons.

Pardine, P., & Napoli, A. (1983). Physiological reactivity and recent life-stress experience. *Journal of Consulting and Clinical Psychology, 51,* 467–469.

Parkes, C. M., & Brown, R. J. (1972). Health after bereavement: A controlled study of young Boston widows and widowers. *Psychosomatic Medicine, 34,* 449–461.

Parkes, K. R. (1984). Locus of control, cognitive appraisal, and coping in stressful episodes. *Journal of Personality and Social Psychology, 46,* 655–668.

Patterson, R. J., & Neufeld, R. W. J. (1987). Clear danger: Situational determinants of the appraisal of threat. *Psychological Bulletin, 101,* 404–416.

Pennebaker, J. W. (1982). *The psychology of physical symptoms.* New York: Springer-Verlag.

Peterson, C. (1988). Explanatory style as a risk factor for illness. *Cognitive Therapy and Research, 12,* 119–132.

Plaut, S. M., & Friedman, S. B. (1981). Psychosocial factors in infectious disease. In R. Ader (Ed.) *Psychoneuroimmunology* (pp. 13–30). New York: Academic Press.

Polefrone, J., & Manuck, S. B. (1988). Effects of menstrual phase and parental history of hypertension on cardiovascular response to cognitive challenge. *Psychosomatic Medicine, 50,* 23–36.

Pynoos, R. S., Frederick, C., Nader, K., Arroyo, W., Steinberg, A., Eth, S., Nunez, F. & Fairbanks, L. (1987). Life threat and posttraumatic stress in school age children. *Archives of General Psychiatry, 44,* 1057–1063.

Radice, M., Alli, C., Avanzini, F., Tullio, M. D., Mariotti, G., Taioli, E., Zussino, A., & Folli, G. (1986). Left ventricular structure and function in normotensive adolescents with a genetic predisposition to hypertension. *American Heart Journal, 111,* 115–120.

Ramirez, A. J., Craig, T. J. K., Watson, J. P., Fentiman, I. S., North, W. R. S., & Rubens, R. D. (1989). Stress and relapse of breast cancer. *British Medical Journal, 298,* 291–293.

Reich, P., DeSilva, R. A., Lown, B., & Murawski, B. J. (1981). Acute psychological disturbances preceding life-threatening ventricular arrhythmias. *Journal of the American Medical Association, 246,* 233–235.

Robinson, N., & Fuller, J. H. (1985). Role of life events and difficulties in the onset on diabetes mellitus. *Journal of Psychosomatic Research, 29,* 583–591.

Rodin, J. (1986). Age and health: Effects of sense control. *Science, 233,* 1271–1276.

Roskies, E., Seraganian, P., Oseasohn, R., Hanley, J. A., Collu, R., Martin, N., & Smilga, C. (1986). The Montreal Type A intervention project: Major findings: *Health Psychology, 5,* 45–70.

Roth, S., & Cohen, L. J. (1986). Approach, avoidance, and coping with stress. *American Psychologist, 41,* 813–819.

Rozanski, A., Bairey, N., Krantz, D. S., Friedman, J., Rosser, K. J., Morrell, M., Hilton-Chalfen, S., Hestrin, L., Bietendorf, J., & Berman, D. S. (1988). Mental stress and the induction of silent myocardial ischaemia in patients with coronary artery disease. *New England Journal of Medicine, 318,* 1005–1012.

Ruch, L. O., Chandler, S. M., & Harter, R. A. (1980). Life

change and rape impact. *Journal of Health and Social Behavior, 21,* 248–260.
Saab, P. G., Matthews, K. A., Stoney, C. M., & McDonald, R. H. (1989). Premenopausal and postmenopausal women differ in their cardiovascular and neuroendocrine responses to behavioral stressors. *Psychophysiology, 26,* 270–280.
Sauter, S. L., Hurrell, J. J., & Cooper, C. L. (Eds.). (1989). *Job control and worker health.* Chichester: John Wiley & Sons.
Schleifer, S. J., Keller, S. E., Camerino, M., Thornton, J. C., & Stein, M. (1983). Suppression of lymphocyte stimulation following bereavement. *Journal of American Medical Association, 250,* 374–377.
Selye, H. (1976). *The stress of life.* New York: McGraw-Hill.
Seraganian, P., Roskies, E., Hanley, J. A., Oseasohn, R., & Collu, R. (1987). Failure to alter psychophysiological reactivity in Type A men with physical exercise or stress management programs. *Psychology and Health, 1,* 195–213.
Shavit, Y., & Martin, F. C. (1987). Opiates, stress and immunity: Animal studies. *Annals of Behavioral Medicine, 9,* 11–15.
Shillitoe, R. W. (1988). *Psychology and Diabetes.* London: Chapman and Hall.
Shore, J. H., Tatum, E. L., & Vollmer, W. M. (1986). Psychiatric reactions to disaster: The Mount St. Helens experience. *American Journal of Psychiatry, 143,* 590–595.
Sinyor, D., Perronet, F., Brisson, G., & Seraganian, P. (1988). Failure to alter sympathoadrenal response to psychosocial stress following aerobic training. *Physiology and Behavior, 42,* 293–296.
Skinner, J. E. (1988). Brain involvement in cardiovascular disorders. In T. Elbert, W. Langosch, A. Steptoe, & D. Vaitl, (Eds.), *Behavioural medicine in cardiovascular disorders* (pp. 229–253). Chichester: John Wiley & Sons.
Sklar, L. S., & Anisman, H. (1981). Stress and cancer. *Psychological Bulletin, 89,* 396–406.
Sklar, L. S., Bruto, V., & Anisman, H. (1981). Adaptation to the tumor-enhancing effects of stress. *Psychosomatic Medicine, 43,* 331–342.
Smith, A. P. (1990). Information processing. In M. Johnston & L. Wallace (Eds.) *Stress and medical procedures* (pp. 58–79), Oxford: Oxford University Press.
Smith, T. W., Turner, C. W., Ford, M. H., Hunt, S. C., Barlow, G. K., Stultz, B. M., & Williams, R. R. (1987). Blood pressure reactivity in adult male twins. *Health Psychology, 6,* 209–220.
Steptoe, A. (1980). Stress and medical disorders. In S. Rachman (Ed.). *Contributions to medical psychology, Vol 2.* (pp. 55–77). Oxford: Pergamon Press.
Steptoe, A. (1984a). Psychophysiological processes in disease. In A. Steptoe & A. Matthews (Eds.) *Health care and human behaviour* (pp. 77–112). London: Academic Press.
Steptoe, A. (1984b). Psychological aspects of bronchial asthma. In S. Rachman (Ed.) *Contributions to medical psychology, Vol 3.* (pp. 7–30). Oxford: Pergamon Press.
Steptoe, A. (1985). Theoretical basis for task selection in cardiovascular psychophysiology. In A. Steptoe, H. Rüddel, & H. Neus (Eds.) *Clinical and methodological issues in cardiovascular psychophysiology* (pp. 6–15). Berlin: Springer-Verlag.
Steptoe, A. (1989). Psychophysiological interventions in behavioural medicine. In G. Turpin (Ed.) *Handbook of Clinical Psychophysiology* (pp. 215–239). Chichester, England: John Wiley & Sons.
Steptoe, A. (1990a). Psychobiological stress responses. In M. Johnston & L. Wallace (Eds.) *Stress and medical procedures* (pp. 3–24). Oxford: Oxford University Press.
Steptoe, A. (1990b). The value of mental stress testing in the investigation of cardiovascular disorders. In L. R. Schmidt, P. Schwenkmezger, J. Weinman, & S. Maes (Eds.) *Health psychology: Theoretic and applied aspects* (pp. 309–329). London: Harwood.
Steptoe, A., & Appels, A. (Eds.) (1989). *Stress, personal control and health.* Chichester: John Wiley & Sons.
Steptoe, A., & Holmes, R. (1985). Mood and pulmonary function in adult asthmatics: A pilot self-monitoring study. *British Journal of Medical Psychology, 58,* 87–94.
Steptoe, A., Moses, J., & Edwards, S. (1990). Age-related differences in cardiovascular reactions to mental stress tests in women. *Health Psychology, 9,* 18–34.
Strehler, E. L., & Mildvan, A. S. (1960). General theory of mortality and aging. *Science, 132,* 14–21.
Suls, J., & Fletcher, B. (1985). The relative efficacy of avoidant and nonavoidant coping strategies: A meta-analysis. *Health Psychology, 4,* 247–288.
Surwit, R. & Feinglos, N. M. (1984). Relaxation-induced improvement in glucose tolerance is associated with decreased plasma cortisol. *Diabetes Care, 7,* 203–204.
Tavazzi, L., Zotti, A. M., & Rondanelli, R. (1986). The role of psychologic stress in the genesis of lethal arrhythmias in patients with coronary artery disease. *European Heart Journal, 7* (Suppl. A), 99–106.
Taylor, J. A., Gatchel, R. J., & Korman, M. (1982). Psychophysiological and cognitive characteristics of ulcer and rheumatoid arthritis patients. *Journal of Behavioral Medicine, 5,* 173–188.
Temoshok, L. (1987). Personality, coping style, emotion and cancer: Towards an integrative model. *Cancer Surveys, 6,* 545–567.
Temoshok, L., Heller, B. W., Sagebiel, R. W., Blois, M. S., Sweet, D. M., DiClemente, R. J., & Gold, M. L. (1985). The relationship of psychosocial factors to prognostic indicators in cutaneous malignant melanoma. *Journal of Psychosomatic Research, 29,* 139–153.

Theorell, T. (1989). Personal control at work and health: A review of epidemiological studies in Sweden. In A. Steptoe & A. Appels (Eds.), *Stress, personal control and health* (pp. 49–64). Chichester: John Wiley & Sons.

Van den Akker, O., & Steptoe, A. (1987). Psychophysiological responses in women with pre-menstrual and menstrual symptoms. *Journal of Psychophysiology, 1,* 149–159.

VanderPlate, C., Aral, S., & Magder, L. (1988). The relationship among genital herpes simplex virus, stress, and social support. *Health Psychology, 7,* 159–168.

Vernon, S. W., & Buffler, P. A. (1988). The status of status inconsistency. *Epidemiologic Reviews, 10,* 65–86.

Visintainer, M., Volpicelli, J., & Seligman, M. (1982). Tumor rejection in rats after inescapable or escapable shock. *Science, 216,* 437–439.

Von Eiff, A. W., & Peikarski, C. (1977). Stress reaction of normotensives and hypertensives and the influence of female sex hormones on blood pressure regulation. *Progress in Brain Research, 47,* 289–299.

Von Holst, D. (1986). Psychosocial stress and its pathophysiological effects in tree shrews. In T. H. Schmidt, T. M. Dembroski, & G. Blümchen (Eds.), *Biological and psychological factors in cardiovascular disease* (pp. 476–490). Berlin: Springer-Verlag.

Walker, B. B., & Sandman, C. A. (1977). Physiological response patterns in ulcer patients: Phasic and tonic components of the electrogastrogram. *Psychophysiology, 14,* 343–400.

Warr, P. (1987). *Work, unemployment, and mental health.* Oxford: Oxford University Press.

Warr, P. V., & Payne, R. L. (1983). Social class and reported changes in behavior after job loss. *Journal of Applied Social Psychology, 13,* 206–222.

Watson, D., & Pennebaker, J. W. (1989). Health complaints: stress, and distress: Exploring the central role of negative affectivity. *Psychological Review, 96,* 234–354.

Weinstein, A. G. (1985). Crying-induced bronchospasm in childhood asthma: Combined pharmacologic and behavioral management. *Annals of Allergy, 54,* 105–108.

Weinstein, A. G. (1987). Familial factors responsible for persistent crying-induced asthma: A case report. *Annals of Allergy, 59,* 256–260.

Weisaeth, L. (1989). The stressors and the post-traumatic stress syndrome after an industrial disaster. *Acta Psychiatrica Scandinavica, 80* (Suppl. 355), 25–37.

Weiss, J. M. (1977). Psychological and behavioral influences on gastrointestinal lesions in animal models. In J. D. Maser & M. E. P. Seligman (Eds.) *Psychopathology: Experimental models* (pp. 232–269). San Francisco: W H Freeman.

Werner, E. E. (1989). High risk children in young adulthood: A longitudinal study from birth to 32 years. *American Journal of Orthopsychiatry, 59,* 72–81.

Williams, R. B., & Barefoot, J. C. (1988). Coronary-prone behavior: The emerging role of the hostility complex. In B. K. Houston & C. R. Snyder (Eds.), *Type A behavior pattern: Research, theory and intervention* (pp. 189–211) New York: Wiley-Interscience.

Zautra, A. J., Okun, M. A., Robinson, S. E., Lee, D., Roth, S. H., & Emmanual, J. (1989). Life stress and lymphocyte alterations among patients with rheumatoid arthritis. *Health Psychology, 8,* 1–14.

CHAPTER 18

PSYCHOPHYSIOLOGY AND BEHAVIORAL ASSESSMENT: IS THERE SCOPE FOR THEORETICAL FRAMEWORKS?

Graham Turpin

The main purpose of this chapter is to evaluate the contribution of psychophysiology to assessment in behavior therapy. To achieve this goal, we will review the domain of psychophysiology, the rationales for its use in behavioral assessment, the techniques employed and its empirical contribution to the advancement of behavior therapy. However, as will be discussed later in the chapter, psychophysiological assessment can be considered to have reached a watershed in its development. This is exemplified by contemporary concerns with "synchrony-desynchrony" (Rachman & Hodgson, 1974) whereby psychophysiological measures demonstrate varying degrees of association/disassociation with more direct behavioral measures. This poses a dilemma for the behavior therapist intent upon employing psychophysiological assessment approaches.

On the one hand, it can be argued that this potentially confusing state of affairs reflects the limited validity and reliability of psychophysiological techniques and hence suggests a cautious approach to further application and development. On the other hand, it could be argued that the time has come for psychophysiologists to shift their attention from empirically oriented research to more theoretically relevant investigations that seek to account for these various disparate relationships between behavior and physiological response.

In keeping with the proposed aim of this volume, a secondary goal of this chapter will be to explore how theoretical frameworks derived from psychophysiological research might clarify this impasse surrounding the current interpretation of psychophysiological measures. In doing so, it is hoped that we will both demonstrate some possible avenues towards the resolution of the "synchrony-desynchrony" problem, and also will suggest that psychophysiological models per se may reveal fresh opportunities for innovation in the practice of behavioral interventions and treatments.

Parts of this chapter previously have been published (Turpin, 1989) and are reproduced by the kind permission of John Wiley and Sons, Chichester, England.

DEFINITIONS

Psychophysiology

It should be recognized that compared to some branches of psychological science represented in this volume, psychophysiology is still a relatively new and developing area. Indeed, its major organization, the Society for Psychophysiological Research, has only been in existence for the last 25 years. Accordingly, some discussion of the domain of psychophysiology and its developing definition is required, together with an examination of its application to the study of psychopathology. These issues have also been recently discussed elsewhere (Turpin, 1989a).

Essentially, psychophysiology is concerned with the application of physiological measurement to the understanding of psychological processes underlying behavior. Previous definitions have emphasized the physiological nature of the dependent variables under study (Stern, 1964) and the tendency to employ human experimental subjects (Sternbach, 1966). It differs from physiological psychology because its major aim is the elucidation of psychological processes, as opposed to the identification of physiological substrates that may subserve behavior. Accordingly, physiological psychology primarily examines the effects of physiological manipulations (i.e., brain lesions, stimulation, etc.) upon behavior, whereas psychophysiology is concerned with the effects of psychological or behavioral manipulations upon physiological activity. With respect to behavior therapy, this distinction, to a degree, is demarcated by the boundary between animal and human subject research. The former tends to be the province of physiological psychology and may be represented by animal models of the physiological basis of behavioral dysfunction (e.g., Eysenck & Kelley, 1987). The latter may be clearly identified with psychophysiological studies of the application of behavior therapy to clinical populations. However, it should be stressed that not all human physiological studies of psychopathology are of an essentially psychophysiological character.

A distinction should be made between psychophysiology and pathophysiology. The latter seeks to identify the physiological locus or marker of psychophysiological dysfunction in human subjects in the absence of psychological factors (Shagass, 1976; Usdin & Hanin, 1982). In contrast, traditional areas of psychophysiological study have included, therefore, the physiological identification of such different behavioral states as sleep, anger, and sexual arousal, and the study of physiological correlates of psychological processes said to underlie such things as conditioning, emotional behavior, arousal, and attention. Typically, psychophysiological measures include changes in electrocortical activity, autonomic nervous system activity and biochemical assays.

(Although cortical measures, such as evoked potentials (EPs), have a central position in contemporary psychophysiological research, I have not included them in this chapter because to date, behavior therapists have failed to exploit their potential. However, recent research on the relationship between affective processing and EPs [e.g., Johnston, Miller, & Burleson, 1986; Klorman & Ryan, 1980; Yee & Miller, 1988] may require a reappraisal of the use of central psychophysiological measures in behavioral assessment.)

Although much psychophysiological research has tended to be of a correlational nature, attempting to identify parallels between inferred psychological processes and observed physiological events, recent theoretical accounts have emphasized the interactional nature of psychophysiological processes. Hence, the distinction between physiological correlate and psychological process becomes blurred since behavioral outcomes are seen as a product of *psychophysiological* processes.

For example, it has been established that specific patterns of heart rate change are associated with different environmental events (cf. Coles, Jennings, & Stern, 1984). In particular, it has been claimed that heart rate slowing or cardiac deceleration is a possible correlate of attention and may reflect the degree and location of attention directed towards environmental stimuli. This relationship between cardiac deceleration and attention has been viewed in several different ways. To begin, deceleration can be seen as a physiological correlate reflecting the operation of orienting; a psychological process said to subserve attention (Graham, 1979). This account does not primarily address either the functional relationship or the physiological mechanism which relates heart rate slowing to enhanced information processing in the form of the orienting response. A complementary account suggests that heart rate slowing accompanies the "intention to note and detect external stimuli" (Lacey & Lacey, 1978, p. 99) and that the physiological response may itself enhance processing via a biological baroreceptor feedback mechanism. Hence, heart rate slowing is viewed both as a component of the process, and also as a product and correlate of the attentional mechanism. Although the Laceys' notion of afferent feedback is a controversial one (Carroll & Anastasiades, 1978), it does illustrate how the relationship between physiological response and psychological process may be integrated within a psychophysiological mechanism. Finally, an alternative perspective has been advanced by Obrist (1981) that relies on the premise that much of cardiac activity is regulated in accord with metabolic demand and consequently motor activity. Cardiac deceleration, therefore, is seen as a physiological concomitant of a behavioral response (i.e., general body quieting) that accompanies changes in attention. Hence, the relationship between cardiac activity and environmental intake is accounted for both at a behavioral and physiological level. Indeed, Obrist (1981) has strongly argued that adequate psychophysiological explanations must take into account physiological substrates and mechanisms. This he has termed as a "psychobiological" approach.

Clinical Psychophysiology

Before discussing the application of psychophysiological to behavior therapy, it is necessary to examine a definition of clinical psychophysiology that can be applied generally to psychopathology. It would appear from the previous definitions that psychophysiological measures can be considered as psychological correlates, psychophysiological processes or psychobiological mechanisms. The distinction between psychophysiological correlates and processes reflects an uneasy separatism between mind and body. Indeed, the problem of dualistic distinctions between psychological and physiological processes is particularly relevant when considering a definition of clinical psychophysiology. Historically, clinical psychophysiology has been associated with so called "functional psychiatric" and "psychosomatic" disorders. Both these areas have suffered from the adoption of dualist principles either in relation to psychoanalytic explanations of psychosomatic disorder (Wittkower, 1977) or the interdisciplinary divisions between psychiatry and medicine (Engel, 1986; Leigh, 1982; cf. Wallace, 1988). There would appear to be two major alternatives to the dualist approach: monist and interactionalist positions. The former attempts to account for both physical and psychological disorder in terms of single elementary processes whether they be based upon operant conditioning (e.g., Engel, 1986) or some undisclosed pathological process as is the case with the medical model (Guze, 1977; but see Tarrier, 1979). The latter approach adopts an interactionalist perspective that is either based upon Systems Theory (Schwartz, 1983) or upon interdisciplinary models that seek to account for physical and psychological well-being and/or disorder at several levels of explanation including the sociological, psychological, and physiological domains of discourse (Engel, 1977; Ohman, 1981a; Weiner, 1977). Given the current trend towards interactionist accounts of psychophysiology that seek to identify both relationships and interactions at a process level between environment and physiology, it would appear that this discipline should be well placed to provide a basis with which to examine "biobehavioral" models of health and disease.

We are still left with the need for a definition of clinical psychophysiology that will reflect the diversity of disciplines that previously have employed psychophysiological techniques. Traditionally, clinical psychophysiology has been approached from several distinct directions. Perhaps the most established application concerns the extension of laboratory-based psychophysiological paradigms to the study of psychopathological groups in psychiatry. A recent overview of the application of psychophysiology to psychopathology in general is to be found in Zahn's (1986) excellent review.

A second area from which clinical psychophysiology has originated involves its application as a collection of clinical assessment instruments in psychotherapy research (Crits-Christoph & Schwartz, 1983; Lacey, 1959; Lang, 1971; Schwartz, 1978; Stern & Plapp, 1969) and behavior therapy, in particular (Haynes & Wilson, 1979; Kallman & Feuerstein, 1986; Ray & Raczynski, 1981; Sturgis & Arena, 1984; Sturgis & Gramling, 1988). A third but related source of influence stems from the psychophysiological foundations of biofeedback and self-regulation (Blanchard & Epstein, 1978; Carroll, 1984; Gatchel & Price, 1979; Olton & Noonberg, 1980).

Finally, the advent of both behavioral medicine and the related disciplines of medical and health psychology have also seen a rapid expansion of the use of psychophysiological techniques for the assessment and treatment of a vast range of physical or nonpsychiatric conditions (Doleys, Meredith, & Ciminero, 1982; Feuerstein, Labbe, & Kuczmierczyk, 1986; Gentry, 1984; Haynes & Gannon, 1981; Surwit, Williams, Steptoe, & Biersner, 1982).

A definition of clinical psychophysiology therefore, should represent these diverse interests. Accordingly, it should be interdisciplinary in nature, linking both biological and social sciences, and should be applied to both psychiatry and medicine. It is proposed, therefore, that clinical psychophysiology is the application of psychophysiological techniques, concepts and theories to the explanation of psychological factors that influence health behaviors and risks. Health, in this context, is taken to mean a state of both physical and psychological well-being.

OVERVIEW OF APPLICATIONS TO BEHAVIOR THERAPY

Despite being in its nascency, psychophysiology has traditionally been associated with the study of psychotherapeutic processes. Indeed, both Jung (see Walrath and Stern, 1981) and Reich (1982) used psychogalvanic responses to examine various psychodynamic concepts. It is not surprising, therefore, that early proponents of the applications of learning theory to psychotherapeutic processes also used psychophysiological indices. For example, Mowrer (1953) extensively employed a measure of palmar sweating in order to assess the physiological correlates of psychological tension from both therapists and patients engaged in psychotherapy.

This emphasis on the use of a correlative approach could be contrasted with other early psychophysiological research in psychiatry that was determined by either psychometric or diagnostic considerations (e.g., Silverman & Powell, 1944; Wenger, 1941). Early attempts using measures such as objective indices of arousal or emotional states (i.e., "affect or arousal meter"; see Lacey, 1959, p. 160) have been reviewed elsewhere (Lang, 1971; O'Kelly, 1953). Ironically, these studies had to confront the crucial problem of dissociation between questionnaire, physiological and behavioral data (Martin, 1961) that also predominates much of contemporary psychophysiological research.

Moreover, it became apparent that these relationships were affected by the context of the clinical interview. Indeed, Lacey (1959, p. 174), in his classic critique, stated that "autonomic responses . . . need to be *interpreted* in terms of the total behavior of the organism" and that the implications of this "are rather serious—even devastating—for those who wish to evaluate the effectiveness of psychotherapy in terms of the course somatic arousal." It will be argued later that this fundamental problem has not altered despite 20 years of further research. However, a possible means of resolution to this issue may be available, which was perhaps conspicuously absent in 1959. This concerns the gradual transformation of psychophysiology from an empirically based inductive discipline to a more theoretically oriented deductive science. The presence of contemporary theoretical frameworks in psychophysiology may provide the means whereby Lacey's emphasis upon interpretation may be brought about.

Given the early recognition of the limitations of the clinical psychophysiological endeavour as applied to psychotherapy, it might be predicted that its use with behavior therapy would be similarly restricted. Moreover, a strict behaviorist orientation might also eschew the role of intervening physiological variables in the assessment of behavioral outcomes (e.g., Wolff & Merrens, 1974). As discussed in Haynes, Falkin, and Sexton-Radeks' (1989) recent review, this evidently has not been the case. They document that the number of articles using psychophysiological measures rose from around 1% in 1965 to about 40% in the 1980s in two leading journals. These authors identified several factors that might account for this upward trend. First, many target areas amenable to behavior therapy have physiological components. Consequently, much research in the area of behavioral medicine will have focused on physiological dysfunctions associated with nonpsychiatric conditions such as hypertension, headache, and diabetes, which would have necessitated the measurement of respective physiological variables such as blood pressure, muscle tension, and blood glucose levels. Second, the search for objective indices of elusive constructs such as "anxiety" have directed behavior therapists towards more broadly-based assessment strategies encompassing physiological, cognitive, and behavioral response channels (cf. Lang, 1968, 1971). Third, a consequence of this "multimodal" approach has been the increasing complexity of causal models. Fourth, many behavioral interventions such as biofeedback, relaxation, and stress management have as their primary goal the modification of physiological dysfunction. Finally, Haynes et al. (1989) also identify technological advances which have usually heralded an expansion of psychophysiological endeavour.

The widespread use of psychophysiology in behavior therapy research may also be indexed by the extensive number of book chapters and reviews dealing with this area (Feuerstein et al., 1986; Haynes &

Wilson, 1979; Haynes et al., 1989; Hollandsworth, 1986; Kallman & Feuerstein, 1986; Lang, 1971; Ray & Raczynski, 1981; Sturgis & Arena, 1984; Sturgis & Gramling, 1988; Turpin, 1989a; Williamson, Waters, & Hawkins, 1986) not to mention similar contributions to biofeedback (e.g., Andrasik & Blanchard, 1983) and behavioral medicine (e.g., Haynes & Gannon, 1981). It is likely that the growth of psychophysiology in relation to clinical research has not been matched by its application to routine clinical practice, especially in Europe. Nevertheless, results from a survey by Feuerstein and Schwartz (1977) suggests that a substantial number of clinical psychology programs approved by the American Psychological Association offered formal training in psychophysiology. Clearly, psychophysiology has achieved a significant position with respect to the fundamental knowledge-base of behavior therapy.

MODELS OF ASSESSMENT

Because this chapter focuses on psychophysiological assessment, it is necessary first to discuss the various assessment models which generally prevail in behavior therapy. This is required in order to identify both the rationales for the inclusion of psychophysiological measures and the criterion by which their contribution to behavior therapy may be evaluated.

Overview of Models of Behavioral Assessment

The use of the term *behavioral assessment* presupposes some unitary collection of assessment techniques, based upon a common rationale and amenable to evaluation via a set of recognized and accepted criteria. However, contemporary accounts of behavioral assessment (e.g., Ciminero, Calhoun, & Adams, 1986; Nelson & Hayes, 1986) reveal a far more complex and disharmonious picture. Substantive issues exist surrounding the agreement as to what constitutes behavioral assessment, its relationship to its psychometric predecessors, and the criteria to be applied in order to evaluate the quality of assessments. It is essential, therefore, to identify, if not resolve, these questions, before attempting any evaluation of the contribution of psychophysiology to assessment.

Despite these contemporary concerns, the essentials of behavioral assessment can still be agreed upon. For example, Barrios (1988, p. 7) suggests that it is based upon "a broad philosophy concerning the purposes, precision and premium of clinical assessment." Nelson and Hayes (1981, p. 3) describe it as "the identification and measurement of meaningful response units and their controlling variables (both environmental and organismic) for the purposes of understanding and altering human behavior." Typically, behavioral assessment concerns the measurement of changes in clinically relevant behaviors as a function of changes in situations and treatments. It is essentially an idiographic approach focusing on change within individual clients and emphasizes the situational determinants of behaviors. The functions of behavioral assessment are summarized as: the selection of target behaviors, the selection of appropriate interventions and the evaluation of treatment outcomes (Nelson & Hayes, 1981). It should be noted that behavioral assessment spans both problem discrimination, specification, formulation, and treatment. Hence, there may be considerable overlap with issues dealt with here and in chapters 17 and 19 of this volume.

Several specific and highly pragmatic models of behavioral assessment have been formulated and typify the "honeymoon period" (cf. Hayes, Nelson, & Jarrett, 1986). For example, Goldfried and Sprafkin's (1976) acronym SORC identified the major areas of analysis as: Stimulus-Organism-Response-Consequence. In addition, various technologies were developed to assess these areas and included: direct behavioral observation, self-monitoring, self-report, and role-play tests (cf. Hersen & Bellack, 1976).

Contemporary reviews of models and methods in behavioral analysis reveal a broadening of these earlier approaches (Barrios, 1988). The choice of a single target problem as the focus of analysis has been superseded by the notion of a "problem space," which may incorporate various target problems. The choice of treatment focus is no longer implicitly determined by such practical considerations as ease of measurement but also by therapeutic priorities assigned by client, significant others, and therapists. Behaviors are not considered necessarily as single symptoms but may also be construed as reflecting membership of syndromes or systems of interdependent clinical problems. The reliance on direct observational measures of overt behaviors has also shifted towards the adoption of more indirect methods such as interviews, questionnaires, and retrospective ratings. The clinical significance of behavior change is no longer evaluated solely in terms of amount of change attributable to the intervention and the degree of client satisfaction. Functional criteria and norm-referenced criteria of the adequacy of intervention end-points are also being sought.

The consequence of these developments is that the determining characteristics of behavioral assessment can no longer be simply summarized. Indeed, it is also no longer valid to identify behavioral assessment by reference to what it is not. It has been customary when describing behavioral assessment to refer to the various ways in which it differs from traditional psychometric approaches. Because this has been discussed at length elsewhere (Barrios, 1988; Barrios & Hartmann, 1986; Cone, 1988), only the major differences will be mentioned. An essential difference was neatly encapsulated by Goldfried's (1977) distinction between behavior as "sign or sample." Psychometric approaches are nomothetic and attempt to infer the presence of stable psychological constructs or traits upon the basis of one or more questionnaire responses. Behavior is, therefore, construed as being relatively stable across time and place. Hence, the psychometric assessment via the use of questionnaire or other psychometric variables (i.e., may include psychophysiological measures) is required as a *sign* or indicator of a particular stable behavioral predisposition, trait or personality. From a clinical perspective, the function of such assessment is to assist the diagnosis, classification, etiology, and prognostication of the problem condition (Barrios, 1988).

Several important differences between these two models, therefore, may be identified. The traditional psychometric approach relies on nomothetic methods, makes inferences about stable trait constructs, and is related to treatment allocation via a clinical inferential process of diagnosis and formulation. In contrast, the behavioral approach stresses idiographic methods, emphasizes the direct measurement of a *sample* of behavior, assumes situational specificity, and is intimately associated with the selection and monitoring of interventions. However, it can be argued that these classical distinctions between the two models may no longer strictly apply. Indeed, several authors have attempted a raprochement between them. For example, Cone (1986, 1988) argues that behavioral assessments may be generally described via *32* different approaches. This is portrayed by a 3-D cube in which the facets include: idiographic versus nomothetic, behavior versus trait, interaction versus noninteraction with situation, intrasubject versus intersubject sources of variation, and inductive versus deductive scientific approaches. Clearly, traditional and strict behavioral assessment models comprise only a minority of the 32 possible combinations. Similarly, the person-situation debate has also influenced contemporary behavioral assessment in the direction of interactionalism (cf. McFall & McDonel, 1986). Hence, organismic factors with possible trait-like characteristics such as biological predispositions, prior learning history, and basic behavioral repertoires (Staats, 1986) may, in conjunction with situational variables, determine behavioral outcomes.

Rationales for Inclusion of Psychophysiology within Behavioral Assessment

It is clear from the previous section that the scope of behavioral assessment can be considered to have widened considerably over the last 25 years. It is interesting to note that in this time, psychophysiological applications have also become more widespread. Moreover, both activities have essentially demonstrated an empirical bias leading to criticisms either in terms of the gap between behavioral research and theory (McFall, 1977; Pierce & Epling, 1980) or the relative atheoretical status of psychophysiology (Gale, 1989). The purpose of this section is to investigate how these two diverse approaches to clinical assessment may be integrated and identify the rationales for their combined application.

Clinical Psychophysiology and Psychopathology

Before attempting to integrate psychophysiology into behavioral assessment, it is necessary to review its general contribution to psychopathology. Turpin (1989b) identified three basic sets of rationales. First, many theories of psychopathology are founded upon experimental research in both psychology and psychophysiology. Hence, psychophysiological measures have been employed to assess the contribution to psychopathology of the following constructs: personality, arousal, stress, emotion, conditioning, information processing, and others. Second, traditional psychiatric research has employed psychophysiological measures to aid discrimination, classification, and diagnosis of psychopathological conditions. Third, psychophysiological measures have been incorporated into clinical assessments and treatments. Clearly, it is the latter two rationales that will principally concern us here. However, it should be stressed that the former rationale concerning psychophysiological/psychological models of psychopathology should not be overlooked or detached from diagnostic or clinical applications. Indeed, the relationship between theory and assessment will be reviewed in the last section of this chapter.

Psychophysiological Approaches to Behavioral Assessment and Treatment

Several different rationales for the application of psychophysiological techniques may be identified (e.g., Haynes et al., 1989; Nay, 1979; Ray & Raczynski, 1981; Turpin, 1989b). Basically, they range from direct applications whereby a target problem has strict physiological referents, as may be the case in many areas of behavioral medicine, to more indirect approaches whereby psychological constructs are inferred on the basis of presumed physiological indices or correlates. The approach is also synonymous with the view that physiological behaviors may also be treated as responses in their own right and presumably may be associated with particular response classes. As such they may have a role to play in the formation of *"behavioral constructs,"* which seek to emphasize interresponse structures and the common behavioral mechanisms presumed to underlie them (cf. Evans, 1986). The selection of physiological measures relative to other responses might be determined either on theoretical grounds or practical considerations. The latter refer to the common belief that physiological measures relative to other measures (e.g., self-report questionnaires) *might* be considered to be objective, sensitive and continuous (Levenson, 1983).

Each of these rationales will be reviewed in the context of the common functions and methods of behavioral assessment. The first application concerns the identification of the target problem that constitutes the basis of initial or pretreatment assessment. In specifying targets and their functional relationships, two distinct areas for psychophysiological assessment may be identified. This is best illustrated by Goldfried and Sprafkin's SORC model. Psychophysiological measures may be adopted either as indices of "O" (organismic/biological predispositions) or as components of "R" (the behavioral response). The former approach will be dealt with later in this section. As stated earlier, physiological measures may be associated with behavioral responses in several ways. Haynes et al. (1989) distinguish between physiological components which constitute the *primary* defining characteristics of the behavioral dysfunction and multiple component approaches as represented by the triple-response approach. In the case of primary dysfunction, they suggest that various physiological behavioral referents can be identified and include: chronic dysfunction (e.g., late stages of hypertension), excessive reactivity (e.g., early stages of hypertension), conditional response (e.g., post-traumatic stress responses), delayed post-stress recovery, and response nonoccurrence (e.g., sexual impotence).

The multiple-component approach described by Haynes et al. (1989) concerns the *secondary* derivation of physiological measures that are not directly related to the behavioral dysfunction but derive from the "three systems" approach advocated by Lang (1971). Faced by the failure to observe simple indicant relationships between physiological and psychological measures (i.e., substitutive measures, to use Lacey's [1959] term), Lang (1971, p. 105) suggested that the emotional response could be viewed as:

> A complex of three measurable systems: verbal-cognitive, overt-motor and physiological (autonomically innervated organs and tonic muscle activity). All systems are modulated by neural centers within the brain, but inter-correlations between their outputs are surprisingly low. From an empirical point of view, the behaviors are partially independent. Nevertheless, these systems are also highly interactive and appear to mutually augment, sustain, or attenuate each other in ways that we are just beginning to understand.

It is important to emphasize that Lang's original account stressed three different neurally mediated systems, each with measurable behavioral outputs, which although empirically partially independent, reflected the interactional nature of the three systems from which they were derived. This working model of emotional response has been developed in several different ways. From a theoretical perspective it has provided the basis for Lang's own Bioinformational Theory of emotional behavior (Lang, 1977, 1979, 1985, 1988). In regards to assessment, it has been developed into a pragmatic taxonomic approach to response selection whereby the three systems have come to represent three independent response modes (Ciminero, 1986; Nay, 1979; Nelson & Hayes, 1981) requiring measurement across a range of emotional behaviors (i.e., not just pertaining to anxiety). With respect to clinical interventions, it has been employed as an explanatory concept (i.e., desynchrony) linking patterns of pretreatment responses to posttreatment outcomes (Rachman & Hodgson, 1974). Accordingly, the notion of "triple response modes" has provided both a structure and a rationale for the inclusion of psychophysiological measures.

Unfortunately, it has also thrown up a series of related issues concerning the "synchrony-desynchrony" problem (e.g., Cone, 1979, 1986; Evans, 1986; Haynes & Wilson, 1979; Hollandsworth, 1986; Hugdahl, 1981). Because these matters will be discussed later in this chapter, they will not be discussed fully here. However, in the context of models of assessment, a particular issue involving the ambiguity that surrounds the identity and consequent measurement of these three modes needs to be addressed. As discussed by Cone (1979) and Evans (1986), there is confusion between the content area said to be associated with each of Lang's proposed systems and methods of measurement. For example, according to Cone (1979), within the physiological domain, sweating might be measured either in terms of direct observation (e.g., he or she is perspiring) or via self-report (e.g., I often perspire). Both these methods can be contrasted to the traditional physiological method of assessment that would employ electrophysiological techniques (e.g., skin conductance measurement). Similarly, Barrios (1988) also provides examples of physiological content area measured using interviews, self-report and self-observation. It becomes clear that the construct system, mode and content area, although prefixed by the same term (i.e., physiological) may come to mean different things. Accordingly, the argument for representing the "physiological mode" of responding does not necessarily lead to the adoption of psychophysiological techniques but may also advocate the use of nonpsychophysiological methods such as direct observation and various autonomic perception questionnaires (Heimberg, Gansler, & Dodge, 1987; Mandler, Mandler, & Uviller, 1958).

Despite these short-comings, the "three system" approach has provided an important impetus for the application of psychophysiology to behavioral assessment. In addition to facilitating the identification of target problems and their subsequent measures, it has also contributed towards the selection of treatment strategies. For example, the distinction between cognitive versus somatic responders on the basis of physiological reactivity is claimed to optimize behavioral outcomes associated with a range of different interventions which have generally been developed to tackle the same category of target problems. Examples of this approach include treatment selection in relation to social phobia (Ost, Jerremalm, & Johansson, 1981), and agoraphobia (Ost, Jerremalm, & Jansson, 1984).

A logical consequence of the inclusion of physiological variables for either primary or secondary assessment of behavioral variables is their subsequent adoption as measures to monitor treatment progress or outcomes. For primary physiological dysfunctions, normalized physiological end-points are a desirable clinical outcome. Hence, it is common to measure variables such as blood pressure and skin temperature in relation to behavioral interventions for hypertension and Raynaud's disease, respectively (Haynes & Gannon, 1981; see also chapter 19). For secondary physiological dysfunctions, physiological variables may also be employed as outcome measures. However, whether these measures are adopted as criterion variables to assess the significance of clinical change is less certain. For example, several large scale outcome studies of agoraphobia have tended to ascribe more importance to behavioral and self-support changes than for physiological changes such as heart rate (cf. Himadi, Boice, & Barlow, 1986). The selection of outcome measures in order to assess the overall impact of the intervention raises a further problem with the "triple response" approach. As Peterson (1984) has pointed out, the arbitrary selection of outcome measures may lead to interpretative problems.

Finally, psychophysiological variables may be adopted as process measures in order to investigate the relationship between the application of intervention and the final clinical outcome (Haynes et al., 1989; Turpin, 1989b). This approach is based on a proposed relationship between intervention related changes in physiological functioning and the nature of the outcome response. In the case of primary uses of psychophysiological measures previously discussed, their status as process measures is self-evident when the focus of a particular intervention is to directly modify the physiological dysfunction. Hence, monitoring the effects of relaxation training or various biofeedback interventions on blood pressure, and its relationship to outcome as indicated by a variety of measures such as blood pressure, medication, and clinic appointments would be an example of a process physiological measure. In the case of the secondary use of physiological measures in conjunction with a "triple response mode" approach to outcome evaluation, particular interventions (e.g., relaxation) may have desired physiological end-points. Once again, physiological process measures may be important for the interpretation of treatment outcomes.

Finally, some interventions for specific disorders are based on the assumption that inferred psychophysiological constructs such as "arousal" may mediate dysfunctional states. Accordingly, desired clinical outcomes might be achieved by using interventions specifically targeted at reducing such states. For example, elevated physiological arousal has been implicated in several disorders such as insomnia (Nicassio & Buchanan, 1981), and asthma (Erskine-Millis & Schonell, 1981), and also in arousal-relapse models of schizophrenic symptoms (Dawson, Nuechterlein, & Lieberman, 1984; Turpin, Tarrier, & Sturgeon, 1988). Psychophysiological process measures, therefore, may provide an invaluable means of assessing the mediational processes said to underlie the use of relaxation training in these conditions (cf. Borkovec, Johnson, & Bloch, 1984).

In discussing physiological process measures, it is apparent that several behavioral interventions are based upon the assumption of modifying physiological states. These include various forms of relaxation training, biofeedback, rebreathing training, and exercise training (Haynes et al., 1989; Steptoe, 1989; Turpin, 1989b). Because the evaluation of psychophysiologically based treatments is the focus of Chapter 19, the topic will not be discussed further.

In summary, various specific rationales may be identified for incorporating psychophysiological measures into behavioral assessment. From a theoretical perspective, all stages of behavioral assessment (i.e., target specification, treatment selection, outcome and process measurement) may *potentially* benefit from their application. However, it should be stressed that in practice psychophysiological measures have been underemployed (cf. Hayes & Nelson, 1986).

Psychophysiological Approaches to Psychometric Assessment

Given the recently perceived relevance of psychometric approaches to behavioral assessment (Cone, 1977, 1986, 1988; Linehan, 1980), it will be necessary to briefly discuss how psychophysiological measures have been adopted as psychometric indices in order to infer stable psychological constructs or traits. Three distinct rationales are identified (cf. Turpin, 1989b).

First, psychophysiological measures have been adopted as indices of biological substrates said to determine various personality characteristics. Examples of this approach include Soviet studies of the personality dimension "strength of nervous system" (e.g., Nebylitsyn & Gray, 1972), psychophysiological studies of Eysenck's personality theory (Claridge, 1967, 1985; Eysenck, 1967), and earlier studies of a proposed psychophysiological trait, Autonomic Balance (Wenger, 1941). Several recent reviews of the application of psychophysiology to personality have been undertaken (Gale & Edwards, 1986; Levenson, 1983).

The second, and perhaps, the major impetus for psychometric approaches has been the search for more objective biological diagnostic markers in psychiatry. Psychiatric diagnosis has been fraught by numerous methodological issues including poorly operationalized criteria and assessment techniques, poor interobserver reliability, limited construct and predictive validity (Morey, Skinner, & Blashfield, 1986). Recognition of these problems has resulted both in attempts to refine the diagnostic process, and the search for so-called "objective indices" of psychophysiological states (Usdin & Hanin, 1982). Psychophysiological measures have been advocated as potential diagnostic markers either as correlates of some underlying biological dysfunction or as objective indicators of psychological dysfunction. The former approach is exemplified by research on possible arousal dysfunctions in anxiety disorders (Lader, 1975). A more recent example is the adoption of electrodermal measures as possible markers of cholinergic dysfunction in affective states (e.g., Thorell, Kjellman, d'Elia, & Kagedal, 1988; Ward & Doerr, 1986). These applications tend toward the use of psychophysiological measures as pathophysiological markers and may be seen as synonymous with other biological markers associated with biological psychiatry. However, one important characteristic of psychophysiological techniques is that they are generally noninvasive.

Psychophysiological measures may also be employed as indices of psychological dysfunction associated with the disorder in question. An obvious example, which has been discussed at length in the previous section, is the use of autonomic measures in conjunction with self-report and behavioral ratings to assess anxiety (Lang, 1968; Rachman & Hodgson, 1974). Similarly, psychophysiological measures have frequently been adopted as correlates of attentional dysfunction in schizophrenia (Venables & Bernstein, 1983; Zahn, 1986).

Before examining the use of psychophysiological markers as discriminative indices, a distinction should be made between the sensitivity and specificity of a marker. Sensitivity refers to the likelihood that the marker will identify specific disorders (i.e., the "hit rate"), whereas specificity concerns the ratio of specific cases identified versus nonrelated cases (i.e., the false alarm rate). Hence, elevated electrodermal activity may be reliably associated with a specific disorder but also evident in numerous other unrelated conditions. This would be an example of high sensitivity but low specificity. With respect to diagnostic discrimination, psychophysiological markers should be both highly sensitive and specific. Low specificity may indicate the presence of some common and hence nonspecific antecedent or consequence of psychopathological dysfunction, such as psychosocial stressors, nonspecific affective changes or psychological discomfort.

Psychophysiological markers may be either employed to discriminate across populations or within populations (Turpin, 1989b). Traditional diagnostic approaches have tended to focus on the former. A classic example is Lader's use of electrodermal habituation rates in order to discriminate between different anxiety disorders (Lader, 1967; Lader & Wing, 1966; Noble & Lader, 1971, 1972). Similar attempts to discriminate people diagnosed as schizophrenic on the basis of "arousal" have fared successfully (e.g., Bernstein, 1967; Depue & Fowles, 1973; Gruzelier & Venables, 1975; Ohman, 1981b). Numerous theoretical and methodological considerations have been invoked to explain the limited utility of psychophysiological assessment to discriminate *between* diagnostic groups or normal controls (Iacono & Ficken, 1989; Turpin, 1989b; Zahn, 1986). Only when the disorder can be characterized *primarily* in terms of physiological dysfunction (e.g., sleep disorders, sexual dysfunction, hypertension) can psychophysiological measures have a *central* role to play in diagnosis. However, the use of psychophysiological diagnostic measures in "primary" dysfunctions such as sexual disorders has not gone uncriticized (Freund & Blanchard, 1989; Nagayama Hall, Proctor, & Nelson, 1988).

Recent psychiatric applications of psychophysiological measures have been directed towards the "subtype" problem within single diagnostic categories. Essentially, three main purposes underlying these applications may be identified: subgroup classification, determination of prognosis, and the prediction of response to treatment. These approaches have been discussed at length elsewhere (Turpin, 1989b) but may be illustrated with respect to schizophrenia. Given the proposed heterogeneity of "the schizophrenias," it is not surprising to observe that clinical subtypes (i.e., good/poor premorbid, acute/chronic, paranoid/nonparanoid) have been claimed to demonstrate psychophysiological differentiation. Similarly, subgroups of people diagnosed schizophrenic may be derived using psychophysiological variables such as electrodermal "responding" or "nonresponding" and can be shown to have different symptom profiles (cf. Venables & Bernstein, 1983). Perhaps of greater interest to behavior therapists, is the possibility that psychophysiological subgroups may demonstrate differential clinical outcomes. For example, slow electrodermal habituation has been associated with slow clinical improvement, electrodermal nonresponding with poorer social outcome and elevated nonspecific electrodermal activity in acutely ill patients with subsequent relapse (cf. Turpin et al., 1988; Turpin, 1989b).

Finally, the third basis for the psychometric use of psychophysiological variables concerns the recent formulation of vulnerability models of psychiatric disorders. These models represent a radical departure from the biomedical disease model that has been the traditional basis for psychiatric research and theory. In some respects, they bear important parallels with contemporary concerns that have attempted to broaden the scope of behavioral assessment. First, they have abdicated total biological determinism in favor of a more eclectic biopsychosocial perspective (Engel, 1977; Ohman, 1981a; Turpin, 1989b but also see Armstrong, 1987; Turpin & Lader, 1986; Turpin et al., 1988; Van Pragg, 1981). For example, Zubin and Spring (1977) identified a variety of biological, social and psychological factors that may be causally related to predispositions for schizophrenia and the subsequent precipitation of schizophrenic episodes. Second, psychiatric disorders are no longer viewed as solely psychophysiological traits which are expressed as disease or syndrome entities. Instead, an *interactional* model is formulated whereby trait-like predispositions or vulnerability are expressed as a function of the interaction with the environment. Hence, vulnerability models may provide a set of theoretical frameworks that might incorporate the recent rapprochement of the situation-person debate within behavioral assessment. In addition, given the biopsychosocial emphasis of vulnerability models, it has been argued that psychophysiological measures may provide noninvasive and theoretically relevant methods in order to assess their impact (Turpin et al., 1988). The use of psychophysiological measures as vulnerability and episode markers in schizophrenia has been discussed at length elsewhere (Dawson et al., 1984; Nuechterlein & Dawson, 1984; Turpin et al., 1988; Turpin, 1989b).

In summary, although behavioral assessment has traditionally distanced itself from psychometric approaches, several parallels may be drawn between the rationales for adopting psychophysiological measures within both these paradigms.

CONTRIBUTION OF PSYCHOPHYSIOLOGY TO BEHAVIORAL ASSESSMENT

Techniques

The successful application of psychophysiology to behavioral assessment requires both knowledge and experience of psychophysiological techniques and paradigms. The purpose of this section is to provide an overview of the methods available. A more detailed discussion of these issues is to be found elsewhere (Turpin, 1989b). Because a comprehensive literature on psychophysiological methodology (Coles, Donchin, & Porges, 1986; Greenfield & Sternbach, 1972; Martin & Venables, 1980) already exists, details of instrumentation and procedures will not be discussed in any great depth. Readers unfamiliar with psychophysiological methods might want to approach either general introductory psychophysiological texts (e.g., Andreassi, 1980; Grings & Dawson, 1978; Stern, Ray, & Davis, 1980) or texts and review articles written specifically for applications of psychophysiology to clinical practice (Cacioppo, Petty, & Marshall-Goodell, 1985; Feuerstein, Labbe, & Kuczmierczyk, 1986; Haynes & Wilson, 1979, Haynes et al., 1989; Hollandsworth, 1986; Kallman & Feuerstein, 1986; Lader, 1975; Lang, 1971; Ray & Raczynski, 1981; Sturgis & Arena, 1984; Sturgis & Gramling, 1988; Turpin, 1989a; Van Praag, Lader, Rafaelsen, & Sacher, 1980; Williamson, Waters, and Hawkins, 1986) and biofeedback (Andrasik & Blanchard, 1983; Blanchard & Epstein, 1978; Reed, Katkin, & Goldband, 1986). General aspects of electronic instrumentation and electrical safety have also been covered elsewhere (Pope, 1978; Rugh, Gable, & Lemke, 1986).

Selection of Measures

Perhaps the most daunting task facing the novice investigator is the choice of a psychophysiological measure or measures (see Turpin, 1989b). This will be governed by several factors. Initial selection will depend upon the kind of rationale underlying the decision to adopt a psychophysiological approach. As discussed in the previous section, choice of measure might result from the observation of some clinically relevant physiological behavior (e.g., blood pressure in hypertension), or via a psychophysiological index of some psychological construct, such as anxiety or attention.

A second factor concerns the physiological context in which the measurement is to be made. It can be argued that the variance attributed to psychophysiological as opposed to physiological influences may be relatively small. Hence, the choice of measures will depend upon identifying other sources of physiological influence that may well determine the sensitivity of the chosen index (see Ohman, 1987; Turpin, 1989b). The need to examine psychophysiological indices within a physiological context should not be oversimplified or understated (Schwartz, 1978).

Practical or clinical considerations may also dictate the adoption of a particular measure (Turpin, 1989b). This will largely depend upon the instrumentation and transducer required for its measurement, together with the nature of the paradigms to be studied. The susceptibility of different measures to movement artifacts will also help determine the choice of measure.

Finally, the scale and the time course of the psychophysiological index to be assessed requires careful consideration. It is common for several different measures to be derived from a single channel of physiological activity. For example, skin conductance activity upon analysis may yield measures of response amplitude, response frequency, nonspecific response frequency and level (Martin & Venables, 1980). These derived measures may all have different functional relationships with the psychological constructs being assessed. Similarly, response derivation is also determined by the time course of events. Heart rate measures can either be obtained as short-term event-locked phasic changes or long-term time-locked tonic changes (Turpin, 1985a). In addition, tonic activity may be represented as changes in the mean and variance of the cardiac data. These different forms of derived measure should not be used interchangeably because they are said to reflect different psychophysiological processes. Similarly, long-term psychobiological changes might be better represented using biochemical as opposed to electrophysiological indices (Fredrickson, 1989; Steptoe, 1987).

Types of Measures

There is a wide range of measures that can be described as constituting a psychophysiological data base and may be classified in a number of ways. First, they may be grouped according to the mode of measurement employed. This would result in invasive and noninvasive electrophysiological measures, biochemical measures, motoric measures (including observed overt behaviors), and self-report measures. Second, measures might be classified according to physiological dimensions underlying either the function or target organ presumed to be under investigation. For example, cardiovascular status might be considered both in terms of cardiac output from the heart and the peripheral resistance encountered within the circulation (Siddle & Turpin, 1980). These physiological variables can in turn be related to a variety of indices including heart rate, left ventricular performance, measures of cardiac impedance, peripheral blood flow, and pulse volume. In addition to functional physiological distinctions, measures may also be classified according to assumed anatomical differences. Hence, psychophysiological measures are frequently subdivided according to central or electrocortical measures on the one hand, and autonomic or peripheral measures on the other. The latter are often further subcategorized into sympathetic and parasympathetic measures.

Finally, psychophysiological indices may be classified with respect to the nature of their presumed psychological significance. For example, psychophysiological indices of attention might include various cortical measures, together with peripheral autonomic measures (see Coles et al., 1986). These latter measures are frequently said to be components of an orienting reflex (Turpin, 1983a). However, although several different measures are said to be associated with attentional processes, examination of the psychophysiological literature strongly suggests that different measures should not be employed interchangeably. For example, orienting is said to be indexed by a number of peripheral autonomic changes including heart rate deceleration, increased skin conductance, and peripheral vaso-constriction. However, even within a simple habituation paradigm consisting of the repetition of an auditory stimulus, different measures will display different response habituation rates (Turpin, 1983a). The use of only a single measure, particularly in the absence of other behavioral data, may lead to erroneous conclusions concerning the psychophysiological process being studied (Turpin, 1986).

Designs and Paradigms

Psychophysiological research has tended to be rooted firmly in the traditions of group designs and accompanying analysis of variance or multivariate statistical procedures. Although this approach has been fruitful for traditional psychophysiological studies, clinical applications necessitate a greater degree of flexibility as regards type of design. In particular, single-case designs (Barlow & Hersen, 1984; Kratochwill, 1978) are probably underrepresented in clinical psychophysiological research. It is likely that the traditional preoccupation with group comparison designs, together with an overcautious expectation of inter- and intrameasure variability, has contributed to the neglect of those potentially useful procedures.

Indeed, several authors have reiterated the potential advantages of single-case methodology in relation to biofeedback (Bandeira, Bouchard & Granger, 1982; Barlow, Blanchard, Hayes, & Epstein, 1977). These include the ability to examine individual versus group mean data, the examination of clinical versus statistical significance, the detailed examination of individual variability and the ethical advantages of single-case innovative procedures. In addition, single-case studies have facilitated the use of psychophysiological procedures to study relatively rare clinical phenomena such as Tourette Syndrome (Surwillo, Shafii, & Barrett, 1978; Turpin & Powell, 1984). Indeed, the continuous nature of psychophysiological measurement makes it an ideal candidate for the adoption of single-case methodology.

Moreover, single-case methodology may provide a means of establishing the *clinical utility* of psychophysiological applications to behavioral assessment (cf. Hayes et al., 1986). In selecting designs for psychophysiological research, the merits of single-case designs should, therefore, also be borne in mind, together with the traditional advantages of comparison group protocols (cf. Kazdin, 1980). Fortunately, there is an increasing amount of literature that has used single-case methodology in relation to blood-injury phobia (e.g., Kozak & Miller, 1985), schizophrenic relapse and expressed emotion (Tarrier & Barrowclough, 1984), mania (Hemsley & Philips, 1975) and depression (Blackburn & Bonham, 1980).

In addition to the traditional limitations of group designs, psychophysiological research has tended to be strongly paradigm-bound. It is important, therefore, to assess how these designs may be adapted for clinical research. The majority of studies have examined differences between clinical populations using existing paradigms such as classical conditioning, orienting and habituation, reaction time, vigilance and signal detection, and recently more complex cognitive tasks such as sentence completion and dichotic listening procedures. Essentially the tasks are relatively simple and require little active or overt participation by the subject so as to allow artifact free collection of psychophysiological data.

Although these paradigms may be of theoretical importance, their divergence from the behavioral assessment of clinical problems should be recognized. Indeed, in the context of individual differences, Gale and Edwards (1986, p. 497) have described many traditional psychophysiological paradigms as " . . . nontasks (i.e., sitting doing nothing); we believe that human subjects in a laboratory do not do or think about nothing, and that experimenters who believe the opposite are misleading themselves." It is likely that the issue of stimulus control is even more apposite when subjects may be acutely psychologically disturbed and preoccupied with obsessional ruminations, hallucinations, delusions, and so forth.

The apparently simple nature of the paradigms used may also lead to the assumption of stimulus equivalence across subjects and conditions as regards task difficulty and requirements. Again this would appear to be an oversimplification. Even the nature of the instructions to "sit and listen/attend" given within a simple habituation task may significantly affect the experimental outcome (Iacono & Lykken, 1979). As in all psychophysiological research, clinical applications require close scrutiny of the experimenter's assumptions and the frequent use of appropriate manipulation checks.

Studies that attempt to examine clinical phenomena per se confront two major problems. The first concerns the restricted nature of the psychophysiology laboratory and the range of activities that can be measured within a space-limited environment and relatively free of movement artifacts (Turpin, 1988). The second problem concerns the availability of clinical populations and access to psychophysiological laboratories. Many laboratories are located away from hospitals and clinics, and present difficulties of enabling clinically distressed subjects to travel to and participate in psychophysiological studies. It is not surprising, therefore, that much clinical psychophysiological research has been essentially of an analogue nature. Either analogue subjects, in the form of so-called "anxious, depressed or phobic" undergraduates, or analogue situations, such as role play or behavioral avoidance tests (cf. Haynes & Wilson, 1979), or sometimes subjects from both groups have been used. Although analogue research may overcome problems due to access to client populations and the need for a limited and restricted psychophysiological environment, problems of validity ensue. Researchers interested in analogue studies should be mindful of the various critiques and recommendations published concerning the validity of this approach (Borkovec & Rachman, 1979; Haynes & Wilson, 1979; Nay, 1986). Nevertheless, analogue studies have enabled the potential extension of psychophysiological hypotheses (e.g., Kartsounis & Turpin, 1987; Ohman, 1981a) to encompass clinical phenomena not easily assessed within the laboratory. Accordingly, they have an important role in clinical psychophysiological research, so long as their findings are treated cautiously and the generalizability to true clinical situations and populations tested.

A final category of paradigm concerns the combined collection of behavioral and psychophysiological data within an appropriate clinic or home environment. This approach requires the use of either portable or ambulatory psychophysiological equipment. The latter approach is discussed in Chapter 19 (see also Turpin, 1985b; Turpin, 1988). Regarding clinic settings, psychophysiological assessments obtained under "resting" or nondysfunctional conditions are probably of limited value (cf. Philips, 1980). Indeed, the use of specific, stressful conditions in order to assess psychophysiological reactivity has been particularly emphasized with respect to behavioral medicine (Steptoe, 1980). If the dysfunctional behavior is infrequent or inappropriate within the clinical setting, situational analogues need to be considered. The alternative is the collection of psychophysiological data in naturalistic settings during ongoing behavior and social interaction, and without the strict "stimulus control" of the psychophysiological laboratory. Although this approach is almost antithetical to the usually well-controlled psychophysiological study, social interactional studies are producing pertinent clinical data (e.g., Levenson & Gottman, 1983; Tarrier, Vaughn, Lader, & Leff, 1978; Turpin, 1983b; Turpin et al., 1988). Social interaction per se would also appear to produce pronounced psychophysiological activation (e.g., Linden, 1987; Lynch, Thomas, Paskewitz, Malinow, & Long, 1982) which would suggest that the new discipline of social psychophysiology (Cacioppo & Petty, 1983) may make important contributions to future research.

Specific Applications

It is not the intention of this chapter to provide an exhaustive review of the applications of psychophysiology to behavior therapy. Numerous authors have recently undertaken this task (e.g., Haynes et al., 1989; Hollandsworth, 1986; Kallman & Feuerstein, 1986; Sturgis & Arena, 1984; Sturgis & Gramling, 1988; Turpin, 1989a). The range of applications can be appreciated by reference to Table 18-1 which has been adapted from Haynes et al. (1989). The table shows psychophysiological measures have been applied to most types of behavioral disorders. The most commonly adopted tend to be, in order of popularity, autonomic (heart rate, peripheral pulse, electrodermal activity), electromyographic, biochemical, and electrocortical measures. Further details concerning these specific applications are provided by Haynes et al. (1989).

EVALUATION AND LIMITATIONS OF PSYCHOPHYSIOLOGICAL MEASURES

Criteria for the Evaluation of Behavioral Assessment

The purpose of this chapter is to provide a critical overview as to how psychophysiological techniques may be applied to behavioral assessment. So far, we have identified the various rationales for employing these methods to *different* models of behavioral assessment, together with a description of some common psychophysiological techniques. Accordingly, it needs to be recognized that in evaluating these applications, different criteria are required for the various models of behavioral assessment to be examined. It is important, therefore, to identify the appropriate criteria with which the quality of different models of behavioral assessment can be assessed. The use of a single criterion such as reliability or validity cannot usefully be applied in order to assess the contribution of psychophysiological measures. The complexity of assessment evaluation is probably best illustrated by a quotation from Hayes, Nelson, and Jarrett (1986, p. 493): "Generic questions about accuracy, reliability, or validity of behavioral assessment techniques are probably meaningless. Assessment data vary, depending on the exact circumstances in which the assessment device is used."

Table 18-1. Representative Psychophysiological Measures in Behavior Therapy

BEHAVIOR DISORDER	MEASURES
Alcoholism	autonomic measures, BA, BAC
Anger	HR
Anxiety disorders	HR, SC, EMG
Asthma	PEFR, TRR, FEV
Convulsive disorders	SMR
Depression	EMG, HR
Diabetes	blood glucose
Eating disorders	calorimetry, RMR, cholesterol, triglycerides
Hypertension	PTT, BP, HR, BVP
Insomnia	EEG, EMG, EOG, HR
Migraine headache	peripheral and cephalic BVPA
Muscle contraction headache	frontal EMG, neck EMG, cephalic BVPA
Post-traumatic stress disorder	HR, SC, cortisol, catecholamines
Raynaud's disease	peripheral BVPA and temperature
Sexual dysfunctions (male)	penile circumference and volume
Sexual dysfunctions (female)	vaginal BVP and BVPA, labial temperature
Sexual disorders	penile volume and circumference
Smoking	CO, SCN, CH, HR
Spasmodic torticollis	EMG
Stuttering	masseter EMG
Tachycardia, premature ventricular contractions	HR and variability
Ulcers	EGG, gastric pH

Note: This list is not fully inclusive of all appropriate measures for all disorders. BA: blood acetaldehyde, BAC: blood alcohol concentration, BP: blood pressure, BVP: blood volume pulse, BVPA: blood volume pulse amplitude, CH: carboxyhemoglobin, CO: carbon monoxide, EEG: electroencephalogram, EGG: electrogastrogram, EMG: electromyogram, EOG: electro-oculogram, FEV: forced expiratory volume, HR: heart rate, SC: skin conductance, SCN: serum thiocynate, SMR: sensory motor rhythm, TRR: total respiratory resistance. (Modified from Table 1, "*Psychophysiological Assessment in Behavior Therapy*" by Haynes et al., 1989. In G. Turpin (Ed.), *Handbook of Clinical Psychophysiology*. New York: John Wiley & Sons. Copyright 1989 by John Wiley & Sons. Reprinted by permission.

The evaluation of different models of assessment have been discussed at length by numerous authors (Barrios, 1988; Barrios & Hartmann, 1986; Cone, 1977, 1986, 1988; Hayes et al., 1986). It would appear that separate sets of criteria should be adopted for different models. Typically, the classical criteria of psychometrics such as standardization, reliability, and validity have been rejected by some authors as inappropriate for behavioral analysis (cf. Hayes et al., 1986). If behavior *as observed,* is considered as a sample of the individual's behavioral repertoire, and that its specific characteristics are determined by the situation, consistency of behavior is not predicted if situations and environmental events are themselves considered to vary. Hence, reliability that essentially is a measure of the consistency of behavior (i.e., across different times, items or observers) is an appropriate criterion. From a psychometric perspective, the error implied by lack of consistency of behavior, is the central focus of functional analysis for the strict behavioral approach. Similarly, if behavior is a sample and not an inferred sign, then questions of validity can also be argued to be inappropriate. However, this disregard for psychometrics has been argued by some (Cone, 1977; Goldfried, 1977) to have resulted in an anarchic state of affairs whereby nonstandardized and imperfect behavioral measures have proliferated resulting in equivocal research findings and a demonstrable lack of differentiation between different interventions.

Various solutions to the choice of appropriate evaluation criteria have been suggested. Barrios (1988) identifies four main approaches that include the traditional psychometric model, generalizability models, accuracy models, and the treatment utility model. The question of nomothetic versus idiographic approaches has also been recently re-examined in relation to behavioral assessment evaluation (Cone, 1988; Hayes et al., 1986). As Cone has emphasized, different criteria need to be derived for idiographic approaches, because psychometric concepts such as reliability and validity have been nomothetically obtained and cannot easily be applied to the single-case methodology. Accordingly, an evaluation of psychophysiological assessment requires that distinctions between different measurement models be explicitly taken into account.

Psychometric Approaches and Group Data

If psychophysiological assessments are to be employed in order to discriminate between groups of subjects, assess for change across a group of subjects over time, or to provide the basis upon which future predictions are to be made, psychophysiological measures should be temporally stable and demonstrate reasonable test-retest reliability across time. Despite early attempts to assess psychophysiological reliability (e.g., Lacey & Lacey, 1962), contemporary psychophysiology has tended to neglect this important area of assessment. Several recently conducted studies (Arena, Blanchard, Andrasik, Cotch, & Myers, 1983; Faulstich et al., 1986; Waters, Williamson, Bernard, Blouin, & Faulstich, 1987) have themselves arrived at equivocal findings concerning the stability of certain psychophysiological measures. It is likely that several measures may be susceptible to specific temporal effects whereby consistency is reduced due to fatigue, habituation, and adaptation to the laboratory environment (cf. Eccles, Marshall, & Barbaree, 1988). In addition, psychophysiological measures frequently give rise to "first-time testing" effects whereby behavior recorded at subsequent sessions is inconsistent with the initial assessment (Whitsett, Robinson, & Kaplan, 1987). These observations would imply that psychophysiological assessments, especially if conducted within laboratory situations, frequently demonstrate significant problems of measurement reactivity (Turpin, 1988, 1989b).

The presence of variations in the temporal consistency of psychophysiological measures suggests that these presumed "objective" measures may be associated with various forms of error. Indeed, reference to most introductory chapters on psychophysiological assessment (e.g., Sturgis & Arena, 1984; Sturgis & Gramling, 1988) clearly identifies the fallacy of considering psychophysiological measures as unbiased and objective indicators of behavior in their own right. Several aspects of the experimental situation need to be considered. First, the personal characteristics of the experimenter (Cacioppo et al., 1985; Gale & Baker, 1981) and therapist (Sturgis & Arena, 1984) may influence the psychophysiological assessment. Second, important subject variables such as age, sex, race, drug abuse (tobacco, alcohol, caffeine, etc.), menstrual cycle, and physical fitness all have profound effects upon physiological parameters (Martin & Venables, 1980; Sturgis & Arena, 1984). Finally, environmental (temperature and humidity), seasonal and diurnal fluctuations may also contribute to systematic errors of measurement.

The above sources of error may also affect situational consistency. Variations in adaptation periods (Hastrup, 1986; Linden & McEachern, 1985), baseline periods (Whitsett et al., 1987), experimental tasks

(Faulstich et al., 1986), and laboratory and field comparisons (McKinney et al., 1985), all strongly suggest a high degree of situational specificity for psychophysiological assessments. Indeed, the presumed situational specificity of psychophysiological measures has been a major rationale for their application to behavioral assessment. However, situational specificity may also affect the determination of temporal specificity if allowances for differences in situational circumstances are not controlled for (cf. Strosahl & Linehan, 1986). This has prompted two discrete approaches to the problems of temporal and situational consistency. The first of these has relied upon the use of standardization whereby *particular* situations (tasks or baselines) are used to assess "resting" and "reactive" values of psychophysiological variables with respect to time. Studies that have examined intertask consistencies and baseline differences (e.g., McKinney et al., 1985) suggest that the search for standardization is an important but difficult challenge. The alternative approach is to adopt the *generalizability model* whereby the systematic effects of time, situations, persons, and their interactions may be studied. Such approaches yield useful data concerning the complexity of psychophysiological assessments and draw attention to naive assumptions underlying the use of single assessment sessions (e.g., Llabre et al., 1988). Moreover, they also emphasize the importance of interactions between person variables and situations. Psychophysiological assessment has been influenced by the notion of "individual response specificity" (Engel, 1960) whereby for certain individuals, psychophysiological profiles may be stable across time. This concept has important implications for both practical assessment as regards the determination of reliability and also for theoretical formulations concerning the etiology of psychosomatic disorder. Recent research into individual response specificity (Robinson, Whitsett, & Kaplan, 1987; Stemmler & Fahrenberg, 1989; Waters et al., 1987) may yield important implications for the selection of response profiles as opposed to single response channels in clinical psychophysiological assessment.

The final psychometric concept that requires brief discussion is that of internal consistency. This refers to the level of consistency between multiple responses or items of the same test. With regard to psychophysiological assessment, internal consistencies could be assessed in a number of ways. First, if a single response channel is considered, for example skin conductance, a series of multiple measurements could be achieved. It is common in psychophysiological assessment to obtain a series of discrete samples from a particular situation or temporal event, and reduce these samples to a representative value such as the mean. Internal consistency, here, would refer to the stability of the samples and might reflect the variance associated with a series of sample values. It could also refer to different methods of quantification/measurement of the underlying variable. For example, electrodermal activity is frequently measured either in terms of conductance or resistance, as an absolute level, in relation to specific response amplitudes, or as numbers of nonspecific responses. These measures could be said to display differing degrees of consistency and also concurrent validity. It is important to recognize that the internal consistency for specific channels may be low, which consequently argues against different parameters being used interchangeably (Turpin, 1989b).

The problem of internal consistency becomes more important, however, when behavioral or physiological constructs are assessed. Hence, if a construct of "physiological arousal" is being assessed, several different physiological parameters might be selected. Unfortunately, inter-response relationships between different psychophysiological measures tend to be low and have led psychophysiologists to abandon general constructs such as arousal or activation (cf. Turpin, 1989b; Venables, 1984). This clearly reflects the limited construct validity of these commonly psychophysiological terms.

Finally, internal consistency has been applied to both psychophysiological and behavioral measures in the form of the "desynchrony problem" (Strosahl & Linehan, 1986). Because this is the focus of the next section of this chapter, we will not discuss this issue in detail here.

Idiographic and Single-Case Approaches

The emergence of studies demonstrating only moderate degrees of temporal stability for psychophysiological variables reveals the limitations of the psychometric approach. First, the experimental determination of distributions and estimates of error associated with absolute values of psychophysiological variables is clearly at an early stage of development. Further research is required in terms of standardization of methods and situations, and also in the extension of these techniques to large, representative, and well-specified samples. Second, although the temporal stability of these measures is important for clinical assessment across time, group comparisons that assess for relative change as opposed to absolute values may experimentally control for the various extraneous factors that contribute to the error of measurement of absolute values. Hence, the application of psychophysiological measures to behavioral assessment across and within clinical groups requires strict experimental control. Third, the relevance of psychometric criteria to the single clinical assessment case needs to be critically examined.

Cone (1988), although a strong advocate of the value of psychometric concepts within behavioral assessment, has drawn attention to the limited generalizability of nomothetic and deductive approaches to the single-case. Because much clinical assessment is by its nature based upon single-cases, the evaluation of an idiographic psychophysiological approach is essential for the scientist-practitioner. Nomothetically derived criteria such as test-retest reliability and concurrent validity may well be misleading. This is illustrated by Hayes et al. (1986) by reference to a hypothetical data set drawn from a series of individual subjects. These subjects are said to demonstrate differences in both intersubject and intrasubject variability. High intrasubject variability across different situations and times might allow sufficient consistency between measures for individual subjects, that meaningful conclusions could be drawn from these hypothetical data. However, when these data are examined nomothetically, low intersubject correlations are found that would otherwise have led to the more cautious conclusion of limited concurrent validity.

Therefore, if psychophysiological measures are to be employed within single-cases, intra- or within subject correlations need to be examined, rather than reliance on nomothetically derived test-retest reliability coefficients. In addition, assessors need to capitalize on the ease of repeated measurements of psychophysiological variables, which if used in conjunction with single-case methodology, may provide an alternative means of evaluating the contribution of psychophysiology to behavioral assessment. The use of single-case designs has already been discussed in this chapter.

Treatment Utility and "Triple Response Mode" Assessment

A final approach to evaluation in behavioral assessment concerns the treatment utility approach (Hayes et al., 1986; Nelson & Hayes, 1981). In evaluating the contribution of any assessment procedure, these authors suggest two functional criteria of particular relevance to behavior therapy. These are *conceptual validity*, which concerns the ability of a specific assessment to contribute to the understanding of behavior, and *treatment validity*, whereby the addition of a particular assessment strategy leads to better (more efficient or effective) treatment. Treatment validity is said to be demonstrated experimentally by using appropriate nomothetic or idiographic methods.

We shall now attempt to apply these new criteria to evaluating psychophysiological measures in behavioral assessment. Indeed, it could be argued that these criteria are synonymous with the "three systems rationale" for the use of psychophysiological assessment (Lang, 1971). As has already been discussed, the routine assessment of physiological variables, in conjunction with cognitive and behavioral response modes, has been justified both in terms of the conceptualization of emotional responding (Lang, 1971) and also the utility of physiological measurement in predicting differential patterns of treatment response (Hodgson & Rachman, 1974; Rachman & Hodgson, 1974).

The first question concerns the contribution of psychophysiology to the increased understanding of behavioral problems. Lang (1968, 1971) has strongly argued against the simple indicand approach to fear assessment whereby a single measure, whether it be self-report, behavioral or physiological, is used to operationalize the fear construct or its accompanying emotional state. Instead, he has advocated that a series of measures are required that reflect the presumed biological systems (verbal-cognitive, overt-motor, and physiological) subserving emotional states. Because these sytems are presumed to be interdependent, all three require assessment to provide a comprehensive account of changes in the emotional state. Within this conceptual framework, physiological measures (autonomic activity, in particular) have been given particular emphasis by Lang. For example, the presence of autonomic activation is frequently interpreted as an indication of adequate processing of fear-related material during exposure treatments (Foa & Kozak, 1986). Absence of such changes may indicate a lack of compliance or degree of cognitive avoidance on behalf of the client, and a subsequent poorer treatment outcome.

Clearly, the addition of psychophysiological measurement has resulted in the general acceptance of broadly based assessment strategies for behavior therapy and a diversification of theoretical models. Indeed, Rachman in the foreword to a recent text on the subject (Hollandsworth, 1986) has stressed the fundamental importance of physiology in the advancement of behavior therapy. However, the widespread recognition of the triple mode assessment approach has not been without its critics. The major area of dissent concerns the conceptual basis of the three systems approach and is discussed in an incisive review by Kozak and Miller (1982). Essentially, these authors question whether the three systems approach should be interpreted either at the level of intervening variables or hypothetical constructs. If the former approach is adopted, each system requires strict operationalization that should result in unambiguous and vigorous empirical definitions of fear in the absence of any unobserved hypothetical process or construct. However, there are a number of problems associated with this essentially methodological behaviorist approach. First, as Hugdahl (1981) has stressed, the diversity of response mode definitions, together with their lack of internal consistency, results in a failure to provide a single definitional focus for fear responding. Hence, the three systems approach, which attempts a *loose* definition of fear responding, does not meet with the strict operational requirements of an intervening variable definition. Moreover, there is a lack of agreement as to how each system should be operationalized and measured. Numerous authors have pointed to ambiguities and inconsistencies in the definition of the three systems, the verbal-cognitive mode being the most troublesome system to explicitly define (Hollandsworth, 1986; Hugdahl, 1981; Kozak & Miller, 1982).

An alternative approach advocated by several authors (Evans, 1986; Kaloupek & Levis, 1983; Kozak & Miller, 1982; Ohman, 1987) is a return to the use of fear as a hypothetical construct, which is imperfectly measured via the three systems model. According to Kozak and Miller (1982) fear should be considered to be a functional emotional state that cannot be directly observed but is inferred from the basis of data collected from a three systems approach. The exact relationship between the inferred construct and observed data base will require continued theoretical developments which should help further define the nature of the construct via empirical hypothesis testing. Indeed, recent developments within the three systems model, notably those undertaken by Lang and his colleagues, reflect this change in direction from the three systems approach as a pragmatic assessment taxonomy to a more theoretically based level of analysis. The contribution of psychophysiological theory to the advancement of the three systems approach will be examined in the next section of this chapter.

Perhaps the greatest support for the use of physiological measures within the three systems approach stems from its use as an explanatory framework, which may uniquely provide new treatment approaches within behavior therapy. This rationale is identical to the criterion of treatment validity proposed by Nelson and Hayes (1981). Essentially, it capitalizes on the fact that although, according to Lang (1971), the three systems interact, their measurable products frequently appear independent leading to unique patterns of differential responding across the three systems.

Accordingly, interventions should be directed at each of these response modes or as Lang stated, "In short, psychotherapy should be a vigorous multisystem training program, tailored to the unique behavioral topography presented by the patient" (Lang, 1971, p. 109).

The major impetus for examining the therapeutic implications of the three systems approach was detailed by Hodgson and Rachman. Rachman and Hodgson (1974) first drew attention to dissociation between fear and avoidance, which they termed *discordance,* and to changes in the pattern of discordance over time, which was referred to as *desynchrony.* They further went on to examine the theoretical implications of synchrony and desynchrony for two-factor learning theory explanations of various types of exposure treatment. In an influential companion article (Hodgson & Rachman, 1974), they then went on to hypothesize a number of factors that might determine the nature of fear synchrony/desynchrony. Essentially, the major predictions made were that discordance would be higher in low emotional arousal but high demand situations and that synchrony would be dependent upon the particular type of intervention employed and the degree of success at follow-up. If these predictions were correctly borne out, then the assessment of synchrony/desynchrony using the three systems approach ought to provide new and important information concerning both target and treatment selection in behavioral assessment.

Accordingly, much research has been devoted to testing these and subsequent predictions from the desynchrony model. However, before reviewing the outcome of these studies, it is necessary to critically examine the validity of the desynchrony concept. The failure to observe high degrees of concordance between fear and avoidance measures is derived from Lang's notion of the loosely coupled three symptoms. However, failure to observe high intercorrelations between measures may arise due to other, nontheoretical factors. Indeed, Hodgson and Rachman (1974) identified range effects, initial level functions, scaling problems and unreliability of measures as having potentially significant decremental effects on inter-response correlations.

The greatest critic, however, of the desynchrony interpretation of low intermeasure correlations is Cone (1979). He argues that differential patterns of correlation between the three so called response modes may reflect a confound between content and method of assessment, rather than a loose coupling of the hypothetical systems described originally by Lang. He argues that any content area represented by the three systems approach may be assessed by several different methods. For example, excess sweating could be measured by self-report, observation or the measurement of autonomic activity. Correlations among measures may not reflect necessarily the interaction, or lack of it, between different systems but communality across similar methods of assessment. Hence, a series of self-report measures from different content areas might be expected to have greater concurrent validity than if *different* methods of assessment had been applied for each content area or system separately. He suggests, therefore, that conclusions regarding the degree of desynchrony might be premature and advocates the use of multitrait-multimethod analysis (cf. Campbell & Fiske, 1959) to estimate true measures of desynchrony. Further discussion of the problem of shared-method variance is provided by Strosahl and Linehan (1986).

Given the above methodological caution of Cone, it should still be possible to assess the treatment validity of the synchrony/desynchrony approach. Two particular questions need to be addressed. First, does the routine use of the three systems approach lead to patterns of desynchrony, and if so, what are their situational determinants? Second, what are the therapeutic implications of patterns of desynchrony for treatment selection and final response outcome?

Several early studies were published purporting to demonstrate patterns of discordance and desynchrony in various different phasic samples (cf. Himadi, Boice, & Barlow, 1985). For example, Mavissakalian and Michelson (1982) report patterns of synchrony/desynchrony in a group of agoraphobic subjects undergoing a standardized walk. Moreover, synchrony became greater with repeated exposures to the walk. Similarly, the effects of emotional arousal and demand characteristics have also been investigated (e.g., Grey, Rachman, & Sartory, 1981; Grey, Sartory, & Rachman, 1979; Kaloupek & Levis, 1983; Matias & Turner, 1986; Sartory, Rachman, & Grey, 1977) but with equivocal and sometimes unexpected results (cf. Himadi et al., 1985). Although the original predictions made by Hodgson and Rachman (1974) have received partial support, the prognostic/therapeutic predictions of the desynchrony model have, perhaps, fared better. For example, the association between synchronous responding and either heart rate response during treatment or more improved post-treatment response (measured using clinical rating scales) was indicated by several agoraphobia treatment studies (Michelson & Mavissakalian, 1985; Michelson, Mavissakalian, & Marchione, 1985; Verimilyia, Boice, & Barlow, 1984).

Similarly, a series of studies by Ost and his colleagues suggested that differential treatment response to either behaviorally or physiologically targeted treatments for social- and claustro-phobia could be obtained if clients were classified as either behavioral or physiological reactors prior to the start of treatment (Ost, Jerremalm, & Johansson, 1981; Ost, Johansson, & Jerremalm, 1982 but also see Jerremalm, Jansson, & Ost, 1986). Indeed, outcome studies published in the early 1980s seem to strongly indicate the treatment validity of triple mode assessment in a variety of phobic disorders. This is illustrated by Himadi et al.'s (1985) optimistic review of three systems assessment for agoraphobia.

Unfortunately, more recent studies have led to some caveats being imposed upon the general utility of triple mode assessment, particularly involving heart rate and agoraphobia. For example, Craske, Sanderson, and Barlow (1987) in a 6 month follow-up study of Vermilyea et al. (1984) failed to observe differences in treatment response between synchronizers and desynchronizers. However, they did replicate an original finding that high heart rate reactors, defined either before or after treatment, were more likely to be treatment responders. Conversely, low heart rate reactors appear to be associated with desynchronizers. Although the results of this reanalysis are disappointing, they point to a potential problem of desynchrony research that employs relatively small sample sizes. The contrasting conclusions arrived at by Vermilyea et al. (1984) and Craske et al. (1987) can be traced to a positive change in follow-up treatment status by two desynchronizers out of a total sample of 21 clients left from the original sample of 28 studied by Vermilyea et al.

Reservations have also been expressed concerning the utility of heart rate in the assessment of agoraphobia. Holden and Barlow (1986) compared agoraphobics and controls participating in a behavioral walk and observed similar decreases in heart rate with repeated exposure. Moreover, the reliabilities of the heart rate measures were also questioned. Accordingly, in their companion article on treatment outcome assessment in agoraphobia, Himadi et al. (1986) are more noticeably cautious concerning the relevance of heart rate monitoring for the measurement of outcome. Similar doubts concerning the adoption of heart rate in agoraphobic assessment have also been raised (Williams, 1985). However, to disregard earlier positive findings at this stage appears premature. Moreover, a recently partially reported large-scale treatment study by Michelson, Mavissakalian, and Marchione (1988) involving 88 agoraphobics has revealed further evidence relating synchrony to improved treatment response.

Finally, one further re-analysis requires comment. Mavissakalian (1987) reported the effects of desynchrony on treatment response in a group of 22 agoraphobic patients. Although neither patterns of synchrony nor pretreatment heart rate predicted therapeutic response, a potentially theoretically important finding emerged. Mavissakalian (1987) defined synchrony/desynchrony in two unusual ways. First, he chose the comparison between heart rate and behavioral avoidance, as opposed to the subjective unit of discomfort scale, commonly used. Second, and of greater relevance, he subdivided desynchronous clients with respect to the specific direction of the desynchrony involved. Using these subgroups, desynchronous clients with high avoidance increase but low heart rate increase, were more likely to be treatment nonresponders. In contrast, subjects with low avoidance increases that were associated with high heart rate increases, were more likely to be treatment responders. These findings suggest that neither heart rate level nor desynchrony per se determine treatment response, but instead, the actual *pattern* of desynchrony is the important factor.

In summary, a review of the treatment validity of three systems assessment suggests that the inclusion of psychophysiological measures has potential for providing specific additional information to facilitate the selection of target problems and behavioral treatments. However, there are several important methodological issues that require urgent attention. These concern the tendency to use relatively small samples largely drawn from agoraphobic populations, the reliance on heart rate as the sole physiological parameter, the determination of criteria for desynchrony and elevated heart rate, the composite nature of criteria for clinical response/nonresponse, and the failure to specify the exact nature of desynchronous responding.

In addition, recent authors have stressed the importance of examining results from desynchrony studies within current theoretical frameworks. For example, the suggestion that heightened autonomic responding is a positive prognostic indicator has been explained in terms of emotional processing and accessing internal fear structures (see Borkovec, 1988; Foa & Kozak, 1986; Lang, 1988).

THEORETICAL CONTRIBUTIONS OF PSYCHOPHYSIOLOGY TO BEHAVIORAL ASSESSMENT

In previous sections of this chapter, the relative bias of both behavioral assessment and psychophysiology towards empiricism and away from theory has been emphasized. However, it will be argued in the final section of this chapter that such a conceptually barren view of clinical psychophysiological assessment is perhaps both misleading and may be counterproductive in the long term. Early investigators (i.e., Lacey, 1959) of the role of psychophysiology in psychotherapeutic assessment emphasized the need to interpret psychophysiological responding within the therapeutic context. Interpretation requires theory, and the need for conceptual models of psychophysiological responding is a pressing requirement for contemporary applications in behavioral assessment. The central questions, therefore, are what are psychophysiological theories, do they exist, and have they utility for the field of behavioral assessment?

Psychophysiological theories can be provisionally defined as psychological explanations or accounts of the interrelations between psychological and physiological variables (see also Levey & Martin, 1987; Miller & Ebert, 1988). Adopting such a wide definition, identifies a relatively broad and rich catch of theoretical explanations. Of particular importance, is the recognition that psychophysiological theories should not be merely identified with the activities of "psychophysiologists" and the products of their activities in the "psychophysiological" literature. Nor should they be equated solely with the mini theories devoted to explaining the behavior of certain psychophysiological indices in the absence of broader psychological contexts. The combined use of psychological and psychophysiological variables has been prevalent for many years in psychological research. Most general areas of psychology, for example, research into emotion (e.g., Plutchik & Kellerman, 1980), social behavior (e.g., Zillmann, 1978), conditioning (e.g., Davey, 1987; Dawson & Schell, 1985), and personality (e.g., Levenson, 1983; Nebylitsyn & Gray, 1972) have all used the psychophysiological approach to advance theoretical developments. Accordingly, these theories are both relevant and pertinent to the need for explanation within behavioral assessment. The use of psychophysiological methods, in conjunction with general psychological approaches to clinically relevant problems has already been overviewed elsewhere (Turpin, 1989b). Suffice it to say that psychophysiology has contributed to the general areas of personality, emotion, social processes, information processing, and learning. The focus of the present discussion will be much more specific and will relate the problem of desynchrony between triple assessment approaches and how psychophysiological theory may help to resolve some of these empirical discrepancies and assist in the provision of more effective assessments and treatments.

The discordance prevalent among measures constituting the triple mode assessment may be interpreted in a number of ways (cf. Kozak & Miller, 1982; Ohman, 1987). For example, a lack of convergence between the three systems can be used to argue against a unitary fear concept and instead support a more amorphous notion of loosely coupled independent fear-related systems (Lang, 1968). This conceptual model either leads to an abandoning of physiological measures in behavioral assessment due to their lack of convergence *or* more importantly, to the routine use of triple mode assessment as a merely pragmatic and inductive solution to a supposedly complex and ill-defined problem. The former response is interestingly similar to arguments *against* the use of psychophysiological measures in social psychology and has been critically discussed by Cacioppo, Petty and Andersen (1988). The latter approach is characterized by Hodgson and Rachman's (1974) proposals that desynchrony may yield important and clinically relevant information concerning treatment selection and outcome.

However, as discussed in the previous section, purely descriptive approaches to identifying the relationship between desynchrony and clinical change are insufficient. Findings derived from this research perspective are frequently equivocal and call into question the adequacy of the desynchrony definition. For example, Mavissakalian (1987) has shown that absolute measures of desynchrony may not predict treatment outcome. Further information concerning elevated heart rate and the *specific pattern* of discordance and desynchronous changes are required in order to yield more meaningful and accurate predictions. However, a solely descriptive desynchrony/three systems approach is unable to account for these more detailed patterns of desynchronous responding.

What is required to resolve the current impasse surrounding desynchrony? The answer is a return to the conceptual status of fear. As Kozak and Miller (1982) argued, we need to distinguish the boundaries between observables and concepts. Indeed, Ohman (1987) has elegantly re-examined the question of the status of hypothetical fear constructs and has convincingly reiterated Kozak and Miller's call for a return to considering the fundamental importance of the role of theory in research concerning fear assessment. Ohman's critique is based essentially upon two arguments. First, the observation of low correlations both between and within the three systems can be attributable to theoretically irrelevant methodological or physiological factors that account for significant proportions of the shared variance. To ignore these sources of variances will necessarily lead to pessimistic conclusions being drawn concerning the lack of convergence between measures (see also Turpin, 1983a; 1989b). Second, it is the relationship between various measures and the hypothetical fear construct itself, and not other convergent measures that should be of central interest. Hence, the discriminant validity of measures should be assessed as opposed to mere convergent validity. To achieve both of these requirements, the interpretation of findings from triple mode assessment needs to be firmly based within relevant theoretical frameworks.

Before attempting to identify the role of psychophysiology in facilitating theoretical models of fear, the central issues underlying the desynchrony problem require to be explicitly stated. First, a distinction should be made between "within" and "between" systems discordance. Within systems discordance refers to a lack of internal consistency for measures purporting to assess the same three-system response mode. From a psychophysiological perspective, this is particularly relevant because even among autonomic measures, such as electrodermal activity and heart rate, discordance will arise across different individuals, situations, and stimuli (Giesen & McGlynn, 1977; Hodgson & Rachman, 1974). Second, between systems discordance has been demonstrated to be widely prevalent, especially within clinical studies. Finally, the relationship between both within and between system discordance to clinical outcome must be addressed.

Within System Discordance: Can Psychophysiological Measures Discriminate Between Emotional States?

Essentially this question concerns the role of undifferentiated arousal versus distinct patterns of peripheral psychophysiological responding in determining the nature of emotional responses. Clearly, this debate has a long and respectable pedigree (e.g., Cannon versus James) and is still relevant to contemporary theories of emotion (cf. Levenson, 1988; Mandler, 1975). On the one hand, nonspecific theories exist that emphasize the role of cognitive appraisal mechanisms (e.g., Lazarus & Folkman, 1984; Reisenzein, 1983; Schacter & Singer, 1962). Whereas, on the other hand, differential theories have ascribed *particular* importance to differentiation within hormonal systems (Ax, 1953), the autonomic system (Ekman, Levenson, & Friesen, 1983; Levenson, 1988) or the motor system (Dimberg, 1988; Ekman, 1982; Leventhal, 1982; Leventhal & Mosbach, 1983). Indeed, recent research on emotional differentiation is strongly suggestive of the ability to discriminate between patterns of emotional response using facial EMG, observational coding of facial expression, and autonomic responding (e.g., Ekman, Levenson, & Friesen, 1983). Such findings have general relevance to the question of situational/stimulus specificity posed by behavioral assessment. Moreover, facial EMG has been applied to clinical questions related to the quantification of depression (Ekman & Fridlund, 1987) and the role of general muscle tension in anxiety (Fridlund, Hatfield, Cottam, & Fowler, 1986). The importance of findings for behavioral assessment should not be overlooked. Indeed, Fridlund et al. argues that anxiety might be characterized not by a general increase in tension but by increased agitation. The implication for treatment, according to Fridlund et al., might be to undermine the rationale for EMG biofeedback techniques, which aim to reduce *general* tension levels.

The possible autonomic differentiation of emotionally relevant stimuli has also been suggested from an alternative psychophysiological perspective. It has been argued that several types of psychophysiologically distinct unconditioned reflexes may be elicited by simple stimuli; these include notably the orienting (OR) and defense response (DR) (Graham, 1979; Sokolov, 1963; Turpin, 1983a; Turpin, 1986). The essential distinction between ORs and DRs is said to be the dimension of stimulus intensity and can be operationalized by psychophysiological measures, notably the heart rate response (Graham, 1979; but also see Turpin, 1983a; 1986). Accordingly, these concepts have been applied to affective stimuli such as phobia-relevant (animal and mutilation) slides by numerous investigators (e.g., Hare & Blevings, 1975; Klorman, Wiessberg, & Wisenfeld, 1977). It is unclear whether this research addresses the elicitation of either fear-relevant or danger-controlling processes (Leventhal, 1970) and also whether such "reflexes" can be distinguished from emotional states (Ekman, Friesen, & Simons, 1985). Moreover, it is also difficult to distinguish between the affective and arousal/intensity properties of the eliciting stimuli. Original models of ORs and DRs were essentially "cold" and relied upon the manipulation of stimulus intensity/energy within the auditory mode (Graham, 1979). However, it is unclear whether it is the affective or arousal dimension that is important in the elicitation of orienting, defense, or startle (SR) because affective encoding has not been satisfactorily incorporated within OR-DR models (cf. Turpin, 1986).

The above distinctions between ORs and DRs have again relevance for behavioral assessors. For example, the presence of phobic responding would appear to distinguish between ORs elicited by nonphobic subjects to potentially phobic/unpleasant material and DRs elicited by phobics to the same material (cf. McNally, 1986). Studies concerning cardiac conditioning and "preparedness" (Cook, Hodes, & Lang, 1986; Hodes, Cook, & Lang, 1985) also lend support to this idea. Moreover, differences may also exist within phobias, animal phobics eliciting DRs consistent with fear/danger responding whereas social phobics eliciting ORs associated with a hypervigilant state of attention (cf. Ohman, Dimberg, & Ost, 1985).

The relative roles of attention, arousal, intensity, and affective salience require detailed examination in relation to OR/SR/DR models. For example, a recent study by Sartory, Eves, and Foa (1987) failed to observe effects for an intensity of phobic material manipulation. Moreover, within session habituation of HR acceleration was observed that might suggest the presence of what Turpin has identified as the "startle" response rather than Graham's definition of "defensive" responding. Lang and colleagues (Greenwald, Cook, & Lang, in press) have also demonstrated that electrodermal and heart-rate responding may be differentiated in terms of affective valence and arousal using nonphobic undergraduate subjects viewing affectively valent slides. Whereas negative affect and heart rate acceleration might be predicted on the basis of phobic DRs, Lang observed the opposite relationship between reported judgements and direction of heart rate responding.

The mechanisms responsible for patterns of autonomic differentiation have also received some attention. For instance, Fowles (1980, 1982, 1984) has argued that differential electrodermal/cardiac responding may be due to specific sensitivities of each system to signals of punishment and reward, as detailed by Gray's (1982) revised two-factor theory of learning. It would be premature to evaluate Fowles' important theoretical contribution to this debate because data from other laboratories unfortunately are not forthcoming (Clements & Turpin, 1987). Another approach to possible mechanisms include information processing models of autonomic responding that have already been discussed (cf. Ohman, 1987). Regarding cardiac response differentiation, the energetic requirements of the cardio-vascular system should not be overlooked. For example, Obrist (1981) has argued that much of the variance associated with cardiac responding can be accounted for by the actual or anticipated metabolic demands of the organism. This he has termed as the *cardiac-somatic coupling* hypothesis, which emphasizes the complementary requirements of metabolic demand and active/passive coping on the interpretation of sympathetic/parasympathetic effects upon the heart. Finally, Lang's *Bioinformational theory* also provides a structure for interpreting possible psychophysiological differences. According to Lang (1985), psychophysiological differences will reflect differences in the presence and accessibility of response propositions that constitute emotional/affective associative networks. Lang's approach will not be reviewed here because it will be discussed in greater detail later in this section.

Finally, the question needs to be addressed as to how these mechanisms can be modified in order to provide the basis of atypical phobic responding. It would appear that these prototypical fear/emotional response patterns are amenable to social modification. For example, Ekman distinguishes between prototypical facial expressions and subsequent cultural modifications dependent upon social display rules (Ekman, 1982). Ohman and colleagues have stressed the importance of adopting an evolutionary perspective to the acquisition of phobic behavior and have suggested that phobic responses represent a form of phylogenetically prepared learning (Ohman, Dimberg, & Ost, 1985). Phobic responses have been said to display more rapid acquisition, greater resistance to extinction, and less susceptibility to cognitive factors such as instructions and expectancies (Seligman, 1971). The psychophysiological literature concerning preparedness is extensive and controversial, and cannot be properly reviewed here (cf. McNally, 1986; Ohman et al., 1985; Ohman, 1986, 1987). Nevertheless, it represents an important contribution to theoretical perspectives of fear acquisition that deserve serious attention from behavioral assessors.

Between System Discordance: The Role of Cognition?

How can dissociations between physiological responding, fear and avoidance behaviors, and verbal reports be explained? In addressing this question it is important to stress again that the focus ought to be upon interactions between underlying systems, as opposed to mere attempts at accounting for the proportion of shared variance among the observed outputs from these hypothetical structures. Until recently, theories of emotion (e.g., Lazarus, 1986; Lazarus & Folkman, 1984) have emphasized the role of cognitive appraisal both in determining the meaning of a situation (primary appraisal) and its associated actions (secondary appraisal). Hence, emotional states and their respective behavioral and physiological components, were viewed as outputs from a system of sequential cognitive processing stages.

Recently, this view of the primacy of cognition has been challenged by Zajonc (1980) who has asserted that the processing of affect may precede or by-pass cognitive appraisal systems and should, therefore, be viewed as an independent or partially independent system. Zajonc's (1980) challenge to the ascendancy of cognitive processes has had important influences on both theories of emotion and behavior therapy. From the emotion perspective, it has emphasized the importance of sensory and motor processes in the determination of emotion (Zajonc & Markus, 1984) and as such is sympathetic to theories that stress somatic factors in emotional responding (e.g., Ekman, 1982; Izard, 1977; Leventhal, 1982). However, it has not gone unchallenged, and has been the focus of several critical replies (Lazarus, 1982, 1984; Zajonc, 1984). To a degree, the debate may be understood as a failure to agree on definitional terms for *cognition* and *affect*. Zajonc (1984) is critical of Lazarus' (1982, 1984) all embracing definition of cognitive processes that lead to a necessary identification of cognition with emotional responding. Lazarus (1984), on the other hand, advocates a more restrictive definiton of emotion that maintains a distinction between sensory and perceptual processes. Other commentators have also emphasized the need to clarify the term *cognition*. For example, Watts (1983) attempts to distinguish between cognitive operations that are characterized by the conscious awareness of their products, and preconscious processing, which he suggests may also be viewed as examples of cognitive activity. Mandler (1982) has questioned the equivalence of subjective experience with conscious processing. Ohman (1987) similarly rejects the simplistic equation of cognition with subjective experience and instead emphasizes the role of pre-attentive mechanisms and the distinction between automatic and controlled processing.

Lang (1977, 1979, 1985) has also identified cognition with the computational transformations associated with information processing in the form of the computer metaphor that distinguishes cognitive software from biological hardware. Importantly, these contemporary accounts of cognition distinguish process from product with respect to the measurement of subjective experiences, attitudes, and beliefs. Hence, a clear distinction should be recognized by the behavioral assessor between *cognitive* approaches to affective processing and *cognitive* therapy as practiced by clinicians.

The problem of integrating cognitive therapy within cognitive models of experimental psychopathology is not the only result of the "Zajonc-Lazarus" debate. Rachman (1981) identified several deliberately speculative implications from the Zajonc (1980) article for behavior therapy. For example, the mere matching of treatments to different discordant fear components as advocated earlier by Hodgson and Rachman (1974) may be inappropriate if affect has primacy over cognition. The "irrationality" of fear responding and Bandura's paradox concerning the increase in cognitive interventions, which appear dependent upon fundamentally behavioral methods, might be explained by the partial independence of affective and cognitive processes. Greenberg and Safran (1984) also have taken advantage of the recent controversy ignited by Zajonc (1980) to advance Leventhal's perceptual-motor theory of emotion as a means of "fusing" the artificial distinctions imposed by the three systems model upon behavior therapy.

The issue that needs to be addressed is the role of psychophysiology in evaluating recent information-processing accounts of emotion. As Ohman (1987) states, these cognitive processes are inferred on the basis of experimental observation. The data upon which these inferences are based are essentially behavioral, as in the form of probe reaction times (e.g., Dawson & Schell, 1985; MacLeod, Mathews & Tata, 1986), and also psychophysiological variables (e.g., Lang, 1979; Ohman, 1987, 1988; Ohman, Dimberg, & Esteves, 1989). Subjective report is a relevant data base but is not necessarily a reflection of inferred processing but rather the result of awareness of the product of processing. Moreover, the reliability of subjective report, given its inability to be subjected to interobserver objectivity (Lang, 1978), may be the least useful source of data for evaluating information-processing models of affect. Performance-based data such as reaction times, recognition, and recall tests are similarly handicapped by the fact that they, too, represent products of the processing chain. Psychophysiological measures on the other hand, given their continuous presence in the stream of data acquisition, may provide unique information, particularly concerning early stages of processing. Obviously, psychophysiology has a role to play in the evaluation of recent models of affect, and this will be illustrated by reference to contemporary theoretical models.

The first example concerns Lang's influential "Bioinformational theory of fear imagery," which has provided a conceptual foundation for several recent models of behavioral change (Lang, 1977, 1979, 1985, 1988). It is perhaps ironic that Lang who was instrumental in, and to some extent saddled with, the widespread adoption of an empirically based three systems approach, has also been influential in advocating a more theoretically based analysis of behavioral problems (Lang, 1977, 1979). Essentially, Lang's Bioinformational Theory has evolved from the observation that inducing emotional/phobic imagery via text processing leads to patterns of physiological responding analogous to activation derived from *in vivo* exposure (Lang, Melamed, & Hart, 1970; Vrana, Cuthbert, & Lang, 1986). To account for this phenomenon, Lang has argued that imagery-invoked responses originate from the accessing of an associative memory network representing stimulus and response propositions concerning previous *in vivo* exposures (Lang, 1979, 1984, 1985, 1988). Space prevents a detailed account of this theory, but the essential features are summarized in Figure 18–1. This model has provided the basis for much experimental research by Lang and his colleagues who have investigated the effects of individual differences in imagery (Miller et al., 1987), the relative importance of response over stimulus-propositions and the potential clinical effects of imagery training (Lang, Levin, Miller, & Kozak, 1983; Lang, Kozak, Miller, Levin, & McLean, 1980), and the use of imagery to discriminate between different diagnostic categories of anxiety disorder (Cook, Melamed, Cuthbert, McNeil, & Lang, in press). Readers interested in a critical appraisal of Lang's theory should consult a recent special issue of *Cognition and Emotion* (Watts & Blackstock, 1987; Lang, 1987).

The central argument of Lang's theory, that fear responding represents consequences of the processing of representations or fear structures, has provided the basis for Foa and Kozak's (1986) model of emotional processing. These authors have extended Rachman's notion of emotional processing that referred to the processes responsible for the decline of emotional responding both within exposure treatment sessions and outside of the session as being within the "real world" of the client. According to Foa and Kozak (1986, p. 22) emotional processing involves "incor-

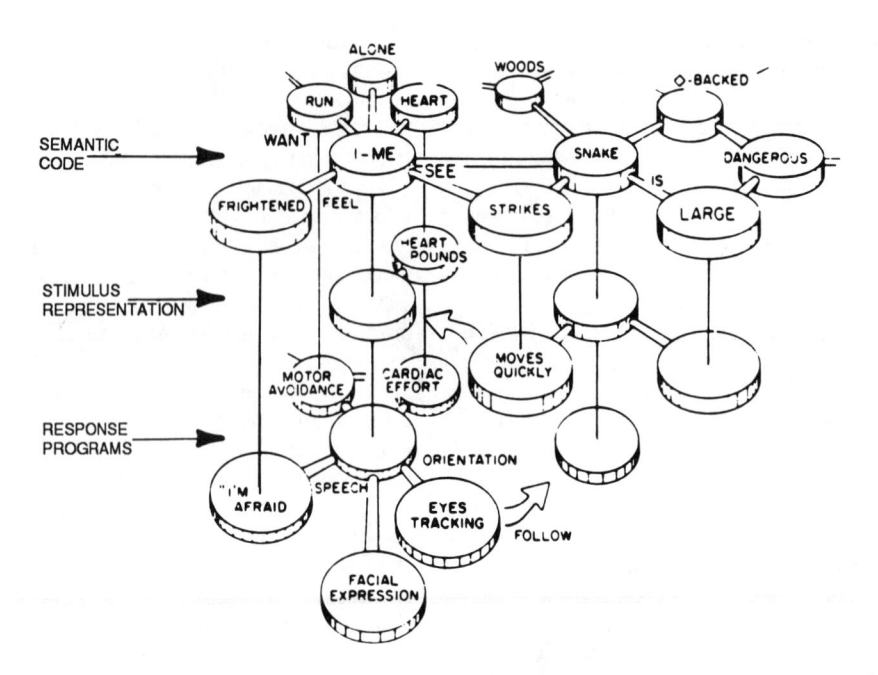

Figure 18.1. Summary of Lang's (1985) Bioinformational Theory of fear processing. From *Anxiety and the Anxiety Disorders* by A. H. Tuma and J. D. Maser (Eds.), 1985, Hillsdale, NJ: Lawrence Erlbaum Associates. Copyright 1982 by Lawrence Erlbaum Associates. Reprinted by permission.

poration of new information into an existing structure" and "allows for either increased or decreased emotional responding." Of particular relevance to the present chapter, Foa and Kozak argue that both within and between session changes in psychophysiological responding provide useful indicators to the extent of processing. In the context of exposure treatments of fear, they suggest that fear reduction results from a re-encoding of the fear stimulus in the absence of fear responding and a change in the meaning of the stimulus-response relationships, particularly with relation to the perceived probability of harm. These processes also result in decreased avoidance and a change in the emotional valance of the stimulus. A recent study (Kozak, Foa, & Steketee, 1988) using physiological measures of habituation provides some support for Foa and Kozak's position.

Finally, psychophysiological measures are beginning to be used in the study of pre-attentive/pre-conscious processes that may subserve emotional disorders. Recent research employing paradigms from cognitive psychology has suggested that emotional disorder may be accompanied by specific and selected biases in attentional and representational mechanisms (see Williams, Watts, MacLeod, & Mathews, 1988). In the case of anxiety disorders, it has been claimed that clients with generalized anxiety disorder may divert attention towards threatening stimuli whereas non-anxious subjects display the opposite allocation of attention away from threatening stimuli (MacLeod, Mathews, & Tata, 1986). In the introduction to this section, we suggested that psychophysiology may provide a means to extend investigations in this area. To date, few investigators have managed to explore this possibility.

A notable exception, however, is Ohman who has attempted to incorporate information-processing models of orienting with pre-attentive models of affective processing. Ohman (1987, 1988, see also Ohman et al., 1989) has suggested that early automatic processing may be responsible for a primary "affective reaction which primes response mobilization systems and initiates controlled processing." To support his claim, Ohman (1988) extensively cites psychophysiological studies that purport to demonstrate autonomic responding in the absence of conscious awareness and presumably result from processing at an unconscious and pre-attentive level. The paradigms reviewed have included subception phenomena, dichotic listening tasks, and the psychophysiology of prosopagnosia. He also draws upon recent empirical studies of nonconscious learning which have used backward masking procedures developed by Marcel (1983) to study the independence of conscious and nonconscious information-processing mechanisms (Ohman et al., 1989). Other recent psychophysiological applications have included heart rate correlates of the effects of mood manipulations on memory (Foa, McNally, & Murdock, 1989), effects of mood upon habituation (Mills & Salkovskis, 1988), and the use of startle probes as an index of affective processing (Vrana, Spence, & Lang, 1988). Although this recent area of enquiry has yet to yield tangible advances in behavioral assessment, the possibility of studying automatic/pre-attentive mechanisms associated with emotional disorders may yield clinical dividends both in assessment and treatment.

CONCLUSION

The role of psychophysiology in behavioral assessment has been described and critically assessed. It has been suggested that progress in this area has been handicapped by a reluctance to consider theoretical models and an over-reliance on empirical observation. Recent theoretical developments in psychophysiology have been identified and their potential for advancing clinical assessment and treatment in behavior therapy will be discussed briefly in relation to the problem of desynchrony across the three systems assessment model.

The central question posed by desynchrony studies is how can the relationship between different patterns of desynchrony and clinical outcome be explained? What is the theoretical significance of elevated heart rate in good treatment responders? What are the processes that subserve good and poor clinical outcomes in behavioral treatments? Similar questions relating to exposure treatments have also been emphasized by Borkovec (1988). For example, what are the necessary conditions for functional exposure? How important is the degree of behavioral avoidance, the presence of cognitive avoidance and distraction, the role of relaxation, coping mechanisms, and worry and mood? In relation to emotional disorders, these are some of the crucial questions that must be resolved before behavior therapy can demonstrate the validity of its frequently claimed high levels of effectiveness.

It can be argued that the previously reviewed theoretical models that have incorporated psychophysiological approaches may promise answers to these key issues. For example, the models of Lang, Foa, and Kozak emphasize the role of representational fear structures which, when accessed, lead to afferent outflow as measured by psychophysiological assessment. Evidence of processing, a precondition for the therapeutic restructuring of these hypothetical structures, is provided by physiological activation (e.g., elevated heart rate). Absence of physiological activation, either during imagery or *in vivo* exposure, may indicate that structures have not been adequately accessed and that clients may be engaging in *countertherapeutic* strategies such as cognitive avoidance and distraction. This information, derived from psychophysiological sources, may be crucial for the appraisal of *therapeutic processing* and subsequent intervention strategies.

Other factors include a degree of relaxation, attentional bias, worry-induced arousal, and subsequent modification of the fear structures (Borkovec, 1988; Foa & Kozak, 1986; Williams et al., 1988, pp. 180–182). Consideration of these factors should lead to testable theoretical *and* clinical hypotheses that can be addressed using contemporary variants of the three-systems assessment approach. The failure to obtain psychophysiological measures will severely limit the scope and potential success of these contemporary approaches.

For example, in a recent re-analysis of exposure treatment for claustrophobic panic patients, Rachman and Levitt (1988) report several interesting relationships between fear habituation as indexed by the decrement in self-reported fear and various self-reported cognitions. Although this is an interesting article in that it lends support to the importance of cognitive variables for self-reported fear decreases, it also raises several questions concerning the relationship of critical fear levels and distraction to processes subsuming fear reduction. The inclusion of psychophysiological variables might well have provided crucial evidence of fear-processing which *might* have resolved some of these more inexplicable findings. From the present data, it is difficult to determine the extent of processing of fear structures and the effectiveness of the various concentration/distraction conditions.

In summary, it is anticipated that the continued use of psychophysiological variables, in conjunction with other assessment methods and used within the framework of contemporary theoretical accounts of emotional disorder, will lead to important advances in behavioral assessment and treatment.

REFERENCES

Andrasik, F., & Blanchard, E. B. (1983). Applications of biofeedback to therapy. In C. E. Walker (Ed.) *Handbook of clinical psychology: Theory, research and practice*. Homewood, IL: Dow-Jones.

Andreassi, J. L. (1980). *Psychophysiology*. London: Oxford University Press.

Arena, J. G., Blanchard, E. B., Andrasik, F., Cotch, P. A., & Myers, P. E. (1983). Reliability of psychophysiological assessment. *Behaviour Research and Therapy, 21*, 447–460.

Armstrong, D. (1987). Theoretical tensions in biopsychosocial medicine. *Social Science and Medicine, 25*, 1213–1218.

Ax, A. F. (1953). The physiological differentiation between fear and anger in humans. *Psychosomatic Medicine, 15*, 433–442.

Bandeira, M., Bouchard, M. A., & Granger, L. (1982). Voluntary control of autonomic responses: A case for a dialogue between individual and group experimental methodologies. *Biofeedback and Self-Regulation, 7*, 317–330.

Barlow, D. H., Blanchard, E. B., Hayes, S. C., & Epstein, L. H. (1977). Single-case experimental designs and clinical biofeedback experimentation. *Biofeedback and Self-Regulation, 2*, 221–239.

Barlow, D. H., & Hersen, M. (1984). *Single-case experimental designs: Strategies for studying behavior change* (2nd ed.). Elmsford, NY: Pergamon Press.

Barrios, B. A. (1988). On the changing nature of behavioral assessment. In A. S. Bellack & M. Hersen (Eds.), *Behavioral assessment: A practical handbook* (3rd ed.) Elmsford, NY: Pergamon Press.

Barrios, B. A., & Hartmann, D. P. (1986). The contributions of traditional assessment: Concepts, issues and methodologies. In R. O. Nelson & S. C. Hayes (Eds.), *Conceptual foundations of behavioral assessment*. New York: Guilford Press.

Bernstein, A. S. (1967). Electrodermal base level, tonic arousal, and adaptation in chronic schizophrenics. *Journal of Abnormal Psychology, 72*, 221–232.

Blackburn, I. M., & Bonham, K. G. (1980). Experimental effects of a cognitive therapy technique in depressed patients. *British Journal of Social and Clinical Psychology, 19*, 353–363.

Blanchard, E. B., & Epstein, L. H. (1978). *A biofeedback primer*. Reading, MA: Addison-Wesley.

Borkovec, T. D. (1988, September). *Treatment of anxiety disorders: The state of the art*. Paper presented at the Third World Congress of Behavior Therapy, Edinburgh, Scotland.

Borkovec, T. D., Johnson, M. C., & Bloch, D. L. (1984). Evaluating experimental designs in relaxation research.
In R. L. Woolfolk & P. M. Lehrer (Eds.) *Principles and practice of stress management*. New York: Guilford Press.

Borkovec, T. D., & Rachman, S. (1979). The utility of analogue research. *Behaviour Research and Therapy, 17*, 253–261.

Cacioppo, J. T., & Petty, R. E. (Eds.). (1983). *Social psychophysiology: A sourcebook*. New York: Guilford Press.

Cacioppo, J. T., Petty, R. E., & Anderson, B. L. (1988). Social psychophysiology as a paradigm. In H. Wagner (Ed.), *Social psychophysiology and emotion: Theory and clinical applications*. Chichester: John Wiley & Sons.

Cacioppo, J. T., Petty, R. E., & Marshall-Goodell, B. (1985). Physical, social and inferential elements of psychophysiological measurement. In P. Karoly (Ed.) *Measurement strategies in health psychology*. New York: John Wiley & Sons.

Campbell, D., & Fiske, D. (1959). Convergent and discriminant validation by the multi-trait-multimethod matrix. *Psychological Bulletin, 56*, 81–105.

Carroll, D. (1984). *Biofeedback in practice*. London: Longman.

Carroll, D., & Anastasiades, P. (1978). The behavioural significance of heart rate: The Laceys' hypothesis. *Biological Psychology, 1*, 249–275.

Ciminero, A. R. (1986). Behavioral assessment: An overview. In A. R. Ciminero, K. S. Calhoun, & H. E. Adams (Eds.), *Handbook of behavioral assessment*. New York: John Wiley & Sons.

Ciminero, A. R., Calhoun, K. S., & Adams, H. E. (Eds.) (1986). *Handbook of behavioral assessment*. New York: John Wiley & Sons.

Claridge, G. S. (1967). *Personality and arousal*. Oxford, Pergamon Press.

Claridge, G. (1985). *Origins of mental illness*. Oxford: Blackwell.

Clements, K., & Turpin, G. (1987). The validity of the Palmer Sweat Index: Effects of feedback-induced anxiety and level of task difficulty on measures of palmar sweating. *Psychophysiology, 24*, 583–584 (Abs).

Coles, M. G. H., Donchin, E., & Porges, S. W. (Eds.) (1986). *Psychophysiology: Systems, processes and applications*. New York: Guilford Press.

Coles, M. G. H., Jennings, J. R., & Stern, J. A. (Eds.) (1984). *Psychophysiological perspectives: Festschrift for Beatrice and John Lacey*. New York: Van Nostrand Reinhold.

Cone, J. D. (1977). The relevance of reliability and validity for behavioral assessment. *Behavior Therapy, 8*, 411–426.

Cone, J. D. (1979). Confounded comparisons in triple response mode assessment research. *Behavioral Assessment, 1*, 85–95.

Cone, J. D. (1986). Idiographic, normothetic and related perspectives in behavioral assessment. In R. O. Nelson & S. C. Hayes (Eds.), *Conceptual foundations of behavioral assessment*. New York: Guilford Press.

Cone, J. D. (1988). Psychometric considerations and the multiple models of behavioral assessment. In A. S. Bellack & M. Hersen (Eds.), *Behavioral assessment: A practical handbook*. (3rd ed.). Elmsford, NY: Pergamon Press.

Cook, E. W. III, Hodes, R. L., & Lang, P. J. (1986). Preparedness and phobia: Effects of stimulus content on human visceral conditioning. *Journal of Abnormal Psychology, 95*, 195–207.

Cook, E. W. III, Melamed, B. G., Cuthbert, B. N., McNeil, D. W., & Lang, P. J. (in press). Emotion imagery and the differential diagnosis of anxiety. *Journal of Consulting and Clinical Psychology*.

Craske, M. G., Sanderson, W. C., & Barlow, D. H. (1987). How do desynchronous response systems relate to the treatment of agoraphobia: A follow-up evaluation. *Behaviour Research and Therapy, 25*, 117–122.

Crits-Christoph, P., & Schwartz, G. E. (1983). Psychophysiological contributions to psychotherapy research: A systems perspective. In A. Gale & J. Edwards (Eds.) *Physiological correlates of human behaviour, Vol. 3: Individual differences and psychopathology*. London: Academic Press.

Davey, G. (1987). *Cognitive processes and Pavlovian conditioning in humans*. Chichester: John Wiley & Sons.

Dawson, M. E., Nuechterlein, K. H., & Lieberman, R. P. (1984). Relapse in schizophrenic disorders: Possible contributing factors and implications for behavior therapy. In M. Rosenbaum, C. M. Franks, & Y. Jaffe (Eds.), *Perspectives on behavior therapy in the eighties*. New York: Springer.

Dawson, M. E., & Schell, A. M. (1985). Information processing and human autonomic classical conditioning. In P. K. Ackles, J. R. Jennings, & M. G. H. Coles (Eds.), *Advances in Psychophysiology, 1*, 89–165. Greenwich, CT: JAI Press.

Depue, R. A., & Fowles, D. C. (1973). Electrodermal activity as an index of arousal in schizophrenics. *Psychological Bulletin, 79*, 233–238.

Dimberg, U. (1988). Facial expressions and emotional reactions: A psychobiological analysis of human social behavior. In H. Wagner (Ed.), *Social psychophysiology: Theory and clinical practice*. Chichester: John Wiley & Sons.

Doleys, D. M., Meredith, R. L., & Ciminero, A. R. (Eds.) (1982). *Behavioral medicine: Assessment and treatment strategies*. New York: Plenum Press.

Eccles, A., Marshall, W. L., & Barbaree, H. E. (1988). The vulnerability of erectile measures to repeated assessments. *Behaviour Research and Therapy, 26*, 179–183.

Ekman, P. (Ed.). (1982). *Emotion in the human face* (2nd ed.). Cambridge: Cambridge University Press.

Ekman, P., & Fridlund, A. J. (1987). Assessment of facial behavior in major affective disorder. In J. D. Maser (Ed.), *Expressive behavior in depression*. Hillsdale, NJ: Lawrence Erlbaum Associates.

Ekman, P., Friesen, W. V., & Simons, R. C. (1985). Is the startle reaction an emotion? *Journal of Personality and Social Psychology, 49*, 1416–1426.

Ekman, P., Levenson, R., & Friesen, W. V. (1983). Autonomic nervous system activity distinguishes among emotions. *Science, 221*, 1208–1210.

Engel, B. T. (1960). Stimulus-response and individual-response specificity. *Archives of General Psychiatry, 2*, 305–313.

Engel, B. T. (1986). Psychosomatic medicine, behavioral medicine, just plain medicine. *Psychosomatic Medicine, 48*, 466–479.

Engel, G. L. (1977). The need for a new medical model: A challenge for biomedicine. *Science, 196*, 129–136.

Erskine-Milliss, J., & Schonell, M. (1981). Relaxation therapy in asthma: A critical review. *Psychosomatic Medicine, 43*, 365–372.

Evans, I. M. (1986). Response structure and the triple-response mode concept. In R. O. Nelson & S. C. Hayes (Eds.) *Conceptual foundations of behavioral assessment*. New York: Guilford Press.

Eysenck, H. J. (1967). *The biological basis of personality*. Springfield, Ill: Charles C Thomas.

Eysenck, H. J., & Kelley, M. J. (1987). The interaction of neurohormones with Pavlovian A and Pavlovian B conditioning in the causation of neurosis, extinction and incubation of anxiety. In G. Davey (Ed.), *Conditioning in humans*. Chichester: John Wiley & Sons.

Faulstich, M. E., Williamson, D. A., McKenzie, S. J., Duchmann, E. G., Hutchinson, K. M., & Blouin, D. C. (1986). Temporal stability of psychophysiological responding: A comparative analysis of mental and physical stressors. *Internal Journal of Neuroscience, 30*, 65–72.

Feuerstein, M., Labbe, E. E., & Kuczmierczyk, A. R. (Eds.) (1986). *Health psychology: A psychobiological perspective*. New York: Plenum Press.

Feuerstein, M., & Schwartz, G. E. (1977). Training in clinical psychophysiology: Present trends and future goals. *American Psychologist, 32*, 560–568.

Foa, E. B., & Kozak, M. J. (1986). Emotional processing and fear: Exposure to corrective information. *Psychological Bulletin, 99*, 20–35.

Foa, E. B., McNally, R., & Murdock, T. B. (1989). Anxious mood and memory. *Behaviour Research and Therapy, 27*, 141–147.

Fowles, D. C. (1980). The three systems arousal model: Implications of Gray's two factor learning theory for heart rate, electrodermal activity and psychopathy. *Psychophysiology, 17*, 87–104.

Fowles, D. C. (1982). Heart rate as an index of anxiety: Failure of a hypothesis. In J. T. Cacioppo & R. E. Petty (Eds.), *Perspectives in cardiovascular psychophysiology*. New York: Guilford Press.

Fowles, D. C. (1984). Arousal: Implications of behavioral thesis of motivation. In M. G. H. Coles, J. R. Jennings, & J. A. Stern (Eds.) *Psychophysiology perspectives: Festschrift for Beatrice and John Lacey*. New York: Van Nostrand Reinhold.

Fredrickson, M. (1989). Psychophysiological and biochem-

ical indices of 'stress' research: Applications to psychopathology and pathophysiology. In G. Turpin (Ed.), *Handbook of Clinical Psychophysiology*. Chichester: John Wiley & Sons.
Freund, K., & Blanchard, R. (1989). Phallometric diagnosis of paedophilia. *Journal of Consulting and Clinical Psychology, 57,* 100–105.
Fridlund, A. J., Hatfield, M. E., Cottam, G. L., & Fowler, S. C. (1986). Anxiety and striate-muscle activation: Evidence from electromyographic pattern analysis. *Journal of Abnormal Psychology, 95,* 228–236.
Gale, A. (1989). Series preface. In G. Turpin (Ed.), *Handbook of Clinical Psychophysiology*. Chichester: John Wiley & Sons.
Gale, A., & Baker, S. (1981). *In vivo* or *in vitro?*: Some effects of laboratory environments with particular reference to the psychophysiology experiment. In M. J. Christie & P. Mellett (Eds.), *Foundations of psychosomatics*. Chichester: John Wiley & Sons.
Gale, A., & Edwards, J. A. (1986). Individual differences. In M. G. H. Coles, E. Donchin, & S. W. Porges (Eds.), *Psychophysiology: Systems, processes and applications*. New York: Guilford Press.
Gatchel, R. J., & Price, K. P. (Eds.) (1979). *Clinical applications of biofeedback: Appraisal and status*. Elmsford, NY: Pergamon Press.
Gentry, W. D. (Ed.) (1984). *Handbook of behavioral medicine*. New York: Guilford Press.
Giesen, J. M., & McGlynn, F. D. (1977). Skin conductance and heart rate responsivity to public speaking imagery among students with high and low self-reported fear: A comparative analysis of "response" definitions. *Journal of Clinical Psychology, 33,* 68–76.
Goldfried, M. R. (1977). Behavioral assessment in perspective. In J. D. Cone, & R. P. Hawkins (Eds.), *Behavioral assessment: New directions in clinical psychology*. New York: Brunner/Mazel.
Goldfried, M. R., & Sprafkin, J. N. (1976). Behavioral personality assessment. In J. T. Spence, R. C. Carson, & J. W. Thibout (Eds.), *Behavioral approaches to therapy*. Morristown, NJ: General Learning Press.
Graham, F. K. (1979). Distinguishing among orienting, defense and startle reflexes. In H. D. Kimmel, E. H. Van Olst, & J. F. Orlebeke (Eds.) *The orienting reflex in humans*. Hillsdale, NJ: Lawrence Erlbaum Associates.
Gray, J. A. (1982). *The neuropsychology of anxiety*. Oxford: Oxford University Press.
Greenberg, L. S., & Safran, J. D. (1984). Integrating affect and cognition: A perspective on the process of therapeutic change. *Cognitive Therapy and Research, 8,* 559–578.
Greenfield, N. S., & Sternbach, R. A. (1972). *Handbook of psychophysiology*. New York: Holt, Reinhart & Winston.
Greenwald, M. K., Cook, E. W. III, & Lang, P. J. (in press). Affective judgement and psychophysiological response: Dimensional covariation in the evaluation of pictorial stimuli. *Journal of Psychophysiology*.

Grey, S. J., Rachman, S., & Sartory, G. (1981). Return of fear: The role of inhibition. *Behaviour Research and Therapy, 19,* 135–143.
Grey, S. J., Sartory, G., & Rachman, S. (1979). Synchronous and desynchronous changes during fear reduction. *Behaviour Research and Theory, 17,* 137–147.
Grings, W. W., & Dawson, M. E. (1978). *Emotions and bodily responses: A psychophysiological approach*. New York: Academic Press.
Gruzelier, J. H., & Venables, P. H. (1975). Evidence of high and low levels of physiological arousal in schizophrenia. *Psychophysiology, 12,* 66–73.
Guze, S. B. (1977). The future of psychiatry: Medicine or social sciences. *Journal of Nervous and Mental Disease, 165,* 225–230.
Hare, R. D., & Blevings, G. (1975). Defensive responses to phobic stimuli. *Biological Psychology, 3,* 1–13.
Hastrup, J. L. (1986). Duration of initial heart rate assessment in Psychophysiology: Current practices and implications. *Psychophysiology, 23,* 15–18.
Hayes, S. C., & Nelson, R. O. (1986). Assessing the effects of therapeutic interventions. In R. O. Nelson & S. C. Hayes (Eds.), *Conceptual foundations of behavioral assessment*. New York: Guilford Press.
Hayes, S. C., Nelson, R. O., & Jarrett, R. B. (1986). Evaluating the quality of behavioral assessment. In R. O. Nelson & S. C. Hayes (Eds.), *Conceptual foundations of behavioral assessment*. New York: Guilford Press.
Haynes, S. N., & Gannon, L. (1981). *Psychosomatic disorders: A psychophysiological approach to etiology and treatment*. New York: Praeger.
Haynes, S. N., & Wilson, C. C. (1979). *Behavioural assessment*. San Francisco: Jossey-Bass.
Haynes, S. N., Falkin, S., & Sexton-Radek, K. (1989). Psychophysiological assessment in behavior therapy. In G. Turpin (Ed.), *Handbook of clinical psychophysiology*. Chichester: John Wiley & Sons.
Heimberg, R. G., Gansler, D., & Dodge, C. S. (1987). Convergent and discriminant validity of the Cognitive-Somatic Anxiety Questionnaire in a social phobic population. *Behavioral Assessment, 9,* 379–388.
Hemsley, D. R., & Philips, C. H. (1975). Models of mania: An individual case study. *British Journal of Psychiatry, 127,* 78–85.
Hersen, M., & Bellack, A. S. (Eds.) (1976). *Behavioral assessment: A practical handbook*. Elmsford, NY: Pergamon Press.
Himadi, W., Boice, R., & Barlow, D. H. (1985). Assessment of agoraphobia: Triple response measurement. *Behaviour Research and Therapy, 23,* 311–323.
Himadi, W. G., Boice, R., & Barlow, D. H. (1986). Assessment of agoraphobia—II. Measurement of clinical change. *Behaviour Research and Therapy, 24,* 321–332.
Hodes, R. L., Cook, E. W., III, & Lang, P. J. (1985). Individual differences in autonomic arousal. Conditioned association or conditioned fear? *Psychophysiology, 22,* 545–560.

Hodgson, R., & Rachman, S. (1974). Desynchrony in measures of fear. *Behaviour Research and Therapy, 12,* 319–326.

Holden, A. E., & Barlow, D. H. (1986). Heart rate and heart rate variability recorded in vivo in agoraphobics and nonphobics. *Behavior Therapy, 17,* 26–42.

Hollandsworth, J. G. (1986). *Physiology and behavior therapy: Conceptual guidelines for the clinician.* New York: Plenum Press.

Hugdahl, K. (1981). The three systems model of fear and emotion—a critical examination. *Behaviour Research and Therapy, 19,* 75–86.

Iacono, W. G., & Ficken, J. W. (1989). Research strategies employing psychophysiological measures: Identifying and using psychophysiological markers. In G. Turpin (Ed.), *Handbook of clinical psychophysiology.* Chichester: John Wiley & Sons.

Iacono, W. G., & Lykken, D. T. (1979). The orienting response: Importance of instructions. *Schizophrenia Bulletin, 5,* 11–14.

Izard, C. E. (1977). *Human emotions.* New York: Plenum Press.

Jerremalm, A., Jansson, L., & Ost, L. G. (1986). Cognitive and physiological reactivity and the effects of different behavioral methods in the treatment of social phobia. *Behaviour Research and Therapy, 24,* 171–180.

Johnston, V. S., Miller, D. R., & Burleson, M. H. (1986). Multiple P3s to emotional stimuli and their theoretical significance. *Psychophysiology, 23,* 684–694.

Kallman, W., & Feuerstein, M. J. (1986). Psychophysiological Procedures. In A. R. Ciminero, K. S. Calhoun, & H. E. Adams (Eds.) *Handbook of behavioral assessment.* New York: John Wiley & Sons.

Kaloupek, D. G., & Levis, D. J. (1983). Issues in the assessment of fear: Response concordance and prediction of avoidance behavior. *Journal of Behavioral Assessment, 5,* 239–260.

Kartsounis, L. D., & Turpin, G. (1987). Effects of induced hyperventilation on electrodermal response habituation to agoraphobia-relevant stimuli. *Journal of Psychosomatic Research, 31,* 401–412.

Kazdin, A. E. (1980). *Research design in clinical psychology.* New York: Harper & Row.

Klorman, R., & Ryan, R. M. (1980). Heart rate, contingent negative variation and evoked potentials during anticipation of affective stimulation. *Psychophysiology, 17,* 513–523.

Klorman, R., Wiessberg, R. P., & Weisenfeld, A. R. (1977). Individual differences in fear and autonomic reactions to affective stimulation. *Psychophysiology, 14,* 45–51.

Kozak, M. J., Foa, E. B., & Steketee, G. (1988). Process and outcome exposure treatment with obsessive-compulsives: Psychophysiology indicators of emotional processing. *Behavior Therapy, 19,* 157–169.

Kozak, M. J., & Miller, G. A. (1982). Hypothetical constructs vs intervening variables: A reappraisal of the three-system model of anxiety assessment. *Behavioral Assessment, 4,* 347–358.

Kozak, M. J., & Miller, G. A. (1985). The psychophysiological process of therapy in a case of injury-scene-elicited fainting. *Journal of Behavior Therapy and Experimental Psychiatry, 16,* 139–145.

Kratochwill, T. R. (1978). *Single subject research: Strategies for evaluating change.* New York: Academic Press.

Lacey, B. C., & Lacey, J. I. (1978). Two-way communication between the heart and the brain. *American Psychologist, 33,* 99–113.

Lacey, J. I. (1959). Psychophysiological approaches to the evaluation of psychotherapeutic process and outcome. In E. I. Rubenstein & M. B. Parloff (Eds.), *Research in psychotherapy.* Washington, DC: American Psychological Association.

Lacey, J. I., & Lacey, B. (1962). The law of initial value and the longitudinal study of autonomic constitution: Reproduceability of autonomic responses and response patterns over a four-year interval. *Annals of the New York Academy of Sciences, 98,* 1257–1290.

Lader, M. H. (1967). Palmer skin conductance measures anxiety and phobic states. *Journal of Psychosomatic Research, 11,* 271–281.

Lader, M. H. (1975). *The psychophysiology of mental illness.* London: Routledge and Kegan Paul.

Lader, M. H., & Wing, L. (1966). *Physiological measures, sedative drugs and morbid anxiety.* London: Oxford University Press.

Lang, P. J. (1968). Fear reduction and fear behavior: Problems in treating a construct. In J. M. Shlien (Ed.), *Research in psychotherapy.* Washington, DC: American Psychological Association.

Lang, P. J. (1971). The application of psychophysiological methods to the study of psychotherapy and behavior modification. In A. E. Bergin & S. L. Garfield (Eds.) *Handbook of psychotherapy and behavior change: An empirical analysis.* New York: John Wiley & Sons.

Lang, P. J. (1977). Imagery in therapy: An information processing analysis of fear. *Behavior Therapy, 8,* 862–886.

Lang, P. J. (1978). Anxiety: Towards a psychophysiological definition. In H. S. Akiskal & W. H. Webb (Eds.), *Psychiatric diagnosis: Exploration of biological predictors.* New York: Spectrum Publications.

Lang, P. J. (1979). A bio-informational theory of emotional imagery. *Psychophysiology, 16,* 495–512.

Lang, P. J. (1984). Cognition in emotion: Concept and action. In C. E. Izard, J. Kagan, & R. B. Zajonc (Eds.), *Emotions, cognition and behavior.* Cambridge: Cambridge University Press.

Lang, P. J. (1985). The cognitive psychophysiology of emotion: Fear and anxiety. In A. H. Tuma & J. D. Maser (Eds.), *Anxiety and the anxiety disorders.* Hillsdale, NJ: Lawrence Erlbaum Associates.

Lang, P. J. (1987). Image as action: A reply to Watts and Blackstock. *Cognition and Emotion, 1,* 407–426.

Lang, P. J. (1988). Fear, anxiety and panic: Context, cognition and visceral arousal. In S. Rachman & J. D.

Maser (Eds.), *Panic: Psychological perspectives*. Hillsdale, NJ: Lawrence Erlbaum Associates.

Lang, P. J., Kozak, M. J., Miller, G. A., Levin, D. N., & McLean, A., Jr. (1980). Emotional imagery: Conceptual structure and pattern of somato-visceral response. *Psychophysiology, 17*, 179–192.

Lang, P. J., Levin, D. N., Miller, G. A., & Kozak, M. J. (1983). Fear behavior, fear imagery, and the psychophysiology of emotion: The problem of affective response integration. *Journal of Abnormal Psychology, 92*, 276–306.

Lang, P. J., Melamed, B. G., & Hart, J. D. (1970). A psychophysiological analysis of fear modification using an automated desensitization procedure. *Journal of Abnormal Psychology, 31*, 220–234.

Lazarus, R. S. (1966). *Psychological stress and the coping process*. New York: McGraw-Hill.

Lazarus, R. S. (1982). Thought on the relations between emotion and cognition. *American Psychologist, 9*, 1019–1024.

Lazarus, R. S. (1984). On the primacy of cognition. *American Psychologist, 39*, 124–129.

Lazarus, R. S., & Folkman, S. (1984). *Stress, appraisal and coping*. New York: Springer.

Leigh, H. (1982). Comment: The role of psychiatry in medicine. *American Journal of Psychiatry, 139*, 1581–1587.

Levenson, R. W. (1983). Personality research and psychophysiology: General considerations. *Journal of Research in Personality, 17*, 1–21.

Levenson, R. W. (1988). Emotion and the autonomic nervous system: A prospectus for research on autonomic specificity. In H. Wagner (Ed.), *Social psychophysiology and emotion: Theory and clinical applications*. Chichester: John Wiley & Sons.

Levenson, R. W., & Gottman, J. M. (1983). Marital interaction: Physiological linkage and affective exchange. *Journal of Personal and Social Psychology, 45*, 587–597.

Leventhal, H. (1970). Findings and theory in the study of fear communications. In L. Berkowitz (Ed.), *Advances in experimental and social psychology, Vol 5*. New York: Academic Press.

Leventhal, H. (1982). The integration of emotion and cognition: A view from the Perceptual-Motor theory of emotion. In M. S. Clark & S. T. Fiske (Eds.), *Affect and cognition*. Hillsdale, NJ: Lawrence Erlbaum Associates.

Leventhal, H., & Mosbach, P. (1983). Perceptual-motor theory. In J. T. Caccioppo & R. E. Petty (Eds.), *Social psychophysiology: A source book*. New York: Guilford Press.

Levey, A. B., & Martin, I. (1987). Theories in psychophysiology: An open forum. *Journal of Psychophysiology, 1*, 3–7.

Linden, W. (1987). A microanalysis of autonomic activity during human speech. *Psychosomatic Medicine, 49*, 562–578.

Linden, W., & McEachern, H. M. (1985). A review of physiological prestress adaptation: Effects of duration and context. *International Journal of Psychophysiology, 2*, 239–245.

Linehan, M. (1980). Content validity: Its relevance to behavioral assessment. *Behavioral Assessment, 2*, 147–159.

Llabre, M. M., Ironson, G. H., Spitzer, S. B., Gellman, M. D., Weidler, D. J., & Schneiderman, N. (1988). How many blood pressure measurements are enough? An application of Generalizability Theory to the study of blood pressure reliability. *Psychophysiology, 25*, 97–106.

Lynch, J. P., Thomas, S. A., Paskewitz, D. A., Malinow, K. L., & Long, J. M. (1982). Inter-personal aspects of blood pressure control. *Journal of Nervous and Mental Disease, 170*, 143–153.

MacLeod, C., Mathews, A., & Tata, P. (1986). Attentional bias in emotional disorders. *Journal of Abnormal Psychology, 95*, 15–20.

Mandler, G. (1975). *Mind and emotion*. New York: John Wiley & Sons.

Mandler, G. (1982). The structure of value: Accounting for taste. In M. S. Clark, & S. T. Fiske (Eds.), *Affect and cognition*. Hillsdale, NJ: Lawrence Erlbaum Associates.

Mandler, G., Mandler, J. M., & Uviller, E. T. (1958). Autonomic feedback: The perception of autonomic activity. *Journal of Abnormal and Social Psychology, 56*, 367–373.

Marcel, A. J. (1983). Conscious and unconscious perception: Experiments on visual masking and word recognition. *Cognitive Psychology, 15*, 197–237.

Martin, B. (1961). The assessment of anxiety by physiological and behavioral measures. *Psychological Bulletin, 58*, 234–255.

Martin, I., & Venables, P. H. (1980). *Techniques in psychophysiology*. Chichester: John Wiley & Sons.

Matias, R., & Turner, S. M. (1986). Concordance and discordance in speech anxiety assessment: The effects of demand characteristics on the tripartite assessment method. *Behaviour Research and Therapy, 24*, 537–546.

Mavissakalian, M. (1987). Trimodal assessment in agoraphobia research: Further observations on heart rate and synchrony/desynchrony. *Journal of Psychopathology and Behavioral Assessment, 9*, 89–98.

Mavissakalian, M., & Michelson, L. (1982). Patterns of psychophysiological change in the treatment of agoraphobia. *Behaviour Research and Therapy, 20*, 347–356.

McFall, R. M. (1977). Theory and method in assessment: The vital link. *Behavioral Assessment, 8*, 3–10.

McFall, R. M., & McDonel, E. C. (1986). The continuing search for units of analysis in psychology: Beyond persons, situations, and their interactions. In R. O. Nelson & S. C. Hayes, (Eds.), *Conceptual foundations of behavioral assessment*. New York: Guilford Press.

McKinney, M. E., Miner, M. H., Ruddel, H., McIlvain,

H. E., Witte, H., Buell, J. C., Eliot, R. S., & Grant, L. B. (1985). The standardization mental stress test protocol: Test-retest reliability and comparisons with ambulatory blood pressure monitoring. *Psychophysiology, 22*, 453–463.

McNally, R. J. (1986). Preparedness and phobias: A review. *Psychological Bulletin, 101*, 283–303.

Michelson, L., & Mavissakalian, M. (1985). Psychophysiological outcome of behavioral and pharmacological treatments of agoraphobia. *Journal of Consulting and Clinical Psychology, 53*, 229–236.

Michelson, L., Mavissakalian, M., & Marchione, K. (1985). Cognitive and behavioral treatments of agoraphobia: Clinical, behavioral and psychophysiological outcomes. *Journal of Consulting and Clinical Psychology, 53*, 913–925.

Michelson, L., Mavissakalian, M., & Marchione, K. (1988). Cognitive, behavioral and psychophysiological treatments of agoraphobia: A comparative outcome investigation. *Behavior Therapy, 19*, 97–120.

Miller, G. A., & Ebert, L. (1988). Conceptual boundaries in psychophysiology. *Journal of Psychophysiology, 2*, 13.

Miller, G. A., Levin, D. N., Kozak, M. J., Cook, E. W., III, McLean, A., & Lang, P. J. (1987). Individual differences in emotional imagery. *Cognition and Emotion, 1*, 367–390.

Mills, I., & Salkovskis, P. M. (1988). Mood and habituation to phobic stimuli. *Behaviour Research and Therapy, 26*, 435–439.

Morey, L. C., Skinner, H. A., & Blashfield, R. K. (1986). Trends in the classification of abnormal behavior. In A. R. Ciminero, K. S. Calhoun, & H. E. Adams (Eds.), *Handbook of behavioral assessment*, (2nd ed.). New York: John Wiley & Sons.

Mowrer, O. H. (Ed.) (1953). *Psychotherapy: Theory and research*. New York: Ronald Press.

Nagayama Hall, G. C., Proctor, W. C., & Nelson, G. M. (1988). Validity of physiological measures of paedophilic sexual arousal in a sexual offender population. *Journal of Consulting and Clinical Psychology, 56*, 118–122.

Nay, W. R. (1979). *Multimethod clinical assessment*. New York: Gardner Press.

Nay, W. R. (1986). Analogue measures. In A. R. Ciminero, K. S. Calhoun, & H. E. Adams (Eds.). *Handbook of behavioral assessment*, (2nd ed.). New York: John Wiley & Sons.

Nebylitsyn, V. D., & Gray, J. A. (1972). *Biological bases of individual behavior*. New York: Academic Press.

Nelson, R. O., & Hayes, S. C. (1981). Nature of behavioral assessment. In M. Hersen & A. S. Bellack (Eds.), *Behavioral assessment: A practical handbook* (2nd ed.). Elmsford, NY: Pergamon Press.

Nelson, R. O., & Hayes, S. C. (Eds.) (1986). *Conceptual foundations of behavioral assessment*. New York: Guilford Press.

Nicassio, P. M., & Buchanan, D. C. (1981). Clinical application of behavior therapy for insomnia. *Comprehensive Psychiatry, 22*, 512–521.

Noble, P. J., & Lader, M. H. (1971). The symptomatic correlates of skin conductance changes in depression. *Journal of Psychiatric Research, 9*, 61–69.

Noble, P. J., & Lader, M. H. (1972). A physiological comparison of "endogenous" and "reactive" depression. *British Journal of Psychiatry, 120*, 541–542.

Nuechterlein, K. H., & Dawson, M. (1984). A heuristic vulnerability/stress model of schizophrenic episodes. *Schizophrenia Bulletin, 10*, 300–312.

Obrist, P. A. (1981). *Cardiovascular psychophysiology: A perspective*. New York: Plenum Press.

Ohman, A. (1981a). The role of experimental psychology in the scientific analysis of psychopathology. *International Journal of Psychology, 16*, 229–321.

Ohman, A. (1981b). Electrodermal activity and vulnerability to schizophrenia: A review. *Biological Psychology, 12*, 87–145.

Ohman, A. (1986). Face the beast and fear the face: Animal and social fears as prototypes for evolutionary analyses of emotion. *Psychophysiology, 23*, 123–145.

Ohman, A. (1987). Psychophysiology of emotion: An evolutionary-cognitive perspective. In P. K. Ackles, J. R. Jennings, & M. G. H. Coles (Eds.), *Advances in psychophysiology, Vol. 2*. Greenwich, CT: JAI Press.

Ohman, A. (1988). Nonconscious control of autonomic responses: A role for Pavlovian conditioning? *Biological Psychology, 27*, 113–136.

Ohman, A., Dimberg, U., Esteves, F. (1989). Preattentive activation of aversive emotions. In T. Archer & L. G. Nilsson (Eds.), *Aversion, avoidance and anxiety: Perspectives on aversively motivated behavior*. Hillsdale, NJ: Lawrence Erlbaum Associates.

Ohman, A., Dimberg, U., & Ost, L. G. (1985). Animal and social phobias: Biological constraints on learned fear responses. In S. Reiss & R. R. Bootzin (Eds.), *Theoretical issues in behavior therapy*. New York: Academic Press.

O'Kelly, L. I. (1953). Physiological changes during psychotherapy. In O. H. Mowrer (Ed.), *Psychotherapy: Theory and research*. New York: Ronald Press.

Olton, D. S., & Noonberg, A. R. (Eds.) (1980). *Biofeedback: Clinical applications in behavioral medicine*. Englewood Cliffs, NJ: Prentice-Hall.

Ost, L. G., Jerremalm, A., & Jansson, L. (1984). Individual response patterns and the effects of different behavioral methods in the treatment of agoraphobia. *Behaviour Research and Therapy, 22*, 697–707.

Ost, L. G., Jerremalm, A., & Johansson, J. (1981). Individual response patterns and the effects of different behavioral methods in the treatment of social phobia. *Behaviour Research and Therapy, 19*, 1–16.

Ost, L. G., Johansson, J., & Jerremalm, A. (1982). Individual response patterns and the effects of different behavioral methods in the treatment of claustrophobia. *Behaviour Research and Therapy, 20*, 445–460.

Peterson, L. (1984). A brief methodological comment on possible inaccuracies induced by multimodal measurement analysis and reporting. *Journal of Behavioral Medicine, 7,* 307–313.

Philips, C. (1980). Recent developments in tension headache research: Implications for understanding and management of the disorder. In S. Rachman (Ed.) *Contributions to Medical Psychology, Vol. 2.* Oxford: Pergamon Press.

Pierce, W. D., & Epling, W. F. (1980). What happened to analysis in applied behavior analysis? *Behavior Analyst, 7,* 1–9.

Plutchik, R., & Kellerman, H. (Eds.). (1980). *Emotion: Theory, research and experience. Vol. 1: Theories of emotion.* New York: Academic Press.

Pope, A. T. (1978). Electrical safety in the use of biofeedback instruments. *Behavior Research Methods and Instrumentation, 10,* 627–631.

Rachman, S. (1981). The primacy of affect: Some theoretical implications. *Behaviour Research and Therapy, 19,* 279–290.

Rachman, S., & Hodgson, R. (1974). Synchrony and desynchrony in fear and avoidance. *Behaviour Research and Therapy, 12,* 311–318.

Rachman, S., & Levitt, K. (1988). Panic, fear reduction and habituation. *Behaviour Research and Therapy, 26,* 199–206.

Ray, W. J., & Raczynski, J. M. (1981). Psychophysiological assessment. In M. Hersen & A. S. Bellack (Eds.), *Behavioral assessment: A practical handbook* (2nd ed.). Oxford: Pergamon Press.

Reed, S. D., Katkin, E. S., & Goldband, S. (1986). Biofeedback and behavioral medicine. In F. H. Kanfer & A. P. Goldstein (Eds.), *Helping people change: A textbook of methods,* (3rd ed.). Elmsford, NY: Pergamon Press.

Reich, W. (1982). *The Bioelectrical investigation of sexuality and anxiety.* New York: Farrar, Straus and Giroux.

Reisenzein, R. (1983). The Schatcher theory of emotion: Two decades later. *Psychological Bulletin, 94,* 236–264.

Robinson, J. W., Whitsett, S. F., & Kaplan, B. J. (1987). The stability of physiological reactivity over multiple sessions. *Biological Psychology, 24,* 129–139.

Rugh, J. D., Gable, R. S., & Lemke, R. R. (1986). Instrumentation for behavioral assessment. In A. R. Ciminero, K. S. Calhoun, & H. E. Adams (Eds.), *Handbook of behavioral assessment,* (2nd ed.). New York: John Wiley & Sons.

Sartory, G., Eves, F., & Foa, E. (1987). Maintenance of within session habituation of the cardiac response to phobic stimulation. *Journal of Psychophysiology, 1,* 21–34.

Sartory, G., Rachman, S., & Grey, S. (1977). An investigation of the relation between fear and heart rate. *Behaviour Research and Therapy, 15,* 435–438.

Schachter, S., & Singer, S. (1962). Cognitive, social and physiological determinants of emotional states. *Psychological Review, 69,* 379–399.

Schwartz, G. E. (1978). Psychobiological foundations of psychotherapy and behaviour change. In S. L. Garfield & A. E. Bergin (Eds.) *Handbook of psychotherapy and behavior change* (2nd ed.). New York: John Wiley & Sons.

Schwartz, G. E. (1983). Social psychophysiology and behavioral medicine: A systems perspective. In J. T. Cacioppo & R. E. Petty (Eds.) *Social psychophysiology: A sourcebook.* New York: Guilford Press.

Seligman, M. E. P. (1971). Phobias and preparedness. *Behavior Therapy, 2,* 307–320.

Shagass, C. (1976). An electrophysiological view of schizophrenia. *Biological Psychiatry, 11,* 3–30.

Siddle, D. A. T., & Turpin, G. (1980). Measurement, quantification and analysis of cardiac activity. In I. Martin & P. H. Venables (Eds.), *Techniques in psychophysiology.* Chichester: John Wiley & Sons.

Silverman, J. J., & Powell, V. E. (1944). Studies on palmar sweating. *Psychosomatic Medicine, 6,* 243–249.

Sokolov, E. N. (1963). *Perception and the conditioned reflex.* Oxford: Pergamon Press.

Statts, A. W. (1986). Behaviorism with a personality: The paradigmatic behavioral assessment approach. In R. O. Nelson & S. C. Hayes (Eds.), *Conceptual foundations of behavioral assessment.* New York: Guilford Press.

Stemmler, G., & Fahrenberg, J. (1988). Psychophysiological assessment: Conceptual, psychometric, and statistical issues. In G. Turpin (Ed.), *Handbook of clinical psychophysiology.* Chichester: John Wiley & Sons.

Steptoe, A. (1980). Stress and medical disorders. In S. J. Rachman (Ed.), *Contributions to medical psychology, Vol. II.* Oxford: Pergamon Press.

Steptoe, A. (1987). The assessment of sympathetic nervous function in human stress research. *Journal of Psychosomatic Research, 31,* 141–152.

Steptoe, A. (1989). Psychophysiological interventions in behavioral medicine. In G. Turpin (Ed.) *Handbook of clinical psychophysiology.* Chichester: John Wiley & Sons.

Stern, J. A. (1964). Toward a definition of psychophysiology. *Psychophysiology, 1,* 90–91.

Stern, J. A., & Plapp, J. M. (1969). Psychophysiology and clinical psychology. In C. D. Spielberger (Ed.), *Current topics in clinical and community psychology, Vol. I.* New York: Academic Press.

Stern, R. M., Ray, W. J., & Davis, C. M. (1980). *Psychophysiological recording.* New York: Oxford University Press.

Sternbach, R. A. (1966). *Principles of psychophysiology.* New York: Academic Press.

Strosahl, K. D., & Linehan, M. M. (1986). Basic issues in behavioral assessment. In A. R. Ciminero, K. S. Calhoun, & H. E. Adams (Eds.), *Handbook of behavioral assessment* (2nd ed.). New York: John Wiley & Sons.

Sturgis, E. T., & Arena, J. G. (1984). Psychophysiological assessment. *Progress in behavior modification, Vol. 17.* New York: Academic Press.

Sturgis, E. T., & Gramling, S. (1988). Psychophysiological assessment. In A. S. Bellack & M. Hersen (Eds.), *Behavioral assessment: A practical handbook* (3rd ed.). Elmsford, NY: Pergamon Press.

Surwillo, W. W., Shafii, M., & Barrett, C. L. (1978). Gilles de la Tourette Syndrome: A 20-month study of the effects of stressful life events and haloperidol on symptom frequency. *Journal of Nervous and Mental Disease, 169,* 812–816.

Surwit, R. S., Williams, R. B., Steptoe, A., & Biersner, R. (Eds.). (1982). *Behavioural treatment of disease.* New York: Plenum Press.

Tarrier, N. (1979). The future of the medical model: A reply to Guze. *Journal of Nervous and Mental Disease, 167,* 71–73.

Tarrier, N., & Barrowclough, C. (1984). Psychophysiological assessment of expressed emotion in schizophrenia: A case example. *British Journal of Psychiatry, 145,* 197–203.

Tarrier, N., Vaughn, C. E., Lader, M. H., & Leff, J. P. (1978). Bodily reactions to people and events in schizophrenia. *Archives of General Psychiatry, 36,* 311–315.

Thorell, L. H., Kjellman, B. F., d'Elia, G., & Kagedal, B. (1988). Electrodermal activity in relation to cortisal dysregulation in depressive patients. *Acta Psychiatrica Scandanavia, 8,* 743–753.

Turpin, G. (1983a). Unconditioned reflexes and autonomic nervous system. In D. Siddle (Ed.) *Orienting and habituation: Perspectives in human research.* Chichester: John Wiley & Sons.

Turpin, G. (1983b). Psychophysiology, psychopathology and the social environment. In A. Gale & J. Edwards (Eds.), *Physiological correlates of human behaviour, Vol. 3: Individual differences and psychopathology.* London: Academic Press.

Turpin, G. (1985a). Quantification, analysis and interpretation of phasic cardiac responses. In D. Papakostopoulos, S. Butler, & I. Martin (Eds.) *Clinical and experimental neuropsychophysiology.* London: Croom Helm.

Turpin, G. (1985b). Ambulatory psychophysiological monitoring: Techniques and applications. In D. Papakostopoulos, S. Butler, & I. Martin (Eds.), *Clinical and experimental neuropsychophysiology.* London: Croom Helm.

Turpin, G. (1986). Effects of stimulus intensity on autonomic responding: The problem of differentiating orienting and defense reflexes. *Psychophysiology, 23,* 1–14.

Turpin, G. (Ed.). (1988, September). *Ambulatory clinical psychophysiological monitoring: Proceedings of a symposium held at the World Congress of Behavior Therapy, Edinburgh, Scotland.* Manuscript submitted for publication.

Turpin, G. (Ed.) (1989a). *Handbook of clinical psychophysiology.* Chichester, England: John Wiley & Sons.

Turpin, G. (1989b). An overview of clinical psychophysiological techniques: Tools or theories? In G. Turpin, (Ed.), *Handbook of clinical psychophysiology.* Chichester: John Wiley & Sons.

Turpin, G. & Lader, M. (1986). Life events and mental disorder: Biological theories of their mode of action. In H. Katschnig (Ed.), *Life events and psychiatric disorders: Controversial issues.* Cambridge: Cambridge University Press.

Turpin, G., & Powell, G. E. (1984). The effects of massed practice and cue-controlled relaxation on tic frequency in Gilles de la Tourette's syndrome. *Behaviour Research and Therapy, 22,* 165–178.

Turpin, G., Tarrier, N., & Sturgeon, D. (1988). Social psychophysiology and the study of biopsychosocial models of schizophrenia. In H. L. Wagner (Ed.) *Social psychophysiology: Theory and clinical applications.* Chichester: John Wiley & Sons.

Usdin, E., & Hanin, I. (Eds.) (1982). *Biological markers in psychiatry and neurology.* Oxford: Pergamon Press.

Van Praag, H. M. (1981). Sociobiological psychiatry. *Comprehensive Psychiatry, 22,* 441–449.

Van Praag, H. M., Lader, M. H., Rafaelsen, O. J., & Sachar, E. J. (Eds.) (1980). *Handbook of biological psychiatry, Part II: Brain mechanisms and abnormal behavior-psychophysiology.* New York: Marcel-Dekker.

Venables, P. H. (1984). Arousal: An examination of its status as a concept. In M. G. H. Coles, J. R. Jennings, & J. A. Stern (Eds.), *Psychophysiological perspectives: Festschrfit for Beatrice and John Lacey.* New York: Van Nostrand Reinhold.

Venables, P. H., & Bernstein, A. S. (1983). The orienting response and psychopathology: Schizophrenia. In D. Siddle (Ed.), *Orienting and habituation: perspectives in human research.* Chichester: John Wiley & Sons.

Vermilyea, J. A., Boice, R., & Barlow, D. H. (1984). Rachman and Hodgson (1974) a decade later: how do desynchronous response systems relate to treatment of agoraphobia? *Behaviour Research and Therapy, 22,* 615–621.

Vrana, S. R., Cuthbert, B. C., & Lang, P. J. (1986). Fear imagery and text processing. *Psychophysiology, 23,* 247–253.

Vrana, S. R., Spence, E. L., & Lang, P. J. (1988). The startle probe response: A new measure of emotion? *Journal of Abnormal Psychology, 97,* 487–491.

Wallace, E. R. (1988). Mind and body: Monistic Dual Aspects Interactionism. *Journal of Nervous and Mental Disease, 176,* 4–21.

Walrath, L. C., & Stern, J. A. (1981). General considerations. In H. M. Van Praag, M. H. Lader, O. J. Rafaelsen, & E. J. Sachar (Eds.), *Handbook of biological psychiatry, Part II: Brain mechanisms and abnormal behaviour-psychophysiology.* New York: Marcel-Dekker.

Ward, N. G., & Doerr, H. O. (1986). Skin conductance: A potentially sensitive and specific marker for depression. *Journal of Nervous and Mental Disease, 174,* 553–559.

Waters, W. F., Williamson, D. A., Bernard, B. A., Blouin,

D. C., & Faulstich, M. E. (1987). Test-retest reliability of psychophysiological assessment. *Behaviour Research and Therapy, 25,* 213–223.

Watts, F. N. (1983). Affective cognition: a sequel to Zajonc and Rachman. *Bahaviour Research and Therapy, 21,* 89–90.

Watts, F. N., & Blackstock, A. J. (1987). Lang's theory of emotional imagery. *Cognition and Emotion, 1,* 391–406.

Weiner, H. (1977). *Psychobiology and human disease.* New York: Elsevier Science.

Wenger, M. A. (1941). The measurement of individual differences in autonomic balance. *Psychosomatic Medicine, 3,* 427–434.

Whitsett, S. F., Robinson, J. W., & Kaplan, B. J. (1987). A comparison of three approaches for the determination of baseline levels of physiological activity. *International Journal of Psychophysiology, 5,* 53–61.

Williams, J. M. G., Watts, F. N., MacLeod, C., & Mathews, A. (1988). *Cognitive psychology and emotional disorders.* Chichester, John Wiley & Sons.

Williams, S. L. (1985). On the nature and measurement of agoraphobia. In M. Hersen, R. M. Eisler, & P. M. Miller (Eds.), *Progress in behavior modification, Vol. 19.* Orlando, Academic Press.

Williamson, D. A., Waters, W. F., & Hawkins, M. F. (1986). Physiologic variables. In R. O. Nelson & S. C. Hayes (Eds.) *Conceptual foundations of behavioral assessment.* New York: Guilford Press.

Wittkower, E. D. (1977). Historical perspective of contemporary psychosomatic medicine. In S. J. Lipowski, D. R. Lipsitt, & P. C. Whybrow (Eds.), *Psychosomatic medicine: Current trends and clinical applications.* New York: Oxford University Press.

Wolff, W. T., & Merrens, M. R. (1974). Behavioral assessment: A review of clinical methods. *Journal of Personality Assessment, 38,* 3–16.

Yee, C. M., & Miller, G. A. (1988). Emotional information processing: Modulation of fear in normal and dysthymic subjects. *Journal of Abnormal Psychology, 97,* 54–63.

Zahn, T. P. (1986). Psychophysiological approaches to psychopathology. In M. G. H. Coles, E. Donchin, & S. W. Porges (Eds.), *Psychophysiology: Systems, processes and applications.* New York: Guilford Press.

Zajonc, R. B. (1980). Feeling and thinking: Preferences need no inferences. *American Psychologist, 35,* 151–175.

Zajonc, R. B. (1984). On the primacy of affect. *American Psychologist, 39,* 117–123.

Zajonc, R. B., & Markus, H. (1989). Affect and cognition: The hard interface. In C. E. Izard, J. Kagan, & R. B. Zajonc (Eds.), *Emotions, cognition and behavior.* Cambridge, Cambridge University Press.

Zillmann, D. (1978). Attribution and misattribution of excitatory reactions. In J. H. Harvey, W. Ickes, & F. R. Kidd (Eds.), *New directions in attribution research, Vol. 2.* Hillsdale, NJ: Lawrence Erlbaum Associates.

Zubin, J., & Spring, B. (1977). Vulnerability: A new view of schizophrenia. *Journal of Abnormal Psychology, 86,* 103–126.

CHAPTER 19

PSYCHOPHYSIOLOGICAL CONTRIBUTIONS TO BEHAVIOR THERAPY

Derek W. Johnston
Paul R. Martin

Psychophysiology has strong links to behavior therapy directed at the treatment of anxiety conditions largely because behavior therapy, as developed by Wolpe (1958), adopted an essentially peripheralist theory of anxiety. Wolpe claimed that anxiety could be reduced when an anxiety provoking stimulus was presented under circumstances that inhibited the expression of anxiety, such as in conjunction with muscular relaxation. It was therefore natural to examine the peripheral manifestations of anxiety. This was most readily done with simple psychophysiological measures such as heart rate or skin conductance. A further pressure in the same direction was the early emphasis on the use of imagery in therapy. There was, and is, no adequate direct measure of mental images and hence physiological responses were one of the few objective tools for studying the process of therapy. In this chapter we will consider the current status of the link between behavior therapy and psychophysiology. The chapter will, of necessity, be highly selective. Its main objective is to stimulate researchers with an interest in psychophysiology, behavior therapy or both. Discussion of terms and references in psychophysiology are included to help orientate readers who have little knowledge of the area, and to provide a follow-up for areas of interest.

The chapter is divided into four sections. The overview discusses the field of psychophysiology, and provides a guide to psychophysiology (including the definition of psychophysiology) and to the published literature. The following subsection focuses on recent theoretical and technical developments in the field. The final subsection provides a historical review of the links between psychophysiology and behavior therapy.

Because it would be impossible to review all of the contributions of psychophysiology to behavior therapy in this chapter, three areas have been chosen for illustrative purposes. The areas are: anxiety, fear, and panic; biofeedback as applied to the cardiovascular system and cardiovascular disorders; and psychophysiological mechanisms of, and biofeedback for, chronic headaches. These areas reflect particular research interests of the authors, but have also been chosen because they provide contrasting examples (e.g., problems from the mental health arena versus behavioral medicine; disorders associated with the autonomic and somatic divisions of the peripheral nervous system; and fields for which psychophysiology has contributed in different ways).

THE FIELD OF PSYCHOPHYSIOLOGY

Although the roots of psychophysiology can be traced back many centuries, the formal development of psychophysiology as a separate discipline began in the 1950s, when a group composed mainly of psychologists met informally under the leadership of R. C. Davis and others (Stern, Ray, & Davis, 1980). In 1960, this group organized the Society for Psychophysiological Research, and in 1964, a newsletter produced by this group was upgraded to become the journal *Psychophysiology*.

A definition of psychophysiology that appeared in the first issue of this journal delineated the field as "any research in which the dependent variable (subject's response) is a physiological measure and the independent variable (the factor manipulated by the experimenter) a behavioral one" (Stern, 1964, p. 90). As the field developed, however, this definition proved too restrictive. Aided by the emergence of biofeedback, it became possible to conduct experiments in which physiological variables were manipulated and behavioral changes measured. Consequently, modern definitions of psychophysiology simply state that it is the study of the relationship between cognition, emotion, behavior, and physiological systems.

Physiological psychologists also study the relationship between physiological and psychological variables, but they usually study the effects of manipulations of the brain or other parts of the nervous system on some aspect of behavior. Much of this research results in permanent tissue damage and so has to be conducted on lower animals. By contrast, psychophysiology is concerned with the study of "intact" humans by noninvasive, usually electrophysiological, methods.

It is surprisingly difficult to gain even the most superficial overview of the field without extensive reading because so few articles are available that serve this function. *The Annual Review of Psychology*, for example, has not published a broad review of psychophysiological research in the last decade, although, the 1983 volume included an article by Hillyard and Kutas entitled "Electrophysiology of Cognitive Processes." Addresses by presidents of learned societies have often been used to critically review progress in the discipline and speculate about future developments but this has not occurred in psychophysiology. Inspection of the last decade of addresses given by successive presidents of the Society for Psychophysiological Research reveal that the speakers have consistently chosen to review their own research programs and develop their theoretical models rather than discussing the field at large. One reason for this dearth of published synoptic comment is probably that the field tends to be fractionalized with different researchers focusing on different physiological systems or devoting all their efforts to investigating particular clinical disorders. The split between researchers with an interest in the central versus the peripheral nervous system is particularly noticeable.

Psychophysiological research is published across a wide range of journals but two journals specializing in psychophysiology have been founded, in addition to *Psychophysiology*. These are the *International Journal of Psychophysiology*, which first appeared in 1983, and the *Journal of Psychophysiology*, first published in 1987.

Also, *Advances in Psychophysiology: A Research Annual* was founded in 1985 to publish reviews and analyses of recent programatic research in psychophysiology. Of course, many other journals (e.g., *Biological Psychology*) and annuals (e.g., *Advances in Behavioral Medicine*) publish overlapping content.

Recent texts of particular note include *Techniques in Psychophysiology* (Martin & Venables, 1980). This manual is an update of their classic work published in 1967. A very authoritative handbook entitled *Psychophysiology: Systems, Processes and Applications* was published by Coles, Donchin, and Porges (1986). This book provides excellent accounts of systems and processes but the section on applications is somewhat limited in scope. Of particular relevance to this chapter is a book by Hollandsworth (1986) entitled *Physiology and Behavior Therapy*. Other psychophysiology texts published in the 1980s include Andreassi (1980), Stern et al. (1980) and Surwillo (1986). Most books on behavioral assessment include a chapter on psychophysiological assessment (e.g., Haynes & Wilson, 1979; Kallman & Feuerstein, 1986; Sturgis & Gramling, 1988).

A trend that has become apparent in the psychophysiological literature has been the move towards integrating the field with other areas of psychological science. This is reflected in the titles of recent books and chapters that include clinical psychophysiology (Turpin, 1989), neuropsychophysiology (Papakostopoulos, Butler, & Martin, 1985), cognitive psychophysiology (Donchin, 1984), developmental psychophysiology (Porges & Fox, 1986), and social psychophysiology (Cacioppo & Petty, 1983). The volume by Gale and Christie (1987) focuses on psychophysiological approaches to human factors and engineering psychology. As in other areas of psychological science, integration with cognitive psychology is a topical issue (Coles, 1989).

Recent Developments in Psychophysiology

Theoretical Developments

The psychophysiological theory that has probably influenced behavior therapy most, is the bioinformational theory of emotional imagery (Lang, 1979). (This theory is also reviewed in the section on anxiety.) The theory that will be discussed briefly is the motivational approach of Fowles (1983, 1986, 1987, 1988). This theory has been chosen because it is recent, clinical potential, and compatibility with the traditional theoretical foundations of behavior therapy.

Fowles' starting point is Jeffrey Gray's learning model, a basic premise of which is that it is important to distinguish between appetitive and aversive motivational systems (Gray, 1975). These are viewed as antagonistic systems that exert an influence on the probability of behavioral responses. The term *appetitive* refers to the motivation associated with appetites such as hunger, thirst, and sex; and it is presumed to be accompanied by a positive hedonistic state. The appetitive motivational system can be called a *behavioral activation system* (BAS) as it is a reward seeking or approach system that responds to positive incentives by activating behavior. In contrast, the aversive motivational system inhibits appetitively motivated behavior in the presence of conditioned stimuli or cues signaling that aversive consequences will occur should the response be made. In view of its primary function of inhibiting behavior, Gray calls the aversive motivational system the *behavioral inhibition system* (BIS).

Fowles (1988) outlines how these motivational constructs can be applied to psychopathology by considering a range of disorders: anxiety, psychopathy, childhood disorders, depression, mania, drug abuse, and schizophrenia. Focusing on depression for illustrative purposes, Fowles argues that dysphoric mood can be viewed as being due to the activation of the BIS in response to uncontrollable punishment, absence of expected rewards, or modification of the neurophysiological substrate. It may also involve a loss of appetitive motivation associated with hopelessness. In contrast, loss of interest or pleasure, poor appetite, loss of energy, and psychomotor retardation all could be attributable to minimal activation of appetitive motivation with subsequent loss of behavioral activation. Hence, Fowles speculates that depression may be associated with activation of aversive motivation and/or a disruption of appetitive motivation.

The physiological component of Fowles' model comes from his empirical work exploring the physiological indices of the two motivational systems. A series of studies by Fowles and his students (reviewed in Fowles, 1988) investigating physiological responses to a continuous motor task demonstrated that heart rate responded to appetitive motivation but not aversive stimulation. In contrast, nonspecific skin conductance fluctuations did not respond to appetitive motivation (although a subsequent study failed to replicate this finding), but did respond to aversive stimulation. Hence, these findings suggest that appetitive motivation can be assessed via heart rate, and aversive motivation via skin conductance.

Fowles' work is at an early stage and has only been applied to a very limited experimental paradigm. However, if his interpretation of his data is accepted, then his paradigm and measures could be used for investigating the application of the motivational model to psychopathology and consequently increasing our understanding of many common disorders. Pursuing the example of depression, laboratory induction of dysphoric mood could be used to investigate whether it is associated with increased aversive motivation, or diminished appetitive motivation. Individuals with various disorders could be compared with control subjects (perhaps before and after treatment of the disorder) in terms of their behavioral activation (as measured by heart rate) and inhibition (as measured by electrodermal activity). Doubtless reality will not conform to this attractively simple scheme but new information and methods of tackling old problems could result from vigorous exploration of Fowles' model.

Technical Developments

Early research in psychophysiology focused on electrodermal activity but this soon gave way to a broader interest in cortical and cardiovascular activity. Most of the techniques are described in Martin and

Venables (1980) authoritative handbook of psychophysiological methods. However, there have been substantial advances in the last decade in both the range of measures that can be taken and the ease of measurement and accuracy of more long established measures. One of the more exciting new developments in the measurement of the activity of the central nervous system (CNS) has been the advent of neuromagnetometry (Beatty, Barth, Richer, & Johnson, 1986). The movement of ions across the membranes of nerve cells generates magnetic as well as electrical fields. In the nervous system, biogenic magnetic fields are not large (at least two orders of magnitude smaller than the fields produced by skeletal or cardiac muscle) but under certain conditions are of sufficient strength to be measured at the surface of the head. "Neuromagnetometry is the study of magnetic fields of the brain; the recording of such fields is termed a magnetoencephalogram (MEG), the magnetic counterpart of the electroencephalogram (EEG)" (Beatty et al., 1986, p. 26). The magnetic response of CNS to sensory stimuli has a wave-shape similar to that of the *event-related potential* (ERP) and has been termed the *event-related field* (ERF). The MEG and EEG reflect different aspects of neuronal function, and hence, provide complementary images of CNS activity.

Within the autonomic nervous system the greatest progress has been made in the continuous noninvasive measurement of blood pressure. A device has been developed and marketed that measures pressure at the finger on a beat by beat basis (Wesseling, Settels, & De Wit, 1986) using a vascular unloading technique. Blood pressure measured in this way correlates satisfactorily with invasive measurement (Parati, Casadei, Groppelli, Di Rienzo, & Mancia, 1989) and its use will greatly aid understanding of the acute effects of psychological and other stimuli on the cardiovascular system.

In addition to the development of new measurement domains, new instrumentation has been developed for recording previously studied systems that provide researchers with novel opportunities for studying the relationships between physiology and behavior. Such advances mean that physiological measurement is no longer restricted to the laboratory. Most physiological responses, such as heart rate, blood pressure, skin conductance, muscle activity, the EEG, and even some blood gases can now be measured in real life settings far from the laboratory or clinic for hours, or even days, on end (e.g., Pilsbury & Hibbert, 1987; Taylor et al., 1982).

This can be done in a variety of ways. The first practical devices, such as the Oxford Medical Systems Medilog recorders, made use of miniaturized analogue tape recorders on which physiological signals could be stored for later offline processing. This method has the advantage that the raw data are available for examination and elimination of the all-to-frequent artifacts that can occur in real life situations. It has the disadvantage, however, of using an electromechanical technology that can be unreliable or require careful maintenance. It also presents the experimenter with an over abundance of data for analysis. Initially, such analyses required dedicated mini computers but most can now be conducted on special low-level processors used in conjunction with more powerful microcomputers, such as those based on the Intel 80286 and 80386 chip or with Vax microcomputers. More recently, solid state digital devices have become available that carry out much of the processing online and store the resulting derived values, such as mean heart rate over a given time, in dynamic memory. This can be read off at a later stage using comparatively simple software. Such recorders are often more robust and reliable than their analogue equivalents but are obviously more sensitive to the effects of artifact because there is only the most limited offline editing facilities and few opportunities to examine the original physiological signal. Such techniques are bound to have a marked effect on the assessment of therapeutic effectiveness and are already influencing theories of the role of physiological responses in the exacerbation of fear and panic, as we shall see in later sections.

In recent years, there have been many developments in the area of data analysis. This has partly evolved from increased use of computers but also reflects a greater awareness of the large amount of information available in psychophysiological recordings much of which had to be ignored in the era of hand measurement from pen and ink charts (Martin & Venables, 1980). Coles, Gratton, Kramer, and Miller (1986) provide a review of analytic techniques for psychophysiological data including the advantages and disadvantages associated with each approach. Their intention is to encourage investigators to enrich their analytic repertoires by including techniques that are either customarily employed in other branches of psychophysiology or not currently in use. One example they offer is the use of principal components analysis that has been used most frequently in the analysis of ERP data, but which they argue is clearly relevant to the analysis of other psychophysiological signals. Another example concerns the use of Multivariate Analysis of Variance (MANOVA). As the authors note, most psychophysiological research involves the multiple measurement of several variables over time and MANOVA has several advantages over Analysis of Variance (ANOVA) in the analysis of such data. MANOVA is beginning to be used more frequently in psychophysiology, in part because of its vigorous promotion by some journals.

The Link Between Psychophysiology and Behavior Therapy

As we have discussed, there is a strong link between behavior therapy and psychophysiology since Wolpe's work on anxiety. However, the knot tying psychophysiology to behavior therapy was tightened when Lang (1971) published his highly influential account of the measurement of fear in which he proposed that fear is represented in three systems, the verbal, the behavioral, and the physiological. For some time, behavior therapy has adopted a much less peripheralist position and imaginal methods have been superseded. As a result the link with psychophysiology started to weaken. However, this has now reversed with some theorists, most notably Lang (1985) and Foa (Foa & Kozak, 1986), arguing forcibly for psychophysiological measurement as an essential tool in the understanding of emotion and the processes underlying exposure based therapies. Separately, there has been a resurgence of interest in peripheralist theories of emotion with a growing emphasis on the role of the patients' detection and interpretation of somatic manifestations of anxiety in determining panic and fearful behavior (Clark, 1986).

Independently of the use of psychophysiological measurement in the study of fear an interest—perhaps even an excessive interest—developed in the use of physiological measurement as a direct vehicle in therapy by providing immediate feedback (biofeedback) of physiological functions. Biofeedback was very much a child of the 1970s and has now largely vanished, at least in areas of traditional concern to behavior therapists; however, it has left a welcome legacy. The possibility of treating physical illness behaviorally became attractive during the brief biofeedback era, and this has led directly to the very healthy offshoot of behavior therapy, behavioral medicine.

In the early days of behavior therapy, psychophysiology was very nonbiological in its orientation. Largely as a result of the persuasive writing and impressive empirical program of Obrist (1981) and the Lacey's (Lacey, 1976), this is no longer so and psychophysiology is now firmly in the biological tradition. Obrist has reminded us that most of the physiological systems we study have very complex innervation. As introductory physiology texts explain, the heart, for example, is controlled by both sympathetic and parasympathetic innervation and circulating hormones, such as adrenaline, which interact in complex ways. Obrist also demonstrated very clearly that even in situations in which psychological processes appear paramount, physiological systems serve, primarily, important metabolic functions.

This is seen most clearly in the cardiovascular system. The easy assumption of early workers that a large heart rate response to a phobic image necessarily meant increased sympathetic arousal may be quite untrue. Such a response might well represent reduced parasympathetic input, perhaps because of the metabolic demands of dealing with the phobic object. Furthermore, in situations in which the phobic response is inactivity, as in blood and injury fears, a reduction in heart rate is quite consistent with fear, whereas in patients with public speaking fears the large heart rate response often found might be independent of the patient's fear, and primarily a product of the metabolic demands of speaking (Lang, Levin, Miller, & Kozak, 1983). This does not mean that psychophysiology has nothing to offer behavior therapy but only that more sophisticated and comprehensive measurement is required to draw persuasive conclusions.

Ideally, many physiological systems should be measured to assess congruence of change across systems and some effort made to measure the metabolic load on the patient at the time of measurement. This is best done through either calorimetry or by measurement of oxygen consumption, but simple measures of activity may often suffice (Anastasiades & Johnston, 1990; Obrist et al., 1975). The other two techniques that aid interpretation of the control mechanisms involved in the physiological responses are the use of pharmacological blockades that selectively block parts of the nervous system so that, for example, the extent that a given change is sympathetically or parasympathetically mediated can be determined (see Freedman et al. [1988] for a very sophisticated use of this approach in the study of biofeedback). Such pharmacological studies are in a very different tradition from behavior therapy; more congenial to some may be recent data analytic techniques that claim to enable one to distinguish between relative contributions of the dual innervation of the heart from study of the variability of heart rate over quite short periods (Akselrod et al., 1981; Pagani et al., 1986). These techniques, based on widely available spectral analytic methods, may offer a convenient route to a deeper understanding of the physiological factors involved in behavioral treatment or, at least temper the over simplistic conclusions that can stem from unwary examination of a polygraph record.

ANXIETY, FEAR, AND PANIC

Three System Theory

Common experience suggests that anxiety and fear have three components, the subjective, the behavioral, and the physiological. In a profoundly influential series of papers (see Lang, 1971), Lang formalized this view and documented that these components are, at best, loosely correlated. As a result, no one measure of fear can be considered as paramount and fear is best considered as a loose coupling of three systems. This "Three System Theory" has influenced assessment of anxiety conditions and, to a lesser extent, the prediction of response to treatment and the matching of patients and therapy.

If fear is represented in the responses of three systems then treatment evaluation that does not adequately assess all three systems may be seriously defective. It is likely that few would dispute that a treatment that only altered some of the components of fear, say markedly reduced subjective fear and phobic avoidance of agoraphobic patients but left patients with markedly elevated heart rates, was at best questionable. In the last 20 years there has been a sustained attempt to incorporate measurement of all three systems in substantial clinical trials in the hope, largely confirmed, that effective treatments would lead to alteration in all three systems (Gelder et al., 1973; Mavissakalian & Michelson, 1982). Because the results from a number of studies appeared to show that all three systems changed in a broadly similar manner and the costs of psychophysiological measurement are high (compared to patient self-rating scales or even a behavioral test) we have previously argued (Mathews, Gelder, & Johnston, 1981) that, although a psychophysiological assessment is desirable, it could at times be omitted. Others have chided us for this (Himadi, Boice, & Barlow, 1985) and argued that the measurement of all three systems is mandatory. Although useful clinical research can be done without psychophysiological measurement, the potential benefits of such assessment has greatly increased in the last few years with the advent of reliable ambulatory recorders for functions such as heart rate, blood pressure, and respiration. Physiological responses can be measured with these devices when the patient is actually in the phobic situation. This has much greater validity than the earlier laboratory-based procedures involving either laboratory analogues or, with complex fears like agoraphobia, imaginal presentation of the feared situation. The second factor that strengthens the case for physiological measurement is the emergence of new treatments that are specifically geared at altering only one of the fear components, such as some forms of cognitive therapy or the new treatments for panic that emphasize the interpretation of bodily symptoms.

If the use of psychophysiological methods in group outcome research is largely uncontentious, the picture is quite different in assessing the process of behavior therapy or in predicting the response to treatment of individual patients. Because the different components of the fear system are thought to be loosely coupled then, as Rachman and Hodgson (Hodgson & Rachman, 1974; Rachman & Hodgson, 1974) pointed out, different systems could change at differing rates during therapy, and change within a patient could be either synchronous, when all three systems show congruous change, or desynchronous, when they do not. They made a number of detailed predictions about the nature and significance of such desynchrony, the most important of which could be interpreted as predicting that patients who show desynchrony at the end of behavioral treatment may do less well subsequently. This intuitively appealing view has not received the empirical support that one might have hoped.

Rachman's group failed to support a number of the detailed predictions on desynchrony during therapy (Grey, Rachman, & Sartory, 1981; Sartory, Rachman, & Grey, 1977) but did find, as predicted, that subjects who combined very high heart rates with no anxiety in the phobic situation had a higher rate of relapse. More recent independent attempts to explore this issue have not supported the prediction convincingly (Craske, Sanderson, & Barlow, 1987). The problem may be primarily methodological. Many of the measures used, particularly the physiological, are of only moderate reliability (Arena, Blanchard, Andrasik, Cotch, & Myers, 1983). The reliability of categorizing patients on the differences between such measures, or, even worse, changes in these measures is likely to be low and may limit effective prediction. Furthermore, all types of desynchrony might not be equally damaging. Rachman (Cox, Hallam, O'Connor, & Rachman, 1983; Rachman, 1978) in his interesting studies of courage, distinguishes between courage, which he defines as carrying out an act when subjectively afraid, a form of desynchrony, and fearlessness in which the dangerous act is conducted without fear, and hence in synchrony. Therapy requires courage from the phobic, and clinical experience suggests that mildly courageous desynchrony is common and need not be associated with relapse.

Another corollary of the three systems approach to fear is that patients may show fear predominantly in one response. This has been used to attempt to fit patient to therapy. Ost (Ost, Jerremalm, & Jansson, 1984; Ost, Jerremalm, & Johanson, 1981; Ost, Johansson, & Jerremalm, 1982), in a model series of studies, characterized patients as either predominantly physiological or behavioral responders and then assigned them to either a physiological or behavioral treatment, for example, relaxation training compared with either assertive training or exposure to the feared situation. He showed, in samples of social phobics, claustrophobic, and agoraphobic patients, that those given treatments consonant with the expression of their fears, fared best. Michelson (1986) extended this by adding the third category of patients with predominantly cognitive fear responses, for which the consonant treatment used was paradoxical intention. With this tripartite classification of patients, he also showed that agoraphobics given a treatment directed at the main aspect of their fear fared best, particularly at follow-up. These findings are important developments in our understanding of fear and its treatment but somewhat surprising because the classification of patients into response type appears fairly crude and of dubious reliability and, more importantly, the therapies studied do not appear sufficiently specific. In particular, many would doubt that relaxation can be regarded as a treatment with predominantly physiological effects (Johnston, 1986; Peveler & Johnston, 1986).

The Bio-Informational Theory of Emotion

Three system theory asserts that fear has three components—subjective, behavioral, and physiological. These components must be represented in memory if they are to be evoked by an appropriate stimulus such as the feared object, some representation of it or information about the likelihood of its imminent occurrence. Lang proposes that emotional information is stored in memory as a series of propositions concerning stimulus, response, and meaning information with connections between each proposition forming an associative network. Stimulus propositions are concerned with the information that makes the feared object recognizable, for example, the snake's skin and coloring; response propositions cover the responses made in the presence of a feared object, for example, running away, sweating, saying to oneself that one is terrified; whereas meaning propositions concern the interpretation of events, their significance, and the consequences for action, for example, a fast heart rate means you are afraid, snakes are dangerous, and so forth. Particularly helpful accounts of this complex model can be found in Lang (1985) and in his response (Lang, 1987) to a critical review by Watts and Blackstock (1987). It is obviously a model of emotion in general but has a peculiar relevance for behavior therapy because the model was developed from Lang's work on systematic desensitization for phobia's and he has chosen to concentrate on phobias in his experimental exploration of his theory.

Emotions occur when the relevant propositions in the associative networks are evoked. This happens most reliably when most propositions are activated, such as when the feared object or situation is presented in reality. However, symbolic representations of the feared object, say in a film or novel, will also evoke fear in as far as the propositions are activated. An image of the object, such as is used in desensitization, will also activate fear propositions, and hence, the emotion of fear. Lang argues that the central feature of an emotion is the production of responses (emotion is defined as an action tendency). Emotion that is experienced without any response, including covert responses, is, in his view, the result of activating only the stimulus elements of the network and, he seems to suggest, is not a true emotion but instead an appraisal of the meaning of these elements, for example, "I would be afraid of such a snake" rather than "I am afraid." This has important applications for exposure-based therapies.

The emphasis on responses has led Lang to concentrate on the nature of the phobic images and the physiological responses evoked by the image. Physiological responses are measured, rather than overt behavior, in the belief that they are less governed by social constraints. Hence, they show reactions even when overt behavior is controlled and apparently unfearful. His concern with responses has led him to carry out a series of experiments on the nature of the image and on the relative power of stimulus and response propositions in evoking evidence of fear. He has shown that subjects trained to invoke response propositions (e.g., my heart races, I am covered in sweat) show greater physiological response to a phobic image than subjects given extensive training in evoking a clear stimulus image, that is, the snake is green with black diamonds and moves with a slithering motion (Lang et al., 1983). One might argue that response training is procedurally much closer to the physiological measures, the main dependent variable is these experiments, than is stimulus training, and hence, the experiments have a bias in favor of confirming the hypothesis. Nevertheless, the markedly greater responses shown in some experiments after response training, the very limited effects of stimulus training, and the finding that response training only affects responding in conjunction with a phobic, rather than a neutral or irrelevant phobic object, all suggest that response training has a powerful effect and maps onto an important aspect of the central representation of fear.

Lang argues that phobias are characterized by particularly tight associative networks and hence strong responses are evoked with only minimal stimuli. A severe phobia has a highly coherent associative network, and hence is invoked with minimal or degraded stimulus input. An interesting offshoot of this contention has been a series of studies comparing the responses of specific phobics, social phobics, and agoraphobics. Clinically one would consider that agoraphobia is the most serious and disabling of these phobias and hence images of scenes that an agoraphobic might consider fear-provoking, should produce the largest responses. In fact specific phobics have the largest physiological responses to phobic images (Cook, Melamed, Cuthbert, McNeil, & Lang, 1988). Lang interprets this as indicating that agoraphobia, and to a lesser extent social phobia, are not represented by tight associative networks with a major response component, but are more diffuse conditions, more akin to generalized anxiety. This is a surprising conclusion given the extensive behavioral avoidance of many agoraphobics and the rather less clear patterns of avoidance of many social phobics. Most current theories of agoraphobia place considerable emphasis on the patients' interpretation of the feared situation and, most critically, their own physiological response. The scripts provided by Cook et al. may not have activated such meaning prototypes. However,

Zander and McNally (1988) systematically varied the content of scripts to cover all three classes of proposition and found that adding the meaning propositions did not increase the agoraphobics' response to the phobic images, which was, as Lang had claimed, very small. In agreement with Lang's earlier findings, the addition of response scripts and training in response production did increase the response to phobic images, albeit rather modestly.

Foa and Kozak (1986) have extended Lang's idea by suggesting that the emotional or phobia prototype has to be evoked during exposure therapy for it to be modified and fear reduced. They suggest that fear reduction occurs when new, corrective, information is incorporated in the fear prototype that is incompatible with it. Following Lang, they maintain that the prototype is active when there is evidence of a response, which is usually physiological, being produced. Their position is elaborated to predict that exposure based therapies are most effective in patients who show large physiological responses to the feared object and show the greatest physiological response reduction (habituation) both within and between therapy sessions. This idea has obvious similarities with Rachman and Hodgson's views on desynchrony between response systems. These predictions have important implications for the conduct of therapy and of our understanding of the mechanism underlying exposure based therapies. Unfortunately, the critical empirical support for Foa and Kozak is, as yet, scanty. In a very early experiment Lang, Melamed and Hart (1970) found that phobics who showed the largest heart rate increase on the first imaging of the phobic image, showed the best behavioral outcome following systematic desensitization. Real-life exposure is more effective because it accesses the prototype more reliably and allows the incorporation of new incompatible information such as, not all snakes bite, or the inevitable result of anxiety in a supermarket is not a heart attack or madness. Techniques that avoid the elicitation of the prototype, as judged by response production, such as distraction, lead to the expected reduction in between-session habituation but not in within-session habituation in both phobics (Sartory, Rachman, & Grey, 1982) and obsessionals (Grayson, Foa, & Steketee, 1982) and are related, as predicted, to the therapeutic outcome (Kozak, Foa, & Steketee, 1988).

It is too early to predict that the bio-informational theory of emotion will greatly alter the practice of behavior therapy, although it may encourage the greater use of psychophysiological methods in therapy. It has, however, already forced us to reconsider old issues, such as the differences between different types of phobias. It will, at the very least, offer a new slant on our understanding of existing therapies.

Preparedness and the Acquisition of Fear

Behavior therapy was once confidently thought to be rooted in learning theory. Although this is true in the most general of ways, there was very little detailed transfer of principles between the learning laboratory and the clinic. Most clinical treatments, at least of phobias, were based on a general belief that such fears were, after Watson and little Albert, acquired through a process of classical conditioning with avoidance maintained by the reinforcing power of fear reduction, as described by Mowrer's (1939) Two Factor Theory. Therapy followed the principles of exposure and counterconditioning as illustrated by Jones (1924) in her efforts to reduce a child's fear of furry objects. It is not clear that recent developments in our understanding of the acquisition of fear will have any greater effect on behavior therapy than did earlier sophistications in learning theory but they may have greater clinical relevance because they are more directly tied to the clinical phenomena. Theorists, as well as clinicians, are also starting to explore the cognitive aspects of fear acquisition, and hopefully extinction, in a way that may tie theory and clinical practice more firmly together.

Early learning theories of the acquisition of phobias did not comment plausibly on one of the most striking features of specific fear: the very limited range of stimuli that provoke irrational fear. Phobic patients are afraid of snakes, of spiders, of rats, but rarely of electric light sockets, lawn mowers, or even guns. Seligman (1971) was the first to attempt to solve this problem by proposing that fearful responses were biologically prepared to be conditioned to particular stimuli as the result of evolutionary pressures.

The main advance in our understanding of this process, however, has come from Ohman and his colleagues with a consistently ingenious program of research on the classical conditioning of autonomic responses to biologically prepared stimuli, such as pictures of snakes or spiders. In numerous studies they have shown that skin conductance and other responses can readily be conditioned to fear relevant stimuli, such as snakes and spiders, and also fear irrelevant stimuli, like flowers or mushrooms, but that the responses conditioned to the fear relevant stimuli are much more resistant to extinction (Fredrikson & Ohman, 1979; Ohman, Eriksson, & Olofsson, 1975; Ohman, Erixon, & Lofberg, 1975). In addition, in Ohman's own studies, responses conditioned to fear irrelevant stimuli can be extinguished by simple cognitive procedures, such as telling the subject that there will be no more shocks, but this is ineffective with responses to the fear relevant stimuli (Hugdahl, 1978; Ohman et al., 1975). Unfortunately, others have failed to replicate this finding (e.g., McNally, 1981), which has obvious parallels with, and implications for, clinical practice.

Ohman views the differences between phobias in a similar way to Lang and sees specific fears of animals and insects as being organized around avoidance and hence action, that is, flight. He sees social fears as being based on submission and hence much less integrated with action. As we have seen, action, or preparation for action, is thought to lead to acceleration in heart rate, whereas the inaction of submission should not. Fredrikson (1981) has confirmed this distinction by showing that patients with specific fears showed the predicted increases in heart rate and skin conductance when exposed to slides of phobic objects whereas social phobics showed a slight decrease in heart rate, combined with the expected increase in skin conductance. Using the conditioning paradigm, Dimberg has shown that socially relevant stimuli may be biologically prepared. Autonomic responses to pictures of angry faces extinguish more slowly than those conditioned to happy faces (Dimberg & Ohman, 1983; Ohman & Dimberg, 1978).

In an effort to explain prepared learning, Ohman (1986) proposes that when incoming stimuli are processed at the pre-attentive (and hence, unconscious level), prepared stimuli are detected and lead to an increase in arousal. Therefore when the stimuli enter awareness the subject is already in a state of heightened arousal which augments other sources of arousal, such as the unconditioned stimulus (UCS) in a classical conditioning paradigm. This in turn facilitates the acquisition of the learned response. The possibility that prepared stimuli are detected pre-attentively was explored by Dimberg and Ohman (see Ohman, 1986). Using backward masking techniques (see MacLeod & Mathews, this volume) it is possible to examine the behavioral effects of stimuli that have not entered conscious awareness. Ohman and Dimberg showed that classically conditioned autonomic responses to fear relevant stimuli could be elicited when the fear stimulus was not detected by the subject.

It is not clear if the pre-attentive processing of feared stimuli relates in a practical way to the treatment of fear. It might be thought that if pre-attentive processes can be harnessed to the acquisition of fear then they might be used to diminish it. Lee, Tyrer, and Horn (1983) in one of a series of studies that, when published, seemed improbable and puzzling, claimed to show greater fear reduction in agoraphobics following subliminal presentation of feared, rather than control stimuli; and the best outcome when fear stimuli were faded in, starting below awareness. This might suggest not only that extinction can occur without awareness but that it avoids some mechanism that interferes with fear reduction, such as some form of active cognitive avoidance. Further work is obviously needed to explore these phenomena both in the laboratory and the clinic.

Panic

The role of awareness is also central to modern views of panic. Panic is the subject of detailed discussion in other chapters (Craske & Barlow, this volume). In this chapter we shall concentrate on the psychophysiological aspects. It is necessary, however, to present briefly the main class of theory that dominates current psychological thinking on panic. Most influential, psychological models of panic are derived from Williams James' (1884) attributional position, that emotions arise through the interpretation of bodily symptoms. This view has a long and controversial history, much of it centered on the limited time that appraisal processes must apparently need if they can be the basis of emotion, and it will be surprising if it finally finds an uncontroversial niche in the explanation and treatment of panic disorder. Nevertheless, it is currently exciting much interest.

The main difference between earlier attributional theories of emotion, and current views of panic, lies in the nature of the attributions and their role. Panic prone individuals are, it is claimed, prone to interpret bodily symptoms catastrophically and these catastrophic interpretations feed back into the system to produce a vicious spiral of autonomic arousal and panic. This type of theory has been expressed most clearly by Clark (1986) who hypothesizes that some stimulus, which can be internal, causes the panic prone individual to feel anxious, this leads to the somatic effects of anxiety such as increased heart rate and sweaty palms, which are detected and interpreted catastrophically as, for example, signs of an imminent heart attack or madness. This leads to escalating anxiety, more bodily symptoms and more catastrophic interpretations. In some versions of this model, particular emphasis is placed on the role of hyperventilation in exacerbating the somatic symptoms of panic (Salkovkis, Jones, & Clark, 1986).

The central, psychophysiological questions are whether panic prone people do misinterpret somatic events in a way that leads to increased fear and autonomic arousal, whether such individuals show markedly increased arousal when panicking or in situations likely to provoke panic and, of course, whether treatments developed to alter catastrophic interpretations do indeed interrupt the hypothesized spiral of autonomic arousal. A subsidiary question is whether hyperventilation is a common feature of panic.

The interpretation of somatic events is best studied in the laboratory. It has been known since the pioneering studies of Pitts and McClure (1967) that panic can be induced in the panic prone by manipulations such as in the infusion of sodium lactate, hyperventilation, and breathing carbon dioxide enriched air. While some have seen this as evidence for biological theories of panic, it is consistent with a cognitive model if it can be shown that those who panic interpret the somatic effects of the various physical stimuli in a catastrophic way, and that they show markedly greater physiological arousal than do panic-free controls.

Evidence on the magnitude of the physiological effects of panic is ambiguous, however it is becoming increasingly clear that expectancy, and presumably interpretation, plays a prominent role in the production of panic, at least in the laboratory. Early studies showed large increases in heart rate in panicking patients, but later ones have shown that the absolute rise in heart rate following lactate infusion and inhalation of carbon dioxide enriched air are the same in the panic prone and controls (Ehlers, Margraf & Roth, 1988; Ehlers et al., 1986). They also found that the increase in autonomic arousal induced by these manipulations is of gradual rather than abrupt onset, as one would expect from a rapidly spiraling panic cycle. These studies were complicated by the fact that panic patients had markedly faster resting heart rates than controls, prior to panic induction, making evaluation of subsequent heart rate change very difficult. Evidence in support of a cognitive model comes from the finding that the panic inducing effect of carbon dioxide (Rapee, Mattik, & Murrell, 1986) and sodium lactate (Van den Hout, 1988) can be markedly reduced by altering the subject's expectations, for example, by explaining the likely physiological effects of carbon dioxide to the subject. This presumably reduces the tendency for catastrophic interpretations. Perhaps more persuasive is a recent study (Ehlers, Margraf, Roth, Taylor, & Birbaumer, 1988) in which the panic prone and controls were given false heart rate feedback suggesting that their heart rate had suddenly increased by 50 bpm. This led to greater increases in anxiety in the panic patients accompanied by increased heart rate, blood pressure, and skin conductance. Although consistent with aspects of the cognitive model, the actual differences in physiological response between panic and controls were rather small. Heart rate, for example, rose by less than 5 bpm.

Panic prone individuals studied in naturalistic situations likely to provoke a panic have not shown reliably greater physiological responsiveness than controls. Roth et al. (1986) found that agoraphobics with panic and controls showed approximately the same elevation in heart rate when walking in a shopping mall, although many of the agoraphobics found this a frightening situation. This appears to contrast with earlier evidence that exposure to feared situations leads to greater increases in heart rate in agoraphobics than does walking in a safe situation (Michelson & Mavissakalian, 1985). The Roth et al. study is one of the few to use a control group and it may be that earlier studies failed to control properly for the physical, and other, nonfear related, effects of walking in a busy street. Rather more positive findings have emerged from studies of the physiological changes actually occurring during natural panic attacks. Taylor et al. (1986) and Freedman, Ianni, Ettedgui, and Puthezhath (1985) have both shown that heart rate is higher during periods when the patient claims to be panicking than at other times when the patient was similarly anxious but did not consider themselves to be panicking. Taylor et al. also showed that the difference was unlikely to be due to physical activity.

In a later study, Margraf, Taylor, Ehlers, Roth, and Agras (1987) examined the physiological correlates of panic in feared situations and spontaneous (nonsituational) panics. Only the situational panics were accompanied by increased heart rate. This, and the finding from these studies of heart rate in real life, that many self-reported panics are not accompanied by detectable autonomic responses, suggests that the somatic component of the cognitive model of panic is only relevant in some patients, or in some panics. Furthermore, even when increases in physiological arousal are found they are, on average, of comparatively small magnitude; much smaller than one might expect from patients' self-reports. Measurement of transcutaneous carbon dioxide during real life panics also suggests that hyperventilation need not accompany panic nor panic accompany hyperventilation (Hibbert & Pilsbury, 1988). Taken together these findings suggest that the interpretive component of the model is more important than the spiraling increase in autonomic arousal. Indeed seen from a psychophysiological perspective, panic disorder seems to be predominantly a cognitive disorder.

If panic attacks are largely cognitive then one might expect that cognitive therapies focusing on disconfirming catastrophic interpretations might be effective. Reports of a number of uncontrolled case series suggest that this is spectacularly so, with Clark, Salkovskis, and Chalkley (1985) and Beck (1988) reporting virtually the complete elimination of panic. Little has been reported on the physiological effects of such treatments and it is possible that little can be expected if the disorder is primarily subjective. Salkovskis et al. (1986) report increases in blood levels of carbon dioxide following a version of cognitive therapy that emphasized controlled breathing, suggesting that patients had reduced hyperventilation.

The role of somatic symptoms and the patient's interpretation of such symptoms is one of the most exciting topics in the behavioral treatment of anxiety disorders at the moment. We can expect extensive new information to appear in the near future. Therefore, it is hard to evaluate the specifically psychophysiological components of current models of panic. However, it is clear that the earlier belief that extreme physiological arousal was a common feature of panic will have to be reviewed. It remains likely, however, that complex misinterpretations of somatic changes that lead to a spiral of increasing anxiety, perhaps independently of physiology, will be seen to play an important role in panic.

BIOFEEDBACK: THE CARDIOVASCULAR SYSTEM AND CARDIOVASCULAR DISORDERS

The most direct attempt to incorporate psychophysiology in the therapeutic process is biofeedback, in which immediate information about the state of a physiological system is fed back to the patient. The patient then uses this information to gain self control over some function, such as the beating of the heart, which was previously outside his or her voluntary control. The idea is simple, elegant, and immensely attractive. Unfortunately, 20 years of, occasionally frenetic, research suggests that biofeedback seldom aids voluntary autonomic control to a clinically useful extent. The role of biofeedback in enhancing the control of the traditionally voluntary, striped muscle system, is more promising. Biofeedback had an obvious appeal for behavior therapists because: it is rooted in the same learning theories; it held the promise of training patients to control autonomic processes closely linked to the anxiety conditions treated by many behavior therapists; and it might enable behavior therapy to extend into the treatment of physical conditions with less obvious behavioral components, such as hypertension. Biofeedback could also be applied within the traditionally voluntary, striped muscle system to increase control of muscles implicated in pain or malfunctioning after disease or injury.

Experimental Studies of Healthy Subjects

Although a number of pioneering papers on biofeedback aided autonomic control appeared in the middle of the 1960s (Brener & Hothersall, 1966; Engel & Hansen, 1966) the main impetus for the biofeedback explosion of the 1970s was the series of studies conducted by Miller and his students (Miller, 1969) purporting to show impressive instrumental learning of very specific, autonomically innervated, responses in curarized rats. Subsequently, many difficulties with this work emerged, the most striking of which concerned failures to replicate (Miller & Dworkin, 1974). Nevertheless, the interest in biofeedback continued to grow.

As far as the practice of behavior therapy is concerned the main questions concerning biofeedback are:

1. Is the self-control of autonomic responses possible?
2. Does biofeedback aid such control?
3. Is such control specific or part of some overall somatic and visceral adjustment?
4. What model best describes the processes of biofeedback?

In considering these questions, we shall concentrate on studies of the cardiovascular system because the most systematic and clinically relevant research was carried out on functions such as heart rate, blood pressure, and to a lesser extent, blood flow. Research on other bodily systems was less interesting, theoretically or clinically, and the findings were seldom strikingly different from those seen in the cardiovascular work.

Is the Self-control of Autonomic Responses Possible?

Numerous studies have shown that some degree of self-control of heart rate (Lang & Twentyman, 1974; Obrist et al., 1975), blood pressure (Fey & Lindholm, 1975; Shapiro, Tursky, Gershon, & Stern, 1969), and blood flow (Roberts, Kewman, & MacDonald, 1973; Surwit, Shapiro, & Feld, 1976) is possible. Most of these studies show that increases in activation, that is, increases in heart rate or blood pressure, can be substantial but that the decreases are much smaller.

Does Biofeedback Aid Such Control?

Determining the extent to which biofeedback is necessary for such control is complex and the answer is still uncertain. Many, but not all investigators, have shown that biofeedback appears to aid increases in activation (e.g., Steptoe, 1976) but most find that it has little or no effect on decreases (Johnston, 1976, 1977a). The effect of biofeedback in producing decreases in cardiovascular functions is confounded with the arousing effects of the feedback task itself, which might well mask the positive effects of feedback. When this is allowed for, for example, by requiring subjects in the nonfeedback self-control condition to monitor a complex biofeedback-like display, modest but reliable differences favoring biofeedback have been found in the control of pulse transit time, a close correlate of systolic blood pressure (Johnston, Lo, & Marie, 1984; Steptoe, 1977). It is hard, however, to believe such control is of clinical value because it represents differences in systolic blood pressure (SBP) of no more than a few millimeters of mercury. The self-control of the vasculature, through feedback of either skin temperature or more direct measures of blood flow, has produced varied results with some claiming that feedback aids control over other methods (Surwit et al., 1976) and others disputing this (Johnston, 1977a; Kluger, Jamner, & Tursky, 1985).

Most biofeedback studies are carried out when the subject is at rest (or as near rest as the biofeedback situation allows) and this may not be a good analogue for most clinical situations where the physiological system and, perhaps, the patient are in a state of increased arousal. This has been investigated by examining the effectiveness of biofeedback in reducing experimentally produced increases in heart rate and blood pressure. De Good and Adams (1976) and Shapiro and colleagues (Reeves & Shapiro, 1982;

Victor, Mainardi, & Shapiro, 1976) have shown that heart rate feedback helps subjects limit the increase in heart rate produced by aversive stimulation but we (Johnston & Ross, 1986) could not train subjects, either with cardiovascular feedback or verbal instructions, to reduce the cardiovascular response to challenging two-person video games. This suggests that feedback may be unhelpful when stress places heavy information-processing demands on the subject. A number of studies have shown that heart rate and blood pressure feedback help subjects limit the cardiovascular responses to dynamic exercise (Goldstein, Ross, & Brady, 1977; Perski & Engel, 1980) to a greater extent than simple verbal instructions of relaxation training (Lo & Johnston, 1984a,b). Biofeedback, however, does not enable subjects to reduce the heart rate or pulse transit time response to isometric exercise (Johnston et al., 1984).

Cardiovascular feedback may lead to larger reductions in heart rate and blood pressure than are possible with other, purely verbal methods. The differences, however, are seldom substantial and are usually found under very specific, tightly controlled, laboratory conditions. This may well limit their applicability to clinical practice.

Is Biofeedback Aided Autonomic Control Specific or Part of Some Overall Somatic and Visceral Adjustment?

Research on the mechanisms of biofeedback aided autonomic control has largely focused on the question of mediation. Many have asked if biofeedback enables direct control of the viscera or if such control is either secondary to alterations in the traditionally voluntary system, that is the striped muscle and respiratory system, or is part of some overall autonomic and somatic adjustment. This question, which is obviously of fundamental theoretical importance, may also be of clinical relevance since, in most conditions of interest, arousal in an autonomically innervated system is dissociated from somatic activity. For example, hypertension is, by definition, higher blood pressure than the patient's current level of activity warrants and the increased heart rate sometimes seen in the very anxious may be dissociated from muscle tension or activity. Direct control of the cardiovascular system would, therefore, appear to offer more therapeutic promise than somatically mediated control.

It has been shown in practically all studies in which somatic activity or respiration was measured, that increases in heart rate or blood pressure are associated with consistent somatic change (Steptoe, 1976; Obrist et al., 1975; Lo & Johnston, 1984a,b), and that when somatic activity is experimentally controlled, heart rate control is also greatly reduced (Obrist et al., 1975). When we (Johnston et al., 1984) previously considered the balance of the evidence, particularly from studies of control during exercise, we concluded that most, if not all, biofeedback aided control of heart rate and blood pressure was associated with changes in muscle activity or respiration and was not due to direct autonomic control. The somatic correlates of blood flow have been less extensively studied in the healthy population but claims have been made for biofeedback aided control of skin blood flow without obvious somatic mediation (Surwit et al., 1976).

What Model Best Describes the Processes of Biofeedback?

Although the earliest biofeedback studies were thought of in terms of instrumental or autonomic conditioning, the dominant model quickly became some version of the motor skills analogy (see Williamson and Blanchard (1979) for a review). This model was stated most explicitly by Lang (1975) who claimed that learning to control the viscera was like learning a motor skill, such as playing darts, and that therefore the processes that control the acquisition of a skill should apply to visceral learning. This model was of potential clinical importance because, if correct, it could guide one towards the most efficient conditions for learning. Lang and his students examined the effects on heart rate control of variables known to determine motor skills learning, such as the quality, frequency, and speed of response of the feedback display (Gatchel, 1974; Lang & Twentyman, 1974). They quickly established that these parameters had some of the predicted effects on learning to increase heart rate but none at all on heart rate decreases, which therefore did not appear to behave like a motor skill.

A fundamental problem for the motor skills model was the finding, reviewed by Johnston (1977b), that equally good control, even of heart rate increases, could be obtained with purely verbal methods, that provided absolutely no feedback on performance. This contrasted with a true motor skill, in which, for example, it is inconceivable that one could play darts without knowing where the dart landed. This, and other, disparities between the effects of feedback on autonomic and skeletal responses, suggested (Johnston, 1977b) that the conventional biofeedback task did not require any skill or any learning, but only effort, and that the main role of feedback was motivational and not informational. This was confirmed in a series of studies in which subjects were set a biofeedback task much more analogous to a situation requiring motor skill. Subjects were required to produce an accurate autonomic response, a small prescribed increase in heart rate. Such a task cannot be done without feedback and is very responsive to the same factors as affect a motor skill, such as the quality and frequency of that feedback (Johnston & Lethem, 1981). The hypothesis that conventional feedback served primarily to motivate subjects was partially supported by the finding (Johnston & Lethem, 1983) that varying the amount of reward affects the magnitude of biofeedback aided heart rate increase but had no effect on the accuracy of heart rate control.

A vast amount of laboratory research was carried out on biofeedback between 1970 and the early 1980s and it is not possible to summarize it fairly and accurately in a few pages. However, the majority of studies within the cardiovascular system suggest that, although feedback may aid control, other simpler methods that do not involve feedback are also effective. When control is achieved it is frequently very closely tied to changes in the systems which we always knew to be under voluntary control, the striped muscle and the respiratory system, and not due to direct control of the viscera. Presumably, because of these disappointing findings the scientific interest in biofeedback has waned so that there has been very little systematic work published for several years, outside very specialist journals.

Clinical Applications

We have argued that biofeedback was attractive to behavior therapists partly because it suggested new approaches to the old problem of anxiety and, more importantly, because it held the promise that biofeedback could be extended to the treatment of the physically ill. Both these propositions turned out to be over optimistic. The findings with healthy volunteers that we have just presented made it very likely, but not inevitable, that feedback of heart rate and blood pressure would have little specific therapeutic power. This is true in the treatment of anxiety, an area where biofeedback had no significant clinical impact nor did it spawn any substantial research. Apart from obvious limitations caused by biofeedback's lack of specific power, problems also arose because of the very peripheralist assumptions that underlie its use in the treatment of anxiety. At least until very recently, the tide of thinking was away from peripheral theories of emotion, and hence, few were attracted to the idea of treating only the peripheral manifestations of a centrally determined fear or anxiety process. Even those who were most committed to a tripartite view of emotion do not seem to have made any substantial attempt to use biofeedback to control the autonomic component, although such a use might provide a purer test of the therapeutic value of such ideas than relaxation training, which some, like Ost, favor.

Attempts to treat cardiovascular disorders have taken three main forms, the treatment of primary hypertension, cardiac arrhythmias, and Raynaud's disease. The first two can be dismissed very summarily. A number of studies using blood pressure feedback failed to show either useful reductions in pressure or superior reductions to apparently simpler relaxation procedures (Blanchard, Miller, Abel, Haynes, & Wicker, 1979; Surwit, Shapiro, & Good, 1978). Occasionally, positive findings have been reported, for example, Glasgow, Gaardner, and Engel (1982) reported that a combination of a very simple form of blood pressure feedback, which patients could use at home, and relaxation was particularly effective in lowering pressure. However, the results were complex and the finding has not been adequately explored in subsequent studies. More recently, Blanchard et al. (1986) have claimed that the use of skin temperature feedback, presumably to reduce sympathetic arousal, led to reductions in blood pressure in hypertensives. This finding does not look secure and needs replication. The treatment of arrhythmias with biofeedback excited interest after an important paper by Weiss and Engel (1971) but failures to replicate the initial findings or to generate useful treatments led to its abandonment.

The treatment of Raynaud's disease with biofeedback is more interesting. Raynaud's disease is a disorder of the peripheral vasculature in which under conditions of cold or, occasionally, emotional stress, extremely painful vasoconstriction occurs, usually in the fingers. Attempts to treat this with temperature and other forms of vascular feedback have had mixed success. Surwit, Pilon, and Fenton (1978) reported that biofeedback and relaxation were equally effective. Guglielmi, Roberts, and Patterson (1982) in a double blind study, found no difference between temperature or electromyographic (EMG) feedback and no treatment. Freedman, Ianni, and Wenig (1983), in a sophisticated study, found that temperature feedback had a greater effect on temperature control in the laboratory and led to larger reductions in the frequency of painful attacks of vasoconstriction, than did relaxation training. In addition, the superior temperature control was not related to detectable changes in various somatic mediators. A further study (Freedman et al., 1988) confirmed that temperature biofeedback was more effective than relaxation training and, in an exemplary investigation of mechanism using receptor and nerve block techniques, showed that temperature feedback led to increases in blood flow through different mechanisms in controls and patients with idiopathic Raynaud's disease. Freedman's major series of papers goes against the general trend of findings on autonomic biofeedback and may suggest that feedback has a role to play in disorders that do not involve functions with dominant somatic linkage, typical of the much studied cardiac system.

Surprisingly, the generally sorry tale of autonomic biofeedback may have a happy ending. A consistent finding in both laboratory and clinical studies is that, even if biofeedback has no special role to play, a modest degree of autonomic self-control is possible. This has led to an enormous upsurge of interest in the use of relaxation based procedures in the treatment of physical conditions, such as hypertension. This work is too recent to say if it will result in useful therapies that find general acceptance but the signs are more promising than for biofeedback. A recent review summarized approximately 25 controlled trials of relaxation based stress management for hypertension (Johnston, 1987), and found that stress management was reliably better than a variety of control procedures and led to twice as great a drop in pressure (Johnston, 1989). Stress management may be the positive legacy of autonomic biofeedback.

CHRONIC HEADACHES: PSYCHOPHYSIOLOGICAL MECHANISMS AND BIOFEEDBACK

Certain types of headaches would seem an obvious candidate for investigation and perhaps treatment by psychophysiologists. After all, headaches were listed in the Diagnostic and Statistical Manual of Mental Disorders, 2nd Edition (DSM-II) as one of the nine categories of 'psychophysiological disorders' (disorders "characterized by physical symptoms that are caused by emotional factors and involve a single organ system, usually under autonomic nervous system inervation," American Psychiatric Association, 1968, p. 46). The involvement of psychophysiologists in headache research has followed a delayed and hesitant path, however, Before reviewing this history, the nature of headaches will be considered briefly.

The International Headache Society has recently published a new headache classification system (Headache classification committee of the International Headache Society, 1988). It is, of course, too early to assess the impact of this system on research and clinical practice. The classification that has dominated the field for the last two or three decades was developed by a Committee of the National Institute of Health (Ad Hoc Committee, 1962). This Committee of six eminent neurologists divided headaches into 15 major types on the basis of pain mechanisms. The three headaches considered to be by far the most common were "vascular headaches of the migraine type," "muscle-contraction headaches" (or tension headaches), and "combined headaches: vascular and muscle-contraction." The pain mechanisms listed were as follows: vascular headache, "cranial arterial distension and dilation are importantly implicated in the pain phase, but cause no permanent changes in the involved vessel" (p. 717); and tension headache, "associated with muscle contraction of skeletal muscles in the absence of permanent structural change, usually as part of the individual's reaction during life stress" (p. 717).

Consideration of these short descriptions of headache mechanisms would lead one to imagine psychophysiologists would have had a field day investigating headache processes. Which blood vessels are involved in migraine pathology, what is the time course of changes, and what stimuli activate the mechanisms? Similar questions can be posed for the alleged muscular mechanism of tension headaches.

Although it was noted previously that psychophysiology began in the 1950s, the first psychophysiological investigations of headaches appeared in the mid 1970s (see Martin, 1980, for a review of the early studies). These studies seem to have been stimulated by the earlier work on biofeedback. Following Miller's seminal work on visceral learning referred to earlier (Miller, 1969), researchers were quick to see the potential application of this conditioning paradigm to the treatment of headaches. The earliest (uncontrolled) studies were of forehead EMG feedback for tension headaches (Budzynski, Stoyva, & Adler, 1970) and hand temperature feedback accompanied by autogenic exercises for migraine (Sargent, Green, & Walters, 1972). As researchers started to "wire-up" headache sufferers in their laboratories for biofeedback training, some began to feel the traditional headache models needed elaboration or perhaps major revision. The result was a series of studies in laboratories around the world aimed at investigating headache mechanisms. The findings from these studies, and from investigations of biofeedback for headaches, are reviewed briefly below. The aim will be to give the reader a feel for the type of research carried out in this area, and what has been achieved so far. This will serve as a basis for an analysis of why greater gains have not been made, and hence avenues for future research. More detailed reviews are available elsewhere (e.g., Adams, Feuerstein & Fowler, 1980; Chapman, 1986; Haynes, Cuevas & Gannon, 1982; Martin, 1986).

Psychophysiological Mechanisms

Psychophysiological investigations of headaches typically involve comparisons between groups of headache sufferers and control subjects. The headache sufferers may consist of a single diagnostic group, or two or three of the common headache categories. Control subjects are usually headache-free individuals but sometimes individuals with other pain problems or disorders; and may or may not be matched with the headache subjects. Some studies involve within subject rather than between subjects comparisons (e.g., headache sufferers during periods of headache versus headache-free). Subjects may be recruited via medical referrals, advertising in the media or through clinics or classes, and there is some evidence that this results in differences between samples (e.g., higher EMG in clinic samples [Belar, Sutton, & Wilson, 1983]). Diagnostic criteria vary from study to study but are most commonly based on the classification of the Ad Hoc Committee (1962).

Experimental subjects are typically compared across at least three experimental conditions (following adaptation) comprising rest, stress, and poststress recovery. Sometimes more than one stress condition is used. Stressors include cognitive tasks such as mental arithmetic (the most commonly used), intellectual problems, and stressful imagery; and physical stressors such as noise stimuli, consumption of ice water, and various means of pain induction (e.g., cold pressor, inflation of an occlusion cuff, Forgione-Barber pain stimulator). Early studies were criticized for using stressors that were unrealistically short (e.g., one minute) so that some recent studies have used more protracted stressors. For example, Gannon, Haynes, Cuevas, and Chavez (1987) required subjects to solve arithmetic problems accompanied by a buzzer for "errors" over a period of one hour.

The physiological variables monitored during such experiments have varied over a wide range. The most common are measures of muscle activity and cephalic vasomotor activity reflecting the postulated muscular and vascular mechanisms of tension headaches and migraines, respectively. EMG activity has been recorded from the forehead, neck, temporalis, trapezius, and occipitalis muscles. More recent studies have advocated other sites. For example, the Schwartz-Mayo model involves placement of one active electrode on the frontalis muscle, the other active electrode on the ipsilateral posterior neck site, and the ground electrode on the side of the neck with the purpose of measuring activity from the occipital area (Nevins & Schwartz, 1985). The Cram-Scan model involves sampling from five different sites (Cram, 1986).

Cephalic vasomotor activity is usually measured via a photoelectric transducer positioned either over the superficial temporal artery or earlobe (which derives its blood supply from a branch of this artery). Other physiological variables that have been measured include heart rate, blood pressure, skin temperature (finger, hand or face), digital blood volume pulse amplitude, electrodermal activity, respiration rate, and forearm EMG. Authors sometimes include rationales for measuring these variables such as to assess generalized psychophysiological arousal but sometimes appear to do it for no special reason.

A recent methodological variation has been to monitor physiological variables while the subject is in a number of different positions (reclining, sitting, and standing) rather than a single position (e.g., Ahles et al., 1988).

Given the diversity of subject samples, paradigms, and measures, it is perhaps not surprising that the findings from these studies have been far from consistent. In many instances, significant differences in one or more studies have not been replicated in others. Occasionally, different investigators have reported diametrically opposite findings. For example, Haynes, Griffin, Mooney, and Parise (1975) found significantly higher forehead EMG during headache periods relative to headache-free periods; Martin and Mathews (1978) reported the reverse.

In view of the inconsistencies and differences between studies, no definitive conclusions can be drawn about headache mechanisms. However, the following four observations are offered:

1. In studies comparing more than one headache group with a control group, differences between the headache and control subjects have usually been more apparent than differences between the different headache groups. Parenthetically, it may be noted that this lack of physiological differences between headache types parallels the literature suggesting the different diagnostic types have overlapping symptomatology (e.g., Drummond & Lance, 1984).
2. There is little evidence to support the muscular mechanism of tension headaches. Most researchers seem to hold the opinion that the traditional model of tension headaches being caused by skeletal muscle tension in the forehead or neck needs to be rejected or at least substantially revised. A couple of studies have suggested, however, that headaches may be associated with elevated muscle tension but that the tension is in the occipital area rather than the more commonly monitored sites (Hudzinski & Lawrence, 1988; Pritchard & Wood, 1983). Given the history of inconsistent findings in this field, only time will tell whether these results will stand the test of replication.
3. Research into the postulated vascular mechanism of migraine has also led to inconclusive results. The balance of evidence is such, however, that we are not aware of any published reports in which investigators argue against some form of vascular dysfunction associated with migraine. In fact, a number of writers have suggested that vascular mechanisms may also be involved in tension headaches (e.g., Gannon et al., 1987).
4. One consistent finding that has emerged is that migraineurs evidence response stereotypy (e.g., Anderson, Stoyva, & Vaughn, 1982; Cohen et al., 1983; Gannon, Haynes, Safranek, & Hamilton, 1981).

Biofeedback

The most widely researched forms of biofeedback with headache sufferers are EMG feedback (usually from the forehead placement, but in some instances the neck or muscle showing the highest resting EMG level) and digital temperature feedback (hand warming). The former has been used predominantly with tension headache sufferers and the latter with migraineurs but both treatments have been used with both types of headaches. A number of investigators have tried training migraineurs to constrict the temporal artery. Occasionally used feedback forms include electroencephalographic feedback (alpha enhancement), skin conductance feedback, and feedback of temporal temperature (on its own or as a differential response to digital temperature).

These treatments are almost invariably accompanied by instructions to carry out some form of home practice to aid transfer of training, and sometimes have involved portable biofeedback devices. Biofeedback has been combined with a number of treatments, particularly the most common alternative of relaxation training. Biodfeedback and relaxation training have been administered both consecutively and concurrently.

Biofeedback has usually involved approximately 10 sessions of simply training subjects to lower or raise the criterion variable. In recent years, some variations on this basic paradigm have emerged. For example, Stout (1985) has developed "homeostatic reconditioning" in which subjects are trained to raise digital temperature after stressful imaginal experiences (vascular recovery conditioning). A number of researchers have been concerned about the expense of biofeedback and have looked for more cost-effective alternatives. One approach to this problem has been to develop treatment packages that use a group format but these have not involved biofeedback. An alternative has been to develop minimal therapist-contact approaches.

The literature on biofeedback for headaches is extensive. A recently published bibliography included 167 such reports (Martin, Marie, & Nathan, 1987). Studies have demonstrated EMG feedback for tension headaches to be significantly superior to noncontingent feedback, a medication placebo control condition, the "most suitable alternative," and more importantly, to a pseudotherapy condition ("meditation"), which the authors were able to demonstrate had equal credibility (Holroyd, Andrasik, & Noble, 1980). A recent meta-analysis of 37 studies reported an average group improvement of 46.0% with EMG feedback compared to 15.3% with noncontingent feedback, and −3.9% with headache monitoring (Holroyd & Penzien, 1986). The 46% improvement rate was lower than the figure of 61% reported by Blanchard, Andrasik, Ahles, Teders, and O'Keefe (1980) in a previous meta-analytic review. The Holroyd and Penzien study emphasized, however, how cautiously the data need to be interpreted as improvement rates with EMG feedback varied from 17% to 87%! (The figure for the lower end of the range reported by Holroyd and Penzien [1986] was 13%. This was based on a study which had applied a logarithmic transformation to its data prior to analysis as scores were positively skewed. Calculating percentage improvement on the basis of untransformed scores [as occurred for the other studies] resulted in a revised figure of 20% so that the lowest percentage improvement [17%] was achieved by another study.)

Analysis revealed that treatment outcome was not related to treatment procedures (e.g., type of intervention, length of treatment, whether or not efforts were made to facilitate transfer of training), nor the research design (e.g., internal validity, explicitness of diagnostic criteria). Treatment outcome was related, however, to characteristics of the subject sample such as age (younger more successful), size of sample, and drop-out rate (better outcome in studies with smaller samples and fewer drop-outs), referral source (superior results with solicited rather than referred subjects), and gender (females more successful).

In comparisons between EMG feedback and alternative treatment procedures, most studies have failed to find significant differences. The meta-analyses referred to above found no differences between EMG feedback, relaxation training and combined feedback and relaxation. Other treatments such as transcendental meditation, hypnotic analgesia, and digital temperature feedback have been compared with EMG feedback, and in almost all cases they have been shown to be equally effective. One exception is a study by Holroyd, Andrasik, and Westbrook (1977) which demonstrated that a cognitively oriented stress coping training program was significantly more effective than EMG feedback in alleviating tension headaches.

Fewer attempts have been made to evaluate digital temperature feedback for migraine in ways that rule out placebo effects. In the meta-analysis by Blanchard et al. (1980), the authors were forced to compare studies of biofeedback with drug trials that included a medication placebo. Given Holroyd and Penzien's findings of extraordinarily large differences in outcome between different studies that are associated with sample characteristics, this strategy is dubious if not invalid. The data seem fairly convincing in their support for the efficacy of digital temperature feedback, however. Hence, the percentage improvement associated with temperature feedback was 57.8%, with temperature feedback plus autogenic training was 65.1%, against 16.5% for medication placebo.

Comparisons of digital temperature feedback with other treatment modalities have usually suggested equal efficacy. Blanchard et al.'s meta-analysis, for example, showed no difference between temperature feedback (with or without autogenic training) and relaxation training. Studies have shown electroencephalographic feedback, temporal temperature feedback, skin conductance feedback, and self-hypnosis to be equal to digital temperature feedback for reducing migraine headaches.

Training in constriction of the temporal artery has been shown to be superior to digital temperature feedback (Elmore & Tursky, 1981; Friar & Beatty, 1976), and more effective than EMG feedback (Bild & Adams, 1980) for migraines. On the other hand, Cohen, McArthur, and Rickles (1980) found no significant differences between this form of feedback and three alternative forms of feedback.

In a recent review of the long term effects of behavioral treatments for chronic headaches, Blanchard (1987) came to the following tentative conclusions (a) the initial improvement obtained with forehead EMG feedback alone for tension headaches deteriorates progressively (but not back to pretreatment levels) at two and three years, (b) in contrast, relief from tension headaches achieved with cognitive therapy or relaxation training (possibly followed by EMG feedback) is maintained for two and four years, respectively, and (c) patients with migraine headaches show good maintenance of headache relief at 12 months regardless of treatment regimen, but migraineurs treated with relaxation and digital temperature feedback progressively deteriorate year-by-year to a four year follow-up point. Since publication of this review, Sorbi, Tellegen, and Du Long (1989) reported a three-year follow-up study of migraineurs treated with relaxation training or stress-coping training. They found that both treatment conditions were associated with good (and equivalent) maintenance. Hence, the currently available evidence suggests that the effects of relaxation training and cognitively oriented stress coping training are long lasting for both tension headaches and migraines, but the effects of biofeedback are of shorter duration. Booster sessions have not been found to improve maintenance (Andrasik, Blanchard, Neff, & Rodichok, 1984).

A number of recent studies have evaluated minimal-contact home-based behavioral treatments for tension headaches and migraines (e.g., Blanchard et al., 1988; Holroyd et al., 1988). The results of these investigations are generally positive suggesting that minimal-contact interventions are not significantly less effective than traditional clinic-based ones. Only a few studies have included biofeedback in their minimal-contrast conditions, however, and those that have, tended to combine it with other approaches such as relaxation training. Hence, the efficacy of biofeedback alone administered in a minimal-contact format is unclear.

Although there is strong evidence that EMG feedback leads to significant improvement in tension headaches, and digital temperature feedback leads to significant improvement in migraines, at least in the short term (12 months), the mechanisms of change are unclear. Numerous studies have shown a poor correspondence between changes in the physiological variable used for feedback and headache improvement. Recent studies have gone further. Andrasik and Holroyd (1980) demonstrated that training tension headache sufferers to *increase* EMG was as effective as training them to decrease EMG. In a similar vein, studies by Kewman and Roberts (1980) and Gauthier, Bois, Allaire, and Drolet (1981) showed that training migraineurs to *decrease* digital temperature was as effective as teaching them to increase digital temperature. How then does one explain that biofeedback for headaches is more than a placebo effect, but does not seem to operate in accordance with the treatment rationale of learned control of physiological responses? (Although the rationale for EMG feedback is clear and uncontentious, the rationale for digital temperature feedback is the subject of some debate [cf. Elmore & Tursky, 1981; Knapp, 1982]). Holroyd and his colleagues (Andrasik & Holroyd, 1980; Holroyd et al., 1984) have answered this question by suggesting that cognitive mechanisms mediate headache change. Specifically, they argue that subjects' perception of success at the biofeedback task (which can be achieved by changes in either direction) leads them to view their headaches as having a more internal locus of control, and increases their feelings of self-efficacy. These cognitive changes are hypothesized to lead to new and more positive efforts to cope with headache-related stress that, in turn, alter psychological and physiological stress-response triggering headaches. Holroyd and his colleagues have presented data supporting this highly plausible model although further research is needed to clarify which are the most critical variables and how they relate to each other.

Summary of Psychophysiological Contributions to Headache Field

The main contribution so far of psychophysiology to the headache field has been its role in stimulating research and development. Prior to the 1970s psychologists had contributed to the headache literature minimally. It was the early biofeedback studies that drew psychologists into the field. In the last two decades psychologists have made significant contributions. Some of these contributions have evolved directly from psychophysiological approaches and have been reviewed in the preceding pages. They include: (a) psychophysiological investigations of mechanisms that have demonstrated that skeletal muscle tension probably does not play a significant role in tension headaches, the differences between tension headaches and migraines are possibly quantitative rather than qualitative with both having a vascular mechanism, and "response stereotypy" may be an etiological factor; and (b) several forms of biofeedback training lead to headache improvement, the treatment effect is more than a placebo response, and is possibly mediated by cognitive changes involving self-efficacy and locus of control. Other contributions did not evolve directly from psychophysiology but were stimulated by the emerging biofeedback literature. These include: (a) important methodological innovations such as the development of headache diaries and pain scales with behavioral-referants; (b) studies related to headache diagnosis and classification; (c) investigations of the relationship between headaches and mood; (d) studies of the personality and behavioral style of headache sufferers; and (e) the development of probably more effective treatment approaches such as cognitively oriented stress coping training (cf. previous section on cardiovascular disorders). How much credit psychophysiology deserves for the success achieved with relaxation training partly depends on whether this form of treatment is viewed as a psychophysiological technique.

On the other hand, it is impossible to escape the conclusion that the potential contributions of psychophysiology to headache research and management are, as yet, largely unfulfilled. The promise of biofeedback as a treatment modality has not been realized. Both EMG feedback and digital temperature feedback have proved no more effective than other treatment approaches that do not require electronic equipment. Long term follow-up studies suggest that maintenance of treatment gains may be more of a problem for biofeedback than other therapies. The place of biofeedback in recently developed less costly approaches such as treatment administered in a group format or minimal therapist-contact, home-based packages has not been established.

Psychophysiological investigations of headaches have had more success in showing what does not cause headaches than what does. A similar conclusion can be drawn in other areas of headache research stimulated by the biofeedback literature. For example, a series of studies have produced findings that fail to support the Ad Hoc Committee's classification system, but convincing alternatives have not been forthcoming.

Why Have Psychophysiological Contributions Not Been More Extensive?

In considering why psychophysiological contributions to the headache literature have not proved more productive, the focus will tend to be on broad issues that have relevance beyond the headache realm (detailed methodological criticisms of the headache literature are available in Thompson and Adams (1984) and Andrasik, Blanchard, Arena, Saunders, and Barron (1982)). For example, the argument could be made that headache research has not chosen to tackle empirical questions in a logically sound sequence (Martin, 1983). The initial and continuing emphasis has been on treatment trials, which is understandable in terms of the humanitarian concern for alleviating suffering, but is questionable on scientific grounds given that so little is understood about headache mechanisms. (How do you train patients to control dysfunctional processes if it is not clear what processes are dysfunctional?) Following the early treatment studies some investigators did resort to laboratory research to elucidate headache processes. Even these studies were perhaps premature, however, because little was known about the controlling variables of headaches. (It is difficult to study physiological mechanisms without knowing how to activate the mechanisms.)

With our current understanding of headaches and treatment mechanisms, why should EMG feedback or digital temperature feedback help headache sufferers other than through nonspecific processes such as the cognitive changes proposed by Holroyd and his colleagues? If specific physiologically mediated benefits are required then the feedback needs to target directly the dysfunctional physiological process. In this context it is interesting to note that the most promising form of feedback appears to be training in constriction of temporal arteries, which probably comes closer to regulating headache mechanisms than alternative forms of feedback. Biofeedback may have to progress, however, beyond simply training subjects to raise or lower a response. For example, the classic view of migraine pathology is a two stage process in which the migraineur initially responds to stressful stimuli with cranial and cerebral vasoconstriction that triggers a rebound phenomenon of cranial and cerebral vasodilation. If this view is correct then merely training subjects to constrict arteries is unlikely to prove adequate. An alternative approach would be to train subjects in both dilation as well as constriction, with further training in when to apply each of these learned skills. It seems unlikely to us that biofeedback will ever again be advocated as the sole treatment modality for chronic headaches, but as our knowledge of pain mechanisms accumulates some form of biofeedback may well be an important component of a treatment package.

What factors have impeded progress in establishing the psychophysiological mechanisms of headaches? Five interrelated points will be discussed briefly here. First, as indicated previously, it is difficult to study mechanisms without knowing what activates the mechanisms. Many studies have investigated the effects of "stress" on headaches but this is only one of numerous stimuli that headache sufferers report precipitate headaches. Other commonly reported stimuli are anxiety, glare, noise, anger, fatigue, eyestrain, alcohol, depression, neck movements, flicker, high temperature, hunger, high humidity, and certain foods. With the exception of noise stimuli, the physiological changes (if they exist) associated with these other stimuli have not been explored. Do the different stimuli trigger the same or different mechanisms?

A second factor is that studies have employed group designs, and headache sufferers have only been partitioned according to traditional diagnostic criteria. Our own work and that of others (e.g., Gannon et al., 1987) shows a great deal of physiological variability, in terms of resting levels and response to stimuli, between subjects. As reviewed, this variability relates poorly to diagnostic status. Hence, what is needed is designs that are more sensitive to individual differences, or the development of classification systems that reflect psychophysiological mechanisms. This second point relates to the first point then, as one possible principle on which to base a classification system might be the patterns of antecedent stimuli that precipitate headaches (Martin, 1985).

A third factor is that most studies investigating headache mechanisms have paid little attention to drugs that might influence the dependent variables. Many medications, for example, influence muscular and vascular activity, and the majority of chronic headache sufferers regularly consume pills. Even nicotine (Stephens, 1977) has been demonstrated to have vasoactive effects and effects upon skeletal muscle tone (Domino, 1973).

A fourth factor concerns the choice of measurement instruments and sites. It was mentioned earlier that recent findings with occipital placements raised the possibility that previous studies were not measuring EMG from the critical site. With respect to vascular variables, psychophysiologists have usually employed superficial placements of sensors to monitor extracranial vascular changes. However, both Blau and Dexter (1981) and Drummond and Lance (1983) concluded that intracranial changes were more important than extracranial changes. This poses a problem for psychophysiologists as there are no noninvasive methods currently available that can be used for measuring the state of dilation of intracranial arteries.

A final factor concerns the tendency in the literature for physiological variables to be measured and analyzed with little appreciation for the underlying physiological systems. For example, some studies have used ultrasonic transducers that measure blood velocity and then claimed this assesses the state of dilation of arteries, which is not the case as velocity is a function of both dilation of arteries and blood pressure. Many studies use photoelectric plethysmographic transducers that measure the amount of blood immediately below them. Changes in this measure could reflect either local vasomotor effects (changes in smooth muscle) or cardiovascular effects (changes in blood pressure), but investigators do not attempt to differentiate these possibilities. This type of problem is well recognized in recent handbooks of psychophysiology (e.g., Coles et al., 1986), but most psychophysiological investigations of headaches continue to appear biologically naive.

CONCLUSION

We have repeatedly emphasized that behavior therapists have recognized for at least 20 years that our therapies are directed at altering behavior, cognition and physiological responses. At various times differing aspects of this trinity have been emphasized. Initially behavior was all; currently the focus is predominantly on cognition. The psychophysiological dimension has never been primary and is never likely to be. However, it is important and must not be lost sight of in any balanced view of the behavioral treatment of a wide range of behavioral and psychophysiological problems.

In this chapter we have sketched the relationship between behavior therapy and psychophysiology and tried to highlight some of the areas where the link has either been most productive or is stimulating most interest at the present. Psychophysiology has increased our understanding of the anxiety disorders, has greatly influenced our procedures for assessing the effectiveness of behavioral treatments and promises to have a major influence on our views of behavior therapy for anxiety related conditions. The increasing sophistication of methods of measurement and analysis hold out great promise for the future. Even more important is the development of dynamic models of the relationship between physiological systems and responses, and behavior and cognition.

The direct role of psychophysiology in the treatment of psychophysiological disorders has proved disappointing. Biofeedback has not proved as uniquely useful as some hoped in the treatment of cardiovascular and other autonomic disorders although it has indicated the considerable potential of various self-control and stress management techniques, such as relaxation training. In the treatment of headache we have argued that although biofeedback has again not proved to be uniquely useful this may be because the correct questions have not been asked.

Psychophysiology is not a theory, it is an area of study defined very largely by its methods. It can provide very expensive, laborious, and frankly tedious answers to the wrong questions. Fortunately, there are signs that the correct questions are being asked more frequently.

REFERENCES

Ad Hoc Committee (1962). Classification of headache. *Journal of American Medical Association, 179,* 717–718.

Adams, H. E., Feuerstein, M., & Fowler, J. L. (1980). Migraine headache: Review of parameters, etiology and intervention. *Psychological Bulletin, 87,* 217–237.

Ahles, T. A., Martin, J. B., Gaulier, B., Cassens, H. L., Andres, M. L., & Shariff, M. (1988). Electromyographic and vasomotor activity in tension, migraine, and combined headache patients: The influence of postural variation. *Behaviour Research and Therapy, 26,* 519–525.

Akselrod, S., Gordon, D., Ubel, F. A., Shannon, D. C., Barger, A. C., & Cohen, R. J. (1981). Power spectrum analysis of heart rate fluctuation: a quantitative probe of beat-to-beat cardiovascular control. *Science, 213,* 220–222.

American Psychiatric Association. (1968). *Diagnostic and statistical manual of mental disorders* (2nd ed.). Washington, DC: Author.

Anastasiades, P., & Johnston, D. W. (1990). A simple activity measure for use with ambulatory subjects. *Psychophysiology, 27,* 89–93.

Anderson, C. D., Stoyva, J. M., & Vaughn, L. J. (1982). A test of delayed recovery following stressful stimulation in four psychosomatic disorders. *Journal of Psychosomatic Research, 26,* 571–580.

Andrasik, F., Blanchard, E. B., Arena, J. G., Saunders, N. L., & Barron, K. D. (1982). Psychophysiology of recurrent headache: Methodological issues and new empirical findings. *Behavior Therapy, 13,* 407–429.

Andrasik, F., Blanchard, E. B., Neff, D. F., & Rodichok, L. D. (1984). Biofeedback and relaxation training for chronic headache: A controlled comparison of booster treatments and regular contacts for long-term maintenance. *Journal of Consulting and Clinical Psychology, 52,* 609–615.

Andrasik, F., & Holroyd, K. A. (1980). A test of specific and nonspecific effects in the biofeedback treatment of tension headache. *Journal of Consulting and Clinical Psychology, 48,* 575–586.

Andreassi, J. L. (1980). *Psychophysiology: Human behavior and physiological response.* New York: Oxford University Press.

Arena, J. G., Blanchard, E. B., Andrasik, F., Cotch, P. A., & Myers, P. E. (1983). Reliability of psychophysiological assessment. *Behaviour Research and Therapy, 21,* 447–460.

Beatty, J., Barth, D. S., Richer, F., & Johnson, R. A. (1986). Neuromagnetometry. In M. G. H. Coles, E. Donchin, & S. W. Porges (Eds.), *Psychophysiology: Systems, processes and applications* (pp. 26–40). New York: Guilford Press.

Beck, A. T. (1988). Cognitive approaches to panic disorder: Theory and therapy. In S. Rachman & J. D. Maser (Eds.), *Panic: Psychological perspectives* (pp. 91–109). Hillsdale, NJ: Lawrence Erlbaum Associates.

Belar, C. D., Sutton, E. P., & Wilson, E. (1983). Tension headache patients: A comparison of a recruited subject sample and a clinic-based subject sample. *Headache, 23,* 240–242.

Bild, R., & Adams, H. E. (1980). Modification of migraine headaches by cephalic blood volume pulse and EMG biofeedback. *Journal of Consulting and Clinical Psychology, 48,* 51–57.

Blanchard, E. B. (1987). Long-term effects of behavioral treatment of chronic headache. *Behavior Therapy, 18,* 375–385.

Blanchard, E. B., Andrasik, F., Ahles, T. A., Teders, S. J., & O'Keefe, D. (1980). Migraine and tension headache: A meta-analytic review. *Behavior Therapy, 11,* 613–631.

Blanchard, E. B., Appelbaum, K. A., Guarnieri, P., Neff, D. F., Andrasik, F., Jaccard, J., & Barron, K. D. (1988). Two studies of the long-term follow-up of minimal therapist contact treatments of vascular and tension headache. *Journal of Consulting and Clinical Psychology, 56,* 427–432.

Blanchard, E. B., McCoy, G. C., Gerardi, M. A., Pallmeyer, T. P., Gerardi, R. J., Cotch, P. A., Siracusa, K., & Andrasik, F. (1986). A controlled comparison of thermal biofeedback and relaxation training in the treatment of essential hypertension: 1: short-term and long-term outcome: *Behavior Therapy, 17,* 563–579.

Blanchard, E. B., Miller, S. T., Abel, C. C., Haynes, M. R., & Wicker, R. (1979). Evaluation of biofeedback in the treatment of essential hypertension. *Journal of Applied Behavioral Analysis, 12,* 99–110.

Blau, J. N., & Dexter, S. L. (1981). The site of pain origin during migraine attacks. *Cephalagia, 1,* 143–147.

Brener, J., & Hothersall, D. (1966). Heart rate control under conditions of augmented sensory feedback. *Psychophysiology, 3,* 23–28.

Budzynski, T., Stoyva, J., & Adler, C. (1970). Feedback-induced muscle relaxation. Application to tension headache. *Journal of Behavior Therapy and Experimental Psychiatry, 1,* 205–211.

Cacioppo, J. T., & Petty, R. E. (Eds.). (1983). *Social psychophysiology: A sourcebook.* New York: Guilford Press.

Chapman, S. L. (1986). A review and clinical perspective on the use of EMG and thermal biofeedback for chronic headaches. *Pain, 27,* 1–43.

Clark, D. M. (1986). A cognitive approach to panic. *Behaviour Research and Therapy, 24,* 461–470.

Clark, D. M., Salkovskis, P. M., & Chalkley, A. J. (1985). Respiratory control as a treatment for panic attacks. *Journal of Behavior Therapy and Experimental Psychiatry, 16,* 23–30.

Cohen, M. J., McArthur, D. L., & Rickles, W. H. (1980). Comparison of four biofeedback treatments for migraine headache: Physiological and headache variables. *Psychosomatic Medicine, 42,* 463–480.

Cohen, R. A., Williamson, D. A., Monguillot, J. E., Hutchinson, P. C., Gottlieb, J., & Waters, W. F. (1983). Psychophysiological response patterns in vascular and muscle contraction headaches. *Journal of Behavioral Medicine, 6,* 93–107.

Coles, M. G. H. (1989). Modern mind-brain reading: Psychophysiology, physiology, and cognition. *Psychophysiology, 26,* 251–269.

Coles, M. G. H., Donchin, E., & Porges, S. W. (1986). *Psychophysiology: Systems, processes and applications.* New York: Guilford Press.

Coles, M. G. H., Gratton, G., Kramer, A. F., & Miller, G. A. (1986). Principles of signal acquisition and analysis. In M. G. H. Coles, E. Donchin, & S. W. Porges (Eds.), *Psychophysiology: Systems, processes and applications* (pp. 183–221). New York: Guilford Press.

Cook, E. W., Melamed, B. G., Cuthbert, B. N., McNeil, D. W., & Lang, P. J. (1988). Emotional imagery and the differential diagnosis of anxiety. *Journal of Consulting and Clinical Psychology, 56,* 734–740.

Cox, D., Hallam, R., O'Connor, K., & Rachman, S. (1983). An experimental analysis of fearlessness and courage. *British Journal of Psychology, 74,* 107–117.

Cram, J. R. (1986). *Clinical EMG: Muscle scanning and*

diagnostic manual for surface recordings. Seattle, WA: Clinical Resources and J. and J. Industries.

Craske, M. G., Sanderson, W. C., & Barlow, D. H. (1987). How do desynchronous response systems relate to the treatment of agoraphobia: A follow-up evaluation. *Behavior Research and Therapy, 25,* 117–122.

De Good, D. E., & Adams, A. S. (1976). Control of cardiac response under aversive stimulation: superiority of a heart rate feedback condition. *Biofeedback and Self-Regulation, 1,* 373–385.

Dimberg, U., & Ohman, A. (1983). The effects of directional facial cues on electrodermal conditioning to facial stimuli. *Psychophysiology, 20,* 160–167.

Domino, E. (1973). Neuropsychopharmacology of nicotine and tobacco smoking. In W. Dunn (Ed.), *Smoking behavior: Motives and incentives.* Washington, DC: Winston.

Donchin, E. (Ed.). (1984). *Cognitive psychophysiology.* Hillsdale, NJ: Lawrence Erlbaum Associates.

Drummond, P. D., & Lance, J. W. (1983). Extracranial vascular changes and the source of pain in migraine headache. *Annals of Neurology, 13,* 32–37.

Drummond, P. D., & Lance, J. W. (1984). Clinical diagnosis and computer analysis of headache symptoms. *Journal of Neurology, Neurosurgery and Psychiatry, 47,* 128–133.

Ehlers, A., Margraf, J., & Roth, W. T. (1988). Interaction of expectancy and physiological stressors in a laboratory model of panic. In D. Hellhammer, I. Florin, & H. Weiner (Eds.), *Neurobiology of human disease* (pp. 379–384). Toronto: Huber.

Ehlers, A., Margraf, J., Roth, W. T., Taylor, C. B., & Birbaumer, N. (1988). Anxiety induced by false heart rate feedback in patients with panic disorder. *Behaviour Research and Therapy, 26,* 1–11.

Ehlers, A., Margraf, J., Roth, W. T., Taylor, C. B., Maddock, R. J., Sheikh, J., Kopell, M. L., McClenahan, K. L., Gossard, D., Blowers, G. H., Agras, W. S., & Kopell, B. S. (1986). Lactate infusions and panic attacks: do patients and controls respond differently. *Psychiatry Research, 17,* 295–308.

Engel, B. T., & Hansen, S. P. (1966). Operant conditioning of heart rate slowing. *Psychophysiology, 3,* 176–187.

Elmore, A. M., & Tursky, B. (1981). A comparison of two psychophysiological approaches to the treatment of migraine. *Headache, 21,* 93–101.

Fey, S. G., & Lindholm, E. (1975). Systolic blood pressure and heart rate changes during three sessions involving biofeedback or no feedback. *Psychophysiology, 12,* 513–519.

Foa, E. B., & Kozak, M. J. (1986). Emotional processing of fear: exposure to corrective information. *Psychological Bulletin, 99,* 20–35.

Fowles, D. C. (1983). Motivational effects on heart rate and electrodermal activity: Implications for research on personality and psychopathology. *Journal of Research in Personality, 17,* 48–71.

Fowles, D. C. (1986). The psychophysiology of anxiety and hedonic affect: Motivational specificity. In B. F. Shaw, Z. V. Segal, T. M. Vallis, & F. E. Cashman (Eds.), *Anxiety disorders: Psychological and biological perspectives* (pp. 51–66). New York: Plenum Press.

Fowles, D. C. (1987). Application of a behavioral therapy of motivation to the concepts of anxiety and impulsivity. *Journal of Research in Personality, 21,* 417–435.

Fowles, D. C. (1988). Psychophysiology and psychopathology: A motivational approach. *Psychophysiology, 25,* 373–391.

Fredrikson, M. (1981). Orienting and defensive reactions to phobic conditioned fear stimuli in phobics and normals. *Psychophysiology, 18,* 456–465.

Fredrikson, M., & Ohman, A. (1979). Cardiovascular and electrodermal responses conditioned to fear-relevant stimuli. *Psychophysiology, 16,* 1–7.

Freedman, R. R., Ianni, P., Ettedgui, E., & Puthezhath, N. (1985). Ambulatory monitoring of panic disorder. *Archives of General Psychiatry, 42,* 244–248.

Freedman, R. R., Ianni, P., & Wenig, P. (1983). Behavioral treatment of Raynaud's disease. *Journal of Consulting and Clinical Psychology, 51,* 539–549.

Freedman, R., Sabharwa, S. C., Ianni, P., Desai, N., Wenig, P., & Mayes, M. (1988). Noneural beta-adrenergic vasodilating mechanism in temperature biofeedback. *Psychosomatic Medicine, 50,* 394–401.

Friar, L. R., & Beatty, J. (1976). Migraine: Management by trained control of vasoconstriction. *Journal of Consulting and Clinical Psychology, 44,* 46–53.

Gale, A., & Christie, B. (Eds.). (1987). *Psychophysiology and the electronic workplace.* Chichester: John Wiley & Sons.

Gannon, L. R., Haynes, S. N., Cuevas, J., & Chavez, R. (1987). Psychophysiological correlates of induced headaches. *Journal of Behavioral Medicine, 10,* 411–423.

Gannon, L. R., Haynes, S. N., Safranek, R., & Hamilton, J. (1980). A psychophysiological investigation of muscle-contraction and migraine headache. *Journal of Psychosomatic Research, 25,* 271–280.

Gatchel, R. J. (1974). Frequency of feedback and learned heart rate control. *Journal of Experimental Psychology, 103,* 274–283.

Gauthier, J., Bois, R., Allaire, D., & Drolet, M. (1981). Evaluation of skin temperature biofeedback training at two different sites for migraine. *Journal of Behavioral Medicine, 4,* 407–419.

Gelder, M. G., Bancroft, J. H., Gath, D. H., Johnston, D. W., Mathews, A. M., & Shaw, P. M. (1973). Specific and non-specific factors in behaviour therapy. *British Journal of Psychiatry, 114,* 323–328.

Glasgow, M. S., Gaardner, K. R., & Engel, B. T. (1982). Behavioral treatment of high blood pressure: II Acute and sustained effects of relaxation and systolic blood pressure biofeedback. *Psychosomatic Medicine, 44,* 155–171.

Goldstein, D. S., Ross, R. S., & Brady, J. V. (1977).

Biofeedback of heart rate during exercise. *Biofeedback and Self-Regulation, 2,* 107–126.
Gray, J. A. (1975). *Elements of a two-process theory of learning.* New York: Academic Press.
Grayson, J. B., Foa, E. B., & Steketee, G. (1982). Habituation during exposure treatment: distraction versus attention focussing. *Behaviour Research and Therapy, 20,* 323–328.
Grey, S. J., Rachman, S., & Sartory, G. (1981). Return of fear: The role of inhibition. *Behaviour Research and Therapy, 19,* 135–143.
Guglielmi, R. S., Roberts, A. H., & Patterson, R. (1982). Skin temperature biofeedback for Raynaud's disease: a double blind study. *Biofeedback and Self-Regulation, 7,* 99–120.
Haynes, S. N., Cuevas, J., & Gannon, L. R. (1982). The psychophysiological etiology of muscle contraction headache. *Headache, 22,* 122–132.
Haynes, S. N., Griffin, P., Mooney, D., & Parise, M. (1975). Electromyographic biofeedback and relaxation instructions in the treatment of muscle contraction headaches. *Behavior Therapy, 6,* 672–678.
Haynes, S. N., & Wilson, C. C. (1979). *Behavioral assessment: Recent advances in methods, concepts and applications.* San Francisco: Jossey-Bass.
Headache classification committee of the International Headache Society (1988). Classification and diagnostic criteria for headache disorders, cranial neuralgias and facial pain. *Cephalalgia, 8* (Suppl. 7).
Hibbert, G., & Pilsbury, D. (1988). Hyperventilation and panic attacks: ambulant monitoring of transcutaneous carbon dioxide. *British Journal of Psychiatry, 153,* 76–80.
Hillyard, S. A., & Kutas, M. (1983). Electrophysiology of cognitive processing. *Annual Review of Psychology, 34,* 33–61.
Himadi, W. G., Boice, R., & Barlow, D. H. (1985). Assessment of agoraphobia: triple response measurement. *Behaviour Research and Therapy, 23,* 311–323.
Hodgson, R., & Rachman, S. (1974). II. Desynchrony in measures of fear. *Behaviour Research and Therapy, 12,* 319–326.
Hollandsworth, J. G. (1986). *Physiology and behavior therapy: Conceptual guidelines for the clinician.* New York: Plenum Press.
Holroyd, K. A., Andrasik, F., & Noble, J. (1980). A comparison of EMG biofeedback and a credible pseudotherapy in treating tension headache. *Journal of Behavioral Medicine, 3,* 29–39.
Holroyd, K. A., Andrasik, F., & Westbrook, T. (1977). Cognitive control of tension headache. *Cognitive Therapy and Research, 1,* 121–133.
Holroyd, K. A., Holm, J. E., Hursey, K. G., Penzien, D. B., Cordingley, G. E., Theofanous, A. G., Richardson, S. C., & Tobin, D. L. (1988). Recurrent vascular headache: Home-based behavioral treatment versus abortive pharmacological treatment. *Journal of Consulting and Clinical Psychology, 56,* 218–223.
Holroyd, K. A., & Penzien, D. B. (1986). Client variables and the behavioral treatment of recurrent tension headache: A meta-analytic review. *Journal of Behavioral Medicine, 9,* 515–536.
Holroyd, K. A., Penzien, D. B., Hursey, K. G., Tobin, D. L., Rogers, L., Holm, J. E., Marcille, P. J., Hall, J. R., & Chila, A. G. (1984). Change mechanisms in EMG biofeedback training: Cognitive changes underlying improvements in tension headaches. *Journal of Consulting and Clinical Psychology, 52,* 1039–1053.
Hudzinski, L. G., & Lawrence, G. S. (1988). Significance of EMG surface electrode placement models and headache findings. *Headache, 28,* 30–35.
Hugdahl, K. (1978). Electrodermal conditioning to potentially phobic stimuli: effects of instructed extinction. *Behaviour Research and Therapy, 16,* 315–321.
James, W. (1884). What is emotion? *Mind, 19,* 188–205.
Johnston, D. W. (1976). Criterion level and instructional effects in the voluntary control of heart rate. *Biological Psychology, 4,* 1–17.
Johnston, D. W. (1977a). Feedback and instructional effects in the voluntary control of digital pulse amplitude. *Biological Psychology, 5,* 159–171.
Johnston, D. W. (1977b). Biofeedback: verbal instructions and the motor skills analogy. In J. Beatty & H. Legewie (Eds.), *Biofeedback and behavior* (pp. 331–341). New York: Plenum Press.
Johnston, D. W. (1986). How does relaxation training reduce blood pressure in primary hypertension. In T. H. Schmidt, T. D. Dembroski, & C. Blumchen (Eds.), *Biological and psychological factors in coronary heart disease* (pp. 550–567). Berlin: Springer-Verlag.
Johnston, D. W. (1987). The behavioral control of high blood pressure. *Current Psychological Research and Reviews, 6,* 99–114.
Johnston, D. W. (1989). Will stress management prevent coronary heart disease: *The Psychologist, 7,* 275–278.
Johnston, D. W., & Lethem, J. (1981). The production of specific decreases in interbeat interval and the motor skills analogy. *Psychophysiology, 18,* 288–300.
Johnston, D. W., & Lethem, J. (1983). Feedback and incentive effects on the decrease of interbeat interval. *Biofeedback and Self-Regulation, 8,* 255–263.
Johnston, D. W., Lo, C. R., & Marie, G. V. (1984). The use of feedback to reduce the cardiovascular response to exercise. In P. Grossman, K. L. Janssen, & D. Vaitl (Eds.), *Cardiorespiratory and cardiosomatic psychophysiology* (pp. 251–261). New York: Plenum Press.
Johnston, D. W., & Ross, A. (1986). *Cardiovascular biofeedback during an active coping task.* Unpublished manuscript.
Jones, M. C. (1924). A laboratory study of fear: The case of Peter. *Pedagogical Seminary, 31,* 308–315.
Kallman, W. M., & Feuerstein, M. (1986). Psychophysio-

logical procedures. In A. R. Ciminero, K. S. Calhoun, & H. E. Adams (Eds.), *Handbook of behavioral assessment* (2nd ed.). New York: John Wiley & Sons.

Kewman, D., & Roberts, A. H. (1980). Skin temperature biofeedback and migraine headaches. *Biofeedback and Self-Regulation, 5*, 327–345.

Kluger, M. A., Jamner, L. D., & Tursky, B. (1985). Comparison of the effectiveness of biofeedback and relaxation training on hand warming. *Psychophysiology, 22*, 162–166.

Knapp, T. W. (1982). Evidence for sympathetic deactivation by temporal vasoconstriction and digital vasodilation biofeedback in migraine patients: A reply to Elmore and Tursky and a new hypothesis. *Headache, 22*, 233–236.

Kozak, M. J., Foa, E. B., & Steketee, G. (1988). Process and outcome of exposure treatment with obsessive-compulsives: psychophysiological indicators of emotional processing. *Behavior Therapy, 19*, 157–169.

Lacey, J. I. (1967). Somatic response patterning and stress: Some revisions of activation theory. In M. H. Appley & R. Trumbell (Eds.), *Psychological stress: Issues in research* (pp. 14–44). New York: Appleton-Century-Crofts.

Lang, P. J. (1971). The application of psychophysiological methods to psychotherapy and behavior modification. In A. E. Bergin & S. L. Garfield (Eds.), *Handbook of psychotherapy and behavior change: an empirical analysis*. New York: John Wiley & Sons.

Lang, P. J. (1975). Acquisition of heart rate control: method, theory and clinical implications. In D. C. Fowles (Ed.), *Clinical applications of psychophysiology*, New York: Colombia University Press.

Lang, P. J. (1979). A bio-informational theory of emotional imagery. *Psychophysiology, 16*, 495–512.

Lang, P. J. (1985). The cognitive psychophysiology of emotion: Fear and anxiety. In A. H. Tuma & J. Maser (Eds.), *Anxiety and the anxiety disorders* (pp. 131–168). Hillsdale, NJ: Lawrence Erlbaum Associates.

Lang, P. J. (1987). Image as action: A reply to Watts and Blackstock. *Cognition and Emotion, 1*, 407–426.

Lang, P. J., Melamed, B. G., & Hart, J. (1970). A psychophysiological analysis of fear modification using an automated desensitization procedure. *Journal of Abnormal Psychology, 76*, 220–234.

Lang, P. J., Levin, D. N., Miller, G. A., & Kozak, M. J. (1983). Fear behavior, fear imagery, and the psychophysiology of emotion: the problem of affective response integration. *Journal of Abnormal Psychology, 92*, 276–306.

Lang, P. J., & Twentyman, C. T. (1974). Learning to control heart rate: binary vs analogue feedback. *Psychophysiology, 11*, 616–629.

Lee, I., Tyrer, P., & Horn, S. (1983). A comparison of subliminal, supraliminal and faded phobic cine-films in the treatment of agoraphobia. *British Journal of Psychiatry, 143*, 356–361.

Lo, C. R., & Johnston, D. W. (1984a). The self-control of the cardiovascular response to exercise using feedback of the product of the interbeat interval and pulse transit time. *Psychosomatic Medicine, 46*, 115–125.

Lo, C. R., & Johnston, D. W. (1984b). Cardiovascular feedback during dynamic exercise. *Psychophysiology, 21*, 199–206.

Margraf, J., Taylor, C. B., Ehlers, A., Roth, W. T., & Agras, W. S. (1987). Panic attacks in the natural environment. *Journal of Nervous and Mental Disease, 175*, 558–565.

Martin, I., & Venables, P. H. (1980). *Techniques in psychophysiology*. Chichester, John Wiley & Sons.

Martin, P. R. (1980). Behavioral management of headaches: A review of the evidence. *International Journal of Mental Health, 9*, 88–110.

Martin, P. R. (1983). Behavioral research on headaches: Current status and future directions. In K. A. Holroyd, B. Schlote, & H. Zenz (Eds.), *Perspectives in research on headaches* (pp. 204–215). Lewiston, NY: Hogrefe.

Martin, P. R. (1985). Classification of headache: The need for a radical revision. *Cephalagia, 5*, 1–4.

Martin, P. R. (1986). Headaches. In N. J. King & A. Remenyi (Eds.), *Health care: A behavioural approach* (pp. 145–157). Sydney: Grune & Stratton.

Martin, P. R., Marie, G. V., & Nathan, P. R. (1987). Behavioral research on headaches: A coded bibliography. *Headache, 27*, 555–570.

Martin, P. R., & Mathews, A. M. (1978). Tension headaches: Psychophysiological investigation and treatment. *Journal of Psychosomatic Research, 22*, 389–399.

Mathews, A. M., Gelder, M. G., & Johnston, D. W. (1981). *Agoraphobia: Nature and treatment*. London: Tavistock.

Mavissakalian, M., & Michelson, L. (1982). Patterns of psychological change in the treatment of agoraphobia. *Behaviour Research and Therapy, 20*, 347–356.

McNally, R. J. (1981). Phobias and preparedness: Instructional reversal of electrodermal conditioning to fear-relevant stimuli. *Psychological Reports, 48*, 175–180.

Michelson, L. (1986). Treatment consonance and response profiles in agoraphobia: the role of individual differences in cognitive, behavioral and physiological treatments. *Behaviour Research and Therapy, 24*, 263–275.

Michelson, L., & Mavissakalian, M. (1985). Psychophysiological outcome of behavioral and pharmacological treatments in agoraphobia. *Journal of Consulting and Clinical Psychology, 53*, 229–236.

Miller, N. E. (1969). Learning of visceral and glandular reponses. *Science, 163*, 434–445.

Miller, N. E., & Dworkin, B. R. (1974). Visceral learning: recent difficulties with curarized rats and significant problems for human research. In P. A. Obrist, A. H. Black, J. Brener, & L. V. DiCara (Eds.), *Cardiovascular psychophysiology: Current issues in response mechanisms, biofeedback, and methodology* (pp. 312–331). Chicago: Aldine.

Mowrer, O. H. (1939). A stimulus response analysis of

anxiety and its role as a reinforcing agent. *Psychological Review, 46,* 553–565.
Nevins, B. G., & Schwartz, M. S. (1985, April). *An alternative placement for EMG electrodes in the study and treatment of tension headaches.* Paper presented at the 16th annual meeting of the Biofeedback Society of America, New Orleans, LA.
Obrist, P. A. (1981). *Cardiovascular Psychophysiology.* New York: Academic Press.
Obrist, P. A., Galosy, R. A., Lawler, J. F., Gaebelin, C. J., Howard, J. L., & Shanks, E. M. (1975). Operant conditioning of heart rate: somatic correlates. *Psychophysiology, 12,* 445–455.
Ohman, A. (1986). Face the beast and fear the face: Animal and social fears as prototypes for evolutionary analyses of emotion. *Psychophysiology, 23,* 123–145.
Ohman, A., & Dimberg, U. (1978). Facial expressions as conditioned stimuli for electrodermal responses: A case of "preparedness?" *Journal of Personality and Social Psychology, 36,* 1251–1258.
Ohman, A., Eriksson, A., & Olofsson, C. (1975). One trial learning and superior resistance of extinction of autonomic responses conditioned to potentially phobic stimuli. *Journal of Comparative and Physiological Psychology, 88,* 619–627.
Ohman, A., Erixon, G., & Lofberg, I. (1975). Phobias and preparedness: phobic versus neutral pictures as conditioned stimuli for human autonomic responses. *Journal of Abnormal Psychology, 84,* 41–45.
Ost, L. G., Jerremalm, A., & Jansson, L. (1984). Individual response patterns and the effects of different behavioral methods in the treatment of agoraphobia. *Behaviour Research and Therapy, 22,* 797–707.
Ost, L. G., Jerremalm, A., & Johansson, J. (1981). Individual response patterns and the effects of different behavioral methods in the treatment of social phobia. *Behaviour Research and Therapy, 19,* 1–16.
Ost, L. G., Johansson, J., & Jerremalm, A. (1982). Individual response patterns and the effects of different behavioral methods in the treatment of claustrophobia. *Behaviour Research and Therapy, 20,* 445–460.
Pagani, M., Lombardi, F., Guzzetti, S., Rimoldi, O., Furlan, R., Pizzinelli, P., Sandrone, G., Malfatto, G., Dell'Orto, S., Piccaluga, E., Turiel, M., Baselli, G., Cerutti, S., & Malliani, A. (1986). Power spectral analysis of heart rate and arterial pressure variabilities as a marker in man and conscious dog. *Circulation Research, 59,* 178–193.
Papakostopoulos, D., Butler, S., & Martin, I. (1985). *Clinical and experimental neuropsychophysiology.* Kent, England: Croom Helm.
Parati, G., Casadei, R., Groppelli, A., Di Rienzo, M., & Mancia, G. (1989). Comparison of finger and intra-arterial blood pressure monitoring at rest and during laboratory testing. *Hypertension, 13,* 647–655.
Perski, A., & Engel, B. T. (1980). The role of behavioral conditioning in the cardiovascular adjustment to exercise. *Biofeedback and Self-Regulation, 5,* 91–104.
Peveler, R., & Johnston, D. W. (1986). Subjective and cognitive effects of relaxation. *Behaviour Research and Therapy, 24,* 413–420.
Pilsbury, D., & Hibbert, G. (1987). An ambulatory system for long-term continuous monitoring of transcutaneous pCO2. *Bulletin of the European Physiopathol Respiration, 23,* 9–13.
Pitts, F. N., & McClure, J. N. (1967). Lactate metabolism in anxiety neurosis. *New England Journal of Medicine, 227,* 1329–1336.
Porges, S. W., & Fox, N. A. (1986). Developmental psychophysiology. In M. G. H. Coles, E. Donchin, & S. W. Porges (Eds.), *Psychophysiology: Systems, processes, and applications* (pp. 611–625). New York: Guilford Press.
Pritchard, D. W., & Wood, M. M. (1983). EMG levels in the occipitofrontalis muscles under an experimental stress condition. *Biofeedback and Self-Regulation, 8,* 165–175.
Rachman, S. (1978). *Fear and courage.* San Francisco: Freeman.
Rachman, S., & Hodgson, R. (1974). I. Synchrony and desynchrony in fear and avoidance. *Behaviour Research and Therapy, 12,* 311–318.
Rapee, R., Mattik, R., & Murrell, E. (1986). Cognitive mediation in the affective component of spontaneous panic attacks. *Journal of Behavior Therapy and Experimental Psychiatry, 17,* 245–253.
Reeves, J. L., & Shapiro, D. (1982). Heart rate biofeedback and cold pressor pain. *Psychophysiology, 19,* 393–403.
Roberts, A. H., Kewman, D. G., & MacDonald, H. (1973). Voluntary control of skin temperature: Unilateral changes using hypnosis and feedback. *Journal of Abnormal Psychology, 82,* 163–168.
Roth, W. T., Telch, M. J., Taylor, C. B., Sachitano, J. A., Gallen, C., Kopell, M. L., McClenahan, K., Agras, S., & Pfefferbaum, A. (1986). Autonomic characteristics of agoraphobia with panic attacks. *Biological Psychiatry, 21,* 1133–1154.
Salkovskis, P. M., Jones, D. R. O., & Clark, D. M. (1986). Respiratory control in the treatment of panic attacks: replication and extension with concurrent measurement of behaviour and pCO2. *British Journal of Psychiatry, 148,* 526–532.
Sartory, G., Rachman, S., & Grey, S. (1977). An investigation of the relation between reported fear and heart rate. *Behaviour Research and Therapy, 15,* 435–438.
Sartory, G., Rachman, S., & Grey, S. J. (1982). Return of fear: the role of rehearsal. *Behaviour Research and Therapy, 20,* 123–133.
Sargent, J. D., Green, E. E., & Walters, E. D. (1972). The use of autogenic feedback training in a pilot study of migraine and tension headaches. *Headache, 12,* 120–124.

Seligman, M. E. P. (1971). Phobias and preparedness. *Behavior Therapy, 2,* 307–320.
Shapiro, D., Tursky, B., Gershon, E., & Stern, M. (1969). Effects of feedback and reinforcement on the control of human systolic blood pressure. *Science, 163,* 588–590.
Sorbi, M., Tellegen, B., & Du Long, A. (1989). Long-term effects of training in relaxation and stress-coping in patients with migraine: A 3-year follow-up. *Headache, 29,* 111–121.
Stephens, R. (1977). Psychophysiological variables in cigarette smoking and reinforcing effects of nicotine. *Addictive Behavior, 2,* 1–7.
Steptoe, A. (1976). Blood pressure control: A comparison of feedback and instructions using pulse transit time feedback. *Psychophysiology, 13,* 528–536.
Steptoe, A. (1977). Voluntary blood pressure reductions measured with pulse transit time: training conditions and reaction to mental work. *Psychophysiology, 14,* 492–498.
Stern, J. A. (1964). Towards a definition of psychophysiology. *Psychophysiology, 1,* 90–91.
Stern, R. M., Ray, W. J., & Davis, C. M. (1980). *Psychophysiological recording.* New York: Oxford University Press.
Stout, M. A. (1985). Homeostatic reconditioning in stress-related disorders: A preliminary study of migraine headaches. *Psychotherapy, 22,* 531–541.
Sturgis, E. T., & Gramling, S. (1988). Psychophysiological assessment. In A. S. Bellack & M. Hersen (Eds.), *Behavioral assessment: A practical handbook* (3rd ed.). Elmsford, NY: Pergamon Press.
Surwillo, W. W. (1986). *Psychophysiology. Some simple concepts and models.* Springfield, IL: Charles C Thomas.
Surwit, R. S., Shapiro, D., & Feld, J. L. (1976). Digital temperature autoregulation and associated cardiovascular changes. *Psychophysiology, 13,* 236–241.
Surwit, R. S., Shapiro, D., & Good, M. I. (1978). Comparison of cardiovascular biofeedback: neuromuscular biofeedback and meditation in the treatment of borderline essential hypertension. *Journal of Consulting and Clinical Psychology, 46,* 252–263.
Surwit, R. S., Pilon, R. N., & Fenton, C. H. (1978). Behavioral treatment of Raynaud's disease. *Journal of Behavioral Medicine, 1,* 323–335.

Taylor, C. B., Kraemer, H. C., Bragg, D. A., Miles, L. E., Rule, B., Savin, W. M., & Debusk, R. F. (1982). A new system for the long-term recording and processing of heart rate and physical activity in outpatients. *Computers and Biomedical Research, 15,* 7–17.
Taylor, C. B., Sheikh, J., Agras, W. S., Roth, W. T., Margraf, J., Ehlers, A., Maddock, R. J., & Gossard, D. (1986). Ambulatory heart rate changes in patients with panic attacks. *American Journal Psychiatry, 143,* 478–482.
Thompson, J. K., & Adams, H. E. (1984). Psychophysiological characteristics of headache patients. *Pain, 18,* 41–52.
Turpin, G. (Ed.). (1989). *Handbook of clinical psychophysiology.* Chichester: John Wiley & Sons.
Van den Hout. (1988). The explanation of experimental panic. In S. Rachman & J. D. Maser (Eds.), *Panic: Psychological perspective* (pp. 237–257). Hillsdale, NJ: Lawrence Erlbaum Associates.
Victor, R., Mainardi, A., Shapiro, D. (1978). Effects of biofeedback and voluntary control procedures on heart rate and perception of pain during the cold pressor test. *Psychosomatic Medicine, 40,* 16–225.
Watts, F. N., & Blackstock, A. J. (1987). Lang's theory of emotional imagery. *Cognition and Emotion, 1,* 391–405.
Weiss, T., & Engel, B. T. (1971). Operant conditioning of heart rate in patients with premature ventricular contractions. *Psychosomatic Medicine, 33,* 301–321.
Wesseling, K. H., Settels, J. J., & De Wit, B. (1986). The measurement of continuous finger arterial pressure noninvasively in stationary subjects. In T. H. Schmidt, T. M. Dembroski, & G. Bluemchen (Eds.), *Biological and psychological factors in cardiovascular disease* (pp. 355–375), Berlin: Springer-Verlag.
Williamson, D. A., & Blanchard, E. B. (1979). Heart rate and blood pressure feedback: II. A review and integration of recent theoretical models. *Biofeedback and Self-Regulation, 4,* 35–50.
Wolpe, J. (1958). *Psychotherapy by reciprocal inhibition.* Stanford: Stanford University Press.
Zander, J. R., & McNally, R. J. (1988). Bio-informational processing in agoraphobia. *Behaviour Research and Therapy, 26,* 421–429.

PART V
CONDITIONING AND LEARNING

CHAPTER 20

SELECTIVE ASSOCIATIONS IN THE ORIGINS OF PHOBIC FEARS AND THEIR IMPLICATIONS FOR BEHAVIOR THERAPY

Michael Cook
Susan Mineka

Research conducted in our laboratory over the past decade has been directed toward the development of a primate model of fears and phobias that is based on long-standing observations concerning the marked fear of snakes exhibited by many primate species. Previous reviews of this research (e.g., Mineka, 1987) have documented significant parallels between snake fear in rhesus monkeys and the symptomatology, etiology, therapy, and prevention of human fears and phobias. The present chapter reviews one important line of recent research generated by this model that attempts to account for the "nonrandom" nature of the distribution of human fears and phobias—an observation that must be explained by any etiological account for human fears and phobias. That is, certain "fear-relevant" stimuli (e.g., snakes, spiders, heights, and water) appear to be the focus of a disproportionately large number of clinical fears and phobias relative to other stimuli such as electrical outlets, guns, and knives, although all of these stimuli may be approximately equivalent in the extent to which they are associated with traumatic experiences, verbal warnings, or both, during ontogeny (De Silva, Rachman, & Seligman, 1977; McNally, 1987; Öhman, Dimberg, & Öst, 1985; Öhman, Fredrikson, Hugdahl, & Rimmö, 1976; Seligman, 1971). This preponderance of clinical phobias involving fear-relevant stimuli has often prompted biologically and ecologically based explanations. Seligman (1971), for example, has proposed that human and nonhuman primates may be evolutionarily predisposed (i.e., "prepared") to easily associate with aversive consequences certain stimuli (e.g., snakes) that may have posed a threat to our early ancestors.

Historically, the most heated issue surrounding observations that many primate species exhibit a marked fear of snakes revolved around the question of whether this fear is "innate" or "spontaneous" (Hebb,

---

Three of the experiments discussed in this chapter were submitted as part of a doctoral dissertation by Michael Cook to the University of Wisconsin-Madison. This research was supported in part by Grants BNS 82-16141 and BNS 85-07340 from the National Science Foundation to Dr. Susan Mineka.

1946; Masserman & Pechtel, 1953), as opposed to being based on some form of learning (Joslin, Fletcher, & Emlen, 1964; Yerkes & Yerkes, 1936). There has never been complete resolution of this controversy, at least in part because it springs from a somewhat misleading theoretical perspective in which the etiology of behavior is viewed as resulting exclusively either from events occurring during ontogeny (e.g., learning) or alternatively from preontogenetic factors (e.g., genetic programs, see Lorenz, 1965). Nevertheless, current evidence seems to substantiate the importance of associative processes (learning) in the acquisition of snake fear for at least some primate species (see Mineka & Cook, 1988, for a review).

Some of the best evidence supporting a role for associative processes in the acquisition of snake fear derives from a number of studies which have demonstrated that wild-reared monkeys tend to exhibit a relatively strong degree of fear in the presence of snakes, whereas their laboratory-born counterparts display little, if any (Joslin et al., 1964; and Mineka, Keir, & Price, 1980, in rhesus monkeys [*Macaca mulatta*]; Murray & King, 1973, in squirrel monkeys [*Saimiri sciureus*]). Such contrasts in behavior have been taken to imply a difference between wild- and laboratory-born monkeys in prior negative experiences with snakes. However, it seemed unlikely that all wild-born monkeys manifesting a fear of snakes had had a direct traumatic incident with snakes. Instead, it was hypothesized that some form of social or observational learning was likely to be involved in the acquisition of this fear. The plausibility of this hypothesis for rhesus monkeys was documented by our initial experiments using a discriminative observational conditioning paradigm (Cook, Mineka, Wolkenstein, & Laitsch, 1985; Mineka, Davidson, Cook, & Keir, 1984). In these experiments, laboratory-reared rhesus monkeys, initially unafraid of snakes, acquired an intense and persistent fear of snakes following short periods of time during which they watched wild-reared conspecifics exhibit an intense fear of snakes.

Of central interest to the present chapter is the question of whether the ease with which snake fear is acquired reflects a selective association. That is, is a fear of snakes acquired more easily than is fear of other more arbitrary neutral objects? In this chapter we will review recent research from our laboratory which strongly supports the proposition that certain objects such as snakes and crocodiles are selectively associable with fear. First, we review the methodological requirements that learning theorists generally agree must be met before it can be concluded that a selective association exists. Next, we review a series of our recent studies using several variants of our traditional observational fear conditioning paradigms in which we demonstrate that monkeys easily associate toy snakes or toy crocodiles with fear, but do not easily associate flowers or a toy rabbit with fear. We also review the results of an experiment using an appetitive discrimination paradigm to demonstrate that monkeys can learn to associate flowers with food at least as easily as they can learn to associate toy snakes with food. Together, these experiments meet the requirements for demonstration of a selective association. Following the review of this series of studies we discuss the implications of selective associations in fear conditioning for understanding the origins of phobic fears in an evolutionary/functional context. Finally, implications of selective associations for the behavioral treatment of phobias and for the prevention of fears are also discussed.

SELECTIVE ASSOCIATIONS: AN OVERVIEW

Before reviewing our research demonstrating that snake fear reflects a selective association, we first review some of the history of interest in the topic of selective associations, and the methodological requirements for demonstrating their existence. Recent interest in the topic of selective associations can perhaps be most clearly traced to the seminal findings of Garcia and Koelling (1966). In their classic experiment, two groups of rats were exposed to a compound conditioned stimulus (CS) consisting of lights, noise, and saccharin-flavored water. For one group, this CS was paired with an electric shock unconditioned stimulus (US) delivered to the paws; for the other group, the CS was paired with an injection of lithium chloride—a US which induces gastrointestinal illness. The nature of the selective association was made manifest by subsequent tests for conditioning: Subjects in the first group associated the exteroceptive lights and noise (but not the interoceptive saccharin taste) with shock. By contrast, subjects in the second group associated the taste (but not the lights and noise) with gastrointestinal illness. This study, along with related findings, stimulated much empirical and theoretical work devoted to understanding phenomena that have been variously subsumed under the terms preparedness, belongingness, selective associations, or biological constraints on learning. (For recent reviews, see Damianopoulos, 1989; Domjan, 1983; Domjan &

Galef, 1983; Johnston & Pietrewicz, 1985; LoLordo, 1979a, 1979b; LoLordo & Droungas, 1989; McNally, 1987; Öhman, 1986, Ohman et al., 1985).

Unfortunately, research in this area has generated a great deal of controversy and confusion, stemming from differences both in terminology and theoretical frameworks. For example, biological "constraints on learning" have been identified both as the failure to learn under certain conditions (Breland & Breland, 1961), as well as the ability to preferentially form certain associations relative to others such as in Garcia and Koelling's experiment (see also Bolles, 1970). Further confusion has been engendered by the frequent failure to logically distinguish between the postulated adaptive value of certain situation-specific types of learning and the mediation of such learning by putative specialized mechanisms (Rozin & Kalat, 1971). In recent years, perhaps in reaction to this confusion, the term selective association has been widely employed as a relatively atheoretical descriptor of certain constraint phenomena; that is, one that eschews attempts to infer the functional nature of these constraints. More specifically, selective associations represent instances of experience-independent association bias in which certain combinations of stimuli are more readily associable (e.g., CS_1-US_1 and CS_2-US_2) than are other combinations (e.g., CS_1-US_2 and CS_2-US_1. Such effects represent apparent violations of what has been termed the equipotentiality premise of general process learning theory—a premise dating back to Pavlov (1927) and Thorndike (1898, see Seligman, 1970). According to this premise, the ease with which associations are learned is independent of the combination of cues, responses, and reinforcers that are employed. (Because our interest in selective associations relates specifically to the observational fear conditioning paradigm we have employed, and because observational fear conditioning, in turn, is generally presumed to be founded at least in part upon Pavlovian learning principles (cf. Berger, 1962; Green & Osborne, 1985), our discussion of selective associations is similarly restricted to Pavlovian examples, although the concept of selective association also has applicability in the instrumental learning domain.)

Historically, research in learning has concentrated on what may be termed "traditional" constraints on the formation of associations such as the salience of the CS, intensity of the US, CS-US delay, etcetera (see Domjan & Galef, 1983). Limitations of this sort have not been considered violations of the equipotentiality premise because they are presumed to operate independently of the specific CS-US combination employed. For example, given two CSs, one of which is more salient than the other, conditioning will more readily occur with the more salient of the two. However, this difference in conditioning is not a function of an interaction between the more salient CS and the US, but is instead solely due to the properties of that CS. In contrast, selective associations, by definition, represent instances that are not explicable by reference to separate stimulus properties, but rather are due to an *interaction* between the specific combination of stimuli used.

Framed in more formal terms, the rate of growth of a given CS-US association can be characterized by separate learning rate parameters for the CS and US (α, or salience, for the CS; and β, possibly related to intensity, for the US). According to the equipotentiality premise, the value of a stimulus' learning rate parameter should remain constant regardless of the identity of the remaining stimulus in the association. In contrast, a selective association is demonstrated when the rate of growth of an association can only be characterized by a single rate parameter unique to the particular CS-US combination under consideration (cf. LoLordo, 1979a, 1979b; Rescorla & Wagner, 1972; Wagner & Rescorla, 1972).

A number of methodological strategies have been proposed for detecting Pavlovian selective associations. The general logic of such strategies is exemplified by the double dissociation paradigm. In this between-groups design, each group receives one combination of a 2 × 2 factorial arrangement of CS and US types. The following pattern of results are indicative of a selective association. First, conditioning must be superior (e.g., faster acquisition, higher asymptotic CR, greater resistance to extinction) for the group receiving CS_1-US_1 than for that receiving CS_2-US_1. Second, the reverse outcome should be found for the remaining two groups: superior conditioning for the CS_2-US_2 group compared to the CS_1-US_2 group (LoLordo, 1979a, 1979b). Such results negate the possibility that the enhanced conditioning in any one group is only a function of the stimulus properties of a specific CS or US. Thus, the superior CS_1-US_1 conditioning and the relatively poor CS_2-US_1 conditioning cannot be attributed to differences between the two CSs on some stimulus dimension such as salience; this is because CS_1 and CS_2 fare much worse and better, respectively, when paired with the alternate reinforcer, US_2. Analogously, the superior CS_1-US_1 conditioning and the relatively poor CS_1-US_2 conditioning cannot be attributed to stimulus differences between the two USs because US$_1$ and US$_2$ fare much worse and better, respectively, when paired with CS$_2$. More recently, LoLordo and Droungas (1989) have stated that this second requirement may be too stringent. It can be argued that compelling evidence for a selective association exists if an equivalent, but nonzero, level of conditioning is seen in both the CS$_2$-US$_2$ and CS$_1$-US$_2$ groups. (If equivalent but zero-level responding, i.e., no conditioning, were found for the two US$_2$ groups, it could be argued that US$_2$ was simply incapable of supporting conditioning to *any* CS.)

As suggested above, a number of theorists have speculated that selective associations may mediate expression of the nonrandom distribution of human fears and phobias. According to these theorists, the greater propensity with which individuals acquire a fear of fear-relevant stimuli such as snakes and spiders (relative to the propensity for acquiring a fear of fear-irrelevant stimuli) is presumed to be a consequence of the fact that such stimuli are selectively associable with aversive outcomes. In keeping with the established definition of a selective association, it must also be demonstrable that the ease with which fear-relevant stimuli are associated with aversive outcomes cannot be attributed to the intrinsic properties of fear-relevant stimuli. That is, one would not expect to see superior conditioning when the fear-relevant CSs were paired with *nonaversive* USs.

Typical human-subject studies examining Pavlovian conditioning to fear-relevant versus fear-irrelevant cues have employed nonphobic subjects, mild shock as the US, and exposure to either fear-relevant CSs (e.g., slides of snakes or spiders) or fear-irrelevant CSs (e.g., slides of flowers or mushrooms). Conditioning is usually indexed by differential (CS+ vs. CS−) electrodermal activity or some other psychophysiological index of fear. Perhaps most consonant with the proposition that the fear-relevant CS/aversive outcome association is selective have been reports showing that, following acquisition, differential responding persists longer in extinction for fear-relevant as opposed to fear-irrelevant cues (e.g., E. Cook, Hodes, & Lang, 1986; Hugdahl, 1978; Hugdahl, Fredrikson, & Öhman, 1977; Öhman, Eriksson, & Olofsson, 1975; Öhman et al., 1976; Öhman et al., 1985; however, see McNally, 1987, for a review of several studies indicating no effect of CS relevance).

By themselves, such studies leave open the possibility that the superior resistance to extinction with fear-relevant CSs is attributable only to their greater salience. In studies attempting to assess this possibility through use of the double dissociation design (Öhman, Fredrikson, & Hugdahl, 1978, Öhman et al., 1976), differences between fear-relevant and fear-irrelevant stimuli were not found when they were used as discriminative cues in a nonaversive reaction-time task. Unfortunately, little, if any, conditioning occurred with either CS in the reaction time task. As noted above, such a pattern of results does not clearly obviate explanations based on differences in CS properties because the control (nonaversive) US may be incapable of supporting conditioning to any CS.

Additionally, the use of human subjects in such studies entails other problems in interpreting conditioning effects. For example, although selective associations supposedly represent *experience-independent* biases in associability, in the case of human subjects it may be impossible to equate the two stimulus classes (fear-relevent vs. fear-irrelevant) in terms of strength of prior associations (Delprato, 1980). This is because all human subjects come to these experiments with prior ontogenetically based associations to the stimuli used as CSs. Further, given the low shock intensities used in these experiments, it is unclear to what extent fear is being measured (Hodes, E. Cook, & Lang, 1985). This problem is at least partly a consequence of ethical constraints against conditioning intense and persistent fears in human subjects. One way to circumvent some of the shortcomings inherent in the human research on selective associations in aversive Pavlovian conditioning is through the use of an animal model that builds on nonhuman primates' reactions to snakes. Because this work involves the training of an intense and persistent fear of a natural predator, it is ethically responsible to conduct this research with monkeys. Such work allows us to study the role of selective associations in fear conditioning in a way that cannot be done in humans. (See Marks, 1977; and Mineka, 1985, 1987, for extended discussions of animal models of fears and phobias.)

OBSERVATIONAL FEAR CONDITIONING PARADIGM

In the present series of experiments, we attempted to provide more compelling evidence for the operation of a selective association in the acquisition of snake fear. These experiments adapted the methodology used in previous studies on snake fear conducted in our laboratory. The purpose of these logically prior studies was not to demonstrate the selective nature of the learning involved, but instead to establish the more basic finding that associative processes could be shown to be involved in the expression of snake fear by primates. Our initial studies were based upon the presumption that one form of learning likely to be involved in the development of snake fear was observational learning. These studies, therefore, used a discriminative observational conditioning paradigm (Cook et al., 1985; Mineka et al., 1984). Naive laboratory-reared (observer) rhesus monkeys (with no pre-experimental exposure to snakes) were first trained to reach rapidly for food placed near neutral objects (wood blocks) in a Wisconsin General Test Apparatus (WGTA; Harlow, 1949). Following the establishment of a baseline of rapid responding, they were administered a series of pretest trials in which food was placed adjacent to a range of stimuli, including a live boa constrictor *(Constrictor constrictor)*, toy snakes, and neutral objects. At pretest, these observers typically showed little fear (i.e., they responded rapidly and exhibited little behavioral distress) regardless of which stimulus was present.

Subsequently, during six discriminative observational conditioning sessions, observers watched wild-reared models react to these stimuli in the same WGTA setting: In the presence of snake stimuli, the models reacted fearfully, failing to reach for food and displaying a relatively large number of fear/disturbance behaviors that frightened monkeys typically exhibit in this context (see Cook et al., 1985; Mineka et al., 1984; Mineka et al., 1980). In the presence of neutral stimuli, however, the models quickly reached for food and displayed few if any fear behaviors. Following these discriminative observational conditioning sessions, the observers were retested alone in the WGTA: In this posttest phase, a majority of observers now displayed an intense fear of snakes (indicated by increased latency to reach for food and increased behavioral distress), demonstrating that fear of snakes could be acquired via observational learning. Evidence that the acquired fear was robust was sustantiated by examination of its persistence: When observers were retested in the WGTA 3 months later, there was no diminution in its intensity. The measurement of fear in two response systems, behavioral avoidance (i.e., latency to reach for food) and behavioral distress, derived from contemporary views that fear is not a unified entity but may instead occur in multiple response systems. Further, considerable discordance may exist among these response systems such that the measurement of fear in one response system may not correlate well with that in another (Lang, 1968, 1971; Mineka, 1979, 1985; Rachman & Hodgson, 1974). In addition, to ascertain that the acquired fear of snakes was not specific to the context in which it had been conditioned (the WGTA), observer reactivity to these stimuli was also examined in a second setting, the Sackett Circus (Sackett, 1970). This apparatus was also used in some of the studies concerned with selective associations. However, results from Circus tests are not presented in the interest of brevity. In general, conclusions drawn from Circus tests were identical to those drawn from the two WGTA measures, latency and behavioral disturbance (see Cook et al., 1985; Cook & Mineka, 1989, in press; Mineka et al., 1984).

Observational Conditioning with Videotaped Models

To explore the issue of whether the rapid and robust acquisition of snake fear through observational conditioning represents a selective association, a number of modifications in the observational conditioning paradigm were necessary. First, the modified paradigm required that observational conditioning of fear to a fear-relevant stimulus be compared with observational conditioning of fear to a fear-irrelevant stimulus such as a flower. Additionally, it was essential that the model's fear performance in the presence of snakes and flowers be equated, given the results of previous research demonstrating that the level of fear acquired by observers is positively correlated with the degree of model disturbance during the conditioning process. Indeed, the level of behavioral distress shown by models to the snakes *during* conditioning accounted for almost 50% of the variance in amount of disturbance exhibited in the presence of snakes by 42 observers *following* conditioning (Mineka & Cook, 1990). Because it was not feasible to equate the fear performance of live models in the presence of snakes and flowers, we decided to use videotapes of fearful models. Editing/splicing techniques could thus be used to produce different versions of the tapes, all of which contained the same footage of fearful model behavior, but in the presence of different stimuli. However, although prior research existed that indicated that various macaque species responded in a socially appropriate manner to color videotapes of conspecifics (Capitanio, Boccia, & Colaiannia, 1985; Lande, Higley, Snowdon, Goy, & Suomi, 1985; Plimpton, Swartz, & Rosenblum, 1981), there was no evidence that rhesus monkeys could acquire a fear of a CS (viz., snakes) by watching videotaped conspecifics. Therefore, a preliminary study was undertaken that was procedurally similar to the observational fear conditioning studies cited above (Cook et al., 1985; Mineka et al., 1984), except videotaped rather than live models were used.

In this study, six laboratory-reared observers watched color videotapes of two models reacting fearfully to real and toy snakes, and nonfearfully in the presence of neutral objects, during six observational conditioning sessions. Posttests and 3-month follow-up tests conducted in the WGTA indicated that the observers acquired a fear of snakes that was comparable in strength and persistence to that acquired by observers in earlier studies who had viewed live models. Figure 20–1 illustrates the results for one of the dependent measures, behavioral avoidance in the WGTA (see Cook & Mineka, in press, for details).

Selective Associations: SN+/FL−, FL+/SN− Experiment

Following this initial demonstration of snake fear acquisition through the use of videotaped models, a further study was conducted that specifically addressed the issue of selective associations. In overview, two observer groups watched videotaped models responding on some trials to toy snakes and on other trials to flowers. The models for one group reacted fearfully to toy snakes, but nonfearfully to flowers. This group was designated SN+/FL− inasmuch as snakes were a CS+ for the US (fearful model behavior), whereas flowers constituted the CS−. In contrast, the models for the second group reacted fearfully to flowers and nonfearfully to toy snakes (FL+/SN−). Preliminary evidence of a selective association would be provided if SN+/FL− observers acquired a fear of snakes, but not of the flowers, and FL+/SN− observers acquired significantly less (or no) fear of flowers (see Cook & Mineka, 1989, in press; Mineka, 1987; Mineka & Cook, 1988, for further details).

As noted earlier, it was critically important to ensure that the behavior of the models for the two groups be identical: That is, the degree of fear displayed by the SN+/FL− models in the presence of the toy snake had to be indistinguishable from the level of fear shown by the FL+/SN− models to the flowers. Furthermore, the nonfearful behavior of the SN+/FL− models in the presence of flowers had to be identical to the nonfearful behavior of the FL+/SN− models to the snakes. This behavioral equivalence was accomplished through splicing (editing) of the videotapes seen by the two groups. The original, unedited videotapes showed models reacting fearfully in the presence of a real snake and a very large toy snake, and nonfearfully when no objects were present. Then, by splicing in the appropriate stimulus objects (toy snakes or flowers), videotapes were produced in which models displayed identical behavior in the presence of different stimuli. In the tapes seen by the SN+/FL− observers, models appeared to react fearfully to the toy snake, and nonfearfully to the flowers,

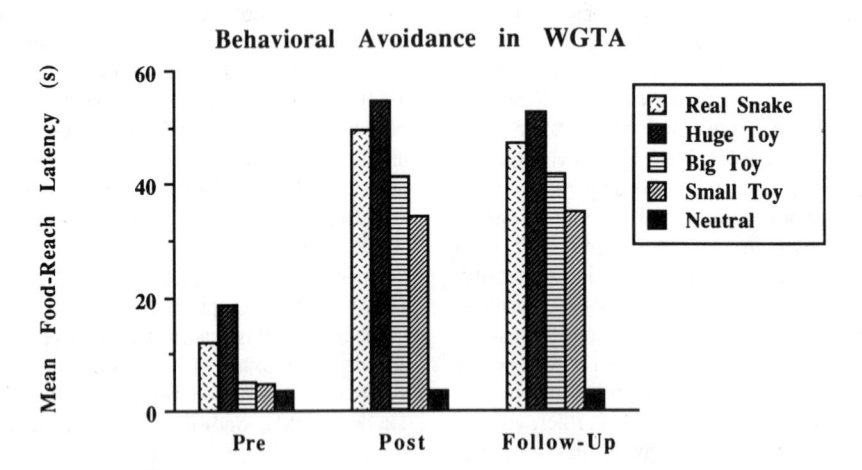

Figure 20.1. Mean observer food-reach latencies (in s) in the Wisconsin General Test Apparatus at pretest, posttest, and follow-up for the live boa constrictor (real snake), three toy snakes (huge, big, and small), and neutral objects (wood blocks). Maximum possible latency = 60 s. From "Selective Associations in the Observational Conditioning of Fear in Rhesus Monkeys" by M. Cook and S. Mineka, in press. Journal of Experimental Psychology: Animal Behavior Processes.

whereas in the tapes seen by the FL+/SN− observers, the same models (displaying the identical behavior) appeared to react nonfearfully to the toy snake and fearfully to the flowers. Furthermore, an attempt was made to roughly equate the two stimulus classes for degree of salience; thus, the toy snakes and flowers were approximately equal in size and length. Moreover, toy rather than real snakes were presented in order to equate the two stimulus classes for movement.

On each of 12 observational conditioning sessions (as compared to 6 sessions in the previous videotape experiment), observers were exposed to either the SN+/FL− or the FL+/SN− tapes. Following observational conditioning, both observer groups were tested alone in the WGTA for fear of flowers and toy snakes. The majority of the 13 SN+/FL− observers acquired a fear of toy snakes, but none acquired a fear of flowers. In contrast, very few of the 13 FL+/SN− observers demonstrated fear of either the toy snakes or flowers following exposure to the videotapes. Figures 20-2 and 20-3 depict the mean results of this experiment for the two WGTA measures, food-reach latency and behavioral disturbance (see Cook & Mineka, in press, for further details).

These results are congruent with the proposition that the association between fear-relevant stimuli and aversive outcomes is selective. That is, it appears relatively easy for rhesus monkeys to associate fear-relevant CSs (snakes) with certain vicariously observed USs, specifically, the fear responses of conspecifics. Subjects observing the fear response of a model to a CS+ were more likely to acquire a fear of that CS+ when it was a toy snake (Group SN+/FL−) than when it was a flower (Group FL+/SN−). Furthermore, the superior conditioning to snake-like stimuli appears to be an associative rather than a nonassociative phenomenon. For example, if selective *sensitization* (a nonassociative process) were responsible for the enhanced snake fear seen in the SN+/FL− observers, then one would also have expected to see enhanced fear of snakes in the FL+/SN− observers, who were also exposed to snake stimuli, albeit explicitly unpaired with the US (LoLordo, 1979a, 1979b).

Selective Associations: FL+SN+ Experiment

A number of theoretical alternatives exist, however, to the proposition that the differential responding found in the SN+/FL−, FL+/SN− study represents a selective association. First, the failure of the FL+/SN− observers to acquire a fear of flowers could stem from the difficulty of the required discrimination. According to this argument, aversive conditioning might be possible with a flower CS+ if a simpler paradigm were instituted in which a FL+ group viewed only fearful model performances in the presence of flowers (i.e., without any CS−[SN−] trials).

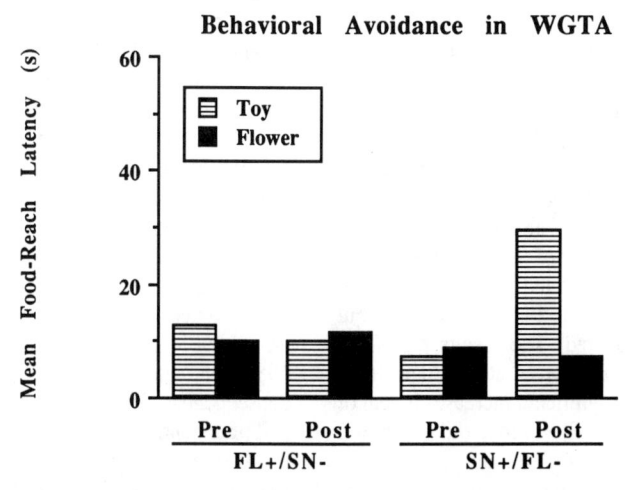

Figure 20.2. Mean food-reach latencies (in s) in the Wisconsin General Test Apparatus for the toy snakes and flowers for the FL+/SN− and SN+/FL− observers at pretest and posttest. Maximum possible latency = 60 s. From "Selective Associations in the Observational Conditioning of Fear in Rhesus Monkeys" by M. Cook and S. Mineka, in press. *Journal of Experimental Psychology: Animal Behavior Processes.*

Fear Behaviors in WGTA

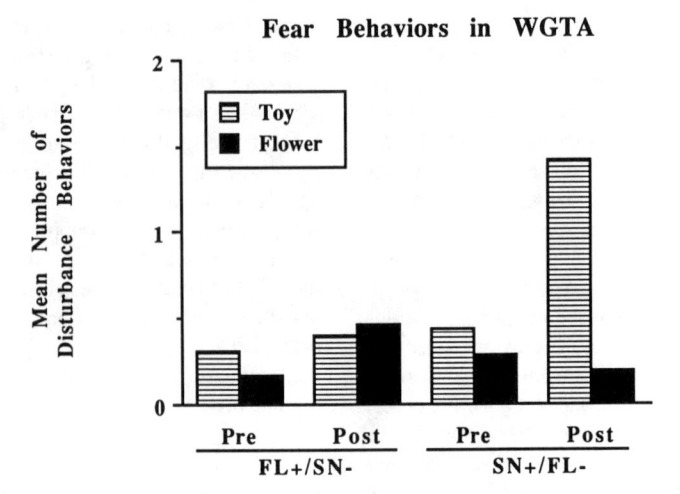

Figure 20.3. Mean number of disturbance behaviors exhibited in the Wisconsin General Test Apparatus for the toy snakes and flowers for the FL+/SN− and SN+/FL− observers at pretest and posttest. Maximum possible disturbance score = 36. From "Selective Associations in the Observational Conditioning of Fear in Rhesus Monkeys" by M. Cook and S. Mineka, in press. *Journal of Experimental Psychology: Animal Behavior Processes.*

At first glance this hypothesis may not seem especially compelling given that the difficulty level of the discrimination was presumably equivalent for the two groups, and yet only one of the two groups (FL+/SN−) failed to exhibit excitatory conditioning to the CS+. However, it is possible that weak long delay conditioning to the snake occurred in the FL+/SN− group (two subjects did show marked fear of snakes in the posttest); this, in turn, could have interfered with the conditioning of fear of the flower stimuli, perhaps through competition for excitatory strength (see Rescorla & Wagner, 1972). Therefore, a follow-up study was conducted both to definitively rule out this alternative hypothesis and, to extend the generality of the previous study by partially replicating its results.

Again, two groups of observers were exposed to videotapes. One group, designated SN+, was exposed to the SN+/FL− tapes of the preceding study, but with the FL− trials deleted. A second group, designated FL+, watched the FL+/SN− tapes, but with the SN− trials deleted. The results paralleled those of the SN+/FL−, FL+/SN− study: At posttest, the SN+ group showed significant increases in fear of the toy snakes, whereas the FL+ group did not show a fear of flowers. Figure 20-4 illustrates these results for WGTA behavioral avoidance. Clearly, they do not support the hypothesis that the failure to observe conditioning to flowers in the FL+/SN− group of the previous experiment was due either to the complexity of the videotape or to competition between flower and snake stimuli for excitatory strength (see Cooke & Mineka, 1989, for details).

Selective Associations: C+/R−, R+/C− Experiment

A second alternative account of the differences in conditionability to snakes versus flowers focuses on the specific stimulus attributes possessed by the toy snakes, but not by the artificial flowers (viz., eyes, forked tongues, sinuous shape). Such properties may have caused observers to discriminate the toy snakes as potentially animate, and hence less predictable/controllable objects (see Cook & Mineka, 1989). Organisms generally prefer, and experience as less stressful, controllable/predictable as opposed to uncontrollable/unpredictable aversive outcomes (e.g., Badia, Harsh, & Abbott, 1979; see Maier & Jackson, 1979; Maier & Seligman, 1976; Mineka & Hendersen, 1985; Overmier, Patterson, & Wielkiewicz, 1980, for general reviews on the various adverse consequences following exposure to unpredictable and/or uncontrollable aversive stimuli). According to this line of reasoning, if observers had learned about the relatively unpredictable/uncontrollable nature of animate stimuli, they may have generalized between such stimuli and the toy snakes presented during observational conditioning, resulting in the snakes acquiring aversive motivational properties for the monkeys. If this were the case, then the differential conditionability of snakes relative to flowers may not represent a biologically based selective association, but would instead be a consequence of these prior experiences (cf. Bandura, in press).

One procedure to discriminate between these two positions would involve examination of fear conditioning to two toy animals (as opposed to a toy animal vs. a flower) that would presumably be matched for the property of "animateness." However, one animal would be fear-relevant, and the other fear-irrelevant. Therefore, a study was conducted that was procedurally analogous to the SN+/FL−, FL+/SN− experiment except that a toy crocodile was the fear-relevant stimulus and a toy rabbit was the fear-irrelevant stimulus (see Cook & Mineka, 1989). For one of two groups (C+/R−), observers watched videotaped models reacting fearfully to a toy crocodile on some trials and nonfearfully when a toy rabbit was present on other trials. For the other group (R+/C−), observers watched videotaped models reacting fearfully to the toy rabbit and nonfearfully to the toy crocodile.

Figure 20-5 summarizes the results of the C+/R−, R+/C− experiment for behavioral disturbance in the WGTA. None of the observers in either group exhibited a fear of the toy rabbit at posttest. In contrast, the majority of the 10 C+/R− observers displayed a fear of the toy crocodile, whereas few of the 10 R+/C− observers displayed behavior indicative of a fear of the crocodile. Thus, subjects observing the conjoint fear response of a videotaped model and a CS+ were more likely to acquire a fear of that CS+ when it was a fear-relevant toy crocodile than when it was a fear-irrelevant toy rabbit. These results argue against an interpretation of the enhanced responding to snake CS+s in the SN+/FL−, FL+/SN− study as stemming primarily from any animate qualities they might possess. Further, they extend the generality of that study by employing different fear-relevant and fear-irrelevant CS.

Although the discriminative conditioning paradigm used in the SN+/FL−, FL+/SN− and C+/R−, R+/C− studies allows an examination of possible sensitization effects, other nonassociative accounts can be advanced to explain the observed effects. Specifically, the fear-irrelevant stimuli may be incapable of supporting excitatory conditioning under any circumstances. That is, despite attempts to equate the salience of the toy snakes and flowers (and of toy crocodile and toy rabbit), the salience of the flowers (and of the rabbit) could be relatively low, whereas that of the snakes (and of the crocodile) could be high (see Mackintosh, 1974, chap. 2). A methodology suitable to examine the plausibility of this hypothesis would be to find an alternative reinforcer capable of supporting a level of conditioning to a videotaped flower stimulus (or rabbit) at least as strong as that to a

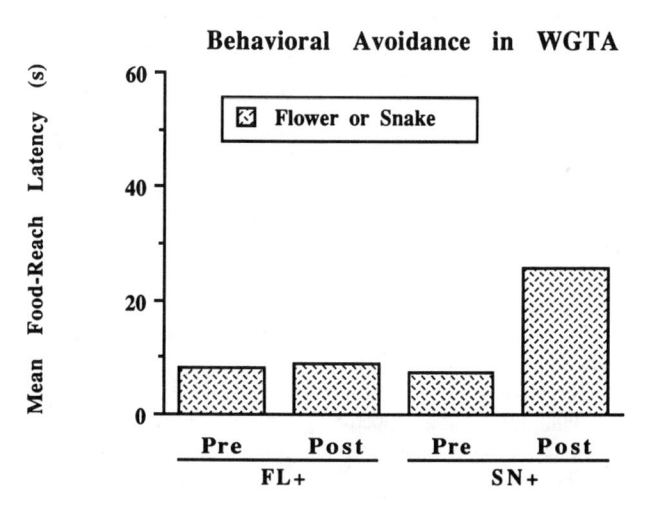

Figure 20.4. Mean food-reach latencies (in s) in the Wisconsin General Test Apparatus in the presence of the CS+ (toy snakes or flowers) for the FL+ and SN+ observers at pretest and posttest. Maximum possible latency = 60 s. From "Selective Associations in the Observational Conditioning of Fear in Rhesus Monkeys" by M. Cook and S. Mineka, in press. *Journal of Experimental Psychology: Animal Behavior Processes.*

Fear Behaviors in WGTA

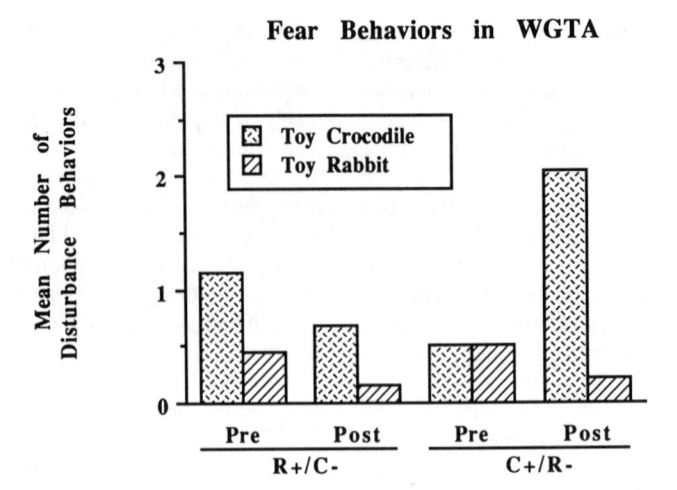

Figure 20.5. Mean number of disturbance behaviors in the Wisconsin General Test Apparatus for the toy crocodile and toy rabbit for the R+/C− and C+/R− observers in pretest and posttest. Maximum possible disturbance score = 36. From "Selective Associations in the Observational Conditioning of Fear in Rhesus Monkeys" by M. Cook and S. Mineka, in press. *Journal of Experimental Psychology: Animal Behavior Processes.*

videotaped snake (or crocodile) (see LoLordo, 1979a, 1979b; LoLordo & Droungas, 1989, for further discussion of these issues). Note that, considered jointly, the SN+/FL−, FL+/SN− design and the alternate-reinforcer design, approximate the double dissociation design discussed above for the detection of potential selective associations. Specifically, a selective association account would be supported if the results of an alternative-reinforcer study revealed that level of responding (or rate of response acquisition) for flower stimuli is as great or greater than that achieved with snake stimuli.

Selective Associations: Appetitive PAN Discrimination Experiment

To explore this hypothesis, an alternative-reinforcer study was designed that used an appetitive rather than aversive reinforcer. In addition, the design was a discriminative operant procedure rather than a Pavlovian observational conditioning procedure. (Extensive pilot work had failed to provide a reliable paradigm for the classical conditioning of an appetitive response in rhesus monkeys. In contrast, see D'Amato, Buckiewicz, & Puopolo, 1981; D'Amato & Safarjan, 1981.) Monkeys were required to solve appetitive, discrete-trial, simultaneous discriminations involving fear-relevant (snake) and fear-irrelevant (flower) stimuli. As in the SN+/FL−, FL+/SN− study, stimuli in the present experiment were videotaped. All subjects were exposed to two general types of discrimination problems, one involving a toy snake S+ and a different toy snake S−, the other involving a flower S+ and a different flower S− (S+ and S− referring to the consistently rewarded and consistently nonrewarded stimuli, respectively).

More specifically, both the snake and flower discriminations were presented as PAN ambiguous-cue problems (which have been solved by a variety of species including rhesus monkeys; e.g., Boyer & Polidora, 1972; Fletcher, Grogg, & Garske, 1968; Leary, 1958; see Cook & Mineka, in press, for a review). PAN problems involve two different stimulus pairs, PA and NA, only one of which is presented on a given trial: On PA trials, a "positive" cue, P, which is consistently rewarded (S+), is presented simultaneously with an "ambiguous" cue, A, which is nonrewarded when paired with P. On NA trials, a "negative" cue, N, which is consistently nonrewarded (S−), is presented simultaneously with the same ambiguous cue, A, which is rewarded when paired with N. The A cue is thus ambiguous because of the conditional nature of the discrimination problem: Whether A is rewarded or nonrewarded depends upon whether it is accompanied by N, or P, respectively. The PAN ambiguous-cue problem was adopted because with a simpler simultaneous discrimination design (involving only S+ vs. S−) any learning which results may be solely a consequence of learning about S+, or solely a consequence of learning about S−. For our purposes, it was critical to demonstrate that monkeys in an appetitive paradigm could learn about the specific videotaped flower and snake stimuli used in the earlier observational fear conditioning fear experiments. (See Cook & Mineka, in press, for a more extended rationale for the use of the PAN problem.)

In the context of the present study, subjects were required to solve two separate PAN problems, one involving videotaped flower stimuli, and a second involving videotaped toy snake stimuli. Figure 20–6 constitutes a representation of these problems. In the snake PAN problem, one toy snake served as P, a different toy snake served as N, and a geometric figure (a square) served as the A cue. In the flower PAN problem, one set of flowers served as P (S+), a different set of flowers served as N (S−), and a geometric figure (a diamond) served as the A cue. The two problems were roughly equated in terms of stimulus content/salience: That is, the shape and size of the two P stimuli (a circular arrangement of mums and a replica of a coiled timber rattlesnake [*Crotalus horridus*]) were similar to one another, as were the shape and size of the two N stimuli (a sinuous toy snake and two artificial flowers). Further, in order to increase the validity of a cross-experiment comparison between this study and the SN+/FL−, FL+/SN− experiment, the two N stimuli were identical (or highly similar, differing only in color) to some of the toy snake and flower stimuli used in the SN+/FL−, FL+/SN− study (see Cook & Mineka, in press, for details.).

On each day of testing, subjects were exposed to either 40, 80, 120, or 160 trials, consisting of an equal number of snake and flower trials. Test sessions continued until subjects either reached response criterion for all problems or were discarded for failing to reach criterion for any of the problems. A given problem (flower-PA, flower-NA, snake-PA, and snake-NA) was considered solved when the subject responded correctly on at least 80% of 30 consecutive problems of that type. Two clear Plexiglas panels covering the screen of the video monitor served as response manipulanda. Each panel covered one of the two stimuli presented on each trial; each stimulus covered approximately one half of the video monitor. A correct response consisted of the subject pressing forward any part of the panel covering the correct stimulus, thereby activating a food treat dispenser. (For extensive additional procedural details, see Cook & Mineka, in press.)

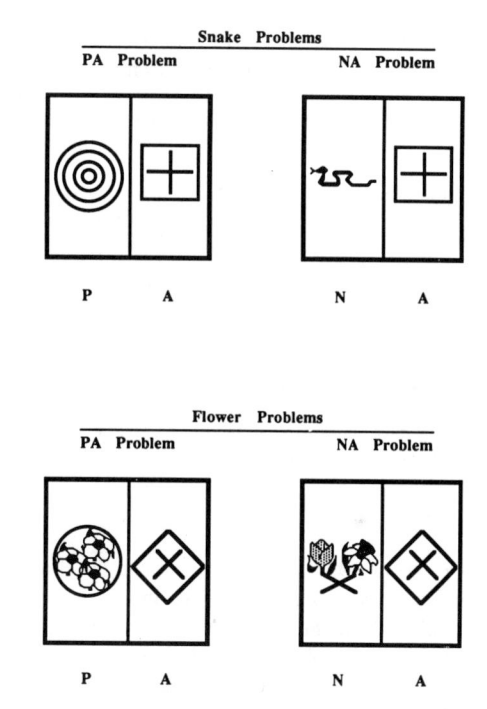

Figure 20.6. Representation of snake and flower PAN problems (stimuli not drawn to scale). For the snake problems (top panels), the concentric circles represent the coiled rattlesnake model and the depiction of a snake (with a forked tongue) represents the sinuous toy snake. For the flower problems (bottom panels), the circle enclosing three flowers represents the circular arrangement of mums and the two flowers, each connected to a straight line, represent the two artificial flowers (including the stems). From "Selective Associations in the Observational Conditioning of Fear in Rhesus Monkeys" by M. Cook and S. Mineka, in press. *Journal of Experimental Psychology: Animal Behavior Processes.*

As one might intuitively expect, the majority of subjects found solution of the discrimination problem difficult or impossible. Of 13 subjects that went through training, only 6 reached the 80% solution criterion on all problems. (None of the remaining 7 subjects achieved criterion for any problems, in spite of receiving an extensive number of trials—over 1000 in all cases. Nor did they show tendencies towards superior performance for particular problems.)

Table 20–1 indicates the number of trials each subject required to reach criterion for each of the problems. The results demonstrate that videotaped flowers are capable of supporting excitatory learning with an appetitive reinforcer. All 6 of the subjects reaching criterion for the problems acquired a discrim-

Table 20-1. Total Number of Trials Required by Subjects to Reach Criterion for Each of the Discrimination Problems

	PA PROBLEMS		NA PROBLEMS	
SUBJECT	SNAKE	FLOWER	SNAKE	FLOWER
AI17	206	430	775	541
AJ81	460	342	671	245
AK16	303	368	340	246
AG21	3216	1266	2869	1235
AG41	1470	2442	1560	2492
AI08	3311	3805	3088	4610

From "Observational Conditioning of Fear to Fear-Relevant versus Fear-Irrelevant Stimuli in Rhesus Monkeys" by M. Cook and S. Mineka, 1989, *Journal of Abnormal Psychology, 98.*

inative operant when flowers constituted the P or N stimuli in the problem. Furthermore, the results failed to reveal any consistent difference across subjects in the rate of solution of flower versus snake discrimination problems. The more important results concern the N stimuli because they were identical or highly similar to the stimuli used in the SN+/FL−, FL+/SN− study. As seen in Table 20-1, for the two NA problems, 4 of the 6 subjects showed faster acquisition on the flower than on the snake subproblem, a nonsignificant difference. For the two PA problems, 2 of the 6 subjects showed faster acquisition on the flower than on the snake subproblem, again, a nonsignificant difference. (See Cook & Mineka, in press, for a more detailed analysis of the results.)

Taken together, the results of the PAN study and the SN+/FL−, FL+/SN− study, strongly imply a differential associability between fear-relevant CSs (as opposed to fear-irrelevant CSs) and vicariously observed USs (i.e., the fear responses of conspecifics). That is, the results of the PAN experiment show that the pattern of the SN+/FL−, FL+/SN− results cannot be easily accounted for by recourse to explanations concerning differential salience or discriminability of the two stimulus classes. If salience of the flowers was very low, whereas that of the snakes was high, one would have predicted PAN problem results analogous to those of the SN+/FL−, FL+/SN− study: subjects should have done significantly better, in terms of trials to achieve criterion, on the snake problems. Because this was not the case, it appears that the differential associability of snakes and reinforcers is specific to aversive rather than appetitive outcomes. That is, the snake-aversive US association is apparently selective.

Partial Overshadowing Experiment

One additional experiment, which used a partial overshadowing design, explored the issue of selective associations (Cook & Mineka, 1987). Given that two CSs are presented simultaneously in association with a US, if the presence during conditioning of one of the CSs—which elicits a CR—causes a failure of the remaining CS to elicit a CR, then overshadowing is said to have occurred (Pavlov, 1927). It was hypothesized that if fear-relevant and fear-irrelevant stimuli were simultaneously presented during observational conditioning, such that models would appear to react fearfully to *both* stimuli, the fear-relevant stimulus would overshadow the fear-irrelevant one. This models the situation for humans that occurs when two or more neutral stimuli are simultaneously present during an observational or a traumatic fear conditioning experience, and yet fear of only one stimulus is acquired.

Explicit support for this prediction derives from a series of experiments on selective associations and overshadowing in pigeons. Pigeons acquire a tone-shock association more rapidly than a light-shock association, and they acquire a light-food association more rapidly than a tone-food association. This outcome suggests that for pigeons tones are fear-relevant (and food-irrelevant) and lights are food-relevant (and fear-irrelevant). More importantly, when a tone/light compound CS was paired with shock, the tone overshadowed the light, and when the same compound was paired with food, the light overshadowed the tone (Shapiro, Jacobs, & LoLordo, 1980; Shapiro & LoLordo, 1982).

In our partial overshadowing experiment, 10 naive laboratory-reared observer monkeys underwent a procedure similar to the observational conditioning procedure outlined above with live models except that during the six observational conditioning sessions they watched the models react fearfully in the joint presence of snakes (fear-relevant) and brightly-colored, artificial flowers (fear-irrelevant) (see Cook & Mineka, 1987, for details; see also Mineka, 1987; Mineka & Cook, 1988). During the various experimental phases, half of the observers witnessed the full range of stimuli (live boa constrictor, toy snakes, flowers, and neutral objects); the remaining observers were exposed to all the stimuli except the real snake. The inclusion of this latter group represented an attempt to equate the flower and snake stimuli for salience. Differential salience of the real snake versus flower stimuli might account for any differences in conditioning (i.e., while the boa constrictor could move, neither the flowers nor the toy snakes could do so). Relative saliences, or intensities, of the component cues has been shown to play a role in at least some overshadowing results, with the more salient CS overshadowing the less salient (Kamin, 1969). (Other factors contributing to overshadowing include the relative "validities" of the cues and prior experience with the cues; Kamin, 1969; Mackintosh, 1983, chap. 4; Wagner, 1969.)

Fear of each element of the compound CS was assessed by presenting snakes and flowers separately to observers during the pretests and posttests. During the pretests, both observer groups reacted with relatively little fear to any of the stimuli: snakes, flowers, or neutral objects. Following conditioning, however, the behavior of most observers indicated an acquired fear of snake stimuli, but not of flower or neutral stimuli. Figure 20–7 illustrates this pretest-to-posttest shift in observer responding to snakes for the behavioral avoidance measure in the WGTA.

By themselves, these results provide only weak evidence for the hypotheses regarding the selective nature of the snake-aversive outcome association (see Mineka & Cook, 1988; Cook & Mineka, 1987, in press, for a discussion of the limitations). For example, although the model was nominally reacting fearfully to both the snake and the flowers, observers may have been able to discern through subtle behavioral/postural cues emitted by the model that the models were reacting only to the snake stimuli. They are, however, perfectly consistent with the results of the series of experiments described earlier using videotaped models demonstrating that selective associations are involved. Furthermore, these results also provide a compelling model for overshadowing of fear-irrelevant cues by simultaneously present fear-relevant cues during observational conditioning of fear. This finding is especially interesting because overshadowing does not always occur with such paradigms. Indeed, sometimes an opposite phenomenon known as *potentiation* occurs. Potentiation refers to findings in which one CS, not conditionable when presented alone with the US, does acquire excitatory strength when it accompanies the US in association with another CS. For example, numerous studies have documented taste-mediated potentiation of odor cues. Odors, not conditionable when paired with induced toxicosis, will often become aversive if presented simultaneously with a taste in association with toxicosis (e.g., Bouton, Jones, McPhillips, & Swartzentruber, 1986; Durlach & Rescorla, 1980; Holder & Garcia, 1987). Consistent with this analysis, the studies reviewed earlier indeed indicated that flower stimuli, like the odor cues in the aforementioned studies, are at best only weakly conditionable when

Behavioral Avoidance in WGTA

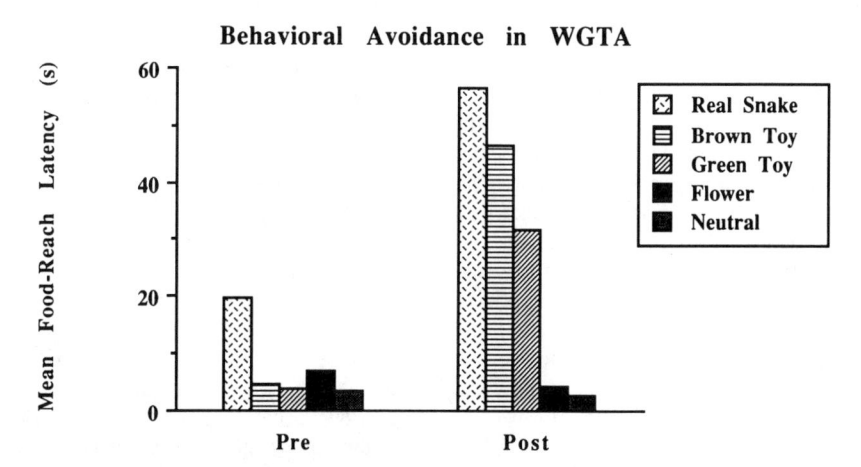

Figure 20.7. Mean food-reach latencies (in s) in the Wisconsin General Test Apparatus for the two observer groups (combined) at pretest and posttest for the live boa constrictor (real snake), toy snakes (brown and green), flowers, and neutral objects (wood blocks). Note that the value for real snake only represents the mean for the group of observers that saw that stimulus; values for all other stimuli represent the weighted average of both observer groups. Maximum possible latency = 60 s. From "Second-Order Conditioning and Overshadowing in the Observational Conditioning of Fear in Monkeys" by M. Cook and S. Mineka, 1987, *Behaviour Research and Therapy*, 25.

presented alone with an aversive US consisting of the fearful reaction of a model. Nevertheless, when presented in combination with snake stimuli, overshadowing rather than potentiation occurred.

Conclusions About Selective Associations and the Origins of Phobic Fears

Taken together, this series of experiments provides strong support for the proposition that human and nonhuman primates selectively associate certain fear-relevant stimuli such as snakes and crocodiles with aversive outcomes. In four separate experiments, superior conditioning was seen when fear-relevant stimuli were paired with a model's fear performance relative to when fear-irrelevant stimuli were paired with the same model's fear performance. The procedures and stimuli in these experiments varied along a number of dimensions (live vs. videotaped models, discriminative conditioning paradigm vs. overshadowing paradigm, snakes and flowers vs. a crocodile and rabbit). The fact that these studies all yielded similar results in spite of these differences strengthens our confidence in the general conclusion. In addition, experiments by Curio, Ernst, and Vieth (1978; see also Curio, 1988) generated analogous results in a very different species, again emphasizing the generality of this effect. In their studies, European blackbirds *(Turdus merula)* exhibited significantly higher levels of mobbing behavior when the alarm cries of a conspecific were paired with the presentation of a predator-like stuffed, noisy friarbird *(Philemon corniculatus)* as opposed to a plastic bottle.

It is critical to note that conclusions about the selective nature of the snake-fear (or crocodile-fear) association derive strongly from the fact that observer monkeys in our studies lacked prior experience with the stimuli employed. That is, selective associations are, by definition, *experience-independent* biases in associability. As stated in the opening paragraphs of this chapter, in human research on this topic it is not possible to determine whether or not differences in conditionability to fear-relevant versus fear-irrelevant stimuli derive from experiential sources. However, in our monkey studies, the fact that differential fear conditioning appeared in the case of snake and crocodile stimuli even though the observers had no experience with any of the fear-relevant or fear-irrelevant stimuli prior to the experiment provides strong support for the notion that selective associations are involved.

The results of the appetitive PAN experiment are also critical in providing support for the contention that the differential associability between fear-relevant stimuli and aversive outcomes is selective. Specifically, the PAN study addresses one possible nonassociative account of the differential responding to fear-relevant stimuli, namely, that parametric differences between the two stimulus classes along some dimension such as salience or discriminability are responsible for the differences in fear conditioning. However, if such parametric differences did, in fact, underlie the observed differences in fear conditioning, then one would expect a similar difference in conditioning in the PAN experiment (i.e., superior performance on snake problems). The fact that we uncovered no clear trends in rate of problem solution as a function of stimulus relevance argues against this nonassociative salience account and simultaneously strengthens the selective association hypothesis. (Curio et al. did not contrast associability of the plastic bottle versus the stuffed friarbird when paired with an appetitive reinforcer. Thus, the possibility remains that the friarbird was simply more salient than was the plastic bottle, and that the friarbird-alarm cry association was not truly selective.)

Unfortunately, not all nonassociative accounts of the failure to observe acquisition of flower fear are eliminated by the present results. For example, it is possible that the rhesus monkeys associated flowers with aversive outcomes in the FL+/SN− and FL+ groups, but that this association was behaviorally "silent" (see Holland, 1977). That is, alternative experimental procedures (e.g., blocking or second-order conditioning) or dependent measures could potentially reveal that conditioning to the "less relevant" stimulus class had occurred. Although we cannot definitively rule out this possibility, we do not consider it to be very plausible. For example, in the SN+/FL− experiment, three dependent measures were used to index fear of the CSs, and all of these measures indicated that, on average, little substantial conditioning to the fear-irrelevant CS occurred (see Cook & Mineka, in press).

Theoretical writing in the area of learning constraints has typically posited ecologically oriented functional accounts of selective associations; that is, learning propensities are presumed to be the product of the process of natural selection, whereby organisms with such propensities are assumed to enjoy greater reproductive success relative to contemporaries who fail to display the behavioral tendencies in question. Seligman's (1970, 1971) theory, for example, postulates that humans are predisposed to associate certain stimuli (e.g., snakes) with aversive consequences because their ancestors who easily acquired these fears possessed a selective advantage compared with contemporaries who did not. Although the present experiments were not specifically designed to address these issues, they do have some implications for the possible validity of such ecologically oriented functional accounts.

First, however, it should be acknowledged that the notion of functionally adaptive, specialized learning abilities in the face of potential predators remains a working hypothesis in need of verification; the possibility exists that such behaviors are, in fact, not adaptive. (See Gould & Lewontin, 1979; Hailman, 1982; and Rowell, 1979, for discussions concerning the tendency to uncritically assume that either morphological or behavioral characteristics are adaptively suited to their environment.) Hypotheses regarding the adaptive function of easily acquired snake fear, for example, rest on the assumption of a predatory relation between snakes and primates. Unfortunately, there appears to be little agreement in the literature regarding the evolutionary impact of predation, in general, on primate behavior. (See Anderson, 1986; and Cheney & Wrangham, 1987, for recent reviews of predation risk for primates.) This uncertainty stems, at least in part, from the paucity of systematic, concrete data on the predation of primates. Thus, although individual field observations support the contention that snakes (and crocodiles) prey upon several primate species (e.g., C. Busse, 1980, personal communication, cited in Anderson, 1986; Heymann, 1987; van Schaik, van Noordwijk, de Boer, & den Tonkelaar, 1983), the relatively sparse and unsystematic nature of the data base makes it difficult to estimate actual predation rates and hence to assess the impact of such predation.

In spite of doubts concerning the impact of predation on primates (and, more specifically, of predation by snakes on primates), a number of scenarios can be advanced to support the hypothesis that snake fear is adaptive. That is, even if one assumes that the relatively low predation rate on primates frequently noted in field studies is an accurate representation of the predator-prey relationship (rather than a reflection of an inadequate data base), low predation risk is not an a priori reason for rejecting the inference that easily acquired snake fear is adaptive. For example, predation by snakes may have been more intense during the phylogenetic past of primate species, resulting in the persistence of antisnake behavior during more recent periods of relaxed selection (see Coss & Owings, 1985; Waddington, 1957). Alternatively, the consequences of a successful predation attempt are so deleterious (i.e., death and the loss of future opportunities to increase one's genetic representation in future generations), that even low rates of snake predation on primates might exert sufficient selective pressure to give rise to antisnake behaviors.

Questions concerning the phylogeny and the adaptive function of behavior might benefit from the adoption of a comparative methodology (cf. Hailman, 1976). Indeed, such an approach has been specifically advocated as a way to investigate selective associations (e.g., Domjan & Galef, 1983; Johnston, 1981). Such an approach could be melded with the present videotape methodology and applied to the more specific question of snake fear in primates. For example, one might contrast two populations of monkeys, one that evolved in an environment free of snakes (or free of dangerous snakes), and another that coevolved with dangerous snakes. If the selective associability of snakes with fear represents an adaptive specialization shaped by natural selection, then one would not expect the species that evolved in the snake-free environment to display a selective association. An elegant series of experiments by Coss and Owings (1985) on antisnake behavior in a variety of ground squirrel species exemplifies this comparative approach. (See Cook & Mineka, in press, for further discussion of these issues.)

Several other general conclusions also can be derived from the results of the studies presented in this chapter. First, although our use of videotape technology was primarily a response to the methodological problem of equating degree of model fear in the presence of different stimuli, the finding that rhesus monkeys were, in fact, capable of acquiring an effective CR when both the CS and US were presented via videotape rather than in vivo is interesting in its own right (Cook & Mineka, 1989, in press). Such an outcome extends the results of prior experimentation from this laboratory using live models (e.g., Cook et al., 1985; Mineka & Cook, 1986; Mineka et al., 1984) by demonstrating that the acquisition of fear through observational conditioning can occur in spite of the degraded "signaling power" of the CS (snakes and crocodiles) and US (the fearful behavior of a conspecific). More generally, these results may have implications for human affective modeling involving mass media presentations such as television (cf. Bandura, in press). In particular, they suggest that previous emphasis on the acquisition of aggressive behaviors through modeling may have overshadowed an equally powerful role that the mass media may play in providing opportunities for the acquisition of new fears. That the observationally acquired fears persisted through a 3-month follow-up period suggests that such observationally acquired fears may be quite persistent (at least in the absence of further nonreinforced exposure to the feared stimulus).

In addition, the significance of the videotape methodology can be viewed from a more practical perspective. Ethologists and comparative psychologists interested in reintroducing endangered primate species into the wild have devoted considerable effort to training their animals to forage for food, climb trees, and other "natural" behaviors. However, little attention has been devoted to the problem of training predator avoidance (see Kleiman et al., 1986; Mittermeier & Cheney, 1987; Snowdon & Savage, 1989). The present experimental methodology may provide an efficient framework through which this can be accomplished. Even if reintroduction of a primate species is not a goal, Snowdon and Savage (1989) have noted that the most conservative criterion that can be adopted in seeking to maintain the psychological well-being of captive populations of animals would be to ensure that their behavioral repertoire mirrors as closely as possible that of their feral counterparts. From this perspective, the present videotape paradigm is again important as an efficient avenue by which fear of predators—a behavioral skill surely possessed by species members in the wild—could be transmitted.

In summary, results from the present series of studies amplifies the results of earlier studies using in vivo models and stimuli by showing that the vicarious transmission of snake fear may also occur in cases where the model and stimuli are videotaped. In addition, use of videotaped stimuli may represent an effective framework that can be used to address (a) the more practical problem of inducing a fear of potential predators in captive populations of primates, and (b) the theoretical issue of the possible role natural selection has played in the expression of snake fear in primates. Finally, and perhaps most importantly, the experimental findings strongly support the hypothesis that certain classes of stimuli (i.e., predator-like stimuli such as snakes and crocodiles) are selectively associable with aversive events.

POSSIBLE IMPLICATIONS OF SELECTIVE ASSOCIATIONS FOR BEHAVIOR THERAPY

In Seligman's original formulation of the preparedness theory of phobias, it was hypothesized that fears that are acquired to prepared stimuli would be considerably more resistant to extinction than would be fears acquired to neutral or unprepared stimuli. The evidence bearing on this proposition is mixed. On the positive side, there is the impressive series of studies by Öhman and his coworkers reviewed earlier demonstrating superior resistance to extinction of electrodermal responses conditioned to prepared CSs relative to unprepared CSs. Although there have been some reported failures to replicate this effect, it has been replicated in a number of different laboratories and so seems to be a reliable, if somewhat elusive, phenomenon (see McNally, 1987, for a review). On the negative side, however, there exists a fair amount of evidence that individuals with phobias of fear-relevant stimuli such as snakes, spiders, or heights do *not*, on average, fare worse in exposure therapy than do individuals with phobias of fear-irrelevant stimuli. For example, De Silva et al. (1977) did a retrospective study of a large sample of phobic patients and found, consistent with the belongingness prediction of preparedness theory, that the majority of the sources of fear were evolutionarily significant (i.e., prepared or fear-relevant). However, they found no consistent differences in therapeutic outcome for prepared versus unprepared phobias. Related findings have been reviewed by McNally (1987). Unfortunately, one weakness of these studies with phobic patients is that it is difficult, if not impossible, to equate phobics with prepared versus unprepared phobias for mode of onset, duration of fear, and intensity of fear. Only when such variables are carefully controlled can one correctly interpret differences (or lack of differences) in rates of fear extinction during exposure therapy (cf. Mackintosh, 1974). Because of this methodological roadblock, the question is likely to remain unanswered for some time.

Given the usefulness of our primate model of phobic fears for understanding selective associations in the origins of fears, we had originally hoped to be able to more carefully assess the question of the relative ease of extinction of fears of fear-relevant (prepared) versus fear-irrelevant (unprepared) objects. Unfortunately, however, it has not been possible to pursue this issue because observer monkeys in this series of experiments did not acquire significant levels of fear of the fear-irrelevant objects. Without comparable levels of fear *acquisition* to the fear-relevant and fear-irrelevant objects, one cannot study possible differences in resistance to *extinction*. Indeed, one of the noteworthy aspects of these findings is that our "preparedness" effects were observed in acquisition rather than in extinction, as has been more typically observed in the human studies of preparedness using an electrodermal conditioning paradigm. The significance of this difference is unclear at the present time, but the possibility must be considered that preparedness or fear-relevance effects may be stronger in acquisition than in extinction when paradigms other than electrodermal conditioning are used. Consistent with this possibility are the results of E. Cook et al. (1986) who found preparedness effects in acquisition rather than extinction when heartrate was used as a dependent measure. In particular, they found that subjects conditioned with fear-relevant CSs showed an acceleratory heart rate CR, whereas subjects conditioned with fear-irrelevant CSs showed a deceleratory CR. The heart rate acceleratory response may be a better index of defensive responding than is the electrodermal response.

In spite of our inability to compare ease of extinction to fear-relevant versus fear-irrelevant CSs, in two studies we did attempt to extinguish snake fear in wild-reared monkeys who were highly similar to the wild-reared models used in our original observational conditioning studies. Earlier reports on snake fear in primates suggested that this fear was relatively easy to extinguish (e.g., Murray & King, 1973, for squirrel monkeys; Schiller, 1952, for chimpanzees; see Mineka et al., 1980, for a review). These studies simply measured how many trials it took for their subjects to reach for a food treat near a snake, and found that this occurred fairly rapidly; these rapid changes in the behavioral avoidance index of fear were taken to mean that the "fear" had "extinguished." There were, however, no measurements made of behavioral or subjective distress, and no follow-up tests to determine if the "fear" remained "extinguished."

Mineka et al. (1980) more carefully examined this issue by subjecting 8 wild-reared monkeys, who all had an intense fear of snakes, to 7 flooding sessions over a 35-day period. Furthermore, they monitored both behavioral avoidance (flood-reach latency) and behavioral distress (fear/disturbance behaviors), as described previously. Consistent with the earlier reports, they found that the wild-reared monkeys all learned fairly rapidly to reach for the food treat on the far side of a live snake; indeed, no monkey took more than 18 trials to meet a criterion of reaching for the food treat in less than 10 seconds on 4 consecutive trials. However, it would be seriously misleading to state that the fear of snakes has been "extinguished" because measures of behavioral distress in the presence of the snake remained high across the seven flooding sessions. More specifically, although there was some within-session decrement of the behavioral distress component of fear, there was complete spontaneous recovery between sessions (i.e., return of fear). Mineka and Keir (1983) reported the results of a 6-month follow-up test on these monkeys, followed by further flooding. Any changes in behavioral avoidance that had occurred during the original 7 flooding sessions disappeared 6 months later, and further flooding still failed to produce any significant changes in behavioral distress. In other words, the fear of snakes in these wild-reared monkeys was extraordinarily resistant to extinction.

This study leaves unresolved the possibility that more rapid and substantial extinction of snake fear could result if wild-reared models were exposed to laboratory-reared monkeys behaving nonfearfully with snakes. That is, there are some suggestions in the human literature that such modeling of nonfearful behavior can produce more fear extinction than does simple exposure to the feared object alone (e.g., Bandura, in press; Bandura, Blanchard, & Ritter, 1969; Bandura, Grusec, & Menlove, 1967; although see Emmelkamp, 1982, for a review suggesting that not all studies show this effect). In a recently completed study, we examined this possibililty by comparing the effectiveness of 15 hour-long sessions of exposure alone with the effectiveness of 15 hour-long sessions of watching nonfearful model monkeys behaving nonfearfully with snakes. There were 5 wild-reared monkeys in each group. No consistent group differences were found; instead, extreme within-group variability was found. Several animals in each group showed a significant decline in fear, several animals showed moderate declines, and several showed no significant decline at all. Thus, there was no evidence that exposure to a nonfearful model potentiated the effects of exposure alone.

What accounts for the apparent difference in our difficulty extinguishing snake fear in wild-reared rhesus monkeys with the relative ease of extinguishing small animal phobias in humans? One obvious possibility is that there are significant differences between the "motivational state" of our monkey subjects and human phobics. That is, the monkeys in these studies have not "chosen" to try and overcome their fear of snakes, bur rather are being forcibly exposed to snakes by the experimenters. By contrast, most human phobics seeking treatment are more motivated to change, usually because the phobia is causing significant distress or interference in their life. Although it is often assumed that exposure is sufficient to mediate extinction of fear, it may be that motivational variables are quite important in cases of very intense fear.

Lack of motivation may, for example, interfere with the important process that Foa and Kozak (1986) have labeled "emotional processing" of the threatening material, which allows for a change in the structure of the fear memory network. Such motivational variables may be less important in the case of mild fears conditioned in the laboratory, where exposure may be sufficient to mediate extinction.

In sum, given the available evidence, it is difficult to know whether intense prepared fears are more resistant to extinction than are intense unprepared fears. This difficulty stems from impediments to performing the requisite experiments using either human or nonhuman primate subjects. Certainly, however, our attempts to extinguish snake fear in wild-reared monkeys demonstrate that there are conditions under which an intense fear of at least one prepared stimulus (snakes) can be extremely resistant to extinction. One possible implication of these results for behavior therapy lies in the suggestion that motivational variables may be quite important in exposure therapy with severe phobias.

There is another possible implication of our results on selective associations for the treatment of phobias. Phobics often do not understand the origins of their phobia(s), and even if they do, they generally feel helpless to control their fear. If a client's phobia is indeed for an object that may be considered "fear-relevant" or "prepared," the therapist may find it useful to educate the client about the role of selective associations in the origins of phobic fears. By understanding the evolutionary/functional pressures that may have led to our high susceptibility to such fears, clients may feel less victimized by their phobias. Also, by better understanding their fears they may be more motivated to try and overcome them.

A final implication of this series of studies for behavior therapy centers on possibilities for preventing the acquisition of fears. Given the relative ease of observational conditioning of some fears in our observer monkeys, one might be surprised that the correlation between parent's fears and their children's fear is not higher than reported (see Emmelkamp, 1982; Marks, 1987, for reviews). However, a major difference between our observer monkeys and many humans undergoing observational fear conditioning experiences lies in the degree of prior experience with the stimulus in question. Other than a brief exposure in a pretest, observer monkeys in our experiments have no prior experience with snakes or crocodiles. Many humans, by contrast, have extensive prior exposure to objects that are later seen in the context of a potential observational conditioning experience.

Mineka and Cook (1986) directly examined the importance of this variable in a study of immunization against the observational conditioning of fear. In this experiment three groups of monkeys received six sessions of observational conditioning of snake fear with live, fearful models. However, prior to these observational conditioning sessions, each group had received one of three different pretreatments. An Immunization group had watched a nonfearful model monkey behaving nonfearfully in the WGTA with snakes for six sessions; a Latent Inhibition group had spent six sessions by themselves in the WGTA with snakes; a Pseudoimmunization control group had spent six sessions watching a nonfearful model monkey behaving nonfearfully in the WGTA with *neutral* objects (wood blocks). The Immunization and Latent Inhibition groups were equated for amount of their prior exposure to snakes, and differed only in whether that exposure was with a nonfearful model or by themselves. The Immunization and Pseudoimmunization groups were equated for their exposure to nonfearful models, and differed only in whether the models were reacting nonfearfully to snakes or to neutral objects.

Results of this experiment were quite striking. The Immunization pretreatment effectively prevented the acquisition of snake fear during the subsequent exposure to a fearful model behaving fearfully with snakes; that is, this group as a whole did not show any changes in snake fear from pretest to posttest. As expected, by contrast, the Pseudoimmunization control group showed strong observational conditioning of snake fear. The results of the Latent Inhibition group were intermediate (not significantly different from the other two groups), but within-group comparisons of responsivity to snakes from pretest to posttest did reveal significant acquisition of snake fear for this group. The results of this experiment clearly show that prior experiences with models behaving nonfearfully with a particular object (even a fear-relevant object) can have a powerful effect on reducing the subsequent impact of later observational fear conditioning experiences. One practical implication of this experiment is that phobic parents who are concerned about passing their phobia onto their children could potentially do some preventative work by having their children exposed to the object(s) of their phobia(s) by nonfearful models.

CONCLUSION

In summary, the present chapter has reviewed how the study of selective associations in fear conditioning promotes an understanding of the etiology and distribution of human fears and phobias. At the present time, however, it is unclear whether fears that are easier to acquire are also more difficult to extinguish, and thus whether the study of selective associations has direct implications for behavior therapy. Nevertheless, it is important to note that fears that are easy to acquire (such as snake fear) can still effectively be prevented through prior exposure to nonfearful models. If the ultimate goal of mental health professionals is prevention, then these findings can be seen as having clear implications for behavior therapy.

REFERENCES

Anderson, C. (1986). Predation and primate evolution. *Primates, 27,* 15–39.

Badia, P., Harsh, J., & Abbott, B. (1979). Choosing between predictable and unpredictable shock conditions: Data and theory. *Psychological Bulletin, 86,* 1107–1131.

Bandura, A. (in press). Social cognitive theory and social referencing. In S. Feinman (Ed.), *Social referencing and social construction of reality.* New York: Plenum Press.

Bandura, A., Blanchard, E., & Ritter, B. (1969). The relative efficacy of desensitization and modeling approaches for inducing behavioral, affective and attitudinal changes. *Journal of Personality and Social Psychology, 13,* 173–199.

Bandura, A., Grusec, J., & Menlove, F. (1967). Vicarious extinction of avoidance behavior. *Journal of Personality and Social Psychology, 5,* 16–23.

Berger, S. (1962). Conditioning through vicarious instigation. *Psychological Review, 69,* 450–466.

Bolles, R. (1970). Species-specific defense reactions and avoidance learning. *Psychological Review, 77,* 32–48.

Bouton, M., Jones, D., McPhillips, S., & Swartzentruber, D. (1986). Potentiation and overshadowing in odor-aversion learning: Role of method of odor presentation, the distal-proximal cue distinction, and the conditionability of odor. *Learning and Motivation, 17,* 115–138.

Boyer, W., & Polidora, V. (1972). An analysis of the solution of PAN ambiguous-cue problems by rhesus monkeys. *Learning and Motivation, 3,* 325–333.

Breland, K., & Breland, M. (1961). The misbehavior of organisms. *American Psychologist, 16,* 681–684.

Capitanio, J., Boccia, M., & Colaiannia, D. (1985). The influence of rank on affect perception by pigtailed macaques *(Macaca nemestrina). American Journal of Primatology, 8,* 53–59.

Cheney, D., & Wrangham, R. (1987). Predation. In B. Smuts, D. Cheney, R. Seyfarth, R. Wrangham, & T. Struhsaker (Eds.), *Primate societies* (pp. 227–239). Chicago: University of Chicago Press.

Cook, E., Hodes, R., & Lang, P. (1986). Preparedness and phobia: Effects of stimulus content on human visceral conditioning. *Journal of Abnormal Psychology, 95,* 195–207.

Cook, M., & Mineka, S. (1987). Second-order conditioning and overshadowing in the observational conditioning of fear in monkeys. *Behaviour Research and Therapy, 25,* 349–364.

Cook, M., & Mineka, S. (1989). Observational conditioning of fear to fear-relevant versus fear-irrelevant stimuli in rhesus monkeys. *Journal of Abnormal Psychology, 98,* 448–459.

Cook, M., & Mineka, S. (in press). Selective associations in the observational conditioning of fear in rhesus monkeys. *Journal of Experimental Psychology: Animal Behavior Processes.*

Cook, M., Mineka, S., Wolkenstein, B., & Laitsch, K. (1985). Observational conditioning of snake fear in unrelated rhesus monkeys. *Journal of Abnormal Psychology, 94,* 591–610.

Coss, R., & Owings, D. (1985). Restraints on ground squirrel antipredator behavior: Adjustments over multiple time scales. In T. Johnston & A. Pietrewicz (Eds.), *Issues in the ecological study of learning* (pp. 167–200). Hillsdale, NJ: Lawrence Erlbaum Associates.

Curio, E. (1988). Cultural transmission of enemy recognition by birds. In T. Zentall & B. Galef (Eds.), *Social learning: Psychological and biological perspectives* (pp. 75–97). Hillsdale, NJ: Lawrence Erlbaum Associates.

Curio, E., Ernst, U., & Vieth, W. (1978). The adaptive significance of avian mobbing: II. Cultural transmission of enemy recognition in blackbirds: Effectiveness and some constraints. *Zeitschrift Tierpsychologie, 48,* 184–202.

D'Amato, M., Buckiewicz, J., & Puopolo, M. (1981). Long-delay spatial discrimination learning in monkeys. *(Cebus apella). Bulletin of the Psychonomic Society, 18,* 85–88.

D'Amato, M., & Safarjan, W. (1981). Differential effects of delay of reinforcement on acquisition of affective and instrumental responses. *Animal Learning and Behavior, 9,* 209–215.

Damianopoulos, E. (1989). Biological constraints revisited: A critique. *Animal Learning and Behavior, 17,* 234–242.

Delprato, D. (1980). Hereditary determinants of fears and phobias. *Behavior Therapy, 11,* 79–103.

De Silva, P., Rachman, S., & Seligman, M. (1977). Prepared phobias and obsessions: Therapeutic outcome. *Behaviour Research and Therapy, 15,* 65–77.

Domjan, M. (1983). Biological constraints on instrumental and classical conditioning: Implications for general process theory. In G. Bower (Ed.), *The psychology of learning and motivation* (Vol. 17, pp. 215–277). New York: Academic Press.

Domjan, M., & Galef, B. (1983). Biological constraints on instrumental and classical conditioning: Retrospect and prospect. *Animal Learning and Behavior, 11,* 151–161.

Durlach, P., & Rescorla, R. (1980). Potentiation rather than overshadowing in flavor-aversion learning: An analysis in terms of within-compound associations. *Journal of*

Experimental Psychology: Animal Behavior Processes, 6, 175–187.

Emmelkamp, P. (1982). *Phobic and obsessive-compulsive disorders: Theory, research, and practice.* New York: Plenum Press.

Fletcher, H., Grogg, T., & Garske, J. (1968). Ambiguous-cue problem performance of children, retardates, and monkeys. *Journal of Comparative and Physiological Psychology, 66,* 477–482.

Foa, E., & Kozak, M. (1986). Emotional processing of fear: Exposure to corrective information. *Psychological Bulletin, 99,* 20–35.

Garcia, J., & Koelling, R. (1966). Relation of cue to consequence in avoidance learning. *Psychonomic Science, 4,* 123–124.

Gould, S., & Lewontin, R. (1979). The spandrels of San Marco and the Panglossian paradigm: A critique of the adaptationist programme. *Proceedings of the Royal Society of London: Series B: Biological Sciences, 205,* 581–598.

Green, G., & Osborne, J. (1985). Does vicarious instigation provide support for observational learning theories? A critical review. *Psychological Review, 97,* 3–17.

Hailman, J. (1976). Uses of the comparative study of behavior. In R. Masterton, W. Hodos, & H. Jerison (Eds.), *Evolution, brain, and behavior: Persistent problems* (pp. 13–22). Hillsdale, NJ: Lawrence Erlbaum Associates.

Hailman, J. (1982). Evolution and behavior: An iconoclastic view. In H. Plotkin (Ed.), *Learning, development, and culture* (pp. 205–254). New York: John Wiley & Sons.

Harlow, H. (1949). The formation of learning sets. *Psychological Review, 56,* 51–65.

Hebb, D. (1946). On the nature of fear. *Psychological Review, 53,* 259–276.

Heymann, E. (1987). A field observation of predation on a moustached tamarin *(Saguinus mystax)* by an anaconda. *International Journal of Primatology, 8,* 193–195.

Hodes, R., Cook, E., & Lang, P. (1985). Individual differences in autonomic response: Conditioned association or conditioned fear? *Psychophysiology, 22,* 545–560.

Holder, M., & Garcia, J. (1987). Role of temporal order and odor intensity in taste-potentiated odor aversions. *Behavioral Neuroscience, 101,* 158–163.

Holland, P. (1977). Conditioned stimulus as a determinant of the form of the Pavlovian conditioned response. *Journal of Experimental Psychology: Animal Behavior Processes, 3,* 77–104.

Hugdahl, K. (1978). Electrodermal conditioning to potentially phobic stimuli: Effects of instructed extinction. *Behaviour Research and Therapy, 16,* 315–321.

Hugdahl, K., Fredrikson, M., & Öhman, A. (1977). "Preparedness" and "arousability" as determinants of electrodermal conditioning. *Behaviour Research and Therapy, 15,* 345–353.

Johnston, T. (1981). Contrasting approaches to a theory of learning. *Behavioral and Brain Sciences, 4,* 125–173.

Johnston, T., & Pietrewicz, A. (1985). *Issues in the ecological study of learning.* Hillsdale, NJ: Lawrence Erlbaum Associates.

Joslin, J., Fletcher, H., & Emlen, J. (1964). A comparison of the responses to snakes of lab- and wild-reared rhesus monkeys. *Animal Behaviour, 12,* 348–352.

Kamin, L. (1969). Predictability, surprise, attention and conditioning. In B. Campbell & R. Church (Eds.), *Punishment and aversive behavior* (pp. 279–296). New York: Appleton-Century-Crofts.

Kleiman, D., Beck, B., Dietz, J., Dietz, L., Ballou, J., & Coimbra-Filho, A. (1986). Conservation program for the golden lion tamarin: Captive research and management, ecological studies, educational strategies, and reintroduction. In K. Benirschke (Ed.), *Primates: The road to self-sustaining populations* (pp. 959–979). New York: Springer-Verlag.

Lande, J., Higley, J., Snowdon, C., Goy, R., & Suomi, S. (1985). Elicitors of parental care in rhesus monkeys [Abstract]. *American Journal of Primatology, 8,* 349.

Lang, P. (1968). Fear reduction and fear behavior: Problems in treating a construct. In J. Shlein (Ed.), *Research in psychotherapy* (Vol. 3, pp. 90–102). Washington, DC: American Psychological Association.

Lang, P. (1971). The application of psychophysiological methods to the study of psychotherapy and behavior modification. In A. Bergin & S. Garfield (Eds.), *Handbook of psychotherapy and behavior change: An empirical analysis* (pp. 75–125). New York: John Wiley & Sons.

Leary, R. (1958). The learning of ambiguous cue-problems by monkeys. *American Journal of Psychology, 71,* 718–724.

LoLordo, V. (1979a). Constraints on learning. In Bitterman, M., LoLordo, V., Overmier, J., & Rashotte, M. (Eds.), *Animal learning: Survey and analysis* (pp. 473–504). New York: Plenum Press.

LoLordo, V. (1979b). Selective associations. In A. Dickinson & R. Boakes (Eds.), *Mechanisms of learning and motivation: A memorial to Jerzy Konorski* (pp. 367–398). Hillsdale, NJ: Lawrence Erlbaum Associates.

LoLordo, V., & Droungas, A. (1989). Selective associations and adaptive specializations: Food aversion and phobias. In S. Klein & R. Mowrer (Eds.), *Contemporary learning theories: Instrumental conditioning theory and the impact of biological constraints on learning* (pp. 145–179). Hillsdale, NJ: Lawrence Erlbaum Associates.

Lorenz, K. (1965). *Evolution and modification of behavior.* Chicago: University of Chicago Press.

Mackintosh, N. (1974). *The psychology of animal learning.* London: Academic Press.

Mackintosh, N. (1983). *Conditioning and associative learning.* New York: Oxford University Press.

Maier, S., & Jackson, R. (1979). Learned helplessness: All of us were right (and wrong): Inescapable shock has multiple effects. In G. Bower (Ed.), *The psychology of learning and motivation: Vol. 13, Advances in theory*

and *research* (pp. 155–218). New York: Academic Press.
Maier, S., & Seligman, M. (1976). Learned helplessness: Theory and evidence. *Journal of Experimental Psychology: General, 105,* 3–46.
Marks, I. (1977). Phobias and obsessions: Clinical phenomena in search of a laboratory model. In J. Maser & M. Seligman (Eds.), *Psychopathology: Experimental models* (pp. 174–213). San Francisco: W H Freeman.
Marks, I. (1987). *Fears, phobias, and rituals: Panic, anxiety, and their disorders.* New York: Oxford University Press.
Masserman, J., & Pechtel, C. (1953). Conflict-engendered neurotic and psychotic behavior in monkeys. *Journal of Nervous and Mental Diseases, 118,* 408–411.
McNally, R. (1987). Preparedness and phobias: A review. *Psychological Bulletin, 101,* 283–303.
Mineka, S. (1979). The role of fear in theories of avoidance, flooding, and extinction. *Psychological Bulletin, 86,* 985–1010.
Mineka, S. (1985). Animal models of anxiety-based disorders: Their usefulness and limitations. In A. Tuma & J. Maser (Eds.), *Anxiety and the anxiety disorders* (pp. 199–244). Hillsdale, NJ: Lawrence Erlbaum Associates.
Mineka, S. (1987). A primate model of phobic fears. In H. Eysenck & I. Martin (Eds.), *Theoretical foundations of behavior therapy* (pp. 81–111). New York: Plenum Press.
Mineka, S., & Cook, M. (1986). Immunization against the observational conditioning of snake fear in rhesus monkeys. *Journal of Abnormal Psychology, 95,* 307–318.
Mineka, S., & Cook, M. (1988). Social learning and the acquisition of snake fear in monkeys. In T. Zentall & B. Galef (Eds.), *Social learning: Psychological and biological perspectives* (pp. 51–73). Hillsdale, NJ: Lawrence Erlbaum Associates.
Mineka, S., & Cook, M. (1990). *Mechanisms involved in the observational conditioning of fear.* Manuscript in preparation.
Mineka, S., Davidson, M., Cook, M., & Keir, R. (1984). Observational conditioning of snake fear in rhesus monkeys. *Journal of Abnormal Psychology, 93,* 355–372.
Mineka, S., & Henderson, R. (1985). Controllability and predictability in acquired motivation. *Annual Review of Psychology, 36,* 495–530.
Mineka, S., & Keir, R. (1983). The effects of flooding on reducing snake fear in rhesus monkeys: 6 month follow-up and further flooding. *Behaviour Research and Therapy, 21,* 527–535.
Mineka, S., Keir, R., & Price, V. (1980). Fear of snakes in wild- and lab-reared rhesus monkeys. *Animal Learning and Behavior, 8,* 653–663.
Mittermeier, R., & Cheney, D. (1987). Conservation of primates and their habitats. In B. Smuts, D. Cheney, R. Seyfarth, R. Wrangham, & T. Struhsaker (Eds.), *Primate societies* (pp. 477–490). Chicago: University of Chicago Press.

Murray, S., & King, J. (1973). Snake avoidance in feral and laboratory-reared squirrel monkeys. *Behaviour, 47,* 281–289.
Öhman, A. (1986). Face the beast and fear the face: Animal and social fears as prototypes for evolutionary analyses of emotion. *Psychophysiology, 23,* 123–145.
Öhman, A., Dimberg, U., & Ost, L-G. (1985). Biological constraints on the learned fear response. In S. Reiss & R. Bootzin (Eds.), *Theoretical issues in behavior therapy* (pp. 123–175). New York: Academic Press.
Öhman, A., Eriksson, A., & Olofsson, C. (1975). One-trial learning and superior resistance to extinction of autonomic responses conditioned to potentially phobic stimuli. *Journal of Comparative and Physiological Psychology, 88,* 619–627.
Öhman, A., Fredrikson, M., & Hugdahl, K. (1978). Orienting and defensive responding in the electrodermal system: Palmar-dorsal differences and recovery rate during conditioning to potentially phobic stimuli. *Psychophysiology, 15,* 93–101.
Öhman, A., Fredrikson, M., Hugdahl, K., & Rimmö, P-A. (1976). The premise of equipotentiality in human classical conditioning: Conditioned electrodermal responses to potentially phobic stimuli. *Journal of Experimental Psychology: General, 105,* 313–337.
Overmier, J., Patterson, J., & Wielkiewicz, R. (1980). Environmental contingencies as sources of stress in animals. In S. Levine & H. Ursin (Eds.), *Coping and health* (pp. 1–38). New York: Plenum Press.
Pavlov, I. (1927). *Conditioned reflexes.* London: Oxford University Press.
Plimpton, E., Swartz, K., & Rosenblum, L. (1981). Responses of juvenile bonnet macaques to social stimuli presented through color videotapes. *Developmental Psychobiology, 14,* 109–115.
Rachman, S., & Hodgson, R. (1974). Synchrony and desynchrony in fear and avoidance. *Behaviour Research and Therapy, 12,* 311–318.
Rescorla, R., & Wagner, A. (1972). A theory of Pavlovian conditioning: Variations in the effectiveness of reinforcement and nonreinforcement. In A. Black & W. Prokasy (Eds.), *Classical conditioning II* (pp. 64–99). New York: Appleton-Century-Crofts.
Rowell, T. (1979). How would we know if social organization were *not* adaptive? In I. Bernstein & E. Smith (Eds.), *Primate ecology and human origins: Ecological influences on social organization* (pp. 1–22). New York: Garland STPM Press.
Rozin, P., & Kalat, J. (1971). Specific hungers and poison avoidance as adaptive specializations of learning. *Psychological Review, 78,* 459–487.
Sackett, G. (1970). Unlearned responses, differential rearing experiences, and the development of social attachments by rhesus monkeys. In L. Rosenblum (Ed.), *Primate behavior: Development in the field and laboratory research* (Vol. 1, pp. 112–140). New York: Academic Press.

Schaik, C. van, Noordwijk, M. van, Boer, R. de, & Tonkelaar, I. den. (1983). The effect of group size on time budgets and social behaviour in wild long-tailed macaques *(Macaca fascicularis)*. *Behavioral Ecology and Sociobiology, 13,* 173–181.

Schiller, P. (1952). Innate constituents of complex responses in primates. *Psychological Review, 59,* 177–191.

Seligman, M. (1970). On the generality of the laws of learning. *Psychological Review, 77,* 406–418.

Seligman, M. (1971). Phobias and preparedness. *Behavior Therapy, 2,* 307–320.

Shapiro, K., Jacobs, W., & LoLordo, V. (1980). Stimulus-reinforcer interactions in Pavlovian conditioning of pigeons: Implications for selective associations. *Animal Learning and Behavior, 8,* 586–594.

Shapiro, K., & LoLordo, V. (1982). Constraints on Pavlovian conditioning of the pigeon: Relative conditioned reinforcing effects of red-light and tone CSs paired with food. *Learning and Motivation, 13,* 68–80.

Snowdon, C., & Savage, A. (1989). Psychological well being of captive primates: General considerations and examples from callitrichids. In E. Siegal (Ed.), *The psychological well being of captive nonhuman primates* (pp. 75–88). Park Ridge, NJ: Noyes.

Thorndike, E. (1898). Animal intelligence: An experimental study of the associative processes in animals. *Psychological Monographs, 2* (4, Whole No. 8).

Waddington, C. (1957). *The strategy of the genes.* London: George Allen Unwin.

Wagner, A. (1969). Stimulus validity and stimulus selection in associative learning. In N. Mackintosh & W. Honig (Eds.), *Fundamental issues in associative learning* (pp. 90–122). Halifax, Nova Scotia: Dalhousie University Press.

Wagner, A., & Rescorla, R. (1972). Inhibition in Pavlovian conditioning: Application of a theory. In R. Boakes & M. Halliday (Eds.), *Inhibition and learning* (pp. 301–336). New York: Academic Press.

Yerkes, R., & Yerkes, A. (1936). Nature and conditions of avoidance (fear) in chimpanzees. *Journal of Comparative Psychology, 21,* 53–66.

CHAPTER 21

A CONTEXTUAL ANALYSIS OF FEAR EXTINCTION

Mark E. Bouton

Extinction, the loss of responding that occurs when a conditioned stimulus (CS) is presented repeatedly without the unconditioned stimulus (US) following conditioning, is a basic fact of learning and a basic tool in behavior therapy. It is often linked to therapies used in the treatment of anxiety disorders, where success appears to depend substantially on exposure to the fear-evoking stimulus (e.g., Barlow, 1988; Foa & Kozak, 1986; Marks, 1978). Although the effects of exposure might be interpreted in several ways (e.g., Barlow, 1988), they are often attributed to extinction: If fear of the evoking stimulus (a CS) is originally due its association with a traumatic US, then exposure to it alone would be expected to extinguish conditioned fear. Historically, extinction theory has been applied most directly to therapies such as systematic desensitization and implosive therapy. But extinction may be relevant to any treatment in which the therapist introduces new learning designed to change a client's cognition or behavior. Like fear extinction, nearly any therapeutic intervention can be viewed as retroactive interference with emotional material.

It is not surprising that basic research on conditioning and extinction has moved forward since the 1950s and 1960s, when behavior therapists first founded their new science. Views of conditioning have changed markedly since then (e.g., Rescorla, 1987). Conditioning is no longer seen as the acquisition of stimulus-response connections. The conditioned response is not assumed to be a unitary reflex, but a component of an adaptively organized system of behaviors and physiological responses (e.g., Bolles & Fanselow, 1980; Holland, 1984; Hollis, 1982; Timberlake, 1983). Learning itself is seen as a process quite separate from actual performance. Theories of conditioning now often invoke concepts such as surprise, stimulus processing, short- and long-term memory, and spreading nodal activation to account for even simple examples of associative learning (e.g., Pearce & Hall, 1980; Wagner, 1978, 1981).

Preparation of this chapter was supported by Grant BNS 86-07208 from the National Science Foundation. I thank Harold Leitenberg, Charles A. Peck, and Dale Swartzentruber for their comments on the manuscript.

Ideas about extinction have also changed. Researchers are now more likely to recognize that conditioned stimuli are behaviorally unstable after extinction (e.g., Bouton, 1988, 1989; Bouton & Bolles, 1985). The research to be reviewed in this chapter suggests that even after fairly prolonged extinction procedures, extinguished fear stimuli can still evoke substantial fear under the right conditions. Instead of destroying the learned basis of fear, extinction leaves at least part of the original learning intact. I have suggested that extinction does not cause unlearning, but instead gives the CS a second, and therefore "ambiguous," meaning (Bouton, 1988; Bouton & Bolles, 1985). The properties of an extinguished CS thus resemble those of an ambiguous word. Note that the meaning of an ambiguous word, and the response it evokes, depends almost by definition on what the context retrieves. Your reaction to someone shouting "Fire!" will be very different in the movie theater and in the shooting gallery. The fear evoked by an extinguished evoking stimulus has the same bi-stable quality. The meaning of the stimulus, and the response it currently evokes, may depend fundamentally on its current context.

The first part of this chapter reviews some of the evidence that supports this view of context and extinction (see also Bouton, 1988). The research involves experiments investigating the rat's fear of tone and light conditioned stimuli associated with mild footshock. "Contexts" were usually provided by the boxes or apparatuses in which the rat was exposed to these events. The results suggest that what the animal "knows" about the context can be a powerful determinant of its fear of the CS after extinction. To put the findings in a broad perspective, the second part of the chapter surveys a wider range of stimuli that can function as contexts, including drug states, emotional states, and time. I will suggest that extinction performance may inherently depend on where, when, and under what conditions the fear stimulus is encountered. Fear can easily recur after extinction because extinction fundamentally involves learning about the context.

CONTEXT, AMBIGUITY, AND RETRIEVAL IN EXTINCTION

Reinstatement of Extinguished Fear

One of the phenomena suggesting that extinction is not due to a loss of the original learning is known as "reinstatement." In the laboratory, fear can first be conditioned by pairing a CS and US several times, and then extinguished by presenting the CS repeatedly alone. Typically, extinction is conducted over several daily sessions. If the US is then presented alone in a separate session, fear can be partially reinstated to the CS when it is tested again 24 hours later (e.g., Bouton, 1984; Bouton & Bolles, 1979b; Bouton & King, 1983; Rescorla & Heth, 1975). Even if fear of the CS has been completely eliminated by extinction, exposure to the US alone can cause it to appear again. The phenomenon can occur after relatively little postextinction exposure to the US; under the right conditions, one US will do (Rescorla & Heth, 1975). And the reinstating effects of the US can last for several days (e.g., Bouton & Bolles, 1979b; Rescorla & Cunningham, 1978). The effect suggests that the potential for even the relatively mild fears created in the laboratory can persist through extinction.

Reinstatement has clinical implications that have been noted by several writers recently (e.g., Jacobs & Nadel, 1985; Mineka, 1985). The most obvious, perhaps, is that exposure to trauma on its own can undo the effects of a successful therapy. Another possible role for reinstatement is in the sudden appearance of phobias after stress. If the effects of an early conditioning experience have been reduced through natural extinction, one might expect them to recur after exposure to separate trauma. Without knowledge of the prior conditioning and extinction history, such fears would probably appear to occur spontaneously, and could be taken as evidence against a conditioning model for anxiety disorders. But armed with knowledge of reinstatement, the conditioning model's account of anxiety disorders may be more interesting than it is sometimes assumed to be. There are actually several conditioning phenomena that would allow fears to appear to develop spontaneously (see Jacobs & Nadel, 1985; Mineka, 1985).

There are several accounts of reinstatement. Pavlov (1927) himself was the first to observe it, and he discussed it in connection with spontaneous recovery and disinhibition, the classic phenomena in which extinguished responding recovers with the passage of time or with exposure to a distractor, respectively. Each of these was assumed to involve the removal of inhibition that had developed in extinction. Rescorla and Heth (1975) studied reinstatement more systematically, and suggested that presenting the US might serve to restrengthen a memory of the US that was weakened in extinction. One problem for this view, however, is that there is little evidence that extinction really weakens the subject's memory of the US. For example, when fear of one CS is extinguished, it has little effect on fear of other stimuli associated with the same US (e.g., Bouton & King, 1983; Richards & Sargent, 1983). From the present perspective, however, a more interesting problem for Rescorla and Heth's hypothesis may be that reinstatement depends substantially on conditioning of the context.

There is strong evidence that reinstatement involves context conditioning. When the US is presented after extinction, it is necessarily presented in a context. Just a few US presentations are sufficient to condition fear of the context; the presence of contextual fear may provide the crucial trigger for reinstated fear of the CS. A number of experiments have produced results that are consistent with this view. Perhaps the most important finding is that the US must be presented in the context in which the CS is to be tested if reinstatement is to occur (Bouton, 1984; Bouton & Bolles, 1979b; Bouton & King, 1983, 1986; Bouton & Peck, 1989). If one compares the effects of USs presented in the test context with identical USs presented in a different context, one finds very little effect of USs presented in the different context (see Figure 21-1). Further, if one measures the strength of contextual fear just prior to testing the CS for reinstatement, individual differences in the strength of contextual fear correlate with, and thus predict, the strength of reinstated fear to the CS (Bouton, 1984; Bouton & King, 1983). It is worth noting, however, that contextual conditioning sufficient to produce reinstatement is often not entirely obvious in performance. We have often had to arrange sensitive tests to confirm its presence. The CS and context may both seem behaviorally quiet by themselves, but in combination they can produce a marked fear response. Contextual fear and residual fear of the CS can combine almost synergistically to produce the reinstatement effect.

In the long run, reinstatement points to the importance of contextual stimuli in determining performance to an extinguished CS. The basic determinant of fear is the context in which the CS occurs. When the extinguished CS is presented in a relatively safe context, it evokes little fear. But when the CS is presented in a dangerous context, it evokes substantial fear. The extinguished CS has this unstable character even after prolonged extinction training. Reberg (1972) and Hendry (1982) both tested fear of an extinguished CS together with another excitor after a very large number of extinction trials. Reberg extinguished a CS for 54 trials beyond a point at which the CS evoked no fear, and then tested it together with a moderate excitor. Hendry ran 96 extinction trials and then tested the CS in compound with another CS that had received the same extinction treatment. In either case, when the extinguished CS was tested together with the other stimulus, it again evoked substantial fear. The potential for fear thus persists long after extinction has removed signs of fear from behavior. In this sense, it is wrong to assume that extinction in the Pavlovian conditioning laboratory is trivially easy to accomplish. Although overt manifestations in performance may go away rapidly, the *potential* for fear seems to persist almost indefinitely.

These considerations may suggest that we should be careful how to think about extinction. It is clearly not appropriate to assume that extinction returns a CS to a state of neutrality. Extinction does reduce fear that is evident in performance. But the extinguished CS is like a chameleon (Bouton, 1988): It tends to take on the color of its background.

Renewal of Extinguished Fear by a Change of Context

There are other extinction phenomena that suggest that the potential for fear persists long into extinction and that the context may be important in bringing it out. If fear is conditioned in one context and then extinguished in another, fear is "renewed" if the extinguished CS is returned to the original conditioning context (e.g., Bouton & Bolles, 1979a; Bouton & King, 1983; Hanford, Mulvaney, & Kelfer, 1980; Lovibond, Preston, & Mackintosh, 1984) or tested in a third context (Bouton & Bolles, 1979a; Bouton & Swartzentruber, 1986). The effect has been shown in both fear conditioning and in appetitive conditioning, where conditioning is produced with food USs (Bouton & Peck, 1989). It can also be observed with several types of contexts (discussed later in this chapter). Like reinstatement, it can occur after quite extensive extinction training. We recently produced a modest fear in rats with 8 CS-US pairings, and then extinguished fear in a second context with 84 CS-alone trials (Bouton & Swartzentruber, 1989, Experiment 2). All overt signs of fear were gone within about 20 extinction trials. But when the CS was returned to the original context, it still evoked a powerful fear response. Once again the potential for fear persisted long into extinction. And once again it was brought out by the context.

The renewal effect is illustrated in Figure 21-2 (Bouton & King, 1983, Experiment 1). In this study, conditioning was conducted in Context A for all groups (not shown); after conditioning, the CS was presented alone repeatedly in Context A for one group

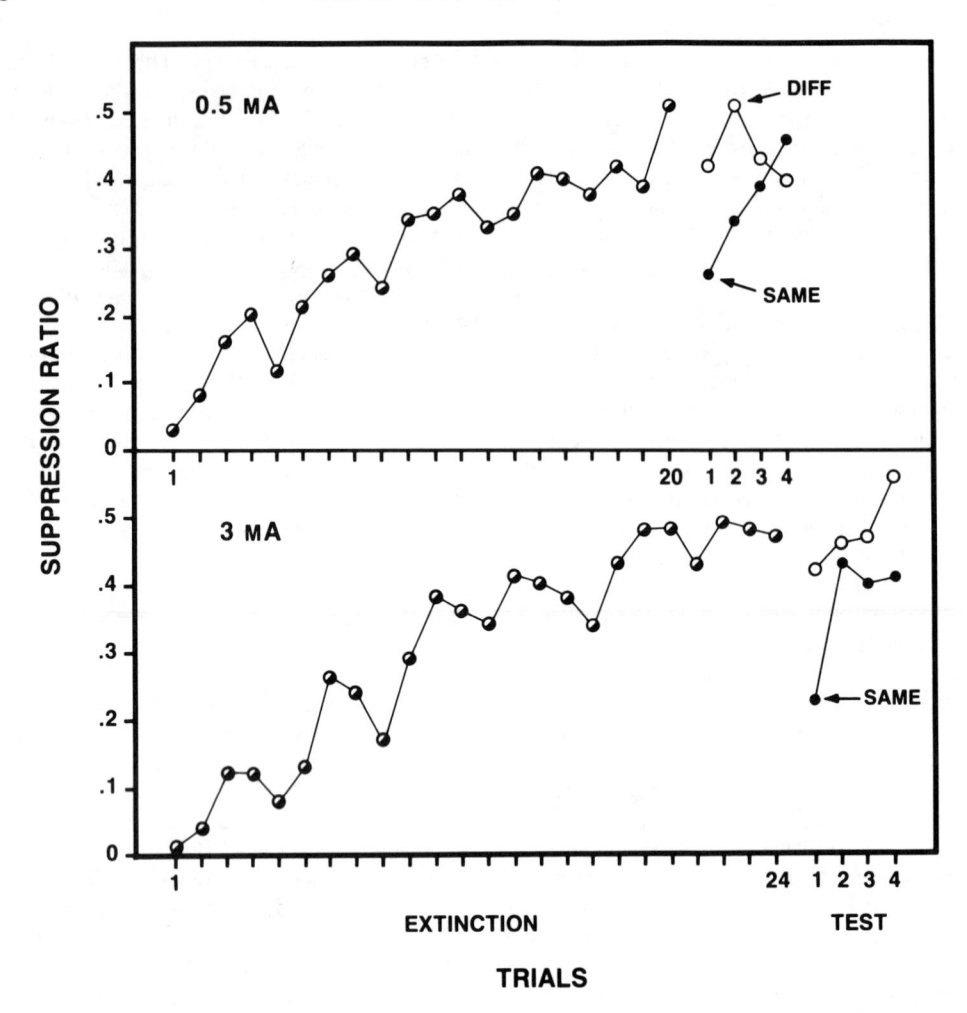

Figure 21.1. Reinstatement of extinguished fear. The y-axis presents the suppression ratio, the standard measure of fear in "conditioned emotional response" studies in which fear is indexed by the CS's ability to suppress an ongoing operant baseline reinforced by food. A ratio of 0 indicates maximal fear of the CS while 0.50 indicates no fear. Both panels show extinction of fear (left) followed by reinstatement testing (right). Conditioning (not shown) involved 12 pairings of the CS with a weak US for the groups in the upper panel and four pairings of the CS with a strong US for the groups in the lower panel. In each panel, Group Same received four USs in the test context 24 h before the reinstatement test; Group Different received the same USs in a different context. Adapted from Bouton (1984, Experiment 4), but reprinted from "Context and Ambiguity in the Extinction of Emotional Learning: Implications for Exposure Therapy" by M. E. Bouton, 1988, *Behaviour Research and Therapy, 26,* 137–149. Copyright 1988 by Pergamon Journals Ltd. Reprinted by permission.

(Group Ext-A), Context B for another (Group Ext-B), or not at all in a final group (Group NE). After extinction was complete, the CS was simply presented on its own again in Context A. A robust renewal of fear is evident in Group Ext-B (at right). The behavior it evoked at the end of extinction would not predict the size or strength of the effect.

It is worth focusing for a moment on the fear evident during the extinction phase itself (at left). At this point one of the groups (Ext-A) was presented with the CS in the conditioning context, whereas the other group (Ext-B) received the CS in a context that differed from the conditioning context. Somewhat surprisingly, the context switch did not reduce fear of the CS. This result, which has been confirmed in a number of other experiments in our own laboratory and in others (e.g., Bouton & Swartzentruber, 1986; Lovibond et al., 1984; Kaye, Preston, Szabo, Druiff, & Mackintosh, 1987), suggests that a fear CS can evoke strong fear regardless of the context. Contrary to popular belief, fear conditioning is very often not specific to its context (see Bouton, 1988, for an expanded discussion). Results like those shown in Figure 21–2 suggest that fear *conditioning* generalizes fairly well across contexts. Fear *extinction*, in contrast, does not. The context is especially important in determining performance to a CS after it has been made ambiguous by extinction.

Learning about Context A and Context B may both contribute to the renewal effect. Renewal is especially strong when testing occurs in the original conditioning context; evidence suggests that we would observe more fear there than in a neutral context (Bouton & Swartzentruber, 1986). But the fact that renewal does occur when testing is conducted in a neutral context suggests that learning about Context B may also be involved. In effect, fear of the CS is released when it is removed from the context of extinction. The contributions of both contexts are easy to explain with mainstream compound conditioning theory (e.g., Rescorla & Wagner, 1972). Context A could become excitatory (associated with the US) during conditioning, and Context B could become a conditioned inhibitor during extinction. However, we have been unable to confirm that A and B have the properties of ordinary excitors and inhibitors (Bouton & King, 1983; Bouton & Swartzentruber, 1986). And strong context associations are often not sufficient to affect CS fear anyway (Bouton, 1984; Bouton & King, 1986).

Instead of simply learning excitation in Context A ("Context A is dangerous") and inhibition in Context B ("Context B is safe"), the subject seems to learn that the meaning of the CS is different in the two contexts ("the CS is dangerous in Context A" and that "the CS is safe in Context B"). The contexts in this sort of procedure effectively "set the occasion for," or retrieve, the corresponding CS-US association (cf. Holland, 1983, 1985; Rescorla, 1985). The ambiguity metaphor is again informative. Contexts disambiguate by selecting associations or meanings, rather than simply being associated with other events. I will return to at least one implication of this mechanism of contextual control at the end of the chapter.

This initial discussion of the renewal effect will end

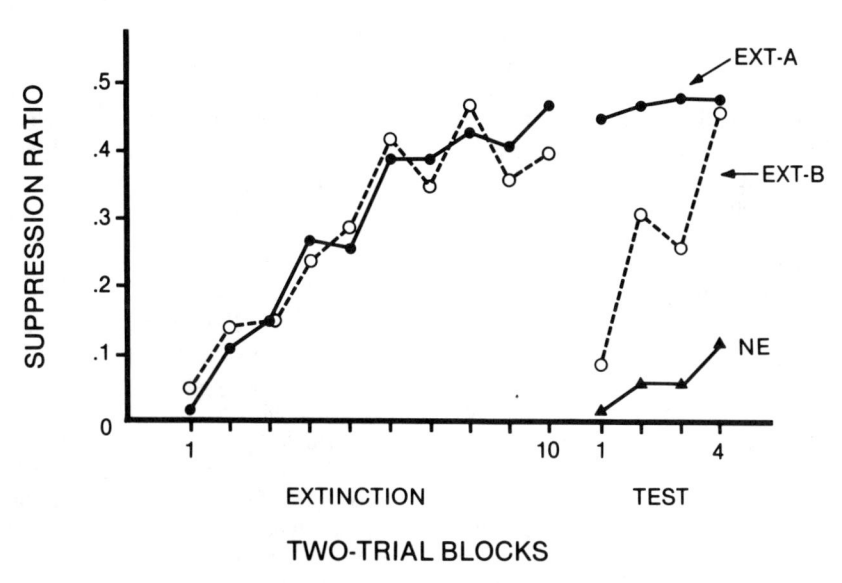

Figure 21.2. The renewal of extinguished fear. Conditioning (not shown) initially occurred in Context A; extinction trials (left) occurred in either Context A (Group Ext-A) or Context B (Group Ext-B). At right, the groups received final tests of the CS in Context A. Group NE had received no previous extinction. From "Contextual Control of the Extinction of Conditioned Fear: Tests for the Associative Value of the Context" by M. E. Bouton and D. A. King, 1983, *Journal of Experimental Psychology: Animal Behavior Processes, 9,* 248–265. Copyright 1983 by the American Psychological Association. Reprinted by permission.

here, although we will return to it in later sections of this chapter. For now, it should be remembered as another indication that (1) the potential for fear persists through extinction and (2) knowledge of the context is involved in its expression. Contextual stimuli play a role that we have come to see as fundamental to the extinction process.

Reacquisition After Extinction

Another phenomenon that supports the view that the original learning persists through extinction is the rate of reconditioning following conditioning. The results of many experiments suggest that conditioned responding reappears rapidly when CS-US pairings are resumed after extinction (e.g., Frey & Butler, 1977; Hoehler, Kirschenbaum, & Leonard, 1973; Konorski & Szwejkowska, 1952; Smith & Gormezano, 1965); a similar effect also occurs in operant conditioning (e.g., Bullock & Smith, 1953). The rapid reemergence of responding suggests that the original learning has been "saved" through extinction. The effect probably boils down to either spontaneous recovery or the renewal effect. For example, many experiments in this literature allowed enough time to elapse between extinction and reconditioning to permit spontaneous recovery to contribute to the responding observed. And many also used "massed" trials (trials occurring close together in time) during the conditioning and reconditioning phases. If aftereffects of recent USs were a part of the conditioning phase, their reintroduction during reconditioning could easily cause renewed conditioned performance. In operant learning, recent reinforcers can demonstrably set the occasion for renewed responding (e.g., Reid, 1958).

Rapid reacquisition is thus consistent with the idea that performance after extinction can be affected by cues in the background. Clearly, any background cue that can retrieve a memory of the conditioning experience would be expected to renew conditioning performance. But it is interesting to note that the retrieval perspective also suggests that a different outcome may be possible under other conditions. If one could create reacquisition conditions that retrieve a memory of extinction, as opposed to conditioning, we might expect to produce the opposite effect. Continued retrieval of an *extinction* memory could actually interfere with reconditioning by continuing to cue extinction performance.

Recent work in my laboratory has documented such slow reacquisition. With relatively extensive extinction training (e.g., 72 or 84 trials), we have observed a rate of reconditioning that is significantly slower than conditioning with a novel CS (Bouton, 1986; Bouton & Swartzentruber, 1989; see Figure 21–3). As I anticipated in my comments above, slow reacquisition occurs primarily when the conditions favor retrieval of a memory of extinction. For example, reconditioning assumes a more rapid rate when CS-US pairings are resumed in a context other than the extinction context (Bouton & Swartzentruber, 1989, Experiment 2); slow reacquisition thus depends on reconditioning occurring in the extinction context. We can also cue extinction performance after reconditioning if the subject is returned to the context uniquely associated with extinction (Bouton & Swartzentruber, 1989, Experiment 3). Extinction performance, and hence slow reacquisition, is strongly controlled by the extinction context.

Interestingly, the CS can still be shown to evoke fear after extinction procedures that generate slow reacquisition. If the CS is tested in the original conditioning context after extinction training that is sufficient to produce slow reacquisition (i.e., 84 trials), conditioned fear is strongly renewed (Bouton & Swartzentruber, 1989, Experiment 2). The CS literally behaves as if it has two separate meanings. One meaning, extinction, is cued by the extinction context and controls slow reacquisition. The other meaning, conditioning, is cued by the conditioning context and controls the renewal effect. The extinguished CS really is like the word "Fire"; its current meaning seems almost completely determined by its current context.

Summary

Extinction is a richer paradigm than many people recognize. The variety of extinction effects we have observed are easily summarized by the view that the CS is disambiguated by contextual retrieval cues. In the laboratory, conditioning and extinction are both learned, and memories of both experiences are retained. The fear evoked by the extinguished CS depends fundamentally on which is currently retrieved. Even after quite extensive extinction training, if the animal encounters the CS under conditions that can retrieve or signal conditioning, conditioned fear will return. This is reinstatement and renewal. But if, in contrast, the prevailing conditions promote retrieval of a memory of extinction, the animal responds as if the CS is currently safe. This is the mechanism

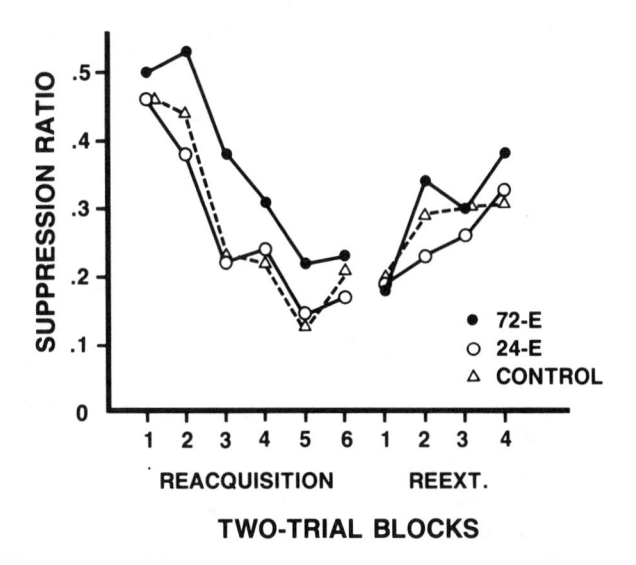

Figure 21.3. Slow reacquisition following extinction. Groups 72-E and 24-E had previously received eight conditioning trials followed by either 72 or 24 extinction trials. Group Control had received no previous conditioning or extinction. From "Slow Reacquisition Following the Extinction of Conditioned Suppression" by M. E. Bouton, 1986, *Learning and Motivation, 17,* 1–15. Copyright 1986 by Academic Press. Reprinted by permission.

behind slow reacquisition, and perhaps extinction performance itself.

The ambiguity view rejects the assumption that extinction, and thus perhaps exposure therapy, erases the initial fear experience from memory. An extinguished CS is accepted for what it is: A behaviorally bi-stable event. The subject or client can be expected to retain memories corresponding roughly to the traumatic and exposure experiences. What is important in determining the continued "success" of extinction is which experience is currently signaled or retrieved. This is the fundamental role of context in extinction and exposure therapy.

A BROAD PERSPECTIVE ON CONTEXT

Thus far the focus has been research using physical contexts provided by different apparatuses housed in different rooms of the laboratory. Such contexts are analogous to the room stimuli manipulated in the literature on human memory, which can also provide strong retrieval cues under some circumstances (e.g., Greenspoon & Ranyard, 1957; Smith, 1979; Smith, Glenberg, & Bjork, 1978). It is worth noting, however, that our use of physical contexts is arbitrary; one would hope that they represent a far wider range of possible background stimuli. At this point it is appropriate to ask whether other kinds of stimuli do provide contexts for conditioning and extinction experiences. The evidence suggests that the perspective developed above can include a fairly wide variety of background cues (see also Spear, 1976, 1978).

Drugs as Interoceptive Contexts

Learning that occurs under the influence of a drug may often fail to transfer to the undrugged condition. Such "state-dependent retention" is typically attributed to a failure to retrieve learned information outside of the original drug state (e.g., Overton, 1978; Spear, 1978; Weingartner, 1978). State-dependent retention has been observed with a variety of drugs in animals (e.g., Overton, 1966) and humans (e.g., Weingartner, 1978). It suggests that one of the many consequences of administering a drug is that it might provide a unique interoceptive context for learning and retention (e.g., Overton, 1985; Spear, 1978; Spear et al., 1980). It is thus reasonable to suspect that fear extinction conducted under the influence of a drug might be state-dependent (e.g., Marks, Viswanathan, Lipsedge, & Garner, 1972; Sartory, 1983). If a drug is combined with exposure therapy, one might expect a renewal effect when the evoking stimulus is encountered in the absence of the drug.

Research on state-dependent retention has usually focused on the retention of acquisition rather than extinction. However, the available data do suggest that state-dependent extinction can occur. Two early studies suggested that extinction under the influence of amobarbital (Barry, Etheredge, & Miller, 1965) and phenobarbital (Bindra, Nyman, & Wise, 1965) might not transfer to the undrugged state. Rats that received extinction combined with the drug showed less evidence of extinction during a final undrugged test than did rats that had received extinction under the influence of a placebo. Similar results have been reported with alcohol (Cunningham, 1979), chlordiazepoxide (librium; Delamater & Treit, 1988; Goldman, 1977; Kamano, 1972; Taub et al., 1977), and diazepam (valium; Gorman, Dyak, & Reid, 1979). Unfortunately, the designs of these experiments often cannot justify concluding that the drug worked as a *context* for extinction. In most cases the drug could have acted by disrupting the learning or "consolidation" of a long-term memory of extinction. Alternatively, because the placebo controls typically received no exposure to the drug at all, the final levels of fear in animals that had received the drug with extinction could have been due to some unconditional (e.g., rebound) effect of previous drug exposure. Two experiments on alcohol (Cunningham, 1979) are a notable exception. Cunningham used a design that equated the experimental and control subjects on overall drug exposure. He found that rats that received fear extinction while inebriated showed renewed fear when tested sober, and further, that a return to the drug state following renewal testing recued extinction performance. Alcohol may thus provide a context that can control fear extinction.

We have recently completed related experiments with chlordiazepoxide (librium) and diazepam (valium) (Bouton, Kenney, & Rosengard, 1990). These benzodiazepine tranquilizers are commonly used in the medical treatment of anxiety (e.g., Sartory, 1983). Our experiments asked whether extinction combined with either drug would be specific to the drug state. In each experiment, a unique chamber (box) provided the CS. The rats initially received eight mild footshocks in the chamber during a 30-minute session conducted in the undrugged state (i.e., after a saline injection). These shocks were sufficient to cause "freezing," a defensive behavior of the rat (e.g., Blanchard & Blanchard, 1969; Bouton & Bolles, 1980; Fanselow, 1980), to occur in the presence of the chamber cues alone. Extinction was then conducted in two 30 minute sessions in which the rats were placed in the chambers for 30 minutes following either drug or saline injections; these sessions were sufficient to reduce fear (i.e., freezing) to near-zero levels. In the last phase, the rats were returned to the chambers after saline injections to test for renewed fear. All sessions were spaced at least 24 hours apart. Throughout the experiments, freezing was scored from videotape (with a time-sampling method) by an observer who was blind to the experimental treatments.

Our initial studies established that both chlordiazepoxide and diazepam can interfere with the success of extinction as determined in the final undrugged test. Figure 21–4 summarizes the test data of two similar but separate experiments. In both studies, fear conditioning was accomplished as described above, and animals received extinction in conjunction with either vehicle injections ("sal") or the drug at various doses. The panels describe freezing in each group during the final undrugged test session. A renewal of fear is suggested by the fact that groups extinguished with the drug showed more freezing in the final test; with both drugs the effect was dose-dependent. In both panels, the dotted line represents freezing of the control (saline) rats at the beginning of the first extinction session. It can be seen that the renewal of fear in the groups given the highest drug doses was fairly complete; freezing in these groups approximated that of the controls at the outset of extinction. In a preliminary way, the results suggest that fear can be renewed when the CS is removed and tested outside of the drug extinction context.

The results of subsequent experiments ruled out relatively uninteresting explanations. One experiment with chlordiazepoxide used a 2 times 2 factorial design (Bouton, Kenney, & Rosengard, 1990, Experiment 2). Half the rats received shock during the initial conditioning session while half did not; half the rats in these two conditions then received "extinction" sessions combined with either drug or saline injections. The extinction procedure was modified so that all groups received equivalent overall exposure to the drug. The two chamber exposure sessions were spaced 48 hours apart; on the intervening days, rats given the drug on the extinction days were given saline in the home cage. Rats given saline on extinction days were given the drug on the intervening days. The actual drug-saline sequence (DSDS and SDSD) was counterbalanced within the groups.

Figure 21–5 illustrates freezing on the final test day. Renewal again occurred in the group that received fear

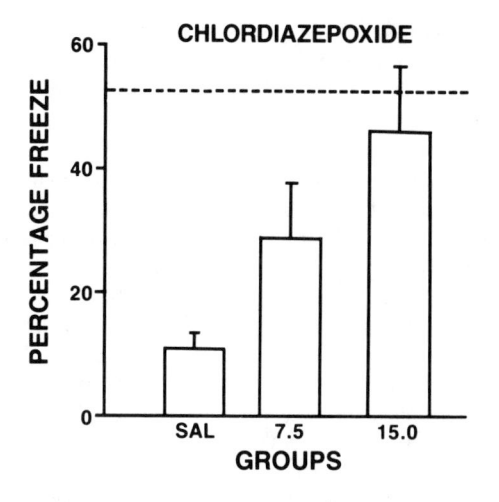

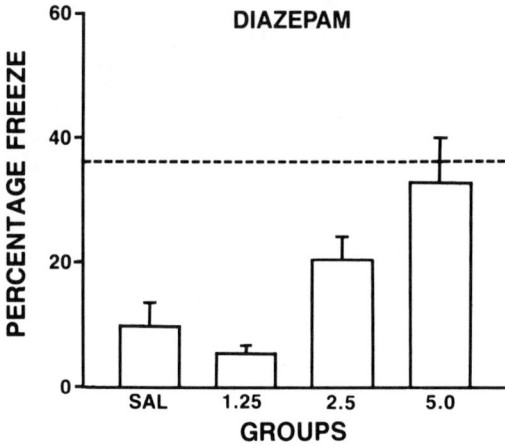

Figure 21.4. Fear during an undrugged test after extinction had been conducted in contexts provided by chlordiazepoxide (librium) or diazepam (valium). Group labels indicate drug dosage administered during extinction (mg/kg); SAL equals vehicle control. The measure of fear is percentage of behavior samples scored by a "blind" observer as freezing. The dashed line indicates freezing of the control group (SAL) at the outset of extinction. Vertical bars indicate standard errors of the mean. From "State-Dependent Fear Extinction with Two Benzodiazepine Tranquilizers" by M. E. Bouton, F. A. Kenney, and C. Rosengard, 1990, *Behavioral Neuroscience, 104,* 44–55. Copyright 1990 by the American Psychological Association. Reprinted by permission.

cause the group shocked but extinguished with saline had received similar drug exposure prior to testing, freezing during testing is not due to some unconditional carry over effect of the drug. Further, mere exposure to the chamber while under the influence of the drug (the no-shock but "extinguished" with drug group) was not sufficient to produce freezing during the final test. The strong fear evident during the test thus depends on the specific combination of drug and fear extinction. Fear extinction did not transfer from the drug context.

Results of another experiment (Experiment 3) suggested that familiarity with the drug does not necessarily reduce the drug's effect on extinction: Rats that received 12 initial exposures to chlordiazepoxide still showed no evidence of extinction transferring outside the drug state. A final study (Experiment 4) confirmed that chlordiazepoxide served as an extinction context rather than disrupting the learning or consolidation of extinction. Rats that had previously had the drug combined with extinction showed less fear in a final

extinction in conjunction with the drug; as before, freezing in the absence of the drug was at a level comparable to that of nondrugged controls at the beginning of extinction (dotted line). Freezing in the three remaining groups was at baseline levels. Be-

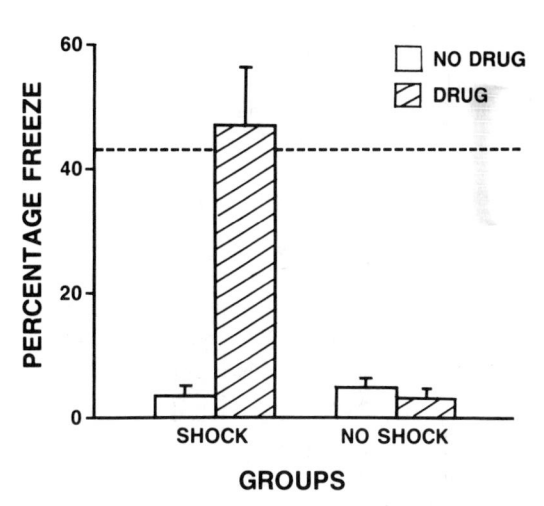

Figure 21.5. Freezing (fear) during a final undrugged test after extinction in the experiment described in the text. "Drug" and "No Drug" refer to the chlordiazepoxide treatment during extinction sessions; "Shock" and "No Shock" refer to the original conditioning treatment. The dashed line represents freezing in the Shock-No Drug group at the outset of extinction. Vertical bars indicate standard errors of the mean. From "State-Dependent Fear Extinction with Two Benzodiazepine Tranquilizers" by M. E. Bouton, F. A. Kenney, and C. Rosengard, 1990, *Behavioral Neuroscience, 104,* 44–55. Copyright 1990 by the American Psychological Association. Reprinted by permission.

drug test than did a group that had never received the drug with extinction (Figure 21–6). Thus, the animals used the drug as a contextual cue for extinction performance.

One interesting feature of the results shown in Figure 21–6 is that the drug did not reduce fear significantly unless it had been previously associated with extinction. Although chlordiazepoxide has a reputation as an anxiolytic, such a failure to reduce fear during a test that followed undrugged conditioning is not uncommon in the animal literature (Fanselow & Helmstetter, 1988; Scobie & Garske, 1970; Stein & Berger, 1969). It may fortuitously suggest that the drug's interference with extinction is not necessarily linked to its suppression of fear during extinction. Because it did not reduce fear demonstrably, the drug's "stimulus" properties, rather than its anxiolytic properties, made it reduce the overall effectiveness of the extinction experience. On the whole, the results provide reasonable support for the view that fear extinction can be specific to a context provided by benzodiazepine tranquilizers.

Our results with rats complement data on humans that suggest that, even in doses that are used clinically, information learned under the influence of a benzodiazepine can be specific to the drug state (e.g., Jensen & Poulsen, 1982). The data obviously recommend caution in combining drugs with exposure therapy. There is also an implication for drug dependence in individuals who ingest drugs to escape anxiety: If some extinction of anxiety ordinarily occurs during natural exposure to the evoking stimulus, state-dependent extinction would "insulate" the person from the beneficial effects of that extinction. Off the drug, the individual would always find his or her anxiety intact; through state-dependent extinction, the basis for drug ingestion could be preserved indefinitely. Much has been written about the implications of state-dependent retention (e.g., see Ho, Richards, & Chute, 1978). For present purposes, however, I would emphasize that the phenomenon expands the contextual analysis of extinction. Whether the context is exteroceptive or interoceptive, extinction can be specific to the context in which it is conducted. Instead of truly unlearning fear in extinction, the subject behaves as if it "attributes" the current safety of the CS to whatever background cues have been correlated with extinction.

Emotional States and Stress

One of the most potent possible contexts that might stimulate relapse is the emotion or affective state that was featured in the original conditioning episode.

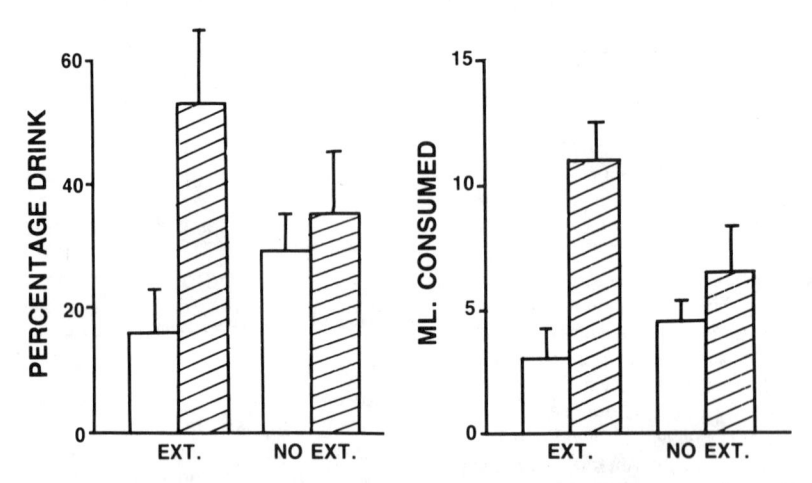

Figure 21.6. Fear during tests conducted with chlordiazepoxide (cross-hatched bars) and without chlordiazepoxide (open bars) in the experiment discussed in the text. The measure of fear is suppression of water drinking as indicated by direct observation of drinking (left) and volume of water consumed (right); in both cases, low scores indicate fear. Vertical bars indicate standard errors of the mean. Group "Ext" had previously received the drug combined with extinction whereas Group "No Ext" had received the drug without extinction. Consistent with a contextual analysis, the drug cued extinction performance in Group Ext. From "State-Dependent Fear Extinction With Two Benzodiazepine Tranquilizers" by M. E. Bouton, F. A. Kenney, and C. Rosengard, 1990, *Behavioral Neuroscience, 104,* 44–55. Copyright 1990 by the American Psychological Association. Reprinted by permission of the publisher.

According to a contextual analysis, if an emotion were a feature of conditioning, it could in principle act as a conditioning context. Thus, if an extinguished evoking stimulus were encountered anew in that emotional state, it could cause a renewal of fear. There are data consistent with a contextual role for emotions and stress. Physiological components of stress, such as the pituitary hormone adrenocorticotrophin (ACTH), are known to retrieve forgotten aversive experiences. For example, ACTH administered in animals just prior to testing can alleviate amnesia for fearful memories that is caused by CO_2 inhalation (Rigter, van Riezen, & de Wied, 1974), deep body cooling (Mactutus, Smith, & Riccio, 1980), and short-term retention deficits following avoidance learning (e.g., Klein, 1972). Riccio and Concannon (1981) have reviewed this literature from the perspective that ACTH provides a contextual stimulus whose presence during testing makes the conditions at retrieval similar to those at learning (see also Izquierdo, 1984, for a possible extension to epinephrine and β-endorphin). Other mechanisms through which stress and stress hormones might cause recovery of forgotten fear memories have been suggested, for example, by Jacobs and Nadel (1985).

ACTH can also cause a renewal-like effect after a brief extinction experience. Richardson, Riccio, and Devine (1984) found that administering the hormone prior to a final test caused recovery of an extinguished avoidance response. Results of a subsequent experiment (Ahlers & Richardson, 1985) suggest that ACTH worked because of its status as a contextual cue associated with conditioning. Dexamethasone, a synthetic glucocorticoid, was administered prior to avoidance training. Among other things, this substance suppresses ACTH release through the pituitary-adrenal negative feedback system. Dexamethasone did not appear to harm initial avoidance learning, but it did eliminate the ability of ACTH to cause renewal when it was introduced later after extinction. Thus, the renewal effect produced by ACTH may depend on its being released during original learning. In a preliminary way, the data suggest that physiological correlates of a traumatic experience may undo the effects of extinction by cueing the original aversive memory. An unresolved issue, however, is that unlike ACTH's reminder effect on simple amnesias, once ACTH is administered after extinction, its cueing effect appears to persist over periods of time longer than its attributes as a "context" should (Ahlers, Richardson, West, & Riccio, 1989; Richardson et al., 1984).

Recent research with humans has also examined the possibility that emotions or affective states can provide contextual retrieval cues (for reviews see Blaney, 1986; Bower, 1981, 1987). In one set of experiments, Bower, Monteiro, and Gilligan (1978) found that happy and sad moods induced by hypnosis in hypnotizable subjects could cause mood-dependent retrieval: Words learned in one mood were best retrieved in the same mood; a mood switch reduced recall. Interestingly, the phenomenon did not occur unless the study involved a design in which different lists were first associated with different mood states. Although the results were replicated in other laboratories with minor variations in procedure (e.g., Schare, Lisman, & Spear, 1984), they have since proven difficult to reproduce (e.g., Wetzler, 1985) even in the original laboratory (e.g., Bower & Mayer, 1985). The difficulty has recently led Bower (1987) to describe the effect as "a will-of-the-wisp that appears or not in different experiments in capricious ways that I do not understand." After a promising start, it thus appears that the retrieval effect of moods induced in the laboratory should be viewed with extreme caution.

It is worth asking, however, whether happy and sad moods in normal college students could ever resemble the kinds of stress and emotions that might precipitate a return of fear in the real world or in the animal laboratory. (One advantage of animal memory studies is that they often do involve nontrivial emotions and material [e.g., Hendersen, 1985].) In this respect, the most striking evidence of emotion-dependent memory in humans may be a study of hospitalized bipolar depressives (Weingartner, Miller, & Murphy, 1977). In this experiment, manic depressives first generated free associates from words and then attempted to recall them four days later; the procedure was repeated at four-day intervals over a long period of time. Because the subjects often went through swings in affect (rated and confirmed by blind observers), they often learned and remembered the material in different affective states. In general, recall was negatively correlated with the degree of mood change between learning and recall. Furthermore, subjects who happened to be tested with each of the four combinations of normal and manic moods produced the classic state-dependent retrieval pattern: Whether the encoding "context" was normal or manic, recall in the same context was better than recall in a different context. Although other affect-dependent cognitive processes might have contributed to the results (Blaney, 1986), this remarkable study begins to suggest that genuine affective states may indeed function as contextual retrieval cues under some conditions. It is not inappropriate to suggest that stress and emotion might cause a renewal of fear by retrieving a fear memory retained after therapy.

The Passage of Time

Our work with physical apparatuses suggests that extinction can be specific to its context (e.g., Bouton & Bolles, 1979a; Bouton & King, 1983). Casually speaking, the data are consistent with the view that extinction involves learning that "the CS is safe here." It is interesting to observe that the natural passage of time may itself provide a sequence of discriminable contexts (Bouton, 1988). If extinction is inherently conditional, as the contextual analysis suggests, then one might expect that extinction would be specific to the *temporal* extinction context; the subject might always learn some version of "the CS is safe *now*." If a temporal extinction context controls extinction performance, then renewed fear should occur when testing occurs in a different temporal context. This is easily demonstrated; if time elapses after extinction, an extinguished response spontaneously recovers (e.g., Pavlov, 1927). In effect, a contextual analysis of extinction provides a new way of viewing spontaneous recovery (cf. Estes, 1955).

Spontaneous recovery suggested to Pavlov that extinction involved inhibition of the original reflex. If inhibition is assumed to be more labile than excitation, then recovery of the extinguished reflex could occur over time. However, there is little evidence to support the idea that extinction depends on the development of inhibition, at least as it is defined today (but see Rescorla, 1979). For example, we have systematically tested the physical extinction context for inhibition with a number of tests; even though the context cues extinction performance, we have never uncovered evidence of inhibition (Bouton & King, 1983; Bouton & Swartzentruber, 1986, 1989). Still, it is worth noting that Pavlov's assumption that inhibition is more labile than excitation may indeed be correct: Fear inhibition controlled by true inhibitory stimuli is indeed forgotten relatively rapidly over time (Hendersen, 1978; Thomas, 1979). This fact itself has clinical implications. If conditioned fear inhibition is present, its relatively rapid dissipation would allow inhibited fear states to be revealed over time (see Hendersen, 1985; Mineka, 1985 for related discussions). The literature on animal learning and memory actually provides a number of mechanisms for the "spontaneous" occurrence of fears (see also Bouton, 1984; Rescorla, 1974).

The spontaneous recovery of extinguished fear has received surprisingly little systematic empirical analysis (see Rescorla & Cunningham, 1978, for an exception). However, in experiments involving multiple daily extinction sessions, a modest recovery is usually observed at the beginning of each day (e.g., see extinction trials 5, 9, and 13 in Figure 21–1). Between-session recovery in extinction may resemble the return of fear that is sometimes observed between sessions of exposure therapy (e.g., Grey, Sartory, & Rachman, 1979; Rachman & Lopatka, 1988). The contextual hypothesis suggests that such recovery may occur because the subject learns in therapy that the stimulus is safe "now." Spontaneous recovery effects are quite consistent with the ambiguity/retrieval view of extinction, and their point is the same as the reinstatement and renewal phenomena discussed earlier. The effects of an extinction procedure are not necessarily permanent. Spontaneous recovery is consistent with the perspective that extinction learning is conditional. All events are learned and remembered against the background of time.

Other Background Stimuli

In some of our current research, we have begun to extend the retrieval analysis of extinction to still other kinds of contextual cues. One of our experiments was designed to ask whether conditioning and extinction performances can be cued by recent presentations of the US, and by the strength of the test context's current association with the US. We used rats in a conditioning preparation in which a brief (10-s) tone was paired with a US consisting of the delivery of two standard food pellets (e.g., Bouton & Peck, 1989). The experiment involved two groups that received three initial "cycles" through conditioning and extinction. The groups' treatments were arranged to make extra food pellets, and the context conditioning they produce, a feature of either the conditioning or extinction phase. For one group, each of the conditioning sessions involved four spaced tone-food pairings plus 28 extra USs delivered during the intertrial intervals. Each of the extinction sessions involved four tones alone and no food. We called this group "Group Hi-Lo," because conditioning was run when the background was full of food (and "high") and extinction was run when the background value low. Group Lo-Hi, the second group, received the reverse treatment: These rats received conditioning sessions without extra pellets, but 28 extra USs were added to the intertrial intervals of each *extinction* session.

The remainder of the experiment examined the effects that context conditioning, and recent food pellets alone, have on responding to the tone in the two groups. If these stimuli control performance as contexts do, they might cue performance appropriate to the phase that featured them. Thus, a "high" background should cue conditioning performance in Group Hi-Lo, but might cue extinction performance in Group Lo-Hi. Similarly, a "low" background should cue extinction performance in Group Hi-Lo, but might cue conditioning performance in Group Lo-Hi. After several phases of conditioning and extinction, both groups received further training in two new physical contexts (boxes) that were different from the one in which the original phases had taken place. Over a series of sessions, each rat received food pellets in Context B and none in Context C. Once the rats had associated B with food but C with none, the tone CS (which had been extinguished most recently) was tested in both contexts. Every rat received the tone in both B and C with the sequence counterbalanced. No pellets were presented during these tests.

The results are shown at left in Figure 21–7. Group Hi-Lo showed more conditioned responding to the tone in food-associated Context B (+) than in the last extinction session (Ext) or in Context C (−). This is the familiar reinstatement effect: With the conditioning and extinction treatments given Group Hi-Lo, the rats once again responded more to an extinguished CS in a context associated with the US. However, for Group Lo-Hi the pattern was different: In these rats, extinguished responding was restored in *both* Contexts B (+) and C (−). Conditioned responding in the negative context is consistent with our prediction; the relative absence of food associations had been a feature of conditioning (not extinction) in this group. However, our idea that food associations in Context B might conversely cue extinction performance was not confirmed with these methods; food associations again appeared to reinstate conditioning performance in Group Lo-Hi despite their connection with extinction. One possibility is that responding was restored in both contexts because all testing occurred without pellets—for the rats in Group Lo-Hi, the presence of extra pellets could have been the most important cue for extinction. In effect, extinction performance could have been specific to the pellet "context."

The right-hand portion of Figure 21–7 illustrates the results of further tests that confirmed such a rule for the added pellets. In this final phase, the rats were returned to the original box in which conditioning and extinction had been conducted, and the tone was

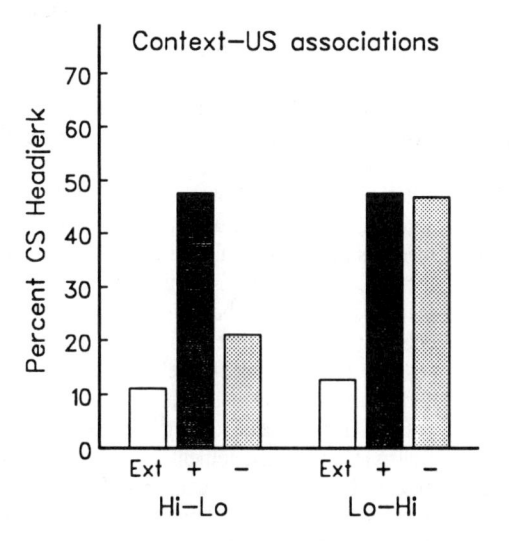

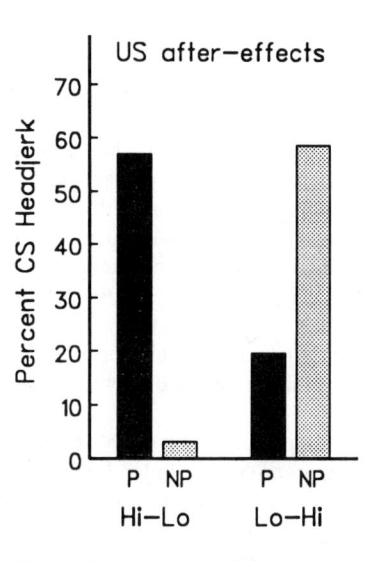

Figure 21.7. Conditioned responding to a tone during the tests described in the experiment discussed in the text. The measure of conditioning was "head jerking," a response of the rat to tones associated with food pellets (e.g., Bouton & Peck, 1989). At left, the tone was tested in contexts associated with the US ("plus") or no US ("minus"). "Ext" indicates performance during the last extinction session. At right, the tone was tested during sessions containing food pellet USs (P) or no food pellets (NP). Group Lo-Hi had previously had context associations and food pellets featured in extinction, whereas Group Hi-Lo had had them featured in conditioning.

tested in sessions containing free food pellets (P) or no pellets at all (NP). (The tone itself was never paired with a pellet.) As before, every rat was tested in both conditions with the sequence counterbalanced. The pellet "context" cued conditioned behavior in Group Hi-Lo. But quite strikingly, the pellet context instead cued extinction behavior in Group Lo-Hi. USs themselves can function to cue responding corresponding to the phase that featured them. Unconditioned stimuli, or their "aftereffects," can provide retrieval contexts.

The results of this experiment are interesting though preliminary. For present purposes, I would emphasize that they begin to suggest that still other types of background stimuli can function as contexts retrieving conditioning performance. When USs are a salient feature of conditioning (Group Hi-Lo), the presence of either USs or their associations to the context can restore extinguished responding. When USs are instead a feature of extinction (Group Lo-Hi), the pattern changes: The *absence* of the US, and perhaps the absence of contextual associations, can restore extinguished responding. The response evoked by an extinguished stimulus is unstable and strongly controlled by a variety of contextual cues.

Summary

A broad range of stimuli and/or events may function as cues controlling extinction and conditioning performance. Although our review has been selective, there is evidence that drugs, emotional states, the passage of time, and other stimuli occurring in the background during conditioning and extinction can assume control over conditioning and extinction performance. Thus, the effects we have observed with our physical "apparatus contexts" may occur with a range of contextual stimuli. It may thus be appropriate to treat *any* background cue that is correlated with aversive conditioning or its extinction as a potential cause for retrieval and recovery of performance appropriate to those experiences.

Although the data clearly favor a broad perspective, some caveats are probably in order. Like many effects in behavioral science, context effects in learning and remembering are rarely complete or all-or-none. The effects of physical context, drugs, and mood states in humans may depend on a number of features of the experimental designs and specifics about the information that is to be retrieved (e.g., Bower, 1987; Eich, 1985; Weingartner, 1978). Note that the same is true for the effects of context in animal learning: Fear extinction is easier to disrupt by a context switch than is simple fear conditioning (e.g., Bouton & King, 1983). Our results consistently suggest that fear of an extinguished CS is especially sensitive to context. That sensitivity suggests that it may be worth bearing the full range of possible contextual stimuli in mind when one considers the success of extinction or exposure therapy.

IMPLICATIONS AND CONCLUSIONS

Basic research on extinction emphasizes the behaviorally unstable nature of an extinguished CS. Animals retain some record of both conditioning and extinction even after prolonged extinction training. Extinction performance, and thus perhaps the success of an exposure therapy, is largely determined by which memory is currently activated or retrieved. If one takes an extinguished CS and creates conditions that retrieve a memory of conditioning, the subject will respond as if it is in conditioning. On the other hand, if conditions retrieve a memory of extinction, the subject will continue to respond as if the evoking stimulus is still in extinction. After extinction, performance depends on which of two available memories is retrieved. The "meaning" of the CS is mixed and ambiguous, and the performance it evokes depends fundamentally on the context provided by place, time, drug state, and other "background" cues.

The implications of this view have been under discussion all along. The most fundamental one is that extinction, and probably any other example of retroactive interference (e.g., Postman, Stark, & Fraser, 1968; Tulving & Psotka, 1971), does not erase, abolish, or destroy the original basis of fear. Learning theorists often distinguish between learning and performance; surely that distinction applies here. The fact that a fear stimulus is behaviorally silent after therapy does not guarantee that it will not cause fear in other settings. Even for the relatively mild fears conditioned and easily extinguished in the animal laboratory, the potential for fear persists long into extinction training. Renewal and reinstatement phenomena have been observed after many extinction trials (Bouton & Swartzentruber, 1989; Hendry, 1982; Reberg, 1972). The ambiguity approach takes such phenomena as central features of extinction.

If the original learning is at least partly retained, then why is fear ever lost? The contextual analysis suggests that the loss of fear occurs in extinction because the subject discriminates, at some level, occasions when the CS is safe from those when it is dangerous. Ambiguity and context are two sides of the same coin; extinction is a context discrimination process. The evidence suggests that the contexts of conditioning and extinction acquire the ability to set the occasion for performance appropriate to either phase (e.g., Bouton, 1990).

A major implication is that the therapist should be alert to contexts that might retrieve conditioning performance. Indeed, therapy might benefit from a focus on such contexts in addition to a focus on the evoking stimulus itself. There is evidence that reinstatement, the recurrence of fear that occurs in a context that is directly associated with the US, can be at least partly undone by extinction exposure to that context (Bouton & Bolles, 1979b, Experiment 2). Thus, reinstatement might be prevented or removed by separate extinction exposure to the problem context. However, the renewal effect that occurs with a context switch following extinction is *not* easily reduced by simple context exposure (e.g., Bouton & King, 1983, Experiment 3; Bouton & Peck, 1989, Experiment 2; see also Bouton & Swartzentruber, 1986, Experiment 3). The mechanism of contextual control may thus determine what treatment will be effective in dealing with it. If the context controls through its direct associations with the US (as in reinstatement), simple exposure to the context may help. But if the context controls by setting the occasion for the meaning of the CS ("The CS is dangerous in Context A" rather than "Context A is dangerous"), other procedures may be more effective. Rescorla (1986) found that an occasion setter's ability to excite responding to a CS was reduced only by extinguishing a separate CS together with it. This kind of result needs to be explored and analyzed more fully. The point is that the therapist may wish to attend to and perhaps "treat" potential relapse contexts, but should be aware that simple exposure to the context alone may not be good enough.

Another direct implication, of course, is that the therapist should pay attention to cues that can potentially signal extinction. What stimuli can the client "attribute" the current safety of the evoking stimulus to during therapy? Can they be made irrelevant? Some evidence with human subjects suggests that learning information in different contexts can improve transfer to still other contexts (Smith, 1982). If such research applies, one might wish to vary the stimuli in the background during exposure. Other evidence suggests that instructing a subject to recall the original training context can enhance memory in a different context (Smith, 1979). Thus, instructions to remember the therapy context might be helpful in reducing fear when it occurs elsewhere. Evidence of drug state-dependent extinction in turn suggests that the therapist might wish to avoid the use of drugs. Where they cannot be avoided, therapy could be conducted with increasingly smaller doses (cf. Sherman, 1967). Finally, in vivo therapy in the problem context should of course be especially effective. Because the loss of fear is inherently a discrimination problem, the therapist should take care to ensure generalization outside the therapy context.

In vivo techniques may be especially effective because the client can learn extinction in a context like that in which the evoking stimulus will be encountered outside of therapy. But note that renewed and reinstated fear might still occur in principle if the CS is encountered in a new way, or if the exposure context itself becomes dangerous again. Interestingly, preliminary data suggest that a less context-specific extinction may be achieved if extinction can be run in the original *conditioning* context (Bouton & King, 1983, Experiment 4). When fear is both conditioned and extinguished in Context A, there is relatively little renewal when the CS is switched and tested in Context B. Richardson, Riccio, and Ress (1988) have reported a similar effect with hormonal contexts. Extinction of a passive avoidance response in combination with ACTH or epinephrine (interoceptive contexts that were presumably part of the original conditioning experience) were especially effective in preventing renewed fear. In the long run, exposure therapy that recreates the original context (if one can be identified) might be more effective than others at preventing renewed fear. Note, however, that even these conditions may not eliminate relapse. Fear extinguished in the original conditioning context is still susceptible to reinstatement when the CS is tested in a dangerous context (e.g., Bouton, 1984; Rescorla & Heth, 1975). It seems safe to assume that no treatment guarantees the unlearning of fear.

The effectiveness of conducting extinction in the conditioning context seems consistent with the view that exposure therapy works best when it provokes maximal fear (e.g., Foa & Kozak, 1986; Rachman, 1980). However, our data confirm that the level of fear per se during therapy may not be the core issue. Although extinction in the conditioning context may be less susceptible to renewal than extinction in a different context, the two procedures do not generate different amounts of fear during extinction (Bouton & King, 1983; Bouton & Swartzentruber, 1986); recall that conditioned fear, unlike fear extinction, generalizes well across contexts (see Figure 21-2). In effect, the amount of fear evoked in extinction is not necessarily an accurate predictor of renewal or relapse. The point is the same as the one I have been developing all along. One should be careful to distinguish what the client does in extinction from what he or she actually learns.

One goal of this chapter has been to illustrate that basic research on conditioning and extinction may still be relevant to the therapeutic enterprise. Learning theory has undergone significant changes since the days when exposure therapies were first introduced, and it continues to provide a fruitful framework for understanding fear and the therapy process. The basic conditioning and extinction paradigms are still analyzed intensively because they are surprisingly rich, and because they are still assumed to be linked to issues outside of the laboratory. As learning theory and behavior therapy continue to change, they should continue to complement one another in new ways.

REFERENCES

Ahlers, S. T., & Richardson, R. (1985). Administration of dexamethasone prior to training blocks ACTH-induced recovery of an extinguished avoidance response. *Behavioral Neuroscience, 99,* 760-764.

Ahlers, S. T., Richardson, R., West, C., & Riccio, D. C. (1989). ACTH produces long-lasting recovery following partial extinction of an active avoidance response. *Behavioral and Neural Biology, 51,* 102-107.

Barlow, D. H. (1988). *Anxiety and its disorders. The nature and treatment of anxiety and panic.* New York: Guilford Press.

Barry, H., Etheredge, E. E., & Miller, N. E. (1965). Counterconditioning and extinction of fear fail to transfer from amobarbital to nondrug state. *Psychopharmacologia (Berl.), 8,* 150-156.

Blaney, P. H. (1986). Affect and memory: A review. *Psychological Bulletin, 99,* 229-246.

Bindra, D., Nyman, K., & Wise, J. (1965). Barbiturate-induced dissociation of acquisition and extinction. Role of movement-initiating processes. *Journal of Comparative and Physiological Psychology, 60,* 223-228.

Blanchard, R. J., & Blanchard, D. C. (1969). Crouching as an index of fear. *Journal of Comparative and Physiological Psychology, 67,* 370-375.

Bolles, R. C., & Fanselow, M. S. (1980). A perceptual-defensive-recuperative model of fear and pain. *Behavioral and Brain Sciences, 3,* 291-323.

Bouton, M. E. (1984). Differential control by context in the inflation and reinstatement paradigms. *Journal of Experimental Psychology: Animal Behavior Processes, 10,* 56-74.

Bouton, M. E. (1986). Slow reacquisition following the extinction of conditioned suppression. *Learning and Motivation, 17,* 1-15.

Bouton, M. E. (1988). Context and ambiguity in the extinction of emotional learning. Implications for exposure therapy. *Behaviour Research and Therapy, 26,* 137-149.

Bouton, M. E. (1990). Context and retrieval in extinction and in other examples of interference in simple associative learning. In L. W. Dachowski & C. F. Flaherty (Eds.), *Current topics in animal learning: Brain, emotion, and cognition.* Hillsdale, NJ: Lawrence Erlbaum Associates.

Bouton, M. E., & Bolles, R. C. (1979a). Contextual control of the extinction of conditioned fear. *Learning and Motivation, 10,* 445-466.

Bouton, M. E., & Bolles, R. C. (1979b). Role of conditioned contextual stimuli in reinstatement of extinguished fear. *Journal of Experimental Psychology: Animal Behavior Processes, 5,* 368-378.

Bouton, M. E., & Bolles, R. C. (1980). Conditioned fear assessed by freezing and by the suppression of three different baselines. *Animal Learning & Behavior, 8,* 429-434.

Bouton, M. E., & Bolles, R. C. (1985). Contexts, event-memories, and extinction. In P. D. Balsam & A. Tomie (Eds.), *Context and learning* (pp. 133-166). Hillsdale, NJ: Lawrence Erlbaum Associates.

Bouton, M. E., Kenney, F. A., & Rosengard, C. (1990). State-dependent fear extinction with two benzodiazepine tranquilizers. *Behavioral Neuroscience, 104,* 44-55.

Bouton, M. E., & King, D. A. (1983). Contextual control of the extinction of conditioned fear: Tests for the associative value of the context. *Journal of Experimental Psychology: Animal Behavior Processes, 9,* 248-265.

Bouton, M. E., & King, D. A. (1986). Effect of context on performance to conditioned stimuli with mixed histories of reinforcement and nonreinforcement. *Journal of Experimental Psychology: Animal Behavior Processes, 12,* 4-15.

Bouton, M. E., & Peck, C. D. (1989). Context effects on conditioning, extinction, and reinstatement in an appetitive conditioning preparation. *Animal Learning & Behavior, 17,* 188-198.

Bouton, M. E., & Swartzentruber, D. (1986). Analysis of the associative and occasion-setting properties of contexts participating in a Pavlovian discrimination. *Journal of Experimental Psychology: Animal Behavior Processes, 12,* 333-350.

Bouton, M. E., & Swartzentruber, D. (1989). Slow reacquisition following extinction. Context, encoding, and retrieval mechanisms. *Journal of Experimental Psychology: Animal Behavior Processes, 15,* 43-53.

Bower, G. H. (1981). Mood and memory. *American Psychologist, 36,* 129-148.

Bower, G. H. (1987). Commentary on mood and memory. *Behaviour Research and Therapy, 25,* 443-455.

Bower, G. H., & Mayer, J. D. (1985). Failure to replicate mood-dependent retrieval. *Bulletin of the Psychonomic Society, 23,* 39–42.

Bower, G. H., Monteiro, K. P., & Gilligan, S. G. (1978). Emotional mood as a context for learning and recall. *Journal of Verbal Learning and Verbal Behavior, 17,* 573–585.

Bullock, D. H., & Smith, W. C. (1953). An effect of repeated conditioning-extinction upon operant strength. *Journal of Experimental Psychology, 46,* 349–352.

Cunningham, C. L. (1979). Alcohol as a cue for extinction: State dependency produced by conditioned inhibition. *Animal Learning & Behavior, 7,* 45–52.

Delamater, A. R., & Treit, D. (1988). Chlordiazepoxide attenuates shock-based and enhances LiCl-based fluid aversions. *Learning and Motivation, 19,* 221–238.

Eich, E. (1985). Context, memory, and integrated item/context imagery. *Journal of Experimental Psychology: Learning, Memory, and Cognition, 11,* 764–770.

Estes, W. K. (1955). Statistical theory of spontaneous recovery and regression. *Psychological Review, 62,* 145–154.

Fanselow, M. S. (1980). Conditional and unconditional components of post-shock freezing. *Pavlovian Journal of Biological Science, 15,* 177–182.

Fanselow, M. S., & Helmstetter, F. J. (1988). Conditional analgesia, defensive freezing, and benzodiazepines. *Behavioral Neuroscience, 102,* 233–243.

Foa, E. B., & Kozak, M. J. (1986). Emotional processing for fear: Exposure to corrective information. *Psychological Bulletin, 99,* 20–35.

Frey, P. W., & Butler, C. S. (1977). Extinction after aversive conditioning: An associative or nonassociative process? *Learning and Motivation, 8,* 1–17.

Goldman, M. S. (1977). Effect of chlordiazepoxide administered early in extinction on subsequent extinction of a conditioned emotional response in rats: Implications for human clinical use. *Psychological Reports, 40,* 783–786.

Gorman, J. E., Dyak, J. D., & Reid, L. D. (1979). Methods of deconditioning persisting avoidance: Diazepam as an adjunct to response prevention. *Bulletin of the Psychonomic Society, 14,* 46–48.

Greenspoon, J., & Ranyard, R. (1957). Stimulus conditions and retroactive inhibition. *Journal of Experimental Psychology, 53,* 55–59.

Grey, S., Sartory, G., & Rachman, S. (1979). Synchronous and desynchronous changes during fear reduction. *Behaviour Research and Therapy, 17,* 137–147.

Hanford, P. V., Mulvaney, D. E., & Kelfer, D. A. (1980). The effect of novel environments on CS extinction in a conditioned suppression paradigm. *Bulletin of the Psychonomic Society, 16,* 341–344.

Hendersen, R. W. (1978). Forgetting of conditioned fear inhibition. *Learning and Motivation, 9,* 16–30.

Hendersen, R. W. (1985). Fearful memories. The motivational significance of forgetting. In F. R. Brush & J. B. Overmier (Eds.), *Affect, conditioning, and cognition: Essays on the determinants of behavior* (pp. 43–54). Hillsdale, NJ: Lawrence Erlbaum Associates.

Hendry, J. S. (1982). Summation of undetected excitation following extinction of the CER. *Animal Learning & Behavior, 10,* 476–482.

Ho, B. T., Richards, D. W. III, & Chute, D. L. (1978). *Drug discrimination and state dependent learning.* New York: Academic Press.

Hoehler, F. K., Kirschenbaum, D. S., & Leonard, D. W. (1973). The effects of overtraining and successive extinctions upon nictitating membrane conditioning in the rabbit. *Learning and Motivation, 4,* 91–101.

Holland, P. C. (1983). "Occasion-setting" in conditional discriminations. In M. L. Commons, R. J. Hernstein, & A. R. Wagner (Eds.), *Quantitative analyses of behavior: Discrimination processes (Vol. 4)* (pp. 183–206). New York: Ballinger.

Holland, P. C. (1984). Differential effects of reinforcement of an inhibitory feature after serial and simultaneous feature negative discrimination training. *Journal of Experimental Psychology: Animal Behavior Processes, 10,* 461–475.

Holland, P. C. (1985). The nature of conditioned inhibition in serial and simultaneous feature negative discriminations. In R. R. Miller & N. E. Spear (Eds.), *Information processing in animals: Conditioned inhibition* (pp. 267–297). Hillsdale, NJ: Lawrence Erlbaum Associates.

Hollis, K. L. (1982). Pavlovian conditioning of signal-centered action patterns and autonomic behavior: A biological analysis of function. *Advances in the Study of Behavior, 12,* 1–64.

Izquierdo, I. (1984). Endogenous state dependency: Memory depends on the relation between the neurohumoral and hormonal states present after training and at the time of testing. In G. Lynch, J. L. McGaugh, & N. M. Weinberger (Eds.), *Neurobiology of learning and memory* (pp. 333–350). New York: Guilford Press.

Jacobs, W. J., & Nadel, L. (1985). Stress-induced recovery of fears and phobias. *Psychological Review, 92,* 512–531.

Jensen, H. H., & Poulsen, J. C. (1982). Amnesic effects of diazepam: "Drug dependence" explained by state-dependent learning. *Scandinavian Journal of Psychology, 23,* 107–111.

Kamano, D. K. (1972). Using drugs to modify the effect of response prevention on avoidance extinction. *Behaviour Research and Therapy, 10,* 367–370.

Kaye, H., Preston, G., Szabo, L., Druiff, H., & Mackintosh, N. J. (1987). Context specificity of conditioning and latent inhibition: Evidence for a dissociation of latent inhibition and associative interference. *Quarterly Journal of Experimental Psychology, 39B,* 127–145.

Klein, S. B. (1972). Adrenal-pituitary influence in reactivation of avoidance-learning memory in the rat after intermediate intervals. *Journal of Comparative and Physiological Psychology, 79,* 341–359.

Konorski, J., & Szwejkowska, G. (1952). Chronic extinction and restoration of conditioned reflexes IV. The dependence of the course of extinction and restoration of conditioned reflexes on the "history" of the conditioned stimulus (the principle of the primacy of the training). *Acta Biologiae Experimentalis, 16,* 95–113.

Lovibond, P. F., Preston, G. C., & Mackintosh, N. J. (1984). Context specificity of conditioning, extinction, and latent inhibition. *Journal of Experimental Psychology. Animal Behavior Processes, 10,* 360–375.

Mactutus, C. F., Smith, R. L., & Riccio, D. C. (1980). Extending the duration of ACTH-induced memory reactivation in an amnesic paradigm. *Physiology & Behavior, 24,* 541–546.

Marks, I. M. (1978). Behavioral psychotherapy of adult neurosis. In S. L. Garfield & A. E. Bergin (Eds.), *Handbook of psychotherapy and behavior change* (2nd ed., pp. 493–589). New York: John Wiley & Sons.

Marks, I. M., Viswanathan, R., Lipsedge, M. S., & Garner, R. (1972). Enhanced relief of phobias by flooding during waning diazepam effect. *British Journal of Psychiatry, 121,* 493–505.

Mineka, S. (1985). Animal models of anxiety-based disorders: Their usefulness and limitations. In A. H. Tuma & J. Maser (Eds.), *Anxiety and the anxiety disorders* (pp. 199–244). Hillsdale, NJ: Lawrence Erlbaum Associates.

Overton, D. A. (1966). State-dependent learning produced by depressant and atropine-like drugs. *Psychopharmacologia (Berl)., 10,* 6–31.

Overton, D. A. (1978). Major theories of state dependent learning. In B. T. Ho, D. W. Richards, & D. L. Chute (Eds.), *Drug discrimination and state dependent learning* (pp. 283–318). New York: Academic Press.

Overton, D. A. (1985). Contextual stimulus effects of drugs and internal states. In P. D. Balsam & A. Tomie (Eds.), *Context and learning* (pp. 357–384). Hillsdale, NJ: Lawrence Erlbaum Associates.

Pavlov, I. P. (1927). *Conditioned reflexes.* London: Oxford University Press.

Pearce, J. M., & Hall, G. (1980). A model for Pavlovian learning: Variations in the effectiveness of conditioned but not of unconditioned stimuli. *Psychological Review, 87,* 532–552.

Postman, L., Stark, K., & Fraser, J. (1968). Temporal changes in interference. *Journal of Verbal Learning and Verbal Behavior, 7,* 672–694.

Rachman, S. (1980). Emotional processing. *Behaviour Research and Therapy, 18,* 51–60.

Rachman, S., & Lopatka, C. (1988). Return of fear. Underlearning and overlearning. *Behaviour Research and Therapy, 26,* 99–104.

Reberg, D. (1972). Compound tests for excitation in early acquisition and after prolonged extinction of conditioned suppression. *Learning and Motivation, 3,* 246–258.

Reid, R. L. (1958). The role of the reinforcer as a stimulus. *British Journal of Psychology, 49,* 202–209.

Rescorla, R. A. (1974). Effect of inflation of the unconditioned stimulus value following conditioning. *Journal of Comparative and Physiological Psychology, 86,* 101–106.

Rescorla, R. A. (1979). Conditioned inhibition and extinction. In A. Dickinson & R. A. Boakes (Eds.), *Mechanisms of learning and motivation: A memorial volume to Jerzy Konorski* (pp. 83–110). Hillsdale, NJ: Lawrence Erlbaum Associates.

Rescorla, R. A. (1985). Conditioned inhibition and facilitation. In R. R. Miller & N. E. Spear (Eds.), *Information processing in animals: Conditioned inhibition* (pp. 299–326). Hillsdale, NJ: Lawrence Erlbaum Associates.

Rescorla, R. A. (1986). Extinction of facilitation. *Journal of Experimental Psychology: Animal Behavior Processes, 12,* 16–24.

Rescorla, R. A. (1987). Pavlovian conditioning: It's not what you think it is. *American Psychologist, 42,* 151–160.

Rescorla, R. A., & Cunningham, C. L. (1978). Recovery of the US representation over time during extinction. *Learning and Motivation, 9,* 373–391.

Rescorla, R. A., & Heth, C. D. (1975). Reinstatement of fear to an extinguished conditioned stimulus. *Journal of Experimental Psychology: Animal Behavior Processes, 1,* 88–96.

Rescorla, R. A., & Wagner, A. R. (1972). A theory of Pavlovian conditioning: Variations in the effectiveness of reinforcement and nonreinforcement. In A. H. Black & W. F. Prokasy (Eds.), *Classical conditioning II. Current research and theory* (pp. 64–99). New York: Appleton-Century-Crofts.

Riccio, D. C., & Concannon, J. T. (1981). ACTH and the reminder phenomena. In J. Martinez, R. A. Jensen, R. B. Messing, H. Rigter, & J. L. McGaugh (Eds.), *Endogenous peptides and learning and memory processes* (pp. 117–142). New York: Academic Press.

Richards, R. W., & Sargent, D. M. (1983). The order of presentation of conditioned stimuli during extinction. *Animal Learning & Behavior, 11,* 229–236.

Richardson, R., Riccio, D. C., & Devine, L. (1984). ACTH-induced recovery of extinguished avoidance responding. *Physiological Psychology, 12,* 184–192.

Richardson, R., Riccio, D. C., & Ress, J. (1988). Extinction of avoidance through response prevention: Enhancement by administration of epinephrine or ACTH. *Behaviour Research and Therapy, 26,* 23–32.

Rigter, H., van Riezen, H., & de Wied, D. (1974). The effects of ACTH- and Vasopressin-analogues on CO_2-induced retrograde amnesia in rats. *Physiology and Behavior, 13,* 381–388.

Sartory, G. (1983). Benzodiazepines and behavioural treatment of phobic anxiety. *Behavioural Psychotherapy, 11,* 204–217.

Schare, M. L., Lisman, S. A., & Spear, N. E. (1984). The effects of mood variation on state-dependent retention. *Cognitive Therapy and Research, 8,* 387–408.

Scobie, S. R., & Garske, G. (1970). Chlordiazepoxide and conditioned suppression. *Psychopharmacologia (Berl.), 16*, 272–280.

Sherman, A. R. (1967). Therapy of maladaptive fear-motivated behavior in the rat by the systematic gradual withdrawal of a fear-reducing drug. *Behaviour Research and Therapy, 5*, 121–129.

Smith, M., & Gormezano, I. (1965). Effects of alternating classical conditioning and extinction sessions on the conditioned nictitating membrane response of the rabbit. *Psychonomic Science, 3*, 91–92.

Smith, S. M. (1979). Remembering in and out of context. *Journal of Experimental Psychology: Human Learning and Memory, 5*, 460–471.

Smith, S. M. (1982). Enhancement of recall using multiple environmental contexts during learning. *Memory & Cognition, 10*, 405–412.

Smith, S. M., Glenberg, A., & Bjork, R. A. (1978). Environmental context and human memory. *Memory & Cognition, 6*, 342–353.

Spear, N. E. (1976). Retrieval of memories: A psychobiological approach. In W. K. Estes (Ed.), *Handbook of learning and cognitive processes: Vol 4. Attention and memory* (pp. 17–90). Hillsdale, NJ: Lawrence Erlbaum Associates.

Spear, N. E. (1978). *The processing of memories. Forgetting and retention*. Hillsdale, NJ: Lawrence Erlbaum Associates.

Spear, N. E., Smith, G. J., Bryan, R., Gordon, W., Timmons, R., & Chiszar, D. (1980). Contextual influences on the interaction between conflicting memories in the rat. *Animal Learning & Behavior, 8*, 273–281.

Stein, L., & Berger, B. D. (1969). Paradoxical fear-increasing effects of tranquilizers: Evidence of repression of memory in the rat. *Science, 166*, 253–256.

Taub, J., Taylor, P., Smith, M., Kelley, K., Becker, B., & Reid, L. (1977). Methods of deconditioning persisting avoidance: Drugs as adjuncts to response prevention. *Psychological Psychology, 5*, 67–72.

Thomas, D. A. (1979). Retention of conditioned inhibition in a bar-press suppression paradigm. *Learning and Motivation, 10*, 161–177.

Timberlake, W. (1983). The functional organization of appetitive behavior: Behavior systems and learning. In M. D. Zeiler & P. Harzem (Eds.), *Advances in analysis of behavior: Vol. 3. Biological factors in learning* (pp. 177–221). Chichester, England: John Wiley & Sons.

Tulving, E., & Psotka, J. (1971). Retroactive inhibition in free-recall: Inaccessibility of information available in the memory store. *Journal of Experimental Psychology, 87*, 1–8.

Wagner, A. R. (1978). Expectancies and the priming of STM. In S. H. Hulse, H. Fowler, & W. K. Honig (Eds.), *Cognitive processes in animal behavior*. Hillsdale, NJ: Lawrence Erlbaum Associates.

Wagner, A. R. (1981). SOP. A model of automatic memory processing in animal behavior. In N. E. Spear & R. R. Miller (Eds.), *Information processing in animals. Memory mechanisms* (pp. 5–47). Hillsdale, NJ: Lawrence Erlbaum Associates.

Weingartner, H. (1978). Human state dependent learning. In B. T. Ho, D. W. Richards III, & D. L. Chute (Eds.), *Drug discrimination and state dependent learning* (pp. 361–382). New York: Academic Press.

Weingartner, H., Miller, H., & Murphy, D. L. (1977). Mood-state-dependent retrieval of verbal associations. *Journal of Abnormal Psychology, 86*, 276–284.

Wetzler, S. (1985). Mood state-dependent retrieval. A failure to replicate. *Psychological Reports, 56*, 759–765.

PART VI
COMMUNITY PSYCHOLOGY AND PREVENTION

CHAPTER 22

INCORPORATING THE ECOLOGICAL PARADIGM INTO BEHAVIORAL PREVENTIVE INTERVENTIONS

Nancy S. Burgoyne
Leonard A. Jason

In the introduction to this text, Martin suggested that the time is ripe for behavior therapy to expand its theoretical and empirical base. The goal of this book is to prompt and guide that expansion. The question of how the field of behavior therapy could most profitably expand should not, however, be purely a question about which conceptual and methodological direction(s) to take. Another crucial, and explicitly orienting question for the field to consider is how the service delivery strategy(s) behavior therapists utilize have influenced the field's development. In both applied research and treatment activities, behavior therapists have primarily targeted populations having manifest disorders and relied on one-to-one or small group intervention strategies (Glenwick & Jason, 1984). In the present chapter we propose that operating predominately within this system restricts behavior therapy's current influence and potential development, and that an alternative, specifically preventive, service delivery strategy offers the field unique options and opportunities to increase its impact, both in terms of scale and social significance.

In this chapter we will first present the compelling rationales for human service delivery professionals, regardless of orientation, to develop a preventive service delivery strategy. Although prevention offers behavior therapy an attractive and socially relevent arena within which to apply it's methods, it also poses substantive challenges. What appears to constrain the alliance between prevention and behavior therapy can best be managed, we propose, by incorporating certain tenets of the ecological paradigm into intervention and research designs. In order to demonstrate the relevance and feasibility of this proposal, we will, by example and description, clarify specifically how the ecological paradigm can enhance behavioral preventive work.

PREVENTION

This chapter advocates for behavior therapists to expand their purview to include what is a relatively new concept in psychology–prevention. Simply put, the goal of prevention in psychology is to reduce the incidence of (psychological) maladjustment. Implementing and demonstrating the efficacy of preventive programs is an exceedingly large and complex task. The rationale for undertaking this strategy is, however, sufficiently compelling to warrant a commitment to it.

The Gap Between Needs and Resources

The number of persons in the United States with serious mental health problems has been estimated at approximately 15%. This figure represents what Albee (1982a) has called "the hard core of the emotionally disturbed" (p. 1043), approximately 25–35 million Americans with overt, incapacitating symptomatology. Kiesler (1985), using somewhat broader criteria, estimated that 15%–35% of the population is in need of mental health services at any one time. In any given year the entire mental health delivery system is capable of providing service to approximately 7 million separate individuals, many of whom are not part of the "hard core" group. In fact, the traditional mental health delivery system actually services fewer than one in five of those with serious mental health problems, an alarmingly small proportion of those in need (Albee, 1982a).

The unmet need for mental health service clearly overwhelms the current mental health system (Felner, Jason, Moritsugu, & Farber, 1983). This is in spite of millions of dollars spent by the federal government to construct and staff community mental health centers in the 1960s and 1970s. The need for service is perhaps most dramatically demonstrated by figures concerning the mental health status of children in the United States. For example, 90% of 3.2 million children in the United States who evidence some major emotional problems receive no treatment (Alpert, 1985), 50% of 7 million children with identifiable learning problems do not receive any assistance (Zigler & Finn, 1982), and estimates of the incidence of childhood victimization range from 25–34% (Swift, 1987). Educated projections suggest that the trend toward increased need for mental health services for both children and adults will continue (Gesten & Jason, 1987).

Our present service delivery system, which targets individuals with manifest disorders and relies predominately on one-to-one or small group intervention strategies, is, and in the forseeable future will be, unable to meet the need for services. Indeed, the gap between mental health needs and resources has become too wide to ever bridge via rehabilitative services (Albee, 1982a). Albee (1982a; 1982b) advises mental health professionals to attend to the logic of the public health dictum that holds that no mass disorder afflicting humankind has ever been eliminated or brought under control by attempting to treat affected individuals.

Prevention in Psychology

Although interest in prevention as an alternative to treatment has a long history, prevention as a service delivery strategy within the mental health system and an established scholarly interest in psychology has evolved primarily over the course of the last 30 years. In the United States, interest in prevention was generated largely in the context of the events and overall Zeigeist of the 1960s. Under the sponsorship of the Joint Commission on Mental Health and Illness in the late 1950s and early 1960s, a number of studies of the distribution of mental health services, the magnitude of mental health problems, the adequacy of mental health resources, and the limitations of then utilized forms of mental health treatment provided the documentation that mental health resources were profoundly inadequate and inequitably distributed. The desire to bridge the gap between needs and resources, as discussed in the previous section, was not the only factor influencing mental health professionals to find alternative strategies for dealing with mental health problems. Concerns about the efficacy of traditional psychotherapy, an increasing tendency to view mental illness as a social problem with environmental underpinnings, and developments in psychiatry and public health (e.g., Caplan, 1964; Lindemann, 1944), which provided early conceptual frameworks for prevention, all contributed significantly to the convergence of thinking and sense of urgency for psychology to develop preventive mental health strategies (Felner et al., 1983).

The model of prevention adopted by psychology was taken largely from the field of public health and influenced by developments in psychiatric epidemiology. Public health practice is characterized by a population focus, that is, the health of entire populations is of concern. The level of analysis is (a) population rather than an individual(s'). The goal of public health practice is to discover means of promoting the well-being of populations while reducing the incidence of (a) disease. The emphasis is on preventing the onset, as opposed to finding a cure, for a disease (Heller, 1984).

In modern public health theories, disease is considered an end product of an interaction between a host, or the person(s) afflicted, a pathological agent(s), or the disease carrier, and the environment (Bloom,

1965). Thus, for public health professionals, effective prevention can occur via the modification of any of these three factors. Small pox, for example, could be prevented by strengthening the host (e.g., immunization); by removing the pathological agent (e.g., spraying infested areas with insecticide to reduce the number of disease-carrying mosquitos), or by modifying the environment (e.g., using window screens or netting to reduce the incidence of bites from disease-carrying insects) (Heller, 1984).

Within the public health model "prevention" is a broad term that includes three conceptually distinct levels: primary, secondary, and tertiary prevention (Goldston, 1977). Tertiary prevention is essentially the equivalent of traditional rehabilitative approaches. Interventions are directed at individuals with an established disorder with the aim of reducing or removing the effects of the disorder. Secondary prevention efforts are directed at individuals or groups determined at risk for, or showing early signs of disorder, but for whom maladaptive behaviors are not ingrained (Felner et. al., 1983). Primary prevention is less easily defined. Cowen's (1983) description, a "group or mass-targeted before-the-fact effort to promote competence or prevent psychological dysfunction in essentially well people" has been considered unreasonably restrictive to some (e.g., Joffee, 1982), yet effectively encapsulates the essential features of primary prevention, if not its entire scope. More simply, however, Felner and Aber (1983) have noted that the goals of primary prevention may be broadly subsumed under either (1) the reduction of new cases of disorders, or (2) the promotion of health-building competencies as protection against dysfunction.

Although the three levels of prevention can be distinguished descriptively, actual interventions tend to be more difficult to identify as absolutely one type of prevention and not another. Indeed, application of the public health model to mental health problems has not been a simple process at either the definitional or practical levels. It is, however, the goals of prevention that have been adapted from the public health model, and the paradigmatic shift this necessitates that provides a distinct challenge and opportunity for psychology in general, and behavior therapists specifically, to expand their field's influence and impact.

PREVENTION AND BEHAVIORISM

Prevention and behaviorism are, at several levels, natural companions. Indeed, a relationship between these fields already exists. Some of the most effective large scale preventive efforts to date have used a behavioral model (Gesten & Jason, 1987). Yet, the majority of preventive interventions have underutilized behavioral technology, and behavior therapy has not, for the most part, included preventive intervention strategies in the field's repertoire. A relationship between behavior therapy and prevention does have common epistemological and empirical ground upon which to build a relationship. Yet, whereas prevention offers behavior therapy sufficient ground for an alliance, and an attractive and interesting arena to apply it's methods, it also poses substantive challenges. For the relationship between behavior therapy and prevention to be most productive and potent, both what allies and what deters an effective interface must be addressed.

Where Behaviorism and Prevention Meet: An Emphasis on Person–Environment Interaction

Behaviorism and prevention share a meaningful alliance. Bogat and Jason (in press), in a critical examination of the historical and philosophical factors that link and separate behaviorism with community psychology, have identified the commonalities. The authors observed that both fields have rallied against the predominant theoretical perspective in 20th century North American psychology, which attributes causation to factors residing within an individual without regard for the role of the social, political, or environmental contexts in individuals' experience of distress. Citing early behaviorists, they observe that the field is well-known for stressing the importance of the context of behavior. Kantor (1958) protested that, "Despite the fact that psychological events always consist of fields, psychologists persist in locating their data in or at the organism" (p. 83). Likewise, Skinner (1971) spoke to the role of the environment in shaping and maintaining behavior, and the early work of applied behaviorists considered the sociological theory and the role of culture in determining behavior (Ullman & Krasner, 1969). Thus behaviorists helped legitimize the study of environments and person-environment interactions (Bogat & Jason, in press).

Prevention advocates express similar, although often more overtly political, discontent with psychoanalytic and medical model formulations of mental health problems. Albee (1982b) challenges the medical model:

To argue that there are a number of separate and discrete mental illnesses each with a separate but undiscovered cause obscures or blocks consideration of the possibility that most emotional disturbance are a result of dehumanization, powerlessness, and (various forms) of victimization ... (p. 1044).

An essential element, then, of both preventive and behavioral ideologies is that the environment exerts significant, if not direct, control over the behavior of individuals. A common value follows from this emphasis; that behavior is adaptive, it adjusts to contingencies that reward and punish it. Whereas behavior therapists are more inclined than preventionists to call behavior "maladaptive" if it is not situation appropriate, this is not equivalent to deeming behavior "deviant" or "pathological." Behavior therapists understand behavior to arise, logically, from the contingencies that shape and maintain it. All behavior, then, is at some level adaptive, albeit inappropriately applied or even asocial according to normal standards. In order to understand behavior, therefore, both behaviorists (e.g., Holland, 1978), and preventionists (e.g., Kelly, 1968) have suggested an investigator ought to analyze the context(s) in which it exists and not, or not exclusively, the individual who exhibits it.

Behaviorists, like preventionists, have always challenged the psychoanalytic and medical model formulations of the nature and etiology of disorder and their means for assessing it. But later in the field's history, behavior therapists, again like preventionists, also protested the rehabilitative strategy the medical system used and mental health professionals had adopted to serve the public. Both fields developed a voice during the 1960s that questioned the efficacy and efficiency of traditional psychoanalytic and client-centered therapy strategies. Specifically, behavior therapists questioned: the generalizability of treatment that did not occur in an individual's natural environment, the likelihood of effecting change in those who were severely and chronically distressed, and the potential for being more effective and cost efficient by treating (individuals) before their distress became severe and embedded (Krasner & Ullman, 1973). Influenced by the socio-political climate, behavior therapists and advocates of prevention in the 1960s and 1970s were asking many of the same questions. Behavior therapists and preventionists did not, however, arrive at all of the same answers.

Where Behavior Therapy and Prevention Depart: Divergent Levels of Analysis and Intervention

The majority of behavior therapists sought to combat the medicalized mental health system by providing more effective and expedient forms of therapy for certain types of problems (e.g., phobias and compulsions), by involving larger systems (e.g., the family, the school) to monitor and control the behavior and rewards of their clients, and by organizing institutional settings (e.g., psychiatric hospitals and mental retardation centers) to maximize socially adaptive behaviors in patients.

A smaller number of behavioral psychologists have applied their technology in community settings to nonclinical problems and issues. Behaviorists' involvement in the schools, for example, has been particularly noteworthy. The development of instructional models derived from both behavior analysis, such as Direct Instruction (Engelmann & Carnine, 1982), and cognitive-behavioral models, such as the various versions of "strategy training" (deBettencourt, 1987; Deshler & Schumaker, 1986; Lloyd, 1980) have been directed at the prevention of academic problems. Yet, whether conducted within the prevailing service delivery system or in alternative settings, behavioral psychologists have tended to direct their efforts toward those with manifest dysfunction, and target their interventions at the level of individual behavior.

The field of prevention has pursued an alternative service delivery system altogether. Given the goal of prevention, to avert mental health problems, intervention must occur prior to the onset of dysfunction. This goal has difficulty being realized through the existing mental health system where mental health professionals typically wait to provide service for those who arrive at their facilities. Prevention necessitates a proactive, competency-based stance, where professionals and paraprofessionals identify potential problems and attempt to amplify the existing resources of citizens and their settings in order to manage them. A preventive approach also expands the target of intervention from individuals and small groups to include as targets the environment(s) that influence them, for example, organizations, institutions, communities (Jason & Bogat, 1983).

Moving to a preventive service delivery strategy has not, however, been simply a matter of applying existing models and methods to larger, nonclinical populations (although this formula has been tried). Within psychology, prevention has sought to develop its own conceptual framework. This framework, although not explicitly formulated, has certain foundational values that have guided its development. Although different authors (e.g., Rappaport, 1977; Sarason, 1981) have emphasized different values, core concerns common among them include: valuing differences within and between groups (e.g., cultural diversity, sexual preference) and enabling groups to pursue self-defined goals; enhancing existing competencies of persons and settings; and developing and supporting organizational and environmental factors that influence behavior.

Implicit in these values is a frame of reference that emphasizes how the social and cultural context affect individual experience. Although behaviorism and prevention are allied in this emphasis, their attention to contextual variables varies considerably (Bogat & Jason, in press). Behaviorists usually focus their attention on setting variables that are directly and demonstrably associated with the target problem. Relevant setting factors for a behavioral intervention are those that can be manipulated to influence the rate of occurrence of the target behavior. Prevention theorists, similar to community psychology theorists, are more process oriented. This orientation leads them to seek to understand the past investigators' attempts to solve current problems, to ascertain different parties' interests and values concerning the problem, to identify ecological-structural problems that might eventually weaken intervention effects, and to uncover relational or interpersonal issues that might complicate the implementation and maintenance of potential solutions. Hence, what constitutes relevant setting factors for a preventive theorist is broad and inclusive.

The difference regarding what levels of context are relevant to target problems reflects a distinction that Bogat and Jason (in press) have discussed in these fields' basic visions of reality. Behaviorists, they note, believe that problems are solvable, that, in time, specific behavioral strategies will be discovered to address what currently appears unsolvable. By contrast, Bogat and Jason (in press) add, the field of prevention tends to be allied with community psychology's view that social problems are inherently paradoxical and therefore are unlikely to have one clear, permanent solution. A solution that is effective during one era, for example, may not be effective for another (Rappaport, 1981).

The differences between prevention and behavior therapy, then, are both pragmatic and paradigmatic. In actuality, the field's have different world views that have led them to divergent foci and problem-solving strategies. Some have suggested (e.g., Rappaport, 1977) that these differences, particularly at the conceptual level, make the marriage of behavioral technology and the goals of prevention untenable. Viewed from another angle, however, the differences between prevention and behavior therapy can easily be seen as complementary. Indeed, evidence from existing behavioral preventive interventions suggests that a relationship between prevention and behaviorism is undeniably possible and potent. An expanded relationship between these fields may, in fact, prove to be reciprocally informative.

Applying Behaviorism to Prevention: Opportunities and Challenges

Behaviorists who have adopted a preventive model have contributed significantly to the progress prevention can claim to have made to date, and in doing so have provided the most convincing argument for behaviorism and prevention to further their relationship. Although preventive ideologists have offered alternative strategies for extending mental health services and have identified neglected time and target points for intervention, behaviorists have contributed organizing designs and methods and a potent technology for behavior change (Jason & Bogat, 1983). Extensive reviews of behavioral preventive and community interventions have been reported elsewhere (e.g., Glenwick & Jason, 1984; Jason & Bogat, 1983), and will not be restated here. It is useful, however, to note through a few examples, the range of behavioral preventive interventions that have been undertaken and the opportunities and challenges they pose.

Much of the work outside of the traditional service delivery system conducted by behavioral psychologists can best be classified within the realm of secondary prevention, that is, identifying and remediating problems in their early stages. This work has frequently taken place in settings other than the mental health clinic. Schools, for example, have been a prime site for behavioral preventive interventions (e.g., Durlak [1977] used paraprofessionals to improve the social and academic skill of second graders who were adapting poorly; and Jason, Ferone, & Soucey [1979] implemented a behavioral school consultation program for acting-out first graders).

Behaviorists have also used primary preventive approaches directed at a variety of populations and concerns within a number of broad areas, including: (a) preventing the onset of specific health-compromising behaviors (e.g., Peterson & Mori [1985] used paraprofessional volunteers to train children in diverse safety responses; Roberts and Turner [1986] increased the use of safety restraints with children at a day care center), (b) enhancing strengths and competencies (e.g., Spivak and Shure [1974] developed a program to train children in social problem solving skills after which more than 50 child and adolescent focused intervention programs have been modeled [Weissberg, 1985]), and (c) assisting individuals facing potentially stressful transitions such as marriage, divorce, school entrance or transfer (e.g., Guerney [1987] provided cognitive behavioral relationship enhancement programs to newly married couples; Jason et al., [in press] have reported on a large-scale effort in progress to assist vulnerable transfer students).

These examples of behavioral preventive interventions are just a small number of successful demonstrations to date. Concern about certain features of some prevention programs has been well noted, especially with regard to the issues raised by secondary prevention and person-centered interventions (e.g., see Glenwick & Jason, 1984; Heller, 1984).

A shift toward higher level interventions has been advocated by a number of behavioral psychologists (e.g., Holland, 1978; Krasner, 1980). Critics, however, have contended that the ideology and technology of behaviorism is inadequate for addressing large-scale, real world problems. Bogat and Jason (in press) have identified the essential arguments against applying behavioral methods to higher-level preventive interventions as, (a) behavioral theory can only describe individual behavior, and therefore, cannot offer information or strategies to effect higher order change, and (b) behavioral technology is potent in certain contained settings with certain clinical problems, but may not be powerful or generalizable enough to be useful in applied settings. Do behavioral psychologists have access to the necessary range of information and reinforcers to effect significant or large scale change (Fawcett, Matthews, & Fletcher, 1980)?

The criticisms are relevant, although not only to behaviorism. Few theories and fewer technologies in psychology could not be accused of similar shortcomings. Psychology has only begun the process of figuring out how to apply what it has learned to larger than micro-level problems. The difficulty of applying behaviorism to preventive efforts may, to a certain extent, be embedded in the problems inherent in large-scale, and/or systems-level change efforts. Behaviorists, in fact, have made substantive efforts to undertake the challenges of community-level change. Many who are skeptical of the feasibility of a relationship between prevention and behaviorism may, in fact, be naive to these efforts, and to advances in behavioral methods that facilitate more complex analyses.

The application of behavioral techniques to larger systems interventions is evidenced by, for example, a volume from the *Journal of Applied Behavior Analysis* documenting the impact of behavior analytic interventions from 1968–1986 on community affairs (Greene, Winett, van Houten, Geller, & Iwata, 1987). The contents of the volume provide examples of interventions and behavioral assessments of community and systems-level problems such as: crime prevention and intervention (e.g., Mayer, Butterworth, Nafpakititis, & Sulzerazaroff, 1983, conducted a program to prevent school vandalism and to improve student discipline); preserving the ecology (e.g., Jacobs, Fairbanks, Poche, & Bailey, 1982, used multiple incentives to encourage carpool formation on a university campus); promoting prosocial behavior in the community (e.g., Hauserman, Walen, & Behling, 1973, reinforced racial integration in the first grade); safety promotion (e.g., Geller, Casali, & Johnson, 1980, tested the generalizability and response maintenance of rewarded safety belt usage in an industrial setting); evaluation of social and governmental programs (e.g., Stokes & Fawcett, 1977, evaluated a municipal policy regarding a refuse-packing program); and citizen and consumer affairs (e.g., Miller & Miller, 1970, reinforced self-help group activities of welfare recipients).

By expanding the levels at which they typically conceptualize and intervene, these behavioral psychologists have extended the reach of their technology, and explored social issues and subject matter that both directly and indirectly impact the psychological and physical health of the population. Such an expansion, however, is not made easily.

Constraints in the Alliance Between Prevention and Behaviorism

Behaviorists have a tendency to attend to a restricted number of directly manipulable contextual factors that impact target behavior. Individuals, however, respond to and must negotiate the demands of a number of contextual factors simultaneously. Some behaviorists have attempted to account for this complexity. McDowell (1988) in his description of Herrnstein's (1970) matching theory, for example, writes, "behavior on a single response alternative is a function not only of reinforcement contingent on that behavior, but also of reinforcement contingent on other behaviors and reinforcement delivered independently of behavior" (p. 95). Behavior is usually considered to be a function of its consequences. But, as experimental analyses conducted on matching theory have found, there appears to be more to the regulation of behavior than just the reinforcement contingent upon it.

Behavioral psychologists who have undertaken preventive interventions at the environmental level could profit from Kantor's (1958) advice to investigators regarding the complex nature of organism-environment interactions and his observation that a contingency control model may not be the most effective or comprehensive way to understand the impact of the environment. Kantor seems also to have foretold the difficulty of applying an unmodified behavioral paradigm to prevention.

Behaviorists (Evans, Meyer, Kurkijian, & Kishi, 1988) have noted that, in the early development of behavior therapy, it was convenient to focus upon the identification of discrete behavioral events, and to de-emphasize the complexity of response repertoires and their interaction with setting factors. It was also convenient to focus on short-term demonstrations because they offer immediate and compelling data to support the success of interventions targeting specific problem behaviors. The emphasis on selectivity and expediency clearly served the field well, judging from the professional and scientific success of behavior modification. However, it also imposed upon the field a number of conceptual and methodological constraints (Evans, et al., 1988). The field has had difficulty demonstrating either the maintenance or generalization of behavior change.

Behavioral psychologists who work within a preventive model, not surprisingly, have been confronted with the same problems and issues that challenge behavior therapists. Indeed, the challenges facing behavioral preventive psychologists overlap extensively with those concerning behavior therapists, for example, social validity, control versus collaboration, maintenance, generalization, side effects, and dissemination (Glenwick & Jason, 1984). Behaviorists, whether behavior therapists, behavior analysts, or behavioral preventionists, who have wrestled with these difficulties have often arrived at a similar conclusion regarding what is needed to overcome the restrictiveness of the behavioral model. What has been called for is a conceptual expansion, which, whether stated explicitly or not, typically involves a shift toward incorporating an ecological or systems perspective into behavioral interventions (e.g., Evans, 1985; Krasner, 1980; Rogers-Warren & Warren, 1977; Voeltz[Meyer] & Evans, 1982; Willems, 1974; Winett, 1985).

Prevention, by the very nature of what it undertakes, has had to seek a paradigm that could address complex social phenomena and accommodate longitudinal designs. Therefore, although all preventive interventions have not been rooted in the ecological model, the field of prevention has consistently emphasized the need to develop conceptual frameworks and empirical methods for understanding how factors within the ecological context facilitate or impede adaptation. The relationship between prevention and behavior therapy is apt to profit most by what benefits each, using the ecological paradigm as an organizing and guiding conceptual structure.

INCORPORATING THE ECOLOGICAL PARADIGM

The argument for incorporating the ecological paradigm into behavioral interventions has been made before (e.g., Willems, 1974). Although the argument is compelling and one we favor, it has been justly criticized for being excessively abstract and unimplementable (Baer, 1974). Clearly, it is not sufficient to call for an "expansion of perspective" without also providing a specific strategy and/or examples of how this might be accomplished. Unfortunately, the ecological paradigm does not lend itself to behavioral specificity or operationalized remedies as well as behaviorism does. It is possible, however, to identify and describe specific ecological principles that can be used in behavioral interventions to enhance and control their impact. Shapiro (1988), for example, offers instructive guidance regarding multidimensional assessments of classroom environments. Evans, et al. (1988) discuss behavioral interrelationships, advocating a movement away from measuring and manipulating behaviors one at a time, toward methods that influence children's entire behavioral repertoires to enhance the relevance and durability of behavior therapy interventions.

It is our intention to demonstrate how behavioral preventive interventions can be similarly enhanced. Incorporating the ecological paradigm actually facilitates the relationship between behaviorism and prevention in such a way that it accesses the strengths and complementarity of the alliance. However, to incorporate the ecological paradigm, it is helpful first to clarify what it means.

The Ecological Paradigm

The development of the ecological paradigm has been part of a larger and relatively recent trend in psychology toward greater acceptance of systems concepts and models. This trend has led many psychologists away from a view of phenomena as isolated entities and toward a greater appreciation of the relational context of phenomena. This movement has been prompted and propelled by psychology's attempts to expand its sphere of application to families, groups, organizations, and communities. Although systems theory and the ecological paradigm have separate origins and parallel, yet distinct, histories, there is considerable overlap between the systems and ecological orientations within psychology at present. They have, in fact, been considered inseparable strands of a single perspective as they are manifested within the discipline (Campbell, Steenbarger, Smith, & Stucky, 1982). References, therefore, to a "systems" (e.g., such as those in the behavior therapy literature) or an "ecological" (e.g., such as those in the behavior analysis literature) orientation are frequently referring to tenets of the same basic perspective. Because the ecological paradigm has, to a certain extent, evolved in the context of the field of prevention, and therefore is closely affiliated with it, we have chosen to refer to it exclusively.

Ecology as a guiding metaphor for prevention has been most conscientiously pursued by James G. Kelly and his colleagues (Kelly, 1966, 1975, 1979, 1985, 1987; Kelly, Snowden, & Munoz, 1977; Trickett, Kelly, & Vincent, 1985). The ecological paradigm is not a specified theory. It is a heuristic, or guiding conceptual framework for understanding behavior in interaction with its social and cultural contexts. Because contexts such as family, school, worksite, hospital or clinic, and community are important mediators of experience, it is central to prevention to develop ways to understand these contexts and their effects on people (Vincent & Trickett, 1983).

Four ecological processes drawn from the study of biology comprise the basic principles of the ecological paradigm as it was originally defined: interdependence, cycling of resources, adaptation, and succession (Kelly, 1968). These four principles will be described in terms of how they offer guidance in conceptualizing the behavior of individuals and the social context; in stimulating research and intervention questions and options; and as a means for averting the problems with side effects, maintenance, and generalization. These problems plague behavior therapy and prevention separately and are potentially compounded in a relationship between them. Whereas each of these principles focuses attention on different aspects of the social context and behavior, they also overlap and complement each other (Trickett & Mitchell, in press). Therefore, although for the sake of clarity and specificity we will discuss each principle and its application to behavioral preventive interventions separately, we caution that applying the principles separately limits the validity of the paradigm and does not serve investigators as well.

Interdependence

The principle of interdependence guides investigators to recognize that any change in one part of an interrelated person-environment system will invariably effect some kind of change in other parts of the system (Vincent & Trickett, 1983). So, if a child's acting-out behavior in school is changed by behavior modification, change will also occur in other areas of the child's life, and/or classroom. The child's acting-out behavior may, for example, have so occupied the teacher's attention that other children received less individual attention. Changing the one child's behavior problem, then, may affect other students' classroom experience and behavior as well. This is not surprising to behaviorists, but such "ripple effects" are rarely systematically documented or controlled for and so the potential for unforeseen outcomes, especially with large scale interventions, is considerable.

The interdependence principle describes behavior as a transaction between the individual and the setting. The effects of transactions are, by definition, reciprocal. Settings influence and shape individuals, and individuals influence and shape environments. Hence, an individual's behavior is inextricably related to the contingencies and demands of the setting(s) that influence it (Vincent & Trickett, 1983).

The interrelatedness of person and setting has been explicitly addressed, although in other terms, by behavior therapists (e.g., Evans et al., 1988). In the context of a discussion about response organization, Evans and colleagues note the paradoxical nature of reciprocal relationships, and in doing so describe, on the level of individual systems of behavior, what is also true about the system that comprises a social setting:

> What makes these relationships seem so paradoxical is our convention of talking about increasing and decreasing behaviors. In actuality, we change only the relative frequency of behaviors within a fixed repertoire. When an appropriate behavior is reduced in frequency, some other behavior must fill the void and replace the excess behavior; this is a question of simple logic, based on the premise that a living organism must always be engaging in behavior (p. 198).

Furthermore, sensitivity to the nature of reciprocal relationships leads Evans and colleagues to observe:

> In terms of collateral effects, a logical conclusion of the present argument is that behavioral events will always fill the void when an excess behavior's probability is reduced. These new probabilities may not be measured, particularly if they are simple extensions of former activities, but they will certainly be present (p. 200).

This observation is as vital to prevention as it is to behavior therapy. Lorion (1983) has remarked with regard to the activities of prevention, that it is inconceivable that an intervention designed to avert or limit the impact of dysfunctional behavior or to generate previously absent inter- or intra-personal skills could not also be capable of causing negative, or unsuspected outcomes. Those who doubt this are alerted to the findings of McCord (1978) who, in a 30 year follow-up of an early secondary prevention project targeting delinquent youth (Powers & Witmer, 1951), found that program participants fared significantly less well than nonprogram controls in terms of rates of alcoholism, psychiatric problems, criminal behavior, and mortality.

The application of the interdependence principle can guide an investigator to anticipate and potentially avoid negative side effects. Although it is never assumed that side effects can be eliminated, given the interactive nature of persons and settings, the ripples that occur through a system during an intervention can be systematically monitored to control for negative events. An example that demonstrates both interdependence and a design strategy to track collateral effects, comes from a study of a behavioral parent training program described in greater detail elsewhere (Liotta, Jason, Robinson, & Lavigne, 1985). The investigators used a behavioral observation system to document changes in support exchanged between a married couple during the training program. Baseline data were collected for 1 month prior to intervention. During the first intervention phase, the mother began involvement in a child-management program and began learning parenting skills. During the second phase, the father was instructed in basic social learning principles and parenting skills.

Changes in reciprocal support over baseline and the first two intervention phases were found, but not as predicted. Reciprocity was defined as the percent of intervals where support was provided in which the provision of support was bidirectional between parents. When only the mother was involved in the parent training (phase one), the mean percent of bidirectional support dropped from 68% to 36%. The mean percentage increased to prior baseline phase levels only when the father was involved in the training.

The most obvious way this study demonstrates interdependence is through the occurrence of unanticipated consequences for the participants. The unanticipated side effect of the intervention was a reduction of support, in this case from father to mother, during one phase of the intervention. Parent training of the mother negatively affected the reciprocity of support in the marital relationship. It appears that during this part of the intervention, the father felt "uncomfortable" with the new parenting techniques the mother was beginning to use. Inclusion of the father in subsequent phases of the intervention eliminated this problem. This is an example of how a behavioral parent training program might inadvertently damage the social support exchanged by couples.

It is also important to recognize how, in a number of ways, the procedures the investigators used to evaluate the effects of their program reflect and assess interdependence. First, choosing to detect changes in a marital relationship concurrent with involvement in a parent training program reflects an awareness that this relationship will be affected by the intervention. It is more typical in preventive interventions to measure only those changes which are directly, or linearly associated with the specified intervention. Measuring social support reflects an awareness that the marital system will be impacted by a change in any part of it (in this case, a change in their relationship as coparents).

It is not sufficient, however, for an investigator to simply acknowledge that there are consequences to change. A measurable indicator must be selected to track relevant, health-influencing consequences and their impact. Investigators must choose to measure changes in behaviors that influence the likelihood that the intervention will be adopted and maintained.

Social support is an appropriate choice both given the significant data accumulated regarding its relationship to various psychological states (Gottlieb, 1983; Heller & Swindle, 1983; Wellman, 1981) and given that the occurrence or lack of occurrence of support between parents will likely impact the effect of a parent training intervention. Choosing to measure *bidirectional* support reflects awareness that effects are reciprocal by nature, and not well accounted for by unidirectional assessments.

Finally, the design of the study permitted collection of data across multiple time points to track the impact of the various phases of the intervention. Had the investigators simply used a pre/post, or pre/post/follow-up design, they would have missed the unanticipated effect entirely. This is of considerable practical importance. Enhancing parenting skills is a common preventive strategy. Programs targeted at one parent, or which, by default may include only one parent of a couple, should be concerned about the potential for undermining the support structure between the parents, the impact of which upon the marriage and the child(ren) is unlikely to be good.

Applying the principle of interdependence, then, can guide the investigator(s) to select a design and measures that will increase feedback about both the direct and indirect effects of an intervention on the participants and the setting in which it occurs. This strategy is one that can assist behavioral psychologists working within a preventive model to monitor and control for side effects.

Cycling of Resources

The cycling of resources perspective leads an investigator to ask: what qualities does the setting, or persons, possess that can be applied or developed to cope with an identified problem? Resources are defined broadly. They can be human, as in the skills of individuals, or a network of social support a group manages to maintain. Resources can be technological, as in expertise, or information, or access to supplies or equipment. Resources can also be built into the social context, as in a socialization process that deters gender or racial bias, or that provides events and settings (e.g., celebrations, rituals) for social and cultural cohesion (Kelly, 1987; Vincent & Trickett, 1983).

This principle leads an investigator to attempt to uncover existing competencies in the environment and "draw them out," per se, or to match individuals with settings that provide the resources they need. The resource perspective assumes that what will serve a person or setting best will be that which has succeeded previously in the setting or for the person. Fawcett et al. (1980) have noted that procedures that are incompatible with local customs and practices may not be adopted, and if adopted, may soon be disgarded the same way biological systems reject foreign objects. Accessing indigenous resources increases the likelihood that an intervention will be maintained.

One way to apply the cycling of resources principle is to use naturally occurring contingencies to modify behavior. This would involve placing or matching individuals with settings that because of the resources available in the setting, facilitate specific desirable behavior patterns (Jason & Glenwick, 1980). An environment that, for example, offers contingencies that reinforce social interaction is a resource for a withdrawn child. Hartup (1979) demonstrated this by significantly increasing the sociability of socially withdrawn preschoolers by exposing them to younger competent children.

An example of using naturalistic contingencies in a behaviorally designed study is provided by Jason, Robson, and Lipshutz (1980). This study modified sharing behaviors in groups of first and third grade children by strategic placement of the children in specific behavior settings. During all intervention sessions triads of children were given play materials and sharing behavior was recorded. During the intervention phase, low sharing children and higher sharing children were placed in triads which contained one low sharing and two higher sharing children. The study's major finding was that rates of sharing in low sharers could be accelerated by placing them in groups where high sharers were playing.

Although small in scope, Jason et al's. (1980) demonstration offers an alternative type of intervention that uses a naturally existing resource, the high capacity for sharing among some children, to promote more cooperative social behavior. It is worth noting that exposure itself to high sharing children was not exclusively responsible for the change in low sharers' behavior. Given that in their normal classrooms, as well as at baseline, low sharers had been exposed to high sharers before, exposure alone appeared insufficient to improve low sharers' performance. The change in the context within which low sharers were exposed to high sharers was of central importance to the intervention's success. The social arrangement (triads engaged in play) created by the investigators facilitated low sharers' opportunity to model high sharers' behavior. It was necessary to both identify the resource (sharing behavior in some children) and create a social setting that provided access to it.

The principle of cycling of resources alerts investigators to seek and develop indigenous person and setting resources that the host environment can reasonably access and use to their advantage. Practically speaking, this must involve intervention procedures that can be realistically integrated into the host setting and/or participants' routine. If, for example, an intervention creates a social setting that provides an opportunity for one group (e.g., low sharers) to learn from the behavior of another more competent group (e.g., high sharers), the social setting (triads engaged in play) must be replicable by the host environment (e.g., the school) in order for effects to be sustained or applied to other children.

An intervention that does not impact (either intentionally or otherwise) the process by which target behaviors are changed, runs the risk of being little more than a demonstration. Instead, it might be possible to integrate the technology into the social and behavioral fabric in a way that its effects will be maintained.

This perspective is crucial to prevention. For preventive efforts to impact sufficient numbers of individuals over sufficient periods of time to deter maladjusted behavior later on, an intervention must be practical for settings and persons to implement and sustain. When behavioral technologies, such as complex motivational systems, require ongoing professional involvement, or an unreasonable portion of the host settings resources, they can rarely be sustained (Fawcett et al., 1980). The principle of cycling of resources, which emphasizes the use of indigenous resources, provides a strategy for effecting change in a way that it is more likely to be maintained.

Succession

The succession principle states that persons and settings are in a constant process of change, and as such require constant adaptation (Kelly, 1968). Therefore, what is true about a person or setting today may not be true tomorrow. Child development is perhaps the most obvious example of succession. Learning to walk, for example, dramatically alters what a child and the setting he or she inhabits must adapt to. On a larger scale, organizations change in response to what the environment demands and provides (Katz & Kahn, 1966). These changes reverberate through the organizational system. Therefore, a preventive intervention designed, for example, to introduce flex-time into the work schedule, must be able to track and respond to the changes the organization will inevitably experience to maintain the feasibility of the intervention for the organization.

The principle of succession leads an investigator to observe behavior over time and design interventions with built-in opportunities for revision. This allows an investigator to respond to changes in the person and the setting. On an individual level, behavioral time series methods lend themselves well to the challenge this poses. This technique was used in a tutoring project that is part of a large scale, ongoing effort to help vulnerable transfer students adjust to a new school setting (Jason et al., in press). The investigators collected ongoing data on childrens' progress during tutoring. The data revealed that one child's progress in mastering a phonetic ladder had slowed. Because this leveling-off was immediately evident to the tutor and supervisor, the intervention techniques were modified and positive results were observed.

Time series data are a hallmark of behavior modification. Data, however, are typically collected over relatively short periods of time and serve as a mechanism to simply track progress and explain outcomes. The principle of succession advises an investigator to observe behavior over longer periods of time and respond to the inevitable changes that occur in person-setting transactions. Preventive interventions may have difficulty maintaining their effects if they are not able to adapt to the changes persons and settings will inevitably manifest over time. A high risk child, for example, may demonstrate important gains in school through a tutoring program. If in the next year, however, the child is placed in a class that is poorly organized or not well-suited to his or her learning style, gains may evaporate as the challenge to simultaneously master the new classroom environment and academic tasks overwhelm the child's adaptive capacity.

Adaptation

The principle of adaptation explains behavior as a result of a continual process of accommodation between persons and their environment. Individuals must constantly revise their coping behavior in response to concurrent, at times competing, contingencies (Vincent & Trickett, 1983). What is adaptive in one setting or for one person is not adaptive in another setting or for another person. The behavior observed in one setting is likely to reflect the negotiation of a combination of environmental pressures to which a person must respond. Trickett (1984) provides an enlightening example of an inner-city school student who, to maintain his "street image," which protected him and gave him social status among his peers, could not regularly attend school or show an interest in it. Once school had ended, however, he would return to be tutored by one of his teachers privately. Being a "good student" would have been maladaptive to this individual's street role, yet not learning to read would also have been maladaptive. The student's response was a particularly ingenious way to manage these conflicting demands. This example argues against drawing inferences about individual or group behaviors that have been assessed in only one setting. The principle of adaptation suggests that behavior is the function of a response to sets of contingencies in several settings (Trickett & Mitchell, in press).

Behavioral data can provide useful documentation of this principle. For example, Jason and Nelson (1980) identified a first grade child having serious acting-out problems. The child was observed during the morning reading period each day. The teacher was located either in front of the entire class or in a small group of 5–8 students. Children, therefore, were located in one of three groupings: in a small group with a teacher, in a large unsupervised group, or in a large group supervised by the teacher. The investigators documented the child's percent of acting-out behaviors over time in each of these three ecological niches. The child evidenced very low levels of misbehavior in closely supervised, small groups. When the group size increased, rates of problem behaviors doubled, and the greatest increases in acting-out behavior occurred in the unsupervised large group. These findings demonstrate that the child's behavior changed according to the setting he occupied. The child's acting-out behavior was a function of how he responded to the contingencies of different settings. The small supervised group setting appears to have facilitated the child's learning best.

The principle of adaptation suggests that matching individuals with settings is a legitimate alternative to directly manipulating an individual's behavior. In the case of education, for example, this principle suggests that investigators pay greater attention to identifying optimal matches between children and their educational environment. As Jason and Nelson (1980) have demonstrated, behavioral preventive investigators can use naturally occurring contingencies, which fit well with the adaptational capacities of a child to produce meaningful behavior change. Given that the contingencies that led to the reduction of acting-out behavior occur naturally in the environment, appropriate placement is likely to help children meet the educational and social expectations of their teachers.

The Impact of the Research Process

Using the ecological principles to guide the creation of more ecologically valid designs and methods is one part of making preventive interventions more relevant and durable. The ecological paradigm also provides a heuristic for how to intervene in a way that will enhance the power, relevance, and durability of interventions. Kelly (1985, 1987) has suggested that the very process by which some research and interventions are carried out can undermine their ability to collect valid information and positively impact participants. For example, a program that teaches adolescents the skills to refuse drugs without recognizing that some adolescents, seeking the approval of their peers, will not want to say "no," will lose some of its potency (Gesten & Jason, 1987). Without engaging the adolescents in a process where they can develop their own resources and skills (e.g., peer support, refusal skills, alternative social behaviors), substance abuse prevention programs are not likely to be durable (Rhodes & Jason, 1988).

Kelly advocates that professionals join in long-term, collaborative relationships with the persons and settings they want to effect. It is by way of these relationships, Kelly contends, that useful research processes may be generated, and in the context of such processes that the resources of a setting may be identified and developed (Kelly, 1987). Kelly specifies the value of this strategy:

> When a professional initiates a process with citizens where the citizens actively co-design service delivery, citizens are validated for taking action that is synonymous with what is known about the practice of good mental health. They are identifying resources, receiving support while creating resources, and having the autonomy and free choice to use these resources for the development of their needs and aspirations (p. 4).

The relevance and long-term effectiveness of behavioral preventive interventions may be limited if the research process has been neglected. Change efforts that are not integrated into the setting are unlikely to produce effects that will last. Kelly (1987) suggests that creating social settings is a potent strategy for effecting long-term change and, as such, should be a goal of preventive research. Places, events, meetings, or gatherings are not, in and of themselves, social settings as Kelly defines them. They may become a social setting, however, if a self-conscious, collaborative process is initiated whereby a value for being resourceful is established and reinforced. By participating and assisting in the creation of social settings, professionals can potentially be included in, and have access to, ongoing change efforts that are a relevant and integral part of a community or group. Ultimately, we may help community members become better problem-solvers who are, therefore, more likely to be effective in dealing with *future* problems (Kelly, 1987).

Behaviorists have a good deal to offer and gain from this process. Social settings imply that there is a commitment on the part of the members to work on problems and enhance their well-being. Behavioral technology, as demonstrated in the last section, can be applied to serve the needs of a social setting quite well. Behaviorists can assist community groups in documenting the effects of their change efforts over time. The feedback generated from tracking data can help members of a social setting revise their strategies as needed. Members might also learn to generate their own data, which may reinforce and expedite their change efforts (e.g., Jason & Zolik, 1981).

Certainly, the most significant advantage of attending to the process of preventive research is that the effects of collaborately defined, produced, and implemented change efforts are more likely to endure. This aspect of the ecological paradigm is central to an effective integration of behaviorism and prevention.

CONCLUSION

In this chapter we have proposed that a preventive service delivery strategy offers behavior therapists unique options and opportunities to increase their field's impact, both in terms of scale and social significance. Behaviorists who have adopted a preventive model have contributed significantly to the progress prevention can claim to have made to date. Yet the application of behaviorism to prevention has been considered untenable by some who contend that the behavioral model is not well-suited to the large-scale, real world problems that prevention seeks to address. Clearly, these fields have different world views that have led them to divergent foci and problem-solving strategies. Present in these differences, however, is a substantive complementarity that enriches the common epistemological and empirical ground upon which these fields have already begun to build an alliance.

The behavioral model, however, does not, in and of itself, appear to provide an adequate conceptual framework to assist psychologists who adopt a preventive service delivery strategy to face the challenges inherent in the work. Behavioral preventive interventions, we have argued in this chapter, can be enhanced by incorporating certain tenets of the ecological paradigm into research and intervention designs. Because social and cultural contexts are important mediators of experience, it has been crucial for prevention to attempt to develop ways to understand transactions between persons and these contexts. The four core principles of the ecological paradigm, interdependence, cycling of resources, adaptation, and succession offer guidance in conceptualizing behavior-in-context and stimulating research designs and questions that are more ecologically valid. The ecological perspective also provides a heuristic for how to intervene in a way that will enhance the power, relevance, and durability of preventive interventions. The paradigm prompts investigators to participate in change efforts that have been collaboratively defined, produced, and implemented by research participants.

The most substantive advantage the ecological paradigm offers behavioral preventive research is the conceptual and practical guidance to engage in a research process that generates intervention effects that last. Incorporating the ecological paradigm actually facilitates the relationship between behaviorism and prevention in a way that accesses the strengths and complementarity of the alliance.

REFERENCES

Albee, G. W. (1982a). Primary prevention: Insights for rehabilitation psychology. *Rehabilitation Psychology, 27*, 13–22.

Albee, G. W. (1982b). Preventing psychopathology and promoting human potential. *American Psychologist, 37*, 1043–1050.

Alpert, J. L. (1985). Change within a profession: Change, future, prevention, and school psychology. *American Psychologist, 40*, 1112–1121.

Baer, D. M. (1974). A note on the absense of santa claus in any known ecosystem: A rejoiner to Willems. *Journal of Applied Behavior Analysis, 7*, 167–170.

Bloom, B. L. (1965). The "medical model," miasma theory and community mental health. *Community Mental Health Journal, 7*, 333–338.

Bogat, G. A., & Jason, L. A. (in press). Dogs bark at those they do not recognize: Towards an integration of Behaviorism and Community Psychology. In J. Rappaport & E. Seidman (Eds.), *Handbook of Community Psychology*. New York: Plenum Press.

Campbell, D. E., Steenbarger, B. N., Smith, T. W., & Stucky, R. J. (1982). An ecological systems approach to evaluation. *Evaluation Review, 6*, 625–648.

Caplan, G. (1964). *Principles of preventive psychiatry*. New York: Basic Books.

Cowen, E. L. (1983). Primary prevention in mental health: Past, present, and future. In R. D. Felner, L. A. Jason, J. N. Moritsugu, & S. S. Farber (Eds.), *Preventive psychology: Theory, research, and practice* (pp. 11–25). Elmsford, NY: Pergamon Press.

deBettencourt, L. U. (1987). Strategy training: A need for clarification. *Exceptional Children, 54*, 24–31.

Deshler, D. D., & Schumaker, J. B. (1986). Learning strategies: An instructional alternative for low achieving adolescents. *Exceptional Children, 52*, 583–589.

Durlak, J. A. (1977). Description and evaluation of a behaviorally oriented school-based preventive mental health program. *Journal of Consulting and Community Psychology, 45*, 80–92.

Engelmann, S., & Carnine, D. W. (1982). *Theory of instruction*. New York: Irvington.

Evans, I. M. (1985). Building systems models as a strategy for target behavior selection in clinical assessment. *Behavioral Assessment, 7*, 21–32.

Evans, I. M., Meyer, L. H., Kurkjian, J. A., & Kishi, G. S. (1988). An evaluation of behavioral interrelationships in child behavior therapy. In J. C. Witt, S. N. Elliott, & F. M. Greshman (Eds.), *Handbook of behavior therapy in education* (pp. 189–215). New York: Plenum Press.

Fawcett, S. B., Matthews, R. M., & Fletcher, R. K. (1980). Some promising dimensions for behavioral community technology. *Journal of Applied Behavior Analysis, 13*, 505–518.

Felner, R. D., & Aber, M. S. (1983). Primary prevention for children: A framework for the assessment of need. In A. Zautra, K. Bachrach, & R. Hess (Eds.), *Prevention in the Human Services, 2, Strategies for needs assessment in prevention* (pp. 109–121). New York: Haworth Press.

Felner, R. D., Jason, L. A., Moritsugu, J. N., & Farber, S. S. (1983). Preventive psychology: Evolution and current status. In R. D. Felner, L. A. Jason, J. N. Moritsugu, & S. S. Farber (Eds.), *Preventive psychology: Theory, research, and practice* (pp. 3–10). Elmsford, NY: Pergamon Press.

Geller, E. S., Casali, J. G., & Johnson, R. P. (1980). Seat belt usage: A potential target for applied behavior analysis. *Journal of Applied Analysis, 13*, 669–675.

Gesten, E. L., & Jason, L. A. (1987). Social and community interventions. *Annual review of psychology, 38*, 427–60.

Glenwick, D. S., & Jason, L. A. (1984). Behavioral community psychology: An introduction to the special issue. *Journal of Community Psychology, 12*, 103–112.

Goldston, S. E. (1977). Defining primary prevention. In G. W. Albee & J. M. Joffee (Eds.), *Primary prevention of Psychopathology: Vol 1. The issues* (pp. 18–23). Hanover, NH: University Press of New England.

Gottlieb, B. H. (1983). *Social support strategies*. Beverly Hills: Sage Publications.

Greene, B. F., Winett, R. A., Van Houten, R., Geller, E. S., & Iwata, B. A. (Eds.), (1987). *Behavior analysis in the community 1968–1986 from the Journal of Applied Analysis*. Lawrence, KS: Society for the Experimental Analysis of Behavior.

Guerney, B. G. (1987). Family relationship enhancement: A skills training approach. In L. Bond & B. Wagner, (Eds.), *Families in transition: Primary prevention programs that work* (pp. 99–134). Beverly Hills: Sage Publications.

Hartup, W. W. (1979). Peer relations and the growth of social competence. In M. W. Kent & J. E. Rolf (Eds.), *Primary prevention of psychopathology, Vol. 3: Social competence in children* (pp. 150–170). Hanover, NH: University Press of New England.

Hauserman, N., Walen, S. R., & Behling, M. (1973). Reinforced radical integration in the first grade: A study in generalization. *Journal of Applied Behavior Analysis, 6*, 193–200.

Heller, K. (1984). Prevention and health promotion. In K. Heller, R. H. Price, S. Reinharz, S. Riger, A. Wandersman, & T. A. D'Aunno (Eds.), *Psychology and community change: Challenges of the future* (pp. 172–226). Homewood, IL: Dorsey Press.

Heller, K., & Swindle, R. W. (1983). Social networks, perceived support, and coping with stress. In R. D. Felner, L. A. Jason, J. N. Moritsugu, & S. S. Farber (Eds.), *Preventive psychology: Theory, research, and practice* (pp. 87–103). Elmsford, NY: Pergamon Press.

Herrnstein, R. J. (1970). On the law of effect. *Journal of the Experimental Analysis of Behavior, 13*, 243–266.

Holland, J. G. (1978). Behaviorism: Part of the problem or part of the solution. *Journal of Applied Behavior Analysis, 11*, 163–174.

Jacobs, H. E., Fairbanks, D., Poche, C. E., & Bailey, J. S. (1982). Multiple incentives in encouraging carpool formation on a university campus. *Journal of Applied Behavior Analysis, 15*, 141–149.

Jason, L. A., Betts, D., Johnson, J., Smith, S., Krueckeberg, S., & Cradock, M. (in press). An evaluation of an orientation plus tutoring school-based prevention program. *Professional School Psychology*.

Jason, L. A., & Bogat, G. A. (1983). Preventive behavioral interventions. In R. D. Felner, L. A. Jason, J. N. Moritsugu, & S. S. Farber (Eds.), *Preventive psychology: Theory, research, and practice* (pp. 128–143). Elmsford, NY: Pergamon Press.

Jason, L. A., Ferone, L., & Soucey, G. (1979). Teaching peer tutoring behaviors in first and third grade classrooms. *Psychology in the Schools, 16*, 261–269.

Jason, L. A., & Glenwick, D. S. (1980). Behavioral community psychology: A review of recent research and applications. *Progress in Behavior Modification, 18*, 85–121.

Jason, L. A., & Nelson, T. (1980). Investigating the relationships between problem behaviors and environmental design. *Corrective Social Psychiatry, 26*, 53–57.

Jason, L. A., Robson, S. D., & Lipshutz, S. A. (1980).

Enhancing sharing behaviors through the use of naturalistic contingencies. *Journal of Community Psychology, 8,* 237–244.
Jason, L. A., & Zolik, E. S. (1981). Characteristics of behavioral community interventions. *Professional Psychology, 12,* 769–775.
Joffee, J. M. (1982). Let a thousand flowers bloom? *Journal of Primary Prevention, 3,* 52–55.
Kantor, A. E. (1958). *Interbehavioral psychology.* Bloomington, IN: Principia Press.
Katz, D. & Kahn, R. L. (1966). *The social psychology of organizations,* New York: John Wiley & Sons.
Kelly, J. G. (1966). Ecological constraints on mental health services. *American Psychologist, 21,* 535–539.
Kelly, J. G. (1968). Toward an ecological conception of preventive interventions. In J. W. Carter, Jr., (Ed.), *Research contributions from psychology to community mental health* (pp. 75–99). New York: Behavioral Publications.
Kelly, J. G. (1975). Community psychology: Some priorities for the immediate future. *Journal of Community Psychology, 3,* 205–209.
Kelly, J. G. (Ed.). (1979). *Adolescent boys in high school: A psychological study of coping adaptation.* Hillsdale, NJ: Lawrence Erlbaum Associates.
Kelly, J. G. (1985). The concept of primary prevention: Creating new paradigms. *Journal of Primary Prevention, 5,* 269–272.
Kelly, J. G. (1987, April). Beyond preventive techniques: Generating social settings for a publics health. Paper presented at the Tenth Erich Lindemann Memorial Lecture. Harvard Medical School, Boston, MA.
Kelly, J. G., Snowden, L. R., & Munoz, R. F. (1977). Social and community interventions. *Annual Review of Psychology, 28,* 223–261.
Kiesler, R. A. (1985). Prevention and public policy. In J. C. Posen & L. J. Soloman (Eds.), *Prevention in health psychology* (pp. 401–413). Hanover, NH: University Press of New England.
Krasner, L. (1980). *Environmental design and human behavior: A psychology of the individual in society.* Elmsford, NY: Pergamon Press.
Krasner, L., & Ullman, L. P. (1973). *Behavior influence and personality: The social matrix of human action.* New York: Holt, Rinehart & Winston.
Lindemann, E. (1944). Symptomatology and the management of acute grief. *American Journal of Psychiatry, 101,* 141–148.
Liotta, R. F., Jason, L. A., Robinson, L., LaVigne, V. (1985). A behavioral approach for measuring social support. *Family Therapy, 12,* 285–295.
Lloyd, J. (1980). Academic instruction and cognitive behavior modification: The need for attack strategy training. *Exceptional Education Quarterly, 1,* 53–63.
Lorion, R. P. (1983). Evaluating preventive interventions: Guidelines for the serious social change agent. In R. D. Felner, L. A. Jason, J. N. Moritsugu, & S. S. Farber (Eds.), *Preventive psychology: Theory, research, and practice* (pp. 251–268). Elmsford, NY: Pergamon Press.
Mayer, G. R., Butterworth, T., Nafpakititis, M., & Sulzer-azaroff, B. (1983). Preventing school vandalism and improving discipline: A three-year study. *Journal of Applied Behavior Analysis, 16,* 355–369.
McCord, J. (1978). A thirty year follow-up of treatment effects. *American Psychologist, 33,* 248–289.
McDowell, J. J. (1988). Matching theory in human environments. *The Behavior Analyst, 11,* 95–109.
Miller, L. K., & Miller, O. L. (1970). Reinforcing self-help group activities of welfare recipients. *Journal of Applied Behavior Analysis, 3,* 57–64.
Peterson, L., & Mori, L. (1985). Prevention of child injury: An overview of targets, methods, and tactics for psychologists. *Journal of Consulting and Clinical Psychology, 58,* 586–595.
Powers, E., & Witmer, H. (1951). *An experiment in the prevention of delinquency: The Cambridge-Somerville Youth Study.* New York: Columbia University Press.
Rappaport, J. (1977). *Community psychology: Values, research, and action.* New York: Holt, Rinehart & Winston.
Rappaport, J. (1981). In praise of paradox: A social policy of empowerment over prevention. *American Journal of Community Psychology, 9,* 1–25.
Rhodes, J. E., & Jason, L. A. (1988). *Preventing substance abuse among children and adolescents.* Elmsford, NY: Pergamon Press.
Roberts, M. C., & Turner, D. S. (1986). Rewarding parents for their children's use of safety seats. *Journal of Pediatric Psychology, 11,* 25–36.
Rogers-Warren, A., & Warren, S. F. (1977). *Ecological perspectives in behavior analysis.* Baltimore: University Park Press.
Sarason, S. B. (1981). An asocial psychology and a misdirected clinical psychology. *American Psychologist, 36,* 827–836.
Shapiro, E. S. (1988). Behavioral assessment. In J. C. Witt, S. H. Elliot, & F. M. Gresham (Eds.). *Handbook of behavior therapy in education* (pp. 67–98). New York: Plenum Press.
Skinner, B. F. (1971). *Beyond freedom and dignity.* New York: Alfred A. Knopf.
Spivak, G., & Shure, M. B. (1974). *Social adjustment of young children.* San Francisco: Josey-Bass.
Stokes, T. F., & Fawcett, S. B. (1977). Evaluating municipal policy: An analysis of a refuse-packing program. *Journal of Applied Behavior Analysis, 10,* 391–398.
Swift, C. (1987). Preventing family violence: Family focused programs. In L. Bond, & B. Wagner, *Families in transition: Primary prevention programs that work* (pp. 252–285). Beverly Hills: Sage Publications.
Trickett, E. J. (1984). Toward a distinctive community psychology: An ecological metaphor for training and the conduct of research. *American Journal of Community Psychology, 12,* 261–279.
Trickett, E. J., Kelly, J. G., & Vincent, T. A. (1985). The

spirit of ecological inquiry in community research. In E. Susskind & D. Klein (Eds.), *Community research: Methods, paradigms, applications*. New York: Praeger.

Trickett, E. J., & Mitchell, R. E. (in press). An ecological metaphor for research and intervention in Community Psychology. In M. S. Gibbs, J. R. Lachenmayer, & T. Siegel, (Eds.), *Community psychology: Theoretical and empirical approaches*, (2nd ed.). New York: Garda Press.

Ullman, L. P., & Krasner, L. (1969). *A psychological approach to abnormal behavior*. Englewood Cliffs, NJ: Prentice-Hall.

Vincent, T., & Trickett, E. J. (1983). Preventive intervention and the human context: Ecological approaches to environmental assessment and change. In R. D. Felner, L. A. Jason, J. N. Moritsugu, & S. S. Farber (Eds.), *Preventive psychology: Theory, research, and practice* (pp. 67–86). Elmsford, NY: Pergamon Press.

Voeltz(Meyer), L. M., & Evans, I. M. (1982). The assessment of behavioral interrelationships in child behavior therapy. *Behavioral Assessment, 4,* 131–165.

Weissberg, R. P. (1985). Developing effective social-problem solving programs for the classroom. In B. Schneider, K. H. Rubin, & J. Ledingham (Eds.), *Peer relationships and social skills* (pp. 225–42). New York: Springer-Verlag.

Wellman, B. (1981). Applying network analysis to the study of support. In B. H. Gottlieb (Ed.), *Social networks and social support* (pp. 171–200). Beverly Hills: Sage Publications.

Willems, E. P. (1974). Behavioral technology and behavioral ecology. *Journal of Applied Behavior Analysis, 7,* 151–165.

Winett, R. A. (1985). Ecobehavioral assessment in health lifestyles: Concepts and methods. In P. Karoly (Ed.), *Measurement strategies in health psychology* (pp. 147–181). New York: John Wiley & Sons.

Zigler, E., & Finn, M. (1982). A vision of child care in the 1980's. In L. A. Bond & J. M. Joffee (Eds.), *Facilitating infant and early childhood development* (pp. 443–465). Hanover, NH: University Press of New England.

CHAPTER 23

EXTENDING APPLICATIONS OF BEHAVIOR THERAPY TO LARGE-SCALE INTERVENTION

Richard A. Winett
Abby C. King
David G. Altman

In this chapter, we will be advocating a substantial redirection for behavior therapy. We will call for larger scale interventions that emphasize prevention and health enhancement, with these interventions based on developmental and ecological perspectives and a new framework and schema for structural and behavior change.

The present volume offers firm evidence that the conceptual and empirical foundations of behavior therapy have greatly expanded in the last 20 years. Likewise, the techniques derived from these foundations and their attendant applications have also diversified. These developments attest to the utility of the paradigm for theoretical advancement and real-world impacts. However, from the perspective of both community psychologists and those health psychologists who identify with the public health field, something elementary and at the very core of the approach has been missing. This missing ingredient, in fact, for some professionals means—at the extreme—that behavior therapy circa 1990 is simply "old wine in a new bottle." For other community and health psychologists, there is at least some question about how innovative the conceptual and technical advancements have been.

A broad panoramic review of behavior therapy over the last two decades reveals that most debate and change has occurred on primarily one side of a major issue. This issue is how various mental health, health, and disability problems should be addressed. Part of the issue is *conceptual and technical*—the focus of debate and change. However, part of the issue pertains to the *service delivery system* itself (Rappaport, 1977, 1987; Rappaport & Chinsky, 1974). Debate and inno-

---

This chapter is based on an invited paper at the American Psychological Association annual meeting, August, 1988, Atlanta, and chapters in R. A. Winett, A. C. King, & D. G. Altman, *Health psychology and public health: An integrative approach;* Elmsford, NY: Pergamon Press. Work on this chapter was partially supported by grants #5 RO1-CA4592602 from the National Cancer Institute and #1 RO1 MH4459901 from the National Institute of Mental Health to the first author; grant #36272 from the National Heart, Lung, and Blood Institute (to William L. Haskell, Ph.D.) for the second author; and grant #87-4614 from the Henry J. Kaiser Family Foundation (to John W. Farquhar, M.D.) for the third author.

vation on the side of the service delivery system has been the core element that has largely been neglected—the missing ingredient.

Behavior therapists, for the most part, have accepted the service delivery system as a given. They have seemingly forgotten or ignored their own history and analysis of the psychotherapy system, repeated analyses by others of the discrepancy between mental health and health needs in the United States and world-wide, resources to meet those needs, and the rich and compelling tradition and impact of other fields that approach problems using different delivery systems.

The first part of this chapter will briefly recount the history of behavior therapy, particularly with regard to its apparent loss of its original reformist mission and the backstaging of its own innovations. The second part of the chapter will examine the issue of health and mental health needs, the ability of present delivery systems to meet those needs, and fundamental innovations that appear to be required. These innovations call for conceptual and technical bases that are the focus of the third section of this chapter. A fourth part will integrate these concepts and strategies using a number of schemas and frameworks. A final section will draw on the material in the fourth part using an extended example to be both more integrative and illustrative.

A BRIEF HISTORY

In the Beginning

No scientific movement can be divorced from the social, political, and economic contexts that mark its beginning. In fact, scientific movements reflect the times (Kuhn, 1970). Behavior therapy of a quarter century ago entered a turbulent world, a world of questioning and change. Behavior therapists displayed a reformist zeal and questioned the efficacy of traditional treatments—namely, psychoanalysis and its derivatives and client-centered therapy. Traditional treatments were construed, and rightly so, as being, at best, minimally effective, while being far too lengthy and overly expensive. It is important to note that when behavior therapists of that era railed against the "medical model," it was not just psychodynamic conceptualization that was the target. Behavior therapists noted how the expensive, rehabilitory fee-for-service psychoanalytic psychiatrists mirrored (or in one of the words of the time, "parodied") all the problems that existed within the real medical system. Thus, treatment was given by a highly trained and expensive professional, in specialized settings removed from the natural environment, to individuals manifesting considerable acute or chronic distress. Behavior therapists of that era, (e.g., Krasner & Ullman, 1973) asked questions such as:

- Are psychiatrists and Ph.D. psychologists the only individuals who can render effective treatment?
- How can people improve when so much of the treatment does not occur in a person's everyday environment?
- Once people are so distressed, what is the likelihood of providing effective treatment?
- If people can be helped before they become so distressed, will not treatment be of shorter duration, less expensive, and more efficient?
- If environmental circumstances contribute so much to problems, should not a good deal of our effort be directed to changing environments?
- If we can change environments, will we be unable to help many people at one time?
- Why not try to help many people improve their daily functioning by moving beyond the purview of psychiatric disorders and treatment in medical establishments to an array of behavioral, social, and economic concerns and community intervention?

Experimental Innovation

It is important to note that in the true spirit of an experimental science, documented efforts were (and are being) made to address each of these questions within the behavioral paradigm. For example:

- Although the debate continues, evidence indicates that paraprofessionals can be effective, if not with every client, technique, and problem—certainly with some clients, techniques, and problems (Hattie, Sharpley, & Rogers, 1984).
- There was once considerable interest, excitement, and some empirical support for the training of various mediators of change in the natural environment. These efforts were not restricted to teachers, parents, or medical personnel, but included a cadre of individuals in often less-than-optimal situations (e.g., Tharp & Wetzel, 1969).
- Although it cannot be said that there have been great breakthroughs using behavior therapy techniques to treat chronic and/or severe problems (e.g., schizophrenia; O'Leary & Wilson, 1987), more recently there are encouraging indications that some behav-

ioral strategies may be effective in prevention or early treatment of problems (Edelstein & Michelson, 1986; see Chapter 22 in this volume). Such primary and secondary prevention efforts may prove to be more cost-beneficial than treatment and rehabilitation.
- A small subfield of researchers associated with behavior therapy has studied the environmental context of the behavior change process from the environmental design (Krasner, 1980) and ecological perspectives (Rogers-Warren & Warren, 1977). Seemingly lost from reference in today's literature are exciting studies which demonstrated how modifying the environmental aspects of different settings could enhance the lives of many present and future inhabitants of diverse settings (e.g., Twordosz, Cataldo, & Risley, 1974).
- There is a collection of methodologically sound studies that have used behavioral principles to address a variety of community problems, e.g., crime prevention, health and safety, preserving the ecology (Greene, Winett, Van Houten, Geller, & Iwata, 1987). These studies show the potential of the behavioral paradigm for facilitating changes within communities, and for redirecting some behavior therapy efforts away from the mire of DSM-III-restricted problems (see Sarason, 1981, for an extended historical analysis of this affiliation). Ironically enough, it has been argued that amelioration of diverse community problems may enhance mental health and health more than traditionally directed services (Winett, 1985).

Thus, both historically and contemporarily, some behavior therapists have shown an inclination to innovate not just on the conceptual and technical side, but also with the service delivery component. These innovations have attempted to reach people in their natural environments, with more preventive interventions, often involving changes in setting, organizational or community structures, and often entailing intervention within new problem domains.

Yet it is safe to say that today much work in behavior therapy still is housed within the traditional service delivery system. The question that must be asked now is, why is that a problem?

THE FUNDAMENTAL ISSUE

Needs and Resources

Virtually paralleling the advent and ascendance of behavior therapy has been a series of studies and analyses (see review in Gesten & Jason, 1987) that have repeatedly made one major point. Current and future mental health and health needs far outstrip the capacities of present delivery systems. That is, needs surpass resources. Thus, when the number of persons in need of service is analyzed, for example, such as substance abusers, elderly persons who are disabled, pregnant teenagers, victims of the AIDS epidemic, it is apparent that current one-to-one rehabilitory services cannot handle the potential case load. The problem is further put into perspective when it is noted that most often discussions and debates in the United States center on policies to cut back or otherwise economize within health delivery systems.

Table 23–1 summarizes additional and projected mental health problems and needs to further substantiate the discrepancy between needs and resources.

Further, when it is also realized that many people in need of service are presently not receiving help, that chronic problems are particularly resistant to treatment, that current services are expensive and providers may not be able to increase case loads, but that the numbers of persons with mental health and health problems will increase in the future, then it becomes apparent that fundamental innovations in service delivery systems must be made. The question is what are the conceptual and strategic foundations of those "fundamental innovations."

Service Delivery Innovations

Part of the basis for change in service delivery systems comes from the generative period of behavior therapy referred to earlier. The second part of the innovation plan rests with community psychology and public health perspectives and tactics. Areas that have received experimentation in behavior therapy include:

1. Training and appropriate use of paraprofessional and various mediators of behavior change.
2. Initial efforts at primary and secondary prevention.
3. An ecological perspective and a focus on environmental change.
4. A concern with addressing diverse community problems not typically under the purview of mental health and health problems and services.

These areas complement basic perspectives, concepts, and strategies within community psychology and public health as well as more recent derivatives that can be called community health promotion and health promotion sciences (Altman & Green, 1987). The major perspective is that much more emphasis

Table 23-1. Examples of Unmet Contemporary and Future Mental Health Problems and Needs in the United States

PROBLEMS/NEEDS	SOURCE
The prevalence rate in the U.S. for severe affective disorders is about 6%, *and* mild to moderate symptomatology rates range from 9–26%.	Munoz, Glish, Soo-Hoo, & Robertson, 1982
The incidence rate of child abuse and neglect in U.S. in 1984 was 1.7 million reported cases. However, it is likely that the actual incidence and prevalence rates for various forms of child abuse, neglect, and psychological maltreatment are much higher.	Hart & Brassard, 1987; Melton & Davidson, 1987
At any given time, 15–35% of the U.S. population needs mental health services.	Kiesler, 1985
Although 3.2 million children in the U.S. show evidence of some major emotional problem, only 10% receive treatment; half of the 7 million children in the U.S. with major learning problems never receive any help.	Gesten & Jason, 1987
By the turn of the 21st century, in the U.S., about 40 million people will have mental health disorders; this estimate may be too conservative because of potential increases from sick and/or dependent elderly and an increase in children from single-parent households.	Gesten & Jason, 1987
Shifts to high technology in the U.S. and other developed countries may cause physical relocations and periods of unemployment, which may result in increased mental health disorders	Dooley, Catalno, & Serxner (1987; general reference)

needs to be placed on primary prevention. Primary prevention from a traditional public health perspective is population-focused and attempts to intervene prior to the onset of problems. A classic and successful example of primary prevention using a "passive" strategy (i.e., not requiring individual behavior change) is fluoridation of the water supply to prevent dental problems. Providing early education and training to children and adolescents to prevent teenage pregnancy and the spread of sexually transmitted diseases (STDs) is an example of an "active" primary prevention strategy, albeit an example that is both controversial and without firm conceptual foundations and complete empirical support (Reppucci, 1987). The considerable interest in smoking prevention, dietary change, and increases in exercise and activity is another example of active primary prevention (Bloom, 1988).

Secondary prevention from a public health perspective entails identification of those individuals who manifest early signs of a disorder and/or otherwise are at high risk for a disorder. The major aspects of secondary prevention are early identification and intervention. Examples of secondary prevention include screening and treatment for hypertension or an unfavorable blood lipid (e.g., cholesterol level) profile. A more psychological example is providing support and training for interested parents-to-be where at least one of the parents reports being abused as a child. Thus, primary prevention is generally community-wide and provides intervention to a population, whereas secondary prevention is more targeted and provides intervention only to those matching certain profiles. Prevention strategies are, however, best viewed as on a continuum with a range of possibilities between primary, secondary, and tertiary (effective rehabilitation) prevention.

Clearly, a complementary continuum is the notion that services can be delivered in a "waiting" or "seeking" mode (Rappaport & Chinsky, 1974; Rappaport, 1977). In a waiting mode, a professional literally waits within traditional settings for clients, usually those who are highly distressed, to present themselves. The waiting mode is, of course, the mode that behavior therapy has become most associated with. In the seeking mode, an individual will often not just work within the confines of an office setting but rather search out problems in the community and work with various community people and organizations. The seeking mode is frequently associated with preventive interventions, although this need not be the case. For example, working with violent youth gangs in the community, or with those gang members who are incarcerated, can be seen as late secondary or tertiary prevention.

A term that fits both preventive and seeking mode interventions is *proactive*. That is, rather than only reacting to problems, even within a preventive stance, being proactive means anticipating problems and intervening. A good example of a preventive, proactive intervention is comprehensive and sustained preretirement training for employees well in advance of retirement time. A reactive approach may involve a crash course in retirement training close to the date of retirement, or stress management training for employees not able to deal with the pressures of retirement.

Table 23–2 summarizes and integrates the points concerning modes of prevention and waiting versus seeking intervention modes.

It is also important to illustrate that conceptual innovation (or lack thereof) is not the same as service delivery innovation. Table 23–3 shows that both traditional conceptualization and innovative conceptualization may be used in different service delivery modes. Our usual goal will be to link conceptual and service delivery innovation.

PERSPECTIVES FOR INNOVATION

This section will focus on two perspectives for innovation, health enhancement, and a developmental/ecological approach, as well as theory and models for structural and behavior change.

Health Enhancement

A major recent perspective involves focusing on strengths and competencies rather than deficits. For most of its history, psychology has had an almost myopic attraction to pathology at the expense of studying health enhancement processes. At the extreme, an entire conceptual and treatment system—

Table 23–2. Prevention and Intervention Modes

INTERVENTION MODE	PREVENTION MODEL		
	PRIMARY	SECONDARY	TERTIARY
Waiting	Usually incompatible with each other but can include, for example, physical exams for everyone with health enhancement advice	Setting up specialized but traditional services for those individuals with high-risk mental health profiles	Most typified by traditional pathology-oriented health and mental health practices
Seeking	Mass media approach to basic health and safety measures for all people	Identifying high-risk individuals through mass public screenings and providing treatment	Finding already highly distressed or chronically disturbed individuals and providing an intervention to more expediently restore functioning

Table 23–3. Conceptual and Services Delivery Bases of Interventions

SERVICE DELIVERY	CONCEPTUAL	
	TRADITIONAL	INNOVATIVE
Waiting	Fee-for-service psychoanalytic therapy	Fee-for service behavior therapy
Seeking	Providing advice based on psychoanalytic theory to TV viewers	Using Social Cognitive Theory as a basis for community health promotion programs

Note: Based on Rappaport, 1977.

psychoanalysis—largely rested on an initial data base of "neurotic" upper middle class women.

More generally, the case has been made for studying and focusing on health enhancement from a number of different quarters, including:

- The strengths, competencies, and empowerment approach of community psychology (Gesten & Jason, 1987; Rappaport, 1987). This approach emphasizes focusing on enhancing skills and resources to enable people to meet and influence the demands of individuals, settings, and institutions.
- The salutogenic approach ("sense of coherence") from Antonovsky (1987) and the concept of "hardiness" from Kobasa (1985), with the notion that certain characteristics can substantially help people positively deal with life's stressors.
- Studies on "invulnerability," that is, individuals with seemingly overwhelming adversity in their lives who not only survive but prosper (Garmezy, 1981; Rosenberg, 1987).

Although none of these three strains of research is well developed, each of them serves as a valuable heuristic. Fascinating insights into human behavior and ideas for program design may be gained by shifting from a pathological to a salutogenic perspective. For example, studying and analyzing how effective people master stress and difficult situations can generate ideas for programs in health enhancement (i.e., template matching; Winett, 1988).

Developmental/Ecological

A developmental/ecological approach most basically involves taking a lifespan approach and studying important settings and systems that impinge on different individuals at different points in their life (e.g., see Bronfenbrenner, 1977). A life span approach attends to predictable milestones and transition points, equally predictable stressors, and skills and resources needed to successfully negotiate these critical milestones and transition points. Examples of important milestones and transition points include the arrival of a child, entry into school, the dawn of adolescence, leaving school, entry into the workforce, unemployment, retirement, and death of a spouse.

Whereas particular skills and resources may be needed at each transition point (e.g., care of a newborn, acquisition of childcare services), importantly, skills and resources throughout life appear to fit into a number of definable categories, such as, how to learn new skills, how to elicit and reciprocate support from others. Thus, although training programs for different transition points may emphasize particular content, the general strategies at different points may be the same or similar (Danish, Galambos, & Laquarta, 1983). Note also that life skills training and the generation of resources nicely fit with the strengths and competencies and the template matching approaches noted previously.

An ecological perspective emphasizes that behavior within environments must be seen as a transactional process, which on the one hand suggests that changes within settings and systems can alter behaviors. Clearly, on the other hand, enhancing people's skills can alter settings and how people negotiate environments. However, too much of psychological conceptualization and intervention inquiry has neglected the possibilities for environmental influence and change. Thus, for example, some of the problems of retirement can be alleviated when there are changes in worksite policies including phased retirement, part-time work, and nonreimbursed positions (Lovett, 1989). In this example, alterations of policies and procedures in the work setting are environmental changes that can influence the lives of many employees within and outside of the worksite (Mullen, 1988). Also within this example, it is clear that the ecological intervention is aimed at a particular life transition point, can be synergistically enhanced by individual skills and resource interventions (preretirement training), and can be a seeking-mode, preventive intervention.

Importantly, an ecological perspective is consistent with public health approaches. Traditionally, public health always has emphasized analyses of environmental determinants of disease, the interaction of environmental determinants, host factors and agents, and environmental modification (Hanlon & Pickett, 1984).

Models for Program Design

Yet another important development has been the search for models for designing and implementing large-scale intervention programs. That is, if the aim is to develop and implement primary and secondary prevention programs, on what basis should this be done? What are the actual design and implementation steps?

The two most prominent approaches have been the PRECEDE model developed by Green (Green & Anderson, 1986), and social marketing (Manoff,

1985). The PRECEDE model involves a step-by-step analysis of existing community problems, prioritization of these problems, analyses of resources to alleviate the problem, barriers and facilitators of change, and potential strategies of change and their probability of success. This seminal model is depicted in Figure 23–1 and has been used in a number of effective health promotion efforts (Green, 1984) such as community hypertension control programs.

Social marketing attempts to take the framework and concepts from commercial marketing and apply them to the world of idea dissemination and social and health behavior change. The major contribution of the framework is the delineation of the key marketing variables, the notion that these variables are interactive, and that effective programs must carefully consider and balance these variables in the design and implementation stages. The key variables are:

- Product—the ideas, behaviors, interactions, or tangible items that are the focus of the program and what people are asked to adopt.
- Price—the social, behavioral, effort, time, and monetary costs for procuring the product.
- Place—the settings in which the program and product are offered.

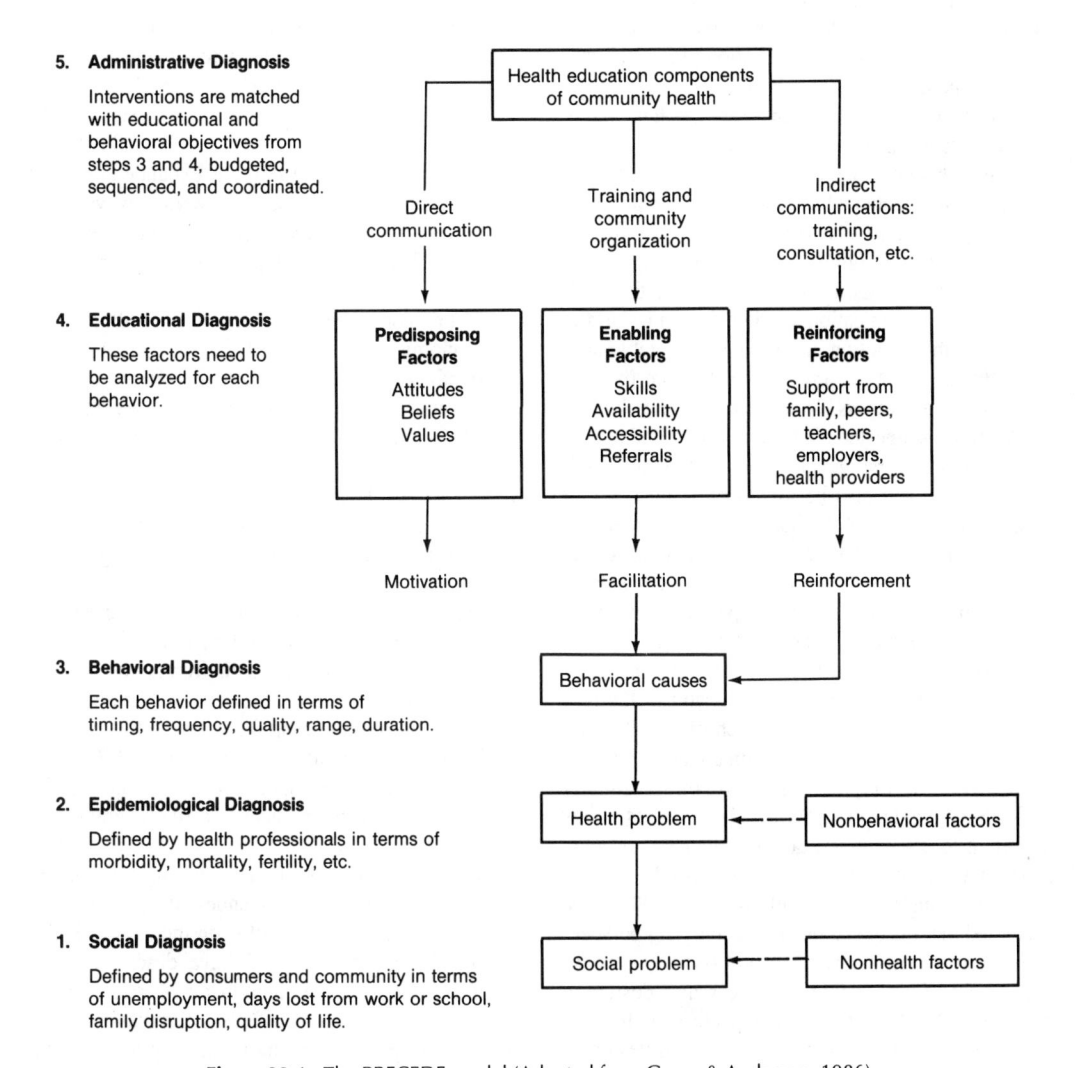

Figure 23.1. The PRECEDE model (Adapted from Green & Anderson, 1986).

- Promotion—the major strategies used to persuade individuals to adopt the product.

A fifth key variable is positioning. By this term it is meant how the product is differentiated from other similar products and the special niche that is developed for the product.

At the heart of the marketing approach is the idea of segmenting audiences (populations) and targeting those segments with particular products, at specific prices, delivered at certain places, by tailored promotion strategies. The interactive notion is found when change in one marketing variable usually leads to changes in other marketing variables. For example, repositioning and redesigning a product while lowering the time and effort to use that product may also suggest that the product's distribution place and promotion strategies should also be altered.

Various formative research methods have been used to develop information pertinent to these major variables. This information is derived from particular population segments and then used to tailor products and strategies to particular segments. Thus, the formative research and design process is interactive.

Social marketing has been used in conjunction with prominent communication models in some of the largest health promotion programs with notable success (Solomon & Maccoby, 1984). Despite the evidence for effectiveness, Winett, King, and Altman (1989) have suggested that PRECEDE and social marketing are "first generation" models that will further evolve and also be joined by other "second generation" models. A limitation of both models is that they tend to be atheoretical. For example, in the PRECEDE model it is not clear once a decision is made to mount a program for a particular problem what concepts and principles guide program development. Likewise, it is far from clear within the social marketing framework what concepts and techniques guide the critical formative research phase. In practice, much has been borrowed from commercial marketing with far too much reliance on potentially misleading verbal reports (Winett, 1986). Thus, if it is important to segment and target audiences, on what conceptual and technical basis is this done?

Winett, King, Altman, and Kramer (1988) have suggested that the developmental/ecological perspectives discussed previously can form one key conceptual schema for targeting audiences and designing programs. Recall that these perspectives will point toward people at transition points and milestones, critical stressors, skills, resources, and key settings and systems in which behaviors are enacted and where populations may be reached, and where aspects of those settings and systems may be altered to facilitate behavior change.

This perspective is illustrated in Figure 23–2, which shows both the concepts "embeddedness" and "interactivity." Embededness means that one level of analysis (e.g., a setting) is encompassed (but not explained) by a succeeding level (e.g., a type of community organization). *Interactivity* means the reciprocity of influence between levels, as when an individual alters a setting but the resulting characteristics of a setting influence the individual's behavior. Bronfenbrenner (1977) has further described these concepts in his seminal work. However, another basis for program design must rest with theory that delineates principles and procedures for change.

Social-cognitive Theory

Recently, Bandura (1986) has expanded on social learning theory in a number of important ways so that the term social-cognitive theory more appropriately describes this approach. These expansions include:

1. A broader delineation of social, cultural, and economic influences on behavior so that "understanding behavior in context" becomes a dynamic and useful part of the theory (e.g., see Bandura, 1986, chapter four, on the diffusion of innovation).
2. Greater explication of cognitive processes (e.g., information processing) so that the theory's reliance on operant and classical conditioning foundations is at best tenuous.
3. Increased movement toward a systems orientation by having the reciprocal interactions of cognitive, affective, behavioral, and environmental domains as well as the notion of the dynamic nature of such interactions as the central part of the theory.
4. Further development of principles of behavior change and, most importantly, the demonstration of their utility in a number of different areas.

Thus, Bandura's paradigm is evolving conceptually and demonstrating many avenues of applications—signs of a paradigm that still is on the ascent (Kuhn, 1970). Winett et al. (1989) have described social cognitive theory as a meta-theory because it has subsumed a number of different theories under its umbrella (e.g., information-processing and learning theories, diffusion theory). They also noted that virtu-

A Developmental/Ecological Perspective

Institutions and Systems
- Economic
- Legal/Regulatory
- Political
- Culture and Tradition

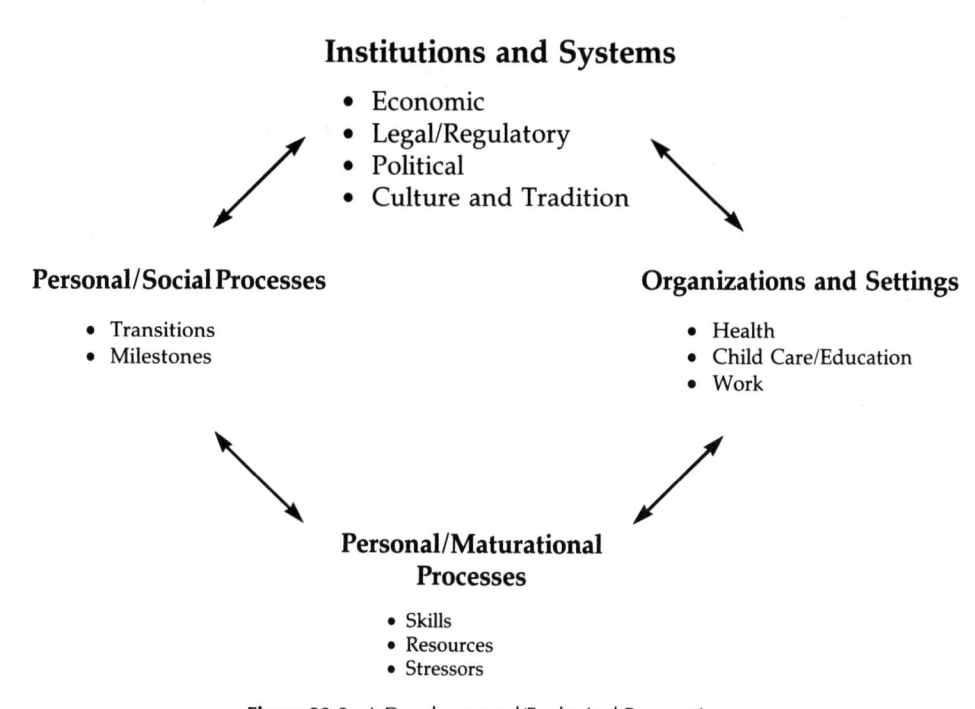

Personal/Social Processes
- Transitions
- Milestones

Organizations and Settings
- Health
- Child Care/Education
- Work

Personal/Maturational Processes
- Skills
- Resources
- Stressors

Figure 23.2. A Developmental/Ecological Perspective.

ally all scientifically based health promotion programs presently rest on social cognitive theory. This last point has its benefits and costs. The benefits are that each program evaluation constitutes a test of the theory. The costs are that other theory and conceptualization for health promotion are neglected.

Multilevel Analysis and Theory

A primary danger of the reliance on social cognitive theory for health promotion programs is that analyses, conceptualization, and intervention primarily remain at the personal and interpersonal levels. Thus, theories of organization and community change, or theories from political science or economics, are rarely foundations for these programs. Not surprisingly, this has meant that few of these programs have involved substantial changes in community structures and legal and regulatory strictures (however, see Farquhar et al., 1990).

Winett et al. (1989) not only pointed out an array of appropriate theories and applications using higher levels of analyses, but also that:

1. An approach that does not include analyses of community and institutional influences and changes in systems is discrepant with a public health approach that has always emphasized the role of the environment in health status.
2. Ecological conceptions are prominently mentioned in the community health promotion literature (and see earlier discussion), but the actualization of these concepts (e.g., analyses and modification of systems) is generally lacking in program design and intervention.
3. More efficacious programs will probably result when interventions are multi-level, that is, combining skill training with organizational change. Indeed, such combinations will probably have synergistic effects.

However, because those working in the field are primarily psychologists and health educators, it would be unexpected for much theory to be other than psychological. The task then is to extend psychological theory and application in a number of fruitful ways, such as, more analysis and change of environmental factors, a point which will be addressed in later sections of this chapter.

INTEGRATION

Major Directions

The argument has been made that behavior therapy can benefit from a re-examination of some of its own history that emphasized service delivery innovation. However, even more so, advancement can come through the examination and use of concepts and strategies from community psychology, public health, health promotion sciences, and community health promotion. The major impetus for innovation is that it has been clear for many years that health and mental health resources as presently used in restorative therapies cannot meet present and future needs. Rather, simply developing new conceptualizations and techniques to fit within prevailing delivery systems is not sufficient.

Major stances, perspectives, and theories that have been discussed for reorienting the goals and means of behavior therapy have included:

- More emphasis on primary and secondary prevention with less emphasis on tertiary prevention. Note that the word "emphasis" does not mean that we are advocating abandonment of all restorative services—surely a mistake of overcorrection.
- More emphasis on proactive seeking mode interventions and less emphasis on reactive waiting mode interventions. Again, it would be a mistake to believe that all problems can be anticipated and planned for well in advance or that many waiting mode services are not useful.
- Taking a salutogenic posture that fosters focusing on health enhancing processes. This does not mean that behavior therapy would relinquish its concern for and duty to treat highly disturbed people, but that much may be gained by shifting away from a narrow focus on pathology.
- A developmental/ecological approach that examines the stressors at key life transition points and milestones and the skills and resources necessary to negotiate those points. The ecological focus forces an analysis of settings and systems, their influence on developmental processes, and the potential modification of settings to facilitate adaptive behaviors.
- A social marketing framework that is useful for designing and implementing programs but that requires additional conceptual and methodological inputs to be more optimal.
- Social cognitive theory that was described as both a meta-theory and still-evolving paradigm, and where its concepts, principles, and procedures have proven to be a remarkably fertile basis for various health promotion programs.
- Multilevel analyses and theory to augment more psychological theory. Particularly needed are theories and analyses that focus more on environmental change.

Table 24–4 summarizes the major directions that have been highlighted to this point. Although at several junctures these points have been addressed in

Table 23-4. Primary Directions for Behavioral Interventions

Timing	Primary and Secondary Prevention; Particular Transitions and Milestones
Scope	Population-focused or Individuals at High Risk; Individual and Environmental Change
Mode	Proactive, Seeking, Multilevel
Emphasis	Health Enhancement, Strengths and Competencies
Targeting	Social Marketing in the Service of Developmental/Ecological Considerations
Concepts	Social Cognitive Theory and Theories for Higher Levels of Analysis
Principles	Psychological Behavior Change and Structural Change

overlapping fashion, the emphasis so far has been more on articulating the points and less on their integration. To better formulate these integrations, an overall framework and exemplar behavior change schema will be presented.

Framework

Winett et al. (1989) have developed a framework for integrating the theoretical and practical strengths of health psychology and public health with the purpose of developing more effective interventions. A framework is useful in establishing a common set of concepts, principles, procedures, and guidelines with which to organize any endeavor. The steps that many frameworks include are:

- Defining a problem through study of a number of data sources.
- Identifying different theories that are useful for understanding the problem while understanding the value bases of different theories.
- Specifying goals for change.
- Designing an intervention.
- Implementing the intervention.
- Assessing a range of impacts of an intervention.

Figure 23–3 is a simple overview depiction of a conceptual and strategic framework that Winett et al. (1989) offered as a first step in integrating the two fields. The key within the framework is multilevel analysis that can often lead to the design of multilevel interventions. Basically, in multilevel analysis a problem is being studied using theory, perspectives, and data which often represent personal and interpersonal levels (the province of psychology) and organizational/environmental and institutional/societal levels (the province of public health). The final result is a synthesis of these contrasting data sources.

For example, understanding how cigarette smoking is acquired by adolescents requires theory, data, and analysis pertaining to:

- Individual beliefs and behaviors; individual repertoires of other health-risk behaviors; individual physiological responses, such as, nicotine addiction.
- Interpersonal influences including peers and family members.
- Organizational and environmental influences including school and community policies and programs and local availability of cigarettes in a variety of settings.
- Institutional and societal influences including laws and regulations concerning advertising, availability, and price.

No one level of analysis is seen as the only essential or correct one, and a general purpose of this aspect of the framework is to see how input from different levels fits together.

The strategic parts of the framework are the steps involved in designing what will typically be multilevel interventions. However, each of the steps also entails contributions from psychology and public health. For example, goals can pertain to both individual change and community organization, and the design of the intervention can incorporate both procedures for individual change and changes within settings (e.g., teaching adolescents procedures to resist smoking and tightening and enforcing school rules and laws about selling cigarettes to minors; Altman, Foster, Rasenick-Douss, & Tye, 1989). Implementing a program can meld techniques from social marketing and community organization to help assure that the intervention is not only well-targeted but is one that will likely be maintained in the community. Sources to assess impacts will also use data from different levels of analysis, for example, individual student smoking rates, numbers of stores refusing to sell cigarettes to minors.

Although the framework can be used for designing any intervention, several key points from prior discussion in this chapter and from Table 23–4 are incorporated in the framework. That is, developmental and ecological perspectives, the use of theories from different disciplines and levels of analysis, larger scale interventions, and the emphasis on behavioral and structural change, all fit within the broader notion of multilevel analysis and multilevel intervention. The framework can also be overlaid with the points pertaining to strengths and competencies, prevention, and seeking mode interventions from community psychology, although this need not be the case. Finally, the framework can be made operational by a variety of persons working alone or in coalitions. These include academics, public health professionals, social workers, educators, business people, or simply concerned citizens.

Although a framework serves an organizational and integrative function, it does not necessarily suggest the specific procedures or processes of behavior

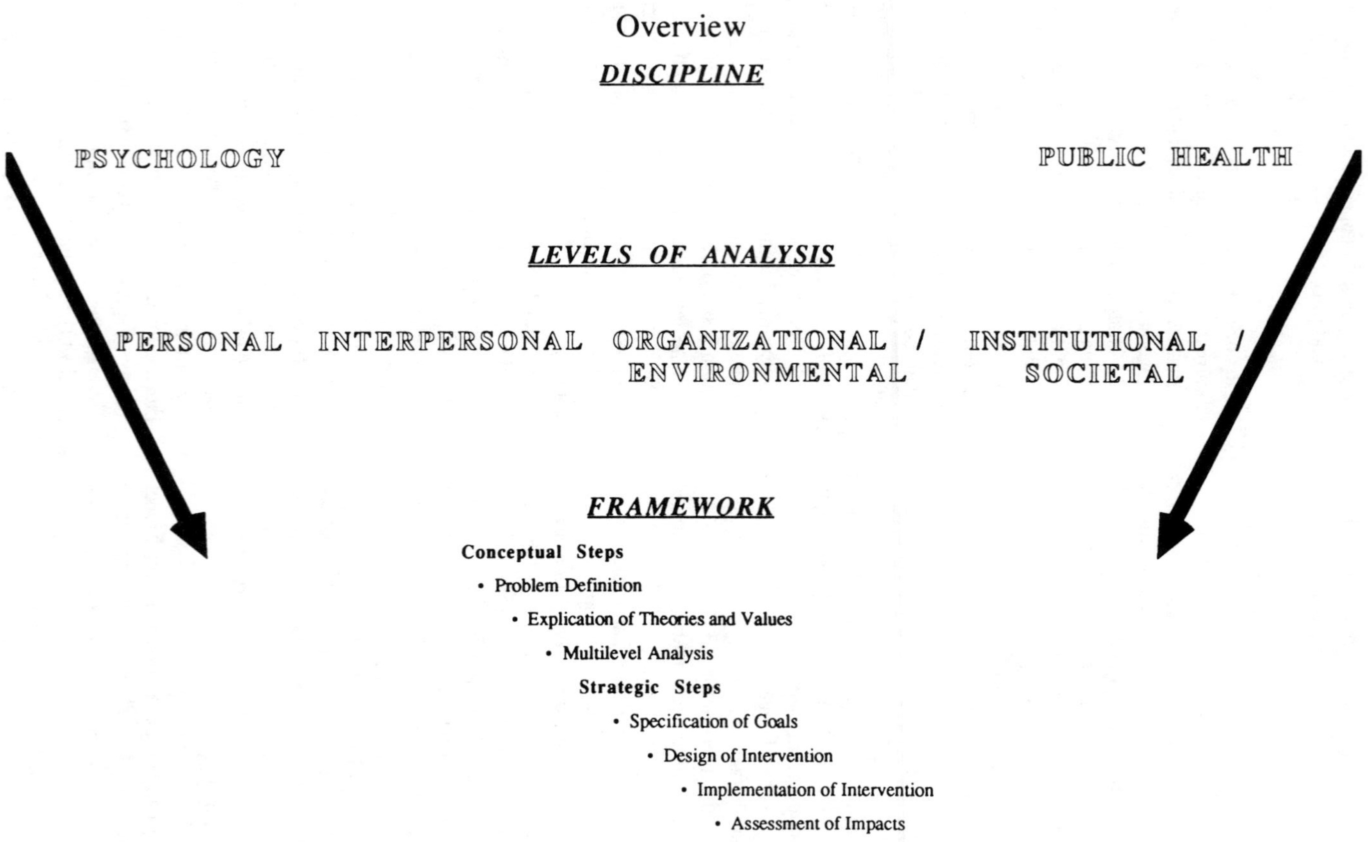

Overview
DISCIPLINE

PSYCHOLOGY

PUBLIC HEALTH

LEVELS OF ANALYSIS

PERSONAL INTERPERSONAL ORGANIZATIONAL / INSTITUTIONAL /
ENVIRONMENTAL SOCIETAL

FRAMEWORK

Conceptual Steps
- Problem Definition
- Explication of Theories and Values
- Multilevel Analysis

Strategic Steps
- Specification of Goals
- Design of Intervention
- Implementation of Intervention
- Assessment of Impacts

Figure 23.3. A Conceptual and Strategic Framework (from Winett, King, & Altman, 1989).

change that need to be part of a program. Therefore, the next section examines one such schema.

Process of Change Schema

Figure 23–4 depicts a process of change schema that has the following elements and emphases:

- The recognition from Bandura (1986) and others that there are different stages of change and that each stage must be properly addressed.
- The notion that change involves the interplays between cognition, performance, and the environment.
- The use of procedures from social cognitive theory but with major emphasis on modeling, goal setting, and real-life practice and corrective feedback.
- The use of these different step-by-step procedures within each stage with the notion that the process of change often requires a number of corrective interactions of steps.
- The notion that behavior change often requires a supportive context at multilevels, that is, interpersonal, community, and cultural, and that without this supportive context initial change is likely to be minimal; also, more than likely, even if initial change is substantial, it will not be maintained.

The process of change schema is meant to be more than a heuristic. Rather, it is meant to be the actual cornerstone for large-scale behavior change campaigns. In the final section, the major points from this chapter, the conceptual and strategic framework, and the process of change schema will all coalesce around one exemplar multilevel analysis and intervention.

EXEMPLAR PROGRAM FOR ADOLESCENTS

Conceptual Steps

In this section, one exemplar program for young adolescents will be painted in broad strokes to illustrate the major points and perspectives and the framework and schema presented in this chapter. In the general area of adolescent health promotion, there have been a number of conceptually sound and empirically based programs, with the best examples being in smoking prevention (Best, Thompson, Santi, Smith, & Brown, 1988) and to a lesser extent the prevention of adolescent pregnancy (Reppucci, 1987).

However, a scientist or practitioner, when reviewing this often disparate literature on adolescent health, and when examining community settings primarily used by adolescents (i.e., schools) or frequently used by adolescents (i.e., shopping malls), will probably be struck by a number of key points:

1. Most programs have tended to focus on one or two risk-taking behaviors (e.g., alcohol and drug use).
2. Theory (e.g., Jessor, 1984) and observation suggest that high-risk behaviors often occur together as a "syndrome" (e.g., alcohol abuse, smoking, reckless driving, unprotected sex).
3. Many high-risk patterns begin early, are forewarnings of more difficult problems in later adolescence, and suggest preventive programs.
4. Many programs have relatively singular, one-level interventions, and some have become unduly simplistic ("Just Say No").
5. Many programs focus on reducing or eliminating high-risk behaviors, but it is unclear what behaviors take the place of these behaviors if the program is "effective."
6. The rationale for targeting certain adolescents in certain ways is unclear.
7. There are few, if any, examples of comprehensive multilevel programs.

A more thorough analysis of these seven points is involved in the conceptual steps of the framework (Figure 23–3). The framework's steps are not linear, but are interactive. For example, an initial problem definition (e.g., the rate of teenage pregnancy in this area is increasing and has reached unacceptable levels) may lead to particular observations (risk-taking behaviors are linked), which start to alter the original problem definition, which can lead to a search for other relevant theories and analyses of risk behaviors from different levels of analysis, another search for more appropriate theories, and a redefining of the problem (a high-risk behavior lifestyle).

The key step involves multilevel analysis where a problem is addressed from different levels of analysis. By way of illustration, only two levels—the personal and organizational/environmental—will be discussed.

At the personal level, theories pertinent to health beliefs (Janz & Becker, 1984), individual cognition and behavior (Bandura, 1986), and human development (Bronfenbrenner, 1977) can be reviewed for ideas concerning the origins and modification of maladaptive behaviors in younger adolescents. Following the emphasis of this chapter, a number of

A Process of Change Schema

Stages

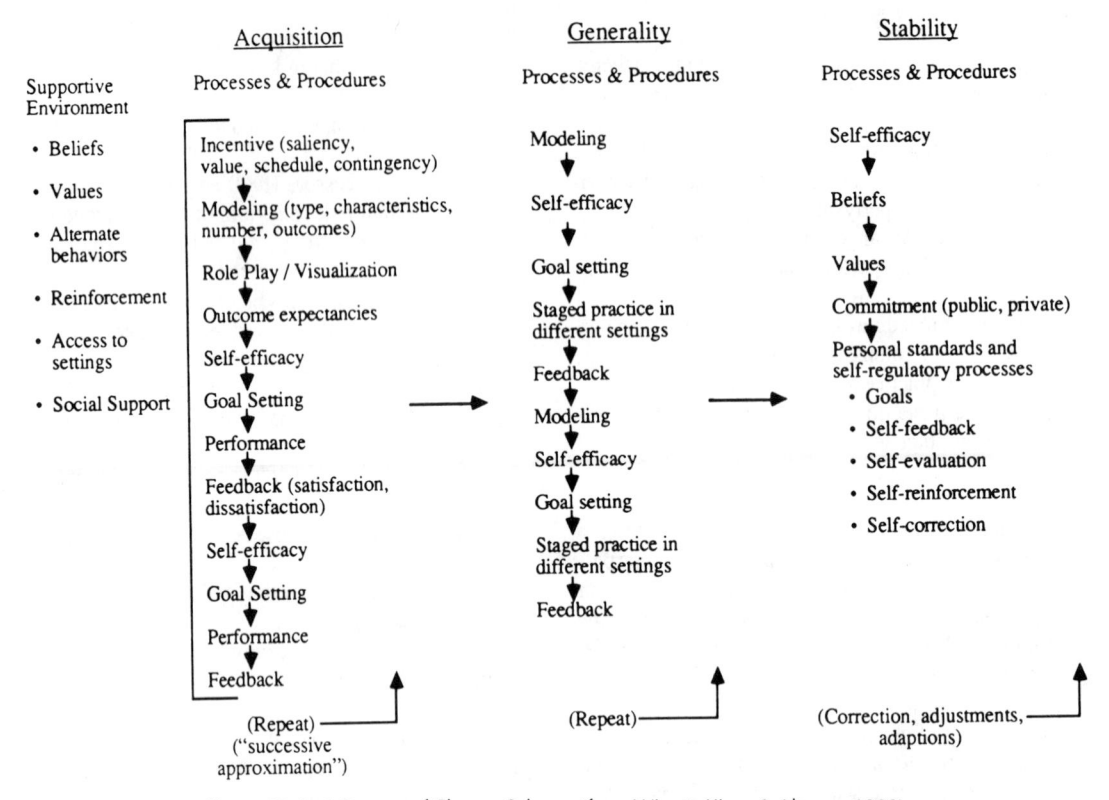

Supportive Environment	Acquisition Processes & Procedures	Generality Processes & Procedures	Stability Processes & Procedures
• Beliefs • Values • Alternate behaviors • Reinforcement • Access to settings • Social Support	Incentive (saliency, value, schedule, contingency) ↓ Modeling (type, characteristics, number, outcomes) ↓ Role Play / Visualization ↓ Outcome expectancies ↓ Self-efficacy ↓ Goal Setting ↓ Performance ↓ Feedback (satisfaction, dissatisfaction) ↓ Self-efficacy ↓ Goal Setting ↓ Performance ↓ Feedback (Repeat) ("successive approximation")	Modeling ↓ Self-efficacy ↓ Goal setting ↓ Staged practice in different settings ↓ Feedback ↓ Modeling ↓ Self-efficacy ↓ Goal setting ↓ Staged practice in different settings ↓ Feedback (Repeat)	Self-efficacy ↓ Beliefs ↓ Values ↓ Commitment (public, private) ↓ Personal standards and self-regulatory processes • Goals • Self-feedback • Self-evaluation • Self-reinforcement • Self-correction (Correction, adjustments, adaptions)

Figure 23.4. A Process of Change Schema (from Winett, King, & Altman, 1989).

points from developmental theory will be highlighted. These points include:

1. Although the existence of qualitatively distinct stages proposed by Piaget and others has been challenged, it does appear appropriate to think of a series of progressive stages and levels (Proctor, 1986) and continuous cognitive developmental trends.
2. These trends involve an increasing capacity to process information and movement from concrete to formal operational thinking (Flavell, 1984).
3. Early adolescence begins around 11 or 12 years of age and lasts until about 14 years of age. This is a period of remarkable physical growth and the development of secondary sexual characteristics. However, the young adolescent's intellectual processes appear to remain largely concrete (Piaget & Inhelder, 1969).
4. This last point is extremely important with regard to high-risk behaviors. The young adolescent shows little future-oriented forethought or planning and little consideration of the long-term consequences of present decisions. Decisions are primarily based on past or present experience.
5. An individual's sense of self is just beginning to form, including their sexual identity and sexuality (Eriksen, 1968). Emotions about sexuality are often confused and ambivalent.
6. There is usually more identification with peer groups and less involvement with parents, particularly concerning many high-risk behaviors.

Thus, early adolescence can be seen as a time of rapid physical change, emotional turbulence, exposure to high-risk situations and models (e.g., in school or from older siblings and peers) but with still relatively immature cognitive processes coupled with less reliance on parental guidance. Patterns established during this period (e.g., absence from school, experimentation with drugs) certainly can set the stage for later adolescence and early adulthood. It is a pivotal time, yet a difficult time, to intervene—the young adolescent is moving beyond parental control, may be tempted to experiment or actually experiment in high-risk behaviors, but may lack the conceptual skills to appreciate the consequences of various actions.

Analyses at the organizational/environmental level are also revealing on two accounts:

1. Early adolescence marks the first time that many children are left home alone for extended periods and are without adult supervision in various community settings (e.g., shopping malls, movies, fast-food restaurants, swimming pools) unattended.
2. There are few settings and activities especially designed for children this age. They no longer fit well into playgrounds but they also do not fit well into middle and later adolescent settings (e.g., parties at different sites, recreational settings dominated by older teens).

Thus, when young adolescents are not at home or at school, it is unclear *where* they should be, much less *what* they should be doing. Coupled with the points from a developmental perspective, a picture emerges of many young adolescents just "hanging around" without parental attention and guidance, and without the abilities to assess the consequences of various risk-taking behaviors.

Clearly, within the conceptual steps of the framework, there would be additional gleaning of theory and data concerning interpersonal influences on young adolescents (e.g., peer groups, salient interpersonal and media-based models) and institutional/societal influences (e.g., laws concerning age/work requirements, legal and economic factors affecting access to cigarettes and other harmful substances, mores concerning intramural sports participation versus the emphasis and status of interscholastic sports). This information would further clarify the context of adolescent risk-taking behaviors and potential points of intervention.

However, and again by way of illustration, the emphasis will rest on the analyses done at the personal and organizational/environmental level. These analyses point toward:

1. Education and skill training geared to particular cognitive ability levels that will teach young adolescents how to cope with their own development, and new and risky situations and how to assess the consequences of particular actions.
2. A focus on alternative behaviors to replace high-risk behaviors (however, the alternative behaviors probably also need to have an element of excitement and risk-taking; e.g., sports participation, rock climbing, entertainment activities).
3. The creation or expansion of settings for young adolescents where such alternative and other behaviors may be enacted.
4. The enhancement (or re-establishment) of parent-child communications.

Note also that these points are consistent with those noted in Table 23-4, "Primary Directions for Behavioral Interventions." That is, the focus is on proactive, preventive interventions that are aimed toward transitions or milestones, with an emphasis on health enhancement, strengths and competencies.

Strategic Steps

The actual design, implementation, and evaluation of programs, that is, the strategic steps, should flow from the conceptual steps. In the present example, this means that the goals not only pertain to changes in a number of early adolescent risk-taking behaviors, but also changes in the environment to foster and maintain these changes. Goals for change in risk-taking behaviors must be within realistic expectations based on current levels of specifiable behaviors, the likelihood of change based on those levels, and current health behavior change literature, and the amount of resources that can be brought to bear on the problem.

The program design should include interventions at multiple levels. In the present example, an educational skill-training intervention, housed in schools, would provide individuals with the knowledge and cognitive and behavioral skills to cope with high-risk situations. This part of the program can follow from other modeling, problem-solving, inoculation programs (e.g., Evans, 1984; Best et al., 1988), but also include other elements. Following the points noted previously, several other key aspects of the program are:

1. All program content must be tailored to the cognitive developmental levels of the adolescents. For

example, training for anticipating consequences of actions is important.
2. New skills and behaviors must be practiced not only with in-class role plays but in structured homework assignments throughout acquisition and generality stages following the steps in the process of change schema (see Figure 23-4). Indeed, the entire curriculum must follow the schema (Winett et al., 1989). For example, there can be small steps involved in homework assignments, practiced previously in the school settings; with practice emphasizing modeling, role playing, and feedback; and specific enactment goals. This process of behavior change is closely linked to antecedent and consequence cognitive change (i.e., outcome expectancies and self-efficacy).
3. The process of change schema not only alerts us to include a substantial maintenance part in the program that emphasizes commitment and value orientation strategies but that behavioral changes require a supportive context (see left-hand side of Figure 23-4).

Two critical environmental supports are parental involvement (affording support and modeling) in the main program and changes within settings to allow new behaviors to be optimally performed. Parental involvement might entail, for example, changes in parental health risk behaviors such as cigarette smoking and increases in healthful parental activities such as involvement in fitness, sports, or cultural activities. Environmental changes can include a much more expanded use of school facilities by students and parents. For a variety of reasons, many schools are empty after 3 p.m., except for a few club members and interscholastic athletes. A fuller expansion of sports and club activities, with some of these activities occurring on evenings and weekends, can facilitate parental involvement. Clearly, some students and parents would pay for these activities. Businesses and other community groups might also sponsor particular activities.

The optimal implementation of the program rests on the use of the social marketing framework and fitting the program into the community so that the program is likely to be maintained by the community. Social marketing alerts us to tailor the program (product) to young adolescents by theme, content, and alternative behaviors; to make sure there are minimal personal, social, and economic costs for participation; to deliver the program in places such as schools that are usually convenient for children and parents (but not always hospitable); and to promote the program in ways appropriate for the target groups (e.g., "hip" or attractive logos, apparel) and which provide distinct positioning.

A key concept for maintenance of the program within the community is reciprocal reinforcement (Jason et al., 1987). That is, all those persons and organizations involved in the program need to benefit in some way. Adolescents and parents may have the opportunity to participate in new activities; community groups and businesses may gain invaluable exposure and good will; schools may acquire additional revenue. It is also appropriate that programs and supporters keep evolving over time. New programs can represent new interests at a particular time, thus increasing participation and adding new sponsors.

The assessment of impacts is an ongoing monitoring process, with assessments conducted at multiple levels. In the present example, person level measures include cognitive measures directed to knowledge about risks of certain behaviors and methods to make decisions, and self-reported and unobtrusive measures of smoking, alcohol consumption, and sexual behavior. Follow-up measures can track program participant involvement in risk-taking behaviors, as well as rates of school dropout and teen pregnancy. Environmental level measures can include numbers of new programs and active participants, numbers of parental participants, and the number and degree of community and commercial sponsors. These assessments can also be done in relationship to the particular goals that have been established (see above) and can be periodically reviewed to modify the overall program.

Where possible, programs can follow true experimental or, more likely, quasi-experimental evaluation designs. Such evaluations would not only be of local interest but would feed back into the knowledge base for subsequent efforts (see Winett et al., 1989; chapter 2).

CONCLUSION

As we noted in the introduction to this chapter, behavior therapy has been characterized by a high level of theoretical, research, and applied innovation. However, over time, this spirit of innovation has mostly focused on what we called the conceptual and technical side of the issue of how to ameliorate health and mental health problems. As long as the service delivery system remains virtually the same and wedded to rehabilitory, fee-for-service approaches, it is unlikely that major impacts in these problems will be made. However, contemporary behavioral theory, principles, and procedures can be linked to a reformist zeal that earlier characterized behavior therapy and perspectives concerning large-scale preventive interventions from community psychology and public health. These include health enhancement and developmental/ecological perspectives and new theory and models for structural and behavior change. When these different concepts and strategies are integrated, they can form a basis for a wide array of proactive programs.

REFERENCES

Altman, D. G., Foster, V., Rasenick-Douss, L., & Tye, J. B. (1989). Reducing the illegal sale of cigarettes to minors. *Journal of the American Medical Association, 261*, 80–83.

Altman, D. G., & Green, L. W. (1988). Interdisciplinary perspectives on behavioral medicine training. *Annals of Behavioral Medicine, 19*(1), 4–7.

Antonovsky, A. (1987). *Unraveling the mystery of health: How people manage stress and stay well*. San Francisco: Jossey-Bass.

Bandura, A. (1986). *Social foundations of thought and action: A social cognitive theory*. Englewood Cliffs, NJ: Prentice-Hall.

Best, A., Thompson, S. J., Santi, S. M., Smith, E. A., & Brown, K. S. (1988). Preventing cigarette smoking among children. In L. Breslow, J. E. Fielding, & L. B. Lave (Eds.), *Annual review of public health, Vol. 9* (pp. 161–202). Palo Alto: Annual Review.

Bloom, B. (1988). *Health psychology: A psychosocial perspective*. Englewood Cliffs, NJ: Prentice-Hall.

Bronfenbrenner, U. (1977). Toward an experimental ecology of human development. *American Psychologist, 32*, 513–531.

Danish, S. J., Galambos, N. L., & Laquarta, I. (1983). Life development intervention: Skill training for personal competence. In R. D. Felner, L. A. Jason, J. N. Moritsugu, & J. S. S. Farber (Eds.), *Preventive psychology: Theory, research, and practice* (pp. 49–66). Elmsford, NY: Pergamon Press.

Dooley, D. D., Catalano, R., & Serxner, S. (1987). Economic development and community mental health. In L. A. Jason, R. E. Hess, R. D. Felner, & J. N. Moritsugu (Eds.), *Prevention: Toward a multidisciplinary approach* (pp. 91–115). New York: Haworth Press.

Edelstein, B. A., & Michelson, L. (Eds.) (1986). *Handbook of prevention*. New York: Plenum Press.

Erikson, E. (1968). *Identity: Youth and crisis*. New York: W W Norton.

Evans, R. I. (1984). A social inoculation strategy to deter smoking in adolescents. In J. D. Matarazzo, S. M. Weiss, J. A. Herd, N. E. Miller, & S. M. Weiss (Eds.), *Behavioral health: A handbook for health enhancement and disease prevention* (pp. 765–774). New York: John Wiley & Sons.

Farquhar, J. W., Fortmann, S. P., Flora, J. A., Taylor, C. B., Haskell, W. L., Williams, P. T., Maccoby, N., & Wood, P. D. (1990). Effects of community-wide education on cardiovascular risk factors. *Journal of the American Medical Association, 264*, 359–365.

Flavell, J. (1984, March). *Cognitive development of adolescents*. Paper presented at Carnegie Corporation of New York Conference on Unhealthful Risk-taking Behaviors in Adolescence, Stanford University, Palo Alto, CA.

Garmezy, N. (1981). Children under stress: Perspectives on antecedents and correlates of vulnerability and resistance to psychopathology. In A. I. Rubin, J. Aronoff, A. M. Barclay, & R. A. Zucker (Eds.), *Further explorations in personality* (pp. 167–193). New York: John Wiley & Sons.

Gesten, E. L., & Jason, L. A. (1987). Social and community interventions. *Annual Review of Psychology, 38*, 427–460.

Green, L. W. (1984). Modifying and developing health behaviors. In L. Breslow, J. A. Fielding, & L. B. Lave (Eds.), *Annual Review of Public Health, Vol. 5* (pp. 215–236). Palo Alto: Annual Reviews.

Green, L. W., & Anderson, C. L. (1986). *Community health* (5th Ed.). St. Louis, MO: C V Mosby.

Greene, B. F., Winett, R. A., Van Houten, R., Geller, E. S., & Iwata, B. A. (1987). *Behavior analysis in the community*. Lawrence, KS: Society for the Experimentation of Behavior.

Hanlon, J. J., & Pickett, G. E. (1984). *Public health: Administration and practice* (8th ed.). St. Louis, MO: C V Mosby.

Hart, S. N., & Brassard, M. R. (1987). A major threat to children's mental health: Psychological maltreatment. *American Psychologist, 42*, 160–165.

Hattie, J. A., Sharpley, C. F., & Rogers, H. J. (1984). Comparative effectiveness of professional and paraprofessional helpers. *Psychological Bulletin, 95*, 534–541.

Janz, N. K., & Becker, M. H. (1984). The health belief model: A decade later. *Health Education Quarterly, 11*, 1–47.

Jason, L. A., Gruder, C. L., Martino, S., Flay, B. R., Warnecke, R., & Thomas, N. (1987). Worksite group meetings and the effectiveness of a televised smoking cessation intervention. *American Journal of Community Psychology, 15*, 57–70.

Jessor, R. (1984). Adolescent development and behavioral health. In J. D. Matarazzo, S. M. Weiss, J. A. Herd, N. E. Miller, & S. M. Weiss (Eds.), *Behavioral health: A handbook for health enhancement and disease prevention* (pp. 69–90). New York: John Wiley & Sons.

Kiesler, C. A. (1985). Prevention and public policy. In J. C.

Rosen & L. J. Soloman (Eds.), *Prevention in health psychology* (pp. 401–413). Hanover, NH: University Press of New England.

Kobasa, S. C. O. (1985). Longitudinal and prospective methods in health psychology. In P. Karoly (Ed.), *Measurement strategies in health psychology* (pp. 235–262). New York: John Wiley & Sons.

Krasner, L. (1980). *Environmental design and human behavior: A psychology of the individual in society*. Elmsford, NY: Pergamon Press.

Krasner, L., & Ullman, L. P. (1973). *Behavior influence and personality: The social matrix of human action*. New York: Holt, Rinehart, & Winston.

Kuhn, T. S. (1970). *The structure of scientific revolutions* (2nd ed.). Chicago, IL: University of Chicago Press.

Lovett, S. B. (1989). Processing of aging: Enhancement of the later years. In R. A. Winett, A. C. King, & D. G. Altman, *Health psychology and public health: An integrative approach* (pp. 349–376). Elmsford, NY: Pergamon Press.

Manoff, R. K. (1985). *Social marketing: Imperative for public health*. New York: Praeger.

Melton, G. B., & Davidson, H. A. (1987). Child protection and society: When should the state intervene? *American Psychologist, 42*, 172–175.

Mullen, P. D. (1988). Health promotion and patient education benefits for employees. In L. Breslow, J. E. Fielding, & L. B. Lave (Eds.), *Annual review of public health, Vol. 9* (pp. 305–332). Palo Alto: Annual Reviews.

Munoz, R. F., Glish, M., Soo-Hoo, T., & Robertson, J. (1982). The San Francisco survey project: Preliminary work toward the prevention of depression. *American Journal of Community Psychology, 10*, 317–329.

O'Leary, K. D., & Wilson, G. T. (1987). *Principles of behavior therapy* (2nd ed.), New York: Holt, Rinehart, & Winston.

Piaget, J., & Inhelder, B. (1969). *The psychology of the child*. New York: Basic Books.

Proctor, S. E. (1986). A developmental approach to pregnancy prevention with early adolescent females. *Journal of School Health, 56*, 313–316.

Rappaport, J. (1977). *Community psychology: Values, research, action*. New York: Holt, Rinehart, & Winston.

Rappaport, J. (1987). Terms of empowerment/exemplars of prevention: Toward a theory for community psychology. *American Journal of Community Psychology, 15*, 121–148.

Rappaport, J. & Chinsky, J. M. (1974). Models for delivery of service from an historical and conceptual perspective. *Professional Psychology, 5*, 42–50.

Reppucci, N. D. (1987). Prevention and ecology: Teenage pregnancy, child sexual abuse, and organized youth sports. *American Journal of Community Psychology, 15*, 1–22.

Rogers-Warren, A. & Warren, S. F. (1977). *Ecological perspectives in behavior analysis*. Baltimore: University Park Press.

Rosenberg, M. S. (1987). New directions for research in the psychological maltreatment of children. *American Psychologist, 42*, 166–171.

Sarason, S. B. (1981). *Psychology misdirected*. New York: Free Press.

Solomon, D. S. & Maccoby, N. (1984). Communication as a model for health enhancement. In J. D. Matarazzo, S. M. Weiss, J. A. Herd, N. E. Miller, & S. M. Weiss (Eds.), *Behavioral health: A handbook for health enhancement and disease prevention* (pp. 209–221). New York: John Wiley & Sons.

Tharp, R. G. & Wetzel, R. (1969). *Behavior modification in the natural environment*. New York: Academic Press.

Twardosz, S., Cataldo, M. R., & Risley, T. R. (1974). Open environment for infant toddler day care. *Journal of Applied Behavior Analysis, 7*, 529–546.

Winett, R. A. (1985). Ecobehavioral assessment in health lifestyles: Concepts and methods. In P. Karoly (Ed.), *Measurement strategies in health psychology* (pp. 147–182). New York: John Wiley & Sons.

Winett, R. A. (1986). *Information and behavior: Systems of influence*. Hillsdale, NJ: Lawrence Erlbaum Associates.

Winett, R. A. (1988). *Ageless athletes*. Chicago: Contemporary Books.

Winett, R. A., King, A. C., & Altman, D. G. (1989). *Health psychology and public health: An integrative approach*. Elmsford, NY: Pergamon Press.

Winett, R. A., King, A. C., Altman, D. G., & Kramer, K. D. (1988, August). *A proactive, developmental/ecological approach to deterring health-risk behaviors in children and adolescents*. In R. I. Evans (Ed.), Deterring health-risk behaviors in children and adolescents. Invited symposium, American Psychological Association, Atlanta, GA.

Winett, R. A., Moore, J. W., Wagner, J. W., Walker, W. B., Hite, L., Leahy, M., & Neubauer, T. (1989). Ongoing National Cancer Institute project using interactive, public access information systems. Virginia Polytechnic Institute and State University, Blacksburg, VA.

CHAPTER 24

CONCLUSION: PSYCHOLOGICAL SCIENCE AND BEHAVIOR THERAPY

Paul R. Martin

The aim of this chapter is to summarize and integrate. The main section of the chapter will consist of a summary of the preceding chapters. Two short sections will follow. The first will focus on anxiety as an example of how clinical topics can be approached from multiple perspectives from psychological science, and the opportunities for integration. The final section will consider the questions and issues raised in the introductory chapter.

DEVELOPMENTAL PSYCHOLOGY

Toward the Integration of Human Developmental and Therapeutic Change

Lerner, Hess and Nitz begin their chapter with a discussion of the concept of development by outlining two contrasting models of development, the "organismic" and "mechanistic" models, the former being more associated with psychoanalytic theories (considered the dominant model) and the latter being more associated with learning theories. These models are then criticized as a prelude to presenting an integrative perspective, *developmental contextualism*. "This perspective, emphasizing the relation between person and context, conceives of development as involving systematic, successive, and "aptive" . . . changes within and across all life periods in the structure, function, and/or content of the person's mental (e.g., cognitive, emotional), behavioral (e.g., activity level, threshold of responsivity), and interpersonal/social (e.g., approach-withdrawal, institutional affiliational) characteristics" (p. 14). From a developmental contextual perspective, maladaptive behavior develops when an inadequate relation exists between an individual and their context.

Lerner et al. go on to explain how the developmental–contextual perspective differs from earlier models. For example, organismic theories have been labeled *predetermined epigenetic* as "in this type of theory biology is seen as the prime mover of development: Intrinsic (e.g., maturational) changes are seen to essentially unfold, and although environmental or experiential variables may speed up or slow down these progressions they can do nothing to alter the sequence or quality (e.g., the structure) of these hereditarily predetermined changes" (p. 16). In contrast, the developmental-contextual perspective adopts a *probabilistic epigenetic* view of development that emphasizes that the influence of the changing context on development is to make the trajectory of development less certain with respect to the applicability of norms to the individual.

The developmental–contextual perspective is summarized in a very complex figure that illustrates the range of variables included in the perspective and the interrelations between them. As Lerner et al. note, it probably would not be possible to do research testing the "model" and in fact developmental contextualism is perhaps better referred to as a perspective than a model. One advantage of the perspective is that it can serve as a guide for the selection of variables for study from the individual and contextual levels depicted. It is possible then to work with "restricted" or "reduced" models (as Lerner and his colleagues do in their research program) whereas the broader perspective reminds investigators of the limits within which they are operating.

Lerner et al. then proceed to discuss one particular model derived from the developmental-contextual perspective, namely the "goodness-of-fit" model. In essence, this model is based on the notion that each context has demands associated with it; if the behavior of an individual is congruent with these demands then this should produce a positive adjustment, but if incongruent then a negative adjustment would be expected. For example, teachers may want minimal distractability in their students so that attention is focused on the lesson. Parents, however, might prefer a moderate level of distractability so that they could draw children away from the television to eat at the table or go to bed. Children who were either generally distractable or generally not distractable would therefore differentially meet the demands of these two contexts. Problems of adjustment to school or home demands might thus develop as a consequence of a child's lack of match or goodness-of-fit in either or both settings.

Lerner et al. go on to review both laboratory and clinical evidence that supports the use of the goodness-of-fit model for understanding the bases of healthy and unhealthy developmental problems, and for designing interventions aimed at optimizing person-context relations across the life span. They point out that from a developmental contextual perspective, the aim of interventions would be to provide individuals with the necessary skills to actively create a good fit for themselves, and thus enhance their own development.

Developmental Psychopathology: An Integrative Framework

Masten and Braswell describe developmental psychopathology as the organizational framework for the study of behavior problems in children and adolescents with the goal of understanding psychopathology in the full context of human development. They begin their chapter by discussing the origins of developmental psychopathology. Although stating that the framework represents the integration of several scientific and clinical traditions, it is interesting to note that the psychoanalytic theories are once again accorded major historical significance (cf. Lerner, Hess & Nitz).

The chapter then proceeds to consider the six evolving tenets of developmental psychopathology. These are: (a) psychopathology occurs in a developing organism; (b) psychopathology is defined by reference to normative problems of development in normative environmental contexts; (c) all psychopathology is influenced by complex interactions of gene expressions and the environmental context of development and behavior; (d) because most forms of psychopathology result from multiple causal influences (sometimes including a necessary but not sufficient cause), rarely from a single cause, it is useful to describe psychopathology in terms of deviant pathways or trajectories of development; (e) the study of adaptation in all its forms, successful and unsuccessful, is important in understanding psychopathology; and (f) the study of deviant development contributes to the study of normative development.

Masten and Braswell then proceed to discuss the implications of this framework for classification, assessment, treatment, prevention, and research. With respect to classification, they advocate a comprehensive system that describes both normal and deviant behavior in the same system. They suggest that such a system would undoubtedly be multifaceted and might include the following areas, axes, or dimensions: cognitive development, academic achievement, social adaptation and development, current mood, known causal influences (organic and environmental), mental disorders, and developmental deviance. Masten and Braswell go on to point out that if a classification system such as this were developed then a much broader view of assessment would need to be adopted. They also stress the need for developmentally appropriate methods of obtaining information such as presenting structured rather than open-ended questions and providing response alternatives, as well as visual referents for responses, when interviewing children younger than 7 years of age.

Masten and Braswell call for a greater recognition of developmental factors in the treatment arena, and note that behavioral interventions with children are usually direct downward extensions of models used with adults. They consider the implications of developmental psychopathology for treatment issues such as deciding whether and when to intervene, the goals of intervention, specific targets of change, concerns with specific behavioral techniques, and the context of treatment. A specific example of a relevant finding in the developmental literature for interventionists, is that children below the age of 6 to 8 years old are unlikely to benefit from self-control training as prior to this age children do not have the ability or, alternatively, the interest in focusing on themselves as an object of evaluation or criticism. An example of a different perspective between developmental psychopathology and behavior therapy is that the former would be more concerned in targeting treatment so as to influence the developmental trajectory of the child rather than seeking only to change specific target behaviors.

Masten and Braswell argue that if psychopathology is conceptualized as a multidetermined path that has gone too far from the spectrum of adaptive pathways identified as normative, then the question of prevention becomes one of knowing when and how to deflect development in such a way that a person's path is turned in more adaptive directions early enough to avoid the worst outcomes. They suggest that the best clues for prevention may come from high risk children who avoid deviance; hence, the need for studying competence and resistance in high risk children, recovery from adversity, and "desistance" or turning away from deviant behavior patterns.

Finally, Masten and Braswell argue for increased collaboration between developmental and behavioral researchers, and outline a number of areas that are in great need of further research.

Developmental Factors in Child Behavioral Assessment

Ollendick and King begin their chapter with a brief overview of child behavioral assessment followed by a discussion of the implications of developmental theory for child behavioral assessment. These sections provide the context for the main agenda of the chapter, which is integrating developmental theory and behavioral assessment. With respect to child behavioral assessment, Ollendick and King point out the changes in perspective that have occurred in recent years. Hence, the early adherence to an operant perspective that placed heavy emphasis on observable events, current behavior, and intraindividual comparisons, with relatively little attention to developmental processes and normative comparisons, has been replaced by an exploratory, hypothesis-testing process in which a range of procedures is used to understand a given child, group, or social ecology and to formulate and evaluate specific intervention strategies. Although Ollendick and King note these changes, it is clear they believe that there is a great need for child behavioral assessment to become more developmentally sensitive; and echoing Masten and Braswell's plea with respect to child treatment approaches, they argue that many current assessment methods are merely downward extensions of those used with adults. With respect to developmental theory, they make the important observation that the contextualist approach that emerged from a synthesis of the organismic and mechanistic models, is remarkably similar to Bandura's social learning theory; both view the human organism as both determining and determined by an active, changing environment.

Ollendick and King use as a starting point for their synthesis, a review of the differences between the developmental and behavioral perspectives. They examine research that blends the developmental and contemporary behavioral assessment perspectives in three primary areas: (a) the development and use of normative guidelines for behavior, (b) the determination of age differences in the patterning of behavior, and (c) the study of continuities versus discontinuities in behavior over time. With respect to this first area, they point out that whereas a major difference between the developmental and behavioral perspectives is the use of a nomothetic versus an idiographic approach, these two approaches are not necessarily incompatible and it is possible to evaluate an individual child's behavior within a normative context. Ollendick and King emphasize that establishing norms is not an easy task as it requires the development of comprehensive data bases describing the behavior of large representative samples of clinic-referred and nonreferred children, including data related to gender, race, socioeconomic status, and culture in addition to age. They go on to give examples of the use of age and gender norms in child behavioral assessment by reference to three instruments. By way of illustration, data are reviewed on the Child Behavior Checklist that demonstrate that 84 of the 118 behavior problem items show significant age effects, for the most part reflecting a linear decrease in prevalence of the item as a problem for ages 4 through 16 years. On the other hand, 19 items show a linear increase in prevalence over age and a few items show nonlinear age trends.

A second difference between the behavioral and developmental perspectives is that the former emphasizes description and quantification of discrete behaviors whereas the latter focuses on identification of patterns of covariation among behaviors. Hence, a second way in which developmental principles can be integrated into child behavioral assessment is to identify age differences in the patterning of behavior. Ollendick and King go on to offer evidence that children of different ages show distinct patterns (i.e., qualitative differences) in their expression of emotions such as anxiety and depression. For example, younger children tend to express anxiety largely through more diffuse activity such as crying, screaming, and flailing; whereas older children tend to express their anxiety by verbal reports of pain and muscular rigidity.

The final way in which Ollendick and King suggest developmental principles can be integrated into child behavioral assessment is to explore the implications of developmental theory for the continuity–discontinuity of behavior. The continuity–discontinuity issue can be addressed from two vantage points. The first is a descriptive one and pertains to whether a behavior seen at one point in time in the life span can be described in the same way as behavior at another point in time. The second is explanatory continuity and refers to whether the same explanations are used to account for behavior over time. For the most part, the behavioral perspective has adopted a continuity position but there are both continuous and discontinuous aspects of development.

Clinical–Childhood Developmental Interface: Implications for Treatment

In the introduction to their chapter, Holmbeck and Kendall begin by suggesting that child-clinical psychologists be cautioned not to endorse the "developmental uniformity myth," that is, to implicitly believe that children aged 5 to 15 years are a homogeneous group, that treatments for one type of child problem are also appropriate for other childhood difficulties, or that treatments for young and latency-aged children should have direct applicability to young adolescents. On this basis, they present an overview of the normative intraindividual developmental changes of childhood and adolescence that are likely to have an effect on therapeutic process, followed by a discussion of the normative developmental changes that take place in the various contexts in which children and adolescents live.

With respect to normative intraindividual changes, three main types are considered (a) physical changes, (b) cognitive and psychological changes, and (c) changes in social role. Normative contextual and environmental changes are reviewed in the following four domains (a) family, (b) peers, (c) school, and (d) work. Holmbeck and Kendall point out that intraindividual changes appear to have an impact on the child's environment or context, and conversely, the environment impacts on intraindividual change (i.e., bidirectional effects occur).

Holmbeck and Kendall begin the major section of their chapter on the implications of developmental psychology for the treatment of children and adolescents with a challenging quote from Michael Rutter in which he argues that the notion of the child as a developing organism has always received lipservice and often much more than that in psychodynamic therapies, but until very recently it has been steadfastly ignored by many behavior therapists. Holmbeck and Kendall then review three types of knowledge that appear to have treatment implications, the first of which is knowledge of developmental norms, levels, and transitions. Knowledge of developmental norms serves as a basis for making sound diagnostic judgments, assessing the need for treatment, and selecting the appropriate treatment. For example, the normal developmental trend of adolescence is toward greater antonymy so that self-control strategies are probably more useful with older adolescents than are behavioral programs where parents are employed as behavior change agents. An example of the importance of developmental level as a moderator of treatment effectiveness was provided in a study of 6-year-olds that showed that self-instructional training led to improvement but only for those children who had reached the concrete operational stage. With respect to developmental transitions, Holmbeck and Kendall point out that confronting multiple life changes simultaneously (e.g., parental divorce combined with change in schools) places children at risk, and that this has obvious implications for preventative efforts.

The second type of knowledge with treatment implications is knowledge of developmental predictors. This field is concerned with what types of behaviors early in childhood predict behavioral disturbance later in childhood, adolescence, or adulthood. Holmbeck and Kendall review a study, for example, that linked severe childhood temper tantrums with problems in adulthood. Hence, childhood tantrums were predictive of divorce, erratic work experience, and downward occupational status in men; and divorce, low occupational status, and ill-tempered parents in women. These data have clear implications for prevention. Holmbeck and Kendall point out the value of considering protective factors that make children less likely to develop problem behaviors as well as risk factors.

The final type of knowledge considered is knowledge of developmental psychopathology. Discussion is limited to the continuity–discontinuity issue in view of the earlier chapter on developmental psychopathology by Masten and Braswell. They point out that there is discontinuity across age in the manifestation of certain disorders but considerable continuity also. An interesting example is depression for which they argue for cognitive continuity and behavioral discontinuity.

Holmbeck and Kendall conclude their section on treatment implications with discussion of two issues derived from the interface of developmental psychology and child/adolescent treatment. The first concerns involving peers in treatment. As the research literature indicates that peer relations provide unique contributions to the development of children and adolescents, peers have been used as behavior change agents. The most common problem studied has been social withdrawal, and peers have been used to help their withdrawn classmates via strategies such as prompting, reinforcement, and modeling.

The second issue concerns the facilitation of normal developmental processes as a treatment strategy, referred to by some as "developmental therapy." Early examples tended to stress facilitation of moral or social reasoning in school and correctional settings. Strategies have also been developed that focus on the modification of mother–infant attachment relationships, formal operations skills during adolescence, identity development, and development of prosocial behavior.

Holmbeck and Kendall conclude their chapter with a section on the implications of their analysis of future research, the training of clinicians who will work with children and adolescents, and the education of teachers and parents.

COGNITIVE PSYCHOLOGY AND NEUROPSYCHOLOGY

Theoretical Cognitive Psychology and Mood Disorders

The main sections of Eysenck's chapter deal with the memory system (divided into structure versus process), and attentional and perceptual phenomena.

Eysenck begins his subsection on structural aspects of memory with a model that argues for three qualitatively different kinds of memory store (a) sensory or modality-specific stores, (b) a short-term memory store, and (c) a long-term memory store. He argues that although the distinction between short-term and long-term memory is valid, the model is oversimplified and the notion of unitary short-term and long-term stores is no longer tenable. After a brief discussion of the "working memory system" as a replacement for a unitary short-term store, the remainder of the subsection focuses on long-term memory.

One distinction discussed is between *episodic* and *semantic memory*. Although cognitive psychologists have been skeptical about the theoretical value of this distinction it seems reasonable that it should be the autobiographical and personal episodic memory that is relevant to mood disorders rather than the more impersonal knowledge based semantic memory, but there are problems with this view. An alternative theoretical distinction is between *procedural* and *declarative knowledge* (knowing how versus knowing that, respectively). The potential clinical utility of this distinction is well illustrated by the case of amnesic patients who typically experience very considerable difficulties with the acquisition and subsequent retention of declarative knowledge, but often exhibit a normal ability to acquire procedural skills. Eysenck concludes his subsection on structural aspects of long-term memory with a discussion of the concepts of *semantic networks* and *schemata,* and their application to understanding mood disorders.

Eysenck's consideration of memory processes is limited to two theoretical approaches one focusing on processes occurring at the time of learning and one more concerned with processes occurring at the time of retrieval. With respect to the first, levels-of-processing theory argues that long-term memory depends very much on the kinds of processing of the to-be-remembered stimulus material that are carried out at the time of acquisition, specifically the depth of processing. Because depth and elaboration of processing are under conscious control to some extent, it follows that the extent to which mood-disordered patients learn and remember threatening or negatively toned stimulus material may well be affected by their decisions concerning the appropriate depth of processing and amount of elaboration.

A theoretical distinction of increasing importance is between *explicit* and *implicit memory*. Implicit memory is revealed when performance on a task is facilitated in the absence of conscious recall whereas explicit memory is revealed when performance on a task requires conscious recollection of previous experience. Eysenck reviews research on amnesia and mood disorders for which this distinction has proved useful. For example, one study failed to observe a negative memory bias in generalized anxiety disorder patients when an explicit memory test (cued recall) was used but detected a bias when an implicit memory test (word-completion) was used.

Eysenck begins his discussion of perception and attention by discussing the very basic theoretical distinction between *data-driven (or bottom-up)* processes and *conceptually driven (or top-down)* processes. Data-driven processes are guided entirely by external stimuli whereas conceptually driven processes depend upon shared knowledge and expectations. Eysenck points out that any differences in perceptual processing between mood disordered patients and normal controls are far more likely to involve conceptually driven than data-driven processes.

Finally, Eysenck discusses the distinction between *automatic* and *attentional* or *controlled processing*. It has been suggested that controlled processes are of limited capacity, require attention, and are used flexibly, whereas automatic processes have no capacity limitations, do not require attention, and are not readily modifiable. The emphasis of cognitive theories of anxiety and depression and therapies for the disorders has been on conscious thoughts and on ways in which these thoughts may be maladaptive. Eysenck adopts the opposite position and argues that it is probable that many conscious processes have automatic processes as antecedents, so that it is necessary to take automatic processes into account to understand conscious processing. He also suggests that nonnormal automatic processes are more likely to be part of a vulnerability factor, whereas nonnormal conscious processes are more likely to reflect current mood state. He argues that much of the available evidence on cognitive vulnerability factors in depression and in anxiety is consistent with this assumption.

Cognitive-experimental Approaches to the Emotional Disorders

In the chapter by MacLeod and Mathews, they review research that has adopted the information-processing paradigm, and used cognitive–experimental research techniques to investigate the cognitive characteristics of anxiety and depression. Until recently the application of the information-processing approach to the study of these emotions was restricted to the investigation of associated cognitive deficits, and it is this research literature that is reviewed first. MacLeod and Mathews conclude that depressed patients do indeed perform poorly, relative to nondepressed control subjects, on a variety of higher level cognitive tasks including abstracting ability, proverb interpretation, and general problem solving ability. Results with anxious subjects have been less straightforward though deficits have been reported in tasks such as anagram task performance, general problem solving, and a wide range of memory tasks. MacLeod and Mathews argue that these impairments appear to be directly related to level of depressed or anxious affect rather than to trait variables. Memory operations are particularly implicated. They argue that those aspects of memory that appear to proceed automatically are relatively preserved in both negative affective states, whereas strategic aspects of memory, particularly those which make heavy demands on processing resources, are most disrupted.

MacLeod and Mathews begin their discussion of the role of cognitive factors in the emotional disorders by discussing two theoretical frameworks (a) Aaron Beck's schema theory, and (b) Gordon Bower's network model. MacLeod and Mathews point out that although these models were developed quite independently from very different data bases, and although they are in many ways dissimilar, they nevertheless make parallel predictions concerning the relationship between affective status, and the processing of affectively valanced information. According to both accounts, an individual's affective status should be associated with pervasive biases favoring emotionally congruent information, throughout the processing continuum (i.e., encoding, comprehension and recall).

MacLeod and Mathews begin their discussion of the evidence for mood congruent information processing by discussing the distinction between *cognitive processes* and *cognitive products*. They argue that most researchers would agree that consciously accessible thoughts and beliefs represent the products of underlying, low level, cognitive processes; and that conscious access may be restricted to cognitive products, whereas the underlying processes themselves defy accurate introspective appraisal. Evidence relevant to cognitive products is reviewed first. MacLeod and Mathews conclude that the content of thought tends to be mood congruent (i.e., depression is characterized by sad thoughts concerning loss and failure; and anxiety by fearful thoughts concerning threat and danger). There is some evidence that depressed subjects are also characterized by dysfunctional attitudes or irrational beliefs that are depressogenic in content. Irrational beliefs have been less extensively evaluated in anxiety but the evidence suggests that high trait anxiety subjects show a pattern of elevated irrational beliefs, relative to low trait anxiety controls, similar to that shown by depressives. MacLeod and Mathews point out, however, that the evidence needs to be viewed with caution as it is based on introspective data.

MacLeod and Mathews review the literature on cognitive processes in depression and anxiety in three sections that focus on attention, comprehension, and memory; and summarize the complex findings in a table. With respect to encoding processes, there is considerable evidence to support mood congruent attentional bias in anxiety but not depression. Anxious subjects selectively attend to threat relevant stimuli. This finding has occurred in a wide range of studies employing objective experimental techniques such as dichotic listening, the dot probe paradigm and the Stroop color naming paradigm. In contrast, there is no convincing evidence for mood congruency effects in perceptual or attentional processes in depressed subjects (i.e., no support for negatively valenced stimuli selectively recruiting processing resources).

With respect to comprehension, there is evidence to support mood congruent interpretive biases in anxiety and depression with anxious subjects distorting the evaluation of risk and interpretation of ambiguous stimuli, and depressed subjects tending towards negative interpretations. Studies of depression have relied exclusively on self-report data, however, although studies of anxiety have used both introspective and more objective measures, so that the findings tend to be open to alternative explanations such as response bias.

Finally, the pattern of results for retrieval processes is the reverse of the one found for encoding processes; there is no convincing evidence for mood congruent retrieval associated with either trait or state anxiety, but a very substantial body of research supporting the existence of mood congruent retrieval biases in both depression as a transient state, and as a more stable personality characteristic. Hence, the hypothesis that anxious subjects will show facilitated memory for threat relevant information has not been supported, but depressed subjects do show retrieval advantages for negatively valenced information.

Contributions of Cognitive Psychology to Assessment and Treatment of Anxiety

Craske and Barlow begin their chapter with a discussion of three issues (a) whether the definition of cognitive processes should include unconscious processes, (b) the primacy of affect or cognition, and (c) the extent to which cognitive processes are a cause or a consequence of anxiety disorders. The first two issues are interrelated as it has been argued that the primacy debate is dependent on how cognition is defined. In discussing the primacy issue, Craske and Barlow outline various models of levels of information processing and Peter Lang's bio-informational model on the way to concluding that the polarity of the debate has lessened as information-processing principles are incorporated more fully into the definitions of cognition and regarded as important components of emotional states. Evidence relevant to the issue of whether cognitive biases predispose to the development of anxiety disorders, or are the consequence of the disorder is briefly reviewed and judged as inconclusive at this stage.

In the following section, Craske and Barlow consider the data pertaining to information-processing biases in anxiety. They start with evidence for the bias in *conscious appraisal* resulting from the assumed processes, the most prominent characteristic of which is perceived threat and danger. This section is organized according to various models and constructs such as *anxiety sensitivity, fear of fear, hypervigilance* and *safety signals*. The first bias in processing considered is *recall biases*. "Mood state dependent retention refers to more accurate recall when recall is assessed during reinstatement of the emotion present at the time of learning, and more accurate recall of information consistent with the original mood than of information inconsistent with the original mood" (p. 156). Craske and Barlow go along with other reviewers in noting that, unlike depression, there was no evidence for the memory biases in anxiety states, but add a couple of caveats to these conclusions. In contrast, quite strong evidence exists for *selectivity of attention* in anxious states with anxious individuals displaying a bias in perceiving mood congruent material.

A process closely related to selective attention is the tendency to *self-focus* following the perception of physiological arousal. Craske and Barlow argue that this self-focus leads to an increased sensitivity to internal experiences and intensification of relevant emotions; and this shift of attention is one component of pathological anxiety. They go on to hypothesize that the self-focus of attention that occurs as a function of arousal associated with negative affect is matched by a *narrowing of attention* that also increases as a function of arousal. This process has been described as consisting of a preoccupation with mood congruent material during emotional reactivity, with the number of cues used decreasing as the emotional intensity increases.

The final section discusses the implications of the reviewed literature for assessment and treatment. Craske and Barlow argue that the inclusion of cognitive biases in the assessment process is needed to enable a complete functional analysis of the presenting problem. Self-report instruments have been developed to assess conscious appraisals of danger and various misinterpretations for different anxiety disorders, but they rely upon accurate self-awareness of biases. Performance-based tasks such as dichotic listening, probe detection latencies, and color naming tasks (as discussed by MacLeod and Mathews) overcome many of the problems associated with self-report inventories. Craske and Barlow point out that the bio-informational model suggests the most sensitive method of assessment is physiological monitoring of responses to different imaginal scenarios but the technology requires further development. Given the tendency to attend to mood congruent stimuli, and for conscious appraisals to differ according to level of state anxiety, assessment while in the presence of the feared stimuli is likely to yield results different from assessment in an office setting.

As Craske and Barlow point out, the obvious treatment implication from the recognition of biased conscious appraisals in anxiety states is to attempt to modify them but this appears to be much more complex than assumed initially. Cognitive restructuring has been used to target the irrational process but few studies have assessed changes in information-processing biases. Marked reductions in the tendency to perceive ambiguous material related to arousal as threatening, with successful treatment of panic disorder, has been reported in a couple of studies, however. In reviewing studies comparing cognitive restructuring and exposure treatments, Craske and Barlow suggest that exposure procedures may be more effective for altering information-processing biases than pure cognitive restructuring. Modification of biases may be best accomplished through behavioral change.

In concluding their chapter, the authors warn that "we must not make the mistake of concluding that the phenomenon of emotion can be reduced to the study of cognition in the same way that some in biology have attempted to reduce behavior to the actions of neurotransmitters" (p. 165). They point out too that cognitive therapy, as currently conceptualized, probably has little to do with the cognitive phenomena that are the subject of cognitive psychology.

Contributions of Cognitive Psychology to Assessment and Treatment of Depression

The chapter by Hollon and Shelton is divided into three main sections (a) cognition and depression, (b) assessment of cognition in depression, and (c) cognition and treatment of depression. The authors begin with a brief discussion of five cognitive theories of depression, particularly focusing on the two considered to have had the greatest impact on research and practice, namely Aaron Beck's cognitive theory, and the helplessness theory of Martin Seligman and colleagues (or hopelessness theory as it is called in its latest revision). The next few subsections are used for delineating conceptual distinctions, discussing network models and describing a framework for evaluating cognitive factors. Two models of accessibility are outlined prior to the authors focusing on a meaning systems perspective of cognitive factors in depression.

This subsection discusses how cognitive processes transform environmental and internal stimuli into cognitive products through the mediation of knowledge structures. One form of knowledge structure is the schema, and of the different types of schema, the one most relevant to depression research is the self-schema. The self-schema of depressives has been shown to differ in a number of ways from the self-schema of nondepressed individuals. For example, self-evaluations are most accurate in the mildly depressed with nondepressives characterized by overly positive self-evaluations and severely depressed individuals characterized by unrealistically negative bias; structural complexity in the self-schema (e.g., multiplicity of roles) seems to decrease vulnerability to depression by buffering against particular failures and losses; and a significant discrepancy between one's "real" and "ideal" self-schema may be associated with greater vulnerability to depression. This first section is concluded with a discussion of the principles of *assimilation* and *accommodation* (when a discrepancy occurs between information presented and existing schemata which is modified?); and the *judgmental heuristics* (discussed in more detail in Schwartz's chapter) that lead to altering information (i.e., assimilation) being the more common process.

The assessment section begins with a review of alternative methods of assessment. These include (a) recording methods—sampling verbal productions generated in relevant contexts (e.g., "think aloud" procedures), (b) endorsement methods—rating or responding to a predetermined set of items (e.g., self-report inventories), (c) production methods—listing thoughts currently in the sensorium (e.g., thought listing), and (d) inferential methods—involving the use of tasks drawn from basic cognitive research in the study of cognitive structures and processes (e.g., category judgments). A number of specific assessment instruments are then discussed with major emphasis on the Automatic Thoughts Questionnaire, Dysfunctional Attitudes Scale and Attributional Styles Questionnaire (noted to be the most successful measure of cognitive-diathesis to date). Hollon and Shelton conclude this section by stating it is clear that differences in cognition and information processing exist between depressed and nondepressed populations, and that these differences can be reliably measured, but it is not so clear whether such differences play any role in the etiology of the disorder.

With respect to treatment, the authors note that the last two decades have seen the development of cognitive and cognitive-behavioral interventions that have evidenced great promise, particularly Beck's cognitive therapy. This approach seeks to ameliorate acute depression and to reduce the risk for subsequent relapse by changing the way people think, but these changes are viewed as taking place not only at the level of cognitive products, but also in terms of underlying structure and processes. There is good evidence supporting the efficacy of cognitive therapy in the treatment of depression (comparable to tricyclic pharmacotherapy), and the prevention of recurrence (comparable to keeping patients on continuation medication), but the data are still not conclusive with regard to precisely how this change is brought about. Hollon and Shelton describe three models of change mechanisms: (a) activation–deactivation involves change in depression by facilitating a switch from an operative schema to a latent nondepressive one; (b) accommodation in which some alteration is made in existing cognition, probably at the level of structure and/or process; and (c) compensation involves the development of skills and strategies that offset the effects of pernicious cognitive proclivities. The authors go on to outline their favored model, the sequential compensation-accommodation, which argues that cognitive therapy might not so much lead depressed patients to think like nondepressives, as to lead them to process information in a very atypical fashion that serves to protect against dysphoric affect and behavioral passivity.

Hollon and Shelton conclude their chapter with a discussion of the practice of cognitive therapy organized according to the seven sequential stages involved in producing change of setting the rationale, training in self-monitoring, behavioral activation, identifying beliefs, evaluating beliefs, uncovering underlying assumptions, and preparing for termination and relapse prevention.

Clinical Decision Making

Schwartz's chapter focuses on the cognitive strategies and heuristics that clinicians use to make everyday judgments. The chapter is divided into four main sections the first of which consists of a hypothetical case history followed by a short quiz. The aim of the quiz is to give readers a first-hand idea of the phenomena studied by decision making researchers. As all clinical relationships begin with an information gathering stage, the second section is concerned with acquiring and interpreting clinical data. Schwartz points out that clinical data are often imprecise and uncertain, and goes on to discuss the sources of uncertainty. Starting with client reports, such reports can be unreliable as a consequence of deception but also as a result of more subtle processes arising out of patients misinterpreting questions, or lack of personal awareness and ignorance. Schwartz goes on to discuss problems with psychological test data, in particular, low predictive validity. He argues that many tests continue to be used despite their low predictive validity as a result of *illusory correlation,* that is, "strength of association" estimates are based on estimates of relationships we believe ought to exist rather than on true empirical covariation. Another source of uncertainty discussed pertains to the fact that prevalence is an important factor influencing the value of test results but one often not taken into account by clinicians. Additional problems arise out of clinicians communicating via verbal labels (e.g., "unlikely," "rare") rather than numbers, which causes ambiguity as different individuals interpret the meaning of the labels quite differently. A final problem discussed in this section is the one of information overload as clinicians have difficulty interpreting and integrating information from many different sources.

Cognitive load can be reduced by simplifying procedures known as *judgment heuristics* and these are the focus of the third section. Judgment heuristics normally lead to good decisions, but under certain circumstances they can lead the decision maker astray (i.e., to biased judgments). The first heuristic discussed is the *availability heuristic* in which easy to imagine events are thought more likely to occur than those that are difficult to imagine or recall. The *representativeness heuristic* refers to the fact that the probability of an event or outcome is estimated by the degree to which it fits an existing cognitive stereotype or schema. Schwartz then discusses six cognitive errors associated with the representativeness heuristic identified by Tversky and Kahneman (a) insensitivity to prior probabilities, (b) insensitivity to sample size, (c) misconceptions about randomness, (d) insensitivity to predictability, (e) the illusion of validity, and (f) misconceptions about statistical regression. Although human information-processing capacity is limited and easily overloaded resulting in the use of judgment heuristics and proneness to error, studies show that the more information available, the more confident decision makers become in the accuracy of their judgments. One particularly interesting form of overconfidence has become known as "hindsight bias" and occurs when our present knowledge is allowed to influence our estimate of the likelihood of previous events. Hindsight bias leads us to overstate our own abilities by convincing us that we "knew it all along."

Attempts to teach people how to avoid cognitive biases have not been notably successful, and for this reason efforts aimed at helping clinicians make better judgments have often involved provision of "decision aids." Such aids are reviewed in the final section of the chapter that begins with a discussion of the clinical versus statistical prediction debate initiated by Paul Meehl. Clinical reasoning was viewed as largely intuitive and certainly nonquantitative whereas the statistical approach was reasoning based on some sort of actuarial formula. The statistical approach uses decision rules, and usually these rules are derived from what has become known as a "linear model." Linear judgment models consist of a set of predictor variables on the one hand and some criterion (the outcome to be predicted) on the other. Usually the predictor variables are weighted via multiple regression analysis so as to maximize the correlation between their weighted sum and the criterion. Although linear models are not theories of cognition (i.e., they do not attempt to mimic decision making processes), they are excellent decision making devices. Indeed, the research literature shows that linear models can often out-perform the human decision makers upon whom they are based, a phenomenon known as "bootstrapping." Linear models may be used to design decision aids, and in medicine they usually take the form of a precisely formulated set of predictor-criterion relationships.

Because of some of the problems associated with linear models such as their inability to suggest new hypotheses or of explaining their own decisions—*expert systems* have been developed that are computer programs that solve problems and give advice by making inferences from the available data. These systems operate interactively and, unlike statistical systems, are easily modified as new knowledge becomes available. Although both linear models and expert systems can serve as decision aids, ultimately the clinicians will have to make a decision, and providing a rational bias for making such choices is the goal of *decision analysis*. Decision analysis is a set of procedures for making decisions under conditions of uncertainty and is based on the notion that clinicians must consider both the probability and the utility (subjective value) of all possible outcomes.

Cognitive Psychology Applied to the Treatment of Acquired Language Disorders

Coltheart begins his chapter by delineating the domain of *cognitive neuropsychology*. He states that it is a branch of cognitive psychology, and its defining feature is the study of relationships between the pattern of impaired performance of brain-damaged individuals on cognitive tasks and what is known about how the tasks are normally carried out. Coltheart points out that many cognitive neuropsychologists have come to be interested in the treatment as well as the theoretical analysis of cognitive impairments after brain damage. According to this approach, an understanding of the causes of cognitive impairment must precede any attempt at treatment. Understanding causes involves discovering the components of the information-processing system that are dysfunctional.

Coltheart illustrates the cognitive neuropsychological approach by reference to an information-processing model of object naming. This model contains five processing components and six pathways for information so that there are $2^{11} - 1 = 16,383$ different ways in which the naming system can be impaired if brain damage can affect any component or pathway. He goes on to argue that the chance of any two patients with a naming difficulty having the same pattern of impairment to the system is extremely small, and hence the chance that the same treatment is appropriate for two patients with naming difficulties is correspondingly small. This is why cognitive neuropsychologists consider that treatment efficacy studies must be individual case studies, a prediliction shared by many behavior therapists.

Coltheart notes that specific information-processing systems are acquired for carrying out specific cognitive functions and that such systems are often localized in specific regions of the brain. He goes on to argue the results of numerous recent reports indicate that it is at least sometimes possible to use cognitive-neuropsychological rehabilitation to rebuild a damaged information-processing system even when the region of the brain that formerly housed that system can no longer function.

Coltheart next proceeds to describe in some depth examples of this kind of rehabilitation. He discusses two patients, both with impairment of reading, though he suggests that the questions he considers can be posed quite generally in relation to the treatment of any kind of acquired cognitive impairment. He begins by describing an information-processing model of reading involving five components. He then outlines how assessment methods from cogitive psychology can be used for differentiating which components have been affected by brain damage. For example, assessing whether patients can read aloud pronounceable nonwords (e.g., vib) determines which of two basic procedures for reading aloud is impaired (the letter-to-sound or whole-word reading procedure). Coltheart emphasizes that the cognitive-neuropsychological approach strives to design interventions such that the results are capable not only of telling us whether the specific rehabilitation method used was responsible for any observed improvement in the patients' performance, but also for providing data relevant to theoretical ideas about normal cognitive processing.

Coltheart points out that cognitive neuropsychology can be used for assessment and design of treatment programs but currently has little to say about methods of treatment. This deficiency arises because cognitive models have not yet advanced to the stage of specifying how the components operate. Hence, assessment is useful in demonstrating which components are intact and therefore inappropriate targets of treatment, but knowing a component is dysfunctional does not provide clues concerning how treatment should proceed.

Behavior Therapy in the Treatment of Neurologically Impaired Adults

The chapter by Wilson starts by noting that whereas, traditionally, treatment of patients with neurological problems has been administered by occupational, speech, and physiotherapists, times are changing and it is now more common to find clinical psychologists and some neuropsychologists attempting to alleviate problems resulting from neurological damage. The first two sections of the chapter describe the common neurological conditions of head injury, cerebral vascular accident, dementia, multiple sclerosis, encephalitis, tumor, and spinal cord injury; and the motor, sensory, behavioral, cognitive, and emotional problems arising from these conditions.

The third section constitutes a brief review of the history of behavioral techniques in the treatment of neurologically impaired adults. Many successful applications are discussed, but Wilson also warns of the potential problems in this area. She argues that the neurological and neuropsychological status of each patient must be taken into account when designing treatment programs as it may be impossible, for example, for many impaired people to remember behavioral contracts, delayed reinforcement or explanations, no matter how carefully structured the program. Another example is provided by relaxation training involving tense-and-release exercises that can cause adverse effects with some hemiparetic, hemiplegic and ataxic patients as the tensing of muscles can trigger or increase spasticity.

The fourth section focuses on assessment of neurological patients. Wilson argues for the benefits of combining neuropsychological and behavioral assessment. Neuropsychological assessment is necessary for determining cognitive strengths and weaknesses that must be taken into account when devising and implementing behavioral programs. On the other hand, this information is not sufficient for designing treatment programs, and behavioral assessment is needed to help identify ways in which impairments are manifested in the behavior of patients, to measure problematic behaviors, and to find out whether intervention strategies are helping to change behaviors beneficially.

The fifth section describes treatment techniques and provides examples of programs for decreasing problem behaviors such as yelling, swearing, and undue apprehension; and increasing positive behaviors such as attending, recognizing, movement, language, and self-care. Behavioral excesses are common after some kinds of neurological damage and behavioral treatment strategies that can be used to reduce or eliminate these include time-out, relaxation and systematic desensitization, stimulus control techniques, extinction, and positive reinforcement. More cognitively oriented approaches have still to make their mark in treatment programs for neurologically impaired people despite their obvious applicability given that, for example, depression is common after head injury, stroke, and other conditions. The techniques that have proved most useful for increasing behaviors include prompting, method of vanishing cues (chaining), expanding rehearsal, positive reinforcement, and Portage (a home-based teaching technique for parents of children with mental handicap).

In the sixth section, Wilson, like Coltheart in the preceding chapter, argues for the importance of single-case experimental designs in the treatment of neurological patients. Reasons for adopting this position include the extreme difficulty in finding homogeneous groups of neurological patients, the rarity of some of the neuropsychological deficits seen in neurological patients, and the frequent need to adjust treatment according to patient progress.

The final section considers the contributions of cognitive psychology and neuropsychology to the treatment of neurological patients. Wilson argues that cognitive psychology is valuable mainly because of its models of functioning, which help conceptualize what is happening in a given disorder, a point well illustrated in Coltheart's chapter. She goes on to suggest that ideas for treatment can come from the cognitive psychologist's explanation of breakdown in memory, reading, perception, or language. One example she offers comes from memory therapy in which cognitive psychology indicates the value of simplifying information, teaching organization strategies, and encouraging deeper levels of processing when there is a need to help patients encode information. It may be advantageous to refer to the findings of encoding specificity and context dependent learning when attempting to increase generalization in therapy programs. Wilson argues that the discipline of neuropsychology has also contributed to the treatment of neurologically impaired patients by increasing our knowledge of the organization of the brain. This point is illustrated by reference to a number of studies that have trained patients to overcome impaired functions by using other areas of the brain left intact. This anatomical reorganization or finding alternative pathways in the brain is little understood, but it has been argued that many systems in the brain are organized in parallel so the brain can cope with damage in part of a system by using other pathways.

SOCIAL PSYCHOLOGY

History and Theories of Social Psychology: Their Relevance to Behavior Therapy

The chapter by Harvey, Burgess, and Orbuch traces various historical developments in the field of social psychology that have been particularly relevant to events unfolding in behavioral theory and practice. The first textbooks in social psychology were published in 1908 and the major journal of the field in the early years appeared in the form of *Journal of Abnormal and Social Psychology* in 1921. As Harvey et al. note, this event signaled the beginning of a fertile alliance between clinical and social psychology that has mushroomed in the last decade.

Harvey et al. provide a relatively full summary of Mead's social behaviorism as they argue that this conception has had an enduring impact in sociological social psychology but has hardly been noticed in previous analyses of the relevance of social psychological theory to behavior therapy. "Like Watsonian radical behaviorism, Mead's approach focused on the observable actions of individuals. However, unlike Watson's position, Mead conceived 'behavior' in broad enough terms to include covert activity. This inclusion was deemed necessary to understanding the distinctive character of human conduct, which Mead considered to be a qualitatively different emergent process as compared to the behavior of nonhumans" (p. 256).

Harvey et al. describe how events around the time of World War II gave impetus to the development of social psychology. These include the emigration of leading social psychologists, such as Fritz Heider and Kurt Lewin, from Germany to the United States to escape Nazi persecution; and the proliferation of research and training programs arising from the war-driven interest in topics such as leadership, group productivity, and morale.

Beginning in the 1940s learning theory entered the field of social psychology. Neal Miller and John Dollard, for example, analyzed aspects of linguistic behavior from a learning perspective, and showed that social imitation plays a central role in the process of learning to talk. Carl Hovland adopted an instrumental learning approach to the study of persuasion processes.

Harvey et al. suggest that the contemporary period in the development of social psychological theories as they relate to behavior therapy began in the late 1950s and early 1960s. The work of Albert Bandura and his colleagues was important because they were learning theorists who had mostly worked with humans rather than nonhumans, and they successfully blended behavioristic and cognitive ideas in their formulation. Bandura contended that novel response patterns can be acquired through observation and that the initiator can successfully imitate the model without performing any overt response and without receiving any direct reinforcement. Around the same period Leon Festinger developed his theories of social comparison and cognitive dissonance that had a major impact because they focused attention on cognitions and a highly cognitive explanation for the workings of reward on behavior.

Cognitive dissonance theory occupied a prominent position in social psychology until the early 1970s at which time attributional approaches were developing and began to become more dominant in stimulating theory and research. One example of those approaches was Daryl Bem's influential analysis of self-perception. Bem viewed himself as a behaviorist "eschewing" reference to internal states as explanatory mechanisms, and his analysis initially was developed to provide an alternative interpretation for phenomena that previously had been interpreted in terms of dissonance theory.

Other early behaviorally oriented social theories include George Homans' Skinnerian analysis of elementary social behavior. Also, explanations of attitude formation and change have been attempted by reference to classical and operant conditioning although this work has become inactive in the last decade with the emphasis on sophisticated cognitive theories.

In the last section of the chapter, Harvey et al. review contemporary developments that are highly congenial to the interface of behavior therapy and social psychology. Two examples of successful research programs developed at this interface are mentioned. The first is Lewinsohn's behavioral analysis of depression that involves a concern with concepts of social interaction. The second example is Jacobson and Margolin's behavioral exchange model of close relationship discord that emphasizes the valence of social interactions. Finally, Harvey et al. identify a number of avenues of exchange between behavior therapy and social psychology that they believe can be pursued profitably. These include the area of social influence and attitude change, self-presentation, and nonverbal behavior.

Psychosocial Determinants of Disorder: Social Support, Coping and Social Skills Interactions

Rolf Peterson begins his chapter with a discussion of how to define and measure social support. He reviews several conceptualizations of the functions of social support including a categorization of seven types of social support: self-value feedback, belief and feeling validation, expression encouragement, information, material aid, task assistance, and network belongingness. Each of these types of support can be measured as objective events, perceived level of support or satisfaction with support received. Peterson notes that most studies measure only a few types of social support or some general global perception of received social support.

Peterson critically reviews a number of studies showing positive associations between social support and adjustment variables such as depression, anxiety, and hostility. Other studies have demonstrated associations between support and rate of recovery from psychiatric problems at least in the absence of major negative life events. Peterson cautions, however, that the direction of causation of association between psychopathology and social support cannot be determined in most studies. Also, the other side of the support issue is that a social support network may produce demands and be a stressor. These negative effects of social support appear to be especially strong when the network contains a conflicted relationship with a "significant other." This might be particularly true for an individual who relies heavily on one or two people for the social support resources.

Peterson also reviews studies of the use of social support as a treatment modality. Studies have demonstrated that increases in social support assist in reducing relapse and hospital re-admissions for psychiatric patients. Formally organized support groups for special crisis and/or illness groups have been shown to be a highly effective procedure for preventing and/or reducing emotional problems. The use of social support as an adjunct or component in multifaceted treatment programs for behavior disorders has increased in recent years although not all the findings are positive.

Peterson then moves on to discuss coping styles and, as with social support, begins with definitional issues. He notes that most studies on coping use one of two definitions. The first defines three major coping dimensions (problem-focused, emotion-focused and appraisal) each with several sub-factors. The second involves an eight dimension scale based on factor analysis: confrontative coping, distancing, self-control, seeking social support, accepting responsibility, escape-avoidance, planful problem-solving, and positive reappraisal.

Several studies suggest coping may be an important factor in psychopathology. For example, it has been demonstrated that severe posttraumatic stress disorder was associated with distancing (denial) and emotion-focused coping (distress reduction), whereas problem-focused coping (problem solving) was associated with less severe posttraumatic stress disorder. Several researchers have warned, however, that rather than particular strategies being more adaptive than others, different strategies may be effective with different demands/situations (e.g., active coping when control over the environment is possible) so that coping style flexibility may be important.

Peterson points out that coping and social support appear to interact. For example, it has been shown that positive family support was associated with a decrease in the use of avoidance coping over time in both a community and patient sample. Peterson goes on to suggest that social skills are a potential determinant of social support availability and possibly coping style. Hence, models that postulate social support and coping as determinants of psychopathology should include, in turn, the role of social skills.

The final section of Peterson's chapter consists of recommendations for research and clinical practice. Peterson argues the time has come to progress beyond demonstrating associations to determining causal relationships and variable interaction patterns. On the applied side, more research is needed on social support treatment and prevention effects with psychiatric and high risk groups. Clinically, a greater emphasis should be placed on assessment of stressors, quality and quantity of social support, and coping strategies; and methods of increasing social support should be considered an important component of treatment planning.

Social Cognition in Behavioral Assessment and Behavior Therapy

Fincham and Bradbury begin their chapter with a discussion of definitions and how the field of social cognition evolved. They argue that social psychology never fully adopted S-R psychology though it was long regarded as the study of social behavior. Cognition pervades social psychology to the extent that modern social psychology might be more accurately described as "cognitive social psychology." The meaning of "cognition" in social psychology has taken on the technical meaning ascribed to it in cognitive psychology and is used to refer to the *cognitive processes* involved in the representation and use of social knowledge in contrast with earlier work in social psychology where the focus was on particular *cognitive contents* (e.g., attitudes, attributions). The concern with cognitive processes was accompanied by a commitment to promote the development of the information-processing metaphor rather than the metaphor that dominated earlier work in social psychology of people as intuitive scientists seeking to understand the causes of behavior. The remainder of the chapter examines the relevance of behavior therapy for research representative of the two dominant conceptual frameworks in social psychology over the last 20 years namely the attribution and information-processing frameworks. Both investigate people's understanding of their social world and constitute examples of the approaches taken prior and subsequent to the influence of cognitive psychology, respectively.

Fincham and Bradbury suggest the attribution approach implies that "a thorough behavioral assessment should include assessment of attributions to determine whether attributions (a) play a role in maintaining the dysfunctional behavior, (b) result from incomplete information, (c) should be the major target of intervention, (d) reflect an attributional style, and (e) are mindless, occur within awareness but remain private, or are communicated to others" (p. 288). They also caution that clinicians need to monitor their own attributions for the client's behavior and evaluate whether they are falling prey to the "fundamental attribution error" (a tendency for the perceiver to attribute effects entirely to persons and thereby underestimate the influence of other factors).

Fincham and Bradbury note that although numerous papers have outlined the implications of the attributional approach for therapy, empirical evaluation of attributionally oriented interventions is rare. They argue that client and therapist are likely to have different causal attributions due to a phenomenon known as "actor-observer difference" (individuals attribute their own reactions to the object world, and those of another, when they differ from their own, to personal characteristics). They suggest that the efficacy of behavior therapy might be enhanced by incorporating explicit discussion of the therapist's explanatory framework into the course of therapy and by careful monitoring of the client's reaction to and acceptance of this framework.

Fincham and Bradbury conclude their section on the attribution approach with a discussion of three issues that they believe will allow the potential contribution of the approach to be realized more fully. The issues pertain to attributional style (current measurement procedures involve averaging so that *variance* in attributions is not tapped); types of attribution (the focus has been on outcomes of action rather than actor's *intentions*); and models of atrributions (Kelley's ANOVA model has had the most impact on clinical research but there are a number of problems with the model that limit its clinical utility).

Fincham and Bradbury's discussion of contributions of the information-processing approach to behavioral assessment begins with the two major themes found in clinical discussion of recent cognitive and social psychological research using this approach: schemata (cognitive structures) and heuristics (cognitive processes). Assessment of schemata is useful because clients usually present in therapy with problems relating to the content of their knowledge structures. The notion that clients' problems may reflect the use of shortcuts or heuristics in processing social information, the products of which are often labeled "errors" or "biases", led to consideration of their clinical relevance.

Fincham and Bradbury go on to argue that although the discussion of schemata and heuristics represents an important clinical application of the information-processing approach, the most valuable contributions of this approach to behavioral assessment have yet to be realized. They include three such contributions. First, although it is recognized that cognitive structures and processes are inexorably linked, discussion of the precise nature of these links is conspicuous in its absence. Cognitive behavioral assessment and therapy have lacked a firm conceptual framework, a weakness that Fincham and Bradbury believe the information-processing approach can potentially address. The second contribution derives from the impressive methodological advances associated with the information-processing approach such as multiple, disparate methods for assessing knowledge structures that go well beyond self-reported cognitions. Third, the information-processing approach can be used to investigate decision making in behavioral assessment.

Fincham and Bradbury point out that the implications of the information-processing approach for behavior therapy are somewhat speculative because little is known about how schemata change or how cognitive processes (heuristics) can be altered. They go on to argue, however, that an information-processing analysis can contribute to behavior therapy in three ways: (a) intervention can result directly from an information-processing assessment (e.g., intensive training on laboratory tasks); (b) intervention may be guided by information-processing findings (e.g., questioning or exercises that will allow clients to negate one knowlege structure while simultaneously confirming a second one); and (c) analysing existing interventions from the perspective of the information-processing approach.

Fincham and Bradbury conclude with some suggestions concerning changes both in the nature of social cognition research conducted within the information-processing approach and its applications that need to occur for the potential of the approach to be realized. One such suggestion is a plea for an ecological perspective whereby the phenomena researched derive from observation and analysis of human functioning in its natural context rather than testing of models. Additional suggestions are for more socially oriented research, and for more clinically motivated research in which the information-processing approach is molded to suit the needs of the clinicians.

Psychotherapy as a Social Process

Christopher Peterson begins his chapter by noting that behavior therapy, like all forms of psychotherapy, depends critically upon the social interaction between the therapist and the client. He argues that, although the importance of the therapist-client relationship is well appreciated, what is not appreciated is that social psychology has much to say about the nature of the relationship.

Peterson starts his discussion of the relationship

between therapist and client by focusing on psychoanalysis as this approach was the first to specify this relationship as critical in determining therapy outcome. Psychoanalytic thinking distinguishes three interacting levels of relationship: transference and countertransference (transference referring to the clients' mental construction of the relationship between themselves and the therapist, this relationship being characterized by the "transfer" of previous thoughts and feelings from earlier relationships); therapeutic alliance (involves the therapist and client joining together in the shared purpose of undertaking therapy); and real relationship (involves ascriptive characteristics of the client and therapist such as sex, age, socioeconomic status, educational background, and ethnicity).

In the next section, Peterson gives an overview of how social psychology conceives relationships. One point he makes is that social psychologists traditionally have favored the use of social analogues (laboratory experiments as a way of creating special social situations) for studying relationships. In discussing theorizing in social psychology he emphasizes the major influence of Kurt Lewin, and the cognitive domination of the field (cf. Fincham & Bradbury). He points out that this is compatible with the "cognizing" of psychoanalytic theory that object relations approaches represent as well as the similar "cognizing" of learning theory by social learning theory. Peterson goes on to discuss three particular models of social beings these pertaining to people as consistency seekers (e.g., cognitive dissonance theory), naive scientists (e.g., attribution theories), and misers (e.g., judgment heuristics).

Next Peterson spells out the implications of his analysis of social psychology for psychotherapy. First, he notes that many of the findings of social psychology apply to early stages of psychotherapy rather than the later stages as therapists and clients do not know each other well in the early stages and necessarily rely on the superficial cues that social psychologists have studied so extensively. Second, social psychology is more obviously relevant to the real relationship between therapist and client and to the therapeutic alliance than to transference and countertransference. Third, social psychology has little to contribute to the *interaction* between therapist and client; and fourth, because much of social psychology is rendered content-free by its reliance on analogue methods its findings are not likely to be informative with respect to the content of therapy.

Peterson then proceeds to argue that many of the established findings from psychotherapy studies make sense from a social psychological perspective. For example, reviewers have concluded that the more similar clients are to therapists in terms of socioeconomic class, education, race, and age, the more likely therapy is to be initiated. Peterson points out that the social psychology of relationships stresses that similarity between people is an important factor in determining whether or not a relationship actually will begin.

The final section of Peterson's chapter addresses specifically behavior modification in the light of social psychology and particularly focuses on attitude change and attitude consistency. Peterson points out that social psychologists have developed several specific strategies for changing attitudes based on the premise that attitudes are a pervasive cause of social behavior so that if they can be changed then a host of behaviors would be efficiently changed in the wake. One method of attitude change is through persuasive communiations (i.e., messages explicitly designed for this purpose). Research has elucidated many of the determinants of whether persuasive communications lead to attitude change. For example, change takes place to the degree the source of the message is perceived as credible, expert, and trustworthy. A second method involves inducing behavior contrary to an attitude so that a state of dissonance arises that can be readily reduced by changing the attitude. A variation of this is to highlight inconsistencies between people's attitudes and values (which are more general than attitudes). A final method that has been used to change prejudiced attitudes is to arrange for people of different races to interact with one another in positive ways.

Peterson notes that although research into attitude change was taking place, other research was undermining its premises by questioning whether attitudes really do lead to behavior. Demonstrations of both consistency and inconsistency between attitudes and behavior were published so that the task became one of determining the conditions under which each occurred. Much has been achieved in this respect and examples include the following. Attitudes stemming from direct experience are more consistent with our behavior than those acquired second hand. Awareness of attitudes promotes behavioral consistency with them. Peterson points out that the identified conditions are quite similar to those that behavior therapists try to create.

PSYCHOBIOLOGY AND PSYCHOPHYSIOLOGY

Psychobiological Processes in the Etiology of Disease

Steptoe's chapter integrates recent developments in the understanding of psychobiological responses into the general framework of disease models based on stress-vulnerability interactions. He begins with a discussion of the five sources of evidence relevant to this objective that include both animal and human studies, and diverse methodologies ranging from laboratory experiments to epidemiological investigations.

The major sections of the chapter outline a stress-coping vulnerability model and the psychobiological pathways to disease both of which are depicted in figures as well as described in the text. The framework derives from transactional models that view stress responses as arising from an interaction between environmental demands on the one hand and the personal and social resources of the individual on the other. The model involves four stages: psychosocial demands and resources; psychobiological stress response; biological vulnerability; and disease. Stage I involves the interaction between demands and resources, and Steptoe discusses the dimensions of each that have been found to influence stress responses. These include the intensity, chronicity, novelty, predictability, complexity, and controllability of demands. The aspects of psychosocial resources considered include cognitive appraisal, psychological coping, prior experience, perceived control, social support, and personality and behavior patterns. The second stage is the psychobiological response systems that provide the pathways through which life stress may influence health and include a number of domains (cognitive, affective, behavioral, autonomic, endocrine, and immunological). Biological vulnerability constitutes the third stage and refers to the constitutional and background health characteristics such as genetic make-up, nutrition, exercise, and age, which determine whether stress responses dissipate without creating any lasting change or increase the risk of ill health.

The remainder of the chapter is devoted to an elaboration of the psychobiological pathways that lead to disease. The discussion begins with a distinction between cognitive-behavioral pathways and physiological pathways, the former referring to cognitive, affective, or behavioral changes that may be elicited as components of stress responses that can influence health independently of any direct actions of the central nervous system on the autonomic, endocrine, or immune systems.

Steptoe goes on to describe six types of processes by which these pathways operate. Beginning with the three processes subsumed under cognitive-behavioral pathways, the first pertains to individuals' responses to signs and symptoms that can lead to inappropriate health-care use. A specific example given is a study which showed delay in seeking treatment was positively correlated with perceived work demands. The second process described is emotional behavior that may precipitate physical pathology such as crying in asthmatic children precipitating symptoms. A final cognitive-behavioral process outlined pertains to health risk behaviors. Steptoe briefly reviews the controversial literature suggesting increases in health risk behaviors such as alcohol consumption and cigarette smoking is associated with stressful life events and chronic stressors.

With respect to physiological pathways, the first process listed refers to psychophysiological hyperreactivity whereby biological reactions in susceptible individuals are larger than those in the remainder of the population, or return to prestress levels is delayed. The second physiological process has been termed "host vulnerability" and concerns alterations in physical vulnerability that might render the person more susceptible to an invasive organism. An obvious example of this process is changes in immune status as a function of psychological stress. The final process discussed is disease stability whereby stress responses can influence disease through modulation of the severity or progression of pre-existing pathology. Studies in recent years have provided an experimental foundation for stress related influences on disease stability by showing that autonomic and neuroendocrine function can fluctuate with daily life experience.

Psychophysiology and Behavioral Assessment: Is There Scope for Theoretical Frameworks?

Turpin's introductory section begins with a discussion of the definitions of psychophysiology and clinical psychophysiology, and concludes with an overview of applications to behavior therapy. In this latter subsection he discusses the problems involved in applying psychophysiology to behavior therapy, but reviews data documenting the large increase in the number of articles using psychophysiological measures (in two leading journals the percentage increased from around 1% in 1965 to about 40% in the 1980s). He goes on to suggest that the growth of psychophysiology in relation to clinical research has not been matched by its application to routine clinical practice, especially in Europe.

The second section starts with a discussion of the assessment models that have been used in behavior therapy namely behavioral assessment and the psychometric approach. Turpin discusses differences between the models but notes the current trend towards raprochement. He then proceeds to review rationales for the inclusion of psychophysiological measures in behavioral assessment and psychometric assessment. Turpin argues that all stages of behavioral assessment may potentially benefit from incorporating psychophysiological measurement; identification of the target problem, which constitutes the basis of initial or pretreatment assessment; selection of treatment strategies; monitoring of treatment progress or outcomes; and process measurement to investigate the relationship between the application of intervention and the final clinical outcome. Because of the recently perceived relevance of psychometric approaches to behavioral assessment, Turpin next discusses the rationales for psychophysiological approaches to psychometric assessment. These include: psychophysiological measures as indices of biological substrates said to determine various personality characteristics; the search for more objective biological diagnostic markers in psychiatry; and the recent formulation of vulnerability models of psychiatric disorders.

The third section briefly discusses methodological considerations in the application of psychophysiology to behavioral assessment. Criteria for choosing between psychophysiological measures are reviewed followed by alternative means of classifying the types of measures available. In considering appropriate designs for clinical research involving psychophysiological measurement, Turpin notes that psychophysiological research has tended to be rooted firmly in the tradition of group designs, but goes on to argue for the value of single-case designs in this area. The section concludes with a table summarizing applications of psychophysiology to behavior therapy showing the types of measures used with different disorders.

The fourth section focuses on evaluation and limitations of psychophysiological measures. Turpin argues evaluation of psychophysiological assessment requires that distinctions between different measurement models be explicitly taken into account. Starting with psychometric approaches, he suggests that if psychophysiological assessments are to be employed to discriminate between groups of subjects over time, or to provide the basis upon which future predictions are to be made, psychophysiological measures should be temporally stable and demonstrate reasonable test-retest reliability across time. On the other hand, if psychophysiological measures are to be employed within idiographic and single-case approaches, intra- or within subject correlations need to be examined rather than reliance on nomothetically derived test-retest reliability coefficients. The third approach to evaluation in behavioral assessment considered by Turpin is the treatment utility approach. This involves two criteria: "conceptual validity," which concerns the ability of a specific assessment to contribute to the understanding of behavior and "treatment validity" whereby the addition of a particular assessment strategy leads to better treatment.

The final section of the chapter considers theoretical contributions of psychophysiology to behavioral assessment. Turpin argues strongly that progress has been handicapped by a reluctance to consider theoretical models and an over reliance on empirical observations. He points out that most general areas of psychology such as research into emotion, social behavior, conditioning, and personality have all used the psychophysiological approach to advance theoretical developments, but he limits his discussion to the problem of desynchrony between triple assessment approaches (verbal-cognitive, overt-motor and physiological). This discussion is divided into "within" and "between" system discordance, the former referring to a lack of internal consistency for measures purporting to assess the same three system mode, the latter referring to a lack of consistency between measures assessing different modes. The subsection on within system discordance particularly focuses on the question of whether psychophysiological measures can discriminate between emotional states, whereas the between system discordance subsection focuses on the question of the role of cognition.

Psychophysiological Contributions to Behavior Therapy

The introductory section of Johnston and Martin begins with an overview of psychophysiology. The history of the field is briefly sketched from its origins in the 1950s, along with the evolving definition of psychophysiology. Major journals and texts are discussed and the trend toward integration with other areas of psychological science is noted. The next subsection focuses on recent developments. Theoretical developments are considered first and a discussion of the motivational approach of Don Fowles follows. A number of technical developments are then reviewed including: the advent of neuromagnetometry (the study of magnetic fields of the brain); progress in the continuous noninvasive measurement of blood pressure; measurement in real life rather than laboratory settings; and new approaches to data analysis. The introductory section concludes with a discussion of the link between psychophysiology and behavior therapy. It is argued that strong links exist largely because behavior therapy, as developed by Wolpe, adopted an essentially peripheralist theory of anxiety. Although behavior therapy moved away from this position, more recently, a resurgence of interest in peripheralist theories of emotion has occurred. The role of biofeedback in stimulating a link is also discussed.

The remaining three major sections of the chapter illustrate contributions of psychophysiology to behavior therapy by focusing on three diverse areas, the first of which is anxiety, fear, and panic. This section begins with a discussion of the "three systems theory." Peter Lang documented that anxiety and fear have three components, the subjective, behavioral and physiological, and that these components are, at best, rather loosely correlated. This theory is discussed in terms of its implications for: assessment (the need to measure all three components); prediction of response to treatment (poor prognosis associated with desynchrony); and matching of patients and therapy (treatment according to most dysfunctional component). The section proceeds with consideration of Lang's bio-informational theory of emotion that proposes that emotional information is stored in memory as a series of propositions concerning stimulus, response and meaning information with connections between each proposition forming an associative network. The theory emphasizes responses, and physiological responses are measured, rather than overt behavior, in the belief that they are less governed by social constraints.

The next issue discussed is preparedness and the acquisition of fear. Johnston and Martin note that Seligman was the first to attempt to solve the problem of the very limited range of situations that provoke irrational fear by proposing that fearful responses were, as the result of evolutionary pressures, biologically prepared to be conditioned to particular stimuli (cf. Cook & Mineka). They go on to discuss how our understanding of this process has been forwarded by research on the classical conditioning of autonomic responses to biologically prepared stimuli such as pictures of snakes or spiders. The section concludes with a review of psychophysiological aspects of current theories of panic. Questions considered include whether panic-prone people do misinterpret somatic events in a way that leads to increased fear and autonomic arousal, and whether such individuals show markedly increased arousal when panicking or in situations likely to provoke panic. Review of the evidence leads to the comment that panic disorder seems to be predominantly a cognitive disorder.

The third section focuses on biofeedback, the most direct attempt to incorporate psychophysiology in the therapeutic process, as applied to the cardiovascular system and cardiovascular disorders. Johnston and Martin point out that numerous studies have shown that some degree of self control of heart rate, blood pressure, and blood flow is possible with biofeedback; however, increases in activation can be substantial but decreases are much smaller. Also, determining the extent to which biofeedback is necessary for such control is complex and the answer is still uncertain. With respect to mechanisms of biofeedback, most, if not all, biofeedback aided control of heart rate and blood pressure seems to be associated with changes in muscle activity or respiration rather than a consequence of direct autonomic control. The motor skills model of biofeedback is discussed but it is argued that the evidence suggests that the role of feedback is motivational not informational. Clinical applications of biofeedback are reviewed and it is noted that results with primary hypertension and cardiac arrhythmias have generally been disappointing (e.g., biofeedback not superior to relaxation training). More positive findings have been reported with Raynaud's disease.

The final section considers psychophysiological contributions with respect to chronic headaches. Review of studies investigating the psychophysiological mechanisms of headaches led to a number of tentative conclusions including: there is little evidence to support the hypothesized muscular mechanism of tension headaches; there is more support for the hypothesized vascular mechanism of migraine although the exact nature of the dysfunctional processes is unclear; and migraineurs appear to demonstrate response stereotypy. Conclusions reached from reviewing studies of biofeedback as a treatment modality for headaches include: several forms of biofeedback lead to improvement which is maintained up to 12 months (the evidence is strongest for EMG feedback for tension headache followed by digital temperature feedback for migraine); the treatment effect is possibly mediated by cognitive changes involving self-efficacy and locus of control; biofeedback is no more effective than alternatives such as relaxation training; and the treatment gains do not seem to be maintained beyond 12 months.

Johnston and Martin argue that it is impossible to escape the conclusion that the potential contributions of psychophysiology to headache research have not been fulfilled, and use their final subsection to consider why this should be so. A number of suggestions are made including the tendency for the literature to concentrate on treatment studies despite the fact that so little is understood about psychophysiological mechanisms, and the tendency for physiological variables to be measured and analyzed with little appreciation for the underlying physiological systems (biological naivety).

CONDITIONING AND LEARNING

Selective Associations in the Origins of Phobic Fears and Their Implications for Behavior Therapy

The chapter by Cook and Mineka reviews one line of recent research generated by their efforts to develop a primate model of fears and phobias based on the long-standing observation concerning the marked fear of snakes exhibited by many primate species. They suggest there are significant parallels between snake fear in rhesus monkeys and the symptomatology, etiology, therapy, and prevention of human fears and phobias; and they argue that any etiological account of human fears and phobias has to explain the "nonrandom" distribution of such fears and phobias (i.e., certain "fear-relevant" stimuli such as snakes, spiders and heights, appear to be the focus of a disproportionately large number of clinical fears and phobias relative to other stimuli such as electrical outlets, guns, and knives; although all of these stimuli may be approximately equivalent in the extent to which they are associated with traumatic experiences, verbal warnings, or both, during ontogeny).

The central concern of the chapter is whether the ease with which snake fear is acquired reflects a *selective association*. Selective associations represent instances of experience-independent association bias in which certain combinations of stimuli are more readily associable than others. A number of theorists have speculated that selective associations may explain the nonrandom distribution of human fears and phobias, as the greater propensity to acquire a fear of fear-relevant stimuli may result from the fact that such stimuli are selectively associable with aversive outcomes. For demonstration of selective associations, it is critical to show, however, that the ease with which fear-relevant stimuli are associated with aversive outcomes cannot be attributed to intrinsic properties of fear-relevant stimuli such as salience (i.e., when such stimuli are paired with nonaversive unconditioned stimuli, superior conditioning would not take place).

Cook and Mineka then proceed to describe an elegant series of experiments on the acquisition of fear. The first two sets of studies were designed simply to demonstrate observational learning of snake fear in naive laboratory-reared rhesus monkeys. The two sets differed in that the first involved live models whereas the second presented models via videotapes so that the models' fear performance could be controlled. The third study specifically addressed the issue of selective associations. In this study, two observer groups watched videotaped models responding on some trials to toy snakes and on other trials to flowers. The models for one group reacted fearfully to snakes, but nonfearfully to flowers; in contrast, the models for the second group reacted fearfully to flowers and nonfearfully to snakes. Preliminary evidence for selective associations was provided by the majority of the first group acquiring a fear of snakes but none acquiring a fear of flowers, whereas in the second group, very few observers demonstrated fear of either snakes or flowers.

The next three studies described were designed to rule out alternative non associative explanations of the above findings. These included: the failure of the second group to acquire a fear of flowers could stem from the difficulty of the required discrimination; differences in conditionability to snakes versus flowers reflect specific stimulus attributes possessed by snakes but not flowers (e.g., eyes, forked tongues); and the flowers may be incapable of supporting excitatory conditioning under any circumstances. The results of all three experiments supported a selective association interpretation of the data. Further support was generated in the final study described in which it was demonstrated that when fear-relevant and fear-irrelevant stimuli were simultaneously presented during observational conditioning, such that models would appear to react fearfully to both stimuli, the fear-relevant stimulus overshadowed the fear-irrelevant one.

Cook and Mineka point out that writers in the area of learning constraints have typically posited ecologically oriented functional accounts of selective associations (i.e., learning propensities are presumed to be the product of natural selection). They discuss some implications of their studies for such hypotheses and go on to suggest how comparative methodologies can be used for testing such hypotheses. Cook and Mineka also discuss the implications of their finding that fear can be learned via videotapes. For example, the mass media may play a role in the acquisition of new fears.

Cook and Mineka conclude with a section on possible implications of selective associations for behavior therapy. They start by pointing out that in Seligman's original formulation of the preparedness theory of phobias, it was hypothesized that fears that are acquired to prepared stimuli would be considerably more resistant to extinction than would be fears acquired to neutral or unprepared stimuli. Review of the relevant evidence led to the conclusion that it provides mixed support. Cook and Mineka discuss the problems involved in researching this issue such as the difficulties of equating phobias with prepared versus unprepared stimuli for mode of onset, duration of fear, and intensity of fear; and in animal studies, the difficulties associated with conditioning significant levels of fear of fear-irrelevant objects. They point out, however, that recent data from their laboratory demonstrate that fears that are easy to acquire can still effectively be prevented through prior exposure to nonfearful models.

A Contextual Analysis of Fear Extinction

Bouton begins his chapter by noting that extinction is a basic tool of behavior therapy. It is often linked to therapies used in the treatment of anxiety disorders where success appears to depend substantially on exposure to the fear-evoking stimulus, but Bouton argues that extinction may be relevant to any treatment in which the therapist introduces new learning designed to change a client's cognition or behavior.

Bouton notes that ideas about conditioning generally, and extinction in particular, have changed markedly since the early days of behavior therapy. Researchers are now more likely to recognize that conditioned stimuli are behaviorally unstable after extinction. The research Bouton reviews suggests that even after prolonged extinction procedures, extinguished fear stimuli can still evoke substantial fear under the right conditions. Bouton suggests that extinction does not cause unlearning, but instead gives the conditioned stimulus (CS) a second, and therefore "ambiguous" meaning. The meaning of the stimulus and the response it currently evokes, may depend fundamentally on its current *context*.

The first part of the chapter reviews some of the evidence from experiments with rats that supports this view of context and extinction. One of the phenomena suggesting that extinction is not due to a loss of the original learning is known as *reinstatement*. Reinstatement involves presentations of the unconditioned stimulus (US) alone in a separate session following extinction. Fear can be partially reinstated to the CS when it is subsequently tested even if fear of the CS had been completely eliminated. The reinstatement phenomenon has important clinical implications as it suggests that exposure to trauma on its own can undo the effects of successful therapy. Also, if the effects of an early conditioning experience have been reduced through natural extinction, one might expect them to recur after exposure to separate trauma. There is strong evidence that reinstatement involves context conditioning as the US must be presented in the context in which the CS is to be tested if reinstatement is to occur.

Bouton goes on to discuss other extinction phenomena that suggest that the potential for fear persists long into extinction and that the context may be important in bringing it out. If fear is conditioned in one context and then extinguished in another, fear is *renewed* if the extinguished CS is returned to the original conditioning context or tested in a third context. Bouton presents evidence suggesting that fear conditioning generalizes fairly well across contexts but fear extinction, in contrast, does not. A third phenomenon that supports the view that the original learning persists through extinction is the rate of recovery following conditioning. The results of many experiments indicate that conditioned responding reappears rapidly when CS-US pairings are resumed after extinction, suggesting that the original learning has been "saved" through extinction. Rate of reacquisition depends on whether reconditioning occurs in a conditioning or extinction context (rapid and slow reacquisition, respectively).

The second part of Bouton's chapter surveys a wide range of stimuli that can function as contexts. The research reviewed in the first part used physical contexts provided by different apparatuses housed in different rooms. Bouton considers next drugs as interoceptive contexts. Learning that occurs under the influence of a drug may fail to transfer to the undrugged condition. Such state-dependent retention has been observed with a variety of drugs in animals and humans, but the available data suggest that state-dependent extinction can also occur (i.e., extinction under the influence of drugs might not transfer to the undrugged state). These data obviously recommend caution in combining drugs with exposure therapy, and suggest the possibility for drug dependence in individuals who ingest drugs to escape anxiety.

Another context considered by Bouton is the emotion or affective state that featured in the original conditioning episode. According to a contextual analysis, if an extinguished evoking stimulus were encountered anew in the same emotional state as was present during conditioning then it could cause a renewal of fear. Bouton reviews data consistent with a contextual role for emotion and stress. For example, the physiological components of stress are known to retrieve forgotten aversive experiences. Mood-dependent retrieval has been demonstrated in mood-induction studies with humans although results have sometimes proved difficult to replicate.

Bouton also suggests that the passage of time may itself provide a sequence of discernible contexts so that extinction may be specific to the temporal extinction context (subjects learn some version of "the CS is safe *now*"). This implies that renewal of fear should occur when testing is carried out in a different temporal context, so that a contextual analysis provides a new way of viewing spontaneous recovery.

Bouton concludes his chapter by discussing the implications of his contextual analysis of fear extinction. One example is that therapists may want to attend to and perhaps "treat" potential relapse contexts, although he warns that simple exposure to the context alone may not be good enough. Another implication is that the therapist should pay attention to cues that can potentially signal extinction. What stimuli can the client "attribute" the current safety of the evoking stimulus to during therapy, and can they be made irrelevant? Finally, in vivo exposure may be especially effective because the client can learn extinction in a context like that in which the evoking stimulus will be encountered outside therapy.

COMMUNITY PSYCHOLOGY AND PREVENTION

Incorporating the Ecological Paradigm into Behavioral Preventive Interventions

Burgoyne and Jason begin their chapter by noting that behavior therapists have primarily targeted populations having manifest disorders and relied upon one-to-one or small group intervention strategies. They "propose that operating predominantly within this system restricts behavior therapy's current influence and potential development, and that an alternative, specifically preventive, service delivery strategy offers the field unique options and opportunities to increase its impact, both in terms of scale and social significance" (p. 457). They suggest that constraints on the alliance between prevention and behavior therapy can best be managed by incorporating certain tenets of the ecological paradigm into intervention and research designs.

Burgoyne and Jason argue for a focus on prevention by indicating a gap between mental health needs and resources. They review evidence, for example, indicating that the traditional mental health delivery system actually services fewer than one in five of those with serious mental health problems, and that the trend toward increased need for mental health services seems likely to continue.

Burgoyne and Jason point out that the model of prevention adopted by psychology was taken largely from the field of public health, and includes three conceptually distinct levels: *primary* (reduction of new cases of disorder or promotion of health building competencies); *secondary* (efforts directed at individuals or groups determined at risk for or showing early signs of disorder); and *tertiary* (equivalent of traditional rehabilitative approaches).

The next section of the chapter focuses on the interface between prevention and behaviorism, and begins by considering what the fields have in common versus where they depart. Two major commonalities are discussed. First, both fields have emphasized the environmental context of behavior rather than models that attribute causation to factors residing within an individual. Second, both fields have questioned the efficacy and efficiency of traditional psychoanalytic and client-centered therapy strategies. However, whereas the majority of behavior therapists sought to combat the medicalized mental health system by providing more effective treatments, by involving larger systems (e.g., families and schools) to monitor and control the behavior of their clients, and by organizing institutional settings to maximize socially adaptive behaviors in patients, the field of prevention has pursued an alternative service delivery system altogether. Prevention necessitates a proactive, competency-based stance, where the goal is to identify potential problems and attempt to amplify existing resources.

Burgoyne and Jason note that behaviorists who have developed a preventive model have contributed significantly to the progress prevention can claim to have made to date, and in doing so have provided the most compelling argument for behaviorism and prevention to further pursue their relationship. Much of the work done outside of the traditional service delivery system conducted by behavioral psychologists can best be classified as secondary prevention although a shift toward higher level interventions has been advocated.

Burgoyne and Jason argue that behaviorists have a tendency to attend to a restricted number of directly manipulable contextual factors that impact target behavior and that this has imposed a number of conceptual and methodological constraints on the field. They suggest that a conceptual expansion is needed that involves a shift toward incorporating an ecological or systems perspective into behavioral interventions.

The ecological paradigm is not a specified theory but rather a heuristic, or guiding conceptual framework for understanding behavior in interaction with its social and cultural contexts. Four ecological processes drawn from the study of biology comprise the basic principles of the ecological paradigm as it was originally defined. The first is *interdependence*, which recognizes that any change in one part of an interrelated person-environment system will invariably effect some kind of change in other parts of the system. This is not surprising to behaviorists, but such "ripple effects" are rarely systematically documented or controlled for and so the potential for unforeseen outcomes, especially with large scale interventions is considerable. The second principle, *cycling of resources*, concerns what qualities the setting, or persons, posses that can be applied or developed to cope with an identified problem. The *succession* principle states that persons and settings are in a constant process of change, and as such require constant adaptations. Preventive interventions may have difficulty maintaining their effects if they are not able to adapt to the changes persons and settings will inevitably manifest over time. The fourth principle, *adaptation*, explains behavior as a result of a continual process of accommodation between persons and their environment. This principle suggests that behavior is the function of a response to sets of contingencies in several settings; one implication is that matching individuals with settings is a legitimate alternative to directly manipulating an individual's behavior.

In the final section, Burgoyne and Jason emphasize the need for collaboration between researchers and persons and settings. Burgoyne and Jason argue that the effects of collaboratively defined, produced and implemented change efforts are more likely to endure.

Extending Applications of Behavior Therapy to Large-scale Intervention

The basic thesis of the chapter by Winett, King, and Altman is similar to that of Burgoyne and Jason and argues that much attention has been given to conceptual and technical issues with respect to how various health and disability problems should be addressed, but *service delivery system* issues have been neglected. They "call for larger scale interventions that emphasize prevention and health enhancement, with these interventions based on developmental and ecological perspectives and a new framework and schema for structural and behavior change" (p. 473).

Winett et al. begin by considering the history of behavior therapy with a view to making the point that it has lost its "original reformist mission." They note that the impetus for the field was not just the absence of effective forms of therapy but criticisms of the health system generally. For example, treatment was administered by highly trained and expensive professionals, in specialized settings removed from the natural environment to individuals manifesting considerable acute or chronic distress.

Winett et al. go on to argue that current and future mental health and health needs far outstrip the capacities of present delivery systems, necessitating service delivery innovation. They discuss the three types of prevention mode, primary, secondary, and tertiary, and call for more primary and secondary prevention, particularly the former. Winett et al. note that primary prevention may use "passive" strategies (i.e., not requiring individual behavior change) such as fluoridation of the water supply to prevent dental problems, or "active" strategies such as providing early education to children and adolescents to prevent teenage pregnancy and the spread of sexually transmitted diseases. They also differentiate two types of intervention mode: *waiting mode* (waiting within traditional settings for clients to present themselves); and *seeking mode* (searching out problems in the community). Winett and colleagues commend the latter mode and emphasize the value of a *proactive* approach in which problems are anticipated rather than reacted to.

The next section of the chapter begins with discussion of two perspectives for innovation. Winett et al. argue for a *health enhancement perspective* that involves focusing on strengths and competencies rather than deficits. Second, they recommend a *developmental/ecological approach* that involves taking a life span approach and studying important settings and systems that impinge on individuals at different points in their lives.

Winett et al. then consider models and theories for large-scale interventions. The two most prominent approaches have been the PRECEDE model and social marketing. Winett et al. note that there is evidence to support the effectiveness of these models but suggest they are "first generation" models that will further evolve and also be joined by other "second generation" models. They particularly criticize the models on the grounds of tending to be atheoretical, and suggest that the developmental/ecological perspective can provide one alternative conceptual schema. Winett et al. also note that virtually all scientifically based health promotion programs presently rest on Albert Bandura's social-cognitive theory. They argue that this has the advantage that each program evaluation constitutes a test of the theory but the costs are that other theory and conceptualization's for health promotion are neglected. Social cognitive theory results in a focus on the personal and interpersonal levels so that the theories of organization and community change, or the theories from political science or from economics, are very infrequently used as foundations for programs geared to health promotion.

The next section begins by reviewing the major directions highlighted so far, and then offers a framework for integrating the theoretical and practical strategies of health psychology and public health with the purpose of developing more effective interventions. The key to the framework is multilevel analysis that can lead to multilevel interventions. Multilevel analysis involves studying a problem using theory, perspectives, and data that often represent personal and interpersonal levels (which is the province of psychology) and organizational/environmental and institutional/societal levels (which is the province of public health).

In the final section of the chapter, Winett et al. discuss an exemplar program for young adolescents to illustrate the major points of the chapter. They start by listing a series of observations on the adolescent health promotion literature: for example, theory and data suggest that high-risk behaviors often occur together as a syndrome; and many high-risk behaviors begin early, are forewarnings of more difficult problems in later adolescence and suggest preventive programs. Winett and colleagues then proceed to illustrate multilevel analysis and intervention by focusing on two levels, the personal and organizational/environmental.

MULTIPLE PERSPECTIVES AND INTEGRATION: THE EXAMPLE OF ANXIETY

Although anxiety is discussed at length in the cognitive psychology section of the Handbook, it also features in most of the other sections reflecting its central position within behavior therapy/clinical psychology. Starting with developmental psychology, perhaps the main question pertaining to anxiety from a developmental perspective is whether there are quantitative and/or qualitative differences in anxiety across the life span. Studies have shown, for example, that different fears and phobias are common for children of different ages. The developmental sequence of fears emerging appears to be fear of strangers (first year of life), fear of animals (2-3), fear of the dark (3-4), school fears (school entry), and evaluative and social fears (middle childhood onwards). Other research has demonstrated qualitative differences in anxiety associated with age. Young children (up to age 6) express anxiety by crying, screaming, needing to be physically restrained, and expressing pain verbally; whereas older children (7-9 years) do not require physical restraint, are more likely to express their anxiety verbally, and show signs of muscular rigidity. Children over 10 years old express anxiety by verbal expression of pain and muscular rigidity.

Anxiety has been investigated extensively from a cognitive perspective. Studies have shown anxiety to be associated with various cognitive deficits that appear to be related to state rather than trait anxiety. Deficits are most apparent in memory but the findings are complex as anxiety can occasionally be associated with a processing advantage in relatively simple cognitive tests. Other research has focused on the cognitive products associated with anxiety. Studies have found that anxiety is associated with an increased prevalence of mood congruent thoughts which, in general, appear to be related to social or physical dangers. There is also some evidence to suggest that high trait anxiety is associated with a pattern of elevated irrational beliefs. More recently, research has investigated cognitive processing in anxiety. Evidence from a wide range of studies has demonstrated mood congruent attentional bias associated with anxiety. That is, at least for individuals high on trait anxiety, state anxiety is associated with selective attention for fear relevant stimuli. There is also considerable evidence to support the existence of an anxiety linked bias in comprehension processes, leading to distortions in the evaluation of risk and in the interpretation of ambiguous stimuli. Although mood congruent retrieval bias has been amply demonstrated for depression, no convincing evidence for such biases in memory processes have been demonstrated for trait or state anxiety.

Contributions to the understanding of anxiety evolving from the social psychological literature include investigations using an attributional approach that stimulated many studies on the phenomenon of misattribution, especially of physiological arousal. For example, snake phobics who were led to believe, via bogus heart rate feedback, that their arousal was low in the presence of snakes relative to a mild shock condition, were more likely to approach snakes than controls not subjected to this manipulation. A quite different line of research from a social psychological perspective has investigated the relationship between anxiety and social support. Anxiety has been shown to be negatively correlated with perceived family support, for example. On the treatment side, social support appears to be a useful adjunct in the treatment of agoraphobia, and social skills training has been shown to be an important treatment modality for social phobias.

One starting point for psychophysiologically oriented research on anxiety has been the three systems analysis that conceptualizes anxiety as having three loosely coupled components (subjective, behavioral, and physiological). Studies have demonstrated that effective treatment tends to lead to alterations in all three systems. Other studies have investigated the hypothesis that patients showing desynchrony at the end of treatment will do less well subsequently, but support for this proposition has been limited. And other studies have explored whether matching type of treatment with most elevated anxiety component produces superior results (e.g., exposure therapy for behavioral responders versus relaxation training for physiological responders). Some data appear to support this matching hypothesis. Other avenues of psychophysiological anxiety research include those investigating theories with physiological components. For example, some theories of panic suggest that panic prone individuals are susceptible to interpreting bodily symptoms catastrophically and these catastrophic interpretations feed back into the system to produce a vicious spiral of autonomic arousal and panic. Psychophysiological research has shown that many self-reported panics are not accompanied by detectable autonomic responses suggesting that the somatic component of the cognitive model of panic is only relevant in some patients, or in some panics.

Learning theory has long played a central role in anxiety research providing a theoretical framework for the development of anxiety disorders and a rationale for treatment techniques. Recent developments in this tradition represented in this Handbook include research evidence suggesting that the "nonrandom" distribution of phobias reflects selective associations. That is, fear-relevant stimuli (e.g., snakes and spiders) are more readily associable with aversive outcomes than fear-irrelevant stimuli (e.g., flowers and rabbits). Other studies have shown that fears which are easy to acquire can be prevented through prior exposure to nonfearful models. An alternative line of research focusing on extinction rather than acquisition suggests that extinction does not cause unlearning but instead gives the conditioned stimulus a second meaning. The meaning of the stimulus and the response it evokes depends on the context in which it is presented (does the context cue the learned response of anxiety or the alternative learned response of no anxiety?). A wide range of stimuli can function as contexts including both external (e.g., physical settings) and internal stimuli (e.g., drug or emotional state).

Considerations such as these emphasize that many areas of psychological science can contribute novel perspectives for theorizing and researching clinical problems. Perhaps what is most interesting and is the essence of this Handbook, however, is that bringing these perspectives together suggests new combinations of approaches that may prove productive. Of course, to a degree, this has already happened. For example, the research mentioned on attributions of physiological arousal draws from the social cognition and psychophysiological literature. Another example is provided by research on preparedness using classical conditioning of autonomic responses.

Other combinations of perspectives do not seem to have been exploited, however. One potentially interesting integration, for example, would be between cognitive and developmental perspectives as they pertain to clinical perspectives. Cognitively oriented psychologists have documented mood congruent information-processing biases but how do these relate to life span development? When do they begin (e.g., related to other developmental changes or environmental events) and how do they develop (e.g., suddenly or gradually)? Another potential integration would be between cognitive and psychophysiological perspectives. Do individual differences in the three components of anxiety relate to individual differences in mood congruent information-processing biases? For example, is it the case that individuals whose maximal anxiety response is in the verbal-cognitive system, demonstrate maximum information-processing biases?

Integrations could involve combining even more perspectives. How, for example, do attributions of physiological arousal relate to life span development?

Of course, bringing together findings from different fields also serves to warn researchers of errors that could easily be made. The research showing qualitative differences in the expression of anxiety across children of different ages, for example, highlights the problem of studying anxiety, from any perspective, in children varying in age, as a measure of anxiety that is appropriate for one age group is potentially inappropriate for other age groups. Another example comes from the cognitive literature on information-processing biases. As noted by Ollendick and King, are younger children really more fearful, as studies have suggested, or might younger children be interpreting test stimuli differently?

QUESTIONS AND ISSUES RAISED IN THE INTRODUCTORY CHAPTER

What Can Psychological Science Offer Behavior Therapy?

The issue of what can psychological science contribute to behavior therapy is the central theme of this Handbook. Potential theoretical and conceptual contributions reviewed in the preceding pages include Lerner's developmental-contextual perspective, Bower's network model of mood and cognition, Lang's bio-informational theory of emotion, Steptoe's stress–coping–vulnerability model of disease and Seligman's theory of preparedness. Perhaps the most impressive methodological contribution could be derived from cognitive psychology where paradigms have been developed for studying mental processes without recourse to (problematic) introspective techniques. Empirical findings of clinical relevance can be found across the spectrum of psychological sciences. Good examples come from the developmental literature where knowledge has accumulated with clear implications for what types of investigative techniques and treatment procedures are appropriate for children of different ages.

No attempt will be made to discuss contributions in more detail here as this would be too repetitive but a few comments on the contributions are offered. The literature reviewed in the proceeding chapters suggests that psychological science has already contributed much to behavior therapy but there is the potential for contributing much more. Some of the theory and research that can be applied in the clinical area has been available, but not fully exploited, for many years. A good example, highlighted by Chris Peterson's social psychological analysis of the psychotherapy process, is the literature on attitude change and attitude behavior consistency. Other theory and research is in an early stage of development. A good example here is provided by the information-processing models of emotional disorders discussed by MacLeod and Mathews.

The unrealized potential of theories and findings from psychological science can be illustrated by further consideration of this latter example. Cognitive psychologists have developed a range of tasks such as the dot probe paradigm, Stroop color naming paradigm, dichotic listening, and various encoding and recall tasks for investigating information processing. Many of these tasks are relatively immune to response bias and can be used for studying processing that is beyond the subject's awareness. Currently, they have been employed in group designs to investigate mood congruent information-processing biases. Clearly, they have the potential for being adapted for direct clinical application whereby they could be used to assess the particular biases of individual clients and monitor progress in reducing such biases.

Implications of Reviewing Psychological Science for the Expanded Domain of Behavior Therapy

It was noted in the introductory chapter that in the early days of behavior therapy the focus was on overt behavior and autonomic processes, but that increasing emphasis has been given to cognitive processes, and some writers have advocated devoting attention to affective processes and unconscious processes. The main criticism of moving away from an exclusive interest in observable events has been that private events cannot be studied in a scientific manner. If the study of mental processes had to rely on introspective techniques then most would agree that a shift from an emphasis on overt to covert processes would indeed involve a loss of scientific rigor. The problems of relying on introspective evidence are outlined briefly in Eysenck's chapter.

As discussed by both Eysenck, and MacLeod and Mathews, however, cognitive psychologists have developed methods of studying mental processes that do not resort to introspection. As MacLeod and Mathews point out "the majority of cognitive-experimental paradigms employ objective behavioral measures, such as response latencies or recall scores, and infer mental processes by relating such data to theoretical models" (p. 117).

These methodological advances can be argued to counter the criticisms offered of expanding the domain to include mental events. In addition to these defences of studying mental processes, positive arguments can be developed with respect to why the field should follow this path. Eysenck, for example, takes issue with those who have concluded that the concept of unconscious processes is largely irrelevant to cognitive therapy by making two important points in relation to the understanding of mood disorders. First, he argues that many conscious processes have automatic processes as antecedents, so that to understand conscious processing it is necessary to focus on automatic or pre-attentive processes also. Second, he suggests that nonnormal automatic processes are more likely to be part of a vulnerability factor for mood disorders, whereas nonnormal conscious processes are more likely to reflect current mood state.

Implications of Reviewing Psychological Science for Integrating Behavior Therapy with Other Schools of Psychotherapy

The introductory chapter also discussed the trend towards integrating behavior therapy with other approaches to psychotherapy, in particular, psychodynamic psychotherapy. It seems difficult to argue with the proposition that any school of psychotherapy that has been practiced by a significant number of professionals over a prolonged period of time will not have developed some important insights into human functioning. Integration offers the promise of pooling this knowledge. The obvious argument against integration is the inherent difficulties involved. The major schools of psychotherapy differ in every conceivable way including: theoretical leanings, philosophical stances, methodological preferences, goals, values, and jargon.

Two points germane to the integration issue seem to emerge from the discussions in this Handbook. First, the gap between behavior therapy and other approaches is narrowing. For example, with the domain of behavior therapy expanding and even moving towards incorporating unconscious processes, the subject matter of behavior therapy and psychoanalysis is more similar. In this respect it is interesting to note parallels between the methods of psychoanalysts and cognitive psychologists as both have used ambiguous stimuli to study processes beyond awareness. Hence, whereas psychoanalysts have used projective techniques (ink blots, pictures, etc), cognitive psychologists have used homophones, words embedded in white noise or presented to an unattended ear, or ambiguous stories.

Second, it seems to the author that full integration will always be an unattainable (and perhaps undesirable) goal. The potential gain from integration, of different schools benefiting from each others' knowledge, may be achieved, however, by indirect means. For example, the chapters in part one on "Developmental Psychology" of this Handbook emphasized that developmental psychology has been strongly influenced by psychoanalysis (and vice versa). Hence, by integrating behavior therapy with developmental psychology (a task that would appear simpler and probably more acceptable to behavior therapists than integrating behavior therapy with psychoanalysis), behavior therapy may gain from some of the insights achieved by the psychoanalytic school.

AUTHOR INDEX

Abbott, B.B., 327, 420
Abel, C.C., 396
Abelson, R.P., 175, 287, 290, 291, 292, 293, 294, 313, 319
Aber, M.S., 459
Abikoff, H., 48
Abramovitz, A., 48
Abrams, D.B., 275
Abramson, L.Y., 132, 169, 170, 172, 180, 181, 186, 265, 278, 288, 291, 326
Achenbach, T.M., 36, 37, 44, 45, 46, 47, 61, 62, 63, 65, 66, 68, 74, 81, 82, 88, 294
Ad Hoc Committee, 397, 398, 402
Adam, T., 88
Adams, A.S., 394
Adams, H.E., 3, 352, 398, 400, 402
Adams, M.R., 334
Adelson, J., 76
Ader, R., 325, 336
Adler, C., 397
Agras, W.S., 393
Ahlers, S.T., 445
Ahles, T.A., 398, 399
Ainsworth, M.D.S., 36, 77
Ajzen, I., 265
Akiskal, H.S., 42

Akselrod, S., 388
Alba, J.W., 107, 123, 172, 177, 187
Albee, G.W., 458, 459
Alden, L.E., 278
Alexander, F., 325
Alexander, L., 156
Alkinson, J.H., 117
Allaire, D., 401
Allan, C.A., 333
Allen, L., 87
Allen, V.L., 15
Alloy, L.B., 170, 172
Allport, E.W., 255, 256
Allport, G.W., 311
Alpert, J.L., 458
Altman, D.G., 475, 480, 483, 484, 486
Alvey, P., 210
Amabile, T.M., 185
Ambrosioni, E., 334
American Psychiatric Association, 36, 44, 45, 67, 397
Amies, P., 164
Anastasiades, P., 350, 387
Ancis, J., 153
Anderson, B.L., 368
Anderson, C., 427
Anderson, C.A., 286

Anderson, C.D., 335, 399
Anderson, C.L., 478, 479
Anderson, D.E., 330
Anderson, E.A., 335
Anderson, J.R., 106, 120, 123, 293
Anderson, K., 153, 180, 286
Anderson, K.O., 337
Anderson, N.H., 297
Anderson, R., 339
Andrasik, F., 337, 352, 358, 362, 399, 400, 401, 402
Andreassi, J.L., 358, 384
Angelakos, E.T., 334
Anisman, H., 326, 327
Antaki, C., 286, 289
Anthony, E.J., 37
Anthony, J., 20
Antonovsky, A., 478
Appels, A., 327
Aral, S., 336
Arena, J.G., 337, 350, 352, 358, 360, 362, 388, 402
Argyle, M., 91
Arizmendi, I.G., 316
Arkes, H.R., 199, 206
Arkowitz, H., 289
Armstrong, D., 357
Arnetz, B.B., 336
Arnoult, L.H., 286
Aronson, E., 261, 262
Arthur, M.W., 77
Asch, S.E., 312
Ashbrook, P.W., 118, 119
Asher, S.R., 78, 86
Atkinson, R.C., 104, 105
August, G., 49
Avitzur, E., 274, 276
Ax, A.L.F., 369
Axelrod, S., 201

Baddeley, A.D., 105, 107, 121, 233, 234, 247
Badia, P., 327, 420
Baer, D.M., 13, 16, 58, 463
Baer, J.S., 275
Baer, P.E., 333
Bagarozzi, D.A., 288
Bagley, C., 338
Bailey, J.S., 462
Bailey, S., 180, 286
Baker, E., 232
Baker, L., 36
Baker, N., 92
Baker, S., 362
Baker, V.L., 266
Ballieux, R.E., 336
Baltes, M.M., 14
Baltes, P.B., 14, 15, 16, 18, 21, 49
Bandeira, M., 359

Bandura, A., 2, 15, 59, 133, 164, 259, 260, 261, 262, 267, 270, 278, 320, 421, 427, 429, 480, 485
Bank, L., 42, 50
Banks, J., 328
Barat, M., 332
Barbaree, H.E., 362
Barber, J.P., 185
Bardwell, R., 42
Barefoot, J.C., 329
Bargh, J.A., 284, 293, 295, 296, 297
Barlow, D.H., 1, 6, 67, 151, 153, 154, 156, 157, 159, 160, 164, 165, 275, 355, 359, 366, 388, 392, 435
Barlow, J.A., 169
Barnes, P.J., 335
Barnes, R.F., 331
Barrera, M., 271, 272, 273
Barrett, C.L., 60, 81, 359
Barrios, B.A., 199, 288, 296, 352, 353, 355, 362
Barron, K.D., 402
Barrowclough, C., 359
Barry, H., 442
Barsky, A.J., 332
Barta, S.G., 179
Barth, D.S., 386
Barth, R.P., 77
Barthe, D.G., 180
Bartlett, F.C., 107, 108, 123, 169, 175
Barton, E.J., 89, 91
Baucom, D.H., 289, 290
Bauer, D., 60
Baum, A., 328
Baumgart, E.P., 180
Baumrind, D., 22, 77
Baxter, M.F., 128
Beach, S.R.H., 288, 289, 291
Beatty, J., 386, 400
Beck, A.T., 4, 107, 110, 111, 122, 126, 127, 131, 143, 151, 152, 154, 169, 170, 171, 172, 173, 174, 175, 176, 178, 180, 181, 182, 183, 185, 186, 187, 278, 289, 294, 298, 393
Beck, D.E., 202
Beck, J.G., 153
Becker, J., 272
Becker, M.H., 485
Becker, W.C., 77
Beekhuis, M.E., 119
Beere, P.A., 334
Behling, M., 462
Behrmann, M., 219
Beitman, B.D., 154
Belar, C.D., 398
Belkin, B., 118
Bell, R.Q., 19, 21, 41, 59
Bell, S.M., 77
Bellack, A.S., 3, 273, 352
Belsky, J., 19, 20, 21, 74, 87, 91
Bem, D.J., 87, 255, 262, 263

Bemis, K.M., 176, 178
Bender, L., 49
Bender, N., 37
Benjamin, C.A., 20
Bental, E., 118
Berent, S., 118
Berger, B.D., 444
Berger, S., 415
Bergin, A.E., 6, 73, 85, 309, 315
Bergman, H.C., 274
Berkman, L.F., 329, 334
Berley, R.A., 266
Bernard, B.A., 362
Berndt, T.J., 78
Bernstein, A.S., 356, 357
Bernstein, D.A., 309
Berry, T., 232
Berwick, D.M., 201
Best, A., 485, 487
Beutler, L.E., 316
Beyth, R., 185
Beyth-Marom, R., 203
Bhrolchain, M.N., 272
Biederman, I., 123
Bierer, L.M., 119, 173
Bierman, K.L., 46, 84, 85, 90, 278
Biersner, R., 351
Biglan, A., 273
Bijou, S.W., 13, 16, 57, 58
Bild, R., 400
Billings, A.G., 276, 278
Bindra, D., 442
Bing, R.F., 335
Bingham, J.L., 120
Biran, M., 163
Birbaum, D.W., 48
Birbaumer, N., 158, 393
Birch, H.G., 19
Birnbaum, A., 160
Bishop, S., 182
Bissonnette, V., 266
Biviano, B., 326
Bjork, R.A., 241, 441
Bjorseth, A., 83
Black, J.P., 293, 294
Blackburn, I.M., 126, 181, 182, 359
Blackstock, A.J., 371, 389
Blanchard, D.C., 442
Blanchard, E.B., 337, 350, 352, 358, 359, 362, 395, 396, 399, 400, 402, 429
Blanchard, R., 357
Blanchard, R.J., 442
Blaney, P.H., 107, 174, 445
Blank, M.A., 123
Blashfield, R.K., 356
Blatt, M., 76
Blau, J.N., 403

Blaxton, T.A., 109
Blehar, M.C., 36
Blevings, G., 369
Bloch, D.L., 356
Bloom, B., 476
Bloom, B.L., 275, 278, 458
Bloomquist, M.L., 49
Blouin, D.C., 362
Bloxom, B.M., 266
Blyth, D.A., 20, 40, 79, 85
Bobbitt, B.L., 83
Boccia, M., 417
Boer, R., de., 427
Bogat, G.A., 459, 460, 461, 462
Bohlin, G., 327
Bohnert, M., 127, 187
Boice, R., 355, 366, 388
Bois, R., 401
Bolles, R.C., 415, 435, 436, 437, 442, 446, 449
Bolton, F.G., Jr., 83
Bond, M.R., 229, 230
Bond, R.N., 295
Bonham, K.G., 359
Booraem, C.D., 231
Booth-Kewley, S., 328
Bootzin, R.R., 3
Border, M., 328
Borduin, C.M., 49
Borgardus, E.S., 256
Borghi, C., 334
Borgida, E., 177, 314
Boring, R., 297
Borkovec, T.D., 121, 158, 165, 340, 356, 360, 367, 373
Borstein, W.H., 48
Boschi, S., 334
Bouchard, M.A., 359
Bouloux, P.M.E., 330
Bouterline-Young, H., 20
Bouton, M.E., 156, 425, 436, 437, 438, 439, 440, 441, 442, 443, 444, 446, 447, 448, 449
Bower, G.H., 4, 106, 107, 122, 123, 128, 130, 131, 132, 133, 138, 153, 156, 157, 174, 177, 293, 445, 448
Bower, T.G.R., 74
Bowers, K.S., 4
Bowlby, J., 36, 41, 42
Boxer, A.M.N., 20, 75
Boyer, W., 422
Bradbury, T.N., 265, 266, 286, 287, 291
Bradford, D.C., 61
Bradley, B., 128, 129, 131, 142
Bradley, C., 337
Bradley, C.F., 180
Bradley, L.A., 337
Brady, J.P., 4
Brady, J.V., 395
Braff, D.L., 117

Branchley, L., 333
Branden, N., 204
Bransford, J.D., 108, 206
Brantley, P.J., 337
Brassard, M.R., 476
Braswell, L., 35, 46, 48, 49, 83, 88
Brazelton, T.B., 19, 24
Bream, L.A., 46
Brehm, J.W., 262
Brehm, S.S., 265, 286, 287, 288, 308
Breiter, H.J., 180
Breland, K., 415
Breland, M., 415
Brener, J., 394
Brenner, N.H., 333
Breslow, L., 334
Breslow, R., 118
Bretherton, I., 36, 41
Brewin, C.R., 103, 112, 286, 289, 291
Brigham, J.C., 317, 319
Bright, P., 127, 161
Brim, O.G., Jr., 14, 15, 29
Brisson, G., 330
British Psychological Society, 228, 230
Broadbent, M.H.P., 124, 137, 141, 142
Broadbent, D.E., 124, 137, 138, 141, 142, 329
Broadbent, K., 107, 128, 129, 139, 142
Broadhurst, A., 3
Brody, D.S., 160, 332
Bromet, E.J., 275
Bronfenbrenner, U., 14, 15, 16, 18, 41, 77, 478, 480, 485
Brooks, D.N., 229, 230, 247
Brooks-Gunn, J., 20, 21, 75
Brown, R.J., 333
Brown, G., 127
Brown, G.W., 272, 273, 326, 327, 328, 333
Brown, J.D., 172
Brown, K.S., 485
Brown, L., 20,
Brown, S.A., 333
Bruning, J.L., 121
Bruto, V., 327
Bryant, G.F., 200
Buchanan, D.C., 356
Buckiewicz, J., 422
Budd, R.J., 333
Budescu, D.V., 200
Budzynski, T., 397
Buffer, P.A., 326
Buffery, A.W.H., 248
Buhrmester, D., 77
Bullock, D.H., 440
Burger, J.N., 329
Burgess, I.S., 135, 141
Burkett, P.A., 229
Burleson, M.H., 349

Burns, D.D., 188
Burstein, E., 295
Burton, L.M., 41
Busch-Rossnagel, N., 14, 15, 16, 17, 21
Bush, D.M., 20, 85
Bush, M.A., 81
Buss, A.H., 19
Buss, R.R., 91
Butler, C.S., 440
Butler, D., 291
Butler, G., 133, 134, 151, 155, 162, 164
Butler, S., 384
Butterfield, E.C., 292
Butterworth, T., 462
Byng, S., 219, 221, 248
Byrne, D., 83
Byrne, D.G., 118
Byrnes, S., 118

Cacioppo, J.T., 179, 265, 266, 318, 358, 360, 362, 368, 385
Calev, A., 119
Calhoun, J.F., 126
Calhoun, K.S., 3, 352
Calvin, A.D., 120
Camerino, M., 336
Campbell, D., 119, 366
Campbell, D.A., 464
Campbell, S.B., 180
Campos, J.J., 19
Canavan-Gumpert, D., 290
Cane, D.B., 132
Cantor, N., 175, 179, 255, 284, 297, 299
Cantwell, D.P., 36, 40
Capage, J.E., 121
Capitanio, J., 417
Caplan, G., 271, 458
Caplan, R.D., 275
Cappe, R.F., 278
Caputo, G.C., 127, 161
Carey, G., 45
Carlsmith, J.M., 261, 262, 318
Carlson, G.A., 40
Carlston, D.E., 123, 284, 293
Carmon, A., 118
Carnine, D.W., 460
Carp, L., 133
Carpenter, P., 121
Carr, E.G., 2
Carr, J., 240
Carr, S., 229
Carroll, D., 350
Carroll, E.M., 274
Carver, C., 159
Casadei, R., 386
Casali, J.G., 462
Caspi, A., 41, 87, 88

AUTHOR INDEX

Catalano, R., 476
Cataldo, M.R., 475
Cautela, J.R., 234
Cebelin, M.S., 338
Cerny, J.A., 57, 58
Chalkley, A.J., 393
Challis, B.H., 138, 139
Chambless, D.L., 126, 154, 155, 161
Champoux, M., 160, 328
Chance, J.E., 123,
Chandler, M., 91
Chandler, M.J., 41
Chandler, S.M., 328
Chapanis, A., 262
Chapanis, N.P., 262
Chapman, J.P., 199, 296
Chapman, L.J., 199, 296
Chapman, M., 49
Chapman, S.M., 398
Chase, W.G., 249
Chassin, L., 120, 127
Cheney, D., 427, 428
Chess, S., 19, 20, 21, 23, 24
Chihara, T., 20
Chilman, C.S., 83
Chinsky, J.M., 473, 476
Chomsky, N., 175
Christensen, P., 126, 180
Christensen-Szalanski, C.M., 202
Christensen-Szalanski, J.J.J., 202, 206, 212
Christie, B., 385
Christie, J.E., 182
Christoff, K.A., 278
Chute, D.L., 444
Cialdini, R.B., 263, 265
Cicchetti, D., 14, 35, 36, 37, 39, 43, 69, 74, 81, 86, 88
Cimbolic, P., 183
Ciminero, A.R., 57, 350, 352, 354
Claridge, G.S., 356
Clark, D., 158, 209
Clark, D.A., 107, 110, 126, 128, 129
Clark, D.M., 138, 142, 387, 392, 393
Clark, D.M.J., 151, 155, 163
Clark, L.A., 45
Clark, M., 133
Clarke, W.R., 335
Clarkson, T.B., 326, 334
Cleary, P.D., 332
Clements, K., 370
Cleminshaw, H.K., 77
Cline, D.W., 40
Clore, G.L., 133
Clum, G.A., 336
Cobb, G., 201
Cobb, S., 271
Cobliner, W.G., 83
Cochran, S.D., 180

Cochrane, S., 180
Cockburn, J., 233, 234
Cohen, A.R., 260, 262, 263
Cohen, D.J., 43
Cohen, F., 336
Cohen, J., 288
Cohen, J.S., 46
Cohen, L.H., 271, 272
Cohen, L.J., 329
Cohen, M.J., 400
Cohen, N., 325
Cohen, N.J., 106, 278
Cohen, P.R., 107, 123
Cohen, R., 2, 49, 83
Cohen, R.A., 399
Cohen, R.M., 119
Cohen, S., 270, 271, 275, 329
Cohler, B.J., 37
Colaiannia, D., 417
Coleman, J.C., 85
Coles, M.G.H., 349, 358, 359, 384, 385, 386, 403
Collector, M.I., 336
Collins, A.M., 123
Collins, F.L., 229
Collins, W.A., 76
Collu, R., 330
Coltheart, M., 216, 219, 221, 222, 223, 247, 248
Colussy, S.A., 119
Compas, B.E., 88, 290
Conant, M.A., 336
Concannon, J.T., 445
Cone, J.D., 58, 60, 66, 236, 353, 355, 356, 362, 364, 366
Connell, M.M., 275
Cook, E., 416
Cook, E.W., 369, 371, 390
Cook, M., 414, 417, 418, 420, 421, 422, 423, 424, 426, 427, 430
Cook, M.L., 126, 181, 185
Cook, S.W., 317
Cooke, D.J., 333
Cooper, C.L., 327
Cooper, C.R., 77
Copeland, A.P., 48
Copeland, J.R., 328
Coppel, D.B., 272
Corbalan, R., 338
Corenthal, C., 180
Cornell, D.G., 118
Corrigan, B., 208
Coryell, W., 180
Coss, R., 427
Costa, F.M., 40
Costa, F.V., 334
Costa, P.T., 329
Cotch, P.A., 362, 388
Cottam, G.L., 369

Cottington, E.M., 329, 334
Coughlan, A.K., 118
Cowan, P.A., 74, 88
Cowen, E.L., 459
Cox, B.J., 153, 157
Cox, D., 389
Cox, G.B., 272
Cox, T., 327
Coyne, J.C., 181, 274, 275, 309
Crago, M., 316
Craig, K.D., 106, 108
Craig, T.J.K., 333
Craighead, L.W., 49, 83
Craighead, W.E., 13, 46, 49, 73, 82, 83
Craik, F.I.M., 104, 179, 247
Cram, J.R., 398
Crandell, C.J., 126
Craske, M.G., 106, 160, 164, 366, 388, 392
Crawford, H.L. 264
Creed, F., 327
Creswell, H.W., 50
Crits-Christoph, P., 350
Crockenberg, S.B., 19, 20
Crocker, J., 184, 294, 297
Croiset, G., 336
Cronholm, B., 118
Cross, K.W., 273
Crossman, R., 84
Cruise, D.G., 118
Cuevas, J., 398
Cullington, A., 164
Cunningham, C.L., 436, 442, 446
Curio, E., 426, 429
Cuthbert, B.C., 371
Cuthbert, B.N., 371, 390
Cutrona, C.E., 180, 290
Cvetkovich, G., 83, 84

D'Amato, M., 422
d'Elia, G., 356
Dahlem, N.W., 271, 272
Damianopoulos, E., 414
Daneman, M., 121
Daniels, D., 26
Danish, S.J., 478
Dantzer, R., 336
Darke, S., 120, 121
Darley, J.M., 186, 258
Davey, G., 367
Davidson, H.A., 476
Davidson, L.M., 328
Davidson, M., 414
Davies, J.K. 339
Davies, M.H., 273
Davies, S., 136
Davis, A., 288
Davis, C.M., 358, 384

Davis, H., 171, 174, 177
Davis, J.M., 182
Davis, K.E., 257, 285
Davis, N., 328
Davis, P., 181
Davis, W., 333
Davison, G.C., 3, 127, 179, 180, 286
Dawes, R.M., 204, 205, 207, 208
Dawson, M.E., 326, 356, 357, 358, 367, 371
De Boo, T., 335
de Mowbray, J., 108
de Partz, M.P. 219
De Silva, P., 413, 428
de Wied, D., 445
De Wit, B., 386
Deanfield, J.E., 338
deBettencourt, L.U., 460
Deffenbacher, J.L., 127
DeFrank, R.S., 333
DeFries, J.C., 41
DeGiovanni, I.S., 48
DeGood, D.E., 394
Delamater, A.R., 442
Delaney, M., 21
deLissovoy, V., 92
DeLongis, A., 274, 275, 276, 329
Delprato, D., 416
Delprato, D.J., 35
deMayo, R., 175, 179, 180
Dembroski, T.M., 329
Demick, J., 14
Dent, J., 175
DePree, J.A., 121
Depue, R.A., 181, 326, 329, 357
Derry, P.A., 105, 107, 129, 131, 142, 171, 179
Derryberry, D., 152
DeRubeis, R.J., 180, 181, 183, 185
Deshler, D.D., 460
DeSilva, R.A., 338
Devine, L., 445
DeWied, D., 336
Dexter, S.L., 403
Di Rienzo, M., 386
Diament, C., 85
Dibona, G.F., 331
Dickman, S., 178
Dickstein, S., 273
Dienstbier, R.A., 328
Dietz, J.R., 330
Dietz, L.S., 337
DiLalla, L.F., 77
Diller, L., 229, 231
Dimberg, U., 369, 370, 371, 391, 413
Ditto, B., 330, 331
Dixon, N.F., 104
Dixon, R., 201
Dixon, R.A., 14, 15, 16

Dobson, K.S., 126, 128, 129, 130, 180, 181
Dodge, C.S., 355
Dodge, K.A., 179
Dodson, J.D., 159
Doerr, H.O., 356
Doherty, M.E., 203
Doleys, D.M., 350
Dollard, J., 259, 260
Domino, E., 402
Domjan, M., 414, 415, 427
Donchin, E., 358, 384
Donnell, C., 126
Donnell, C.D., 131, 155, 163
Donnellan, A.M., 43
Donnelly, E.F., 117
Donovan, J.E., 40
Dooley, D., 476
Dornic, S., 121
Dorward, J., 153, 157
Douglas, R.M., 336
Douvan, E., 76
Dow, M.G., 126, 132, 278
Drabman, R.S., 57
Drolet,M., 401
Droungas, A., 415, 416, 422
Drown, D., 291
Drugan, R., 336
Druian, P., 291
Druiff, H., 439
Drummond, P.D., 399, 403
Du Bois, P., 336
Du Long, A., 400
Duhe, A., 290
Dunkel-Schetter, C., 270, 271, 275, 276, 277
Durham, R.L., 120
Durlach, P., 425
Durlak, J.A., 461
Dusenbury, L., 277
Dweck, C., 288
Dworkin, B.R., 394
Dyak, J.D., 442

Eames, P.G., 230, 231
Eardley, D.A., 175
East, P.L., 20, 21, 26
Easterbrook, J.A., 120, 159, 160
Easton, C.R., 127
Eastwood, J., 333
Eastwood, M.A., 333
Eaves, G., 126, 175, 180
Ebbesen, P., 338
Ebert, L., 367
Eccles, A., 362
Ecton, R.B., 81, 82
Eddy, D.M., 204
Edelbrock, C.S., 44, 45, 59, 60, 61, 62, 63, 64, 65, 66, 68, 82, 88

Edelstein, B.A., 475
Edgar, M., 83
Edwards, J.A., 356, 360
Edwards, S., 331
Edwards, W., 206
Eelen, P., 3
Egberg, N., 338
Eggeraat, J.G., 163
Ehlers, A., 136, 141, 152, 158, 162, 392, 393
Ehrman, M., 338
Eich, E., 156, 448
Eidelson, J.I., 127
Eingartner, H., 119
Einhorn, H.J., 207
Eisenberg, L., 41, 81
Eiser, J.R., 333
Ekman, P., 369, 370
Elder, G.H., Jr., 15, 20, 41, 87
Elkin, I., 182
Elkind, D., 75
Ellard, J.H., 272, 273
Ellis, A., 176, 186, 289
Ellis, A.W., 216, 218, 219
Ellis, H.C., 118, 119
Ellis, H.D., 118, 119
Elmore, A.M., 400, 401
Elstein, A.S., 210
Emery, G., 4, 107, 111, 122, 151, 154, 182, 187, 278, 289
Emlen, J., 414
Emmelkamp, P., 429, 430
Emmelkamp, P.M.G., 163, 200
Emmerich, W., 16
Engel, B.T., 330, 350, 363, 394, 395, 396
Engel, G.L., 350, 357
Engelmann, S., 460
Ennis, K.E., 233
Enright, R.D., 75, 90. 91
Epling, W.F., 353
Epstein, L.H., 350, 358, 359
Erdly, W.W., 272
Ericsson, K.A., 104, 178, 249
Erikson, E., 486
Erikson, E.H., 13, 16, 39, 40, 58, 76
Eriksson, A., 391, 416
Erixon, G., 391
Ernst, U., 426
Erskine-Milliss, J., 356
Erwin, P.G., 119
Esler, M., 326
Estes, W.K., 446
Esteves, F., 371
Eth, S., 38
Etheredge, E.E., 442
Ettedgui, E., 393
Eunson, K.M., 182
Evans, I.M., 57, 61, 67, 68, 354, 355, 365, 463, 464, 465

Evans, L., 161
Evans, M.D., 180, 182, 183, 184, 185
Evans, R.L., 487
Eves, F., 369
Eysenck, H.J., 1, 2, 3, 117, 349, 356
Eysenck, M. W., 103, 105, 108, 109, 110, 111, 112, 113, 120, 121, 134, 142, 152, 153, 154, 157, 159, 160, 164, 329

Fahrenberg, J., 330, 363
Fairbanks, D., 462
Falconer, S., 249
Falkin, S., 351
Falkner, B., 334
Fanselow, M.S., 435, 442, 444
Farber, S.S., 458
Farina, A., 286
Farley, G.K., 271, 272
Farquhar, J.W., 481
Farr, R., 284
Faulstich, M.E., 337, 362, 363
Faust, D., 206
Fawcett, S.B., 462, 467
Fazio, R., 258
Fazio, R.H., 179, 186
Featherman, D.L., 15, 18
Feindler, E.L., 81, 82
Feinglos, N.M., 340
Feinman, S., 19
Feld, J.L., 394
Feldman, M.P., 3
Feldman, P.M., 127, 179
Feldman-Summers, S., 83
Feldon, J., 328
Feldstein, M., 271
Felner, R.D., 458, 459
Fenton, C.H., 396
Fernaeus, S.E., 121
Ferone, L., 461
Ferrari, M., 46, 48
Ferry, D.R., 338
Festinger, L., 260, 261, 262, 267, 313, 318
Feuerstein M., 350, 351, 352, 358, 360, 384, 398
Fey, S.G., 394
Feyno, G., 208
Ficken, J.W., 357
Finch, A.J., 120
Fincham, F.D., 265, 266, 285, 287, 288, 290, 291
Fineberg, H.V., 201, 212
Fink, H.H., 120
Finn, M., 458
Fiore, J., 272, 273
Fisch, H.U., 208
Fischhoff, B., 185, 202, 203, 206
Fish, B., 37
Fishbein, M., 265
Fisher, J.D., 286

Fisher, W.A., 83
Fiske, D., 366
Fiske, S.T., 177, 293, 296, 297, 313
Fitchett, D., 338
Flavell, J., 486
Flavell, J.H., 75
Fleeson, J., 77, 87
Fleming, I., 328, 337
Fletcher, B., 164, 329
Fletcher, G.J.O. 285, 286
Fletcher, H., 414, 422
Fletcher, R.K., 462
Flocco, R., 271, 272
Flor, H., 334
Florin, I., 333
Flum H., 274, 276
Foa, E.B., 3, 131, 135, 141, 155, 163, 164, 165, 200, 364, 367, 369, 371, 372, 373, 387, 390, 430, 435, 449
Fogarty, S.J., 128, 130, 179
Folkman, S., 270, 276, 277, 278, 327, 329, 369, 370
Folkow, B.S., 335
Follick, M.J., 338
Fontaine, O., 3
Foorman, S., 272
Ford, M.J., 333
Forgas, J.P., 128, 132, 284, 285, 299
Forsythe, C.J., 290
Foss, D.J., 123
Foster, S.L., 89, 236
Foster, V., 483
Forsterling, F., 286, 288, 291
Foulds, G.A., 119
Fowler, J.L., 398
Fowler, R.C., 40
Fowler, S.C., 369
Fowles, D.C., 357, 369, 385
Fox, B.H., 338
Fox, J., 127, 209
Fox, J.J., 89, 90
Fox, N.A., 385
Foy, D.W., 274
Frame, C.L., 179, 278
France, C., 330, 331
Francis, G., 66, 67, 68
Frankenhaeuser, M., 326
Franklin, J., 181
Franklin, Y., 112
Franks, C.M., 2, 3, 5, 6, 265, 266, 284, 300
Franks, J.J., 108
Frary, R.B., 61, 63
Fraser, J., 448
Fredrikson, M., 330, 334, 335, 358, 391, 413, 416
Freedman, R.R., 387, 393, 396, 397
Freeman, S.J., 274
Freud, A., 44
Freud, S., 13, 16, 58, 310

AUTHOR INDEX

Freund, K., 357
Frey, P.W., 440
Friar, L.R., 400
Frick, P., 278
Fridlund, A.J., 369
Friedlander, M.L., 202
Friedman, A., 108
Friedman, S.B., 326, 328, 336
Friend, R., 161
Friesen, W.V., 369
Frith, C.D., 118, 129
Fuller, J.H., 339
Funnell, E., 223
Furman, W., 35, 46, 47, 48, 74, 77, 81, 83, 85, 86, 90, 91
Furth, H.G., 80

Gaardner, K.R., 396
Gable, R.S., 358
Gagne, R.M., 69
Galambox, J.A., 123
Galambox, N.L., 20, 478
Galanter, E., 258
Gale, A., 353, 356, 360, 362, 385
Galef, B., 415, 427
Gallagher, D., 129
Gallagher, R., 127, 161
Galvin, K.S., 286, 290
Gambrill, E.D., 3
Gammage, P., 333
Ganellen, R.J., 127
Ganiere, D.M., 91
Gannon, L.R., 328, 337, 351, 352, 355, 398, 399, 402
Gansler, D., 355
Garber, J., 36, 38, 44, 47, 175, 176, 177, 186, 297, 298
Garcia, J., 414, 415, 425
Garcia, K.A., 48
Gardner, H., 232, 314
Garfield, S.L., 73, 85, 126, 180, 309, 315, 316
Garfinkel, B.D., 42
Garfinkel, P.E., 40
Garmetzy, L.B., 333
Garmezy, N., 36, 37, 38, 42, 45, 74, 88, 278, 478
Garner, D.M., 42
Garner, R., 441
Garske, G., 444
Garske, J., 422
Gasiewski, E., 84
Gatchel, R.J., 335, 350, 395
Gauthier, J., 401
Gelder, M., 164
Gelder, M.G., 388
Gelfand, D.M., 35, 47, 50, 61, 74, 81, 85, 86, 91
Geller, E.S., 462, 475
Geller, V., 135
Genest, M., 178
Gentry, W.D., 332, 351

Georgoudi, M., 15
Gerdt, C., 119
Gerrig, R.J., 138
Gershon, E., 394
Gesell, A.L., 13, 16
Gesten, E.L., 458, 459, 468, 475, 476
Gianutsos, J., 247
Gianutsos, R., 247
Gibbs, G., 108
Gibbs, J.C., 90
Giddings, C.W., 288
Giesen, J.M., 368
Gifford, R.K., 314
Giles, D.E., 180
Gillespie, J.F., 81
Gilligan, C., 76, 81
Gilligan, S.C., 123
Gilligan, S.G., 107, 445
Gilmore, J.B., 4, 260, 262
Gilmore, N., 338
Ginsburg, H., 75
Guiliano, T., 159
Glagov, S., 334
Glaser, R., 330
Glasgow, L., 336
Glasgow, M.S., 396
Glasgow, R., 2
Glasgow, R.E., 275
Glass, C.R., 178, 293
Glass, R., 127
Gleave, J., 234
Glen, A.I.M., 182
Glenberg, A., 441
Glenwick, D.S., 457, 461, 462, 463, 466
Glish, M., 476
Glisky, E.L., 240, 241, 247
Glowinski, A.J., 209
Godden, D., 247
Godstein, A.J., 123
Goering, P., 274
Goffman, E., 266
Goldband, S., 358
Goldried, M.R., 3, 4, 127, 179, 293, 294, 296, 297, 352, 353, 354, 362
Goldman, M.S., 442
Goldstein, A., 3
Godlstein, A.J., 154
Goldstein, A.P., 265
Goldstein, D.S., 326, 395
Goldstein, G., 233
Goldstein, M.J., 37
Goldstein, M.N., 218
Goldston, S.E., 459
Goll, S., 236
Gollin, E.S., 14
Golombek, H., 40
Gong-Guy, E., 180

Good, M.I., 396
Goodall, E., 236
Goodkin, R., 231
Goodman, G., 275, 278
Goodman, J., 48
Goodson, J.D., 332
Goodwin, F.K., 117
Gordon, D.E., 75, 91
Gordon, P.C., 299, 300
Gordon, S.E., 295
Gordon, W.A., 229
Goren, E.R., 85
Gorham, D.R., 117
Gorman, J.E., 442
Gormezano, I., 440
Gormly, J., 120
Gotlib, I.H., 132, 138, 139, 142, 181, 309
Gottesman, I.I., 38, 41
Gottfredson, D.K., 126, 180
Gottlieb, B.H., 466
Gottlieb, G., 14, 16, 17, 18, 59
Gottman, J.M., 78, 360
Gould, S., 14, 427
Goy, R., 417
Gracely, E.J., 155
Graesser, A.C., 108, 123
Graf, P., 109, 113, 141, 142, 247
Graham, F.K., 349, 369
Graham, N.N.H., 336
Graham, S., 198
Gramling, S., 350, 352, 358, 360, 362, 384
Grandits, G.A., 329
Granger, L., 359
Gratton, G., 386
Gray, J., 229
Gray, J.A., 328, 356, 367, 369, 385
Gray, W.M., 84
Grayson, J.B., 164, 390
Graziano, A.M., 48
Green, D.W., 123
Green, E.E., 397
Green, G., 415
Green, L.W., 475, 478, 479
Green, T.M., 80
Greenberg, G., 15
Greenberg, G.D., 278
Greenberg, L.S., 371
Greenberg, M.S., 131
Greenberg, M.T., 87, 88
Greenberg, R.C., 122
Greenberger, E., 79
Greene, B.F., 462, 475
Greene, R.W., 58
Greenfield, N.S., 358
Greenson, R.R., 310
Greenspan, S., 39, 44
Greenspoon, J., 4, 265, 441

Greenwald, M.K., 369
Greenwood, C.R., 90
Greer, S., 337, 338
Greiger, R., 289
Grey, S., 446
Grey, S.J., 366, 388, 390
Griffin, P., 398
Griffin, T., 196, 198, 206, 208, 212
Griffs, S.S., 123
Grings, W.W., 358
Grippaldi, R., 120
Grogg, T., 422
Groom, D.H., 118
Groppelli, A., 386
Gross, Y., 229
Grosscup, S.L., 265
Grossman-McKee, D., 127
Grote, B., 83
Grotevant, H.D., 77
Group for the Advancement of Psychiatry, 37
Gruber, B.L., 336
Gruen, R., 276
Grusec, J., 429
Gruzelier, J.H., 357
Guenther, R.K., 156
Guerney, B.G., 462
Guglielmi, R.S., 396
Guidubaldi, J., 77
Guilmette, T.J., 206
Gumbrecht, G., 331
Gumpert, P., 290
Gunnar, M., 160, 328
Gunnar, M.R., 41
Gurman, A.S., 89
Gursky, D.M., 154, 155, 161
Guttman, L., 256
Guyre, P.M., 330
Guze, S.B., 350

Haemmerlie, F.M., 263
Hagerman, S.M., 293, 296, 297
Haggerty, R., 336
Hailman, J., 427
Hains, A., 75
Halal, M., 128
Halberstadt, L.J., 180, 326
Hale, W.D., 118
Halevy, J., 274
Hall, F.M., 326
Hall, G., 435
Hall, G.S., 16
Hall, N.R., 336
Hallam, R., 389
Halligan, P., 233
Hamburg, B., 20
Hamburg, B.A., 74, 77, 79, 83, 84
Hamburger, V., 16

Hamilton, D.I., 66,
Hamilton, D.L., 284, 314
Hamilton, E.W.; 132, 180
Hamilton, J., 399
Hamilton, V., 123
Hamley-Van-der-Velden, E., 274
Hammen, C.L., 132, 175, 179, 180, 181, 185
Hammond, A., 234
Hammond, K.R., 207, 208
Hampe, E., 60, 81
Hancher-Kvam, S., 273
Hanford, P.V., 437
Hanin, I., 349, 356
Hanley, J.A., 330
Hanlon, J.J., 478
Hansen, S.P., 394
Hanson E., 78
Hanson, C.L., 38
Hanson, D.R., 49
Hanson, S.L., 337
Harburg, E., 329
Hardiman, P., 201
Harding, K., 273
Hardy, J.D., 272
Hare, R.D., 369
Harkness, A.R., 206
Harkness, S., 14, 15, 20, 22, 23
Harlow, H., 417
Harness, B.Z., 118
Harrell, T.H., 126, 180
Harrigan, J.A., 337
Harris, D.B., 16
Harris, J. E., 234
Harris, M., 274
Harris, S.L., 46, 48, 61, 67, 85
Harris, T., 272, 326, 327, 328
Harsh, J., 420
Hart, D., 84
Hart, J., 390
Hart, J.D., 371
Hart, K., 206
Hart, S.N., 476
Harter, R.A., 328
Harter, S., 26, 27, 47, 76, 82, 84
Hartmann, D.P., 61, 66, 353, 362
Hartup, W.W., 76, 78, 466
Harvey, D., 180
Harvey, J.H., 262, 263, 266, 286, 290
Hasher, L., 107, 119, 123, 172, 177, 187
Hasking, G., 326
Hastie, R., 285, 293, 294
Hastrup, J.L., 362
Hatcher, J., 275
Hatfield, F.M., 216, 219
Hatfield, M.E., 369
Hattie, J.A., 474
Hatzenbuehler, L.C., 48, 81

Haugtuedt, C., 164
Hauser, S.T., 76, 80
Hauserman, N., 462
Havighurst, R.J., 39
Hawkins, M.F., 352, 358
Hawley, K., 236
Hawton, K., 41
Hayes, D.S., 48
Hayes, J.R., 275, 276
Hayes, S.C., 6, 352, 354, 356, 359, 361, 362, 364, 365
Hayes-Roth, B., 176
Hayes-Roth, F., 209
Haynes, J., 120
Haynes, M.R., 396
Haynes, R.B., 200
Haynes, S.N., 350, 351, 352, 354, 355, 356, 358, 360, 361, 384, 398, 399
Hays, R.B., 272, 274
Headache classification committee of the International Headache Society, 397
Headen, S., 275
Heagerty, A.M., 335
Hebb, D., 413
Hechtman, L.T., 38
Hedman, M., 326
Heider, F., 169, 258, 259, 261, 265, 267, 284, 285, 289, 290, 292
Heijnen, C.J., 336
Heilman, K.M., 240
Heimberg, R.G., 355
Heller, J.F., 121
Heller, K., 265, 271, 277, 278, 458, 459, 462, 466
Helmstetter, F.J., 444
Helsel, W.S., 63
Helson, H., 264
Hemsley, D.R., 139, 359
Hendersen, R.W., 445, 446
Henderson, R., 420
Hendry, J.S., 437, 448
Henggeler, S.W., 49, 83
Henker, B., 44
Henn, F.A., 42
Henry, G.M., 118
Henry, J.P., 330
Henry, R.L., 338
Herjanic, B., 46
Hernstein, R.J., 463
Hersen, M., 3, 6, 57, 58, 59, 60, 61, 62, 64, 66, 273, 278, 352, 359
Hersh, S.P., 336
Hess, L.E., 13, 21
Heth, C.D., 436, 437, 449
Hetherington, E.M., 15, 74, 77
Hewlett, J.H.G., 118
Hewstone, M., 286, 292
Heymann, E., 427
Hibbert, G., 386, 393

Hibbert, G.A., 111, 127
Higgins, E.T., 76, 171, 175, 284, 293, 295, 296, 297, 299
Higgins, R.L., 286
Higley, J., 417
Higuchi, S., 335
Hill, C.A., 297
Hill, J.P., 74, 75, 76, 77, 78, 80, 82, 89
Hill, M.G., 256, 286
Hill, R.A., 127
Hillyard, S.A., 384
Hilton, D., 292
Himadi, W.G., 355, 366, 367, 388
Himmelhock, J.M., 273
Hiorns, R. 233
Hirsch, C.S., 338
Hirschfeld, R.M.A., 182
Hitch, G.J., 121
Hjemdahl, P., 338
Ho, B.T., 444
Hoare, A., 201
Hobbs, S.A., 277
Hockenbury, D., 277
Hodes, R., 416
Hodes, R.L., 369
Hodges, W.F., 120
Hodgson, R., 348, 354, 356, 364, 365, 366, 368, 371, 388, 390, 417
Hodgson, R.J., 153
Hoehler, F.K., 440
Hoffman, M.A., 289
Hoffman, M.L., 76, 77
Hoffman, P.J., 208
Hoffman, W.J., 50
Hogarth, R.M., 204
Hoier, T.S., 58, 60, 66
Holahan, C.J., 277
Holbrook, N.J., 330
Holden, A.E., 366
Holder, M., 425
Hollaender, J., 333
Holland, A.L., 233
Holland, J.G., 460, 462
Holland, P., 426
Holland, P.C., 435, 439
Hollandsworth J.G., Jr., 279
Hollandsworth, J.G., 352, 355, 358, 360, 364, 384
Holliday, J.E., 330
Hollis, K.L., 435
Hollon, S.D., 4, 126, 143, 171, 175, 176, 177, 178, 179, 180, 181, 182, 183, 184, 185, 186, 187, 293, 294, 297, 298
Holloway, W., 154, 155
Hollows, S.E., 118
Holmbeck, G.N., 73, 76, 77, 78, 80, 82, 84, 89
Holmes, R., 337
Holroyd, K.A., 399, 400, 401, 402

Holt, R.R., 212
Holter, J.B., 331
Holtzworth-Munroe, A., 288
Holyoak, K.J., 299, 300
Homans, E.C., 263, 264
Honzik, M.P., 87
Hops, H., 66
Horn, S., 392
Hornstra, G., 338
Horowitz, F.D., 70
Horowitz, L.M., 278
Horowitz, M.J., 329
Horrocks, J., 201
Horton, A.M., 231
Hothersall, D., 394
House, J.S., 256, 271, 332
Houston, B.K., 127, 335
Hovland, C., 317
Hovland, C.I., 259, 260, 262, 264
Howard, B.L., 89, 90
Howard, D., 216
Howard, J.W., 207
Howard, K.I., 317
Howard, K.I., 82
Howell, C.T., 46
Hubbard, M., 185
Hudson, L.M., 84
Hudzinski, L.G., 399
Hugdahl, K., 355, 365, 391, 413, 416
Hughes, H., 4
Hull, J.G., 329
Hultsch, D.F., 14
Huntzinger, R.M., 68
Hurlburt, R.T., 179
Hurrell, J.J., 327
Hutchinson, M., 181
Hynd, G.W., 278
Hyson, R., 336

Iacono, W.G., 357, 360
Ianni, P., 393, 396
Ickes, W., 266, 286, 290
Ince, L.P., 230, 231
Ingram, R.E., 126, 171, 174, 293, 297, 298, 300
Inhelder, B., 486
Insko, C.A., 265
Isen, A.M., 133, 174
Ito, N., 335
Ivey, A.E., 74, 91
Iwata, B.A., 462, 475
Iwawaki, S., 20
Izard, C.E., 37, 82, 370
Izquierdo, I., 445

Jacklin, C.N., 65
Jackson, R., 420
Jacobs, H.E., 462

AUTHOR INDEX

Jacobs, M.K., 275, 278
Jacobs, W., 424
Jacobs, W.J., 436, 445
Jacobson, N.S., 265, 266, 288, 289
James, W., 392
Jamner, L.D., 394
Janis, I.L., 260, 262, 264, 317
Janoff, D.S., 286
Jansson, L., 355, 366, 389
Janz, N.K., 485
Jarrett, R.B., 352, 361
Jarvik, M.E., 118
Jason, L.A., 457, 458, 459, 460, 461, 462, 463, 465, 466, 467, 468, 469, 476, 488
Jaspars, J.M., 286, 292
Jemmott, J.B., 336
Jenkins, C.D., 333
Jenkins, J.J., 15, 172
Jenkins, R.I., 42
Jenkins, R.R., 20
Jennings, D., 326
Jennings, J.R., 349
Jensen, H.H., 444
Jerremalm, A., 355, 366, 389
Jessor, R., 40, 485
Joffee, J.M., 459
Johansson, J., 355, 366, 389
Johnson, E.H., 329
Johnson, J., 120
Johnson, J.E., 326
Johnson, M.C., 356
Johnson, M.H., 118, 174, 297
Johnson, M.K., 179
Johnson, R.A., 386
Johnson, R.P., 462
Johnson, W.G., 286
Johnson-Laird, P.N., 108, 141
Johnston, D.W., 340, 387, 388, 389, 394, 395, 396, 397
Johnston, T., 415, 427
Johnston, V.S., 349
Jones, C.R., 295
Jones, D., 425
Jones, E., 219
Jones, E.E., 257, 266, 285, 289
Jones, G.N., 337
Jones, M., 153
Jones, M.C., 391, 392
Jones, R.D., 290
Jones, R.J., 126
Jones, S., 126
Jones, W.H., 277
Jorgensen, R.S., 335
Jorgensen, S.R., 84
Joslin, J., 414
Jovanovic, J., 21
Joyce, C.R.B., 208
Judd, C.M., 284

Julius, M., 329
Jungerman, H., 206

Kagan, A.R., 325
Kagan, J., 14, 15, 29, 284
Kagedal, B., 356
Kahn, R.L., 467
Kahneman, D., 133, 156, 169, 176, 177, 178, 184, 201, 202, 203, 205, 212, 294, 314
Kalat, J., 415
Kallman, W., 350, 352, 358, 360
Kallman, W.M., 384
Kaloupek, D.G., 365, 366
Kamano, D.K., 442
Kamarck, T., 275
Kamin, L., 425
Kandel, D., 76
Kanfer, F.H., 6, 293, 296, 297
Kanner, A.D., 276
Kanner, L., 38
Kanouse, D.E., 290
Kantor, A.E., 459, 463
Kaplan, B., 15
Kaplan, B.H., 332
Kaplan, B.J., 362, 363
Kaplan, G.A., 326
Kaplan, J.R., 326, 330, 334
Kardes, F.R., 179
Kartsounis, L.D., 360
Kassirer, J.P., 210
Katkin, E.S., 358
Katon, W., 153
Katz, A.N., 138
Katz, D., 467
Katz, E.R., 62, 65, 66, 68, 69, 81,
Kauffman, M.B., 14, 17, 18
Kavanagh, D.L., 133
Kaye, H., 439
Kaye, K., 85
Kazdin, A.E., 1, 3, 5, 6, 43, 44, 47, 66, 283, 359
Keating, D.P., 75
Keating, D.P.A., 83
Keefe, F.J., 276
Keighly, M., 201
Keir, R., 414, 429
Kelfer, D.A., 437
Keller, S.E., 336
Kellerman, H., 367
Kellerman, J., 62, 81
Kelley, H., 263
Kelley, H.H., 260, 262, 264, 285, 286, 291, 314, 317
Kelley, J., 77
Kelley, K.W., 336
Kelley, M.J., 349
Kelly, J.G., 460, 464, 467, 468, 469
Kemeny, M.E., 336
Kenardy, J., 161

AUTHOR INDEX

Kendall, P.C., 4, 13, 29, 46, 48, 49, 73, 74, 75, 76, 81, 82, 83, 85, 86, 88, 89, 90, 91, 120, 126, 176, 178, 179, 180, 185, 187, 293, 300
Kennelly, K., 121
Kenney, F.A., 442, 443, 444
Kenny, D.A., 183
Kern, L., 203
Kern, M.J., 338
Kershner, J., 278
Kessler, R.C., 270, 276, 277
Kewman, D.G., 394, 401
Kickbusch, I., 339
Kidd, R.F., 286
Kiecolt-Glaser, J.K., 326, 330, 336
Kiesler, C.A., 476
Kiesler, D.J., 73
Kiesler, R.A., 458
Kihlstrom, J.F., 176, 255, 293, 294, 295, 296
Killen, J.D., 90
King, A.C., 480, 484, 486
King, D.A., 436, 437, 439, 445, 446, 448, 449
King, J., 414, 429
King, N.J., 57, 61, 63, 66
Kirsch, I., 126, 127, 164
Kirschenbaum, D.S., 440
Kishi, G.S., 463
Kjellman, B.F., 356
Klee, S., 132
Klee, S.H., 181
Kleiman, D., 428
Kleman, R.M., 181
Klein, D.F., 182
Klein, D.N., 273
Klein, R., 171
Klein, S.B., 445
Kleinmuntz, B., 207, 210
Klerman, G.L., 116
Klinger, E., 179
Klorman, R., 349, 369
Kluger, M.A., 394
Knapp, T.W., 401
Knill-Jones, R., 210
Kniskern, D.P., 89
Knox, W.J., 120
Kobasa, S.C.O., 478
Kocsis, J., 118
Koelling, R., 414, 415
Koepke, J.P., 335
Koepsell, T.D., 202
Kohlberg, L., 76
Kohn, M., 45
Kolb, D.A., 47
Koman, S.L., 85, 89
Konold, C., 201
Konorski, J., 440
Koons, P.B., 120
Kopel, S.A., 289

Kopp, C.B., 42
Korchin, S., 159
Korman, M., 335
Korn, S., 23, 24, 25
Koslowski, B., 19
Kosslyn, S.M., 284
Kovacs, M., 81, 85, 170, 181, 182
Kowalski, D.J., 108
Kozak, M., 164, 165, 430
Kozak, M.J., 359, 364, 365, 367, 368, 371, 372, 373, 387, 390, 435, 449
Kozielecki, J., 201, 204
Kozuh, G.F., 121
Krakow, J.B., 42
Kramer, A.F., 386
Kramer, D.D., 480
Krames, L., 119, 174
Krane, R.V., 138, 139
Krantz, D.S., 326
Krantz, S.E., 132, 180, 181, 185, 274, 276
Krasner, L., 1, 2, 6, 266, 459, 460, 462, 463, 474, 475
Kratochwill, T.R., 359
Krauss, S.P., 181
Kriss, M.R., 171, 178, 179, 293, 294, 297, 298
Kucher, J.S., 21
Kuczmierczyk, A.R., 350, 358
Kues, J.R., 337
Kuhn, T.S., 474, 480
Kuiper, N.A., 105, 107, 129, 131, 142, 171, 172, 173, 174, 175, 177, 179, 180, 181, 278, 299
Kuipers, A.C.M., 163
Kuller, L.H., 332, 334
Kumar, D., 334
Kuo, Z.Y., 15, 18
Kurdek, L.A., 77
Kurkijian, J.A., 463
Kushner, H., 334
Kutas, M., 384

L'Abate, L., 89
Labbé, E.E., 350, 358
Lacey, B.C., 349, 350, 362
Lacey, J.I., 349, 350, 351, 354, 362, 367, 387
Lachman, J.L., 292, 293
Lachman, R., 292, 293
Lachman, S.J., 325
Ladd, G.W., 86
Lader, M.H., 116, 356, 357, 358, 360
Lahey, B.B., 278
Laird, J.D., 128, 130
Laitsch, K., 414
Lalljee, M., 290, 291, 292
Lamal, P., 4
Lamb, M.E., 77
Lambert, G., 326
Lampi, L.A., 86
Lancater, J.B., 83, 84

Lance, J.W., 399, 403
Lancee, W., 274
Landau, R.J., 179, 293, 294, 296
Landauer, T.K., 241
Lande, J., 417
Landerman, L.R., 332
Landolf-Firtsche, B., 127
Lane, H., 230
Lane, J.W., 128, 130
Lane, R.S., 332
Lang, P.J., 153, 350, 351, 352, 354, 355, 356, 358, 364, 365, 366, 367, 368, 369, 370, 371, 372, 373, 385, 387, 388, 389, 390, 391, 394, 395, 416, 417
Langer, E.J., 287
Langer, J., 58, 69
Langlois, J.H., 27
Lanyon, R.I., 208, 209
LaPiere, R.T., 319, 320
Lapsley, D.K., 91
Laquarta, I., 478
Larkin, K., 42
Larner, S., 119
LaRosa, J.F., 42, 50
Larsen, A., 42
Larson, D.W., 112, 176, 180
Larsson, P.T., 338
Last, C.G., 67
Lau, J., 210
Laude, R., 127, 187
Laudenslager, M., 336
Lauer, R.M., 335
LaVigne, V., 465
Lawrence, G.S., 399
Layden, M.A., 290
Lazarus, A.A., 1, 2, 48
Lazarus, R.S., 183, 187, 270, 276, 277, 278, 327, 329, 369, 370, 371
Lazlo, J., 201
Leary, M.R., 265, 286
Leary, R., 422
Leavy, R.L., 274
Leddo, J., 292
Ledwidge, B., 4
Lee, I., 392
Lee, J., 338
Lee-Painter, S., 21
Leeper, R., 169
Leff, J.P., 360
Lehmanb, D.R., 272, 273
Lehrman, D.S., 18
Leigh, H., 350
Leight, K.A., 118, 119
Lemke, R.R., 358
Lemmens, W.A.J., 335
LeMoal, M., 336
Lenat, D.B., 209
Lenders, J.W.M., 335

Leon, M.R., 120
Leonard, D.W., 440
Lepper, M.R., 185
Lerner, J.V., 14, 15, 20, 21, 22, 25, 26, 29, 92
Lerner, R.M., 13, 14, 15, 16, 17, 18, 19, 20, 21, 22, 25, 26, 27, 28, 29, 40, 41, 46, 58, 59, 61, 66, 68, 69, 73, 92
Lesser, G.S., 76
Lester, D., 172
Lester, G.W., 289
Lethem, J., 396
Levenson, R.W., 334, 354, 356, 360, 367, 369
Leventhal, H., 369, 370, 371
Levey, A.B., 325, 367
Levi, L., 325
Levin, D.N., 371, 387
Levine, F., 288
Levine, J.A., 77
Levine, J.L., 181
Levis, D.J., 3, 365, 366
Levitt, K., 165, 373
Levy, S.M., 338
Lewin, K., 258, 259, 267, 284, 312, 313, 316, 317
Lewin, R.J.P., 126
Lewinsohn, P.M., 112, 176, 180, 265
Lewis, M., 19, 21, 69
Lewis, P., 119
Lewko, J.H., 79
Lewontin, R., 427
Liben, L.S., 14
Lieberman, R.P., 278
Lichtenstein, E., 275
Lichtenstein, S., 202
Lieber, C.S., 333
Lieberman, M.A., 271, 274
Lieberman, R.P., 356
Liepman, H., 240
Light, K.C., 335
Likert, R., 256
Likona, T., 78
Lilienfeld, A., 198
Lincoln, N.B., 231, 242
Lindberg, G., 208
Lindemann, E., 458
Linden, W., 360, 362
Lindenthal, J.J., 333
Lindholm, E., 394
Lindsley, O.R., 1
Linehan, M.M., 356, 363, 366
Linville, P.W., 171
Liotta, R.F., 465
Lippmann, M., 338
Lipsedge, M.S., 441
Lipshutz, S.A., 466
Lishman, W.A., 128
Lisman, S.A., 445
Litrownick, A.J., 293

Litt, M.D., 160, 329
Livingstone, M.G., 230
Llabre, M.M., 363
Lloyd, C., 272
Lloyd, G.C., 128
Lloyd, J., 460
Lo, C.R., 394, 395
Locke, E.A., 5
Lockhart, R.S., 104, 108, 179, 247
Loeber, R., 42, 47
Loehlin, J.C., 41
Loevinger, J., 76
Lofberg, I., 391
Loftus, E.F., 123, 178
Loftus, G.R., 178
Logan, G.D., 111
LoLordo, V., 415, 416, 422, 424
Lombardi, W.L., 295
London, P., 1
Long, J.M., 360
Longo, D.J., 336
Lopatka, C., 156, 165, 446
Lopez, A., 286
Lorayne, H., 248
Lorcia, M., 118
Lord, C.G., 185
Lorenz, K., 414
Lorenz, M., 155
Lorion, R.P., 465
Lourie, I.S., 81
Lourie, R.S., 39, 44
Lovaas, O.I., 74
Lovett, S.B., 478
Lovibond, P.F., 437, 439
Lown, B., 338
Lucas, J.A., 153
Luchetta, T., 328
Lumry, A., 126, 180
Lumsdaine, A.A., 317
Lundberg, G.D., 198
Lundberg, U., 326
Luria, A.R., 48, 230, 240
Lusso, F.M., 326
Lustman, P.J., 182
Lykken, D.T., 360
Lyman, D.R., 89
Lynch, J.P., 360
Lynch, M.E., 20, 80
Lyons, J.S., 273

Maccoby, E.E., 65, 78, 90
Maccoby, N., 77, 92, 480
MacCorquodale, K., 103
MacDonald, H., 394
MacDonald, M.L., 6
MacDonald, M.R., 105, 107, 171, 173, 174
MacDougall, J.M., 329

Mackey, S., 242
Mackintosh, N., 425, 428
Mackintosh, N.J., 437, 439
MacLeod, A.K., 119
MacLeod, C., 111, 123, 126, 134, 136, 137, 138, 139, 141, 142, 152, 158, 159, 162, 329, 371, 372
Mactutus, C.F., 445
Maddux, J.E., 286
Magaro, P.A., 118, 174, 293, 297
Magder, L., 336
Magnusson, D., 14, 15, 16
Mahoney, L.T., 335
Mahoney, M.J., 4, 35, 49, 117, 169, 178, 186
Maier, S., 336, 420
Main, M., 19
Mainardi, A., 395
Maisto, S.A., 206
Malinow, K.L., 360
Mancia, G., 386
Mandler, G., 109, 121, 141, 142, 355, 369, 370
Mandler, J.M., 355
Manly, P.C., 180
Manne, S.L., 277
Manoff, R.K., 478
Manuck, S.B., 326, 331, 334
Marcel, A.J., 373
Marchione, K., 163, 366, 367
Margalit, B., 136
Margolin, G., 265, 289
Margraf, J., 136, 152, 158, 162, 392, 393
Marie, G.V., 394, 399
Marks, I., 116
Marks, I.M., 416, 430, 435, 441
Marks, T., 175, 179
Markus, H., 175, 179, 284, 295, 296, 299, 313, 370
Marlow, L., 80
Marmot, M.G., 334
Marrow, A.J., 258
Marshall, J.C., 222
Marshall, M.M. 229
Marshall, W.L., 362
Marshall-Goodell, B., 358
Martello, J., 119
Martens, B.K., 46
Martin, B., 351
Martin, D., 77, 84
Martin, D.J., 265, 266
Martin, F.C., 336
Martin, I., 3, 325, 358, 362, 367, 384, 397
Martin, J.A., 77, 92
Martin, M., 138, 158, 162
Martin, P.R., 2, 4, 385, 386, 398, 399, 402
Martinage, D.P., 229
Mash, E.J., 2, 47, 57, 60, 61, 66
Masserman, J., 414
Masten, A.S., 35, 36, 37, 38, 40, 42, 45, 74, 88, 278
Masters, J.C., 3

AUTHOR INDEX

Mastria, M.A., 286
Mathews, A., 103, 109 110, 113 123, 128, 129, 131, 133, 134, 136, 137, 139, 141, 142, 151, 152, 153, 154, 155, 157, 158, 159, 160, 162, 164, 293
Mathews, A.M., 329, 371, 372, 388, 398
Matias, R., 366
Matson, J.L., 63
Matthews, K.A., 330, 331, 332, 334, 335
Matthews, R.M., 462
Matthews, W.S., 20
Mattick, R., 152
Mattik, R., 392
Matuzas, W., 127
Mavissakalian, M., 163, 366, 367, 368, 388, 393
Maxeiner, M.E., 179
May, J., 109, 113, 142
Mayer, G.R., 462
Mayer, J.D., 130, 445
Mayol, A., 175, 179
McAlister, A.L., 90
McArdle, S., 328
McArthur, D.L., 400
McCann, C.D., 139
McCarthy, R., 218
McCartney, K., 16, 18, 19, 41, 87
McCaul, K.D., 164
McClure, J.N., 392
McConaughy, S.H., 44, 46
McCord, J., 465
McDaniel, L.K., 337
McDonald, M.R., 119
McDonald, R.H., 331
McDonel, E.C., 353
McDougall, W., 256, 311
McDowell, J., 128, 129
McDowell, J.J., 463
McEachern, H.M., 362
McFall, R.M., 353
McFarlane, J.W., 87
McGillis, D., 285
McGlynn, F.D., 368
McGuire, W.J., 317
McHale, S.M., 83
McInnis, E. T., 293
McKay, G., 270
McKenna, F.P., 135, 158
McKinlay, W.W., 229
McKinney, B., 275
McKinney, K.L., 20
McKinney, M.E., 363
McKinney, W.T., 42
McKnight, G.T., 337
McLachlan, A.L., 138
McLean, A., 371
McLoughlin, R.T., 333
McMahon, R.B., 180
McMahon, R.J., 35, 46

McMichael, A.J.,332
McNally, R.J., 131, 135, 141, 153, 154, 155, 163, 369, 370, 373, 390, 391, 413, 415, 416, 428
McNeal, E.T., 183
McNeil, B.J., 212
McNeil, D.W., 371, 390
McPhillips, S., 425
McQueen, D.V., 339
Mead, G.H., 255, 256, 257, 258, 267
Mednick, S.A., 37
Meehl, P.E., 103, 169, 207, 208, 297
Meichenbaum, D.H., 4, 46, 48, 143, 176, 188
Meinhardt, K., 272
Melamed, B.G., 371, 390
Melin, B., 326
Melton, G.B., 476
Mendez, O., 20, 23
Menlove, F., 429
Menzies, R., 169
Meredith, R.L., 350
Merluzzi, T.V., 178, 293, 296
Mermelstein, R., 275
Merrens, M.R., 351
Mersch, P.P., 163
Mesibov, G.B., 38
Metalsky, G.I., 169, 180, 326
Metz, J.R., 278
Meyer, J.W., 13
Meyer, L.H., 463
Meyer, R., 336
Meyers, A., 49, 83
Meyers, A.W., 49
Michael, C.C., 181
Michaud, B., 336
Michela, J.L., 286
Michelson, L., 163, 366, 367, 388, 389, 393, 475
Mikulincer, M., 274, 276
Mildvan, A.S., 331
Miller, C.L., 278
Miller, D., 75
Miller, D.R., 349
Miller, E., 119, 231, 248
Miller, F.D., 126, 291
Miller, G.A., 258, 349, 359, 365, 367, 368, 371, 386, 387
Miller, H., 445
Miller, I.W., 126, 132, 181, 187
Miller, L.C., 60, 81
Miller, L.K., 462
Miller, N.E., 259, 260, 394, 397, 442
Miller, O.L., 462
Miller, P.H., 75
Miller, P.M., 333
Miller, R.S., 265, 286
Miller, S., 330
Miller, S.M., 69, 160, 332
Miller, S.T., 396

Miller, W.G., 231
Miller, W.R., 118
Mills, I., 373
Mills, J., 261
Milner, M., 335
Mineka, S., 160, 328, 413, 414, 416, 417, 418, 420, 421, 422, 423, 424, 426, 427, 429, 430, 436, 446
Minsky, M., 175
Minuchin, P.P., 79
Miranda, J., 126
Mirels, H.L., 265, 286
Mirkin, M.P., 85, 89
Mischel, W., 15, 179
Mitchell, C.M., 77
Mitchell, R.E., 464, 468
Mittermeier, R., 428
Miura, S., 129
Mizes, J.S., 127
Moffat, N., 231
Mogg, K., 109, 112, 113, 131, 132, 136, 141, 142, 157
Monjan, A.A., 336
Monroe, S.M., 271, 272, 274, 326, 329
Monteiro, K.P., 445
Montemayor, R., 78
Montgomery, R.L., 263
Mooney, D., 398
Moore, D., 77
Moos, R.H., 274, 276, 277, 278, 328
Moreland, R.L., 295
Moreno, J.L., 256, 266
Morey, L., 206
Morey, L.C., 356
Morgan, M., 333
Mori, L., 462
Moritsugu, J.N., 458
Mormede, P., 336
Moroz, M., 4
Morris, C.D., 108
Morris, J.B., 182
Morris, L., 119
Morris, T., 338
Morrison, D.M., 84
Mortimore, P., 79
Morton, J., 124
Mosbach, P., 369
Moscovici, S., 299
Moscovitch, M., 247
Moses, J., 331
Moskowitz, A.J., 210
Mowrer, O.H., 47, 351
Mowrer, W.M., 47
Mueller, J.H., 120, 121
Mueser, K.T., 274, 278
Mull, H.K., 128
Mullen, P.D., 478
Mulvaney, D.E., 437
Mulvey, E.P., 42, 50

Mumby, M., 164
Munck, A., 330
Munoz, R.F., 176, 464, 476
Munson, P., 121
Murawski, B.J., 338
Murdock, T.B., 131, 373
Murphy, D.L., 117, 118, 119, 445
Murphy, E., 333
Murphy, G., 236
Murphy, G.E., 126, 180, 181, 182
Murphy, R., 330
Murray, S., 414, 429
Murrell, E., 152, 392
Mussen, P.H., 20
Mussi, A., 334
Myers, J.K., 333
Myers, P.E., 362, 388

Nadel, J.A., 335
Nadel, L., 436, 445
Nafpakititis, M., 462
Nagayama Hall, G.C., 357
Nagel, E., 14
Najavits, L., 182
Nakamura, C.Y., 63
Nakamura, G.V., 123
Nakamura, M., 335
Nakao, M.A., 201
Nannis, E.D., 74, 84
Napoli, A., 337
Nasby, W., 176, 293, 294, 295, 296
Nathan, P.R., 399
Navon, D., 136
Nay, W.R., 354, 360
Naydin, V.L., 230
Neale, J.M., 198
Nebylitsyn, V.D., 356, 367
Neely, J.H., 124
Neff, D.F., 400
Neimark, E.E., 75
Neisser, U., 137, 175, 293, 294, 299
Nelson, G., 291
Nelson, G.M., 357
Nelson, K., 123
Nelson, P., 153
Nelson, R.O., 6, 57, 67, 352, 354, 356, 361, 364, 365
Nelson, T., 468
Nesselroade, J.R., 15
Neufeld, R.W.J., 327
Neunabert, D.J., 180
Nevins, B.G., 398
Newell, A., 201
Newman, I.M., 50
Nezworksi, T., 74, 87, 91
Nezworski, M.T., 35, 49
Nicassio, P.M., 356
Nietzel, M.T., 309

Niles, W.J., 75, 76, 90
Nisbett, R.E., 104, 117, 126, 128, 169, 174, 175, 176, 177, 178, 184, 185, 286, 289, 294, 314
Nitz, K., 13, 21, 26
Noam, G.G., 76, 84, 91
Noble, H., 81
Noble, J., 399
Noble, P.J., 357
Noonberg, A.R., 350
Noordwijk, M., van., 427
Norman, G.R., 200
Norman, W.H., 126, 132, 181
Norton, G.R., 153, 157
Novikoff, A.B., 15, 18
Nuechterlein, K.H., 326, 356, 357
Nulty, D.D., 139
Ninn, J.D., 130, 131, 156
Nutter, R.W., 118
Nyman, K., 442

O'Brien, G.T., 158
O'Connor, K., 389
O'Grady, D., 278
O'Hara M.W., 180
O'Keefe, D., 399
O'Kelly, L.I., 351
O'Leary, K.D., 2, 3, 474
O'Neil, M., 209
O'Reilly, M., 208
Oatley, K., 141
Obrist, P.A., 335, 350, 370, 387, 394
Oehman, A., 14, 15, 16
Oei, T.P., 161
Offer, D., 82
Ohman, A., 327, 350, 357, 358, 360, 365, 368, 369, 370, 371, 372, 373, 391, 413, 415, 416, 428
Olinger, L.J., 171, 174, 180
Oliver, J.M., 180
Ollendick, T.H., 48, 57, 58, 59, 60, 61, 62, 63, 64, 65, 66, 68, 81
Olofsson, C., 391, 416
Olson, D.H., 77
Olson, J.M., 299
Olson, L.M., 91
Olsson, G., 338
Olton, D.S., 350
Omessi, E., 291
Onesti, G., 334
Ooms, T., 83
Opper, S., 75
Orlinsky, D.E., 317
Orvis, B.R., 291
Osborn, C.E., 127, 179
Osborn, E.L., 48
Osborne, J., 415
Oseasohn, R., 330
Osgood, C.E., 261

Oskamp, S., 205
Ost, L.G., 355, 366, 369, 370, 389, 396, 413
Ostrom, T.M., 284, 300
Ostrov, E., 82
Ottati, V.C., 293
Ottoson, J., 118
Ouston, J., 79
Overcast, T.D., 120
Overmier, J., 420
Overton, D.A., 441
Overton, W.F., 13, 14, 16, 17, 75, 76
Owen, S., 328
Owings, D., 427
Oxley, D., 272, 274

Pagani, M., 388
Page, M.M., 264
Pagel, M.D., 272, 273, 274
Pagliocca, P.M., 77
Paige, K.E., 20
Pallack, M.S., 121
Palmquist, W., 75
Papakostopoulos, D., 384
Papini, D.R., 80
Parati, G. 386
Pardine, P., 337
Parise, M., 398
Park, B., 284
Parke, R., 23
Parke, R.D., 74
Parker, J.G., 78, 86
Parkes, C.M., 333
Parkes, K.R., 329
Parkin, A.J., 106
Parkinson, L., 127, 135, 141, 157
Parks, C., 178, 181
Pasahow, R.J., 169
Paskewitz, D.A., 360
Passingham, R., 248
Patnoe, S., 258
Patterson, G.R., 42, 46, 50
Patterson, J., 420
Patterson, K.E., 219, 222
Patterson, R., 396
Patterson, R.J., 327
Pauker, S.G., 210, 212
Paul, R., 43
Paulauskas, S.L., 81, 85
Paulman, R., 121
Pavlov, I.P., 415, 416, 422, 424, 436, 437, 446
Pavlova, Z., 198
Payne, R.W., 118
Pearce, J.M., 435
Pearlin, L.I., 276
Pechtel, C., 414
Peck, C.D., 437, 446, 447, 449
Peeters, R., 173

AUTHOR INDEX

Peikarski, C., 331
Pellegrini, D.S., 42
Pennebaker, J.W., 329, 332, 339
Penzien, D.B., 399, 400
Pepper, M.P., 333
Pepper, S.C., 15
Perlmutter, M., 15
Perronet, F., 330
Perrotta, P., 273
Perry, C.L., 90
Perry, J.D., 77
Perski, A., 395
Persons, J.B., 126
Persons, R.W., 231
Pestrak, V.A., 84
Peters, R.DeV., 35, 46
Petersen, A.C., 20, 74, 75, 77, 79, 81
Peterson, C., 88, 126, 176, 180, 181, 185, 287, 289, 329
Peterson, L., 35, 47, 50, 61, 74, 85, 86, 91, 355, 462
Peterson, R.A., 154, 155, 270, 275, 276, 278
Peterson, R.F., 57
Pettinati, H.M., 118
Pettingale, K.W., 338
Petty, R.E., 179, 265, 266, 318, 358, 360, 368, 385
Petzel, S.V., 40
Petzel, T., 120
Peveler, R., 389
Pfeffer, C.R., 41
Philips, C., 359, 360
Phillips, E.L., 277
Phillips, J.S., 46, 47
Piaget, J., 14, 15, 58, 59, 75, 78, 176, 486
Piasecki, J.M.,
Pichert, J.W., 337
Pickar, D., 119
Pickett, G.E., 478
Pickles, A.J., 131
Pierce, W.D., 353
Pietrewicz, A., 415
Pietromonaco, P., 295
Pilon, R.N., 396
Pilsbury, D., 386, 393
Pine F., 74
Pinkerton, S.S., 4
Pittman, F.S., 89
Pittman, T.S., 121, 266
Pittner, M.S., 126
Pitts, F.N., 392
Plapp, J.M., 350
Platt, J.J., 82
Plaut, S.M., 326
Pleban, R., 284
Pleck, J.H., 77
Plienis, A.J., 278
Plimpton, E., 417
Plomin, R., 19, 26, 41

Plutchik, R., 367
Poche, E.E., 462
Pokorny, A.D., 333
Polefrone, J., 331
Polidora, V., 422
Pollatsek, A., 201
Pollen, O.F., 4
Pomerleau, O.F., 4
Pope, A.T., 358
Poppen, P.J., 5
Porges, S.W., 358, 384, 385
Post, R.M., 117 118, 119, 173, 174
Postman, L., 448
Poulsen, J.C., 444
Powell, G.E., 230, 236, 359
Powell, M., 139
Powell, M.C., 179
Powell, V.E., 351
Powers, E., 465
Powers, M.D., 43, 61, 67
Preston, G., 439
Preston, G.C., 437
Pribram, K.H., 258
Price, K.P., 350
Price, R.H., 270
Price, V., 414
Pritchard, D.W., 399
Procidano, M.,271
Proctor, S.E., 486
Proctor, W.C., 357
Prujinsky, T., 121
Psotka, J., 448
Puopolo, M., 422
Purkel, W., 48
Puthezhath, N., 393
Pynoos, R.S., 38, 327

Quillian, M.R., 123

Rabinowitz, S.H., 338
Rachman, S., 127, 135, 141, 153, 155, 156, 157, 160, 165, 348, 354, 356, 360, 364, 365, 366, 368, 371, 373, 388, 389, 390, 413, 417, 446, 449
Raczynski, J.M., 350, 352, 354, 358
Radice, M., 335
Radloff, L.S., 172
Rae, D.S., 172
Rafaelsen, O.J., 358
Raimy, V., 298
Rakover, S., 126
Ramirez, A.J., 326, 338
Ranyard, R., 441
Rao, P.A., 126
Rapee, R., 392
Rapee, R.M., 152, 153, 160
Rappaport, J., 461, 473, 476, 477, 478
Rappoport, J.A., 163
Raps, C.S., 181

Rasenick-Douss, L., 483
Raskind, M., 331
Ray, A., 286
Ray, C., 135
Ray, R.S., 46, 47
Ray, W.J., 350, 352, 354, 358, 384
Rayner, R., 246
Read, P.B., 37, 82
Read, S., 290, 292
Reberg, D., 437, 448
Rectanus, E., 328
Reed, M.R., 293
Reed, S.D., 358
Reese, H.W., 13, 16, 75
Reeves, J.L., 394
Rehm, L.P., 129, 170, 172, 180
Reich, P., 338
Reich, W., 46, 351
Reid, L.D., 442
Reid, R.L., 440
Reisenzein, R., 369
Reiss, S., 3, 154, 155, 161
Reppucci, N.D., 476, 485
Rescorla, R.A., 415, 420, 425, 435, 436, 437, 439, 446, 449
Resnick, H.S., 274
Ress, J., 449
Reus, V.I., 118
Revelle, W., 120
Revenstorf, D., 288
Reynolds, P., 326
Rhodes, J.E., 468
Rhodes, W.A., 288
Rholes, W.S., 128, 130, 181, 295
Ricci, J.A., 229
Riccio, D.C., 445, 449
Rich, C.L., 40
Rich, S.A., 241
Richards, A., 110, 112, 134
Richards, D.W., 444
Richards, M., 75
Richards, R.W., 437
Richardson, D.C., 284
Richardson, R., 445, 449
Richer, F., 386
Rickel, A.U., 86
Rickles, W.H., 400
Ricks, D.F., 337
Ricks, D.F., 5
Riecken, H., 314
Riegel, K.F., 14, 15, 18
Rigter, H., 445
Rimm, D.C., 3
Rimmo, P.A., 413
Rincover, A., 6
Rips, L.J., 123
Riskind, J.H., 127, 128, 130, 174, 181

Risley, T.R., 475
Ritter, B., 429
Roberts, A.H., 394, 396, 401
Roberts, M.C., 462
Robertson, I., 229
Robertson, J., 476
Robertson, W.O., 200
Robin, A.L., 89
Robins, C., 179, 293, 297
Robins, L., 89
Robinson, E., 121
Robinson, J.W., 362, 363
Robinson, L., 465
Robinson, N., 339
Robson, M., 291
Robson, S.D., 466
Rock, D.L., 206
Rodichok, L.D., 400
Rodick, J.D., 49, 83
Rodin, J., 286, 331
Rodrigez, I.A., 118
Rodriguez, A., 81
Rodriguez, M., 81
Roediger, H.L., 109
Rogers, H.J., 474
Rogers, P.J., 179
Rogers, T.B., 179
Rogers-Warren, A., 463, 475
Rokeach, M., 318
Rolf, J.E., 37
Romanczyk, R.G., 85
Ronan, K., 126
Rondanelli, R., 338
Roper, B.L., 61
Rosch, E., 179
Rose, R.M., 333
Rose, S., 273
Rosen, G.M., 2
Rosenbaum, M., 2, 6, 265, 266
Rosenberg, J., 118
Rosenberg, M.S., 478
Rosenberg, S.J., 275, 276
Rosenblum, L., 19, 21, 417
Rosengard, C., 442, 443, 444
Rosenstiel, A.K., 276
Rosenthal, R., 15
Rosenwein, R., 286
Roskies, E., 330, 340
Rosnow, R., 15
Ross, A., 395
Ross, A.O., 6
Ross, E.A., 256, 311
Ross, E.D., 230
Ross, J.C., 201
Ross, J.M., 286
Ross, L., 76, 126, 169, 174, 175, 176, 184, 185, 186, 188, 287, 288, 290, 294, 301

Ross, M., 285, 286, 291
Ross, R.S., 395
Ross, S.M., 126, 180, 186
Roth, D., 129
Roth, S., 329
Roth, W.T., 136, 158, 392, 393
Rothbart, M.K., 152
Rothblum, E.D., 270, 276, 277
Rowell, T., 427
Roy-Byrne, P.J., 119
Roy-Byrne, P.P., 173, 174
Royal College of Physicians, 228
Rozanski, A., 338
Rozin, P., 415
Ruble, D.N., 20, 21, 75, 76
Ruch, L.O., 328
Rudy, T.E., 293
Ruehlman, L.S., 169, 172, 173, 175, 176, 177, 275
Rugh, J.D., 358
Ruhf, L., 274
Rush, A.J., 4, 107, 122, 126, 152, 175, 180, 181, 182, 278, 289
Russel, D., 290
Russell, C.S., 77
Russell, M.L., 130
Russell, P.N., 131
Russell, P.W., 119
Russo, J., 153
Russo, T.J., 75, 91
Rutter, M., 36, 37, 38, 41, 42, 51, 74, 76, 79, 81, 82, 88, 89
Ryan, E., 75
Ryan, P., 336
Ryan, R.M., 349
Ryan, S., 336
Ryle, G., 106
Ryon, N.B., 180

Saab, P.G., 331
Sacco, W.P., 111
Saccuzzo, D.P., 117
Sachar, E.J., 358
Sackett, D.L., 200
Sackett, G., 417
Safarjan, W., 422
Safran, J.D., 371
Safranek, R., 399
Salge, R.S., 153
Salkovskis, P.M., 373, 392, 393
Salovey, P., 107, 179, 196, 293, 294, 295, 297
Sameroff, A., 17, 20, 41
Sanbonmatsu, D.M., 179
Sander, L.W., 39
Sanderson, W.C., 160, 366, 388
Sandler, I.M., 272, 273
Sandman, C.A., 335
Santi, S.M., 485

Santilli, N.R., 80
Santisteban, G.A., 326
Santostefano, S., 39, 81
Sarason, S.B., 121, 461, 475
Sarbin, T.R., 15
Sargent, D.M., 437
Sargent, J.D., 397
Sarkissian, J., 83
Sartory, G., 366, 369, 388, 390. 441, 442, 446
Saunders, N.L., 402
Sauter, S.L., 327
Savage, A., 428
Saville, P.D., 206
Sayers, S.L., 290
Scarr, S., 16, 18, 19, 41, 87
Schacter, D.L., 108, 109, 142, 240, 241, 247
Schacter, S., 152, 153, 314, 369
Schaefer, E., 157
Schaik, C., van., 427
Schare, M.L., 445
Scheff, T., 257
Scheier, M.F., 159
Schell, A.M., 367, 371
Scherer, M.W., 63
Schiller, P., 429
Schleifer, S.J., 336
Schleser, R., 49, 83
Schneider, R.M., 173
Schneider, W., 111
Schneider-Rosen, K., 74
Schneirla, T.C., 14, 17, 18, 21
Schoen, L.S., 327
Schoenfeld, P., 274
Schonell, M., 356
Schooler, C., 276
Schoomaker, E.B., 201
Schopler, E., 38
Schorin, M.Z., 84
Schroeder, H.E., 48, 81
Schuerman, J.A., 236
Schul, Y., 275, 295
Schulman, L.F., 210
Schulsinger, F., 37
Schultz, L.H., 84
Schumaker, J.B., 460
Schwab, J., 21, 26
Schwartz, G.E., 350, 352, 358
Schwartz, M.S., 398
Schwartz, N., 133
Schwartz, S., 196, 198, 206, 208, 212
Schwitzgebel, R., 47
Scobie, S.R., 444
Scott, C., 287
Scott, W.A., 265
Seacat, G.F., 231
Searleman, A., 232
Sebby R.A., 80

Sechrest, L.B., 265
Segal, Z.V., 112
Seligman, M.E.P., 88, 169, 170, 172, 176, 180, 278, 287, 291, 312, 336, 370, 391, 413, 415, 420, 426, 428
Selman, R.L., 78, 80, 81, 84, 89, 90
Selye, H., 329
Semenza, C., 218
Semmel, A., 172, 180
Seraganian, P., 330
Serxner, S., 476
Settels, J.J., 386
Sewitch, T.S., 127
Sexton-Radek, K., 351
Shaffer, D., 36, 40
Shafii, M., 359
Shagass, C., 349
Shalker, T.E., 133
Shallice, T., 216
Shantz, C.U., 76
Shapiro, D., 394, 395, 396
Shapiro, D.A., 291
Shapiro, E.K., 79
Shapiro, E.S., 463
Shapiro, J.L., 129
Shapiro, K., 424
Sharpley, C.F., 474
Sharrock, R., 118, 119, 131, 135, 158, 161
Shaver, K.G., 286, 291
Shaver, P., 135
Shavit, Y., 336
Shaw, B., 180
Shaw, B.F., 4, 107, 112, 122, 126, 128, 129, 130, 174, 180, 181, 182, 278, 289
Shea, T.M., 182
Sheldon, W.H., 26
Shelton, D., 328
Sherif, M., 317
Sherman, A.R., 449
Sherman, S.J., 284, 293, 298
Sherrod, L.R., 15
Shevrin, H., 178
Shewell, C., 219
Shields, J., 41
Shiffrin, R.M., 104, 105, 111
Shiffrin, W., 173
Shillitoe, R.W., 334
Shimizu, D., 272
Shirk, S.R., 74, 75, 81, 83, 84, 85, 86, 91
Shore, J.H., 327
Showers, C., 284, 299
Shure, M.B., 82, 462
Siddle, D.A.T., 359
Sides, J.K., 165, 340
Siegel, J.M., 332, 334
Siegel, S.E., 62, 81
Silberman, E.K., 117, 118, 119, 174

Sillan, J., 20, 23
Silverberg, S.B., 76, 77, 82
Silverman, J.A., 175, 180
Silverman, J.J., 351
Silverman, J.S., 175, 180
Simmons, R.G., 20, 21, 40, 79, 85
Simon, H.A., 104, 178, 201
Simons, A.D., 126, 180, 182
Simons, R.C., 369
Singer, J., 152
Singer, J.A., 107
Singer, S., 369
Sinyor, D., 330
Sipprelle, R.C., 274
Sisson, J.C., 201
Skilbeck, W.M., 286
Skinner, B.F., 1, 3, 58, 81, 246, 262, 263, 459
Skinner, E.A., 49
Skinner, H.A., 356
Skinner, J.E., 338
Sklar, L.S., 326, 336
Slaymaker, F., 120
Slife, B.D., 129, 130
Sloan, R.D., 127
Slovic, P., 156, 169, 201, 202, 294
Slugoski, B.R., 292
Smallberg, S.A., 119
Smith, A.P., 329
Smith, D.A., 108
Smith, E.A., 485
Smith, E.R., 126, 291
Smith, J., 295
Smith, M., 440
Smith, R., 337
Smith, R.L., 445
Smith, S.M., 441, 449
Smith, T.W., 126, 272, 286, 288, 330, 464
Smith, W.C., 440
Smith, W.P., 262
Snowden, L.R., 464
Snowdon, C., 417, 428
Snyder, C.R., 286, 288
Snyder, M., 297
Sokolov, E.N., 369
Solnik, J.V., 6
Solomon, D.S., 480
Solomon, H.C., 1
Solomon, L.J., 270, 276, 277
Solomon, Z., 274, 276
Solyom, C., 160
Sonne, J.L., 286
Soo-Hoo T., 476
Sorbi, M., 400
Sorell, G.T., 20
Sorensen, B., 15
Sostrin, S.V., 198
Soucey, G., 461

Sox, H.E., 212
Spanier, G.B., 17, 19, 20, 21
Spear, N.E., 441, 445
Speers, M.A., 174, 175, 179, 293, 294, 297
Speicher, C.E., 330
Speltz, M.L., 87, 88
Spence, E.L., 373
Spence, J.T., 120
Spence, K.W., 120
Spiegelhalter, D., 210
Spielberger, C.D., 120
Spivack, G., 82
Spivak, G., 462
Sprafka, S.A., 210
Sprafkin, J.N., 352, 354
Sprenkle, D.H., 77
Spring, B., 357
Sprinthall, N.A., 76
Sprock, J., 117
Squire, L.R., 106, 109
Sroufe, L.A., 36, 38, 39, 41, 42, 43, 46, 51, 77, 87, 88
Srull, T.K., 293, 295
St. Lawrence, J.S., 278
Staats, A.W., 264
Staats, C.K., 264
Stabb, S.D., 278
Stampp, M.S., 241
Stark, K., 448
Stark, K.D., 88
Statts, A.W., 353
Steele, B.F., 92
Steenbarger, B.N., 464
Steer, R.A., 127
Stein, B.S., 108
Stein, L. 444
Stein, M., 336
Steinberg, L.D., 76, 77, 79, 80, 82, 85
Steiner, S.C., 271, 272, 275
Steinmetz, J.L., 112, 180, 185
Steketee, G., 372, 390
Steketee, G.S., 164
Stemmler, G., 363
Stephens, P.M., 326
Stephens, R., 402
Steptoe, A., 325, 326, 327, 328, 330, 331, 334, 337, 340, 351, 356, 358, 360, 394, 395
Stern, J.A., 349, 350, 351, 384
Stern, M., 394
Stern, R.M., 358, 384
Sternbach, R.A., 349, 358
Sternberg, D.E., 118
Sternberg, R.J., 179
Stevenson, R., 130
Stevenson, R.J., 156
Stewart, R.L., 309
Stinson, L., 266

Stockman, S.J., 202
Stokes, T.F., 462
Stoltenberg, C.D., 286
Stomgren, L.S., 118
Stone, D.B., 50
Stoney, C.M., 331
Storms, M.D., 286
Stout, M.A., 399
Stouthamer-Loeber, M., 47
Stoyva, J.M., 335, 397, 399
Strack, F., 185
Strain, P.S., 89, 90
Strauman, T., 171
Strauman, T.J., 278
Strauss, C.C., 67, 278
Strayhorn, J.M., 89
Street, L., 164
Strehler, E.L., 331
Streitman, S., 37, 38
Streuning, E.L., 288
Strickland, B.R., 118
Strong, S.R., 286, 288
Strongman, K.T., 131
Stroop, J.R., 135, 139
Strosahl, K.D., 363, 366
Strupp, H., 6
Stuart, I.R., 83
Stucky, R., 464
Sturgeon, D., 356
Sturgis, E.T., 350, 352, 358, 360, 362, 384
Suarez, R., 118
Sullivan, H.S., 78, 311
Suls, J., 164, 329
Sulzerazaroff, B., 462
Summerton, J., 160, 332
Sundberg, N.D., 233
Sunderland A., 234
Suomi, S., 417
Super, C.M., 14, 15, 20, 22, 23
Surwillo, W.W., 359, 384
Surwit, R.S., 340, 351, 394, 395, 396
Sutterfield, S.J., 75
Sutton, E.P., 398
Sutton, R.S., 317
Sutton-Simon, K., 127
Swales, J.D., 335
Swallow, S.R., 278
Swan, G.E., 6
Swann, W.B., Jr., 297
Swartz, K., 417
Swartzentruber, D., 425, 437, 439, 440, 446, 448, 449
Sweeney, P.D., 180, 286, 289
Swift, C., 458
Swindle, R.W., 466
Swindle, R.W., Jr., 277
Syme, S.L., 334

Szabo, L., 439
Szegda, M., 128
Szwejkowska, G., 440

Takeshita, A., 335
Talbot, E., 334
Talbott, R., 230
Tallman, K., 160
Talwar, R., 21, 26, 27
Tanguay, P.E., 44, 45
Tannenbaum, P.H., 261
Tanner, J., 74
Tarrier, N., 350, 356, 359, 360
Tasto, D.L., 81
Tata, P., 111, 136, 137, 139, 157, 371, 372
Tatum, E.L., 327
Taub, D.B., 326
Taub, J., 442
Tavazzi, L., 338
Taylor, B., 20, 75
Taylor, C.B., 158, 386, 393
Taylor, E.B., 273
Talyor, G.P., 231
Taylor, J.A., 335
Taylor, R., 128, 130, 179
Taylor, S.E., 172, 177, 184, 263, 293, 294, 296, 297, 313, 314
Teasdale, J.D., 125, 128, 129, 130, 138, 142, 170, 179, 278, 291
Teasdale, J.P., 175
Teders, S.J., 399
Teglasi, H., 289
Telch, M.J., 90, 153
Tellegen, A., 42, 45
Tellegen, B., 400
Temoshok, L., 329, 333, 337
Terdal, L.G., 47, 57, 60, 61, 66
Terr, L.C., 92
Thackwray, D., 49
Tharp, R.G., 474
Thase, M.E., 273
Thelen, E., 41
Theorell, T., 327
Thibaut, J.W., 263, 264
Thien, T., 335
Thoits, P.A., 271, 277
Thomas, A., 19, 20, 21, 23, 24, 25
Thomas, D.A., 446
Thomas, R.L., 118
Thomas, S.A., 360
Thompson, J.K., 402
Thompson, K., 119, 173
Thompson, L.W., 129
Thompson, M., 332
Thompson, S.J., 485
Thorell, L.H., 356

Thoresen, C.E., 5
Thorndike, E., 415
Thorndyke, P.W., 123, 176
Thornton, J.C., 336
Thurston, H., 335
Thurstone, I.L., 256
Timberlake, W., 435
Tisdelle, D.A., 278
Tobach, E., 14, 15, 16, 17, 18
Tobin-Richards, M.H., 20, 75
Tolman, E.C., 103
Tonkelaar, I., den., 427
Tooke, W., 266
Tota, M.E., 295
Toth, E., 338
Toth, S.L., 81
Towbes, L.C., 271, 272
Treit, D., 442
Trexler, L., 172, 229
Trezise, L., 131, 135, 158, 161
Trickett, E.J., 464, 466, 467, 468
Triplett, N., 256
Trunell, G., 85
Tsai, M., 83
Tsujimoto, R.N., 179
Tsvetkova, L.S., 230
Tubman, J., 13
Tugwell, P., 200
Tulley, R., 337
Tulving, E., 105, 173, 179, 241, 247, 448
Tuma, A.H., 37
Tuma, J.M., 2
Turiel, E., 78
Turk, D.C., 174, 175, 178, 179, 196, 293, 294, 295, 297, 334
Turner, D.S., 462
Turner, J., 339
Turner, R.H., 169
Turner, S.M., 3, 366
Turpin, G., 349, 352, 354, 355, 356, 357, 358, 359, 360, 361, 362, 363, 368, 369, 370, 384
Tursky, B., 394, 400, 401
Tversky, A., 133, 156, 169, 177, 178, 201, 202, 203, 212, 294, 314
Twardosz, S., 475
Twentyman, C.T., 394, 395
Tye, J.B., 483
Tyler, L. E., 233
Tyrer, P., 392

Uhlenhuth, E.H., 127
Ullman, L.P., 459, 460, 474
Unruh, W.R., 171, 174, 177
Urbain, E.S., 76
Urberg, K.A., 84
Urey, J.R., 49

Usdin, E., 349, 356
Uviller, E.T., 355
Uzzell, B.P., 229

Valins, S., 286
Vallacher, R.R., 284
Van Cleave, E.F., 20, 85
Van den Akker, O., 331
van den Broek, M.D., 131
Van den Hout, 392
van den Hout, M.A., 158
Van Houten, R., 462, 475
Van Praag, H.M., 357, 358
van Riezen, H., 445
Van Treuren, R.R., 329
VanderPlate, C., 336
Vaughn, B.E., 42
Vaughn, C.E., 360
Vaughn, L.J., 335, 399
Vega, W., 272
Veldhuis, H.D., 336
Velten, E., 130
Venables, P.H., 356, 357, 358, 362, 363, 384, 386
Vermilyea, J.A., 366
Vernon, S.W., 326
Verrier, R.L., 338
Victor, R., 395
Vieth, W., 426
Villanova, P., 181
Vinarskaya, E.N., 230
Vincent, T., 464, 466, 467
Vinokur, A., 275
Virnelli, S., 329
Visintainer, M., 336
Viswanathan, R., 441
Vitaliano, P.P., 153
Vitkus, J., 277
Voeltz (Meyer), L.M., 463
Voeltz, L.M., 61, 67, 68
Vollmer, W.M., 327
Volpicelli, J., 336
von Baeyer, C., 172, 180
von Bertalanffy, L., 14, 16
Von Eiff, A.W., 331
von Eye, A., 21
Von Holst, D., 326
Vrana, S.R., 371, 373
Vrba, E., 14
Vygotsky, L., 48, 179

Wachtel, P.L., 4
Waddel, M.T., 275
Waddington, C., 427
Waddington, C.H., 41
Wagener, J.J., 128
Wagner, A., 415, 420, 425
Wagner, A.R., 160, 435, 439

Wagner, B.M., 290
Waldman, I.N., 117
Walen, S.R., 462
Walker, B.B., 335
Walker, H.M., 66
Wall, S., 36
Wallace, C.J., 274, 278
Wallace, E.R., 350
Wallerstein, J., 77
Wallsten, T.S., 200, 206
Walrath, L.C., 351
Walters, E.D., 397
Walters, R.H., 260
Wandersman, A., 5
Wang, P.L., 233
Wapner, S., 14
Ward, N.F., 356
Warheit, G., 272, 273
Warr, P.V., 333
Warren, E.W., 118, 135
Warren, R.M., 110
Warren, R.P., 110
Warrent, S.F., 463, 475
Warrington, E.K., 218, 247
Washburn, M.F., 128
Wasserman, T.H., 48
Wasylenki, D., 274
Waterman, D.A., 209
Waters, E., 36, 41, 42, 46, 51, 77
Waters, R.H., 169
Waters, W.F., 352, 358
Waters, W.G., 362, 363
Watkins, J.T., 181
Watson, D., 45, 161, 289, 329, 332
Watson, J.B., 246
Watson, M., 337
Watson, S.M., 49
Watt, N.F., 37
Watts, F., 286
Watts, F.N., 118, 119, 123, 131, 135, 141, 152, 158, 161, 370, 371, 372, 389
Weary, G., 256, 265, 286
Weaver, R., 126, 180
Webster-Stratton, C., 49
Wechsler, D., 118
Weckowicz, T.E., 118
Wegner, D.M., 159
Wegner, D.M., 284
Wehrspann, W., 278
Weigel, C. 271
Weinberg, J., 231
Weinberg, S., 200
Weiner, B., 286, 290, 291, 292
Weiner, H., 350
Weinert, E., 15
Weingartner, H., 117, 118, 119, 173, 174, 176, 441, 445, 448

Weinman, J., 109, 131, 136, 157
Weinstein, A.G., 333
Weinstein, M.C., 201, 212
Weintraub, S., 198
Weisaeth, K., 327
Weisenfeld, A.R., 369
Weiskrantz, L., 104, 247
Weiss, G., 38, 88
Weiss, J.M., 326, 331
Weiss, T., 396
Weissberg, R.P., 462
Weissenberger, J., 175, 181
Weissman, A., 172, 175, 180, 181
Weissman, A.N., 126
Weissman, M.W., 116
Well, A.D., 201
Wellman, B., 466
Wells, C.F., 83
Wells, J.A., 332
Wenar, C., 69
Wenger M.A., 351, 356
Wenig, P., 396
Wenrich, W.W., 4
Werner, E.E., 328
Werner, E.E., 37, 42
Werner, H., 69
Wernick, M.J., 333
Wertlieb, D., 271
Wertman, B.B., 198
Wesseling, K.H., 386
West, C., 445
West, S.G., 169
Westbrook, T., 400
Westney, O.E., 20
Wetzel, R., 474
Wetzel, R.D., 181, 182
Wetzler, S., 445
Whalan, G., 130, 156
Whalen, C.K., 44
Whalley, L., 182
Whisman, M.A., 127
White, J.D., 123
White, P.A., 126
White, S.H., 16
Whitehead, A., 118
Whitlow, J.W., Jr., 160
Whitsett, S.F., 362, 363
Wicker, A.W., 319
Wicker, R., 396
Wickless C., 126, 127
Wielgus, M.S., 119
Wielkiewicz, R., 420
Wiessberg, R.P., 369
Wilcox, L.E., 49
Wilensky, R., 292
Wilkinson, I.M., 181
Willems, E.P., 463

Willemsen, J.J., 335
Williams, C.D., 47
Williams, C.L., 82
Williams. J.M.G., 107, 123, 128, 129, 134, 139, 141, 142, 152, 153, 156, 157, 158, 159, 372, 373
Williams, R., 158
Williams, R.B., 329, 351
Williams, S.L., 163, 367
Williamson, D.A., 337, 352, 358, 362, 395
Willis, P.W., 335
Wilson, B.A., 229, 230, 231, 233, 234, 235, 236, 240, 246, 247, 248, 249
Wilson, C.C., 350, 352, 355, 358, 360, 384
Wilson, E., 398
Wilson, G.T., 2, 3, 4, 5, 6, 163, 283, 284, 296, 300, 474
Wilson, T.D., 104, 117, 126, 128, 175, 178, 180
Windle, M., 20, 21, 25, 27
Wine, J., 121
Winett, R.A., 462, 463, 475, 478, 480, 481, 483, 484, 486, 488
Winfrey, L.P., 297
Wing, L., 357
Wingate, D.L., 334
Winocur, G., 247
Winters, K.C., 198
Wise, C.M., 337
Wise, J., 442
Witmer, H., 465
Witt, J.C., 46
Wittkower, E.D., 350
Wolchik, S.A., 275
Wolf, M.M., 66
Wolff, W.T., 351
Wolkenstein, B., 286, 414
Woll, S.B., 108
Wolpe, J., 1, 2, 5, 116, 117, 383, 387
Wood, J.V., 286
Wood, M.M., 399
Wood, R.L., 230, 231, 234, 236
Wortman, C.B., 270, 271, 272, 273, 275, 277
Wortmann, R.L., 206
Wozney, K., 157
Wrangham, R., 427
Wyatt, R.J., 117
Wyer, R.S., 284, 293, 295
Wynne, L.C., 37

Yamanda, K., 128
Yarkin, R.L., 266
Yates, A.J., 2, 4
Yee, C.M., 349
Yerkes, A., 414
Yerkes, R., 414
Yerkes, R.M., 159
Young, A., 216, 218, 219
Young, D., 40

Young, L.D., 337
Young, P.F., 121
Young, W.E., 121
Youngren, M.A., 265
Youniss, J., 78
Yule, W., 240

Zabski, S., 21
Zacks, R.T., 119
Zaffy, D.J., 121
Zahn, T.P., 350, 356, 357
Zaidel, E., 232
Zajonc, R.B., 4, 152, 187, 284, 296, 299, 313, 370, 371
Zander, J.R., 153, 390
Zarantonello, M, 120, 122
Zarins, C.K., 334
Zatz, S., 120, 127

Zautra, A.J., 277, 337
Zegans, O.S., 336
Zekoski, E.M., 180
Zettin, M., 218
Zigler, E., 458
Zillmann, D., 367
Zimbardo, P.G., 286
Zimet, G.D., 271, 272, 273
Zimet, S.G., 271, 272
Zimmerman, M., 180
Zolik, E.S., 469
Zotti, A.M., 338
Zubin, J., 357
Zurif, E.B., 232
Zuroff, D.C., 119
Zwemer, W.A., 127

SUBJECT INDEX

Academic:
  achievement, 27–28, 45
  competence, 27
Accommodation, 176–177, 183, 184, 498, 499
Accuracy:
  models of, 362
  predictive, 204–205
  retrospective, 204–205
Acting-out behavior, 464, 468
Action research, 313, 317
Action tendencies, 153, 154, 157, 160, 164, 165, 389
Activation–deactivation model of change, 183, 499
Activation or integration, 141–143
Activity scheduling, 187
Actor–observer differences, 289, 505
Adultocentrism, 84
Affective development, 79
Affective therapy, 165
Age differences, 63–67
Aggression, 260
Agoraphobia, 127, 131, 135, 156, 161, 164, 275, 355, 366, 367, 388, 389, 390, 392, 393
Agoraphobia Cognitions Questionnaire, 161
AIDS, 83, 228
Alcohol:
  as a context for extinction, 442
  use as a response to stress 333
Alzheimer's disease, 242, 273, 326
American Psychiatric Association, 36, 44, 45
Amnesia, 106, 109, 212, 240–241, 247, 495, 496
Anger control, adolescents, 81
Anorexia: 88
Anxiety. (*See also* Agoraphobia, Extinction, Fear of fear, Generalized anxiety disorder, Hypervigilance, Lang's Bioinformational theory of emotion, Obsessional disorder, Panic disorder, Preparedness, Safety signal perspective of agoraphobia, Selective associations, Separation anxiety disorder, Social phobia, Spider phobia, Three systems theory)
  anxiety sensitivity, 154–155, 497
  attention processes in, 135–138, 140, 157–161, 497, 514
  automatic processes in, 111
  in children and adolescents, 62–69, 89, 494, 514
  cognitive deficits in, 120–122, 496, 514
  cognitive processes in, 130–132, 133–138, 140, 151–165, 497
  cognitive products in, 127–128, 496–497, 514
  cognitive vulnerability factor for, 111–113
  comprehension processes in, 133–135, 140, 154–156, 497, 514
  contextual analysis of fear extinction, 435–450
  implications of cognitive psychology for assessment of, 161–163
  implications of cognitive psychology for treatment of, 163–165
  memory processes in, 109–110, 130–132, 140, 156–157, 497, 514
  multiple perspectives from psychological science, 514–516
  neurological impairment associated with, 230, 236, 237–238
  prevalence of, 116, 153
  psychophysiological assessment of, 356, 357, 364–367
  and social support, 272, 515
  and working memory, 121–122
Anxiety Sensitivity Index, 154–155, 161
Appetitive motivational system, 385
Applied behavior analysis, 5
Apraxia, 239–240
Aptive changes, 14, 17, 18
Arrhythmicity of behavior, 23–24
Artificial intelligence, 207, 293
Assertive training, 389
Assimilation, 176–178, 498
Associative networks, 106–107, 123–125, 153, 156, 171–172, 370, 371, 389–390, 495
Asthma, 328, 333, 334–335, 336, 337, 339, 356
Attachment:
  attachment-based skill training, 87, 91
  mother-infant relationships, 77, 87
  theory, 36, 41
Attention:
  and cardiac deceleration, 349–350, 359
  narrowing of, 159–161
  selectivity of, 157–159, 162, 163, 164
  self-focussed, 159–161, 164
  theoretical constructs, 110–113
Attention deficit hyperactivity disorder (ADHD), 88
Attentional processes. *See* Controlled processes
Attitudes:
  behavior consistency 319–320, 506
  change methods, 313–319, 506
  change processes, 266, 318
  and cognitive dissonance, 261–262
  formation by classical conditioning, 264, 503

547

formation by operant conditioning, 264–265, 503
maladaptive or dysfunctional, 175, 180
and self-perception, 262–263
value confrontation, 318, 506
Attractiveness, physical, 27–28
Attribution therapy, 288–289
Attributional approach (AA) to social cognition:
clinical applications, 286–290
description, 285–286
Attributional Styles Questionnaire (ASQ), 180–181, 184, 499
Attributions:
models of, 291–292
style, 287, 290
types of, 290–291
Automatic processes, 111–114, 119, 121, 122, 152, 158, 173, 178, 298, 370, 372, 373, 391–392, 496, 517
Automatic Thoughts Questionnaire (ATQ), 111, 126, 179–180, 184, 499
Autonomic balance, 356
Autonomic differentiation, 369
Autonomic perception, 158, 162, 355
Autonomic Perception Questionnaire, 158
Aversive motivational system, 385

Backward masking techniques, 373, 391
BASIC ID, 5
Beck Depression Inventory, 136, 139
Beck's cognitive theory of depression, 170, 278, 498
Beck's schema theory of mood and cognition, 107, 122, 123, 124–126, 130, 132, 134, 135, 137, 138, 140, 141, 154, 496
Behavior checklists, 44, 45
Behavior modification. (*See* Behavior therapy)
Behavior therapy:
affect in, 4
applications to large-scale interventions, 473–489
associations of, 2, 3
and attributional approach, 288–290, 505
cognitive processes in, 4
definition of, 2–3, 5–6, 283–284
developmental principles in, 81
domain of, 4, 516–517
history of, 1–2, 474–475
implications of selective associations for, 413–431, 510–511
and information processing approach, 297–298, 505
journals, 1
multimodal, 5
new directions in, 3–5
psychophysiological contributions to, 351–352, 383–403, 509
and prevention, 457–469, 473
and social psychology, 255–267, 317–320, 506
stress–coping–vulnerability model and, 339–340
theoretical and empirical foundations of, 1–7
in the treatment of neurologically impaired adults, 227–249, 501–502
unconscious processes in, 4
Behavioral activation system (BAS), 385
Behavioral assessment:
and attributional approach, 286–288
child, 57–58, 493–494
criteria for the evaluation of, 361–362
decision making in, 199–200
differences with psychometric assessment, 353
and information processing approach, 293–297
models of, 352–353
of neurological patients, 233–236, 501
psychophysiology and, 348–374, 508
and social support, 275, 279
theoretical contributions of psychophysiology to, 367–373
Behavioral Inattention Test (BIT), 233
Behavioral inhibition system (BIS), 385
Behavioral medicine, 4, 286, 326, 341, 350, 351, 352, 354, 360, 387
Behavioral observation systems, 65, 69, 465
Behavioral recording methods, 235–236
Behavioral treatment strategies:
for decreasing behaviors in the neurologically impaired, 236–238, 501–502
for increasing behaviors in the neurologically impaired, 238–246, 501–502
Behavioral-exchange model of close relationship discord, 265–266, 503
Behaviorism, 5, 117, 256–258, 284, 459–463, 502, 512–513
Belongingness, 414, 428
Benzodiazapine tranquilizers as a context for extinction, 442–444
Bereavement:
as a factor promoting health-risk behaviors, 333
and immune status, 336
and social support, 273
Berkeley Guidance Study, 87
Biofeedback, 340, 352, 387, 393–397, 399–401, 402, 403, 509
Biological constraints on learning, 414–415
Biological model of development, 16
Biopsychosocial perspective, 357
Blindsight, 104
Bone marrow aspirations (BMAs), 65, 66, 69
Bootstrapping, 208, 500
Bottom-up processes, 110, 124, 295, 496
Bower's network model of mood and cognition, 106–107, 122, 123–126, 130, 132, 134, 135, 137, 138, 140, 141, 156, 496
Brain function therapy, 248

Cancer, 329, 337–338
Carbon dioxide enriched air inhalation, 392
Cardiac-somatic coupling hypothesis, 370

SUBJECT INDEX

Cardiac arrhythmias, 338, 396, 509
Cardiac deceleration, 349–350
Cerebral palsy, 242–244
Chaining or method of vanishing cues, 240–241, 247
Child abuse, 92, 476
Child Behavior Checklist (CBC), 62–63, 66–67, 68, 493–494
Childhood temper tantrums, 87, 494
Chlordiazepoxide (librium), as a context for extinction, 442–444
Chumship, 78
Chunking, 187
Circular functions, 21, 25, 27
Classification scheme of parenting, 77
Client-centered therapy, 460, 474, 512
Cognition, definition of, 152, 370
Cognitive Bias Questionnaire (CBQ), 132, 185
Cognitive Competency Test, 233
Cognitive consistency, theories of, 261, 313–314
Cognitive development level and treatment, 83–85
Cognitive misers, people as, 285, 294, 314, 506
Cognitive neuropsychology:
    definition of, 216–217, 500
    and rehabilitation, 217–225, 501
    and treatment methods, 225–226, 501
Cognitive processes, 126, 171, 176, 284, 496
Cognitive products, 126, 171, 175–176, 496
Cognitive psychology:
    and assessment and treatment of anxiety, 151–165
    and assessment and treatment of depression, 169–189
    definition of, 103, 500
    interface with social psychology, 284–285
Cognitive psychophysiology, 384
Cognitive Response Test (CRT), 181, 184
Cognitive restructuring, 163, 164, 236, 278, 498
Cognitive structures. (*See* Knowledge structures)
Cognitive styles, 160
Cognitive therapy, 111, 143, 163, 164, 165, 180, 182–189, 289, 371, 388, 393, 400, 498, 499, 517
Cognitive triad, 170
Cognitive-behavior modification, 4, 5, 236, 296
Cognitivism, 117, 143
Collaborative empiricism, 185
Communication, 259–260
Community psychology, 459, 461, 473, 475, 478, 482, 483, 489
Comparative psychology, 427, 428
Comparison levels, 264
Compensation model of change, 183, 499
Competence, 37, 42, 46, 48, 50, 278, 459, 460, 461, 462, 477, 478, 487, 493, 512, 513
Computer simulation, 293
Concentration problems, 234
Concept formation, 299
Conceptually driven processes. (*See* Top-down processes)
Concrete operational period, 75, 83, 84, 486, 494
Conditioning:

classical or Pavlovian, 116, 156, 264–265, 391, 415, 416
compound, 439
context, 437, 447
instrumental or operant, 116, 259–260, 264–265, 395, 415, 440
intereoceptive, 154
verbal, 265
Conduct problems, 87
Confirmatory bias, 199
Conscious processes. (*See* Controlled processes)
Consistency seekers, people as, 313–314, 506
Contextualist philosophy, 15
Continuity-discontinuity of behavior:
    in antisocial behavior, 89
    in attention deficit hyperactivity disorder, 88
    behavioral continuity, 88, 495
    cognitive continuity, 88, 495
    cumulative continuity, 87
    in depression, 88, 89
    descriptive continuity, 68–69, 494
    explanatory continuity, 69, 494
    interactional continuity, 87
    in schizophrenia, 89
Contraceptive use, knowledge, attitudes and behavior, 84
Controlled processes, 111–113, 152, 173, 178, 184, 298, 370, 372, 373, 496, 517
Conversation of gestures, 257
Coping Strategies Questionnaire, 276
Coping style:
    dimensions of, 276, 504
    interaction with social support, 277, 504
    and level of depression, 276
    and posttraumatic stress disorder, 276, 504
    sex differences, 276–277
    and stress, 276
    and types of demand, 277
Coronary artery atherosclerosis, 326, 330, 334
Coronary heart disease, 329, 331, 334, 336, 338
Counter-attitudinal behavior, 318
Counterconditioning, 48, 261, 391
Countertransference, 310, 311, 315, 506
Courage, 389
Crandell Cognition Checklist (CCC), 111, 126
Crime prevention and intervention, 462
Criterion-referenced approach, 61

Data-driven processes. *See* Bottom-up processes
Decision analysis, 210–212, 500
Decision making:
    applications of information processing approach to behavioral assessment, 296–297
    clinical, 196–213
Decision models and decision aids, 206–213, 500
Decision tree, 201–211
Deep structure, 175, 176, 183, 184, 187

SUBJECT INDEX

Defense response (DR), 369
Deliberate processes. *See* Controlled processes
Delinquent adolescents, 90–91
Demands, psychosocial, 327, 507
Dementia, 241–242
Depression. *See also* Beck's cognitive theory of depression; Cognitive triad; Depressogenic attributional style; Depressotypic schemata; Depressotypic thinking; Helplessness; Hopelessness theory of depression; Kuiper's self-schema theory of depression; Rehm's self-control theory of depression; Seligman's helplessness theory of depression
  access bias in, 173–174, 177
  assessment of cognition in, 178–182
  associated with neurological impairment, 230, 236
  attention processes in, 138–140, 497
  attributional styles in, 170, 172, 176, 289
  automatic cognitive processes in, 111, 119
  bipolar, 445
  cognition and the treatment of, 182–189
  cognitive deficits in, 117–120, 122, 174, 496
  cognitive errors in, 170, 173, 176, 178
  cognitive or knowledge structures in, 174–175
  cognitive processes in, 128–130, 132–133, 138–140, 176, 497
  cognitive products in, 126–127, 175–176, 496
  cognitive theories of, 170–171
  cognitive vulnerability factor for, 111–113
  comprehension processes in, 132–133, 140, 497
  continuity–discontinuity in, 88, 89, 495
  and coping style, 276
  in children and adolescents, 67, 81
  a framework for evaluating cognitive factors in, 172–173
  a meaning systems perspective on cognitive factors in, 174–177, 498
  memory deficits in, 118–119
  memory processes in, 109, 128–130, 140, 497
  motivational approach to, 385
  an operational perspective on cognitive factors in, 171
  prevalence of, 116
  reinforcement and, 265
  self-references in, 171, 172
  and social support, 272, 273, 274, 275
  strategic cognitive processes in, 119
Depressogenic attributional style, 170, 180
Depressotypic schemata, 173
Depressotypic thinking, 173
Desistance, 42, 43, 50, 493
Desynchrony, 365–367, 368, 373, 388–389, 508, 515
Development-stage specific therapies, 81
Developmental antecedents of maladaptation, 86, 87, 88
Developmental contextual perspective, 14–29, 59, 491–492
Developmental lines, 44
Developmental manual, 44, 46
Developmental milestones, 74, 478

Developmental norms and treatment, 82, 494
Developmental predictors, using knowledge of, 86–88, 494
Developmental psychopathology:
  definition of, 35, 74, 492
  implications for assessment, 46, 492–493
  implications for classification and diagnosis, 43–46, 492
  implications for prevention, 50, 493
  implications for treatment, 46–50, 81–82, 88–89, 493
  tenents for, 37–43, 492
  origins of, 36–37
Developmental psychophysiology, 384–385
Developmental tasks, 39–40, 45, 46, 48
Developmental therapy, 91, 495
Developmental trajectories, 17, 41, 48, 50, 492, 493
Developmental transitions:
  multiple, 85, 494
  and treatment, 85–86, 478, 494
  as a window for viewing developmental processes, 41
Diabetes, 335, 336, 337, 339
Diagnostic and Statistical Manual (DSM), 36–37, 38, 43–45, 68, 397, 475
Dialectical models of development, 14, 15
Diazepam (valium) as a context for extinction, 442–443
Direct instruction, 460
Discordance:
  between system, 368, 370–373, 417, 508
  definition of, 365, 366
  within system, 368–370, 508
Discrimination learning, 261
Disease:
  pathways to, 331–338, 507
  psychobiological processes in the etiology of, 325–341, 507
  stability, 336–338, 340, 507
Disinhibition, 436
Distractability, 160
Divergent perspectives hypothesis. *See* Actor–observer differences
Divorce, child adjustment to, 83, 88
Downward arrow technique, 188
Drug dependence, 444
Dyadic interaction, 266
Dysfunctional Attitudes Scale (DAS), 126, 180, 184, 499
Dyslexia, acquired, 222–224, 249

Ecological perspective, 15, 18, 21, 26, 44, 46, 47, 298–299, 413, 426–427, 457–469, 473, 475, 478, 480, 481, 483, 489, 505, 513, 514
Ecological processes:
  adaptation, 467–468, 513
  cycling of resources, 466–467, 513
  interdependence, 464–466, 513
  succession, 467, 513
Effortful processes. *See* Controlled processes
Ego development, 76, 80

Egocentrism, 75, 84, 91
Elaboration, 108–109, 141–143, 157, 160
Elementarism, 14
Elementary social behavior, 263
Embeddedness:
  in community context, 25
  definition of, 480
  historical, 16
  mutual, 17
  in social context, 18, 20, 21
Emotional behavior, mediating role between stress and health, 333
Empowerment approach, 478
Environmental design, 475
Epigenetic development:
  predetermined, 16, 59, 491
  probabilistic, 16–18, 29, 492
Epigenetic landscape, 41
Equipotentiality:
  of intervention techniques across life, 29
  premise of general process learning theory, 415
Ethnotheory, 22–23
Ethology, 428
Event-related field (ERF), 386
Event-related potential (ERP), 386
Evolutionary perspective to acquisition of phobic behavior, 370, 391
Exercise, 330
Expanding rehearsal, 241–242
Expert systems, 209–210, 500
Exposure therapy, 163, 164, 165, 372, 373, 389, 390, 428, 430, 441, 446, 448, 449, 450, 498
Externalizing problems, 68, 67, 88
Extinction:
  background stimuli as contexts for fear, 446–448
  of biologically prepared stimuli, 391, 428–430
  contextual analysis of fear extinction, 435–450, 511–512, 515
  drugs as interoceptive contexts for fear, 441–444, 449, 511
  emotional states and stress as contexts for fear, 444–446, 512
  as a major way of modifying behavior, 261
  passage of time as contexts for fear, 446, 512
  reacquisition after, 440, 511
  for reducing aggression, 236
  reinstatement of extinguished fear, 436–437, 440, 446, 447, 448, 449, 511
  renewal of extinguished fear, 437–440, 442, 446, 448, 449, 511

False heart rate feedback, 393
Family therapy, 85, 230, 298
Fear of fear, 154, 497
Fear of Negative Evaluation scale, 161
Fear Survey Schedule for Children, Revised (FSSC-R), 63–64, 68–69

Fear. *See* Anxiety
Festinger's theory of cognitive dissonance, 261–263, 313–314, 503
Field theory, 258, 312
Flooding, 116, 429
Formal operational thinking, 75, 84, 91, 486
Formative research methods, 480
Fowles motivational approach to psychophysiology and psychopathology, 385
Frames, 175
Functional analysis, 62
Fundamental attribution error, 287–288, 504

Gender differences, 63–65, 67
Generalizability models, 362, 363
Generalized anxiety disorder, 109–110, 113, 127, 131, 132, 136, 137, 142, 158, 372, 496
Genital herpes infection, 336
Gestalt psychology, 259, 284, 312
Goodness of fit model, 21–29, 492

Habituation, 160, 164
Hardiness, 478
Head injury, 219, 228, 229, 230, 231, 234, 235, 236–237
Headaches:
  biofeedback for, 399–401, 402, 509–510
  and changes in mood, 337
  classification of, 397, 402
  psychophysiological contributions to, 401–403
  psychophysiological mechanisms, 398–399, 401, 402, 509
  stress-related reactions, 334
Health enhancement, 473, 447–478, 482, 487, 489, 513
Health promotion, 475, 480, 481, 482, 485, 514
Health psychology, 473, 483, 514
Health-risk behavior, 333, 507
Helplessness, 160
Heuristics:
  anchoring with adjustment, 178
  availability, 156, 177, 201–202, 294, 295, 296, 500
  cognitive or judgment, 133, 173, 184, 201–206, 294, 297, 314, 498, 499–500, 505
  representativeness, 178, 202–205, 298, 500
Hindsight bias, 206, 500
Homeostasis, 44
Homeostatic reconditioning, 399
Hopelessness Scale (HS), 181, 184
Hopelessness theory of depression, 170, 498
Hyperreactivity, psychophysiological, 334–335, 340, 507
Hypertension, 326, 329, 330, 331, 333, 334, 335, 340, 395, 396, 397, 479, 509
Hyperventilation, 392–393
Hypervigilance, 155, 497

Identity crises, 76
Identity formation, 76

Idiographic approach, 60–61, 62, 352, 353, 362, 363–364, 493
Illusory correlation, 178, 199, 202, 296, 499
Imagery, 48, 383, 387
Imitation, 259, 260–261
Immune status and stress, 336, 338
Implosive therapy, 435
In vivo exposure, 48, 449, 512
Individual-response specificity, 330, 363
Individuality:
  behavioral, 19, 21–23
  physical, 20–23, 27
Inferences, 177, 178
Information overload, 201, 499
Information processing approach (IPA) to social cognition:
  clinical applications, 293–298
  description, 292–293
Insensitivity:
  to predictability, 204–205, 500
  to prior probabilities, 202–203, 500
  to sample size, 203–204, 500
Insomnia, 356
Interactivity, 480
Internalizing problems, 63, 67, 88
Interoceptive:
  awareness, 158
  conditioning, 154
  contexts, 441–444
  feared stimuli, 160
Intervening variables, 103, 365
Intervention mode:
  seeking, 476–477, 478, 482, 483, 513
  waiting, 476–477, 482, 513
Introspection, 104, 106, 117, 128, 516–517
Intuitive or naive scientists, people as, 285, 314, 504, 506
Invulnerability, 478
Irrational Beliefs Test (IBT), 126
Irritable bowel syndrome, 333, 334
Isomorphism, 181–182, 184

Judgments, 169, 173, 177, 178, 183, 196–213, 294, 295, 296, 297

Knowledge:
  declarative, 106, 495
  procedural, 106, 495
  structures, 171, 174–175, 292, 294–297, 300, 498, 505
Kuiper's self-schema theory of depression, 171

Labeling effects, 288
Lang's bioinformational theory of emotion, 153–154, 156, 162, 164, 354, 370, 371, 372, 385, 389–391, 509
Law of effect, 81, 260
Learning approach to social behavior, 259, 502

Letter-sound rule system, 219–221, 226, 501
Life skills training, 478
Life span perspective, 15–16, 17, 18, 478, 513
Lifespace, 312–313, 315, 316
Linear models, 208–209, 210, 212, 500
Locus of control, 274, 275, 329, 401, 510
Longitudinal perspective, 16

Maladaptive functioning, 14, 17, 18
Mand, 262
Marital discord, 265–266, 286, 287, 289, 290, 291, 326, 336
Marital stress, 83
Mastery and pleasure, 187
Mastery, experience of, 160, 172
Matching theory, 463
Mechanistic model of development, 13–14, 16, 17, 58–59, 70, 491, 493
Media role in acquisition of fears, 427–428
Medical model, 459–460, 474
Melanomas, 332
Memory:
  episodic, 105–106, 173, 495
  explicit, 109–110, 113, 142, 495–496
  implicit, 109–110, 113, 142, 495–496
  levels-of-processing theory of, 108–109, 495
  long-term, 104–109, 160, 495
  multistore model of, 104
  processes of, 108–110, 495
  representations of, 160–161
  semantic, 105–106, 173, 495
  sensory, 104, 495
  short-term, 104–105, 160, 495
  structural aspects of, 104–108, 495
  therapy, 247, 502
  working memory system, 105, 107, 121–122, 495
Menarche, 20–21
Mental health needs and resources, 458, 475–477, 512, 513
Mental health system, 458, 460, 461, 512
Mentalism, 117, 128
Metacognition, 75, 298
Mind, 257
Minded behavior, 257
Minnesota Multiphasic Personality Inventory (MMPI), 209
Misattribution, 286–287, 515
Mnemonics, 221–222, 226, 247–248
Modeling, 48, 90, 232, 260–261, 413–431, 510–511
Mood congruity, 156, 157
Moral development, 76, 79, 90
Moral reasoning. See Moral development
Morality:
  autonomous, 78
  heteronomous, 78
Morphological processing during reading, impaired, 222–224
Motivation, 314–315

SUBJECT INDEX

Motor skills analogy of biofeedback, 395, 509
Multilevel analysis and theory, 481–482, 483, 484, 485, 514
Multimethod assessment, 58
Multiple regression analysis, 208
Multitrait-multimethod analysis, 366
Myocardial infarction, 332, 338

Naive psychology, 285–286, 290
Naturalistic contingencies, use of, 466, 468
Neobehavioristic mediational S-R model, 5
Network therapy, 274, 279
Neurological conditions:
  behavioural assessment of, 233–236, 501
  behavioral techniques in the treatment of 230–233, 501
  prevalence, 228
  problems faced by people with, 229–230
Neuromagnetometry, 386
Neuropsychology:
  assessment in, 233
  and behavior therapy, 231
  definition of, 216, 233
  and knowledge of the organization of the brain, 248
Neuropsychophysiology, 384
New York Longitudinal Study (NYLS), 23–25
Niche:
  developmental, 22
  ecological, 468
  niche-picking, 87
Nodes:
  emotion, 106–107, 124–125, 171, 173
  memory, 123
Nomothetic approach, 60–61, 62, 353, 362, 364, 493
Nonconscious processes. *See* Automatic processes
Nondeliberate processes. *See* Automatic processes
Nonverbal behavior, 266
Normative contextual and environmental changes:
  changes in family relations, 77–78
  changes in peer relations, 78–79
  effects of the school context, 79
  effects of working, 79–80
Normative intra-individual changes:
  changes in social role, 76–77
  cognitive and psychological changes, 75–76
  physical changes, 74–75
Normative-developmental perspective, 60
Nutrition, 330

Object naming, 217–218, 500
Object relations approaches, 315
Observational conditioning. *See* Modeling
Observational learning. *See* Modeling
Obsessional disorder, 135, 390
Ontogeny, 14, 16, 17, 21, 413, 414
Operant parent training skills, 87
Organismic model of development, 13–14, 16, 17, 58–59, 70, 491, 493

Orienting response (OR), 349, 359, 369
Overconfidence in decision making, 205–206
Overshadowing, 424–426, 510

Pain, 156, 164, 198, 212, 276, 334
Panic disorder, 127, 132, 136, 153–154, 155, 156–157, 158, 162, 163, 392–393, 498, 509, 515
Paradigms:
  discriminative observational conditioning, 414, 417, 421
  dot probe, 136–137, 138, 158, 162, 497
  double dissociation, 415, 416, 422
  ecological, 457, 463–469
  habituation, 359
  information processing, 117, 128, 143, 496
  lexical decision, 138–139
  in psychophysiology, 359–360
  Stroop color naming, 135–136, 158, 162, 497
Paraprofessionals as change agents, 462, 474, 475
Pardoxical intention, 389
Parent training program, 465–466
Path analysis, 25–28, 277
Patterning of behaviors, 66–68
Peer acceptance, 86, 90
Peers, involvement in child and adolescent treatment, 89–90, 92, 495
Pennsylvania Early Adolescent Transitions Study (PEATS), 25–29
Perception. *See* Attention
Perceptual threshold, 162
Performance based tasks, 162
Person prototype or persona, 175
Personality in relation to clinical disorders, 328–329
Perspective-taking, 76, 90–91
Persuasive communications, 317–318, 506
Pharmacotherapy, 180, 182, 184
Phonics, 220, 226
Phylogeny, 427
Physiological psychology, 349, 384
Piaget's theory:
  of children's morality, 78
  of cognitive development, 59, 75
Plasticity, 13, 16, 17, 29
Plateau and cliff effect, 210
Portage, 244–245
Posttraumatic stress disorder (PTSD), 274, 276, 327, 504
Potentiation, 425–426
Preattentive processes. *See* Automatic processes
PRECEDE model, 478–480, 514
Prediction, clinical versus statistical, 207–208
Pregnancy, adolescent, 83–84
Preoperational period, 75, 83
Preparedness, 369, 370, 391–392, 413, 414, 428–430, 509, 511, 515
Prevention:
  of acquisition of fears, 430
  of adolescent pregnancy, 485

and behaviorism, 459–463, 512–513
for children about to experience multiple transitions, 85, 494
implications of developmental psychopathology for, 50, 493
primary, 459, 462, 476–477, 478, 482, 512, 513
in psychology, 458–459
of reinstatement of fears, 449
of relapse, 188–189, 449
secondary, 459, 461, 462, 465, 476–477, 478, 482, 512, 513
of smoking, 485
tertiary, 459, 476–477, 482, 512, 513
Primacy of affect versus cognition, 152–153, 370–371, 497
Proactive interventions, 476–477, 482, 487, 489, 512, 513
Problem space, 352
Process of change schema, 485–486, 488
Prompting, 239–240
Propositions:
  meaning, 153, 162, 164, 165, 389–390
  response, 153, 162, 164, 370, 371, 389–390
  stimulus, 153, 162, 164, 371, 389–390
Protective factors, 88
Pseudodiagnosticity, 203
Psychiatric classification, 36–37
Psychoanalysis, 309–310, 311, 315, 459–460, 474, 477, 491, 492, 506, 512, 517
Psychobiology, 325, 350
Psychometric assessment:
  differences with behavioral assessment, 353
  and group data, 362–363
  psychophysiological approaches to, 356–358
Psychophysiological assessment:
  ambulatory recording, 386, 388
  designs and paradigms, 359–360
  evaluation and limitations of, 361–367
  internal consistency of, 363
  selection of measures, 358
  situational consistency of, 362–363
  temporal stability of, 362–363
  types of measures, 358–359
Psychophysiological disorders. See Psychosomatic disorders
Psychophysiological markers:
  as discriminative indices, 357
  sensitivity of, 356–357
  specificity of, 356–357
Psychophysiology:
  applications to behavior therapy, 351–352, 383–403
  and behavioral assessment, 348–374, 508
  clinical, 350–351, 353–354, 384
  definition of, 349–350, 384
  journals and texts, 384
  technical developments in, 385–387
  theoretical developments in, 385

Psychosomatic disorders, 325, 350, 363, 397
Psychotherapy:
  client variables in, 316
  concerns about efficacy, 458
  definition of, 309
  integrationism in, 4–5, 517
  process variables in, 317
  psychophysiological assessment in, 350, 351, 367
  as a social process, 308–320
  and social psychology, 315–317
  therapist variables in, 316–317
Pubertal development, 74–75, 80
Public health, 458–459, 473, 475–476, 478, 481, 482, 483, 484, 489, 512, 514
Punishment, 48, 236, 260, 265, 266

Quadriplegia, 244–245

Rational emotive therapy, 289
Raynaud's disease, 396–397, 509
Reading errors:
  morphological, 222
  semantic, 222
  visual, 222
Reading, models of, 219–221, 225–226, 247, 248, 501
Real relationship, 310, 315, 506
Reattribution as an adjunctive therapy technique, 289
Recall. See Memory
Reciprocal determinism, 5
Reciprocity, symmetrical, 78
Reductionism, 14
Regularity of behavior. See Rhythmicity of behavior
Rehm's self-control theory of depression, 170–171
Reinforcement:
  positive, 48, 232, 236, 242–244, 260–261, 265, 266
  reciprocal, 488
  vicarious, 260
Relapse prevention, 188–189, 449
Relations:
  bidirectional, 17
  between organismic and contextual processes, 17–18
  peer, 25–26
  in psychopathology, 14, 15
  reciprocal, 16
  between temperament and problem behaviors, 20
  temperament-psychosocial functioning, 26
Relaxational training, 165, 232, 236, 238, 278, 279, 340, 355, 356, 389, 396–397, 399, 400, 401, 403, 501, 510
Research Diagnostic Criteria, 36
Resilience, 37, 42, 330
Resistance in therapy, 297, 298
Resources:
  cycling of, 466–467
  generation of, 478
  psychosocial, 327–329, 507
Responders, cognitive versus somatic, 355

SUBJECT INDEX

Response–response relationships, 61, 67, 68
Response stereotypy, 399, 401, 509
Retrieval. *See also* Memory
 active, 157
 passive, 157
 problems of, 478
Reward. *See* Reinforcement, positive
Rheumatoid arthritis, 235, 328, 335, 337
Rhythmicity of behavior, 23–24, 27
Ripple effects, 464–465, 513
Risk research, 37, 88
Rivermead Behavioral Memory Test (RBMT), 233
Role-taking, 257
 skills, 83

Sackett Circus tests, 417
Safety signal perspective of agoraphobia, 156
Salutogenic approach, 478, 482
Schemata, 107–108, 123–125, 154, 155, 156, 158–159, 160, 162, 170, 172, 173, 174–175, 182, 183, 294, 297, 298, 495, 505
Schizophrenia, 37, 41–42, 274, 297, 356, 357
Scientist-practitioner split, 6–7
Scripts, 175, 292
Selective associations:
 history of interest in, 414–415
 methodological requirements for demonstration of, 415–416
 in origins of phobic fears, 413–431, 510–511, 515
Self, 257
Self-concept, 76
Self-control:
 development of, 260–261
 training in adolescents, 82, 494
 training in children, 47, 493
Self-efficacy, 133, 160, 278, 327, 329, 401, 486, 510
Self-esteem, 76, 79, 84, 170, 329
Self-help groups. *See* Support groups
Self-instructional training, 48–49, 83, 494
Self-monitoring, 187
Self-perception, 262–263, 503
Self-presentation, 266
Self-schemata, 105–106, 171, 172, 173–174, 175, 177, 498
Self-serving bias in attribution, 315
Seligman's helplessness theory of depression, 170, 498
Selman's theory of the growth of interpersonal understanding, 78, 80, 90
Semantic networks. *See* Associative networks
Sensorimotor period, 75
Sensorimotor processes. *See* Automatic processes
Separation anxiety disorder, 67–68
Sequential compensation–accommodation model of change, 183–185, 499
Service delivery strategies, 457–458, 460, 461, 468, 469, 473–477, 482, 488–489, 512–513
Sex education, 84, 85

Sexual abuse, 83
Sexual disorders, 357
Sharing behavior, modification of, 466
Single-case studies, 218, 223, 246–247, 359, 362, 363–364, 502
Smoking, cigarettes,
 prevention, 485
 as a response to stress, 333
 treatment of, 275
 understanding acquisition, 483
Social act, 257–258
Social adaptation, 45
Social analogue, 311–312, 315, 506
Social behavior, 311–312
Social behaviorism, 256–258, 502
Social cognition:
 attributional approach to, 258, 285–292, 504–505
 and behavior therapy, 288–290, 297–298, 505
 and behavioral assessment, 286–288, 293–297, 504
 definition of, 284–285
 history of, 284–285
 information processing approach to, 292–300, 505
 models of, 313–314
Social cognitive development, 75–76
Social competence, 46, 61, 62, 272
Social interaction, 264, 265, 300–301, 360
Social learning theory, 5, 59, 260–261, 315, 480, 493
Social marketing, 478–480, 482, 483, 488, 514
Social network. *See* Social support
Social phobia, 127, 135, 161, 162, 164, 278, 355, 366, 369, 389, 390, 391
Social psychology:
 and behavior modification, 317–320
 characteristics of, 315
 definition of, 255–256, 311
 history of, 256–260, 284, 502
 journals, 256–265
 links with clinical psychology, 256, 265, 286, 308
 and psychotherapy research, 315–317
 of relationships, 313–315
 theorizing in, 312–313
Social psychophysiology, 385
Social relationships, 311
Social skills:
 children in training, 47, 85, 90, 91
 general psychiatric problems, training for, 278
 negative social behaviors, training for, 278
 and psychopathology, 277–278, 504
 schizophrenics, training in, 274, 278
 shyness and social phobias, training for, 278
Social support:
 buffer interaction effect hypothesis of, 271, 272, 275, 329
 changes in as a side effect of treatment, 465–466
 and coping style, 276–277, 504
 definition of, 271–272, 503
 direct main effect hypothesis of, 271, 272, 275, 329

measurement of, 271, 272
and mortality, 334
and psychopathology, 272–275, 503
as a treatment modality, 274, 278, 279, 503
Social-cognitive games, 90
Social-cognitive theory, 480–481, 482, 485, 514
Socialization, 257
Sodium lactate infusion, 392
Spider phobia, 131, 135–136, 158, 161
Spoken word production, 219–221
Spontaneous recovery, 436, 440, 446
Startle response (SR), 369
State dependent retention:
   drug, 441–444, 511–512
   mood, 156, 157, 174, 445, 497
Statistical regression, 205, 500
Stimulus–Organism–Response–Consequence (SORC) model, 352, 354
Stimulus control, 236
Storm and stress beliefs, 82
Strategic processes, 119, 121, 122
Strategy training, 460
Stress:
   biological vulnerability to, 330–331, 507
   as a context for extinction, 444–446
   and coping style, 276, 329
   in families of head injured, 230
   and immune status, 336, 338
   management, 278–279, 340, 397, 403
   responses, psychobiological, 329–330, 507
   and social support, 271, 272, 273, 274
   stress–coping–vulnerability models, 327–331, 507
Stressor-support specificity model of buffering, 271–272
Stroke, 222, 228, 229, 230, 231, 232, 234, 236, 237–238
Structural/behavioral model of development, 70
Subjective expected utility (SEU), 207, 210–212
Success therapy, 187
Sullivan's theory of the development of peer relations, 78
Support groups:
   formal, 275, 278, 279, 503
   self-help, 275, 278, 462
Surface structure, 175, 176, 183, 188
Systematic desensitization, 1, 48, 81, 116, 233, 236, 238, 390, 435
Systems theory, 41, 350, 464

Tact, 262
Teleology, 13–14
Temperament, 19–20, 21, 23–27
Template matching, 478
Test of Functional Communication for Aphasic Adults, 233
Theories:
   of emotion, 369, 370, 371, 387, 392
   psychophysiological, 367–373
   role of, 3

Therapeutic alliance, 310, 311, 315, 506
Therapist–client relationship, 308, 309–311
Thought sampling techniques, 161, 179
Three systems theory, 354–355, 364–367, 371, 373, 387, 388–389, 508, 509, 515
Time out, 236
Time series methods, 467
Top-down processes, 110, 124, 293, 295, 496
Topological psychology, 258
Tourette syndrome, 359
Training in child/adolescent clinical psychology, 92
Transference, 309–310, 315, 506
Transformational rules, 175, 176
Treatment utility model, 362, 364–367
Type A behavior, 340

Uncertainty:
   judgment under, 177, 294
   prevalence and, 200
   sources of, 198, 499
Unconscious processes. See Automatic processes
Uncontrollability, perceived, 160, 163
Uninformity myth:
   developmental, 73, 81, 494
   patient, 73
   therapist, 73

Validity:
   of analogue research, 360
   conceptual, 364, 508
   concurrent, 363, 364, 366
   construct, 363
   convergent, 296
   discriminant, 368
   ecological, 233, 469
   external, 299
   illusion of, 204–205, 500
   psychological test, 198–199
   social, 66
   treatment, 364, 365, 366, 367, 508
Verbal behavior, 262, 266
Vigilance:
   for danger, 156, 157
   for safety, 155–156
Visceral learning, 395, 397
Visual word recognition, impaired, 219–222, 223, 225–226
Vividness bias, 314
Vulnerability:
   biological, 330–331
   host, 335, 340, 507
   models of psychiatric disorders, 357
   to mood disorders, 111–114, 496, 517

Ways of Coping Questionnaire, 276
Wisconsin General Test Apparatus (WGTA), 417, 418, 419, 420, 421, 422, 425, 430
Withdrawn children, treatment for, 89–90, 466
World Health Organization, 45

Yerkes-Dodson law of relationship between arousal and performance 159
Yohimbine, 158

ABOUT THE EDITOR AND CONTRIBUTORS

ABOUT THE EDITOR

Paul R. Martin, DPhil, is director of the Clinical Psychology Unit and director of the Adoption Research and Counseling Service at the University of Western Australia. His interests are in the fields of behavior therapy, health psychology, and psychophysiology. The major focus of his research activities has been to develop a new model of chronic headaches based on functional characteristics rather than symptomatology. He has received a number of grants from the National Health and Medical Research Council to support his headache research program. He is on the editorial board of *Behaviour Change* and *International Review of Health Psychology*. Dr. Martin is a past president of the Australian Behaviour Modification Association.

ABOUT THE CONTRIBUTORS

David G. Altman, PhD, is senior research scientist and associate director of the Health Promotion Resource Center at the Stanford Center for Research in Disease Prevention, Stanford University School of Medicine. His primary research interests include community health promotion, tobacco control, and public health advocacy.

David H. Barlow, PhD, is professor in the Department of Psychology at the State University of New York at Albany, co-director of the Center for Stress and Anxiety Disorders, and director of the Phobia and Anxiety Disorders Clinic. He has published over 150 articles and chapters and nine books, mostly in the areas of anxiety disorders, sexual problems, and clinical research methodology. Recent books include *Clinical Handbook of Psychological Disorders: A Step-by-Step Treatment Manual, Psychological Treatment of Panic* (with Cerny), and *Anxiety and its Disorders: The Nature and Treatment of Anxiety and Panic*. The major objective of his work for the last ten years has been the development of new treatments for anxiety disorders, and he was recently awarded a merit award from the National Institute of Mental Health.

Mark E. Bouton, PhD, is associate professor of psychology at the University of Vermont. He has published articles on a number of topics in learning, but his primary research interest is the role of context and memory processes in Pavlovian conditioning. A recent sabbatical leave to the University of Cambridge was supported by a fellowship from the United Kingdom Fulbright Commission and by a James McKeen Cattell Sabbatical Award.

Thomas N. Bradbury, PhD, is assistant professor of psychology at the University of California at Los Angeles and is the author of numerous research articles and book chapters on affective and cognitive aspects of marital interaction. He is co-editor of *The Psychology of Marriage*. His theoretical and research interests include factors that contribute to the development and remediation of marital dysfunction.

Lauren Braswell, PhD, is a psychologist with North Memorial Medical Center's Child Guidance Clinic in Minneapolis, Minnesota. She is an instructor for the child clinical training program at the University of Minnesota. Her research and publications have addressed treatment outcome and process considerations with attentionally disordered children. With Philip Kendall, she coauthored *Cognitive-Behavioral Therapy with Impulsive Children*.

Mary L. Burgess, MA, is a doctoral candidate in social psychology at the University of Iowa and is an associate editor for *Representative Research in Social Psychology*. Her research interests include examining the effects of anxiety and mood on the cognitive processing of social information and on intergroup relations. She has also published a paper on the detection of prejudiced behavior.

Nancy S. Burgoyne, MA, is a doctoral candidate in the clinical/community psychology program at DePaul University, and a research associate at the University of Illinois, Institute for Juvenile Research. She is currently investigating the impact of community variables on Mexican families in cultural transition.

Max Coltheart, PhD, is professor of psychology and coordinator of the clinical psychology program at Macquarie University. He was editor of the *British Journal of Psychology* from 1979 to 1983. He founded the journal *Cognitive Neuropsychology* in 1984, and is currently its editor-in-chief. Books he has written or edited include *Deep Dyslexia, Surface Dyslexia, The Cognitive Neuropsychology of Language, Language Processing in Children and Adults,* and *The Psychology of Reading*. He was president of the Experimental Psychology Society from 1985 to 1987, received the President's Award of the British Psychological Society in 1987. His interests are in cognitive neuropsychology and in the computational modeling of cognition.

Michael Cook, PhD, is a research associate in the Department of Rehabilitation Medicine at the University of Wisconsin–Madison. He received his PhD in psychology from the University of Wisconsin in 1988. In 1990, he received the Outstanding Dissertation Award from APA's Division 12 (Section 3) for portions of the work described in this chapter. He has published in the area of fear conditioning, observational learning, and selective associations.

Michelle G. Craske, PhD, is assistant professor of psychology in the clinical psychology program at the University of California, Los Angeles. She has published many articles and chapters in the area of anxiety disorders, and is currently a member of the DSM-IV anxiety disorders work group subcommittee for revision of the diagnostic criteria surrounding panic disorder and simple phobia.

Michael W. Eysenck, PhD, is professor of psychology at Royal Holloway and Bedford New College, University of London. He was the founding editor of *The European Journal of Cognitive Psychology,* and is the author of *Attention and Arousal: Cognition and Performance* and *Happiness: Facts and Myths*.

Frank D. Fincham, PhD, is associate professor of psychology at the University of Illinois at Urbana–Champaign. He is an associate editor of *Cognition and Emotion,* sits on the editorial boards of several journals in social and clinical psychology, and is co-editor of the books *Attribution Theory and Research, The Psychology of Marriage,* and *Cognition in Close Relationships*. The recipient of several professional awards, including a Rhodes Scholarship and the Gerald R. Miller Award for early career achievements, his interests center on marital dysfunction and on the relation between marital conflict and children's adjustment.

John H. Harvey, PhD, is professor of psychology at the University of Iowa. Previously he was at Vanderbilt and Texas Tech Universities. His major focus is on attribution theory, especially as applied to dynamics in close relationships. He has been co-editor (with

Ickes and Kidd) of the three-volume series *New Directions in Attribution,* coauthor (with Weary) of *Perspectives on Attributional Processes,* coauthor (with Kelley and others) of *Close Relationships,* coauthor (with Weary and Stanley) of *Attribution,* coauthor (with Weber and Orbuch) of *Interpersonal Accounts: A Social Psychological Perspective,* and co-editor (with Orbuch and Weber) of *Attributions, Accounts and Close Relationships.* He was also founding editor of the *Journal of Social and Clinical Psychology.*

Laura E. Hess, PhD, is a research associate in the Center for the Study of Child and Adolescent Development at the Pennsylvania State University. In the Fall of 1990, Dr. Hess will begin a two-year position as a postdoctoral fellow in the Center for Psychology and Human Development at the Max Planck Institute for Human Development and Education in Berlin. Her research interests include examination of the relationships between family structural and functional change and early adolescent adjustment across home, school, peer, and community contexts.

Steven D. Hollon, PhD, is professor of psychology in the clinical psychology program at Vanderbilt University. He received his PhD from the Florida State University in 1977. He has published numerous articles regarding the role of cognitive factors in depression, and its treatment and subsequent prevention. With Philip Kendall, he co-edited *Cognitive-Behavioral Interventions: Theory, Research and Procedures* and *Assessment Strategies for Cognitive-Behavioral Interventions.* He is an associate editor of *Journal of Abnormal Psychology* and a former editor of *Cognitive Therapy and Research.*

Grayson N. Holmbeck, PhD, is assistant professor of psychology in the clinical psychology program at Loyola University of Chicago. His current research and publications are in biological maturation and family relations during adolescence, developmental psychopathology of adolescence, chronically ill adolescents, sequential analyses of family interaction, and personality assessment. He sits on the editorial boards of *Child Development,* the *Journal of Adolescent Research* and the *Journal of Early Adolescence.*

Leonard A. Jason, PhD, is professor of psychology at DePaul University. He is a fellow of the Division of Community Psychology of the American Psychological Association. He has published over 160 articles and chapters on varied topics including substance abuse prevention, school-based interventions, program evaluation, smoking cessation, and behavioral assessment. Dr. Jason is on the editorial board of several professional journals, including *The American Journal of Community Psychology, Professional Psychology,* and the *Journal of Applied Behavioral Analysis.* He is co-editor of *Prevention: Towards a Multidisciplinary Approach, Preventive Psychology: Theory, Research, and Practice,* and *Behavioral Community Psychology: Progress and Prospects.*

Derek W. Johnston, PhD, is a member of the Medical Research Council External Scientific Staff, based in the psychology department at St George's Hospital Medical School, University of London. His primary research interests are in stress management and prevention of coronary heart disease, the cardiovascular effects of stress, the cognitive effects of stress management, and cognitive and behavioral treatments for anxiety disorders. He is associate editor of the *British Journal of Clinical Psychology* and a past chair of the British Association for Behavioural Psychotherapy.

Philip C. Kendall, PhD, is professor of psychology and head of the Division of Clinical Psychology at Temple University. He is editor of *Cognitive Therapy and Research* and associate editor of *Journal of Consulting and Clinical Psychology.* The author of numerous research papers and monographs, Dr. Kendall authored *Child and Adolescent Therapy: Cognitive-Behavioral Procedures* and *The Stop and Think Workbook,* and has also coauthored *Clinical Psychology: Scientific and Professional Dimensions* (with Ford), *Cognitive Behavioral Therapy for Impulsive Children* (with Braswell), and *Annual Review of Behavior Therapy* (with Franks, Wilson and Foreyt). He is president of the Association for Advancement of Behavior Therapy. His interests lie in cognitive-behavioral assessment and treatment, especially with children.

Abby C. King, PhD, is senior research scientist at the Stanford Center for Research in Disease Prevention, Stanford University School of Medicine. Her research interests and publications are in the areas of health promotion and disease prevention with middle- and older-aged adults. She is a consulting editor for a number of journals in the health field, and is on the editorial board of *Health Psychology.* She is director of the Stanford-Sunnyvale Health Improvement

Project, and is coauthor (with Winett and Altman) of *Health Psychology and Public Health: An Integrative Approach.*

Neville J. King, PhD, is senior lecturer in the faculty of education at Monash University. His major clinical and research interests are child and adolescent fears and anxiety disorders. He is coauthor (with Hamilton and Ollendick) of *Children's Phobias: A Behavioural Perspective* and co-editor (with Remenyi) of *Psychology for the Health Sciences* and *Health Care: A Behavioural Approach.* He was founding editor of *Behaviour Change* and serves on the editorial board of several behavioral journals.

Richard M. Lerner, PhD, is professor of child and adolescent development at the Pennsylvania State University. He is the author or editor of more than 20 books and over 150 articles and chapters. Dr. Lerner is editor of the *Journal of Research on Adolescence,* associate editor of *International Journal of Behavioral Development,* and co-editor of the annual series *Life-Span Development and Behavior.* He was a fellow at the Center for Advanced Study in the Behavioral Sciences, and is a fellow of the American Psychological Association, and the American Association for the Advancement of Science. Dr. Lerner has written extensively about philosophical and theoretical issues in human development, and is noted for his research on childen's and adolescents' personality and social development.

Colin MacLeod, DPhil, is lecturer in psychology at the University of Western Australia. His major research and clinical activities have focused on the emotional disorders, with a central emphasis on the development of appropriate information-processing models to account for such conditions. Dr. MacLeod is coauthor (with Williams, Watts, and Mathews) of the recent book *Cognitive Psychology and the Emotional Disorders.*

Ann S. Masten, PhD, is assistant professor of Child Psychology at the Institute of Child Development, University of Minnesota. She was awarded a three-year McKnight-Land Grant Professorship by the University of Minnesota in 1988. Her research and publications focus on competence, stress, and resilience. She is co-editor (with Rolf, Cicchetti, Nuechterlein and Weintraub) of *Risk and Protective Factors in the Development of Psychopathology.*

Andrew M. Mathews, PhD, was until recently professor and chair of the department of psychology at St. George's Hospital Medical School, University of London, and is now professor of psychology at Louisiana State University. His published research has covered many different aspects of anxiety, and he is coauthor of *Agoraphobia: Nature and Treatment, Essential Psychology for Medical Practice,* and *Cognitive Psychology and the Emotional Disorders.*

Susan Mineka, PhD, is professor of psychology in the clinical psychology program at Northwestern University. She has published widely on animal models of fear, anxiety, and depression. Much of her recent work with primates has focused on selective associations in the observational conditioning of phobic fears. Her current research interests are focused on cognitive and behavioral approaches to the etiology and therapy for anxiety disorders. She is currently the editor of the *Journal of Abnormal Psychology.*

Katherine Nitz, MS, is pursuing her doctoral degree in child clinical psychology at the George Washington University. She is also a predoctoral fellow for the Section on Social and Emotional Development in the Laboratory of Comparative Ethology at the National Institute of Child Health and Human Development. Her research interests include testing of a goodness-of-fit model of person–context relations with regard to early adolescent temperament.

Thomas H. Ollendick, PhD, is professor of psychology and director of clinical training at Virginia Polytechnic Institute and State University. His major clinical and research interests focus on the understanding, assessment, and treatment of child behavior disorders from a social learning perspective. The coauthor of *Clinical Behavior Therapy with Children* and *Child Behavior Assessment,* he is president of the American Psychological Association's Section in Clinical Child Psychology.

Terri L. Orbuch, PhD, is assistant professor of sociology at the University of Michigan—Ann Arbor. Her major research interests include relationship loss, account-making in response to severe stress, and sexuality. She has been author of *Introduction to Sociology,* coauthor (with Harvey and Weber) of *Interpersonal Accounts: A Social Psychological Perspective,* editor of *Relationship Loss: Theoretical*

Perspectives, and co-editor (with Harvey and Weber) of *Attribution, Accounts and Close Relationships.*

Christopher Peterson, PhD, is professor of psychology at the University of Michigan. He is affiliated with the Clinical Psychology Area. He has a long-standing interest in the cognitive determinants of adjustment and well-being, both physical and psychological. He is a consulting editor for the *Journal of Abnormal Psychology.* His most recent book is *Optimism and Health.*

Rolf A. Peterson, PhD, is professor of psychology and director of the clinical psychology training program at the George Washington University. He has published in the areas of stress and social support, perception of illness, and anxiety sensitivity. He coauthored *Abnormality: Experimental and Clinical Approaches.* He recently coauthored the *Anxiety Sensitivity Index Manual* and the *Illness Effects Questionnaire Manual.* He was recently elected chair of the Council of Directors of Health Psychology Training programs.

Steven Schwartz, PhD, is professor and head of the psychology department at the University of Queensland. He has previously held positions at the University of Texas, the University of Western Australia, and Harvard University. He has been a NATO, WHO, and Royal Society Exchange fellow. He is coauthor, (with Griffin) of *Medical Decision Making* and coauthor (with Johnston) of *Psychopathology of Childhood.*

Mary Shelton, BA, is an advanced graduate student in the department of psychology and human development at Vanderbilt University. A developmental psychopathologist, her interests are in the relation of cognition and depression across the life span.

Andrew Steptoe, DPhil, is professor of psychology at St George's Hospital Medical School, University of London. His current research interests include psychophysiological processes in health and illness, and patterns of health-related beliefs, and behavior. He is a past president of the Society for Psychosomatic Research, and a co-chair of the Steering Committee of the International Society of Behavioral Medicine. Recent publications include *Essential Psychology for Medical Practice* (with Mathews), and *Stress, Personal Control, and Health* (co-edited with Appels).

Graham Turpin, PhD, is senior lecturer in the department of psychology, Sheffield University and the course director of the clinical psychology program. In 1984, he was the recipient of the Distinguished Scientific Award for an Early Career Contribution to Psychophysiology from the Society for Psychophysiological Research. He is an associate editor of the *Journal of Psychophysiology.* His major academic research interests concern the application of psychophysiology to clinical psychology. He is editor of the *Handbook of Clinical Psychophysiology.*

Barbara Wilson, PhD, is a reader in rehabilitation studies in the University of Southampton (Faculty of Medicine). She is a clinical psychologist working mostly with clients who have sustained brain injury in adult life through head injury, stroke, encephalitis, or anoxia. Her research interests are in the development of new assessment and treatment procedures for cognitive problems arising from brain injury. She is the senior author of the *Rivermead Behavioural Memory Test* and has published over 50 articles on rehabilitation. She is co-editor of *Clinical Management of Memory Problems* and author of *Rehabilitation of Memory.*

Richard A. Winett, PhD, is professor of psychology and director of the Center for Research in Health Behavior, at Virginia Polytechnic Institute and State University. He received his PhD in clinical psychology from the State University of New York at Stony Brook. His major interests are in health psychology, public health, and preventive medicine, and he is coauthor of *Health Psychology and Public Health: An Integrative Approach.*